The Year's Work
in English Studies
Volume 82

OXFORD

UNIVERSITY PRESS

Great Clarendon Street, Oxford OX2 6DP, UK

Oxford University Press is a department of the University of Oxford.
It furthers the University's objective of excellence in research, scholarship,
and education by publishing worldwide in

Oxford New York

Athens Auckland Bangkok Bogotá Buenos Aire Cape Town
Chennai Dar es Salaam Delhi Florence Hong Kong Istanbul Karachi
Kolkata Kuala Lumpur Madrid Melbourne Mexico City Mumbai Nairobi
Paris São Paulo Shanghai Taipei Tokyo Toronto Warsaw

Oxford is a registered trade mark of Oxford University Press
in the UK and in certain other countries

Published in the United States
by Oxford University Press Inc., New York

British Library Cataloguing in Publication Data

Data available

ISSN 0084-4144
ISBN 0-19-853081-1

1 3 5 7 9 10 8 6 4 2

Typeset by Hope Services (Abingdon) Ltd
Printed in Great Britain
on acid-free paper by
Biddles Ltd.,
Guildford and King's Lynn

The English Association

The object of The English Association is to promote the knowledge and appreciation of English language and its literatures.

The Association pursues these aims by creating opportunities of co-operation among all those interested in English; by furthering the recognition of English as essential in education; by discussing methods of English teaching; by holding lectures, conferences, and other meetings; by publishing several journals, books, and leaflets; and by forming local branches overseas and at home.

Publications

The Year's Work in English Studies. An annual narrative bibliography which aims to cover all work of quality in english studies published in a given year. Published by Oxford University Press.

The Year's Work in Critical and Cultural Theory. An annual narrative bibliography which aims to provide comprehensive cover of all work of quality in critical and cultural theory published in a given year. Published by Oxford University Press.

Essays and Studies. A well-established series of annual themed volumes edited each year by a distinguished academic. The 2003 volume is *Victorian Women Poets* edited by Alison Chapman and published by D.S. Brewer.

English. This internationally-known journal of the Association is aimed at teachers of English in universities and colleges, with articles on all aspects of literature and critical theory and an extensive reviews section. Three issues per year.

Use of English. The longest-standing journal for English teachers in schools and colleges. Three issues per year.

English 4–11. Designed and developed by primary English specialists to give practical help to primary and middle school teachers. Three issues per year.

Membership

Membership information can be found at http://www.le.ac.uk/engassoc or please write to The English Association, University of Leicester, University Road, Leicester LE1 7RH, UK or email: engassoc@le.ac.uk.

The Year's Work
in English Studies

Subscriptions for Volume 82

Institutional (combined rate to both *The Year's Work in English Studies* and *The Year's Work in Critical and Cultural Theory*): UK and Europe £197, USA and rest of world $315.

Personal rates: as above.

Online Access

For details please email Oxford University Press Journals Customer Services on: jnls.cust.serv@oup.co.uk.

Order Information

Payment is required with all orders and may be made by: cheque (made payable to Oxford University Press), National Girobank (account 500 1056), credit card (Mastercard, Visa, American Express), UNESCO coupons.

Bankers: Barclays Bank plc, PO Box 333, Oxford, UK. Code 20–65–18, account 00715654.

Please send orders to: Journal Subscriptions Department, Oxford University Press, Great Clarendon Street, Oxford OX2 6DP, UK. Tel: +44 (0)1865 353907, fax: +44 (0)1865 353485, jnl.orders@oupjournals.org.

Back Issues

The current volume and the two previous are available from Journals Subscriptions Department, Oxford University Press, Great Clarendon Street, Oxford OX2 6DP, UK. Tel:+44 (0)1865 353907, fax:+44 (0)1865 353485, jnl.orders@oupjournals.org. Earlier volumes can be obtained from the Periodicals Service Company, 11 Main Street, Germantown, NY 12526, USA. Tel:+1 (518) 537 4700, fax: +1 (518) 537 5899.

Electronic Notification of Contents

The Table of Contents email alerting service allows anyone who registers his or her email address to be notified via email when new content goes online. Details are available at http://www3.oup.co.uk/ywes/etoc.html.

Advertising

Enquiries should be made to Helen Pearson, Oxford Journals Advertising, PO Box 347, Abingdon SO, Oxford OX14 5AA, UK; tel/fax: +44 (0)1235 201904, email: helen@oxfordads.com.

Contents

Brookes University; Paul Poplawski, University of Leicester; John
Nash, Trinity College, Dublin; Nancy Paxton, Northern Arizona
University; John Brannigan, University College Dublin; Maggie
B. Gale, University of Birmingham; Malcolm Page, Simon Fraser
University; Jo Gill, University of Exeter; Fran Brearton, Queen's
University Belfast

Abbreviations

1. Journals, Series and Reference Works

1650–1850	*1650–1850 Ideas, Aesthetics, and Inquiries in the Early Modern Era*
A&D	*Art and Design*
A&E	*Anglistik und Englishunterricht*
AAA	*Arbeiten aus Anglistik und Amerikanistik*
AAAJ	*Accounting, Auditing and Accountability Journal*
AAR	*African American Review*
ABäG	*Amsterdamer Beiträge zur Älteren Germanistik*
ABC	*American Book Collector*
ABELL	*Annual Bibliography of English Language and Literature*
ABM	*Antiquarian Book Monthly Review*
ABQ	*American Baptist Quarterly*
ABR	*American Benedictine Review*
ABSt	*A/B: Auto/Biography Studies*
AC	*Archeologia Classica*
Academy Forum	*Academy Forum*
AcadSF	Academia Scientiarum Fennica
ACar	*Analecta Cartusiana*
ACH	*Australian Cultural History*
ACLALSB	*ACLALS Bulletin*
ACM	*Aligarh Critical Miscellany*
ACS	*Australian–Canadian Studies: A Journal for the Humanities and Social Sciences*
Acta	Acta (Binghamton, NY)
AdI	*Annali d'Italianistica*
ADS	*Australasian Drama Studies*
AEB	*Analytical and Enumerative Bibliography*
Æstel	*Æstel*
AF	*Anglistische Forschungen*
AfricanA	*African Affairs*
AfrSR	*African Studies Review*
AgeJ	*Age of Johnson: A Scholarly Annual*
Agenda	*Agenda*
Agni	*Agni Review*
AH	*Art History*
AHR	*American Historical Review*
AHS	*Australian Historical Studies*
AI	*American Imago*

AICRJ	American Indian Culture and Research Journal
AIQ	American Indian Quarterly
AJ	Art Journal
AJGLL	American Journal of Germanic Linguistics and Literatures
AJL	Australian Journal of Linguistics
AJP	American Journal of Psychoanalysis
AJPH	Australian Journal of Politics and History
AJS	American Journal of Semiotics
AKML	Abhandlungen zur Kunst-, Musik- and Literaturwissenschaft
AL	American Literature
ALA	African Literature Association Annuals
ALASH	Acta Linguistica Academiae Scientiarum Hungaricae
Albion	Albion
AlexS	Alexander Shakespeare
ALH	Acta Linguistica Hafniensia; International Journal of Linguistics
Alif	Journal of Comparative Poetics (Cairo, Egypt)
ALitASH	Acta Literaria Academiae Scientiarum Hungaricae
Allegorica	Allegorica
ALR	American Literary Realism, 1870–1910
ALS	Australian Literary Studies
ALT	African Literature Today
Alternatives	Alternatives
AmasJ	Amerasian Journal
AmDram	American Drama
Americana	Americana
AmerP	American Poetry
AmerS	American Studies
AmLH	American Literary History
AmLS	American Literary Scholarship: An Annual
AMon	Atlantic Monthly
AmPer	American Periodicals
AmRev	Americas Review: A Review of Hispanic Literature and Art of the USA
Amst	Amerikastudien/American Studies
AN	Acta Neophilologica
Anaïs	Anaïs
AnBol	Analecta Bollandiana
ANF	Arkiv för Nordisk Filologi
Angelaki	Angelaki
Anglia	Anglia: Zeitschrift für Englische Philologie
Anglistica	Anglistica
Anglistik	Anglistik: Mitteilungen des Verbandes Deutscher Anglisten
AnH	Analecta Husserliana
AnL	Anthropological Linguistics
AnM	Annuale Mediaevale
Ann	Annales: Économies, Sociétés, Civilisations

ANQ	*ANQ: A Quarterly Journal of Short Articles, Notes and Reviews* (formerly *American Notes and Queries*)
AntColl	*Antique Collector*
AntigR	*Antigonish Review*
Antipodes	*Antipodes: A North American Journal of Australian Literature*
ANZSC	*Australian and New Zealand Studies in Canada*
ANZTR	*Australian and New Zealand Theatre Record*
APBR	*Atlantic Provinces Book Review*
APL	*Antwerp Papers in Linguistics*
AppLing	*Applied Linguistics*
APR	*American Poetry Review*
AQ	*American Quarterly*
Aquarius	*Aquarius*
AR	*Antioch Review*
ArAA	*Arbeiten aus Anglistik und Amerikanistik*
Arcadia	*Arcadia*
Archiv	*Archiv für das Stadium der Neueren Sprachen und Literaturen*
ARCS	*American Review of Canadian Studies*
ArdenS	Arden Shakespeare
ArielE	*Ariel: A Review of International English Literature*
ArkQ	*Arkansas Quarterly: A Journal of Criticism*
ArkR	*Arkansas Review: A Journal of Criticism*
ArQ	*Arizona Quarterly*
ARS	Augustan Reprint Society
ARSR	*Australian Religion Studies Review*
ArtB	*Art Bulletin*
Arth	*Arthuriana*
ArthI	*Arthurian Interpretations*
ArthL	*Arthurian Literature*
Arv	*Arv: Nordic Yearbook of Folklore*
AS	*American Speech*
ASch	*American Scholar*
ASE	*Anglo-Saxon England*
ASInt	*American Studies International*
ASoc	*Arts in Society*
Aspects	*Aspects: Journal of the Language Society* (University of Essex)
AspectsAF	*Aspects of Australian Fiction*
ASPR	*Anglo-Saxon Poetic Records*
ASSAH	*Anglo-Saxon Studies in Archaeology and History*
Assaph	*Assaph: Studies in the Arts (Theatre Studies)*
Assays	*Assays: Critical Approaches to Medieval and Renaissance Texts*
ASUI	*Analele Stiintifice ale Universitatii 'Al.I. Cuza' din Iasi (Serie Noua), e. Lingvistica*

ATQ	*American Transcendental Quarterly: A Journal of New England Writers*
AuBR	*Australian Book Review*
AuFolk	*Australian Folklore*
AuFS	*Australian Feminist Studies*
AuHR	*Australian Humanities Review*
AuJL	*Australian Journal of Linguistics*
AUMLA	*Journal of the Australasian Universities Language and Literature Association*
AuS	*Australian Studies*
AuSA	*Australian Studies* (Australia)
AusCan	*Australian–Canadian Studies*
AusPl	*Australian Playwrights*
AusRB	*Australians' Review of Books*
AuVSJ	*Australasian Victorian Studies Journal*
AuWBR	*Australian Women's Book Review*
AvC	*Avalon to Camelot*
AY	*Arthurian Yearbook*
BakhtinN	*Bakhtin Newsletter*
BALF	*Black American Literature Forum*
BAReview	*British Academy Review*
BARS Bulletin	*British Association for Romantic Studies Bulletin & Review*
BAS	*British and American Studies*
BASAM	*BASA Magazine*
BathH	*Bath History*
BayreuthAS	Bayreuth African Studies
BB	*Bulletin of Bibliography*
BBCS	*Bulletin of the Board of Celtic Studies*
BBCSh	BBC Shakespeare
BBN	*British Book News*
BBSIA	*Bulletin Bibliographique de la Société Internationale Arthurienne*
BC	*Book Collector*
BCan	*Books in Canada*
BCMA	*Bulletin of Cleveland Museum of Art*
BCS	*B.C. Studies*
BDEC	*Bulletin of the Department of English* (Calcutta)
BDP	*Beiträge zur Deutschen Philologie*
Belfagor	*Belfagor: Rassegna di Varia Umanità*
BEPIF	*Bulletin des Itudes Portugaises et Brésiliennes*
BFLS	*Bulletin de la Faculté des Lettres de Strasbourg*
BGDSL	*Beiträge zur Geschichte der Deutschen Sprache und Literatur*
BHI	*British Humanities Index*
BHL	*Bibliotheca Hagiographica Latina Antiquae et Mediae Aetatis*
BHM	*Bulletin of the History of Medicine*
BHR	*Bibliothèque d'Humanisme et Renaissance*

BHS	*Bulletin of Hispanic Studies*
BI	*Books at Iowa*
Bibliotheck	*Bibliotheck: A Scottish Journal of Bibliography and Allied Topics*
Biography	*Biography: An Interdisciplinary Quarterly*
BIS	*Browning Institute Studies: An Annual of Victorian Literary and Cultural History*
BJA	*British Journal of Aesthetics*
BJCS	*British Journal of Canadian Studies*
BJDC	*British Journal of Disorders of Communication*
BJECS	*British Journal for Eighteenth-Century Studies*
BJHP	*British Journal for the History of Philosophy*
BJHS	*British Journal for the History of Science*
BJJ	*Ben Jonson Journal*
BJL	*Belgian Journal of Linguistics*
BJPS	*British Journal for the Philosophy of Science*
BJRL	*Bulletin of the John Rylands* (University Library of Manchester)
BJS	*British Journal of Sociology*
Blake	*Blake: An Illustrated Quarterly*
BLE	*Bulletin de Littérature Ecclésiastique*
BLJ	*British Library Journal*
BLR	*Bodleian Library Record*
BN	*Beiträge zur Namenforschung*
BNB	*British National Bibliography*
BoH	*Book History*
Bookbird	*Bookbird*
Borderlines	*Borderlines*
Boundary	*Boundary 2: A Journal of Postmodern Literature and Culture*
BP	*Banasthali Patrika*
BPMA	*Bulletin of Philadelphia Museum of Art*
BPN	*Barbara Pym Newsletter*
BQ	*Baptist Quarterly*
BRASE	Basic Readings in Anglo-Saxon England
BRH	*Bulletin of Research in the Humanities*
Brick	*Brick: A Journal of Reviews*
BRMMLA	*Bulletin of the Rocky Mountain Modern Language Association*
BSANZB	*Bibliographical Society of Australia and New Zealand Bulletin*
BSE	*Brno Studies in English*
BSEAA	*Bulletin de la Société d'Études Anglo-Américaines des XVIIe et XVIIIe Siècles*
BSJ	*Baker Street Journal: An Irregular Quarterly of Sherlockiana*
BSLP	*Bulletin de la Société de Linguistique de Paris*
BSNotes	*Browning Society Notes*

BSRS	*Bulletin of the Society for Renaissance Studies*
BSSA	*Bulletin de la Société de Stylistique Anglaise*
BST	*Brontë Society Transactions*
BSUF	*Ball State University Forum*
BTHGNewsl	*Book Trade History Group Newsletter*
BTLV	*Bijdragen tot de Taal-, Land- en Volkenhunde*
Bullán	*Bullán*
BunyanS	*Bunyan Studies*
BuR	*Bucknell Review*
BurlM	*Burlington Magazine*
BurnsC	*Burns Chronicle*
BWPLL	Belfast Working Papers in Language and Linguistics
BWVACET	*Bulletin of the West Virginia Association of College English Teachers*
ByronJ	*Byron Journal*
CABS	Contemporary Authors Bibliographical Series
CahiersE	*Cahiers Élisabéthains*
CAIEF	*Cahiers de l'Association Internationale des Études Françaises*
Caliban	*Caliban* (Toulouse, France)
Callaloo	*Callaloo*
CalR	*Calcutta Review*
CamObsc	*Camera Obscura: A Journal of Feminism and Film Theory*
CamR	*Cambridge Review*
CanD	*Canadian Drama / L'Art Dramatique Canadienne*
C&L	*Christianity and Literature*
C&Lang	*Communication and Languages*
C&M	*Classica et Medievalia*
CanL	*Canadian Literature*
CAnn	*Carlyle Annual*
CanPo	*Canadian Poetry*
CapR	*Capilano Review*
CARA	Centre Aixois de Recherches Anglaises
Carib	*Carib*
Caribana	*Caribana*
CaribW	*Caribbean Writer*
CarR	*Caribbean Review*
Carrell	*Carrell: Journal of the Friends of the University of Miami Library*
CASE	Cambridge Studies in Anglo-Saxon England
CaudaP	*Cauda Pavonis*
CBAA	*Current Bibliography on African Affairs*
CBEL	*Cambridge Bibliography of English Literature*
CCRev	*Comparative Civilizations Review*
CCrit	*Comparative Criticism: An Annual Journal*
CCTES	*Conference of College Teachers of English Studies*
CCV	*Centro de Cultura Valenciana*
CDALB	*Concise Dictionary of American Literary Biography*

CDCP	Comparative Drama Conference Papers
CDIL	*Cahiers de l'Institut de Linguistique de Louvain*
CdL	*Cahiers de Lexicologie*
CE	*College English*
CEA	*CEA Critic*
CEAfr	*Cahiers d'Études Africaines*
CE&S	*Commonwealth Essays and Studies*
CentR	*Centennial Review*
Cervantes	*Cervantes*
CFM	*Canadian Fiction Magazine*
CFS	*Cahiers Ferdinand de Saussure: Revue de Linguistique Générale*
Chapman	*Chapman*
Chasqui	*Chasqui*
ChauR	*Chaucer Review*
ChauS	*Chaucer Studion*
ChauY	*Chaucer Yearbook*
ChH	*Church History*
ChildL	*Children's Literature*
ChiR	*Chicago Review*
ChLB	*Charles Lamb Bulletin*
CHLSSF	*Commentationes Humanarum Litterarum Societatis Scientiarum Fennicae*
CHR	*Camden History Review*
CHum	*Computers and the Humanities*
CI	Critical Idiom
CILT	Amsterdam Studies in the Theory and History of the Language Sciences IV: Current Issues in Linguistic Theory
Cinéaste	*Cinéaste*
CinJ	*Cinema Journal*
CIQ	*Colby Quarterly*
CISh	Contemporary Interpretations of Shakespeare
Cithara	*Cithara: Essays in the Judaeo-Christian Tradition*
CJ	*Classical Journal*
CJE	*Cambridge Journal of Education*
CJH	*Canadian Journal of History*
CJIS	*Canadian Journal of Irish Studies*
CJL	*Canadian Journal of Linguistics*
CJR	*Christian–Jewish Relations*
CK	*Common Knowledge*
CL	*Comparative Literature* (Eugene, OR)
CLAJ	*CLA Journal*
CLAQ	*Children's Literature Association Quarterly*
ClarkN	*Clark Newsletter: Bulletin of the UCLA Center for Seventeenth- and Eighteenth-Century Studies*
ClassW	*Classical World*
CLC	*Columbia Library Columns*
CLIN	*Cuadernos de Literatura*

ClioI	*Clio: A Journal of Literature, History and the Philosophy of History*
CLQ	*Colby Library Quarterly*
CLS	*Comparative Literature Studies*
Clues	*Clues: A Journal of Detection*
CMCS	*Cambridge Medieval Celtic Studies*
CML	*Classical and Modern Literature*
CN	*Chaucer Newsletter*
CNIE	*Commonwealth Novel in English*
CogLing	*Cognitive Linguistics*
Cognition	*Cognition*
ColB	*Coleridge Bulletin*
ColF	*Columbia Forum*
Collections	*Collections*
CollG	*Colloquia Germanica*
CollL	*College Literature*
Comitatus	*Comitatus: A Journal of Medieval and Renaissance Studies*
Commentary	*Commentary*
Commonwealth	*Commonwealth*
Comparatist	*Comparatist: Journal of the Southern Comparative Literature Association*
CompD	*Comparative Drama*
CompLing	*Contemporary Linguistics*
ConfLett	*Confronto Letterario*
ConL	*Contemporary Literature*
Connotations	*Connotations*
ConnR	*Connecticut Review*
Conradian	*Conradian*
Conradiana	*Conradiana: A Journal of Joseph Conrad Studies*
ContempR	*Contemporary Review*
Coppertales	*Coppertales: A Journal of Rural Arts*
Cosmos	*Cosmos*
CP	*Concerning Poetry*
CQ	*Cambridge Quarterly*
CR	*Critical Review*
CRCL	*Canadian Review of Comparative Literature*
CRev	*Chesterton Review*
CRevAS	*Canadian Review of American Studies*
Crit	*Critique: Studies in Modern Fiction*
CritI	*Critical Inquiry*
Criticism	*Criticism: A Quarterly for Literature and the Arts*
Critique	*Critique* (Paris)
CritQ	*Critical Quarterly*
CritT	*Critical Texts: A Review of Theory and Criticism*
CrM	*Critical Mass*
CRNLE	*CRNLE Reviews Journal*
Crossings	*Crossings*
CRUX	*CRUX: A Journal on the Teaching of English*

CS	*Critical Survey*
CSASE	Cambridge Studies in Anglo-Saxon England
CSCC	*Case Studies in Contemporary Criticism*
CSELT	Cambridge Studies in Eighteenth-Century Literature and Thought
CSLBull	*Bulletin of the New York C.S. Lewis Society*
CSLL	*Cardozo Studies in Law and Literature*
CSML	Cambridge Studies in Medieval Literature
CSNCLC	Cambridge Studies in Nineteenth-Century Literature and Culture
CSPC	Cambridge Studies in Paleography and Codicology
CSR	Cambridge Studies in Romanticism
CSRev	*Christian Scholar's Review*
CStA	*Carlyle Studies Annual* (previously *CAnn*)
CTR	*Canadian Theatre Review*
Cuadernos	*Cuadernos de Literatura Infantil y Juvenil*
CulC	*Cultural Critique*
CulS	*Cultural Studies*
CUNY	*CUNY English Forum*
Current Writing	*Current Writing: Text and Reception in Southern Africa*
CV2	*Contemporary Verse 2*
CVE	*Cahiers Victoriens et Edouardiens*
CW	*Current Writing: Text and Perception in Southern Africa*
CWAAS	*Transactions of the Cumberland and Westmorland Antiquarian and Archaeological Society*
CWS	*Canadian Woman Studies*
DA	*Dictionary of Americanisms*
DAE	*Dictionary of American English*
DAEM	*Deutsches Archiv für Erforschung des Mittelalters*
DAI	*Dissertation Abstracts International*
DAL	*Descriptive and Applied Linguistics*
D&CN&Q	*Devon and Cornwall Notes and Queries*
D&S	*Discourse and Society*
Daphnis	*Daphnis: Zeitschrift für Mittlere Deutsche Literatur*
DC	Dickens Companions
DerbyM	*Derbyshire Miscellany*
Descant	*Descant*
DFS	*Dalhousie French Studies*
DHLR	*D.H. Lawrence Review*
DHS	*Dix-huitième Siècle*
Diac	*Diacritics*
Diachronica	*Diachronica*
Dialogue	*Dialogue: Canadian Philosophical Review*
Dickensian	*Dickensian*
DicS	*Dickinson Studies*
Dictionaries	*Dictionaries: Journal of the Dictionary Society of North America*
Dionysos	*Dionysos*

Discourse	*Discourse*
DisS	*Discourse Studies*
DLB	*Dictionary of Literary Biography*
DLN	*Doris Lessing Newsletter*
DM	*Dublin Magazine*
DMT	Durham Medieval Texts
DNB	*Dictionary of National Biography*
DOE	*Dictionary of Old English*
Dolphin	*Dolphin: Publications of the English Department* (University of Aarhus)
DOST	*Dictionary of the Older Scottish Tongue*
DownR	*Downside Review*
DPr	*Discourse Processes*
DQ	*Denver Quarterly*
DQR	*Dutch Quarterly Review of Anglo-American Letters*
DQu	*Dickens Quarterly* '
DR	*Dalhousie Review*
Drama	*Drama: The Quarterly Theatre Review*
DrS	*Dreiser Studies*
DS	*Deep South*
DSA	*Dickens Studies Annual*
DU	*Der Deutschunterricht: Beiträge zu Seiner Praxis und Wissenschaftlichen Grundlegung*
DUJ	*Durham University Journal*
DVLG	*Deutsche Viertejahrsschrift für Literaturwissenschaft und Geistesgeschichte*
DWPELL	*Dutch Working Papers in English Language and Linguistics*
EA	*Études Anglaises*
EAL	*Early American Literature*
E&D	*Enlightenment and Dissent*
E&S	*Essays and Studies*
E&Soc	*Economy and Society*
EAS	*Essays in Arts and Sciences*
EASt	*Englisch Amerikanische Studien*
EBST	*Edinburgh Bibliographical Society Transactions*
EC	*Études Celtiques*
ECan	*Études Canadiennes/Canadian Studies*
ECCB	*Eighteenth Century: A Current Bibliography*
ECent	*Eighteenth Century: Theory and Interpretation*
ECF	*Eighteenth-Century Fiction*
ECI	*Eighteenth-Century Ireland*
ECIntell	*East-Central Intelligencer*
ECLife	*Eighteenth Century Life*
ECon	*L'Époque Conradienne*
ECr	*L'Esprit Créateur*
ECS	*Eighteenth-Century Studies*
ECSTC	Eighteenth-Century Short Title Catalogue

ECW	*Essays on Canadian Writing*
EDAMN	*EDAM Newsletter*
EDAMR	*Early Drama, Art, and Music Review*
EDH	*Essays by Divers Hands*
EdL	*Études de Lettres*
EdN	*Editors' Notes: Bulletin of the Conference of Editors of Learned Journals*
EDSL	*Encyclopedic Dictionary of the Sciences of Language*
EEMF	Early English Manuscripts in Facsimile
EHR	*English Historical Review*
EI	*Études Irlandaises* (Lille)
EIC	*Essays in Criticism*
EinA	*English in Africa*
EiP	*Essays in Poetics*
EIRC	*Explorations in Renaissance Culture*
Éire	*Éire-Ireland*
EiTET	*Essays in Theatre / Études Théâtrales*
EJ	*English Journal*
EJES	*European Journal of English Studies*
ELangT	*ELT Journal: An International Journal for Teachers of English to Speakers of Other Languages*
ELet	*Esperienze Letterarie: Rivista Trimestrale di Critica e Cultura*
ELH	*English Literary History*
ELing	*English Linguistics*
ELL	*English Language and Linguistics*
ELN	*English Language Notes*
ELR	*English Literary Renaissance*
ELS	*English Literary Studies*
ELT	*English Literature in Transition*
ELWIU	*Essays in Literature* (Western Illinois University)
EM	*English Miscellany*
Embl	*Emblematica: An Interdisciplinary Journal of English Studies*
EMD	*European Medieval Drama*
EME	*Early Modern Europe*
EMedE	*Early Medieval Europe* (online)
EMLS	*Early Modern Literary Studies* (online)
EMMS	*Early Modern Manuscript Studies*
EMS	*English Manuscript Studies, 1100–1700*
EMu	*Early Music*
EMW	Early Modern Englishwomen
Encyclia	*Encyclia*
English	*English: The Journal of the English Association*
EnT	*English Today: The International Review of the English Language*
EONR	*Eugene O'Neill Review*
EPD	*English Pronouncing Dictionary*

ER	*English Review*
ERLM	*Europe-Revue Littéraire Mensuelle*
ERR	*European Romantic Review*
ES	*English Studies*
ESA	*English Studies in Africa*
ESC	*English Studies in Canada*
ESQ	*ESQ: A Journal of the American Renaissance*
ESRS	*Emporia State Research Studies*
EssaysMedSt	*Essays in Medieval Studies*
ET	*Elizabethan Theatre*
EWhR	*Edith Wharton Review*
EWIP	*Edinburgh University, Department of Linguistics, Work in Progress*
EWN	*Evelyn Waugh Newsletter*
EWPAL	*Edinburgh Working Papers in Applied Linguistics*
EWW	*English World-Wide*
Excavatio	*Excavatio*
Exemplaria	*Exemplaria*
Expl	*Explicator*
Extrapolation	*Extrapolation: A Journal Science Fiction and Fantasy*
FC	*Feminist Collections: A Quarterly of Women's Studies Resources*
FCEMN	*Mystics Quarterly* (formerly *Fourteenth-Century English Mystics Newsletter*)
FCS	*Fifteenth-Century Studies*
FDT	Fountainwell Drama Texts
FemR	*Feminist Review*
FemSEL	*Feminist Studies in English Literature*
FH	*Die Neue Gesellschaft / Frankfurter Hefte*
Fiction International	*Fiction International*
FiveP	*Five Points: A Journal of Literature and Art* (Atlanta, GA)
FJS	*Fu Jen Studies: Literature and Linguistics* (Taipei)
FLH	*Folia Linguistica Historica*
Florilegium	*Florilegium: Carleton University Annual Papers on Classical Antiquity and the Middle Ages*
FMLS	*Forum for Modern Language Studies*
FNS	*Frank Norris Studies*
Folklore	*Folklore*
FoLi	*Folia Linguistica*
Forum	*Forum*
FranS	*Franciscan Studies*
FreeA	*Free Associations*
FrontenacR	*Revue Frontenac*
Frontiers	*Frontiers: A Journal of Women's Studies*
FS	*French Studies*
FSt	*Feminist Studies*
FT	*Fashion Theory*
FuL	*Functions of Language*

Futures	*Futures*
GAG	Göppinger Arbeiten zur Germanistik
GaR	*Georgia Review*
GBB	*George Borrow Bulletin*
GBK	*Gengo Bunka Kenkyu: Studies in Language and Culture*
GEGHLS	*George Eliot–George Henry Lewes Studies*
GeM	*Genealogists Magazine*
Genders	*Genders*
Genre	*Genre*
GER	*George Eliot Review*
Gestus	*Gestus: A Quarterly Journal of Brechtian Studies*
Gettysburg Review	*Gettysburg Review*
GG@G	*Generative Grammar in Geneva* (online)
GHJ	*George Herbert Journal*
GissingJ	*Gissing Journal*
GJ	*Gutenberg-Jahrbuch*
GL	*General Linguistics*
GL&L	*German Life and Letters*
GlasR	*Glasgow Review*
Glossa	*Glossa: An International Journal of Linguistics*
GLQ	*A Journal of Lesbian and Gay Studies* (Duke University)
GLS	*Grazer Linguistische Studien*
GR	*Germanic Review*
Gramma	*Gramma: Journal of Theory and Criticism*
Gramma/TTT	*Tijdschrift voor Taalwetenschap*
GrandS	*Grand Street*
Granta	*Granta*
Greyfriar	*Greyfriar Siena Studies in Literature*
GRM	*Germanisch-Romanische Monatsschrift*
GSE	Gothenberg Studies in English
GSJ	*Gaskell Society Journal*
GSN	*Gaskell Society Newsletter*
GURT	*Georgetown University Round Table on Language and Linguistics*
HamS	*Hamlet Studies*
H&T	*History and Theory*
HardyR	*Hardy Review*
Harvard Law Review	*Harvard Law Review*
HatcherR	*Hatcher Review*
HBS	Henry Bradshaw Society
HC	*Hollins Critic*
HCM	*Hitting Critical Mass: A Journal of Asian American Cultural Criticism*
HE	*History of Education*
HEAT	*HEAT*
Hecate	*Hecate: An Interdisciplinary Journal of Women's Liberation*
HEdQ	*History of Education Quarterly*

HEI	History of European Ideas
HeineJ	Heine Jahrbuch
HEL	Histoire Épistémologie Language
Helios	Helios
HEng	History of the English Language
Hermathena	Hermathena: A Trinity College Dublin Review
HeyJ	Heythrop Journal
HFR	Hayden Ferry Review
HistJ	Historical Journal
History	History: The Journal of the Historical Association
HistR	Historical Research
HJR	Henry James Review (Baton Rouge, LA)
HL	Historiographia Linguistica
HLB	Harvard Library Bulletin
HLQ	Huntingdon Library Quarterly
HLSL	(online)
HNCIS	Harvester New Critical Introductions to Shakespeare
HNR	Harvester New Readings
HOPE	History of Political Economy
HPT	History of Political Thought
HQ	Hopkins Quarterly
HR	Harvard Review
HRB	Hopkins Research Bulletin
HSci	History of Science
HSE	Hungarian Studies in English
HSELL	Hiroshima Studies in English Language and Literature
HSJ	Housman Society Journal
HSL	University of Hartford Studies in Literature
HSN	Hawthorne Society Newsletter
HSSh	Hunganan Studies in Shakespeare
HSSN	Henry Sweet Society Newsletter
HT	History Today
HTR	Harvard Theological Review
HudR	Hudson Review
HumeS	Hume Studies
HumLov	Humanistica Lovaniensia: Journal of Neo-Latin Studies
Humor	Humor: International Journal of Humor Research
HUSL	Hebrew University Studies in Literature and the Arts
HWJ	History Workshop
HWS	History Workshop Series
Hypatia	Hypatia
IAL	Issues in Applied Linguistics
IAN	Izvestiia Akademii Nauk SSSR (Moscow)
I&C	Ideology and Consciousness
I&P	Ideas and Production
ICAME	International Computer Archive of Modern and Medieval English
ICS	Illinois Classical Studies

IEEETrans	*IEEE Transactions on Professional Communications*
IF	*Indogermanische Forschungen*
IFR	*International Fiction Review*
IGK	*Irland: Gesellschaft und Kultur*
IJAES	*International Journal of Arabic-English Studies*
IJAL	*International Journal of Applied Linguistics*
IJBEB	*International Journal of Bilingual Education & Bilingualism*
IJCP	*International Journal of Corpus Linguistics*
IJCT	*International Journal of the Classical Tradition*
IJECS	*Indian Journal for Eighteenth-Century Studies*
IJES	*Indian Journal of English Studies*
IJL	*International Journal of Lexicography*
IJPR	*International Journal for Philosophy of Religion*
IJSL	*International Journal of the Sociology of Language*
IJSS	*Indian Journal of Shakespeare Studies*
IJWS	*International Journal of Women's Studies*
ILR	*Indian Literary Review*
ILS	*Irish Literary Supplement*
Imago	*Imago: New Writing*
IMB	*International Medieval Bibliography*
Imprimatur	*Imprimatur*
Indexer	*Indexer*
IndH	*Indian Horizons*
IndL	*Indian Literature*
InG	*In Geardagum: Essays on Old and Middle English Language and Literature*
Inklings	*Inklings: Jahrbuch für Literatur und Ästhetik*
Ioc	*Index to Censorship*
Inquiry	*Inquiry: An Interdisciplinary Journal of Philosophy*
Interlink	*Interlink*
Interpretation	*Interpretation*
Interventions	*Interventions: The International Journal of Postcolonial Studies*
IowaR	*Iowa Review*
IRAL	*IRAL: International Review of Applied Linguistics in Language Teaching*
Iris	*Iris: A Journal of Theory on Image and Sound*
IS	*Italian Studies*
ISh	*Independent Shavian*
ISJR	*Iowa State Journal of Research*
Island	*Island Magazine*
Islands	*Islands*
Isle	*Interdisciplinary Studies in Literature and Environment*
ISR	*Irish Studies Review*
IUR	*Irish University Review: A Journal of Irish Studies*
JAAC	*Journal of Aesthetics and Art Criticism*
JAAR	*Journal of the American Academy of Religion*

Jacket	*Jacket*
JADT	*Journal of American Drama and Theatre*
JAF	*Journal of American Folklore*
JafM	*Journal of African Marxists*
JAIS	*Journal of Anglo-Italian Studies*
JAL	*Journal of Australian Literature*
JamC	*Journal of American Culture*
JAmH	*Journal of American History*
JAmS	*Journal of American Studies*
JArabL	*Journal of Arabic Literature*
JAS	*Journal of Australian Studies*
JAStT	*Journal of American Studies of Turkey*
JBeckS	*Journal of Beckett Studies*
JBS	*Journal of British Studies*
JBSSJ	*Journal of the Blake Society at St James*
JCAKSU	*Journal of the College of Arts* (King Saud University)
JCanL	*Journal of Canadian Literature*
JCC	*Journal of Canadian Culture*
JCF	*Journal of Canadian Fiction*
JChL	*Journal of Child Language*
JCL	*Journal of Commonwealth Literature*
JCP	*Journal of Canadian Poetry*
JCPCS	*Journal of Commonwealth and Postcolonial Studies*
JCSJ	*John Clare Society Journal*
JCSR	*Journal of Canadian Studies / Revue d'Études Canadiennes*
JCSt	*Journal of Caribbean Studies*
JDECU	*Journal of the Department of English* (Calcutta University)
JDHLS	*D.H. Lawrence: The Journal of the D.H. Lawrence Society*
JDJ	*John Dunne Journal*
JDN	*James Dickey Newsletter*
JDTC	*Journal of Dramatic Theory and Criticism*
JEBS	*Journal of the Early Book Society*
JEDRBU	*Journal of the English Department* (Rabindra Bharati University)
JEGP	*Journal of English and Germanic Philology*
JEH	*Journal of Ecclesiastical History*
JELL	*Journal of English Language and Literature*
JEn	*Journal of English* (Sana'a University)
JEngL	*Journal of English Linguistics*
JENS	*Journal of the Eighteen Nineties Society*
JEP	*Journal of Evolutionary Psychology*
JEPNS	*Journal of the English Place-Name Society*
JES	*Journal of European Studies*
JETS	*Journal of the Evangelical Theological Society*
JFR	*Journal of Folklore Research*
JGE	*Journal of General Education*
JGenS	*Journal of Gender Studies*

JGH	*Journal of Garden History*
JGN	*John Gower Newsletter*
JH	*Journal of Homosexuality*
JHI	*Journal of the History of Ideas*
JHLP	*Journal of Historical Linguistics and Philology*
JHP	*Journal of the History of Philosophy*
JHPrag	*Journal of Historical Pragmatics*
JHSex	*Journal of the History of Sexuality*
JHu	*Journal of Humanities*
JHuP	*Journal of Humanistic Psychology*
JIES	*Journal of Indo-European Studies*
JIL	*Journal of Irish Literature*
JIPA	*Journal of the International Phonetic Association*
JIWE	*Journal of Indian Writing in English*
JJ	*Jamaica Journal*
JJA	*James Joyce Annual*
JJB	*James Joyce Broadsheet*
JJLS	*James Joyce Literary Supplement*
JJQ	*James Joyce Quarterly*
JL	*Journal of Linguistics*
JLH	*Journal of Library History, Philosophy and Comparative Librarianship*
JLLI	*Journal of Logic, Language and Information*
JLP	*Journal of Linguistics and Politics*
JLS	*Journal of Literary Semanitcs*
JLSP	*Journal of Language and Social Psychology*
JLVSG	*Journal of the Longborough Victorian Studies Group*
JMemL	*Journal of Memory and Language*
JMEMS	*Journal of Medieval and Early Modern Studies*
JMGS	*Journal of Modern Greek Studies*
JMH	*Journal of Medieval History*
JML	*Journal of Modern Literature*
JMMD	*Journal of Multilingual and Multicultural Development*
JMMLA	*Journal of the Midwest Modern Language Association*
JModH	*Journal of Modern History*
JMRS	*Journal of Medieval and Renaissance Studies*
JNLH	*Journal of Narrative and Life History*
JNPH	*Journal of Newspaper and Periodical History*
JNT	*Journal of Narrative Technique* (formerly *Technique*)
JNZL	*Journal of New Zealand Literature*
Jouvert	*Jouvert: A Journal of Postcolonial Studies*
JoyceSA	*Joyce Studies Annual*
JP	*Journal of Philosophy*
JPC	*Journal of Popular Culture*
JPCL	*Journal of Pidgin and Creole Languages*
JPhon	*Journal of Phonetics*
JPJ	*Journal of Psychology and Judaism*
JPrag	*Journal of Pragmatics*

JPRAS	*Journal of Pre-Raphaelite and Aesthetic Studies*
JPsyR	*Journal of Psycholinguistic Research*
JQ	*Journalism Quarterly*
JR	*Journal of Religion*
JRAHS	*Journal of the Royal Australian Historical Society*
JRH	*Journal of Religious History*
JRMA	*Journal of the Royal Musical Association*
JRMMRA	*Journal of the Rocky Mountain Medieval and Renaissance Association*
JRSA	*Journal of the Royal Society of Arts*
JRUL	*Journal of the Rutgers University Libraries*
JSA	*Journal of the Society of Archivists*
JSaga	*Journal of the Faculty of Liberal Arts and Science* (Saga University)
JSAS	*Journal of Southern African Studies*
JScholP	*Journal of Scholarly Publishing*
JSem	*Journal of Semantics*
JSoc	*Journal of Sociolinguistics*
JSSE	*Journal of the Short Story in English*
JTheoS	*Journal of Theological Studies*
JVC	*Journal of Victorian Culture*
JWCI	*Journal of the Warburg and Courtauld Institutes*
JWH	*Journal of Women's History*
JWIL	*Journal of West Indian Literature*
JWMS	*Journal of the William Morris Society*
JWSL	*Journal of Women's Studies in Literature*
KanE	*Kansas English*
KanQ	*Kansas Quarterly*
KB	*Kavya Bharati*
KCLMS	King's College London Medieval Series
KCS	*Kobe College Studies* (Japan)
KJ	*Kipling Journal*
KN	*Kwartalnik Neoflologiczny* (Warsaw)
KompH	*Komparatistische Hefte*
Kotare	*Kotare: New Zealand Notes and Queries*
KPR	*Kentucky Philological Review*
KR	*Kenyon Review*
KSJ	*Keats–Shelley Journal*
KSR	*Keats–Shelley Review*
Kuka	*Kuka: Journal of Creative and Critical Writing* (Zaria, Nigeria)
Kunapipi	*Kunapipi*
KWS	*Key-Word Studies in Chaucer*
L&A	*Literature and Aesthetics*
L&B	*Literature and Belief*
L&C	*Language and Communication*
L&E	*Linguistics and Education: An International Research Journal*

Landfall	*Landfall: A New Zealand Quarterly*
L&H	*Literature and History*
L&L	*Language and Literature*
L&LC	*Literary and Linguistic Computing*
L&M	*Literature and Medicine*
L&P	*Literature and Psychology*
L&S	*Language and Speech*
L&T	*Literature and Theology: An Interdisciplinary Journal of Theory and Criticism*
L&U	*Lion and the Unicorn: A Critical Journal of Children's Literature*
Lang&S	*Language and Style*
LangF	*Language Forum*
LangQ	*USF Language Quarterly*
LangR	*Language Research*
LangS	*Language Sciences*
Language	*Language* (Linguistic Society of America)
LanM	*Les Langues Modernes*
LATR	*Latin American Theatre Review*
LaTrobe	*La Trobe Journal*
LB	*Leuvense Bijdragen*
LBR	*Luso-Brazilian Review*
LCrit	*Literary Criterion* (Mysore, India)
LCUT	*Library Chronicle* (University of Texas at Austin)
LDOCE	*Longman Dictionary of Contemporary English*
LeedsSE	*Leeds Studies in English*
Legacy	*Legacy: A Journal of Nineteenth-Century American Women Writers*
L'EpC	*L'Epoque Conradienne*
LeS	*Lingua e Stile*
Lexicographica	*Lexicographica: International Annual for Lexicography*
Lexicography	*Lexicography*
LFQ	*Literature/Film Quarterly*
LH	*Library History*
LHY	*Literary Half-Yearly*
Library	*Library*
LibrQ	*Library Quarterly*
LIN	*Linguistics in the Netherlands*
LingA	*Linguistic Analysis*
Ling&P	*Linguistics and Philosophy*
Ling&Philol	*Linguistics and Philology*
LingB	*Linguistische Berichte*
LingI	*Linguistic Inquiry*
LingInv	*Linvisticæ Investigationes*
LingP	*Linguistica Pragensia*
Lingua	*Lingua: International Review of General Linguistics*
Linguistics	*Linguistics*
Linguistique	*La Linguistique*

LiNQ	*Literature in Northern Queensland*
LIT	*LIT: Literature, Interpretation, Theory*
LitH	*Literary Horizons*
LitI	*Literary Imagination*
LitR	*Literary Review: An International Journal of Contemporary Writing*
LittPrag	*Litteraria Pragensia: Studies in Literature and Culture*
LJCS	*London Journal of Canadian Studies*
LJGG	*Literaturwissenschaftliches Jahrbuch im Aufrage der Görres-Gesellschaft*
LJHum	*Lamar Journal of the Humanities*
LMag	*London Magazine*
LockeN	*Locke Newsletter*
LocusF	*Locus Focus*
LongR	*Long Room: Bulletin of the Friends of the Library* (Trinity College, Dublin)
Lore&L	*Lore and Language*
LP	*Lingua Posnaniensis*
LPLD	*Liverpool Papers in Language and Discourse*
LPLP	*Language Problems and Language Planning*
LR	*Les Lettres Romanes*
LRB	*London Review of Books*
LSE	Lund Studies in English
LSLD	Liverpool Studies in Language and Discourse
LSoc	*Language in Society*
LSp	*Language and Speech*
LST	Longman Study Texts
LTM	Leeds Texts and Monographs
LTP	*LTP: Journal of Literature Teaching Politics*
LTR	*London Theatre Record*
LuK	*Literatur und Kritik*
LVC	*Language Variation and Change*
LWU	*Literatur in Wissenschaft und Unterricht*
M&Lang	*Mind and Language*
MÆ	*Medium Ævum*
MAEL	Macmillan Anthologies of English Literature
MaComère	*MaComère*
MagL	*Magazine Littéraire*
Mana	*Mana*
M&H	*Medievalia et Humanistica*
M&L	*Music and Letters*
M&N	*Man and Nature / L'Homme et la Nature: Proceedings of the Canadian Society for Eighteenth-Century Studies*
Manuscripta	*Manuscripta*
MAR	*Mid-American Review*
Margin	*Margin*
MarkhamR	*Markham Review*
Matatu	*Matatu*

Matrix	*Matrix*
MBL	*Modern British Literature*
MC&S	*Media, Culture and Society*
MCI	Modern Critical Interpretations
MCJNews	*Milton Centre of Japan News*
McNR	*McNeese Review*
MCRel	*Mythes, Croyances et Religions dans le Monde Anglo-Saxon*
MCV	Modern Critical Views
MD	*Modern Drama*
ME	*Medieval Encounters*
Meanjin	*Meanjin*
MED	*Middle English Dictionary*
Mediaevalia	*Mediaevalia: A Journal of Mediaeval Studies*
MedPers	*Medieval Perspectives*
MELUS	*MELUS: The Journal of the Society of Multi-Ethnic Literature of the United States*
Meridian	*Meridian*
MESN	*Mediaeval English Studies Newsletter*
MET	Middle English Texts
METh	*Medieval English Theatre*
MFF	*Medieval Feminist Forum* (formerly *Medieval Feminist Newsletter*)
MFN	*Medieval Feminist Newsletter* (now *Medieval Feminist Forum*)
MFS	*Modern Fiction Studies*
MH	*Malahat Review*
MHL	Macmillan History of Literature
MHLS	*Mid-Hudson Language Studies*
MichA	*Michigan Academician*
MiltonQ	*Milton Quarterly*
MiltonS	*Milton Studies*
MinnR	*Minnesota Review*
MissQ	*Mississippi Quarterly*
MissR	*Missouri Review*
Mittelalter	*Das Mittelalter: Perspektiven Mediavistischer Forschung*
MJLF	*Midwestern Journal of Language and Folklore*
ML	*Music and Letters*
MLAIB	*Modern Language Association International Bibliography*
MLing	*Modelès Linguistiques*
MLJ	*Modern Language Journal*
MLN	*Modern Language Notes*
MLQ	*Modern Language Quarterly*
MLR	*Modern Language Review*
MLRev	*Malcolm Lowry Review*
MLS	*Modern Language Studies*
MMD	Macmillan Modern Dramatists
MMG	Macmillan Master Guides

MMisc	*Midwestern Miscellany*
MOCS	*Magazine of Cultural Studies*
ModA	*Modern Age: A Quarterly Review*
ModET	*Modern English Teacher*
ModM	*Modern Masters*
ModSp	*Moderne Sprachen*
Mo/Mo	*Modernism/Modernity*
Monist	*Monist*
MonSP	*Monash Swift Papers*
Month	*Month: A Review of Christian Thought and World Affairs*
MOR	*Mount Olive Review*
Moreana	*Moreana: Bulletin Thomas More* (Angers, France)
Mosaic	*Mosaic: A Journal for the Interdisciplinary Study of Literature*
MoyA	*Moyen Age*
MP	*Modern Philology*
MPHJ	*Middlesex Polytechnic History Journal*
MPR	*Mervyn Peake Review*
MQ	*Midwest Quarterly*
MQR	*Michigan Quarterly Review*
MR	*Massachusetts Review*
MRDE	*Medieval and Renaissance Drama in England*
MRTS	Medieval and Renaissance Texts and Studies
MS	*Mediaeval Studies*
MSC	Malone Society Collections
MSE	*Massachusetts Studies in English*
MSEx	*Melville Society Extracts*
MSh	Macmillan Shakespeare
MSNH	Mémoires de la Société Néophilologique de Helsinki
MSpr	*Moderna Språk*
MSR	Malone Society Reprints
MSSN	*Medieval Sermon Studies Newsletter*
MT	*Musical Times*
MTJ	*Mark Twain Journal*
MusR	*Music Review*
MW	*Muslim World* (Hartford, CT)
MysticsQ	*Mystics Quarterly*
Mythlore	*Mythlore: A Journal of J.R.R. Tolkein, C.S. Lewis, Charles Williams, and the Genres of Myth and Fantasy Studies*
NA	*Nuova Antologia*
Names	*Names: Journal of the American Name Society*
NAmR	*North American Review*
N&F	*Notes & Furphies*
N&Q	*Notes and Queries*
Narrative	*Narrative*
Navasilu	*Navasilu*
NB	*Namn och Bygd*
NCaS	New Cambridge Shakespeare

NCBEL	*New Cambridge Bibliography of English Literature*
NCC	*Nineteenth-Century Contexts*
NCE	Norton Critical Editions
NCFS	*Nineteenth-Century French Studies*
NCL	*Nineteenth-Century Literature*
NConL	*Notes on Contemporary Literature*
NCP	*Nineteenth-Century Prose*
NCS	New Clarendon Shakespeare
NCSR	New Chaucer Society Readings
NCSTC	Nineteenth-Century Short Title Catalogue
NCStud	*Nineteenth-Century Studies*
NCT	*Nineteenth-Century Theatre*
NDQ	*North Dakota Quarterly*
NegroD	*Negro Digest*
NELS	*North Eastern Linguistic Society*
Neoh	*Neohelicon*
Neophil	*Neophilologus*
NEQ	*New England Quarterly*
NERMS	*New England Review*
NewA	*New African*
NewBR	*New Beacon Review*
NewC	*New Criterion*
New Casebooks	New Casebooks: Contemporary Critical Essays
NewComp	*New Comparison: A Journal of Comparative and General Literary Studies*
NewF	*New Formations*
NewR	*New Republic*
NewSt	*Newfoundland Studies*
NewV	*New Voices*
NF	*Neiophilologica Fennica*
NfN	*News from Nowhere*
NFS	*Nottingham French Studies*
NGC	*New German Critique*
NGS	*New German Studies*
NH	*Northern History*
NHR	*Nathaniel Hawthorne Review*
NJL	*Nordic Journal of Linguistics*
NL	*Nouvelles Littéraires*
NL&LT	*Natural Language and Linguistic Theory*
NLH	*New Literary History: A Journal of Theory and Interpretation*
NLitsR	*New Literatures Review*
NLR	*New Left Review*
NLS	*Natural Language Semantics*
NLWJ	*National Library of Wales Journal*
NM	*Neuphilologische Mitteilungen*
NMAL	*NMAL: Notes on Modern American Literature*
NMer	New Mermaids

NMIL	*Notes on Modern Irish Literature*
NMS	*Nottingham Medieval Studies*
NMW	*Notes on Mississippi Writers*
NN	*Nordiska Namenstudier*
NNER	*Northern New England Review*
Nomina	*Nomina: A Journal of Name Studies Relating to Great Britain and Ireland*
NoP	*Northern Perspective*
NOR	*New Orleans Review*
NorfolkA	*Norfolk Archaeology*
NortonCE	Norton Critical Edition
Novel	*Novel: A Forum on Fiction*
NOWELE	*North-Western European Language Evolution*
NPS	New Penguin Shakespeare
NR	*Nassau Review*
NRF	*La Nouvelle Revue Française*
NRRS	*Notes and Records of the Royal Society of London*
NS	*Die neuren Sprachen*
NSS	New Swan Shakespeare
NTQ	*New Theatre Quarterly*
NVSAWC	*Newsletter of the Victorian Studies Association of Western Canada*
NwJ	*Northward Journal*
NWR	*Northwest Review*
NWRev	*New Welsh Review*
NYH	*New York History*
NYLF	New York Literary Forum
NYRB	*New York Review of Books*
NYT	*New York Times*
NYTBR	*New York Times Book Review*
NZB	*New Zealand Books*
NZListener	*New Zealand Listener*
OA	Oxford Authors
OB	*Ord och Bild*
Obsidian	*Obsidian II: Black Literature in Review*
OBSP	Oxford Bibliographical Society Publications
OED	*Oxford English Dictionary*
OENews	*Old English Newsletter*
OET	Oxford English Texts
OH	*Over Here: An American Studies Journal*
OHEL	Oxford History of English Literature
OhR	*Ohio Review*
OLR	*Oxford Literary Review*
OPBS	*Occasional Papers of the Bibliographical Society*
OpenGL	Open Guides to Literature
OpL	*Open Letter*
OPL	Oxford Poetry Library
OPLiLL	*Occasional Papers in Linguistics and Language Learning*

OPSL	*Occasional Papers in Systemic Linguistics*
OralT	*Oral Tradition*
Orbis	*Orbis*
OrbisLit	*Orbis Litterarum*
OS	Oxford Shakespeare
OSS	Oxford Shakespeare Studies
OT	*Oral Tradition*
Outrider	*Outrider: A Publication of the Wyoming State Library*
Overland	*Overland*
PA	*Présence Africaine*
PAAS	*Proceedings of the American Antiquarian Society*
PacStud	*Pacific Studies*
Paideuma	*Paideuma: A Journal Devoted to Ezra Pound Scholarship*
PAJ	*Performing Art Journal*
P&C	*Pragmatics and Cognition*
P&CT	*Psychoanalysis and Contemporary Thought*
P&L	*Philosophy and Literature*
P&P	*Past and Present*
P&R	*Philosophy and Rhetoric*
P&SC	*Philosophy and Social Criticism*
PAPA	*Publications of the Arkansas Philological Association*
Papers	*Papers: Explorations into Children's Literature*
PAPS	*Proceedings of the American Philosophical Society*
PAR	*Performing Arts Resources*
Parabola	*Parabola: The Magazine of Myth and Tradition*
Paragraph	*Paragraph: The Journal of the Modern Critical Theory Group*
Parergon	*Parergon: Bulletin of the Australian and New Zealand Association for Medieval and Renaissance Studies*
ParisR	*Paris Review*
Parnassus	*Parnassus: Poetry in Review*
PastM	Past Masters
PaterN	*Pater Newsletter*
PAus	*Poetry Australia*
PBA	*Proceedings of the British Academy*
PBerLS	*Proceedings of the Berkeley Linguistics Society*
PBSA	*Papers of the Bibliographical Society of America*
PBSC	*Papers of the Biographical Society of Canada*
PCL	*Perspectives on Contemporary Literature*
PCLAC	*Proceedings of the California Linguistics Association Conference*
PCLS	*Proceedings of the Comparative Literature Symposium* (Lubbock, TX)
PCP	*Pacific Coast Philology*
PCRev	*Popular Culture Review*
PCS	Penguin Critical Studies
PEAN	*Proceedings of the English Association North*

PE&W	*Philosophy East and West: A Quarterly of Asian and Comparative Thought*
PELL	*Papers on English Language and Literature* (Japan)
Pequod	*Pequod: A Journal of Contemporary Literature and Literary Criticism*
Performance	*Performance*
Peritia	*Peritia: Journal of the Medieval Academy of Ireland*
Persuasions	*Persuasions: Journal of the Jane Austen Society of North America*
Philosophy	*Philosophy*
PHist	*Printing History*
Phonetica	*Phonetica: International Journal of Speech Science*
PHOS	Publishing History Occasional Series
PhRA	*Philosophical Research Archives*
PhT	*Philosophy Today*
PiL	*Papers in Linguistics*
PIMA	*Proceedings of the Illinois Medieval Association*
PinterR	*Pinter Review*
PJCL	*Prairie Journal of Canadian Literature*
PLL	*Papers on Language and Literature*
PLPLS	*Proceedings of the Leeds Philosophical and Literary Society, Literary and Historical Section*
PM	*Penguin Masterstudies*
PMHB	*Pennsylvania Magazine of History and Biography*
PMLA	*Publications of the Modern Language Association of America*
PMPA	*Proceedings of the Missouri Philological Association*
PNotes	*Pynchon Notes*
PNR	*Poetry and Nation Review*
PoeS	*Poe Studies*
Poetica	*Poetica: Zeitschrift für Sprach- und Literaturwissenschaft* (Amsterdam)
PoeticaJ	*Poetica: An International Journal of Linguistic-Literary Studies* (Tokyo)
Poetics	*Poetics: International Review for the Theory of Literature*
Poétique	*Poétique: Revue de Théorie et d'Analyse Littéraires*
Poetry	*Poetry* (Chicago)
PoetryCR	*Poetry Canada Review*
PoetryR	*Poetry Review*
PoetryW	*Poetry Wales*
POMPA	*Publications of the Mississippi Philological Association*
PostS	*Past Script: Essays in Film and the Humanities*
PoT	*Poetics Today*
PP	Penguin Passnotes
PP	*Philologica Pragensia*
PPMRC	*Proceedings of the International Patristic, Mediaeval and Renaissance Conference*
PPR	*Philosophy and Phenomenological Research*

PQ	*Philological Quarterly*
PQM	*Pacific Quarterly* (Moana)
PR	*Partisan Review*
Pragmatics	*Pragmatics: Quarterly Publication of the International Pragmatics Association*
PrairieF	*Prairie Fire*
Praxis	*Praxis: A Journal of Cultural Criticism*
Prépub	*(Pré)publications*
PRev	*Powys Review*
PRIA	*Proceedings of the Royal Irish Academy*
PRIAA	Publications of the Research Institute of the Abo Akademi Foundation
PRMCLS	*Papers from the Regional Meetings of the Chicago Linguistics Society*
Prospects	*Prospects: An Annual Journal of American Cultural Studies*
Prospero	*Prospero: Journal of New Thinking in Philosophy for Education*
Proteus	*Proteus: A Journal of Ideas*
Proverbium	*Proverbium*
PrS	*Prairie Schooner*
PSt	*Prose Studies*
PsyArt	*Psychological Study of the Arts* (hyperlink journal)
PsychR	*Psychological Reports*
PTBI	Publications of the Sir Thomas Browne Institute
PubH	*Publishing History*
PULC	*Princeton University Library Chronicle*
PURBA	*Panjab University Research Bulletin (Arts)*
PVR	*Platte Valley Review*
PWC	*Pickering's Women's Classics*
PY	*Phonology Yearbook*
QDLLSM	*Quaderni del Dipartimento e Lingue e Letterature Straniere Moderne*
QI	*Quaderni d'Italianistica*
QJS	*Quarterly Journal of Speech*
QLing	*Quantitative Linguistics*
QQ	*Queen's Quarterly*
QR	*Queensland Review*
QRFV	*Quarterly Review of Film and Video*
Quadrant	*Quadrant* (Sydney)
Quarendo	*Quarendo*
Quarry	*Quarry*
QWERTY	*QWERTY: Arts, Littératures, et Civilisations du Monde Anglophone*
RadP	*Radical Philosophy*
RAL	*Research in African Literatures*
RALS	*Resources for American Literary Study*
Ramus	*Ramus: Critical Studies in Greek and Roman Literature*

R&L	*Religion and Literature*
Raritan	*Raritan: A Quarterly Review*
Rask	*Rask: International tidsskrift for sprong og kommunikation*
RB	*Revue Bénédictine*
RBPH	*Revue Belge de Philologie et d'Histoire*
RCEI	*Revista Canaria de Estudios Ingleses*
RCF	*Review of Contemporary Fiction*
RCPS	*Romantic Circles Praxis Series* (online)
RDN	*Renaissance Drama Newsletter*
RE	*Revue d'Esthétique*
ReAL	*Re: Artes Liberales*
REALB	*REAL: The Yearbook of Research in English and American Literature* (Berlin)
ReAr	*Religion and the Arts*
RecBucks	*Records of Buckinghamshire*
RecL	*Recovery Literature*
RECTR	*Restoration and Eighteenth-Century Theatre Research*
RedL	*Red Letters: A Journal of Cultural Politics*
REED	Records of Early English Drama
REEDN	*Records of Early English Drama Newsletter*
ReFr	*Revue Française*
Reinardus	*Reinardus*
REL	*Review of English Literature* (Kyoto)
RELC	*RELC Journal: A Journal of Language Teaching and Research in Southeast Asia*
Ren&R	*Renaissance and Reformation*
Renascence	*Renascence: Essays on Values in Literature*
RenD	*Renaissance Drama*
Renfor	*Renaissance Forum* (online)
RenP	*Renaissance Papers*
RenQ	*Renaissance Quarterly*
Rep	*Representations*
RePublica	*RePublica*
RES	*Review of English Studies*
Restoration	*Restoration: Studies in English Literary Culture, 1660–1700*
Rev	*Review* (Blacksburg, VA)
RevAli	*Revista Alicantina de Estudios Ingleses*
Revels	Revels Plays
RevelsCL	Revels Plays Companion Library
RevelsSE	Revels Student Editions
RevR	Revolution and Romanticism, 1789–1834
RFEA	*Revue Française d'Études Américaines*
RFR	*Robert Frost Review*
RG	*Revue Générale*
RH	*Recusant History*
Rhetorica	*Rhetorica: A Journal of the History of Rhetoric*
Rhetorik	*Rhetorik: Ein Internationales Jahrbuch*

RHist	*Rural History*
RHL	*Revue d'Histoire Littéraire de la France*
RHT	*Revue d'Histoire du Théâtre*
RIB	*Revista Interamericana de Bibliografia: Inter-American Reviews of Bibliography*
Ricardian	*Ricardian: Journal of the Richard III Society*
RL	Rereading Literature
RLAn	*Romance Languages Annual*
RLC	*Revue de Littérature Comparée*
RLing	*Rivista di Linguistica*
RLit	*Russian Literature*
RLM	*La Revue des Lettres Modernes: Histoire des Idées des Littératures*
RLMC	*Rivista di Letterature Moderne e Comparate*
RLT	*Russian Literature Triquarterly*
RM	*Rethinking Marxism*
RMR	*Rocky Mountain Review of Language and Literature*
RM	*Renaissance and Modern Studies*
RMSt	*Reading Medieval Studies*
Romania	*Romania*
RomN	*Romance Notes*
RomQ	*Romance Quarterly*
RomS	*Romance Studies*
RoN	*Romanticism on the Net*
ROO	*Room of One's Own: A Feminist Journal of Literature and Criticism*
RORD	*Research Opportunities in Renaissance Drama*
RPT	Russian Poetics in Translation
RQ	*Riverside Quarterly*
RR	*Romanic Review*
RRDS	Regents Renaissance Drama Series
RRestDS	Regents Restoration Drama Series
RS	*Renaissance Studies*
RSQ	*Rhetoric Society Quarterly*
RSV	*Rivista di Studi Vittoriani*
RUO	*Revue de l'Université d'Ottawa*
RUSEng	*Rajasthan University Studies in English*
RuskN	*Ruskin Newsletter*
RUUL	*Reports from the Uppsala University Department of Linguistics*
R/WT	*Readerly/Writerly Texts*
SAC	*Studies in the Age of Chaucer*
SAD	*Studies in American Drama, 1945–Present*
SAF	*Studies in American Fiction*
Saga-Book	*Saga-Book (Viking Society for Northern Research)*
Sagetrieb	*Sagatrieb: A Journal Devoted to Poets in the Pound–H.D.– Williams Tradition*

SAIL	Studies in American Indian Literatures: The Journal of the Association for the Study of American Indian Literatures
SAJL	Studies in American Jewish Literature
SAJMRS	South African Journal of Medieval and Renaissance Studies
Sal	Salmagrundi: A Quarterly of the Humanities and Social Sciences
SALCT	SALCT: Studies in Australian Literature, Culture and Thought
S&S	Sight and Sound
SAntS	Studia Anthroponymica Scandinavica
SAP	Studia Anglica Posnaniensia
SAQ	South Atlantic Quarterly
SAR	Studies in the American Renaissance
SARB	South African Review of Books
SatR	Saturday Review
SB	Studies in Bibliography
SBHC	Studies in Browning and his Circle
SC	Seventeenth Century
Scan	Scandinavica: An International Journal of Scandinavian Studies
ScanS	Scandinavian Studies
SCel	Studia Celtica
SCER	Society for Critical Exchange Report
Schuylkill	Schuylkill: A Creative and Critical Review (Temple University)
SCJ	Sixteenth Century Journal
SCL	Studies in Canadian Literature
ScLJ	Scottish Literary Journal: A Review of Studies in Scottish Language and Literature
ScLJ(S)	Scottish Literary Journal Supplement
SCN	Seventeenth-Century News
ScottN	Scott Newsletter
SCR	South Carolina Review
Screen	Screen (London)
SCRev	South Central Review
Scriblerian	Scriblerian and the Kit Cats: A Newsjournal Devoted to Pope, Swift, and their Circle
Scripsi	Scripsi
Scriptorium	Scriptorium: International Review of Manuscript Studies
SD	Social Dynamics
SDR	South Dakota Review
SECC	Studies in Eighteenth-Century Culture
SECOLR	SECOL Review: Southeastern Conference on Linguistics
SED	Survey of English Dialects
SEDERI	Journal of the Spanish Society for Renaissance Studies (Sociedad Española de Estudios Renacentistas Ingleses)
SEEJ	Slavic and East European Journal

SEL	*Studies in English Literature, 1500–1900* (Rice University)
SELing	*Studies in English Linguistics* (Tokyo)
SELit	*Studies in English Literature* (Tokyo)
SELL	*Studies in English Language and Literature*
Sem	*Semiotica: Journal of the International Association for Semiotic Studies*
Semiosis	*Semiosis: Internationale Zeitschrift für Semiotik und Ästhetik*
SER	*Studien zur Englischen Romantik*
Seven	*Seven: An Anglo-American Literary Review*
SF&R	Scholars' Facsimiles and Reprints
SFic	*Science Fiction: A Review of Speculative Literature*
SFNL	*Shakespeare on Film Newsletter*
SFQ	*Southern Folklore Quarterly*
SFR	*Stanford French Review*
SFS	*Science-Fiction Studies*
SH	*Studia Hibernica* (Dublin)
ShakB	*Shakespeare Bulletin*
ShakS	*Shakespeare Studies* (New York)
Shandean	*Shandean*
Sh&Sch	*Shakespeare and Schools*
ShawR	*Shaw: The Annual of Bernard Shaw Studies*
Shenandoah	*Shenandoah*
SherHR	*Sherlock Holmes Review*
Shiron	*Shiron*
ShJE	*Shakespeare Jahrbuch* (Weimar)
ShJW	*Deutsche Shakespeare-Gesellschaft West Jahrbuch* (Bochum)
ShLR	*Shoin Literary Review*
ShN	*Shakespeare Newsletter*
SHR	*Southern Humanities Review*
ShS	*Shakespeare Survey*
ShSA	*Shakespeare in Southern Africa*
ShStud	*Shakespeare Studies* (Tokyo)
SHW	*Studies in Hogg and his World*
ShY	*Shakespeare Yearbook*
SiAF	*Studies in American Fiction*
SIcon	*Studies in Iconography*
SidN	*Sidney Newsletter and Journal*
Signs	*Signs: Journal of Women in Culture and Society*
SiHoLS	*Studies in the History of the Language Sciences*
SiM	*Studies in Medievalism*
SIM	*Studies in Music*
SiP	Shakespeare in Performance
SiPr	Shakespeare in Production
SiR	*Studies in Romanticism*
SJS	*San José Studies*
SL	*Studia Linguistica*

SLang	*Studies in Language*
SLCS	*Studies in Language Companion Series*
SLI	*Studies in the Literary Imagination*
SLJ	*Southern Literary Journal*
SLRev	*Stanford Literature Review*
SLSc	*Studies in the Linguistic Sciences*
SMC	*Studies in Medieval Culture*
SMed	*Studi Medievali*
SMELL	*Studies in Medieval English Language and Literature*
SMLit	*Studies in Mystical Literature* (Taiwan)
SMRH	*Studies in Medieval and Renaissance History*
SMS	*Studier i Modern Språkvetenskap*
SMy	*Studia Mystica*
SN	*Studia Neophilologica*
SNNTS	*Studies in the Novel* (North Texas State University)
SO	*Shakespeare Originals*
SOA	*Sydsvenska Ortnamnssällskapets Årsskrift*
SoAR	*South Atlantic Review*
Sociocrit	*Sociocriticism*
Socioling	*Sociolinguistica*
SocN	*Sociolinguistics*
SocSem	*Social Semiotics*
SocT	*Social Text*
SohoB	Soho Bibliographies
SoQ	*Southern Quarterly*
SoR	*Southern Review* (Baton Rouge, LA)
SoRA	*Southern Review* (Adelaide)
SoSt	*Southern Studies: An Interdisciplinary Journal of the South*
Soundings	*Soundings: An Interdisciplinary Journal*
Southerly	*Southerly: A Review of Australian Literature*
SovL	*Soviet Literature*
SP	*Studies in Philology*
SPAN	*SPAN: Newsletter of the South Pacific Association for Commonwealth Literature and Language Studies*
SPAS	*Studies in Puritan American Spirituality*
SPC	*Studies in Popular Culture*
Spectrum	*Spectrum*
Speculum	*Speculum: A Journal of Medieval Studies*
SPELL	*Swiss Papers in English Language and Literature*
Sphinx	*Sphinx: A Magazine of Literature and Society*
SpM	*Spicilegio Moderno*
SpNL	*Spenser Newsletter*
Sprachwiss	*Sprachwissenschalt*
SpringE	*Spring: The Journal of the e.e. cummings Society*
SPub	*Studies in Publishing*
SPWVSRA	*Selected Papers from the West Virginia Shakespeare and Renaissance Association*
SQ	*Shakespeare Quarterly*

SR	*Sewanee Review*
SRen	*Studies in the Renaissance*
SRSR	*Status Report on Speech Research* (Haskins Laboratories)
SSEL	Stockholm Studies in English
SSELER	Salzburg Studies in English Literature: Elizabethan and Renaissance
SSELJDS	Salzburg Studies in English Literature: Jacobean Drama Studies
SSELPDPT	Salzburg Studies in English Literature: Poetic Drama and Poetic Theory
SSELRR	Salzburg Studies in English Literature: Romantic Reassessment
SSEng	*Sydney Studies in English*
SSF	*Studies in Short Fiction*
SSL	*Studies in Scottish Literature*
SSR	*Scottish Studies Review*
SSt	*Spenser Studies*
SStud	*Swift Studies: The Annual of the Ehrenpreis Center*
Staffrider	*Staffrider*
StaffordS	*Staffordshire Studies*
STAH	*Strange Things Are Happening*
STGM	Studien und Texte zur Geistegeschichte des Mittelalters
StHR	*Stanford Historical Review*
StHum	*Studies in the Humanities*
StIn	*Studi Inglesi*
StLF	*Studi di Letteratura Francese*
StQ	*Steinbeck Quarterly*
StrR	*Structuralist Review*
StTCL	*Studies in Twentieth-Century Literature*
StTW	*Studies in Travel Writing*
StudWF	*Studies in Weird Fiction*
STUF	*Sprachtypologie und Universalienforschung*
Style	*Style* (De Kalb, IL)
SUAS	*Stratford-upon-Avon Studies*
SubStance	*SubStance: A Review of Theory and Literary Criticism*
SUS	*Susquehanna University Studies*
SussexAC	*Sussex Archaeological Collections*
SussexP&P	*Sussex Past & Present*
SVEC	*Studies on Voltaire and the Eighteenth Century*
SWPLL	*Sheffield Working Papers in Language and Linguistics*
SWR	*Southwest Review*
SwR	*Swansea Review: A Journal of Criticism*
Sycamore	*Sycamore*
Symbolism	*Symbolism: An International Journal of Critical Aesthetics*
TA	*Theatre Annual*
Tabu	*Bulletin voor Taalwetenschap, Groningen*
Takahe	*Takahe*
Talisman	*Talisman*

T&C	*Text and Context*
T&L	*Translation and Literature*
T&P	*Text and Performance*
TAPS	*Transactions of the American Philosophical Society*
TCBS	*Transactions of the Cambridge Bibliographical Society*
TCE	*Texas College English*
TCL	*Twentieth-Century Literature*
TCS	*Theory, Culture and Society: Explorations in Critical Social Science*
TCWAAS	*Transactions of the Cumberland and Westmorland Antiquarian and Archaeological Society*
TD	*Themes in Drama*
TDR	*Drama Review*
TEAS	Twayne's English Authors Series
Telos	*Telos: A Quarterly Journal of Post-Critical Thought*
TennEJ	*Tennessee English Journal*
TennQ	*Tennessee Quarterly*
TennSL	*Tennessee Studies in Literature*
Te Reo	*Te Reo: Journal of the Linguistic Society of New Zealand*
TexasSLL	*Texas Studies in Language and Literature*
Text	*Text: Transactions of the Society for Textual Scholarship*
TH	*Texas Humanist*
THA	*Thomas Hardy Annual*
Thalia	*Thalia: Studies in Literary Humor*
ThC	*Theatre Crafts*
Theater	*Theater*
TheatreS	*Theatre Studies*
Theoria	*Theoria: A Journal of Studies in the Arts, Humanities and Social Sciences* (Natal)
THES	*Times Higher Education Supplement*
Thesis	*Thesis Eleven*
THIC	*Theatre History in Canada*
THJ	*Thomas Hardy Journal*
ThN	*Thackeray Newsletter*
ThoreauQ	*Thoreau Quarterly: A Journal of Literary and Philosophical Studies*
Thought	*Thought: A Review of Culture and Ideas*
Thph	*Theatrephile*
ThreR	*Threepenny Review*
ThS	*Theatre Survey: The American Journal of Theatre History*
THSLC	*Transactions of the Historic Society of Lancashire and Cheshire*
THStud	*Theatre History Studies*
ThTop	*Theatre Topics*
THY	*Thomas Hardy Yearbook*
TiLSM	*Trends in Linguistics: Studies and Monographs*
TiP	*Theory in Practice*
Tirra Lirra	*Tirra Lirra: The Quarterly Magazine for the Yarra Valley*

TJ	*Theatre Journal*
TJS	*Transactions* (Johnson Society)
TkR	*Tamkang Review*
TL	*Theoretical Linguistics*
TLR	*Linguistic Review*
TLS	*Times Literary Supplement*
TMLT	*Toronto Medieval Latin Texts*
TN	*Theatre Notebook*
TNWSECS	*Transactions of the North West Society for Eighteenth Century Studies*
TP	*Terzo Programma*
TPLL	*Tilbury Papers in Language and Literature*
TPQ	*Text and Performance Quarterly*
TPr	*Textual Practice*
TPS	*Transactions of the Philological Society*
TR	*Theatre Record*
Traditio	*Traditio: Studies in Ancient and Medieval History, Thought, and Religion*
Transition	*Transition*
TRB	*Tennyson Research Bulletin*
TRHS	*Transactions of the Royal Historical Society*
TRI	*Theatre Research International*
TriQ	*TriQuarterly*
Trivium	*Trivium*
Tropismes	*Tropismes*
TSAR	*Toronto South Asian Review*
TSB	*Thoreau Society Bulletin*
TSLang	Typological Studies in Language
TSLL	*Texas Studies in Literature and Language*
TSWL	*Tulsa Studies in Women's Literature*
TTR	*Trinidad and Tobago Review*
TUSAS	Twayne's United States Authors Series
TWAS	Twayne's World Authors Series
TWBR	*Third World Book Review*
TWQ	*Third World Quarterly*
TWR	*Thomas Wolfe Review*
TYDS	*Transactions of the Yorkshire Dialect Society*
Typophiles	Typophiles (New York)
UCrow	*Upstart Crow*
UCTSE	*University of Cape Town Studies in English*
UCWPL	*UCL Working Papers in Linguistics*
UDR	*University of Drayton Review*
UE	*Use of English*
UEAPL	*UEA Papers in Linguistics*
UES	*Unisa English Studies*
Ufahamu	*Ufahamu*
ULR	*University of Leeds Review*
UMSE	*University of Mississippi Studies in English*

Untold	*Untold*
UOQ	*University of Ottawa Quarterly*
URM	*Ultimate Reality and Meaning: Interdisciplinary Studies in the Philosophy of Understanding*
USSE	*University of Saga Studies in English*
UtopST	*Utopian Studies*
UTQ	*University of Toronto Quarterly*
UWR	*University of Windsor Review*
VCT	Les Voies de la Création Théâtrale
VEAW	Varieties of English around the World
Verbatim	*Verbatim: The Language Quarterly*
VIA	*VIA: The Journal of the Graduate School of Fine Arts* (University of Pennsylvania)
Viator	*Viator: Medieval and Renaissance Studies*
Views	*Viennese English Working Papers*
VIJ	*Victorians Institute Journal*
VLC	*Victorian Literature and Culture*
VN	*Victorian Newsletter*
Voices	*Voices*
VP	*Victorian Poetry*
VPR	*Victorian Periodicals Review*
VQR	*Virginia Quarterly Review*
VR	*Victorian Review*
VS	*Victorian Studies*
VSB	*Victorian Studies Bulletin*
VWM	*Virginia Woolf Miscellany*
WAJ	*Women's Art Journal*
WAL	*Western American Literature*
W&I	*Word and Image*
W&L	*Women and Literature*
W&Lang	*Women and Language*
Wasafiri	*Wasafiri*
WascanaR	*Wascana Review*
WBEP	Wiener Beiträge zur Englischen Philologie
WC	World's Classics
WC	*Wordsworth Circle*
WCR	*West Coast Review*
WCSJ	*Wilkie Collins Society Journal*
WCWR	*William Carlos Williams Review*
Wellsian	*Wellsian: The Journal of the H.G. Wells Society*
WEn	*World Englishes*
Westerly	*Westerly: A Quarterly Review*
WestHR	*West Hills Review: A Walt Whitman Journal*
WF	*Western Folklore*
WHASN	*W.H. Auden Society Newsletter*
WHR	*Western Humanities Review*
WI	*Word and Image*
WLA	*Wyndham Lewis Annual*

WL&A	War Literature, and the Arts: An International Journal of the Humanities
WLT	World Literature Today
WLWE	World Literature Written in English
WMQ	William and Mary Quarterly
WoHR	Women's History Review
WolfenbütteleB	Wolfenbüttele Beiträge: Aus den Schätzen der Herzog August Bibliothek
Women	Women: A Cultural Review
WorcesterR	Worcester Review
WORD	WORD: Journal of the International Linguistic Association
WQ	Wilson Quarterly
WRB	Women's Review of Books
WS	Women's Studies: An Interdisciplinary Journal
WSIF	Women's Studies: International Forum
WSJour	Wallace Stevens Journal
WSR	Wicazo Sa Review
WTJ	Westminster Theological Journal
WTW	Writers and their Work
WVUPP	West Virginia University Philological Papers
WW	Women's Writing
WWR	Walt Whitman Quarterly Review
XUS	Xavier Review
YCC	Yearbook of Comparative Criticism
YeA	Yeats Annual
YER	Yeats Eliot Review
YES	Yearbook of English Studies
YEuS	Yearbook of European Studies/Annuaire d'Études Européennes
YFS	Yale French Studies
Yiddish	Yiddish
YJC	Yale Journal of Criticism: Interpretation in the Humanities
YLS	Yearbook of Langland Studies
YM	Yearbook of Morphology
YNS	York Note Series
YPL	York Papers in Linguistics
YR	Yale Review
YULG	Yale University Library Gazette
YWES	Year's Work in English Studies
ZAA	Zeitschrift für Anglistik und Amerikanistik
ZCP	Zeitschrift für celtische Philologie
ZDA	Zeitschrift für deutsches Altertum und deutsche Literatur
ZDL	Zeitschrift für Dialektologie und Linguistik
ZGKS	Zeitschrfit für Gesellschaft für Kanada-Studien
ZGL	Zeitschrift für germanistische Linguistik
ZPSK	Zeitschrift für Phonetik, Sprachwissenshaft und Kommunikationsforschung
ZSpr	Zeitschrift für Sprachwissenshaft

ZVS   *Zeitschrift für vergleichende Sprachforschung*

Volume numbers are supplied in the text, as are individual issue numbers for
journals that are not continuously paginated through the year.

2. Publishers

AAAH	Acta Academiae Åboensis Humaniora, Åbo, Finland
AAH	Australian Academy of Humanities
A&B	Allison & Busby, London
A&R	Angus & Robertson, North Ryde, New South Wales
A&U	Allen & Unwin (now Unwin Hyman)
A&UA	Allen & Unwin, North Sydney, New South Wales
A&W	Almqvist & Wiksell International, Stockholm
AarhusUP	Aarhus UP, Aarhus, Denmark
ABC	ABC Enterprises
ABC CLIO	ABC CLIO Reference Books, Santa Barbara, CA
Abbeville	Abbeville Press, New York
ABDO	Association Bourguignonne de Dialectologie et d'Onomastique, Dijon
AberdeenUP	Aberdeen UP, Aberdeen
Abhinav	Abhinav Publications, New Delhi
Abingdon	Abingdon Press, Nashville, TN
ABL	Armstrong Browning Library, Waco, TX
Ablex	Ablex Publishing, Norwood, NJ
Åbo	Åbo Akademi, Åbo, Finland
Abrams	Harry N. Abrams, New York
Academia	Academia Press, Melbourne
Academic	Academic Press, London and Orlando, FL
Academy	Academy Press, Dublin
AcademyC	Academy Chicago Publishers, Chicago
AcademyE	Academy Editions, London
Acadiensis	Acadiensis Press, Fredericton, New Brunswick, Canada
ACarS	Association for Caribbean Studies, Coral Gables, FL
ACC	Antique Collectors' Club, Woodbridge, Suffolk
ACCO	ACCO, Leuven, Belgium
ACP	Another Chicago Press, Chicago
ACS	Association for Canadian Studies, Ottawa
Adam Hart	Adam Hart Publishers, London
Adam Matthew	Adam Matthew, Suffolk
Addison-Wesley	Addison-Wesley, Wokingham, Berkshire
ADFA	Australian Defence Force Academy, Department of English
Adosa	Adosa, Clermont-Ferrand, France
AEMS	American Early Medieval Studies
AF	Akademisk Forlag, Copenhagen
Affiliated	Affiliated East–West Press, New Delhi

AFP	Associated Faculty Press, New York
Africana	Africana Publications, New York
A–H	Arnold–Heinemann, New Delhi
Ahriman	Ahriman-Verlag, Freiburg im Breisgau, Germany
AIAS	Australian Institute of Aboriginal Studies, Canberra
Ajanta	Ajanta Publications, Delhi
AK	Akadémiai Kiadó, Budapest
ALA	ALA Editions, Chicago
Al&Ba	Allyn & Bacon, Boston, MA
Albatross	Albatross Books, Sutherland, New South Wales
Albion	Albion, Appalachian State University, Boone, NC
Alderman	Alderman Press, London
Aldwych	Aldwych Press
AligarhMU	Aligarh Muslim University, Uttar Pradesh, India
Alioth	Alioth Press, Beaverton, OR
Allen	W.H. Allen, London
Allied Publishers	Allied Indian Publishers, Lahore and New Delhi
Almond	Almond Press, Sheffield
AM	Aubier Montaigne, Paris
AMAES	Association des Médiévistes Angliciste de l'Enseignement Supérieur, Paris
Amate	Amate Press, Oxford
AmberL	Amber Lane, Oxford
Amistad	Amistad Press, New York
AMP	Aurora Metro Press, London
AMS	AMS Press, New York
AMU	Adam Mickiewicz University, Posnan
Anansi	Anansi Press, Toronto
Anderson-Lovelace	Anderson-Lovelace, Los Altos Hills, CA
Anma Libri	Anma Libri, Saratoga, CA
Antipodes	Antipodes Press, Plimmerton, New Zealand
Anvil	Anvil Press Poetry, London
APA	APA, Maarssen, Netherlands
APH	Associated Publishing House, New Delhi
APL	American Poetry and Literature Press, Philadelphia
APP	Australian Professional Publications, Mosman, New South Wales
Applause	Applause Theatre Book Publishers
Appletree	Appletree Press, Belfast
APS	American Philosophical Society, Philadelphia
Aquarian	Aquarian Press, Wellingborough, Northants
ArborH	Arbor House Publishing, New York
Arcade	Arcade Publishing, New York
Archon	Archon Books, Hamden, CT
ArchP	Architectural Press Books, Guildford, Surrey
ArdenSh	Arden Shakespeare
Ardis	Ardis Publishers, Ann Arbor, MI
Ariel	Ariel Press, London

Aristotle	Aristotle University, Thessaloniki
Ark	Ark Paperbacks, London
Arkona	Arkona Forlaget, Aarhus, Denmark
Arlington	Arlington Books, London
Arnold	Edward Arnold, London
ArnoldEJ	E.J. Arnold & Son, Leeds
ARP	Australian Reference Publications, N. Balwyn, Victoria
Arrow	Arrow Books, London
Artmoves	Artmoves, Parkdale, Victoria
ASAL	Association for the Study of Australian Literature
ASB	Anglo-Saxon Books, Middlesex
ASECS	American Society for Eighteenth-Century Studies, c/o Ohio State University, Columbus
Ashfield	Ashfield Press, London
Ashgate	Ashgate, Brookfield, VT
Ashton	Ashton Scholastic
Aslib	Aslib, London
ASLS	Association for Scottish Literary Studies, Aberdeen
ASU	Arizona State University, Tempe
Atheneum	Atheneum Publishers, New York
Athlone	Athlone Press, London
Atlas	Atlas Press, London
Attic	Attic Press, Dublin
AuBC	Australian Book Collector
AucklandUP	Auckland UP, Auckland
AUG	Acta Universitatis Gothoburgensis, Sweden
AUP	Associated University Presses, London and Toronto
AUPG	Academic & University Publishers, London
Aurum	Aurum Press, London
Auslib	Auslib Press, Adelaide
AUU	Acta Universitatis Umensis, Umeå, Sweden
AUUp	Acta Universitatis Upsaliensis, Uppsala
Avebury	Avebury Publishing, Aldershot, Hampshire
Avero	Avero Publications, Newcastle upon Tyne
A-V Verlag	A-V Verlag, Franz Fischer, Augsburg, Germany
AWP	Africa World Press, Trenton, NJ
Axelrod	Axelrod Publishing, Tampa Bay, FL
BA	British Academy, London
BAAS	British Association for American Studies, c/o University of Keele
Bagel	August Bagel Verlag, Dusseldorf
Bahri	Bahri Publications, New Delhi
Bamberger	Bamberger Books, Flint, MI
B&B	Boydell & Brewer, Woodbridge, Suffolk
B&J	Barrie & Jenkins, London
B&N	Barnes & Noble, Totowa, NJ
B&O	Burns & Oates, Tunbridge Wells, Kent

B&S	Michael Benskin and M.L. Samuels, Middle English Dialect Project, University of Edinburgh
BAR	British Archaelogical Reports, Oxford
Barn Owl	Barn Owl Books, Taunton, Somerset
Barnes	A.S. Barnes, San Diego, CA
Barr Smith	Barr Smith Press, Barr Smith Library, University of Adelaide
Bath UP	Bath UP, Bath
Batsford	B.T. Batsford, London
Bayreuth	Bayreuth African Studies, University of Bayreuth, Germany
BBC	BBC Publications, London
BClarkL	Bruccoli Clark Layman
BCP	Bristol Classical Press, Bristol
Beacon	Beacon Press, Boston, MA
Beck	C.H. Beck'sche Verlagsbuchandlung, Munich
Becket	Becket Publications, London
Belin	Éditions Belin, Paris
Belknap	Belknap Press, Cambridge, MA
Belles Lettres	Société d'Édition les Belles Lettres, Paris
Bellew	Bellew Publishing, London
Bellflower	Belflower Press, Case University, Cleveland, OH
Benjamins	John Benjamins, Amsterdam
BenjaminsNA	John Benjamins North America, Philadelphia
BennC	Bennington College, Bennington, VT
Berg	Berg Publishers, Oxford
BFI	British Film Institute, London
BGUP	Bowling Green University Popular Press, Bowling Green, OH
BibS	Bibliographical Society, London
Bilingual	Bilingual Press, Arizona State University, Tempe
Bingley	Clive Bingley, London
Binnacle	Binnacle Press, London
Biografia	Biografia Publishers, London
Birkbeck	Birkbeck College, University of London
Bishopsgate	Bishopsgate Press, Tonbridge, Kent
BL	British Library, London
Black	Adam & Charles Black, London
Black Cat	Black Cat Press, Blackrock, Eire
Blackie	Blackie & Son, Glasgow
Black Moss	Black Moss, Windsor, Ontario
Blackstaff	Blackstaff Press, Belfast
Black Swan	Black Swan, Curtin, UT
Blackwell	Basil Blackwell, Oxford
BlackwellR	Blackwell Reference, Oxford
Blackwood	Blackwood, Pillans & Wilson, Edinburgh
Bl&Br	Blond & Briggs, London
Blandford	Blandford Press, London

Blaue Eule	Verlag die Blaue Eule, Essen
Bloodaxe	Bloodaxe Books, Newcastle upon Tyne
Bloomsbury	Bloomsbury Publishing, London
Blubber Head	Blubber Head Press, Hobart
BM	Bobbs-Merrill, New York
BMP	British Museum Publications, London
Bodleian	Bodleian Library, Oxford
Bodley	Bodley Head, London
Bogle	Bogle L'Ouverture Publications, London
BoiseSUP	Boise State UP, Boise, Idaho
Book Guild	Book Guild, Lewes, E. Sussex
BookplateS	Bookplate Society, Edgbaston, Birmingham
Boombana	Boombana Press, Brisbane, Queensland
Borealis	Borealis Press, Ottawa
Borgo	Borgo Press, San Bernardino, CA
BostonAL	Boston Athenaeum Library, Boxton, MA
Bouma	Bouma's Boekhuis, Groningen, Netherlands
Bowker	R.R. Bowker, New Providence, NJ
Boyars	Marion Boyars, London and Boston, MA
Boydell	Boydell Press, Woodbridge, Suffolk
Boyes	Megan Boyes, Allestree, Derbyshire
Bran's Head	Bran's Head Books, Frome, Somerset
Braumüller	Wilhelm Braumüller, Vienna
Breakwater	Breakwater Books, St John's, Newfoundland
Brentham	Brentham Press, St Albans, Hertfordshire
Brepols	Brepols, Turnhout, Belgium
Brewer	D.S. Brewer, Woodbridge, Suffolk
Brewin	Brewin Books, Studley, Warwicks
Bridge	Bridge Publishing, S. Plainfield, NJ
Brill	E.J. Brill, Leiden
Brilliance	Brilliance Books, London
Broadview	Broadview, London, Ontario and Lewiston, NY
Brookside	Brookside Press, London
Browne	Sinclair Browne, London
Brownstone	Brownstone Books, Madison, IN
BrownUP	Brown UP, Providence, RI
Brynmill	Brynmill Press, Harleston, Norfolk
BSA	Bibliographical Society of America
BSB	Black Swan Books, Redding Ridge, CT
BSP	Black Sparrow Press, Santa Barbara, CA
BSU	Ball State University, Muncie, IN
BuckUP	Bucknell UP, Lewisburg, PA
Bulzoni	Bulzoni Editore, Rome
BUP	Birmingham University Press
Burnett	Burnett Books, London
Buske	Helmut Buske, Hamburg
Butterfly	Butterfly Books, San Antonio, TX
CA	Creative Arts Book, Berkeley, CA

CAAS	Connecticut Academy of Arts and Sciences, New Haven
CAB International	Centre for Agriculture and Biosciences International, Wallingford, Oxfordshire
Cadmus	Cadmus Editions, Tiburon, CA
Cairns	Francis Cairns, University of Leeds
Calaloux	Calaloux Publications, Ithaca, NY
Calder	John Calder, London
CALLS	Centre for Australian Language and Literature Studies, English Department, Universty of New England, New South Wales
Camden	Camden Press, London
C&G	Carroll & Graf, New York
C&W	Chatto & Windus, London
Canongate	Canongate Publishing, Edinburgh
Canterbury	Canterbury Press, Norwich
Cape	Jonathan Cape, London
Capra	Capra Press, Santa Barbara, CA
Carcanet	Carcanet New Press, Manchester, Lancashire
Cardinal	Cardinal, London
CaribB	Caribbean Books, Parkersburg, IA
CarletonUP	Carleton UP, Ottawa
Carucci	Carucci, Rome
Cass	Frank Cass, London
Cassell	Cassell, London
Cavaliere Azzurro	Cavaliere Azzurro, Bologna
Cave	Godfrey Cave Associates, London
CBA	Council for British Archaeology, London
CBS	Cambridge Bibliographical Society, Cambridge
CCEUCan	Centre for Continuing Education, University of Canterbury, Christchurch, New Zealand
CCP	Canadian Children's Press, Guelph, Ontario
CCS	Centre for Canadian Studies, Mount Allison University, Sackville, NB
CDSH	Centre de Documentation Sciences Humaines, Paris
CENS	Centre for English Name Studies, University of Nottingham
Century	Century Publishing, London
Ceolfrith	Ceolfrith Press, Sunderland, Tyne and Wear
CESR	Société des Amis du Centre d'Études Supérieures de la Renaissance, Tours
CETEDOC	Library of Christian Latin Texts
CFA	Canadian Federation for the Humanities, Ottawa
CH	Croom Helm, London
C–H	Chadwyck–Healey, Cambridge
Chambers	W. & R. Chambers, Edinburgh
Champaign	Champaign Public Library and Information Center, Champaign, IL
Champion	Librairie Honoré Champion, Paris

Chand	S. Chand, Madras
ChelseaH	Chelsea House Publishers, New York, New Haven, and Philadelphia
ChLitAssoc	Children's Literature Association
Christendom	Christendom Publications, Front Royal, VA
Chronicle	Chronicle Books, London
Chrysalis	Chrysalis Press
ChuoUL	Chuo University Library, Tokyo
Churchman	Churchman Publishing, Worthing, W. Sussex
Cistercian	Cistercian Publications, Kalamazoo, MI
CL	City Lights Books, San Francisco
CLA	Canadian Library Association, Ottawa
Clarendon	Clarendon Press, Oxford
Claridge	Claridge, St Albans, Hertfordshire
Clarion	Clarion State College, Clarion, PA
Clark	T. & T. Clark, Edinburgh
Clarke	James Clarke, Cambridge
Classical	Classical Publishing, New Delhi
CLCS	Centre for Language and Communication Studies, Trinity College, Dublin
ClogherHS	Clogher Historical Society, Monaghan, Eire
CLUEB	Cooperativa Libraria Universitaria Editrice, Bologna
Clunie	Clunie Press, Pitlochry, Tayside
CMAP	Caxton's Modern Arts Press, Dallas, TX
CMERS	Center for Medieval and Early Renaissance Studies, Binghamton, NY
CML	William Andrews Clark Memorial Library, Los Angeles
CMST	Centre for Medieval Studies, University of Toronto
Coach House	Coach House Press, Toronto
Colleagues	Colleagues Press, East Lansing, MI
Collector	Collector, London
College-Hill	College-Hill Press, San Diego, CA
Collins	William Collins, London
CollinsA	William Collins (Australia), Sydney
Collins & Brown	Collins & Brown, London
ColUP	Columbia UP, New York
Comedia	Comedia Publishing, London
Comet	Comet Books, London
Compton	Compton Press, Tisbury, Wiltshire
Constable	Constable, London
Contemporary	Contemporary Books, Chicago
Continuum	Continuum Publishing, New York
Copp	Copp Clark Pitman, Mississuaga, Ontario
Corgi	Corgi Books, London
CorkUP	Cork UP, Eire
Cormorant	Cormorant Press, Victoria, BC
Cornford	Cornford Press, Launceston, Tasmania
CornUP	Cornell UP, Ithaca, NY

Cornwallis	Cornwallis Press, Hastings, E. Sussex
Coronado	Coronado Press, Lawrence, KS
Cosmo	Cosmo Publications, New Delhi
Coteau	Coteau Books, Regina, Saskatchewan
Cowley	Cowley Publications, Cambridge, MA
Cowper	Cowper House, Pacific Grove, CA
CPP	Canadian Poetry Press, London, Ontario
CQUP	Central Queensland UP, Rockhampton
Crabtree	Crabtree Press, Sussex
Craftsman House	Craftsman House, Netherlands
Craig Pottoon	Craig Pottoon Publishing, New Zealand
Crawford	Crawford House Publishing, Hindmarsh, SA
Creag Darach	Creag Durach Publications, Stirling
Cresset	Cresset Library, London
CRNLE	Centre for Research in the New Literatures in English, Adelaide
Crossing	Crossing Press, Freedom, CA
Crossroad	Crossroad Publishing, New York
Crown	Crown Publishers, New York
Crowood	Crowood Press, Marlborough, Wiltshire
CSAL	Centre for Studies in Australian Literature, University of Western Australia, Nedlands
CSLI	Center for the Study of Language and Information, Stanford University
CSP	Canadian Scholars' Press, Toronto
CSU	Cleveland State University, Cleveland, OH
CTHS	Éditions du Comité des Travaux Historiques et Scientifiques, Paris
CUAP	Catholic University of America Press, Washington, DC
Cuff	Harry Cuff Publications, St John's, Newfoundland
CULouvain	Catholic University of Louvain, Belgium
CULublin	Catholic University of Lublin, Poland
CUP	Cambridge UP, Cambridge, New York, and Melbourne
Currency	Currency Press, Paddington, New South Wales
Currey	James Currey, London
CV	Cherry Valley Edition, Rochester, NY
CVK	Cornelson-Velhagen & Klasing, Berlin
CWU	Carl Winter Universitätsverlag, Heidelberg
Da Capo	Da Capo Press, New York
Dacorum	Dacorum College, Hemel Hempstead, Hertfordshire
Daisy	Daisy Books, Peterborough, Northampton
Dalkey	Dalkey Archive Press, Elmwood Park, IL
D&C	David & Charles, Newton Abbot, Devon
D&H	Duncker & Humblot, Berlin
D&M	Douglas & McIntyre, Vancouver, BC
D&S	Duffy and Snellgrove, Polts Point, New South Wales
Dangaroo	Dangaroo Press, Mundelstrup, Denmark
Dawson	Dawson Publishing, Folkestone, Kent

DawsonsPM	Dawsons Pall Mall
DBAP	Daphne Brasell Associates Press
DBP	Drama Book Publishers, New York
Deakin UP	Deakin UP, Geelong, Victoria
De Boeck	De Boeck-Wesmael, Brussels
Dee	Ivan R. Dee Publishers, Chicago, IL
De Graaf	De Graaf, Nierwkoup, Netherlands
Denoël	Denoël S.A.R.L., Paris
Dent	J.M. Dent, London
DentA	Dent, Ferntree Gully, Victoria
Depanee	Depanee Printers and Publishers, Nugegoda, Sri Lanka
Deutsch	André Deutsch, London
Didier	Éditions Didier, Paris
Diesterweg	Verlag Moritz Diesterweg, Frankfurt am Main
Dim Gray Bar Press	Dim Gray Bar Press
Doaba	Doaba House, Delhi
Dobby	Eric Dobby Publishing, St Albans
Dobson	Dobson Books, Durham
Dolmen	Dolmen Press, Portlaoise, Eire
Donald	John Donald, Edinburgh
Donker	Adriaan Donker, Johannesburg
Dorset	Dorset Publishing
Doubleday	Doubleday, London and New York
Dove	Dove, Sydney
Dovecote	Dovecote Press, Wimborne, Dorset
Dovehouse	Dovehouse Editions, Canada
Dover	Dover Publications, New York
Drew	Richard Drew, Edinburgh
Droste	Droste Verlag, Düsseldorf
Droz	Librairie Droz SA, Geneva
DublinUP	Dublin UP, Dublin
Duckworth	Gerald Duckworth, London
Duculot	J. Duculot, Gembloux, Belgium
DukeUP	Duke UP, Dublin
Dundurn	Dundurn Press, Toronto and London, Ontario
Duquesne	Duquesne UP, Pittsburgh
Dutton	E.P. Dutton, New York
DWT	Dr Williams's Trust, London
EA	English Association, London
EAS	English Association Sydney Incorporated
Eason	Eason & Son, Dublin
East Bay	East Bay Books, Berkeley, CA
Ebony	Ebony Books, Melbourne
Ecco	Ecco Press, New York
ECNRS	Éditions du Centre National de la Recherche Scientifique, Paris
ECW	ECW Press, Downsview, Ontario
Eden	Eden Press, Montreal and St Albans, VT

EdinUP	Edinburgh UP, Edinburgh
Edizioni	Edizioni del Grifo
EEM	Eastern European Monographs, Boulder, CO
Eerdmans	William Eerdmans, Grand Rapids, MI
EETS	Early English Text Society, c/o Exeter College, Oxford
1890sS	Eighteen-Nineties Society, Oxford
Eihosha	Eihosha, Tokyo
Elephas	Elephas Books, Kewdale, Australia
Elibank	Elibank Press, Wellington, New Zealand
Elm Tree	Elm Tree Books, London
ELS	English Literary Studies
Ember	Ember Press, Brixham, South Devon
EMSH	Éditions de la Maison des Sciences de l'Homme, Paris
Enitharmon	Enitharmon Press, London
Enzyklopädie	Enzyklopädie, Leipzig
EONF	Eugene O'Neill Foundation, Danville, CA
EPNS	English Place-Name Society, Beeston, Nottingham
Epworth	Epworth Press, Manchester
Eriksson	Paul Eriksson, Middlebury, VT
Erlbaum	Erlbaum Associates, NJ
Erskine	Erskine Press, Harleston, Norfolk
EscutchP	Escutcheon Press
ESI	Edizioni Scientifiche Italiane, Naples
ESL	Edizioni di Storia e Letteratura, Rome
EUFS	Éditions Universitaires Fribourg Suisse
EUL	Edinburgh University Library, Edinburgh
Europa	Europa Publishers, London
Evans	M. Evans, New York
Exact Change	Exact Change, Boston
Exile	Exile Editions, Toronto, Ontario
Eyre	Eyre Methuen, London
FAB	Free Association Books, London
Faber	Faber & Faber, London
FAC	Fédération d'Activités Culturelles, Paris
FACP	Fremantle Arts Centre Press, Fremantle, WA
Falcon Books	Falcon Books, Eastbourne
FALS	Foundation for Australian Literary Studies, James Cook University of North Queensland, Townsville
F&F	Fels & Firn Press, San Anselmo, CA
F&S	Feffer & Simons, Amsterdam
Farrand	Farrand Press, London
Fay	Barbara Fay, Stuttgart
F–B	Ford–Brown, Houston, TX
FCP	Four Courts Press, Dublin
FDUP	Fairleigh Dickinson UP, Madison, NJ
FE	Fourth Estate, London
Feminist	Feminist Press, New York
FictionColl	Fiction Collective, Brooklyn College, Brooklyn, NY

Field Day	Field Day, Derry
Fifth House	Fifth House Publications, Saskatoon, Saskatchewan
FILEF	FILEF Italo–Australian Publications, Leichhardt, New South Wales
Fine	Donald Fine, New York
Fink	Fink Verlag, Munich
Five Leaves	Five Leaves Publications, Nottingham
Flamingo	Flamingo Publishing, Newark, NJ
Flammarion	Flammarion, Paris
FlindersU	Flinders University of South Australia, Bedford Park
Floris	Floris Books, Edinburgh
FlorSU	Florida State University, Tallahassee, FL
FOF	Facts on File, New York
Folger	Folger Shakespeare Library, Washington, DC
Folio	Folio Press, London
Fontana	Fontana Press, London
Footprint	Footprint Press, Colchester, Essex
FordUP	Fordham UP, New York
Foris	Foris Publications, Dordrecht
Forsten	Egbert Forsten Publishing, Groningen, Netherlands
Fortress	Fortress Press, Philadelphia
Francke	Francke Verlag, Berne
Franklin	Burt Franklin, New York
FreeP	Free Press, New York
FreeUP	Free UP, Amsterdam
Freundlich	Freundlich Books, New York
Frommann-Holzboog	Frommann-Holzboog, Stuttgart
FS&G	Farrar, Straus & Giroux
FSP	Five Seasons Press, Madley, Hereford
FW	Fragments West/Valentine Press, Long Beach, CA
FWA	Fiji Writers' Association, Suva
FWP	Falling Wall Press, Bristol
Gale	Gale Research, Detroit, MI
Galilée	Galilée, Paris
Gallimard	Gallimard, Paris
G&G	Grevatt & Grevatt, Newcastle upon Tyne
G&M	Gill & Macmillan, Dublin
Garland	Garland Publishing, New York
Gasson	Roy Gasson Associates, Wimbourne, Dorset
Gateway	Gateway Editions, Washington, DC
GE	Greenwich Exchange, UK
GIA	GIA Publications, USA
Girasole	Edizioni del Girasole, Ravenna
GL	Goose Lane Editions, Fredericton, NB
GlasgowDL	Glasgow District Libraries, Glasgow
Gleerup	Gleerupska, Lund
Gliddon	Gliddon Books Publishers, Norwich
Gloger	Gloger Family Books, Portland, OR

GMP	GMP Publishing, London
GMSmith	Gibbs M. Smith, Layton, UT
Golden Dog	Golden Dog, Ottawa
Gollancz	Victor Gollancz, London
Gomer	Gomer Press, Llandysul, Dyfed
GothU	Gothenburg University, Gothenburg
Gower	Gower Publishing, Aldershot, Hants.
GRAAT	Groupe de Recherches Anglo-Américaines de Tours
Grafton	Grafton Books, London
GranB	Granary Books, New York
Granta	Granta Publications, London
Granville	Granville Publishing, London
Grasset	Grasset & Fasquelle, Paris
Grassroots	Grassroots, London
Graywolf	Graywolf Press, St Paul, MI
Greenhalgh	M.J. Greenhalgh, London
Greenhill	Greenhill Books, London
Greenwood	Greenwood Press, Westport, CT
Gregg	Gregg Publishing, Surrey
Greville	Greville Press, Warwick
Greymitre	Greymitre Books, London
GroC	Grolier Club, New York
Groos	Julius Groos Verlag, Heidelberg
Grove	Grove Press, New York
GRP	Greenfield Review Press, New York
Grüner	B.R. Grüner, Amsterdam
Gruyter	Walter de Gruyter, Berlin
Guernica	Guernica Editions, Montreal, Canada
Guilford	Guilford, New York
Gulmohar	Gulmohar Press, Islamabad, Pakistan
Haggerston	Haggerston Press, London
HakluytS	Hakluyt Society, c/o British Library, London
Hale	Robert Hale, London
Hall	G.K. Hall, Boston, MA
Halstead	Halstead Press, Rushcutters Bay, New South Wales
HalsteadP	Halstead Press, c/o J. Wiley & Sons, Chichester, W. Sussex
Hambledon	Hambledon Press, London
H&I	Hale & Iremonger, Sydney
H&L	Hambledon and London
H&M	Holmes & Meier, London and New York
H&S	Hodder & Stoughton, London
H&SNZ	Hodder & Stoughton, Auckland
H&W	Hill & Wang, New York
Hansib	Hansib Publishing, London
Harbour	Harbour Publishing, Madeira Park, BC
Harman	Harman Publishing House, New Delhi
Harper	Harper & Row, New York
Harrap	Harrap, Edinburgh

HarrV	Harrassowitz Verlag, Wiesbaden
HarvardUP	Harvard UP, Cambridge, MA
Harwood	Harwood Academic Publishers, Langhorne, PA
Hatje	Verlag Gerd Hatje, Germany
HBJ	Harcourt Brace Jovanovich, New York and London
HC	HarperCollins, London
HCAus	HarperCollins Australia, Pymble, New South Wales
Headline	Headline Book Publishing, London
Heath	D.C. Heath, Lexington, MS
Heinemann	William Heinemann, London
HeinemannA	William Heinemann, St Kilda, Victoria
HeinemannC	Heinemann Educational Books, Kingston, Jamaica
HeinemannNg	Heinemann Educational Books, Nigeria
HeinemannNZ	Heinemann Publishers, Auckland (now Heinemann Reed)
HeinemannR	Heinemann Reed, Auckland
Helm	Christopher Helm, London
Herbert	Herbert Press, London
Hermitage	Hermitage Antiquarian Bookshop, Denver, CO
Hern	Nick Hern Books, London
Heyday	Heyday Books, Berkeley, CA
HH	Hamish Hamilton, London
Hilger	Adam Hilger, Bristol
HM	Harvey Miller, London
HMSO	HMSO, London
Hodder, Moa, Beckett	Hodder, Moa, Beckett, Milford, Auckland, New Zealand
Hodge	A. Hodge, Penzance, Cornwall
Hogarth	Hogarth Press, London
HongKongUP	Hong Kong UP, Hong Kong
Horsdal & Schubart	Horsdal & Schubart, Victoria, BC
Horwood	Ellis Horwood, Hemel Hempstead, Hertfordshire
HoughtonM	Houghton Mifflin, Boston, MA
Howard	Howard UP, Washington, DC
HREOC	Human Rights and Equal Opportunity Commission, Commonweath of Australia, Canberra
HRW	Holt, Reinhart & Winston, New York
Hudson	Hudson Hills Press, New York
Hueber	Max Hueber, Ismaning, Germany
HUL	Hutchinson University Library, London
HullUP	Hull UP, University of Hull
Humanities	Humanities Press, Atlantic Highlands, NJ
Huntington	Huntington Library, San Marino, CA
Hutchinson	Hutchinson Books, London
HW	Harvester Wheatsheaf, Hemel Hempstead, Hertfordshire
HWWilson	H.W. Wilson, New York
Hyland House	Hyland House Publishing, Victoria
HyphenP	Hyphen Press, London
IAAS	Indian Institute of Aveanced Studies, Lahore and New Delhi

Ian Henry	Ian Henry Publications, Hornchurch, Essex
IAP	Irish Academic Press, Dublin
Ibadan	Ibadan University Press
IBK	Innsbrucker Beiträge zur Kulturwissenschaft, University of Innsbruck
ICA	Institute of Contemporary Arts, London
IHA	International Hopkins Association, Waterloo, Ontario
IJamaica	Institute of Jamaica Publications, Kingston
Imago	Imago Imprint, New York
ImperialWarMuseum	Imperial War Museum Publications, London
IndUP	Indiana UP, Bloomington, IN
Inkblot	Inkblot Publications, Berkeley, CA
IntUP	International Universities Press, New York
Inventions	Inventions Press, London
IonaC	Iona College, New Rochelle, NY
IowaSUP	Iowa State UP, Ames, IA
IOWP	Isle of Wight County Press, Newport, Isle of Wight
IP	In Parenthesis, London
Ipswich	Ipswich Press, Ipswich, MA
IrishAP	Irish Academic Press, Dublin
ISI	ISI Press, Philadelphia
Italica	Italica Press, New York
IULC	Indiana University Linguistics Club, Bloomington, IN
IUP	Indiana University of Pennsylvania Press, Indiana, PA
Ivon	Ivon Publishing House, Bombay
Jacaranda	Jacaranda Wiley, Milton, Queensland
JadavpurU	Jadavpur University, Calcutta
James CookU	James Cook University of North Queensland, Townsville
Jarrow	Parish of Jarrow, Tyne and Wear
Jesperson	Jesperson Press, St John's, Newfoundland
JHall	James Hall, Leamington Spa, Warwickshire
JHUP	Johns Hopkins UP, Baltimore, MD
JIWE	JIWE Publications, University of Gulbarga, India
JLRC	Jack London Research Center, Glen Ellen, CA
J-NP	Joe-Noye Press
Jonas	Jonas Verlag, Marburg, Germany
Joseph	Michael Joseph, London
Journeyman	Journeyman Press, London
JPGM	J. Paul Getty Museum
JT	James Thin, Edinburgh
Junction	Junction Books, London
Junius-Vaughan	Junius-Vaughan Press, Fairview, NJ
Jupiter	Jupiter Press, Lake Bluff, IL
JyväskyläU	Jyväskylä University, Jyväskylä, Finland
Kaibunsha	Kaibunsha, Tokyo
K&N	Königshausen & Neumann, Würzburg, Germany
K&W	Kaye & Ward, London
Kangaroo	Kangaroo Press, Simon & Schuster (Australia), Roseville,

	New South Wales
Kansai	Kansai University of Foreign Studies, Osaka
Kardo	Kardo, Coatbridge, Scotland
Kardoorair	Kardoorair Press, Adelaide
Karia	Karia Press, London
Karnak	Karnak House, London
Karoma	Karoma Publishers, Ann Arbor, MI
KC	Kyle Cathie, London
KCL	King's College London
KeeleUP	Keele University Press
Kegan Paul	Kegan Paul International, London
Kenkyu	Kenkyu-Sha, Tokyo
Kennikat	Kennikat Press, Port Washington, NY
Kensal	Kensal Press, Oxford
KentSUP	Kent State University Press, Kent, OH
KenyaLB	Kenya Literature Bureau, Nairobi
Kerosina	Kerosina Publications, Worcester Park, Surrey
Kerr	Charles H. Kerr, Chicago
Kestrel	Viking Kestrel, London
K/H	Kendall/Hunt Publishing, Dubuque, IA
Kingsley	J. Kingsley Publishers, London
Kingston	Kingston Publishers, Kingston, Jamaica
Kinseido	Kinseido, Tokyo
Klostermann	Vittorio Klostermann, Frankfurt am Main
Kluwer	Kluwer Academic Publications, Dordrecht
Knopf	Alfred A. Knopf, New York
Knowledge	Knowledge Industry Publications, White Plains, NY
Kraus	Kraus International Publications, White Plains, NY
KSUP	Kent State UP, Kent OH
LA	Library Association, London
LACUS	Linguistic Association of Canada and the United States, Chapel Hill, NC
Lake View	Lake View Press, Chicago
LAm	Library of America, New York
Lancelot	Lancelot Press, Hantsport, NS
Landesman	Jay Landesman, London
L&W	Lawrence & Wishart, London
Lane	Allen Lane, London
Lang	Peter D. Lang, Frankfurt am Main and Berne
LehighUP	Lehigh University Press, Bethlehem, PA
LeicAE	University of Leicester, Department of Adult Education
LeicsCC	Leicestershire County Council, Libraries and Information Service, Leicester
LeicUP	Leicester UP, Leicester
LeidenUP	Leiden UP, Leiden
Leopard's Head	Leopard's Head Press, Oxford
Letao	Letao Press, Albury, New South Wales
LeuvenUP	Leuven UP, Leuven, Belgium

Lexik	Lexik House, Cold Spring, NY
Lexington	Lexington Publishers
LF	LiberFörlag, Stockholm
LH	Lund Humphries Publishers, London
Liberty	Liberty Classics, Indianapolis, IN
Libris	Libris, London
LibrU	Libraries Unlimited, Englewood, CO
Liguori	Liguori, Naples
Limelight	Limelight Editions, New York
Lime Tree	Lime Tree Press, Octopus Publishing, London
LincolnUP	Lincoln University Press, Nebraska
LITIR	LITIR Database, University of Alberta
LittleH	Little Hills Press, Burwood, New South Wales
Liveright	Liveright Publishing, New York
LiverUP	Liverpool UP, Liverpool
Livre de Poche	Le Livre de Poche, Paris
Llanerch	Llanerch Enterprises, Lampeter, Dyfed
Locust Hill	Locust Hill Press, West Cornwall, CT
Loewenthal	Loewenthal Press, New York
Longman	Addison Longman Wesley, Harlow, Essex
LongmanC	Longman Caribbean, Harlow, Essex
LongmanF	Longman, France
LongmanNZ	Longman, Auckland
Longspoon	Longspoon Press, University of Alberta, Edmonton
Lovell	David Lovell Publishing, Brunswick, Australia
Lowell	Lowell Press, Kansas City, MS
Lowry	Lowry Publishers, Johannesburg
LSUP	Louisiana State UP, Baton Rouge, LA
LundU	Lund University, Lund, Sweden
LUP	Loyola UP, Chicago
Lutterworth	Lutterworth Press, Cambridge
Lymes	Lymes Press, Newcastle, Staffordshire
MAA	Medieval Academy of America, Cambridge, MA
Macmillan	Macmillan Publishers, London
MacmillanC	Macmillan Caribbean
Madison	Madison Books, Lanham, MD
Madurai	Madurai University, Madurai, India
Maecenas	Maecenas Press, Iowa City, Iowa
Magabala	Magabala Books, Broome, WA
Magnes	Magnes Press, The Hebrew University, Jerusalem
Mainstream	Mainstream Publishing, Edinburgh
Maisonneuve	Maisonneuve Press, Washington, DC
Malone	Malone Society, c/o King's College, London
Mambo	Mambo Press, Gweru, Zimbabwe
ManCASS	Manchester Centre for Anglo-Saxon Studies, University of Manchester
M&E	Macdonald & Evans, Estover, Plymouth, Devon
M&S	McClelland & Stewart, Toronto

Maney	W.S. Maney & Sons, Leeds
Mansell	Mansell Publishing, London
Manufacture	La Manufacture, Lyons
ManUP	Manchester UP, Milwaukee, WI
Mardaga	Mardaga
Mariner	Mariner Books, Boston, MA
MarquetteUP	Marquette UP, Milwaukee, WI
Marvell	Marvell Press, Calstock, Cornwall
MB	Mitchell Beazley, London
McDougall, Littel	McDougall, Littel, Evanston, IL
McFarland	McFarland, Jefferson, NC
McG-QUP	McGill-Queen's UP, Montreal
McGraw-Hill	McGraw-Hill, New York
McIndoe	John McIndoe, Dunedin, New Zealand
McPheeG	McPhee Gribble Publishers, Fitzroy, Victoria
McPherson	McPherson, Kingston, NY
MCSU	Maria Curie Sk³odowska University
ME	M. Evans, New York
Meany	P.D. Meany Publishing, Port Credit, Ontario
Meckler	Meckler Publishing, Westport, CT
MelbourneUP	Melbourne UP, Carlton South, Victoria
Mellen	Edwin Mellen Press, Lewiston, NY
MellenR	Mellen Research UP
MercerUP	Mercer UP, Macon, GA
Mercury	Mercury Press, Stratford, Ontario
Merlin	Merlin Press, London
Methuen	Methuen, London
MethuenA	Methuen Australia, North Ryde, New South Wales
MethuenC	Methuen, Toronto
Metro	Metro Publishing, Auckland
Metzler	Metzler, Stuttgart
MGruyter	Mouton de Gruyter, Berlin, New York, and Amsterdam
MH	Michael Haag, London
MHRA	Modern Humanities Research Association, London
MHS	Missouri Historical Society, St Louis, MO
MI	Microforms International, Pergamon Press, Oxford
Micah	Micah Publications, Marblehead, MA.
MichSUP	Michigan State UP, East Lansing, MI
MidNAG	Mid-Northumberland Arts Group, Ashington, Northumbria
Mieyungah	Mieyungah Press, Melbourne University Press, Carlton South, Victoria
Milestone	Milestone Publications, Horndean, Hampshire
Millennium	Millennium Books, E.J. Dwyer, Newtown, Australia
Millstream	Millstream Books, Bath
Milner	Milner, London
Minuit	Éditions de Minuit, Paris

MIP	Medieval Institute Publications, Western Michigan University, Kalamazoo
MITP	Massachusetts Institute of Technology Press, Cambridge, MA
MLA	Modern Language Association of America, New York
MlM	Multilingual Matters, Clevedon, Avon
MLP	Manchester Literary and Philosophical Society, Manchester
Modern Library	Modern Library (Random House), New York
Monarch	Monarch Publications, Sussex
Moonraker	Moonraker Press, Bradford-on-Avon, Wiltshire
Moorland	Moorland Publishing, Ashbourne, Derby
Moreana	Moreana, Angers, France
MorganSU	Morgan State University, Baltimore, MD
Morrow	William Morrow, New York
Mosaic	Mosaic Press, Oakville, Ontario
Motilal	Motilal Books, Oxford
Motley	Motley Press, Romsey, Hampshire
Mouton	Mouton Publishers, New York and Paris
Mowbray	A.R. Mowbray, Oxford
MR	Martin Robertson, Oxford
MRS	Medieval and Renaissance Society, North Texas State University, Denton
MRTS	MRTS, Binghamton, NY
MSUP	Memphis State UP, Memphis, TN
MtAllisonU	Mount Allison University, Sackville, NB
Mulini	Mulini Press, ACT
Muller	Frederick Muller, London
MULP	McMaster University Library Press
Murray	John Murray, London
Mursia	Ugo Mursia, Milan
NAL	New American Library, New York
Narr	Gunter Narr Verlag, Tübingen
Nathan	Fernand Nathan, Paris
NBB	New Beacon Books, London
NBCAus	National Book Council of Australia, Melbourne
NCP	New Century Press, Durham
ND	New Directions, New York
NDT	Nottingham Drama Texts, c/o University of Nottingham
NEL	New English Library, London
NELM	National English Literary Museum, Grahamstown, S. Africa
Nelson	Nelson Publishers, Melbourne
NelsonT	Thomas Nelson, London
New Endeavour	New Endeavour Press
NeWest	NeWest Press, Edmonton, Alberta
New Horn	New Horn Press, Ibadan, Nigeria
New Island	New Island Press
NewIssuesP	New Issues Press, Western Michigan University
NH	New Horizon Press, Far Hills, NJ

N-H	Nelson-Hall, Chicago
NHPC	North Holland Publishing, Amsterdam and New York
NicV	Nicolaische Verlagsbuchhandlung, Berlin
NIE	La Nuova Italia Editrice, Florence
Niemeyer	Max Niemeyer, Tübingen, Germany
Nightwood	Nightwood Editions, Toronto
NIUP	Northern Illinois UP, De Kalb, IL
NUSam	National University of Samoa
NLA	National Library of Australia
NLB	New Left Books, London
NLC	National Library of Canada, Ottawa
NLP	New London Press, Dallas, TX
NLS	National Library of Scotland, Edinburgh
NLW	National Library of Wales, Aberystwyth, Dyfed
Nodus	Nodus Publikationen, Münster
Northcote	Northcote House Publishers, Plymouth
NortheasternU	Northeastern University, Boston, MA
NorthwesternUP	Northwestern UP, Evanston, IL
Norton	W.W. Norton, New York and London
NorUP	Norwegian University Press, Oslo
Novus	Novus Press, Oslo
NPF	National Poetry Foundation, Orono, ME
NPG	National Portrait Gallery, London
NPP	North Point Press, Berkeley, CA
NSP	New Statesman Publishing, New Delhi
NSU Press	Northern States Universities Press
NSWUP	New South Wales UP, Kensington, New South Wales
NT	National Textbook, Lincolnwood, IL
NUC	Nipissing University College, North Bay, Ontario
NUP	National University Publications, Millwood, NY
NUSam	National University of Samoa
NUU	New University of Ulster, Coleraine
NWAP	North Waterloo Academic Press, Waterloo, Ontario
NWP	New World Perspectives, Montreal
NYPL	New York Public Library, New York
NYUP	New York UP, New York
OakK	Oak Knoll Press, New Castle, DE
O&B	Oliver & Boyd, Harlow, Essex
Oasis	Oasis Books, London
OBAC	Organization of Black American Culture, Chicago
OberlinCP	Oberlin College Press, Oberlin, OH
Oberon	Oberon Books, London
O'Brien	O'Brien Press, Dublin
OBS	Oxford Bibliographical Society, Bodleian Library, Oxford
Octopus	Octopus Books, London
OdenseUP	Odense UP, Odense
OE	Officina Edizioni, Rome
OEColl	Old English Colloquium, Berkeley, CA

Offord	John Offord Publications, Eastbourne, E. Sussex
OhioUP	Ohio UP, Athens, OH
Oldcastle	Oldcastle Books, Harpenden, Hertfordshire
Olms	Georg Olms, Hildesheim, Germany
Olschki	Leo S. Olschki, Florence
O'Mara	Michael O'Mara Books, London
Omnigraphics	Omnigraphics, Detroit, MI
Open Books	Open Books Publishing, Wells, Somerset
Open Court	Open Court Publishing, USA
OpenUP	Open UP, Buckingham and Philadelphia
OPP	Oxford Polytechnic Press, Oxford
Orbis	Orbis Books, London
OregonSUP	Oregon State UP, Corvallis, OR
Oriel	Oriel Press, Stocksfield, Northumberland
OrientUP	Oriental UP, London
Ortnamnsarkivet	Ortnamnsarkivet i Uppsala, Sweden
Orwell	Orwell Press, Southwold, Suffolk
Oryx	Oryx Press, Phoenix, AR
OSUP	Ohio State UP, Columbus, OH
OTP	Oak Tree Press, London
OUCA	Oxford University Committee for Archaeology, Oxford
OUP	Oxford UP, Oxford
OUPAm	Oxford UP, New York
OUPAus	Oxford UP, Melbourne
OUPC	Oxford UP, Toronto
OUPI	Oxford UP, New Delhi
OUPNZ	Oxford UP, Auckland
OUPSA	Oxford UP Southern Africa, Cape Town
Outlet	Outlet Book, New York
Overlook	Overlook Press, New York
Owen	Peter Owen, London
Owl	Owl
Pace UP	Pace University Press, New York
Pacifica	Press Pacifica, Kailua, Hawaii
Paget	Paget Press, Santa Barbara, CA
PAJ	PAJ Publications, New York
Paladin	Paladin Books, London
Palgrave	Palgrave, NY
Pan	Pan Books, London
PanAmU	Pan American University, Edinburgh, TX
P&C	Pickering & Chatto, London
Pandion	Pandion Press, Capitola, CA
Pandora	Pandora Press, London
Pan Macmillan	Pan Macmillan Australia, South Yarra, Victoria
Pantheon	Pantheon Books, New York
ParagonH	Paragon House Publishers, New York
Parnassus	Parnassus Imprints, Hyannis, MA
Parousia	Parousia Publications, London

Paternoster	Paternoster Press, Carlisle, Cumbria
Patten	Patten Press, Penzance
Paulist	Paulist Press, Ramsey, NJ
Paupers	Paupers' Press, Nottingham
Pavilion	Pavilion Books, London
PBFA	Provincial Booksellers' Fairs Association, Cambridge
Peachtree	Peachtree Publishers, Atlanta, GA
Pearson	David Pearson, Huntingdon, Cambridge
Peepal Tree	Peepal Tree Books, Leeds
Peeters	Peeters Publishers and Booksellers, Leuven, Belgium
Pelham	Pelham Books, London
Pembridge	Pembridge Press, London
Pemmican	Pemmican Publications, Winnipeg, Canada
PencraftI	Pencraft International, Ashok Vihar II, Delhi
Penguin	Penguin Books, Harmondsworth, Middlesex
PenguinA	Penguin Books, Ringwood, Victoria
PenguinNZ	Penguin Books, Auckland
Penkevill	Penkevill Publishing, Greenwood, FL
Pentland	Pentland Press, Ely, Cambridge
Penumbra	Penumbra Press, Moonbeam, Ontario
People's	People's Publications, London
Pergamon	Pergamon Press, Oxford
Permanent	Permanent Press, Sag Harbor, NY
Perpetua	Perpetua Press, Oxford
Petton	Petton Books, Oxford
Pevensey	Pevensey Press, Newton Abbot, Devon
PH	Prentice-Hall, Englewood Cliffs, NJ
Phaidon	Phaidon Press, London
PHI	Prentice-Hall International, Hemel Hempstead, Hertfordshire
PhilL	Philosophical Library, New York
Phillimore	Phillimore, Chichester
Phoenix	Phoenix
Piatkus	Piatkus Books, London
Pickwick	Pickwick Publications, Allison Park, PA
Pilgrim	Pilgrim Books, Norman, OK
PIMS	Pontifical Institute of Mediaeval Studies, Toronto
Pinter	Frances Pinter Publishers, London
Plains	Plains Books, Carlisle
Plenum	Plenum Publishing, London and New York
Plexus	Plexus Publishing, London
Pliegos	Editorial Pliegos, Madrid
Ploughshares	Ploughshares Books, Watertown, MA
Pluto	Pluto Press, London
PML	Pierpont Morgan Library, New York
Polity	Polity Press, Cambridge
Polygon	Polygon, Edinburgh
Poolbeg	Poolbeg Press, Swords, Dublin

Porcepic	Press Porcepic, Victoria, BC
Porcupine	Porcupine's Quill, Canada
PortN	Port Nicholson Press, Wellington, NZ
Potter	Clarkson N. Potter, New York
Power	Power Publications, University of Sydney
PPUBarcelona	Promociones y Publicaciones Universitarias, Barcelona
Praeger	Praeger, New York
Prestel	Prestel Verlag, Germany
PrestigeB	Prestige Books, New Delhi
Primavera	Edizioni Primavera, Gunti Publishing, Florence, Italy
Primrose	Primrose Press, Alhambra, CA
PrincetonUL	Princeton University Library, Princeton, NJ
PrincetonUP	Princeton UP, Princeton, NJ
Printwell	Printwell Publishers, Jaipur, India
Prism	Prism Press, Bridport, Dorset
PRO	Public Record Office, London
Profile	Profile Books, Ascot, Berks
ProgP	Progressive Publishers, Calcutta
PSUP	Pennsylvania State UP, University Park, PA
Pucker	Puckerbrush Press, Orono, ME
PUF	Presses Universitaires de France, Paris
PurdueUP	Purdue UP, Lafayette, IN
Pushcart	Pushcart Press, Wainscott, NY
Pustet	Friedrich Pustet, Regensburg
Putnam	Putnam Publishing, New York
PWP	Poetry Wales Press, Ogmore by Sea, mid-Glamorgan
QED	QED Press, Ann Arbor, MI
Quarry	Quarry Press, Kingston, Ontario
Quartet	Quartet Books, London
QUT	Queensland University of Technology
RA	Royal Academy of Arts, London
Rainforest	Rainforest Publishing, Faxground, New South Wales
Rampant Lions	Rampant Lions Press, Cambridge
R&B	Rosenklide & Bagger, Copenhagen
R&L	Rowman & Littlefield, Totowa, NJ
Randle	Ian Randle, Kingston, Jamaica
RandomH	Random House, London and New York
RandomHAus	Random House Australia, Victoria
Ravan	Ravan Press, Johannesburg
Ravette	Ravette, London
Reaktion	Reaktion Books, London
Rebel	Rebel Press, London
Red Kite	Red Kite Press, Guelph, Ontario
Red Rooster	Red Rooster Press, Hotham Hill, Victoria
Red Sea	Red Sea Press, NJ
Reed	Reed Books, Port Melbourne
Reference	Reference Press, Toronto
Regents	Regents Press of Kansas, Lawrence, KS

Reichenberger	Roswitha Reichenberger, Kessel, Germany
Reinhardt	Max Reinhardt, London
Remak	Remak, Alblasserdam, Netherlands
RenI	Renaissance Institute, Sophia University, Tokyo
Research	Research Publications, Reading
RETS	Renaissance English Text Society, Chicago
RH	Ramsay Head Press, Edinburgh
RHS	Royal Historical Society, London
RIA	Royal Irish Academy, Dublin
RiceUP	Rice UP, Houston, TX
Richarz	Hans Richarz, St Augustin, Germany
RICL	Research Institute for Comparative Literature, University of Alberta
Rivers Oram	Rivers Oram Press, London
Rizzoli	Rizzoli International Publications, New York
RobartsCCS	Robarts Centre for Canadian Studies, York University, North York, Ontario
Robinson	Robinson Publishing, London
Robson	Robson Books, London
Rodopi	Rodopi, Amsterdam
Roebuck	Stuart Roebuck, Suffolk
RoehamptonI	Roehampton Institute London
Routledge	Routledge, London and New York
Royce	Robert Royce, London
RS	Royal Society, London
RSC	Royal Shakespeare Company, London
RSL	Royal Society of Literature, London
RSVP	Research Society for Victorian Periodicals, University of Leicester
RT	RT Publications, London
Running	Running Press, Philadelphia
Russell	Michael Russell, Norwich
RutgersUP	Rutgers UP, New Brunswick, NJ
Ryan	Ryan Publishing, London
SA	Sahitya Akademi, New Delhi
Sage	Sage Publications, London
SAI	Sociological Abstracts, San Diego, CA
Salamander	Salamander Books, London
Salem	Salem Press, Englewood Cliffs, NJ
S&A	Shukayr and Akasheh, Amman, Jordon
S&D	Stein & Day, Briarcliff Manor, NJ
S&J	Sidgwick & Jackson, London
S&M	Sun & Moon Press, Los Angeles
S&P	Simon & Piere, Toronto
S&S	Simon & Schuster, New York and London
S&W	Secker & Warburg, London
Sangam	Sangam Books, London
Sangsters	Sangsters Book Stores, Kingston, Jamaica

SAP	Scottish Academic Press, Edinburgh
Saros	Saros International Publishers
SASSC	Sydney Association for Studies in Society and Culture, University of Sydney, New South Wales
Saur	Bowker-Saur, Sevenoaks, Kent
Savacou	Savacou Publications, Kingston, Jamaica
S-B	Schwann-Bagel, Düsseldorf
ScanUP	Scandinavian University Presses, Oslo
Scarecrow	Scarecrow Press, Metuchen, NJ
Schäuble	Schäuble Verlag, Rheinfelden, Germany
Schmidt	Erich Schmidt Verlag, Berlin
Schneider	Lambert Schneider, Heidelberg
Schocken	Schocken Books, New York
Scholarly	Scholarly Press, St Clair Shores, MI
ScholarsG	Scholars Press, GA
Schöningh	Ferdinand Schöningh, Paderborn, Germany
Schwinn	Michael Schwinn, Neustadt, Germany
SCJP	Sixteenth-Century Journal Publications
Scolar	Scolar Press, Aldershot, Hampshire
SCP	Second Chance Press, Sag Harbor, NY
Scribe	Scribe Publishing, Colchester
Scribner	Charles Scribner, New York
Seafarer	Seafarer Books, London
Seaver	Seaver Books, New York
Segue	Segue, New York
Semiotext(e)	Semiotext(e), Columbia University, New York
SePA	Self-Publishing Association
Seren Books	Seren Books, Bridgend, mid-Glamorgan
Serpent's Tail	Serpent's Tail Publishing, London
Sessions	William Sessions, York
Seuil	Éditions du Seuil, Paris
7:84 Pubns	7:84 Publications, Glasgow
Severn	Severn House, Wallington, Surrey
SF&R	Scholars' Facsimiles and Reprints, Delmar, NY
SH	Somerset House, Teaneck, NJ
Shalabh	Shalabh Book House, Meerut, India
ShAP	Sheffield Academic Press
Shearwater	Shearwater Press, Lenah Valley, Tasmania
Sheba	Sheba Feminist Publishers, London
Sheed&Ward	Sheed & Ward, London
Sheldon	Sheldon Press, London
SHESL	Société d'Histoire et d'Épistemologie des Sciences du Langage, Paris
Shinozaki	Shinozaki Shorin, Tokyo
Shinshindo	Shinshindo Publishing, Tokyo
Shire	Shire Publications, Princes Risborough, Buckinghamshire
Shoal Bay Press	Shoal Bay Press, New Zealand
Shoe String	Shoe String Press, Hamden, CT

SHP	Shakespeare Head Press
SIAS	Scandinavian Institute of African Studies, Uppsala
SIL	Summer Institute of Linguistics, Academic Publications, Dallas, TX
SIUP	Southern Illinois University Press
Simon King	Simon King Press, Milnthorpe, Cumbria
Sinclair-Stevenson	Sinclair-Stevenson, London
SingaporeUP	Singapore UP, Singapore
SIUP	Southern Illinois UP, Carbondale, IL
SJSU	San Jose State University, San Jose, CA
Skilton	Charles Skilton, London
Skoob	Skoob Books, London
Slatkine	Éditions Slatkine, Paris
Slavica	Slavica Publishers, Columbus, OH
Sleepy Hollow	Sleepy Hollow Press, Tarrytown, NY
SLG	SLG Press, Oxford
Smith Settle	Smith Settle, W. Yorkshire
SMUP	Southern Methodist UP, Dallas, TX
Smythe	Colin Smythe, Gerrards Cross, Buckinghamshire
SNH	Société Néophilologique de Helsinki
SNLS	Society for New Language Study, Denver, CO
SOA	Society of Authors, London
Soho	Soho Book, London
SohoP	Soho Press, New York
Solaris	Solaris Press, Rochester, MI
SonoNis	Sono Nis Press, Victoria, BC
Sorbonne	Publications de la Sorbonne, Paris
SorbonneN	Publications du Conseil Scientifique de la Sorbonne Nouvelle, Paris
Souvenir	Souvenir Press, London
SPA	SPA Books
SPACLALS	South Pacific Association for Commonwealth Literature and Language Studies, Wollongong, New South Wales
Spaniel	Spaniel Books, Paddington, New South Wales
SPCK	SPCK, London
Spectrum	Spectrum Books, Ibadan, Nigeria
Split Pea	Split Pea Press, Edinburgh
Spokesman	Spokesman Books, Nottingham
Spoon River	Spoon River Poetry Press, Granite Falls, MN
SRC	Steinbeck Research Center, San Jose State University, San Jose, CA
SRI	Steinbeck Research Institute, Ball State University, Muncie, IN
SriA	Sri Aurobindo, Pondicherry, India
Sri Satguru	Sri Satguru Publications, Delhi
SSA	John Steinbeck Society of America, Muncie, IN
SSAB	Sprakförlaget Skriptor AB, Stockholm
SSNS	Scottish Society for Northern Studies, Edinburgh

StanfordUP	Stanford UP, Stanford, CA
Staple	Staple, Matlock, Derbyshire
Starmont	Starmont House, Mercer Island, WA
Starrhill	Starrhill Press, Washington, DC
Station Hill	Station Hill, Barrytown, NY
Stauffenburg	Stauffenburg Verlag, Tübingen, Germany
StDL	St Deiniol's Library, Hawarden, Clwyd
Steel Rail	Steel Rail Publishing, Ottawa
Steiner	Franz Steiner, Wiesbaden, Germany
Sterling	Sterling Publishing, New York
SterlingND	Sterling Publishers, New Delhi
Stichting	Stichtig Neerlandistiek, Amsterdam
St James	St James Press, Andover, Hampshire
St Martin's	St Martin's Press, New York
StMut	State Mutual Book and Periodical Source, New York
Stockwell	Arthur H. Stockwell, Ilfracombe, Devon
Stoddart	Stoddart Publishing, Don Mills, Ontario
StPB	St Paul's Bibliographies, Winchester, Hampshire
STR	Society for Theatre Research, London
Strauch	R.O.U. Strauch, Ludwigsburg
Studio	Studio Editions, London
Stump Cross	Stump Cross Books, Stump Cross, Essex
Sud	Sud, Marseilles
Suhrkamp	Suhrkamp Verlag, Frankfurt am Main
Summa	Summa Publications, Birmingham, AL
SUNYP	State University of New York Press, Albany, NY
SUP	Sydney University Press
Surtees	R.S. Surtees Society, Frome, Somerset
SusquehannaUP	Susquehanna UP, Selinsgrove, PA
SussexAP	Sussex Academic Press
SussexUP	Sussex UP, University of Sussex, Brighton
Sutton	Alan Sutton, Stroud, Gloucester
SVP	Sister Vision Press, Toronto
S–W	Shepheard–Walwyn Publishing, London
Swallow	Swallow Press, Athens, OH
SWG	Saskatchewan Writers Guild, Regina
Sybylla	Sybylla Feminist Press
SydneyUP	Sydney UP, Sydney
SyracuseUP	Syracuse UP, Syracuse, NY
Tabb	Tabb House, Padstow, Cornwall
Taishukan	Taishukan Publishing, Tokyo
Talonbooks	Talonbooks, Vancouver
TamilU	Tamil University, Thanjavur, India
T&F	Taylor & Francis Books
T&H	Thames & Hudson, London
Tantivy	Tantivy Press, London
Tarcher	Jeremy P. Tarcher, Los Angeles
Tartarus	Tartarus Press

Tate	Tate Gallery Publications, London
Tavistock	Tavistock Publications, London
Taylor	Taylor Publishing, Bellingham, WA
TaylorCo	Taylor Publishing, Dallas, TX
TCG	Theatre Communications Group, New York
TCP	Three Continents Press, Washington, DC
TCUP	Texas Christian UP, Fort Worth, TX
TEC	Third Eye Centre, Glasgow
Tecumseh	Tecumseh Press, Ottawa
Telos	Telos Press, St Louis, MO
TempleUP	Temple UP, Philadelphia
TennS	Tennyson Society, Lincoln
TexA&MUP	Texas A&MUP, College Station, TX
Text	Text Publishing, Melbourne
TextileB	Textile Bridge Press, Clarence Center, NY
TexTULib	Friends of the University Library, Texas Tech University, Lubbock
The Smith	The Smith, New York
Thimble	Thimble Press, Stroud, Gloucester
Thoemmes	Thoemmes Press, Bristol
Thornes	Stanley Thornes, Cheltenham
Thorpe	D.W. Thorpe, Australia
Thorsons	Thorsons Publishers, London
Times	Times of Gloucester Press, Gloucester, Ontario
TMP	Thunder's Mouth Press, New York
Tombouctou	Tombouctou Books, Bolinas, CA
Totem	Totem Books, Don Mills, Ontario
Toucan	Toucan Press, St Peter Port, Guernsey
Touzot	Jean Touzot, Paris
TPF	Trianon Press Facsimiles, London
Tragara	Tragara Press, Edinburgh
Transaction	Transaction Publishers, New Brunswick, NJ
Transcendental	Transcendental Books, Hartford, CT
Transworld	Transworld, London
TrinityUP	Trinity UP, San Antonio, TX
Tsar	Tsar Publications, Canada
TTUP	Texas Technical University Press, Lubbock
Tuckwell	Tuckwell Press, East Linton
Tuduv	Tuduv, Munich
TulaneUP	Tulane UP, New Orleans, LA
TurkuU	Turku University, Turku, Finland
Turnstone	Turnstone Press, Winnipeg, Manitoba
Turtle Island	Turtle Island Foundation, Berkeley, CA
Twayne	Twayne Publishing, Boston, MA
UAB	University of Aston, Birmingham
UAdelaide	University of Adelaide, Australia
UAlaP	University of Alabama Press, Tuscaloosa
UAlbertaP	University of Alberta Press, Edmonton

UAntwerp	University of Antwerp
UArizP	University of Arizona Press, Tucson
UArkP	University of Arkansas Press, Fayetteville
UAthens	University of Athens, Greece
UBarcelona	University of Barcelona, Spain
UBCP	University of British Columbia Press, Vancouver
UBergen	University of Bergen, Norway
UBrno	J.E. Purkyne University of Brno, Czechoslovakia
UBrussels	University of Brussels
UCalgaryP	University of Calgary Press, Canada
UCalP	University of California Press, Berkeley
UCAP	University of Central Arkansas Press, Conway
UCapeT	University of Cape Town Press
UChicP	University of Chicago Press
UCDubP	University College Dublin Press
UCL	UCL Press (University College London)
UCopenP	University of Copenhagen Press, Denmark
UDelP	University of Delaware Press, Newark
UDijon	University of Dijon
UDur	University of Durham, Durham, UK
UEA	University of East Anglia, Norwich
UErlangen-N	University of Erlangen-Nuremberg, Germany
UEssex	University of Essex, Colchester
UExe	University of Exeter, Devon
UFlorence	University of Florence, Italy
UFlorP	University of Florida Press
UFR	Université François Rabelais, Tours
UGal	University College, Galway
UGeoP	University of Georgia Press, Athens
UGhent	University of Ghent
UGlasP	University of Glasgow Press
UHawaiiP	University of Hawaii Press, Honolulu
UIfeP	University of Ife Press, Ile-Ife, Nigeria
UIllp	University of Illinois Press, Champaign
UInnsbruck	University of Innsbruck
UIowaP	University of Iowa Press, Iowa City
UKanP	University of Kansas Press, Lawrence, KS
UKL	University of Kentucky Libraries, Lexington
ULavalP	Les Presses de l'Université Laval, Quebec
ULiège	University of Liège, Belgium
ULilleP	Presses Universitaires de Lille, France
ULondon	University of London
Ulster	University of Ulster, Coleraine
U/M	Underwood/Miller, Los Angeles
UMalta	University of Malta, Msida
UManitobaP	University of Manitoba Press, Winnipeg
UMassP	University of Massachusetts Press, Amherst
Umeå	Umeå Universitetsbibliotek, Umeå

UMichP	University of Michigan Press, Ann Arbor
UMinnP	University of Minnesota Press, Minneapolis
UMirail-ToulouseP	University of Mirail-Toulouse Press, France
UMIRes	UMI Research Press, Ann Arbor, MI
UMissP	University of Missouri Press, Columbia
UMP	University of Mississippi Press, Lafayette
UMysore	University of Mysore, India
UNancyP	Presses Universitaires de Nancy, France
UNCP	University of North Carolina Press, Chapel Hill, NC
Undena	Undena Publications, Malibu, CA
UNDP	University of Notre Dame Press, Notre Dame, IN
UNebP	University of Nebraska Press, Lincoln
UNevP	University of Nevada Press, Reno
UNewE	University of New England, Armidale, New South Wales
UnEWE, CALLS	University of New England, Centre for Australian Language and Literature Studies
Ungar	Frederick Ungar, New York
Unicopli	Edizioni Unicopli, Milan
Unity	Unity Press, Hull
Universa	Uilgeverij Universa, Wetteren, Belgium
UNMP	University of New Mexico Press, Albuquerque
UNorthTP	University of North Texas Press
UNott	University of Nottingham
UNSW	University of New South Wales
Unwin	Unwin Paperbacks, London
Unwin Hyman	Unwin Hyman, London
UOklaP	University of Oklahoma Press, Norman
UOslo	University of Oslo
UOtagoP	University of Otago Press, Dunedin, New Zealand
UOttawaP	University of Ottawa Press
UPA	UP of America, Lanham, MD
UParis	University of Paris
UPColardo	UP of Colorado, Niwot, CO
UPennP	University of Pennsylvania Press, Philadelphia
UPittP	University of Pittsburgh Press, Pittsburgh
UPKen	University Press of Kentucky, Lexington
UPMissip	UP of Mississippi, Jackson
UPN	Université de Paris Nord, Paris
UPNE	UP of New England, Hanover, NH
Uppsala	Uppsala University, Uppsala
UProvence	University of Provence, Aix-en-Provence
UPValéry	University Paul Valéry, Montpellier
UPVirginia	UP of Virginia, Charlottesville
UQDE	University of Queensland, Department of English
UQP	University of Queensland Press, St Lucia
URouen	University of Rouen, Mont St Aignan
URP	University of Rochester Press

USalz	Institut für Anglistik und Amerikanstik, University of Salzburg
USantiago	University of Santiago, Spain
USCP	University of South Carolina Press, Columbia
USFlorP	University of South Florida Press, Florida
USheff	University of Sheffield
Usher	La Casa Usher, Florence
USPacific	University of the South Pacific, Institute of Pacific Studies, Suva, Fiji
USQ, DHSS	University of Southern Queensland, Department of Humanities and Social Sciences
USydP	University of Sydney Press
USzeged	University of Szeged, Hungary
UtahSUP	Utah State UP, Logan
UTampereP	University of Tampere Press, Knoxville
UTas	University of Tasmania, Hobart
UTennP	University of Tennessee Press, Knoxville
UTexP	University of Texas Press, Austin
UTorP	University of Toronto Press, Toronto
UTours	Université de Tours
UVerm	University of Vermont, Burlington
UVict	University of Victoria, Victoria, BC
UWalesP	University of Wales Press, Cardiff
UWAP	University of Western Australia Press, Nedlands
UWarwick	University of Warwick, Coventry
UWashP	University of Washington Press, Seattle
UWaterlooP	University of Waterloo Press, Waterloo, Ontario
UWI	University of the West Indies, St Augustine, Trinidad
UWiscM	University of Wisconsin, Milwaukee
UWiscP	University of Wisconsin Press, Madison
UWoll	University of Wollongong
UYork	University of York, York
Valentine	Valentine Publishing and Drama, Rhinebeck, NY
V&A	Victoria and Albert Museum, London
VanderbiltUP	Vanderbilt UP, Nashville, TE
V&R	Vandenhoeck & Ruprecht, Göttingen, Germany
Van Gorcum	Van Gorcum, Assen, Netherlands
Vantage	Vantage Press, New York
Variorum	Variorum, Ashgate Publishing, Hampshire
Vehicule	Vehicule Press, Montreal
Vendome	Vendome Press, New York
Verdant	Verdant Publications, Chichester
Verso	Verso Editions, London
VictUP	Victoria UP, Victoria University of Wellington, New Zealand
Vieweg	Vieweg Braunschweig, Wiesbaden
Vikas	Vikas Publishing House, New Delhi
Viking	Viking Press, New York

VikingNZ	Viking, Auckland
Virago	Virago Press, London
Vision	Vision Press, London
VLB	VLB Éditeur, Montreal
VP	Vulgar Press, Carlton North, Australia
VR	Variorum Reprints, London
Vrin	J. Vrin, Paris
VUUP	Vrije Universiteit UP, Amsterdam
Wakefield	Wakefield Press
W&B	Whiting & Birch, London
W&N	Weidenfeld & Nicolson, London
Water Row	Water Row Press, Sudbury, MA
Watkins	Paul Watkins, Stanford, Lincsolnshire
WB	Wissenschaftliche Buchgesellschaft, Darmstadt
W/B	Woomer/Brotherson, Revere, PA
Webb&Bower	Webb & Bower, Exeter
Wedgestone	Wedgestone Press, Winfield, KS
Wedgetail	Wedgetail Press, Earlwood, New South Wales
WesleyanUP	Wesleyan UP, Middletown, CT
West	West Publishing, St Paul, MN
WHA	William Heinemann Australia, Port Melbourne, Victoria
Wheatsheaf	Wheatsheaf Books, Brighton
Whiteknights	Whiteknights Press, University of Reading, Berkshire
White Lion	White Lion Books, Cambridge
Whitston	Whitston Publishing, Troy, NY
Whittington	Whittington Press, Herefordshire
WHP	Warren House Press, Sale, Cheshire
Wiener	Wiener Publishing, New York
Wildwood	Wildwood House, Aldershot, Hampshire
Wiley	John Wiley, Chichester, New York and Brisbane
Wilson	Philip Wilson, London
Winter	Carl Winter Universitätsverlag, Heidelberg, Germany
Winthrop	Winthrop Publishers, Cambridge, MA
WIU	Western Illinois University, Macomb, IL
WL	Ward Lock, London
WLUP	Wilfrid Laurier UP, Waterloo, Ontario
WMP	World Microfilms Publications, London
WMU	Western Michigan University, Kalamazoo, MI
Woeli	Woeli Publishing Services
Wolfhound	Wolfhound Press, Dublin
Wombat	Wombat Press, Wolfville, NS
Wo-No	Wolters-Noordhoff, Groningen, Netherlands
Woodstock	Woodstock Books, Oxford
Woolf	Cecil Woolf, London
Words	Words, Framfield, E. Sussex
WP	Women's Press, London
WPC	Women's Press of Canada, Toronto
WSUP	Wayne State UP, Detroit, MI

WVUP	West Virginia UP, Morgantown
W-W	Williams-Wallace, Toronto
WWU	Western Washington University, Bellingham
Xanadu	Xanadu Publications, London
YaleUL	Yale University Library Publications, New Haven, CT
YaleUP	Yale UP, New Haven, CO and London
Yamaguchi	Yamaguchi Shoten, Kyoto
YorkP	York Press, Fredericton, NB
Younsmere	Younsmere Press, Brighton
Zed	Zed Books, London
Zell	Hans Zell, East Grinstead, W. Sussex
Zena	Zena Publications, Penrhyndeudraeth, Gwynedd
Zephyr	Zephyr Press, Somerville, MA
Zomba	Zomba Books, London
Zwemmer	A. Zwemmer, London

Preface

The Year's Work in English Studies is a narrative bibliography that records and evaluates scholarly writing on English language and on literatures written in English. It is published by Oxford University Press on behalf of the English Association.

The Editors and the English Association are pleased to announce that this year's Beatrice White Prize has been awarded to Alan J. Fletcher for *Drama and the Performing Arts in Pre-Cromwellian Ireland: A Repertory of Sources and Documents from the Earliest Times until c.1642* published by Boydell & Brewer (ISBN 0 8599 1573 5).

The authors of *YWES* attempt to cover all significant contributions to English studies. Writers of articles can assist this process by sending offprints to the journal, and editors of journals that are not readily available in the UK are urged to join the many who send us complete sets of current and back issues. These materials should be addressed to The Editors, *YWES*, The English Association, The University of Leicester, University Road, Leicester LEI 7RH, UK.

Our coverage of articles and books is greatly assisted by the Modern Language Association of America, who annually supply proofs of their *International Bibliography* in advance of the publication of each year's coverage.

The views expressed in *YWES* are those of its individual contributors and are not necessarily shared by the Editors, Associate Editors, or the English Association.

We would like to acknowledge a special debt of gratitude to Gill Mitchell and Carole Bookhamer for their efforts on behalf of this volume.

The Editors

I

English Language

TERESA FANEGO, CAMILLA VASQUEZ, JEROEN VAN DE
WEIJER, BETTELOU LOS, WIM VAN DER WURFF, BEÁTA
GYURIS, JULIE COLEMAN, PAUL CULLEN, LIESELOTTE
ANDERWALD, ANDREA SAND, PETRA BETTIG AND CLARA
CALVO

This chapter has twelve sections: 1. General; 2. History of English Linguistics; 3. Phonetics and Phonology; 4. Morphology; 5. Syntax; 6. Semantics; 7. Lexicography, Lexicology and Lexical Semantics; 8. Onomastics; 9. Dialectology and Sociolinguistics; 10. New Englishes and Creolistics; 11. Pragmatics and Discourse Analysis; 12. Stylistics. Section 1 is by Teresa Fanego; section 2 is by Camilla Vasquez; section 3 is by Jeroen van de Weijer; sections 4 and 5 are by Bettelou Los and Wim van der Wurff; section 6 is by Beàta Gyuris; section 7 is by Julie Coleman; section 8 is by Paul Cullen; section 9 is by Lieselotte Anderwald; section 10 is by Andrea Sand; section 11 is by Petra Bettig; section 12 is by Clara Calvo.

1. General

The *Routledge Encyclopedia of Translation Studies*, published in 1998 but not reviewed in *YWES*, is now available in paperback. Drawing on the expertise of over ninety contributors from more than thirty countries, this impressive reference work, edited by Mona Baker, is an invaluable tool for anyone with an academic or professional interest in translation. The individual entries are organized into two parts. Part 1 covers the key concepts, ideas, movements and trends of the discipline, with topics including drama, poetry and literary translation, Bible and Shakespeare translation, corpora in translation studies, discourse analysis and translation, semiotic approaches, and many others. Part 2 presents an overview of national histories of translation in some thirty major cultural and linguistic communities worldwide. Irrespective of the unavoidable brevity of treatment, these histories offer interesting insights into the variety of activities that have been subsumed at different times under the general heading of 'translation', the role of the translator and/or interpreter as it has been conceived by different communities, and the range of incentives that have led to periods of intensive translation activity across the ages.

Moving on to work on a different, but equally global, area, we note the publication of David Crystal's *Language and the Internet*, a book that will surely be frequently referred to on many future occasions. Crystal investigates both the role of language on the Internet and the effect of the Internet on language. To this end, he looks at four Internet-using situations which he assumes are likely to contain distinctive linguistic features, namely email, chat groups, virtual worlds—imaginary environments which people can enter to engage in text-based fantasy social interaction—and the World Wide Web. Each of these is discussed in detail in a separate chapter, and this allows Crystal to show that the Internet is not a homogeneous linguistic medium but rather a collection of distinct dialects, although there are a few properties which different Internet situations seem to share, such as the frequent use of acronyms (e.g. DNS 'domain name system', W3C 'World Wide Web Consortium', etc.), distinctive graphology and spelling practices (e.g. plural -*z* rather than -*s* to refer to pirated versions of software, as in *downloadz* or *filez*) and a distinctive lexicon (*netizens, netties, illegal operation, hyperlink, ecruiting*, etc.). With respect to the impact which the Internet is making on language, Crystal stresses the fact that 'Netspeak'—the kind of language used on the Internet in its different situations—though displaying some similarities with both speech and writing, is fundamentally different from them and must therefore be considered as a genuine new medium of communication. It is in this sense that the electronic revolution of the last few decades can be said to be bringing about a linguistic revolution; as Crystal aptly notes, 'from now on we must add a further dimension to comparative enquiry: "spoken language vs. written language vs. sign language vs. computer-mediated language". Netspeak is a development of millennial significance. A new medium of linguistic communication does not arrive very often, in the history of the race' (pp. 238–9).

Among the publications on corpus linguistics that have come out this year, Elena Tognini-Bonelli's *Corpus Linguistics at Work* deserves mention in this section. The book offers a discussion of the main theoretical, methodological and application issues related to corpus work. After two introductory chapters, Tognini-Bonelli addresses in chapter 3 questions such as the definition of what a corpus is, the representativeness of the texts included in any given corpus and the sampling criteria used in their selection. Chapters 4 and 5 go on to discuss the two main approaches to corpus work, namely the 'corpus-based' approach, which starts with a set of explicit rules and uses corpus data to validate and quantify these rules, and the 'corpus-driven' approach, which, by contrast, builds up the rules step by step in the presence of the corpus evidence. The specific applications where the corpus-driven approach is exemplified are language teaching and contrastive linguistics, which are covered in two separate chapters (respectively 2 and 7) containing interesting observations on pairs such as *largely/broadly*, English *in (the) case of / Italian nel caso di*, or English *real/Italian vero*. Two further chapters (8 and 9) explore the Contextual Theory of Meaning, proposed by J.R. Firth and used by Tognini-Bonelli as the central frame for corpus-driven work. Notions such as 'collocation' and 'colligation', which are basic to the corpus-driven approach, are discussed as they were first put forward by Firth. The concluding chapter 10 argues explicitly for the setting up of Corpus-Driven Linguistics as a discipline of its own on the grounds that it has a distinctive set of goals (to make exhaustive and explicit connections between the occurrence and distribution of language items in text, and the meanings created by the text), a unique methodology, a set of theoretical and descriptive categories for articulating the body of the research and an accumulating body of knowledge which is particular to this domain of enquiry.

A number of collective volumes on important linguistic topics have appeared during 2001. One of them is Tomasello and Bates, eds., *Language Development: The Essential Readings*, which brings together nineteen representative and significant writings illustrating the contribution of child language research to developmental cognitive science. Two of the contributions—by Jeffrey L. Elman on 'Connectionism and Language Acquisition' (pp. 295–306), and Barbara Clancy and Barbara Finlay on 'Neural Correlates of Language Learning' (pp. 307–30)—were specially commissioned for the volume; the rest are articles published elsewhere between 1989 and 2001. The readings are organized into four parts, selected so as to provide a perspective on biological and computational approaches to language learning (part 4) and on basic phenomena in language development, from speech perception (part 1), through first words (part 2), to the development of grammar (part 3). The contributions having to do with English come mostly in part 3 and are written from a coherent theoretical perspective that is broadly compatible with Cognitive-Functional or Usage-Based Linguistics, as expounded in e.g. Langacker's *Foundations of Cognitive Grammar* [1987–91] or Croft's *Explaining Language Change: An Evolutionary Approach* [2000]. They include Michael Tomasello's 'The Item-Based Nature of Children's Early Syntactic Development' (pp. 168–86), which discusses experimental studies conducted with young children speaking English, French or Spanish and shows that young children's early multi-word productions are highly concrete, that is to say, they are based on particular words and phrases, not on innate and abstract linguistic categories, parameters or rules. Thus, for example, a child learning Spanish might be very good with the first person form of a verb, as in *te amo* 'I love you', but not know the other forms of that same verb—suggesting that his verb knowledge does not consist of totally abstract and verb-general rules. In 'An Exploration into Children's Use of Passives' (pp. 226–47), Nancy Budwig finds that young children's earliest passive utterances tend to involve verbs that rank high in transitivity and could be construed as having agent/patient arguments, but are nevertheless used in sequences where the agent is not overtly expressed, such as *it got broken* (the *get*-passive) and *I don't want it to be played with* (the *be*-passive). Budwig makes the important point that, while the discourse function in children's speech of these two types of passives is similar in that they both serve to background the agent, the two passive auxiliaries were used contrastively: *be*-passives were typically used to refer to events in which the agent is unknown, generic or irrelevant to the discourse; *get*-passives, on the other hand, were most often used to focus on negative outcomes. Finally, the paper by Lois Bloom, Matthew Rispoli, Barbara Gartner and Jeremie Hafitz, 'Acquisition of Complementation' (pp. 248–66), describes children's acquisition of verb complements, for example *I think Mommy's making punch*. The authors demonstrate that children's earliest utterances of this type all revolve around a very small set of main verbs (*think, know, look, see*) involving psychological states or attitudes towards external events, and which thus have a clear and delimited set of discourse functions. Similar conclusions are reached by Holger Diessel and Michael

Tomasello in 'The Acquisition of Finite Complement Clauses in English: A Corpus-Based Analysis' (*CogLing* 12[2001] 97–141).

A mainstay of functional linguistics has been the claim that frequency and repetition affect and, ultimately, bring about form in language. Some of the findings of recent research along these lines are represented in Bybee and Hopper, eds., *Frequency and the Emergence of Linguistic Structure*. The nineteen original articles included in the volume are organized thematically into three parts dealing with patterns of occurrence of morphosyntactic structures in natural conversation (part 1), and with the effects of frequency of use on change and structure at the word (part 2) and phrasal (part 3) levels. Since the individual papers are discussed in later sections of this chapter, we simply note here the importance of most of the contributions.

The collection of essays in Andersen, ed., *Actualization: Linguistic Change in Progress* consolidates Alan Timberlake's insightful observation [1977] that linguistic change is typically actualized step by step, any structural innovation being introduced, accepted and generalized over time in one grammatical environment after another. The volume contains an introductory section and two articles by the editor himself, plus eight papers by invited contributors. The focus is chiefly on morphological and syntactic change, except for Kristin Bakken's 'Patterns of Restitution of Sound Change' (pp. 59–78), which offers an account of the progression in Norwegian of certain sound changes involving lateral consonants. The morphosyntactic issues dealt with are the rise of English *wh*-relatives and of periphrastic *do* (by Alexander T. Bergs and Dieter Stein, pp. 79–93), the drift from accusative to ergative structures in Indian languages (by Vit Bubenik, pp. 95–118), the use of *thou* and *you* in Shakespeare's works (by Ulrich Busse, pp. 119–42), the development from clauses of a new category of locative terms in Northern Iroquoian (by Marianne Mithun, pp. 143–68), the loss of case in Old French and concomitant changes in word order (by Lene Schøsler, pp. 169–85), and the loss of object agreement in the participles of Romance compound tenses (by John Charles Smith, pp. 203–23). As regards Andersen's two contributions, the paper 'Markedness and the Theory of Change' (pp. 21–57) departs from Timberlake's claim that in actualization processes markedness must be understood with reference to the particular linguistic change involved, in the sense that changes will be actualized earlier in those environments which are unmarked, or more natural contexts for the change, and later in environments which are marked, or less natural contexts for the change. Andersen, by contrast, tries to define markedness in an independently motivated way and argues that, as a linguistic innovation gains currency and is generalized in a language, 'the process of actualization conforms to [a] Principle of Markedness Agreement in that the innovated element is favored first of all in marked environments, if the innovated element is marked, but in unmarked environments if it is unmarked' (p. 31). In the closing paper in the volume, 'Actualization and the (Uni)Directionality of Change' (pp. 225–48), he describes the place of actualization in a theory of linguistic change.

I conclude this section with Grabes, ed., *Innovation and Continuity in English Studies: A Critical Jubilee*, a collective volume commemorating the fiftieth anniversary of the International Association of University Professors of English (IAUPE). It contains twenty specially commissioned contributions, fourteen written by literary scholars and six by linguists. Among the latter are survey articles by

Yoshihiko Ikegami on 'English Studies in Japan' (pp. 239–50), Norman Blake on 'The History of the English Language' (pp. 251–66), Matti Rissanen on 'Variation, Change and New Evidence in the Study of the History of English' (pp. 267–73), and Arne Zettersten on 'English Lexicography at the Turn of the Millennium' (pp. 315–29). Also included are articles by Dieter Kastovsky and Hans Sauer on rather more specific topics. In 'Local and Global-Typological Changes in the History of English' (pp. 275–87), Kastovsky notes that individual, local changes sometimes move in the same direction over centuries, producing a combined cumulative effect the final result of which may be an incipient typological change, a drift. Hans Sauer, in turn, offers an exhaustive discussion of 'The Old English Suffix -ell-ill-oll-ull-l (> ModE -le, cf. beetle, girdle, thistle) as Attested in the Épinal–Erfurt Glossary' (pp. 289–313).

2. History of English Linguistics

In 'Lowth's *Short Introduction to English Grammar* (1762) Reprinted' Ingrid Tieken-Boon Van Ostade examines a series of letters from Robert Lowth written to his publishers, Robert and James Dodsley (*PubH* 49[2001] 83–95). Building on her previous work on Lowth's famous eighteenth-century grammar, Tieken-Boon Van Ostade uses these letters to shed light on the publishing history of its various editions. She provides important insights into the nature of Lowth's involvement with the grammar in later editions, including his contributions to processes of revision and proof-reading, and even his suggestions for typesetting and the quality of paper to be used. Tieken-Boon Van Ostade observes that Lowth's authorial interest in the grammar began to wane subsequent to the first two editions. She attributes this fading interest to two possible causes: his ascent to the position of bishop of London in 1777 and the fact that, after the first two editions, the publishers owned the copyright to his grammar. She makes the important point that, after James Dodsley's death, part of the copyright of Lowth's grammar was taken over by the publishers of another major grammar—that of Lindley Murray. Moreover, Tieken-Boon Van Ostade notes the great profitability of Lowth's grammar, at a time when there was 'a great interest among the general public for practical grammars of English' (p. 90).

Adam Beach also remarks on the 'tremendous expansion of linguistic projects' in Britain during this period, the middle of the eighteenth century (p. 118). In 'The Creation of a Classical Language in the Eighteenth Century: Standardizing English, Cultural Imperialism and the Future of the Literary Canon' (*TexasSLL* 43[2001] 117–41), Beach situates the standardization of English within a context of '"internal" cultural imperialism' over the British Isles, arguing that standardization of the language was essential 'in order to teach it, forcibly or otherwise, to the citizens located at the nation's periphery' (p. 118). The notion of 'classic, standardized' languages contrasted with 'primitive or savage' languages figured prominently, Beach argues, in the writings of Thomas Sheridan, Samuel Johnson, Lord Monboddo, Hugh Blair and Adam Smith. Beach suggests that Johnson's dream for his work was to permanently 'fix' the English language, thereby stopping any changes resulting from 'time and chance' and elevating it to the status of a classical language. A concomitant process to the standardization of English was securing a national literary tradition. Beach concludes by mentioning the process of cultural imperialism in the colonial context of India. He notes that while, at first, in India, Johnson's dream of a 'frozen' standard English seemed to have been realized, in reality 'no standardized language can be exported to another culture and exist in a pure form' (p. 133). In this article, Beach offers a new perspective on the conceptualization and use of standard English as a tool in British imperial expansion.

In another article addressing an eighteenth-century topic, 'Origins and Development of English Dictionaries: Nathaniel Bailey and Samuel Johnson', Bob Jordan provides a cursory overview of English lexicography (*ModET* 10[2001] 15–19). Focusing his discussion on eighteenth-century dictionaries, Jordan remarks on some similarities and differences between Bailey's dictionary and Johnson's. In particular, Jordan compares how the two lexicographers defined a small set of common words.

Biographers Beverly Collins and Inger Mees trace Daniel Jones's transformation from prescriptive to descriptive phonetician in 'Daniel Jones, Prescriptivist R.(I.)P' (*ES* 82[2001] 66–73). Responding to Crowley's (1989) claims of Jones holding 'prescriptivist and gender-biased views', Collins and Mees present a well-constructed counter-argument, pointing out that Crowley's evidence, taken selectively from Jones's earlier years, does not accurately represent Jones's views later in life. Collins and Mees observe that, while Jones's *Pronunciation of English* [1909] contained pronouncements about 'uneducated speech', 'vulgarisms', etc., he eventually 'got to dislike this book intensely' (p. 66), ultimately rewriting it completely some forty years later. According to the authors, 'by 1914 Jones was ashamed of the prescriptivism of his earliest efforts' (p. 68), and later works, such as his *Outline of English Phonetics* [1918], take a more objective approach to pronunciation. They include further evidence which seems to suggest that Jones himself did not have the intention of promoting 'this particular style of pronunciation [RP] as a standard' (p. 67). Collins and Mees attribute some of Jones's change in attitude to his debates with his contemporary, Poet Laureate Robert Bridges, who held quite 'pedantic views on pronunciation' without having any real expertise in the area (p. 68). Finally, in response to Crowley's claims of Jones's alleged sexism, they note that Jones provided many professional opportunities for women in his phonetics department, at a time in which women had quite restricted access to academic positions.

In a previously overlooked article from 2000, Ingrid Tieken-Boon Van Ostade reports on a workshop held at the Tenth International Conference on English Historical Linguistics (*EJES* 4[2000] 211–16). The topic of this workshop was the potential for applying social network analysis, as developed by the sociolinguists Lesley and Jim Milroy, to the field of English historical linguistics, specifically to examine and to explain the processes of historical language change as well as language maintenance. Tieken-Boon Van Ostade refers to a number of existing studies (among them Terttu Nevalainen [1996] and Susan Wright [1994]), which illustrate the usefulness of such an approach in producing 'new insights into the social mechanism of linguistic change' (p. 216). Indeed, Tieken-Boon Van Ostade's discussion suggests the enormous promise of social network analysis in addressing and understanding the history of standard English.

3. Phonetics and Phonology

As for segmental phonology, Cemil Orhan Orgun, 'English *r*-Insertion in Optimality Theory' (*NL&LT* 19[2001] 737–49), draws on so-called 'Sympathy Theory' to explain the effect of intrusive *r* in such forms as *draw[r]ing*, *Wanda[r] arrived*, etc., where the accent described is the Boston dialect of American English, and which has been used in the literature as a counter-argument to a non-derivational OT approach. The same analysis could be applied to many other varieties of English of course. It will have to be seen whether later Optimality approaches that supersede the Sympathy framework can also handle this phenomenon based on Orgun's insightful analysis.

W. Leo Wetzels and Joan Mascaró's 'The Typology of Voicing and Devoicing'(*Language* 77[2001] 207–44) is an important contribution towards the 'arity' (i.e. binarity vs. unarity) of distinctive features, in particular of [voice], which the authors argue to be binary at all levels of representation, contrary to much earlier work. The argument rests partly on the basis of data such as that from Yorkshire English, which has a voice assimilation process in which all voiced obstruents become voiceless before a voiceless consonant across word boundaries (e.g. *be*[tt]*ime* for *bedtime*; *su*[pk]*ommittee*; *live performance* with [fp]). In such cases a rule which spreads [-voice] best accounts for the facts. Also with respect to voicing, S.P. Whiteside and J. Marshall, 'Developmental Trends in Voice Onset Time: Some Evidence for Sex Differences' (*Phonetica* 58[2001] 196–210), find evidence for differences in Voice Onset Time, which is arguably the most important phonetic cue for distinguishing between phonologically 'voiceless' and phonologically 'voiced' plosives in English, and found differences between boys and girls, especially in the 9–11 age group and for the alveolar plosives. A third study that considers perception of voicing in English is José R. Benkí's 'Place of Articulation and First Formant Transition Patterns both Affect Perception of Voicing in English' (*JPhon* 29[2001] 1–22).

The fourth issue of *Journal of Phonetics* [2001] is entirely devoted to phonation types, an excellent choice for a thematic issue. One study in this enjoyable issue is on glottalization in American English—Laura Redi and Stefanie Shattuck-Hufnagel, 'Variation in the Realization of Glottalization in Normal Speakers' (*JPhon* 29[2001] 407–29)—in which the authors find a great deal of variation across speakers in both the degree of glottalization and its acoustic characteristics. It turns out that glottalization is used especially at the end of higher-level prosodic units.

Lisa M. Lavoie's *Consonant Strength: Phonological Patterns and Phonetic Manifestations* is a book-length phonetic study of consonant weakening, or lenition. In English, intervocalic /t/ and /d/ are subject to intervocalic weakening ('flapping') in many dialects, as in *water, writer, rider*. She argues that the role of the position in the word (initial, medial, final) and lexical stress (pre-stress, as in /t/ in *boutíque*, or non-pre-stress, as in /t/ in *bóoty*) has been underestimated in previous studies, and provides a careful study of these aspects for a number of languages, focusing on Mexican Spanish and American English (other varieties appear in passing). She shows that the primary acoustic correlate of weakening is shorter duration. This study could be compared to the study by David Patterson and Cynthia M. Connine on 'Variant Frequency in Flap Production'(*Phonetica* 58[2001] 254–75), which investigates the distribution of allophones of /t d/ in a large conversational database, establishing the prevalence of flapping in medial position in American English, and also paying attention to vowel length.

With respect to syllable structure, Jessica A. Barlow, 'Individual Differences in the Production of Initial Consonant Sequences in Pig Latin' (*Lingua* 111[2001] 667–96), experimentally investigates the representation of consonant sequences in English, focusing on complex onsets with glides (as in *cute*) and complex onsets with *s* (as in *spoon*). In the former case, the question is whether the glide belongs to the onset or is in fact part of a diphthong in the nucleus of the syllable, and in the second case the question is whether *s* is incorporated in the syllable structure at all, and, if so, whether it forms a complex segment with the consonant immediately following.

A number of papers deal with metrical phonology, intonation or rhythm. Nigel Fabb, 'Weak Monosyllables in Iambic Verse and the Communication of Metrical Form' (*Lingua* 111[2001] 771–90), shows that non-prominent syllables are regularly distributed in verse. Key to an understanding of these regularities is the organization of the verse line. The problem in terms of a generative (rule) approach, Fabb argues, is that it makes a distinction between ungrammatical (unmetrical) and grammatical (metrical) lines and it is not well suited to rules which are violable to a limited extent and which add to the recognizability of certain verse forms.

Elizabeth Couper-Kuhlen, in 'Interactional Prosody: High Onsets in Reason-for-the-Call Turns' (*LSoc* 30[2001] 29–53), investigates the intonational characteristics of special telephone conversations, viz. where listeners are calling in to a radio programme. Apart from its general findings, this study underscores that it is important to include prosodic analysis in this domain of pragmatics. Also on radio talk in the same volume is Nikolas Coupland, 'Dialect Stylization in Radio Talk' (*LSoc* 30[2001] 345–75), which deals with English-language national radio broadcasts in Wales. In such broadcasts, several stereotypical phonetic features of Welsh English, especially monophthongization of the diphthongs (ei) and (ou), creates a sense of 'Welshness'.

Alan Cruttenden's 'Mancunian Intonation and Intonational Representations' (*Phonetica* 58[2001] 53–80) claims to be one of the first descriptions of intonational systems other than RP or General American. Its specific properties are claimed to necessitate a radical change in the standard 'Tones and Break Index' (ToBI) system of representing intonation. Intonation in another variety of English is investigated in Janet Fletcher and Jonathan Harrington's 'High-Rise Terminals and Fall-Rise Tunes in Australian English' (*Phonetica* 58[2001] 215–29), which researches statement intonation in AusE, which is often perceived as being phonetically identical to yes/no question intonation. It turns out that there are subtle phonetic distinctions between the two. The article also investigates the consequences of this for the ToBI analysis of AusE. David Deterding, 'The Measurement of Rhythm: A Comparison of Singapore and British English' (*JPhon* 29[2001] 217–30), continues the debate whether Singapore English is (or is more like) a syllable-timed language compared to British English, which is (or is more like) a stress-timed one.

Also with regard to language variation, Paul Boersma and Bruce Hayes's 'Empirical Tests of the Gradual Learning Algorithm' (*LingI* 32[2001] 45–86) deals with a variety of phenomena such as the distribution of clear and dark /l/ in various American English dialects, focusing on very interesting forms in this respect such as *Greeley, feely,* and *grayling.* Boersma and Hayes show that the Gradual Learning

Algorithm proposed by Boersma makes exactly the right predictions in these and other cases.

Nicola J. Woods, 'Internal and External Dimensions of Language Change: The Great Divide? Evidence from New Zealand English' (*Linguistics* 39[2001] 973–1007), deals specifically with the shift of the diphthong in *mouth* in NZE (while commenting also on the same shift in Canadian English), and investigates the interplay between external/social forces and internal/structural factors. One of the conclusions is that particular social situations motivate change; internal dimensions may determine which sounds will shift and in what direction. Barbara M. Horvath and Ronald J. Horvath, in 'A Multilocality Study of a Sound Change in Progress: The Case of /l/ Vocalization in New Zealand and Australian English' (*LVC* 13[2001] 37–57), examine the phenomenon of /l/ vocalization in nine Australian and New Zealand cities, with an eye on specific geographical effects and spatial diffusion. Jan Tent, 'Yod Deletion in Fiji English: Phonological Shibboleth or L2 English?' (*LVC* 13[2001] 161–91), investigates the deletion of /j/ in non-primary stressed /Cju/ syllables (as in *occupation, fabulous*), which appears to be one of the few phonological markers of this variety. It is also a source of recurrent mistakes in L2 learners of English, which is the reason why Tent carefully investigates it in his article.

The first issue of the new *International Journal of English Studies*, published at the University of Murcia, provides perspectives on interlanguage, in the realms of phonetics and phonology. A number of papers in this issue deal with the acquisition of English by Spanish learners, for example, Francisco Gutiérrez-Diez, 'The Acquisition of English Syllable Timing by Native Spanish Speakers Learners of English. An Empirical Study' (*IJES* 1[2001] 93–113), M.L. García Lecumberri, 'Native Language Influence in Learners' Assessment of English Focus' (*IJES* 1[2001] 53–71), and J.A. Mompeán-González, 'A Comparison between English and Spanish Subjects' Typicality Ratings in Phoneme Categories: A First Report' (*IJES* 1[2001] 115–56). There are also papers dealing with contrastive phonetics and phonology: Paul Tench, 'An Applied Interlanguage Experiment into Phonological Misperceptions of Adult Learners' (*IJES* 1[2001] 257–76), on Korean and English; Kari Sajavaara and Hannele Dufva, 'Finnish–English Phonetics and Phonology' (*IJES* 1[2001] 241–56), on Finnish and English; and Wiktor Gonet, 'Obstruent Voicing in English and Polish: A Pedagogical Perspective' (*IJES* 1[2001] 73–92), on Polish and English. Finally, attention should be drawn to two more general papers in this issue: Charles Reiss, 'L2 Evidence for the Structure of the L1 Lexicon' (*IJES* 1[2001] 219–39), and the review article by Juan Antonio Cutillas-Espinosa, 'Learning the Phonology of a Language: An Optimality Theory Approach' (*IJES* 1[2001] 277–98).

Finally, the new volume by Ewen and van der Hulst, *The Phonological Structure of Words*, is a very clear introductory textbook which includes a host of material, in most cases also discussed elsewhere, dealing with the main categories of phonological representation: segments, features, syllables and higher prosodic units (feet and words). In chapter 1 the authors deal, among other things, with *i*-umlaut in OE, which is used to illustrate autosegmental spreading of phonological features. Chapter 2, on features, focuses again on the 'arity' question (see above), i.e. the issue whether features are binary or unary (single-valued). Chapter 3 (on syllables) may be the most interesting for the general learner, since it contrasts a number of different theories on the topic of the syllable, including a clear exposition of such concepts as government and licensing in Government Phonology. Chapter 4 mainly deals with stress, and ends with a comparison between the stress systems of Dutch and English. Every chapter ends with suggestions for further reading; there are no exercises. It is rather a pity that OT did not make it into the book at all, except for a few sentences in the epilogue, where Ewen and van der Hulst argue that their textbook mainly deals with 'representational' issues, while OT deals with the question how phonology operates. It is a pity that the relation between the two spheres of research, i.e. in the realms of underspecification or syllable structure, is not explored. One book, though not a textbook, which does offer an inroad into precisely these questions is *Segmental Phonology in Optimality Theory: Constraints and Representations*, by Linda Lombardi. This volume offers a number of studies of segmental phenomena cast in the OT framework. It is divided into three parts: the content of representations, the content of constraints, the structure of the grammar. Lombardi's own contribution in part 1 on the difference in representation of place of articulation and of voice is a well-written exposé of her position on 'arity' and underspecification.

4. Morphology

We start with matters inflectional. Gregory T. Stump's *Inflectional Morphology: A Theory of Paradigm Structure* presents Paradigm Function Morphology (PFM), a formal framework for morphological analysis which identifies morphology as an autonomous linguistic level in its own right, not as a subsystem of syntax or phonology. PFM associates a particular set of morpho-syntactic properties with a particular cell in a paradigm by means of realization rules (rules of exponence and rules of referral), which allows generalizations not only over the inflectional expression in a group of cells in a paradigm but also over an individual cell in a series of different paradigms. A language paradigm function is defined in terms of its realization rules. The realization rules are organized in 'blocks', with each block representing a particular slot in a word's sequence of inflectional affixes, so that a word's inflectional form is made up of a combination containing no more than one realization rule from any one block. A central tenet of PFM is the Pāninian Determinism Hypothesis, which states that rule competition is in all cases resolved by Pānini's Principle that the narrowest applicable rule in any particular block overrides the other rules, and is never stipulated on a language-specific basis, i.e. by rule-ordering.

Further inflections can be found in *Transactions of the Philological Society* 99:ii[2001], a special issue on the topic of paradigms. It starts with a reprint of the classic 'In Defence of WP' (*TPS* 99[2001] 171–200) by the late R.H. Robins (originally published in *TPS* 57[1959]), in which the traditional conception of morphology as consisting of words arranged in paradigms is contrasted with morpheme-based approaches, such as Item-and-Arrangement and Item-and-Process, which were being explored in American structuralism at the time. Given the paucity of paradigms in (Modern) English, the other papers in this issue understandably focus on other languages (Latin, German, Slavic and Yimas), with the single exception of 'Paradigmatic Derivation' (*TPS* 99[2001] 211–22) by James

P. Blevins. He shows that a mechanism of lexeme-preserving derivation could account for English forms such as *man-eating*, which otherwise appear to present a bracketing paradox. Two specimens of high-flight modern theory confronting inflectional facts are Peter Ackema's 'On the Relation between V-to-I and the Structure of the Inflectional Paradigm' (*TLR* 18[2001] 233–63) and Martin Neef's 'A Non-Universal Approach to English Inflectional Morphology' (*Linguistics* 39[2001] 1149–70). Both employ constraints *à la* Optimality Theory to derive the facts, but for Ackema they are violable and the facts concern richness of agreement in relation to verb position, while for Neef, the job is done by inviolable constraints that derive the forms of the plural and possessive in English. A programmatic sketch of a theory still to be further developed is presented by Sylvain Neuvel and Rajendra Singh in 'Vive la Différence! What Morphology is About' (*FoLi* 35[2001] 313–20). They argue against a view of morphology based on partial similarities and instead advocate an approach in terms of differences, specifically differences that are exploited in more than one pair of words.

Matters derivational form the main topic of Laurie Bauer's *Morphological Productivity*. It brings together twenty years' work in the field and tries to answer the question: what exactly is morphological productivity, how does it work and what does it have to say about what makes some endings more productive than others? After a detailed overview of the various ways in which the concept of productivity has been defined over the years (chapter 2), and a discussion of fundamental notions such as lexicalization, transparency, regularity, markedness and naturalness, default, and analogy (chapter 3), the focus moves to psycholinguistic findings in chapter 4 (storage, production and comprehension). Chapter 5 examines various attempts at measuring productivity and chapter 6 discusses a number of examples that illustrate some aspects of productivity discussed earlier in the book: (1) the vagaries of the reflexes of Proto-Germanic *-dōm* illustrate the diachronic dimension and show that restrictions on the bases of endings can change, as can patterns of productivity; (2) the nominalization of colour words (?*purpleness* versus *whiteness*) demonstrates the limits of constraints on bases; here familiarity, length, and etymological origin all play a part and productivity appears to be a gradient phenomenon; (3) nominalization endings, from the least successful (*-th, -ency, -ancy* etc.) to the most successful (*-ment, -ion* and conversion), exemplify competing derivational endings—neither corpus-based nor dictionary-based measures of productivity are without flaws, and the conclusion is that we still have no reliable measure of productivity; (4) agentive and non-agentive *-er* exemplifies the question of exactly what should be considered the same process when we are measuring the productivity of a process. Chapter 7 wraps up the discussion and moves on to productivity in syntax and phonology.

Another general issue in the domain of complex words is addressed in Jennifer Hay's 'Lexical Frequency in Morphology: Is Everything Relative?' (*Linguistics* 39[2001] 1041–70). She finds fault with the standard view that high-frequency complex words are accessed as wholes and not easily decomposed; instead, she argues that, given a reasonable processing model, we would expect decomposition to be unproblematic if the base word is even more frequent than the complex (as in the pair *firm–infirm*, but not *sane–insane*). Apart from frequency, there is also of course 'The Contribution of Semantic Transparency to the Morphological Decomposition of Prefixed Words' (*FoLi* 35[2001] 285–97), in which Alissa

Melinger argues, on the basis of psycholinguistic experiments, that decomposability is greater for prefixes that are semantically transparent (as in *recede* but not *receive*). Differences between listed and productively formed items are also relevant to Heinz Giegerich's 'Synonymy Blocking and the Elsewhere Condition: Lexical Morphology and the Speaker' (*TPS* 99[2001] 65–98); here it is the exact nature of the elsewhere condition and its effects that comes in for close scrutiny.

Several specific suffixes have received special attention this year. Göran Kjellmer, in 'Why *Weaken* but not **Strongen*? On Deadjectival Verbs' (*ES* 82[2001] 154–71), concludes on the basis of corpus research that the success rate of individual adjectives in forming verbs depended on the etymology and derivational history of the adjectival class they belong to, and on the frequency of the adjective in relation to other adjectives in the same class. A third significant factor was the existence of an established alternative to the hypothetical derivation ('blocking'). Semantic factors such as dynamicity did not appear to play a significant role. Mark Aronoff and Sungeun Cho consider 'The Semantics of -*ship* Suffixation' (*LingI* 32[2001] 167–73). Interestingly, it turns out that this suffix only combines with stage-level predicates (cf. *apprenticeship* vs. ?*womanship*); its specific meaning depends on the most salient stage-level property of the base (cf. *friendship*, which designates a relation, with *penmanship*, which designates a skill). Elzbieta Górska studies 'Recent Derivatives with the Suffix -*less*: A Change in Progress within the Category of English Privative Adjectives' (*SAP* 36[2001] 189–202). She contrasts paperless offices and cordless phones with acid-free paper and focus-free cameras, using a cognitive grammatical approach to tease out the differences between these two privative elements (which involve the concept of 'desirable state'). A zero suffix is commonly postulated for words such as *bag*, *hammer*, *kiss* and *dance* used in both verbal and nominal functions, but Patrick Farrell, in 'Functional Shift as Category Underspecification' (*ELL* 5[2001] 109–30), argues that the phenomenon is best analysed as involving semantic underspecification rather than the operation of a category-changing rule. The lexical semantic representations of such words include event schemas that are compatible with either noun or verb meanings. Support is found in distributional and neurolinguistic evidence. Finally, Stefan Th. Gries, in 'A Corpus-Linguistic Analysis of English -*ic* vs. -*ical* Adjectives (*ICAME* 25[2001] 65–108) investigates such pairs as *numeric/numerical* and shows that many of them are not as synonymous as has been claimed. His sophisticated collocation techniques throw up strange anomalies. With *egoist*-, for example, the -*ic* affix predominates overwhelmingly over -*ical*, but for *egotist*- it is just the other way around.

Compounding remains somewhat less popular among morphological scholars, but in 'A Corpus-Based Study of Compounding in English' (*JEngL* 29[2001] 101–23) Laurie Bauer and Antoinette Renouf show that there is no real justification for this. Using data from a BrE corpus, they show that productive patterns may break principles that have been laid down as absolute in the literature: right-headedness, the claim that English compounding does not allow internal inflections and claims involving synthetic compounding. The same authors write about 'Contextual Clues to Word-Meaning' (*IJCL* 5[2000] 231–58), an investigation of the way in which people unravel the meaning of innovative words. On the basis of a corpus study, they find that the degree of support provided by the context is generally low, with the morphological structure of the new word providing the most efficient starting-point for deducing its meaning. Compounding also features in 'Compounding and Inflection in Language Impairment: Evidence from Williams Syndrome (and SLI)' (*Lingua* 111[2001] 729–57) by Harald Clahsen and Mayella Almazan, who argue from evidence of the overgeneralization of regular plural -*s* in compounds by sufferers of Williams Syndrome compared to production of the same compounds by children with Specific Language Impairments that this specific impairment of the lexical system supports the theoretical distinction between listed lexical entries and a rule-based computational component.

Straddling synchronic and diachronic morphology is Andrew Carstairs-McCarthy's 'Umlaut as Signans and Signatum: Synchronic and Diachronic Aspects' (in Booij and van Marle, eds., *Yearbook of Morphology 1999*, pp. 1–24). The author first presents the idea that both stem and affix encode information about each other (e.g. in *whiten*, -*en* is a signans of an obstruent-final stem, while that final obstruent is a signatum of -*en*), and then shows how this idea can shed light on that happy hunting ground for morphologists, German Umlauted plurals and their history. In the same book (which is a theme volume on the topic of diachronic morphology, with Martin Haspelmath acting as guest editor), there is Damaris Nübling's 'The Development of "Junk": Irregularization Strategies of HAVE and SAY in the Germanic Languages' (pp. 53–74). This consists of a survey of the changes leading to the irregularities in modern languages (e.g. [sez] and [sed] in English), and an explanation in terms of economy (the development of short forms for high-frequency items) moderated by a tendency towards distinctiveness (needed to protect the identity of forms growing shorter and shorter). Guy Deutscher writes 'On the Mechanisms of Morphological Change' (*FLH* 22[2001] 41–8), where he contrasts the proliferation and confusion of terms for morphological change (proportional analogy, four-part analogy, extension, levelling, back-formation, hypercorrection, regular change, sporadic change, etc.) with the neat systematization of syntactic change given by A. Harris and L. Campbell [1995], who recognize only three mechanisms (cf. *YWES* 76[1997] 65–6). He then goes on to suggest that the same three mechanisms of reanalysis, extension and borrowing are also sufficient to account for morphological change.

Morphology in the early periods of English has also inspired some scholars. Alfred Bammesberger writes on '-*Um* (>-*On*) as Marker of the Instrumental Singular in Old English and Old Frisian' (*Neophil* 85[2001] 287–90). He suggests that this ending, found in *on meolcum* and a few other phrases, goes back to an old dual, expressing the meaning 'and suchlike' (as in *welig on meolcum and on hunige*, where the phrase *on hunige* was at some point added to specify the indeterminate co-ordinate). Another puzzling OE ending is investigated in Kenneth Shields, 'On the Origin of Old English *Uncet* and *Incit*' (*NM* 102[2001] 211–16); he suggests that these first-/second-person dual accusatives should not be compared with *wit/git* or *usic/eowic* (with subsequent dissimilation), but feature the descendant of an archaic IE non-singular marker -(*e*)*t*. Hans Sauer has written quite a mouthful in 'The Old English Suffix -*el/-il/-ol/-ul/-l* (>ModE -*le*, cf. *beetle, girdle, thistle*) as Attested in the Épinal-Erfurt Glossary' (in Grabes, ed., pp. 289–313); he shows that there are forty-six types of this noun-forming family of suffixes in the material, and analyses their meanings, cognates and probable time of formation. Jun Terasawa's 'The Scarcity of Formations in -*ere* in Old English Poetry' (*Anglia* 119[2001] 193–206) demonstrates that this derivational suffix, precursor of ModE -*er*, is rare in OE verse, which mainly uses *-end* and *-a* to denote personal agents, but is reasonably frequent in OE prose. A comparison of *-ere* in the works of two contemporary prose writers, Ælfric and Wulfstan, shows up noticeable differences. Hans Platzer's '"No sex, please, we're Anglo-Saxon?" On Grammatical Gender in Old English' (*Views* 10[2001] 34–47) shows, on the basis of agreement and anaphoric reference for both native and loan words, that OE inanimates still had grammatical gender, while animates largely followed a system of natural gender. Alfred R. Wedel, in 'Alliteration and the Prefix *ge-* in Cynewulf's *Elene*' (*JEGP* 100[2001] 200–10), shows how Cynewulf exploited the semantic/aspectual contribution of *ge-* in his verse. Unprefixed forms present background information, while prefixed forms are reserved for major events.

A development starting in the OE period is analysed in Jerzy Weßna's 'Suppletion for Suppletion, or the Replacement of *Eode* by *Went* in English' (*SAP* 36[2001] 95–110). He does not speculate on why, in dropping the suppletive past tense *eode*, the verb 'go' adopted the new suppletive *went*, but instead carefully traces the replacement process, finding that *went* probably did not spread from the north to the south (though this is the standard view), that the two forms coexisted for a long time, and that the specifically northern form *yode* did not survive long. The OE system of strong verbs and their development is studied in Marcin Krygier's 'Reconsidering the History of the English Verbal System' (*SAP* 36[2001] 51–9). He argues that strong verb class membership had become opaque in OE, being centred on just a few gravity points (such as the historical class 1), and that this led to various shifts in the OE period and the complete collapse of the system later. The origin and spread of the plural marker *-(e)s* is discussed in Antonio Bertacca's 'Naturalness, Markedness and the Productivity of the Old English *a*-declension' (*SAP* 36[2001] 73–93). Rather than attributing the spread of this marker to analogy, Bertacca appeals to principles of Natural Morphology and markedness (e.g. the relevant inflectional class was highly frequent; it was transparent since it had word-based rather than stem-based marking; and, unlike other classes, its plural marker was unambiguous). Plural markings at a somewhat later stage are the topic of Joanna Kopaczyk's 'The Scots–Northern English Continuum of Marking Noun Plurality' (*SAP* 36[2001] 131–40); she finds that in the period 1375–1525, Northern English does not share the strong Scottish preference for *-is/-ys* and also behaves somewhat differently in the case of irregular plurals.

An eModE phenomenon has been investigated by Julia Schlüter, who explains 'Why *Worser* is Better: The Double Comparative in 16th- to 17th-Century English (*LVC* 13[2001] 193–208). In data from the *OED* and a corpus of Early English prose fiction (of 9.6 million words), it turns out that the form *worser* is strongly preferred over *worse* in attributive use when a stressed syllable immediately follows (so that rhythmic alternation is optimized)—what we have here then is an example of phonologically conditioned allomorphy, with the condition targeting not the base but the word that happens to follow. The eModE period may also have been the time when the suffix *-y/-ie* first arose, as argued by Kenneth Shields, writing 'On the Origin of the English Diminutive Suffix *-y*, *-ie*' (*SAP* 36[2001] 141–4). He suggests it derives from the word *baby*, itself a specimen of caretaker speech (mimicking the preference in child speech for the sound *-ie*) based on the original form *babe*.

5. Syntax

(a) Modern English

A first item that we would recommend to our readers this year is Aronoff and Rees-Miller, eds., *The Handbook of Linguistics*. This is a non-technical but authoritative volume on what is known about human language, which presupposes no prior knowledge of linguistics. The book includes chapters on the world's languages, writing, the history of linguistics, field linguistics, phonetics and phonology, the lexicon, typology, formal semantics, pragmatics, discourse analysis, first and second language acquisition, sign languages, neurolinguistics, and clinical and forensic linguistics. Chapter 1, 'Origins of Language' by Andrew Carstairs-McCarthy, is an overview of what we know about the evolution of the language ability in humans. It reports an interesting suggestion by R. Dunbar (made in *Grooming, Gossip and the Evolution of Language*, London: Faber [1996]), that language evolved as an efficient alternative to social grooming—cementing social relationships is still one of its major functions today. Chapter 5, 'Historical Linguistics' by Brian D. Joseph, provides an overview of some of the issues of that field: how do changes spread, what are the mechanisms of change, why does language change happen? Chapter 9, 'Morphology' by Andrew Spencer, gives an overview of inflection, derivation and compounding, item-and-arrangement theory, concatenative and non-concatenative morphology, and complex predicates (thus providing the general introduction to the topic of morphology that we did not find among the items reviewed in section 4). Chapter 11, 'Syntax' by Mark Baker, makes the point that, although steady progress has been made in programming computers to play chess, there is still no computer system that matches the ability of an average 10-year-old to judge, generate and interpret English sentences, in spite of the huge resources devoted to this problem. However, the syntax of natural languages is not only vaster than anyone imagined, it is also more uniform. Some of the items introduced by Baker (phrase structure rules, transformations, the interpretation of pronouns) are taken up again in the next two chapters—'Generative Grammar' by Thomas Wasow and 'Functional Linguistics' by Robert D. Van Valin Jr.—but from two different perspectives, the latter including a discussion of the differences between formal and functional approaches. The next chapter, 'Typology' by William Croft, also considers mainly syntactic phenomena. The chapter on Computational Linguistics by Richard Sproat, Christer Samuelsson, Jennifer Chu-Carroll, and Bob Carpenter looks at the technical problems of parsing and annotation, computing discourse structure, and computational morphology and phonology. What shines through here is the extreme complexity of the models required for these various linguistic levels (e.g. see the figure of 'The transducer for a small fragment of Spanish verbal morphology' on p. 628), which brings home (if home it needs to be brought) the stunning complexity of human language.

Further depth in the area of syntax can be found in Baltin and Collins, eds., *The Handbook of Contemporary Syntactic Theory*, which provides researchers and students with an overview of the current state of research in syntax, mostly with a GB or minimalist flavour. The chapters are grouped by area of grammar: derivation versus representation (chapters by Joan Bresnan, Chris Collins, Howard Lasnik and Luigi Rizzi), movement (chapters by Ian Roberts, Höskuldur Thráinsson, Akira Watanabe and Mark R. Baltin), argument structure and phrase structure (chapters by

Jeffrey S. Gruber, John Bowers, Hiroyuki Ura, Naoki Fukui, Mark C. Baker and Kyle Johnson), functional projections (chapters by Adriana Belletti, Raffaella Zanuttini, Judy B. Bernstein and Giuseppe Longobardi), the interface with interpretation (chapters by Anna Szabolcsi, Eric Reuland and Martin Everaert, and Andrew Barss), and the external evaluation of these syntactic concepts (chapters by Anthony Kroch about syntactic change and by Janet Dean Fodor about setting syntactic parameters).

Another excellent work specifically aimed at students of linguistics is Robert D. Van Valin Jr.'s *An Introduction to Syntax*. Although it also covers 'the basics', it probably works best for students who are not absolute beginners. Apart from being clear and well written, its great strength is that it presents the standard tools for syntactic analysis—semantic roles, grammatical relations, lexical categories, dependency relations, constituent structure and the relation between syntax and lexicon—in the context of samples from many different languages, and encourages readers to puzzle out their own analyses of natural language data in the exercises provided after every chapter. The final chapter presents an overview of generative syntactic theories: Relational Grammar, Lexical-Functional Grammar, Government-Binding Theory (including a section on the Minimalist Program) and Role and Reference Grammar, with exercises intended to bring out each theory's strengths and weaknesses.

A work chock-full of cross-linguistic facts and surprising observations and insights is Talmy Givón's two-volume *Syntax: An Introduction*. It covers all the basic formal syntactic phenomena and concepts but simultaneously provides an introduction to the functional study of syntax, explaining and illustrating both of these approaches with sentences from a host of typologically very diverse languages. The result may be hard going for some students, and we can see the point of Givón's warning that 'the book presupposes a teacher who is either well versed in the material, or is willing to immerse her/himself in it' (p. 42). But working one's way through it is an educational experience that will give students an unmistakable sense of having widened their linguistic horizons, which is something not many books can achieve. Givón starts off with a chapter on the main characteristics of the functional typological approach, and then goes on to devote attention to the following topics: words and morphemes; simple clauses and argument structure; grammatical relations and case; word-order typologies; tense, aspect and mood; negation; pronouns and agreement; definiteness; noun phrases; verbal complementation; detransitives (reflexives, reciprocals, middles, passive, inverse); relative clauses; contrastive focus; marked topics; non-declaratives; and, finally, interclausal coherence (co-ordination and subordination, adverbial clauses; control and chaining).

A general work of a different type is David Crystal's *Language and the Internet*, a wonderful, well-written book that presents an in-depth investigation into the effects of the new medium on the English language. Far from sounding the death knell of English or any other language, the author views the Internet as a potential source of creativity and enrichment. Apart from providing a historical usage guide to the vocabulary of *flames*, *lurkers*, *troll*, *spam* and the like, and many statistics relating to the medium, his main aim is to identify the characteristics of 'Netspeak', the language of the Web. Crystal situates Netspeak somewhere on a sliding scale between spoken and written language on the basis of formal criteria, although it has to be broken down further according to the environment in which it is used: web pages, email, chat groups or virtual worlds. As email increasingly takes over the functions of the traditional letter, and comes to be used for official invitations, contracts and other formal messages, it is rapidly developing beyond its earlier image where informality was *de rigueur*. The communicative unit is, increasingly, the 'exchange', with replies to earlier messages not starting with the acknowledgement that there has been a previous message ('in answer to your letter of … ') but barging right in with the actual response: 'Fine by me'/'Yes, I think you're right'/'He'll meet you at the station' etc. An even greater immediacy of response is seen in the language of chat groups, where the limitations of the medium lead to certain adaptations: greetings ('hello everyone') are better not responded to because this would flood the screen, the order of the various replies gets mixed up because of the inevitable 'lag', and most users evolve a single-sentence style in order to achieve more of the real-time dynamics of ordinary conversation. Finally, in the language of virtual worlds the maintenance of discourse coherence is compromised even more, and conversational adaptations become almost surreal, witness the 'losing' routine one virtual world evolved as the equivalent of the repair sequences that arise in face-to-face communications when two people speak at once. Another example is the 'gag' command that player Q can resort to in order to make player P's obnoxious messages invisible on Q's screen, with player P's communicative isolation dawning on him as more and more players follow Q's example. A final example is the authorial split between the on-screen character in the virtual world and its off-screen human controller, dismissively referred to by the players as 'the typist'.

If virtual worlds are places where colourless green ideas can indeed exist, and sleep furiously (Crystal, p. 191), one wonders what the logicians discussed in Gaskin, ed., *Grammar in Early Twentieth-Century Philosophy*, would make of such a world. Its ten essays not only discuss the ideas of philosophers and logicians such as Husserl, Russell, Wittgenstein and Frege, but also show the extent to which modern linguistic theory is indebted to them. There is a lot of clearing of brushwood and debunking of myths that have been perpetuated in textbooks and other surveys which do not take the trouble to check their sources. In his contribution, 'Categories, Construction, and Congruence: Husserl's Tactics of Meaning' (pp. 54–73), Peter Simons examines the impact of Husserl's work on semantics, which was the basis of later developments in categorial grammar. Stewart Candlish, in 'Russell and Bradley: Grammar, Ontology, and Truth' (pp. 116–41), dispels some myths about the development of Russell's thought that 'have soaked deeply into the collective memory of subsequent philosophers' (p. 130), not least because of Russell's own not particularly rational way of dismissing other views. Russell was also prone to charge his predecessors with beliefs they did not actually hold; Alex Oliver, in 'A Few More Remarks on Logical Form' (pp. 142–62), refutes his claim that logicians were misled by grammar and so treated 'I met Jones' and 'I met a man' as having the same form; after showing that many of the mechanisms needed to make this equation between 'I' and 'a man'—the concept of the noun phrase, for instance— were not in place yet in traditional grammar, Oliver argues that, in fact, Russell and other heroes of modern logic committed the same mistake in their own works—as do all of us, Oliver says, unable to free ourselves from the notion that logic is somehow primary, and not just another cultural artefact. There are three essays on

Wittgenstein: 'Logical Syntax in the *Tractatus*' by Ian Proops (pp. 163–81); 'Wittgenstein on Grammar, Meaning, and Essence' by Bede Rundle (pp. 182–98); and 'Nonsense and Necessity in Wittgenstein's Mature Philosophy' by Richard Gaskin (pp. 199–217). The volume concludes with 'Carnap's Logical Syntax' by Gary Ebbs (pp. 218–37) and 'Heidegger and the Grammar of Being' by Graham Priest (pp. 238–51).

There are also several textbook introductions to English linguistics and/or grammar. Shirley Russell's *Grammar, Structure and Style: A Practical Guide to Advanced Level English Language* is a course-book offering a clear and well-thought-out introduction to linguistics at AS- and A-level English, with a bias towards aspects which provide a solid background for the analysis and evaluation of written and spoken English. The material is divided into two parts, 'The Structures of English', and 'Language and the Social Context', each of which is further subdivided into two chapters. Chapter 1, 'Language and Speech', contains sections on the features of spoken versus written language, an introduction to discourse and conversation analysis, gender-specific and age-specific features, intonation patterns, language acquisition, phonetics, accents and dialects. Chapter 2, 'Language and Grammar', contains a brief history of the vocabulary of English, loan words, grammar and syntax, including that of earlier stages of the language with a discussion of (the loss of) inflections, a short course in parsing and sentence analysis (into clauses, but not into constituent functions, and with a strong emphasis on its usefulness in composition), and an interesting section on 'breaking the rules' in advertising and in literary writing. Chapter 3, 'Language and Society', looks at gender issues, the language of the media, the language of literature, including the uses of metaphor and irony. Chapter 4, 'Language Development', presents a brief overview of the history of English from the fifteenth century onwards, including a section on 'Current Trends in Language Use' which deals with political correctness, jargon, euphemisms and neologisms. The book ends with a third, practical, section on the 'Analysis and Evaluation of Prose' and 'Directed Writing'.

English: An Essential Grammar by Gerald Nelson offers a first, practical, introduction to traditional grammatical analysis, with chapters on constituent functions, words and word classes, phrases and their functions in the clause, complex sentences, and a final chapter on word-formation and spelling, which includes British and American spelling variants and problem spellings. The emphasis is on grammar as an aid to writing. There is an appendix on irregular verbs, and a glossary. Also aimed at beginners is Kim Ballard's *The Frameworks of English: Introducing Language Structures*, but this book offers a more theoretical account, in which the student progresses from word classes to word-formation, inflection, phrases, clauses, sentences, and discourse, followed by chapters on phonetics and phonology, segmental and suprasegmental phonology. As in Nelson, there are no exercises but there is a glossary.

Kersti Börjars and Kate Burridge have written a zestful book, *Introducing English Grammar*, which deals with syntactic structure, some issues in morphology, and matters of language use. There are ten chapters (all with exercises) on the following topics: the nature of grammar; the structure of sentences (covering word structure, constituency, and tree diagrams); grammatical functions; sentence types (declarative, interrogative, imperative, exclamative, and echoes); the verb phrase (verb strings, tense, auxiliaries and verb classes); NPs (determiners, modifiers and complements); clauses within clauses (finite, non-finite and subjectless); issues beyond the sentence (information packaging, discourse strategies such as fronting, extraposition, and clefts); and grammar at work (on such topics as speech vs. writing, e-speak, and occupational varieties). Most example sentences and passages are taken from *The Big Issue* (a magazine sold by the homeless); some of these are several times weirder than any made-up examples could ever hope to be.

We have seen two works on English grammar aimed at second-language learners. John Shepheard's *Teach Yourself English Grammar* contains fifty-four units of five pages each, dealing with all the familiar problem areas (not very surprisingly, thirty-six of the units are devoted to the correct use of tense, aspect and modal verbs). The explanations and tips given in each unit are brutally brief, but the many clear example sentences and exercises (asking for matching, listing, filling in, making sentences and spotting errors; a key is provided) and the 'Grammar Summaries' at the back of the book make it a useful work for any beginner who has somehow acquired a rudimentary understanding of the language and is forced to continue by teaching themselves. For intermediate to advanced learners, there is a new edition of *An A–Z of English Grammar and Usage* by Geoffrey Leech, Benita Cruickshank and Roz Ivanič. Here, clearly laid out and formulated information can be found on grammatical patterns, their meaning, use and frequency, stylistic associations, and mistakes often made with them. In the *c.* fifty pages devoted to the letter *I*, to give just one example, there are entries (containing many cross-references) for all of the following: *I*; idiom; *i.e.*; *if* (four pages); *if only*; imperative; *in*; *indeed*; indefinite article; indefinite pronoun; independent clause; indirect command; indirect object; indirect question; indirect speech and thought (three and a half pages); indirect statements; infinitive; infinitive clause; inflection; informal; *-ing*; *-ing* clause; *instead* (*of*); instructions; instrument; *into*; intonation; intransitive verb; inversion; invitations; irregular plurals; irregular verbs; *-ise, -ize*; *it*; and *it*-patterns.

Next, we turn to work describing or developing specific theories or models of syntax. An older model is examined in Sigfrido Di Giorgi's 'Jespersen's Formalism: Problems and Extensions' (*ELL* 5[2001] 131–58), where the syntactic formalism of Jespersen's *Analytic Syntax* is reformulated in terms of the Backus metalinguistic formulas (J.W. Backus [1959]) used in the description of the syntax of programming languages. Di Giorgi concludes that Jespersen's Grammar is well able to hold its own as regards descriptive adequacy and explanatory power when compared to more modern systems. Such a modern system is described in Kempson, Meyer-Viol and Gabbay, *Dynamic Syntax: The Flow of Language Understanding*, which presents an ambitious formal model of syntax, based on the assumption that syntactic structures are interpretable by the hearer and that this process of interpretation, though complex, can be modelled. The work, which draws on the specialized fields of each of its three authors—linguistics, logic and computation—presents a further formalization of Gabbay [1996], and the emphasis is on the process of establishing the interpretation, not on the structure itself. The annotated binary-branching trees that are gradually built up reflect the partial nature of the information at every stage, with the gap between input specifications of individual lexical items and the output content getting smaller and smaller with each new tree: an emergent logical form. As the linear string to be decoded proceeds from left to right in natural language, so do the trees. The authors discuss the workings and implications of this formal model with data from relativization, *wh*-questions, crossover phenomena and quantification. Its showcase is the handling of long-distance dependencies, which is the bugbear of most formal theories, but poses no problem to a system geared to parsing in which underspecified projections can be updated at a later stage by introducing an unfixed node from some top node of the right type, which is eventually merged with a fixed position in the emergent tree structure.

The model of lexical-functional grammar is well served this year with two book-length introductions. Yehuda N. Falk's *Lexical-Functional Grammar: An Introduction to Parallel Constraint-Based Syntax* sets out the main ideas and principles of the theory in some 200 pages (including exercises), paying special attention to differences with government-and-binding theory and minimalism. The explanations provided are clear and systematic, making this an excellent work for newcomers to the theory. After chapters dealing with the characteristic lexical-functional constructs of constituent structure, functional structure, argument structure, and the relations between them, the student is shown how a grammar with this kind of architecture can deal with phenomena like control (which subsumes raising), long-distance dependencies, and anaphora. In discussing these topics, Falk also makes clear that in some cases different practitioners of the theory have explored different approaches. An appendix contains all the rules of English grammar dealt with in the book, yielding a mini-grammar of the language.

For teachers, it will be difficult to choose between Falk's book and Joan Bresnan's *Lexical-Functional Syntax*, a new addition to the Blackwell Textbooks in Linguistics. This too is an excellent pedagogical work; the fact that the author is one of the chief creators of the model that she presents further increases its value as a textbook. The theory is built up from the simplest beginnings, with Bresnan taking sufficient time over explanations of the various grammatical concepts, mechanisms and their motivations. The book's fourteen chapters are arranged in four parts, which deal with the overall architecture of UG, the formal model (involving argument, constituent and functional structures and their constraints), variation in constituent structure, and issues involving functional structure (binding, predication, control). A fifth part contains exercises, for some of which solutions are provided. Altogether, a very wide range of languages and phenomena is dealt with, making clear that lexical-functional grammar must be regarded as a serious competitor to principles-and-parameters theory not only in terms of the relative maturity of the model but also in terms of the range of phenomena that it has been able to shed light on.

More strictly functionalist approaches receive attention in several articles. Alan Huffman writes about 'The Linguistics of William Diver and the Columbia School' (*WORD* 52[2001] 29–68), presenting a survey of Diver's ideas that went into later theories of functionalism. Among these are an emphasis on the need for empirical motivation for distinguishing language-specific from universal phenomena or principles, and a view that grammatical structure arises from communicative needs, regulated by general human traits such as the capacity for inference and the preference for expending least effort in achieving a certain goal. However, it is clear that functionalism is far from being a unified approach, and in 'The Prague School and North American Functionalist Approaches to Syntax' (*JL* 37[2001] 101–26), Frederick J. Newmeyer lays bare the profound theoretical differences between the two schools of thought mentioned in his title. He explains why the impact of the former on the early development of the latter did not last, but also why there has recently been productive collaboration between scholars of the two approaches. Information about recent thinking within the school of Praguian Functional Generative Description is given in Peter Sgall's 'Functional Generative Description, Word Order and Focus' (*TL* 27[2001] 3–19). On the basis of some relatively simple word order and focus facts (e.g. the two possible orderings of the adjuncts in *Jim went by bus to a small town*), Sgall proposes certain new mechanisms in the theory (e.g. the use of dependency-based complex node labels, and the use of a hierarchy of activation for elements in the stock of shared knowledge between speaker and listener). Hallidayan grammar is represented in G. David Morley's 'Reaffirming the Predicator and Verbal Group in Systemic Grammar' (*WORD* 52[2001] 339–55). Morley considers the verbal group, comparing its analysis in early systemic grammar with that in M.A.K. Halliday's *Introduction to Functional Grammar* [1994] and that in R. Fawcett's recent work; he argues for retaining the category of Predicator, with elements of the verb group being constituents of the predicate. The relation between lexicon and syntax is studied in Peter Harder's 'The Lexico-Syntactic Symbiosis in a Functional Perspective' (*NJL* 24[2001] 232–40). The ways in which the lexicon is viewed in generative grammar and construction grammar are contrasted and it is proposed that the lexicon should be seen as a mediator between syntax (which presupposes—and is presupposed by—the lexicon) and encyclopedic knowledge.

Much more about this topic can be found in Doris Schönefeld's *Where Lexicon and Syntax Meet*. The overall aim of this work is to assess the plausibility of views about lexicon–syntax interaction in several linguistic models (the functional grammar developed by Simon Dik; Hallidayan grammar; government-binding and the minimalist model; lexical-functional grammar; head-driven phrase structure grammar; and cognitive linguistics). The approach taken is to confront each of these theories with findings from the study of language-processing, which suggest that the construction of syntactic structure starts after the first lexical item has been accessed and then proceeds incrementally as more lexical items are accessed; frequent collocations can trigger certain syntactic expectations, and well-entrenched syntactic fragments may be recalled as units. These findings are complemented with some new psycholinguistic experiments on self-repairs, overlap, and collocations. The conclusion is that most linguistic models suffer from various kinds of implausibility with regard to the relation between lexicon and syntax; the model that tallies best with the psycholinguistic evidence turns out to be Ronald Langacker's cognitive grammar.

As usual, the principle-and-parameters version of generative grammar has sparked off a lot of work. We have not seen any textbook introduction to the theory this year, but there are three monographs and a host of articles to report on. In a general piece, 'Nature, Nurture and Universal Grammar' (*Ling&P* 24[2001] 139–86), Stephen Crain and Paul Pietroski offer a helpful update of the arguments underlying the UG debate and a clarification of the issues involved. After these fundamentals, readers might like to know about the state of the art in the currently dominant principles-and-parameters model, i.e. minimalism. They could then profitably turn to Norbert Hornstein's clear and well-written *Move! A Minimalist Theory of Construal*. One of the things this book offers is a description of the reasons for the shift from government-based theories to minimalist approaches that has been gradually taking place over the past ten years, and the kinds of analysis that this shift has led to. After this, Hornstein takes minimalist considerations one step further, and shows how various construal processes (operating in control, parasitic gaps, and binding) could be eliminated from the theory, because their effects automatically follow from a movement analysis of the phenomena. This means that the theory as a whole is simplified (it in fact looks like a classic case of Ockham's razor) but of course there is a cost, in that changes need to be made in our thinking about movement. Thus, movement into a theta-marked position must be allowed, movement from A-bar positions into A-positions needs to be admitted, and a phrase must be able to move out of its sub-tree into an unconnected sub-tree (which only at a later point gets integrated with the original sub-tree). This latter mechanism was first developed in a 1995 Ph.D. thesis by Jairo Nunes, who reports on his findings in his article 'Sidewards Movement' (*LingI* 32[2001] 303–44), which very nicely complements Hornstein's book. Nunes first decomposes movement into copying, merging, chain formation and chain reduction, and then shows how sideways movement can be viewed as a result of merging. Subsequently, he applies this mechanism to the analysis of trace deletion, cases of apparent non-cyclicity (as in Chomsky's analysis of sentences like *Which claim that John made was he willing to discuss*), parasitic gaps and across-the-board extractions.

More on the minimalist model can be found in Alexandrova and Arnaudova, eds., *The Minimalist Parameter*, a collection of papers presented at a 1997 Ottawa conference. As the editors put it, the volume contains 'numerous proposals consistent with or alternative to tendencies it [i.e. minimalism] follows or anticipates' (p. vii). Taken together, the twenty papers yield a good picture of the theory, the opportunities created by it, the aspects of it requiring further development or clarification, and the alternative directions currently being pursued. Some of the papers deal exclusively with facts from other languages, but most discuss issues in English syntax or have direct implications for them. Dennis Bouchard's 'Integral Minimalism' (pp. 3–32) discusses compositionality within the NP, focusing on different types of adjectives in English and French. Susan Powers contributes 'A Minimalist Account of Phrase Structure Acquisition' (pp. 33–50), suggesting that the transition from one-word to two-word to multi-word utterances (*ball*; *see ball*; *girl see ball*) reflects the growth of phrase markers, and is comparable to the derivational steps in the generation of a sentence in the adult grammar. Hiroyuki Ura offers 'A Theory of Grammatical Functions in the Minimalist Program' (pp. 51–64) employing the notion of multiple feature checking to split up properties—in the case of the subject, these include the ability to control PRO and the ability to bind a reflexive. Sharon Armon-Lotem does some 'Checking on Checking' (pp. 65–76), suggesting that all checking is done after Spell-Out; overt movement is reanalysed as being due to requirements of Phonetic Form. Masanori Nakamura writes 'On the Role of Interpretability' (pp. 101–12), in which the aim is to assimilate the analysis of empty subject *it* to the analysis of empty subject *there* by also requiring *it*-associates (CPs) to replace *it* at LF, making *it* an LF-affix just like *there*. The analysis of head movement is the topic of Takashi Toyoshima's 'Head to Spec Movement' (pp. 115–36), where it is proposed that head movement does not involve adjunction, but movement into an extra specifier position of the target head. Bernadette Plunkett has studied 'Attract and Covert Merge: Predicting Interrogative Variation' (pp. 159–74); she provides a minimalist account of differences between English and French in the area of *wh*-questions. In 'Covert

F(eature)-Movement and the Placement of Arguments' (pp. 175–90), Artemis Alexiadou and Elena Anagnostopoulou address the cross-linguistic variation in the acceptability of postverbal subjects in (in)transitive clauses. Andrew Simpson writes 'On Covert Movement and LF' (pp. 191–204), arguing that there is no room or need for the level of LF in minimalist theory. Kerstin Hoge has looked at '*That*-t Effects in English and Yiddish' (pp. 233–48); she presents an ECP-less minimalist analysis employing an access constraint. Satoshi Oku has developed 'A Minimalist Theory of LF Copy' (pp. 281–94); here VP ellipsis is analysed as involving LF-copying (of the entire set of features or a subset). Finally, Juan Romero-Morales and Norberto Moreno-Quibén consider 'A/A-bar Movement and Attract-F' (pp. 295–308), deriving the absence of reconstruction effects in cases of A-movement from properties of Attract-F.

Many of the topics just mentioned have also attracted minimalist attention from other scholars. Thus, Cedric Boeckx, in 'Scope Reconstruction and A-Movement' (*NL&LT* 19[2001] 503–48), re-examines arguments against A-movement reconstruction and argues that A-moving quantifiers do not usually exhibit reconstruction effects because arguments are interpreted in the position where their uninterpretable Case feature is erased. Facts of A-bar quantifier raising are investigated by Benjamin Bruening in 'QR Obeys Superiority: Frozen Scope and ACD' (*LingI* 32[2001] 233–73). The starting point is the (unexpected) lack of ambiguity in sentences such as *I gave a child each doll* and *Ozzy gave somebody everything that Belinda did*. Bruening argues that these cases of frozen scope do have quantifier raising, but that ambiguity is absent because the principle of shortest movement or superiority is obeyed. Quantifier scope is also addressed (again) by Susumo Kuno, Ken-ichi Takami and Yuru Wu in 'Response to Aoun and Li' (*Language* 77[2001] 134–43). Continuing last year's debate (see *YWES* 81[2002] 24), they still refuse to accept J. Aoun and Y.A. Li's syntactic account and attempt to refute two pieces of criticism against their own expert system analysis of the facts. Unexpected binding by a quantifier (as in *Somebody in every city loves its weather* and *I took every book and put it back on the shelf*, where the quantifier does not c-command the pronoun) is the topic of Valentina Bianchi's 'Antisymmetry and the Leftness Condition: Leftness as Anti-C-Command' (*SL* 55[2001] 1–38). She reformulates the linear leftness condition that has been proposed as a solution to these cases, turning it into an anti-c-command principle, whereby the pronoun or a category containing it cannot asymmetrically c-command the variable.

Cedrik Boeckx and Sandra Stjepanović investigate head movement in 'Head-ing toward PF' (*LingI* 32[2001] 345–55).Their starting point is Chomsky's conjecture that head movement is a PF phenomenon, for which they provide evidence coming from pseudo-gapping (as in *He ate the cookies and she did the chocolate*). They note several problems in Howard Lasnik's earlier analysis of pseudo-gapping, and suggest PF movement would solve them. Though assuming a somewhat different overall model (that of Distributed Morphology) David Embick and Rolf Noyer, in 'Movement Operations after Syntax' (*LingI* 32[2001[555–95), also argue for the existence of PF movement; among the facts discussed is *do*-support. Lasnik himself contributes 'A Note on the EPP', in which he uses facts from pseudo-gapping but also VP ellipsis and sluicing (the phenomenon in which an interrogative clause is reduced to a *wh*-phrase, as in *Jack called, but I don't know {when/how/why/where from}*) to arrive at the conclusion that the Extended Projection Principle cannot be reduced to feature checking. He suggests that the approach of Boeckx and Stjepanović may solve the problems raised by this conclusion.

Jason Merchant's *The Syntax of Silence: Sluicing, Islands, and the Theory of Ellipsis* argues that sluicing examples are derived by applying two operations for which there is independent evidence: (1) a movement rule that extracts the *wh*-phrase from an IP in interrogative structures, and (2) a deletion of the remaining IP. The investigation takes in plenty of other phenomena: the commonly assumed structural isomorphism condition imposed on deleted structures is shown to be untenable, and is replaced by a focus condition on ellipsis sites which also eliminates the need for a separate theory of 'vehicle change'. Chapter 2 discusses the licensing conditions of operation (2) above. Chapter 3 examines data from twenty-four languages, which leads to a generalization about the form-identity required between the sluiced *wh*-phrase and its antecedent. Chapter 4 evaluates earlier accounts of sluicing and finds that they fail to account for the island insensitivity or for the form-identity generalizations established in the previous chapter. Chapter 5 argues that a deletion account of sluicing captures the facts of the form-identity generalizations. The island insensitivity in the crucial cases can be argued away, leaving only cases where no syntactic island is violated. The analysis supports a division between syntactic islands such as relative clauses and adjuncts, and PF-effects such as COMP-trace phenomena, certain co-ordinate structures, and left-branch effects.

The investigation of *wh*-movement has yielded some further results. Norvin Richards in *Movement in Language: Interactions and Architectures* investigates its properties in natural language. He identifies three basic *wh*-strategies: (1) all *wh*-elements move overtly to a clause-initial position; (2) overt movement is restricted to one *wh*-phrase only per clause, the others remaining *in situ*; and (3) all *wh*-phrases remain *in situ*, i.e. no overt movement at all. His investigation into the behaviour of multiple overt movement, scrambling, cliticization and object shift leads him to posit that syntactic derivation takes place cyclically. The computational system tries to avoid checking the same constraint in the same portion of the structure more than once (what Richards calls the Principle of Minimal Compliance). Gosse Bouma, Robert Malouf and Ivan Sag, in 'Satisfying Constraints on Extraction and Adjunction' (*NL&LT* 19[2001] 1–65), present a feature-based theory of complement, adjunct and subject extraction, including a new account of the *that*-trace effect. Hiroyuki Ura investigates 'Local Economy and Generalized Pied-Piping' (*TLR* 18[2001] 169–91), suggesting that pied-piping is constrained by economy (in particular, minimality); evidence comes from that classic puzzle of syntactic analysis, **Who$_i$ has not yet been decided {to belit will be} told t$_i$ that Mary has left*.

An entire volume on parasitic gaps has appeared, appropriately called *Parasitic Gaps*, edited by Peter W. Culicover and Paul M. Postal. The volume contains four major parts. The first is historical, and consists of an introductory chapter by Peter Culicover (pp. 3–68) charting the work that has been done so far on the construction, followed by a reprinted version of Elisabet Engdahl's seminal 1983 paper 'Parasitic Gaps', (pp. 69–97) and ending with Katherine É. Kiss's 'Parasitic Gaps revisited' (pp. 99–124), an updated version of her 1985 article 'Parasitic Chains' in *The Linguistic Review*. The second part considers the identifying characteristics of P-gaps. Elisabet Engdahl's chapter 'Versatile Gaps' (pp. 127–45) discusses the relation between P-gaps and category restrictions, anaphoric elements, referentiality and island facts. Jamal Ouhalla's 'Parasitic Gaps and Resumptive Pronouns' (pp. 147–79) investigates the question whether parasitic gaps are null pronouns, and if so, whether they are instances of resumptive pronouns. 'Parasitic Gaps in English: Some Overlooked Cases and their Theoretical Implications' (pp. 181–222), by Robert D. Levine, Thomas E. Hukari and Michael Calcagno, disputes the view that P-gaps are all of the category NP and that P-gaps have inherently pronominal properties. Paul M. Postal, in 'Further Lacunae in the English Parasitic Gap Paradigm' (pp. 223–49), checks the evidence for these alleged pronominal characteristics by looking at the conditions under which P-gaps are licensed. The third part focuses on pseudo-gaps. Paul M. Postal's 1994 *LingI* paper 'Parasitic and Pseudoparasitic Gaps' is reprinted as chapter 8 (pp. 253–313), and argues that only cases in which the extracted phrase is to the left of its associated gap represent true P-gaps. Andreas Kathol's 'On the Non-Existence of True Parasitic Gaps in Standard German' (pp. 315–38) argues on the basis of Postal's findings that German lacks true P-gaps. Part 4 deals with a variety of factors that limit the occurrence of genuine P-gaps. Christine Tellier, in 'On Some Distinctive Properties of Parasitic Gaps in French' (pp. 341–67), considers four major contrasts between French and English P-gaps and relates the differences to their different tense and agreement systems. Alan Munn, in 'Explaining Parasitic Gap Restrictions' (pp. 369–92), investigates the relation between P-gaps and logical concepts such as individual variable as well as the link between P-gaps and co-ordination and pronouns. Christopher Kennedy's 'VP-deletion and "Nonparasitic" Gaps' (pp. 393–402), a reprint of his 1997 *LingI* article, argues that some cases do not involve P-gaps 'inside' elided VPs or indeed any P-gaps at all but ordinary pronouns. 'Missing Parasitic Gaps' by Paul M. Postal (pp. 403–17) refines Kennedy's argumentation and shows that, ultimately, English does exhibit P-gaps 'inside' elided VPs. In another parasitic gap piece, 'Chain Composition and Uniformity' (*NL&LT* 19[2001] 67–107), Soowon Kim argues, against the standard analysis, that parasitic gaps are licensed at LF.

We saw above that Hornstein would like to reduce control to movement. Peter W. Culicover and Ray Jackendoff respond by saying that 'Control Is Not Movement' (*LingI* 32[2001] 493–512). They are sorry that the resulting simplification of the grammar (which would make it possible to do away with PRO and the theta-criterion) cannot go through, but see too many obstacles for the reduction to be successful (having to do with PRO in adjuncts and in noun complements, control properties of verbs like *promise*, and the shift of control found in *He asked to be allowed to leave*). In 'Null Case and the Distribution of PRO' (*LingI* 32[2001] 141–66), Roger Martin also presents an analysis of control without movement. He argues that control (but not raising) infinitivals contain a head T that checks null case and provides various kinds of evidence for the presence of T in control structures. Idan Landau, in 'Control and Extraposition: The Case of Super-Equi' (*NL&LT* 19[2001] 109–52), proposes a solution to the (cross-linguistic) asymmetric control relations in extraposition cases seen in *Mary knew that it disturbed John [PRO to perjure himself/*herself]* versus *Mary knew that it damaged John [PRO to perjure himself/ herself]* and to the fact that non-extraposed parallels with gerunds do not show this asymmetry. We slip in here also the one piece on accusative-plus-infinitive constructions (*They considered him to be intelligent*) that we have seen this year, Concha Castillo's 'The Configuration of ECM Structures' (*SL* 55[2001] 113–39).

The embedded subject is argued to have a T-feature needing to be checked against the head of TP (note that this makes the structure dangerously similar to Martin's analysis of control); many languages have an infinitival TP lacking the required feature, making ECM impossible. Perception verbs are different in lacking TP altogether.

Lingua 111 incorporates a special issue on the effects of morphological case, with Helen de Hoop, Olaf Koeneman, Iris Mulder and Fred Weerman as guest editors, which includes the following two papers: Eric Haeberli, 'Deriving Syntactic Effects of Morphological Case by Eliminating Abstract Case' (*Lingua* 111[2001] 279–313), which offers a theoretical explanation in a minimalist framework for the often observed link between rich morphological case systems and relatively free word order, and Joan Maling, 'Dative: The Heterogeneity of the Mapping among Morphological Case, Grammatical Functions, and Thematic Roles' (*Lingua* 111[2001] 419–64), which concludes on English, German and Icelandic evidence that mapping thematic roles to their relative positions in a theta-grid is not enough to ensure a good result; lexical rules need to have access to the content of the thematic roles.

Locative or stylistic inversion is the subject of two articles. Heizo Nakajima's 'Verbs in Locative Constructions and the Generative Lexicon' (*TLR* 18[2001] 43–67) shows that, in addition to unaccusatives like *arise* or *appear*, the construction also allows real unergatives, as in *On the third floor worked two young women*. In all cases, the verb must contain a sub-eventual structure designating a result state; this can be achieved through co-composition with a locative or directional phrase. Peter W. Culicover and Robert D. Levine, in 'Stylistic Inversion in English: A Reconsideration' (*NL&LT* 19[2001] 283–310), show that the phenomenon comprises two distinct constructions, with different derivations: 'light inversion' as in *Into the room walked Robin* and 'heavy inversion', which requires the postverbal subject to be heavy: *Into the room walked ... ROBIN!* Such constructions crop up, too, further on in the same volume in the ongoing debate (reported in *YWES* 81[2002] 23) concerning the contention of S. Lappin et al. [2000] that the uncritical adoption of the Minimalist Program had little to do with its intrinsic superiority over earlier theories. This contention is hotly contested once more by Eric Reuland, in 'Confusion Compounded' (*NL&LT* 19[2001] 879–85), Ian Roberts, in 'Who Has Confused What? More on Lappin, Levine and Johnson' (*NL&LT* 19[2001] 887–90), and Juan Uriagereka, in 'Cutting Derivational Options' (*NL&LT* 19[2001] 891–900). In their reaction to these views, 'The Revolution Maximally Confused' (*NL&LT* 19[2001] 901–19), Shalom Lappin, Robert D. Levine and David E. Johnson discuss these inversion constructions, too, and their view is that what is relevant in these constructions is appropriateness in focal position, not intonation or heaviness requirements.

Complex predicates feature prominently in William Snyder's 'On the Nature of Syntactic Variation: Evidence from Complex Predicates and Complex Word-Formation' (*Language* 77[2001] 324–42). Snyder proposes that there is a parameter involving the availability or non-availability of such constructions (e.g. *paint the house red*, *pick up a book*, *make somebody leave*, *put something on the table*, and also endocentric root compounds). Cross-linguistic and acquisitional data support the patterning of the data predicted by this analysis. In 'An Idiomatic Argument for Lexical Decomposition' (*LingI* 32[2001] 183–92), Norvin Richards finds complexity in items such as *get* and *give* in the idioms *get the boot* and *give somebody the boot*. Assuming that idioms form a syntactic unit leads to an analysis along the lines of 'X cause Y [have the boot]' and 'X become [have the boot]'; similar decomposition is found in other *give* items (*give X the creeps, give birth to X*). Jingqi Fu, Thomas Roeper and Hagit Borer, in 'The VP within Process Nominals: Evidence from Adverbs and the VP anaphor *Do-So*' (*NL&LT* 19[2001] 549–82), offer evidence that such nominals contain a VP, implying that there is syntactic verbal structure within derivational morphology. Thomas Stroik's 'On the Light Verb Hypothesis' (*LingI* 32[2001] 362–9) identifies the helping verb *do* (*yes, he does so*) as an instantiation of the head v of the functional projection vP (with the element *so* being its VP complement). Further functional projections are postulated by K.A. Jayaseelan in 'IP-Internal Topic and Focus Phrases' (*SL* 55[2001] 39–75), the relevant structure being TopP* – FocP – vP. In pseudo-gapping cases, such as *Mary hasn't dated Bill but she has Harry*, for example, *Harry* has moved to this FocP (since it has contrastive stress), after which the inner VP is deleted. In *They did it themselves*, *themselves* is also in FocP, but here the inner VP is subsequently preposed. Finally, Olaf Koeneman and Ad Neeleman, in 'Predication, Verb Movement and the Distribution of Expletives' (*Lingua* 111[2001] 189–233), argue that predication theory has a significant contribution to make when it comes to capturing the distribution of expletives, including expletives in Transitive Expletive Constructions, and V-to-I movement. Predication theory also forces an analysis of NP-raising as predicate formation.

Next, we turn to corpus linguistics, which has yielded a textbook, a monograph, an edited volume, and several other papers. The textbook is McEnery and Wilson's *Corpus Linguistics: An Introduction*, which now appears in a second edition. This updated version remains a clear and useful guide for beginning students, who can learn from it about both the conceptual underpinnings of corpus work and also its concrete possibilities and practices. There are chapters on early corpus work and the impact of the Chomskyan revolution; the meaning of the word 'corpus'; handling quantitative data; the use of corpora; corpora and language engineering; a case study of sublanguages (IBM manuals, the Canadian Hansard, and a fiction corpus); and recent and future developments. The authors have included exercises (a key is provided) and the book also contains lists of corpora and useful software. With his or her appetite whetted by all this material, the student can therefore proceed by striking out alone. Guidance on the further journey is provided by Elena Tognini-Bonelli in her *Corpus Linguistics at Work* (volume 6 in Benjamins' Studies in Corpus Linguistics series, which is shaping up nicely). The book addresses issues and implications of corpus work, both practical and theoretical (having to do with our view of language, in the spirit of John Sinclair's dictum that 'Language looks quite different when you see a whole lot of it all at once'). A distinction is made between corpus-based approaches, where the corpus is merely viewed as a repository of examples to be used for theoretical purposes, and corpus-driven ones, where the theory is fully accountable to corpus data. Such approaches are shown to form a discipline of their own, with distinctive goals, philosophical standpoints, methods, and categories. A great deal of attention is also paid to extended units of meaning (items within their context) and the theories of meaning in terms of which such units are best analysed (here, the Firthian concepts of collocation and colligation are important). On the practical side, there are chapters on criteria for corpus composition, on corpora, in language teaching, and on corpora in cross-linguistic work (where they can be useful for teaching, contrasting, and translating).

Further possibilities for corpora in teaching are described in the papers in Ghadessy, Henry and Roseberry, eds., *Small Corpus Studies and ELT: Theory and Practice* (another very useful volume in the Studies in Corpus Linguistics series). Robert de Beaugrande writes about 'Large Corpora, Small Corpora, and the Learning of Language' (pp. 3–38), arguing the need for using 'real' English in classrooms, and giving several examples of how corpora, small and large, can be made to yield instructive material (such as data on the use of the word *language* in the British National Corpus as compared with linguistic texts; or data on the patterns that the verb *see* enters into—rarely expressing direct perception as in *I see something there*, and frequently expressing stance and attitude, as in *I/they don't see that … /him doing it/him as …*). Paul Nation contributes 'Using Two Small Corpora to Investigate Learner Needs' (pp. 31–45), which is mainly on vocabulary. Mike Scott says it all in his title, 'Comparing Corpora and Identifying Keywords, Collocations, Frequency Distributions through the WordSmith Tools Suite of Computer Programs' (pp. 47–67). John Flowerdew's 'Concordancing as a Tool in Course Design' (pp. 71–92; a reprint from 1993, which we missed at the time) includes titbits of grammatical information such as the greater frequency of PPs with attributive rather than predicative function and the various placement options of the word *then*. Alex Henry and Robert Roseberry offer ideas on 'Using a Small Corpus to Obtain Data for Teaching a Genre' (pp. 93–133), the two genres being (spoken) introductions of guest speakers and letters of application; they describe their overall structure and lexico-grammatical patterning, suggesting specific uses in teaching. Marina Bondi studies 'Small Corpora and Language Variation: Reflexivity across Genres' (pp. 135–74), comparing economics textbooks and journal abstracts with regard to the use of argumentative expressions (i.e. claims, concessions, proofs, beliefs, etc.). Vincent B.Y. Ooi considers 'Investigating and Teaching Genres Using the World Wide Web' (pp. 175–203), focusing on personal ads and their lexical-grammatical properties (e.g. the words *old* and *sense*). Peter H. Ragan presents thoughts about 'Classroom Use of a Systemic Functional Small Learner Corpus' (pp. 207–36) and provides an analysis of a corpus of instructions written by native and non-native speakers. Old corpus cracks Geoff Barnbrook and John Sinclair have joined up to write 'Specialised Corpus, Local and Functional Grammars' (pp. 237–76), in which their aim is to develop a complete grammar of the definitions found in the *Collins Cobuild Students' Dictionary*. As they point out, such a grammar can play an important role in quality control and the making of new dictionaries.' Ann Lawson writes about 'Collecting, Aligning and Analysing Parallel Corpora' (pp. 279–309), providing information about how to make a corpus containing translations of the same text, using the example of Plato's *Republic*. Geoff Thompson's 'Corpus, Comparison, Culture: Doing the Same Thing Differently in Different Cultures' (pp. 311–34) looks at English and Chinese tourist brochures as well as English and Swiss job ads, and finds numerous differences in grammatical choices. Mohsen Ghadessy and Yanjie Gao write about 'Small Corpora and Translation: Comparing Thematic Organization in Two Languages' (pp. 335–59), a study of Hallidayan theme in news commentary in English and Chinese. Lynne Flowerdew considers 'The Exploitation of Small Learner Corpora in EAP Materials Design' (pp. 363–79), discussing the uses of such corpora and making some caveats.

Christopher Tribble investigates 'Small Corpora and Teaching Writing' (pp. 383–408), advocating a genre-based approach and using lexical, grammatical and textual features of promotional leaflets on the World Wide Web as an example.

Two more papers on corpus findings that we would like to mention here have appeared in *ICAME*. Although the collocation results reported by John Newman and Sally Rice in 'English SIT, STAND, and LIE in Small and Large Corpora' (*ICAME* 25[2001] 109–34) are in themselves not particularly remarkable (*lay down* appears predominantly conjoined with expressions for 'sleep' etc.), they do make interesting reading from the perspective of the cross-linguistic tendency for aspectual expressions to develop out of such posture verbs, as the authors point out: the first beginnings of the inchoative aspect often developed by STAND verbs can be underpinned by the tendency they found for the English past tense *stood up* to occur co-ordinated with verbs that represent a new activity undertaken after the change in posture. With *sit down*, the -*ing*-form is more frequent and the activity is simultaneous with rather than consecutive to holding or changing the posture, again reminiscent of the cross-linguistic tendency of SIT to develop into a progressive marker. Margareta Westergren Axelsson and Angela Hahn, in 'The Use of the Progressive in Swedish and German Advanced Learner English: A Corpus-Based Study' (*ICAME* 25[2001] 5–30), demonstrate that there have been changes in the use of the progressive in English in recent decades which have not made it into learners' grammars yet.

Three other articles discuss general points of corpus work. Gerhard Leitner, in 'Lexical Frequencies in a 300 Million Word Corpus of Australian Newspapers: Analysis and Interpretation' (*IJCL* 5[2000] 147–78), uses this corpus to discuss the dangers of generalizing corpus findings beyond the data actually found there, and the problem of whether the corpus is truly representative. Wolfgang Teubert, in 'Corpus Linguistics and Lexicography' (*IJCL* 6[2001] 125–53), discusses the danger of corpus linguistics in its present state getting bogged down in technical details of standardizing coding and tagging instead of concentrating on the question of how the analysis of corpora may contribute to our knowledge of language and establishing it as a discipline in its own right. Evelyne Viegas, in 'The Propagation of Core Lexicons Using On-Line Language Resources and Savoir Faire' (*IJCL* 5[2000] 133–45), describes an experiment to extend a semantics-based core lexicon with paradigmatic relations and to predict the syntactic behaviour of verbs from their semantics, the results of which are relevant for the construction of a multi-purpose multilingual lexical knowledge base at minimal cost.

After all these general works, theory-bound contributions, and corpus concerns, we will now report on the year's work on the various elements of the clause, starting with NPs, then moving on to subjects, verb groups and their properties, complements, adjuncts, and finally complex constituents, mopping up anything else that we meet on the way. Hana Filip, in 'Nominal and Verbal Semantic Structure: Analogies and Interactions' (*LangS* 23[2001] 453–501), examines parallels in semantic structure between NPs and VPs and argues on the basis of data from English, Slavic, German and Finnish that these interactions are semantically motivated and best described within a constraint-based framework. NPs with a surprising article have been studied by Göran Kjellmer in '"It's a interesting book": On the Use of the Indefinite Article Before a Vowel in English' (*NM* 102[2001] 307–15). It turns out *a* used before a vowel occurs in 0.4 per cent of all possible cases in the Cobuild Corpus, with informal spoken texts having the highest frequencies; among the reasons for its use may be selection of this form before the following noun has been selected, or it may be a survival from earlier English (as is certainly the case in Scottish English). Jeanette K. Gundel, Nancy Hedberg and Ron Zacharski's 'Definite Descriptions and Cognitive Status in English: Why Accommodation is Unnecessary' (*ELL* 5[2001] 273–95) tries a solution in terms of the Givenness Hierarchy framework. They support their analysis by a corpus investigation. Richard Epstein, in 'The Definite Article, Accessibility, and the Construction of Discourse Referents' (*CogLing* 12[2001] 333–78), proposes that the basic meaning of the definite article cannot be adequately defined in terms of familiarity or unique identifiability. Its function is better described as signalling the availability of an access path through a configuration of mental spaces or cognitive domains.

Adjectives inside NPs form the topic of Artemis Alexiadou's 'Adjective Syntax and Noun Raising: Word Order Asymmetries in the DP as the Result of Adjective Distribution' (*SL* 55[2001] 217–48), where English/French/Greek patterns in adjective position are analysed as involving possible base-generation of the adjective as a predicative in a relative. More clearly predicative adjectives are the topic of Winfried Lechner's 'Reduced and Phrasal Comparatives' (*NL&LT* 19[2001] 683–735), which examines the relationship between phrasal comparatives (*John is older than Mary*) and clausal comparatives (*John is older than Mary is*). Nouns turning into adjectives are investigated in 'Gradience and Linguistic Change' by David Denison (in Brinton, ed., *Historical Linguistics 1999*, pp. 119–44). Looking at words that appear to waver between adjectives and nouns in recent English (*a very fun party, an extremely Oxbridge accent*) Denison investigates the boundaries between word classes and the consequences for linguistic analysis. Christopher Kennedy, in 'Polar Opposition and the Ontology of "Degrees"' (*Ling&P* 24[2001] 33–70), argues on the basis of the distribution and interpretation of antonymous adjectives that 'degrees' must be modelled as intervals on a scale rather than as points. Carita Paradis, in 'Adjectives and Boundedness' (*CogLing* 12[2001] 47–65), examines the characteristic of boundedness in adjectives from a cognitive perspective. Boundedness is a high-level schematic domain mode, which is abstract in the sense that it configures a wide range of different content domains, but at the same time highly concrete in that it is associated with basic experience of countability, aspectuality and gradability. The property of boundedness is not fixed but context-dependent and can be manipulated.

'Proximal and Distal Demonstratives', by Simon Botley and Tony McEnery (*JEngL* 29[2001] 214–33), presents evidence against the claim that the former tend to be used with antecedents that are closer in textual and cognitive space than the antecedents of the latter. The preliminary work of corpus annotation that made this exploration of demonstratives possible is described in 'Demonstratives in English' (*JEngL* 29 [2001] 7–33), by the same authors. Sun-Young Oh's 'A Focus-Based Study of English Demonstrative Reference with Special Reference to the Genre of Written Advertisements' (*JEngL* 29[2001] 124–48) argues that focus is the deciding factor that explains why the use of demonstratives is so different in different discourse types (speech, writing, advertisements, etc.). Francis Cornish, in '"Modal" *that* as Determiner and Pronoun: The Primacy of the Cognitive-Interactive Dimension' (*ELL* 5[2001] 297–315), investigates the 'modal' use of the demonstrative *that*, i.e. the choice of *that* rather than the expected *this* or *it* to refer to a referent that has been evoked in the immediately prior discourse, as in *I'm not going to the Eisteddfod this year. Work does not allow that* (Cornish' real-life example 10, p. 303). He argues that the principles underlying this use are social and cognitive and do not have anything to do with proximity or attention focus. J. Dever, in 'Complex Demonstratives' (*Ling&P* 24[2001] 271–330), presents a formal analysis of the syntax and semantics of complex demonstratives such as *that man in the corner* (in which a nominal head is both pre- and postmodified). Makoto Kanazawa, in 'Singular Donkey Pronouns are Semantically Singular' (*Ling&P* 24[2001] 383–403), argues against the idea that *it in Every farmer who owns a donkey beats it* (which can be paraphrased as *Every farmer who owns a donkey beats the donkey or donkeys he owns*) is semantically numberless.

Simple subjects have not received a great deal of attention, but there is Marcel den Dikken on '"Pluringulars", Pronouns and Quirky Agreement' (*TLR* 18[2001] 19–41). He considers cases like *The identity of the participants are to remain a secret, The committee have decided* and *The poor are having a hard time*, suggesting that in some cases there could be an invisible pronoun *pro* inducing plural agreement. Ellen Thompson, 'Temporal Dependency and the Syntax of Subjects' (*JL* 37[2001] 287–312), explores the interface between the syntactic and semantic representation of natural language by looking at temporal dependency of gerundive relative clauses, which, she claims, requires syntactic locality at LF.

After the subject comes the verb, and that has tense, aspect and mood. Ronald W. Langacker, in 'The English Present Tense' (*ELL* 5[2001] 251–72), offers a solution to the well-known problem that this category is not adequately analysed as indicating present time: present-time events often cannot be expressed in the present tense, and the present tense is also used to express non-present events. Langacker suggests 'coincidence with the time of speaking' is a more adequate characterization provided the conceptual factors involved are taken into account. Frank Brisard, in '*Be going to*: An Exercise in Grounding' (*JL* 37[2001] 251–85), investigates the semantics of *be going to* in a cognitive framework and concludes that it features a paradoxical but pragmatically plausible interpretation of the future as non-given, yet present. In 'The Syntax of Complex Tenses' (*TLR* 18[2001] 125–67), Marit Julien argues that every clause has two tense projections, one being [± Past] and the other one [± Future]; other tenses require a bi-clausal structure. A comparison with Reichenbachian and similar analyses is included. Also theoretical in outlook is Miguel Leith and Jim Cunningham's 'Aspect and Interval Tense Logic' (*Ling&P* 24[2001] 331–81); it defines a 'computationally tractable' model of J. Halpern and Y. Shoham's interval tense logic which is tested on a core set of aspectual structures. A descriptive piece is Devyani Sharma's 'The Pluperfect in Native and Non-Native English: A Comparative Corpus Study' (*LVC* 13[2001] 343–73). Comparison of the Brown, LOB and Kolhapur corpora shows that American English employs the fewest pluperfects (which are often accompanied by an adverbial locating the event in time) and that Indian English has most pluperfects (often with present perfect and past meanings) and fewest adverbials. John M. Anderson, in 'Modals, Subjunctives, and (Non-)Finite-ness' (*ELL* 5[2001] 159–66), re-examines the concept of finiteness by looking at morphological and periphrastic subjunctives in English. Finite verbs could be said to license embedding (sentencehood), a syntactic property which could be labelled 'syntactic finiteness'. Morphological properties may, but need not, coincide with syntactic finiteness, and keeping the two kinds of finiteness—syntactic and morphological—distinct may lead to new insights into the syntax and morpho-syntax of the English modals.

The second edition of F.R. Palmer's *Mood and Modality* (first published in 1986) draws on data from a wide variety of languages. After an introductory chapter, there are three chapters on modal systems; chapter 2 on propositional modality (epistemic, evidential, interrogative, negative, and discourse), chapter 3 on event modality (deontic, dynamic, imperative and jussive, and purposive), and chapter 4 on modal verbs (possibility, necessity and negation). The next three chapters deal with mood: chapter 5 investigates the indicative and subjunctive and their uses, chapter 6 realis and irrealis (joint and non-joint systems) and the relation of this system to various propositional modalities (speculative and deductive, interrogative, negative, reported, presupposed, conditional and habitual past). Chapter 7 discusses the extent of overlap between irrealis and subjunctive, and which other structures can express irrealis. Irrealis can also be expressed by the past tense (chapter 8).

Maurizio Gotti and Marina Dossena have edited *Modality in Specialized Texts*. In their introduction (pp. 9–18), they sketch the various types of modality, discuss the crucial role of modality in specialized texts (since it determines the overall understanding), and give an overview of the following chapters. Among these we note Irma Taavitsainen on English medical writings in the period 1375–1750, when markers of evidentiality develop in scientific writing (pp. 21–52); Gabriella del Lungo Camiciotti on the decline in the expression of volition in late ME wills (pp. 71–88); Maurizio Gotti on the meanings of *will* and *shall* in eModE statutes (pp. 89–112); Marina Dossena on adverb(ial)s with modal and intensifying meanings in eModE legal texts (pp. 113–32); Roberta Facchinetti on conditionals in eModE (pp. 133–50); Giuliana Garzone on modality and performative discourse in PDE legal texts (pp. 153–74); Giuliana Diani on modality and speech acts in British Acts of Parliament (pp. 175–92); Ken Hyland on hedges and boosters in research articles (pp. 291–310); Davide Simone Giannoni on deontics in 'Instructions to the Authors' of English academic journals (pp. 311–40); Polly Walsh on modals in concluding paragraphs in *The Economist* (pp. 361–78); Belinda Crawford Camiciottoli on learners' errors in understanding modality in economic texts (pp. 379–96); and Pauline Webber, Huon Snelgrove and Philippa Mungra on modality in medical texts (pp. 399–416). The detailed analyses in these chapters show clearly how uses of modality are determined by matters such as context, purpose, and topic.

Next is negation. Chung-Hye Han writes about 'Force, Negation and Imperatives' (*TLR* 18[2001] 289–325). She contrasts the grammaticality of negated imperatives in English with their ungrammaticality in Greek and other languages, attributing this to an incoherent phrase structure in Greek (and other) negated imperatives, where IMP would end up being c-commanded by NEG. Jennifer Smith studies double negation in 'Negative Concord in the Old and New World: Evidence from Scotland' (*LVC* 13[2001] 109–34). She distinguishes several negative concord contexts, and finds that data from north-east Scotland and New York show the phenomenon in only one context (postverbal indeterminates, as in *He didn't say nothing/no word*), while other US varieties have it also elsewhere (and therefore appear to have extended the original pattern). Göran Kjellmer, in 'No Work will Spoil a Child: On Ambiguous Negation, Corpus Work, and Linguistic Argument' (*IJCL* 5[2000] 121–32), reports on the ambiguity as seen in the string in the title, which is ambiguous between 'not to work will spoil a child' and 'no work of any kind will spoil a child'. The results of corpus work, which reveal that the second interpretation is far more frequent in such cases than the first one, is used to argue for a synthesis between using intuitions and corpus data in linguistic research.

We have arrived at complements to the verb. Elizabeth Ritter and Sara Thomas Rosen, in 'The Interpretive Value of Object Splits' (*LangS* 23[2001] 425–51), report the existence of two classes of direct objects in a range of different languages. Such 'splits' are evident from differences in case marking, position, or verb-agreement properties, and invariably correlate with specificity and indefiniteness, or with delimitation or boundedness of the event. They are best accounted for by assuming an object feature [Quantization]. In 'The Real-World Colour of the Dative Alternation' (*LangS* 23[2001] 525–50), Marjolein Groefsema argues that the fact that the dative alternation is only seen with some verbs (*John gave the book to Mary/ John gave Mary the book*) and not with others (*John donated the painting to a museum/ *John donated a museum the painting*) can be accounted for if we accept that these two subcategorization frames have different semantics which do not fit all dative verbs. Adele Goldberg, in 'Patient Arguments of Causative Verbs Can Be Omitted: The Role of Information Structure in Argument Distribution' (*LangS* 23[2001] 503–24), shows that themes with low discourse prominence can be left out, in which case the activity comes to be perceived as atelic (either iterative or generic); an example is *The chef-in-training chopped and diced all afternoon* (p. 506). Rong-Rong Kao, in 'Where Have the Prepositions Gone? A Study of English Prepositional Verbs and Input Enhancement in Instructed SLA' (*IRAL* 39[2001] 195–215), reports that Japanese EFL learners (1) use the null-preposition construction, (2) generally prefer preposition stranding over pied piping, but (3) employ more pied piping in relative clauses than in *wh*-questions, and considers various explanations and their implications for EFL or ESL teaching. A fundamental insight into the status of prepositions is provided by Karen Froud, in 'Prepositions and the Lexical/Functional Divide' (*Lingua* 111[2001] 1–28), who argues on the basis of data from an aphasic patient whose deficits only affect his use of functional categories that prepositions apparently belong in the functional domain, even though they are traditionally classified as the fourth major lexical category.

Some verbs have received individual attention this year. Joybrato Mukherjee, in 'Principles of Pattern Selection' (*JEngL* 29[2001] 295–314), builds on F. Hunston and G. Francis's *Pattern Grammar* ([2000]; discussed in *YWES* 81[2002] 18–19) in his study of the argument structure of the verb *provide*. John Newman has written 'A Corpus-Based Study of the Figure and Ground in Sitting, Standing, and Lying Constructions' (*SAP* 30[2001] 203–16). Data from the Bank of English show that the subject of these verbs is predominantly human and they are usually followed by specific types of PP; a cognitive profile for the verbs is developed. The general mechanism of argument linking appears in Nikolas Gisborne's 'The Stative/ Dynamic Distinction and Argument Linking' (*LangS* 23[2001] 603–28), where it is argued that the stative/dynamic contrast can be derived through the linking of semantic relations, offering support for Jackendoff's [1990] semantic tiering hypothesis.

Resultatives (as in *The pond froze solid* and *The dog barked him awake*) crop up in several contributions. Malka Rappaport Hovav and Beth Levin propose 'An Event Structure Account of English Resultatives' (*Language* 77[2001] 766–97).

They survey and criticize current syntactic analyses and instead propose a semantic one, based on principles of well-formed event structure and its mapping to syntax. Stephen Wechsler and Bokyung Noh's 'On Resultative Predicates and Clauses: Parallels between Korean and English' (*LangS* 23[2001] 391–423) offers an HPSG analysis of these structures and shows that the apparent differences between the two languages disappear if it is realized that English tends to use secondary predication where Korean prefers clausal subordination. Claudia Brugman's 'Light Verbs and Polysemy' (*LangS* 23[2001] 551–78) argues that the light verbs which are assumed to head complex predicates are not empty of lexical content but are systematically related to their main-verb counterparts, and make their own, systematic contribution to the construction. A special grammaticalized case of a resultative construction is discussed in Jochen Zeller's 'How Syntax Restricts the Lexicon: Particle Verbs and Internal Arguments' (*LingB* 188[2001] 459–92), which argues that the object in a particle-verb construction is not selected by the verb but by the particle. Syntactically, the particle heads a phrase which occupies the object position of the verb, an analysis reminiscent of the Small Clause.

There is now a paperback version of Alsina, Bresnan and Sells, eds., *Complex Predicates* ([1997]; missed by us on first publication). Two types of account can be given of these constructions: they may be treated just like complementation patterns, but taking the form of a single word, or they may be viewed as instances of a special predicate composition mechanism. On English, the volume contains a contribution by Edwin Williams, 'Lexical and Syntactic Complex Predicates' (pp. 13–28); here, some small clauses are argued to be lexical (e.g. *wipe clean, put together,* prepositional passives) while others are syntactic (e.g. *consider strange*). Samuel J. Keyser and the late Ken Hale write 'On the Complex Nature of Simple Predicators' (pp. 39–65); as in their earlier work, they basically decompose everything that can be decomposed (so that *to shelve* becomes 'cause to make X be on shelf'); this has implications for several principles of grammar, as they make clear. Adele Goldberg, in 'Making One's Way Through the Data' (pp. 151–73), argues that a sentence such as *He dug his way out of the prison* has a meaning of motion that cannot be derived from its components but that inheres in the construction as such. Paul Kiparsky has some 'Remarks on Denominal Verbs' (pp. 473–99), and argues against Hale and Keyser's syntactic decomposition, preferring a semantic theory of the process (for causatives/inchoatives and zero objects).

Adverbs and adverbials have not sparked a great deal of work. Joseph Taglicht, in 'Actually, There's More to it Than Meets the Eye' (*ELL* 5[2001] 1–16), presents an analysis of the syntax, semantics, pragmatics and phonology of the word *actually*. Constraints on the use of *actually* as a propositional modifier (as opposed to its other disjunctive use as a discourse modifier) rely heavily on the feature 'assertive/non-assertive', which, Taglicht argues, is required not just for *actually* but for all structures that denote propositions, irrespective of their syntactic form. Other aspects of the same word are examined in Rebecca Clift's 'Meaning in Interaction: The Case of *Actually*' (*Language* 77[2001] 245–91). It is shown that clause-final and initial position of this word are both available for the functions of informing, topic movement and self-repair, but in systematically different ways (having to do with features such as 'other-' vs. 'self-directed' and disjunctive or non-disjunctive topic change). Adele E. Goldberg and Farrell Ackerman write on 'The Pragmatics of Obligatory Adjuncts' (*Language* 77[2001] 798–814), addressing sentences such as *This house was built *(last year)*. Rejecting an analysis by J. Grimshaw and S. Vikner based on event structure (*YWES* 74[1995] 31), they propose that the adjunct is needed because every utterance must have a focus (= new information); the same principle, a subcase of H.P. Grice's maxim of quantity, makes middles without an adjunct impossible (*This car drives *(like a bomb)*).

There are a few items on relations between clausal constituents. John A. Hawkins, in 'Why are Categories Adjacent?' (*JL* 37[2001] 1–34), argues on the basis of distance computations of dependency relations in many different languages that the answer involves processing efficiency. The erosion of morphological marking in the history of English obscures dependency relations, and leads to greater emphasis on adjacency of dependent elements. There is a special 'Anaphora' issue of the *Australian Journal of Linguistics* this year (21:i[2001]). The emphasis is on topic-chaining of the type popularized by Talmy Givón and featuring the use of zero, bound pronouns, independent pronouns, definite NPs and referential indefinite NPs to mark co-reference across clauses. Most of the papers are on languages other than English, but we mention here Lesley Stirling's 'The Multifunctionality of Anaphoric Expressions: A Typological Perspective' (*AuJL* 21:i[2001] 7–23), which shows that the use of a marked form signals the start of a new discourse unit, and Keith Allan's 'From *A* to *The*' (*AuJL* 21:i[2001] 73–82), where a semantic analysis is provided of chaining, as in *I met a man last month; when I saw the man again last week* ... Classical binding phenomena are investigated in 'Primitives of Binding' (*LingI* 32[2001] 439–92) by Eric Reuland, who builds on earlier work by himself and T. Reinhart (see *YWES* 71[1992] 41) but now provides a minimalist version of their proposal. Crucially, he assumes an economy principle counting interpretative steps.

Complex sentences featuring *it* as a dummy subject have been investigated by Philip H. Miller in 'Discourse Constraints on (Non-)Extraposition from Subject in English' (*Linguistics* 39[2001] 683–701). He notes that extraposition of sentential subjects (e.g. *It is impossible that he said so/to say so*) is obligatory if the subject represents new information; old and inferrable information may remain non-extraposed (the choice depending on the discourse status of the predicate). In '"It comes time": A Look at Existential *It*' (*ES* 28[2001] 328–35) Göran Kjellmer investigates the innovation *It came time to leave*, which he shows by corpus figures to be on the rise, particularly in American English. The innovation does not signal any change in syntax as it only shows up in this one phrase as a fixed expression, and may be either a historical dialectal survival or due to language contact, or a combination of both.

'The Acquisition of Finite Complement Clauses in English: A Corpus-Based Analysis' (*CogLing* 12[2001] 97–141), by Holger Diesel and Michael Tomasello, charts the production of such clauses in the speech of seven children aged 1;2 to 5;2. The complement clauses of the younger children are typically tacked on to imperfect main clauses whose main function appears to be that of an epistemic marker, attention-getter, or marker of illocutionary force. The fact that these embryonic main clauses invariably contain verbs from a limited list supports the conclusion that these constructions are 'constructional islands' and are not yet licensed by a general schema or rule. David Adger and Josep Quer write about 'The Syntax and Semantics of Unselected Embedded Questions' (*Language* 77[2001] 107–33). They note that some predicates allow an embedded question only in negative and interrogative contexts (*Was it clear if he was happy or not?* and *It wasn't clear if ...* versus **It was clear if he was happy or not*) and argue that such questions contain a determiner-like functional projection which is licensed only in negative polarity contexts.

John Anderson writes on 'Raising Control' (*SL* 55[2001] 77–111), in which he builds on his notional theory of categories to analyse control as sharing many properties with raising. Various types of matrix predicate are discussed, as is control in adjuncts. Helen Goodluck considers 'The Nominal Analysis of Children's Interpretation of Adjunct PRO Clauses' (*Language* 77[2001] 494–509), which concerns the well-known problem of children with adjunct PRO (yielding readings like *Fred hugged Sue$_i$ before PRO$_i$ leaving the room*). Goodluck provides experimental evidence for the idea that children attach the adjunct correctly but interpret it as a PP; she also notes that some children acquire the adult analysis earlier than is usually thought.

Gerald P. Delahunty looks at 'Discourse Functions of Inferential Sentences' (*Linguistics* 39[2001] 517–45). He argues for a broad range of interpretations of sentences like *It isn't that his brainpower is weak* (inferentials, aka sentential-focus clefts), which can express an explanation, interpretation but also cause, reason, result or consequence. Delahunty analyses *it is that* as an expletive matrix. Monika Doherty's 'Cleft-Like Sentences' (*Linguistics* 39[2001] 607–38) is concerned with sentences like *The question is what we should do*, *The way we make a cake is by ...* , and *The reason I did it is that ...* ; their discourse functions are discussed and a comparison is made with similar sentences and discourse functions in German. Mats Johansson considers 'Clefts in Contrast: A Contrastive Study of *It* Clefts and *Wh* Clefts in English and Swedish Texts and Translations' (*Linguistics* 39[2001] 547–82), finding various differences between the languages with regard to (preferred) functions and frequencies of the two constructions. In 'A Framework for the Analysis of Cleft Constructions' (*Linguistics* 39[2001] 463–516), Knud Lambrechts adopts Otto Jespersen's view of clefts whereby *it is ... that/who* is semantically empty but pragmatically focus-inducing. The function of clefts can then be seen to mark as focal an argument that might otherwise taken to be non-focal, or vice versa for a predicate. *Wh*-clefts, reverse *Wh*-clefts and *Wh*-amalgams (*What he should do is he should leave at once*) are also analysed.

We have seen only two items on relative clauses. Hongyin Tao and Michael J. McCarthy, in 'Understanding Non-Restrictive *Which*-Clauses in Spoken English, Which is Not an Easy Thing' (*LangS* 23[2001] 651–77), conclude on the basis of a corpus of spoken English that such clauses fall into three types: 'expansion', 'evaluation' and 'affirmation'. In turn-taking, *which*-clauses are used as turn extensions, following a response token from the listener. Han-Sook Lee offers 'English Free Relative Constructions: A Constraint-Based Approach' (*HEng* 12[2001] 237–60). After a survey of free relative properties (such as their obligatory finiteness, the option of preposition deletion as in *I'll live in whatever town you live*, the matching effect, and the absence of stacking as in **Whoever was on the boat whoever had been on the island ...*) and a critical discussion of earlier analyses, Lee proposes a new one, whereby free relatives form a construction *sui generis*, of the head-adjunct phrase type.

Adverbial clauses, finally, have only been studied by Renaat Declerck and Susan Reed in two joint items, one small and one big. The smaller of the two is 'Some Truths and Nontruths about *Even If*' (*Linguistics* 39[2001] 203–55). They discuss earlier analyses of the interpretation of *even if* conditionals but find them fragmentary or overgeneralized, and present their own conclusions about *even if* in the form of thirteen main findings, all having to do with the precise interpretation of various kinds of *even if* clauses. The same two authors also present a 500+-page description and analysis of English conditionals in general, entitled *Conditionals: A Comprehensive Empirical Analysis*. No theoretical analysis is given here; instead, conditional facts are categorized according to criteria such as type of subordination, possible-world interpretation, use of the tenses and modals, etc. The result is a much fuller taxonomy of the types and meanings of conditional clauses than was available before. There are chapters on the range of conditional subordinators, on terminology (also conveniently gathered in a glossary at the back of the book), on the possible-world typology of conditionals, on the use of the tenses, on the use of modals, on the three canonical conditional tense patterns (*If he comes/came/had come* ...), on the relation between theoretical world and actual world, on the typology of case-specifying conditionals (i.e. where the *if*-clause specifies when the content of the main clause is valid or actualized), on rhetorical conditionals (*If you want to know* ...), on syntactically marked conditionals (anacolutha, incomplete/reduced/implicit conditionals, etc.) and on sufficient versus necessary conditions. In other words: here is everything you ever wanted to know about English conditionals.

(b) Early Syntax
We begin with some general works on language change. The third edition of Jean Aitchison's *Language Change: Progress or Decay?* has added two new chapters on grammaticalization and semantic change, and has generally updated the suggestions for further reading. We will concentrate here on the additions. Chapter 2 now mentions Nostratic, population typology, glotto-chronology and mass comparison. Chapter 3 updates Labov's famous study of New York /r/ by reporting on a follow-up by J. Fowler [1986]. Chapter 5 now incorporates a section on 'Jocks versus Burnouts', two subcultures in a Detroit high school (P. Eckert [1989, 2000]). Chapter 6 ends with a few critical notes on the assumption that all changes follow an S-curve pattern, and introduces the idea that what is usually called 'lexical diffusion' could also be interpreted as an instance of analogical change, as words copy each other's sound patterns. The problems with S-curves figure again briefly in chapter 7 where A. Kroch's constant rate hypothesis is mentioned. In chapter 11, the section on 'Other Natural Tendencies' has been enlarged, with a paragraph on how speakers automatically filter out distortions but mentally correct what they hear only if they notice that something needs correcting; the section on iconicity in language has also been extended. Chapter 12 updates the study of the use of *be* as a habitual marker by Texas teenagers, and chapter 13 extends the section on chain shifts by adding changes in progress in 'Estuary English' and the American Northern Cities Shift. Chapter 14 includes a section on age-grading. Chapter 15 adds sections on 'The Origin Of Human Language' and 'From Words To Grammar', extends the section on Tok Pisin and crops the one on the existence of a bioprogram. Chapter 16 adds code-switching and provides some tentative figures for dying languages on the planet. The final chapter remains unchanged.

The second part of William Labov's *Principles of Linguistic Change: Social Factors* (volume 1, *Internal Factors*, appeared in 1994) builds on decades of careful fieldwork conducted for the Philadelphia Project and the *Atlas of North American*

English. The book is divided into four parts: 'The Speech Community', which tackles the sociolinguistic description of a speech community, the indicators of its social class, and the identification of its linguistic variables, stable or otherwise; 'Social Class, Gender, Neighbourhood and Ethnicity'; 'The Leaders of Linguistic Change', including social networks and a discussion of the gender paradox; and 'Transmission, Incrementation, and Continuation', which investigates whether, and how, children acquire their parents' variants and at what age a speaker's lect stabilizes (which, as it turns out, could be as late as 50). The first chapter examines the many, often conflicting, explanations that have been put forward over the years for linguistic (phonological) change. Not only are there competing explanations for each phenomenon, but most explanations can predict the opposite of what actually happened. The explanatory power of the 'ease of effort' theory, or the optimization of rule systems, or the maximization of semantic transparency is limited. The 'prestige' explanation, too, whether overt or covert, needs further qualification: linguistic structure and social structure are isolated domains, which do not bear upon each other, and it is not any particular sound that receives stigma or prestige, but rather the use of a particular allophone for a particular phoneme.

The question the book tries to answer, therefore, changes from 'Why does language change?' to 'Who are the leaders of language change?' and the investigation becomes more and more detailed as its focus homes in increasingly on the minutiae of social networks and individual speakers. This extremely painstaking, laborious method pays off in that it allows important insights into the mechanism of language change and its diffusion through a community that would never have emerged otherwise. To name just one of these insights, it allows a resolution of the 'gender paradox': women have long been known to be both more conservative than men in that they use more standard variants, and at the same time more progressive because they adopt new variants more quickly. It emerges from the detailed Philadelphia data that the women who deviate from the established norms are not the same women who conform to them. The women who have been identified as the leaders of linguistic change (members of the upper working class or skilled workforce with a dense network of local ties and a broad range of connections outside the local neighbourhood) are in fact a special set: as adolescents, they were non-conforming and resisted adult authority, but as adults their strong-mindedness allowed them to achieve a respected social and economic position in their local networks. Altogether this is a wonderful, rich book whose findings provide new insights into many old problems.

A probabilistic perspective on change is offered by Ronald R. Butters in 'Chance as Cause of Language Variation and Change' (*JEngL* 29[2001] 201–13). He argues convincingly that a chance/chaos model of linguistic change is an important supplement to functional and social explanations: 'drift' is not a mysterious process but subject to the laws of probability. Hans-Jürgen Diller, in 'Genre in Linguistic and Related Discourses' (in Diller and Görlach, eds., *Towards a History of English as a History of Genres*, pp. 3–43) first discusses the role of genre in literary and linguistic studies, then attempts to discern some order in the terminological jungle of genres, registers and text types, and finally discusses the role of genre in language change. A methodology for systematically comparing genres/text types is developed in Manfred Görlach's 'A History of Text Types: A Componential Analysis' (in Diller and Görlach, eds., pp. 47–88). Having compiled a list of *c.*2,100 ModE words for text types, Görlach shows how these could be classified using functional-situational features like [± conventional], [± homogeneous], [± written], [± formal], [± technical], [± original], [topic], [type of speech act], [field], [status], [length], and so on. The nature of the features is discussed at some length, as is the influence of the historical dimension. In another general paper on change, Matti Rissanen considers 'Variation, Change and New Evidence in the Study of the History of English' (in Grabes, ed., *Innovation and Continuity in English Studies*, pp. 267–73), taking a variationist perspective and discussing the exact types of variation encountered, the uses of corpora and the work along these lines being carried out at the Helsinki Research Unit for Variation and Change in English.

Three papers, all in Andersen, ed., *Actualization*, consider the actualization of change from the perspective of markedness. Henning Andersen himself contributes a 'Position Paper: Markedness and the Theory of Change' (pp. 21–57). After discussing the ways in which the term markedness can and has been used (here Roman Jakobson comes in for quite of bit of criticism), Andersen proposes the principle of markedness agreement, which basically says that marked goes with marked and unmarked with unmarked. This leads to certain predictions about typical contexts and pathways of change. In a second paper in the volume, Andersen deals with 'Actualization and the (Uni)Directionality of Change' (pp. 225–48). After comparing the notion of actualization with concepts such as reanalysis, extension, adoption, the output of underlying grammar, the output of usage rules, and markedness, Andersen argues that the output of the underlying grammar is unmarked, and will in the long run win out over the output of usage rules (which is marked). Alexander T. Bergs and Dieter Stein apply these ideas to 'The Role of Markedness in the Actuation and Actualization of Linguistic Change' (in Andersen, ed., pp. 79–93), suggesting that a formally marked *signifiant* tends to correlate with a cognitively marked *signifié*. A PDE example would be inversions like *Into the room came the teacher*, where a marked, salient meaning is expressed through a marked word order. Historical examples include the introduction of *who* as a relative marker in ME, which was initially used only for God, saints, noblemen and other worthies, and the rise of *do*-periphrasis, which started out as a marker of conspicuousness (e.g. having *God* as a subject, or occurring in the language of business letters).

In general contributions on change, the main impetus still comes from ideas related to grammaticalization. Tania Kuteva's *Auxiliation: An Enquiry into the Nature of Grammaticalization* builds on the framework for auxiliaries put forward by Heine. After a short introduction and historical overview, the book offers a cognitive-semantic analysis of auxiliation and argues that cross-linguistic similarities are best accounted for by recourse to the conceptual-semantic structure underlying auxiliation: the grammatical meanings expressed by auxiliaries are conceptualized in terms of non-grammatical notions in a motivated way. Kuteva offers a number of detailed grammaticalization paths in chapter 2, and argues that the underlying mechanism is not always loss of meaning ('bleaching'), but can also involve specification, a narrowing of meaning. Chapter 3 examines claims that the development of auxiliaries in a language is triggered by some functional need in the Tense-Mood-Aspect system of a language, with as its test case the development in North Germanic of auxiliaries of the progressive based on bodily posture. The best counter-evidence to functional need claims comes from those languages that already have a perfectly serviceable progressive and still go on to develop bodily-posture auxiliaries, reflecting a basic cognitive urge of human beings for variety of expression. Chapter 4 presents a case study involving the identification of a 'particularly evasive grammatical morpheme' that emerges again and again during the auxiliation process quite independently in related and unrelated languages: the expression for *being on the verge of V-ing (but did not V)* which Kuteva names the 'avertive'. The message here is that to get data on the cutting edge of grammaticalization one may have to cast one's net wide and consider structures that are not as clear-cut as the typical grammaticalization show-cases. Chapter 5 examines auxiliation in discourse context, building on the assumption from Relevance Theory that hearers use both conceptual and procedural knowledge until the resulting interpretation meets their expectation of relevance. This is a clear, well-written and well-argued work which contributes to the grammaticalization literature not only by presenting many concrete data that show the same grammaticalization processes happening again and again in widely disparate languages, but also by its careful scrutiny of some of the basic tenets of grammaticalization theory that tend to be taken for granted.

Werner Abraham, in 'How Far Does Semantic Bleaching Go? About Grammaticalization that Does Not Terminate in Functional Categories' (in Faarlund, ed., *Grammatical Relations in Change*, pp. 15–63), supports his case with modal verbs, modal particles and infinitival *to*. Minoji Akimoto, in 'How Far has *Far From* Become Grammaticalized?' (in Brinton, ed., *Historical Linguistics 1999*, pp. 1–11) establishes a grammaticalization chain for *far from* following the general semantic change of propositional > textual > interpersonal/emotive/subjective. Östen Dahl looks at 'Grammaticalization and the Life Cycles of Constructions' (*Rask* 14[2001] 91–133), making comparisons with life-cycles in fashion, disease and the economy, and suggesting that routinization and loss of information value is what triggers reduced expression. Richard D. Janda, in 'Beyond "Pathways" and "Unidirectionality": On the Discontinuity of Language Transmission and the Counterability of Grammaticalization' (*LangS* 23[2001] 265–340), discusses the status of the notion grammaticalization (primitive or derived?) in the light of the discontinuous transmission of language.

There is also quite a lot of grammaticalization-bashing going on. Lyle Campbell, in 'What's Wrong with Grammaticalization?' (*LangS* 23[2001] 113–61), argues that there are serious problems with grammaticalization theory. In his view, grammaticalization represents an interesting intersection of various sorts of change but has no independent status of its own and cannot be evoked as a mechanism of linguistic change. Brian D. Joseph comes to the same conclusion in 'Is There Such a Thing as Grammaticalization?' (*LangS* 23[2001] 163–86): grammaticalization is as much an epiphenomenon as lexical diffusion. He warns that adherents of unidirectionality are so eager to dismiss counter-examples that it almost seems as if they use unidirectionality as a defining characteristic of grammaticalization, thereby running the risk of circularity. A somewhat similar charge is made by Hyeree Kim in 'Remarks on the Unidirectionality Principle of Grammaticalization' (*FLH* 22[2001] 49–65). Pointing to counter-examples such as grammatical markers becoming content words (*to up the ante*), clitics and affixes turning into words (*wiltow>wilt thou*; *-es>his*; *-ism>ism*), Kim argues that grammaticalizationists sometimes appear to look only at cases fitting their theory, making the whole model unfalsifiable. Frederick J. Newmeyer, in 'Deconstructing Grammaticalization' (*LangS* 23[2001] 187–229), makes a similar point to Joseph: grammaticalization is a cover term for certain syntactic, semantic and phonetic changes which all have independent status.

Next, we turn to items dealing with (specific periods in) the history of English. Barbara A. Fennell's *A History of English: A Sociolinguistic Approach* is a student textbook, divided up in the traditional chronological periods, but it suffers somewhat from the conflict between the need to present information clearly and the desire to present it concisely. This has led to the inclusion of many statements with terms such as 'correlative conjunction' or 'phonemicization' without any hint of what they might mean (the latter concept also crops up as 'phonologize', to add to the student's confusion). This general user-unfriendliness also shows up in the omission of a map in the discussion of the 'Rhenish Fan', of isoglosses indicating the extent of the second consonant shift. The sociolinguistic focus is very limited in the first half of the book, for obvious reasons, and does not come into its own until the discussion of eModE. In a book purporting to focus on the social aspects of language change, one would expect some discussion of people's attitudes towards language change, but there is only a single remark tucked away as an aside on p. 161, that 'no linguistic token is inherently prestigious or stigmatized, but rather becomes so by convention'. The second half of the book is decidedly stronger, with a discussion of the features of 'Estuary English' and immigrant English, and the globalization of English. In 'The History of the English Language' (in Grabes, ed., pp. 251–66), Norman F. Blake reflects on the reasons why there is so far only one multi-volume history of the English language (the Cambridge set) while there are many such works on English literature. The following factors may have played a role in this: the study of the English language was/is often equated with the study of OE and ME; popular ideas about standard English discouraged the study of different varieties, which made progress in understanding the history of English difficult; linguistics was for a long time focused on the study of phonology alone.

The history of one variety of English is described in Poplack and Tagliamonte's *African American English in the Diaspora*, a work that is the fruit of twenty years of research on the origin of African American Vernacular English (AAVE). The authors' hypothesis is that underlying grammatical structure can be deduced from the distribution and conditioning of competing variants, in this case the expression of tense and aspect. The quantitative patterning of these variants may be consistent with English grammar (standard or dialectal, early or modern), creole grammar (basilectal or mesolectal) or both, and each of these possibilities is investigated. After analysing the expression of tense and aspect in the speech of more than a hundred people in three isolated 'diaspora' enclaves in Canada and the Caribbean in this way, the authors conclude that AAVE is a direct descendant of colonial British English and not a creole or a relexified African language. Their quantitative methodology ensures that this conclusion is not based on casual correspondences between varieties, but on statistically validated results. This methodology, then, combines the methods of (comparative) historical linguistics and variationist sociolinguistics. The statistical results are backed up by detailed historical research into migration and population patterns that led to the establishment of these diaspora enclaves and to contemporary AAVE. Early AAVE was different from the surrounding White dialects, but not as different as AAVE is today. AAVE innovated its most distinctive features on its own, with little help from either creoles or English. Labov speculates, in his foreword to the book, that it was not until the Great Migration of African Americans to the great cities that the social conditions were created in which distinctly different dialects could arise.

Issues in the study of Old English are addressed in Rodrigo Pérez Lorido's 'The *Anglo-Saxon Chronicle*: The Annalistic Style as Evidence of Old English Syntax' (in Diller and Görlach, eds., pp. 127–43). It is pointed out that the *Chronicle* has been under a cloud as a witness of OE syntax, but it is also shown—through an examination of patterns of co-ordination and verb deletion—that its language does not differ very much from that of other OE texts. Interesting from the perspective of the language contact situation in the Danelaw is Donald N. Tuten's 'Modeling Koineization' (in Brinton, ed., pp. 325–36), which shows that the new variety that may result from such a contact situation is not a mere reduction to the least common denominator but may lead to the introduction of novel features not found in the original varieties. Language contact, this time between English and Celtic, also figures in Theo Vennemann's 'Atlantis Semitica: Structural Contact Features in Celtic and English' (in Brinton, ed., pp. 351–69), in which he argues that English, Insular Celtic and Semitic form a single *sprachbund*-like group of languages, supporting this with three cross-linguistically rare features that they all share: verbal nouns, certain agreement features and the internal possessor construction as in *He cut off his head*, contrasting with its Germanic equivalent *He cut him off the head*.

Some further social background to language change can be found in 'Language and Society in Twelfth-Century England' by Tim William Machan (in Taavitsainen, Nevalainen, Pahta, and Rissanen, eds., *Placing Middle English in Context*, pp. 43–65), which investigates the social background to English–Norman French bilingualism in twelfth-century England, and in 'Standard Language in Early Middle English?' by Jeremy Smith (in Taavitsainen et al., eds., pp. 125–39), who attempts to clarify what is meant by the notion of standardization and to assess how far standardization was achieved during the transition from OE to ME, focusing on the AB dialect. Roger Lass's 'Language Periodization and the Concept "Middle"' (in Taavitsainen et al., eds., pp. 7–41) discusses the logic of period taxonomies of which 'Middle English' is an example in the context of the periodization of other Germanic languages. 'Syntactic Constraints on Code-Switching in Medieval Texts', by Herbert Schendl (in Taavitsainen et al., eds., pp. 67–86), concludes that such constraints are probabilistic rather than categorical; in this as in many other respects they are not very different from those in modern speech.

There are two chapters about the *Linguistic Atlas of Early Middle English* (*LAEME*). Margaret Laing's 'Never the Twain Shall Meet. Early Middle English: The East–West Divide' (in Taavitsainen et al., eds., pp. 97–124) sets out some of the challenges of working on *LAEME* and suggests how some of the apparently intractable problems can be solved. Keith Williamson, in 'Changing Spaces: Linguistic Relationships and the Dialect Continuum' (in Taavitsainen et al., eds., pp. 141–79), proposes an enhancement of the fit technique used in the making of *LAEME* and shows how it bears up when tested with both modern dialect and Middle English data. In 'Normalizing the Word Forms in the *Ayenbite of Inwyt*' (in Taavitsainen et al., eds., pp. 181–97), Manfred Markus addresses the question of how and to what extent texts can be normalized to produce machine-readable corpora, with Dan Michel's *Ayenbite of Inwyt* as its demonstration text. 'Linguistic

Commercialism in and around the *Paston* and *Cely Letters*: An *OED* and Corpus-Based Approach' (*JEngL* 29[2001] 162–78), by the same author, discusses methodological questions of corpus research and the rise of commercial terms. We also mention here Dieter Kastovsky's 'Local and Global-Typological Changes in the History of English: Two Complementary Perspectives' (in Grabes, ed., 275–87), where two local changes, the adoption of French loans and the loss of unstressed syllables (itself due to the fixing of initial stress in Germanic), are argued to have had far-reaching consequences for the global typology of the language as a whole.

There are also several items for the later periods. Irma Taavitsainen considers 'Language History and the Scientific Register' (in Diller and Görlach, eds., 187–202): she finds that scientific (especially medical) writing had already started to develop in the fourteenth-century central Midlands. The influences on and of such writing are also traced. Young-Joo Lee investigates 'The Influence of the Tyndale Bible's English on Modern English: A Study Based on Genesis 3: 1–7' (*HEng* 12[2001] 179–97). A few constructions (some word orders, the pattern *the* N *of the* N, and the use of *and*) in the Tyndale Bible, the Authorized Version and a modern American version are compared, and it turns out that the three texts are quite similar. Claudia Claridge, in 'Structuring Text: Discourse Deixis in Early Modern English Texts' (*JEngL* 29[2001] 55–71), tabulates the use of discourse-deictic elements in various registers and genres using the Lampeter Corpus (1640–1740). Douglas Biber's 'Dimensions of Variation Among 18th-Century Speech-Based and Written Genres' (in Diller and Görlach, eds., pp. 89–109) investigates several eighteenth-century genres using his multidimensional approach, i.e. he tries to establish what linguistic features tend to co-occur in what genres. A comparison with twentieth-century material shows up broad similarity in the functions associated with specific (groups of) features; one striking difference is that the eighteenth-century material does contain a spoken–written dimension of variation, something that Biber's own work has shown to be absent from PDE. Another difference is that, over the past two centuries, expository genres have become more literate and personal writing more spoken-like.

There is more—much more, in fact—on the eighteenth century in Manfred Görlach's *Eighteenth-Century English*. This book brings to completion Görlach's project of single-handedly describing the history of English after 1500, which had already given us his study of eModE and of nineteenth-century English (see *YWES* 80[2001] 50), not to mention a host of articles on more specific topics. The present work has the same format as the two earlier volumes: after an introduction (describing sources, periodization, social, political, cultural, economic and literary developments, grammar books, education, notions of correctness, and standardization), there are chapters on varieties (spoken and written, dialectal, social, colloquial, gender-based, regional, creolistic and foreign), spelling and pronunciation (printed spellings, handwriting, typefaces, punctuation, changes in pronunciation, standardization), inflections (a short chapter, on nouns, adjectives, pronouns and verbs), syntax (covering topics such as negation, *do*-periphrasis, word order, participles, phrasal verbs, tense, aspect, modality, complex sentences, Latinity and much more), lexis (social and regional variation, word-formation, changes in meaning), and text types and style (genres, text-typical variation, stylistic conventions). These are followed by 111 sample texts of one to two pages, on topics in the field of language, culture, literature and non-English English. In the chapters themselves, there are 255 shorter extracts illustrating the various points dealt with. To complete this impressive book, there are 100 study questions (some simple, some more challenging, and some requiring a degree of *Gründlichkeit* that we have never seen in our own students), a word index, topic index and name index.

Developments in one text type in the nineteenth and twentieth centuries form the topic of Sabine Gieszinger's *The History of Advertising Language: The Advertisements in 'The Times' from 1788 to 1996*. Based on an analysis of 540 texts, this starts with an overview of earlier research on advertising language, sketches some historical background (economic conditions, the media, *The Times*, the role of advertising agencies), and then launches into a detailed description of the material and the changes observable in it, paying attention to formal, semantic and functional aspects. All the obvious points (such as length of ads, structural elements, references to the producer and reader, use of adjectives, language play, relation between text and pictures) are covered, as are a host of other ones; there can be little that has escaped Gieszinger's eye. The overall conclusion with respect to diachronic development is that there has been an increase in uniformity of the text type, but at the same time a growth in individuality when it comes to the realization of the various expected and possible constituent parts of the ad.

We now turn to studies on the different elements of the clause, starting with nominal groups. Alfred Bammesberger has looked at two nominal groups in an OE text, both marked with dative case, and reports on them in 'The Syntactic Analysis of *Beowulf*, Lines 4–5' (*NM* 102[2001] 131–3). He suggests that they are not, as is commonly assumed, parallel; instead, the first one is instrumental and the second one an indirect object. Gwang-Yoon Goh, in 'Genitive in *Deor*: Morphosyntax and Beyond' (*RES* 52[2001] 485–99), argues that the unexpected genitive *þisses* used in the refrain of that poem (*þæs ofereode þisses swa mæg* 'that passed away, so may this') was intended to express a low degree of affectedness. More about the genitive is to be found in Anette Rosenbach's 'The English *S*-Genitive: Animacy, Topicality, and Possessive Relationship in a Diachronic Perspective' (in Brinton, ed., pp. 277–92), which investigates the diachronic factors underlying the selection of the *s*- or the *of*-genitive. There are two articles on the loss of case in Scandinavian that are of interest to the Middle English syntactician: John Ole Askedal, in '"Oblique Objects", Structural and Lexical Case Marking: Some Thoughts on Case Assignment in North Germanic and German' (in Faarlund, ed., pp. 65–97), notes the Scandinavian move towards positionally rather than morphologically marked grammatical functions and argues against the idea that this was triggered by loss of case-marking. The second article is Muriel Norde's 'The Loss of Lexical Case in Swedish' (in Faarlund, ed., pp. 241–72), which discusses the mechanisms that led to the decline of inflectional case-marking; the decline was slowed down by a tendency to maintenance. We see here the conflicting interests of the speaker and the hearer, or ease of production versus ease of perception. While case is apparently interesting, adjectives have been neglected this year, with only one item. 'The Adjective *Weary* in Middle English Structures: A Syntactic-Semantic Study', by Saara Nevanlinna (in Taavitsainen et al., eds., pp. 339–56), examines the geographical, diachronic, and textual distribution of the various complements of this adjective: the prepositional phrase with *of*, *with*, *in* or *for*, the *to*-infinitive, the bare infinitive, the gerund, and the past participle, the prefixed forms of which (*of*-, *for*-) were later reanalysed as prepositional phrases. With Päivi Pahta, Saara Nevanlinna has also written about a phenomenon usually associated with NPs, i.e. apposition. In 'On Markers of Expository Apposition' (*NOWELE* 39[2001] 3–51), they trace the history of markers such as *i.e.*, *namely*, *viz.*, *that is*, *yea*, *nay*, *marry*, *as much to say as*, and so on, providing information on the use of each marker and sketching a general framework for their analysis.

Pronouns feature in Michiko Ogura's 'Late West-Saxon Forms of the Demonstrative Pronouns as Native Prototypes of *They*' (*N&Q* 246[2001] 5–6), which offers evidence that the ModE pronouns *they*, *their* and *them*, usually ascribed to ON influence, may in part have been a native development of demonstratives. Ulrich Busse's 'The Use of Address Pronouns in Shakespeare's Plays and Sonnets' (in Andersen, ed., 119–42) is an investigation of the replacement of *thou* by *you*. In Shakespeare's works, the use of *you* shows a notable increase after 1597; somewhat surprisingly, the comedies (and also prose passages in other plays) feature relatively little *thou*; the sonnets, on the other hand, have high proportions of *thou*. 'Towards Personal Subjects in English: Variation in Feature Interpretability', by Elly van Gelderen (in Faarlund, ed., pp. 137–57), adduces evidence for a slight person split in OE and eME: third-person pronouns remain impersonal longer than first- and second-person pronouns. This is linked to different rates of loss of morphological Case.

The mighty flood of work on tense, mood and aspect that we have reported over the years has dwindled to a mere trickle this year. The only item exclusively devoted to this topic is 'Using the Past to Explain the Present: Tense and Temporal Reference in Early African American English', by James A. Walker (*LVC* 13[2001] 1–35). The author finds fault with the narrow focus on the alternation between *-s* and zero marking on verbs in much work, and sets out to describe in a more comprehensive manner the various forms carrying present meaning in AAVE. Data are drawn from African Nova Scotia English, Samaná English and the Ex-Slave Recordings, which turn out to have similar conditioning of the variants and to resemble earlier stages of English rather than a creole. Marianne Hundt, in 'What Corpora Tell Us about the Grammaticalisation of Voice in *Get*-Constructions' (*SLang* 25[2001] 49–88), charts the rise of the *get*-passive by paying particular attention to the frequencies of its syntactic patterns in diachronic corpora. Causative *get* (*get* + NP + Ved/to V) turned out to play a significant role in this development, whereas the use of *get* as a lexical verb was not affected (a further instance of layering in grammaticalization).

Internal arguments of verbs are investigated in Luis Iglesias-Rábade's 'Composite Predicates in Middle English with the Verbs *Nimen* and *Taken*' (*SN* 73[2001] 143–63), which discusses the history of such combinations as *take a seat*, *take care* with data from corpora and the *MED*. Data from the Helsinki Corpus are used by Teresa Moralejo-Gárate in 'Composite Predicates and Idiomatisation in Middle English: A Corpus-Based Approach' (*SAP* 36[2001] 171–87), which looks at such combinations as *make accord*, *make amend*, *make end*, and *make joy* in ME. Fixation of these phrases had already set in at that time: there is limited use of adjectives, some combinations have an obligatory plural, and article usage is not entirely free. Michiko Ogura looks at 'Verbs Used Reflexively in Old and Middle English' (*NM* 102[2001] 23–36). A comparison of the West Saxon gospels with the Wyclif Bible shows that the use of the simple pronoun with reflexive function declines, but the use of *himself* etc. doesn't increase much, leading to fewer reflexive constructions. Other texts continue using simple pronouns reflexively.

Adverbial markers expressing attitude or modality are investigated in two articles. Marina Dossena writes '*The Cruel Slaughtyr that vas Cruelly Exsecutit*: Intensification and Adverbial Modality in the Helsinki Corpus of Old Scots—A Preliminary Overview' (*NM* 102[2001] 287–301). Eighteen different modal adverbs are examined, attention being paid to their distribution across text types and the kind of modal meaning that they express. Various corpora have been used by Elly van Gelderen, in 'The Syntax of Mood Particles in the History of English' (*FLH* 22[2001] 301–30), which considers a broad spectrum of such words, but focuses on *though, ac/eac* (in OE and ME), *now* and *then*. These turn out not to be highly frequent in the data; their preferred position in the clause shifts from medial (OE) to peripheral.

Word order plays a role in several contributions. 'Are Old English Conjunct Clauses Really Verb-Final?', by Kristin Bech (in Brinton, ed., pp. 49–62), examines the by now accepted view that OE *and/ac* clauses tend to be verb-final, and proposes an explanation on pragmatic grounds. Masayuki Ohkado studies 'The Position of Subject Pronouns and Finite Verbs in Old English' (*FLH* 22[2001] 255–76), suggesting that subject pronouns are clitics to the right of the complementizer position (as argued by A. van Kemenade [1987]); this would explain the absence of elements intervening between the complementizer position and subject pronouns. Mary Blockley, in 'Subordinate Clauses without απο Κοινου in Old English Verse, Chiefly in *Beowulf* and Chiefly *Nu* and *Swa*' (*SN* 73[2001] 4–10), argues that it is possible, contrary to many remarks in the literature, to tell these adverbs apart from their homophonous conjunctions. Mieko Ogura's 'Perceptual Factors and Word Order Change in English' (*FLH* 22[2001] 233–53) attributes the change from OV to VO in the history of English to the perceptual problems caused by sequences consisting of an object containing a relative clause followed by the verb, which would lead to centre-embedding. The Peterborough Chronicle [1070–1154] is indeed shown to have very few such constructions, instead preferring VO or extra-position of the relative clause (which Ogura in fact takes to reflect an earlier paratactic construction). Gwang-Yoon Goh, in 'The Advent of the Prepositional Passive: An Innovation of Middle English?' (*ES* 82[2001] 203–17) argues for a negative answer to this question, his point being that OE had prepositional passives too, or at least structures that were functionally equivalent to the prepositional passive, but with the preposition incorporated into the verb.

Infinitival issues have sparked off several papers too. Concha Castillo writes 'On the Non-Expressed Object of Old English Infinitives' (*SAP* 36[2001] 111–29). The author considers constructions like purpose and relative infinitivals, tough-movement and the *to*-infinitive clauses in OE of the type surviving in the BrE fossil *He is to blame*, arguing that the non-expressed object in all these cases is small *pro* (also found in sentences such as *het hiene þa niman* 'he then ordered *pro* to take him'). Evidence comes from the absence of an overt relative marker in infinitival relatives and the non-existence of subject infinitival relatives; the changes in ME are also identified. D. Gary Miller, in 'Subject and Object in Old English and Latin Copular Deontics' (in Faarlund, ed., pp. 223–39), links the development of the *he-is-to-blame* construction to similar developments in other languages, and provides a coherent account of the different markings of the thematic object (nominative or accusative) and the consequences of the reanalysis of the agentive dative in similar constructions as a quirky subject. Matthew Whelpton explores the semantics of the infinitive in examples like *John hung his coat up, only to realize that he had to go out again* (p. 313) in his article 'Elucidation of a Telic Infinitive' (*JL* 37[2001] 313–37) and argues that these derive from the properties of the predicate heading this infinitive, which he identifies as TELOS, representing a relation between events. Dirk Noël, in 'The Passive Matrices of English Infinitival Complement Clauses' (*SLang* 25[2001] 255–96), argues that the preference for passive ECM-constructions with English verbs such as *believe*, which appears to be due to information-structural reasons, could also be a concomitant effect of a grammaticalization process, with the string *is believed to* increasingly functioning as a modal verb.

Anne Österman takes us 'From *There* to *Where*: The Development of Relative and Conjunctive Adverbs in Middle English' (*NOWELE* 38[2001] 65–107), i.e. she shows us how relatives like *the place THERE the king lay slain* turn into *the place WHERE the king lay slain*. *Where* overtakes *there* in frequency in the Helsinki Corpus around 1400 (though some text types are more conservative than others), and the facts seem amenable to a grammaticalization account. 'WHICH and THE WHICH in Late Middle English: Free Variants?', by Helena Raumolin-Brunberg (in Taavitsainen et al., eds., pp. 209–25), concludes that the distribution of these forms cannot be shown to be determined by grammatical, textual, social, geographical or register factors. The only thing that can be said is that the longer form is favoured by the London wool merchant community in the fifteenth century and by women in general.

Finally, there are some items on adverbial clauses. Thomas Kohnen writes about 'Text Types as Catalysts for Language Change: The Example of the Adverbial First Participle Construction' (in Diller and Görlach, eds., 111–24), investigating sentences like *He came in, looking rather grim* in the period 1100–1700. He traces the spread of the construction across text types, identifies its most common functions (which tend to differ from one text type to another), and accounts for the pattern of diffusion by pointing out that some text types arose later than others, and that some are closer to Italian and French (the presumed source of the construction) than others. Mariá José López-Couso and Belén Méndez-Naya, in 'On the History of *If-* and *Though*-Links with Declarative Complement Clauses' (*ELL* 5[2001] 93–107), argue that such clauses should be analysed as complements rather than as adjuncts. An investigation of the diachronic part of the Helsinki Corpus reveals the factors that have influenced the selection of these clauses over the regular complement-clause linkers *that* and *zero* from OE to the present. Going back further in time, Jürg Rainer Schwyter writes 'On Conjunction *þeah* (*þe*): Law II Cnut 72.1 and II Cnut 75' (*Neophil* 85[2001] 291–6); he identifies two cases of *þeah* being not concessive but just conditional (i.e. being equivalent to *if*), and suggests that this was in fact the original meaning of the word. Rafał Molencki has written 'Counterfactuals in the Different Manuscripts of the *Cursor Mundi*' (*MN* 102[2001] 11–22), tracing the development in the use of tense and modals in this clause type and finding that the southern manuscripts are more progressive than the northern ones. '"My mother, whenever she passed away, she had pneumonia": The History and Functions of *Whenever*', by Michael B. Montgomery and John M. Kirk (*JEngL* 29 [2001] 234–49), traces the various meanings of this conjunction in AmE to its use in Ulster English.

6. Semantics

Dahl, ed., *Tense and Aspect in the Languages in Europe*, contains the results of one area of investigation carried out in the framework of a major European project on language typology (Typology of Languages in Europe—EUROTYP). The volume presents an impressive survey of the tense and aspect systems of the languages of Europe in the form of individual papers, supplemented by some fascinating theoretically oriented works, whose aim is to emphasize distinctions which are sometimes blurred in this field of research. The volume consists of five parts, three of which, 'Future Time Reference', 'The Perfect', and 'The Progressive', are devoted to the three 'focal areas' identified by the research group within the topic area. Each part starts with a general overview of the particular phenomenon in the languages under investigation, written by Östen Dahl ('The Grammar of Future Time Reference in European Languages', pp. 309–28), Jouko Lindstedt ('The Perfect: Aspectual, Temporal and Evidential', pp. 365–83), and Pier Marco Bertinetto, Karen H. Ebert and Casper de Groot ('The Progressive in Europe', pp. 517–58). These are followed by studies on individual languages or language families. The first part of the volume, entitled 'General Papers', is devoted to more synthetizing and theoretically oriented contributions. Östen Dahl's 'The Tense-Aspect Systems of European Languages in a Typological Perspective' (pp. 3–25) sets the scene for the studies to follow, and defines the most important concept of the research reported on in the volume, that of *gram*, which originates from joint work by the author with Joan Bybee. According to Dahl, grams are the basic units of description of tense and aspect, and exemplified by things like the progressive in English or the *passé simple* in French. Notions such as tense, aspect and mood are seen as ways of characterizing the semantic content of grams. In their contribution 'Aspect vs. Actionality: Why They Should be Kept Apart' (pp. 189–225), Pier Marco Bertinetto and Denis Delfitto suggest that a distinction should be made between the category of 'aspect', which refers to the specific (global vs. partial) perspective adopted by the speaker, and that of 'actionality', which specifies particular properties of the type of event described, in terms of such oppositions as: punctual–durative, telic–atelic, static–dynamic etc., and which normally lacks overt morphological marking. In 'The Type-Referring Function of the Imperfective' (pp. 227–64), Eva Hedin claims that the opposition between imperfective and perfective aspect can be captured in terms of the type-token distinction: 'the imperfective is used when reference is made to situations as types, when they are considered in a non-temporal perspective as abstractions not existing in time but corresponding to the denotative content of some verbal expression', while 'the Perfective ... is used when reference is made to situations as tokens, as instantiations of situations in time' (p. 228). The fifth part of the volume is devoted to case studies on individual languages.

Another large-scale empirical study of (various manifestations of) a construction whose interpretational possibilities have been at the centre of attention of semanticists for a considerable length of time now is Renaat Declerck and Susan Reed's book entitled *Conditionals*. This work is based on an extensive corpus study, and owes its existence to the fact that the authors were dissatisfied with the number of dimensions which are normally used in differentiating the various types of conditionals from each other in English, and the number of semantic/pragmatic functions which are normally ascribed to a particular construction. The authors show that previous theoretical approaches to conditionals are partly incomparable since they only make use of (non-identical) subsets of the possible distinctions. It is to be hoped that as a result of the careful distinctions put forward capturing the syntactic and semantic differences between conditionals, and the wide range of data presented, this impressive volume will serve as a reference work on conditionals for more theoretically oriented future research as well, as intended by the authors.

María Ángeles Gómez-González's *The Theme–Topic Interface: Evidence from English*, provides a thoroughgoing survey on the use of two terms which commonly appear in studies on information structure (or information-packaging), namely, 'topic' and 'theme'. Gómez-González shows that there are essentially three different types of interpretation given to these terms in various approaches. According to the semantic one, the notions of topic/theme reflect discourse relevance or aboutness, the informational approach defines them in terms of givenness, while the syntactic approach identifies topic/theme with sentence-initial position. Having set up the above typology, the author provides a detailed analysis and critique of the interpretations of the above terms within three functionalist theories, the Prague school approach, Systemic Functional Grammar, and Functional Grammar. In the last part of the book, the results of a survey of the Lancaster/IBM Spoken English Corpus are provided, whose aim was to investigate how the syntactically defined 'themes' are mapped onto new vs. given information within the sentence, and how they fare in terms of aboutness.

A new textbook introducing undergraduate or postgraduate students to the field is Keith Allan's *Natural Language Semantics*. The author believes that linguistic meaning is cognitively and functionally motivated, and that 'language provides a set of underspecified clues that need to be expanded by semantic and pragmatic inferences based on knowledge of the lexicon and grammar but heavily reliant upon encyclopedic knowledge and awareness of the conventions for language use' (p. xi). In order to be able to illustrate the various factors which play a role in semantic interpretation, Allan breaks away from the tradition of presenting only the formal, the cognitive, the traditional, or the pragmatics-based approaches to the specification of meaning in an introductory textbook, an effort that deserves respect. The book provides a detailed discussion of the aims of formal semantic approaches to the study of meaning, as well as those of frame-semantics, the componential analysis of meaning, cognitive semantics, Jackendoff's conceptual semantics, Role and Reference Grammar, Ensemble Theory, Grice's theory of conversational implicatures, and Speech Act Theory. In addition, under the pretext of presenting analyses of phenomena that lie on the borderline between semantics and other subdisciplines of linguistics, such as idioms, sound symbolism, connotation, and jargon, the volume provides detailed discussions on several other subfields of linguistics such as lexicology, lexicography, onomastics, morphology (including even definitions of 'morpheme', 'root' and 'stem'), and many more. As a consequence, the reader has the impression that instead of being an introduction to semantics, this extremely long and condensed work aspires to become an introduction to linguistics as a whole, from the point of view of a semanticist. Although the author strives to make the material more accessible to students by including exercises, a summary of the key terms at the end of each chapter, and pointers to further reading, he sometimes uses concepts that are left undefined (e.g.

'implicature', p. 22), or introduces definitions which he does not make use of in the rest of the work (e.g. of 'ratified participant', 'bystander', 'eavesdropper', pp. 18–19). On the whole, the book seems to put more emphasis on presenting definitions, data, and theoretical frameworks and less on showing the reader interesting problems which have been or could be handled with the above tools. In spite of these drawbacks, Allan's work definitely remains a valuable reference collection on possible approaches to the study of semantics.

Hana Filip, *Aspect, Eventuality Types and Nominal Reference*, offers a new and intriguing explanation for the interactions between the interpretations of NPs and VPs, which have already been observed and discussed within various theoretical frameworks. On the one hand, the quantificational properties of NPs may influence the aspectual properties of VPs, as the contrast between the sentences *Mary ate a sandwich in an hour/?for an hour* vs. *Mary ate soup/blueberries ??in an hour/for an hour* shows. On the other hand, the perfective and imperfective operators and verbal affixes may influence the quantificational and (in)definite interpretations of NPs appearing without any articles or quantifiers, for example those frequently found in Slavic languages such as Czech. Filip proposes that the thematic structures of verbs greatly influence the above types of interaction, since in prototypical cases they only apply to episodic verbal predicates with Incremental Theme arguments, and that within a constraint-based (or unification-based) framework the above interactions can be given a unified analysis. The essence of the proposal is that the verb and the Incremental Theme NP are each assumed to specify information about one linguistic object, the complex verbal predicate or a sentence. Languages can vary according to whether they include the relevant information (*quantization* vs. *cumulativity*) on the verb or on the NP, although, naturally, there are always built-in constraints that ensure that the information carried by the verb and the NP is compatible.

Kenesei and Harnish, eds., *Perspectives on Semantics, Pragmatics, and Discourse: A Festschrift for Ferenc Kiefer*, contains some fascinating new research on all three subdisciplines mentioned in the title. Among the contributions discussing semantic problems, the following three papers deserve close attention. Barbara H. Partee and Vladimir Borschev's 'Some Puzzles of Predicate Possessives' (pp. 91–117) claims that not all possessives are arguments of nouns, since there exist predicate possessives which cannot be considered remnants of elliptical NPs, but have to be assigned the semantic type of $<e, t>$. Zoltán Gendler Szabó, in 'Adjectives in Context' (pp. 119–46), proposes a method by which the meaning of context-dependent adjectives like *green* in the sentence *That leaf is green* can be captured in a way which preserves compositionality, by treating them as predicate modifiers. Johan van der Auwera and Bert Bultinck's 'On the Lexical Typology of Modals Quantifiers, and Connectives' (pp. 173–86) investigates the parallels and differences between the meanings of the modals for *necessity* and *possibility*, *all* and *some*, the connectives *and* and *or*, and their negations. They claim that, while there is almost complete semantic similarity between expressions from the above three domains, which can be represented in a three-layered scalar square, on the lexical semantic level they differ significantly.

Epistemic Modality, Language and Conceptualization: A Cognitive Pragmatic Perspective, by Jan Nuyts, is a study of the linguistic manifestations of epistemic modality, that is, 'the speaker's evaluation of the likelihood of a state of affairs, as expressed in language' (p. xv). On the basis of an intensive corpus study, Nuyts investigates what factors determine the choice between the following four possible structures, which can be used to express epistemic modality in Dutch, German and English: modal adverbs, predicatively used modal adjectives, mental space predicates, and modal auxiliaries. He argues that, besides the epistemic qualification, the following four factors co-determine the choice between expression types: (inter)subjective evidentiality, performativity vs. descriptivity, information structure, and discourse strategy. On the basis of the empirical findings, he feels justified in arguing for a non-linguistic view of conceptualization.

Nirit Kadmon's *Formal Pragmatics*, one of the most intriguing publications from last year, discusses phenomena and research topics which are currently assumed to lie on the borderline between the semantics and pragmatics of natural language, and which have been discussed extensively in the framework of model-theoretic approaches. In the author's opinion, semantics is what is concerned with 'literal meaning' only, while pragmatics is concerned with language use, and what is beyond the literal meaning. The above distinction thus does not coincide with the distinction between 'what is in the grammar' (i.e. what is conventional) and 'what is outside the grammar', which has traditionally been assumed to underlie the division between the two disciplines. Part 1, entitled 'Dynamic Semantics, Definites, and Indefinites', is concerned with the Kamp-Heim approach to the semantics of definite and indefinite NPs. Part 2 introduces and evaluates some recent and less recent accounts on presupposition projection, accommodation, and the triggering of presuppositions. Part 3 provides a survey and evaluation of various approaches concerned with explaining the function and interpretation of prosodically marked focus, its scopal properties, presuppositions, and discussion of possible amendments to these theories. The author offers a new constraint on the use of 'complex focal structures with contrastive topics in English', which has the potential of being extendable to other languages as well. Its precise, thorough discussion of the claims made in previous studies and its ingenious proposals turn the volume into an excellent reference book for the most influential ideas of present-day semantics/ pragmatics, a superb textbook for advanced students of semantics and pragmatics, and an important contribution to the field in its own right.

Two other excellent volumes which discuss topics on the interface between syntax and semantics/pragmatics and between semantics and philosophy are the last ones to be mentioned here. Cole, Hermon, and Huang, eds., *Long-Distance Reflexives*, investigates the syntactic and discourse/pragmatic properties of long-distance reflexives, i.e. those forms which can be used as local reflexives but can also take antecedents outside their local domain, and thus appear as exceptions to Binding Theory in several typologically unrelated languages such as the Mandarin and Teochew dialects of Chinese, Hindi/Urdu, Riau Indonesian, Norwegian, Turkish, Kannada, Chechen, Ingush, Icelandic, and English. The individual studies reported on in the book seem to lead to the following general conclusions. Long-distance reflexives do not constitute a homogeneous class from a syntactic point of view, since there are long-distance bound anaphors, forms which are used as reflexives locally and as pronominals non-locally, and forms which are primarily bound anaphors, but which can be used non-locally under specific syntactic and discourse conditions, mostly when the reflexive is in a non-argument position, and when the antecedent satisfies logophoric conditions (i.e. is a subject of a verb of saying or thinking, and the long-distance reflexive is used to indicate co-reference with this subject). The role of discourse in determining whether a form which in most environments functions as a bound anaphor can be used as a pronominal, or whether long-distance bound anaphors are possible, varies, however, from language to language (and even across dialects of the same language). The second publication is the second edition of Donald Davidson's *Inquiries into Truth and Interpretation*, which appeared first in 1984, and contains the author's influential essays on the philosophy of language, which are centred around the problem of what it is for words to mean what they do. Davidson argues in these papers that we would only have a philosophically instructive answer to the above question if a theory of meaning could be constructed which was holistic, i.e. one that would provide an interpretation of all utterances (either actual or potential, produced by one speaker or a group of speakers), and that would be verifiable without knowledge of the detailed propositional attitudes of the speaker.

One of the most fundamental assumptions in contemporary semantics is the Principle of Compositionality, traditionally attributed to Gottlob Frege but never explicitly articulated by him. A special issue of the *Journal of Logic, Language and Information*, edited by Peter Pagin and Dag Westerståhl, is devoted to the question of in what form the principle was actually held by Frege, and to some of the implications for the organization of grammar. The editors formulate the principle in their 'Editorial' (*JLLI* 10[2001] 1–5) in the following way: 'The meaning of a complex expression is determined by the meaning of its parts and the "mode of composition".' The contributions to the volume include Wilfrid Hodges's 'Formal Features of Compositionality' (*JLLI* 10[2001] 7–28), which addresses the question of which partical semantics have Fregean extensions; Herman Hendriks's 'Compositionality and Model-Theoretic Interpretation' (*JLLI* 10[2001] 29–48), which investigates the implications of the principle of compositionality for the organization of the grammar; and Tim Fernando's 'Ambiguous Discourse in a Compositional Context: An Operational Perspective' (*JLLI* 10[2001] 63–86), which discusses the compositionality problem for discourses, as well as the papers 'Did Frege Believe Frege's Principle?' (*JLLI* 10[2001] 87–114), by Francis Jeffry Pelletier, and 'Frege, Contextuality, and Compositionality', by Theo M. V. Janssen (*JLLI* 10[2001] 115–36), which deal with the issue of where Frege makes reference to the Principle of Compositionality and to the Context Principle ('Never ask for the meaning of a word except in the context of a sentence') in his published and unpublished texts, and what interpretations have been given to these texts by others.

The semantics of definite and indefinite NPs received special attention in several papers published in 2001. Jeanette K. Gundel, Nancy Hedberg and Ron Zacharski argue, in 'Definite Descriptions and Cognitive Status in English: Why Accommodation is Unnecessary' (*ELL* 5[2001] 273–95), that the fact that the addressee is able to assign a unique representation to a definite description without previous familiarity with the referent is not to be explained by resorting to accommodation, but in terms of the Givenness Hierarchy proposed by Gundel et al. [1993].

A special issue of the *Journal of Semantics*, edited by Paul Dekker and Christopher Piñón, was dedicated to the purpose of investigating the semantics of indefinites. Paul Dekker's 'Dynamics and Pragmatics of "Peirce's Puzzle"' (*JSem* 18[2001] 211–41) proposes a semantic/pragmatic explanation based on Gricean principles for 'Peirce's Puzzle', which is concerned with the fact that certain pairs of natural-language sentences, such as *Someone wins $1,000 if everyone takes part* versus *Someone wins $1,000 or someone will not take part* have identical representations in terms of first-order logic, although their intuitive interpretations are different. Kerstin Schwabe and Klaus von Heusinger's 'On Shared Indefinite NPs in Coordinate Structures' (*JSem* 18[2001] 243–69), investigates the issue of why the referential options of indefinite NPs in shared co-ordinate structures vary in German with respect to the information status (topicality or focusing) of the indefinite. In 'Specific Indefinites and the Information Structure Theory of Topics' (*JSem* 18[2001] 271–97), Paul Portner and Katsuhiko Yabushita discuss the relationship between topicality and the specificity of indefinites on the basis of Japanese data. The contribution by Ariel Cohen, 'On the Generic Use of Indefinite Singulars' (*JSem* 18[2001] 183–209), claims that the reason why the distribution of indefinite singular generics is much more restricted than that of bare plural generics (the latter can either express the way things are or be a rule or regulation, but the former can only have the second interpretation) is that bare plurals, referring to a kind, are acceptable topics, but bare singulars are not. The information structure of sentences, or the interpretation of topics/foci has also been discussed in various other publications. In 'Secondary Topic as a Relation in Information Structure' (*Linguistics* 39[2001] 1–49), Irina Nikolaeva discusses the concept of secondary topic (functionally similar to Enric Vallduv's 1990 'tail'), and argues that there is a language, Ostyak (Uralic), where this notion receives a systematic syntactic expression. Joachim Jacobs's thought-provoking paper, 'The Dimensions of Topic-Comment' (*Linguistics* 39[2001] 641–81), argues, on the basis of German data, that the constructions which have been claimed to encode topic-comment structure in natural language do not share one functional (semantic or pragmatic) feature (e.g. aboutness), but only the property that they show some semantic similarity to prototypical instances of topic-comment constructions. A special issue of *Linguistics*, edited by Monica Doherty, is devoted to the discourse functions of cleft sentences. In 'A Framework for the Analysis of Cleft Constructions' (*Linguistics* 39[2001] 463–516) Knud Lambrecht proposes a framework for the discourse functional analysis of clefts. He argues that the above construction manifests an example of a division of labour between the matrix and the subordinate clause: while the predicate of the relative clause assigns a semantic role to the shared argument, the matrix predicate assigns it the pragmatic role of focus.

Gerhard Jäger's study, 'Topic-Comment Structure and the Contrast between Stage-Level and Individual-Level Predicates' (*JSem* 18[2001] 83–126) investigates the interrelation between two fascinating topics of research, and argues that it is impossible to provide a uniform explanation for all the linguistic phenomena that have traditionally been considered to be sensitive to the contrast between stage-level and individual-level predicates. The paper argues that the ability of a predicate to admit a weak construal of its subject, which has been linked to the above contrast, is determined by independent factors, which include the topic-focus construal of the clause as well. Still on the issue of the stage-level/individual-level contrast, Yoshiki Ogawa, 'The Stage/Individual Distinction and (In)alienable Possession' (*Language* 77[2001] 1–25), proposes to extend the distinction beyond verbal and adjectival predicates, to (underived) nominal predicates, and argues on the basis of data from several languages that the set of stage-level predicates is identical to the set of relational ones, which points towards the possibility of eliminating one distinction, and thus towards the simplification of the grammar.

The semantic interpretation of quantificational NPs is investigated in Lisa Matthewson's paper 'Quantification and the Nature of Crosslinguistic Variation' (*NLS* 9[2001] 145–89), which argues, on the basis of data from St'át'imcets (Lillooet Salish), against the view that the general pattern of creating generalized quantifiers (in the nominal domain) follows the same strategy in all languages as it does in English. In English, determiners are regarded as expressions having the semantic type of a function which takes the denotation of common noun phrases having type <e,t> as its argument, resulting in expressions which have the type of a generalized quantifier, <<e,t>, t>. Matthewson proposes that, if the generalized quantifiers are to be created in a cross-linguistically uniform way, they should preferably follow the pattern observed in Lillooet, where a quantificational element appears as sister to a full DP containing an overt plural determiner, which is assigned a denotation of type *e*, and shows that a reanalysis of many English constructions (e.g., partitives, non-partitive *all-* and *most-*phrases, etc.) is possible in terms of the above pattern. Manfred Krifka's 'Quantifying into Speech Acts' (*NLS* 9[2001] 1–40) comes with an explanation for the phenomenon that quantified NPs in questions may have an interpretation according to which the NP is quantified into the question; i.e. a question like *Which dish did every guest bring?* may have the following reading: 'For every guest x: which dish did x bring?'. Krifka argues that the above types of interpretation are cases of quantifying into speech acts, and that the reason why only universal quantifiers, i.e. quantifiers based on conjunction, can scope out of questions is that the only general operation applicable to speech acts is conjunction. Still on the topic of quantification in natural language, Ariel Cohen's study on 'Relative Readings of *Many*, *Often*, and Generics' (*NLS* 9[2001] 41–67) provides a uniform characterization of what he refers to as the *relative* proportional reading of the determiners *many* and *few*, *often* and *seldom*, and generics, which exist in addition to their cardinal and proportional readings. The relative proportional reading of the sentence 'Many/few ψs are φs' is true if and only if the proportion of φs among ψs is greater/smaller than the proportion of φs among contextually given alternatives to ψ.

Two papers are concerned with the semantics of donkey pronouns, like the *it* in *Every farmer who owns a donkey beats it*. In 'E-type Anaphora as NP-deletion' (*NLS* 9[2001] 241–88), Paul Elbourne proposes that donkey pronouns are to be regarded as definite articles, which are followed by an NP undergoing deletion in the phonology. In 'Singular Donkey Pronouns are Semantically Singular' (*Ling&P* 24[2001] 383–403), Makoto Kanazawa argues against the view that syntactically singular donkey pronouns are semantically numberless, building on the observation, among others, that the above donkey sentence has the following paraphrase: *Every farmer who owns a donkey beats the donkey or donkeys he owns*. Still on the interpretation of pronouns, in 'Exhaustivity in Dynamic Semantics: Referential and Descriptive Pronouns' (*Ling&P* 24[2001] 621–57), Robert van Rooy defends the view that pronouns should always be interpreted exhaustively, by claiming that they are used either referentially, referring to the unique speaker's referents of their antecedent indefinites, or descriptively, denoting the exhaustive set of individuals to which the description in the antecedent clause applies. He presents a formal representation of the above ideas in terms of dynamic semantics.

The paper 'Discourse Parallelism, Ellipsis, and Ambiguity' (*JSem* 18[2001] 1–25), by Nicholas Asher, Daniel Hardt and Joan Busquets, proposes a simple recovery mechanism for ellipsis, according to which the recovered material and the antecedent should be subject only to the general discourse constraints on parallelism, which can account for a wide range of puzzles concerning ellipsis, formalized in the framework of Segmented Discourse Representation Theory. A new approach to the problem of how to predict the interpretation possibilities for elliptical or anaphoric quantificational expressions is put forth in 'Optimality Theoretic Semantics' (*Ling&P* 24[2001] 1–32) by Petra Hendriks and Helen de Hoop, who suggest that there is a set of general, ranked but violable (i.e. soft) constraints governing interpretation, most of which have been proposed independently in the literature. Whenever speakers assign interpretations to the above types of structure, they do it in such a way that they try to adhere to the stronger, higher-ranked constraints, even violating the lower-ranked ones if this helps satisfy the stronger ones.

In 'Disjunction and Alternativeness' (*Ling&P* 24[2001] 597–619), Mandy Simons proposes that the natural language connective *or* has the truth-conditions of inclusive disjunctions, and that the requirement that the disjuncts should constitute related but disjunct alternatives is a condition on felicitous use, and derivable in a systematic way from general (Gricean) principles of conversation.

Sandro Zucchi and Michael White's paper 'Twigs, Sequences and the Temporal Constitution of Predicates' (*Ling&P* 24[2001] 223–70) launches two possible accounts for a problem which arises for all existing accounts concerned with the influence of NP-types on the aspectual class of predicates: whereas the application of *for*-adverbial phrases is restricted to *non-quantized* event predicates like *drink wine* (where the property of being non-quantized means that the events of drinking wine can have subevents which satisfy the same description, i.e. which are also events of drinking wine)—in contrast to such phrases as *drink a bottle of wine*, which are quantized—there are certain types of NP (such as *a twig*, *a quantity of wine*, or *a sequence*), which make the event predicate they appear in non-quantized, and yet they do not allow modification with a *for*-adverbial phrase. Thus *??John wrote a sequence of ten minutes*, *??John drank a quantity of milk for an hour* are as marked as *??John wrote a letter for an hour*, which contains a quantized event predicate. Similarly, on the interpretation of NPs, Giuseppe Longobardi, in 'How Comparative is Semantics? A Unified Parametric Theory of Bare Nouns and Proper Names' (*NLS* 9[2001] 335–69), proposes an interesting distinction between Romance and English bare (plural and mass) common nouns, according to which Romance bare common nouns are a type of indefinites (to be represented as variables which are either existentially or generically bound in particular contexts), while the English instantiations of the category are ambiguous between a referential (kind-denoting) interpretation and the above quantificational one.

Two publications discuss the semantics of reciprocals. In 'Reciprocals are Definites' (*NLS* 9[2001] 69–138), Sigrid Beck shows that elementary reciprocal sentences have four different semantic readings, and she provides a compositional analysis of these readings, which is based on the assumption that reciprocal sentences are a kind of relational plural, and the reciprocal expression is an anaphoric plural indefinite. Yoad Winter's 'Plural Predication and the Strongest Meaning Hypothesis' (*JSem* 18[2001] 333–65) extends a principle originally proposed for the interpretation of reciprocals, the Strongest Meaning Hypothesis of Dalrymple et al. [1994, 1998], to complex predicates that are composed of lexical predicates that hold of atomic entities, by claiming that the meaning of such complex predicates is the truth-conditionally strongest meaning that does not contradict the lexical properties of the simple predicates themselves. Hana Filip and Gregory N. Carlson's paper 'Distributivity Strengthens Reciprocity, Collectivity Weakens it' (*Ling&P* 24[2001] 417–66), however, argues against the validity of the Strongest Meaning Hypothesis, since in their opinion it does not predict correctly the interactions of the reciprocal with distributive and collective operators in Czech.

In addition to the works reviewed in a more systematic fashion above, the following papers deserve a brief mention: Renaat Declerck and Susan Reed's comprehensive description of the interpretation of *even if* conditionals ('Some Truths and Nontruths about *even if*', *Linguistics* 39[2001] 203–55), Maria Bittner's proposal for a dynamic Bridging Theory ('Surface Composition and Bridging', *JSem* 18[2001] 127–77), Claudia Maienborn's study ('On the Position and Interpretation of Locative Modifiers', *NLS* 9[2001] 191–240) which puts forward that there are three types of locative modifiers within the verbal domain differing from a syntactic and semantic point of view, and Matthew Whelpton's characterization of the interpretation of modifier infinitives in English, which express the outcome of the event denoted by the verb, as in the example *John hung his coat up, only to realize that he had to go out again*, in a Davidsonian event-semantics (*JL* 37[2001] 313–37).

7. Lexicography, Lexicology and Lexical Semantics

R.R.K. Hartmann's *Teaching and Researching Lexicography* distinguishes between *lexicography* 'as a practical and professional activity' (p. 12) and *dictionary research* or *metalexicography*. He argues that lexicography is not exclusively a linguistic discipline, but rather a multidisciplinary pursuit, which may eventually come to belong to the field of reference science. This would include reference works like directories and atlases as well as dictionaries. In the section on dictionary research, Hartmann offers seven perspectives on dictionary history, and characterizes these approaches as universal-anthropological, diachronic-linguistic, cultural-historical, genre-specific, genealogical, personal-biographical, and historiographic. He also looks at dictionary criticism, structural and typological perspectives on dictionaries, and the user perspective, offering a list of numbered perspectives for each. These overviews of dictionary research are useful in their own right, but also include references to detailed studies belonging to each category. Throughout the volume, Hartmann summarizes his position in clearly stated principles. For example: 'Principle 5.2 Dictionary typology: Whether dictionary typologies are based on shape and content ("phenomenological classification") or activity contexts ("functional classification"), the dimensions chosen depend on their purpose' (p. 69). The third section of the book deals with issues, methods, and case studies, and draws upon Hartmann's broad and distinguished career in lexicography and dictionary research. A directory of information sources follows, including discussion groups, dictionary archives, associations, dictionary research centres, text corpora, and selected websites. The last chapter is a glossary of terms used in lexicography and dictionary research. The directory and glossary will be invaluable to anyone beginning or continuing research in this area. R.R.K. Hartmann has also republished in paperback, with Gregory James, their *Dictionary of Lexicography*, which first appeared in 1998 (see *YWES* 79[2000] 67). The paperback edition of this invaluable work includes updated bibliographic references. Michael Rundell asks whether we are 'Teaching Lexicography or Training Lexicographers' (*Kernerman Dictionary News* 9[2001] 17–18), and concludes that, although a foundation in lexicography can be provided in universities, the only way to become a lexicographer is by writing dictionaries.

There were no large-scale dictionary studies this year, but the 'Distribution of Glosses in MSS of the Wycliffite Gospel of John' allows Saara Nevanlinna to reconstruct the text's manuscript transmission (*NM* 102[2001] 173–83). In 'The Renaissance Lexicographers Hulœt and Baret' (*N&Q* 48:ii[2001] 114–17), David W. Porter argues that the orthography of both names is influenced by a 'reformed, phonetic spelling' (p. 117). John Considine discusses 'Narrative and Persuasion in Early Modern English Dictionaries' (*RES* 52[2001] 195–206), and argues that early dictionaries and phrasebooks were intended to be read more or less consecutively, and that they had political as well as linguistic functions. In 'Authorship of *A Dictionarie French and English* (London, 1571)' (*N&Q* 48[2001] 231–3), David W. Porter provides further support for the case for Claudius Hollyband. Julie Coleman looks at the first English slang dictionary, and identifies 'Some of the Sources of B.E.'s *New Dictionary of the Terms Ancient and Modern of the Canting Crew*' (*N&Q* 48[2001] 400–1). Helen Berry looks at a flash glossary in 'Rethinking Politeness in Eighteenth-Century England: Moll King's Coffee House and the Significance of "Flash Talk"' (*TRHS* 11[2001] 65–81). Simon Beattie discusses an eighteenth-century writer on Scots lexicology in 'The Other John Sinclair' (*EnT* 17:ii[2001] 37–8). Andrew Ball considers the *OED*'s changing treatment of a maligned eighteenth-century author in 'A Resuscitated Reputation: The Case of Eliza Haywood' (*OED News* Sept.[2001]). In 'Twelve Notes on the Canadian *Oxford Dictionary*' (*Verbatim* 26:i[2001] 16–17), John Considine discusses some inadequacies of the dictionary, but concedes that it is, on the whole, an excellent work. In 'The Coming Boom in English Lexicography: Some Thoughts about the World Wide Web (Part One)' (*Kernerman Dictionary News* 9[2001] 1–2), Charles M. Levine argues that spell-checkers will not make dictionaries obsolete, and that the ubiquity of English on the World Wide Web will actually expand the market for ESL/EFL dictionaries. 'Why Bud Weiser Can Sell Cars (But Not Beer)' (*Verbatim* 26:iii[2001] 3–4) is Shawn M. Clankie's consideration of the relationship between lexicographers and corporate lawyers. Ian Brookes looks at words in the 1901 edition of Chambers dictionary that were omitted in 2001, in 'Some Words that Escaped from the Chambers Dictionary' (*Verbatim* 26:iii[2001] 21–3). Fred R. Shapiro shows how useful electronic access to *Harper's Weekly* can be in antedating *OED* first citations, in 'HarpWeek: Full-Text Searching of History' (*Verbatim* 26:iv[2001] 15–16). In 'It's Earlier Than You Think ... ' (*OED News* Sept.[2001]), Graeme Diamond looks at surprising antedatings uncovered for *OED*3.

Yukio Tono's *Research on Dictionary Use in the Context of Foreign Language Learning* is an exploration of how research into dictionary use can improve dictionary design and clarify issues in language learning. The volume begins by surveying the literature of user-oriented dictionary research, and dates the beginnings of systematic study to the early 1980s. Tono summarizes research on dictionary use in language learning, on the needs of L2 dictionary users, and on the analysis of their dictionary-using skills. Methodological considerations in dictionary-user research are also covered in some detail. The second section of the volume is a collection of Tono's own papers in the field. Some have been published before; most deal with Japanese EFL learners. Tono concludes, contrary to the findings of earlier studies, that there is a positive correlation between dictionary use and reading comprehension; that unskilled dictionary users tend to turn to a dictionary more quickly and with less success; that dictionary users benefit from training in dictionary skills, but that dictionaries should also be designed with incompetent dictionary users in mind. L2 learners tend to choose the first translation equivalent in their dictionary, with skilled users employing grammatical as well as semantic information to discount this first choice where it is not appropriate. Inserting a menu at the beginning of an entry helped unskilled users to pick the correct alternative. Of other ways of helping the dictionary user navigate entries, guide-words (which are placed after the headword) were found to be more useful than signposts (which are distributed throughout the entry). Tono also considers how far information about incorrect usage is helpful to L2 learners. Kazuo Dohi looks at the work of an influential American lexicographer in 'Dr Thorndike's Influence in Learners' Dictionaries' (*Dictionaries* 22[2001] 153–62), with particular reference to word, construction, and meaning frequency. Alice Yin Wa Chan and Andrew Taylor review dictionary reviews in 'Evaluating Learner Dictionaries: What the Reviews Say' (*IJL* 14[2001] 163–80), and argue that reviews should be evaluative and should involve study of target users' use of the dictionary. In 'The Use of Grammatical Information in Learners' Dictionaries' (*IJL* 14[2001] 97–121), Paul Bogaards and Willem A. van der Kloot consider the usefulness and usability of systems for providing grammatical information. Pedro A. Fuertes-Olivera and Marisol Velasco-Sacristán provide 'A Critical Comparison of the Macrostructure and Microstructure of Two Bilingual English–Spanish Dictionaries of Economics' (*IJL* 14[2001] 31–55).

A template is beginning to emerge for introductions to lexicology in terms of content and structure (see the reviews of Geoffrey Hughes's *A History of English Words* and Howard Jackson and Etienne Zé Amvela's *Words, Meaning and Vocabulary*, *YWES* 81[2002] 72). Robert Stockwell and Donka Minkova's *English Words: History and Structure* does not conform to it. Instead, this introduction to the origins and structure of English words, concentrates largely on those derived from Latin and Greek. It assumes no background knowledge and is accessibly written. The entertaining chapter on word origins covers neologisms, blending, various forms of acronyms, derivation, compounding, eponyms, and imitative forms. An introduction to comparative philology sets the scene for a discussion of the vocabulary of English since the early Modern English period. Where this differs from other introductions to lexicology is in the emphasis on phonology and morphology, which are introduced as disciplines dealing with units smaller than words. Minkova and Stockwell then discuss the rules of predictable allomorphy and consider the fossilized allomorphy that can obscure relationships between etymological cognates. The chapter on semantic change concentrates on its obscuration of the meaning of loan words, and suggests methods for determining the sense of unfamiliar classical words. This is followed by a guide to the pronunciation of classical words in English. An appendix gives an overview of the dictionaries currently available and advises users about the most appropriate purchase for their purposes. Exercises are available online. David Singleton's *Language and the Lexicon* is another fascinating introduction to a variety of approaches to the study of vocabulary. He has chapters on the relationship between lexis and syntax, morphology, meaning, phonology and orthography, and linguistic variation. Other chapters deal with collocation, lexical acquisition, dictionaries, and lexical change. Examples are drawn from a wide variety of languages, and each chapter ends with further reading and discussion topics. It is a comprehensive and readable introduction to the study of the lexicon. He concludes that 'after decades upon decades of being treated by most language specialists as the least interesting aspect of language, words have returned to the very centre of linguists' field of vision' (p. 238). Anthony R. Davis's *Linking by Types in the Hierarchical Lexicon* is aimed at a more specialist audience. He concentrates on the relationship between the syntactic arguments of verbs and the participant roles in situations, and provides an overview of previous research. He draws four main conclusions: 'The hierarchical lexicon, and multiple inheritance generally, provide the mechanisms for a nonprocedural constraint-based linking theory'; 'Regularities in mapping between semantic roles and syntactic arguments provide evidence for a level of lexical semantic representation'; 'Proto-role attributes group classes of entailments that behave identically for purposes of argument structure and syntax; they extract the semantic information relevant for linking'; and 'Linking constraints can be kept simple because each one is a partial specification of the mapping between lexical semantics and subcategorization; the structure of the lexical hierarchy ensures that the constraints applicable to a given predicator will indeed apply' (p. 277).

In an etymological exploration, Fred R. Shapiro looks at 'The Humble Origins of the Chad' (*Verbatim* 26:ii[2001] 17), a term for the incompletely punched holes in ballot papers, which arose frequently in discussions of contested counts in the 2001 American presidential election. Anatoly Liberman examines another uncertain etymology in 'Skip to the Loo: *Loo* in its (Indo-)European Context' (*Verbatim* 26:iii[2001] 1–3). Ari Hoptman offers 'A Possible Origin of *Flash Flood*' (*Verbatim* 26:iv[2001] 11–12). In 'Some Recent *OED* Releases: A Tale of Two Treats' (*OED News* Mar.[2001]), Peter Gilliver looks at the etymology of *marzipan*. Tania Styles explains how etymologies are being revised for *OED*3 in 'Confections à la Mode: Revising the *OED*'s Etymologies' (*OED News* Dec.[2001]). In 'Dictionary Etymologies of South Asian Loanwords into English: Some Suggestions for Improvement' (*Dictionaries* 22[2001] 145–52), Michael C. Shapiro considers some 'subtly inaccurate etymologies' (p. 152). Fred R. Shapiro discusses the origin of the term *bug* with reference to computer failures in 'George Orwell, Meet Regis' (*Verbatim* 26:i[2001] 20–1). Nick Humez looks at 'Eponymous Ailments' (*Verbatim* 26:iii[2001] 11–15): conditions named after the doctor that identified them. Deborah Schaffer looks at 'The Story of *e*-' (*EnT* 17:iv[2001] 22–6), as in *e-mail*. The prefix is sometimes used humorously in words like *e-cology* and *e-tail* (as opposed to *retail*). *Eco-* receives Brad Benz's attention in '*Eco* and the New Millennium: Current Coverage of *eco-* in Dictionaries' (*Dictionaries* 22[2001] 163–70). He concludes that definitions tend to be too narrowly based on etymology and to take insufficient account of usage. Heinz J. Giegerich investigates 'Synonymy Blocking and the Elsewhere Condition: Lexical Morphology and the Speaker' (*TPS*

99[2001] 65–98), and proposes a revised version of the Elsewhere Condition to account for homonymy blocking.

Piotr Sadowski considers 'The Sound-Symbolic Quality of Word-Initial *gr*-Clusters in Middle English Alliterative Verse' (*NM* 102[2001] 37–47), and concludes that alliteration is not merely a feature of prosody, but is inseparable from semantic content. Gillian Evans discusses the changing representation of pronunciation in the three editions of the *OED* in 'It's the Way You Say It: Pronunciation in the *OED*' (*OED News* Dec.[2001]). In 'Medical Malapropisms: What Doctors Say, What Patients Hear' (*Verbatim* 26:iii[2001] 6–10), Roger Smith lists miscommunications arising from the use of technical language to laypeople. 'Spelt as it Sounds' (*Verbatim* 26:iii[2001] 23–4) is David Galef's inelegantly entitled piece on words commonly respelt phonetically, like <vittles> for *victuals*. In 'Noncing the Indefinite Article, or, Do you have a Nuncle?' (*Verbatim* 26:iii[2001] 27), Thomas L. Bernard examines shifting word boundaries. Dennis Mills's 'An Alphabetaphile's Outrage' (*Verbatim* 26:ii[2001] 9–11) considers the lack of names for letters in English, except *aitch* for <h> and the now obsolete *izzard* for <z>. Barry Baldwin looks at words beginning with <x> in 'X Files' (*Verbatim* 26:ii[2001] 20–1) and <z> in 'Catching Some Zees' (*Verbatim* 26:iii[2001] 17).

In 'How to Understand *Understand*' (*NM* 102[2001] 185–99), John Newman looks at semantic motivations for OE *understandan*. Kenneth Shields proposes that the suffix *-et/-it* was archaic in Old English in 'On the Origin of Old English *Uncet* and *Incit*' (*NM* 102[2001] 211–16). In 'Is Old English *Hryre* "Perishable" Reliably Attested?' (*N&Q* 48[2001] 215–16), Alfred Bammesberger argues that it is not, which has implications for the category of short-stem *i*-adjectives in Old English. Bammesberger also concludes that 'The Meaning of Old English *Eowend(e)*' (*N&Q* 48[2001] 371–2) is 'testicles'. Carole Hough finds place-name evidence to support the interpretation 'dairy' for 'Middle English *Deye* in a Fifteenth-Century Cookery Book' (*NM* 102[2001] 303–5). Susan Yager finds that *folk* has neutral or occasionally positive connotations for Chaucer, but that *peple* is generally negative, in 'Chaucer's *Peple* and *Folk*' (*JEGP* 100[2001] 211–23). Heli Tissari takes a prototype-semantic approach to '*Affection, Friendship, Passion* and *Charity*: A History of Four "Love Lexemes" since the Fifteenth Century' (*NM* 102[2001] 49–76). In '*Innuendo* in the Restoration' (*JEGP* 100[2001] 22–39), Alan Roper traces the history of the development of the term from law-Latin into politics and thence into general use. John Spurn's 'A Profane History of Early Modern Oaths' (*TRHS* 11[2001] 37–63) is an exploration of the interrelation between profane and solemn oaths. In 'Denaturized Profanity in English' (*Verbatim* 26:ii[2001] 22–5), Ralph H. Emerson looks at terms like *gosh* and *lor*. Rebecca Clift's 'Meaning in Interaction: The Case of *Actually*' (*Language* 77[2001] 245–91) concludes that the syntactic flexibility of *actually* is exploited for interactional ends, but also constrains that interaction. David Galef discusses terms falling into obsolescence in 'Plain Talk of the Case of the Vanishing Vocabulary' (*Verbatim* 26:i[2001] 21–3).

Stephan Gramley's *The Vocabulary of World English* is an examination of the unity and variety of the vocabulary of English. Gramley is unusual in including grammatical as well as lexical words. He introduces some basic areas of lexicological study: etymology, semantics, register, loss and gain of vocabulary, language contact, and social context. Case studies, exercises, and projects are included to help the beginner understand these areas of study. Case studies include a consideration of the connotations of colour terms for speakers of different varieties of English, the use of ritual insults in a Western novel, and the Irish influence on Irish English. Exercises include a comparison of the terms used with reference to British and American educational systems, a study of a selection of loan words found in Australian, New Zealand and South African English, and an examination of rhyming slang terms. Suggested projects range from a study of how English terms are used in advertisements in a French newspaper to a questionnaire-based study of the use of slang terms. This is a well-written and imaginative introduction to the field. The inclusion of slang, and the vocabulary of internet chat-rooms, rap, and reggae is likely to recommend this book to students, but will, unfortunately, mean that it will date quickly. W.S. Ramson's 'Anna Wierzbicka and the Trivialization of Australian Culture' (*AJL* 21[2001] 181–94) is a discussion of what he sees as her 'flagrant abuse of the principles of historical lexicography' (p. 182), specifically her choice of key-words to represent Australian identity. Her response follows: 'Australian Culture and Australian English: A Response to William Ramson' (*AJL* 21[2001] 195–214). James Morton looks briefly at Australian slang (*ABM* Mar.[2001] 7; May[2001] 7). John H. Felts's 'Lapsed Language of Appalachia' (*Verbatim* 26:i[2001] 25–7) looks at dialect terms from the North Carolina mountains. James Morton considers slang terms derived from American nightlife (*ABM* Feb.[2001] 12) and the Old West (*ABM* Aug.[2001] 7, Sept.[2001] 7). Ronald R. Butters argues that a vulgar interpretation is historically unfounded in '"We didn't realize that lite beer was supposed to suck!" The Putative Vulgarity of "X sucks" in American English' (*Dictionaries* 22[2001] 130–44). Jennie Price explains the treatment of world English in *OED*3 in 'Varieties of English: World English and the *OED*' (*OED News* June[2001]), and Penny Silva looks specifically at South African English in 'Making it Click: Working on South African Words in the *OED*' (*OED News* Dec.[2001]). Antonio Lillo presents a forty-six-item glossary of 'The Rhyming Slang of the Junkie' (*EnT* 17:ii[2001] 39–45), 'almost entirely reliant on written sources' (p. 40). James Morton looks at obsolete slang (*ABM* Nov.[2001] 8) and catch-phrases (*ABM* Oct.[2001] 7). In 'Playing Upon Words' (*NM* 102[2001] 339–56 and 451–68), Eric Stanley concludes that, although various categorizations of wordplay are possible, the fundamental distinction is between playing on sounds and senses. He finds a close relationship between wordplay and rhyme because the demands of the form force the poet into linguistic self-awareness. Jessy Randall explores Rowling's wordplay and word-invention in 'Wizard Words: The Literary, Latin, and Lexical Origins of Harry Potter's Vocabulary' (*Verbatim* 26:ii[2001] 1–7). 'Baddabing, Baddabang' (*Verbatim* 26:iv[2001] 19–22) is Nick Humez's exploration of ablaut reduplications, such as *chit-chat* and *ding-dong*.

8. Onomastics

Two volumes in the EPNS Survey series were published this year. The third part of Margaret Gelling's *The Place-Names of Shropshire* covers Telford New Town, the northern part of Munslow Hundred, and the Franchise of Wenlock. Treatment of the major names is minimal, usually just a pocket definition, as the reader is referred to the first volume (see *YWES* 71[1992] 161) for full discussion, but we have here nevertheless a tremendous assemblage of early material and careful interpretation.

In the introduction, Gelling provides a useful assessment of the question of settlement, especially continuity of settlement, as illuminated by the place names. She also draws attention to the occurrence of certain items of particular lexicographical interest, including such rare place-name elements as OE *cwelm* 'spring', *salegn* 'willow copse', *weax* 'wax', ME *balne* 'bath', and *enche* 'servant', as well as noting evidence for a specific local sense of ME *pirle* 'spring' and for the survival of OE *halh*/ME *hale* 'nook' as a living term as late as the sixteenth century. Meanwhile, Kenneth Cameron's *The Place-Names of Lincolnshire* reaches its sixth part, covering the Wapentakes of Manley and Aslacoe, and thus embarking on the names of the West Riding of Lindsey. Once again, the wealth of data is truly impressive and the standard of scholarship impeccable. The interpretations of major names hold few surprises as they have been recently treated by Cameron in *A Dictionary of Lincolnshire Place-Names* [1998] (*YWES* 79[2000] 75–6), but some changes of opinion can be detected: a firm case is now made for preferring OE *beorg* 'hill' to *bearu* 'grove' as the generic in Alkborough, and we have a fuller discussion of the first element of Glentham which leads to a rejection of OE *glente* 'kite'.

An important regional study outside the EPNS series is *A Dictionary of London Place Names* by A.D. Mills, covering some 1700 names within the Greater London Boroughs and the City of London. The entries are models of their kind for a 'popular' reference work, engagingly and clearly written (with the minimum of abbreviations) and scholarly, supported when possible by a range of early spellings (though with regrettably few sources stated). The introduction is thorough, indeed surprisingly extensive in its range of topics, and the maps are effective. The provision of a list of elements is particularly welcome and unusually full; even the quickest glance will reveal any number of rare or unique place-name elements (note for instance OE *ludgeat* 'postern', ME *berdcherver* 'barber', *knightridere* 'mounted knight', *menouresse* 'Franciscan nun', *neckercher* 'neckerchief', *paternostrer* 'maker of rosaries').

A number of papers concerned with place names appear in Graham-Campbell, Hall and Parsons, eds., *Vikings and the Danelaw: Select Papers from the Proceedings of the Thirteenth Viking Congress, Nottingham and York, 21–30 August 1997*. In an analysis of place-name evidence for Scandinavian settlement, Gillian Fellows-Jensen's 'In the Steps of the Vikings' (pp. 279–88), divides 'England' (in effect the Danelaw) into four zones, within each of which she notes and discusses in some detail the different frequencies of occurrence of the Old Scandinavian generics *bý* 'settlement' and *þorp* 'secondary settlement', and of the so-called Grimston hybrids. Tania Styles looks at 'Scandinavian Elements in English Place-Names: Some Semantic Problems' (pp. 289–98), examining ME *appel-garth* 'orchard' and ON *bryggja*/OE *brycg* 'bridge, jetty'. Through a detailed exploration of the difficulties involved in separating English, Scandinavian and Anglo-Scandinavian origins, senses, sounds and spellings in these terms, she provides a valuable assessment of the value, limitations and complexities of place-name evidence. David Stocker and Paul Everson, in 'Five Towns Funerals: Decoding Diversity in Danelaw Stone Sculpture' (pp. 223–43), discuss, *inter alia*, how place-name interpretations do or do not fit with the picture of settlement history indicated by their examination of tenth/eleventh-century monuments in parts of the Danelaw, while other chapters in the same volume also make some use of place names; David N. Parsons, 'How Long did the Scandinavian Language Survive in

England? Again', offers some interesting thoughts on Grimston hybrids (pp. 299–312, at pp. 308–9), and Kevin Leahy and Caroline Paterson's 'New Light on the Viking Presence in Lincolnshire: The Artefactual Evidence' (pp. 181–202) includes evidence both onomastic and dialectal to boot.

Traces of Vikings are apparent in the names assembled in Sylvia Laverton's *Shotley Peninsula: The Making of a Unique Suffolk Landscape*, a study of nine parishes in south-east Suffolk which form a well-defined peninsula between the rivers Orwell and Stour. Laverton augments a detailed survey of archaeological sources with an investigation of the area's onomastic evidence (including minor names and personal names) to produce a useful account of settlement development from Iron Age to Norman Conquest.

In this year's *Journal of the English Place-Name Society*, the highly problematic Suffolk place name Hinderclay is tackled by Kathryn Lowe, in 'Elders and Betters: Hinderclay in Suffolk' (*JEPNS* 33[2001] 15–20), whose admirably meticulous manuscript analysis demonstrates that the name is to be derived not from OE **hyldre* 'elder-tree' + *clēa* 'claw' but from an OE masculine personal name **Hild(e)rīc* + *lēah* 'woodland clearing'. W.A.R. Richardson examines in detail a problematic group of coastal place names off Selsey Bill, Sussex, making particular use of early sailing charts, in 'The Owers, *Les Ours*, *Weembrug* and "The Old City": Place-Names, History and Submarine Archaeology' (*JEPNS* 33[2001] 55–114). Andrew Breeze, 'The Name of the River Tiddy' (*JEPNS* 33[2001] 5–6), interprets the river name Tiddy in Cornwall as 'the soaker', related to Cornish **teudhi* 'to melt'. Carole Hough's 'Postscript to Pitchcombe' (*JEPNS* 33[2001] 14) adds a note on dialect *pitch* 'short steep hill' to her earlier article [2000] on 'The Place-Name Pitchcombe' in Gloucestershire (*YWES* 81[2002] 79). María Auxiliadora Martín Díaz's 'A Two-Fold Development for Old English *æ* in 12th- and 14th-Century Kentish Place-Names' (*JEPNS* 33[2001] 21–54) is a fuller version of her earlier piece [2000] 'Old English æ in Middle Kentish Place-Names: a Geographical Approach' (*YWES* 81[2002] 81). The maps and most of the (curiously brief) text are familiar from the previous article, but we are now presented, in a series of tables, with the data upon which the analysis rests. Sadly, the same major criticism applies: this commendable undertaking is in reality a job half done, neglecting entirely the material in J.K. Wallenberg's *Kentish Place-Names* [1931]. The journal also includes two articles analysing the street-name types of a single town. G. Hilton charts and discusses changes in categories of twentieth-century street names in 'The Evolution of Street-Naming in Kenilworth, Warwickshire' (*JEPNS* 33[2001] 7–13), while Audrey Rosset and Henry Daniels, in 'Mixing and Matching: A Study of the Woking Street-Namestock' (*JEPNS* 33[2001] 115–46), examine the street names of Woking in Surrey, classifying and tabulating their findings according to category and frequency.

Nomina contains a carefully argued piece by Diana Whaley on 'Trusmadoor and Other Cumbrian "Pass" Words' (*Nomina* 24[2001] 77–95), which reveals that rarest of lexical items, a word of Cumbric. The term in question, *trus*, is cognate with Welsh *drws* 'door' and is applied to Lakeland passes at Trusmadoor in Cumberland and Truss Gap in Westmorland. Anthony R. Rowley's note on 'Stirton' (*Nomina* 24[2001] 97–9), a hamlet in the West Riding of Yorkshire, points out that the place name (OE *strt tūn* 'farmstead on a Roman road') confirms the route of a postulated Roman road between Skipton and Ingleton. Prompted by Carole Hough's recent suggestion [1998] that OE *hearpe* and *hearpere* might mean 'nightingale' in certain place names (*YWES* 79[2000] 78), Mary C. Higham makes a good case for the plausibility, in Lancashire at least, of the interpretation of the elements as 'harp' and 'harper', first by presenting evidence for an archetypal harp shape readily applicable in transferred senses, and secondly by establishing the status of harpers in medieval society and investigating their landholdings ('Harper's Lands', *Nomina* 24[2001] 67–76). Gillian Fellows-Jensen, 'The Mystery of the *bý*-Names in Man' (*Nomina* 24[2001] 33–46), looks at the place names containing Old Scandinavian *bý* 'settlement' on the Isle of Man, addressing the curiously frequent parallel formations in northern England and southern Scotland, which raise many questions, not least of analogy, chronology and language contact. She is, after much cogitation, 'inclined to see inspiration for their occurrence in Man ... in north-west England'. *Nomina* includes one article on an anthroponymic topic, David Postles's '"Gender Trouble" (Judith Butler): Describing English Women in the Twelfth and Thirteenth Centuries' (*Nomina* 24[2001] 47–66), an analysis of referents for women in medieval documents, and one piece on literary onomastics, W.F.H. Nicolaisen's '"A change of place is a change of fortune": Place-Names as Structuring Devices in Chaim Bermant's Novels' (*Nomina* 24[2001] 5–15).

Locus Focus once again offers a wide range of notes and queries on the place names of Sussex, including two articles by Richard Coates: a very tentative Brittonic solution to the name '*Biohchandoune* in Ferring Charter S1178/Kelly 13' (*LocusF* 5:ii[2001] 13–15), and 'A New Resource, *Literature Online* and Some Sussex Place-Names with Literary Mentions' (*LocusF* 5:ii[2001] 15–25), a demonstration of the wealth of literary mentions of place names which electronically searchable databases can throw up. Coates also provides an annotated transcription of a mid-nineteenth-century manuscript on South Downs topographical terms, in 'John Dudeney's Topographical Vocabulary' (*LocusF* 5:i[2001] 13–18), and John Townsend discusses the curious transferred name 'Bergen-op-Zoom, Ashurst' (*LocusF* 5:i[2001] 19–20). Elsewhere, Gabor Thomas, 'Hamsey near Lewes, East Sussex' (*SussexAC* 139[2001] 123–32, at 127), reconsiders the attribution of the tenth-century *witan* meeting-place *æt Hamme wiþ Læwe* to Hamsey, and Paul Cullen, 'The Place-Name Evidence', explores the archaeological significance of the Sussex place names Wickham and Comps (in Butler and Lyne, eds., *The Roman Pottery Production Site at Wickham Barn, Chiltington, East Sussex*, p. 66), supporting the identification of Wickham Barn with *wichama in ciltinne* in an eighth-century charter.

A number of pieces on English place names appeared in *Notes and Queries* this year. Warning against accepting *Anglo-Saxon Chronicle* accounts of eponymous heroes at face value, Carole Hough argues that the name 'Netley Marsh (Hampshire)' (*N&Q* 48[2001] 211–13) does not incorporate that of a British king *Natan*[*leod*], as recently defended by Andrew Breeze (in Coates and Breeze, eds., *Celtic Voices, English Places*, pp. 97–9; see *YWES* 81[2002] 77–8). In other notes, Hough prefers the interpretation 'land endowed for the maintenance of the church clock' to 'beetle croft' for the Cheshire field name 'Clock Croft' (*N&Q* 48[2001] 9–10); discusses the onomastic evidence for 'ME *paved* in a Cheshire Field-Name' (*N&Q* 48[2001] 371); and suggests ME *werod* 'a pack of wolves' (or its ancestor OE *weorod* in this otherwise unrecorded sense) as the first element of Wuerdle, in 'Old English *weorod* in Wuerdle, Lancashire' (*N&Q* 48[2001] 7–9). In 'English Place-

Names in *Marn-*, *Marl-*' (*N&Q* 48[2001] 6–7), Gillis Kristensson suggests OE *(ge)m re* 'boundary' + *ærn* 'house' as the first part of Marnham in Nottingham, Marnhull in Dorset, and Marlcliff on the Warwickshire/Worcestershire boundary, appealing to early haplology (and some analogy) to explain the historical spellings, and rightly noting the locations of these places on boundaries, but without discussing quite what a 'boundary house' might be. He also looks at 'The Place-Name Owermoigne Again' (*N&Q* 48[2001] 102–3), amplifying his earlier interpretation [2000] of this Dorset name as 'terror ridge' (*YWES* 81[2002] 82), unfortunately with no reference to the recent detailed discussions by Richard Coates (*YWES* 74[1997]) or in Coates and Breeze, eds., pp. 100–5 (see *YWES* 81[2002] 77–8, 82), the latter including a rebuttal of Kristensson's solution.

Northern History includes some items of onomastic interest. Gillian Fellows-Jensen's review article 'J. McN. Dodgson and the Place-Names of Cheshire' (*NH* 38[2001] 153–7) looks not only at the great man and his work but also at discussions of Cheshire names published by others since Dodgson's death. John Blair, 'Beverley, *Inderauuda* and St John: A Neglected Reference' (*NH* 38[2001] 315–16), provides evidence to support the identification of Bede's *Inderauuda* 'in the wood of the Deirans' with Beverley in the East Riding of Yorkshire. In 'A Paston Letter of 1461 and "Coroumbr", Yorkshire' (*NH* 38[2001] 316–17), Andrew Breeze suggests that *Coroumbr* is Knaresborough in the West Riding of Yorkshire, though the phonological difficulties are worryingly understated. David Postles, 'Defining the "North": Some Linguistic Evidence' (*NH* 38[2001] 27–46), addresses the long-standing problem of how to interpret the apparently 'northern' phenomenon of *-son* and *-doghter* bynames and surnames, and in so doing questions the extent of the 'North', arguing from the distribution of name-types against a precise isogloss.

There is but one book on personal names to report this year. Silvio Brendler's *Beiträge zur Geschichte der englischen und chinesischen Anthroponomatik / Contributions to the History of English and Chinese Anthroponomastics* includes a chapter on the pioneering work of Charlotte Mary Yonge, author of *History of Christian Names* [1863], and her influence on later scholarship: 'Charlotte Mary Yonge als Namenforscherin: Zum hundertsten Todestag einer viktorianischen Anthroponomastin' (pp. 12–29). Two chapters address aspects of English surname studies: 'On the Study of Isle of Wight Surnames: A Retrospective' (pp. 40–9) is a useful summary of the scattered contributions to the subject over four centuries, while 'On the Lexicography of English Surnames (LES): Some Problems and Prospects' (pp. 30–9) is a critique and typology of surname dictionaries coupled with an assessment of current and future desiderata. The appeal for renewed and concerted efforts towards systematic surname investigation is understandably heartfelt. Brendler's blend of theoretical and practical approaches to anthroponymic research works well, and these thoroughly researched historical contributions are to be welcomed. One aspect of surname study which looks set to expand is the involvement of genetics. Mark A. Jobling's 'In the Name of the Father: Surnames and Genetics' (*Trends in Genetics* 17[2001] 353–7) can be recommended as a valuable review article which examines recent studies of the correlation between Y chromosomes and patrilineal hereditary surnames, and looks ahead to likely future developments. Meanwhile, the unsuspecting onomast should perhaps be warned that Thomas W. Sheenan's *Dictionary of Patron Saints' Names* is not in any sense a work of etymological scholarship, but rather a handlist to provide 'Catholic connections with almost any possible given name' (and there are some ingenious matches!).

To return to toponymy, the booklet *Vanishing Hexham Street and Place Names* by Colin Dallison and David Jennings, though not offering any linguistic interpretation, deserves a mention as a worthwhile enterprise, comprising a list of lost or changing names in Hexham (Northumberland), arranged in 'Then' and 'Now' columns for purposes of identification, compiled from sources which include the personal memories of local townsfolk. Harold Fox's study of *The Evolution of the Fishing Village: Landscape and Society along the South Devon Coast, 1086–1550*, contains useful sections on 'cellar settlements' and 'cabins', which examine a range of terms found in different parts of Britain for temporary habitations (pp. 129–38, 178–81). Place- and personal names and their interpretation naturally feature prominently throughout Sean Miller's *Charters of the New Minster, Winchester* and Gillis Kristensson's *A Survey of Middle English Dialects, 1290–1350. The Southern Counties*, vol. 1: *Vowels (except Diphthongs)*.

Karl Inge Sandred's 'East Anglian Place-Names: Sources of Lost Dialect' (in Fisiak and Trudgill, eds., *East Anglian English*, pp. 39–61) surveys the linguistic layers that make up English place names, drawing examples from Norfolk and Suffolk—a useful contribution, since the place names of these counties have been relatively little studied. Sandred dwells especially on Scandinavian influence, and includes a special section on the minor names of Norwich. To conclude he gives examples of a range of non-standard terms (many of them Norse in origin) common in East Anglian names. The same author's 'Norwich: Uppkomsten av en Medeltida Stad' (*Ortnamnssällskapets i Uppsala Årsskrift* [2001] 44–65) presents an excellent historical overview of Norwich through its place names, based on the extensive material in Sandred's EPNS volume *The Place-Names of Norfolk: Part One* [1989] covering the names of the city's streets, markets, buildings, districts, watercourses and so on. The approach is broadly chronological, always with an eye to setting Norwich in a wider English context. An English summary is included ('The Rise of a Medieval Town'), though it hardly does the Swedish text justice, being little more than a contents list to the EPNS volume. A further article by Sandred, 'English *stead*: A Changeable Place-Name Element in a Changing Community' (*SN* 73[2001] 164–70), examines various aspects of OE *stede* 'place', thus revisiting the subject of his book *English Place-Names in -stead* [1963], and ably reasserts a number of his earlier arguments in the light of subsequent discussion of the term.

In 'Place-Name Evidence for an Anglo-Saxon Animal Name: OE *pohha/*pocca "Fallow Deer"' (*ASE* 30[2001] 1–14), Carole Hough examines a corpus of names which have hitherto been interpreted as containing OE *pohha/pocca* 'pouch, bag', making the crucial observation that the word in question occurs overwhelmingly as the qualifier rather than generic in place names, and in combination with elements (e.g. OE *hl pe* 'leap') suggestive of an animal term. In another well-argued piece, 'Domesday Land-Holdings and the Place-Name *Freeland*' (*SN* 73[2001] 137–42), Hough investigates the place name Freeland in Sussex and comparable field names in Berkshire and the West Riding of Yorkshire, relating them to forms of tenure in their Domesday parishes; she derives the names from an OE technical term *frēoland applied to 'land owned independently but under the jurisdiction of an overlord', represented in Domesday Book by Latin *libera terra* and similar phrases. Elsewhere, Hough convincingly re-establishes 'The Non-Celtic Origin of *meguines* *paed* in Kent' (*NOWELE* 38[2001] 109–13), and in a discussion of 'Old English *pottere*' (*Neophil* 85[2001] 621–4) she reconsiders the name *potteres lege* in a tenth-century Staffordshire charter, suggesting that OE **pottere* may alternatively be explained as a bird-name, while not ruling out the traditional interpretation 'potter'.

John Insley contributes seven articles to this year's three instalments of Beck, Geuenich and Steuer, eds., *Reallexikon der Germanischen Altertumskunde*, each containing much valuable onomastic material, beginning in volume 17 (*Kleinere Götter–Landschaftsarchäologie*) with a substantial survey of heathen names, analysing in detail place names which contain god names and terms for shrines ('Kultische Namen: England', pp. 425–37), followed by a similarly thorough account of the names of Anglo-Saxon kingdoms and districts ('Länder- und Landschaftsnamen: England', pp. 569–79). In volume 18 (*Landschaftsrecht–Loxstedt*) Insley investigates the names and history of Lindsey in Lincolnshire (pp. 471–9), and in volume 19 (*Luchs–Metrum*) he examines Lyminge in Kent (pp. 58–69), the province of the *Meonware* in Hampshire ('Meanware', pp. 473–6), the *Anglo-Saxon Chronicle*'s Sussex battle-site *Mearcredes burna* (pp. 477–80), and the historical and onomastic evidence for the kingdom of Mercia (pp. 548–64). Though full justice cannot be done to these *Reallexikon* entries here, it should be emphasized that they are not mere snippets but hefty pieces of sound scholarship and erudition. Missed last year were Insley's contributions to volume 15 (*Hobel–Iznik*), surveying the *Hwicce* (pp. 287–95), *Hwinca* (p. 296), *Iclingas* (pp. 320–3), and *Ipswich* (pp. 480–3).

OE *burh* 'stronghold' receives some varied attention this year. In 'Bedford: An Alfredian burh?' (*Bedfordshire Archaeology* 24[2001] 40–6), Alan Crawley and Ian Freeman make the interesting suggestion that the place name *Aldermanbury* in Bedford might, like Aldermanbury in the City of London, be associated with Ethelred, alderman of Mercia under King Alfred. Mark Blackburn, '*Metheltun* not *Medeshamstede*: An Anglo-Saxon Mint at Melton Mowbray Rather than Peterborough Abbey' (*British Numismatic Journal* 70[2001] 143–5), makes a convincing case for identifying the Anglo-Saxon mint-name MEÐELTV, and its truncated form MEÐ, with Melton Mowbray in Leicestershire rather than Peterborough (called *Medeshamstede* before becoming simply *Burh*) in Northamptonshire, thus providing us with the first pre-Conquest evidence for the place name; as a corollary he reconsiders whether such mint-signatures as BVR might refer to Peterborough. Andrew Reynolds, 'Avebury: A Late Anglo-Saxon *burh*?' (*Antiquity* 75[2001] 29–30), examines the nature of the *burh* of Avebury in Wiltshire. Note also that Sara María Pons Sanz's analysis of 'Aldredian Glosses to Proper Names in the *Lindisfarne Gospels*' (*Anglia* 119[2001] 173–92), as well as being of general onomastic interest, may also begin to offer insights into tenth-century usage of individual terms such as *burh*.

A few other scattered articles should be noted here. Arnold H.J. Baines, 'Beating the Bounds: Rogationtide at Waddesdon' (*Records of Buckinghamshire* 41[2001] 143–64), examines in admirable detail the Bounds Book of a Buckinghamshire parish, including much of onomastic interest in a piece which can also be recommended for its excellent introductory survey of bounds-beating. David Graham establishes the locations of 'The Cricklestone and Thor's Stone: Parish Boundary Markers on Thursley Common' (*Surrey Archaeological Collections* 88[2001] 337–41), partially explaining the name Cricklestone and revealing Thor's

Stone to be a late nineteenth-century 'romantic' coinage. Andrew Breeze proposes the Brittonic ancestor of Welsh *pedryal* 'rectangle, square' (used of some archaeological feature) as the etymon of 'The Name of the River Petteril' (*Transactions of the Cumberland and Westmorland Antiquarian & Archaeological Society* 101[2001] 195–6). To explain Bede's place name *Maelmin* (i.e. Milfield in Northumberland), the second element of which is Brittonic *mīn 'brink, edge', the same author, in 'The Name of *Maelmin*, near Yeavering' (*Archaeologia Aeliana* 29[2001] 31–2), proposes Brittonic *mal 'decayed, rotten', though curiously without mention of the Brittonic *mail 'prince' proposed in Coates and Breeze, eds., *Celtic Voices, English Places* [2000], p. 323 (*YWES* 81[2002] 77–8). In other scattered pieces Breeze discusses a further selection of names in the north of England in 'The British-Latin Place-Names *Arbeia, Corstopitum, Dictim*, and *Morbium*' (*Durham Archaeological Journal* 16[2001] 21–5); 'Great Dinnod, a Boundary Stone near Danby, Eskdale' (*Transactions of the Yorkshire Dialect Society* 20[2001] 37–9); and, in the south, in '*Durnovaria*, the Roman Name of Dorchester' (*Somerset and Dorset Notes and Queries* 35[2001] 69–72) and 'Does Lamorna in Cornwall mean "Valley of Murders"?' (*Devon and Cornwall Notes and Queries* 38[2001] 261–2). Onomastic discussion plays a large part in Harald Kleinschmidt's '*Nomen* and *Gens*: The Germanic Settlement in Britain and the Genesis of the English' (*Archives* 105[2001] 97–111); in particular he makes use of, and in some cases seeks to explain, the group names of the Germanic migrants to Britain, investigating which collective identities already existed among the migrants and how those identities changed after migration.

A handful of items missed last year merit notice. Gillian Fellows-Jensen's account of 'Vikings in the British Isles: The Place-Name Evidence' (*Acta Archaeologica* 71[2000] 135–46) is a valuable review of recent research into Scandinavian place names in England and Scotland. Andrew Fleming locates and explains some tricky names in the North Riding of Yorkshire in 'A Lost Swaledale Vaccary and a Palimpsest of Place-Names' (*Northern History* 36[2000] 159–62). Finally, David N. Parsons and Patrick Sims-Williams, eds., *Ptolemy: Towards a Linguistic Atlas of the Earliest Celtic Place-Names of Europe* [2000] contains two chapters relating to England: David N. Parsons discusses the manifold problems involved in 'Classifying Ptolemy's English Place-Names' (pp. 169–78), and presents the tabulated and mapped results of his cautious handling of the material, while Patrick Sims-Williams includes names from the English borders in his consideration of 'Degrees of Celticity in Ptolemy's Names: Examples from Wales' (pp. 1–15).

9. Dialectology and Sociolinguistics

This year's publications on dialectology and sociolinguistics have a strong focus on theory. In the field of general publications, a notable shift towards more macro-sociolinguistic concerns is visible this year. We will begin with some good news: the classic *Foundations in Sociolinguistics* by Dell Hymes has been reprinted. Although the original is from 1974, it has lost none of its vitality and is now available again to a new generation of sociolinguists. A wide definition of sociolinguistics is also the basis of Mesthrie, ed., *The Concise Encyclopedia of Sociolinguistics*, which is based on the Pergamon *Encyclopedia* [1994], edited by R.E. Asher (see *YWES* 75[1996] 1–2). Its contributions range so widely over the field that the table of contents takes up eighteen pages alone, and the reviewer may be forgiven for not going into the details of every article here. Although classical sociolinguists will also find much of interest here (for example very good background articles on 'Social Class' (M.W. Macy, pp. 362–9), 'Social Networks' (Lesley Milroy, pp. 370–6) or 'Sociolinguistics and Language Change' (Jim Milroy, pp. 389–91), the ten sections of the book provide a much wider overview. 'The Foundations of Society and Language', for example, also introduces the reader to the 'Ecology of Language' (J.M.Y. Simpson, pp. 30–1) and the 'Sociolinguistics of Sign Language' (C. Lucas, pp. 89–92); section 2, 'Language and Interaction' has contributions ranging from the intriguingly titled 'Antilanguage' (p. 109) to 'Speech Act Theory' (pp. 197–208), indicating that this section touches on pragmatics. Section 3 borders on stylistics, and the more narrowly sociolinguistic section 4, 'Language Variation and Change: Dialects and Social Groups' mentioned above also covers an unexpected—and fascinating—topic, 'Forensic Phonetics and Sociolinguistics' (by Paul Foulkes and J.P. French, pp. 329–32). 'Language Contact' and 'Language, Power and Inequality' are perhaps more predictable section headings, as are 'Language Planning, Policy, Practice' and 'Language Education'. Section 9 deals with 'Methods in Sociolinguistics' from 'Attitude Surveys' (H. Schuman, pp. 761–5) via 'Corpus Linguistics' (M. Sebba and S.D. Fligelstone, revised by W.A. Kretzschmar, pp. 765–9) and 'Fieldwork Ethics' (Barbara Johnstone, pp. 781–4) to 'Statistics' (David Sankoff, pp. 828–34). Completely unconventional is section 10, which presents 'The Profession', listing 'Endangered Languages Projects (An Inventory)' (L.A. Grenoble and L.J. Whaley, pp. 835–8), 'Internet Resources for Sociolinguistics' (Andrea Deumert, pp. 838–40), 'Professional Associations' (Rajend Mesthrie, pp. 840–2) and surveying 'Sociolinguistics Journals' (Nikolas Coupland, pp. 842–4). The last (unnumbered) section gives profiles of eighty-eight notable sociolinguists, appraising their contribution to the field, which makes the encyclopedia an invaluable resource for students and researchers alike.

Linguistic Anthropology is the title of a reader edited by Alessandro Duranti, who also gives an excellent overview of the 'History, Ideas, and Issues' (pp. 1–38) of the field. The contributions are grouped into four parts, of which the first part, 'Speech Community and Communicative Competence', might be the most interesting to micro-sociolinguists. Part 2, 'The Performance of Language: Acts, Events, and Activities', also clearly marks a new trend towards which sociolinguistics as a field is turning. Contributions include classic studies by John G. Gumperz, Dell Hymes and Benjamin Lee Whorf, but more recent papers can also be found. As they have all appeared before, individual contributions will not be singled out here. Alessandro Duranti is also the editor of *Key Terms in Language and Culture*, a highly original collection of seventy-five almost lexicon-like 1,000-word entries on concepts from 'Acquisition' to 'Writing' (in alphabetical order) by some of the leading anthropologists in the field. While most contributions touch more narrowly sociolinguistic concerns only marginally, chapters such as 'Variation', 'Gender', 'Identity' or 'Community' are relevant to both research communities and may constitute good entrance points to particular topics.

Another classic volume has re-emerged, namely Giles and Robinson, eds., *The New Handbook of Language and Social Psychology*. Completely and thoroughly revised, this volume is now a collection of papers at the programmatic forefront of the field. Of the thirty-two new contributions, only a few can be mentioned here. In part 1, 'Theoretical Perspectives', Carolyn A. Shepard, Howard Giles and Beth A. Le Poire give an updated account of 'Communication Accommodation Theory' (pp. 33–56) which might also be of interest to more variationist sociolinguists. Parts 2 to 4 really concentrate on the ethnography of speaking, with topics such as 'Face to Face' or 'Social Relations'. In part 5, 'Social Categories', Linda Coates and Trudy Johnson's 'Towards a Social Theory of Gender' (pp. 451–86) calls for a study of gender that views gender not as a property inherent to individuals but 'as a product of interaction' (pp. 451–86, at 455). Nikolas and Justine Coupland argue, in 'Language, Ageing and Ageism' (pp. 465–86), that ageing is a social (and, specifically, a linguistic) construct that masks gerontophobia. We note here another study on the topic of gender by Suzanne Romaine, which presents 'A Corpus-Based View of Gender in British and American English' (in Hellinger and Bussmann, eds., *Gender Across Languages*, vol. 1, pp. 153–75). It focuses on forms of address and on generic *he*, pointing out that English is (still) a gendered language, with British English lagging behind American English in language reform.

A highly original contribution to the general field is Coupland, Sarangi and Candlin, eds., *Sociolinguistics and Social Theory*. In 'Introduction: Sociolinguistic Theory and Social Theory' (pp. 1–26) Coupland provides an overview of sociolinguistic work in three frameworks: social theory as social structure (Labov-style sociolinguistics), social theory as social action perspectives (ethno-methodological approaches) and integrationist approaches, and suggests that 'the future theoretical shape of sociolinguistics will be determined by how sociolinguists orient to integrationist social theories' (p. 15). Srikant Sarangi discusses the role of language in the work of Habermas, Foucault and Bourdieu in 'A Comparative Perspective on Social Theoretical Accounts of the Language–Action Interrelationship' (pp. 29–60). Jonathan Potter and Derek Edwards suggest, in 'Sociolinguistics, Cognitivism, and Discursive Psychology' (pp. 88–103), that neither cognition nor reality should be accepted as given, but treated as constructed in and through discourse. In part 2, Per Linell contrasts 'Dynamics of Discourse or Stability of Structure: Sociolinguistics and the Legacy from Linguistics' (pp. 107–26) and sees inherent problems in the acceptance by linguistics of dynamics, change, vagueness and openness (for structural, historical and technical reasons). Frederick Erickson gives an example for 'Co-membership and Wiggle Room: Some Implications of the Study of Talk for the Development of Social Theory' (pp. 152–81), an instance where a tutor does not behave as gatekeeper towards one of his students, thanks to co-membership. Part 3, 'Language, Ideology and Social Categorization', has another interesting contribution on age by Nikolas Coupland, 'Age in Social and Sociolinguistic Theory' (pp. 185–211), recalling his contribution to Giles and Robinson, eds., noticed above. Coupland critically assesses the role of age in more traditional sociolinguistic studies and claims that 'the experience of ageing lies in how changing social conditions ... interact with historical cohort experiences' in discourse (p. 204). Lesley Milroy deals with 'The Social Categories of Race and Class: Language Ideology and Sociolinguistics' (pp. 235–60), comparing in particular the standard language ideology in the UK with the US. Whereas 'non-standard dialect' in the UK mainly indicates class differences, class differences in the US are masked by race, such that the most criticized and least accepted dialect is AAVE—this difference of course has important consequences for applied linguistic concerns. Finally, Ben Rampton gives a fascinating account of 'Language Crossing, Cross-Talk, and Cross-Disciplinarity in Sociolinguistics' (pp. 261–96), accounting for the use of Stylized Asian English in terms of ritual and liminality. This collection closes with 'Retrospective Commentaries' (part 4): Celia Roberts assesses '"Critical" Social Theory: Good to Think with or Something More?' (pp. 323–33); John Wilson asks: 'Who Needs Social Theory Anyway?' (pp. 334–49); and Srikant Sarangi and Christopher N. Candlin call for sociolinguists to break out of their current theoretical framework, in '"Motivational Relevancies": Some Methodological Reflections on Social Theoretical and Sociolinguistic Practice' (pp. 350–88), aptly summing up the gist of this collection. Also on a theoretical theme, Alison Sealey and Bob Carter advocate sociological realism approaches for sociolinguistic studies in 'Social Categories and Sociolinguistics: Applying a Realist Approach' (*IJSL* 152[2001] 1–19). They point out that in particular the usual 'independent' variables of sociolinguistic research—age, gender, ethnicity, class—are themselves theoretical constructs and are often used in a circular way in correlation with linguistic variables. One possible way out is to analyse language variation as case-driven, taking account of language as having features of emergence and complexity.

On a more practical level, Newman and Ratliff, eds., *Linguistic Fieldwork*, introduces the student to basic questions of ethnomethodology. Although written from an ethnographic perspective, the basic rules are surely valid for more purely sociolinguistic fieldwork as well. In particular the chapter on 'Monolingual Field Research' by Daniel L. Everett (pp. 166–88) seems intuitively relevant for sociolinguists too, even if the advice that 'the linguist should work with the people, hunt with the people, fish with the people, and farm with the people' (p. 177) will perhaps not be as strictly adhered to in urban sociolinguistic studies as the author might wish [ϑ].

Moving briefly to textbooks, Janet Holmes has updated her *Introduction to Sociolinguistics* [1992], and the second edition now contains a new chapter on 'Language, Cognition and Culture' (pp. 317–41) dealing with linguistic relativism, as well as new sections on the construction of gender through language. The accessible text is replete with exercises, and the solutions have now been separated from the exercises, an innovation many teachers will no doubt welcome.

The field of historical sociolinguistics has become so established that it is making its way into introductory textbooks. Herbert Schendl, in his very short *Historical Linguistics*, devotes a whole chapter to 'Socio-Historical Linguistics and Historical Pragmatics' (pp. 81–5), and Barbara A. Fennell has written her *History of English* wholly from a sociolinguistic point of view, as the subtitle indicates—which seems to mean that Fennell tries to put the speakers at the centre of her overview, always relating change to the socio-historical background, and in particular trying to answer the actuation problem. Perhaps a little unexpected for a 'history' of a language, Fennell devotes roughly half of the volume to PDE, dealing with varieties of English in Britain (e.g. RP and English in Scotland, Ireland and Wales, as well as immigrant varieties), English in the United States (discussing British–American divergence, but also giving an overview of the American English dialects, including up-to-date features such as the Northern Cities Vowel Shift and the Southern Vowel Shift) and World-Wide English. This last chapter is really an introduction to the socio-historical circumstances that introduced English to the various former colonies across the world, rather than an overview of specific linguistic features of these varieties. Nevertheless, this new addition to the many histories of the English language will no doubt prove very valuable as concise background information for students and teachers of sociolinguistics alike.

Jean Aitchison in the third edition of her *Language Change: Progress or Decay?* [1981, 1991] has added a chapter on the (hot) new topic of grammaticalization, and one on new approaches to the change of meaning, and also in general puts the speaker at the centre of her accessible overview; in view of the fact that variationist sociolinguistics is always also concerned with change in progress, it is warranted to mention Aitchison's accessible introduction to the field in the context of this section. Ronald R. Butters adds an interesting twist to the debate in his discussion of 'Chance as Cause of Language Variation and Change' (*JEngL* 29[2001] 201–13). Pure chance, coupled with individuals' desire to 'talk like the people around you' leads to a surprisingly good model of language variation and change. This basically takes account of Sapir's notion of 'drift', but new models of chaos theory show that random variations do not have to cancel each other out, but can lead to qualitative changes. The interest in historical sociolinguistics is also testified by the publication of the first online journal for this (sub)discipline, *Historical Sociolinguistics and Sociohistorical Linguistics*, edited by Ingrid van Tieken Boon-Ostade. In its first edition, Irene van Baalen asks: 'Male and Female Language: Growing Together?' (*HSL/SHL* 1[2001] no pagination). Van Baalen finds no significant differences in the use of hedging devices between men and women on the TV show 'Ruscoe on five' and in the absence of historical studies concludes that male and female language have indeed become more similar. (Spot the non sequitur?)

Regional varieties have received comparatively less attention this year. One of the few exceptions for Britain is East Anglia, thanks to Fisiak and Trudgill, eds., *East Anglian English*. While the majority of contributions are historical in nature, present-day dialectologists will also find much of interest. As probably the most famous East Anglian sociolinguist, Peter Trudgill is eminently qualified to define 'Modern East Anglia as a Dialect Area' (pp. 1–12). Indeed he also proposes the Spanish Inquisition as a major factor in the development of one of the most distinctive features of this dialect area, 'Third-Person Singular Zero: African-American English, East Anglian Dialects and Spanish Persecution in the Low Countries' (pp. 179–86). Ken Lodge discovers 'The Modern Reflexes of Some Middle English Vowel Contrasts in Norfolk and Norwich' (pp. 205–15), and David Britain bids us 'Welcome to East Anglia!' discussing 'Two Major Dialect "Boundaries" in the Fens' (pp. 217–42), i.e. the /U-V/ and the /a-aː/ split that runs across the Fenland and that does not only distinguish north from south England, but also East Anglia from the Midlands. Finally, Pat Poussa deals with 'Syntactic Change in North-West Norfolk' (pp. 243–59), discussing in particular the use of *that* as an anaphoric pronoun, and *what*-relatives. The contributions confirm the status of East Anglia as a distinct dialect area from the rest of south-east England until quite recently. Most of Peter Trudgill's work on this dialect area can in fact also be found in his *Sociolinguistic Variation and Change*, a collection of his more recent papers, which have all been published before (although some of them are 'substantially revised'). The contributions are grouped into sections—'Sociohistorical Linguistics', 'Dialect Change', 'Language Contact', 'Language Creation and

Death', and 'Englishes'—although many could equally well go into the neighbouring section, and indeed about half of the chapters deal with East Anglian data in one way or another. As all have appeared before, they will not be reviewed here in detail again.

Teenagers in the London metropolis provide the data central to Andersen and Fretheim, eds., *Pragmatic Markers and Sociolinguistic Variation*, long announced and finally out this year. On the basis of COLT (the Bergen Corpus of London Teenage Language), Andersen investigates two pragmatic features in great detail: the use of *innit* as an invariant tag and as an invariant follow-up, and the use of *like* in all its facets. Invariant *innit* (i.e. *innit* not following a third-person singular subject with a present-tense verb) in London seems to be a local innovation, according to Andersen due to the multi-ethnic setting. It has spread to young adults, as comparisons with the London BNC-material reveal, but only marginally so. *Like* on the other hand seems to be an imported innovation from the US and is used exclusively by adolescents, in fact mainly by white girls. Surprisingly, of all 'new' uses of *like*, the quotative use is relatively rare (it only accounts for 7 per cent of all 'new' *likes*—more on quotatives below), which might testify to its relatively late appearance in the grammaticalization chain. Whether the strong emergence of *like* does constitute the initial stages of language change, or whether we are observing only a severe case of age-grading is not, however, discussed in detail in Andersen's work. Another study on non-standard grammar is Lieselotte Anderwald's '*Was/ were* Variation in Non-Standard British English Today' (*EWW* 22[2001] 1–21). Based on spoken material from the BNC, Anderwald finds that negation in particular is an important factor in the choice of a non-standard past-tense form of *be*, and that the most widespread pattern (*was* for all persons combined with *weren't* for all persons) has remorphologized the standard English number distinction as a distinction of polarity.

For the north of England, Sali Tagliamonte presents an analysis of '*Come/Came* Variation in English Dialects' (*AS* 76[2001] 42–61) in the city of York. Based on her corpus of ninety-two speakers, Tagliamonte finds that past tense *come* is as frequent here as in other varieties, but she attributes it to, among other things, former contact with Scandinavian languages. Dominic Watt and Jennifer Tillotson contribute 'A Spectrographic Analysis of Vowel Fronting in Bradford English' (*EWW* 22[2001] 269–302), an innovative phenomenon for Bradford that is, however, well documented for East Yorkshire, Tyneside and Humberside. Watt and Tillotson discard internal explanations and speculate that fronting of /o/ (as in *goat*) represents a 'northern' identity. Catherine M. Sangster investigates 'Lenition of Alveolar Stops in Liverpool English' (*JSoc* 5[2001] 401–12), i.e. strong affrication of /p t k/, but, contrary to textbook statements, her instrumental analysis reveals no absolute neutralization with fricatives or affricates. Instead, through differences in length of friction, phonemic differences are maintained. Patrick Honeybone looks at the same subject from the reverse angle, i.e. those instances of 'Lenition Inhibition in Liverpool English' (*ELL* 5[2001] 213–45), where lenition does not occur. According to his impressionistic analysis, this is due to prosodic (in word-initial position or before a stressed vowel) or melodic reasons (after a consonant).

Nikolas Coupland, in addition to his various contributions on age (see above), also enlightens us on Welsh English, or, more specifically, on its stylized use, in 'Dialect Stylization in Radio Talk' (*LSoc* 30[2001] 345–75). Coupland's analysis of the use of stylized Welsh (monophthongization of (ou) and (ei), prosodic and paralinguistic features) by two radio presenters shows that stylization occurs in particular in contexts of verbal 'cartooning' (p. 366). Stylization serves as de-authentication of the speaker without discrediting the variety—raising the general question of how authentic dialect speech is, potentially rocking the foundations of sociolinguistic variationist studies.

Ronald Macaulay comments on 'You're Like "Why Not?" The Quotative Expressions of Glasgow Adolescents' (*JSoc* 5[2001] 3–21), leading us back to the most frequently analysed phenomenon this year. Macaulay's study of male and female 13–14-year olds (in 1997) indicates that *like* as a quotative marker has reached Glasgow, where it is used in 14 per cent of all cases of quotations, mostly by middle-class girls. Macaulay postulates a chain of development for *like*: *go* > *go like that* > *be like that* > *be like* > *be* (all these quotatives are attested in his material), but the evidence for this kind of evolution is not all that conclusive. Macaulay himself speaks of the possibility of some 'distortion in the transmission' (p. 17), and indeed this seems the more likely explanation. Jennifer Smith deals with another grammatical variable in 'Negative Concord in the Old and New World: Evidence from Scotland' (*LVC* 13[2001] 109–34). The relic dialect of Buckie (in north-east Scotland) shows very high ratios of negative concord (almost 70 per cent), but a restricted distribution across linguistic contexts. In this it is similar to other British varieties, but different from most American ones. Smith considers socio-historical reasons and concludes that negative concord in extended contexts constitutes an American innovation.

One of the most impressive studies, and indeed one of the few monographs out this year, is Kevin McCafferty's *Ethnicity and Language Change: English in (London)Derry, Northern Ireland*. McCafferty carefully picks apart the 'myth of non-sectarianism' (which claims that ethnicity does not play a role in linguistic variation) in the most segregated city in Northern Ireland and shows how the Protestant and Catholic communities diverge in ongoing linguistic changes, no doubt due to both residential and activity segregation. McCafferty's detailed studies of five phonological variables (/or/-raising, /Er/-centring, /e/-diphthongization, <th>-elision, and /V/) show that the Protestants, in the minority in (London)Derry but in the majority in Northern Ireland as a whole, orient towards the wider Ulster developments and converge with them, while the Catholics tend to preserve the older, rural forms longer, resisting Belfast innovations in particular. The local innovation (<th> realized as a lateral approximant—thus *other* comes out as *oller*), on the other hand, is led by the Catholics. McCafferty's lucid account shows in particular that ethnicity also plays an important role for linguistic features, contrary to received sociolinguistic wisdom.

Anyone interested in an introduction to *English in North America* should turn to the Cambridge History of the English Language, volume 6, edited by John Algeo, which has a strong focus on British English–American English contrasts, but also gives an overview of the traditional dialect work done in this field. Of particular interest to dialectologists will be Michael Montgomery's contribution on the possibility of discovering 'British and Irish Antecedents' (pp. 86–153), where he calls for meticulous methodological work, Lee Pederson giving an overview of the four major (traditional) American 'Dialects' (pp. 253–90), based on the various atlas projects, and Salikoko S. Mufwene's introduction to 'African-American English' (pp. 291–324), incidentally the only contribution which briefly mentions the name of William Labov. Otherwise modern sociolinguistic studies, which have surely contributed greatly to our understanding of 'English in North America', are completely missing from the pages of this book, and readers will leaf through it without ever encountering more recent dialectal developments like the Northern Cities Shift or the Southern Shift.

A much more popular—and, indeed, up-to-date—overview is provided by Alan Metcalf in *How We Talk: American Regional English Today* [2000] from last year. Metcalf proceeds region by region and even state by state, with a brief appendix on ethnic variation as well, presenting mainly lexicographical differences but making an effort to represent phonetic differences as well as grammatical ones. Although replete with stereotypes and often rather flippant, the book tries to do justice to the great variability that we find in American dialects and even some of the regularities that underlie the different developments. As Metcalf does not presuppose any knowledge of linguistics, this book might serve as a very basic introduction to some regional dialects. The last chapter may be very useful in that Metcalf lists films featuring dialect speakers and evaluates their authenticity.

Anything but flippant is the long-awaited second volume of William Labov's monumental *Principles of Linguistic Change*—although it has to be said that the phrase 'phonetic change' might be more accurate here, as only phonetic variables, in fact almost exclusively vowels, are investigated. Volume 2 deals with the social factors of his Project on Linguistic Variation and Change in Philadelphia (LVC) in the most scrupulously detailed way imaginable. Space precludes a detailed discussion here, but one of the most striking results is that Labov claims to have solved the gender paradox—namely the fact that although women generally orient towards the more standard forms, they lead in new and vigorous (non-standard) changes. At least for Philadelphia, in moving from large-scale statistical analyses to detailed neighbourhood studies Labov is able to show that the innovative leading women are also otherwise unconventional and nonconformist (not just linguistically), so that the gender paradox is really a function of statistics.

Patricia Cukor-Avila and Guy Bailey raise a potentially troubling methodological question about 'The Effects of the Race of the Interviewer on Sociolinguistic Fieldwork' (*JSoc* 5[2001] 254–70). They find, however, that this can be ameliorated by other factors such as familiarity with the interviewee or peer group recording.

Moving to more fine-grained regional studies, Naomi Nagy posits '"Live Free or Die" as a Linguistic Principle' (*AS* 76[2001] 30–41) in New Hampshire. Based on a questionnaire study, the article finds that the area closest to Boston is in fact most different from the metropolis linguistically, no doubt for attitudinal reasons. Charles Boberg moves east of the Connecticut river and defines 'The Phonological Status of Western New England' (*AS* 76[2001] 3–29), a rather little-studied area so far. As this area provided the main input to migration into the Inland North area, a phonological analysis may also shed light on the origins of the Northern Cities Shift, which, according to Boberg, 'clearly lie on the banks of the lower Connecticut River' (p. 27). Benjamin Torbert 'Trac[es] Native American Language History through Consonant Cluster Reduction: The Case of Lumbee English' (*AS* 76[2001] 361–87). Although nothing is known of the ancestral language of the Lumbee (in Robeson County, North Carolina), the high incidence of prevocalic consonant cluster reduction, especially by older speakers, points to transfer from a language that did not permit extensive consonant clusters. Also on a southern and a historical theme, Edgar W. Schneider and Michael B. Montgomery are 'On the Trail of Early Non-Standard Grammar: An Electronic Corpus of Southern U.S. Antebellum Overseers' Letters' (*AS* 76[2001] 388–410). This new corpus contains material from 1794 to 1876 by little-educated men. A sample analysis suggests that many grammatical features now typical of the South may be relatively recent innovations (after the Civil War), as Bailey [1997] has already claimed (*YWES* 78[1999] 103–4). The defining (phonetic) characteristic of the South is the subject of Valerie Fridland's 'The Social Dimension of the Southern Vowel Shift: Gender, Age and Class' (*JSoc* 5[2001] 233–53). Her data from Memphis, Tennessee suggest that the back and the front high and mid-vowels pattern differently in shifting and that we are dealing here with two shifts rather than one. The stereotypical shift of /E/ and /ey/ seems to be used by Memphis middle-class men as a 'marker of local self-identification' (p. 243), whereas /I/ and /iy/ seem not to shift at all. The non-stereotypical back vowels, on the other hand, are involved in a vigorous shift: /uw/ especially for men, /U/ and /ow/ for women. Another stereotype of the South, absence of postvocalic /r/, is investigated by Thomas Schöneweitz in 'Gender and Postvocalic /r/ in the American South: A Detailed Socioregional Analysis' (*AS* 76[2001] 259–85). Based on the data in LAGS, the article finds that rhotic /r/ is more common among female, white, younger, highly educated, middle-class speakers, and that the South seems to be changing towards the national rhotic pattern. Michael B. Montgomery and John M. Kirk give an example of a rather striking use of *whenever* in '"My mother, whenever she passed away, she had pneumonia": The History and Functions of *Whenever*' (*JEngL* 29[2001] 234–49). This example from southern Appalachia is paralleled by similar uses in Northern Ireland and Scotland, and indeed considering the settlement history this link is not surprising. However, descriptions of this use of *whenever* for *when* are missing from historical dialect descriptions, leaving much room for further investigation.

Moving far west to a variety little studied, Rachelle Waksler discovers 'A New *All* in Conversation' (*AS* 76[2001] 128–38) in the speech of San Francisco teenagers. Although this is used mostly as a quotative (in about 68 per cent of all cases), other uses include quantification over an adjective phrase or a prepositional phrase. Waksler presents a unified analysis of *all* as a 'marker of unique characterization' (p. 135), which also accounts for the use as a quotative.

The study of the history of AAVE is again well represented this year with Shana Poplack and Sali Tagliamonte continuing their investigation of early AAE in *African American English in the Diaspora*. The two diaspora African American communities of Samaná (in the Dominican Republic) and Nova Scotia provide the database for their analyses of past, present and future tenses. They find that zero past tense forms pattern in the same way as in British dialects, present tense -*s* (or absence thereof) is not a feature of hypercorrection, but is also paralleled in British dialects, and that *gonna* again shows the same constraints hierarchy as in other varieties. For all three features they conclude that, rather than from a creole origin, AAVE must have developed from British dialect sources. Nevertheless, it should not be forgotten that, conservative as these diaspora varieties may be, they at best offer 'an indirect view of what earlier states of AAE might have looked like' (p. 13), as Walker in the following contribution rightly points out. James A. Walker's 'Using the Past to Explain the Present: Tense and Temporal Reference in Early

African American English' (*LVC* 13[2001] 1–31) similarly deals with tense and aspect in the history of this variety. His cross-variety analysis (of creoles, standard and non-standard English dialects) unearths enormous variability, as well as similarities, which cautions against using aspect as a diagnostic of AAVE origin. His detailed investigation of the two diaspora varieties (the same as in Poplack and Tagliamonte above) and the Ex-Slave Recordings confirms that -*s* is associated with habituality, zero is linked to duration, and stative verbs are shown to disfavour progressives.

Linking the historical debate with more contemporary concerns is the aim of Lanehart, ed., *Sociocultural and Historical Contexts of African American English*. Salikoko S. Mufwene identifies this variety with its speakers in 'What is African American English?' (pp. 21–51), including Gullah in AAE but excluding more creole, pidgin and Caribbean varieties, supported by a questionnaire study. Guy Bailey traces 'The Relationship between African American and White Vernaculars in the American South: A Sociocultural History and some Phonological Evidence' (pp. 53–92). While many features are shared between the two varieties, no doubt due to increased contact of blacks and whites after the Civil War, Bailey singles out in particular the Southern Shift that seems to be a predominantly white development. Patricia Cukor-Avila does a similar analysis for grammatical features in 'Co-existing Grammars: The Relationship between the Evolution of African American and White Vernacular English in the South' (pp. 93–127). Her data from Springville, Texas, show that copula absence in particular has been subject to change over the last fifty years.

Reviving the creolist camp, David Sutcliffe carefully listens to 'The Voice of the Ancestors: New Evidence on 19th-Century Precursors to 20th-Century African American English' (pp. 129–68) and finds many 'attestations of a creole-like vernacular in the ex-slave recordings' (p. 129) where none were transcribed before, features that have been edited out of the published transcripts. Mary B. Zeigler has 'Something to *Shout* about: AAVE as a Linguistic and Cultural Treasure' (pp. 169–85), investigating the meaning of AAVE *shout*, whereas Marcyliena Morgan discusses '"Nuthin' but a G Thang": Grammar and Language Ideology in Hip Hop Identity' (pp. 187–209), and indeed the construction of identity is the pivotal concern of the next contributions. Denise Troutman gives examples of 'African American Women: Talking that Talk' (pp. 211–37), and Arthur K. Spears postulates 'Directness in the Use of African American English' (pp. 239–59) as an important tool also for educators. Educational concerns similarly move Toya A. Wyatt, who presents an overview of 'The Role of Family, Community, and School in Children's Acquisition and Maintenance of African American English' (pp. 216–80), and Michèle Foster. Foster shows in 'Pay Leon, Pay Leon, Pay Leon Paleontologist: Using Call-and-Response to Facilitate Mastery and Literacy Acquisition among African American Students' (pp. 281–98) how the use of well-known AAVE verbal strategies can help children master school skills. William Labov reports on the good results of his Individualized Reading Program in 'Applying our Knowledge of African American English to the Problem of Raising Reading Levels in Inner-City Schools' (pp. 299–317), except where final consonant clusters are concerned. Here, obviously, more dialect-specific tasks are required. John Baugh stresses that it takes educators, parents and students together to make a successful student in 'Applying Linguistic Knowledge of African American English to Help Students Learn and

Teachers Teach' (pp. 319–30), and Walt Wolfram is 'Reconsidering the Sociolinguistic Agenda for African American English: The Next Generation of Research and Application' (pp. 331–62). Apart from hotly debated issues in the research community, trying to change the general public's attitudes towards AAVE (or indeed any non-standard variety) clearly remains one of the most urgent tasks for sociolinguists.

Concluding our overview for this year, on a grammatical theme, Walter Edwards investigates 'Aspectual d@n in African American Vernacular English in Detroit' (*JSoc* 5[2001] 413–27). His exemplary, also terminologically careful, discussion of a number of examples shows that unstressed preverbal d@n is equivalent to the standard English present perfect with its various meanings, and indeed in variation with it. It is, however, used slightly more often than StE *have ... Ven* to expressive a negative attitude or criticism.

10. New Englishes and Creolistics

A number of publications this year deal with English as a world language with a focus on the New Englishes. Stephan Gramley's *The Vocabulary of World English* and Robert Hendrickson's *World English: From Aloha to Zed* are concerned with its lexicon. While Hendrickson's book consists merely of a collection of about 3500 words and phrases, mainly taken from American and British English, Gramley combines an introduction to the study of the lexicon (basic word-formation, semantics, pragmatics and lexicology) and the diachronic aspects of the English lexicon with an introduction to the New Englishes. In each chapter, the theoretical concepts are illustrated with case studies from various parts of the English-speaking world, with special attention given to Australia, New Zealand, South Africa, West Africa, India and Singapore. The book also includes many exercises, projects for further research and a glossary, which make it an excellent choice as an introductory textbook for the study of the English lexicon.

Anthea Fraser Gupta discusses 'Realism and Imagination in the Teaching of English' (*WEn* 20[2001] 365–81), touching upon a number of issues concerning the standardization and teaching of Englishes spoken in countries belonging to Kachru's outer and expanding circle and arguing in favour of a comparative approach based on various text-types as in the *International Corpus of English* project. Along similar lines, Barbara Seidlhofer suggests 'Closing a Conceptual Gap: The Case for a Description of English as a Lingua Franca' (*IJAL* 11[2001] 133–58), proposing a research framework in which a corpus-based linguistic description of English as a lingua franca plays a central role. Yasukata Yano looks at 'World Englishes in 2000 and Beyond' (*WEn* 20[2001] 119–31), outlining the future development of EFL and ESL-varieties of English. In this context, the collection edited by Anne Burn and Caroline Coffin, *Analysing English in a Global Context: A Reader* also deserves mention. It is primarily designed for TEFL and TESOL instructors and students, but Parts One and Two address many issues which are relevant to the discussion about the role of English as a world language; they are written in a concise format by experts in the field, such as Braj B. Kachru, David Graddol, David Crystal and Alastair Pennycook. Wendy Baker offers an analysis of five varieties of English (Indian, West African, Anglo-American, Mexican

American and British) from the angle of 'Gender and Bilingual's Creativity' (*WEn* 20[2001] 321–39) using Biber's multidimensional approach.

Phenomena of language contact also receive much scholarly attention. The most important contribution is without doubt Sarah G. Thomason's *Language Contact: An Introduction*. Thomason explores all imaginable types of language contact, multilingualism (both of individuals and of nations), contact-induced language change and types of mixed languages in a systematic way. She supplements the theoretical discussion with many examples, often drawn from her own research, and a number of more detailed case studies on the linguistic situation in India, South Asia, the Pacific Northwest, the Sepik River Basin in Papua New Guinea, as well as some others. The book also contains chapters on endangered languages and language death, which are also of interest to linguists involved in the New Englishes. Several appendices, a fairly comprehensive glossary and ample suggestions for further reading in each chapter make Thomason's book an excellent choice as a textbook for advanced students or as a starting point for language contact research. Salikoko S. Mufwene's monograph *The Ecology of Language Evolution* also addresses the topic of language contact, albeit from a different angle. The most interesting chapter for those concerned with the New Englishes, 'The Legitimate and Illegitimate Offspring of English' (pp. 106–25), deals with the contact history of English, pointing out instances of language contact and substrate influence which are often overlooked or downplayed in the study of the English language. Section V, 'Language Contact', of the *Concise Encyclopedia of Sociolinguistics* (Meshtrie, ed., cf. Section 9 above for further details) provides useful general reference on the topic, featuring well-researched entries on keywords such as the 'New Englishes' (B. Kachru, pp. 519–24), 'Native Speaker' (A. Davies, pp. 512–19), 'Migrants and Migration' (A.M. Pavlinic, pp. 504–9), 'Language Maintenance, Shift and Death' (R. Meshtrie, pp. 493–8), 'Borrowing' (J. Heath, pp. 432–42) or 'Codeswitching' (P. Auer, pp. 443–6, K.M. McCormick, pp. 447–54, S. Gross, pp. 454–6, R. Bhatt, pp. 456–61).

Turning now to studies concerned with individual New Englishes, we will begin with the Southern hemisphere. David Blair and Peter Collins present a substantial collection of papers on *English in Australia*, covering the structure of standard AusE (Section A) as well as the variation encountered in it (Section B). The editors' introduction (pp. 1–13) covers the contents of the individual contributions under the aspect of an Australian linguistic identity. Three contributions deal with AusE phonology: Felicity Cox and Sallyanne Palethorpe look at 'Vowel Change: Synchronic and Diachronic Evidence' (pp. 17–44), comparing small speech samples from the 1960s and the 1990s and a larger sample from the 1990s by means of spectrographic analysis. Both sets of data display vowel changes, especially for the vowels in HAD, HODE and HADE. Laura Tollfree reports on 'Variation and Change in Australian English Consonants: Reduction of /t/' (pp. 45–67) and Toni Borowsky discusses 'The Vocalisation of Dark *l* in Australian English' (pp. 69–87). Jane Simpson's study of 'Hypocoristics of Place-Names' (pp. 89–112), Mark Newbrook's survey of 'Syntactic Features and Norms in Australian English' (p. 113–32) and Pam Peters' account of 'Corpus Evidence on Australian Style and Usage' (pp. 163–78) cover grammatical aspects of AusE. The development of the AusE lexicon is the topic of Bruce Moore's 'Australian English and Indigenous Voices' (pp. 133–49) and Susan Butler's 'Australian English: An Identity Crisis' (pp. 151–61). The following ethnic varieties are introduced in Section B: 'Torres Strait English' by Anna Shnukal (pp. 181–200), 'Aboriginal English' by Ian Malcolm (pp. 201–22), 'Ethnic Varieties of Australian English' by Michael Clyne, Edina Eisikovits and Laura Tollfree (pp. 223–38) and the AusE of recent immigrant groups by Scott Kiesling (pp. 239–57). Barbara M. Horvath and Ronald J. Horvath trace 'Short A in Australian English: A Geolinguistic Study' (pp. 341–55), which represents one of the first attempts to chart regional variation in AusE. The last group of papers is concerned with diachronic variation in AusE, from pronunciation (Colin Yallop, pp. 287–302) to language attitudes (David Bradley and Maya Bradley, pp. 271–86 and Arthur Delbridge, pp. 303–16). The volume is an important contribution to the study of AusE, especially with regard to sociolinguistic and diachronic variation.

There are also quite a number of articles this year on Southern hemisphere varieties, which often compare NZE with AusE or set off both against British or American English. Donn Bayard, Cynthia Gallois, Ann Weatherall and Jeffery Pittam wonder about 'Pax Americana? Accent Attitudinal Evaluations in New Zealand, Australia and America' (*JSoc* 5[2001] 22–49) because several hundred college students in these countries preferred the General American accent over RP, NZE and AusE. Barbara M. Horvath and Ronald J. Horvath discuss 'A Multilocality of a Sound Change in Progress: The Case of /l/ Vocalisation in New Zealand and Australian English' (*LVC* 13[2001] 37–57), evaluating the potential of the multi-locality approach to distinguish universal linguistic change from geographically conditioned change. Richard B. Baldauf Jr. is 'Speaking of Science: The Use by Australian University Science Staff of Language Skills' in Ammon, ed., *The Dominance of English as a Language of Science: Effects on Other Languages and Language Communities*, pp. 139–65), examining the use of English versus other languages in business and university settings. Anne Pauwels is concerned with 'Non-sexist Language Reform and Generic Pronouns in Australian English' (*EWW* 22[2001] 105–19) and 'Spreading the Word: The Case of the New Courtesy Title *Ms* in Australian English' (in Hellinger and Bußmann, eds., *Gender Across Languages: The Linguistic Representation of Women and Men. Vol 1.*, pp. 137–51), revealing that generic *he* has decreased in favour of *they*, while *Ms.* is slowly gaining ground in AusE usage. Janet Holmes provides 'A Corpus-Based View of Gender in New Zealand English' (in Hellinger and Bußmann, eds., pp. 115–35), looking at features such as *Ms*, generic *man*, lexical items like *chairperson* and gender-specific morphological markings, e.g. *actress*, in British, Australian and New Zealand corpora. Nicola Daly and Paul Warren think that speakers are 'Pitching it Differently in New Zealand English: Speaker Sex and Intonation Patterns' (*JSoc* 5[2001] 85–96), providing acoustic analyses of pitch range and dynamism in the speech of five male and six female speakers of NZE in a variety of tasks, which clearly show that female speakers indeed display higher values for range and dynamism. Nicola J. Woods discusses 'Internal and External Dimensions of Language Change: The Great Divide? Evidence from New Zealand English' (Linguistics 39[2001] 973–1007), re-examining the dichotomy between internal and external explanations and proposing a conciliatory approach based on an intergenerational analysis of the NZE MOUTH diphthong. Andrea Sudbury, finally, introduces a little-known variety, 'Falkland Islands English: A Southern Hemisphere Variety?' (*EWW* 22[2001] 55–80), discussing its phonological, grammatical and lexical features in comparison to other Southern hemisphere varieties, and comes to the conclusion that Falkland Islands English shares a number of variables with AusE, NZE and SAE.

Many publications this year deal with Indian English and the linguistic make-up of South Asian regions. Tamara M. Valentine analyses 'Cross-Cultural Discourse in World Englishes' (in Abbi, Gupta and Kidway, eds., *Linguistic Structure and Language Dynamics in South Asia: Papers from the Proceedings of SALA XVIII Roundtable*, pp. 223–40) on the basis of conversations between Indian and American speakers of English. Devyani Sharma studies 'The Pluperfect in Native and Non-Native English: A Comparative Corpus Study' (*LVC* 13[2001] 343–73), drawing on the Kolhapur Corpus of Written Indian English, the Brown Corpus of Written American English and the LOB Corpus of Written British English, all dating from the 1960s and 1970s, to verify impressionistic claims on the innovative uses of the past perfect in Indian English. Jean D'Souza has revised and updated her assessment of 'Indian English: The Reality behind the Myths' (in Abbi, Gupta and Kidwai, eds., pp. 241–55), which first appeared in *EWW* 18[1997] (cf. *YWES* 78[1997] 114). She also aims at 'Contextualizing Range and Depth in Indian English' (*WEn* 20[2001] 145–59), using these notions developed by Kachru to show that English is an Indian language and that the norms of its standard variety are a matter to be decided by its Indian speakers. Shobhana L. Chelliah likewise deals with linguistic norms in her article 'Constructs of Indian English in Language 'Guidebooks'' (*WEn* 20[2001] 161–77), in which she compares eleven Indian 'Common Errors in English' textbooks with similar EFL textbooks published in Great Britain and the United States, concluding that the teaching materials provided in India are of poor quality and will not help Indians to attain high levels of proficiency in English. Two publications examine the complex linguistic situation in Northeast India and the role of English in the areas under investigation. Selma K. Sonntag looks at 'The Politics of Linguistic Sub-Alternity in North India' (in Abbi, Gupta and Kidwai, eds., pp. 207–22), while Anne Hvenenkilde offers a detailed account of 'Kinship Systems and Language Choice among Academics in Shillong, Northeast India' (*IJAL* 11[2001] 174–93), showing that due to a number of social factors, English is moving from the work sphere into the family sphere in this group. Tariq Rahman gives an account of 'English-Teaching Institutions in Pakistan' (*JMMD* 22[2001] 242–61), highlighting the various ways of transmission of this South Asian variety. For Southeast Asia, Jerzy Smolicz, Iluminado Nical and Margaret Secombe report on 'English as the Medium of Instruction for Science and its Effects on the Languages of the Philippines' (in Ammon, ed., pp. 205–26), presenting a survey of the language use and attitudes of 152 Filipino students.

Singapore English is well represented this year. Boa Zhiming attributes 'The Origins of Empty Categories in Singapore English' (*JPCL* 16[2001] 275–319) to topic prominence and changes in pro-drop and wh-movement rules due to the influence of the Chinese substrate. Mian Lian Ho and Irene F.H. Wong come to the conclusion that 'The Use of *Ever* in Singaporean English' (*WEn* 20[2001] 79–87) results from an interplay of the Hokkien and Malay substrates and the syntax and semantics of the superstrate. Rani Rubdy examines the possible effects of 'Creative Destruction: Singapore's Speak Good English Movement' (*WEn* 20[2001] 341–55) on the future of Colloquial Singapore English or Singlish, which has recently become a marker of a joint Singaporean identity but is shunned by the government for economic reasons. Singapore English is one of the varieties under analysis in Long Peng and Jean Ann's article on 'Stress and Duration in Three Varieties of English' (*WEn* 20[2001] 1–27), in which they illustrate how syllable type and vowel duration influence stress placement in L2 varieties of English.

Shanta Nair-Venugopal studies 'The Sociolinguistics of Code Choice in Malaysian Business Settings' (*IJSL* 152[2001] 21–52) on the basis of an ethnographic analysis of oral presentations in two different organizations, showing that an indigenized variety of Malaysian English is on the rise even in formal settings. Rodolfo Jacobson reports on 'Aspects of Scholarly Language Use in Malaysia: Switching Codes in Formal Settings' (in Ammon, ed., pp. 177–92) between English and Malay, which even gave rise to the new term 'holey English', i.e. English with gaps.

Similarly, William Y. Wu, Dennis W.K. Chan and Björn H. Jernudd look at 'English in Science Communication in Hong Kong: Educational Research Output' (in Ammon, ed., pp. 193–203) on the basis of two scholarly journals on education, published between 1991 and 1999, coming to the conclusion that Chinese-related content tends to trigger the use of Chinese as the language of publication. Stephen Evans and Christopher Green are concerned with 'Language in Post-Colonial Hong Kong: The Roles of English and Chinese in the Public and Private Sectors' (*EWW* 22[2001] 247–68), using a variety of methods to tabulate the relevance of English and Chinese in various domains and to identify factors influencing language choice in the workplace. Winnie Cheng and Martin Warren discuss 'The Use of Vague Language in Intercultural Conversations in Hong Kong' (*EWW* 22[2001] 81–104), identifying motivations for native and non-native speakers of English to use vague language, such as to achieve informality, to close lexical or conceptual gaps or for reasons of politeness. Finally, Jackie F.K. Lee reports on the 'Functions of *Need* in Australian English and Hong Kong English' (*WEn* 20[2001] 133–43) when used as an auxiliary or a lexical verb, based on corpus analysis and elicitation data.

Two studies by Jan Tent provide important information on a less well-known variety, namely Fiji English. In the first, Tent has compiled 'A Profile of the Fiji English Lexis' (*EWW* 22[2001] 209–45) identifying the various sources of the Fiji English lexicon, which include Fijian, Hindi, various Polynesian languages and Indian English. Her second article is concerned with 'Yod Deletion in Fiji English: Phonological Shibboleth or L2 English?' (*LVC* 13[2001] 161–91), based on an elicitation study designed to test the presence of the glide in /Cju/ syllables, which tends to be deleted by Fijian speakers of English.

Moving on to the African Englishes, we note the publication of Hans–Georg Wolf's book-length study of *English in Cameroon*. Wolf begins by placing Cameroon English (CamE) in the wider context of West African English and then proceeds to untangle the complex socio-historical developments which led to the present linguistic situation, which is discussed with a focus on the Anglophone speech community. This detailed socio-political account is followed by two shorter chapters illustrating the unique features of Cameroon English, mainly based on a lexical analysis of a computer-readable text-corpus containing approximately 890,000 words. Wolf also attempts to reveal the cultural concepts underlying the use of certain standard English words, such as 'ancestors', 'witch' or 'spirit', in CamE by comparing their occurrences in the Cameroon corpus to those in the Brown Corpus of American English. The two corpora used are unfortunately not entirely compatible, but the cultural model analysis presented in chapter 5 is nevertheless convincing. This analysis also forms the basis of Hans-Georg Wolf and Augustin Simo Bobda's discussion of 'The African Cultural Model of Community in English Language Instruction in Cameroon: The Need for More Systematicity' (in Pütz, Niemeier and Dirven, eds., *Applied Cognitive Linguistics II: Language Pedagogy*, pp. 225–59). Paul Mbufong argues in favour of a bigger role of 'Pidgin English in Anglophone Cameroon Education' (*EnT* 17[2001] 52–4) because it is the L1 of the majority of anglophone Cameroonians.

Alfred J. Matiki addresses 'The Social Significance of English in Malawi' (*WEn* 20[2001] 201–18), documenting the dominance of English over the other official language, Chichewa, and suggesting remedial measures to ensure the majority's participation in national affairs. Kari Dako looks at 'Ghanaisms: Towards a Semantic and a Formal Classification' (*EWW* 22[2001] 23–53), providing a long list of lexical items taken from English and local sources. Efurosibina Adegbija and Janet Bello's study of 'The Semantics of 'Okay' (OK) in Nigerian English' (*WEn* 20[2001] 89–98) is an excellent illustration of how English lexical items are semantically and pragmatically adapted in an African context, thus causing misunderstandings in the communication with foreigners. Nigerian English is also one of the varieties studied in Long Peng and Jean Ann's article on 'Stress and Duration in Three Varieties of English' discussed above. Augustin Simo Bobda provides a large-scale survey of 'East and Southern African Accents' (*WEn* 20[2001] 269–84), singling out characteristic features in the pronunciation of English in Sudan, Somalia, Kenya, Uganda, Tanzania, Zambia, Malawi, Zimbabwe, South Africa, Swaziland, Lesotho, Botswana and Namibia. Paul Skandera reports on 'Research into Idioms and the International Corpus of English' (in Mair and Hundt, eds., *Corpus Linguistics and Linguistic Theory: Papers from the 20th International Conference on English Language Research on Computerized Corpora, Freiburg im Breisgau 1999*, pp. 339–53), comparing the British and the Kenyan subcomponents of the corpus.

The bulk of publications on English in Africa is again concerned with SAE. Jan Bernsten discusses 'English in South Africa: Expansion and Nativisation in Concert' (*LPLP* 25[2001] 219–35), focusing on the more recent domains of SAE. Vivian De Klerk and Gary Barkhuizen report on 'Language Usage and Attitudes in a South African Prison: Who Calls the Shots?' (*IJSL* 152[2001] 97–115), showing that the eleven-language policy of the government has utterly failed in this particular type of institution with the result that Xhosa and English predominate. This is also reflected in Margaret Probyn's account of 'Teachers' Voices: Teachers' Reflections on Learning and Teaching through the Medium of English as an Additional Language in South Africa' (*IJBEB* 4[2001] 249–66), in which she studies the classroom behaviour of five teachers in English-medium schools and analyses their communicative strategies, such as code-switching between English and Xhosa. 'Ethnicity and Language Crossing in Post-Apartheid South Africa' (*IJSL* 152[2001] 75–95) is the topic of Nkonko M. Kamwangamalu's article, in which he uses Rampton's concept of 'linguistic crossing' to explain South Africans' linguistic choices in a multilingual setting.

To round off the discussion of English in Africa, I would like to mention a publication that I missed in last year's review. Ayo Bamgbose's book *Language and Exclusion: The Consequences of Language Policies in Africa* offers a detailed account of how language policies favouring former colonial languages such as English and French exclude the majority of the population from political participation, literacy and education. The book is written in an accessible style and offers a wealth of examples drawn from a large number of African countries.

A number of contributions to the festschrift for Robert LePage (in Christie, ed., *Due Respect: Papers on English and English-Related Creoles in the Caribbean in Honour of Professor Robert LePage*) deal with Caribbean English, e.g. Velma Pollard's account of '"A Singular Subject Takes a Singular Verb" and Hypercorrection in Jamaican Speech and Writing' (pp. 97–107), demonstrating how 3rd person sg. *–s* and PAST *–ed* have become markers of 'Englishness' in the most formal register of Creole speakers and are therefore often used hypercorrectly. Pollard investigates ways of improving teaching materials and methods to remedy this situation. Monica Taylor addresses 'English in the English-Speaking Caribbean: Questions in the Academy' (pp. 108–21), discussing the question of what is to be standard English in the Caribbean. Two contributions are based on conversation analysis. Kathryn Shields-Brodber looks at 'Contrapuntal Conversation and the Performance Floor' (pp. 208–18), identifying a specifically Caribbean kind of performance-oriented simultaneous speech, which she compares to musical counterpoint. Valerie Youssef's contribution is devoted to 'Working out Conversational Roles through Questioning Strategies' (pp. 219–46) on the basis of a small Trinidadian sample. Youssef points out gender differences in the use of questions and the importance of culture-specific interaction types, such as *picong* among Trinidadian males. Interestingly, the contrapuntal analysis is strongly rejected in Jack Sidnell's article on 'Conversational Turn-Taking in a Caribbean English Creole' (*JPrag* 33[2001] 1263–90), which is based on data from the Guyanese continuum and stresses the orderly turn-taking patterns of the conversations analysed.

Shondel J. Nero's qualitative study of *Englishes in Contact: Anglophone Caribbean Students in an Urban College* is situated at the intersection of standard American English, standard Caribbean English and English-lexicon Creoles from the Caribbean. Nero presents an in-depth analysis of four college students who recently emigrated to New York from Jamaica and Guyana, based on a corpus of their writing in various text-types and a number of interviews. In addition to the morpho-syntactic, orthographic and discourse analysis of the data, Nero also addresses the status of English-based creoles in the education system of various anglophone countries, questions of assessment and placement, the role of language attitudes in pedagogy and the relationship between language and identity.

A much larger number of publications deal with pidgins and creoles, both from the Caribbean and elsewhere. Beginning with those of a general or theoretical nature, I would like to point out the paperback edition of *Language Creation and Language Change: Creolization, Diachrony, and Development* edited by Michel DeGraff. The focus of this substantial volume, which links creolization with language change and language acquisition in a generative framework, is best summarized in DeGraff's introduction 'Creolization, Language Change and Language Acquisition: A Prolegomenon' (pp. 1–46) and his final chapter on 'Creolization, Language Change and Language Acquisition: An Epilogue' (pp. 473–543). Important contributions include Derek Bickerton's study on 'How to Acquire Language without Positive Evidence: What Acquisitionists Can Learn from

Creoles' (pp. 49–74), in which he elaborates his language bioprogram hypothesis. Salikoko S. Mufwene in turn comments 'On the Language Bioprogram Hypothesis: Hints from Tazie' (pp. 95–127). By comparing this hypothesis to acquisition data produced by his daughter at between 20 and 30 months of age, he arrives at a reinterpretation of the model based on the concept of markedness. John S. Lumsden also compares 'Language Acquisition and Creolization' (pp. 129–57), establishing parallels to L2-acquisition by concentrating on the processes of relexification, functional category ellipsis and reanalysis. Adrienne Bruyn, Pieter Muysken and Maaike Verrips concentrate on a single syntactic feature, namely 'Double-Object Constructions in the Creole Languages: Development and Acquisition' (pp. 329–73), which occur also in creoles whose Romance language lexifiers do not exhibit this feature. They identify three different kinds of 'dative' constructions and compare data from a large number of creoles to acquisition data from Dutch and French children, concluding that there is no simple UG explanation for the presence or absence of this feature.

We also welcome the publication of *Creolization of Language and Culture*, the English edition of Robert Chaudenson's 1992 classic on the French-lexifier creoles, *Des îlês, des hommes, des langues: essai sur la créolisation linguistique et culturelle*, which has not only been translated into English, but also revised in collaboration with Salikoko S. Mufwene. Since Chaudenson's theory of gradual basilectalization figures prominently in the work of francophone creolists, it is high time for it to become available also to the anglophone linguistic community. Chaudenson develops a socio-historical model of creolization, which also includes music, cuisine, folk medicine and oral literature. He assumes that most French-lexifier creoles originated as only partially restructured varieties of informal or regional French in 'homestead colonies' with a relatively even demographic distribution between colonizers and slaves and were restructured more drastically only in cases where this relationship was changed in favour of a larger slave population ('plantation society', e.g. Haiti). This view is contrary to most models of creole genesis proposed by anglophone creolists, who assume the presence of a more basilectal variety in the beginning, which may decreolize in prolonged contact with the lexifier.

The individual chapters of Salikoko S. Mufwene's book *The Ecology of Language Evolution* are mainly revised versions of previously published articles and papers. He uses pidgin and creole developments to illustrate his general ideas about language ecology and language evolution, arguing that pidgins and creoles are not structurally different from other varieties and that only the socio-historical circumstances of their formation set them apart from other languages. This is discussed at length in Chapter 2, 'The Founder Principle in the Development of Pidgins and Creoles'. Chapter 5 illustrates 'What Research on the Development of Creoles Can Contribute to Genetic Linguistics', while Chapter 7 uses his integrative approach to interpret the linguistic developments that account for the present situation on the African continent, 'Past and Recent Population Movements in Africa: Their Impact on its Linguistic Landscape'. All in all, the book is a useful resource for those interested in an overview of Mufwene's recent work, tying in his interest in pidgins and creoles with his views on linguistic theory, which runs along similar lines as Peter Mühlhäusler's and Alwin Fill's ecolinguistics.

Sarah G. Thomason's book on *Language Contact: An Introduction*, reviewed in more detail in the section on New Englishes above, also contains a substantial chapter on 'Contact Languages I: Pidgins and Creoles' (pp. 157–95). Thomason defines pidgins and creoles and their distinctive structural features and discusses current models of creole genesis, including Chaudenson's gradualist approach. Thomason's book thus also serves as an excellent starting point for the study of pidgins and creoles. Other useful introductory references to this field include the key entries in the *Concise Encyclopedia of Sociolinguistics* (Meshtrie, ed.) concerning pidgins and creoles, for example 'Contact Languages' (S. G. Thomason, pp. 461–4), 'Intertwined Languages' (P. Muysken, pp. 481–3), 'Jargons' (P.Mühlhäusler, pp. 483–5), 'Language Transfer and Substrates' (T. Odlin, pp. 499–503) and 'Pidgins and Creoles' (L. Todd, pp. 524–30, J. Aitchinson, pp. 530–6, F.C.V. Jones, pp. 536–8). Peter Mühlhäusler's contribution on 'Pidginization' (in Haspelmath *et al*., eds., *Language Typology and Universals: An International Handbook. Vol. 2.*, pp. 1648–55) and Pieter Muysken's article on 'Creolization' (in Haspelmath *et al*., eds., pp. 1656–67) can also be used as brief introductions to the field. A concise introduction to the characteristics of 'The Creole Languages of the Caribbean' by Pieter Muysken can also be found in *A History of Literature in the Caribbean, Vol. 2: English- and Dutch-Speaking Regions* (Arnold, ed., pp. 399–414).

Linguistic Typology (5[2001]) has devoted an entire double issue to the very interesting question whether creoles are indeed a distinguishable structural language type. John McWhorter's in-depth answer to this question is affirmative, and he claims that 'The World's Simplest Grammars Are Creole Grammars' (125–66). After having argued in favour of a structurally identifiable creole prototype (McWhorter (2000) in Neumann-Holzschuh and Schneider, eds., *Degrees of Restructuring in Creole Languages*, cf. *YWES* 81[2002] 87), McWhorter proceeds to present a metric of grammatical complexity, which measures the presence of marked phonemes and/or a tonal system, the grammaticalization of fine-grained semantic or pragmatic distinctions and the amount of inflectional morphology. In order to prove that creoles are indeed simpler than older languages, he compares Saramaccan to the Northeast Causasian language Tsez and the Tibeto-Burman language Lahu, which both turn out to be more complex than Saramaccan. Finally, he lists fourteen grammatical features, ranging from ergativity to grammatical gender, which he claims are absent from all creole languages. His contribution is followed by eleven comments from creolists (e.g. Jacques Arends, Pieter Muysken, Michel DeGraff, Claire Lefebvre) and typologists (e.g. Östen Dahl, Wolfgang U. Wurzel), and a final response by the author. While the majority of these comments is largely in favour of McWhorter's model but suggest a number of alterations or additions, Lefebvre (pp. 186–213) and DeGraff (pp. 213–311) strongly attack McWhorter's hypothesis, while Umberto Ansaldo and Stephen J. Matthews (311–25) and David Gil (325–71) provide counterexamples taken from Chinese and Riau Indonesian respectively to McWhorter's claims concerning the presence or absence of particular features in creoles and older languages.

A number of contributions to *Creolization and Contact* (Smith and Veenstra, eds.) are also concerned with theoretical issues of creolization. Claire Lefebvre discusses the role of 'Relexification in Creole Genesis and Its Effects on the Development of the Creole' (pp. 9–42), elaborating her claim that Haitian Creole can be regarded as a relexified version of Fongbe. Anthony P. Grant deals with

'Language Intertwining: Its Depiction in Recent Literature and Its Implications for Theories of Creolisation' (pp. 81–111), while Marten Mous addresses the specific aspect of 'Paralexification in Language Intertwining' (pp. 113–23). Pieter C. Muysken looks at 'The Origin of Creole Languages: The Perspective of Second Language Learning' (pp. 157–73) based on data from Negerhollands. Jeff Siegel examines 'Koine Formation and Creole Genesis' (pp. 175–97), using data from overseas varieties of Hindi, mainly Fiji Hindi, and discussing its implications for creole genesis. Silvia Kouwenberg evaluates the relevance of the notion of 'Convergence and Explanations in Creole Genesis' (pp. 219–47), discussing its different uses in historical linguistics and creolistics and warns against the 'return of the Cafeteria Principle through the back door' (pp. 242–3) of 'convergence'. Sarah G. Thomason writes on 'Contact-Induced Language Change and Pidgin/Creole Genesis' (pp. 249–62), summarizing some of the main points from her book reviewed above.

Michel DeGraff attacks the general consensus in creolistics that creole languages have little or no morphology. In his contribution 'Morphology in Creole Genesis: Linguistics and Ideology' (in Kenstowicz, ed., *Ken Hale: A Life in Language*, pp. 53–121) he provides counter-evidence to this belief from Haitian Creole, attributing the lack of research in this area to (neo-)colonial ideologies. This question is also addressed by Ingo Plag, who offers a short note on 'The Nature of Derivational Morphology in Creoles and Non-Creoles' (*JPCL* 16[2001] 153–60). Claire Lefebvre's columns are concerned with the creole lexicon. In the first, she deals with 'Multifunctionality and the Concept of the Lexical Entry' (*JPCL* 16[2001] 107–45) and in the second, she elaborates 'On the Semantic Opacity of Creole Languages' (*JPCL* 16[2001] 321–54). Lefebvre's theory of relexification is also elaborated further in her account of 'The Interplay of Relexification and Levelling in Creole Genesis and Development' (*Linguistics* 39[2001] 371–408), in which she illustrates the effect of dialect levelling when several substrate languages are present in creole genesis, concentrating on 3rd person plural pronouns and plural markers, reflexives and demonstratives in Haitian Creole.

Carol Myers-Scotton applies the theoretical models developed in her research on code-switching and bilingualism (4-M Model, Abstract Level Model) to creole genesis and arrives at 'Implications of Abstract Grammatical Structure: Two Targets in Creole Formation' (*JPCL* 16[2001] 217–73), claiming that creole genesis is based on a universal 'innate linguistic architecture' (p. 264). Liu Haitao compares 'Creoles, Pidgins, and Planned Languages: Language Evolution under Special Conditions' (*Interface* 15[2001] 121–77), pointing out interesting parallels between the two groups. Large-scale comparative work is presented by Philip Baker and Magnus Huber, who analyse the earliest known attestations of 'Atlantic, Pacific and World-Wide Features in English-Lexicon Contact Languages' (*EWW* 22[2001] 157–208), identifying a number of world-wide features which were most likely spread in both the Atlantic and the Pacific region through anglophone sailors, traders or missionaries.

The anglophone creoles of the Caribbean receive ample scholarly attention. Silvia Kouwenberg and Darlene LaCharité examine 'The Iconic Interpretations of Reduplication: Issues in the Study of Reduplication in Caribbean Creole Languages' (*EJES* 5[2001] 59–80), showing convincingly that there is a continuum of iconic and opaque reduplications in Caribbean creoles. Kouwenberg and LaCharité have also co-authored a study on 'The Mysterious Case of Diminutive *Yala-Yala*' (in Christie, ed., pp. 124–34) in Jamaican Creole, investigating a specific case of adjective reduplication with an attenuated meaning. In the same volume, Donald Winford provides 'A Comparison of Tense/Aspect Systems in Caribbean English Creoles' (pp. 155–83) based on fieldwork and elicitation data. Hubert Devonish writes 'On the Sierra-Leone – Caribbean Connection: Hot on the Trail of "Tone-Shifted" Items in Anglo-West African' (pp. 184–205), discussing the occurrence of tone-shifts in bi-syllabic lexemes in Caribbean and West African creoles. Lawrence D. Carrington reports on 'The Status of Creole in the Caribbean' (pp. 24–36), looking at domains ranging from politics and government to the Performing Arts and the music industry. Finally, Dennis R. Craig reviews language policies and their implementation in Caribbean school systems in 'Language Education Revisited in the Commonwealth Caribbean' (pp. 61–78), pointing out that not much progress has been made since the 1970s.

Two book-length publications about Jamaican Creole also deserve mention. A revised second edition of Velma Pollard's *Dread Talk: The Language of Rastafari* was published in 2000, but did not reach me in time for the last volume. Although the book also contains chapters on Rastafarian language in St. Lucia, Barbados and in a global context, its main focus is Jamaica. Pollard traces the development of the Rastafarian movement and concentrates on the discussion of the Dread Talk lexicon, since its phonology and morpho-syntax are very much like Jamaican Creole. Although most of the transcribed examples date from the 1970s, Pollard has included a number of recent bibliographic sources, which enhance the status of her monograph as the most comprehensive scholarly work on Dread Talk.

Rocky R. Meade's study of the *Acquisition of Jamaican Phonology* is a comprehensive and well-founded account of the phonological development of children growing up in a creole continuum situation in comparison to monolingual children. Meade examined the linguistic development of twenty-four Jamaican children aged 1,0 to 2,8 over a two-year period. The children were divided into two groups according to the education level of their primary caregivers. Using a modified OT-approach, Meade found that all children had very similar acquisition patterns, but the average age of acquisition varied between the two groups. The phonemes restricted to the acrolectal end of the continuum were acquired late or not at all. Meade stresses the fact that a large number of children do not acquire acrolectal Jamaican English phonology at home. His findings from Jamaica also have cross-linguistic parallels, especially in the order of acquisition of the different syllable types, which is an indication of linguistic universals in language acquisition. Acoustic research on the phonology of adult Jamaican speakers is presented by Alicia Bedford Wassink, who looks at 'Theme and Variation in Jamaican Vowels' (*LVC* 13[2001] 135–50) to determine the role of vowel length versus vowel quality in the Jamaican continuum. Dhanis Jaganauth conducted a study of a Jamaican Creole verb and complementizer, describing 'The Use of *Se* in Jamaican' (in Christie, ed., pp. 135–54). Finally, Beverley Bryan presents an interesting contrastive study on the use of creole in classrooms in Kingston and London, 'Defining the Role of Linguistic Markers in Manufacturing Classroom Consent' (in Christie, ed., pp. 79–96).

Moving on to the creoles of Surinam, we find Norval Smith's contribution 'Voodoo Chile – Differential Substrate Effects in Saramaccan and Haitian' (in

Smith and Veenstra, eds., pp. 43–80), in which he compares the different results of creolization in the Surinam creoles and Haitian Creole of what is basically the same substrate, Eastern Gbe, but with two different lexifiers, English and French. He arrives at the conclusion that the Surinam creoles exhibit both universal features (along the lines of Bickerton's Language Bioprogram Hypothesis) and substrate features (along the lines of Lefebvre's relexification theory), but the substrate features present in the Surinam creoles are not all shared by Haitian Creole. In the same volume, Jacques Arends provides a micro-level analysis of the socio-historical background in creole genesis, examining 'Social Stratification and Network Relations in the Formation of Sranan' (pp. 291–308). Ingo Plag and Birgit Alber look at 'Epenthesis, Deletion and the Emergence of the Optimal Syllable in Creole: The Case of Sranan' (*Lingua* 111[2001] 811–40), using an OT approach to show that these two processes are interrelated. They also argue that universals, substrate and superstrate influence interact in creole genesis in a systematic way. Bettina Migge reports on 'Communicating Gender in the Eastern Maroon Creole of Suriname' (in Hellinger and Bußmann, eds., pp. 85–104), analysing gender-marked nouns in the creole commonly referred to as Ndyuka.

A more comprehensive approach to gender is taken by Geneviève Escure, who looks at 'Belizean Creole: Gender, Creole, and the Role of Women in Language Change' (in Hellinger and Bußmann, pp. 53–83). Escure not only discusses gender-marking in nominal reference and proverbs, but also the expression of gender in a pronoun system that does not distinguish grammatical gender and the role of women in linguistic change, which is illustrated by the case of the copula and the past tense. A sociolinguistic study of the town of Danigra, Belize, was conducted by Donna M. Bonner, who reports on 'Garifuna Children's Language Shame: Ethnic Stereotypes, National Affiliation, and Transnational Immigration as Factors in Language Choice in Southern Belize' (*LSoc* 30[2001] 81–96), showing that Belizean Creole is gaining ground at the expense of the Garifuna language. Valerie Youssef investigates 'Age-Grading in the Anglophone Creole of Tobago' (*WEn* 20[2001] 29–46), looking at the range of Creole and Standard English tense and aspect markers used by speakers of different age groups in the village of Bethel, Tobago. Interestingly, the more educated speakers in the younger age group preferred mesolectal forms over the acrolectal forms used in the older group's public variety. Rounding off the section on Caribbean creoles, I would like to mention Kean Gibson's monograph *Comfa Religion and Creole Language in a Caribbean Community*, which places Guyanese Creole in the context of the Comfa religion. Although Gibson's focus is the history and current practises and beliefs of Comfa, he devotes one chapter to the Guyanese Creole continuum and likens it to a "Continuum of Comfa" (p. 217), which also plays an important role in the construction of Guyanese identity.

Moving on to the pidgins and creoles spoken in the Pacific region, we note a paucity of publications dealing with this area. Miriam Meyerhoff takes 'Another Look at the Typology of Serial Verb Constructions: The Grammaticalization of Temporal Relations in Bislama (Vanuatu)' (*OLin* 40[2001] 247–68), pointing out that some Bislama serial verb constructions do not fit into the categories developed for other creoles and that the non-past vs. past distinction is encoded differently from standard English. Meyerhoff has also worked on the 'Dynamics of Differentiation: On Social Psychology and Cases of Language Variation' (in Coupland, Sarangi and Candlin, eds., *Sociolinguistics and Social Theory*, pp. 61–87;

this book is discussed in more detail in the previous section on Sociolinguistics) on the basis of her Bislama data, concentrating on the analysis of inclusive pronouns, apologies and null subjects. Stephen Levey reports on 'Relative Clauses and Register Expansion in Tok Pisin' (*WEn* 20[2001] 251–67), showing that the emergence of information-oriented literate genres has led to new relative constructions employing *husat* and *we* as relativizers.

The final paragraph of this section is devoted to the creolist approach to AAVE. Studies with a more sociolinguistic or dialectological orientation are included in the previous section on Sociolinguistics and Dialectology. Thus, Shana Poplack and Sali Tagliamonte's book *African American English in the Diaspora* is discussed in greater detail there. However, since the authors address the creole origin hypothesis explicitly (cf. chapters 6.2, 7.3 or 8.5) and present evidence strongly in favour of a dialectal rather than a creole origin of AAVE, based on their diachronic data of Early AAE from the American Ex-Slave Recordings and data from linguistic enclaves in Nova Scotia and on the Samaná Peninsula, their work also deserves mention here. Poplack and Tagliamonte concentrate their analysis on the tense and aspect system, comparing Early AAE data with varieties of British and Canadian English. They conclude that all the putative creole features of the AAVE tense and aspect system can be traced back to non-creole dialectal sources. However, they do not use any creole data in their comparative analysis. A different analysis of the Ex-Slave Recordings is presented in David Sutcliffe's contribution on 'The Voice of the Ancestors: New Evidence on 19th-Century Precursors to 20th-Century African American English' (in Lanehart, ed., *Sociocultural and Historical Contexts of African American English*, pp. 129–68, see also previous section), in which he compares Early AAE and Gullah, identifying a number of 'overt creole features' (p. 151) which had been edited out in earlier transcriptions. His argument runs more along the lines of Alexander Kautzsch and Edgar W. Schneider (cf. *YWES* 81[2000] 91), who suggest different degrees of creolization on the Atlantic Seaboard and further inland.

11. Pragmatics and Discourse Analysis

Last year in this section only journal articles could be reviewed. Therefore, books which appeared in the year 2000 will be discussed here together with this year's publications. A survey of the work published on pragmatics and discourse analysis must begin with Schiffrin, Tannen, and Hamilton, eds., *The Handbook of Discourse Analysis*. The handbook was compiled to bring together work following different approaches to discourse analysis, and thus to offer a comprehensive view of this heterogeneous field. The individual chapters are not restricted to a discussion of the current situation, but look back on developments that have taken place in all the relevant areas and give an outlook on possible future perspectives. The forty-one chapters are organized into four parts: 'Discourse and Linguistics', 'The Linking of Theory and Practice in Discourse Analysis', 'Language, Context, and Interaction', and 'Discourse across Disciplines'.

The popularity of discourse analysis is reflected in the number of textbooks published. Wetherell, Taylor and Yates, eds., *Discourse Theory and Practice: A Reader*, is written for advanced students of the social sciences and goes together with another volume entitled *Discourse as Data: A Guide for Analysis*, with a focus on methodology. The first part of the reader is dedicated to the presentation of different approaches to discourse analysis and their development. Parts 2, 3 and 4 are collections of material published in the 1980s and 1990s, and concentrate on 'Social Interaction', 'Minds, Selves and Sense-Making', and 'Culture and Social Relations'. The editors give an introduction to each part to guide the students through the individual readings, and in a concluding chapter they discuss the differences and relationships between the approaches to discourse research presented in this book.

As the title indicates, Linda A. Wood and Rolf O. Kroger are concerned with methodological issues in *Doing Discourse Analysis: Methods for Studying Action in Talk and Text* [2000]. The first part introduces the reader to various approaches to and the concerns and aims of discourse analysis. The authors then discuss the nature of discourse data, the collection and preparation of data for analysis, and various analytical strategies and techniques. The last part of the book deals with the evaluation of discourse research and the writing of research reports.

Deborah Cameron's introduction to discourse analysis is restricted to *Working with Spoken Discourse*. This book is addressed to undergraduate students with little or no previous knowledge of discourse analysis and is therefore more pedagogically oriented. Cameron adds illustrative examples to the discussion of different approaches to discourse research, and students find a number of 'activities' which are as a rule meant to be done in groups. These small tasks are provided to help students understand and reflect on the issues presented in the book. The last chapter offers information on how students can design their own projects.

The structure of Michael Hoey's *Textual Interaction: An Introduction to Written Discourse Analysis* [2000] is quite different from that of the above-mentioned books. He does not, for instance, offer an introduction to the theoretical background or to the various approaches to discourse analysis. Instead, he immediately begins with the study of a wide variety of texts, the analysis of which becomes more complex as the reader learns more and more about methods and techniques. Comments on relevant work and suggestions for further reading are given at the end of each chapter, however. Hoey continually stresses the aspect of interactivity between readers and writers of texts, and he demonstrates this aspect not only in the text passages he analyses but also in the dialogic style in which the whole book is written and which should make it very attractive for students.

In *Talking at Cross-Purposes: The Dynamics of Miscommunication* [2000], Angeliki Tzanne writes on the creation and development of misunderstandings. Referring to other work on miscommunication, she argues against a tendency to concentrate exclusively on the differences in the linguistic and/or cultural backgrounds of the discourse participants as a possible source of misunderstandings, and focuses instead on dynamic factors such as those features of the linguistic, social, and physical context of the discourse situation which the participants in the conversation consider relevant to the interpretation of utterances. Among the features investigated are shifts in the roles participants adopt during conversation and the politeness strategies they employ.

In *The Music of Everyday Speech: Prosody and Discourse Analysis*, Ann Wennerstrom's aim is to supply discourse researchers with an accessible account of prosody. Considering the integral part it plays in the interpretation of spoken texts, prosody has, Wennerstrom claims, been too often neglected in the analysis of discourse. The book accordingly begins with a theoretical part, in which the author introduces and explains the model of prosody that is to be applied to discourse in the second part. This second part consists of chapters on 'Intonation, Mental Representation, and Coherence', 'Prosody as a Discourse Marker', 'Intonation and Speech Act Theory', 'Prosody in the Study of Conversation', 'Prosody in Oral Narratives', and 'Prosody in Second-Language Discourse'. Each chapter includes several examples illustrating how prosodic features might be investigated and how discourse analysis would benefit from such an investigation.

In her book *Analysing the Language of Discourse Communities* [2000], Joan Cutting investigates the use of implicit language by members of an academic discourse community—six students attending a twelve-month Masters course in Applied Linguistics. Her data are taken from casual conversations among the students, which were recorded at regular intervals during the course. Cutting analyses different features of implicitness and the development of the use of implicit language as the individuals participating in the study gradually form a social group with a continually growing amount of shared knowledge. To this investigation of implicitness and the influence of shared knowledge on language use within a social group she adds an analysis of the functions of implicit language.

Elly Ifantidou begins her study of *Evidentials and Relevance* with a survey of literature on evidentiality. Then, using speech-act theory, H.P. Grice's work on meaning and communication, and relevance theory, she sets out to investigate evidentials, focusing on the following aspects: the interaction between linguistically encoded and pragmatically inferred evidential information, the classification of evidentials as truth-conditional or non-truth-conditional, and the contribution of evidentials to explicit or implicit communication. Roy Gardner's *When Listeners Talk: Response Tokens and Listener Stance* investigates the contributions listeners make to talk-in-interaction, in particular the use of response tokens as continuers, acknowledgements, newsmarkers, and change-of-activity tokens. After an initial discussion of the typical uses of the response tokens *Mm hm* and *Uh huh* (continuers), *Yeah* and *Mm* (acknowledgements), *Oh* and *Right* (newsmarkers), and *Okay* and *Alright* (change-of-activity tokens), Gardner focuses on the token *Mm*, examining the environments in which it occurs and its possible intonational contours.

Rose and Kasper, eds., *Pragmatics in Language Teaching*, is a collection of articles on the relationship between language learning in a classroom setting and the development of pragmatic competence in a second language. The first part includes two papers and offers a review of research into interlanguage pragmatics. The following eight chapters focus on the acquisition of pragmatic knowledge, and the remaining three chapters on its assessment.

Marianne Celce-Murcia and Elite Olshtain's *Discourse and Context in Language Teaching: A Guide for Language Teachers* [2000] begins with a brief introduction to aspects of pragmatics and discourse analysis which the authors consider relevant to language learning. The next two parts are concerned with language knowledge (phonology, grammar, and vocabulary) and the four language skills (listening, reading, writing, speaking), always including a discussion of the interrelationships with discourse. The presentation of the individual issues is very much practically oriented: the authors point out typically occurring difficulties and suggest teaching strategies. The concluding part of the book deals with the impact the adoption of a discourse perspective has on curriculum design, materials development, assessment, and teacher training. The chapter on assessment is a contribution by guest author Elana Shohamy.

Gender issues have been taken up in Christine Christie's *Gender and Language: Towards a Feminist Pragmatics* [2000] and Clare Walsh's *Gender and Discourse: Language and Power in Politics, the Church and Organisations*. Christie explores the advantages the adoption of a pragmatic perspective can bring to research into language use in general and to feminist research in particular. She offers a brief introduction to speech act theory, Grice's co-operative principle, politeness theory and relevance theory, and discusses a number of feminist studies, pointing out how these benefited, or might have benefited, from using the insights of pragmatics. Following a feminist approach to critical discourse analysis, Clare Walsh develops an analytical framework which she then uses to investigate the discursive strategies employed by women who enter traditionally male-dominated 'communities of practice'. She discusses the available options—acceptance of the prevailing, male-oriented, discourse practices, rejection and an attempt to change them, or strategic shifts between those two positions—and the risk of a negative evaluation of the adopted discourse style (whichever it is) as weak and ineffectual, aggressive and unfeminine, or inconsistent and insincere. Following this, Walsh analyses data presented in case studies on women Labour MPs at Westminster, the Northern Ireland Women's Coalition, and women priests in the Church of England. A fourth case study explores the discursive practices of the Women's Environmental Network in comparison to those of non-gender-specific groups.

Several collections of articles were published in the area of pragmatics and discourse analysis. Among them is Weigand and Dascal, eds., *Negotiation and Power in Dialogic Interaction*. The papers collected in this book are contributions to the International Conference on Pragmatics and Negotiation at Tel Aviv University and the Hebrew University of Jerusalem in 1999. The term 'negotiation' is used to refer to a specific discourse type as well as to an activity the participants in any type of discourse engage in. The first part, which comprises seven articles, is entitled 'Negotiation, Mediation and Power'. The four papers included in the second part investigate 'Means of Negotiation' (such as irony or silence). In the third part, again consisting of seven papers, 'Objects of Negotiation' (topic, relevance, social relationships, among others) are examined.

Sarangi and Coulthard, eds., *Discourse and Social Life* [2000], collects a number of papers to 'offer a mapping of the current field of discourse studies by inviting leading "discourse practitioners" to situate themselves in this growing intellectual landscape and to illustrate their concerns with data of their choice' (p. xv). Contributors are Srikant Sarangi ('Activity Types, Discourse Types and Interactional Hybridity: The Case of Genetic Counselling'), Ruqaiya Hasan ('The Uses of Talk'), Geoffrey Leech ('Same Grammar or Different Grammar? Contrasting Approaches to the Grammar of Spoken English Discourse'), Theo van Leeuwen ('The Construction of Purpose in Discourse'), Robert B. Kaplan ('Contrastive Rhetoric and Discourse Analysis: Who Writes What to Whom? When? In What Circumstances?'), Celia Roberts ('Professional Gatekeeping in Intercultural Encounters'), Greg Myers ('Becoming a Group: Face and Sociability in Moderated Discussions'), Ron Scollon ('Methodological Interdiscursivity: An

Ethnographic Understanding of Unfinalisability'), Henry Widdowson ('Critical Practices: On Representation and the Interpretation of Text'), Norman Fairclough ('Dialogue in the Public Sphere'), Ruth Wodak ('Recontextualization and the Transformation of Meanings: A Critical Discourse Analysis of Decision Making in EU Meetings about Employment Policies'), Nikolas Coupland and Justine Coupland ('Relational Frames and Pronominal Address/Reference: The Discourse of Geriatric Medical Triads'), Sally Candlin ('New Dynamics in the Nurse-Patient Relationship'), Yon Maley ('The Case of the Long-Nosed Potoroo: The Framing and Construction of Expert Witness Testimony'), and Malcolm Coulthard (Whose Text Is It? On the Linguistic Investigation of Authorship).

Most of the papers in Coulthard, Cotterill and Rock, eds., *Dialogue Analysis VII: Working with Dialogue. Selected Papers from the 7th IADA Conference, Birmingham 1999* [2000] are studies of spoken language. The data are taken from various settings, among them the courtroom, the clinic, and the classroom. Other contributions use written, mainly fictional, texts as data for analysis, and there are also theoretical papers on various aspects of the analysis of dialogue.

The pragmatic markers investigated in the eleven papers collected in Andersen and Fretheim, eds., *Pragmatic Markers and Propositional Attitude* [2000], are taken from a wide range of languages. In most of the studies a relevance-theoretic perspective is adopted to examine one or more pragmatic markers in a single language, or a number of markers in more than one language. Gisle Andersen is concerned with the use of *like* and claims that it may be employed by a speaker to indicate that an utterance is not the identical representation of the speaker's thought or that an expression used in an utterance might not be the most appropriate one. Thus the use of *like* allows speakers to distance themselves from (part of) the propositional content of their utterances. Regina Blass investigates the similarities and differences in the use of the English marker *after all*, German *ja* and *doch*, and Hausa *mana*, *ashe* and *lalle*. Sara W. Smith and Andreas H. Jucker focus on the interactional role of *actually*. They suggest that speakers use *actually* as a means of indicating that the following utterance will not be consistent with the hearer's expectations. The other contributors discuss pragmatic markers used in Norwegian (Thorstein Fretheim), Japanese (Seiko Fujii, Tomoko Matsui, Satoko Suzuki), Greek (Elly Ifantidou), Amharic and Swahili (Steve Nicolle), Gascon (Claus D. Pusch) and Hungarian (Ildikó Vaskó).

Lawrence Schourup proposes 'Rethinking *well*' (*JPrag* 33[2001] 1025–60). His investigation of the discourse marker is based on Dwight Bolinger's *Intonation and its Uses: Melody and Grammar in Discourse* [1989], which is discussed in some detail in the article. Schourup then analyses *well* in connection with parenthetical and non-parenthetical discourse connectives, illocutionary adverbs and 'mental state' interjections. He argues for a classification of *well* as a 'mental state' interjection which implies an act of consideration on the part of the speaker.

In 'Cooperating with Grice: A Cross-Disciplinary Metaperspective on Uses of Grice's Cooperative Principle' (*JPrag* 33[2001] 1601–23), Kenneth Lindblom claims that the full analytical power of Grice's co-operative principle has not yet been understood. The reason for this is, according to Lindblom, that there are different units of analysis in discourse (utterance, social interaction, and social context), but that discourse analysts, typically limiting their research to just one of these units, evaluate the co-operative principle from this limited perspective and therefore do not see the 'whole picture'. To change this unsatisfactory state of affairs requires, Lindblom claims, 'a fully articulated account of the CP—an account that uses the CP consistently to describe discourse as utterance, as social interaction and as social context' (p. 1620).

The analyses in the following articles all make use of politeness theory. Soledad Pérez de Ayala, 'FTAs and Erskine May: Conflicting Needs? Politeness in Question Time' (*JPrag* 33[2001] 143–69), and Sandra Harris, 'Being Politically Impolite: Extending Politeness Theory to Adversarial Political Discourse' (*D&S* 12[2001] 451–72) both use the adversarial discourse of Question Time in the House of Commons as a source of data. Pérez de Ayala investigates the influence of Erskine May's rules on discourse contributions. The rules protect the MP's private face while leaving their public face relatively open to attack. Harris examines discourse in Prime Minister's Question Time. She finds that most contributions to discourse are intentionally and explicitly face-threatening (or face-enhancing) and stresses the fact that FTAs practically never disrupt interpersonal relationships, because systematic impoliteness is expected by MPs in the context of adversarial political debate. Dennis Kurzon analyses 'The Politeness of Judges: American and English Judicial Behaviour' (*JPrag* 33[2001] 61–85), using appellate court opinions as data. The results of his analysis show that impoliteness is a common feature where judges disagree with their colleagues or with lower court judges; it is, however, far more frequent among American than among English judges. In 'Self-Politeness: A Proposal' (*JPrag* 33[2001] 87–106), Rong Chen argues that self-politeness should be included in the study of politeness because not only the hearer's face is vulnerable but also the speaker's. According to the model of self-politeness proposed by Chen, speakers have a choice of four superstrategies (baldly, with redress, off record, withhold the S(elf)FTA), which can be realized in various output strategies.

A conversation-analytic approach is adopted in the following studies. Steven E. Clayman examines 'Answers and Evasions' (*LSoc* 30[2001] 403–42) in broadcast news interviews. He starts by pointing out that interviewees are seen to be under an obligation to give a 'proper' answer, but that giving a 'proper' answer might not be in the best interests of the interviewee, given the adversarial nature of questions in interviews. Clayman discusses overt and covert strategies available to interviewees to resist questions, and investigates in two case studies how these strategies are implemented. Paul Dickerson's 'Disputing with Care: Analysing Interviewees' Treatment of Interviewers' Prior Turns in Televised Political Interviews' (*DisS* 3[2001] 203–22) provides an analysis of the differences in attitude towards challenging moves in interviews and everyday conversations. Dickerson discusses the forms challenging moves may take and the environments in which they occur. He points out that challenging moves are rarely used without mitigating action and that they never challenge the entire interview structure. He also emphasizes that neither interviewer nor interviewee takes steps to ward off disagreement because disagreement is an expected feature in interviews. In her examination of 'Questions, Control and the Organization of Talk in Calls to a Radio Phone-In' (*DisS* 3[2001] 119–43), Joanna Thornborrow focuses on the various stages of a call to a phone-in programme such as call opening or question sequence. She compares the patterns displayed at these stages with the corresponding stages in 'ordinary' telephone calls. In their article 'In the Heat of the Sequence: Interactional Features Preceding

Walkouts from Argumentative Talk' (*LSoc* 30[2001] 611–38), Ian Dersley and Anthony J. Wootton investigate complaint sequences to identify features which contribute to the result of one of the parties walking out on the other. In view of an ongoing extension of the advisory role of pharmacists unaccompanied by information on how such a role could be filled, Alison Pilnick calls for research on the nature of face-to-face interaction between pharmacists and their clients and contributes the article 'The Interactional Organization of Pharmacist Consultations in a Hospital Setting: A Putative Structure' (*JPrag* 33[2001] 1927–45), in which she examines a sample conversation from a larger corpus and develops a sequence structure of encounters between pharmacists and their patients.

12. Stylistics

This year has not been particularly fruitful for stylistics monographs but Jonathan Culpeper's *Language and Characterisation: People in Plays and Other Texts* makes up for it by providing a full-length study of character and characterization in (mostly) literary texts. The fact that it foregrounds dramatic texts in its title is also to be welcomed, since stylistic analyses of plays have not been exactly abundant in the field. Culpeper is particularly interested in exploring how a character is constructed in the reader's mind through language, and to this end he builds an interdisciplinary framework which combines pragmatics, literary stylistics, cognitive psychology and social cognition. This framework enables him to pursue answers to three related issues: how the prior knowledge readers bring to a text influence their perception of character; how readers make inferences about characters from the text; and which textual features contribute to characterization. This exploration is conducted through a combination of social schemata, impression formation and attribution theory with self- and other-presentation, conversational implicature and politeness theory. The structure of the book is neat: an introductory chapter entitled 'Modelling Characterization' is followed by two clearly differentiated sections, 'Characterization and the Mind' and 'Characterization and the Text', each of which foregrounds one of the two strands—social cognition and linguistics—which Culpeper succeeds in bringing together. The last chapter amply shows this through a systematic examination and innovative analysis of Katherina in *The Taming of the Shrew*, which rescues this character from its received view as a mere shrew and farcical stereotype, presenting it as much rounder than Shakespearean criticism has ever been capable of offering. Texts dealt with in the course of this study range from the overwhelming presence of Shakespeare's plays to poetry, fiction, films, advertising, newspapers and jokes. Characters discussed range from the personifications of abstract virtues found in medieval morality plays to the Teletubbies, and this wide spectrum of texts and characters enhances the value of this study.

Three books which are by now seminal texts in stylistics have been re-edited, testifying to the health of the discipline: Guy Cook's *The Discourse of Advertising*, Michael Toolan's *Narrative: A Critical Linguistic Introduction* and Katie Wales's *A Dictionary of Stylistics*. The degree of revision to be found in each of them varies, but all contain new material. Cook has thoroughly revised all the chapters of his study on the language of advertising and has also added a considerable amount of new advertising material. The introduction has been enlarged, advertising is no longer seen as a discourse-type but as a genre, and the relation between ads and literary texts is given prominence. Most of the revision in other chapters is directed towards bringing the book in line with contemporary trends in communication, including e-mail and the Internet. It is a shame, though, that on some occasions, rather than adding more examples and new ads to those in the original edition, the old material has been replaced. Proud owners of the first edition, therefore, will be wise not to chuck their old copies away, but this revised edition cannot be ignored by anyone working on the linguistic/stylistic analysis of advertising. Michael Toolan's revised edition of his influential critical linguistic introduction to narrative has also been brought into line with recent developments in communication, as the chapter on media narrative shows, since it has been updated and enlarged, incorporating new sections on hard news reporting in newspapers and on online reporting on the Internet. His revision also reaches deeper in that the layout and structure of some chapters has been improved, and readers who are familiar with the first edition will see that substantially new material can be found in sections on narrativity, modes of narration, suspense, film narratives and gender. The further reading, notes and exercises sections have been considerably revised and updated too. For some, the term 'introduction' will seem a misnomer when applied to this book—its range and depth make it suitable reading for sophisticated readers as well as undergraduates. This new edition ensures that Toolan's book will remain the staple, standard introduction to narrative for some years to come. Katie Wales's dictionary of stylistics is surely so well known to readers of this section that it is probably unnecessary to stress the fact that its wide range of entries also makes it a dictionary of rhetoric, literary terms, fundamental notions in grammar, discourse, sociolinguistics and critical theory. Most changes introduced in this new edition are called for by the transformation of stylistics and related disciplines in the last ten years. It now includes entries on cognitive linguistics, schema theory, relevance theory and politeness. Existing entries have been transformed to accommodate developments; for example, the entry for 'critical linguistics' has been considerably enlarged to create room for 'critical discourse analysis', and in most cases bibliographical references have been updated. For those familiar with the first edition, this new one will be a record of the most salient new directions stylistics research has followed in the last decade; for those not yet acquainted with it—and for future generations of students and researchers—it is bound to become an invaluable work of reference.

Unlike 2000, 2001 was a good year for pedagogical stylistics. The Intertext series continues to provide concise and useful introductions to specific registers and language varieties. In *The Language of Speech and Writing*, Sandra Cornbleet and Ronald Carter have produced a very neat guide to the differences between written and spoken discourse, which, although aimed at A-level students and first-year undergraduates, will not disappoint more advanced readers. It has a very appealing range of texts, including e-mail messages, some of which may end up being plundered by teachers for further analysis. As a textbook, it is extraordinarily user-friendly without doing away with depth of thought; it has a well-contrived structure that introduces the nature of speech and writing and then descends to practical analysis of written and spoken varieties in alternating chapters. The book is rounded off by two unexpected chapters which contain much food for thought: one on the reasons for and consequences of choosing one channel rather than another for conveying information, and another on the cross-fertilization of the two modes of language, which alerts students to the presence of features of spoken language in written texts. Francesca Pridham's *The Language of Conversation* can be used as a companion volume to *The Language of Speech and Writing*, since it expands the range of spoken varieties discussed by paying attention to jokes and oral narratives. It also reaches further than its sister volume as it aims to make students familiar with basic concepts from pragmatics, conversation analysis, discourse analysis and politeness theory, including H.P. Grice's co-operative principle, adjacency pairs, exchange structure, discourse markers and the distinction between positive and negative face. Schemata and frame theory are also used to introduce students to the existence of a great variety of conversational genres. The final chapter, entitled 'Spoken Language in Written Texts', should perhaps have been given a more transparent title since it is exclusively concerned with literary texts. Still, it is a much-needed and well-placed chapter, which analyses the representation of spoken language in poetry (Steve Waling's 'What She Said'), the novel (*Sense and Sensibility*) and drama (*Othello*). *The Language of Drama* is, in fact, the topic of Keith Sanger's contribution to the Intertext series; a very necessary introductory volume, which will, one hopes, entice students to continue to explore the stylistics of dramatic texts on their own. The recurrent presence of two well-known *Viz* characters, Crispin and Natasha Critic, in strips specially conceived by John Fardell for the opening of each chapter, will no doubt alert students to the hours of fun and pleasure that reward the brave practitioner of stylistic analysis. Sanger's course-book overlaps at times with Pridham's, just as Pridham's sometimes overlaps with Cornbleet and Carter's but this is no shortcoming; rather, it suggests that these textbooks might provide an interesting threesome for a course on spoken discourse. Character presentation, soliloquy, rhythm and sound, and the absence of a narrator are all given room in this volume, which closes with a wink to cinema adaptations of canonical texts such as, once again, Austen's *Sense and Sensibility*. However, the range of texts under examination is one of the assets of this compact introduction to dramatic language; the reader is exposed to some of the most canonical texts— including the best-known monologues in *Macbeth*, *Hamlet* and *Othello*—but televisions soaps and radio drama are also dealt with in examples from *Coronation Street* and *The Archers*. Other texts analysed include Samuel Beckett's *Waiting for Godot*, Edward Bond's *Saved*, Jim Cartwright's *Road*, Caryl Churchill's *Fen*, Brian Friel's *Dancing at Lughnasa*, Arthur Miller's *Death of a Salesman*, Peter Shaffer's *Lettice and Lovage* and Tom Stoppard's *The Real Inspector Hound*. On the whole, this is a very manageable introduction that will whet the student's appetite for the linguistic analysis of drama. This year's output of Intertext volumes is completed by Tim Shortis with *The Language of ICT: Information and Communication Technology*, an exciting and comprehensive introduction to a variety which is increasingly shaping our use of language. Shortis shows that ICT language is not just a matter of expanding the lexicon and coping with a bunch of new technical coinages but, rather, that it is a far-reaching phenomenon affecting the whole linguistic spectrum, from graphology to semantics (conceptual metaphors) and discourse (spoken vs. written modes; jargon and anti-languages). He also manages to produce a textbook which succeeds in fulfilling very thoroughly the Intertext series' aim of describing the linguistic features and stylistic patterns found in a given language variety and relating this description to the social context in which text-production takes place. On top of this, through having to describe a rapidly evolving language variety such as ICT, Shortis foregrounds the fact that language is inevitably subject to change, something which other Intertext volumes tend to neglect, dealing with linguistic description as if varieties existed in an ahistorical, merely synchronic limbo. Shortis writes in a clear, precise, didactic prose without sacrificing intellectual depth or linguistic sophistication, and his elegant, engaging writing style is the best proof that ICT is not the herald of the disintegration of English. With chapters on the nature of the electronic text and how it allows new ways of reading and writing, the emergence of new patterns of punctuation, spelling and use of graphological symbols as a result of the spread of CMC (computer-mediated communication), the representation of ICT in advertising and media, the purpose of ICT and its identity-conferring function for specific social groups (not ignoring gender distinctions), the ways in which vocabulary change reflects and shapes how people think and relate to each other, how word-formation can be analysed and new words tracked and studied as lexicographers do, how ICT language is mediated by imagery and metaphor, it is clear that Shortis's textbook has a far wider audience than could be gathered from its title. Rather than simply offering a course-book on a very specific language variety, it provides an extraordinarily stimulating text for language study and future research. In fact, being equipped with a good glossary, a helpful appendix with guidelines on how to research the language of ICT, a companion website students can surf at leisure (netting-it.com) and a bibliography which is much longer than the usual brief reading lists found in other Intertext volumes, this new addition to the series cannot fail to encourage research.

Adrian Beard's *Texts and Contexts: Introducing Literature and Language Study* is a practical, efficient and very stimulating textbook which is not exclusively concerned with linguistic approaches to literary texts but will be of great use to those teaching stylistic courses, since it contemplates language as one of several 'contexts' students can explore when analysing, commenting on, discussing and interpreting a literary text. These contexts—the writer, the text, the reader, the readings (of critical schools and theories) and the language—are presented as different angles from which texts can make their multiple, fluid meanings available. By paying attention to each of these contexts in turn, Beard constructs a framework which empowers students and helps them to build a measure of critical confidence. The book's structure is student-friendly and clear: the first chapter introduces the 'texts and contexts' framework and the next two chapters illustrate the framework of analysis; the middle part of the book applies the framework in several chapters dealing with narrative and poetic and dramatic texts (including a chapter on Shakespeare co-authored with Margaret Walker); the book closes with a chapter on intertextuality which draws examples from different genres, and a final chapter that brings together most of the critical/theoretical issues introduced in the course of the book through a thorough analysis of Thomas Hardy's 'The Going'. From a stylistics point of view, one of the attractive qualities of this book is that it offers a way of integrating awareness about linguistic issues in commentaries on literary texts in literature courses and shows how any attempt to teach critical/theoretical ways of analysing texts is more rewarding if it takes language and linguistics into account.

Keith Sanger's contribution to the Intertext series is not the only stylistics book which has recently focused on the language of plays. Drama, or rather Shakespeare, has received an unusual amount of attention this year. Adamson, Hunter, Magnusson, Thompson and Wales, eds., *Reading Shakespeare's Dramatic Language: A Guide*, a collection of essays in the Arden Shakespeare series, provides a useful companion on language and style for readers of the plays. The editors claim in their preface that their 'main purpose is to make Shakespeare's language and his uses of language more accessible to modern readers' (p. xi), and they have achieved this without being merely didactic or ignoring recent critical trends in Shakespeare studies, since the relation of Shakespeare's language to rhetoric, performance and history is by no means neglected. The guide has a structure which enables different readers to select particular areas of interest: part 1 approaches language from the perspective of literary criticism; part 2 deals with language from the perspective of linguistics; part 3 looks at language from the perspective of the student or reader, and contains a glossary of rhetorical terms illustrated with examples taken from Shakespeare's plays and a further reading list, which has been conscientiously annotated, but which merely seems to duplicate the further reading entries placed at the end of individual chapters. Part 1 offers chapters on Shakespeare's 'heightened' language (Ann Thompson), rhetoric and decorum (Lynne Magnusson), the grand style (Sylvia Adamson), metre and scansion (George T. Wright), and puns and parody (Walter Nash), plus four chapters on specific issues such as description (William C. Carroll), narrative (David Scott Kastan), persuasion (Lynette Hunter) and dialogue (Lynne Magnusson). This first part closes with three chapters on: character (Pamela Mason), language in the theatre (Peter Lichtenfels), and language in performance (Keir Elam). Part 2 provides the linguistic scaffolding for this guide, with chapters on sociolinguistic variety (Katie Wales), grammar (Sylvia Adamson), word-formation (Terttu Nevalainen) and sound (Roger Lass). Although on the whole it is very good value for money and will not disappoint its readers, this guide to Shakespeare's 'dramatic' language might have cast its net slightly wider in the linguistic section, where the absence of discourse analysis, pragmatics, and cognitive approaches to metaphor—areas in which recent stylistic criticism of Shakespeare has been reasonably fruitful—is to be deplored.

Similarly focused on Shakespeare's language, Ross McDonald's *Shakespeare and the Arts of Language* has more in common with part 1 than part 2 of *Reading Shakespeare's Dramatic Language* since its approach is not primarily linguistic. McDonald's aim is to foreground the importance of language for a full understanding of Shakespeare's work, given that it is Shakespeare's deployment of the 'arts of language'—more than his contribution to plot, characterization or theme—that creates the distinctive nature of his dramatic world. To support this, McDonald explores words in Shakespeare's plays, the rhetorical traditions in which they are immersed, the imagery they create, their metaphoric and symbolic functions and the importance of wordplay. Blank verse, with its rhythmic permutations, and the variety shown in the use and function of prose, together with Shakespeare's changing views on language, complete this account of the pre-eminence of the word in Shakespeare's art. Written in a very clear, elegant prose, which is highly informative without being demanding, this new addition to the Oxford Shakespeare Topics series will not disappoint readers looking for a way into Shakespeare's language that may enhance their enjoyment of the plays.

Two books not centrally concerned with literary texts or linguistic approaches to literature which are nevertheless bound to be of interest to readers of this section are Michael Hoey's *Textual Interaction: An Introduction to Written Discourse Analysis* and Susan Ehrlich's *Representing Rape: Language and Sexual Consent*. Hoey's *Textual Interaction* is a very personal contribution to the study of written discourse, which takes as its departure point a conception of the text as a site of interaction where author, writer, audience and reader meet. Chapter 2 describes how interaction in texts take place; chapter 3 deals with the large-scale hypotheses readers construct for texts; chapter 4 focuses on the hierarchical organization of texts, illustrated with an analysis of *Goldilocks and the Three Bears*; in chapter 5, Hoey discusses what he calls 'Cinderella' texts (i.e. texts that are neglected in other accounts of written discourse, such as shopping lists or statutes) and the text as 'colony'; in chapter 6 he offers a matrix analysis for a Borges short story ('Death and the Compass'); chapters 7 and 8 introduce several 'culturally popular patterns' for the organization of texts, such as Problem–Solution, Problem–Response, Goal–Achievement, Opportunity-Taking, Desire Arousal–Fulfilment, and Gap in Knowledge-Filling, and chapter 9 presents Question–Answer patterns. The volume ends with a brief conclusion, which presents texts as a set of questions: the author makes guesses at the questions the reader would like to see answered and the reader tries to anticipate the questions that the author aims to answer. This personal account of written discourse mixes conventional and unconventional instances of academic prose, turning itself into a testing ground for the approach it presents. In *Representing Rape*, Ehrlich has produced a well-researched and theoretically informed study of legal language which places under the microscope courtroom discourse in rape and sexual assault trials and shows the extent to which linguistic practice actively constructs (rather than merely revealing) speakers' social identities. It also shows how the linguistic construction of reality in this type of criminal trial disadvantages women and contributes to the perpetuation of rape myths. After a rather concise introduction, the first chapter exposes the theoretical framework on which the study is based, which draws on Foucauldian conceptions of discourse, feminist linguistics, sociolinguistics and feminist legal studies. Chapters 2 to 5 contain a case study of the trial of the same male subject (a student) in two different settings: a university tribunal and a criminal court. The roles played by transitivity and agency in the reporting of events, questions asked of complainants and the ideological assumptions which lie behind them, conversational implicature and miscommunication are all analysed, leading Ehrlich to the conclusion that the limiting nature of institutional legal discourse, which prevents witnesses from asking questions or initiating turns, shows how individuals and events are constructed and constrained by a discursive practice. *Representing Rape* is priority reading for anyone interested in feminist linguistics, legal discourse, critical discourse analysis, systemic-functional grammar, pragmatics and conversational analysis, but also for those who want to see the critical thinking of Foucault, Bakhtin and Bourdieu tested on naturally occurring data.

In a stimulating essay which is bound to be polemical, 'Parody and Style' (*PoT* 22[2001] 25–39), Seymour Chatman challenges the status of parody as the most typically postmodern genre and advocates a restrictive use of the term, which reserves it for its non-satirical use, i.e. the one that encodes praise for the original. Unreliability in narrative has been studied in two articles by Jean-Jacques Weber. A reasonably reliable narrator is shown to become unreliable as the narrative progresses through his refusal to grow ideologically after being exposed to post-colonial Congo's independence process in 'Reliability and Commitment in Ronan Bennett's *The Catastrophist*' (*AAA* 26[2001] 3–11). In 'The Unreliable Readers of Sam Selvon's *Moses Ascending*' (*LWU* 34[2001] 135–42), it is not only the narrator but two 'internal' readers built into the narrative frame who prove unreliable, and Weber shows how, although their narrative function is to alert 'external', real-world readers to ideological pitfalls (such as the prejudice against non-standard varieties of English), the author of a recent article on this novel has failed to take his cue. Two other articles on narrative and narratology which readers of this section may find of interest are Ralf Schneider's 'Toward a Cognitive Theory of Literary Character: The Dynamics of Mental-Model Construction' (*Style* 35[2001] 607–39) and Richard Walsh's 'Fabula and Fictionality in Narrative Theory' (*Style* 35[2001] 592–606).

Parliamentary language is the object of Soledad Pérez de Ayala's 'FTAS and Erskine May: Conflicting Needs? Politeness in Question Time' (*JPrag* 33[2001] 143–69), an enlightening study of how face-redressing politeness strategies interact with Erskine May's code of linguistic behaviour for British MPs, making it acceptable that they pose threats to each other's Public Face during the highly aggressive parliamentary sessions known as 'Question Time'. The discourse of Australian eco-resorts and eco-tours (whale-watching, bird-watching, eco-walking) is dissected by Peter Mühlhäusler and Adrian Peace in 'Discourse of Ecotourism: The Case of Fraser Island, Queensland' (*L&C* 21[2001] 359–80) to show that perceived environmental protection can be a linguistic construction, built sometimes through metaphor, the semantic bleaching of the prefix *eco-* or the reconciliation of economic interest and moral beliefs. The discourse of tourism also provides subject-matter for Arsenio Jesús Moya Guijarro and José Ignacio Albentosa Hernández's 'Points of Departure in News Items and Tourist Brochures: Choices of Theme and Topic? (*Text* 21[2001] 347–71), who have found empirical evidence that news items and tourist brochures differ in their topical and thematic organization, since news items show a preference for new topical entities in sentence-initial position whereas in tourist brochures, shaped by the persuasive function, new topics tend to be postponed to engage the reader's attention.

The language of advertising has received attention in Ingrid Piller's 'Identity Constructions in Multilingual Advertising' (*LSoc* 30[2001] 153–86) and Paul Simpson's '"Reason" and "Tickle" as Pragmatic Constructs in the Discourse of Advertising' (*JPrag* 33[2001] 589–607). Piller dissects a corpus of German press and television advertisements which incorporate English words or sentences in their copy and discusses the social identities constructed in these advertisements with the help of the Bakhtinian concept of dialogism and narratological notions of point of view. Simpson provides linguistic criteria for accommodating Bernstein's non-linguistic distinction between 'reason' and 'tickle' advertisements (i.e. adverts which provide a reason or motive for purchase and adverts which arouse humour, emotion or mood) within models used in current pragmatics and systemic-functional linguistics. Empirical stylistics has also produced two interesting studies this year. In 'Psychological Differences of Reception between Literary (Fictive) and Historiographical (Nonfictive) Texts' (*JLS* 30[2001] 147–65), Lászlo Halász reports on two studies which show that naive subjects detected the literariness of both literary and historiographical narrative texts, although they could identify these texts as belonging to two different text types: fictive and non-fictive. Chanita Goodblatt contributes to a greater understanding of the strategies deployed by reading subjects in the reading process in 'Adding an Empirical Dimension to the Study of Poetic Metaphor' (*JLS* 30[2001] 167–80), a study of the cognitive process that enables readers to comprehend poetic metaphor, which integrates in its theoretical framework Gestalt psychology and the Interaction theory of metaphor.

Elżbieta Chrzanowska-Kluczewska approaches the study of poetic language through Wittgensteinian language games in 'Semantic and Pragmatic Language-Games in Poetry' (*JLS* 30[2001] 181–97) and concludes that it is possible to distinguish several kinds of language game: semantic games of the author, pragmatic games of the reader, and autonomous games of the text. In 'Fictions, Fantasies, and Fears: The Literary Foundations of the Cloning Debate' (*JLS* 30[2001] 37–52), Brigitte Nerlich, David D. Clarke and Robert Dingwall show how the media debate about cloning and genetic engineering (genetically modified food in particular) has been strongly influenced by the language of science fiction. They argue that the use of images and metaphors from science fiction films and narratives, such as *Frankenstein* and *Gattaca*, both feeds and mirrors the general public's fear of a process of biological hybridization which threatens to blur the distinction between humans, animals, plants and machines.

George Lakoff and Mark Johnson's cognitive theory of metaphor continues to engage the attention of those who practise stylistics. Proof of this is that cognitive approaches are overwhelmingly present in this year's volume of *Language and Literature*. In 'Allegory: Conceptual Metaphor in History' (*L&L* 10[2001] 5–19), Peter Crisp approaches Western allegory as a surface manifestation of conceptual metaphor, offers a history of the term, explores Prudentian allegories such as *The Pilgrim's Progress* and defends the idea that allegorical discourse is governed both by universal constraints and specific socio-historical contexts. Cognitive theory of metaphor is also the basis for Roberto Bertuol's analysis of Cavendish's poem 'The Circle of the Brain Cannot be Squared' in 'The *Square Circle* of Margaret Cavendish: The 17th-Century Conceptualization of Mind by Means of Mathematics' (*L&L* 10[2001] 21–39). Bertuol shows how the conceptual metaphor 'the universe is mathematics' explains Cavendish's use of the poetic metaphor 'squaring the circle' in order to argue that human desire to control 'irrationalia' (such as female nature and fancy) is doomed to failure. In 'The Concept of America in the Puritan Mind' (*L&L* 10[2001] 195–209), Szilvia Csábi applies the notions of conceptual metaphor and blending developed by Lakoff, Johnson, M. Turner and G. Fauconnier to prose works by American Puritans in order to examine how America is conceptualized in biblical terms as both the promised land and a desolate, dangerous wilderness, and how Puritans regarded their immigration experience as enacting a business deal, all of which are sub-metaphors of a master metaphor, 'The settlement of America is the movement of the Jews from Egypt to Israel'. Although not concerned with literary texts, Francisco José Ruiz de Mendoza Ibáñez and Lorena Pérez Hernández's 'Metonymy and the Grammar: Motivation, Constraints and Interaction' (*L&C* 21[2001] 321–57) will be of interest to those working on the stylistic application of cognitive linguistics because it provides an enlightened discussion of the constraints that metonymy as a conceptual phenomenon and the grammatical system impose on each other.

A special issue of *Language and Literature* (*L&L* 10:ii[2001]) is devoted to 'Literary Dialectic Analysis with Computer Assistance'. Although the issue's primary aim is to show how computers can be of great use in the analysis of literary dialectal varieties, students of American literature in general and Mark Twain's oeuvre in particular, as well as those interested in African American Vernacular English (AAVE), ought to welcome it as a windfall. It opens with a theoretically oriented article by William A. Kretzschmar Jr., 'Literary Dialectic Analysis with Computer Assistance: An Introduction' (*L&L* 10:ii[2001] 99–110), which shows the advantages of the LinguaLinks software for the analysis of dialect in literary texts. This is followed by three articles on Mark Twain's best-known novels. In 'Jim's Language and the Issue of Race in *Huckleberry Finn*' (*L&L* 10:ii[2001] 111–28), Lisa Cohen Minnick puts LinguaLinks to use and shows that Mark Twain's realistic characterization of Jim owes a great deal to the phonological and grammatical features of AAVE present in Jim's speech. Using the same software and applying it to works by the same author, Susan Tamasi's 'Huck Doesn't Sound Like Himself: Consistency in the Literary Dialect of Mark Twain' (*L&L* 10:ii[2001] 129–44) examines dialectal consistency in Huck's speech to conclude that Twain's consistency in the use of some dialectal features does not preclude variation in his representation of his character's speech. Unlike the other articles on Twain's work, in '"I'm going to see what's going on here": A-Prefixing in *The Adventures of Huckleberry Finn*' (*L&L* 10:ii[2001] 145–57), Lamont Antieau concentrates on a single linguistic feature, *a*-prefixing in present participles, and suggests that in *Huckleberry Finn* Twain resorts to *a*-prefixing when representing the non-standard speech of several characters. Dialect in Harriet Beecher Stowe's canonical novel is submitted to quantitative, computerized concordance analysis with WordSmith tools by Allison Burkette in 'The Use of Literary Dialect in *Uncle Tom's Cabin*' (*L&L* 10:ii[2001] 158–70) enabling her to show Stowe's linguistic accuracy in the representation of the speech of Aunt Chloe, George and Mr Haley and support recent findings about the close relationship between AAVE and South White Vernacular English. The issue is rounded off by Betsy Barry's '"It's hard fuh me to understand what you mean, de way you tell it": Representing Language in Zora Neale Hurston's *Their Eyes Were Watching God*' (*L&L* 10:ii[2001] 171–86), which submits to analysis phonetic and phonological differences in pronunciation as represented through respelling to assess if they are purely fictional stylistic devices or if they accurately reproduce southern American dialectal features.

The representation of spoken discourse in narrative has been the object of attention in two articles. In 'Style-Shifting in Edith Wharton's *The House of Mirth*' (*L&L* 10[2001] 61–77), David Herman discusses how the communicative styles adopted by Wharton's characters in a given context help to locate them as gender subjects and construct their social identities. In 'The French *Théorie de l'énonciation* and the Study of Speech and Thought Presentation' (*L&L* 10[2001] 243–62), Sophie Marnette offers an integrated model for reported discourse in literary texts by combining Geoffrey Leech and Mick Short's well-known framework with the notion of split subject developed by O. Ducrot and D. Maingeneau. Also concerned with narrative is Teresa Bridgeman's 'Making Worlds Move: Re-Ranking Contextual Parameters in Flaubert's *Madame Bovary* and Céline's *Voyage au bout de la nuit*' (*L&L* 10[2001] 41–59), which draws on Paul Werth's cognitive model of text worlds and Monika Fludernik's work on schemata for an analysis of the author–audience relation in two novels which transformed readers' perceptions of narrative conventions. The psychological effects of narrative perspective on readers is the subject of Willie Van Peer and Henk Pander Maat's 'Narrative Perspective and the Interpretation of Characters' Motives' (*L&L* 10[2001] 229–41). Van Peer and Pander Maat show how narrative point of view (and internal focalization in particular) is responsible for the degree of sympathy readers feel for characters and for readers' choices in the interpretation of character behaviour.

Drama continues to receive little attention in the journals, but it is not completely neglected. Habib Abdesslem applies P. Brown and S. Levinson's politeness model to C. Hampton's *The Philanthropist* in 'Politeness Strategies in the Discourse of Drama: A Case Study' (*JLS* 30[2001] 111–38), and in 'The Play off the Stage: The Writer–Reader Relationship in Drama' (*L&L* 10[2001] 79–93), Zongxin Feng and Dan Shen foreground the relation between reader and writer in dramatic texts, showing that it is a more complex, multidimensional relation than in other kinds of text with the help of a stylistic analysis of Ionesco's *The Lesson*.

A number of articles in this year's volume of *Language and Literature* deal with political discourse, poetry and authorial attribution tests. Michael Pearce has examined a Labour party broadcast released during the 1997 general election campaign in 'Getting Behind the Image: Personality Politics in a Labour Party Election Broadcast' (*L&L* 10[2001] 211–28), disclosing the use of Tony Blair's biography in propaganda discourse through an analysis of pronominal choice and linguistic markers of hesitation such as repetition, hedges and pauses. In a wide-raging diachronic study, which looks into the factors motivating poetic change, 'Adverbial Function in English Verse: The Case of *Thus*' (*L&L* 10[2001] 291–306), Gareth Twose and C.B. McCully trace the history of *thus* as metrical filler since Chaucer, and show how its high frequency in sixteenth- and seventeenth-century epic poetry (Spenser and Milton) is followed by a noticeable decline in the following centuries, providing evidence for a link between linguistic function and poetic style. Peter Dixon and David Mannion offer a stylometric study of three essays attributed to the author of *Chinese Letters* in 'Goldsmith and the *Public Ledger*' (*L&L* 10[2001] 307–23) and conclude with the help of samples from Goldsmith's works and four control authors that only one of the essays can be attributed to him.

Before I round off this section, I would like to draw attention to two final matters. Lesley Jeffries takes issue with the work of Guy Cook [1994] and Elena Semino [1997] on schema theory in 'Schema Affirmation and White Asparagus: Cultural Multilingualism among Readers of Texts' (*L&L* 10[2001] 325–43), and puts forward that literary texts do not always challenge readers' schemata. He defends this point of view by means of the analysis of two poems, Fleur Adcock's 'Against Coupling' and Sujata Bhatt's 'White Asparagus', which can be seen as either schema-refreshing or schema-reinforcing depending on the particular reader response of different individuals. Elena Semino has taken up the editors' offer to provide a response in 'On Readings, Literariness and Schema Theory: A Reply to Jeffries' (*L&L* 10[2001] 345–55). In past years, debates on relevance theory or critical discourse analysis have found a convenient home for the exchange of divergent views on a given topic in the pages of this journal, so let us hope practitioners of schema theory will take advantage of this opportunity. As in previous years, Geoff Hall continues to provide, in 'The Year's Work in Stylistics:

2000' (*L&L* 10[2001] 357–68), a very insightful overview, which I find both extraordinarily useful and stimulating.

Books Reviewed

Abbi, Anvita, R. S. Gupta, Ayesha Kidwai, eds. *Linguistic Structure and Language Dynamics in South Asia: Papers from the Proceedings of SALA XVIII Roundtable*. Motilal Banarsidass Delhi. [2001] pp. xxi + 409. Rupees 895 ISBN 8 1208 1765 6.

Adamson, Sylvia, Lynette Hunter, Lynne Magnusson, Ann Thompson, and Katie Wales, eds. *Reading Shakespeare's Dramatic Language: A Guide*. ArdenSh. [2001] pp. xii + 321. pb £12.99 ISBN 1 9034 3629 X.

Aitchison, Jean. *Language Change: Progress or Decay?* 3rd edn. Cambridge Approaches to Linguistics. CUP. [2001] pp. xi + 312. hb £35 ($54.95) ISBN 0 5217 9155 3, pb £12.95 ($19.95) ISBN 0 5217 9155 3.

Alexandrova, Galina M., and Olga Arnaudova, eds. *The Minimalist Parameter: Selected Papers from the Open Linguistics Forum, Ottawa, 21–23 March 1997*. CILT 192. Benjamins. [2001] pp. x + 360. €86.22 ISBN 9 0272 3699 2.

Algeo, John, ed. *English in North America*. Cambridge History of the English Language 6. CUP. [2001] pp. 662. £74.82 ISBN 0 5212 6479 0.

Allan, Keith. *Natural Language Semantics*. Blackwell. [2001] pp. xix + 529. hb £60 ISBN 0 6311 9296 4, pb £19.99 ISBN 0 6311 9297 2.

Alsina, Alex, Joan Bresnan, and Peter Sells, eds. *Complex Predicates*. CSLI Lecture Notes 64. CSLI. [1997] pp. vi + 514. pb $20.95 ISBN 1 5758 6046 5.

Ammon, Ulrich, ed. *The Dominance of English as a Language of Science: Effects on Other Languages and Language Communities*. MGruyter. [2001] pp. xiii + 478. €130.89 ISBN 3 1101 6647 X.

Andersen, Gisle, and Thorstein Fretheim, eds. *Pragmatic Markers and Propositional Attitude*. Pragmatics & Beyond ns 79. Benjamins. [2000] pp. viii + 273. €83 ($83) ISBN 9 0272 5098 7 (Eur.), ISBN 1 5561 9797 7 (US).

Andersen, Henning, ed. *Actualization: Linguistic Change in Progress*. CILT 219. Benjamins. [2001] pp. 250. €77.14 ($77) ISBN 9 0272 3726 3 (Eur.), ISBN 1 5881 1081 8 (US).

Arnold, A. James, ed. *A History of Literature in the Caribbean. Vol. 2: English- and Dutch-Speaking Regions*. Benjamins. [2001] pp. viii + 672. €200 ISBN 9 0272 3448 5, $182 ISBN 1 5881 1041 9.

Aronoff, Mark, and Janie Rees-Miller, eds. *The Handbook of Linguistics*. Blackwell. [2001] pp. xvi + 824. £85 ISBN 0 6312 0497 0.

Baker, Mona, ed. *Routledge Encyclopedia of Translation Studies*. Routledge. [1998, 2001] pp. xix + 654. hb £135 ISBN 0 4150 9380 5, pb £25.99 ISBN 0 4152 5517 1.

Ballard, Kim. *The Frameworks of English: Introducing Language Structures*. Palgrave. [2001] pp. xiii + 301. pb £15.99 ISBN 0 3336 5913 9.

Baltin, Mark, and Chris Collins, eds. *The Handbook of Contemporary Syntactic Theory*. Blackwell Handbooks in Linguistics. Blackwell. [2001] pp. xii + 860. £85 ISBN 0 6312 0507 1.

Bamgbose, Ayo. *Language and Exclusion: The Consequences of Language Policies in Africa*. LIT. [2000] pp. 150. pb €19.90 ISBN 3 8258 4775 6.

Bauer, Laurie. *Morphological Productivity*. Cambridge Studies in Linguistics 95. CUP. [2001] pp. xiii + 245. £42.50 ISBN 0 5217 9238 X.

Beard, Adrian. *Texts and Contexts: Introducing Literature and Language Study*. Routledge. [2001] pp. viii + 165. hb £60 ISBN 0 4152 5350 0, pb £10.99 ISBN 0 4152 2987 1.

Beck, Heinrich, Dieter Geuenich, and Heiko Steuer, eds. *Reallexikon der Germanischen Altertumskunde (Begründet von Johannes Hoops)*, 2nd edn. Vol. 15: *Hobel–Iznik*. Gruyter. [2000] pp. vi + 610. $288 ISBN 3 1101 6469 6.

Beck, Heinrich, Dieter Geuenich, and Heiko Steuer, eds. *Reallexikon der Germanischen Altertumskunde (Begründet von Johannes Hoops)*, 2nd edn. Vol. 17: *Kleinere Götter–Landschaftsarchäologie*. Gruyter. [2001] pp. vi + 634. €288, sFv461 ($317) ISBN 3 1101 6907 X.

Beck, Heinrich, Dieter Geuenich, and Heiko Steuer, eds. *Reallexikon der Germanischen Altertumskunde (Begründet von Johannes Hoops)*, 2nd edn. Vol. 18: *Landschaftsrecht–Loxstedt*. Gruyter. [2001] pp. vi + 633. $288 ISBN 3 1101 6950 9.

Beck, Heinrich, Dieter Geuenich, and Heiko Steuer, eds. *Reallexikon der Germanischen Altertumskunde (Begründet von Johannes Hoops)*, 2nd edn. Vol. 19: *Luchs–Metrum*. Gruyter. [2001] pp. vi + 642. $288 ISBN 3 1101 7163 5.

Blair, David, Peter Collins, eds. *English in Australia*. VEAW G26. Benjamins. [2001] pp. vi + 366. €113.45 ISBN 9 0272 4884 2.

Booij, Geert, and Jaap van Marle, eds. *Yearbook of Morphology 1999*. Kluwer. [2001] pp. 321. €140.50 ISBN 0 7923 6631 X.

Börjars, Kersti, and Kate Burridge. *Introducing English Grammar*. Arnold. [2001] pp. xiii + 311. hb £45 ISBN 0 3406 9172 7, pb £14.99 ISBN 0 3406 9173 5.

Brendler, Silvio. *Beiträge zur Geschichte der englischen und chinesischen Anthroponomatik / Contributions to the History of English and Chinese Anthroponomastics*. Baar. [2001] pp. 60. €30.50 pb ISBN 3 9355 3601 1.

Bresnan, Joan. *Lexical-Functional Syntax*. Blackwell Textbooks in Linguistics 16. Blackwell. [2001] pp. ix + 446. hb $73.95 ISBN 0 6312 0973 5, pb $41.95 ISBN 0 6312 0974 3.

Brinton, Laurel J., ed. *Historical Linguistics 1999: Selected Papers from the 14th International Conference on Historical Linguistics, Vancouver, 9–13 August 1999*. CILT 215. Benjamins. [2001] pp. xii + 389. €115 ISBN 9 0272 3722 0.

Burns, Anne, Caroline Coffin, eds. *Analysing English in a Global Context: A Reader*. Routledge. [2001] pp. xii + 276. hb €65 ISBN 0 4152 4115 4, pb €18.99 ISBN 0 4152 4116 2

Butler, Chris, and Malcolm Lyne. *The Roman Pottery Production Site at Wickham Barn, Chiltington, East Sussex*. BAR British Series 323. Archaeopress. [2001] pp. vi + 98. pb £22 ISBN 1 8417 1242 6.

Bybee, Joan, and Paul Hopper, eds. *Frequency and the Emergence of Linguistic Structure*. TSLang 45. Benjamins. [2001] pp. vii + 492. hb €124.79 ISBN 9 0272 2947 3, pb €43.11 ISBN 9 0272 2948 1.

Cameron, Deborah. *Working with Spoken Discourse*. Sage. [2001] pp. 216. hb £60 ISBN 0 7619 5772 3, pb £17.99 ISBN 0 7619 5773 1.

Cameron, Kenneth, in collaboration with John Field and John Insley. *The Place-Names of Lincolnshire*, pt. 6: *The Wapentakes of Manley and Aslacoe*. EPNS 77. [2001] pp. xviii + 228. £30 ISBN 0 9048 8962 9.

Celce-Murcia, Marianne, and Elite Olshtain. *Discourse and Context in Language Teaching: A Guide for Language Teachers*. CUP. [2000] pp. 288. hb £47.30 ISBN 0 5216 4055 5, pb £17.80 ISBN 0 5216 4837 8.

Chaudenson, Robert. Salikoko S. Mufwene, rev. and trans. Sheri Pargman, Sabrina Billings, Michelle AuCoin, trans. *Creolization, Language and Culture*. Routledge. [2001] pp. xiii + 340. pb €19.99 ISBN 0 4151 4593 7.

Christie, Pauline, ed. *Due Respect: Papers on English and English-Related Creoles in the Caribbean in Honour of Professor Robert LePage*. UWI Jamaica. [2001] pp. xvi + 256. $20 ISBN 9 7664 0105 5.

Christie, Christine. *Gender and Language: Towards a Feminist Pragmatics*. EdinUP. [2000] pp. 224. pb £15.95 ISBN 0 7486 0935 0.

Cole, Peter, Gabriella Hermon, and C.-T. James Huang, eds. *Long-Distance Reflexives*. Syntax and Semantics 33. Academic. [2001] pp. xlvii + 378. £79.95 ISBN 0 1261 3533 9.

Cook, Guy, *The Discourse of Advertising*, 2nd edn. Routledge. [2001] pp. xii + 256. hb £55 ISBN 0 4152 3454 9, pb £16.99 ISBN 0 4152 3455 7.

Cornbleet, Sandra, and Ronald Carter, *The Language of Speech and Writing*. Routledge. [2001] pp. x + 129. pb £9.99 ISBN 0 4152 3167 1.

Coulthard, Malcolm, Janet Cotterill, and Frances Rock, eds. *Dialogue Analysis VII: Working with Dialogue. Selected Papers from the 7th IADA Conference, Birmingham 1999*. Beiträge zur Dialogforschung 22. Niemeyer. [2000] pp. ix + 443. pb $106 ISBN 3 4847 5022 7.

Coupland, Nikolas, Srikant Sarangi, Christopher N. Candlin, eds. *Sociolinguistics and Social Theory*. Pearson Education. [2001] pp. xvi + 399. pb $28.99 ISBN 0 5823 2783 0.

Coupland, Nikolas, Srikant Sarangi and Christopher N. Candlin, eds. *Sociolinguistics and Social Theory*. Longman. [2001] pp. 410 £18.99 ISBN 0 5823 2783 0.

Crystal, David. *Language and the Internet*. CUP. [2001] pp. ix + 272. £13.95 ISBN 0 5218 0212 1.

Culicover, Peter W., and Paul Postal, eds. *Parasitic Gaps*. Current Studies in Linguistics. MITP. [2001] pp. 496. $60 ISBN 0 2620 3284 8.

Culpeper, Jonathan, *Language and Characterisation: People in Plays and Other Texts*. Longman. [2001] pp. xvi + 328. pb £17.99 ISBN 0 5823 5753 5.

Cutting, Joan. *Analysing the Language of Discourse Communities*. Elsevier. [2000] pp. 192. €81 ISBN 0 0804 3893 8.

Dahl, Östen, ed. *Tense and Aspect in the Languages of Europe*. Empirical Approaches to Language Typology 20, EUROTYP 6. MGruyter. [2000] pp. xii + 846. €253 ISBN 3 1101 5752 7.

Dallison, Colin, and David Jennings. *Vanishing Hexham Street and Place Names*. Hexham Local History Society. [2001] pp. 15. pb £1.50 ISBN 0 9527 6152 1.

Davidson, Donald. *Inquiries into Truth and Interpretation*. OUP. [2001] pp. xxiii + 296. hb £30 ISBN 0 1992 4628 9, pb £14.99 ISBN 0 1992 4628 9.

Davis, Anthony R. *Linking by Types in the Hierarchical Lexicon*. CSLI. [2001] pp. viii + 312. $22.95 ISBN 1 5758 6224 7.

Declerck, Renaat, and Susan Reed. *Conditionals: A Comprehensive Empirical Analysis.* Topics in English Linguistics 37. MGruyter. [2001] pp. xviii + 536. €91.59 ISBN 3 1101 7144 9.

DeGraff, Michel, ed. *Language Creation and Language Change: Creolization, Diachrony, and Development.* [1999 hb, 2001 pb] MIT. pp. x + 573. $42 ISBN 0 2620 4168 5.

Diller, Hans-Jürgen, and Manfred Görlach, eds. *Towards a History of English as a History of Genres.* AF 298. Winter. [2001] pp. x + 230. pb €36 ISBN 3 8253 1240 2.

Duranti, Allesandro, ed. *Key Terms in Language and Culture.* Blackwell. [2001] pp. 504. £50 ISBN 0 6312 2665 6

Duranti, Allesandro, ed. *Linguistic Anthropology.* Blackwell. [2001] pp. 504. £60 ISBN 0 6312 2110 7.

Ehrlich, Susan, *Representing Rape: Language and Sexual Consent.* Routledge. [2001] pp. x + 174. hb £55 ISBN 0 4152 0521 2, pb £16.99 ISBN 0 4152 0522 0.

Ewen, Colin J., and Harry van der Hulst. *The Phonological Structure of Words. An Introduction.* Cambridge Textbooks in Linguistics. CUP. [2001] pp. xiii + 274. pb £15.95 ISBN 0 5213 5914 7.

Faarlund, Jan Terje, ed. *Grammatical Relations in Change.* Studies in Language Companion Series 56. Benjamins. [2001] pp. viii + 326. €110 ISBN 9 0272 3058 7.

Falk, Yehuda N. *Lexical-Functional Grammar: An Introduction to Parallel Constraint-Based Syntax.* Lecture Notes 126. CSLI. [2001] pp. xv + 237. pb $22 ISBN 1 5758 6340 5.

Fennell, Barbara A. *A History of English: A Sociolinguistic Approach.* Textbooks in Linguistics 17. Blackwell. [2001] pp. xi + 284. hb £55 ISBN 0 6312 0072 X, pb £16.99 ISBN 0 6312 0073 8.

Filip, Hana. *Aspect, Eventuality Types, and Nominal Reference.* Outstanding Dissertations in Linguistics. Garland. [1999] pp. ix + 312. £45 ISBN 0 8153 3271 8.

Fisiak, Jacek, and Peter Trudgill, eds. *East Anglian English.* Brewer. [2001] pp. xii + 264. pb £55 ISBN 0 8599 1571 9.

Fox, Harold. *The Evolution of the Fishing Village: Landscape and Society along the South Devon Coast, 1086–1550.* Leopard's Head. [2001] pp. 236. £13.50 ISBN 0 9049 2043 7.

Gardner, Rod. *When Listeners Talk: Response Tokens and Listener Stance.* Pragmatics and Beyond ns 92. Benjamins. [2001] pp. xxii + 281. €98 ($98) ISBN 9 0272 5111 8 (Eur.), ISBN 1 5881 1093 1 (US).

Gaskin, Richard, ed. *Grammar in Early Twentieth-Century Philosophy.* Routledge. [2001] pp. 272. £60 ISBN 0 4152 2446 2.

Gelling, Margaret, in collaboration with H.D.G. Foxall. *The Place-Names of Shropshire,* pt. 3: *Telford New Town, the Northern Part of Munslow Hundred and the Franchise of Wenlock.* EPNS 76. [2001] pp. xxiv + 299. £30 ISBN 0 9048 8960 2.

Ghadessy, Mohsen, Alex Henry, and Robert L. Roseberry, eds. *Small Corpus Studies and ELT: Theory and Practice.* Studies in Corpus Linguistics 5. Benjamins. [2001] pp. xxiii + 419. €125 ($114) ISBN 9 0272 2275 4 (Eur.), ISBN 1 5881 1035 4 (US).

Gibson, Keane. *Comfa Religion and Creole Language in a Caribbean Community.* SUNYP. [2001] pp. xvii + 244. pb $22.95 ISBN 0 7914 4960 2.

Gieszinger, Sabine. *The History of Advertising Language: The Advertisements in 'The Times' from 1788 to 1996.* Münchener Universitäts-Schriften 23. Lang. [2001] pp. xiv + 363. pb £33 ISBN 3 6313 7835 1.

Giles, Howard, and W. Peter Robinson, eds. *The New Handbook of Language and Social Psychology.* John Wiley. [2001] pp. 688. £105 ISBN 0 4714 9096 2.

Givón, Talmy. *Syntax: An Introduction*, vol. 1. Benjamins. [2001] pp. xvii + 500. pb €33 ISBN 9 0272 2578 8.

Givón, Talmy. *Syntax: An Introduction.* vol. 2. Benjamins. [2001] pp. x + 406. hb €79.87 ISBN 9 0272 2579 6, pb €27.23 ISBN 9 0272 2580 X.

Gómez-González, María Ángeles. *The Theme-Topic Interface: Evidence from English.* Pragmatics and Beyond, ns 71. Benjamins. [2001] pp. xxiv + 434. €95 ISBN 9 0272 5086 3 (Eur.), ISBN 1 5561 9949 X (US).

Görlach, Manfred. *Eighteenth-Century English.* Sprachwissenschaftliche Studienbücher. Winter. [2001] pp. xvi + 392. pb €36 ISBN 3 8253 1072 8.

Gotti, Maurizio, and Marina Dossena, eds. *Modality in Specialized Texts.* Linguistic Insights 1. Lang. [2001] pp. 421. £38 ISBN 3 9067 6710 8.

Grabes, Herbert, ed. *Innovation and Continuity in English Studies: A Critical Jubilee.* University of Bamberg Studies in English Linguistics 44. Lang. [2001] pp. xix + 353. pb £30 ISBN 3 6313 8372 X.

Graham-Campbell, James, Richard Hall, Judith Jesch, and David N. Parsons, eds. *Vikings and the Danelaw: Select Papers from the Proceedings of the Thirteenth Viking Congress, Nottingham and York, 21–30 August 1997.* Oxbow. [2001] pp. xiii + 368. £40 ISBN 1 8421 7047 3.

Gramley, Stephan. *The Vocabulary of World English.* Arnold. [2001]. pp. 310. £17.99 ISBN 0 3407 4072 8.

Gramley, Stephan. *The Vocabulary of World English.* Arnold. [2001] pp. xiv + 323. hb £50 ISBN 0 3407 4071 X, pb £17.99 ISBN 0 3407 4072 8.

Hartmann, R.R.K. *Teaching and Researching Lexicography.* Longman. [2001] pp. xii + 211. pb £14.99 ISBN 0 5823 6977 0.

Hartmann, R.R.K., and Gregory James. *Dictionary of Lexicography.* Routledge. [2001] pp. xviii + 176. £19.99 ISBN 0 4151 4144 3.

Haspelmath, Martin, Ekkehard König, Wulf Oesterreicher and Wolfgang Raible, eds. *Language Typology and Universals: An International Handbook. Vol. 2.* MGruyter. [2001] pp. 1002. €398 ISBN 3 11 017154 6.

Hellinger, Marlis, Hadumod Bußmann, eds. *Gender Across Languages: The Linguistic Representation of Women and Men. Vol 1.* Benjamins. [2001] pp. xiv + 319. hb €83 ISBN 9 0272 1840 4, pb €33 ISBN 9 0272 1841 2.

Hellinger, M., and H. Bussmann, eds. *Gender Across Languages*, vol. 1. John Benjamins. [2001] ISBN 1 5881 1082 6.

Hendrickson, Robert. *World English: From Aloha to Zed.* Wiley. [2001] pp. 281. $24.95 ISBN 0 4713 4518 0.

Hoey, Michael. *Textual Interaction: An Introduction to Written Discourse Analysis.* Routledge. [2001] pp. xviii + 203. hb £65 ISBN 0 4152 3168 X, pb £18.99 ISBN 0 4152 3169 8.

Holmes, Janet. *Introduction to Sociolinguistics.* Longman. [2001] pp. 417. £19.99 ISBN 0 5823 2861 6.

Hornstein, Norbert. *Move! A Minimalist Theory of Construal*. Generative Syntax. Blackwell. [2001] pp. viii + 248. pb £19.99 ISBN 06312 2361 4.

Hymes, Dell. *Foundations in Sociolinguistics*. CUP. [repr. 2001] pp. 175. £14.95 ISBN 0 5213 1113 6.

Ifantidou, Elly. *Evidentials and Relevance*. Pragmatics and Beyond ns 86. Benjamins. [2001] pp. xxii + 225. €80 ($80) ISBN 9 0272 5105 3 (Eur.), ISBN 1 5881 1032 X (US).

Kadmon, Nirit. *Formal Pragmatics*. Blackwell. [2001] pp. ix + 430. hb £55 ISBN 0 6312 0120 3, pb £19.99 ISBN 0 6312 0121 1.

Kempson, Ruth, Wilfried Meyer-Viol, and Dov Gabbay. *Dynamic Syntax: The Flow of Language Understanding*. Blackwell. [2001] pp. xii + 348. hb £60 ISBN 0 6311 7612 8, pb £19.99 ISBN 0 6311 7613 6.

Kenesei, István, and Robert M. Harnish, eds. *Perspectives on Semantics, Pragmatics, and Discourse: A Festschrift for Ferenc Kiefer*. Pragmatics and Beyond, ns 90. Benjamins. [2001] pp. xxi + 348. €110 ISBN 9 0272 5109 6 (Eur.), ISBN 1 5881 1053 2 (US).

Kenstowicz, Michael, ed. *Ken Hale: A Life in Language*. MIT. [2001] pp. xi + 480. hb $75 ISBN 0 2621 1257 4, pb $30 ISBN 0 2626 1160 0.

Kristensson, Gillis. *A Survey of Middle English Dialects, 1290–1350. The Southern Counties*, vol. 1: *Vowels (except Diphthongs)*. LundU. [2001] pp. 141. pb £24.90 ISBN 9 1796 6586 1.

Kuteva, Tania. *Auxiliation: An Enquiry into the Nature of Grammaticalization*. OUP. [2001] pp. viii + 209. £45 ISBN 0 1982 9974 5.

Labov, William. *Principles of Linguistic Change*, vol. 2: *Social Factors*. Language in Society 29. Blackwell. [2001] pp. xviii + 572. pb. £19.99 ISBN 0 6311 7916 X.

Lanehart, Sonja L., ed. *Sociocultural and Historical Contexts of African American English*. Benjamins. [2001] pp. xviii + 373. hb €105 ISBN 9 0272 4885 0, pb €45 ISBN 9 0272 4886 9.

Lanehart, Sonja L., ed. *Sociocultural and Historical Contexts of African American English*. Benjamins. [2001] pp. 371. £39.95 ISBN 1 5881 1046 X.

Laverton, Sylvia. *Shotley Peninsula: The Making of a Unique Suffolk Landscape*. Tempus. [2001] pp. 160. pb £14.99 ($24.99) ISBN 0 7524 1937 4.

Lavoie, Lisa M. *Consonant Strength: Phonological Patterns and Phonetic Manifestations*. Outstanding Dissertations in Linguistics. Garland. [2001] pp. xix + 214. $70 ISBN 0 8153 4044 3.

Leech, Geoffrey, Benita Cruickshank, and Roz Ivanič. *An A–Z of English Grammar and Usage*, 2nd edn. Longman. [2001] pp. xv + 636. pb £12.99 ISBN 0 5824 0574 2.

Lombardi, Linda, ed. *Segmental Phonology in Optimality Theory. Constraints and Representations*. CUP. [2001] pp. vii + 300. £45 ISBN 0 5217 9057 3.

Mair, Christian, Marianne Hundt, eds. *Corpus Linguistics and Linguistic Theory: Papers from the 20th International Conference on English Language Research on Computerized Corpora, Freiburg im Breisgau 1999*. Rodopi. [2000] pp. vii + 395. €91 ($91) ISBN 9 0420 1493 8.

McCafferty, Kevin. *Ethnicity and Language Change: English in (London)Derry, Northern Ireland*. Benjamins. [2001] pp. 255. £50 ISBN 9 0272 1838 2.

McDonald, Ross. *Shakespeare and the Arts of Language*. OUP. [2001] pp. x + 211. hb £25 ISBN 0 1987 1170 0, pb £12.99 ISBN 0 1987 1171 9.

McEnery, Tony, and Andrew Wilson. *Corpus Linguistics*, 2nd edn. Edinburgh Textbooks in Empirical Linguistics. EdinUP. [2001] pp. x + 235. pb ££15.95 ISBN 0 7486 1165 7.

Merchant, Jason. *The Syntax of Silence: Sluicing, Islands, and the Theory of Ellipsis*. Oxford Studies in Theoretical Linguistics 1. OUP. [2001] pp. xiii + 262. hb £47.50 ISBN 0 1992 4373 5, pb £18.99 ISBN 0 1992 4372 7.

Meade, Rocky Ricardo. *The Acquisition of Jamaican Phonology*. Foris LOT. [2001] pp. xiii + 265. pb €18.20 ISBN 9 0769 1206 8.

Meshtrie, Rajend, ed. *Concise Encyclopedia of Sociolinguistics*. Elsevier. [2001] pp. xxviii + 1031. €237 ISBN 0 0804 3726 5.

Mesthrie, Rajend, ed. *Concise Encyclopaedia of Sociolinguistics*. Elsevier. [2001] $244 ISBN 0 8004 3726 5.

Metcalf, Alan. *How We Talk: American Regional English Today*. Houghton Mifflin. [2000] pp. 206. £8.73 ISBN 0 6180 4362 4.

Miller, Sean, ed. *Charters of the New Minster, Winchester*. Anglo-Saxon Charters IX. OUP for BA. [2001] pp. lxvii + 244. £45 ISBN 0 1972 6223 6.

Mills, A.D. *A Dictionary of London Place Names*. OUP. [2001] pp. lxiii + 276. pb £7.99 ISBN 0 1928 0106 6.

Mufwene, Salikoko S. *The Ecology of Language Evolution*. CUP. [2001] pp. xviii + 255. hb €40 ISBN 0 5217 9138 3, pb €14.95 ISBN 0 5217 9475 7.

Nelson, Gerald. *English: An Essential Grammar*. Routledge. [2001] pp. ix + 176. £45 ISBN 0 4152 2449 7.

Nero, Shondel J. *Englishes in Contact: Anglophone Caribbean Students in an Urban College*. Hampton Press. [2001] pp. 171. $19.95 ISBN 1 5727 3325 X.

Newman, Paul, and Martha Ratliff, eds. *Linguistic Fieldwork*. CUP. [2001] pp. 300. £45 ISBN 0 5216 6049 1.

Norvin Richards. *Movement in Language: Interactions and Architectures*. OUP. [2001] pp. xii + 326. pb £22.99 ISBN 0 1992 4651 3.

NuytsJan, . *Epistemic Modality, Language, and Conceptualization: A Cognitive Pragmatic Perspective*. Human Cognitive Processing 5. Benjamins. [2001] pp. xix + 428. €110 ISBN 9 0272 2357 2 (Eur.), ISBN 1 5561 9983 X (US).

Palmer, Frank R. *Mood and Modality*, 2nd edn. Cambridge Textbooks in Linguistics. CUP. [2001] pp. xxi + 236. hb £45 ($64.95) ISBN 0 5218 0035 8, pb £15.95 ($22.95) ISBN 0 5218 0479 5.

Parsons, David N., and Patrick Sims-Williams, eds. *Ptolemy: Towards a Linguistic Atlas of the Earliest Celtic Place-Names of Europe*. CMCS. [2000] pp. ix + 188. pb £12 ISBN 0 9527 4783 9.

Pollard, Velma. *Dread Talk: The Language of Rastafari*. UWI Press. [2000] pp. xv + 117. JA$700 ISBN 9 7681 2568 3.

Poplack, Shana, and Sali Tagliamonte. *African American English in the Diaspora*. Blackwell. [2001] pp. xx + 293. pb £16.99 ISBN 0 6312 1266 3.

Pridham, Francesca. *The Language of Conversation*. Routledge. [2001] pp. x + 96. pb £9.99 ISBN 0 4152 2964 2.

Pütz, Martin, Susanne Niemeier and René Dirven, eds. *Applied Cognitive Linguistics II: Language Pedagogy*. MGruyter. [2001] pp. xxv + 263. € 84 ISBN 3 1101 7222 4.

Robinson, W. Peter, and Howard Giles, eds. *The New Handbook of Language and Social Psychology*. Wiley. [2001] pp. xx + 668. £95 ISBN 0 4714 9096 2.

Rose, Kenneth R., and Gabriele Kasper, eds. *Pragmatics in Language Teaching.* Cambridge Applied Linguistics. CUP. [2001] pp. 380. hb £41.20 ISBN 0 5218 0379 9, pb £16.40 ISBN 0 5210 0858 1.

Russell, Shirley. *Grammar, Structure, and Style: A Practical Guide to Advanced Level English Language*, rev. edn. OUP. [2001] pp. 284. pb £11.50 ISBN 0 1983 1478 7.

Sanger, Keith. *The Language of Drama.* Routledge. [2001] pp. xiv + 97. pb £9.99 ISBN 0 4152 1423 8.

Sarangi, Srikant, and Malcolm Coulthard, eds. *Discourse and Social Life.* Longman. [2000] pp. 344. pb £19.99 ISBN 0 5824 0468 1.

Schendl, Herbert. *Historical Linguistics.* OUP. [2001] pp. 144. £7.90 ISBN 0 1943 7238 3.

Schiffrin, Deborah, Deborah Tannen, and Heidi E. Hamilton, eds. *The Handbook of Discourse Analysis.* Blackwell Handbooks in Linguistics. Blackwell. [2001] pp. 872. £85 ISBN 0 6312 0595 0.

Schönefeld, Doris. *Where Lexicon and Syntax Meet.* Trends in Linguistics 135. Mouton. [2001] pp. vi + 332. €88 ISBN 3 1101 7048 5.

Sheenan, Thomas W. *Dictionary of Patron Saints' Names.* Our Sunday Visitor Publishing Division. [2001] pp. 595. pb $19.95 ISBN 0 8797 3539 2.

Shepheard, John. *English Grammar.* Teach Yourself. H&S. [2001] pp. xiv + 300. pb $11.95 ISBN 0 3407 8019 3.

Shortis, Tim. *The Language of ICT: Information and Communication Technology.* Routledge. [2001] pp. xii + 116. pb £9.99 ISBN 0 4152 2275 3.

Singleton, David. *Language and the Lexicon: An Introduction.* Arnold. [2001] pp. xii + 244. hb £40 ISBN 0 3407 3173 7, pb £14.99 ISBN 0 3407 3174 5.

Smith, Norval, Tonjes Veenstra, eds. *Creolization and Contact.* CLL 23. Benjamins. [2001] pp. vi + 323. €110 ISBN 9 0272 5245 9.

Stockwell, Robert, and Donka Minkova. *English Words: History and Structure.* CUP. [2001] pp. xi + 208. hb £37.50 ISBN 0 5217 9012 3, pb £13.95 ISBN 0 5217 9362 9.

Stump, Gregory T. *Inflectional Morphology: A Theory of Paradigm Structure.* Cambridge Studies in Linguistics 93. CUP. [2001] pp. xvi + 308. £45 ($64.95) ISBN 0 5217 8047 0.

Taavitsainen, Irma, Terttu Nevalainen, Päivi Pahta, and Matti Rissanen. *Placing Middle English in Context.* Topics in English Linguistics 35. Mouton. [2001] pp. x + 518. €128 ISBN 3 1101 6780 8.

Thomason, Sarah. *Language Contact: An Introduction.* EdinUP. [2001] pp. x + 310. pb €16.95 ISBN 0 7486 0719 6.

Tognini-Bonelli, Elena. *Corpus Linguistics at Work.* Studies in Corpus Linguistics 6. Benjamins. [2001] pp. xi + 223. €56.72 ISBN 9 0272 2276 2.

Tomasello, Michael, and Elizabeth Bates, eds. *Language Development: The Essential Readings.* Essential Readings in Developmental Psychology. Blackwell. [2001] pp. viii + 375. hb £60 ISBN 0 6312 1744 4, pb £17.99 ISBN 0 6312 1745 2.

Tono, Yukio. *Research on Dictionary Use in the Context of Foreign Language Learning.* Niemeyer. [2001] pp. xii + 257. €68 ISBN 3 4843 9106 5.

Toolan, Michael. *Narrative: A Critical Linguistic Introduction*, 2nd edn. Routledge. [2001] pp. xii + 260. hb £60 ISBN 0 4152 3174 4, pb £16.99 ISBN 0 4152 3175 2.

Trudgill, Peter. *Sociolinguistic Variation and Change*. EdinUP. [2001] pp. 224 £16.99 ISBN 0 7486 1515 6.

Tzanne, Angeliki. *Talking at Cross-Purposes: The Dynamics of Miscommunication*. Pragmatics & Beyond ns 62. Benjamins. [2000] pp. xiv + 263. €95 ($95) ISBN 9 0272 5076 6 (Eur.), ISBN 1 5561 9940 6 (US).

Van Valin, Robert D. Jr. *An Introduction to Syntax*. CUP. [2001] pp. xvi + 239. hb £40 ($59.95) ISBN 0 5216 3199 8, pb £14.95 ($22.95) ISBN 0 5216 3566 7.

Wales, Katie. *A Dictionary of Stylistics*. Longman. [2001] pp. viii + 429. pb £22.99 ISBN 0 5823 1737 1.

Walsh, Clare. *Gender and Discourse: Language and Power in Politics, the Church and Organisations*. Real Language Series. Longman. [2001] pp. 256. pb £17.99 ISBN 0 5824 1892 5.

Weigand, Edda, and Marcelo Dascal, eds. *Negotiation and Power in Dialogic Interaction*. Benjamins. [2001] pp. viii + 303. €95 ($95) ISBN 9 0272 3721 2 (Eur.), ISBN 1 5881 1047 8 (US).

Wennerstrom, Ann. *The Music of Everyday Speech: Prosody and Discourse Analysis*. OUPAm. [2001] pp. 338. hb £50 ISBN 0 1951 4321 3, pb £20 ISBN 0 1951 4322 1.

Wetherell, Margaret, Stephanie Taylor, and Simeon J. Yates. *Discourse as Data: A Guide for Analysis*. Sage. [2001] pp. 344. hb £55 ISBN 0 7619 7157 2, pb £17.99 ISBN 0 7619 7158 0.

Wetherell, Margaret, Stephanie Taylor, and Simeon J. Yates. *Discourse Theory and Practice: A Reader*. Sage. [2001] pp. 416. hb £60 ISBN 0 7619 7155 6, pb £19.99 ISBN 0 7619 7156 4.

Wolf, Hans-Georg. *English in Cameroon*. CSL 85. MGruyter. [2001] pp. viii + 359. €84 ISBN 3 1101 7053 1.

Wood, Linda A., and Rolf O. Kroger. *Doing Discourse Analysis: Methods for Studying Action in Talk and Text*. Sage. [2000] pp. 256. hb £62 ISBN 0 8039 7350 0, pb £23 ISBN 0 8039 7351 9.

II

Old English Literature

STACY S. KLEIN AND MARY SWAN

This chapter has ten sections: 1. Bibliography; 2. Manuscript Studies, Palaeography and Facsimiles; 3. Social, Cultural and Intellectual Background; 4. Literature: general; 5. The Exeter Book; 6. The Poems of the Vercelli Book; 7. The Junius Manuscript; 8. The *Beowulf* Manuscript; 9. Other Poems; 10. Prose. Sections 1, 2, 3 and 10 are by Mary Swan; sections 4 and 5–9 are by Stacy S. Klein.

1. Bibliography

The *Old English Newsletter* 34:iii[Spring 2001] includes conference news; a report on a new, funded, project, 'Investigating Eleventh-Century English', at the Centre for Anglo-Saxon Studies, University of Manchester; and notes on some new essay collections. The sixteenth progress report of the Fontes Anglo-Saxonici project (*OENews* 34:iii[2001] 7–9) is contributed by Peter Jackson, and the second annual report on the Anglo-Saxon Plant Name Survey by C.P. Biggam is included (*OENews* 34:iii[2001] 9–11). A group of scholars from the University of Malaga describe 'CALLOE: A Pedagogical Tool for the Learning of Old English' (*OENews* 34:iii[2001] 12–20). This volume also contains Abstracts of Papers in Anglo-Saxon Studies. Volume 34:iv[Summer 2001] contains the Old English Bibliography for 2000 and the Research in Progress listings. Volume 35:i[Fall 2001] includes notes on forthcoming conferences, reports on the *Dictionary of Old English*, the Friends of the *DOE* Fundraising Campaign, the 2001 International Society of Anglo-Saxonists Conference at Helsinki, and the 2001 National Endowment of the Humanities Summer Seminar at the British Library. The following articles are also included: '*Circolwyrde 2001*: New Electronic Resources for Anglo-Saxon Studies' by Martin K. Foys (*OENews* 35:i[2001] 20–3), 'Standard Old English and the Study of English in the Eleventh Century' by Donald Scragg (*OENews* 35:i[2001] 24–6), which is a description of the funded project announced in volume 34:iii; 'The Evidence of the Copy' by Karen Thompson (*OENews* 35:i[2001] 27–33), which focuses on 'association copies'—copies of printed editions or studies of Anglo-Saxon texts with significant annotations by early modern scholars—describes eight such books, and makes a case for the importance of a permanent catalogue record of them; and 'Michael Crichton, Ibn Fadlan, Fantasy Cinema: *Beowulf* at the Movies' by Hugh Magennis (*OENews* 35:i[2001] 34–8).

Anglo-Saxon England 30[2001] 247–314 contains the bibliography for 2000.

2. Manuscript Studies, Palaeography and Facsimiles

A major resource for Anglo-Saxon manuscript studies is published this year in the form of Helmut Gneuss's *Handlist of Anglo-Saxon Manuscripts*. This is the final version of the work whose early stages were published as 'A Preliminary List of Manuscripts Written or Owned in England up to 1100' (*ASE* 9[1981]). The book lists 947 manuscripts, summarizing their contents and giving information on their date, origin and provenance. The volume's indices list authors and texts, and shorter Latin poems.

Another important resource for the study of Anglo-Saxon manuscripts is R.M. Thomson's *A Descriptive Catalogue of the Medieval Manuscripts in Worcester Cathedral Library*. Thomson's immensely thorough and scholarly cataloguing of this library gives Anglo-Saxonists their first clear insight into the extent of its pre- and early post-Conquest English holdings, which include three fragments from one of the three Pandects ordered by Ceolfrith of Wearmouth-Jarrow (BL Add. 37777, 45025 and Loan 81), which might have been given to Worcester by King Offa of Mercia in 780. At least twenty-three books in Old English also survive from the library, which makes it a particularly interesting site for students of Old English textual production.

Three volumes of the Anglo-Saxon Manuscripts in Microfiche Facsimile series are reviewed this year. The first, *Anglo-Saxon Gospels* (volume 3), with descriptions by Roy M. Liuzza and A.N. Doane, was published in 1995 but not reviewed in *YWES*. It includes manuscripts BL Cotton Nero D.iv; Otho C.I, v.1 + B.x, f.51; Royal 1 A.xiv; Bodleian Auct. D.2.19; Bodl. 441; Eng. bib. c.2; and Hatton 38. The accompanying booklet includes full codicological descriptions of each manuscript, and notes on its history and contents. *Latin Manuscripts with Anglo-Saxon Glosses* (volume 5), with descriptions by Peter J. Lucas, A.N. Doane and I.C. Cunningham, was published in 1997, and includes ten manuscripts. *Deluxe and Illustrated Manuscripts Containing Technical and Literary Texts* (volume 9 [2001]), with descriptions by A.N. Doane and Tiffany J. Grade, also includes ten manuscripts.

Early Anglo-Saxon illuminated manuscripts are the subject of new work this year. The Early English Manuscripts in Facsimile series issues the first part of its twenty-eighth volume, the splendid *The Codex Aureus: An Eighth-Century Gospel Book*, edited by Richard Gameson. The high-quality full-colour facsimile of the gospel of Matthew in manuscript Stockholm, Royal Library A. 135 is preceded by a thorough and detailed analysis of the manuscript's date, origin, text, dimensions, structure and preparation, script, artwork, and history. In all, this volume provides scholars with an important scholarly study of the manuscript and, in the form of the facsimile, accessible images to prompt further work. The second and final part of this facsimile, containing the gospels of Mark, Luke and John, is to be published soon.

New work on the Book of Cerne and its connections is published this year in David Howlett's examination of 'Hiberno-Latin Syllabic Poems in the Book of Cerne' (*Peritia* 15[2001] 1–21), which reconstructs the text of these poems and argues that they were composed in seventh-century Ireland by several poets, or by Irish- or Welsh-speaking poets. Howlett notes that Æthelwald of Lindisfarne, whom he believes to be the compiler of the Book of Cerne, is 'a direct inheritor of seventh-century Irish literary traditions' (p. 21).

Catherine E. Karkov examines 'Broken Bodies and Singing Tongues: Gender and Voice in the Cambridge, Corpus Christi College 23 *Psychomachia*' (*ASE* 30[2001] 115–36), and in particular the way in which the texts of the *Psychomachia* and the *Peristephanon* relate to each other, how the reading of both texts is affected by their presence side by side in Corpus 23, and the reader's relationship to the texts. Karkov analyses the texts and illustrations, focuses on the gendering of violence in both, and suggests that 'the absence of a female audience, the nature of the imagery, and the fact that the illustrated manuscript appears only in the wake of the Benedictine Reform, suggest that we might relate the production of the manuscripts to the curtailing of female power within the church' (p. 136).

Rediscovered Anglo-Saxon manuscript fragments from an eleventh-century mass lectionary manuscript believed to have been written by the scribe Eadwig Basan are described by Rebecca Rushworth in 'The Prodigal Fragment: Cambridge, Gonville and Caius College 734/782a' (*ASE* 30[2001] 137–44). Rushworth describes the fragments, the script and the text, concludes that the scribe may not be Eadwig Basan, and stresses the significance of the fragments as a rare example of an Anglo-Saxon mass lectionary.

3. Social, Cultural and Intellectual Background

From *YWES* 81 onwards, publications on pre-Conquest Anglo-Latin prose are being reviewed in the 'Prose' section along with Old English prose.

Mark A. Handley investigates the religious context of Britain in the period immediately before and after the Anglo-Saxon arrival, in 'The Origins of Christian Commemoration in Late Antique Britain' (*EMedE* 10[2001] 177–99), through a consideration of the approximately 250 Christian inscriptions in western Britain dating from before *c.* ad 700. Handley argues against the common belief that these inscriptions are the result of contact with Gaul, and proposes instead connections with widespread epigraphic practice in late antiquity in places including Spain, Italy and North Africa. He also makes a case for an earliest date of the late fourth century, rather than 420–40 as usually given, and suggests in conclusion that fourth- and fifth-century Britain was more Christian than is generally thought.

The religious culture of early Anglo-Saxon England is the subject of two essays in Thompson, ed., *Monasteries and Society in Medieval Britain* (published in 1999 but not previously reviewed in *YWES*), the proceedings of the 1994 Harlaxton Symposium. Sarah Foot's 'The Role of the Minster in Earlier Anglo-Saxon Society' (pp. 35–58) examines the Anglo-Saxon Church and its relation to the secular world, religious families, the founding of minsters, minsters as central places, and the spiritual role of the minster. Foot compares minster families with secular ones, and notes that 'the relationship between aristocracy and monasticism is crucial to our understanding of the nature of the early Anglo-Saxon church' (pp. 57–8). David Rollason's focus is on 'Monasteries and Society in Early Medieval Northumbria' (pp. 59–74). He summarizes the 'minster hypothesis'—the idea that monasteries exercised pastoral functions like other sorts of churches—and then considers whether it can be shown to apply to Northumbria. He finds little supporting evidence for a network of minster parishes in texts from Anglo-Saxon Northumbria, and suggests that, in the case of some important later medieval churches, the apparent evidence for their status as pre-Viking minsters is in fact evidence of their later importance, and argues for a more complex and drawn-out process of the development of church structure.

A second edition of Knowles, Brooke, and London, eds., *The Heads of Religious Houses England and Wales. I: 940–1216*, with new material by C.N.L. Brooke, is published this year. Corrigenda and addenda are indicated with an asterisk in the pages reproducing the first edition, which itself is printed here with minor corrections, and an additional bibliography is also included.

Anglo-Saxon England in a European context is given some attention this year. McKitterick, ed., *The Early Middle Ages: Europe 400–1000*, includes discussion of things Anglo-Saxon in several sections, including the introduction and the chapter on 'Politics', both by McKitterick, and chapters on 'Society' by Chris Wickham, 'The Economy' by Jean-Pierre Devroey, 'Religion' by Mayke de Jong, 'Culture' by Ian Wood, and 'Europe and the Wider World' by Jonathan Shepard. The volume also contains useful suggestions for further reading and chronologies and maps. Ian Wood's *The Missionary Life: Saints and the Evangelisation of Europe, 400–1050* contains much of relevance to Anglo-Saxon literary culture in terms of its Continental ecclesiastical connections. Part 2 of Wood's study, 'The Anglo-Saxons and their Legacy', discusses Boniface, Mainz and Fulda, Alcuin and Echternach, Utrecht and Münster, and Hamburg and Bremen, and includes analysis of a range of hagiographical texts to investigate how Anglo-Saxon missionaries saw their own work and what effect they had on the communities in which they operated.

The political context of Anglo-Saxon literature is, as usual, the subject of much new work. Higham and Hill, eds., *Edward the Elder, 899–924*, is a collection of essays which were originally given as papers at a 1999 conference at the Manchester Centre for Anglo-Saxon Studies to mark the eleventh centenary of Edward's accession. The collection constitutes a very valuable grouping of textual, historical, archaeological and art-historical scholarship. It contains 'Edward the Elder's Reputation: An Introduction' by Nick Higham; 'What is Not Known about the Reign of Edward the Elder' by James Campbell; 'Edward as Ætheling' by Barbara Yorke; 'Edward, King of the Anglo-Saxons' by Simon Keynes; 'The Coinage of Edward the Elder' by Stewart Lyon; 'The West Saxon Tradition of Dynastic Marriage: With Special Reference to Edward the Elder' by Sheila Sharpe; 'View from the West: An Irish Perspective on West Saxon Dynastic Practice' by Alex Woolf; 'Gloucester and the New Minster of St Oswald' by Carolyn Heighway; 'Ælfwynn, Second Lady of the Mercians' by Maggie Bailey; 'Edward the Elder's Danelaw' by Lesley Abrams; 'The Shiring of Mercia—Again' by David Hill; 'Edward the Elder and the Re-establishment of Chester' by Simon Ward; 'The North-West Frontier' by David Griffiths; 'A Kingdom Too Far: York in the Early Tenth Century' by Richard Hall; 'The (Non)submission of the Northern Kings in 920' by Michael R. Davidson; 'The Northern Hoards: From Cuerdale to Bossall/ Flaxton' by James Graham-Campbell; 'Edward the Elder and the Churches of Winchester and Wessex' by Alexander R. Rumble; 'Dynastic Monasteries and Family Cults: Edward the Elder's Sainted Kindred' by Alan Thacker; '*On þa wæpnedhealfe*: Kingship and Royal Property from Æthelwulf to Edward the Elder' by Patrick Wormald; 'The Junius Psalter Gloss: Tradition and Innovation' by Mechtild Gretsch; 'The Embroideries from the Tomb of St Cuthbert' by Elizabeth Coatsworth; and 'Endpiece' by Nick Higham.

One event—the alleged submission by Welsh, Scottish and Scandinavian rulers to Edgar at Chester in 973—generates two articles this year. David E. Thornton's 'Edgar and the Eight Kings, AD 973: *Textus et Dramatis Personae*' (*EMedE* 10[2001] 49–79) edits and analyses the relevant sections of texts recording this event, argues that the episode in which the other rulers row Edgar up and down the Dee is a post-Conquest addition, and raises the possibility that the Chester meeting was a peace summit. Julia Barrow responds to Thornton in 'Chester's Earliest Regatta? Edgar's Dee-Rowing Revisited' (*EMedE* 10[2001] 81–93), and proposes that the event in question was an egalitarian ritual for making peace treaties. To support this interpretation, Barrow traces classical Carolingian and Ottonian parallels, and highlights the particular political imperatives of the Benedictine Reform and post-Conquest periods, which might have encouraged this sort of portrayal of Edgar.

Anglo-Norse culture, literary and otherwise, receives more attention this year, in the form of one collection of essays and one separate article. Graham-Campbell, Hall, Jesch and Parsons, eds., *Vikings and the Danelaw: Select Papers from the Proceedings of the Thirteenth Viking Congress, Nottingham and York, 21–30 August 1997*, is a rich source of new work on the topic. It contains the following contributions: 'Defining the Danelaw' by Katherine Holman; 'In Search of the Vikings: The Problems and the Possibilities of Interdisciplinary Approaches' by D.M. Hadley; 'The Conversion of the Danelaw' by Lesley Abrams; 'Repton and the "great heathen army", 873–4' by Martin Biddle and Birthe Kjølbye-Biddle; 'Boundaries and Cult Centres: Viking Burial in Derbyshire' by Julian D. Richards; 'Pagan Scandinavian Burial in the Central and Southern Danelaw' by James Graham-Campbell; 'Expansion and Control: Aspects of Anglo-Scandinavian Minting South of the Humber' by Mark Blackburn; 'Anglo-Scandinavian Urban Development in the East Midlands' by Richard Hall; 'Lincoln in the Viking Age' by Alan Vince; 'New Light on the Viking Presence in Lincolnshire: The Artefactual Evidence' by Kevin Leahy and Caroline Patterson; 'The Strange Beast that is the English Urnes Style' by Olwyn Owen; 'Five Towns Funerals: Decoding Diversity in Danelaw Stone Sculpture' by David Stocker and Paul Everson; 'The Southwell Lintel, its Style and Significance' by Philip Dixon, Olwyn Owen and David Stocker; 'Finding the Vikings: The Search for Anglo-Scandinavian Rural Settlement in the Northern Danelaw' by Julian D. Richards; 'In the Steps of the Vikings' by Gillian Fellows-Jensen; 'Scandinavian Elements in English Place-Names: Some Semantic Problems' by Tania Styles; 'How Long Did the Scandinavian Language Survive in England? Again' by David N. Parsons; 'Scaldic Verse in Scandinavian England' by Judith Jesch; 'Eddic Poetry in Anglo-Scandinavian Northern England' by John McKinnell; 'Representations of the Danelaw in Middle English Literature' by Thorlac Turville-Petre; and 'Hereward, the Danelaw and the Victorians' by Andrew Wawn. Matthew Townend offers a further insight into late Anglo-Norse courtly poetic culture in 'Contextualizing the *Knútsdrápur*: Skaldic Praise-Poetry at the Court of Cnut' (*ASE* 30[2001] 145–79). Through a close discussion of the relevant texts, Townend shows them to come from an Anglo-Norse milieu rather than a wholly Scandinavian one, posits 'a thriving Scandinavian culture at the higher levels of court society' (p. 174) in Cnut's Winchester, and makes a convincing case for the Old Norse poems as 'just as much a part of Anglo-Saxon England's literary history as, say, Latin works composed at the time' (pp. 178–9).

A comprehensive study of one Anglo-Saxon kingdom is offered in Brown and Farr, eds., *Mercia: An Anglo-Saxon Kingdom in Europe*. The collection is divided into five parts, and opens with an introduction by Brown and Farr. Part 1, 'The Mercian Polity: Church and State', contains the following essays: 'The Origins of Mercia' by Barbara Yorke; 'The Tribal Hidage and the Ealdormen of Mercia' by Peter Featherstone; 'Political Women in Mercia, Eighth to Early Tenth Centuries' by Pauline Stafford; 'The Mercian Church: Archaeology and Topography' by David Parsons; and 'Hagiography and Literature: The Case of Guthlac of Crowland' by Jane Roberts. Part 2, 'Parallel Cultures', contains 'Wales and Mercia, 613–918' by T.M. Charles-Edwards; 'The Verturian Hegemony: A Mirror in the North' by Alex Woolf; 'Abbesses, Minor Dynasties and Kings *in clericatu*: Perspectives of Ireland, 700–850' by Edel Bhreathnach; and 'Carolingian Contacts' by Janet L. Nelson. Part 3, 'The Material Culture of Mercia', contains 'The Archaeology of Mercia' by Martin Welch; 'Mercia: Landscape and Environment' by Della Hooke; 'Mercians: The Dwellers on the Boundary' by David Hill; 'The Growth of Market Centres and Towns in the Area of the Mercian Hegemony' by Alan Vince; 'Mercian London' by Robert Cowie; and 'Mercian Coinage and Authority' by Gareth Williams. Part 4, 'The Visual Culture of Mercia', contains 'Constructing Iconographies: Questions of Identity in Mercian Sculpture' by Jane Hawkes; 'Classicism of Southumbrian Sculpture' by Richard Jewell; 'Metalwork of the Mercian Supremacy' by Leslie Webster; and 'Mercian Manuscripts? The "Tiberius" Group and its Historical Context' by Michelle P. Brown. Part 5, 'Mercia in Retreat', contains 'Military Institutions and Royal Power' by Gareth Williams, and 'Mercia and Wessex in the Ninth Century' by Simon Keynes.

Two new volumes in the extremely useful Anglo-Saxon charters project are published this year. S.E. Kelly's *Charters of Abingdon Abbey*, parts 1 and 2, forms volume 8 of the series. Part 1 of this set discusses the abbey, its archive, the manuscripts and their authenticity, and endowments, and edits charters 1–50. Part 2 edits charters 51–151 and closes with appendices, including lists of lost charters and detached bonds, and indices. Sean Miller edits *Charters of New Minster, Winchester*, in volume 9 of the series. The introductory section of the volume includes discussion of the history of New Minster Winchester and its archive, the *Liber Abbatiae* and its sources, the authenticity of the charters, and the endowment of the New Minster. Editorial notes, a list of charters and a concordance are provided before the edition of the charters, which includes extensive and useful comments. The appendix to the volume gives Middle English and Latin translations in the *Liber Abbatiae*, and the volume closes with indices, a Latin glossary, and a Diplomatic Index.

Andrew Wareham examines 'The Transformation of Kinship and the Family in Late Anglo-Saxon England' (*EMedE* 10[2001] 375–99) by tracing the early stages of the family as a small unit in which descent runs almost exclusively through the male line. He suggests that this might be connected to links between aristocratic and monastic practices, and examines late Anglo-Saxon wills to show how the 'model for the lay family's behaviour arose from monastic concerns' (p. 399).

Nicholas Howe's Toller Lecture [1999] was published last year as 'An Angle on this Earth: Sense of Place in Anglo-Saxon England' (*BJRL* 82[2000] 3–27). Howe investigates 'how England was written as a place' (p. 9) by tracing early medieval etymologies of 'Angle', including Bede's, and examining texts by Gildas and Ælfric, the *Marvels of the East*, and the Anglo-Saxon world map in manuscript BL Cotton Tiberius B.v. His exploration of this particular cultural geography concludes with a reminder that 'memory survives in place' (p. 27).

Anglo-Saxon overseas settlement is the subject of Vera Orschel's 'Mag nEó Sacsan: An English Colony in Ireland in the Seventh and Eighth Centuries' (*Peritia* 15[2001] 81–107). The colony in question is the Anglo-Saxon monastery of Mag nEó in Connacht, which was founded in the early 670s as a result of the Synod of Whitby. Orschel examines the motivation behind this foundation, and the contacts it cultivated, with reference to Bede and Alcuin.

Carole Hough publishes another contribution to the study of Anglo-Saxon law this year in 'Two Kentish Laws Concerning Women: A New Reading of Æthelbert 73 and 74' (*Anglia* 119[2001] 554–78). Æthelbert 73 is usually read as referring to sexual or financial wrongdoing by a free woman, and 74 as a reference to compensation for injury to an unmarried girl. Hough re-evaluates these clauses and proposes that they are related, and that they concern physical assault committed by adult freeborn women and unmarried freeborn girls.

Andrew Breeze examines 'The Name of *Maelmin*, Near Yeavering' (*Archaeologia Aeliana* 29[2001] 31–2), which is referred to by Bede. Breeze summarizes the argument for this being a site two miles from Yeavering, and suggests a Celtic etymology for the name, which means that it translates as 'decayed (river-)bank, marshy edge' (p. 32). Carole Hough offers 'Place-Name Evidence for an Anglo-Saxon Animal Name: OE *pohha/*pocca* "Fallow Deer"' (*ASE* 30[2001] 1–14), and counters the suggestion that place-name use of this element may derive from OE *pohha, pocca* 'pouch, bag'. Hough shows that, in fact, this meaning of the word may be associated with OE *pocc* 'spot', and may be a reference to a fallow deer, and probably a male one.

R.I. Page's 'The Provenance of the Lancashire Runic Ring' (*N&Q* 48[2001] 217–19) examines the seventeenth- and eighteenth-century evidence for the find-site and shows that the apparent Manchester location is not certain.

Passing reference to Anglo-Saxon textual evidence, in particular the *Regularis Concordia* and the *Leofric Missal*, is made by Mark Spurrell in 'The Procession of Palms and West-Front Galleries' (*Downside Review* 119[2001] 125–44).

4. Literature: General

Pulsiano and Treharne, eds., *A Companion to Anglo-Saxon Literature*, provides a wide-ranging set of essays on all aspects of literary production in Anglo-Saxon England. Its first section, 'Contexts and Perspectives', contains 'An Introduction to the Corpus of Anglo-Saxon Vernacular Literature' by Elaine Treharne and Phillip Pulsiano; 'An Introduction to the Corpus of Anglo-Latin Literature' by Joseph P. McGowan; 'Transmission of Literature and Learning: Anglo-Saxon Scribal Culture' by Jonathan Wilcox; 'Authorship and Anonymity' by Mary Swan; 'Audience(s), Reception, Literacy' by Hugh Magennis; and 'Anglo-Saxon

Manuscript Production: Issues of Making and Using' by Michelle P. Brown. Part 2, 'Readings: Cultural Framework and Heritage', contains 'The Germanic Background' by Patrizia Lendinara; 'Religious Context: Pre-Benedictine Reform Period' by Susan Irvine; 'The Benedictine Reform and Beyond' by Joyce Hill; 'Legal and Documentary Writings' by Carole Hough; 'Scientific and Medical Writings' by Stephanie Hollis; and 'Prayers, Glosses and Glossaries' by Phillip Pulsiano. Part 3, 'Genes and Modes', contains 'Religious Prose' by Roy M. Liuzza; 'Religious Poetry' by Patrick W. Conner; 'Secular Prose' by Donald G. Scragg; 'Secular Poetry' by Fred C. Robinson; and 'Anglo-Latin Prose' by Joseph P. McGowan. Part 4, 'Intertextualities: Sources and Influences', contains 'Biblical and Patristic Learning' by Thomas Hall; 'The Irish Tradition' by Charles D. Wright; 'Continental Germanic Influences' by Rolf Bremmer; and 'Scandinavian Relations' by Robert E. Bjork. Part 5, 'Debates and Issues', contains 'English in the Post-Conquest Period' by Elaine Treharne; 'Anglo-Saxon Studies: Sixteenth to Eighteenth Centuries' by Timothy Graham; 'Anglo-Saxon Studies in the Nineteenth Century: England, Denmark, America' by J.R. Hall; 'Anglo-Saxon Studies in the Nineteenth Century: Germany, Austria, Switzerland' by Hans Sauer; 'By the Numbers: Anglo-Saxon Scholarship at the Century's End' by Allen Frantzen; and 'The New Millennium' by Nicholas Howe. Suggestions for further reading and an index complete the volume.

This year has seen the publication of the third edition of Pope, ed., *Eight Old English Poems*, revised by R.D. Fulk. Originally published as *Seven Old English Poems* [1966], the major change to the new edition is the addition of an eighth poem, *The Wife's Lament*. Fulk has also made minor textual corrections to the other seven poems in light of improved readings from manuscript facsimiles, rewritten the essay on Old English versification, composed a new translation of Bede's account of Cædmon, and updated the critical apparatus and bibliography.

Peter Dendle's *Satan Unbound: The Devil in Old English Narrative Literature* traces the narrative significance of the devil, the most frequently appearing character in Old English literature. In lucid readings that attend to source study, intertextual analysis, and cultural contextualization, Dendle moves through a variety of Old English texts, and reveals that the devil performs a wide range of narrative and thematic functions that have little to do with human sin. Dendle argues that 'the devil is above all an ontological symbol: his primary purpose is to challenge the saints in an ongoing debate that questions and strives to legitimize the justice of God's rule by force' (p. 3). Narrative conceptualizations of the demonic thus 'provide extended enquiries into the construction of reality (after their own fashion), far more obviously than they provide moral guidance for the spiritual aspirant' (pp. 3–4).

In *Anglo-Saxon Audiences*, Eugene Green uses modern semantic theory and rhetorical analysis to consider how Anglo-Saxon kings, poets, and homilists attempted to direct the minds of Anglo-Saxon audiences. Green discusses royal law codes from the ninth to the eleventh centuries, *Beowulf*, a variety of Old English shorter poems, and select homilies by Ælfric and Wulfstan. He considers how Anglo-Saxon audiences thought about the future, and argues that Anglo-Saxon readers were not wholly receptive to the social directives imposed upon them by vernacular writings.

Shari Horner's *The Discourse of Enclosure: Representing Women in Old English Literature* argues that representations of women and femininity in Old English literature were powerfully shaped by the material conditions and institutional discourses of female monastic enclosure. Responding to prevalent critical views of women in Old English literature as 'strong, independent, eloquent, sometimes martial figures' (p. 16), particularly when contrasted with women in post-Conquest literature, Horner argues that we can nevertheless identify 'a simultaneous and marked tendency to circumscribe and confine the female figures of early English literature that is analogous to early medieval cultural constraints on female religious' (pp. 16–17). *The Discourse of Enclosure* offers lucid close readings of *Beowulf*, the female-voiced Old English elegies, *Juliana*, and Ælfric's lives of female saints. It also makes a case for renewed attention to female enclosure as one of the defining conceptual frameworks of Anglo-Saxon texts, and for a more expansive understanding of enclosure's literal and figural dimensions.

In *Paradise, Death and Doomsday in Anglo-Saxon Literature*, Ananya Jahanara Kabir considers 'the rarely noted conjunction of two much-discussed concepts: paradise, and the soul's condition in the interim period between death and Judgment Day' (p. 1). Drawing on techniques of literary analysis and source study, Kabir traces the concept of what she terms 'interim paradise' from its early appearances in Augustinian exegesis and apocryphal writings through its later incantations in the works of Bede, Boniface, Ælfric, and Anglo-Saxon poets. She argues for interim paradise as a 'necessary, influential and ideologically charged concept during the early Middle Ages, and within Anglo-Saxon England in particular' (p. 12), and suggests that changing depictions of interim paradise in these texts offer a unique angle from which to consider such ostensible oppositions as orthodoxy and heterodoxy, learned and popular sensibilities, Latin and vernacular writings, and prose and verse.

Jun Terasawa considers 'The Scarcity of Formations in -*ere* in Old English Poetry' (*Anglia* 119 [2001] 193–206]. She shows that the *Beowulf*-poet frequently resorts to words in -*a* and -*end* to denote personal agents, as in such compounds as *æsc-wiga* and *gar-wigend*, but only once uses a derivative in -*ere*, i.e. *leassceaweras*. Terasawa then examines possible reasons for the scarcity of -*ere* formations in poetry and their greater prevalence in prose texts, and concludes by briefly examining Ælfric's frequent use of words with -*ere* formations and Wulfstan's greater hesitancy to do so.

Alfred Bammesberger considers 'The Meaning of Old English *eowend(e)*' (*N&Q* 48[2001] 371–2). He proposes that this *hapax legomenon* is accurately translated as 'testicles', and that it appears in a regulation prescribing castration as a punishment for rape.

Thomas D. Hill's '"When the leader is brave ... ": An Old English Proverb and its Vernacular Context' (*Anglia* 119[2001] 232–6) compares the statements in the *Anglo-Saxon Chronicle* 1003 entry, a letter by Alcuin, and the Alfredian translation of the Regula Pastoralis, and also offers another close example from Durham Proverb 31. He suggests that the wordier *Chronicle* and Regula Pastoralis versions might be back-formations from oral proverbs like the Durham one, and also highlights the centrality of the tension between the 'old heroic ideals and the harsh necessities demanded by the reality of war' (p. 236).

Ursula Zender's 'A Metrical Comparison of *Beowulf* and the Old English Riddles of the Exeter Book' (in Honegger, ed., *Authors, Heroes and Lovers*, pp. 27–46) rests on the assumption that both texts were probably composed in the first half of the eighth century. Zender surveys theories of metre, applies them to *Beowulf* and the riddles, and argues that the riddles only deviate from the metre of *Beowulf* in order to express their different genre.

This year marks the issuing in paperback of Nicholas Howe's *Migration and Mythmaking in Anglo-Saxon England*. First published in 1989 by YaleUP, the book argues that 'the Anglo-Saxons honored the ancestral migration as the founding and defining event of their culture' (p. xvii), and examines the migration myth in Bede, Boniface, Wulfstan, *Exodus*, and *Beowulf*. *Migration and Mythmaking* has become standard reading for scholars concerned with questions of cultural dislocation, historical remembrance, myths of origin, and nationalism in pre-modern culture. The paperback edition includes a new introduction by the author which considers 'how the political and cultural arguments of *Migration and Mythmaking* intersect with the claims made by theorists of nationalism and communal identity in the 1990s' (p. x).

Michael Schmidt's *The Story of Poetry*, volume 1: *English Poets and Poetry from Cædmon to Caxton* is an anthology of medieval English poetry. The book is focused mainly on Middle English poetry, but includes translations of *The Dream of the Rood* (by Charles Schmidt), and of *The Seafarer, The Wanderer, The Ruin*, five Old English riddles, the opening of *Beowulf*, and Grendel's attack on Heorot (all by Edwin Morgan). The book is divided into two parts: the first consists of brief chapters that provide contextualization for the poems; the second contains the poems.

5. The Exeter Book

'Exeter's Relics, Exeter's Books' (in Roberts and Nelson, eds., *Essays on Anglo-Saxon and Related Themes in Memory of Lynne Grundy*, pp. 117–56) is the subject of a substantial new study by Patrick W. Conner. Having edited and discussed the primary documentation for Exeter's relics in a previous study, Conner re-examines this documentation in the light of other Exeter documents to determine Exeter's ability to produce such a manuscript as the Exeter Book. He argues that Æthelstan sought relics as avidly as he did deluxe manuscripts, that he may have commissioned the core of the Leofric Missal for use at Exeter, and that Exeter's relics provide crucial evidence that it had the means to have a scriptorium actively producing books.

Lara Farina's 'Before Affection: *Christ I* and the Social Erotic' (*Exemplaria* 13[2001] 469–96) reassesses evidence for eroticism in Old English literature by analysing images of Mary and Christ in *Christ I*. Farina argues that modern readers have missed depictions of eroticism in Anglo-Saxon texts by looking for them within such private spaces as the inner recesses of the psyche and material enclosures. She shows that *Christ I* enables a social eroticism in its readers, who are encouraged to engage in sustained longing for Christ that would have been experienced collectively. The essay draws on both contemporary theory and studies in the history of sexuality to elucidate the problems of identifying eroticism in cultures so removed from our own.

Mercedes Salvador argues that we ought not to accept 'A Case of Editorial Hypercorrection in Exeter Riddle 35 (8b)' (*ANQ* 14:iii[2001] 5–11). Salvador considers Riddle 35 in relation to the two other extant versions of this riddle, the so-called 'Leiden Riddle' and the Latin version (no. 33) of Aldhelm's *enigmata*, and argues that the riddler intentionally used *amas* in Riddle 35 as a kind of wordplay, and that the emendation of *amas* to *am*, or to any other singular form, is unnecessary. Ian J. Kirby examines 'The Exeter Book, Riddle 60' (*N&Q* 48[2001] 219–20) and proposes that Riddle 60 does not refer to a rune staff, reed pen, reed flute, or any number of other previously suggested solutions, but to an inscription, most likely in runes, on a rock or boulder situated close to a high water mark, which may have functioned as a way marker or an indicator of warning to mariners who could understand its coded message.

Gwang-Yoon Goh examines 'Genitive in *Deor*: Morphosyntax and Beyond' (*RES* 52[2001] 485–99). Focusing on the problem of the so-called '*Deor*-genitive', that is, the poem's repeated use of the genitive pronouns *þæs* and *þisses* with the verb *ofergan*, Goh offers possible explanations for this usage, and suggests that it contributes to the poem's general attempt to convey a sense of the inevitability of misfortunes and the need to patiently endure them.

Peter Orton's 'To Be a Pilgrim: The Old English *Seafarer* and its Irish Affinities' (in Kay and Sylvester, eds., *Lexis and Texts in Early English: Studies Presented to Jane Roberts*, pp. 213–23), reassesses evidence for possible Irish influences on *The Seafarer*. He discusses contemporary Latin terms for pilgrimage in England and Ireland and posits that the relatively restricted usage of such terms in England suggests that the English learned about ascetic exile from the Irish rather than vice versa. Erick Keleman also takes up the topic of exile in his study of '*Clyppan* and *Cyssan*: The Formulaic Expression of Return from Exile in Old English Literature' (*ELN* 38:iii[2001] 1–19). Keleman traces the thirteen occurrences of the alliterating pair *clyppan* and *cyssan* in the Old English corpus and demonstrates that the pair usually appears as part of a type-scene marking the real or imagined return of a exile or traveller, and is generally accompanied by profound religious significance. Keleman argues that the religious connotations of the pair *clyppan* and *cyssan*, which occurs in *The Wanderer*, problematizes any attempt to read the poem solely through the lens of secular experience or Germanic-heroic cultural paradigms.

Glenn Wright examines the Middle English secular lyric '"Now springs the spray" and *The Wife's Lament*' (*ANQ* 14:iii[2001] 11–14), and points out that lines 9–10 of 'Now springs the spray' resemble the Old French 'L'autrier defors Picarni', which has typically been seen as the Middle English lyric's closest analogue, less closely than they do lines 52–3 of *The Wife's Lament*. Wright suggests that we ought not to discount the possibility that '*The Wife's Lament* represents a discrete elegiac subgenre that survived the Conquest and influenced the English appropriation of the *chanson d'aventure* form' (p. 12).

In 'The Thief in the Night: An Error in a Textual Note From Klinck's *Old English Elegies*' (*ELN* 38:iii[2001] 19–20), Ruth Carroll reconsiders Anne Klinck's textual note to lines 15a–16a of *Resignation*, which Klinck believes allude to 'Christ's comparison of the Devil to a thief who comes in the night (Matthew 24:43 and Luke 12:39)' (Klinck, *The Old English Elegies*, p. 189, cited in Carroll, p. 19). Carroll points out that these biblical passages compare not the Devil but the Son of Man to a thief.

Daniel Paul O'Donnell considers 'Fish and Fowl: Generic Expectations and the Relationship between the Old English *Phoenix*-Poem and Lactantius's *De ave phoenice*' (in Olsen, Harbus, and Hofstra, eds., *Germanic Texts and Latin Models: Medieval Reconstructions*, pp. 157–71). He argues that *De ave phoenice* presented the *Phoenix*-poet with 'a Latin text that described the habits and features of the phoenix in a comprehensive but hopelessly out of date fashion ... [and] he therefore was forced to seek a generic model for his translation in order to make it intelligible as natural history to contemporary readers' (p. 159). O'Donnell contends that the *Phoenix*-poet found such a model in the *Physiologus* tradition.

6. The Poems of the Vercelli Book

Éamonn Ó Carragáin has published two substantial articles on individual poems in the Vercelli Book this year. In 'The Annunciation of the Lord and his Passion: A Liturgical Topos from Saint Peter's on the Vatican in *The Dream of the Rood*, Thomas Cranmer and John Donne' (in Roberts and Nelson, eds., pp. 339–81), Ó Carragáin traces the liturgical topos of unity between the Passion and Incarnation, and the tradition of celebrating both on 25 March. He considers the progression from death to new birth as a central conceptual framework for the *Dream*, the Ruthwell Cross, and writings by Cranmer and Donne, and concludes that 'the Anglo-Saxon poetic and artistic development of the *topos* was inspired by the liturgical thought, in the 670s, of the monks of St. Martin's on the Vatican hill, whose duty it was to provide the liturgy at the body of Saint Peter' (p. 377).

In 'Cynewulf's Epilogue to *Elene* and the Tastes of the Vercelli Compiler: A Paradigm of Meditative Reading' (in Kay and Sylvester, eds., pp. 187–201), Ó Carragáin argues that the epilogue to *Elene* provides a paradigm of meditative reading in which fear of the Lord leads to rumination on texts, and ultimately to prayer. Ó Carragáin then examines advice on reading in the Vercelli homilies, and concludes that Cynewulf and the compiler of the Vercelli Book shared a similar view of devotional reading and its attendant work of sifting out meaning from texts. Both viewed this kind of reading as a preparation for the Last Judgement when, in turn, the mind of God would sift out and test all human souls.

Ivan Herbison examines 'Generic Adaptation in *Andreas*' (in Roberts and Nelson, eds., pp. 181–211). Herbison argues that the long-recognized incongruity between the style and the subject matter of *Andreas* is symptomatic of a more fundamental problem: the tension between the inherited narrative's depiction of Andrew and the poet's attempt to develop a hagiographical representation of him as *imago Christi* and *miles Christi*.

In 'A Mind for Hagiography: The Psychology of Resolution in *Andreas*' (in Olsen, Harbus, and Hofstra, eds., pp. 127–40), Antonina Harbus examines *Andreas* as a 'poetic enunciation of the psychology of reluctance and resolution' (p. 128). Focusing on the poet's emphasis on Andrew's mental reorientation and psychological fortification, Harbus suggests that the poet's newfound attention to the mind has the broader goal of drawing Anglo-Saxon readers 'to contemplate the wider significance of the text off the page, specifically their own personal reactions to the poem at hand' (p. 140).

Karin Olsen examines 'Cynewulf's *Elene*: From Empress to Saint' (in Olsen, Harbus, and Hofstra, eds., pp. 141–56). Olsen questions whether *Elene* is 'as autonomous or even as characteristically Germanic as some critics like to believe' and argues that 'Cynewulf's representation of the empress reflects his own orthodox attitudes towards women, attitudes that lead him to alter the status and qualities attributed to the empress in the Latin versions of the legend' (p. 142).

Alfred R. Wedel examines 'Alliteration and the Prefix *Ge-* in Cynewulf's *Elene*' (*JEGP* 100[2001] 200–10). Wedel compares the past-tense *ge*-compounded verbal forms in *Elene* with their unprefixed counterparts in order to determine the function of the unstressed prefix. He suggests that the prefix *ge-* occasionally served to fill in a needed unstressed syllable to achieve a specific stress pattern, but more often as a means for Cynewulf to signal the relative importance of events in the poem: unprefixed verbal forms were used for background information, and prefixed verbal forms reserved for major events.

7. The Junius Manuscript

The past year has been unusually fruitful for studies of the Junius manuscript. The major work of the year is Catherine Karkov's *Text and Picture in Anglo-Saxon England: Narrative Strategies in the Junius 11 Manuscript*. The Junius manuscript is the only one of the four poetic codices that is illustrated, and has often been studied either for its literary texts or for the style and iconography of its drawings. Karkov is the first to undertake an in-depth study of the interrelations between the manuscript's texts and drawings. She argues that 'a significant number of the Junius 11 drawings have a typological function, yet they work in a slightly different way from the psalter illustrations, combining symbolic and literal content to create a visual narrative that both illustrates the poetic text and translates it into a new pictorial language' (p. 8). She suggests further that 'the need to read and interpret properly is one of the central themes of the manuscript' and that stylistic similarities between the poetic and pictorial narratives 'help us to create a unified reading that bridges the gap between the verbal and the visual' (p. 9).

There have also been a good number of shorter articles, many of which focus on *Exodus*. In 'Ring Composition and the Digressions of *Exodus*: The "Legacy" of the "Remnant"' (*ES* 82[2001] 289–307), Phyllis Portnoy proposes a new reading of *Exodus* based on the poet's use of ring composition. Although widely recognized as a structural device in such poems as *Beowulf* and *The Battle of Maldon*, ring composition has never been noted in *Exodus*; Portnoy argues that it 'serves to incorporate and integrate—but also to demarcate—digressive episodes' (p. 290). In 'Theme in *Exodus*: Grammatical Meaning and Spoken Syntax in Old English Poetry' (in Kay and Sylvester, eds., pp. 129–42), Rosemary Huisman examines various clauses in *Exodus* that begin with a verb and have no explicit subject. Huisman argues that such clauses are 'grammatically meaningful' (p. 129), and discusses the interpretative possibilities for one clause. She concludes that 'the language of the whole text suggests choices of cohesion and syntax ... more characteristic of spoken language than written' (p. 129), and that the poem's oral origins persist in many of its grammatical features. Alfred Bammesberger comments on 'Old English *Ingere* and *Gere* in *Exodus*' (*RES* 52[2001] 327–30). He proposes that *ingere* in *Exodus* 33a is correctly understood as the adverb *gere* prefixed by the intensifying *in-*, and that the manuscript reading *ingere* is not in need of emendation.

Glenn M. Davis examines 'Changing Senses in *Genesis B*' (*PQ* 80[2001] 113–31), with particular attention to the poet's emphasis on the heightened senses of hearing, taste and touch that accompany Eve's newfound vision. Davis argues that the poet's expansive account of Eve's altered bodily senses not only conveys the well-known patristic theme of information transmitted through the senses leading to sin, but also serves as a lesson to readers that 'the senses can be active, yet covert, participants in deception' (p. 126).

In '"*Hwalas ðec herigað*": Creation, Closure and the *Hapax Legomena* of the OE *Daniel*' (in Kay and Sylvester, eds., pp. 105–16), J.-A. George discusses the frequency of *hapax legomena* in *Daniel*, *Genesis A* and *B*, and *Exodus*. She then explores the thematic significance of three particular *hapax legomena* in *Daniel*, and argues that *Daniel* is complete as it stands.

8. The *Beowulf* Manuscript

This year has seen the publication of a new edition of Michael Alexander's *Beowulf: A Verse Translation*, originally published in 1973. The new edition contains a revised text, new introduction and notes, updated suggestions for further reading, and a reorganization of introductory material that 'reflects changes in understanding' (p. xii). The three genealogical tables now immediately follow the introduction, and the map appears at the end of the text to ensure that '*Beowulf* now seems a poem less about physical history and more about human nature and its ancestry' (p. xii).

In '*Desecto Capite Perfido*: Bodily Fragmentation and Reciprocal Violence in Anglo-Saxon England' (*Exemplaria* 13[2001] 399–432), John Edward Damon considers images of decapitation and dismemberment in *Beowulf* in relation to similar images in other Old English texts. He concludes that these literary images point to a cultural system of reciprocal violence in which severed heads and body parts performed a crucial symbolic function.

Frederick M. Biggs examines 'The Naming of Beowulf and Ecgtheow's Feud' (*PQ* 80[2001] 95–112). Biggs argues that the *Beowulf*-poet's delay in naming Beowulf is a strategy designed 'to place greater weight on Hrothgar's, rather than Beowulf's, explanation of his journey, which depends on an account of a feud involving Beowulf's father, Ecgtheow' (p. 95). Biggs suggests that the poet's invocation of Ecgtheow's feud, in which ties of kin are either not specified or shown to be weak, is used to suggest that 'the Danes and the Geats confront similar problems, related ... to succession' (p. 95), and 'rather than cleansing Heorot, he [Beowulf] may leave it much as he found it, in danger of Hrothulf's treachery' (p. 107).

As in most years, Alfred Bammesberger offers helpful textual notes on difficult lines. In 'The Syntactic Analysis of *Beowulf*, lines 4–5' (*NM* 102[2001] 131–3), he argues that *sceapena þreatum* ought to be understood not as a variation on *monegum mægþum* but as an instrumental. The phrase is thus correctly translated as 'together with his troops of warriors' and refers to Scyld Scefing's own men, not enemy tribes. In 'Further Thoughts on *Beowulf*, Line 1537a: *Gefeng þa be [f]eaxe*' (*N&Q* 48[2001] 3–4), Bammesberger supports the suggestion previously made by Max Rieger and Eric Stanley that *eaxle* in line 1537a should be emended to *[f]eaxe*, and that Beowulf is thus attacking Grendel's mother by grabbing her hair rather than her shoulder. Bammesberger also examines 'The Half-Line *þenden hyt sy* (*Beowulf* 2649b)' (*ANQ* 14:iii[2001] 3–5), and lends support to the proposal made by both J.M. Kemble and Fr. Klaeber that *hyt* ought to be emended to *h[a]t*.

Other brief analyses of difficult words and phrases have also appeared. In '*Beowulf* 1763 *adl oððe ecg*: A Corruption of *adl oððe ece*' (*N&Q* 48[2001] 97–8), Matti Kilpiö suggests that *ecg* be emended to *ece*. Gale R. Owen-Crocker, in '"Gracious" Hrothulf, "Gracious" Hrothgar: A Reassessment' (*ELN* 38:iv[2001] 1–7), questions Klaeber's translation of *glæd* as 'gracious'. She examines the five occurrences of *glæd* in *Beowulf* and argues that a translation of 'appreciative' is more appropriate to the passages in which *glæd* appears.

Augustine Thompson suggests a need for 'Rethinking Hygelac's Raid' (*ELN* 38:iv[2001] 9–16), and offers a brief examination of the literary sources that recount it: *Beowulf*, Gregory of Tours's *Historia Francorum* 3:3, the anonymous *Liber Historiae Francorum* 19, and a passage from a marvel collection, *Liber Monstrorum* 3. Thompson also considers the areas in which these texts circulated and their interrelationships.

Mary Blockley studies 'Subordinate Clauses Without απο κοινου in Old English Verse, Chiefly in *Beowulf* and Chiefly *nu* and *swa*' (*SN* 73[2001] 4–10). Blockley considers the problems of syntax that arise when attempting to interpret such ambiguous headwords as *nu* and *swa* in *Beowulf*, and she examines the extent to which we can determine if these headwords introduce subordinate clauses or main clauses.

9. Other Poems

Daniel Paul O'Donnell examines 'Junius's Knowledge of the Old English Poem *Durham*' (*ASE* 30[2001] 231–45), focusing on Donald Fry's claim to have discovered a seventeenth-century transcription by Francis Junius that represents a third medieval manuscript of *Durham*. O'Donnell argues that Fry is not correct, for far from being the sole surviving transcription of a now lost third medieval copy of *Durham*, Junius's transcription is merely a corrected copy of a flawed seventeenth-century edition. It is thus 'of no value' (p. 240) in establishing the text of the Old English poem, but may be of much interest to historians of Anglo-Saxon studies for what it tells us about Junius's knowledge of Old English orthography and verse.

Craig Ronalds and Margaret Clunies Ross consider '*Thureth*: A Neglected Old English Poem and its History in Anglo-Saxon Scholarship' (*N&Q* 48[2001] 359–70). They provide a modern translation of this little-known eleven-line poem, examine its critical history, and argue that *Thureth* merits further study from both a literary and a lexical standpoint.

'Phonology and Meter in the Old English Macaronic Verses' (*SP* 98[2001] 273–91) is the subject of a study by Christopher M. Cain. Cain's main concern is to ascertain what Old English macaronic verse can tell us about the state of Latin in late

Anglo-Saxon England. He questions whether the imposition of native Germanic metrical strictures on Latin words effects their nativization in a manner that more closely resembles phonological nativization as manifested in early Old English borrowings from Latin, or as manifested in later borrowings. Cain concludes that 'the Latin off-verses of the Old English macaronic poems demonstrate a prosodic structure consistent with that of the late Latin borrowings into Old English' (p. 290).

In 'Alfred's Verse Preface to the *Pastoral Care* and the Chain of Authority' (*Neophil* 85[2001] 625–33), Nicole Guenther Discenza argues that the Verse Preface to Alfred the Great's *Pastoral Care* completes the preceding Prose Preface's work of explaining the Anglo-Saxon *translatio studii*. By positioning himself as the last link in a chain of learning that moves from the Hebrews to the Greeks to the Romans and finally to the English, and by making use of church language, Alfred justifies his claim to authority over religious as well as lay people. The article draws on Pierre Bourdieu's work on legitimate language and symbolic capital to further illuminate Alfred's strategic use of language to assert authority.

'The *Timaeus* in Old English' (in Kay and Sylvester, eds., pp. 255–67) is the subject of a study by Paul E. Szarmach. He begins from the well-known premise that the twenty-eight hexametric lines that comprise III.m.9 of Boethius' *De Consolatione Philosophiae* transmit ideas that are found in Plato's *Timaeus*. Szarmach then examines Alfred's poetic rendition of these lines and considers the cultural implications of Alfred's attempt to express classical Platonic thought in Old English.

In 'The Genre of the Sutton Brooch Verses' (*N&Q* 48[2001] 375–7), E.V. Thornbury considers the inscription on the inner rim of the late tenth- or early eleventh-century silver brooch found near Sutton, Isle of Ely. He posits that 'the form of the Sutton brooch verse … is best explained by postulating the influence of legal formulae on the formulae used by engravers' (p. 377).

10. Prose

From *YWES* 81 onwards, publications on pre-Conquest Anglo-Latin prose are reviewed in this section along with Old English prose.

Old English and Anglo-Latin religious prose continues to generate new work. Three of the four essays in Scragg, ed., *Ælfric's Lives of Canonised Popes*, come from papers given at the International Congress on Medieval Studies at Kalamazoo in 2000 in connection with a project to prepare a new collaborative edition of all Old English Saints' Lives. The first essay, 'Ælfric and Gregory the Great', by Mechtild Gretsch, was commissioned especially for the volume to complete coverage of Ælfric's lives of canonized popes. In her essay, Gretsch sets out what Alfred knew about Gregory's life and the development of his cult, what of this knowledge he thought it appropriate to offer to his audience, and how he presents Gregory as a model for late Anglo-Saxon Christians at a time of spiritual and political uncertainty. In 'Ælfric's Two Homilies for May 3: The Invention of the Cross and the Martyrdom of Pope Alexander and SS Eventius and Theodolus', Susan Rosser addresses the question of why Ælfric included as his second item for this day a homily on three martyrs who do not seem to have been widely venerated in Anglo-Saxon England. Rosser examines Ælfric's sources for the two 3 May homilies, and considers the possibility that Ælfric's intended audience for the second series of *Catholic Homilies* was slightly different than that for his first, that he may have been influenced by the wishes of his patrons, and that he was simply attracted to the stories themselves as expressions of the need for spiritual strength in the face of enemy threat. Scott DeGregorio's 'Ælfric, *Gedwyld*, and Vernacular Hagiography: Sanctity and Spirituality in the Old English Lives of SS Peter and Paul' compares Ælfric's homily for the *Natale* of Peter and Paul with the earlier Old English homily Blickling 15 which draws on the same main source, the *Passio sanctorum apostolorum Petri et Pauli*. DeGregorio shows how the Blicking homily emphasizes the apostles' human weakness, while Ælfric edits his source to remove such emphasis and to present a more straightforward portrait. Joyce Hill's subject is 'Ælfric's Homily for the Feast of St Clement', and she sets out to investigate why Ælfric composed 'such a curious homily' (p. 99) for this feast. She argues that, in the first part of the homily, Ælfric constructs a 'missionary-conversion narrative' (p. 105), and concludes that the perception of the homily as one which seems to fall into two relatively unrelated parts was apparently shared by Anglo-Saxon copyists, and that a rationale for this split subject matter has still to be found.

Old English preaching texts receive further attention in Winfried Rudolf's 'Style and Composition of Napier XVIII: A Matter of Person or a Matter of Purpose?' (in Honegger, ed., pp. 107–49). Rudolf addresses the question of why this homily reworks its Ælfrician source, and examines the viability of the identification of individual authorial style—Wulfstanian or other. He then turns to a detailed study of Napier XVIII, 'De Falsis Deis', and from this concludes that, rather than seeking to identify a single author, 'we should rather pay attention to the variety of methods of composition and the intertextuality of those versions thematically linked with each other' (p. 136). In 'An Anonymous Homily for Palm Sunday, *The Dream of the Rood*, and the Progress of Ælfric's Reform' (*N&Q* 48[2001] 377–80), Aidan Conti examines homily HomS 18, versions of which also survive in the other Ælfrician manuscripts Bodley 340 and CCCC 162. Conti analyses this homily as a translation of the gospel reading for the day, and focuses on its errors of translation and interpretation, and its similarity to *The Dream of the Rood* in terms of the apocryphal detail of the cross bowing down to Joseph and Nichodemus. He notes the links of content between Bodley 340 and the Vercelli Book, suggests that homily was composed at a centre with access to *The Dream of the Rood*, in the south of England before the Benedictine Reform, and that corrections of errors in manuscript versions of the homily are the result of the Reform.

In 'Bede's Commentaries on Luke and Mark and the Formation of a Patristic Canon' (in Echard and Wieland, eds., *Anglo-Latin and its Heritage: Essays in Honour of A.G. Rigg on his 64th Birthday*, pp. 17–26), Berenice M. Kaczynski examines Bede's system of marginal references to his authorities, 'an innovation in the history of the manuscript book' (p. 23) which is replicated by some copyists of Bede's works, and also looks at the continuing influence of his arrangement of the Fathers Ambrose, Augustine, Gregory and Jerome into a group of four.

A good quantity of new work on Aldhelm is published this year. Scott Gwara's Corpus Christianorum edition of and introduction to the prose *De Virginitate* will be a major resource for future scholarship on this text. The edition is in two volumes, the first of which contains a substantial introduction, including discussion of Alcuin's political and intellectual career, the *Prose de Virginitate*, glossed manuscripts of the text, the transmission of the Old English and Latin glosses, bibliography and indices, and also notes on how to use the edition, which is published in the second volume. Sinéad O'Sullivan analyses 'The Image of Adornment in Aldhelm's *De Virginitate*: Cyprian and his Influence' (*Peritia* 15[2001] 48–57) and shows how Alcuin presents adornment as a complex image, linked to virginity, with outer (worldly sin) and inner (purity of the soul) states. She shows Alcuin to be drawing on traditions, and in particular the work of Cyprian, and also making his own innovative, spiritual, version of this image. G.T. Dempsey's focus is on a different Aldhelmian innovation: 'Aldhelm of Malmesbury's Social Theology: The Barbaric Heroic Ideal Christianised' (*Peritia* 15[2001] 59–80). Dempsey argues that Aldhelm creates a new, Christianized heroic ideal for Anglo-Saxon men and women through his focus on virginity as a struggle during life, and suggests that Aldhelm's popularity was partly due to his appeal to a monastic and aristocratic audience.

Mary Alberi examines 'The Better Paths of Wisdom: Alcuin's Monastic "True Philosophy" and the Worldly Court' (*Speculum* 76[2001] 896–910) with regard to the competing pull for Alcuin of monastic life and courtly duties. Alberi draws on Alcuin's *Disputatio de vera philosophia* and his letters to show how he sets out his monastic 'true philosophy' for the renewal of the Frankish kingdom in the face of Carolingian authority.

Andy Orchard's 'Old Sources, New Resources: Finding the Right Formula for Boniface' (*ASE* 30[2001] 15–38) aims to redress the lack of recent scholarly attention on the Bonifatian correspondence as literature by exploring its links with other Old English and Anglo-Latin literature. Orchard examines formulae and other patterns used in a range of Boniface's letters and shows how these works cast light on the mission in their echoing of the expressions of longing and loss in found in other Anglo-Saxon texts.

Studies of the Bible in Anglo-Saxon England continue to multiply. The second volume of R.M. Liuzza's EETS edition of *The Old English Version of the Gospels* was published in 2000, but not covered in *YWES* 81. It complements volume 1's edition by providing notes and glossary. The notes are an important piece of scholarship in their own right, since they are not organized as a line-by-line commentary on the edited text, but are rather a series of thematically structured analyses, which consider such central topics as the Latin original of the Old English Gospels, the work of translation, authorship, orthography and language, and transmission. Liuzza also supplies an index of biblical passages discussed in the notes to help the reader to find specific references, a glossary, and a Latin–Old English word list. The two volumes of Liuzza's edition form a major work of interpretation and analysis, and a huge body of material for future study.

Lynne Long's survey, *Translating the Bible from the 7th to the 17th Century*, includes the following chapters on Anglo-Saxon topics: 'From Bede to Alfred', 'The Practice of Glossing: The Writings of Ælfric', and 'The Continuity of Religious Prose'. The central questions addressed are the status of the vernacular, changing influences and pressures, orality and literacy, and the practicalities of translation.

The health of King Alfred and its depiction in Anglo-Latin prose are the subject of two articles this year. Paul Kershaw seeks connections between 'Illness, Power and Prayer in Asser's *Life of King Alfred*' (*EMedE* 10[2001] 201–24), and finds echoes of Carolingian ideas of rulership in Asser's account of Alfred's mysterious illness. Kershaw examines the relationship between royal authority and religious belief, Alfred's daily round of prayers, and Continental parallels for this being done by lay noblemen, and he suggests that the teachings of Gregory the Great might have motivated Alfred's actions in his illness. David Pratt's examination of 'The Illnesses of King Alfred the Great' (*ASE* 30[2001] 39–90) as described by Asser aims to uncover 'the ideals and expectations of the society within which Alfred was operating' (p. 40). Like Kershaw, Pratt sees Alfred's preoccupation with his bodily suffering in the context of lay devotion, and he too traces Carolingian connections and differences in the presentation of lay piety. Pratt examines the vocabulary of Anglo-Saxon medical texts in comparison with that of Asser, tracks Alfred's devotional response to his illness, supports the 'modern diagnosis' (p. 72) of Crohn's disease, and concludes that 'the Alfredian "ministerial" disciplines that resulted were not a sign of weakness, but rather served to assert the king's own bodily and political power' (p. 89).

Stephen J. Harris engages with the ongoing debate on the origins of English national identity in 'The Alfredian World History and Anglo-Saxon Identity' (*JEGP* 100[2001] 482–510). He examines Bede's *Historia Ecclesiastica* in its Latin and Old English versions, and Anglo-Saxon genealogies, argues that the view that English national identity originates in the works of Alfred does not take into account the production of the Alfredian *Orosius*, and proposes instead a Germanic religious-ethnic identity transmitted to Anglo-Saxon England by Carolingian contacts in Alfred's court.

In 'The Social Context of Narrative Disruption in *The Letter of Alexander to Aristotle*' (*ASE* 30[2001] 91–114), Brian McFadden highlights the 'chilling resonance' (p. 91) for the English of the narrative of monstrous force and 'the anxieties caused by tenth- and early eleventh-century Viking invasions, the Benedictine Reform, and eschatological concerns provoked by the coming millennium' (p. 91). McFadden also notes that all of the texts in the *Beowulf* manuscript are concerned with struggles whose outcome for the powerful figure is uncertain.

Roy Michael Liuzza's 'Anglo-Saxon Prognostics in Context: A Survey and Handlist of Manuscripts' (*ASE* 30[2001] 181–230) opens with a summary of the sorts of scholarly attention paid to date to prognostic texts and the manuscripts in which they survive, and then turns to a survey of the texts themselves and their manuscript distribution, for which he groups the texts into a number of categories. This analysis enables Liuzza to demonstrate that prognostic texts are not, as some Anglo-Saxon and many modern scholars believed, folkloric survivals from pre-Christian belief systems, but rather are central to the Benedictine Reform. The handlist of relevant manuscripts forms the appendix to Liuzza's article.

Sara María Pons Sanz's study of 'Aldredian Glosses to Proper Names in the *Lindisfarne Gospels*' (*Anglia* 119[2001] 173–92) leads her to question the belief that Aldred left most proper names unglossed, and to show instead that he paid careful attention to glossing them as accurately as possible, in some cases in order to give information about the meaning of the Bible. Christine Franzen adds two new articles to her body of work on the Worcester 'Tremulous Hand' scribe. She comments 'On the Attribution of Copied Glosses in CCCC MS 41 to the "Tremulous Hand" of Worcester' (*N&Q* 48[2001] 373–4), and concludes that the glosses in question are not by the Tremulous Hand at any stage of that scribe's career, and that the Tremulous Hand did not do any work in CCCC 41. In 'The Cerne "Trembling" Hand and the Tremulous Hand of Worcester' (*N&Q* 48[2001] 374–5) Franzen takes as her starting-point Michelle Brown's observation of a 'correcting, trembling' hand in the Book of Cerne (MS Cambridge, University Library L1.1.10), which might be the Worcester hand. On the basis of her examination of the relevant corrections, Franzen states that she is certain that some of them are not by the Worcester hand, and is fairly confident that one other is not either.

Two new books add to the range of scholarly work on the *Anglo-Saxon Chronicle*. Another volume in the collaborative edition of the *Chronicle* is published this year. *The Anglo-Saxon Chronicle*, volume 5: *MS C*, edited by Katherine O'Brien O'Keeffe, contains a full edition of the contents of the text of the *Chronicle* in MS C, London, British Library, Cotton Tiberius B.i, written in the mid-eleventh century. The edition is preceded by a detailed account of the manuscript's composition and history—including an examination of the evidence for its origin, and in particular the commonly held view that it was written at Abingdon—its textual relationships and language, and a bibliography. Thomas A. Bredehoft's *Textual Histories: Readings in the 'Anglo-Saxon Chronicle'* is a wide-ranging examination of the *Chronicle*, its context and effects. With chapters covering 'The Common Stock Genealogies', 'Cynewulf and Cyneheard in the Context of the Common Stock', 'The Post-Alfred Annals', 'The *Chronicle* Poems', and 'Latin in the *Chronicle*', a conclusion which considers 'The Ends of the *Chronicle* and the End of Anglo-Saxon History', and an appendix which presents diplomatic transcriptions of the texts of Annal 755, Bredehoft offers a coherent discussion of the *Chronicle* as historical record and as evidence for Anglo-Saxon literate practice.

Anglo-Saxonism is again the subject of some new work this year. Peter Lucas considers 'Cotton MS Domitian A. viii, The F-Version of the *Anglo-Saxon Chronicle* and William Camden' (*N&Q* 48[2001] 98–9), and offers support for the argument that Camden had this manuscript and almost certainly owned it, in the form of evidence in a statement by James Ussher, and also Camden's use of the manuscript in his sixth edition of *Britannia*.

Books Reviewed

Alexander, Michael. *Beowulf: A Verse Translation*, rev. edn. Penguin. [2001] pp. lxvi + 137. pb £ 5.99 ($10) ISBN 0 1404 4788 1.

Bredehoft, Thomas A. *Textual Histories: Readings in the 'Anglo-Saxon Chronicle'*. UTorP. [2001] pp. 229. £50 ($70) ISBN 0 8020 5850 1.

Brown, Michelle, and Carol Farr, eds. *Mercia: An Anglo-Saxon Kingdom in Europe*. LeicUP. [2001] pp. xiv + 386. £75. ISBN 0 7185 0231 0.

Dendle, Peter. *Satan Unbound: The Devil in Old English Narrative Literature*. UTorP. [2001] pp. xi + 196. hb $50 ISBN 0 8020 4839 0, pb $22.95 ISBN 0 8020 8369 2.

Doane, A.N., and Tiffany J. Grade. *Deluxe and Illustrated Manuscripts Containing Technical and Literary Texts*. Anglo-Saxon Manuscripts in Microfiche Facsimile 9. MRTS. [2001] pp. x + 96. £76 ($120) ISBN 0 8669 8267 1.

Echard, Siân, and Gernot R. Wieland, eds. *Anglo-Latin and its Heritage: Essays in Honour of A.G. Rigg on his 64th Birthday*. Brepols. [2001] pp. xviii + 280. €50 ISBN 2 5035 0838 3.

Gameson, Richard, ed. *The Codex Aureus: An Eighth-Century Gospel Book*, pt. 1. EEMF 28. Rosenkilde & Bagger. [2001] pp. 103 + 134 pp. plates. hb €1,297 ISBN 8 7423 0533 0, pb €1,112 ISBN 8 7423 0531 4.

Gneuss, Helmut. *Handlist of Anglo-Saxon Manuscripts: A List of Manuscripts and Manuscript Fragments Written or Owned in England up to 1100*. MRTS. [2001] pp. 188. £24 ($28) ISBN 0 8669 8283 3.

Graham-Campbell, James, Richard Hall, Judith Jesch and David N. Parsons, eds. *Vikings and the Danelaw: Select Papers from the Proceedings of the Thirteenth Viking Congress, Nottingham and York, 21–30 August 1997*. Oxbow. [2001] pp. xiii + 368. £40. ISBN 1 8421 7047 3.

Green, Eugene. *Anglo-Saxon Audiences*. Lang. [2001] pp. ix + 235. $55.95 ISBN 0 8204 4550 9.

Gwara, Scott, ed. *Aldhelmi Malmesbiriensis: Prosa De Virginitate*, 2 vols. Corpus Christianorum Series Latina 124. Brepols. [2001] pp. 399 and 761. pb €150 and €147 ISBN 2 5030 1242 6 (vol. 1), 2 5030 1244 2 (vol. 2).

Higham, N.J., and D.H. Hill, eds. *Edward the Elder, 899–924*. Routledge. [2001] pp. xvi + 320. pb £16.99. ISBN 0 4152 1497 1.

Honegger, Thomas, ed. *Authors, Heros and Lovers: Essays on Medieval Literature and Language*. Peter Lang. [2001] pp. xx + 251. ISBN 3 9067 6638 1.

Horner, Shari. *The Disclosure of Enclosure: Representing Women in Old English Literature*. SUNYP. [2001] pp. viii + 207. hb $62.50. ISBN 0 7914 5009 0, pb $21.95. ISBN 0 7914 5010 4.

Howe, Nicholas. *Migration and Mythmaking in Anglo-Saxon England*. UNDP. [2001] pp. xxi + 198. $17.95 ISBN 0 2680 3463 X.

Kabir, Ananya Jahanara. *Paradise, Death and Doomsday in Anglo-Saxon Literature*. CSASE 32. CUP. [2001] pp. xi + 210. $70 ISBN 0 5218 0600 3.

Karkov, Catherine E. *Text and Picture in Anglo-Saxon England: Narrative Strategies in the Junius 11 Manuscript*. CSASE 31. CUP. [2001] pp. xii + 225. $70 ISBN 0 5218 0069 2.

Kay, C.J. and L.M. Sylvester eds., *Lexis and Texts in Early English: Studies Presented to Jane Roberts*. Rodopi. [2001] pp. 315 £40 ISBN 9 0420 1001 0.

Kelly, S.E., ed. *Charters of Abingdon Abbey*, pt. 1. Anglo-Saxon Charters 8. OUP. [2001] pp. 437. £55 ISBN 0 1972 6217 1.

Kelly, S.E., ed. *Charters of Abingdon Abbey*, pt. 2. Anglo-Saxon Charters 8. OUP. [2001] pp. 477. £55 ISBN 0 1972 6221 X.

Knowles, David, C.N.L. Brooke and Vera C.M. London, eds., with new material by C.N.L. Brooke. *The Heads of Religious Houses England and Wales. I: 940–1216*, 2nd edn. CUP. [2001] pp. xlvii + 360. £47.50 ISBN 0 5218 0452 3.

Liuzza, R.M., ed. *The Old English Version of the Gospels*, vol. 2: *Notes and Glossary*. EETS os 314. OUP [2000] pp. xxii + 369. £45 ISBN 0 1972 2313 3.

Liuzza, Roy M., and A.N. Doane. *Anglo-Saxon Gospels*. Anglo-Saxon Manuscripts in Microfiche Facsimile 3. MRTS [1995] pp. ix + 34. £76 ($120) ISBN 0 8669 8183 7.

Long, Lynne. *Translating the Bible from the 7th to the 17th Century*. Ashgate. [2001] pp. vii + 230. £40 ISBN 0 7546 1411 5.

Lucas, Peter J., A.N. Doane and I.C. Cunningham. *Latin Manuscripts with Anglo-Saxon Glosses*. Anglo-Saxon Manuscripts in Microfiche Facsimile 5. MRTS [1997] pp. viii + 51. £76 ($120) ISBN 0 8669 8217 5.

McKitterick, Rosamond, ed. *The Early Middle Ages: Europe, 400–1000*. Short Oxford History of Europe. OUP. [2001] pp. 326. hb £35 ISBN 0 1987 3173 6, pb £12.99 ISBN 0 1987 3172 8.

Miller, Sean, ed. *Charters of New Minster, Winchester*. Anglo-Saxon Charters 9. OUP. [2001] pp. 312. £45 ISBN 0 1972 6223 6.

O'Brien O'Keeffe, Katherine, ed. *The Anglo-Saxon Chronicle: A Collaborative Edition*, vol. 5: *MS C*. Brewer. [2001] pp. cxxi + 150. £45 ($75) ISBN 0 8599 1491 7.

Olsen, K. E., A. Harbus and T. Hofstra, eds. *Germanic Texts and Latin Models: Medieval Reconstructions*. Mediaevalia Groningana 2. Peeters. [2001] pp. vi + 240. pb £32.95 ISBN 9 0429 0985 4.

Pope, John C, ed. *Eight Old English Poems*, 3rd edn. Revised by R.D. Fulk. Norton. [2001] pp. xvi + 243. pb $18.45 ISBN 0 3939 7605 X.

Pulsiano, Phillip, and Elaine Treharne, eds. *A Companion to Anglo-Saxon Literature*. Blackwell. [2001] pp. xviii + 529. £80 ISBN 0 6312 0904 2.

Roberts, Jane, and Janet Nelson, eds. *Essays on Anglo-Saxon and Related Themes in Memory of Lynne Grundy*. KCL Centre for Late Antique and Medieval Studies. [2000] pp. viii + 590. £30 ISBN 0 9522 1199 8.

Schmidt, Michael. *The Story of Poetry*, vol. 1: *English Poets and Poetry from Cædmon to Caxton*. W&N. [2001] pp. viii + 496. $15.86 ISBN 0 2976 4703 2.

Scragg, Donald, ed. *Ælfric's Lives of Canonised Popes*. *OEN* Subsidia 30. Medieval Institute, Western Michigan University. [2001] pp. 112. $10.

Thompson, Benjamin, ed. *Monasteries and Society in Medieval Britain: Proceedings of the 1994 Harlaxton Symposium*. Paul Watkins. [1999] pp. 380. £49.50 ISBN 1 8716 1588 7.

Thomson, R.M. *A Descriptive Catalogue of the Medieval Manuscripts in Worcester Cathedral Library*. Brewer. [2001]. pp. xlviii + 256 + 56 pp. plates. £95 ISBN 0 8599 1618 9.

Wood, Ian. *The Missionary Life: Saints and the Evangelisation of Europe, 400–1050*. Longman. [2001] pp. 320 £17.99 ISBN 0 5823 1213 2.

III

Middle English: Excluding Chaucer

NICOLE CLIFTON, KENNETH HODGES, JURIS LIDAKA,
MICHAEL SHARP, MARION TURNER, GREG WALKER AND
K.S. WHETTER

This chapter has ten sections: 1. General and Miscellaneous; 2. Women's Writing; 3. Alliterative Verse and Lyrics; 4. The *Gawain*-Poet; 5. *Piers Plowman*; 6. Romance; 7. Gower, Lydgate and Hoccleve; 8. Malory and Caxton; 9. Middle Scots Poetry; 10. Drama. Section 1 is by K.S. Whetter, with additional material by Juris Lidaka and Greg Walker; section 2 is by Marion Turner; section 3 is by Nicole Clifton; section 4 is by Michael Sharp; section 5 is by Nicole Clifton; sections 6 and 7 are by Juris Lidaka; section 8 is by Kenneth Hodges; section 9 is by Michael Sharp; section 10 is by Greg Walker.

1. General and Miscellaneous

To begin, once again, with manuscripts and texts. The form, layout and indexes of Schmidt, ed., *Handlist XVII: Manuscripts in the Library of Gonville and Caius College*, are the same as those in the rest of the *Index of Middle English Prose*. There is thus an introduction to the collection, a summary list of contents which gives both library shelfmark and a Middle English prose index number, a fuller list detailing folio numbers and opening and closing lines of each entry, and indexes of macaronics, incipits, explicits and rubrics. Gonville and Caius has been receiving manuscripts, incunabula and books since its foundation, and—whether by accident or design—enjoyed a reputation from early on for caring for its manuscripts. Schmidt cites Christopher Brooke's (1996) estimation that more than 300 of the college's manuscripts have been there since its inception. From early on 'the collection was divided between a working library and a lending library', with the majority of manuscripts stored separately. Vernacular texts are 'incidental' to many of the manuscripts, but of the Middle English materials, medical items and recipes dominate (e.g. MS 84/166 *passim*; MS 147/197 *passim*; MS 190/223 *passim*; MS 457/395 *passim*). There are also, *inter alia*, various zodiacal items (e.g. MS 84/166 items 11–13, 23–7; MS 336/725 items 3, 26), Wycliffite Gospels (MS 179/212), a

Wycliffite New Testament (MS 343/539), an *Apocalypse of Jesus* (MS 231/117), a *Life of St Katherine* (MS 390/610 item 3), and an *Ancrene Riwle* (MS 234/120).

Still on the subject of early books is William Proctor Williams and William Baker's '*Caveat Lector*: English Books 1475–1700 and the Electronic Age' (*AEB* 12[2001] 1–29). Ralph Hanna's 'Analytical Survey 4: Middle English Manuscripts and the Study of Literature' (*NML* 4[2001] 243–64), meanwhile, surveys the state of Middle English manuscript study, noting that codicology is dominated by articles because of a lack of agreement about methodology. Hanna urges the integration of 'manuscript and literary study' and the recognition of the importance of manuscript culture. He also emphasizes the links between codicology and enumerative study and surveys the major guides, catalogues and facsimiles. Manuscripts are also the focus of A.S.G. Edwards's 'Editing and Manuscript Form: Middle English Verse Written as Prose' (*ESC* 27[2001] 15–28). Edwards examines the forces—cultural, linguistic, geographic, metrical, traditional, contextual—which influenced the copying of Middle English verse as prose. He concludes by emphasizing that modern, regularized editions of medieval verse are, in many cases, being untrue to their manuscript presentation. Readers seeking details of medieval texts in Susan Hockey's *Electronic Texts in the Humanities: Principles and Practice* [2000] will mostly be disappointed. No mention is made, for instance, of the *Electronic Beowulf*, and the discussions of both the CD-ROM edition of Chaucer's *Wife of Bath's Prologue* and the *Middle English Compendium* are fairly generalized. Instead, Hockey offers a professional survey and evaluation of humanities computing and electronic editions and the tools available for generating electronic texts. Some of the information and caveats which come across here may be useful to medievalists, though the technologically savvy may find little that is new. There are chapters on electronic texts in general, locating, creating and acquiring electronic texts, encoding, concordance and retrieval programs, literary and linguistic analysis, stylometry and attribution studies, textual criticism and the tools and techniques available for generating electronic editions, dictionaries and lexical databases, and recommendations for the future.

In Thomson, ed., *A Descriptive Catalogue of the Medieval Manuscripts in Worcester Cathedral Library*, R.M. Thomson describes 285 complete medieval manuscripts and very many fragments, almost all from bindings, most having been in Worcester in the Middle Ages. From medieval pressmarks and similar evidence, Thomson notes that at least seventy volumes are missing, nineteen of these being Old English homiliaries; those remaining may represent less than a third of the library as it once was. Michael Gullick provides descriptions of the bindings, for about 125 of them are medieval, and one is even pre-Conquest. The manuscripts catalogued thus provide valuable information about the library and its history, about medieval bindings, and about monastic education at Oxford and book production there, numerous scribbles by monks who name themselves (plus the Tremulous Hand, who unfortunately does not give his name), many manuscripts with Old and Middle English texts, and a strong tradition of local production of texts and manuscripts, with many still unstudied and some even unique. Contents in English include Rolle, Hilton, an Ælfric written by the Tremulous Hand, and a Wycliffite New Testament. There are some acknowledged drawbacks that may not readily reveal themselves to a hasty user. Among the indices, incipits are not given when they are already included in about fifteen *incipitaria* that should be available in large research collections. This saves a tremendous amount of space, but adds a bit to a researcher's task. The catalogue includes all complete manuscripts described in the catalogue by Floyer and Hamilton [1906], but not the newer ones and fragments in Ker's *Medieval Manuscripts in British Libraries*. After the manuscript, incipit, and general indices are fifty plates illustrating the library, bindings, hands, pressmarks, and more. [JL]

Although not strictly Middle English, one facsimile published this year is R.M. Thomson's *Bury Bible*. Produced at Bury St Edmunds in the 1130s, the *Bury Bible* is a superb example of Romanesque art. This slightly less than full-size facsimile is not available for review owing to its price, but according to the publisher's website 'Thomson provides a full discussion of the manuscript's production and its place among English manuscripts and art, together with photographs of comparable material'. There are chapters on the book, its context, the artist (Master Hugh, whom Thomson identifies as a professional artist with knowledge of Byzantine art), and the miniatures. The colour illuminations are based on photographs taken by the HUMI project at the University of Keio, and are given high praise by the publisher; the outstanding proof the reviewer was sent of a full-size plate more than justifies this praise.

As the subtitle of Tamarah Kohanski's *Book of John Mandeville* makes clear, this is an edition of Mandeville's *Book* based on Pynson's *c*.1496 incunabulum, itself 'based on a Defective [version] manuscript' of Mandeville. Kohanski's title reflects Pynson's colophon rather than the more common *Mandeville's Travels* or *Travels of Sir John Mandeville*. For Kohanski, 'book' is also less prescriptive and less suggestive of a journey or travel diary, allowing readers to decide for themselves the nature of this encyclopedic work, which juggles 'geography, history, romance, propaganda, satire, and a multitude of other generic patterns'. Following Iain Higgins's *Writing East* (UPennP [1997]), Kohanski argues against the 'best text' trend in Mandeville editions, arguing instead that scholars embrace the *Book*'s variant versions, receptions and readings. Hence the choice of the Pynson incunabulum as base text, though such a decision also privileges the 'constant state of flux' enjoyed (or suffered) by medieval popular texts. Kohanski thus hopes to secure for the Defective versions greater scholarly scrutiny than they currently enjoy. The text itself is clearly laid out with a generous left-hand margin. Kohanski claims to have modernized the text, but this is only partially the case: *u* and *v* have been normalized, in-text references have been supplied for biblical quotations, and marginal cross-references are supplied to the Cotton MS chapter divisions. Marginal notes allowing readers quickly to locate, say, 'the Amazons' or 'the Land of Murkiness' have also been added to ease cross-referencing with other editions or manuscripts. Punctuation and capitalization, however, are medieval, not modern, including slashes for commas and sentences which end without full stops or begin without capitals. (Mandeville is also the focus of an article mentioned below.)

A.S.G. Edwards and T. Takamiya, 'A New Middle English Carol' (*MÆ* 70[2001] 112–15), an important but brief article, presents an edition of an unrecorded Nativity carol now in the possession of Professor Takamiya. Mostly conventional, the carol is unusual in its unique use of *Chorus* to signify the refrain. It thus testifies to, and helps modern readers to appreciate, the medieval sense of form.

Neil Cartlidge renders an impressive edition of *The Owl and the Nightingale*, which together with translation takes up barely a fifth of the whole volume. The closely packed and well-reasoned introduction is nearly as long, ranging from authorship through reception, sources and contexts, and transmission to textual matters of language, palaeography (even identifying the location of wynns), and editorial treatment of the text, taken from BL MS Cotton Caligula A.ix. A peculiar omission is any discussion of the translation, which attends the text in parallel columns and is much more hypotactic than the Middle English text. Thanks to the narrow columns, some long, solid blocks of the modernization are not unduly hard on the eyes; the Middle English is occasionally broken to maintain some cross-column coordination, but additional paragraphing and line-referencing would have helped. The explanatory notes are longer than the text, but well worth that. They are followed by a short group of appendices with references to, texts of, or texts and translations of source and analogue materials, which should perhaps have been only texts or texts and translations. This is followed by extensive textual and linguistic notes, and then by a lengthy classified bibliography that is a marvel of thoroughness, though difficult to refer to from the short references in the introduction and two groups of notes because the short references do not indicate which portion of the bibliography will carry the full information. A longish glossary closes the volume. In all, as Cartlidge predicts at the beginning, the book walks a fine line, balancing the needs and interests of generalists with those of specialists, but it is thorough enough to serve many uses. [JL]

A number of EETS titles have again been reprinted. As reprints they are unavailable for review, but readers may be interested in the renewed availability of, *inter alia*, *Mum and the Sothsegger*, edited by M. Day and R. Steele, *Quatrefoil of Love*, edited by I. Gollancz and M.M. Weale, and *The Owl and the Nightingale*, edited by J.H.G. Grattan and G.F.H. Sykes. Further details can be found at <http://www.boydell.co.uk/EETS.HTM>.

Kathryn Kerby-Fulton and Maidie Hilmo have edited a collection of essays on *The Medieval Professional Reader at Work: Evidence from Manuscripts of Chaucer, Langland, Kempe, and Gower*, which suggests 'some methods and approaches for the recovery of medieval reader response from manuscript evidence of a kind still too often ignored'. The medieval professional reader is defined as the person responsible for 'prepar[ing] a text for the reading public'. Such a person might be scribe, illustrator, editor, or something else, but obviously had considerable impact on medieval texts and culture. Following Kerby-Fulton and Denise Despres's *Iconography and the Professional Reader* (UMinnP [1998]), medieval reading is given five functions: mnemonic, meditative, performative, self-reflexive, or dissenting. As a whole, the collection is well laid out, and includes a number of black and white reproductions of manuscript illustrations and pages, including several of the Ellesmere miniatures, but it lacks an index, list of illustrations or list of manuscripts discussed.

Ashley and Clark, eds., *Medieval Conduct*, expands the notion of courtesy book beyond the typical prose treatise for courtly etiquette to include various texts 'systematizing a society's codes of behavior'. Hence the title *conduct* book. Throughout, the contributors are concerned to explore the intersections of text, history, culture and practice, and a number of essays highlight the dialogic and subversive potential of conduct books. Material is considered from Italy, Germany, France and England, mostly from the fourteenth and fifteenth centuries. Of those essays relevant to this section, Anna Dronzek highlights what we can learn about the gendered nature of the medieval education of children from, *inter alia*, 'The Good Wife Taught her Daughter', 'The Good Wyfe wold a Pylgremage', *The Book of the Knight of the Tower* (the French text of which is discussed by Roberta Krueger in chapter 3), 'The Babees Book', 'Lerne or be Lewde', 'The ABC of Aristotle', 'Urbanitatis', and 'The Lytylle Childrenes Book', while Ruth Nissé focuses on the fifteenth-century Norwich Lollard trials to highlight connections between devotional conduct and Lollard rejection of images. Other Middle English texts are examined by Claire Sponsler, who reveals the programme of moderated consumption and self-governance in Lydgate's 'Dietary', and Mark Addison Amos, who argues that Caxton's *Book of Courtesy* suggests that manners and morals are related, thus offering the increasingly powerful urban mercantile elite manners by which to validate their claims to some degree of social nobility. The occasional cross-references (usually to the introduction) would have benefited from the inclusion of page references, and Nissé stretches the notion of what constitutes a conduct manual rather too far, but the volume will interest scholars of conduct literature, class, gender and religion.

Middle English courtesy books also appear in Alessandra Petrina's 'Children's Literature and Children's Education in Late Medieval England' (in Tosi, ed., *Hearts of Lightness: The Magic of Children's Literature*, pp. 27–45), the only chapter on a medieval subject in the book. In a collection of essays designed in part to rebut various fallacies regarding children's literature, Petrina attempts to 'profile ... a medieval child' and his or her reading material. Since a paramount concern of children's education was manners, they read courtesy books. It is an interesting chapter, but many of Petrina's conclusions are insufficiently supported by her evidence, and too little attention is given to orality. The volume as a whole would also have benefited from an index.

As Wendy Scase's introduction makes clear, all of the essays in *New Medieval Literatures* 4[2001] 'explore nation, identity, and otherness', though some do so more obviously than others. Of the relevant papers, David Lawton's 'The Surveying Subject and the "Whole World" of Belief: Three Case Studies' (pp. 9–37), focuses on (1) the frame, rider and text of the Hereford Map, (2) the first-person pronouns in *Mandeville's Travels*, a text which is 'as much map as ... text' and whose first-person pronouns reflect the pronouns of its various sources, and (3) John Leland's 'remapping [of] the textuality and landscape of past and present'. James H. Landman, 'Pleading, Pragmatism, and Permissible Hypocrisy: The "Colours" of Legal Discourse in Late Medieval England' (pp. 139–70), examines John Fortescue's shift from Lancastrian to Yorkist as an example of the medieval legal doubling of pragmatism and principle. Theresa D. Kemp, 'The *Knight of the Tower* and the Queen in Sanctuary: Elizabeth Woodville's Use of Meaningful Silence and Absence' (pp. 171–88), highlights the ways in which Elizabeth Woodville's commissioning of Caxton's *Book of the Knight of the Tower* 'enabled her ... to assert her dynastic legitimacy'. Kemp's paper leads naturally to Carroll Hilles's 'Gender and Politics in Osbern Bokenham's *Legendary*' (pp. 189–212), for Hilles highlights the ways in which Bokenham's 1440s *Legendys of Hooly Wummen* 'uses female piety to develop a rhetoric of political dissent' undermining Lancastrian authority and supporting York. Two other papers are linked by their examination of political prophecy: Lesley Coote and Tim Thornton's 'Merlin, *Erceldoune*, Nixon: A Tradition of Popular Political Prophecy' (pp. 117–37), and Ruth Nissé's

'Prophetic Nations' (pp. 95–115). Coote and Thornton note that various 'popular prophecies' are, with the notable exception of Geoffrey's *Prophetiae Merlini*, in English. Their foci are the *Prophetiae*, the Nixon prophecies, and *Thomas of Eceldoune*, and what they reveal of orality, nationalism, and (least successfully, in my opinion) the influence of 'non-élite groups' on English identity. Since Nissé compares the presentation of geopolitical, apocalyptic prophecy and reform in *Eulogium Historiarum* and Walter Brut's Latin response to heresy charges, her focus is less obviously Middle English, but the Lollards' concern with the vernacular and both texts' concern with the English nation make it worth mentioning here. As with earlier volumes, *NML* 4 closes with an analytical survey, in this case, Hanna's survey of Middle English codicology, mentioned above.

In general religious matters, Thomas D. Hill, '"The Ballad of St Stephen and Herod": Biblical History and Medieval Popular Religious Culture' (*MÆ* 70[2001] 240–9), examines the origins of the late medieval ballad in the title, and argues that it 'clearly displays the tendency of medieval popular religion to reshape "historical" [biblical] narrative to conform to the conventions and expectations of traditional or "folk" narrative'. Andrew Taylor, 'Translation, Censorship, Authorship and the Lost Work of Reginald Pecock' (in Blumenfeld-Kosinski, *et al.*, eds., *The Politics of Translation in the Middle Ages and the Renaissance*, pp. 143–60), looks at Bishop Reginald Pecock's fifteenth-century English theological writings. Generally 'conventional and … dull', Pecock's work translates and popularizes 'professional discourse' and represents the final attempt before Tyndale 'to create a vernacular theology in England'. Nonetheless, says Taylor, Pecock is not Lollard—at least, not entirely. It may be added that the entire Blumenfeld-Kosinksi volume explores translation's sociopolitical, cultural and 'systemic' contexts, as well as the voice of the individual translator. The introduction surveys various aspects of medieval European translation, and although it has nothing explicitly on Middle English, it does address the political connotations of Anglo-Saxon and Anglo-Norman translations in England, in addition to what Blumenfeld-Kosinksi sees as the linguistic polemics of the Hundred Years War. The volume is well laid out, but lacks an index, and pages 151–2 appear twice. Biblical translation is also the subject of Su Fang Ng's 'Translation, Interpretation, and Heresy: The Wycliffite Bible, Tyndale's Bible, and the Contested Origin' (*SP* 98[2001] 315–38). Ng argues that what is important about the possible continuities between Lollardy and the Reformation is the ongoing 'subversiveness of translation'. Rather less convincing is the claim that 'translation is also subversive because it challenges the claim to an "original" and to an "origin"'.

Two new articles discuss the *South English Legendary*. O.S. Pickering, '*South English Legendary* Style in Robert of Gloucester's *Chronicle*' (*MÆ* 70[2001] 1–18), examines stylistic similarities and a shared outspokenness common to both the *South English Legendary* and Robert of Gloucester's *Chronicle*, and concludes not that Robert of Gloucester borrowed from the *South English Legendary*, but rather that he is in all likelihood its 'outspoken reviser'.

Instead of a *South English Legendary*, Thomas R. Liszka argues for 'The *South English Legendaries*' (in Liszka and Walker, eds., *The North Sea World in the Middle Ages: Studies in the Cultural History of North-Western Europe*, pp. 243–80). He surveys the origin of the title in modern scholarship and the lack of any particular title in medieval England. Arguing from the manuscripts' selection of contents and their organization, as well as from titles of individual items as given in the manuscripts (there are fifteen appendices listing contents and titles), Liszka determines that the *SEL* was not perceived as a fixed work but as an open collection, that items may have circulated in booklets or in isolated form, and that the calendric order seems far less 'original' than a loose one based on Church history: materials before Christ and Mary, followed by materials on Christ and Mary, and finally lives of the saints. The lack of a perceived form allowed the manuscripts to develop in many ways, not chaotically but in response to immediate circumstances. [JL]

Malcolm Richardson, 'The Fading Influence of the Medieval *Ars Dictaminis* in England after 1400' (*Rhetorica* 19[2001] 225–47), links the decline in English *ars dictaminis* to the fact that fifteenth-century letters were influenced more by (brief) royal epistles than dictaminal rhetoric. Towards the middle to end of the century, even this format was abandoned by the middle classes, as well as by the rising number of lawyers.

David Salter, *Holy and Noble Beasts: Encounters with Animals in Medieval Literature*, examines 'the representation of animals' in thirteenth- and fourteenth-century romance and *vitae*, 'with a view to uncovering the range of attitudes towards the animal kingdom that were current at the time'. A recurring question posed by Salter is whether the representations of animals reflect a genuine interest in animals *per se* or merely an anthropocentric allegory. Thus he emphasizes that human identity and values in romance and *vitae* are often measured by and defined against animal–human interaction. Two-thirds of the book is devoted to romance, with the remainder focused on animals in hagiography, particularly in stories of St Francis of Assisi and (in chapter 1) Colantonio's *St Jerome and the Lion*. Emphasizing the 'multiplicity of representations of, and attitudes towards, animals and nature ... in medieval literature', Salter argues that Francis's relations with animals reflect his purity and God's favour. However, Francis alternately views animals as divinely created for human use and as creatures deserving reverence as a sign of respect for God's creations. The *vitae* quotations are all given in modern English. This makes the book more accessible, though some specialists will perhaps lament the fact that the Latin or Italian original is never offered even in footnotes.

Corinne Saunders's *Rape and Ravishment in the Literature of Medieval England* is a large book with a wide scope. Since it is covered elsewhere, I restrict myself here to some general comments. Saunders's introduction surveys modern theories of rape in order (rightly, in my opinion) to highlight the differences between medieval and modern notions of rape. A key concern throughout is the connection between rape and abduction. The dominant focus is the fourteenth century, but Saunders also examines Anglo-Saxon and post-Conquest rape laws, the Church's views on ravishment, narratives of rape in hagiographic literature, rape in romance, ravishment in Malory's *Morte Darthur*, and the more nuanced portrait of rape in Chaucer. Chapter 4 steps outside the medieval period to look at classical narratives well told and well known in the Middle Ages: the rape of Lucretia and the Sabine women, and the abduction of Helen of Troy. These stories, says Saunders, are 'myths of origin for social upheaval ... and they focus the two faces of ravishment, rape and abduction'. Different contexts and narratives produce different emphases. Hagiography, for instance, highlights sexual assault and bodily pollution, whereas historical narratives focus on rape as abduction. Saunders defines the 'medieval understanding of "rape" [as] the exercise of the will to control and possess another human being'. Throughout, Saunders is widely read in both primary and secondary material, and several chapters have both general and theoretical discussions as well as readings of particular texts or documents. Anglo-Saxon, Latin and Anglo-Norman material is quoted in the original with translations, and difficult Middle English words are glossed in the margins. Saunders occasionally refutes an argument with questions when more forceful (and deserved) scepticism would improve the clarity of her prose and thesis, but this is an important work for those interested in medieval rape.

Relations between the sexes are also the subject of Burger and Kruger, eds., *Queering the Middle Ages*. The introduction questions 'straight (teleological) narration, causal explanations, and schemes of periodization'. Hence the contributors offer new and destabilizing views of the Middle Ages and medieval sexuality and a concomitant examination of how such a view affects queer theory and the (post)modern. The volume is divided into three sections, each of which closes with a response essay. The essays cover medieval Italian, Spanish, French and English literature, but some are less helpful than others. *Pace* Karma Lochrie, for instance, I question how helpful Bill Clinton's sexual shenanigans are 'for understanding the incoherence in medieval representations of heterosexuality'. A concern about rigid periodization is laudable, but a volume on the Middle Ages would be better served—here and elsewhere—by medieval evidence. Of the Middle English papers, Glenn Burger juxtaposes Chaucer's *Miller's Tale* and John Preston's [1992] gay porn anthology in an attempt to renegotiate the relationship between pre- and postmodern and to show why queer readers might need Chaucer, while Garrett P.J. Epp, in one of the finer essays in the volume, focuses on the *Tretise of Miraclis Pleyinge* [*c*.1400] and its criticism of what its authors see as the lechery inspired by representations of Christ's body in Passion plays. *Inter alia*, Larry Scanlon's response to part 3 links Oscar Wilde and George Lyman Kittredge. Claire Sponsler's essay both is and is not concerned with medieval England, since she examines Froissart's 'theatricalized' account of the deposition of Edward II and the sexual reasons behind Edward's downfall. The essay as a whole is good, but the conclusion flatly contradicts itself. Overall, the volume is well laid out, and the prose is generally clear.

The *Roman de la Rose* is hardly a Middle English item, but its stature as a vernacular text and its influence upon medieval English literature are great. According to Alastair Minnis's *Magister amoris: The 'Roman de la Rose' and Vernacular Hermeneutics*, medieval literary theory played a large role in the creation and reception of *Roman de la Rose*. A key figure within medieval literary theory is Ovid, 'an *auctor* of pre-eminent significance for vernacular poetics' and a *magister amoris* whose treatment of sexuality and human behaviour became a model for Jean de Meun and for medieval European vernacular hermeneutics. Like Ovid, his medieval followers, including Jean de Meun, are ambiguous, hence the varied responses to the *Rose*. Indeed, 'no clear route through the [*Rose*] is visible or perhaps even possible'. It is Minnis's contention that the complexity of the *Rose* is not due to botched artistry. On the contrary, Jean de Meun was setting himself up as medieval successor to Ovid, including succeeding to the contentious office of master of love. This, it is emphasized, includes a bluntness, even bawdiness, of speech consonant with Roman and medieval theories of satire, as well as certain 'homoerotic possibilities'. Minnis places the result in the context of medieval literary theory in order to emphasize the *Rose*'s 'true embarrassment of riches'. Minnis's wit and learning are evident throughout, and *Magister amoris* will interest scholars of *Roman de la Rose*, medieval literary theory, and European vernacular hermeneutics. (Jean de Meun's sexual concerns are also discussed by Susan Schibanoff in *Queering the Middle Ages*, mentioned above.)

The fourteenth-century Welsh poet Dafydd ap Gwilym, the most prolific, and perhaps best known of the medieval bards, is sure to reach a still wider audience as a result of Gwyn Thomas's excellent new collection, *Daffyd ap Gwilym: His Poems*. Delightfully produced by the University of Wales Press, this paperback edition of texts translated into lively, idiomatic English gives the non-Welsh speaker new access to the poems in a highly readable form. A brief introduction presents the reader with accounts of the poet, his life and milieu, and an insight into the complex rules of *cynghanedd*, the 'harmonies' underlying the system of metrics upon which Welsh fixed-metre verse is based. But it is the poems themselves that are the best introduction to Dafydd and his world. They provide detailed exemplification of the importance of patronage to bardic culture (a series of panegyrics and elegies, satires and poems of thanks chart the shifting relation between poet—or his fictional surrogates—and a number of patrons), of the centrality of love, sexual rivalry, and the natural world, to the poet's work. The publication of the scurrilous, scabrous, verses 'To his Pecker'—a possibly spurious addition to the canon—with their injunctions to his 'stiff conger eel' (allegedly 'longer than a man's thigh') regarding its 'awkward itching' (pp. 317–18), justifies the price of the volume on its own. [GW]

Helen Barr's *Socioliterary Practice in Late Medieval England* is a broad and engaging survey of its subject, which explores language, literature, and culture as mediated in and through a range of canonical and non-canonical texts of the Ricardian period and beyond. Conservative social commentaries in *Wynnere and Wastoure*, Hoccleve, and Chaucer are the subject of a stimulating opening chapter. Chaucer's works recur in later chapters, where the Prologue to *The Legend of Good Women* (read in relation to Richard II's royal image) and *The Nun's Priest's Tale* (and the 1381 rising) take centre stage. *Pearl*, *Mum and the Sothsegger*, John (or was it Thomas?) Clanvowe's *The Book of Cupid, Richard the Redeless*, and Lydgate's *The Churl and the Bird* are also the subject of sustained analysis. [GW]

The archival reconstruction undertaken in Vincent Gillespie's edition of the *Registrum* of the Bridgetine house of Syon, published with an edition of 'The Libraries of the Carthusians' by A.I. Doyle as *Syon Abbey: With the Library of the Carthusians*, is singularly impressive. The *Registrum* (Cambridge Corpus Christi College MS 141) is an early sixteenth-century catalogue drawn up in the hand of the Syon librarian Thomas Betson (d. 1516). In addition to editing the text, tracking down elusive references, and adding information from other sources, Gillespie uses the reconstructed contents of the list as the basis of a cultural history of the brethren in the half-century before the dissolution. As well as a brief history of the house from its foundation by Henry V in 1415, he considers the impact upon it of various intellectual and cultural forces: the advent of print, the humanist new learning, and the early Reformation controversies, all of which are reflected in the library's acquisition of books. The volume also contains, *inter alia*, Betson's own index, lists of 'class marks reconstructed from the Index and from erasure', donors of books to Syon, and a conspectus of class marks. Added to this are Doyle's excellent accounts of the surviving records of books in the Carthusian houses of Hinton, London, Witham, and a further unidentified house. [GW]

Another valuable research tool for scholars and students of the history of the book is provided by the ongoing project under the general editorship of Kathleen Scott to publish *An Index of Images in English Manuscripts from the Time of Chaucer to Henry VIII*. The first two volumes, covering the manuscripts in the Bodleian Library, Oxford, are now published (a third and final Bodleian volume was due to follow in 2002). The first, dealing with MSS Additional to Digby, is edited by Scott herself, Ann E. Nichols, Michael T. Orr, and Lynda Dennison; the second, covering MSS Dodsworth to Marshall, by Scott, Nichols, Martha W. Driver, and Dennison. Once the third volume completes the set, these books will add up to a comprehensive index of images in Bodleian manuscripts, including marginalia, diagrams, tables, coats of arms, and pictorial notations as well as illuminations and illustrations *per se*. Some (but alas not all) of the more interesting images described are reproduced in black and white plates at the back of the book. [GW]

2. Women's Writing

Three essays in the excellent Daybell, ed., *Early Modern Women's Letter Writing, 1450–1700* comprise some of the most innovative and informative work on women's writing in Middle English published in 2001. Daybell writes in his introduction (pp. 1–15) that this volume 'shows that women's letter-writing during the late medieval and early modern periods was a very much larger and more socially diversified area of female activity than has generally been assumed' (p. 3), and the book amply demonstrates the truth of this assertion. The first three essays deal with letter-writing in the fifteenth century; subsequent articles focus on the sixteenth, seventeenth, and eighteenth centuries, so that the volume places medieval Englishwomen within a larger trajectory of female self-expression. The essays pertinent here are Roger Dalrymple's 'Reaction, Consolation and Redress in the Letters of the Paston Women' (pp. 16–28); Jennifer C. Ward's 'Letter-Writing by English Noblewomen in the Early Fifteenth Century' (pp. 29–41); and Alison Truelove's 'Commanding Communications: the Fifteenth-Century Letters of the Stonor Women' (pp. 42–58). They deal with a fascinating range of sources: letters written as early as 1392 are cited by Ward (p. 30), who focuses on the development of women's letter-writing in the early 1400s, while Dalrymple and Truelove each focus on a family archive—the Pastons and the Stonors. Truelove's selection includes letters by figures such as Alice Chaucer and Elizabeth Woodville, both of whom were connected with the Stonor family. The three essays complement each other: all, for example, discuss the intersection between oral and written culture in women's letters. Ward comments on the oral communications added to letters via the bearer (p. 33), Dalrymple discusses the oral and literary qualities of the texts and their opposition to oral gossip and rumour (p. 24), describing the ways in which Margaret Paston had faith in 'the written word as redressive' (p. 23), and Truelove explores the idea that women have been 'innovators in linguistic changes' (p. 53) because they adopt new, colloquial forms more quickly than men, demonstrating that this is borne out in women's greater use of terms such as 'you' rather than 'ye', or 'which' rather than 'the which' in the letters under consideration (p. 53). She also points out that the fact that many letters by women were dictated actually places the 'authors' firmly in a scholarly tradition, as the origin of letter-writing as a scholarly practice was dictation (p. 55). The scholarly and literary aspects of the letters of the Paston women are crystallized in a letter by Agnes Paston, strikingly described by Dalrymple as proceeding 'in cadences which are biblical and Chaucerian by turns' (p. 21). These essays are an invaluable resource for anyone interested in women's writing in Middle English, and will hopefully stimulate more work on medieval women's letters.

The Paston letters are also briefly discussed in Peter Fleming's *Family and Household in Medieval England*, in particular letters about the love lives of the Paston women—including the subjects of Margery Paston's notorious marriage (pp. 28–9) and of Margery Brew's valentines to her lover and husband-to-be, John Paston (pp. 35–6). There are some brief references to the Pastons—whose letters are characterized as 'rambling and stylistically stultifying' (p. 245)—in Malcolm Richardson, 'The Fading Influence of the Medieval *Ars Dictaminis* in England after 1400' (*Rhetorica* 19[2001] 225–47).

Reflecting the huge upsurge in interest in Margery Kempe over the last decade, much work was published in 2001 on this extraordinary medieval woman. Indeed, she has now reached the heady heights symbolized by a Norton Critical Edition: Staley, ed., *The Book of Margery Kempe: A New Translation, Contexts, Criticism*. Aspects of this book will make it a useful teaching tool: it includes a sensible range of contextual material (excerpts from *Arundel's Constitutions, The Meditations on the Life of Christ, The Shewings of Julian of Norwich, The Book of St. Bride*, and *The Life of Marie d'Oignies*) and a good mix of crucial critical essays (by Clarissa Atkinson, Lynn Staley, Karma Lochrie, David Aers, Kathleen Ashley, Gail McMurray Gibson, Sarah Beckwith, Caroline Walker Bynum, and Nicholas Watson) plus an introduction, map, and bibliography. However, it is difficult to see the point of translating this text, which is relatively accessible in its original form, and it is to be hoped that the arrival of this edition does not tempt students to neglect the Middle English text itself. The translator seems to be aware of the problems of translating this text: the edition includes a 'Kempe Lexicon', which explains that some of Kempe's vocabulary—including words such as 'creature' 'dalliance' 'ghostly' 'homely' and 'kind'—cannot adequately be translated, and the translation itself does keep much of the word order and tone of the original.

Sarah Salih's *Versions of Virginity in Late Medieval England*, a book which challenges Caroline Walker Bynum's conception of medieval women and argues that virginity is 'itself a sexuality' (p. 10), deals at length with *The Book of Margery Kempe*. Salih argues that the *Book* is 'both a record of the process of remaking a virgin, and itself one of the techniques used to do so' (p. 170). She contextualizes Kempe's bid for virginity, claiming that 'no one is ever born a virgin, in the full sense' (p. 242) according to certain medieval thinkers, citing Aquinas's assertion that the virginity of those who lack the intention to remain virgins is no virginity at all (p. 203). Thus Kempe, 'never was a virgin until Christ made her into one' (p. 203), and Salih ultimately suggests that Kempe might 'not just be *like* a virgin, but herself the paradigm of virginity on earth' (p. 241). Salih makes many useful observations—such as the idea that Kempe's wearing of white clothes might signify liminality rather than virginity (p. 220)—and has a knack for neat phrases, terming Kempe a 'female urban hermit' (p. 168) in search of 'Martyrdom by slander' (p.

213) and as one of a group of women 'winning battles for their bodies' (p. 181). This book is an important contribution both to the study of Margery Kempe and to the study of gender in medieval Europe more generally.

Corinne Saunders also includes a brief examination of Margery Kempe and her attitude to virginity and chastity in the excellent *Rape and Ravishment*, discussing Kempe's obsessive fear of rape (p. 147). Kempe's sexuality and sociality is productively discussed in a debate between Amy Hollywood and Carolyn Dinshaw about the way in which Kempe is 'queer'. This appears in 'History's Queer Touch: A Forum on Carolyn Dinshaw's *Getting Medieval: Sexualities and Communities*' (*JHSex* 10[2001] 165–212). Most of the seven articles in this forum (by Elizabeth A. Castelli, Rosemary Drage Hale, Amy Hollywood, Mark D. Jordan, Ann Pellegrini, Angela Zito, and Carolyn Dinshaw) include some discussion of Kempe.

Kempe's interest in Bridget of Sweden is explored by Catherine S. Akel in '"A schort tretys and a comfortybl ... ": Perception and Purpose of Margery Kempe's Narrative' (*ES* 82[2001] 1–13). (Kempe and Bridget of Sweden are also discussed in Julia Mortimer, 'Reflections in *The Myroure of Oure Ladye*: The Translation of a Desiring Body' (*MysticsQ* 27[2001] 58–76), which focuses mainly on Bridget, with only brief references to Kempe.) Akel's article also discusses the hostile reception of Kempe's text in the 1930s, contrasting this with the respectful, engaged, early annotations on the *Book*. The annotations on the manuscript of *The Book of Margery Kempe* are the subject of a substantial essay by Kelly Parsons, 'The Red Ink Annotator of *The Book of Margery Kempe* and his Lay Audience' (in Kerby-Fulton and Hilmo, eds., pp. 143–216). Parsons argues that the annotations 'support a strong argument in favour of a lay audience for the *Book*' (p. 144) discussing the Carthusians' pastoral care of wealthy patrons and of their servants (p. 145) and the evidence that books changed hands between Mount Grace and the outside world from the mid-fifteenth century (p. 145). The existence of a recipe written into the book in the late fifteenth or early sixteenth century, containing exotic ingredients anathema to the Carthusians' lifestyle, is cited as evidence pointing towards lay ownership or prolonged use (pp. 153–4). Parsons specifically suggests that the annotations 'seem to have been tailored for female consumption' (p. 147) and that the text was being 'customized for female use' (p. 153). This illuminating article also provides listings of all the red ink annotations, corrections and rubrications in the manuscript.

The twentieth-century editing of the *Book* is the focus of two pieces in *MFF* 31[2001], a second special issue on 'Feminist Legacies', dealing with biography. It contains two articles on Hope Emily Allen: John C. Hirsh, 'Hope Emily Allen, the Second Volume of the *Book of Margery Kempe*, and an Adversary' (*MFF* 31[2001] 11–17) and Marea Mitchell, '"The ever-growing army of serious girl students": The Legacy of Hope Emily Allen' (*MFF* 31[2001] 17–29). These articles form a tribute to one of the pioneers of the study of women's writing in Middle English. Four other articles on Margery Kempe, covering the central issues of performative gender, literacy, mercantilism, and desire have been published this year. Clare Bradford's 'Mother, Maiden, Child: Gender as Performance in *The Book of Margery Kempe*' (in Devlin-Glass and McCredden, eds., *Feminist Poetics of the Sacred: Creative Suspicions*, pp. 165–81) uses the work of Judith Butler to comment on Kempe's ambiguous subversion of gender identities. Cheryl Glenn's 'Popular Literacy in the Middle Ages: *The Book of Margery Kempe*' (in Trimbur, ed., *Popular Literacy:*

Studies in Cultural Practices and Poetics, pp. 56–73) presents Kempe as a worthy object of study for literacy scholars. Terming Kempe 'an attempted escapee from the merchant class' (p. 135), and suggesting that she had internalized the rhetoric of anti-mercantilism, Roger A. Ladd discusses the text in the context of estates satire in 'Margery Kempe and her Mercantile Mysticism' (*FCS* 26[2001] 121–41). Finally, in 'The Savior of her Desire: Margery Kempe's Passionate Gaze' (*Exemplaria* 13[2001] 39–66), Lisa Manter uses film theory and psychoanalysis to analyse desire, the gaze, and Christ's masculinity, asserting that Kempe 'demands that Christ become the impossible sign—the male body without phallic power that will allow for the fulfillment of her desiring gaze' (p. 66).

Sadly, Julian of Norwich has continued to receive far less attention than Margery Kempe. Paul F. Reichardt's article '"Speciall sainctes": Julian of Norwich, John of Beverley, and the Chronology of the *Shewings*' (*ES* 82[2001] 385–92), puts forward an explanation for the inclusion of John of Beverley in Julian's list of saints in the Long Text but not in the Short: Reichardt ultimately suggests that Julian's healing occurred on John's feast day. Kevin J. Magill discusses the divine perspective in the *Revelations*, and argues against some of the work of Oliver Davies, in 'The Transformation of Vision in the *Revelations* of Julian of Norwich' (*Magistra* 7[2001] 97–110). Two books including extended discussions of Julian have a 2001 imprint: Kerrie Hide, *Gifted Origins to Graced Fulfilment: The Soteriology of Julian of Norwich* (permanently out of print) and Tarjei Park, *Selfhood and 'Gostly Menyng' in Some Middle English Mystics: Semiotic Approaches to Contemplative Theology* (not yet available). The year 2001 also saw the publication of an ambitious new edition of Julian's Showings: Reynolds and Holloway, eds., *Julian of Norwich: Showing of Love, Extant Texts and Translation*. This luxury linen-bound volume, beautifully illustrated, with detailed notes and appendices, aims 'to give each letter, each word, each line, each folio, of the extant manuscripts of Julian of Norwich's *Showing of Love* diplomatically' (p. xiii). The edition is a true labour of love, and shows evidence of much knowledge of and devotion to Julian's work. Four different versions of Julian's text are printed (MSS Westminster Cathedral, Paris, BN Anglais 40, London, BL Sloane 2499, and London, BL Amherst), three with facing-page translations. The edition includes useful tools such as a glossary for Sloane 2499, which preserves a Norfolk dialect, appendices of cross-references and scriptural references, a table of dates, and a bibliography. There are eighteen colour illustrations of folios from the manuscripts, and each version is provided with a detailed introduction. Somewhat problematically, Holloway vehemently argues for the Short Text as the latest version of Julian's text (pp. 689–97), without giving enough space to opposing points of view, resulting in a manifestly biased view of the texts. More attention to differing critical viewpoints would have made this a stronger and more useful edition.

Female religious experience in its heretical manifestation can be found in the records of the Norwich heresy trials, in the words of women such as Margery Baxter and Hawisia Moon (although, as with many letters by women and indeed with *The Book of Margery Kempe*, the female author is masked by a scribe of dubious reliability and veracity). In 'Grace Under Pressure: Conduct and Representation in the Norwich Heresy Trials' (in Ashley and Clark, eds., pp. 207–25), Ruth Nissé discusses Baxter's attack on oaths and idolatry and her praise of Moon and of

William White. This excellent article contains particularly insightful comments on the Lollards' attitude to guilds and to pilgrimage.

Female spirituality is also the subject of Nancy Bradley Warren's *Spiritual Economies: Female Monasticism in Later Medieval England*, which deals with the relationships and conflicts between 'material, symbolic, textual, political, and spiritual economies' (p. viii). Warren is interested not only in 'breach[ing] the cloister wall' but also in breaching other boundaries 'particularly those demarcating the sacred and the secular, the material and the symbolic, the literary and the historical' (p. viii). This assured and interesting book deals with a variety of sources written by women, including *The Book of Margery Kempe* (pp. 92–110), letters, such as one by Joan Ketteryche to John Paston (p. 62), and accounts recorded by treasuresses (p. 65). The volume contains many useful insights: in the case of Ketteryche, for example, Warren describes the way in which she 'mobilizes textual practices for material gain' (p. 62) and discusses her techniques for exploiting her own identity as a bride of Christ. Warren's discussion of the Carthusians' admiration for Kempe (pp. 108–10) chimes with the essays by Akel and Parsons mentioned above.

More generally, two books on medieval women which touch on women's writing have been reissued this year. Margaret Wade Labarge's *Women in Medieval Life* [1986] was published as a Penguin Classic for the first time in 2001, and Eileen Power's *Medieval Women* [1975] was reissued by the Folio Society with a new (very short) foreword and illustrations. Margery Kempe and Julian of Norwich also make cameo appearances alongside a diverse range of women in Reichardt, ed., *Catholic Women Writers: A Bio-Bibliographical Sourcebook*. [MT]

3. Alliterative Verse and Lyrics

The seventh volume of the Annotated Bibliographies of Old and Middle English Literature, *The Middle English Lyric and Short Poem*, by Rosemary Greentree, is remarkably comprehensive. In her introduction, Greentree attempts to define the Middle English lyric, comments on trends in criticism and individual scholars, and discusses some of the individual lyrics and groups of lyrics that have drawn scholarly attention. The bibliography itself begins with nineteenth-century editions and works of criticism, and is complete up to the end of 1995. The annotations are neutral summaries of contents and approaches. Spot-checking entries against online databases such as the MLA bibliography and ITER revealed more lacunae in the databases than errors in Greentree; the rare errors I found would not prevent a scholar locating the article in question.

Two essays in Cooney, ed., *Nation, Court and Culture: New Essays on Fifteenth-Century English Poetry*, deal with lyrics. Tony Davenport, in 'Fifteenth Century Complaints and Duke Humphrey's Wives' (pp. 129–52), analyses a Findern lyric showing a solitary, anxious figure with reference to Hoccleve, Lydgate and Chaucer, establishing the tradition of the complaint, before studying two Lydgatian complaints on behalf of or in the voice of the duke's wives. In 'Fifteenth Century Lyrics and Carols' (pp. 168–83), Douglas Gray suggests seeing 'traditional' and 'individual/autobiographical' as ends of a spectrum.

Piotr Sadowski studies 'The Sound-Symbolic Quality of Word-Initial *gr*-Cluster in Middle English Alliterative Verse' (*NM* 102[2001] 37–47). Building on the research of linguists Hinton and Anderson, Sadowski argues that words beginning with *gr*- in Middle English cluster into six major groups of overlapping meaning: words relating to *grasping* or *greediness*; words referring to above-ground natural processes; words associated with the underground, such as *grave* and *grub*; agricultural words, especially those associated with milling, such as *grind*; words signifying negative or painful emotions, such as *grisli*; and finally words associated with sadness, pain and lament, such as *greven* and *grucchen*.

Other literary essays on alliterative poetry include 'Life against Death in *Death and Liffe*' (*C&L* 50[2001] 207–24), in which Lyell Asher finds that Life's victory is dispersed through the poem. Life's final triumph relies on atmosphere and implication as much as on argument and doctrine. Asher comments on the effulgence of the world depicted, showing Life as so positive that Death's negativity is predetermined. In 'Metaphysical Wit in a Fourteenth-Century English Complaint Lyric' (*N&Q* 48[2001] 380–2), Angela Woollam argues that Carleton Brown's glosses and emendations to a four-line lyric from Oxford, Merton College 248 must be revised; 'tort and fort' is 'a legal formula' and 'shoren' should stand, meaning 'shorn', not be emended to 'sworen' (p. 381). The personified defendants have sheared the oath, thus depriving law of its overcoat. James I. McNelis writes 'A Note on the Index of Middle English Verse 3910.5: A Misidentified Envoy to *The Master of Game*' (*N&Q* 47[2000] 171–2). In Rome, Venerabile Collegio Inglese, Libri 1405, the envoy in fact follows Edward, second duke of York's *Master of Game*, not Twiti's *The Art of Hunting*, as *IMEV* has it. McNelis adds that no two manuscripts have the same envoy; 'the verse envoys were presumably scribal in origin' (p. 172).

Among essays with a historical slant, Matti Peikola examines the form of the Ave Maria learned by the narrator of *Pierce the Ploughman's Creed*, in '"And after all, myn Aue-Marie almost to the ende": *Pierce the Ploughman's Crede* and Lollard Expositions of the *Ave Maria*' (*ES* 81[2000] 273–92). Peikola argues that the phrase 'almost to the end' functions as a 'hotlink' to 'an issue more fully explicated elsewhere in Lollard texts' (p. 277). The word 'Jesus' was an addition that granted sixty days' indulgence to the speaker; Wycliffites, however, objected to adding words to Scripture. Peikola appends the text of the indulgence from Cambridge, Trinity College MS R.3.21, fo. 216[v]. Jana Mathews, in 'The Case for Misprision in *Wynnere and Wastoure*' (*N&Q* 46[1999] 317–21), resists the association of *Wynnere and Wastoure* with the 1352 Statute of Treasons, arguing that 'pese to distourb' is a commonplace found both earlier and later than the statute. In the poem, the king's herald elaborates on the king's order not to fight, turning it into an accusation of treason; but Wynnere and Wastoure, apparently, will forfeit only goods and offices, not their lives, corresponding to the fourteenth-century treatment of misprision, then a petty crime. In '*The Parlement of the Thre Ages* and Martorell, Spain' (*N&Q* 47[2000] 295–6), Andrew Breeze identifies Martorell with the 'Mawtryple' of line 546 of *Parlement*, and the river Llobregat with 'Flagot' of line 542. Daniel Wakelin clarifies the 'local references' of *IMEV* 3566 in 'Lightning at Lynn, 1363: The Origins of a Lyric in MS Sloane 2593' (*N&Q* 48[2001] 382–5). A Lynn Franciscan who continued the Bury St Edmunds chronicle noted, along with the pestilences and wind of the lyric, a 'double lightning strike' of 6 July 1363 (p. 383); Wakelin suggests several possible owners of the manuscript.

4. The *Gawain*-Poet

Sarah Stanbury's lovely edition of *Pearl* is the one new edition of the *Gawain*-poet's work published in 2001. This slim and affordable volume should give teachers good incentive to include *Pearl* on syllabuses of early English courses, together with, or even instead of, the oft-taught *Sir Gawain and the Green Knight*. Stanbury's edition is sufficiently scholarly for undergraduates and beginning graduate students—there are over thirty pages of notes at the end of the edition, which attend to both textual and interpretative issues—without being mired in an excess of daunting and distracting annotation. Difficult words are glossed in the margin and difficult passages are translated at the bottom of the page. The latter are selectively and judiciously chosen (where other editors have often felt compelled to translate extensively, which often means 'needlessly' or 'erroneously' or both). Her introduction is simple and elegant, covering the expected historical background and themes of the poem with an insight and energy rarely seen in editors' introductions. Her linking of *Pearl* to the work of contemporary authors such as Gloria Naylor and J.K. Rowling is particularly inspired.

Dieter Mehl provides a useful introduction to the *Gawain*-poet in chapter 5 of his *English Literature in the Age of Chaucer* ('The *Gawain*-Poet'). While Mehl is a little more given to uncritical praise, cheerleading, and defensiveness than the *Gawain*-poet needs or warrants, his chapter will certainly help first-time readers get their bearings and appreciate the poems more than they might on their own. He follows a brief, general discussion of MS Cotton Nero A.x and its historical contexts with interpretative summaries of each poem in the manuscript. His schematic outlines of *Cleanness* and *Pearl* are particularly useful, given that these two poems lack the clear narrative arcs of *Patience* and *Gawain*, and are thus more challenging for students to conceptualize.

J.A. Burrow has written a slim introduction to the work of the *Gawain*-poet as his contribution to Northcote House's extensive Writers and their Work series. *The 'Gawain'-Poet* offers charming and provocative chapters on each poem, as well as chapters on the poet's reception and publication history, his identity/anonymity, and an 'Interchapter' on alliterative verse generally. The great problem with this book is its thinness. One feels that Burrow was constrained by strict length requirements; his choice of focus occasionally feels capricious (given how little he can cover in a book that is only fifty-eight pages long, excluding notes) and his insights rarely have enough space to develop into convincing arguments. Much of these short chapters is given over to summarizing, which, while useful to first-time students and undeniably entertaining, crowds out all but the most rudimentary analysis.

In *The Politics of 'Pearl': Court Poetry in the Age of Richard II*, John M. Bowers offers a substantial and highly anticipated book-length study of *Pearl* and its relationship to late fourteenth-century court politics in England. Expanding on earlier articles, Bower brings forth a wealth of evidence to suggest that, far from being the most ahistorical of the Cotton Nero poems (as traditional scholarship would have it), *Pearl* contains multiple textual 'traces' of its historicity, particularly its engagement with political issues central to the Ricardian court of the mid-1390s. Bowers argues forcefully and convincingly that the religious iconography of *Pearl*—'religious images such as the Lamb of God, biblical symbols such as the Pearl of Great Price, and specific saints such as St. John the Baptist'—cannot and should not be interpreted solely with reference to its biblical context in Revelation; rather, it must also be understood as resonant with the iconography of Richard's court, an iconography cultivated in various works of art dating from the 1390s (several of which, including a detail from the Wilton diptych, Bowers reproduces at the beginning of his book). This resonance, he argues, suggests that the *Pearl*-poet represents a delicate satire of Ricardian power, in which 'royal materialism' is called into question even as the monarchy itself appears validated by heavenly comparison. Bowers explains the difference between the subtle satire of *Pearl* and the more overt and direct satire of *Sir Gawain and the Green Knight* by calling attention to the likelihood that the two poems are products of different times in Richard's reign, with *Gawain* being written when the Ricardian reign was in its infancy and northern interests were marginal, and *Pearl* being written at a time when 'Cheshiremen' (from the *Pearl*-poet's own home region) were in much higher royal favour.

In *Poetry Does Theology: Chaucer, Grosseteste, and the 'Pearl'-Poet*, Jim Rhodes argues that England's development of a strong secular poetic tradition in the fourteenth century resulted in a 'complex and problematical' relationship between theology and poetry, with Chaucer and his contemporaries tending to refract theological issues through various narrative lenses rather than address those issues directly (as, he argues, English poetry more frequently did in the early part of the century). Like Bowers, Rhodes argues that the *Pearl*-poet's work does not stand as far apart from the socially conscious and critical work of Chaucer and Langland as scholars have suggested. But where Bowers alleges the *Pearl*-poet's active engagement with political and historical issues, Rhodes sees in the poet an interrogator of theological doctrine whose critique of ecclesiastical corruption and priestly incompetence has affinities with certain reformist discourse, including that found in Wycliffite writing. Rhodes adduces evidence from the three biblical poems of MS Cotton Nero as well as *Saint Erkenwald* in order to show that, contrary to critical opinion, the *Pearl*-poet was not an 'apologist for the theological status quo,' but a thoughtful poet whose visionary poetry and redactions of biblical stories reconceptualized the relationship of God to humankind in a humanity-affirming way.

In chapter 4 of her *Sovereign Fantasies: Arthurian Romance and the Making of Britain*, entitled '"In contrayez straunge": Sovereign Rivals, Fantasies of Gender, and *Sir Gawain and the Green Knight*', Patricia Clare Ingham situates *Sir Gawain and the Green Knight* in the context of internal colonialism and Anglo-Welsh difference. She begins by noting how British history is elaborated at the beginning of *Gawain*, not only with the familiar invocation of Roman origins, but with the near-complete elision of France, Britain's 'most recent colonizer'. Ingham suggests that this elision is in the service of the poem's primary concern with internal difference, specifically with the relationship between British and Welsh identities. She reads Gawain's 'failure' as a form of enduring Celtic resistance to English cultural hegemony, and suggests that the poem ultimately refuses an imperial and hierarchical distinction between civilized England and wild Wales. Concomitant to this is Ingham's argument that the poem's concern with the ability to accommodate cultural difference is gendered: heterosexual women are associated with the limitations of passions and human attachment, while heterosexual men are associated with the capacity for autonomy and the ability to cross borders.

Aside from the chapter in Rhodes's book, there was but one notable contribution to scholarship on *Cleanness* in 2001. In 'Medicine as Metaphor in the Middle English *Cleanness*' (*ChauR* 35[2001] 260–80), Jeremy J. Citrome tries to reconcile two recent critical approaches to the poem, one which sees it in historiographical terms as a reflection of the shift from Old to New Testament, and the other which sees it as defined by its concerted attention to corporeality (particularly sodomy). Situating sodomy within the terms of medieval medical discourse, Citrome argues that the eschatology of *Cleanness* is expressed through medical metaphor, whereby the Incarnation, the arrival of Christ, represents a 'cure' for the 'sickness' of humanity, represented by sodomy. Medical metaphors are, for Citrome, a way in which the poet connected the familiar quotidian problems of 'plague, bloodshed, and starvation' with the universal concept of salvation history.

The bulk of the articles published in 2001 focus exclusively on *Sir Gawain and the Green Knight*. In '*Luf-talkyng* and Middle English Romance' (in Diller, ed., *Towards a History of English as a History of Genres*), Thomas Honegger considers the uniqueness of the quality and scope of courtly amatory discourse in *Sir Gawain and the Green Knight* as it compares to the rest of the field of Middle English romances. While subtlety and playfulness in amatory dialogue between the sexes had its place in the earlier French romance tradition, *Gawain* stands alone among English romances in its engagement and refinement of *luf-talkyng*. Honegger's approach is oddly schematic and statistically driven; the article comes complete with an appendix in which Honegger counts not only the number of lines, but the number of *words*, in each encounter between Gawain and 'Lady Bertilak'.

Catherine S. Cox makes the provocative suggestion, in 'Genesis and Gender in *Sir Gawain and the Green Knight*' (*ChauR* 35[2001] 378–90), that *Gawain* engages not only Christian but 'Jewish exegetical modes' (though the meaning of this phrase is never well defined). Cox suggests that there is a fundamental conservatism at work in the poem's ending, where the appropriation of the garter represents an eradication of 'the potential contagion of Gawain-as-Other', and that this conservatism is somehow in the service of an orthodox Christianity that would deny or at least repress its origins in Judaism. Her argument seems to rest on the notion of intertextual affiliation between the scene of temptation in *Gawain* and the 'Hebrew Genesis/Bereshit creation and expulsion sequences', rather than on any notion of the *Gawain*-poet's intentional invocation of Jewish tradition. Convoluted language occasionally makes the finer points of Cox's argument difficult to follow. Jeremy Lowe, on the other hand, writes in a mercifully clear fashion about the ways in which film theory can illuminate our understanding of *Gawain*. In 'The Cinematic Consciousness of *Sir Gawain and the Green Knight*' (*Exemplaria* 13[2001] 67–97), Lowe claims that classical and psychoanalytic film theory, overdetermined by directorial intent and protagonist subjectivity respectively, are inadequate to elucidate a poem such as *Sir Gawain*, which 'resists closure'. Lowe turns instead to Deleuze and Guattari's *Anti-Oedipus*, Deleuze's work on cinema, and the film theory of Steven Shaviro to explore the 'decentered freeplay' at the heart of the reading experience and the pleasure a reader might take in the interplay between identification and non-identification with Gawain. His claim that there is a 'logic of capitalism' at work in Gawain is a bit strained, but his call for new readings that go beyond questions of Gawain's identity to focus on the constantly 'shifting relationships' of the poem is exciting.

Derek Brewer is having none of this decentred freeplay. According to his 'A Supernatural Enemy in Green in *Sir Gawain and the Green Knight*' (in Davidson and Chaudhri, eds., *Supernatural Enemies*), 'finally ... the onus of meaning comes back to Gawain. He is the centre'. Brewer's article explores the significance of the Green Knight's greenness, without coming to any hard conclusions. It must be nice to be at a point in your career when you can make sweeping and frank yet true statements like '[the Green Knight's] greenness has been the subject of many interpretations, mostly wrong, or at least not wholly right'. For Brewer, the Green Knight represents death, and his greenness suggests a range of implications, which include, possibly, the 'non-existence' of implications. The most that Brewer can say definitively is that green is not natural, and that it bespeaks the supernatural quality of the knight, to which the supernatural power of the Virgin Mary is opposed. Conor McCarthy, in '*Sir Gawain and the Green Knight* and the Sign of *trawþe*' (*Neophil* 85[2001] 297–308), is concerned with the resonances of the word *trawþe*, particularly as it connects the description of Gawain's armour to his later behaviour during his various tests. McCarthy suggests that Gawain's failure to exemplify absolute *trawþe* (that is, fidelity to his pledged word) contributes to the poem's overarching critique of 'the value of renown'.

Finally, 2001 saw the publication of two new articles that attempt to connect *Sir Gawain and the Green Knight* to a particular historical figure or context. Leo Carruthers, in 'The Duke of Clarence and the Earls of March: Garter Knights and *Sir Gawain and the Green Knight*' (*MÆ* 70[2001] 66–79), uses the 'Hony soit qui mal pence' motto, which concludes *Sir Gawain* in the MS, as a springboard for a larger discussion of the Order of the Garter. He then alleges that the poet 'intended ... to flatter a noble patron, one who desired to gain admission into the highly exclusive Order of the Garter'. Citing a reference to 'þe duk of Clarence' in the list of knights gathered around Gawain before his departure, Carruthers argues that this reference is an allusion to the real duke of Clarence, Lionel of Antwerp, Edward III's 'second surviving son'. He argues further that this allusion was intended to flatter Roger Mortimer, fourth earl of March, the grandson of Lionel and, Carruthers alleges, 'the literary patron for whom the *Gawain*-poet wrote'. Ann R. Meyer, in 'The Despensers and the *Gawain* Poet: A Gloucestershire Link to the Alliterative Master of the Northwest Midlands' (*ChauR* 35[2001] 413–29), argues that the *Gawain*-poet had a close association with Edward and Thomas Despenser and with Tewkesbury Abbey, whose iconography and architecture celebrate the Despenser family. Meyer points out that *Pearl* seems to draw on works found in the library of Eleanor of Castile, many of whose books must have found their way into the Despenser family through marriage. Though no definitive claim is made about the *Gawain*-poet's particular relationship to the Despensers, Meyer notes suggestive parallels between the aesthetic of the poet and the aesthetic of Tewkesbury Abbey, with its 'mingling of secular portraits and sacred iconography' and its 'gestures of humility and worship set within the frameworks of lavish decoration and ostentatious display'.

5. *Piers Plowman*

Mary Clemente Davlin's *The Place of God in 'Piers Plowman' and Medieval Art* focuses on the 'extensive, explicit poetry about God' (p. 1) and the guiding question

'Where?' in *Piers*. Davlin characterizes her study as both formalist and historicist (p. 3), examining the poem's language in the context of both religious art and liturgical and theological language. After the introduction, chapter 2 studies 'Heaven and Earth: Horizontal and Vertical Views'; chapter 3 considers 'God's Body', the various physical manifestations taken by Jesus and other representations of God in *Piers*, and chapter 4, 'Within', looks at descriptions, metaphors and other language placing God within the human heart and humans living within God's love. Chapter 5 examines 'God in the Community', and the final chapter, 'Imagining the Place and Presence of God', details the paradoxes of the poem's placement of God. Davlin emphasizes Langland's understanding of divine love as familial or communal rather than erotic: 'God is brother, mother, mediator, king, father, and companion ... union with God is described as healing, nurture, purification, the security of being held, the rapture of nursing, dwelling in God's house' (p. 170). Explicating the paradox of simultaneously being within God and holding God in one's heart, Davlin juxtaposes the 'universal human experience of pregnancy in the family' with that of taking the Eucharist, showing that common experiences shape Langland's view of spirituality as much as do religious language and thought (p. 123). Twenty-five illustrations, largely from manuscripts but some from church art, suggest the visualizations that Langland tried to express in words. Although Davlin states in the introduction that illustrations come from the twelfth to fifteenth centuries, some indication of individual dates would have been welcome. Despite close examination of illustrations and references to artworks not reproduced in this volume, close readings take precedence over art history.

D. Vance Smith's *The Book of the Incipit: Beginnings in the Fourteenth Century* is challenging, intriguing, and provocative. Smith certainly succeeds in showing the importance of the idea of beginnings in medieval philosophy, emphasizing this point by calling his chapters 'Incipit', 'Initium', 'Exordium', 'Thema', 'Origo', 'Conditora', and 'Principium'. And it is true that *Piers Plowman* has multiple beginnings, a construction that contributes to the difficulty of the poem, so that an exposition of the medieval theories that might inform this construction is helpful in coming to a new understanding of Will's difficulties with beginnings. This book has three main threads: modern theory, medieval philosophy, and Langland's poem. At times they are successfully braided together, but at other points analysis of Langland's text seems uncomfortably patched into a more abstract argument. Since, in Smith's formulation, medieval theological and philosophical thinking frequently seems to anticipate twentieth-century 'theory', I began to question whether the discussions of theory were in fact necessary, or whether the two medieval threads might combine more successfully without them. Certainly Smith's misapprehension of the nature of the Heisenberg indeterminacy principle (which states that it is impossible accurately to measure position and momentum at the same time; it is a statement about physics, not logic) detracts from his presentation of medieval logicians' discussions of beginnings and endings, and the problem of determining at what point a beginning or an ending takes place. Many elements of this book are thought-provoking and valuable, particularly the emphasis on the kinds of work done (or supposed to be done) by the medieval author before beginning to write, and Smith's attention to the ideas of genealogical beginning.

Dee Dyas surveys *Pilgrimage in Medieval English Literature, 700–1500*, to conclude that the primary meaning of 'pilgrimage' in the Middle Ages was not 'travel' but 'life as pilgrimage', which may be categorized as 'inner' if practised by monastics and 'moral' for those in the active life. In chapter 9, on *Piers Plowman*, she suggests that the narrator's characterization of himself as a 'shep' underlines his spiritual lostness. She also interprets the scene of Piers tearing the pardon as showing that, just as Piers gives up a travelling pilgrimage in favour of interior pilgrimage, so he destroys the written pardon 'while maintaining the hope which Truth intended to communicate' (p. 159). The Seven Deadly Sins appear in many texts as obstacles or dangers on the road of inner or moral pilgrimage.

Kathleen Hewett-Smith, in editing *William Langland's 'Piers Plowman': A Book of Essays*, has collected a number of remarkable studies. Andrew Galloway's 'Making History Legal: *Piers Plowman* and the Rebels of Fourteenth-Century England' (pp. 7–39) looks less at 1381 than at the legal battles of previous decades, to which, Galloway asserts, the poem responds. The essay divides into three parts: '*Piers Plowman* and the Justice of Antiquity', which considers the poem's conflict with and assertion of legal history and tradition; '*Piers Plowman* and the Conflicts before 1381', which examines passages that seem to refer to conflicts between tenants and religious landlords; and 'Thomas Walsingham and the Dialogue of Legal History at St. Albans', in which he rebuts Steven Justice's view that Walsingham did not understand the importance of various aspects of the rebellious townsmen's behaviour. A lesser scholar might have separated and padded these sections into three separate articles; Galloway's solid, concentrated argumentation builds to an impressive conclusion. Joan Baker and Susan Signe Morrison's 'The Luxury of Gender: *Piers Plowman* B.9 and *The Merchant's Tale*' (pp. 41–67) is reprinted from *YLS* 12[1998]. Stephen H.A. Shepherd readdresses the problem of Langland's multiple genres, specifically of whether he alludes to romance, in 'Langland's Romances' (pp. 69–81). After reviewing similar attempts, he turns to manuscript contexts for help, showing that *Piers* tends to appear with romances of historical and didactic interest, often those that portray a virtuous non-Christian, which he connects to Langland's attention to Trajan. He suggests the Pseudo-Turpin Chronicle, in some version, as a possible source for the explanation by Imaginatif of the different orders in heaven. Shepherd admits that much of this essay is speculative. In 'The Langland Myth' (pp. 83–99), C. David Benson suggests that, as the 'facts' of Langland's 'life' are mostly owing to Skeat's assertions rather than to rigorous research and argument, it may be time to try some other approaches, despite the 'sophisticated editing and powerful critical interpretations' that Skeat's 'myth' has inspired (p. 84). He points out that editors of *Piers* describe a 'more chaotic' manuscript situation than a neat A–B–C progression, and suggests—in line with Jill Mann's claim that A was a revision for a non-Latinate audience—that all the various versions of *Piers* might be intended for different audiences. Though I can see the attraction of painting Langland as a scholar reworking his conference papers into articles and job talks, I confess to some scepticism here. But Benson's main point is really to demand serious argument, along the lines of Mann's (and Traugott Lawler's response), for what most critics and editors have chosen simply to accept.

Stephen A. Barney, in 'Langland's Mighty Line' (pp. 103–17), compares Chaucer's and Langland's poetics, surveying their 'characteristic line-work' (p. 104) in different categories: those of similar meanings; 'Chidynges and Knavyssh Speche' (p. 111); and 'High Seriousness' (p. 116). He shows that 'often Chaucer's satire operates by indirection, Langland's by derision' (p. 105), while emphasizing the energy of Langland's lines and his 'clerkly indifference to the marks of upper class discourse' (p. 112). The middle section is strongest; one could wish for more explanation in the last part, where Barney finds that Langland's great lines speak for themselves. Sister Mary Clemente Davlin, also in the comparative mode, considers 'Chaucer and Langland as Religious Writers' (pp. 119–41). Langland, she points out, is 'the *only* poet we have (with the possible exception of Milton) who dares to probe at length the nature of God' (p. 122). In this densely footnoted article, Davlin applies Walter Ong's distinction between affective and wit poetry, concluding that Chaucer tends to work in the affective tradition, while Langland's 'puns, paradoxes, and shifts in scene … like puzzles, demand effort from the reader to bring meaning together' (p. 130), producing religious feeling through intellect rather than emotion. 'The Power of Impropriety: Authorial Meaning in *Piers Plowman*', by James Simpson (pp. 145–65), focuses on the 'personification of will' and on how 'the developing logic of that personification … creates a communal authorial position' (p. 148). He sees personification as performing analysis, which analysis ultimately leads to control or dismissal of the concept personified. Unlike 'Gower' or 'Hoccleve', who are personified authors, 'Will' prefers 'inclusive and anonymous discursive spaces', so that the 'poem's authorship ideally becomes its readership' (p. 154). Simpson reads Will's punning or riddling statement of identity as defining 'an authorial "longe wille", a *longanimis* common will' (p. 163), so that the narrator speaks for the entire land.

Elizabeth Robertson offers 'Measurement and the "Feminine" in *Piers Plowman*: A Response to Recent Studies of Langland and Gender' (pp. 167–92). She sees gender in *Piers* not as 'luxury' (as Baker and Morrison do) but as a 'central mode of analysis' (p. 168). Langland uses the 'feminine' to explore the problems of excess and need in the poem. Robertson uses Kristeva's concept of feminine abjection and Irigaray's theories of mimicry and feminine fluids to show that Langland's 'use of gender … plays with … essentialist notions of the feminine' (p. 170). She looks specifically at Gluttony and Mede to show that their gender association is fluid, and concludes that Langland 'posits a relationship between men and women that is one of mutuality rather than subservience' (p. 192). 'Inventing the Subject and the Personification of Will in Piers Plowman: Rhetorical, Erotic, and Ideological Origins and Limits in Langland's Allegorical Poetics', by James Paxson (pp. 195–231), pursues the argument of Paxson's previous work (looking at '"bodies" of rhetorical figures' (p. 198)) by borrowing Carolyn Dinshaw's tactic of comparing a modern film and a medieval text. He juxtaposes *Piers* B.XX and the 1998 *Meet Joe Black* to show 'how our modern culture appropriates, defines, misreads, intersects with, and projects onto things medieval its own narrative myths of subject formation and public (or corporative) activity' (p. 198). He discusses Elde as a personification who engages in sodomy with Will, and Anima as a vagina; he also considers wordplay on long/land and king/kind. He finds that 'queerness in medieval literature may be yoked to allegorical personification itself' (p. 202). The final essay, by Kathleen Hewett-Smith, '"Nede ne hath no lawe": Poverty and the De-stabilization of Allegory in the Final Visions of *Piers Plowman*' (pp. 233–53), considers medieval and present-day theories or models of allegory. She gives a close reading of Need that shows how Langland's 'allegorical poetics' clarify his 'theme of poverty' (p. 234). The allegory from passus XVII onwards no longer focuses on actions but is more intellectual and schematic, showing metaphor at work. Langland here tries to revalue poverty as morally significant, rather than a social problem; this revaluation cannot hold, as material reality reasserts itself. Need appears as '*experience* rather than ... authority' (p. 244); nothing in Need's speech suggests a moral value to poverty.

Will's Vision of Piers Plowman, Do-well, Do-better, and Do-best: A Lemmatical Analysis of the Vocabulary of the A, B, and C Versions as Presented in the Athlone Editions, with Supplementary Concordances of the Latin and French Macaronics, assembled by Joseph Wittig, is one of those books whose title is so complete that the book scarcely needs further comment. The author emphasizes that it is not a glossary, but considers semantics, orthography, dialect and, for some words, morphology.

Claire Marshall's *William Langland: Piers Plowman*, in the Writers and their Work series, begins with a basic introduction to and narrative synopsis of the poem. Three chapters follow: the first focuses on Langland's attempt to express God's truth in human language, and how through allegory Langland's language signifies on multiple levels; the second explores the symbolism of the ploughman and his material community; the third traces 'Will', the fragmented speaking self, through various episodes involving his name to his encounter with Piers at the Tree of Charity. Marshall argues that apocalyptic language both demonstrates the difficulty of establishing a subjective self in a world where the mediating forces of subjectivity—representatives of the Church—are corrupt, and allows the possibility of reconciliation with God. The aim of this short book appears to be to introduce *Piers Plowman* to students, but it is certainly not a handbook.

The recent focus on manuscripts and readers continues with Carl James Grindley's 'Reading *Piers Plowman* C-Text Annotations: Notes toward the Classification of Printed and Written Marginalia in Texts from the British Isles, 1300–1641' (in Kerby-Fulton and Hilmo, eds., pp. 73–141). Grindley proposes three basic types of marginalia, with multiple sub-types of each, and transcribes all the marginalia in Huntington Library MS HM 143 and BL MS Additional 35157, respectively MSS X and U of the C-text. Grindley consulted fifty-four other manuscripts of a wide variety of texts and genres in order to create his taxonomy. Though he raises some arguments against aspects of his scheme and hopes that other scholars will refine it, it will certainly help to impose some order on discussions of marginalia, not only in *Piers* but in other works as well.

Richard J. Goldstein, in '"Why calle ye hym Crist, siþen Iewes called hym Iesus?": The Disavowal of Jewish Identification in the *Piers Plowman* B-text' (*Exemplaria* 13[2001] 215–52), uses terms from psychoanalysis to help explain Langland's ideas about Jews and salvation history. The medieval question of how Judaism could survive after Christ embodies contemporary doubt. Goldstein suggests that, because Langland assimilates a Jewish concern with righteousness, he identifies with the Jews, therefore feels guilty, therefore represses his awareness that he has identified with the Jews, and so Jews, subjected to projected guilt, appear in a negative light. He reviews Langland's use of anti-Jewish stereotypes and looks closely at passages in passus XVIII and XIX.

Addressing his article 'Visionary Eschatology: *Piers Plowman*' (*Modern Theology* 16[2000] 3–17) primarily to students of theology, David Aers argues that Langland's poem opposes Joachite eschatology. Aers provides an interpretative summary of the action of the poem, terming Passus I–XV 'the poet's search for the resources of reformation in the polity and church' (p. 6). Aers discusses Will's wish to taste the fruit of charity, the Harrowing of Hell, and the Good Samaritan and 'semyvif', concluding, darkly, that for Langland 'the church is not, emphatically not, the kingdom of God' (p. 13). Will keeps the faith by remaining in the compromised Church of passus XX, trusting in Christ's various promises. A.S.G. Edwards suggests, in a study of 'Two *Piers Plowman* Manuscripts from Helmingham Hall' (*TCBS* 11[1999] 421–6), that London, Society of Antiquaries 687 and Cambridge, Newnham College 4, may have belonged to Helmingham Hall, Suffolk.

In '"For coueitise after cros; þe croune stant in golde": Money as Matter and Metaphor in *Piers Plowman*' (in Perry, ed., *Material Cultures and Cultural Materialisms in the Middle Ages and Renaissance*, pp. 59–74), Joerg O. Fichte traces a circular movement of monetary imagery through *Piers*. From its material and usually negative treatment in the *Visio*, it dissolves into 'insubstantial metaphors' that fail to 'neutralize' its influence (p. 60). In the *Vita*, characters present the proper use of money, to be used in charity to store up treasure in heaven, but in the end, when 'the poem returns to historical reality' (p. 79), cupidity is stronger than charity.

R. Carter Hailey, in '"Geuyng light to the reader": Robert Crowley's Editions of Piers Plowman (1550)' (*PBSA* 95[2001] 483–502), suggests that the vocabulary and metre of *Piers*, not censorship, prevented its early publication. Hailey studies the title pages, texts and notes of Robert Crowley's three 1550 editions, noting that Crowley 'attempts to present an accurate ... critical edition of the poem, within the limits of his understanding of that process' (p. 501).

In 'Recounting Riches: Personification and Performance in the *Roman de la Rose* and *Piers Plowman*' (*Arcadia* 35[2000] 254–63], Madeleine Kasten uses the notion of performativity developed by philosopher John L. Austin to explore the differences between types of allegorized characters. As illustration, she compares Langland's Meed to Richece from the *Roman*. The internal ambiguities in Richece's portrait are not developed, while Langland exploits such contradictions as the two uses or natures of Meed. Though Richece appears only 'as a subject and object of narrative (self-)description', Meed 'perform[s] her internal difference' (p. 263).

In 'Marriage and Mede in Passus 2 to 4 of Piers Plowman' (*NMS* 44[2000] 152–66], Conor McCarthy argues that Langland 'attack[s] the financial motivation' for marriage (p. 152). He characterizes Favel's enfiefment of Mede and False as a jointure, considers problems of consent and potential incest, and discusses the roles of Civil, Simony, and Coveitise. He suggests that Mede's personification as female owes as much to common-law restrictions on women's property and financial rights as it does to grammar, though he nowhere considers the status of the 'femme sole'.

William E. Rogers, in 'Spiritual Love and the Hard Counsel of Need: *Piers Plowman* C.XXII.1–50' (in Ridyard, ed., *Earthly Love, Spiritual Love, Love of the Saints*, pp. 269–81), explores first the rhetorical justification of Need and then the implications of this 'term that anchors various arguments of self-justification' (p. 276). His examination of the rhetorical aspects of Need borders on the philosophical and leads naturally to his conclusion that God himself, in the incarnated Jesus, is needy; thus, 'we participate in God's love when we interpret ourselves as yearning and incomplete' (p. 279). In '*Piers Plowman* B.V.379: A Syntactic Note' (*N&Q* 47[2000] 18–20), Matsuji Tajima argues that 'shewynge' in this line should be understood as a verbal noun followed by its object, rather than as a participle or participial adjective.

Noting the contrast in prestige between Latin and the vernacular, Ming-tsang Yang argues, in 'Signs in Translation: Plowing and Pilgrimage in *Piers Plowman*' (*NTU Studies in Language and Literature* 9[June 2000] 1–20), that Langland participates in a 'self-conscious ... solemnization of vernacular composition' (p. 6), writing partly in order to develop English vocabulary for 'contemporary theological and social issues' (p. 7). Yang sees 'radical implications' (p. 10) in Langland's valorization of a ploughman, and explores some of these: equating the work of ploughman, scribe/writer, and pilgrim invites the reader to join the search for Truth beyond the limitations of the vernacular sign.

Volume 15 of the *Yearbook of Langland Studies* continues to publish essays from the 1999 International Langland Conference, in Asheville, NC, along with response papers. In 'What Then Does Langland Mean? Authorial and Textual Voices in Piers Plowman' (*YLS* 15[2001] 3–13), C. David Benson discusses the difficulty of determining any (not just an authorial) authoritative voice in *Piers*. The poem's debates are 'genuine ... without resolution' (p. 6). Speakers rarely have 'recognizable voices' (p. 7): even Trajan's eruption loses its initial distinctiveness; Hunger is self-contradictory; Jesus' apparent claim of universal salvation conflicts with other authorities in the poem, including the Athanasian Creed. Christ's words remain 'mysterious' (p. 11). Edwin D. Craun, in '"Ye, by Peter and by Poul!": Lewte and the Practice of Fraternal Correction' (*YLS* 15[2001] 15–25), uses 'late medieval debates over the proper conditions for fraternal correction' (p. 18)—public rebuke of sin in a community—to illumine Lewte's stance on this issue. He finds Petrine as well as Pauline support for inferiors correcting superiors, and shows that Lewte's only stipulation on such correction is that the sin must be overt, not private. David C. Fowler responds (*YLS* 15[2001] 26–9) that Craun gives a 'striking model' (p. 26) for applying the ethics of speech to *Piers*. Fowler raises five questions regarding Craun's position vis-à-vis other critics, and notes the frequency of Will's shifts in attitude. Lawrence M. Clopper, also in response to Craun (*YLS* 15[2001] 30–2), sees Will as irreverent in his correction of his confessor; it is not just a question of speaking publicly but also of whether Will can publish writing against friars. Clopper revisits Craun's comparison of Will and Margery Kempe, to Will's disadvantage.

Lawrence M. Clopper, writing on 'Langland and Allegory: A Proposition' (*YLS* 15[2001] 35–42), challenges 'the notion of "levels" within allegorical representation' (p. 41) through application of medieval philosophical realism, in which concepts—'universals'—already really exist; they are not on some other plane of reality, separate from concrete individual objects. In this view, 'the literal' does not 'frustrate the allegorical' (p. 36). Langland's ploughman thus always points 'to St. Peter', but never ceases to be 'an English plowman' (p. 41). Ann Astell's response (*YLS* 15[2001] 43–6) points out that personification and allegory are not the same thing, although she agrees that allegory was a mode of composition, not only of interpretation. She suggests that distinguishing among 'four topical arguments' (p. 44) defined by Cicero and Boethius would strengthen Clopper's argument. In his own response (*YLS* 15[2001] 47–57), James J. Paxson asks whether medievalists are 'sick of allegory' (p. 47); then, assuming that we are, offers a 'get-well card' combining 'Clopper's foregrounding of a plausible Langlandian realism with alternative postmodern approaches for understanding Langland's literary dream universe' (p. 49). The main alternative is 'contemporary cognitive science' (p. 51).

In 'The Essential (Ephemeral) William Langland: Textual Revision As Ethical Process in *Piers Plowman*' (*YLS* 15[2001] 61–84), Alan J. Fletcher explores the 'ethical imperative' (p. 62) of Langland's revisions, by way of comparison to preachers' multiple versions of sermons. Fletcher studies C.V and its connection between preaching and contrition, contemporary preaching practices and their echoes in *Piers*, and 'textual conversion' (p. 77) as it figures moral conversion. He concludes by suggesting that sermons in London, BL MS Additional 41321 respond to *Piers Plowman*. In response, Wendy Scase (*YLS* 15[2001] 85–8) notes that, while preaching is '*essentially ephemeral*' (p. 85, her emphasis), the manuscripts that mix different versions of *Piers* show that scribes wanted to offer 'a full, complete and finished edition rather than [a] provisional product' (p. 87). She suggests further that contrasts between *Piers* and sermons may be as revealing as similarities. Judith Dale's response (*YLS* 15[2001] 89–94) identifies 'a conceptual slippage between poet and product' (p. 89), and explores the autobiographical section of C.V through a comparison with Julian of Norwich as another revising religious writer who 'develop[s] the text by modifying the role that the narrator plays' (p. 93). The poem's lack of closure illustrates the impossibility of perfect penitence.

Anna Baldwin, in 'Patient Politics in *Piers Plowman*' (*YLS* 15[2001] 99–108), takes Patience as a model for dealing with a country's enemies as well as with an individual's poverty or other problems. She suggests that the Saturday and Wednesday of B.XIII.154–5 referred to significant days in the expiration of the 1375 treaty of Bruges, and that C.XVII.233–7 criticize the Despenser Crusade. Where Baldwin finds it 'difficult to determine' whether Langland regards this approach 'as a practical policy or an impossible ideal' (p. 101), Fiona Somerset, in her response (*YLS* 15[2001] 109–14), sees Patience as incompatible with quotidian affairs. Summerset characterizes Patience's 'peace policy' as 'a riddle' (p. 109), whose answer implies that Patience's will must conform to the will of those in power, and thus is unlikely to effect change. Contemporary Wycliffite writings use similar 'extremism of expression' to 'different ends' (p. 112).

In '*Piers Plowman* and the Subject of the Law' (*YLS* 15[2001] 117–28), Andrew Galloway juxtaposes work by Anne Middleton and Richard Firth Green on 'cultural-legal-literary history' (p. 118) to explore the case of Peace vs. Wrong, in passus IV, through the minor characters Warren Wisdom and Witty, who, Galloway argues, in A and B represent the world of 'humbler litigants seeking settlement and reconciliation' (p. 123) in contrast to the higher social world of royal justice. In C, however, they join with Wrong, as Langland makes 'the king's justice' less problematic but contests 'the authority of that justice' (p. 127). David Lawton responds (*YLS* 15[2001] 129–33) by encouraging a search 'for historical explanations' for Langland's 'legal vocabulary' (p. 129), and picks up Middleton's term 'crossover discourse' to explore further. Lawton wonders if Green's terms of a change 'from orally based folklaw to literate centralized law' (p. 130) are suitable for Galloway's purposes; he finds it more important that both the B and C versions of Peace vs. Wrong are subordinated to the 'Meed allegory' (p. 132), and thinks that, to Meed, folklaw would be as good as centralized law. She can be defeated only by invoking the Last Judgement. Louise Bishop, in her response to Galloway (*YLS*

15[2001] 134–9), identifies 'two patterns of authority and resistance' in the work of Middleton, Green and Galloway, one linear, the other reciprocal, 'where poetic and administrative texts' share vocabulary (p. 135); she revisits the relationship of Warren Wisdom and Witty by exploring the implications of Peace—related to *otium*—having to act, of the relationship between law and labour, and of a comparison of Wit and Study to the earlier pair of characters.

Anne Scott treats Langland's study of charity to the poor and the question of the ethical and spiritual value of poverty in her '"Nevere noon so nedy ne poverer deide": *Piers Plowman* and the Value of Poverty' (*YLS* 15[2001] 141–53). She surveys the 'intellectual and social' contexts (p. 142) surrounding his treatment of alms-giving and the suffering of the poor. Although distinctions were customarily made between the deserving and undeserving poor, and Langland echoes these, he 'insists that poverty, whether patiently borne, voluntarily chosen or endured as inevitable, has, in itself, the power to save' (p. 152). Bruce W. Hozeski's response (*YLS* 15[2001] 154–7) outlines Scott's essay and notes a slippage between 'religious themes and social satire' (p. 156). Joan Baker's response (*YLS* 15[2001] 158–65) focuses on four issues: '(1) the livery of poverty; (2) commercial charity; (3) human agency; and (4) divine bargains' (p. 159). Of these, the livery of poverty receives the most attention; Baker points out that one reason for Langland's insistence on helping all the poor is that schemes like Ambrose's, which begin with family and work outwards, risk entirely neglecting 'the unaffiliated poor subsisting on the margins of society' (p. 161).

Joseph S. Wittig discusses '"Culture Wars" and the Persona in *Piers Plowman*' (*YLS* 15[2001] 167–95). Wittig recognizes that Piers has been 'appropriated by the agendas of its readers' since 1381 (p. 167), but queries some appropriations by Middleton, Hanna and Scase that see Langland questioning political, religious and/ or economic authority. Wittig's own view is based in 'traditional moral theology and canon law … according to which the poet seeks to disguise that he is himself an authoritative voice' (pp. 167–8). Wittig reads the 'autobiography' of C.V as both a disguise of the 'authoritative' poet's voice and as a 'mirror … [of] audience response' (p. 183), thus prompting that audience to a similar examination of conscience. He appends a translation of C.V.5–108 and citations for words related to 'loller' and 'loll'. In response (*YLS* 15[2001] 196–200), Gregory J. Wilsbacher argues that the Dreamer's self-questioning is motivated by 'the poet's … uncomfortable engagement and interaction with' his 'social and political realities' (p. 196), though Wilsbacher agrees with some of Wittig's remarks about Middleton's essay. Wilsbacher objects to the term 'culture wars', which for him suggests a 'younger generation' that sees a 'public and political Langland' and an older generation's 'private and religious Langland' (p. 197). He suggests that the "political Langland" may be an 'effort to make the poem matter within contemporary English departments, to both students and administrators' (pp. 199–200).

Thomas D. Hill has two short explicative essays in this volume. In '" Dumb David": Silence and Zeal in Lady Church's Speech, *Piers Plowman* C.2.30–40' (*YLS* 15[2001] 203–11), he treats Holy Church's association of David with muteness (C.II.39–40), finding the usual gloss—that books, as dumb objects, cannot lie—problematic. He suggests instead that line C.II.39 is 'an early version of a proverb … in early modern English' (p. 204), adds Bracton's comments on the legal position of the mute with regard to promises, notes that in Psalm 38 David twice refers to himself as dumb, and adds the witness of various commentators on the Psalms. Hill also addresses 'The Problem of Synecdochic Flesh: *Piers Plowman* B.9.49–50' (*YLS* 15[2001] 213–18), the question being why Langland glosses *caro* as 'man with a soul' (B.IX.50). In John 1:14, 'Verbum caro factum est', '*caro* must mean more than "flesh" since ... Jesus had a human soul as well as a human body' (p. 215). Thus the synecdoche, which is crucial for understanding the Latin quotation of B.XVIII.409a.

6. Romance

This has proved a busy year. The Early English Text Society issued Rhiannon Purdie's massive edition of the A-version of *Ipomadon*, not available otherwise except for Kölbing's edition in 1889 and D.M. Andersen's doctoral dissertation in 1968. The only copy of this version is in Chetham's Library, Manchester, MS Chetham 8009, copied probably in London in the last quarter of the fifteenth century, but the poem could be as early as the very end of the fourteenth century, Purdie favouring the last decade, partly on the basis of costume terms. The manuscript's contents make it seem to be an educational collection, with a bilingual *Liber Catonis* and 'A Good Boke of Kervyng and Nortur', and Purdie has previously argued for female ownership, which seems *prima facie* likely since the first four works are lives of Sts Dorothy, Anne, and Katherine and an Assumption of St Mary. This is complicated by the presence of 'The Namys of Wardeyns and Balyffys' of London from 1189 to 1217, but since this is followed by the 'Ballad of a Tyrannical Husband' (evidently not published since 1843 in the *Reliquiae Antiquae*) its presence could be explained in other ways. *Ipomadon* is in twelve-line tail-rhyme stanzas, much better handled than Chaucer's satirical six-line ones, and Purdie concludes that the poet's dialect was ultimately West Riding, though interestingly the *Ipomadon* scribe in this manuscript 'left almost no discernible linguistic layer on the texts he copied' (p. xlix), with at least a south-western layer in between. In good EETS tradition, the linguistic section is done in careful detail, but considerable effort has also been spent on analysing the relationship with the Anglo-Norman original and its versions, and more. The text is nicely set out with textual variants at the bottom of each page, and this is followed by explanatory notes and a sizeable glossary.

W.R.J. Barron and S.C. Weinberg have issued a revised version of their edition and translation *Layamon's Arthur: The Arthurian Section of Layamon's 'Brut'*, with some pages appearing to have been reset, such as p. 28, where line 9775 has been corrected from 'Vðer þe ald' to 'Vðer þe alde', a definite metrical improvement. Similarly, the translation has been reviewed, so that on p. 41 it departs from a fairly awkward literal 'fell to the ground a youthful Arthur', repeating 'fell them to the ground' just two lines above, to a clear and more idiomatic 'kill the youthful Arthur'. The introduction has been revised in places, with footnotes replacing endnotes and much improved formatting. Notes at the end seem unchanged except for the commentary note on p. 69, but the select bibliography has been substantially improved. W.R.J. Barron has also issued a revised version of *The Arthur of the English: The Arthurian Legend in Medieval English Life and Literature* (see *YWES*

80[1999] 165–6). The central text seems unchanged, including the notes, but some nine items have been added to the bibliography and the index seems at least reformatted. However, there is a new 'postscript'—John J. Thompson's 'Authors and Audiences', a very learned and readable ramble among those but also among the scribes, who often provide our main information about audiences. A similar emphasis on English appropriation of the legend lies in John P. Brennan's 'Rebirth of a Nation? Historical Mythmaking in Layamon's *Brut*' (*EssaysMedSt* 17[2001] 19–33), which follows others in believing Layamon intended to turn Wace's work into a national epic, using Merlin's prophecy that Arthur would return to help the English, the tales of Rouwenne and Layamon's careful distinction between the English and the Saxons, and the refounding of London by King Lud.

A different approach to recreating audiences is through consideration of performance, as in Linda Marie Zaerr's 'Meter Change as a Relic of Performance in the Middle English Romance *Sir Beues*' (*Quidditas* [formerly *JRMMRA*] 21[2000] 105–26), which finds that the manuscripts betray a shift in values from performance to text. That is, the earlier versions are more flexible in form but later ones are more fixed or regular; the variety works better for performance, while the fixity shows a text-based perception. The jump from tail rhyme to couplets may not even be noticed in aural reception, especially since syntactic links can split two couplets into a triplet that may be perceived as a partial tail rhyme or even an extended one. Metrical elasticity can have the same effect in an oral context. This understanding of performance can elucidate formal features of other works as well, whose editors and critics have been hard pressed to explain satisfactorily their variety and inconsistency.

Wheeler and Tolhurst, eds., *On Arthurian Women: Essays in Memory of Maureen Fries*, contains a wide variety of contributions on both medieval and modern women, as shown by the sections 'On Arthurian Women' and 'On Women Arthurians'. In the first section, Guenevere is discussed in Rebecca S. Teal's 'Guenevere's Tears in the Alliterative *Morte Arthure*: Doubly Wife, Doubly Mother, Doubly Damned' (pp. 1–9), Beverly Kennedy's 'Malory's Guenevere: A "trew lover"' (pp. 11–34), and Edward Donald Kennedy's 'Malory's Guenevere: "A woman who had grown a soul"' (pp. 35–43). A different Elaine is inspected in James Noble's 'Gilding the Lily (Maid): Elaine of Astolat' (pp. 45–57) and Elizabeth S. Sklar's 'Malory's Other(ed) Elaine' (pp. 59–70). Sorceresses are the topics of Sue Ellen Holbrook's 'Elemental Goddesses: Nymue, the Chief Lady of the Lake, and her Sisters' (pp. 71–88) and 'From Niniane to Nimüe: Demonizing the Lady of the Lake' (pp. 89–101). Morgan is the concern of Michael W. Twomey's 'Morgan le Fay at Hautdesert' (pp. 103–19), Lorraine Kochanske Stock's 'The Hag of Castle Hautdesert: The Celtic Sheela-na-gig and the *Auncian* in *Sir Gawain and the Green Knight*' (pp. 121–48), and Dorsey Armstrong's 'Malory's Morgause' (pp. 149–60). A miscellaneous group of women is treated in Jo Goyne's 'Arthurian Wonder Women: The Tread of Olwen' (pp. 161–6), Margaret Jewett Burland's 'Chrétien's Enide: Heroine or Female Hero?' (pp. 167–86), and Susann T. Samples's 'Belacane: Other as Another in Wolfram Von Eschenbach's *Parzival*' (pp. 187–98), before we turn to potential villainesses with Ellen L. Friedrich's 'The Beaten Path: Lancelot's Amorous Adventure at the Fountain in *Le Chevalier de la Charrette*' (pp. 199–212), Melanie McGarrahan Gibson's 'Lyonet, Lunete, and Laudine: Carnivalesque Arthurian Women' (pp. 213–27), Janet Knepper's 'A Bad

Girl Will Love You to Death: Excessive Love in the Stanzaic *Morte Arthur* and Malory' (pp. 229–43), Maud McInerney's 'Malory's Lancelot and the Lady Huntress' (pp. 245–57), and Charlotte A.T. Wulf's 'Merlin's Mother in the Chronicles' (pp. 259–70). The first section segues into the second by focusing on 'The Modern Gaze' with Donald L. Hoffman's 'Hard(l)y Tristan' (pp. 271–82), Kathleen Coyne Kelly's '"No—I am out—I am out of my Tower and my Wits": The Lady of Shalott in A.S. Byatt's *Possession*' (pp. 283–94), Alan Lupack's 'Women Illustrators of the Arthurian Legends' (pp. 295–311), and Kevin J. Harty's 'A Note on Maureen Fries, Morgan le Fay, and Ugo Falena's 1911 Film *Tristano e Isotta*' (pp. 313–18).

The second part turns to female Arthurians: Rachel Bromwich on 'The "Mabinogion" and Lady Charlotte Guest (1812–1921)' (pp. 321–34), Norris J. Lacy on 'Jessie Laidlay Weston (1850–1928)' (pp. 335–42), Henry Hall Peyton II on 'The Loomis Ladies: Gertrude Schoepperle Loomis (1882–1921), Laura Hibbard Loomis (1883–1960), Dorothy Bethurum Loomis (1897–1987)' (pp. 343–7), Sue Ellen Holbrook on 'The Quickening Force: Vida Dutton Scudder (1861–1954) and Malory's *Le Morte Darthur*' (pp. 349–68), Chris Grooms on '"The Girl from Cumbria" A Tribute to Rachel Bromwich' (pp. 369–74), Sigmund Eisner on 'Helaine Newstead: "A giant in her field"' (pp. 375–79), Elspeth Kennedy on herself in 'How I Became (and Continue To Be) an Arthurian Woman Scholar' (pp. 381–85), Fanni Bogdanow also on herself in 'From Holocaust Survivor to Arthurian Scholar' (pp. 387–94), Martin B. Shichtman on 'Valerie Lagorio' (pp. 395–98), and finally Donald L. Hoffman on 'Maureen Fries: Teacher, Scholar, Friend' (pp. 399–402), followed by a list of her published works (pp. 403–8). As one might predict, with such a large number of submissions there is great variety in quality, but as a whole the collection is informative and a useful addition to the shelves.

A different collection is Carley, ed., *Glastonbury Abbey and the Arthurian Tradition*. The contributions, many by Carley himself or in collaboration, have all been published elsewhere before, but have been gathered in one convenient (though large) volume. A very few are revised significantly, but most have at best minor updates; having them all indexed together is definitely an added value, though the general index is selective and mainly for names, texts, and a few places. The opening 'Background' section contains Aelred Watkin's 'The Glastonbury Legends' (*ArthL* 15[1997] 77–91), followed by two 'Departure Points': Antonia Gransden's 'The Growth of the Glastonbury Traditions and Legends in the Twelfth Century' (*JEH* 27[1976] 337–58) and Valerie M. Lagorio's 'The Evolving Legend of St. Joseph of Glastonbury' (*Speculum* 46[1971] 209–31).

A section on 'Arthur's Death and Burial at Glastonbury' contains Charles T. Wood's 'Guenevere at Glastonbury: A Problem in Translation(s)' (*ArthL* 16[1998] 23–40); Richard Barber's 'The *Vera Historia de Morte Arthuri* and its Place in Arthurian Tradition' (*ArthL* 1[1981] 62–77); Michael Lapidge's 'The *Vera Historia de Morte Arthuri*: A New Edition' with translation, incorporating information about manuscripts not available for his 'An Edition of the *Vera Historia de Morte Arthuri*' (*ArthL* 1[1981] 79–93), with an addendum on the manuscript circulation by Richard Barber; Richard Barber's 'Was Mordred Buried at Glastonbury? Arthurian Tradition at Glastonbury in the Middle Ages' (*ArthL* 4[1985] 37–63), with an appendix giving relevant extracts from the major texts oddly at the end of the volume, before the indices; Ceridwen Lloyd-Morgan's 'From Ynys Wydrin to

Glasynbri: Glastonbury in Welsh Vernacular Tradition' (in L. Abrams and J.P. Carley, eds., *The Archaeology and History of Glastonbury Abbey* (Woodbridge [1991]), pp. 301–15); John Carmi Parsons's 'The Second Exhumation of King Arthur's Remains at Glastonbury, 19 April 1278' (*ArthL* 12[1993] 173–7; see *YWES* 74[1995] 119–20); John A. Goodall's 'The Glastonbury Abbey Memorial Plate Reconsidered' (*Antiquaries Journal* 66[1986] 364–7); Michelle Brown and James P. Carley's 'A Fifteenth-Century Revision of the Glastonbury Epitaph to King Arthur' (*ArthL* 12[1993] 179–91; see *YWES* 74[1995] 120); Neil Wright's 'A New Arthurian Epitaph?' (*ArthL* 13[1995] 145–9); John Withrington's 'The Arthurian Epitaph in Malory's *Morte Darthur*' (*ArthL* 7[1987] 103–44; see *YWES* 68[1989] 164–5); E.D. Kennedy's 'John Hardyng and the Holy Grail' (*ArthL* 8[1989] 185–206; see *YWES* 70[1991] 200); Felicity Riddy's 'Glastonbury, Joseph of Arimathea and the Grail in John Hardyng's Chronicle' (in L. Abrams and J.P. Carley, eds., *The Archaeology and History of Glastonbury Abbey* [Woodbridge, 1991], pp. 317–31); James P. Carley's 'A Grave Event: Henry V, Glastonbury Abbey, and Joseph of Arimathea's Bones' (in M.B. Shichtman and J.P. Carley, eds., *Culture and the King: The Social Implications of the Arthurian Legend* (Albany [1994]), pp. 129–48); and James P. Carley's 'The Discovery of the Holy Cross of Waltham at Montacute, the Excavation of Arthur's Grave at Glastonbury Abbey, and Joseph of Arimathea's Burial' (*ArthL* 4[1985] 64–9).

The section on 'Romances and Chronicles' has James P. Carley's 'A Fragment of *Perlesvaus* at Wells Cathedral Library' (*Zeitschrift für romanische Philologie* 108[1992] 35–61); James P. Carley's 'A Glastonbury Translator at Work: *Quedam narracio de nobili rege Arthuro* and *De origine gigantum* in their Earliest Manuscript Contexts' (*NFS* 30:ii[1991] 5–12); James P. Carley and Julia Crick's 'Constructing Albion's Past: An Annotated Edition of *De Origine Gigantum*' (*ArthL* 13[1995] 41–114); and Ruth Evans's 'Gigantic Origins: An Annotated Translation of *De Origine Gigantum*' (*ArthL* 16[1998] 197–211).

Finally, 'Other Texts' presents both parts of Jeanne Krochalis's '*Magna Tabula*: The Glastonbury Tablets' (*ArthL* 15[1997] 93–183 and 16[1998] 41–82); and James P. Carley and Martin Howley's 'Relics at Glastonbury in the Fourteenth Century: An Annotated Edition of British Library, Cotton Titus D.vii, fols. 2^r–13^v' (*ArthL* 16[1998] 83–129). Thereafter follow the appendix to Richard Barber's article on Mordred's burial, a general index to the whole collection, and a manuscript index.

In '*Sir Orfeo* and the Flight from the Enchanters' (*SAC* 22[2000] 141–77), Alan J. Fletcher seeks to explain the gallery of the mad and nearly dead, frozen in time, taken for display in fairyland. He finds a path to the answer through knowledge of three discourses, which he examines carefully with regard to the elements of the gallery: late medieval Christianity, astrology, and fairyland. Each could have been applied to help explain the gallery, but each fails to do so, leaving the events and text in chaos; the discourses themselves thereby also seem to be 'taken'. Sir Orfeo is able to escape fairyland by harping, a performative act which has its own artistic and moral values. In a similar fashion, Fletcher seems to say, performance—providing also a union of *nomen* and *res*—can provide a moral refuge against chaos for the audience.

Caroline D. Eckhardt finds a shortened version of the well-known romance of 'Havelok the Dane in *Castleford's Chronicle*' (*SP* 98[2001] 1–17). In this version, Havelok is called by a patronymic Birkebaineson, consistent with some other versions of the narrative. The chronicle version shares some details thought to be unique innovations of the Middle English romance, but Eckhardt finds that both must be relying on a tradition otherwise unattested. Discussing *Havelok* itself, Ananya J. Kabir's 'Forging an Oral Style? *Havelok* and the Fiction of Orality' (*SP* 98[2001] 18–48) concludes that, despite the guise of popular fiction, the romance's oral narrative and realism are deliberate artefacts aimed at a courtly audience, with a kind of nostalgic, retrospective wish-fulfilment. Turning to a different romance, Myra Seaman looks at 'Engendering Genre in Middle English Romance: Performing the Feminine in *Sir Beves of Hamtoun*' (*SP* 98[2001] 49–75). The popularity of *Beves* has been generally overturned in modern critical estimation, which also prefers its heroines passive. To counter that, Seaman focuses on Josian's active roles and qualities, including an education and a self-awareness that allow her to exceed socially prescribed limitations.

Several articles considered the relationship between works and their audiences. Dana M. Symons, 'Does Tristan Think, or Doesn't He? The Pleasures of the Middle English *Sir Tristrem*' (*ArthI* 11:iv[2001] 3–22), hopes to find the grounds for popular pleasure through a contrast with the literary version, taking her starting point from Thomas of Britain's frequently introspective Tristan as opposed to the Middle English hero, who loves Ysonde with all his might, as does his dog Hodain, once all three have taken the love potion, and then at length reviewing critical dissatisfaction with this later romance. Not surprisingly, the answer is in a shift from process and description to result, and from thought to action, with the focus on what Symons calls 'spectacle and episodic movement'. The details that may seem odd are no doubt simply elements of parody, again entertaining those whose tastes do not include more serious fare. Stephen D. Powell's 'Models of Religious Peace in the Middle English Romance *Sir Isumbras*' (*Neophil* 85[2001] 121–36) observes how, though the poet and audience had the patent belief that non-Christians must be converted even if by force of arms, the poem nevertheless has an undercurrent of alternative views which tolerate some religious coexistence with Muslims (conflated to a degree with Jews). And in '"Talkyng of cronycles of kinges and of other polycyez": Fifteenth-Century Miscellanies, the *Brut* and the Readership of *Le Morte Darthur*' (*ArthL* 18[2001] 125–41), Raluca Radulescu surveys reading preferences among the rising gentry and in London mercantile circles, politically conscious groups with a taste for chronicles, chivalric texts, and history, especially the *Brut*, to speculate how those preferences and some aspects of the *Brut* might have influenced Malory's rendition of Arthur and his court. Radulescu therefore takes some care to show how the Middle English *Brut* came to reflect the concerns of these readers in the fifteenth century, with some notes on correspondences and differences in Malory.

A different way of looking at romances and their social relationships is Noël James Menuge's *Medieval English Wardship in Romance and Law*. The prime romances including wardship are *King Horn*, *Horn Child*, *Havelok the Dane*, *Beues of Hamtoun*, *William of Palerne*, and *Gamelyn*, ranging across the thirteenth century and late into the fourteenth century; legal works include principal treatises from the late twelfth to mid-thirteenth centuries and cases in the Year Books (fourteenth and early fifteenth centuries). Menuge examines both carefully for how they separately and together illuminate a patriarchal social system valuing the father, who in all these cases needs be absent, and attempt to provide a surrogate for him; she also looks at issues such as primogeniture vs. partible inheritance, waste, majority and legal age (with exile as symbolic of minority), consent and marriage (especially with regard to female wards), and the problem of female guardians, especially maternal ones.

Partly historical, partly morphological, partly manuscript study, socioeconomics, and more is Carol M. Meale's 'Romance and its Anti-Type? *The Turnament of Totenham*, the Carnivalesque, and Popular Culture' (in Minnis, ed., *Middle English Poetry: Texts and Traditions*, pp. 103–27). She observes that there is a record of some kind of performance 'de la Tornment de Totyngham' and wonders at audience, its reception, and the very reputation of Tottenham. In casting about for answers in this heavily footnoted article she ranges very widely indeed, with much to inform us about Tottenham, the manuscripts and their owners or readers, and what this work and others on the edge of social propriety reveal about social mores and the limits of irreverence. With *The Turnament* itself having been staged, Meale notes that there are other references to performances of more typical romances; thus it would no doubt be fruitful to investigate romance and drama, not just romance and hagiography, to understand more fully the breadth and variety of popular culture.

Adding to prior discussions of parodic elements, Rebecca A. Davis's 'More Evidence for Intertextuality and Humorous Intent in *The Weddynge of Syr Gawen and Dame Ragnell*' (*ChauR* 35[2000–1] 430–9) discusses connections between the *Weddynge* and its analogues in the opening call to attention, the Loathly Lady's appearance, the marriage day, the name Dame Ragnell, Gawain's defence of Arthur, and the closing prayer. On the other hand, Yin Liu's 'Clothing, Armour, and Boundaries in *Sir Perceval of Galles*' (*Florilegium* 18:ii[2001] 79–92) looks at how the poet's attention to detail belies his work as a critique or parody of chivalry; instead, he affirms it, particularly through physical and symbolic details of clothing and armour, which represent 'boundaries between socially constructed spaces' (p. 81), just as walls help distinguish the castle from the wilderness. That is, the comically ignorant Perceval needs more than martial prowess to become a knight: he must learn the nature, use, and even words for the outer trappings that visibly display the nature of the knight within them.

Some attention is given to language issues. In 'The Text of *Sir Perceval of Galles*' (*MÆ* 70[2001] 191–203), Ad Putter untangles six cruces to show that its 'loose grammar' and 'labored diction' are our misunderstandings: 'armour' (l. 139) means feats of arms, not armour itself; the buck passage (ll. 302–4) is metaphorical and alludes to Perceval's hunting skills; 'menevaire' (l. 409) is miniver, a high-quality squirrel fur used on robes for the well-to-do; 'sprongen of a stane' (l. 1043) is a proverbial expression of isolation; 'aughte' (l. 1490) is 'owed'; and 'wete' (l. 1614) is an infinitive of 'know', here meaning 'be able to'. Second, Thomas Honegger briefly (though with some data appended) examines '*Luf-talkyng* and Middle English Romance' (in Jürgen and Görlach, eds., *Towards a History of English as a History of Genres*, pp. 159–82), looking at general 'verbal amatory interaction' in 'works that are generally referred to as *Middle English romances*' (p. 159), meaning *Sir Gawain and the Green Knight*, *The Grene Knight* (an abbreviation of that in tail rhyme, *c*.1500), *Ywain and Gawain* vs. Chrétien's *Yvain*, and *Guy of Warwick*. Sophisticated dialogues, he discovers, are rare and their significance evidently lies in their courtliness; with the exception of *Sir Gawain and the Green Knight*, the romances are not interested in romantic love, and do not exhibit any evolution from a simple to a more complex *luf-talkyng*.

Several works have concentrated recently on the late romance *Huon of Bordeaux*. First, M.I. Cameron's 'Such Joy at Heart: Lord Berners' *Huon of Bordeaux*' (*Florilegium* 16[1999] 107–230) finds John Bourchier, Lord Berners, comparable to Malory in his wistful retrospectiveness, but Bourchier's prose translation of a French text is more free, having a lively, conversational style that matches a minstrel's jollity. Second, Joyce Boro's 'The Textual History of *Huon of Burdeux*: A Reassessment of the Facts' (*N&Q* 48[2001] 233–7) follows up on N.F. Blake's leads in 'Lord Berners: A Survey' (*M&H* 2[1971] 124–5; see *YWES* 53[1974] 137). Only two copies of the romance survive, as well as a record of a third; Boro reviews the evidence to argue for a history of four printed editions, part of the argument relying upon realizing that the 1601 edition refers to Francis, Lord Hastings, earl of Huntingdon 1545–61.

Although not directly on romances, Glenn Wright' 'Churl's Courtesy: *Rauf Coilyear* and its English Analogues' (*Neophil* 85[2001] 647–62) examines how romances and tales influenced *The Taill of Rauf Coilyear* in depicting social relations among classes. The king-and-commoner stories have already been discussed as analogues, but Wright reviews them and adds the Middle English Gawain romances, especially *Syre Gawene and the Carle of Carelyle*, for their use of a menacing outsider who tests the aristocratic figure. In combining the two kinds of source or analogue, the poet is able to examine class and especially 'courtesy' in a novel way, pointing to reason and fairness as the best determiners of proper treatment across class boundaries.

7. Gower, Lydgate and Hoccleve

(a) Gower

A.S.G. Edwards and T. Takamiya announce and describe 'A New Fragment of Gower's *Confessio Amantis*' (*MLR* 96[2001] 931–6), which is now in the Takamiya Collection in Tokyo. In addition to a few corrections to the *Index of Middle English Verse*, they edit the text of the fragment because of its importance: though most recently a binding fragment, it was originally part of the Stafford Gower. Another manuscript is described by Kate Harris in 'The Longleat House Extracted Manuscript of Gower's *Confessio Amantis*' (in Minnis, ed., *Middle English Poetry*, pp. 77–90). Longleat MS 174 is mainly a medical manuscript with an apparently London-based core around 1459–71 with many accretions perceived as scientific lore, added at various times as late as the sixteenth and seventeenth centuries. The extract comes from Book VII, lines 1281–438, complete with the Latin apparatus, being the section on the fifteen stars from the *Education of Alexander*. Harris provides a detailed description of the manuscript and its development, and includes some comparison between how Gower is used here and in Sloane 3847, a collection of alchemical and necromantic texts from the fifteenth to the seventeenth centuries.

Siân Echard also considers manuscript evidence in 'Dialogues and Monologues: Manuscript Representations of the Conversation of the *Confessio Amantis*' (in Minnis, ed., *Middle English Poetry*, pp. 57–75). Looking at the *ordinatio* with special attention to speech markers, Echard notes that the presence, placement, or absence of markers influences how the work is perceived: as narrative, drama, story collection, or a confessional dialogue akin to the *Consolation of Philosophy*. The conclusion is that Gower, who attempted to control the physical appearance of the manuscripts, intended the design to focus on the confessional model, particularly because the markers designate mainly *Confessor*, not Genius, and *Amans*, and formulae are generally based on *confessio* and *opponit*.

A different use of manuscript evidence is Kathryn Kerby-Fulton and Steven Justice's 'Scribe D and the Marketing of Ricardian Literature' (in Kerby-Fulton and Hilmo, eds., *The Medieval Professional Reader at Work*, pp. 217–37). Though Parkes and Doyle identified a good number of important manuscripts as having been written by Scribe D, Kerby-Fulton and Justice look instead at their nature and their apparent audience among the politicians, lawyers, and high-ranking civil servants of Ricardian and early Lancastrian Westminster, noting the curious shift from Langland to Gower and thus D's evidently keen awareness of his clients' interests. They analyse the Taylor Gower manuscript to show how Scribe D's role is probably more that of an entrepreneur of vernacular literature, and consider secular exemplarity as a key reason for Gower and Trevisa as D's main output. One of the Gower portraits in the Taylor Gower shows the author pointing to a book cupboard; this motif in several D manuscripts appears to come from its use in manuscripts illuminated at Herman Scheerre's elite shop, whose patrons or early owners shared high political and legal status.

Theory directs several articles this year. First, Miriamne Ara Krummel's 'The *Tale of Ceïx and Alceone*: Alceone's Agency and Gower's 'Audible Mime'' (*Exemplaria* 13[2001] 497–528) considers how this tale 'explores the social validity of woman's psychological centrality in a fiction that points to experienced reality' (p. 502), in having Ithecus, Panthasas, and Morpheüs enact an audible mime and in freeing Alceone from other versions' use of her as a subaltern. Second, in a more structured article, 'Sins of Omission: Transgressive Genders, Subversive Sexualities, and Confessional Silence in John Gower's *Confessio Amantis*' (*Exemplaria* 13[2001] 529–51), Diane Watt reviews instances of cross-dressing and their relationship to femininity and effeminacy, lesbian sex, and the absence of male sodomy, to find that Gower shared the penitential focus on male sexuality, so that while female transgressiveness is explored but not condemned, male homosexuality is curiously taboo. James T. Bratcher notes that the 'Tale of Three Questions' at the end of Book I of the *Confessio Amantis* may have no identifiable source, but one ballad is a distant analogue: 'Gower and Child, No. 45, "King John and the Bishop"' (*N&Q* 48[2001] 14–15).

(b) Lydgate

The TEAMS Middle English Texts series issued a new edition of *The Siege of Thebes*, edited by Robert R. Edwards from BL MS Arundel 119. A brief introduction reviews Lydgate's predecessors more than his probably immediate political purpose, then surveys critical reception before a brief overview of main themes; this is followed by a good discussion of the textual history and Edwards's editorial activities, and by a select bibliography. As with other TEAMS editions, the text is well spaced, with line numbers on the left and glosses on the right. Pointing hands indicate the location of marginalia in the original; these are produced in the notes (the Latin ones are not translated, though translating the common *nota* would seem superfluous), but Edwards does not discuss their authorship. The explanatory notes are generally sufficient, the textual notes are quite detailed, and there is a basic glossary. One of the manuscripts is discussed by Priscilla J. Bawcutt in 'The Boston Public Library Manuscript [f. med. 94] of John Lydgate's *Siege of Thebes*: Its Scottish Owners and Inscriptions' (*MÆ* 70[2001] 80–94), a manuscript written by Stephen Dodesham *c*.1430–60, perhaps early, but in Scottish hands by the end of the century, apparently owned by Mariota Lyle of Renfrewshire. By the middle of the sixteenth century it passed through various other hands, including Duncan Campbell's, who owned other manuscripts of singular interest. He may have written one of several short verses added to the manuscript; all are Scottish, including a snippet from Gower, and Bawcutt edits them with commentary. Departing from the usual critical assessment of Lydgate's prologue as demonstrating his incompetence is Scott-Morgan Straker's 'Deference and Difference: Lydgate, Chaucer and the *Siege of Thebes*' (*RES* 52[2001] 1–21). Instead, Straker takes a fresh look and considers it a case of intentional inversion, given Lydgate's desire to shift to a moral high ground. His self-creation delivers a product different from that requested by the Host, an emblematic patron, and thus acts as a counsellor, whose advice seems fated to be ignored.

A few articles take fairly practical views of Lydgate's works. In 'Text as Performance: Toward a More Authentic Experience of the Lydgate Canon' (*Florilegium* 17[2000] 21–43), Anita Helmbold chastises us for our modern silent reading, which is responsible for determining that Lydgate is dull, even though we tacitly admit many of his works were for performance—visual and oral—in pageants, mummings, or picture poems. She reviews the evidence that troubadour songs survive as poems without musical notes, and that poems, including Lydgate's, were performed with music, to argue that we should be more consciously mindful of the performative nature of his works, in order to appreciate them. And Claire Sponsler's 'Eating Lessons: Lydgate's "Dietary" and Consumer Conduct' (in Ashley and Clark, eds., *Medieval Conduct*, pp. 1–22) reviews the social and popular aspects of eating, dressing, and living in general. The audience seems to have consisted of adult males interested in maintaining a healthy lifestyle, no doubt well-off enough to have sufficient leisure and livelihood to engage in a variety of foods and activities. She surveys some of the manuscript evidence for readership, and considers how the *Dietary* might have fitted into the beginnings of the consumer society around the second quarter of the fifteenth century, with reference to some theoretical studies. In 'New Perspectives on Lydgate's Courtly Verse' (in Cooney, ed., *Nation, Court and Culture*, pp. 95–115), Sue Bianco works from Jauss's theory that we must understand a poet's contemporary readership to understand that poet's works. Thus, Lydgate's *dits amoreux* were expected to have puns, visual allusions, anagrams, acrostics, and other wordplay that would identify the real people inhabiting the poems. Therefore, 'Complaynt of a Lovered Lyfe' may well be about Henry Bolingbroke and addressed to the Percys of Northumberland, and the 'Temple of Glas' is about Henry's marriage to Joan of Navarre. Though these conclusions seem odd in this summary, readers must consider the argument as presented in Bianco's article to more fully evaluate its strengths and qualifications.

Some of Lydgate's other classical works attract attention too, particularly the *Troy Book*. Robert R. Edwards unfolds 'Lydgate's *Troy Book* and the Confusion of Prudence' (in Liszka and Walker, eds., *The North Sea World in the Middle Ages*, pp.

52–69) to show, first, the larger and more immediate intellectual and literary understandings of prudence that Lydgate inherited, and second, an important distinction between prudence and cunning or trickery, in that both apply thought to action but the latter does so with no focus upon honour. The development of the *Troy Book* poses examples of each against the other, with a larger concern that distinguishes pagan from Christian prudence: when ideals are grounded in this world, even prudence can lead to disaster. Reception of the past continues in Martha W. Driver's 'Medievalizing the Classical Past in Pierpont Morgan MS M 876' (in Minnis, ed., *Middle English Poetry*, pp. 211–39), where the illustrations for Lydgate's *Troy Book* and the romance *Generides* depict the ancients modernized, with contemporary arms, armour, ships, and heraldic devices. As in other, less obvious, cases, such fictionalized picturing is memorial, not factual. Even contemporary funerary practices are reflected in the displayed effigy of Hector, visible by his tomb.

Lynn Shutters, in 'Truth, Translation, and the *Troy Book* Women' (*Comitatus* 32[2001] 69–98), begins with the observation that Lydgate's view of women in the *Troy Book* is usually seen as anti-feminist because critics generally consider only Criseyde. Matching a larger theme of truthfulness vs. falsehood, however, Lydgate's women also parallel successionary lines and thus Lancastrian legitimacy and authority. The 'dublinesse' of Criseyde, Medea, and Helen is opposed by the 'stedfastnes' and 'trowth' of Penthesilia, Penelope, Cassandra, Hecuba, and Polyxena, with the addition of Katharine of Valois. However, there is a problem in that the 'good' women suffer while the false ones successfully adapt to their changed environments, as Katharine would have had to when translated to England. Shutter does not find an answer to this, but offers the suggestion that Lydgate's 'gendering duplicity female' lets him explore safely 'the fluidity of such categories and the anxiety with which they were regarded in Lancastrian England' (p. 98). Scott Lightsey's 'Lydgate's Steed of Brass: A Chaucerian Analogue in *Troy Book* IV' (*ELN* 38[2001] 33–40) has an interesting observation we hope can be carried further. When Lydgate calls his mechanical horse a 'stede of bras', he intends his readers to think of the one with exactly the same name in Chaucer's *Squire's Tale*, and he draws his description from there for more than simple convenience, for otherwise he uses Guido della Collonne. Both Lydgate and Chaucer emphasize the steed as a man-made device, controlled by various pins. More importantly, both include a moral note of deception in the crafting of the engine; for us, this indicates as well how carefully Lydgate was reading Chaucer.

Andrew Breeze's 'Sir John Paston, Lydgate, and *The Libelle of Englyshe Polycye*' (*N&Q* 48[2001] 230–1) looks at how Paston's booklist of 1479, though fragmentary, indicates that the book he lent Midelton apparently included Lydgate's *Horse, Goose and Sheep*, probably his *Guy of Warwick*, and his *Fabula duorum mercatorum*; these and other works the Pastons owned point to 'John Paston's part in the formulation of national policy'. John J. Thompson's 'Reading Lydgate in Post-Reformation England' (in Minnis, ed., *Middle English Poetry*, pp. 181–209) looks not at readers of Lydgate but at the printing of the *Fall of Princes* by both John Wayland and Richard Tottel in 1554, with deeper investigation into their business and legal lives and into the political environment.

(c) Hoccleve

Hot on the heels of Burrow's edition (see *YWES* 80[2001] 173) comes Roger Ellis's edition of Thomas Hoccleve's *'My Compleinte' and Other Poems*, using the holograph manuscripts as much as possible for the Series Poems and six other poems ('Conpleynte paramont', 'La male regle', 'Balade ... H. Somer', 'Balade ... Robert Chichele', 'De beata Virgine', and 'L'epistre de Cupide'). Although Ellis occasionally discusses the marginal glosses and specifies that many, if not most, originated with Hoccleve, he does not reproduce them with the texts and includes only a few in the discursive notes, despite the contrary implication of his observation that 'they are well worth persevering with' (p. 2). Perhaps he was ruled by the feeling that 'marginal glosses are, it must be admitted, marginal to most readers' interests' (p. 23), unlike *ordinatio* and many textual matters. Ellis supplies the kind of helpful discussion that EETS editions are not usually intended for, guiding students through general matters and more specific difficulties. Each text is accompanied by marginal glosses of hard words and phrases and by short explanatory, textual, and source notes at the end. The book ends with appendices containing the extra stanzas for the 'Conpleynte paramont', comparisons with selected sources and analogues, glosses to a part of the Series in two manuscripts, more notes on textual relationships in three works in non-holograph manuscripts, selected variants from non-holograph manuscripts, and a longish bibliography.

Textual matters are also discussed by Christina von Nolcken in 'Almost Hoccleve's Own: J.A. Burrow and the Editing of Hoccleve's Poetry' (*N&Q* 48[2001] 224–9). This is a review article not only of Burrow's EETS edition of the *Complaint and Dialogue* but also of Blythe's TEAMS edition of the *Regiment of Princes* (see *YWES* 80[2001] 172–3), discussing the editorial history of Blythe's *Regiment*, the double novelties of separating accidentals from substantives (common in post-medieval editing practice) and then recreating those accidentals from scratch, as it were, given the lack of holographic texts for these portions of the poems. She concludes that both editions, especially that of Burrows, greatly illuminate Hoccleve's metrical practice, particularly because his historical unstressed final *-e* was almost immediately misrepresented by scribes to whom it essentially meant nothing.

There is further work on textual or historical backgrounds. Lee Patterson surveys 'Beinecke MS 493 and the Survival of Hoccleve's *Series*' (in Babcock and Patterson, eds., *Old Books, New Learning: Essays on Medieval and Renaissance Books at Yale*, pp. 80–92). Dated by Malcolm Parkes to the third quarter of the fifteenth century, this manuscript is typical in grouping the Series Poems with Lydgate's *Daunce of Machabre* and Hoccleve's *Regiment of Princes*. Patterson also proposes that John Carpenter-Clerk of London, one of the executors of Dick Whittington's will, and a dedicatee of one of Hoccleve's ballades, had a hand in supporting Hoccleve and his verse. Patterson even suggests that in 1442 Carpenter may have willed Bodleian MS Arch. Selden supra 53, which resembles Beinecke MS 493, to the Guildhall. John J. Thompson's 'Thomas Hoccleve and Manuscript Culture' (in Cooney, ed., *Nation, Court and Culture*, pp. 81–94) briefly discusses how Hoccleve's autobiographical headings in the autograph Huntington Library MS HM 111 reveal a typical fifteenth-century recycling of poems into new anthologies, as well as promoting him as a poet for an influential elite. His works also circulated alongside selections from Chaucer, and we are reminded of his own activities in the London book trade.

Separately, Lee Patterson discusses the poet's introspection, in '"What is me?": Self and Society in the Poetry of Thomas Hoccleve' (*SAC* 23[2001] 437–70). Hoccleve's self-absorption is exactly that—not a pose used for other purposes—and the Series is an attempted talking cure, doomed to fail if for no reason other than its inability to find selections appropriate to the dedicatees. Other works, including earlier ones, also betray a political or social tactlessness, for he is seeking to de-fragment his individuality in a culture requiring selfless conformity in support of a cult of personality. Hoccleve's difficulty must have been compounded by his migrating from rural homogeneity to the national and international heterogeneity of London, where money speaks loud and many become 'spiritually lost in the anonymity of the metropolis'. An awareness of how one is seen by others is deemed to be politically wise in J.A. Burrow's 'Hoccleve and the "Court"' (in Cooney, ed., *Nation, Court and Culture,* pp. 70–80), where Burrow describes the degree to which Hoccleve's office was a courtly one and thus how Hoccleve would have had access to those in power. His verse even shows that he considered himself as being in court, and it bears the right signs: princely advice, not *fin amour*, and a constant concern about one's status in the eyes of others, a necessity in a competitive political court environment.

Happily this year proves that there is more to Hoccleve than worrying about money or public image. W.A. Davenport gives a short but interesting survey of antiphrasis in 'Thomas Hoccleve's *La Male Regle* and Oxymoron' (*ES* 82[2001] 497–506). Hoccleve uses it frequently in the early portion of the work, where he recounts his misspent youth, but it gives way to more 'appropriate pairings' of nouns with adjectives after he is counselled. Similar pairings of 'bad' adjectives with 'good' nouns occur in various love poems and satirical passages, in Chaucer and elsewhere. It might have been equally informative to examine some of Lydgate's works; though his *Ballade per Antiphrasim* may not be the best choice, the paradoxes in 'Tyed with a Lyne' and elsewhere are curiously reminiscent of Hoccleve's oxymora. J.A. Burrow examines 'Scribal Mismetring' (in Minnis, ed., *Middle English Poetry*, pp. 169–79) between the Durham autograph of Hoccleve's *Dialogue* and five scribal copies, which unfortunately represent a 'Variant Original' different from the Durham autograph. Hoccleve, as noted above, did not write orthographic, silent *es* and even elided them when desired; the scribes seemed not to understand this and misrepresented his strict decasyllabic lines. Curiously, Gower's decasyllables are not so readily corrupted in some manuscripts, and Chaucer's use has yet to be determined.

But that does not mean that investigations of Hoccleve's cashflow have become passé. In 'Hoccleve and the Apprehension of Money' (*Exemplaria* 13[2001] 173–214), Robert J. Meyer-Lee finds financial stress inseparable from Hoccleve's poetic self-consciousness, hypothesizing that this results from a shift from feudalism to capitalism around 1350–1426. The monetary spills over into the linguistic in several ways, such as the pre-emptive deferrals of the Series Poems, resembling the delays Hoccleve experienced regarding his financial health, money itself becoming a major social as well as personal issue. And Sarah Tolmie's 'The *Prive Sclence* of Thomas Hoccleve' (*SAC* 22[2000] 281–309) is a free-ranging survey of passages in the *Regement of Princes* that lend themselves to punning interpretation encircling the materiality of language and the immateriality of Hoccleve's power, purse, and position. She foregrounds silence, vacuity, and implied threats in a frame spanning from willed (as it were) goods to good will.

A different way of looking at Hoccleve's relationship to society is propounded by Nicholas Perkins in *Hoccleve's 'Regiment of Princes': Counsel and Constraint*. By the time of the *Regiment*, there was a good tradition of officialdom trying to restrain (if not control) speech and thus thought, even as the pinnacle of government was expected to listen and to a great degree respect and obey the advice of those below him. Perkins uses his first two chapters to describe this double-edged sword, as found in bureaucratic, historical, and literary texts. Counsel given is never specific to any immediate situation, no matter how specific complaints after the fact could be (as in the Articles against Richard II). The king is to abstract universal rules of behaviour and government from his readings. Not surprisingly, Hoccleve uses the common medieval metaphor of the state as a human body, but Jacobus de Cessolis' *De ludo scaccorum* is more Hoccleve's source for form and content than Ægidius Romanus. Perkins also surveys the manuscript heritage for clues to the *Regiment*'s reception history.

Ethan Knapp's *The Bureaucratic Muse: Thomas Hoccleve and the Literature of Late Medieval England* revises some of his earlier articles (see *YWES* 80[2001] 171–2) and adds material to argue that Hoccleve's autobiography grows out of the impersonality of the bureaucracy, as revealed in his *Formulary*, in that bureaucrats must identify what is personal and subjective in order to eliminate it, leading to the lowly clerk's insecurity, as in 'La male regle'. Similarly, bureaucracy replaces personal authority with a persona. By extension, eliminating a voice leads to the elimination of a gendered authority, and we see cross-gendering traversed several times in Hoccleve's translation of Christine de Pizan's *Epistre au Dieu d'Amours*. The *Regement of Princes* shows the topoi of bureaucracy and authority in two ways. First, documents ensure that an individual's actions and intents may survive his life, yet the clerks' jobs made them keenly aware of the effects writing had on their bodies and health, with no consolation from their textuality. Second, the fact of writing a claim to inherit office or authority may confer it, as in Hoccleve's attempt to connect himself with paternal Chaucer. His religious works also reflect a minor bureaucrat's sceptical adoption of authoritative positions, made metaphoric through his use of images and sight. Hoccleve's *Series* reflects the difficulties of the individual, yet represents writing by committee, with multiple voices and styles joined in one work.

8. Malory and Caxton

Two books of interest to Malory scholars were published in 2001. Elizabeth Edwards's *The Genesis of Narrative in Malory's 'Morte Darthur'* focuses on Balin, the Grail, and Arthur's death. She claims that the structure of the work is based not on plot or character but on symbol. Drawing on Saussure's claim that loss helps to create symbols by preserving connections between objects and ideas after the original explanations have leached away, she argues that Malory amplifies the symbolic impact of his sources by his abbreviation and his preference for the physical signifiers (swords, grails, and so on) over the abstract signified. She pays particular attention to Balin, Gareth, the Grail, and Arthur's death. The interesting ideas more than make up for the occasionally dense prose.

Wheeler and Tolhurst, eds., *On Arthurian Women: Essays in Memory of Maureen Fries*, is an engaging, occasionally aggravating, collection of essays with much of interest to Malory scholars; it also includes biographies of ten female Arthurian scholars at the end, which provide an interesting bit of intellectual history. Essays on Malory include Maud Burnett McIerney's 'Malory's Lancelot and the Lady Huntress', Janet Knepper's 'A Bad Girl Will Love You To Death: Excessive Love in the Stanzaic *Morte Arthur* and Malory', Melanie McGarrahan Gibson's 'Lyonet, Lunete, and Laudine: Carnivalesque Arthurian Women', Dorsey Armstrong's 'Malory's Morgause', Sue Ellen Holbrook's 'Elemental Goddesses: Nymue, the Chief Lady of the Lake, and her Sisters', Elizabeth Sklar's 'Malory's Other(ed) Elaine', James Noble's 'Gilding the Lily (Maid): Elaine of Astolat', and Beverly Kennedy's 'Malory's Guinevere: A "trew lover"'. Also included is Edward Donald Kennedy's 'Malory's Guinevere: "A woman who had grown a soul"', originally printed in *Arthuriana*. As the titles suggest, many of the works focus on desire and its dangers, especially when it is women who are desiring. Sklar gives a sympathetic reading of Galahad's mother. Edward Donald Kennedy's sympathetic reading of Launcelot and Guinevere as a pair of lovers struggling to find a way to grace other than through the Grail is ultimately more convincing than Beverley Kennedy's continued insistence that their love was almost perfectly chaste. Armstrong makes an interesting (but overstated) case for Morgause's disruptive desires having greater consequences than is commonly acknowledged.

Several articles discuss the role of emotion, magic, and the divine in Malory. Bonnie Libby explores Merlin's various roles in the early part of Malory's book in 'The Dual Nature of Merlin in the *Morte Darthur*' (*MedPers* 16[2001] 63–73). Felicia Ackerman edits a special issue of Arthurian on 'Philosophical and Emotive Issues in Malory' (*Arthuriana* 11:ii[2001]). In her essay, '"Every Man of Worshyp": Emotion and Characterization in Malory's *Le Morte Darthur*' (32–42), Ackerman argues that the emotional flatness and inconsistency many see in Malory's characters comes from his presenting only what we routinely see from those around us—action and speech—without the internal description of thoughts or feelings found in more modern novels, and that perceptive readers can use the details given to reconstruct emotionally plausible characters. Beverly Kennedy suggests that an exploration of the relation between human choice and divine providence underlies much of *Le Morte Darthur* ('The Idea of Providence in Malory's *Le Morte Darthur*', 5–19). Virginity is not an undisputed value even in the Grail quest, according to Karen Cherewatuk who argues in 'Born-Again Virgins and Holy Bastards: Bors and Elyne and Lancelot and Galahad' that Bors and Launcelot in many ways gain status for fathering good sons out of wedlock (52–64). Peter R. Schroeder's contribution notes that Malory usually understates moments of extreme emotion, creating a contrast with the often excessive swooning and weeping in moments when the emotions are simpler ('Saying but Little: Malory and the Suggestion of Emotion', 43–51). Kevin T. Grimm argues in 'the Love and Envy of Sir Palomides' (65–74) that Palomides is a 'thematic character' who embodies the two main forces that Drive Malory's 'Tale of Trystram', love and envy. Mark Ricciardi argues that in the Winchester MS Arthur's war with Rome emphasizes fellowship while in Caxton it emphasizes the king's individual heroism; in neither case is it merely brutal violence being celebrated "'Se What I Shall Do as for my Trew Parte": Fellowship and Fortitude in Malory's *Noble Tale of King Arthur and the Emperor Lucius'*, 20–31).

In addition to Ricciardi, two other critics touch on textual issues. Elizabeth Sklar, in 'Re-Writing Malory: Vinaver's *Selected Tales*' (*Arthuriana* 11:iv[2001] 53–63), argues that Vinaver tries to make a 'modern' version of Malory, and that, among other changes, he presents a darker, more sexualized love between Guinevere and Launcelot. P.J.C. Field, 'Malory's Own Marginalia' (*MÆ* 70[2001] 226–39) argues that the marginal comments in the Winchester manuscript are not the products of the scribes but original to Malory.

Kathy Cawsey, 'Merlin's Magical Writing: Writing and the Written Word in *Le Morte Darthur* and the English Prose *Merlin*' (*Arthuriana* 11:iii[2001] 89–101), looks at the power of writing in late medieval Arthurian literature, associated both with magicians and scribes, and often breaking the frame of the story to let writings of the characters become the actual textual tradition that records those acts. Angela Gibson, in 'Malory's Reformulation of Shame' (*Arthuriana* 11:iv[2001] 64–76), argues that Malory uses shame to mark the revelation of private affairs as worse than the affairs themselves, thereby creating a legitimate space for privacy in the very public world of Arthur's court.

Malory serves as a point of comparison in Paul Robichaud's 'The Undoing of All Things: Malorian Language and Allusion in David Jones' *In Parenthesis*' (*Renascence* 53:ii[2001] 149–65). I have not seen Kathy Cawsey's 'The Hanged Man: Lancelot and Guinevere in Malory's *Morte Darthur*' (*BAS* 7[2001] 93–102).

9. Middle Scots Poetry

Bateman, Crawford and McGonigal, eds., *Scottish Religious Poetry: An Anthology*, contains a significant amount of pre-modern verse not only in Middle Scots (by such notables as Henryson and Dunbar), but in Latin, Gaelic, and even Old Norse. The book is not intended to be scholarly; rather, it serves to introduce the general reader to the great variety of religious expression in Scotland, from the early Middle Ages to the present. In this respect, it is an admirable anthology.

Dieter Mehl, in 'Middle Scots Poetry' (chapter 8 of his *English Literature in the Age of Chaucer*), ably surveys the most important Middle Scots poetry, including *The Kingis Quair*, *The Book of the Houlat*, and the works of Robert Henryson, William Dunbar, and Gavin Douglas. His summaries and analyses of poems are often far too brief to offer significant insight, but his overarching picture of the period is comprehensive and provides a useful road map for the undergraduate or beginning graduate student, and his scholarship is remarkably up to date.

A relatively wide variety of Middle Scots poetry scholarship appeared in 2001, with articles published not only on the Makars (Henryson, Dunbar, Douglas), but also on less often examined poems of the fifteenth century. Karin Fuog has written two articles on *The Kingis Quair*. The first, 'Weaving Words and Steering by Stars: Punning in *The Kingis Quair*' (*ELN* 38[2001] 20–33), argues that there are two puns in *The Kingis Quair*, one on stere/sterre ('steer' and 'star') and the other on word/ werd ('word' and 'fate'), and that these work, in counter-Boethian fashion, to suggest a reconciliation of the earthly and the divine. In her other article, 'Placing

Earth at the Center of the Cosmos: *The Kingis Quair* as Boethian Revision' (*SSL* 32[2001] 140–9), Fuog furthers her argument that *The Kingis Quair* challenges rather than simply echoes Boethian philosophy. She suggests that, although *The Kingis Quair* takes its Ptolemaic view of the universe, with the 'earth at the center of the cosmos', from Boethius's *Consolation of Philosophy*, it values earth's position far differently, according it a place of primary importance, in contrast with Boethius, who saw it as the lowest place in the hierarchy of the cosmos. Glenn Wright's 'Churl's Courtesy: *Rauf Coilyear* and its English Analogues' (*Neophil* 85[2001] 647–62) offers compelling evidence that *Rauf Coilyear*, a fifteenth-century Middle Scots folktale in which a collier and King Charlemagne 'sample each other's hospitality', sets forth an 'ethical' vision of class relations that other poems featuring the 'king-and-the-commoner' plot do not. Wright suggests that *Rauf* has been influenced by a previously unrecognized set of analogues: the '*Gawain* group' of Middle English romances, in which exclusionary regimes of class hierarchy and privilege are brought up for critique by the eruption of a disruptive alien element that forces a recognition that 'courtesy' does not belong by nature to nobility alone.

Several studies of Henryson's poetry came out in 2001, the most important of which is chapter 4 of Kathleen Forni's *The Chaucerian Apocrypha: A Counterfeit Canon*, entitled 'The Apocrypha and Chaucer's Reception: Much Ado about Henryson. Forni first points out that Shakespearean critics, from the eighteenth century to the Second World War, tended to blame Henryson's *Testament of Cresseid* for distorting Chaucer's nuanced and sympathetic portrait of Criseyde and thus providing Shakespeare (in the form of the *Testament*, which was then ascribed to Chaucer himself) with a heroine unworthy of his genius. Forni convincingly demonstrates how denigration of the Henryson poem vis-à-vis Chaucer's poem stems from a distinctly modern understanding of (and investment in) Chaucer's canonicity, and how this understanding of Henryson's poem differs from the pre-modern understanding, which accepted the *Testament* as a valuable part of the Criseyde tradition even after that poem was dissociated from Chaucer. Two articles in *Studies in Scottish Literature* address issues in Henryson's other major poems, *Orpheus and Eurydice* and the *Fables*. In 'Some Comments on the Moralitas of Robert Henryson's "Orpheus and Eurydice"' (*SSL* 32[2001] 1–12), Dietrich Strauss purports to 'do away with' the lack of critical consensus concerning the 'essence' of the poem's 'message' by arguing in detail that the poem and *moralitas* are not at all 'complementary' (in their sources and rhyme patterns, *inter alia*), and then asserting that only one conclusion can follow: the *moralitas* was not written by Henryson. He suggests, rather, that it was appended by someone who perhaps objected to the way the poem ended. The argument is fascinating, but relies far too much on the presumptive genius of Henryson in arguing that no one who handled moral poetry so ably in the *Fables* and wrote narrative poetry so beautifully in *Testament* could have produced the clunky appendage that is the *moralitas* of *Orpheus and Eurydice*. Strauss's claim that Henryson was 'forgotten' by 1508 when Chepman and Myllar printed *Orpheus*, which allowed for a spurious addition to the poem to go unnoticed, neglects the most obvious evidence that Henryson did indeed have a certain measure of fame: Dunbar's reference to him in his catalogue of Scottish poets in *Lament for the Makars* (1505). To be fair, however, it should be noted that Strauss died before this article was properly completed; it is possible that in revisions he would have strengthened his bold but ultimately unconvincing argument. Arnold Clayton Henderson also takes up the question of Henryson's moralizing bent, this time in reference to the *Fables*. In 'Having Fun with the Moralities: Henryson's *Fables* and Late-Medieval Fable Innovation' (*SSL* 32[2001] 67–87), Henderson, somewhat defensively, argues that Henryson is not a 'boring' moralizer but an innovative adapter of the classical fabular tradition in which he works. He compares Henryson to Odo of Cheriton, a thirteenth-century English preacher, in his accommodation of Christian exegetical and fabular discourses.

Douglas Gray, in 'Gavin Douglas and "the gret prynce Eneas"' (*EIC* 51[2001] 18–34), argues that Douglas's translation of Virgil's *Aeneid* is itself an 'original' creation worthy of greater acclaim and critical attention. In this article, which is more summary and appreciation than criticism, Gray demonstrates the specific ways in which Douglas responded powerfully and imaginatively to the subtleties of the Virgilian text. Gray is particularly impressed by Douglas's rendering of Virgil's delicately balanced treatment of 'scenes of pathos'; he notes that Douglas's preferred translation for Latin *pius* is 'reuthful', which 'seems to emphasize Aeneas's "reuth", that human emotion, rather than his sense of "the command of the goddis"'.

Finally, two new articles add to the literature on the textual history of Middle Scots poetry. Alastair J. Mann, in 'The Anatomy of the Printed Book in Early Modern Scotland' (*Scottish Historical Review* 80[2001] 181–200), contains an abundance of useful historical information on the early history of printing in Scotland. He compares this early history to that of English printing, noting that, although most early Scottish reading material came from France, in its early printing habits Scotland shared with England both a penchant for literary nationalism and a taste for religious literature. Priscilla Bawcutt, in 'The Boston Public Library Manuscript of John Lydgate's *Siege of Thebes*: Its Scottish Owners and Inscriptions' (*MÆ* 70[2001] 80–94), continues her fascinating work on book and manuscript ownership in early modern Scotland. Bawcutt considers the relationship of the Lydgate manuscript to later Scottish vernacular writing by examining the various owners' inscriptions, particularly six pieces of Middle Scots verse (which include excerpts from the Scottish translator/historian John Bellenden and from Gower's *Confessio Amantis*). According to Bawcutt, these inscriptions have a lot to tell scholars about the Scottish reception of both native and English poetry, including the fact that 'Gower was being carefully read in Scotland'; this strengthens the possibility that references to 'moral Gower' by 'poets such as Douglas and Dunbar' quite possibly arise from direct familiarity with Gower's work rather than a familiarity only with the phrase 'moral Gower' from Chaucer's *Troilus and Criseyde*.

10. Drama

In the absence of a REED volume to welcome this year, drama records are nonetheless well served by the appearance of Alan J. Fletcher's magisterial edition of source-texts and commentary, *Drama and the Performing Arts in Pre-Cromwellian Ireland: A Repertory of Sources and Documents from the Earliest Times until c.1642*. Initially planned as a contribution to the REED series, Fletcher's volume is a conscious companion piece to the Toronto project's work, thereby 'unofficially' extending the coverage of REED and RED:S to include all the pre-modern drama records produced in these islands. Nearly two decades in the making, the book is a magnificent achievement, transcending the provision of a definitive volume of the drama records to offer the foundations of a cultural history of performance in medieval and early modern Ireland. In addition to the sections, familiar to readers of the REED volumes, on the historical, geographical, and archival contexts of the records, there are copious notes and an all-too-brief introduction to the Gaelic and English traditions of performance. Among the treasures of the volume is a fascinating account of documents describing the arrangement of musicians and other entertainers in royal halls *c.*700, which bespeaks a highly complex and diverse performance culture—in theory at least—at a very early period. The records themselves, drawn from Irish, Latin, French, and English texts ranging from chronicles, prose narratives, and verse to more conventional documentary sources, are arranged alphabetically, and each is well annotated (and where necessary translated). Generous appendices print proclamations, play prologues, and other accounts that describe or mention performance at greater length. Clearly a labour of love as well as a work of great scholarship, this volume, weighing in at nearly 650 pages, is no little room, but it offers near-infinite riches for readers to explore and delight in.

A number of the essays in the stimulating collection, Davidson, ed., *Gesture in Medieval Drama and Art*, deal with medieval British material. Jody Enders's 'Of Miming and Signing: The Dramatic Rhetoric of Gesture' (pp. 1–25) examines in a pan-European context the links between the gestural speech acts described in classical rhetorical manuals, those performed by priests in the Christian liturgy, and those that may have been made by actors in the religious plays. Davidson's own essay, 'Gesture in Medieval British Drama' (pp. 66–127), offers an overview and prospectus for the study of dramatic gesture, focusing on the religious drama and the Cycle plays in particular. Barbara D. Palmer examines a specific kind of gestural rhetoric in 'Gestures of Greeting: Annunciations, Sacred and Secular' (pp. 128–57), and Natalie Crohn Schmitt uses insights gained from the celebrated 1998 Toronto production of the York Cycle to illuminate 'The Body in Motion in the York *Adam and Eve in Eden*' (pp. 158–77). The rhetorical culture of early Renaissance drama is also illuminated, albeit from a different angle, by two excellent new translations of every Tudor humanist's favourite Roman, Cicero. Oxford University Press has published both *On the Ideal Orator*, edited by James M. May and Jakob Wisse, and *On Obligations*, edited by P.G. Walsh. Each text is accompanied by a useful introduction and detailed critical and textual notes, along with select bibliographies of further reading, and each conveys well a sense of both the style and the substance of Cicero's writings. The religious reformers' attempts to establish links between Ciceronian rhetoric, Erasmian reform and their own doctrinal project are well illustrated in Douglas H. Parker's edition of William Roye's *An Exhortation to the Diligent Studye of Scripture and An Exposition on the Seventh Chaptre of the Pistle to the Corinthians*. Parker's edition supplies original-spelling texts of both of these works, the first a translation of Erasmus's *Paraclesis*, the second a commentary by Martin Luther, originally printed together in 1529 to further Roye's own evangelical and anti-clerical campaign.

Victor Scherb takes the religious drama as his subject in his engaging monograph *Staging Faith: East Anglian Drama in the Later Middle Ages*. Following Gail McMurray Gibson's ground-breaking study of the same region, *Theatre of Devotion* [1989], Scherb seeks to illuminate the mutually informative connections between performance practice and religious belief in the East Anglian region. Arguing that religious drama was an important part of how East Anglians understood—and literally 'saw'—their faith, Scherb illustrates the symbolic and iconic effects that the surviving play texts seem to envisage through close reading of dramatic text and cultural context. Inevitably somewhat conjectural in its treatment of questions of staging, this study nonetheless offers some fruitful suggestions about East Anglians' financial, cultural, and spiritual investment in the drama they produced, patronized, or witnessed. Religious culture in provincial England is also the subject of Richard Hoyle's historical study, *The Pilgrimage of Grace and the Politics of the 1530s*, which ranges across issues of popular piety, regional particularism, and devotion to local cults, shrines, and the material culture of the parish. Unlike a number of the more lurid conspiracy theorists, Doyle presents the pilgrimage as a spontaneous rising in defence of local religious culture (broadly defined), a conclusion that will resonate with a good deal of recent work on the religious drama of the period. There is also some material on the religious drama, chiefly relating to John Bale's plays of the 1530s, in Benjamin Griffin's *Playing the Past: Approaches to English Historical Drama, 1385–1600*. But, despite the generous chronology suggested in the title, the bulk of the book deals with the last two decades of the sixteenth century.

Ros King's edition of *The Workes of Richard Edwards: Politics, Poetry and Performance in Sixteenth-Century England* provides an excellent addition to both the stock of scholarly editions of pre-Shakespearean plays and our knowledge of courtly performances in the Tudor period. In addition to Edwards's *Damian and Pythias*, printed in a lightly modernized text with critical and textual notes at the foot of the page, King also prints all of the author's surviving poems (both those confidently ascribed to him and those whose authorship is conjectural) and a biographical account of Edwards himself, his historical and cultural background, and a description of the staging of the lost play *Palamon and Arcyte*, performed in Oxford before Elizabeth I. There is also an appendix in which Edwards's songs are set out with tablature for voice and keyboard. As a comprehensive account of all that is known about Edwards and his fragmentary oeuvre (much of which was not known until King discovered it) this edition is very much to be welcomed.

Very different in both style and approach is the latest volume in Stanford University Press's Figurae: Reading Medieval Culture series. First published in German in 1974 as *Funktion und Struktur: Die Ambivalenzen der Geistlichen Spiels*, Rainer Warning's study of medieval religious drama has now been made more widely available in an English translation by Steven Rendall as *The Ambivalences of Medieval Drama*. As Hans Ulrich Gumbrecht notes in a new foreword, Warning's book, whether in English or German, is a demanding read, growing as it does very clearly from the particular, and now decidedly remote-seeming, intellectual climate prevailing in Germany in the late 1960s. While there is a good deal of interest in the book's analysis of the significance of the Mass and of motifs of Christ as scapegoat in the drama, its heavily theorized approach to the plays as ritual, and its insistence on the identification of archetypes of pan-European religious culture, tend to reduce the relevance of many of the discussions for an understanding of any particular cycle or play. Warning is unapologetic about the book's very different focus to most contemporary drama criticism. And theatre historians should perhaps be advised that his arguments are more often with sociological and cultural theorists than they are with scholars of performance or literary critics, which reflects his primary agenda. Tellingly he declares in a new afterword that, 'if I had to write the book again today, I would probably reflect more explicitly on the relationship between a functional approach and the theory of the social imaginary' (pp. 252–3).

As well as containing essays on Tudor poetry and prose, and the drama of the playhouse period, all written by members of the Tudor Symposium, Pincombe, ed., *The Anatomy of Tudor Literature*, contains a piece by Peter Happé, 'Subversion in *The Towneley Cycle*: Strategies for Evil' (pp. 11–23), which explores the contribution of the Wakefield Master to the Towneley text, and discusses his (or possibly her?) treatment of evil, violence, and punishment in the context of the cycle as a whole. The articles in the latest volume of *Medieval English Theatre* 22[2001 for 2000] continue that journal's high standard of engagement with both the material and the intellectual contexts of early performance. In 'The "Now" of "Then"' (*METh* 22[2001 for 2000] 3–12), David Mills revisits the Chester Play of *Antichrist*, suggesting persuasively how it reflects both a distinctive sense of history and the contemporary religious politics of this evangelically influenced city. In 'The York Plays and the Feast of Corpus Christi: A Reconsideration' (*METh* 22[2001 for 2000] 13–32), Pamela M. King examines the relationship between liturgy and drama, between the feast, guild, and procession of Corpus Christi and the York Cycle, offering stimulating readings of the *Nativity* pageant (in the light of the elevation of the eucharistic host) and other moments in the cycle when echoes of liturgical and para-liturgical vocabulary and motifs inform and punctuate the drama.

More theoretical in its focus is Janette Dillon's 'Performance Time: Suggestions for a Methodology of Analysis' (*METh* 22[2001 for 2000] 33–57), which explores the limitations of the idea of a binary division between 'real' and 'performance' time as a means of describing the complex temporal effects in medieval drama. Taking the Croxton *Play of the Sacrament* as her central example, Dillon examines the ways in which parallel senses of time are kept in play at key moments in the text and performance. Like King, she usefully explores these in the context of the fusion of universal history and the special contemporary moment created in the sacrament of the Eucharist. Greg Walker's short article, '"Faill nocht to teme your bleddir": Passing Time in Sir David Lindsay's *Ane Satyre of the Thrie Estaitis*' (*METh* 22[2001 for 2000] 52–8) examines time in a more practically pressing context, discussing the links between the numerous references to duration, the passing of time, drinking, bladders, and urination in Lindsay's panoramic drama. Thomas Pettitt's '"This man is Pyramus": A Pre-history of the English Mummers' Plays' (*METh* 22[2001 for 2000] 70–99) goes in search of the elusive origins of the mummers' plays, arguing suggestively that they might be located in the elite household entertainments of the later medieval period, and that such entertainments are reflected in Peter Quince's troupe's production of 'Pyramus and Thisbe' as performed in *A Midsummer Night's Dream*. In 'Lollards Stop Play? A Curious Case of Non-Performance in 1505' (*METh* 22[2001 for 2000] 100–11), Joanna Mattingly examines the records of an abortive 'play' scheduled for performance at Cookham, Berkshire in that year, arguing that the Lollard sympathies of a number of those involved in the production may have prompted an unwillingness to perform the play.

The title of Paulette Marty's article, 'The Coventry Hock Tuesday Play: Its Origins and Relationship to Hocktide' (*METh* 22[2001 for 2000] 112–26) gives a clear summary of the content of her article, which explores fruitfully the not immediately self-evident connections between the Coventry combat play and the Hocktide festival. In 'Drama and Entertainment in Peebles in the Fifteenth and Sixteenth Centuries' (*METh* 22[2001 for 2000] 127–44), Eila Williamson also combines archival, literary, and practical research to good effect, using both the burgh records and literary texts such as *The Thre Prestis of Peblis* and *Peblis to the Play* to illustrate the rich and diverse dramatic culture of this part of Scotland. Sarah Carpenter and Graham Runnalls's 'The Entertainments at the Marriage of Mary Queen of Scots and the French Dauphin François, 1558: Paris and Edinburgh' (*METh* 22[2001] 145–61) offers a detailed and scholarly account of the ceremonies and festivities marking the royal betrothal, comparing and contrasting what seems to have been a tightly controlled courtly and aristocratic production in Paris with a more bourgeois, civic (and conceivably even popular) event in Edinburgh. Finally, demonstrating *METh*'s commitment to the contemporary 'now' as well as the historicized 'then', the issue is completed by Yoshimichi Suematsu's illustrated 'Report on the Children's Kabuki in Tonami and Lomatsu, Japan' (*METh* 22[2001] 59–69).

In addition to some excellent articles on Dutch, German, Italian, and Portuguese plays, *European Medieval Drama* 4[2001 for 2000] also contains a number of engaging pieces on the British drama. In 'Performing Passion Plays in France and England' (*EMD* 4[2001] 57–76), Peter Happé draws illuminating parallels between the content and conditions for Passion plays in the two countries. Bob Godfrey's '*Everyman* Reconsidered' (*EMD* 4[2001 for 2000] 155–68) also looks at staging and the wider cultural context(s) of performances, both in the modern theatre and in the early sixteenth century, suggesting a plausible location for the initial production of the play in a church, and noting some interesting resonances between the play's central scenes and religious imagery. Janette Dillon's 'What Sacrament? Excess, Taboo, and Truth in the Croxton *Play of the Sacrament* and Twentieth-Century Body Art' (*EMD* 4[2001 for 2000] 169–79) also mediates between medieval and modern dramatic performances and values, comparing and contrasting aspects of Croxton's highly corporeal play with the modern work *I'm Not Your Babe* by Franko B, and drawing out the implied notions of the 'real' and the 'represented' in the acts of violence, suffering, and bodily damage performed in each work. Finally, on a still more practical level, Richard Rastall offers an ingenious solution to the problem of presenting the disembodied voice of God in the Cycle plays in 'The Construction of a Speaking Tube for Late-Medieval Drama' (*EMD* 4[2001 for 2000] 231–44).

Richard Rastall is also responsible for a much more substantial publication this year, the monograph *Minstrels Playing: Music in Early English Religious Drama*. A companion piece to his excellent *The Heaven Singing* ([1996]: see *YWES* 77[1998] 201–2), this volume takes up the framework outlined in the earlier volume and adds substantial flesh to its bones in the form of detailed accounts of individual plays. The first (and by far the largest) section examines the biblical plays, providing substantial introductions to each cycle before examining the manuscript stage-directions and those allusions in the text that indicate the presence of music or song, the use of Latin and liturgical material (which also might have been sung) in the cycles, as well as any documentary evidence for the nature or modes of performance, and a list of cues for music and other aural effects. In addition to the usual Cycle plays, Rastall also discusses the Norwich Grocers' Play, the Cornish *Ordinalia*, and *Creation of the World*, and the remaining miscellaneous biblical plays, thus providing comprehensive coverage of the genre as a whole. The same pattern is employed in the second section, dealing with the Saints Plays and Miracle Plays (*The Conversion of St Paul, Mary Magdalen*, the Cornish *Life of St. Meriasek*, the Croxton *Play of the Sacrament*, and two fragmentary texts, the Cambridge Prologue (Cambridge University Library Mm, 18 f. 628), and the Durham Prologue (Durham Cathedral, Dean and Chapter Muniments 1.2 Archidiac. Dunelm. 60.dorse)). The third section is similarly arranged and deals with the Moralities (*The Castle of Perseverance, Wisdom, Mankind*, and the incomplete texts of *The Pride of Life, Dux Moraud*, the Reynes Extracts, and the Winchester Dialogues). Finally an invaluable fourth section considers modern productions, offering in essence a blueprint and historically informed 'action plan' for anyone seeking to produce a medieval religious play with musical content on the modern stage.

Books Reviewed

Ashley, Kathleen, and Robert L.A. Clark, eds. *Medieval Conduct*. Medieval Cultures 29. UMinnP. [2001] pp. xx + 241. hb $54.95 ISBN 0 8166 3575 7, pb $19.95 ISBN 0 8166 3576 5.

Babcock, Robert G., and Lee Patterson, eds. *Old Books, New Learning: Essays on Medieval and Renaissance Books at Yale. Yale University Library Gazette*, occasional supplement 4. Beinecke Rare Book and Manuscript Library. [2001] pp. iv + 188. $25 ISBN 0 8457 3142 4.

Barr, Helen. *Socioliterary Practice in Late Medieval England*. OUP. [2001] pp. 229. £35 ISBN 0 1981 1242 4.

Barron, W.R.J., ed. *The Arthur of the English: The Arthurian Legend in Medieval English Life and Literature*, rev. edn. UWalesP. [2001] pp. xviii + 422. pb £35 ISBN 0 7083 1477 5.

Barron, W.R.J., and S.C. Weinberg, eds. *Layamon's Arthur: The Arthurian Section of Layamon's 'Brut'*. UExe. [2001] pp. lxxii + 290. pb £14.99 ISBN 0 8598 9685 4.

Bateman, Meg, Robert Crawford and James McGonigal, eds. *Scottish Religious Poetry: An Anthology*. St Andrew's Press. [2001] pp. xxvii + 330. £14.99 ISBN 0 7152 0775 X.

Blumenfeld-Kosinski, Renate, *et al.*, eds. *The Politics of Translation in the Middle Ages and the Renaissance*. MRTS 233. MRTS and UOttawaP. [2001] pp. 230. pb £22 ($25) ISBN 0 8669 8275 2 (MRTS), ISBN 0 7766 0527 5 (UOttawaP).

Bowers, John M. *The Politics of 'Pearl': Court Poetry in the Age of Richard II*. Brewer. [2001] pp. xvii + 236. $75, £50. ISBN 0 8599 1599 9.

Burger, Glenn, and Steven F. Kruger, eds. *Queering the Middle Ages*. Medieval Cultures 27. UMinnP. [2001] pp. xxiv + 318. hb £34.50 ISBN 0 8166 3403 3, pb £14 ISBN 0 8166 3404 1.

Burrow, J.A. *The 'Gawain'-Poet*. WTW. Northcote. [2001] pp. 70. pb £8.99 ISBN 0 7463 0878 7.

Carley, James P., ed. *Glastonbury Abbey and the Arthurian Tradition*. Brewer. [2001] pp. xii + 646. £75 ($130) ISBN 0 8599 1572 7.

Cartlidge, Neil, ed. *The Owl and the Nightingale: Text and Translation*. UExe. [2001] pp. liv + 202. pb £14.99 ISBN 0 8598 9690 0.

Cooney, Helen, ed. *Nation, Court and Culture: New Essays on Fifteenth-Century English Poetry*. FCP. [2001] pp. 191. $75 ISBN 1 8518 2566 5.

Davidson, Clifford, ed. *Gesture in Medieval Drama and Art*. EDAM Monographs 28. MIP. [2001] pp. xi + 239. hb $30 ISBN 1 5804 4028 2, pb $15 ISBN 1 5804 4029 0.

Davidson, Hilda Ellis, and Anna Chaudhri, eds. *Supernatural Enemies*. Carolina Academic Press. [2001] pp. xiii + 226. $40 ISBN 0 8908 9711 5.

Davlin, Mary Clemente, OP. *The Place of God in 'Piers Plowman' and Medieval Art*. Ashgate. [2001] pp. ix + 208 + 25 ills. $74.95 ISBN 0 7546 0270 2.

Daybell, James, ed. *Early Modern Women's Letter Writing, 1450–1700*. Palgrave. [2001] pp. xiv + 213. £47.50 ISBN 0 3337 1472 5.

Devlin-Glass, Frances, and Lyn McCredden, eds. *Feminist Poetics of the Sacred: Creative Suspicions*. OUP. [2001] pp. xiii + 268. hb £32.50 ISBN 0 1951 4468 6, pb £16.99 ISBN 0 1951 4469 4.

Diller, Hans-Jørgen, ed. *Towards a History of English as a History of Genres*. AF. CWU. [2001] pp. 230. pb _36 ISBN 3 8253 1240 2.

Dyas, Dee. *Pilgrimage in Medieval English Literature, 700–1500*. Brewer. [2001] pp. vii + 288. £50 ($90) ISBN 0 8599 1623 5.

Edwards, Elizabeth. *The Genesis of Narrative in Malory's 'Morte Darthur'*. Arthurian Studies 43. Brewer [2001] pp. x + 201. £40 ($75) ISBN 0 8599 1596 4.

Edwards, Robert R., ed. *John Lydgate: The Siege of Thebes*. MIP. [2001] pp. x + 196. pb $11 ISBN 1 5804 4074 6.

Ellis, Roger, ed. *'My Compleinte' and Other Poems*. By Thomas Hoccleve. UExe. [2001] pp. x + 294. hb £47.50 ISBN 0 8598 9700 1, pb £15.99 ISBN 0 8598 9701 X.

Fleming, Peter. *Family and Household in Medieval England*. Palgrave. [2001] pp. viii + 162. hb £47.50 ISBN 0 3336 1078 4, pb £15.99 ISBN 0 3336 1079 2.

Fletcher, Alan J. *Drama and the Performing Arts in Pre-Cromwellian Ireland: A Repertory of Sources and Documents from the Earliest Times until c.1642*. Brewer. [2001] pp. xiii + 624. £90 ISBN 0 8599 1573 5.

Forni, Kathleen. *The Chaucerian Apocrypha: A Counterfeit Canon*. UFlorP. [2001] pp. xviii + 260. $55 ISBN 0 8130 2427 7.

Gillespie, Vincent, ed., with additional material by A.I. Doyle. *Syon Abbey: With the Library of the Carthusians*. Corpus of British Medieval Library Catalogues 9. BL in association with BA. [2001] pp. lxxiii + 819. £115 ISBN 0 7123 4731 3.

Greentree, Rosemary. *The Middle English Lyric and Short Poem*. Annotated Bibliographies of Old and Middle English Literature 7. Brewer. [2001] pp. x + 570. £55 ISBN 0 8599 1621 9.

Griffin, Benjamin. *Playing the Past: Approaches to English Historical Drama, 1385–1600*. Brewer. [2001] pp. xiii + 193. £40 ISBN 0 8599 1615 4.

Hewett-Smith, Kathleen, ed. *William Langland's Piers Plowman: A Book of Essays*. Routledge. [2001]. pp. viii + 261. $90 ISBN 0 8153 2804 4.

Hide, Kerrie. *Gifted Origins to Graced Fulfilment: The Soteriology of Julian of Norwich*. Liturgical Press. [2001] pp. 256. pb $24.95 ISBN 0 8146 5093 7 (permanently out of print).

Hockey, Susan. *Electronic Texts in the Humanities: Principles and Practice*. OUP [2000]. pp. xii + 218. hb £45 ISBN 0 1987 1194 8, pb £13.99 ISBN 0 1987 1195 6.

Hoyle, Richard. *The Pilgrimage of Grace and the Politics of the 1530s*. OUP. [2001] pp. xvi + 487. £30 ISBN 0 1982 0874 X.

Ingham, Patricia Clare. *Sovereign Fantasies: Arthurian Romance and the Making of Britain*. UPennP. [2001] pp. 288. £35 ($49.95) ISBN 0 8122 3600 9.

Jürgen, Hans, and Manfred Görlach, eds. *Towards a History of English as a History of Genres*. AF 298. Winter. [2001] pp. x + 230. _36 ISBN 3 8253 1240 2.

Kerby-Fulton, Kathryn, and Maidie Hilmo, eds. *The Medieval Professional Reader at Work: Evidence From Manuscripts of Chaucer, Langland, Kempe, and Gower*. ELS Monographs 85. UVict. [2001] pp. 239. pb $26 ISBN 0 9206 0477 3.

King, Ros. ed. *The Workes of Richard Edwardes: Politics, Poetry, and Performance in Sixteenth-Century England*. RevelsCL. MUP. [2001] pp. xiv + 269. £45 ISBN 0 7190 5299 8.

Knapp, Ethan. *The Bureaucratic Muse: Thomas Hoccleve and the Literature of Late Medieval England*. PSUP. [2001] pp. x + 210. $40 ISBN 0 2710 2135 7.

Kohanski, Tamarah, ed. *The Book of John Mandeville: An Edition of the Pynson Text with Commentary on the Defective Version*. MRTS 231. MRTS. [2001] pp. lviii + 134. £24 ISBN 0 8669 8273 6.

Labarge, Margaret Wade. *Women in Medieval Life*. Penguin Classic History. Penguin. [2001] pp. xiv + 271. pb £4.99 ISBN 0 1413 9046 8.

Liszka, Thomas R., and Lorna E.M. Walker, eds. *The North Sea World in the Middle Ages: Studies in the Cultural History of North-Western Europe*. FCP. [2001] pp. 302. £45 ISBN 1 8518 2561 4.

Marshall, Claire. *William Langland: Piers Plowman*. WTW. Northcote. [2001]. pp. 123. $21 ISBN 0 7463 0860 4.

May, James M., and Jakob Wisse, eds. *On the Ideal Orator*. By Cicero. OUP. [2001]. pp. x + 374. hb £32 ISBN 0 1950 9197 3, pb £15.99 ISBN 0 1950 9198 1.

Mehl, Dieter. *English Literature in the Age of Chaucer*. Literature in English. Longman. [2001] pp. xii + 252. pb $24 ISBN 0 5824 9299 8.

Menuge, Noël James. *Medieval English Wardship in Romance and Law*. Brewer. [2001] pp. viii + 150. £40 ($75) ISBN 0 8599 1632 4.

Minnis, Alastair. *Magister amoris: The 'Roman de la Rose' and Vernacular Hermeneutics*. OUP. [2001] pp. xvi + 352. £50 ISBN 0 1981 8754 8.

Minnis, Alastair, ed. *Middle English Poetry: Texts and Traditions, Essays in Honour of Derek Pearsall*. Brewer. [2001] pp. xvi + 304. £50 ISBN 1 9031 5309 3.

Park, Tarjei. *Selfhood and 'Gostly Menyng' in Some Middle English Mystics: Semiotic Approaches to Contemplative Theology*. Mellen. [2001] pp. 196. $79.95 ISBN 0 7734 7507 9.

Parker, Douglas H., ed. *An Exhortation to the Diligent Studye of Scripture and an Exposition on the Seventh Chaptre of the Pistle to the Corinthians*. By William Roye. UTorP. [2001] pp. 243. £40 ISBN 0 8020 4818 8.

Perkins, Nicholas. *Hoccleve's 'Regiment of Princes': Counsel and Constraint.* Brewer. [2001] pp. xii + 236. £35 ($60) ISBN 0 8599 1631 6.

Perry, Curtis, ed. *Material Cultures and Cultural Materialisms in the Middle Ages and Renaissance.* Arizona Studies in the Middle Ages and the Renaissance 5. Brepols. [2001] pp. xxiv + 246. $50 ISBN 2 5035 1074 4.

Pincombe, Michael, ed. *The Anatomy of Tudor Literature.* Ashgate. [2001] pp. vii + 235. £40 ISBN 0 7546 0243 5.

Power, Eileen. *Medieval Women,* ed. M.M. Postan, introd. Maxine Berg, foreword Emmanuel Le Roy Ladurie. Folio Society. [2001] pp. xlv + 130. £17.95.

Purdie, Rhiannon, ed. *Ipomadon.* EETS os 316. OUP. [2001] pp. lxxxx + 366. £45 ($80) ISBN 0 1972 2319 2.

Rastall, Richard. *Minstrels Playing: Music in Early English Religious Drama II.* Brewer. [2001] pp. xxi + 549. £60 ISBN 0 8599 1585 9.

Reichardt, Mary R., ed. *Catholic Women Writers: A Bio-Bibliographical Sourcebook.* Greenwood. [2001] pp. xxix + 424. £79.95 ISBN 0 3133 1147 1.

Reynolds, Sister Anna Maria, and Julia Bolton Holloway, eds. *Julian of Norwich: Showing of Love, Extant Texts and Translations.* SISMEL. UFlorence. [2001] pp. xvi + 848. _191.09 ISBN 8 8845 0095 8.

Rhodes, Jim. *Poetry Does Theology: Chaucer, Grosseteste, and the 'Pearl'-Poet.* UNDP. [2001] pp. xi + 324. hb $54.95 ISBN 0 2680 3869 4, pb $24.95 ISBN 0 2680 3870 8.

Ridyard, Susan J., ed. *Earthly Love, Spiritual Love, Love of the Saints.* Sewanee Mediaeval Colloquium. [1999] $60 ISBN 0 9187 6947 7.

Salih, Sarah. *Versions of Virginity in Late Medieval England.* Brewer. [2001] pp. ix + 278. £45 ISBN 0 8599 1622 7.

Salter, David. *Holy and Noble Beasts: Encounters with Animals in Medieval Literature.* B&B. [2001] pp. viii + 168 + 2 plates. £35 ISBN 0 8599 1624 3.

Saunders, Corinne. *Rape and Ravishment in the Literature of Medieval England.* B&B. [2001] pp. vii + 343. £50 ISBN 0 8599 1610 3.

Scherb, Victor L. *Staging Faith: East Anglian Drama in the Later Middle Ages.* FDUP. [2001] pp. 273. £30 ISBN 0 8386 3878 3.

Schmidt, Kari Anne Rand, ed. *The Index of Middle English Prose, Handlist XVII: Manuscripts in the Library of Gonville and Caius College, Cambridge.* B&B. [2001] pp. xxvi + 176. £35 ISBN 0 8599 1611 1.

Scott, Kathleen L., Ann E. Nichols, Michael T. Orr, and Lynda Dennison, eds. *An Index of Images in English Manuscripts from the Time of Chaucer to Henry VIII,* fascicle I: *The Bodleian Library, Oxford, MSS Additional–Digby.* HM. [2000]. pp. 140 + 24 b/w plates. £35 ISBN 1 8725 0115 X.

Scott, Kathleen L., Ann E. Nichols, Martha W. Driver, and Lynda Dennison, eds., *An Index of Images in English Manuscripts from the Time of Chaucer to Henry VIII,* fascicle II: *The Bodleian Library, Oxford, MSS Dodsworth–Marshall.* HM. [2001]. pp. 172 + 24 b/w plates. £35 ISBN 1 8725 0117 6.

Smith, D. Vance. *The Book of the Incipit: Beginnings in the Fourteenth Century.* UMinnP. [2001] pp. xiii + 295. $34.95 ISBN 0 8166 3760 1.

Staley, Lynn, ed. and trans. *The Book of Margery Kempe: A New Translation, Contexts, Criticism.* Norton. [2001] pp. xxii + 305. pb £7.95 ISBN 0 3939 7639 4.

Stanbury, Sarah, ed. *Pearl.* TEAMS Middle English Texts. MIP. [2001] pp. viii + 112. $10 ISBN 1 5804 4033 9.

Thomas, Gwyn, ed. and trans., *Dafydd ap Gwilym: His Poems*. UWalesP. [2001]. pp. xxxiv + 318. pb £12.99 ISBN 0 7083 1664 6.

Thomson, R.M., ed. *The Bury Bible*. B&B and Yushodo. [2001] pp. 76 + 49 colour and 31 b/w plates. £395 ISBN 0 8511 5855 2.

Thomson, R.M., ed. *A Descriptive Catalogue of the Medieval Manuscripts in Worcester Cathedral Library*. Brewer. [2001] pp. xlviii + 312. £95 ISBN 0 8599 1618 9.

Tosi, Laura, ed. *Hearts of Lightness: The Magic of Children's Literature*. Cafoscarina. [2001] pp. 198. pb €10.33. ISBN 8 8886 1318 8.

Trimbur, John, ed. *Popular Literacy: Studies in Cultural Practices and Poetics*. UPittP. [2001] pp. x + 322. £33.50 ISBN 0 8229 4136 8.

Walsh, P.G., ed. *On Obligations*. By Cicero. OUP. [2001] pp. ix + 218. £40 ISBN 0 1992 4018 3.

Warning, Rainer. *The Ambivalence of Medieval Drama*, trans. Steven Rendall. Figurae: Reading Medieval Culture. StanfordUP. [2001] pp. xvii + 308. £40 ISBN 0 8047 3791 6.

Warren, Nancy Bradley. *Spiritual Economies: Female Monasticism in Later Medieval England*. UPennP. [2001] pp. xi + 276. £38.50 ($55) ISBN 0 8122 3583 5.

Wheeler, Bonnie, and Fiona Tolhurst, eds. *On Arthurian Women: Essays in Memory of Maureen Fries*. Scriptorium. [2001] pp. xvi + 408. $39.95 ISBN 0 9651 8771 3.

Wittig, Joseph. *Will's Vision of Piers Plowman, Do-well, Do-better, and Do-best: A Lemmatical Analysis of the Vocabulary of the A, B, and C Versions as Presented in the Athlone Editions, with Supplementary Concordances of the Latin and French Macaronics*. Athlone. [2001] pp. xvi + 874. $325.

IV

Middle English: Chaucer

VALERIE ALLEN AND MARGARET CONNOLLY

This chapter has four sections: 1. General; 2. *Canterbury Tales*; 3. *Troilus and Criseyde*; 4. Other Works. The ordering of individual tales and poems within the sections follows that of the *Riverside Chaucer*.

1. General

Mark Allen and Bege K. Bowers continue to do stalwart service in co-ordinating the production of 'An Annotated Chaucer Bibliography 1999' (*SAC* 23[2001] 615–93); for the electronic version consult the New Chaucer Society webpage: <http://ncs.rutgers.edu>. Also published in *Studies in the Age of Chaucer* and of general interest to Chaucerians is Paul Strohm's presidential address to the New Chaucer Society, 'Rememorative Reconstruction' (*SAC* 23[2001] 3–16) in which he characteristically ponders the boundaries between literature and history, and commends the society's breadth of interest, which is reflected in the title of its journal. Indeed this year's volume of *Studies in the Age of Chaucer* is a bumper issue containing, in addition to the bibliography, Strohm's address, and the usual feast of reviews, the biennial Chaucer lecture, a colloquium on the Cambridge History of Mediaeval Literature, and no fewer than twelve articles, nine of which are reviewed in various locations below.

Andrew James Johnston has written a substantial study of the age in which Chaucer wrote in *Clerks and Courtiers: Chaucer, Late Middle English Literature and the State Formation Process*. His thesis is essentially that Chaucer belonged to neither of the dominant social formations of his time, and was thus obliged to try to create his own space. Rejecting a great deal of what others have claimed as Chaucer's proper social context, Johnston offers a new social paradigm against which to measure the type of literature that developed in London around 1400. Influenced by the work of Norbert Elias and Pierre Bourdieu, he calls this paradigm the 'state formation process', and argues that the new social group that this spawned, a veritable 'fourth estate' of clerks (p. 19), provided the means by which Chaucer's poetic consciousness was shaped. Chaucer is taken as a starting point, and Johnston considers parts of his work in some detail. From the *Canterbury Tales* he selects the tales of the Squire and the Franklin, showing how they illustrate changing aristocratic attitudes and conflicts within the gentle classes; by contrast, the prologues to the tales told by the Man of Law and the Clerk reveal both clerkly ambitions and insecurities. He also analyses the two stories told by Chaucer himself, looks more briefly at the *Legend of Good Women*, and gestures towards *Troilus and Criseyde* by contemplating the famous frontispiece to Cambridge, Corpus Christi College MS 61. However, it is not his intention is to give a thorough reading of Chaucer's works, and instead he devotes much of the space in the second half of the book to a study of Chaucer's contemporaries and successors, amongst them Gower, Usk, Scogan, Hoccleve, and Pecock. This is an interesting, if dense, read, which is strongly argued throughout, and which is to be commended for its sustained effort to understand the shifting nature of late medieval English society.

Quite a rash of student guides to Chaucer has appeared this year, some new, some not so new. In the latter category is the reissue of Muriel Bowden's *A Reader's Guide to Geoffrey Chaucer*, first published in 1964 (*YWES* 45[1966] 80) and now released by a different press. The book is a simple reprint, with no explanations or modern additions. It shows its age visually in terms of a dated typeface and in layout, with comparatively long chapters unbroken by subdivisions. Oddly though, Bowden's contextual approach is one which has again become fashionable, though she defines context more narrowly than would now be thought acceptable, being concerned 'only with those facts which influenced Chaucer to write as he did' (p. 4), and in general there is rather too much talk about timeless genius to suit the modern critic. Students might be better off with Rob Pope's *How to Study Chaucer*, first published in 1988 (*YWES* 69[1990] 181), and now offered in a fresh edition with new sections that review key terms and the arguments of contemporary critical debates, and with an updated guide to further reading. Better still, and also completely new, is Gillian Rudd's *The Complete Critical Guide to Geoffrey Chaucer*. Like Bowden, Rudd aims to contextualize Chaucer for the modern reader, devoting the first quarter of the book to 'life and contexts', covering both personal biography and social, literary, and historical topics such as war, chivalry, plague, and philosophy. Unlike Pope and Bowden, Rudd eschews the Robinson-derived arrangement of Chaucer's works, which privileges the *Canterbury Tales*, preferring to deal with them in their supposed chronological order. Approximately the same amount of space is devoted to the *Canterbury Tales* as to all the other works put together, which is about the best balance that could be hoped for in a brief student guide. The last section is devoted to criticism, and here Rudd attempts a survey of the most influential critical approaches, inevitably sketchy but bolstered by a generous bibliography. If inspired to read more, students could go on to consult Corinne Saunders's *Chaucer*, issued as the inaugural volume in the Blackwell Guides to Criticism series. This study combines consideration of Chaucer's writing with an examination of the development of Chaucer criticism. Beginning with a summary of Chaucer's life and works, and an assessment of the main strands of Chaucer criticism, Saunders tackles the potentially amorphous subjects of Chaucer's reading and audience before approaching the poetry itself. In the main part of the book she gives a useful overview of each of the three main areas of Chaucer's work that a student is likely to encounter (the dream visions, *Troilus and Criseyde*, and the *Canterbury Tales*), and then offers a selection of critical extracts from twentieth-century critical essays. She finishes with an extensive bibliography in which the items that she judges most useful are flagged, and which includes listings of audiotapes, video recordings, CD-ROMs and websites.

Appearing last year was *Chaucer's England*, by Diana Childress, who provides an informative and accessible introduction and covers a surprising amount of ground for such a slim volume. Some interesting details (for example, halfpennies and farthings were originally pennies broken in halves and quarters) lend colour to what is often inevitably general and predictable information for a publication of this sort—the Ptolemaic universe, the four humours, the three estates, the Black Death, the Peasants' Revolt, etc.; the material, however, is imaginatively explained and well synthesized with allusions to Chaucer's text, which are subordinated to the structure of chapters organized around general topics such as 'learning' and 'social hierarchy'. Feature insets include a description of different kinds of horses, from stots to destriers; the ranks within the three estates, from the vagrant to the king; calculation of time; and rules of endowment and inheritance. A time chart at the beginning of the volume covers the main events of fourteenth-century England and of Chaucer's life (no mention of Cecily Chaumpaigne here!); four pages of works consulted and a short list of popular films and books at the end complete the critical apparatus. The main shortcoming of the book is the minimalism of the footnotes and references, making it frequently difficult to use the material for further research or to track down details.

Dieter Mehl continues the long line of introductory surveys with *English Literature in the Age of Chaucer*, one chapter of which is dedicated to our poet. The picture that emerges of Chaucer, in contrast to Shakespeare, a 'snapper-up of unconsidered trifles' (p. 8), is of one who prized erudition highly; in a short section dealing with what Chaucer read and translated, Mehl argues for the poet's non-partisan imagination, which, while perhaps giving his work more lasting appeal, makes it difficult for a modern reader to identify with. Further short sections on the *Book of the Duchess*, *Parliament of Fowls*, *House of Fame*, and *Legend of Good Women* continue the interest in translation, and offer thorough, if safe, introductions to the literary backgrounds of the poems. *Troilus and Criseyde* merits a longer section, and the rest goes to the Canterbury poem. Perhaps for the sake of space, Mehl avoids offering summaries or detailed considerations of individual tales, keeps the discussion focused on dominant themes around which they can be grouped, and emphasizes the open-ended nature and meaning of the poem. Not surprisingly, discussion of the manuscripts and the ordering of the tales are not mentioned, although the important work done in recent years on matters codicological ought by rights to touch the beginner as well as the scholar.

SunHee Kim Gertz contributes to the Transitions series with a volume on *Chaucer to Shakespeare, 1337–1580*. This survey differentiates itself from other historical overviews by its reliance on semiotic and rhetorical theory, enabling the author to speak of the Order of the Garter as both metaphor (*translatio*) and as a cultural sign that Gertz compares to the commissioned portrait of Hitler dressed as a knight. Embedded into a discussion of Vološinov's semiotics and his critique of Saussure, a short section on the Wife of Bath emphasizes the 'multiaccentuality' (p. 84) of her discourse, implying that the individual's utterance is never univocal but shot through with the dissonant voices of her society. Moral judgements of Criseyde's behaviour are sidestepped in a short section on *Troilus and Criseyde*, where the heroine is read as a rhetorical sign: embodying *translatio*, Criseyde is endlessly transferable, a blank text to be constantly (re)written upon. Occasionally Gertz's Latin needs some double-checking ('red' being the correct translation of *rubor* rather than *rubeo*, p. 54), but maybe the slips are an occupational hazard of such wide-ranging coverage.

Yet another wide sweep is achieved in Currie, ed., *The 1300s: Headlines in History*. This series, Headlines in History, devotes one volume to each century of the second millennium, from 1000 to 2000. The brief chapter on Chaucer is an excerpt from S.S. Hussey, *Chaucer: An Introduction* (*YWES* 52[1973] 110–11), and focuses on biographical detail rather than interpretation of his work. Perhaps a more recent review of his life could have been used. The book offers the usual historical overview for the Chaucer scholar; a welcome addition is three chapters on 'The Fourteenth Century Outside Europe', the West African 'Mali Empire', and 'The Ming Dynasty'. This material attests to the established interest in non-Western cultures and their effect on occidental life, an interest reflected in Schildgen's book, reviewed below, and in the Prioress's anti-semitism. The plethora of survey material on Chaucer's background, while useful and informative, does bear witness to the poverty of undergraduates' acquaintance with medieval culture.

Stephen Knight's essay 'Chaucer: *The Canterbury Tales*' appears as the first of fifteen studies in Rylance and Simons, eds., *Literature in Context* (pp. 1–14). It is good to see medieval literature included, however briefly, in this volume which is aimed at pre-university students and which spans English literature from Chaucer to Toni Morrison. The essay is subdivided into what Knight deems the five most pertinent contexts that need to be considered when confronted by a pre-modern literary work: history, religion, society, literature, and language. These might seem to be rather broad categories, and ones which are difficult to disentangle; this division also makes the essay sound rather dull, which it definitely is not—the writing is lively, and the examples are well chosen for an audience who may know little or nothing of Chaucer's work. With a nice illustration of the pilgrims at the beginning and a brief list of further reading at the end (works carefully selected to be accessible and appealing to beginners), Knight is doing his best to promote medieval literature outside the academy.

Kathryn Jacobs looks at the legal side of marriage in a full-length study of *Marriage Contracts from Chaucer to the Renaissance Stage*. The larger part of her book is devoted to marriage in the Middle Ages, as seen through the lens of Chaucer's major works. Her first three chapters take their evidence primarily from the *Canterbury Tales* to explore the disruptions caused by adultery and neglect; the consequences of choosing a private or public wedding ceremony; and the influence of the marriage contract on extramarital sexual unions. These chapters have all previously been published in article form (for the first two, see *YWES* 76[1997] 180) and (*YWES* 80[2001] 194). Her fourth chapter focuses on widows, traditionally regarded pejoratively as libidinous and outspoken; by contrast she finds Chaucer's treatment of such women respectful and sympathetic, and credits his portrayal of the attractive Criseyde as deeply influential on the later widows of the Renaissance stage. She concludes that the complexities of fourteenth-century marriage law influenced Chaucer's representation of both married and unmarried relationships.

A broader consideration of the law is offered by Mary Flowers Braswell, *Chaucer's 'Legal Fiction': Reading the Records*, a study that emerges out of the appreciation of how intimately Chaucer knew and wrote about the law and how little literary critics know of the topic. In a critical climate where current interest is fixed on Chaucer's shady side—most notoriously his *raptus* of Cecily Chaumpaigne but also his troubles with debtors—Chaucer was more often than not on the right side of the law and indeed would have acted as juror in his capacity as Controller of the Port of London. His knowledge, Braswell argues, is more extensive than is allowed by Joseph Hornsby in his book-length study of Chaucer and law (*YWES* 69[1990] 178), and she sets her case out in the first chapter, noting his involvement as violator, victim, witness, and Justice of the Peace, and moving beyond biographical record to illustrate the highly theatrical aspect of litigation and the narrativistic aspect of case-law. Having established the links between the legal and the literary, in chapter 2 Braswell applies the concept of legal fame, of the necessity of being *de bone fama* to the *House of Fame*, where Fame is depicted as a capricious judge. The Leet rolls, which were registers of Manor Courts, are offered in chapter 3 as a non-literary alternative inspiration for some of the Canterbury portraits—the unscrupulous reeve, unhygienic cook and light-fingered miller—and these legal exemplars extend into the characterization of the Franklin's, Reeve's and Shipman's tales. The *Calendar of Plea and Memoranda Rolls* even refers to a Roger of Ware, who broke curfew. Braswell avoids putting Chaucer into any ideological straitjacket, for this was a man who broke the law, sought justice from it, and served it. What she does call for is a more intimate knowledge of the legal texts with which Chaucer was daily involved.

The issue of rape has attracted a significant amount of attention this year. Corinne Saunders has written substantially on the topic in her book *Rape and Ravishment in the Literature of Medieval England*, setting herself many questions about the definition of the act and public understanding of it in the Middle Ages. Rather ambitiously she aims at both a generalist and specialist audience, and takes a broad approach to the issue, beginning with an analysis of the changing status of rape in Anglo-Saxon and post-Conquest law before turning to consider the matter in the quite different context of canon law. Once the legal ground has been established, she investigates how rape, ravishment, violation, and abduction are treated in literature, devoting separate chapters to the genres of hagiography and romance, and another chapter to an examination of the classical paradigms of rape and abduction: Lucretia and Helen of Troy. The final two chapters are allocated to particular authors, Sir Thomas Malory and Chaucer. Her discussion of the latter incorporates all the possible rape victims in Chaucer's works, from his reworking of unfortunate classical figures to the equally unfortunate, though sometimes also hilarious, women found on the Canterbury pilgrimage. The scope of this book's coverage in terms of literature is impressive, as is its in-depth treatment of the topic, and the discussion remains thoughtful and lucid throughout. More briefly, Louise Sylvester also offers her thoughts on rape in 'Reading Narratives of Rape: The Story of Lucretia in Chaucer, Gower and Christine de Pizan' (*LeedsSE* 31[2000] 115–44), focusing on reader response to the male and female sexual roles posited by romance and romantic texts, and on notions of a female masochism that is erotic, rather than psychological.

Robertson and Rose, eds., contains thirteen essays on *Representing Rape in Medieval and Early Modern Literature*. Four of the contributors to this volume discuss Chaucer. In 'Reading Chaucer Reading Rape' (pp. 21–60) Christine Rose explores Chaucer's uses of rape as a trope, demonstrating how in several of the

Canterbury Tales which feature rape (those told by the Reeve, Wife of Bath, Man of Law, and Physician), the focus tends to be on contention between men rather than sexual violence directed against women. Virginia's rape is also discussed by Robin L. Bott in '"O, keep me from their worse than killing lust": Ideologies of Rape and Mutilation in Chaucer's *Physician's Tale* and Shakespeare's *Titus Andronicus*' (pp. 189–211). Bott focuses on the consequences of rape, comparing the argument made in Chaucer's text—that the woman must be killed to prevent her rape—with the early modern text's insistence that the woman be killed *after* her rape (neither 'solution' ever defensible in English law). She recognizes rape as a political event and finds it intrinsically connected in these stories with homosocial rivalry. The medieval definition of *raptus*, which could mean both forced coitus and abduction, is considered by Elizabeth Robertson in her contribution 'Public Bodies and Psychic Domains: Rape, Consent, and Female Subjectivity in Geoffrey Chaucer's *Troilus and Criseyde*' (pp. 281–310). She compares Criseyde with other important classical heroines who were raped—Lucretia and Helen of Troy—and finds Criseyde to be a potential victim of both types of *raptus*. For Christopher Cannon's essay 'Chaucer and Rape: Uncertainty's Certainties' (pp. 255–79; reprinted from *SAC* 22[2000]), see *YWES* 81[2002] 238.

Another volume honouring Derek Pearsall has appeared this year: Minnis, ed., *Middle English Poetry: Texts and Traditions, Essays in Honour of Derek Pearsall*. Perhaps unsurprisingly, given the interests of the volume's honoree, most of the sixteen contributions are concerned with the manuscripts of Middle English poetry. Three essays cover the *Canterbury Tales* and one is devoted to the *Legend of Good Women*, but there is plenty of incidental reference to Chaucer throughout the volume. In the first of the Chaucerian offerings, Estelle Stubbs focuses on 'Clare Priory, the London Austin Friars and Manuscripts of Chaucer's *Canterbury Tales*' (pp. 17–26). She traces a complex network of possible connections between individual friars and lay members of their houses' extended communities, suggesting that the innate links between the provincial priories and the metropolis could have provided a climate conducive for manuscript production. The steady accumulation of fragments of evidence, more convincing in bulk than individually, leads Stubbs to the conclusion that the Augustinians, both friars and canons, were somehow involved in the transmission of certain *Canterbury Tales* manuscripts, though she cannot be sure how or why. The difficulty of stating for certain who might have been responsible for what is also faced by Elizabeth Solopova in her analysis of 'The Survival of Chaucer's Punctuation in the Early Manuscripts of the *Canterbury Tales*' (pp. 27–40). She questions the view that punctuation in the Ellesmere and Hengwrt manuscripts is entirely scribal, arguing that it is simpler to assume that Chaucer himself introduced both iambic pentameter and its punctuation into English poetry. She also points out that, if this conclusion is accepted, modern editors had better pay sharper attention to the punctuation in these early witnesses. Editorial matters are the concern of Charlotte C. Morse, who discusses two monumental editions in 'What the *Clerk's Tale* Suggests about Manly and Rickert's Edition—and the *Canterbury Tales* Project' (pp. 41–56). Having worked on the *Clerk's Tale* for the Variorum Chaucer, and thus become very familiar with the scholarship of Manly and Rickert, Morse professes herself tired of such major undertakings, identifying the very real danger inherent in grandiose editorial schemes: 'tired, old, or dead' editors tend not finish their work (p. 41). She outlines a number of areas where Manly and Rickert's work is unhelpful in its opacity or lacunae, noting that the project will advance the investigation of Chaucer's metrics as well as making the evidential basis for all textual readings clearer. She also identifies similarities and differences between the two enterprises, noting for example that though both are committed to the recension method of editing, the project assumes that the *Canterbury Tales* descends from a single lost original, whereas the early editors believed that multiple copies of the tales were already in circulation by the time of Chaucer's death. The afterlife of Chaucer's works is also addressed by Julia Boffey with respect to dream poetry in '"Twenty thousand more": Some Fifteenth- and Sixteenth-Century Responses to *The Legend of Good Women*' (pp. 279–304). Boffey notes other recent work on the poem's reception and offers some new lines of enquiry, in particular focusing on the number of women Chaucer managed to write about before abandoning his unfinished work. She discusses a poem copied by John Shirley in MS Bodley Ashmole 59, which has nine stanzas and which recalls nine worthy women, though their identities are not quite those apostrophized by Chaucer. Another nine-stanza poem lauding another nine women, in Trinity College Cambridge, MS R.3.19, is included in an appendix, and various visual representations of female worthies are also identified. Boffey's intriguing idea is that the masculine precedent of the Nine Worthies may have somehow channelled into the reception of Chaucer's poem over the course of the fifteenth and early sixteenth centuries. Some nice illustrations accompany this essay.

In another testimony to a scholar, a large volume brings together a number of essays, fourteen of which directly involve Chaucer: Yeager and Morse, eds., *Speaking Images: Essays in Honor of V.A. Kolve*. Opening his discussion with an image of a 'billowing wind' John V. Fleming considers the *Summoner's Tale* in 'The Pentecosts of Four Poets' (pp. 111–41), and notes in particular the association of a sweet odour not only with sanctity in general but also with the feast of Pentecost, as when red petals were dropped from the ceiling of the church to evoke the Holy Spirit. Through mention of a 'Whitsun farthing' or 'pentecostal', which was an ecclesiastical tax in England payable at Pentecost, Fleming discerns an allusion to simony, suggesting a link between Chaucer's tale and *Inferno* XIX. Whether or not simony is a conscious concern for Chaucer here, Fleming rightly points out what a close reader of Dante Chaucer was. Next, Marjorie Curry Woods observes that Chaucer would most likely have first encountered the women who would subsequently become the heroines of the *Legend of Good Women* in classroom texts: 'Boys Will Be Women: Musings on Classroom Nostalgia and the Chaucerian Audience' (pp. 143–66). Something of schoolboy nostalgia can therefore be assumed in the poem. Indeed, two of the most widely praised legends, of Dido and of Thisbe, are especially emblematic of schoolboy experience. Citing Augustine's own affective and youthful reaction to Dido, Woods suggests that the male-dominated schoolroom produced both an intense emotional investment in these stories about women and—perhaps paradoxically, perhaps not—misogyny. Certainly this would explain the mixture of pathos and anti-feminism present in Chaucer's poem. In 'Chaucer, Suicide, and the Agencies of Memory: Troilus and the Death Drive' (pp. 185–204), R. James Goldstein makes a connection between classical memory training and the suicide topos. Most notoriously in the *Legend of Good Women* and in Dorigen's complaint in the *Franklin's Tale*, Chaucer draws from a remembered storehouse of famous pagan suicides. Goldstein sees in the conflict between the noble suicide and Christian prohibition against death by one's own hand something of a repressed death drive (à la Freud), and cites *Troilus* as the main text where this drive is both expressed and repressed. Certainly Pandarus's no-nonsense and cynical sense of survival undercuts and trivializes Troilus's gloom; nonetheless, Goldstein, quoting Kolve's own comments upon the poem, finds a 'humanist sympathy' (p. 194) in the treatment of Troilus's melancholic despair. Terry Jones begins his consideration of 'The Image of Chaucer's Knight' (pp. 205–36) with the ironic reflection that Kolve, a Junior Fellow at Oxford in 1962, was the very first victim of Jones's then 'half-baked' thoughts about the Knight. Many years and drafts later, Kolve receives this revision. The premise remains the same, and in the essay he focuses on clues to the Knight's nature based on his physical appearance. Citing contemporary exhortation to dress according to one's station, Jones observes that not only do the Knight's lack of coat-armour and his shabby array look bad, they are also suspiciously similar to the casual dress and light armour of John Hawkwood's White Company, the group with which Jones has long associated Chaucer's Knight. As further evidence, Jones notes the parallels between the Ellesmere miniature of the Knight and the monument of Hawkwood in the Duomo in Florence. In 'Speaking Images in Chaucer's "Miller's Tale"' (pp. 237–53), Jill Mann considers the apotropaic intention of Alison when she moons at Absolom through the window. Whatever Alison actually means by the gesture, Mann rejects the idea that the female body is univocal and 'irreducible ... against a "courtly and artificial language"' (p. 247). Her discussion explores the many meanings female exposure may assume, as well as the intense physicality of Chaucer's poem. It is telling, however, that she eschews the term 'realism', and emphasizes rather the polysemous aspect of matter in the phrase 'speaking images'. In a long essay, 'Playing Parts: Fragments, Figures, and the Mystery of Love in "The Miller's Tale"' (pp. 255–99), Barbara Nolan develops Kolve's description of the misdirected kiss as synecdoche into a consideration of the part–whole relationship that synecdoche exploits—a relationship that ultimately has to do with (partial) signs and (whole) signifieds, that is, with the question of meaning itself. Chaucer's tale has long been cited as a triumph of literalism, with no higher or 'whole' meaning (the pun on Middle English 'hole' is not lost on Nolan), but she places it firmly in a wider debate, demonstrating how the tale supplies a way of (not) thinking about the materiality of parts and signs and the immateriality of wholes. This is one of the more thoughtful essays on the *Miller's Tale* to appear in recent years. Noting the discrepancy between critical reaction to the Pardoner and to his Partner, John M. Bowers's project is 'Queering the Summoner: Same-Sex Union in Chaucer's *Canterbury Tales*' (pp. 301–24). The Summoner, argues Bowers, is queer by being bisexual, a sexual orientation that undoes the very idea of sexual orientation. By claiming that the Summoner does not simply behave bisexually but '*is* bisexual' (p. 314), Bowers problematizes Foucault's historical and ontological distinction between medieval sodomites, defined only by their acts, and modern homosexuals, defined by their nature.

Turning more historical and political, the volume continues with Glending Olson's essay on the *Clerk's Tale*, 'The Marquis of Saluzzo and the Marquis of Dublin' (pp. 325–45). To a court audience from the 1380s to the end of Richard II's reign, Chaucer's tale could not fail to remind them of Robert de Vere, marquis of

Dublin. The capricious behaviour of Walter, marquis of Saluzzo, offers a telling analogy with de Vere, popularly regarded as one of Richard's ill-chosen and immature counsellors. Further support is inadvertently lent to his case by Charlotte C. Morse, who, in 'Griselda Reads Philippa de Coucy' (pp. 347–92) draws a parallel between the shabby treatment of both Griselda and Philippa, wife of Robert de Vere, who divorced her in the 1380s. As niece of Thomas, duke of Gloucester, Philippa was politically connected, and her divorce at least seemed to provide her uncle, leader of the Appellants, with just cause to rebel against the king. Morse's treatment is meticulously detailed, and offers strong evidence for the political resonance of Chaucer's tale. She leaves open any final interpretation of Griselda's plight (and, by analogy, of Philippa's), but her treatment certainly explains for us how gripping and popular the Griselda story was to Chaucer and his contemporaries.

Katheryn L. Lynch notes rampant allusion to gluttony in 'The Pardoner's Digestion: Eating Images in the *Canterbury Tales*' (pp. 393–409), thereby at once supplying a contrast to the Parson, who inveighs against the vice in his own sermon. Lynch also considers the theological resonance to the image of feasting, nourishment, and feeding from the word. Where the Parson's words offer spiritual sustenance, those of the Pardoner turn to waste and chaff. Henry Ansgar Kelly, in 'The Pardoner's Voice, Disjunctive Narrative, and Modes of Effemination' (pp. 411–44), ranges through the myriad sexual possibilities in the goat/gelding/mare image applied to the pilgrim—simultaneously under-sexed and over-sexed, a fop, an exhausted womanizer, a castrate, and a number of other options. It is not very clear to which medical portrait Kelly is most wedded, but the Pardoner's effeminacy is never in doubt, and what Kelly does suggest is that being effeminate need in no way impair the pilgrim's ability to perform—indeed his appetite seems voracious and well exercised. Stephen Knight offers some interesting insights into 'Places in the Text: A Topographicist Approach to Chaucer' (pp. 445–61). We ask too little about the actual places mentioned in Chaucer's work, suggests Knight, although the topographicism he promotes is not to be confused with tourist trips. Where the tourist experience centres around the individual wanderer, the sense of place Knight argues for in the *Canterbury Tales* is non-subjective, ultimately other-worldly, and patterned. The Canterbury trajectory is both highly teleological and yet rooted in the local—Harbledown, and at a precise moment of the day—and Knight speaks directly about how the cathedral fills the horizon in the village in the April sun. In one sense Knight is arguing for a return to the material experience of place in Chaucer's work, yet, careful not to err by going to the other extreme, he remains open to the symbolic and figurative meanings of place. Place is also considered by Derek Pearsall, in 'The "Roving Eye" Point of View in the Medieval Perception of Landscape' (pp. 463–77). The roving eye refers to the difference between medieval and Renaissance perspective: where a medieval person would walk all the way around a cathedral, a Renaissance viewer would look for a vantage point from which to take it in. Eschewing any overly simplified divisions between periods and perspective, Pearsall nonetheless argues for a medieval lack of constraint, which enables the viewer to reconstitute a landscape each time it is viewed. Chaucer's text figures infrequently, although Pearsall does attribute the same freedom to Chaucer, whose narrator in the *Book of the Duchess* conveys a sense of spontaneity and informality when describing scenes, rather than the premeditated 'taking in' of a prospect. Finally, editor R.F. Yeager compares the two poets in 'John Gower's

Images: "The Tale of Constance" and "The Man of Law's Tale"' (pp. 525–57); perhaps unsurprisingly, Yeager finds Chaucer's images much more intensely visual and affective, describing Gower's portraiture as minimalist by comparison. This is a fine collection (and for its size and presentation very reasonably priced) although in a number of cases the material covered tends to review and recapitulate scholars' previous work rather than contribute new research. That said, this is a fitting tribute to Kolve's career and scholarship.

In a chapter entitled 'Eulogies and Usurpations: Father Chaucer in the *Regement of Princes*' (pp. 107–27), which appears in his book-length study of Hoccleve, *The Bureaucratic Muse: Thomas Hoccleve and the Literature of Late Medieval England*, Ethan Knapp develops ideas of Chaucer's literary paternity (*YWES* 80[2001] 192). Paul Price, in 'Trumping Chaucer: Osbern Bokenham's *Katherine*' (*ChauR* 36[2001] 158–83) argues that Bokenham joins many other so-called 'dull' fifteenth-century poets in being deferential to their literary forebears, but that Bokenham's rejection of the Chaucerian tradition is far from deferential. The essay's focus is on Bokenham, and it does not go into detail in elaborating how Chaucer gets trumped.

Carolyn P. Collette and Vincent J. DiMarco's discussion of 'The Matter of Armenia in the Age of Chaucer' (*SAC* 23[2001] 317–58) is largely concerned with Armenia Minor (also known as Lesser Armenia or Cilician Armenia). They argue that, despite the presence of Levon VI at the court of Richard II, Armenia figured in the popular imagination and in the literature of late medieval England as a doomed country, a realm robbed of its future by the failures of its monarchs. Chaucer's awareness of Armenia and of contingent events central to her precarious independence and ultimate fall may be traced through references in his portrait of the Knight; in the crusading/conversion romance ideologies of the *Squire's Tale*; in elements of the tales of the Man of Law and the Monk; and in the figure of Anelida in *Anelida and Arcite*. Collette and DiMarco argue that collectively this demonstrates that Chaucer's writing is more subtly allusive to international events than has generally been recognized.

Mary Clemente Davlin compares 'Chaucer and Langland as Religious Writers' (in Hewett-Smith, ed., *William Langland's 'Piers Plowman': A Book of Essays*, pp. 119–41), finding pathos a stronger characteristic of Chaucer's religiosity than of Langland's. Where Langland focuses on doctrinal essentials, Chaucer's interest seems more rooted in miracles, pilgrimages, and female sanctity. Given these criteria, the Man of Law's and Prioress's tales epitomize Chaucer's religious impulse. Davlin compares the distinction between the two poets to Walter Ong's distinction between Latin hymns of affect and of wit. The difference is also reflected stylistically in their writing, with Chaucer addressing his audience directly and frequently, while Langland adopts a more general and distanced voice.

Although no reference to it is made in the title, 'Langland's Mighty Line' (in Hewett-Smith, ed., pp. 103–17), Chaucer's own mighty line is well represented by Stephen A. Barney. Chaucer is better at couplets, and a master of euphemism, and hence of obscenity. Langland's verse, on the other hand, is more direct, more muscular, and, obviously, more alliterative. Barney's claim is that Langland at his best is better than Chaucer at his best, though one might respond that comparisons are odious.

The biennial Chaucer lecture given in London in July 2000 is published this year. The speaker, Carolyn Dinshaw, strikes an autobiographical note in her study of

'Pale Faces: Race, Religion, and Affect in Chaucer's Texts and their Readers' (*SAC* 23[2001] 19–41), by drawing comparisons between Chaucer's characters, his nineteenth-century editors, and her own family background. She begins by exploring the semantic range of the word 'pale', noting various instances of the term in Chaucer's writing, before turning to look in particular at the *Man of Law's Tale* and the pale figure of Custance. She argues that this tale, with its range of cultural contact and conflict between East and West, must have seemed especially relevant to the early editors of Middle English texts whose own age was one of empire, and she then traces some interesting connections between British imperial enterprise in India and the editorial work of both the Chaucer Society and the Early English Text Society. One of the twentieth-century critics mentioned by Dinshaw is Margaret Schlauch [1898–1986], whose career is considered in more detail by Laura Mestayer Rogers in a short essay, 'Embarking with Constance: Margaret Schlauch' (*MFF* 31[2001] 36–43). Fascinated by the strange way in which life can end up imitating art, Rogers focuses on Schlauch's Chaucerian work, particularly her pioneering feminist reading of *Chaucer's Constance and Accused Queens* which was first published in 1927, reprinted in 1969 (*YWES* 51[1972] 116). Parallels between Schlauch's life and her scholarship were recently noted by Sheila Delany, whose work Rogers acknowledges and expands here. The work of another early twentieth-century Chaucerian is taken up by Chauncey Wood, who considers Chaucer's characterization in 'John Matthews Manly: Some Old Light on Chaucer Being an Exposition of the "Abhorrent Doctrine" and the "More Abhorrent Doctrine"' (*MedPers* 15[2000] 1–10). The doctrines mentioned in the title are those techniques of characterization (photographic realism and composition by compilation), which were rejected by Manly, who argued instead that Chaucer worked by observing real people. Wood contends that observation was an important idea in late fourteenth-century art, offering an analysis of the figures in the Wilton diptych to support his point.

Laura L. Howes draws attention to the idea of walking in '"The Slow Curve of the Footwalker": Narrative Time and Literary Landscapes in Middle English Poetry' (*Soundings* 83[2001] 165–81). Taking examples from *Sir Orfeo* and *Sir Gawain and the Green Knight* as well as *The Book of the Duchess*, she argues that a sense of the pedestrian experience is crucial to an understanding of medieval space. The essay makes a good companion piece to Pearsall's essay in the Yeager and Morse collection. However, walking was not the only means of getting about in the Middle Ages, as Betsy Bowden acknowledges in her essay 'Transportation to Canterbury: The Rival Envisionings by Stothard and Blake' (*SiM* 11[2001] 73–111). Her analysis of the works of the two artists focuses largely on their treatment of the pilgrims' horses, and she argues that their differing interpretations of the nature of Chaucer's work (and, indeed, the Middle Ages in general) may be detected through their different renderings of these equestrian elements. The controversy surrounding these two nineteenth-century artistic works is explored in another essay published this year, 'Blake v. Cromek: A Contemporary Ruling' (*MP* 99[2001] 66–77), by J.B. Mertz. Mertz cites some contemporary evidence from the papers of the antiquarian Francis Douce (1757–1834) to demonstrate that Blake's version of *Sir Jeffrey Chaucer and the nine and twenty Pilgrims on their Journey to Canterbury* was regarded as the more accurate historical representation. And Chaucer's reception in the eighteenth century is charted by Glenn Wright in 'Geoffrey the Unbarbarous:

Chaucerian "Genius" and Eighteenth-Century Antimedievalism' (*ES* 82[2001] 193–202). Wright suggests that Chaucer's high profile at the start of the eighteenth century, when Dryden championed him as a great wit, led—paradoxically—to his identification with the anti-medievalism of the Enlightenment. Accordingly Chaucer does not feature very strongly in the neo-medievalism that emerged towards the end of the century until his rehabilitation through William Godwin's biography.

Gaylord, ed., *Essays on the Art of Chaucer's Verse*, is a mixed collection of old and new pieces. Having written a seminal article, 'Scanning the Prosodists: An Essay in Metacriticism' in 1976 (*YWES* 58[1979] 111), which is reprinted here, Gaylord now returns to the topic of Chaucer's prosody to survey responses to his work and to review the subsequent development of the subject. Dismissing aspersions cast upon prosodic analysis as bean-counting, Gaylord unashamedly puts form back in the aesthetic debate. After a rather disjointed introduction which gives an overview of each contribution, but which does not attempt to link them together into a coherent discussion, Gaylord places two historical essays at the head of the collection: Thomas Tyrwhitt's 'Essay on the Language and Versification of Chaucer. Part the Third' is extracted from his *Poetical Works of Geoffrey Chaucer* [1798], and George Saintsbury's essay on 'Chaucer's Prosody' formed part of his *History of English Prosody from the Twelfth Century to the Present Day* [1906–10]. The Tyrwhitt excerpt is designed to highlight his emphasis on Chaucer's classical heritage and his exhortation to editors to restore to Chaucer's occasionally fractured lines 'their just number of syllables' (p. 33). Stylish and written with verve, Saintsbury's essay both persuades, so musical and sure is his ear, and provokes doubt, for the only evidence for the 'great staple meter of the *Canterbury Tales*' (p. 67) is the self-evident given that 'it is *there*'. Saintsbury's appeal to taste and the unambiguous evidence of the ear *in fine* is nothing other, observes Gaylord, than mere 'fudge' (p. 9). Gaylord's analysis of these two pieces is clear and helpful, and with his own essay these help to set the boundaries of the collection. Three other reprints are admitted to this initial 'historical and theoretical' section. Gaylord includes Derek Pearsall's study of 'Chaucer's Meter: The Evidence of the Manuscripts'; Steven R. Guthrie's 'Prosody and the Study of Chaucer: A Generative Reply to Halle and Keyser'; and Stephen A. Barney's investigation of 'Chaucer's *Troilus*: Meter and Grammar' (*YWES* 75[1996] 190). In part 2, the shortest section, the essays combine history and theory with close reading. James I. Wimsatt's analysis of 'Natural Music in Middle French Verse and Chaucer' is reprinted here, but the other two contributions are newly commissioned. Richard H. Osberg writes about various of the *Canterbury Tales* in '"I kan nat geeste": Chaucer's Artful Alliteration', examining the ornamentation of Chaucer's verse and setting his use of this technique in the context of the fourteenth-century alliterative revival. While the essay does its job in terms of historical overview, it offers little by way of any attempt to understand how prosodic analysis relates to Chaucer criticism of the twenty-first century. In the second of the new essays in this section Emerson Brown Jr. considers 'The Joy of Chaucer's Lydgate Lines', pondering the problem of those broken-backed lines in Chaucer's poetry which cannot be explained away by emendation. The five essays in part 3 all offer practical exemplifications of prosody. In the first of the two new contributions, 'Theme, Prosody, and Mimesis in the *Book of the Duchess*', Winthrop Wetherbee explores a range of effects such as pacing, enjambment, and the use of hypermetrical lines to show that in this early work Chaucer was deliberately experimenting with material inherited from his Continental models and sources. Charles A. Owen Jr.'s study of 'Chaucer's Witty Prosody in the General Prologue' also stresses Chaucer's love of experimentation, this time evident in his later work. The rest of the essays in this final section are reprints: 'The Making of *Troilus and Criseyde*', by David Wallace (*YWES* 66[1987] 164–5); 'Comic Meter in the *Miller's Tale*', by Howell Chickering (*YWES* 76[1997] 184); and Stephen Knight's essay the *Nun's Priest's Tale*. As an exercise in republishing this is more purposeful than most, and this collection will certainly facilitate future research into Chaucer's prosody. However, it is surprising that Gaylord does not offer any sort of conclusion or any pointers for the future; such would have been welcome, but as it is the volume rather peters out with a list of works cited.

The business of editing Chaucer's works and medieval texts in general continues to provoke debate. In a thought-provoking article '"I endowed thy purposes": Shakespeare, Editing, and Middle English Literature' (*Text* 13[2000] 9–25) Tim W. Machan argues that Shakespearean textual criticism has had an adverse influence on the editing of Chaucerian and other Middle English texts. He contends that Anglo-American editorial theories have been developed largely in response to Shakespeare's works, and that such theories are inappropriate for the editing of Middle English literature because texts from the earlier period are very different. While not proposing an entirely new theory, Alex Jones tries to refine an old one in 'The Properties of a Stemma: Relating the Manuscripts in Two Texts from *The Canterbury Tales*' (*Parergon* 18[2001] 35–53). He uses the work of Manly and Rickert, though he is critical of their handling of the relationships of those manuscripts supposed to be closest to Chaucer's archetype. At this crucial point, he claims, the biological model fails because it is insufficiently general—'it is a question of *metric*' (p. 41). Jones tries to illustrate his point by investigating the relations of twelve *Canterbury Tales* manuscripts, but his 'optimum solution' (p. 44) as to which is most authoritative isn't quite convincing, and overall he fails to guide the lay reader through a bewildering array of mathematical workings.

In the debate over the best manuscript witness for the *Canterbury Tales* Jill Mann fears that the balance has swung too far in the direction of the Hengwrt manuscript, and in 'Chaucer's Meter and the Myth of the Ellesmere Editor of *The Canterbury Tales*' (*SAC* 23[2001] 71–107) she attempts to dispel some of the criticisms that have been levelled at Ellesmere. By paying close attention to the metre of Chaucer's poem and comparing variant readings between the two manuscripts, she is able to dismiss the notion that Ellesmere was revised and improved by 'an intelligent person, who was certainly not Chaucer' (p. 75), an idea which originated with Manly and Rickert. Noting how enthusiastically the 'mythical beast' (p. 107) of the Ellesmere editor has been adopted by Norman Blake, Mann cautions that this is a suspiciously convenient way to elevate the status of Hengwrt, and warns that the beast may have a prolonged existence in the thickets of the *Canterbury Tales* project. Writing about the latter in 'The One Text and the Many Texts' (*L&LC* 15[2000] 5–14), Peter Robinson argues that electronic editions should include reconstructed editorial texts rather than simply reproducing all the source materials. After a brief survey of the history of electronic editions, and an equally brief examination of three actual editions which have to accommodate very large numbers of variant texts (the *Canterbury Tales*, Dante's *Commedia* and the Greek New Testament), Robinson concludes that reliance on a base text is essential. However, this reconstructed text need not be regarded as the precise representation of the lost original; rather, the privileged text should be one that best explains all the extant documents and may be seen therefore principally as a convenience to the user. In 'Cultural Capital: Selling Chaucer's *Works*, Building Christ Church, Oxford' (*ChauR* 36[2001] 149–57), Sarah A. Kelen draws our attention to a little-known fact, that profits from the 1721 edition of Chaucer by John Urry were to be used to contribute to the completion of the college's quadrangle. The essay contains interesting details about the fortunes of the edition (it flopped) and discussions about requiring students entering the college in the 1730s to purchase a volume, but Kelen does not draw any real conclusion about Chaucer as cultural capital. Franciscus Junius, seventeenth-century Dutch philologist and best known in Anglo-Saxon studies as bequeather of the Junius manuscripts at the Bodleian Library, was also an avid reader of Chaucer, recounts Rolf H. Bremmer Jr., in 'Franciscus Junius Read Chaucer: But Why? And How?' (*SiM* 11[2001] 37–72). His annotated copy of Speght's edition shows that the activity was more than a pastime for the philologist, and Bremmer posits a tentative thesis that Urry may actually have seen Junius's marked-up copy prior to compiling his own edition.

Modern criticism has come to rely on a fixed notion of Chaucer's canon, give or take some perennial anxieties about the authorship of certain works. But until the early nineteenth century readers knew a very different Chaucer, one who was believed to have written many more works, and whose reputation and identity had been constructed accordingly. Kathleen Forni explores this phenomenon of *The Chaucerian Apocrypha: A Counterfeit Canon*, concentrating on what she terms the 'folio canon', that is, those presumably spurious works which appeared between 1532 and 1721 in the editions of Thynne, Stow, Speght, and Urry. She does a great service to other scholars by including both a comprehensive list of the so-called Chaucer works that are found in these folio editions, and also a list of the manuscripts that contain the apocryphal texts. The focus of her book is the bibliographical and critical history of the complex symbiotic relationship between the canon and the apocrypha. In the early chapters she considers the material genesis of the apocrypha by examining those manuscript sources still extant which may have been used by the folio editors; she wonders whether the editors really believed that what they printed was Chaucer's, and how much their selections were influenced by the social and political concerns of their own era. The specific texts that she discusses are Usk's *Testament of Love*, the *Plowman's Tale*, Henryson's *Testament of Cresseid*, and the *Flower and the Leaf*. These individual case studies allow her to challenge the modern assumption that the apocrypha ruined Chaucer's early reputation. She is also able to demonstrate that attribution and evaluation are inextricably linked; once disattributed and expelled from the Chaucer canon, the critical fate of most of the spurious works was to sink without trace (the exception being the *Testament of Cresseid*). Earlier versions of chapters 3 and 5 appeared in article form in 1997 (*YWES* 78[1999] 233); the publication this year of Forni's more sustained argument on this topic is very welcome.

Two essays in Gutjahr and Benton, eds., *Illuminating Letters: Typography and Literary Interpretation*, have a bearing on Chaucer. In the first, '*Peirs Plouhman* [*sic*] and the "formidable array of blackletter" in the Early Nineteenth Century' (pp.

47–67), Sarah A. Kelen considers Thomas Dunham Whitaker's edition of *Piers Plowman* [1813], arguing that, in an era of anxiety about Catholic emancipation, Whitaker was intimidated by the poem's Catholicism and tried to distance it from his Protestant readership by presenting it in blackletter type, a chronologically alien typeface. By contrast, she notes that Chaucer's works had been modernized and made more accessible both linguistically, through Dryden's versions of some of the *Canterbury Tales*, and by their appearance in a whiteletter typeface in Urry's edition of 1721. Editors usually hope to bring their work to a wider audience, but Kelen shows that the visual format of a book may be used to limit its readership. This is also the argument made in the next essay, 'Typography and Gender: Remasculating the Modern Book' (pp. 71–93), where Megan L. Benton focuses on two texts, Chaucer's *Canterbury Tales* and Walt Whitman's *Leaves of Grass*. These 'serious' works attracted the attention of reforming printers who aimed to combat the feminization of reading they believed had resulted from mass printing. William Morris's deluxe edition of Chaucer [1896] is usually regarded as a work of fine craftsmanship, which apes the splendour of the medieval illuminated manuscript. Benton argues that productions such as this from the Kelmscott Press were part of a nineteenth-century backlash against frothy modern typefaces, and that they may be viewed as misogynistic creations, designed to appeal to gentleman readers, affordable only by such, and intended to be kept in the privacy and security of the aristocratic library.

Studies in Bibliography 52[1999] carried two items of interest not previously noted. Daniel W. Mosser offers some 'Corrective Notes on the Structures and Paper Stocks of Four Manuscripts Containing Extracts from Chaucer's *Canterbury Tales*' (*SB* 52[1999] 97–114), tackling four manuscripts whose collation has previously been dismissed as impossible: BL MSS Arundel 140, Harley 2382, and Sloane 1009, and Magdalene College, Cambridge, Pepys 2006. This detailed essay contains a great deal of preliminary information that will be very useful to other scholars. New information about Chaucer is also offered in a shorter article, 'Back at Chaucer's Tomb: Inscriptions in Two Early Copies of Chaucer's *Workes*' (*SB* 52[1999] 89–96), where Joseph A. Dane and Alexandra Gillespie record their discovery of two transcriptions of Chaucer's epitaph in sixteenth-century books at the Huntington Library and the Harry Ransom Humanities Research Centre at the University of Texas. And Alexandra Gillespie offers further bibliographical conclusions, this time about 'Caxton's Chaucer and Lydgate Quartos: Miscellanies from Manuscript to Print' (*TCBS* 12[2000] 1–25). Her discussion covers the eleven volumes of English verse printed by Caxton at Westminster in 1476, two of which were works by Chaucer. She finds that Caxton's quartos had a dual function: they supplied the market for English poetry with cheap pamphlets, but they were also the components of the first printed poetic miscellanies in England. Indeed, the history of Chaucer's works in the early modern period, especially their passage through the early presses, continues to attract a good deal of attention. In this regard Satoko Tokunaga examines 'The Sources of Wynkyn de Worde's Version of "The Monk's Tale"' (*The Library* 7th series, 2[2001] 223–35), and argues that de Worde's 1498 edition was not merely a reprint of Caxton's second edition of the 1480s. Identifying differences between the two editions, including changes in tale order and textual variants, which are particularly apparent from the *Prioress's Tale* onwards,

Tokunaga concludes that de Worde rather arbitrarily conflated both Caxton's second edition and a manuscript in order to produce a complete text.

In 'Tyrwhitt's Urry's Chaucer's *Works*: The Tracks of Editorial History' (*BLJ* 25[1999] 180–7), Sarah A. Kelen identifies the annotations in a copy of John Urry's 1721 edition of Chaucer's *Works* (BL 642.m.1) as belonging to the hand of Thomas Tyrwhitt. Her analysis of the marginal comments draws out their significance: Tyrwhitt can be seen making progress towards his own edition, and already here displays an interest in identifying the source texts of Chaucer's works.

Some essays that have appeared this year in volumes dedicated to the history of the language or linguistics offer interesting points about forms of speech in Chaucer's works. First, Norman Blake examines the evidence offered by 'Fabliaux and Other Literary Genres as Witnesses of Early Spoken English' (in Diller and Görlach, eds., *Towards a History of English as a History of Genres*, pp. 145–57). Perhaps not surprisingly given the focus on fabliaux, the elements of spoken English that are considered here are those that would shame polite company. Blake gives Chaucer the dubious credit of importing such terms into the language of belles-lettres, and notes that, although we associate such 'cherles termes' with the lower classes, Chaucer actually puts 'rude' words into the mouths of characters of varying social status. The links between social rank and linguistic use are also explored by Gabriella Mazzon, who considers 'Social Relations and Forms of Address in the *Canterbury Tales*' (in Kastovsky and Mettinger, eds., *The History of English in a Social Context: A Contribution to Historical Sociolinguistics*, pp. 135–68). Mazzon hopes to extend our understanding of the distinction between *you* and *thou* as modes of address (more technically, between Y-forms and T-forms). She finds that singular Y-forms are already very common in Chaucer's work, and that their usage cuts across social distinctions. Some interesting points arise from the special categories of speech she examines, for example, T-forms are apparently *de rigueur* when speaking to a corpse, but Y-forms should be used when addressing pagan gods. Other findings, such as the differing forms of address used when courting and within marriage, are less surprising and tend to reinforce concepts of authority and gender, but ultimately Mazzon finds that the choice between the two forms is not merely a matter of social relationship; in Chaucer's English, it seems, forms of address could be manipulated as a politeness strategy, just as they were in early modern English, as is apparent from the works of Shakespeare. Laurel J. Brinton also works back from a Shakespearean model in her examination of 'The Importance of Discourse Types in Grammaticalization: The Case of *Anon*' (in Herring, van Reenen, and Schøsler, eds., *Textual Parameters in Older Languages*, pp. 139–62). She notes that, of eighty-four occurrences of the term in *Troilus and Criseyde*, the majority are clustered in Book II, the section of the poem that has the highest proportion of narration to direct discourse. Further examination reveals that in narration *anon* functions as a pragmatic marker with textual meaning, whereas in dialogue it may be used as mere filler.

Taavitsainen, Nevalainen, Pahta, and Rissanen, eds., *Placing Middle English in Context*, a volume of twenty-three essays, contains three pieces specifically concerned with Chaucer. In the first, 'Chaucer's spelling and the manuscripts of the *Canterbury Tales*' (pp. 199–207) Simon Horobin considers scribal attitudes to Chaucer's orthography. He is able to demonstrate that fifteenth-century scribes respected Chaucerian spelling forms despite the emergence of standard written

English during the period in which they were writing. His findings also contribute to ongoing revisions of our understanding of the development of London English. A second essay by Andreas H. Jucker investigates a more particular aspect of Chaucer's language: 'Slanders, Slurs and Insults on the Road to Canterbury: Forms of Verbal Aggression in Chaucer's *Canterbury Tales*' (pp. 369–89). Jucker argues that four main types of verbal aggression can be discerned in Chaucer's work, namely direct, embedded, mediated, and indirect, and that Chaucer achieved such unpleasantness by a large range of stylistic means. Another type of bad language is explored by Leslie Arnovick in the third essay, '"Whoso thorgh presumpcion ... mysdeme hyt": Chaucer's Poetic Adaptation of the Medieval "Book Curse"' (pp. 411–24). This focuses on lines 80–102 of the *House of Fame* where Chaucer appropriates the ancient genre of the 'book curse'. Arnovick discusses the discourse origins of the book curse and Chaucer's poetic adaptation of this tradition. A fourth essay, by Donka Minkova, 'Middle English prosodic innovations and their testability in verse' (pp. 431–59), which is concerned with variable stress in spoken Middle English, includes among its rhyme evidence considerable reference to *Troilus and Criseyde*.

Susan Yager looks at *Boece*, *Troilus and Criseyde* and the *Canterbury Tales* in considering 'Chaucer's *Peple* and *Folk*' (*JEGP* 100[2001] 211–23). Although apparent synonyms, Yager argues for their semantic difference, *folk* being unmarked and occasionally positive, and *peple* generally negatively marked. In *Boece*, the word *peple* usually translates Latin *uulgus* or *populus*, implying people of the baser sort; in *Troilus and Criseyde*, the heroine is concerned with what 'goosissh poeple' may think, while *folk*, the more common term in the poem, can refer to nations, lovers, or warriors; and in the Canterbury poem, the association of *peple* with lewdness and ignorance tends to be stronger in Chaucer than in his sources.

Finally we note M.J. Toswell's review article, 'Chaucer's Pardoner, Chaucer's World, Chaucer's Style: Three Approaches to Medieval Literature' (*CollL* 23[2001] 155–62), which covers recent work by Lillian Bisson, Charles Muscatine (*YWES* 80[2001] 161–2), and Robert Sturges.

2. Canterbury Tales

R. Allen Shoaf's book-length study of *Chaucer's Body: The Anxiety of Circulation in the 'Canterbury Tales'* both returns to themes in which he has long been interested—the circulation of money and language (*YWES* 64[1985] 144)—and develops new arguments. Shoaf's writing is highly distinctive; with its dense wordplay and swift switches between critical and personal commentary, it is often difficult to abstract into a formal thesis. Circulation develops in the book as an all-embracing aesthetic concept that describes not only Chaucer's social role (he circulated throughout Europe and between court and the 'middle' classes) but also his literary activities as a translator/circulator of texts. In many ways, the concept of circulation sums up the productive position of the 'middle' and can be usefully compared to the 'ethos of the in-between' discussed three years ago (*YWES* 79[2000] 198); Shoaf's discussion of the *Man of Law's Tale* in chapter 1 revisits an earlier essay (*YWES* 72[1993] 132), and his fourth chapter, on the *Franklin's Tale*, comes from another previous essay (*YWES* 67[1988] 184). In a vein of thinking strikingly like that of Barbara Nolan (see the *Miller's Tale* below), Shoaf considers the fragmented nature of metonymy and the way in which it makes partial that which used to be whole. One of the most stimulating applications of the idea is in chapter 3, 'Etym-Alchemy', where, in the *Canon's Yeoman's Tale*, the poet, who 'sweats at the crucible of language' (p. 60) emerges as an alchemist of words rather than gold (coins). Just as alchemy is partial, because it never reaches its goal, so Chaucer's poetic is one of unfinishedness and fragmentation. The poet-alchemist who looks, however, to complete his project produces only dead language, for there is 'no "philosopher's etymon," no *elixir verbi*, that will reduce a word to one enduring proper substantive' (p. 65). Language is always tainted and in circulation. Revising Harold Bloom's 'anxiety of influence' to a Chaucerian 'anxiety of circulation', Shoaf portrays the poet in chapter 5 as a 'grant translateur', as 'late', always coming after the writers whose texts he swiped, anxious about the circulation of his reputation, name and fame; and it is this anxiety that explains why, throughout his corpus, Chaucer never mentions Boccaccio. Although Shoaf's work is overtly committed to theory, which for him is 'above all resistance' (p. 11), what emerges from this book is a profound pleasure in Chaucer's text and an awareness of the richness of his language—qualities that theoretically minded critics are often accused of lacking.

In *Species, Phantasms, and Images: Vision and Medieval Psychology in the 'Canterbury Tales'*, Carolyn Collette tackles the knotty subject of medieval faculty psychology. Chapters 3, on the *Franklin's Tale*, and 4, on the *Physician's Tale*, appeared in earlier forms (*YWES* 73[1994] 163) and (*YWES* 76[1997] 194) respectively. Most of chapter 1 is expository, and here Collette introduces us to the key terms of her title. The operation of *species* is of particular moment in love. Collette contrasts modern depictions of love as primarily an active event with the medieval understanding of the process whereby the lover is overwhelmed by having internalized the *species* of the beloved (it is from this essentially passive nature of sensory perception that we derive the name 'passion'). The involvement of the will in the 'imagining' of the beloved is not, however, in abeyance, and much of the subsequent analysis centres on the psychological agency of Chaucer's characters. Collette's main focus is on the role of vision in the operation of the imagination, which leads naturally, in her second chapter, to a consideration of the dramatic sighting of Emily by Palamon and Arcite in the *Knight's Tale*. These lovers indulge in a limited vision of things, and it is significant that Chaucer excises the moment of Arcite's higher vision when drawing from Boccaccio, reserving the moment for Troilus. In chapter 5, alchemy is discussed as philosophically relevant to faculty psychology because the science deals with the inner nature of things and their outer appearance; physical sight, which is needed to identify the moment of alchemical transmutation, can lead one astray. Collette's discussion of the *Second Nun's Tale* and, in the final chapter, of the *Parson's Tale* turns from the physical and psychological processes of sight emphasized in the earlier chapters to a higher form of seeing synonymous with understanding.

Critical interest in the non-Christian other, most particularly the Jew and the Muslim, so evident over the past few years, is again apparent in Brenda Deen Schildgen's study of *Pagans, Tartars, Moslems, and Jews in Chaucer's 'Canterbury Tales'*. Seeking a space between totalizing and fragmenting views of the tales, Schildgen sees in Chaucer a more local and pragmatic ethical approach to the cultural other and connects it to Habermas's 'discourse ethics'. The consensus of the 'compaignye' required by the Host to embark on the Canterbury game suggests to Schildgen an inclusive ethos, open to cultural difference. The fourteenth century, in contrast to the twelfth and thirteenth, emerges as a pan-continental world with Chaucer firmly as a man of his age. By setting many of his stories in the past, Chaucer brackets present political concerns and opens up a space for a more tolerant reception of difference; indeed, the Squire in his tale ignores contemporary negative depictions of the Tartar in favour of a festive inclusiveness that marginalizes history. Christianity is portrayed in an equally pluralistic way, with the rifts between the 'Christian' pilgrims evident from the beginning. Schildgen finds Chaucer anti-hegemonic, whether speaking of Christian or infidel. With all this benign tolerance, what then to do with the *Prioress's Tale*? In chapter 6 Schildgen neither denies the tale's anti-semitism nor argues that Chaucer satirizes her; rather, she shows how anachronistic and simply dichotomous the tale's world-view is. Would this have been self-evident to Chaucer's audience? It remains unclear how Chaucer really has set himself at any distance from the Prioress's prejudices. (These are questions Patterson more convincingly addresses; see below.) Although Schildgen's book covers some interesting ground, discussion is often weighted with general literary and cultural history for its own sake, leaving the reader with no clear sense of its connection to Chaucer's text. The links, for example, between the Squire and Epicureanism, Cambyuskan's gifts and Islamic science, and the narrator of the tale and popular Averroism are forced. Nonetheless, her portrayal of Chaucer's literary secularism, cultural curiosity and pragmatic ethic seems apposite.

In *Poetry Does Theology: Chaucer, Grosseteste, and the Pearl-Poet*, Jim Rhodes confronts the boundaries between the medieval and the modern, for which poetry is a thoroughly secular discourse and cannot really 'do' theology. In the fourteenth century, however, the two discourses were more intertwined, and the *Nun's Priest's Tale* well exemplifies a humanistic crisis in truth and language. The narrator expresses humorous confusion over traditionalist vs. 'new' theories of predestination and free will—concerns that gave fourteenth-century English theological debate its distinctive cast. Unable to remain within exclusively theological discourse, this man of the cloth turns to art to transmute theology, and to *ars poetica* to articulate the language of redemption. The tale opens up a space of 'play' where right interpretations are tested and upended—'mulier est hominis confusio'. The Prioress is presented by Rhodes as an incomplete embodiment of *caritas*, limited by her anti-semitism (the discussion makes an interesting companion to Besserman's discussion; see below). In contrast, the *Second Nun's Tale* reverses the exclusion of the infidel and embraces the pagan other. The next couple treated is the Reeve and Pardoner. In a 'revisionist' reading of the Reeve, Rhodes presents him as a preacher of sorts (his hair is shorn like a priest's), and the tale he tells is actually more sympathetic to marriage and community than is that of the Miller. In the Pardoner, Rhodes sees a preacher who missed the opportunity to use fiction for self-reflection and understanding; rather, he offers a canned performance-piece, goading the Host into his violent rebuke. Instead of interpreting the Pardoner's humiliation as complete, Rhodes sees his silence as a kind of awakening, which leads to a redeemed vision of 'compaignye', implied by the subsequent kiss of peace and his remaining on the pilgrimage. Theological issues are thus ever present, even in secular contexts, and Rhodes offers Chaucer's redemptive 'play world' (p. 7) as an indication of the extent to which theology was being secularized and becoming more lay-oriented in the fourteenth century.

Whether by design or by accident, none of the essays in Myles and Williams, eds., *Chaucer and Language: Essays in Honour of Douglas Wurtele*, deals with Chaucer's other works in any depth. Here are ten essays, all on Chaucer, from the editors and seven other scholars; David Williams supplies a précis of each essay in a short introduction. The first, by Robert Myles, addresses 'Chaucer and Character: The Heresies of Douglas Wurtele', and defiantly, or rather defensively, explains Wurtele's heresy as an adherence to character individualism (individuality being identified by Myles as a deviation from the norms of type) and to authorial intentionality—old-fashioned literary ideals not in vogue today. The late Beverly Kennedy contributes the second essay, '"Withouten oother compaignye in youthe": Verbal and Moral Ambiguity in the *General Prologue* Portrait of the Wife of Bath', in which she attempts to salvage Chaucer's text from the disambiguating proclivities of editors. Chaucer, she argues, himself intended textual *ambiguitas* as an object lesson in the difficulty of making moral judgements based on partial evidence. Medieval readers, that is, were to disagree and debate about the Wife's moral nature as avidly as they do today. Chauncey Wood takes a more jaundiced view of 'The Wife of Bath and "speche daungerous"', arguing that her apparently reasonable argument is undercut by her mincing euphemisms for male and female genitalia. The euphemisms originate from the *Roman de la Rose*; just as the refined terms preferred by the narrator of the *Roman* belie the sordidness of his intent and action, so the Wife's euphemisms expose the weakness of her arguments. Wood himself admits that the satire 'depends on the reader's knowledge of other texts' (p. 42), so tough luck if you haven't read the *Roman de la Rose*. E.C. Ronquist next considers the relationship between virtue and the good life in 'The Franklin, Epicurus, and the Play of Values'. Echoing many of Kennedy's sentiments about the ambiguity of Chaucer's utterance, Ronquist suggests that the reconciliation of goodness and happiness is an ongoing concern in the poet's work, and that in the view represented by the Franklin, pleasure need not be sacrificed to virtue. In keeping with Ronquist's view of Chaucer as a constructive pragmatist who delays resolution to some future date, the evidence is 'mixed' (p. 54) and one position can never be final. Glenn Burger continues his quest to queer the Middle Ages by 'Mapping a History of Sexuality in *Melibee*'. By preferring the term 'mapping' to 'tracing', Burger alludes to Gilles Deleuze and Félix Guattari's project in *A Thousand Plateaus*, where mapping suggests a more contingent drawing of historical lines ever open to reconstruction. Melibee learns a more flexible (and by implication less homophobic) kind of masculinity in taking Prudence's advice. Continuing discussion of the same tale, Christine Jones writes about 'Chaucer after the Linguistic Turn: Memory, History, and Fiction in the Link to *Melibee*'. The 'linguistic turn' refers to a change in the view of language, from seeing it as a transparent medium reflecting an external reality to an utterance that constitutes in part its own object, which is another way of saying that the world comes into being through language, that the world is a text. Rather than setting up Chaucer as the mouthpiece of a nominalism that ultimately discounts the connection between language and reality, Jones locates him somewhere in between. Without presenting language as unproblematic and transparent, the link to Melibee does express a faith that language can truthfully describe reality, that (objective) history is not merely (subjective) fiction. The essays are well ordered here, for the earlier discussion about ambiguity in language develops into a discussion about realism and nominalism, issues close to Myles's heart (*YWES* 75[1996] 168–9). In 'Chaucer's Clerk, on the Level?' Victor Yelverton Haines discerns witty games played by both Chaucer and his Clerk about medieval Christian concepts of testing and promise-keeping. Griselda emerges as a wily semiotician, able to slip around promises with irony and sarcasm because she was never really free to refuse Walter's marriage proposal in the first place. Robert Myles also considers the 'Confusing Signs: The Semiotic Point of View in the *Clerk's Tale*'. He begins his discussion with a consideration of the Augustinian distinction between natural signs (*signa naturalia*; e.g. smoke as sign of fire) and designated or given signs (*signa data*). The former are involuntary, the latter voluntary and learned. Walter's big mistake is to assume that phenomena are either one or the other. He misunderstands signs and himself abuses them in his constant discrepancy between word and intent; worst of all, he never really learns differently. Patrick J. Gallacher turns to 'Sense, Reference, and Wisdom in the *Merchant's Tale*', arguing that the tale represents an enquiry into and a partial rejection of his own (nominalist) scepticism. January's finale, in which sense and reference are entirely ruptured (he agrees that the reality of May and Damian doing it up a tree was only an illusion), represents the ridiculous extreme of nominalism. The Merchant has learned not to be January. If the reader hasn't got the point by this stage in the volume that Chaucer had little truck with nominalism, it is made again in the final essay, by David Williams, '"Lo how I vanysshe": The Pardoner's War against Signs'. St Augustine counselled against confusing the carnal (or literal) and the spiritual (or allegorical)—that is, of valorizing the sign over the signified—but that is exactly what the Pardoner does. His sterility is expressed in his devaluation of signs and relics; his tale, where life is anti-eucharistically transubstantiated into death, represents no less than the destruction of literature. Such is the world where the distinction between *res* and *verbum* is not carefully, assiduously protected against the depradations of nominalism.

Scott-Morgan Straker defends Lydgate's poem from charges of (bad) imitation in 'Deference and Difference: Lydgate, Chaucer, and the *Siege of Thebes*' (*RES* 52[2001] 1–21), arguing that Lydgate portrays himself in his prologue as an inversion of Chaucer's Monk, thereby redeeming the authority of monasticism. Lydgate's Host is less tolerant of edifying tales than is Chaucer's counterpart, and, drawing from the Prologue to Chaucer's *Clerk's Tale*, Lydgate stages a resistance to his Host's insistence on a secular tale. Teasing out the political implications of this move, Straker notes Lydgate's affirmation of ecclesiastical integrity in the face of monarchical pressure.

We have too long neglected 'The Influence of Plautus and Latin Elegiac Comedy on Chaucer's Fabliaux', argues Kathleen A. Bishop (*ChauR* 35[2001] 294–317). Although Chaucer could feasibly have had direct access to Plautus, the playwright's influence is more probably mediated to Chaucer through the Latin *comoediae*, plays written in twelfth-century France, and often featuring in grammar syllabi for young scholars. Sex and money, along with verbal dexterity, are elements common to Chaucer and Plautus, as are the jealous, stingy *senex amans* and the duplicitous, lustful woman.

In view of his contribution to Chaucer studies as an editor, Skeat's own Chaucerian imitations have been largely ignored, but James D. Johnson takes a look at 'Walter W. Skeat's *Canterbury Tale*' (*ChauR* 36[2001] 16–27), the *Deyer's Tale*, which was his longest and most ambitious imitative composition. Defending the tale's literary interest as both an intelligent imitation and a telling insight into Skeat's imagination, Johnson demonstrates how it is thoroughly grounded in medieval traditions and in works known to Chaucer. Most especially, it exploits the poet's fascination with mechanical *mirabilia* and *automata*, phenomena explored elsewhere this year.

Thomas Farrell's discussion of 'Philological Theory in *Sources and Analogues*' (*MedPers* 15[2000] 34–48) centres on the *Clerk's Tale*, and in particular on the work of J. Burke Severs in editing Petrarch's *Epistolae Seniles* XVII.3, the *Historia Griseldis*. Farrell and Amy Goodwin are re-editing the *Clerk's Tale* for *Sources and Analogues II*, and Farrell here outlines the alternative kind of work they intend to do, which includes producing a rather different edition of Petrarch's tale.

Chaucer's three most hypocritical churchmen—the Pardoner, the Friar, and the Summoner—feature in Fiona Somerset's article '"Mark him wel for he is on of þo": Training the "lewed" Gaze to Discern Hypocrisy' (*ELH* 68[2001] 315–34). The main part of this essay covers the substantial body of instructive literature written by the clergy for the laity, which (falsely) promises knowledge and discernment, especially on the crucial topic of knowing how to sort the wheat from the chaff when it comes to men of the Church. Chaucer gives Somerset a pretext for her discussion, and becomes the focus of her conclusion.

Drawing primarily from the Squire's and Franklin's tales and referring to the booming trade in mechanical knick-knacks that entertained and validated European nobility, Scott Lightsey notes the shift from supernatural *admiratio* to mundane *curiositas* in 'Chaucer's Secular Marvels and the Medieval Economy of Wonder' (*SAC* 23[2001] 289–316). In his travels, Chaucer would have seen or heard tell of *automata* such as those at castle Hesdin, or the astronomical clocks in Padua (by Jacopo di Dondi) and in Salisbury Cathedral. In the *Squire's Tale*, Chaucer subjects the *mirabilia* of traditional romance to empirical enquiry into their mechanical causation, while in the *Franklin's Tale* he subjects them to the mundaneness of economic exchange. Joseph D. Parry, 'Interpreting Female Agency and Responsibility in *The Miller's Tale* and *The Merchant's Tale*' (*PQ* 80[2001] 133–67), finds that these issues are central to both tales. The two stories play out a process of revenge and retribution administered by Absolom in the *Miller's Tale* and Pluto and Proserpina in the *Merchant's Tale*, yet neither Alison nor May is punished for her adultery, raising the question of whether the women trump the system or so lack agency that they are exempted from accountability.

Maidie Hilmo's long essay 'Framing the Canterbury Pilgrims for the Aristocratic Readers of the Ellesmere Manuscript' (in Kerby-Fulton and Hilmo, eds., *The Medieval Professional Reader at Work: Evidence from Manuscripts of Chaucer, Langland, Kempe, and Gower*, pp. 14–71), sees the miniatures in the Ellesmere manuscript as a visual guide to the reading process. After an extended analysis of the Knight's illustration, Hilmo's discussion focuses on a handful of the pilgrim portraits, arguing that some figures are elevated to make them suitable models for an aristocratic family circle (the Prioress, the Wife of Bath, and the Squire), while others (the Merchant, Miller, Cook, and Summoner), are mocked in order to confirm the social attitudes of the elite audience. She thus credits the production team of

Ellesmere with trying to stylize, elevate, decorate and sanitize Chaucer's text. This essay is generously illustrated with sixteen plates.

W. Rothwell asks in what sense the Prioress's French is non-Parisian, in 'Stratforde Atte Bowe Re-visited' (*ChauR* 36[2001] 184–207). In a welcome and timely reconsideration of the matter, Rothwell rejects the usual assumption that Chaucer's phrase in the *General Prologue* was designed to raise smirks in his audience at the Prioress's expense. While acknowledging how bastardized the French spoken in England had become in the fourteenth century in comparison to Parisian French, Rothwell rightly observes that the Anglicization of French was inevitable and was not a mark of uncouthness (except to a Parisian). Defending the sophistication of fourteenth-century trilingual writers in England, Rothwell suggests that Chaucer's allusion to Stratford Atte Bowe simply refers to the Prioress's insularity and limited horizons.

In 'Absolon as Barber-Surgeon' (*ChauR* 35[2001] 391–8), Kathryn Walls notes the conflict of interest between Absolon's double role as parish clerk and barber. As the former, he is forbidden to shed blood; as the latter, he is required to do so. Her essay emphasizes the centrality of his barber-surgeon profession, from the emblematic colours of his clothes to his fastidiousness about bodily smells, with which a man of his trade would be thoroughly familiar. Glenn Burger's 'Shameful Pleasures: Up Close and Dirty with Chaucer, Flesh, and the Word', appears in a section of Burger and Kruger, eds., *Queering the Middle Ages* (pp. 213–35), the intention of which is to realign the 'rhizomatic' relations between medieval and postmodern. Burger interprets the Canterbury narrator's apology for the upcoming *Miller's Tale* as a moment of shameful complicity on his part between the scurrility of the tale and the pilgrims' sensibilities. Burger finds this a 'productive middle' for the 'postmodern queer reader' whose own identity is so much in question. Robert Boenig points out the tactile nature of psaltery, nimbly played by 'hende' Nicholas, who also knows how to finger Alison's body, in 'Musical Instruments as Iconographical Artifacts in Medieval Poetry' (in Perry, ed., *Material Culture and Cultural Materialisms in the Middle Ages and Renaissance*, pp. 1–15). His comments provide a supplement to ideas developed last year (*YWES* 81[2002] 249). S.C.P. Horobin sets '*Phislophye* in *The Reeve's Tale* (Hg 4050) in Answer to *Astromye* in *The Miller's Tale* (3451)' (*N&Q* 48[2001] 109–10). Horobin leaves open the question of whether 'astromye' is a malapropism or an acceptable spelling variant, but suggests that the Reeve's reference to 'phislophye', a spelling that occurs only in Hengwrt, may be a deliberate misnomer in quitting of the Miller's 'cherles termes'.

In the *Reeve's Tale*, Britton J. Harwood attempts a reconciliation between the 'two great hermeneutics of suspicion' (p. 1)—Marxist and Freudian—to achieve a 'Psychoanalytic Politics: Chaucer and Two Peasants' (*ELH* 68[2001] 1–27). By a fairly convoluted line of association, Harwood interprets the humiliation of the miller in the tale as an unconscious acting out of the notorious downfall of Michael de la Pole. In de la Pole, a merchant's son made gentle, Chaucer finds a gratifying self-representation. Chaucer's awareness of de la Pole as historical object of the tale is repressed, Harwood argues, by a series of displacements: on to Symkyn, as humble peasant with aspirations beyond his station; on to the northern students, given de la Pole's northern origins; and on to the Reeve, whose close-cropped hair evokes de la Pole's attempt at disguise through shaving his head. The aggression with which Chaucer handles Symkyn's downfall only masks the uneasiness of Chaucer's own status as the upwardly mobile son of a vintner. Harwood psychoanalyses the tale as if it were a dream which can incorporate simultaneously contradictory elements. Highly theoretical and ideologically driven, the essay at once both vexes and illuminates, producing a rich and textured analysis that will stand as an effective rebuttal (or illustration) of Patterson's arguments about the Pardoner, reviewed below. In 'J.R.R. Tolkien as a Philologist: A Reconsideration of the Northernisms in Chaucer's *Reeve's Tale*' (*ES* 82[2001] 97–105), S.C.P. Horobin analyses the orthography, phonology, morphology and dialect vocabulary of the *Reeve's Tale* in order to demonstrate that, despite what Tolkien thought, later scribes did get the joke, and that they sought to preserve the northern differences of Chaucer's text.

Elizabeth Robertson reconsiders the relationship between Christian and Islamic representations in 'The "elvyssh" Power of Constance: Christian Feminism in Geoffrey Chaucer's *The Man of Law's Tale*' (*SAC* 23[2001] 143–80). Where much recent criticism has exposed a caricature of the Islamic as monstrously other, Robertson, not disagreeing with such stereotypical depiction in Chaucer's tale, nevertheless argues for Christianity as also radically other. Constance is described from the Syrians' point of view, and thereby she embodies a racial and gendered 'elvishness' that arouses both desire and repulsion. By choosing a woman as arch-representative of Christianity, Chaucer makes Christianity strange unto itself, separating Constance's religious character from the masculinist power-brokering of institutionalized religion. This is a thoughtful reading, which connects Constance's strangeness with Chaucer's own elvish poetics and his similarly enigmatic attitude towards corrupted orthodoxy and Lollard reform.

A.C. Spearing notes how critical understanding of Chaucer is dominated by 'Narrative Voice: The Case of Chaucer's *Man of Law's Tale*' (*NLH* 32[2001] 715–46). Concentration on narrative voice has led to the general opinion that the Man of Law is an unreliable narrator and that Chaucer has little but contempt for him. For Spearing, the attribution of certain voices to certain pilgrims is largely a matter of convention (churls tell churls' tales, knights narrate romances, etc.); not only does this loosen the relation between what we know about pilgrims from other parts of the *Canterbury Tales* and the tales they themselves tell, but Spearing also suggests that we may jettison the very sense of there being a speaking individual as such. The Man of Law as speaking individual, unloved and unadmired by contemporary critics, has become an obstacle to a full appreciation of the unanswerable and unironic metaphysical questions posed in the tale about suffering.

Yvonne Yaw finds 'Students' Study Guides and the Wife of Bath' (*ChauR* 35[2001] 318–32), in particular Cliffs Notes and MAX Notes, at best an over-simplification and at worst a falsification. It is a pity that Yaw did not include a British study guide such as York Notes for comparison with these American publications. Cliff Notes suggest that the Wife loved none of her husbands, they imply that Jankyn read aloud his stories about wicked wives only once, and they omit any reference to the deafness she sustained as a result of Jankyn's blow. MAX Notes omit any reference at all to Jankyn beating her. The cumulative impact of such inaccuracies is to represent the Wife as less sympathetic than she need be. Yaw concludes the essay with a more textually accurate synopsis of her own. In 'Gofraidh Fionn Ó Dálaigh's Analogue to Geoffrey Chaucer's *Wife of Bath's Tale*'

(*ChauR* 48[2001] 110–12), Michael Terry notes the following relevant narrative: an old man, being kind to a strange child, is rewarded with a return to youth. His wife no longer recognizes him, but when she is subjected to several questions about love is also rewarded with youth. The trial by question and the gift of youth as a reward for good behaviour are the salient points of connection between the tales of Chaucer and of Ó Dálaigh, who pre-dated Chaucer by a few decades.

Kathy Lavezzo considers 'Chaucer and Everyday Death: *The Clerk's Tale*, Burial, and the Subject of Poverty' (*SAC* 23[2001] 255–87), noting that, despite superficial appearances of death as the great leveller, death in the late Middle Ages, not unlike today, was a sure index of one's status and income in life—a connection implied in the tale's vocabulary, for 'cheste' and 'cofre' mean both coffin and strongbox. While the *dance macabre* did facilitate democratic ideals and social satire, such as we see in the 1381 chant 'When Adam delved and Eve span ... who was then a gentleman?', Griselda shows a more subtle kind of peasant resistance to the oppression by Walter, which centres upon the burial of her children. She does not oppose their deaths, but draws the line at their bodily exposure. This concern for the care of the corpse is shared by the guilds, suggesting that Griselda's anxiety over the burial of her children bespeaks a material resistance more class-based and politicized than has hitherto been appreciated. In Philippe de Mézières's wish for Richard in 1395 that he may find a wife like Griselda, Michael Hanrahan, in '"A straunge succesour sholde take youre heritage": The *Clerk's Tale* and the Crisis of Ricardian Rule' (*ChauR* 35[2001] 335–50), argues for a subtext of political urgency in Chaucer's tale. Parallels are traced between the tyrannical Walter and Richard, whose growing obsession with royal prerogative was matched only by his pressing need for an heir, and between the various scandals that surrounded Anne of Bohemia, Richard's first queen, and the 'scandal' of Griselda's low estate.

In 'The Luxury of Gender: *Piers Plowman* B.9 and *The Merchant's Tale*' (in, Hewett-Smith, ed., pp. 41–67), Joan Baker and Susan Signe Morrison argue that January's excursus on marital bliss is a caricature of Wit's preaching. Where Langland subordinates gender concerns to other social and moral imbalances in the 'unkynde similitude' of an asymmetrical marriage, Chaucer brings them to the fore by depicting January's excessive self-love as the basis for his 'love' of May and by implying rape through the presence of Pluto, champion of blind January and rapist of Proserpina. Although 'kyndely' similitude is possible in terms of age and class, gender for Chaucer constitutes a permanent element of difference within the marriage bond.

In 'Flying Sources: Classical Authority in Chaucer's *Squire's Tale*' (*ELH* 68[2001] 287–313), Craig A. Berry reviews the depiction of Chaucer as a 'lewd compilator', arguing for a more serious form of imitation. The tale's flying brass horse is a work of art in its own right and Cambyuskan's court cannot agree on whether it is more like Pegasus or the Trojan horse; just so Chaucer's poem. The body of the essay is devoted to elaborating the analogies between the poem and Pegasus and the poem and the Trojan horse: the allusion to Pegasus both asserts and performatively contradicts the notion of freedom from sources, while, with the mask of the Squire, Chaucer simulates Sinon's lack of rhetorical control. The tale, Berry argues, enacts *in parvo* many of the Chaucerian narrative concerns writ large in the *Canterbury Tales*.

There's no way round it. If we want to understand the *Franklin's Tale*, we need to accept that chivalric ideals and wifely obedience might have been values unironically admired by Chaucer, argues Gerald Morgan in 'Experience and the Judgement of Poetry: A Reconsideration of the *Franklin's Tale*' (*MÆ* 70[2001] 204–25). The essay mostly comprises a close reading of the tale, with contemporary sources (fourteenth-century marriage vows, Aquinas, Froissart, etc.) to support his argument, namely, that the marriage of Dorigen and Arveragus is one founded on honour, equality, love, generosity, and wifely obedience. While Morgan makes a persuasive case, *in fine* he offers one way of reading the tale, but—as some of the other equally persuasive and less benign readings suggest—not the only way.

Lee Patterson lays down a sharp, even absolute, opposition between historicism and psychoanalysis in 'Chaucer's Pardoner on the Couch: Psyche and Clio in Medieval Literary Studies' (*Speculum* 7[2001] 638–80). Read against an earlier essay in which he recuperates empiricism as a working model of historical enquiry (*YWES* 77[1998] 211), his argument here has culminated in a bleak choice between the heavy responsibilities of historical enquiry and the Freudian 'spell' under which we view the external world, both of the present and the past, through the 'pudendascope' of psychoanalysis. The liberal option, namely that of retaining psychoanalysis as one hermeneutic model amongst many, only fudges the issue, for the authority of psychoanalysis lies primarily in Freud's claims for it as an empirical science. Patterson reads sodomy and eunuchry as symbols of the Pardoner's spiritual sterility manifested in his simony and in his failure to 'sow God's seed in the field of holy mother's church'. It is not that the Pardoner is not a sodomite or eunuch; it is rather that sexuality (of whatever ilk) is not the determining centre of his personality. What drives his nature is spiritual lack. His false relics can only parody the co-presence of spiritual and material reality that authentic relics enact. Few would take issue with Patterson's scrupulous reading of the Pardoner. To what extent that reading positively ousts the possibility of translating the sacred/profane category into the psychoanalytic, or at least of juxtaposing them in meaningful ways, is very much less decisive. Elizabeth Allen asks what was so threatening about the Pardoner to a late medieval audience. In 'The Pardoner in the "dogges boure": Early Reception of the *Canterbury Tales*' (*ChauR* 36[2001] 91–127), she notes the rough treatment he receives in the pseudo-Chaucerian *Interlude and Tale of Beryn*, in which the Pardoner, having pilfered tokens from the Beckett shrine and unsuccessfully propositioned Kit the tapster, is beaten up and spends the night literally in the dog house. Allen notes how the violence in Chaucer's Host is modified and made reasonable in the Interlude so as to make the Pardoner get only what he deserves. Where Chaucer resisted judgement, the Interlude thoroughly punishes and exiles a character who indulges in excessive appetite.

Bruce Holsinger's *Music, Body, and Desire in Medieval Culture: Hildegard of Bingen to Chaucer* contains some important insights into the Pardoner in the *General Prologue*. In addition, 'The Pardoner's Polyphonic Perversity: A Chaucerian Coda' is set into a chapter discussing sodomy and polyphony. Holsinger notes that the narrator of the *General Prologue* casts aspersions on the Pardoner's sexuality only after he has heard the duet sung with the Summoner; he then notes the parallel between such sexual anxiety and a contemporary anxiety about same-sex polyphonic singing. It is not that corrupted sexuality is the cause of flamboyant, effeminate music, but rather that the perversion of the sobriety of sacred music has led to the corruption of everything else, including sex. The discussion develops into a consideration of the inherent musicality of the Chaucerian (sexual and scatological) body, and indicates in miniature the forceful case Holsinger makes throughout the book for the primacy of music. Re the Pardoner, it is striking that both Holsinger and Patterson interpret his doubtful sexuality more as symptom than as cause. It is no accident that in the same year come two powerful displacements of the Pardoner's sexuality onto other categories of being, be it spiritual or musical. Chapter 5, on violence and music in the *Prioress's Tale*, is developed from an essay originally published in *New Medieval Literatures* (*YWES* 78[1999] 251).

In 'Ideology, Antisemitism, and Chaucer's *Prioress's Tale*' (*ChauR* 36[2001] 48–72), Lawrence Besserman offers little by way of a new reading of the tale but lots by way of discussing the ideological agendas of contemporary readings of it. He questions the value of categorizing Chaucer as either politically correct or non-politically correct in relation to the tale's anti-semitism, and contends that too many readings today are driven by 'contentious social and political ends' that are simply irrelevant to the text. The main target of his critique is an essay by Louise Fradenburg (*YWES* 70[1989] 225), and in particular one unfortunate footnote, which, Besserman argues, beneath an apparent evenhandedness discloses exactly the 'libelous Christian anti-semitism' that Fradenburg in her article initially set out to expose. Besserman's larger point is that anti-semitism is simply the other side of a repugnance for Christianity, and that we are too preoccupied today with projecting our own ideological bugbears and blind spots to be able to read closely. This is strong stuff, and we can look forward to some ripostes in future years. Taking a very different approach, Lee Patterson historicizes the anti-semitism of the tale in '"The living witnesses of our redemption": Martyrdom and Imitation in Chaucer's *Prioress's Tale*' (*JMEMS* 31[2001] 507–60). Patterson discusses Jewish ritual martyrdom—most notably the *kiddush hashem* of 1146—as resistance to the purges enacted by Christians. Christian responses were mixed, sometimes even more vicious in their caricaturing of Jewish violence, but often ambivalent and disgusted at the brutality of Christians. The original version of the story of the little clergeon is a twelfth-century response to the *kiddush hashem* of 1146. Arguing that the Marian miracle tales were not generally anti-semitic, Patterson notes that the story of the little clergeon was one of the two popular ones that were extravagantly so. From his travels in Spain, Chaucer could well have been acquainted with the *kiddush hashem* and Patterson suggests that Chaucer's choice of this story, heavily larded as it is with every anti-semitic slur in the book, enforces a sense of the history from which the Prioress is trying to escape into the 'absolutism of the eternal' (p. 512). In a tale so much about learning by rote and empty mimicry of the voices of others, Chaucer's audience cannot not question the intolerance and ignorance the Prioress demonstrates.

Mari Pakkala-Weckström draws from historical pragmatics to analyse 'Prudence and the Power of Persuasion: Language and *Maistrie* in the *Tale of Melibee*' (*ChauR* 35[2001] 399–412). Differing from linguistic pragmatics, which analyses shades of meaning in spoken language, historical pragmatics relies on written sources. By paying attention to markers such as *ye*/*thou* forms of address, Pakkala-Weckström shows that Prudence employs strategies of politeness and respectfulness to achieve the 'maistrie' for which the couple struggles. Her politeness is a veneer, however, as such strategies diminish the more Prudence's discourse gains in authority. Her comments can usefully be compared with those of Mazzon (reviewed in section 1 above), with reference to Y-forms and T-forms.

Scott Norsworthy picks up the Host's reference to the Monk as a cellarer in 'Hard Lords and Bad Food-Service in the *Monk's Tale*' (*JEGP* 100[2001] 313–32). Norsworthy contrasts the idealized picture of hospitality and nurture of the cellarer given in the Rule of St Benedict with the unsavoury abuses of power exercised by cellarers in late medieval England, and notes the implied connection between this latter reality and the Monk's interest in dictatorial power that he displays in his tale.

George Kane turns to Chaucer's only explicit allusion to the Peasants' Revolt, four lines of the *Nun's Priest's Tale*, in 'Language as Literature' (in Kay and Sylvester, eds., *Lexis and Texts in Early English: Studies Presented to Jane Roberts*, pp. 161–71). Here Kane rejects accusations that Chaucer's allusion in the lines to the massacre of the Flemings in London was unfeeling. Suggesting Chaucer's emotional involvement, Kane both notes the poet's close connections with London and the very sites of violence and argues that the poem's mock-heroism requires a discrepancy between style and content that could be mistaken for lack of feeling. What detracts from the essay is a spleenful assertion of 'old-fashioned literary examination' over 'the procrustean imposition of New Historicist preconceptions' (these are the last words of his essay). Such mannered antagonism between the historicist and the stylistic is both dated and crude, and most of all jars in a volume designed to celebrate a colleague's scholarship.

Eileen S. Jankowski sounds an eschatological note in '*Chaucer's Second Nun's Tale* and the Apocalyptic Imagination' (*ChauR* 36[2001] 128–48). Generally agreed upon as the beginning of the end of the Canterbury poem, the tale, with its frustrating lack of narrative development and of 'muchel speche', tends to be treated as a preface to the *Parson's Tale*. Jankowski observes, however, that the *Second Nun's Tale* in many ways goes beyond the *Parson's Tale*, which is so preoccupied with earthly repentance and confession, to move us to a point beyond pilgrimage; it exhibits, in other words, an apocalyptic imagination.

The sunny portrait of Apollonian power is tarnished somewhat in Michael Kensak's consideration of 'Apollo *exterminans*: The God of Poetry in Chaucer's *Manciple's Tale*' (*SP* 98[2001] 143–57). He detects a lesser tradition of a violent Apollo, deriving possibly from Ovid's *Metamorphoses*. In addition, Alain de Lille, in the *Anticlaudianus*, depicts an Apollo insufficient for the task of concluding Phronesis's voyage. As the *Parson's Tale* follows the *Manciple's Tale*, the Apollonian poetry of natural man must yield to the poetics of eternity.

Katherine Little opens her discussion of 'Chaucer's Parson and the Specter of Wycliffism' (*SAC* 23[2001] 225–53) with some general comments on the concerns of Lollard reform, which was focused primarily on preaching and confession. In offering a Parson who preaches about confession, Chaucer shows himself a close reader, if not necessarily a supporter, of Lollard concerns. In contrast to Gower, who carefully distances his anticlericalism from any taint of Wycliffism, Chaucer seems unbothered by any such association. Rather, Little argues, Chaucer implies a certain hopelessness about the Parson's reformist ideals. Where Wycliffism betrays an 'interpretative cul-de-sac' (p. 243) in its preaching about preaching, Chaucer's Parson reaches a dead end in his attempt to put sin into language; the discussion of the sinning 'I' degenerates into an empty catalogue of sins.

James McNelis finds some 'Parallel Manuscript Readings in the CT Retraction and Edward of Norwich's *Master of Game*' (*ChauR* 36[2001] 87–90). In the prologue to this hunting manual, written by Edward of Norwich, second duke of York, reference is made to the *Legend of Good Women*, a work also mentioned in the *Retraction*. Since Edward actually misquotes the *Legend*, McNelis infers that he did not have a text of the poem to hand and that he was quoting from memory, but also suggests that he may well have been consulting a copy of the *Retraction*. Since one of the manuscripts of the *Master of Game* dates from approximately 1406 (New Haven, Yale, Beinecke 163 (the Wagstaff Miscellany)), it suggests that a copy of the *Canterbury Tales* may have been circulating as early as this date; or, if the *Retraction* is post-Chaucerian, it means it was written within a few years of Chaucer's death.

3. *Troilus and Criseyde*

There continues to be a significant lack of critical interest in *Troilus and Criseyde*. One of the few relatively extended treatments of the poem is to be found in Lawrence Besserman's discussion of '"Priest" and "Pope," "Sire" and "Madame": Anachronistic Division and Social Conflict in Chaucer's *Troilus*' (*SAC* 23[2001] 181–224). In his long essay Besserman takes the set of terms mentioned in his title and traces their use in *Troilus and Criseyde* and, to a lesser extent, in the *Canterbury Tales*, arguing that their deployment reveals Chaucer's covert engagement with contentious late medieval English religious, political and social controversies. He takes both the narrator and Pandarus to be priestly figures, and claims that their representation as such shows the deep influence of clerical culture on an ostensibly secular love story. He also detects a general movement from mirth to doctrine in the poem, mirroring that endemic in the structure of the *Canterbury Tales*, by charting the conversion of the priest and pope of lovers at the beginning into the lay preacher who addresses the audience at the end.

In a briefer note on the poem, Kathryn Walls draws attention to 'Chaucer's *Troilus and Criseyde* l. 540–875' (*Expl* 59[2001] 59–62) to argue that Pandarus has known all along that his niece is the object of Troilus's affections. And Lori Ann Pearson suggests that Troilus's sorrow is not double but threefold in a rather basic discussion 'The Triple Sorrow of Chaucer's Troilus' (*InG* 20[1999] 89–99). Tison Pugh asks about the presence of a 'Queer Pandarus? Silence and Sexual Ambiguity in Chaucer's *Troilus and Criseyde*' (*PQ* 80[2001] 17–35), and prefers the term 'homosocial', which leaves the question mark permanently over the relationship between Pandarus and Troilus. It is the silences of Pandarus and what is not said rather than what is that for Pugh 'queers' the encounters between the two men and renders them non-heteronormative. Pugh also reads the poem in tandem with contemporary anxiety about the 'homosocial' relationship between Richard II (playing Troilus) and Robert de Vere (playing Pandarus), whom Thomas Walsingham explicitly accused of sharing 'obscene intimacies'. Since we have already entertained the possibility of Robert de Vere being Walter of the *Clerk's Tale* (see Olson, section 1 above), not to mention Richard II being Walter (see Hanrahan, section 2), the point is less which character de Vere represents than that one detects him there in the first place. Considered alongside the interpretations of

Morse and of Harwood, these readings demonstrate a not unreasonable but nonetheless telling urge to read contemporary politics in Chaucer's poetry.

Turning from the attention she has been giving of late to the Canterbury pilgrims, Laura F. Hodges now considers 'Sartorial Signs in Troilus and Criseyde' (*ChauR* 35[2001] 223–58). Where Criseyde's 'costume rhetoric' displays her as a beautiful widow, that of Troilus marks him out as a warrior, while the hood alluded to in the phrase 'game in myn hood' (II.1110), which bears association with trickery, becomes the signature costume image for Pandarus. Book III, where Criseyde consummates her love, sees a jettisoning of the widow rhetoric, and reduces the marital Troilus to a lover sitting in his underwear. By Book V, Criseyde's transition to romance heroine is signalled by hair no longer hidden under widow's garb but displayed and adorned with gold thread. There is some interesting material in the essay, which expounds the sartorial array of the characters more fully than any critical edition would; for example, the angelic imagery of Criseyde described in Book I in her widow's weeds is explained by sumptuous sheen of the samite she wears. Hodges's exposition, however, is often an interpretative reading of sartorial detail that needs little commentary.

With reference to Gertz's consideration of Criseyde as sign, a similar textual metaphor is noted by Victoria Warren in '(Mis)Reading the "Text" of Criseyde: Context and Identity in Chaucer's *Troilus and Criseyde*' (*ChauR* 36[2001] 1–15). Warren accuses Troilus of reading Criseyde's face 'new critically' rather than discursively, that is, of assuming her to be author of her own identity rather than a construct of multiple and conflicting functions. Blinded by his own self-absorption, Troilus cannot recognize the vulnerability of her position as a woman, a vulnerability which, when she is in the Greek camp, she protects by the use of practical survival skills, i.e. accepting Diomede as her new lover.

4. Other Works

In '"Dreme he barefot, dreme he shod": Chaucer as a Performer of Dream Visions' (*ES* 81[2000] 506–12), Ebbe Klitgård delicately explores Chaucer's use of communicative strategies and seeks to convince us that the dream visions were originally performance poems. Nicole Lassahn looks closely at the relationship between the *Book of the Duchess* and Guillaume de Machaut's *Dit de la fonteinne amoureuse* as part of her discussion of 'Literary Representations of History in Fourteenth Century England: Shared Technique and Divergent Practice in Chaucer and Langland' (*Essays in Medieval Studies* 17[2001] 49–64). She argues that a knowledge of the French poem, and in particular what Machaut has to say about the poet–patron relationship, is crucial to an understanding of the historical content of Chaucer's dream vision. Machaut's influence cannot be doubted, but Lassahn's conclusions may be unnecessarily complicated by her rejection of the assumption that the primary audience for the *Book of the Duchess* was John of Gaunt and his circle. Less controversially Delmar C. Homan writes on 'Loss, Grief, Reminiscence, and Popular Culture in Chaucer's *Book of the Duchess*' (*Publications of the Medieval Association of the Midwest* 7[2000] 63–83), arguing that the plot of Chaucer's poem parallels the process of grief therapy and reminiscence, and that this structure, with its techniques of coping with loss, is an example of lasting popular culture. Her essay touches upon the use of number symbolism, and applauds the healing creativity of the narrator/dreamer. Robert A. Watson offers a long discussion of Chaucer's philosophy in 'Dialogue and Invention in the *Book of the Duchess*' (*MP* 98[2001] 543–76). In a forthcoming longer work Watson argues that Chaucer's philosophy, often associated with nominalism and scepticism, should more properly be termed 'Ciceronian Platonism'; in the present article he tries to identify the earliest signs of the poet's interest in such ideas by a close reading of the dream vision. Guillemette Bolens and Paul Beckman Taylor continue a discussion of 'Chess, Clocks, and Counsellors in Chaucer's *Book of the Duchess*' (*ChauR* 35[2001] 281–93) which they began in 1998 (*YWES* 79[2000] 222). In the *fers*, the Black Knight has lost not only a queen but also a counsellor, for he wrongly took her as a gift of Fortune rather than of grace. Just as a pawn may be promoted to a queen, so the narrator, playing *poun errant*, promotes himself to the position of counsellor, thereby remedying the loss the Knight has sustained. The time-marking bell that enters and ends the dream implies an orderly and providential time that counters the random spinning of Fortune's wheel which has dominated the Black Knight's life. This second essay develops the image of the clock, both offering technical information and considering the literary significance of the clock, which, for example, provided Froissart with the controlling metaphor of *Orloge amoureus*. The essay also provides a convenient expansion on the *mirabilia* mentioned in Scott Lightsey's article (section 2 above).

Gregory K. Jember offers 'Two Notes on Chaucer and Cultural Tradition' (*InG* 19[1998] 1–17), exploring the 'clashing rocks' or 'Symplegades' motif in the northern Germanic tradition and then demonstrating two manifestations of this motif in Chaucer's dream poems. His first example, from the *Book of the Duchess*, is more convincing than his second, from the *House of Fame*. Another note, this time by Tony Davenport, attempts to elucidate the reference to St Leonard in 'Chaucer's *House of Fame*, 111–18: A Windsor Joke?' (*N&Q* 48[2001] 222–4). Davenport suggests that the pilgrimage to St Leonard mentioned in these lines refers to the eponymous hermitage two miles west of Windsor Castle, and notes that in the fourteenth century Sir Bernard Brocas had successfully petitioned Pope Innocent VI to grant indulgences to those who visited the hermit's chapel. In '"A man of gret auctorite": The Search for Truth in Textual Authority in Geoffrey Chaucer's *The House of Fame*' (*BJRL* 81[1999] 155–65), Robert Clifford argues that the poem shows the arbitrariness of the distinction between truth and fiction, and that it criticizes the concept of authorities. He concludes that Chaucer ultimately found the pseudo-experience of the dream vision unfulfilling, and thus chose to abandon the form in his later work.

Michael Hagiioannu compares 'Giotto's Bardi Chapel Frescoes and Chaucer's *House of Fame*: Influence, Evidence, and Interpretations' (*ChauR* 36[2001] 28–47). Much of the earlier part of the essay is devoted to a review of Chaucer's acquaintance with Italian art and the significance of Giotto's frescos, specifically the new awareness of empirical observation as the basis for individual experience and knowledge. The narrator's interpretation of pictures on a wall and his frequent reference to the seeing 'I' mimic the experience of 'reading' frescos. Like Dante and Giotto, however, Chaucer in the poem explores and exposes the limits of such a temporal and local perspective. Ruth Evans indulges in a spot of retrospective science fiction in 'Chaucer in Cyberspace: Medieval Technologies of Memory and

The House of Fame' (*SAC* 23[2001] 43–69), imaging Chaucer at his computer with all the virtual resources available to modern scholars. Using Derridean and Freudian theories she re-examines the *House of Fame*, interrogating its obsession with late medieval technologies of memory and archiving, and offering many imaginative modern analogies in an attempt to understand the poem's complexities. Thus the house of fame itself is described as 'something like a vast telephone exchange or switchboard' (p. 57), and the twiggy structure of the house of rumour is identified as a model of the internet within which may be heard the noise of cyberspace.

The theories of Freud and Lacan are more frequently applied to modern writing than to medieval literature, an imbalance that Britton J. Harwood seeks to redress in his essay 'Same-Sex Desire in the Unconscious of Chaucer's *Parliament of Fowls*' (*Exemplaria* 13[2001] 99–135). Harwood believes that 'an unwillingness to take up the psychoanalytic tradition ... needlessly handicaps us in reading what is difficult in "olde bokes"' (p. 135), and that psychoanalytic criticism can reveal the presence of an unconscious homoerotic wish in Chaucer's poem. An even more novel and less charted approach to the poem, that of ecocriticism, is taken by Lisa J. Kiser in 'Chaucer and the Politics of Nature' (in Armbruster and Wallace, eds., *Beyond Nature Writing: Expanding the Boundaries of Ecocriticism*, pp. 41–56). Focusing on the vexed binary of nature and culture, Kiser argues that Chaucer's Nature is largely a social construction serving dominant social ideologies, and whose primary function is to preserve social hierarchies; she is remote from the lower orders she herself has created and her advocacy of female interests is only a mirage.

Catherine Sanok's detailed argument in 'Reading Hagiographically: *The Legend of Good Women* and its Feminine Audience' (*Exemplaria* 13[2001] 323–54), is concerned with the politics of reading but not with real-life women readers of the poem. She begins by suggesting that the association between women and saints' legends was largely a late medieval cultural fiction, and that this is an important and neglected context for understanding Chaucer's poem. She subsequently finds that the critical reception of the poem as a satire has been influenced by medieval anti-feminist hermeneutics, and that the poem's hagiographic reference (explicitly aimed at an inscribed female audience), establishes the validity of another reading. In 'A Curious Error? Geoffrey Chaucer's *Legend of Hypermnestra*' (*ChauR* 36[2001] 73–86), Gila Aloni ponders why Chaucer switched the names of the fathers of Hypermnestra and Lyno, her groom, when he adapted Ovid's story. He also reduced the number of daughters from fifty to one, thereby radically altering the nature of the relationship between Hypermnestra and her father. Fixed between two men, Hypermnestra's position as a commodity of exchange between men is highlighted. As for the change of paternal names, Aloni suggests that Chaucer wants to destabilize male fixity and reveal male transactability. Possibly, but maybe the switch of names was just a mistake.

Chaucer's merits as a translator are considered by W.A. Davenport in 'Ballades, French and English, and Chaucer's "Scarcity" of Rhyme' (*Parergon* 18[2001] 181–201). Davenport challenges the notion that Chaucer was linguistically deficient when it came to translating French ballades into English, and refuses to put the blame of the English language either. Another of Chaucer's shorter poems that is also a translation, *An ABC*, has been criticized in the past as being too derivative and too pious. Its cause is taken up this year by William A. Quinn in an essay entitled 'Chaucer's Problematic *Priere: An ABC* as Artifact and Critical Issue' (*SAC*

23[2001] 109–41). Quinn attributes the poem's comparative critical neglect to post-Reformation anti-Catholic prejudice, and insists on reminding us that this is a prayer as well as a lyric. He argues that its visual and aural achievements deserve more attention, and also suggests that 'Priere de Nostre Dame' would be a better title than the somewhat juvenile *An ABC*.

Books Reviewed

Armbruster, Karla, and Kathleen R. Wallace, eds. *Beyond Nature Writing: Expanding the Boundaries of Ecocriticism*. UPVirginia. [2001] pp. x + 372. hb $75 ISBN 0 8139 2013 2, pb $22.50 ISBN 0 8139 2014 0.

Bowden, Muriel. *A Reader's Guide to Geoffrey Chaucer*. SyracuseUP. [2001] pp. viii + 212. pb £14.50 ($19.95) ISBN 0 8156 0696 6.

Braswell, Mary Flowers. *Chaucer's 'Legal Fiction': Reading the Records*. FDUP. [2001] pp. 170. $36.50 ISBN 0 8386 3917 8.

Burger, Glenn, and Stephen Kruger, eds. *Queering the Middles Ages*. Medieval Cultures 27. UMinnP. [2001] pp. xxiii + 318. hb $49.95 ISBN 0 8166 3403 3, pb $19.95 ISBN 0 8166 3404 1.

Childress, Diana. *Chaucer's England*. Linnet. [2000] pp. xvii + 137. $25 ISBN 0 2080 2489 1.

Collette, Carolyn P. *Species, Phantasms, and Images: Vision and Medieval Psychology in the 'Canterbury Tales'*. UMichP. [2001] pp. ix + 208. $50 ISBN 0 4721 1161 2.

Currie, Stephen, ed. *The 1300s: Headlines in History*. Greenhaven. [2001] pp. 272. hb $44.95 ISBN 0 7377 0534 5, pb $28.70 ISBN 0 7377 0533 7.

Diller, Hans-Jürgen, and Manfred Görlach, eds. *Towards a History of English as a History of Genres*. Winter. [2001] pp. ix + 230. ISBN 3 8253 1240 2.

Forni, Kathleen. *The Chaucerian Apocrypha: A Counterfeit Canon*. UPFlor. [2001] pp. xviii + 260. £45.95 ($55) ISBN 0 8130 2427 7.

Gaylord, Alan T. *Essays on the Art of Chaucer's Verse*. Routledge. [2001] pp. viii + 449. $100 ISBN 0 8153 2951 2.

Gertz, SunHee Kim. *Chaucer to Shakespeare, 1337–1580*. Palgrave. [2001] pp. xi + 248. hb $55 ISBN 0 3337 2198 5, pb $21.95 ISBN 0 3337 2199 3.

Gutjahr, Paul C., and Megan L. Benton, eds. *Illuminating Letters: Typography and Literary Interpretation*. UMassP. [2001] pp. ix + 198. $34.95 ISBN 1 5584 9288 7.

Herring, Susan C., Pieter van Reenen, and Lene Schøsler, eds. *Textual Parameters in Older Languages*. Benjamins. [2000] pp. x + 448. $95 ISBN 9 0272 3702 6 (Eur.), ISBN 1 5561 9973 2 (US).

Hewett-Smith, Kathleen M., ed. *William Langland's 'Piers Plowman': A Book of Essays*. Medieval Casebooks 30. Routledge. [2001] pp. 261. $90 ISBN 0 8153 2804 4.

Holsinger, Bruce. *Music, Body, and Desire in Medieval Culture: Hildegard of Bingen to Chaucer*. StanfordUP. [2001] pp. xviii + 472. hb $65 ISBN 0 8047 3201 9, pb $24.95 ISBN 0 8047 4058 5.

Jacobs, Kathryn. *Marriage Contracts from Chaucer to the Renaissance Stage*. UPFlor. [2001] pp. viii + 181. £50.50 ($59.95) ISBN 0 8130 2102 2.

Johnston, Andrew James. *Clerks and Courtiers: Chaucer, Late Middle English Literature and the State Formation Process*. Winter. [2001] pp. 410. ISBN 3 8253 1234 8.

Kastovsky, Dieter, and Arthur Mettinger, eds. *The History of English in a Social Context: A Contribution to Historical Sociolinguistics*. MGruyter [2000] pp. xviii + 484. $131.15 ISBN 3 1101 6707 7.

Kay, Christian J., and Louise M. Sylvester, eds. *Lexis and Texts in Early English: Studies Presented to Jane Roberts*. Rodopi. [2001] pp. xiii + 302. $53 ISBN 9 0420 1001 0.

Kerby-Fulton, Kathryn, and Maidie Hilmo, eds. *The Medieval Professional Reader at Work: Evidence from Manuscripts of Chaucer, Langland, Kempe, and Gower*. UVict. [2001] pp. 239. $26 ISBN 0 9206 0477 3.

Knapp, Ethan. *The Bureaucratic Muse: Thomas Hoccleve and the Literature of Late Medieval England*. UPennP. [2001] pp. x + 210. $40 ISBN 0 2710 2135 7.

Mehl, Dieter. *English Literature in the Age of Chaucer*. Pearson. [2001] pp. xii + 252. $24 ISBN 0 5824 9299 8.

Minnis, A.J., ed. *Middle English Poetry: Texts and Traditions. Essays in Honour of Derek Pearsall*. Boydell. [2001] pp. xv + 304 £50 ISBN 1 9031 5309 3.

Myles, Robert, and David Williams, eds. *Chaucer and Language: Essays in Honour of Douglas Wurtele*. McG-QUP. [2001] pp. xxi + 250. $65 ISBN 0 7735 2182 8.

Perry, Curtis, ed. *Material Culture and Cultural Materialisms in the Middle Ages and Renaissance*. Arizona Studies in the Middle Ages and the Renaissance 5. Brepols. [2001] pp. xxiv + 246. $50 ISBN 2 5035 1074 4.

Pope, Rob. *How to Study Chaucer*, 2nd edn. St Martin's Press. [2001] pp. xi + 223. pb £10.99 ($17.95) ISBN 0 3337 6283 5.

Rhodes, Jim. *Poetry Does Theology: Chaucer, Grosseteste, and the Pearl-Poet*. UNDP. [2001] pp. xi + 324. hb $54.95 ISBN 0 2680 3869 4, pb $24.95 ISBN 0 2680 3870 8.

Robertson, Elizabeth, and Christine M. Rose, eds. *Representing Rape in Medieval and Early Modern Literature*. Palgrave. [2001] pp. ix + 453. £32.50 ISBN 0 3122 3648 4.

Rudd, Gillian. *The Complete Critical Guide to Geoffrey Chaucer*. Routledge. [2001] pp. xiii + 200. hb $80 ISBN 0 4152 0241 8, pb $19.95 ISBN 0 4152 0242 6.

Rylance, Rick, and Judy Simons, eds. *Literature in Context*. Palgrave. [2001] pp. xxix + 244. hb $55 ISBN 0 3338 0390 6, pb $22.95 ISBN 0 3338 0391 4.

Saunders, Corinne. *Chaucer*. Blackwell. [2001] pp. xi + 356. hb £60 ISBN 0 6312 1711 8, pb $29.95 ISBN 0 6312 1712 6.

Saunders, Corinne. *Rape and Ravishment in the Literature of Medieval England*. B&B. [2001] pp. vii + 343. £50 ($90) ISBN 0 8599 1610 3.

Schildgen, Brenda Deen. *Pagans, Tartars, Moslems, and Jews in Chaucer's 'Canterbury Tales'*. UFlorP. [2001] pp. 183. $59.95 ISBN 0 8130 2107 3.

Shoaf, R. Allen. *Chaucer's Body: The Anxiety of Circulation in the 'Canterbury Tales'*. UFlorP. [2001] pp. xvi + 162. $55 ISBN 0 8130 2423 4.

Taavitsainen, Irma, Terttu Nevalainen, Päivi Pahta, and Matti Rissanen, eds. *Placing Middle English in Context*. MGruyter. [2000] pp. x + 518. $142.25 ISBN 3 1101 6780 8.

Yeager, Robert F., and Charlotte C. Morse, eds. *Speaking Images: Essays in Honor of V.A. Kolve*. Pegasus. [2001] pp. xvii + 650. $90 ISBN 1 8898 1826 7.

V

The Sixteenth Century: Excluding Drama after 1550

ROS KING AND JOAN FITZPATRICK

This chapter has three sections: 1. General; 2. Sidney; 3. Spenser. Section 1 is by Ros King; sections 2 and 3 are by Joan Fitzpatrick.

1. General

Recent work on the sixteenth century continues two essential undertakings: making a far greater range of texts more widely available in either facsimile or edited form, and complicating our responses to the literature and culture of the period. We are beginning to insist on a more subtle approach to religious difference, and are countering the notion that a sense of the self was a late Renaissance invention. The Ashgate series, The Early Modern Englishwoman: A Facsimile Library of Essential Works, reflects these issues. The general editors' aim, outlined in the preface, is to 'remedy one of the major obstacles to the advancement of feminist criticism of the early modern period, namely the limited availability of the very texts upon which the field is based', and to include a range of texts 'both by women and for and about them'. The texts for each volume are selected, and prefaced in a short introductory note, by a leading scholar. Anne Lake Prescott (*Elizabeth and Mary Tudor*) points out that the translation by the 11-year-old Princess Elizabeth of *Le Miroir de l'âme pécheresse* by Marguerite of Angoulême [1531] had political as well as religious significance since it insists that 'only God, not human willpower, has saving force', and that the theology faculty at the Sorbonne had therefore attempted to have it censored. The text might well also have had personal significance for the young princess: 'Margaret tells God gratefully that he forgives his unfaithful "wife", whereas human kings would send them to be executed'. This volume also prints a series of poems predicated on the letters of Elizabeth's name and the translation by her sister Mary, in conjunction with Nicholas Udall and perhaps her chaplain, of Erasmus's *Paraphrase ... upon the gospel of sainct John*, although the introduction does not further contribute to the debate about how much of this work was actually by Mary.

In the same series, Valerie Wayne (*Anne Cooke Bacon*) presents various important translations by Anne Bacon, including that of one of the most seminal texts of the English Reformation, John Jewel's *An Apologie or answere in defence of the Churche of Englande*. Written originally in Latin, this text must owe its influence amongst the laity to the strength, clarity and facility of Bacon's English: 'We affirme togither with the auncient fathers, that the body of Christe is not eaten but of the good and faithfull, and of those that are endued with the spirit of Christe. Their doctrine is, that Christes very bodie effectually, & as they speake, really and substantially, may not only be eaten of the wicked and unfaithful men, but also (which is monstrous to be spoken) of myse and dogges' (Mii^v). Lee Cullen Khanna (*Early Tudor Translators: Margaret Beaufort, Margaret More Roper and Mary Basset*) has made a selection that presents these well-educated women, the first of whom was the mother of Henry VII, as patrons as well as practitioners of the essential godly task of the translation of devotional treatises. If there is a criticism to be made of this important series, however, it is that the texts, once selected, are left to fend for themselves. One is left wanting more in the way of contextualization: longer introductions, and even some finding tools—index or annotated contents pages—to help one get around the texts, most of which, as reproductions of sixteenth-century black letter, are physically demanding to read.

G.W. Pigman III's edition of George Gascoigne's *A Hundreth Sundrie Flowres* has similar problems, although for opposite reasons. This is an immensely scholarly edition, with copious and rigorous annotation of one of the most interesting of little-known and neglected writers. Pigman has evidently been absolutely immersed in this material for some years, but his own familiarity with it, evidenced by his system of abbreviation and referencing, does not contribute to a reader-friendly volume. One fears that this book, on its own, may not contribute to a wider reawakening of interest in its subject, which would be a shame. Gascoigne's work is interesting on a number of distinct levels. He was a colourful character, chronically in debt and embroiled in the law, who regarded himself as a soldier who also wrote, and who, rather engagingly, scattered his garden at home with inscriptions that likened the life of man to the cycle of the gardening year. He was a member of the English forces sent to aid the Dutch Revolt, and writes extraordinary eyewitness descriptions in verse of military life. His near shipwreck on one occasion, and his graphic representation of what he sees as the perfidy of the Dutch captain who endangered him—including snatches of Dutch speech—are grippingly recounted. He also had an active theoretical interest in the development of English literature, which resulted practically in his translation of *Jocasta*—the first classical tragedy to appear in English—and in *Certayne notes of Instruction concerning the making of verse or ryme in English*, although he protests 'I holde a preposterous order in my traditions, but as I sayed before, I wryte moved by good wil, and not to shewe my skill' (p. 461). Pigman's edition unpicks the difficult question of the relationship between *A Hundreth Sundrie Flowres* [1573] and *The Posies of George Gascoigne Esquire* [1575], which raises interesting questions about the concept of authorship and the nature of book production in the period. The earlier publication presents the shorter poems as if they were a collection by different authors. The later book reprints most of the same material, including the two plays (*Jocasta* and *Supposes*), the prose work, *The Adventures of Master F.J.*, and the shorter poems, although it gives these in a different order, with different titles, and drops the pretence of their multiple authorship. A few other works are added. With the exception of *Adventures*, there is little revision to any of these texts, but the difference in presentation means that the two books appear as fundamentally different and 'not merely two editions of the same book'. *Flowres* is 'an anthology by diverse gentlemen without patent moral intent' while *Posies* is 'a record of Gascoigne's wasted youth, a warning to others which marks the reformation of this prodigal son' (p. li). Pigman takes *Flowres* as his copy text, and follows this with the additions from the *Posies*. Gascoigne is a poet to whom we should pay more attention, while the literature that resulted in so many different languages from the Dutch Revolt demands an interdisciplinary study.

A collection of essays edited by A.J. Piesse, *Sixteenth-Century Identities*, starts with a self-styled 'subversive' essay by Douglas Gray ('Finding Identity in the Middle Ages'), which, given the weight of strident opinion that it seeks to counter, is admirably restrained and careful. It is followed by two essays which explore the identity through topographical naming of the English countryside: Victor Watts, 'English Place-Names in the Sixteenth Century: The Search for Identity', and John Scattergood, 'John Leland's Itinerary and the Identity of England'. Leland's work was based as much on literary researches as on direct observation made on various travels across the country, but either way his object was the construction of a geo-historical identity for the kingdom. He wrote to Cromwell in the light of the Act for the Dissolution of Smaller Monasteries in 1536 asking for permission to acquire for the royal library the manuscripts they housed as a 'great profit to students and honour to this realm'. According to Bale, this also served to ensure that 'the scriptures of God might therby be more purely taught then afore in the Romish popes time' (Scattergood, pp. 61 and 63). Leland was evidently aware that the appearance of the land was fundamentally affected by its ownership and the use to which it was put and that the dissolution of the monasteries was having a profound effect on the identity of the country, not just culturally, but also physically. His seemingly haphazard—because never completed—project thus preserves a picture of England at a time of radical change. Ciaran Brady's essay in the same collection, 'New English Ideology in Ireland and the Two Sir William Herberts', then proposes a reassessment of William Herbert's Latin manuscript, *Croftus*, concerning the settlement of Ireland. He seeks to reconcile what others have seen as the contradictory nature of Herbert's (ultimately non-influential) treatise. Herbert, who was also a landholder in Wales, wanted to apply to Ireland the imposition of English law that was the essential feature of the union with Wales. Persuasively, Brady argues that Herbert deplored the cruelty of the English soldiery in Ireland and that his ambitious proposal for two generously funded universities to be financed by a special tax levied on Irish villages was an attempt to extend colonial control more humanely and justly than was possible through military occupation: 'Through taxation, which would be the means of defeudalising, demilitarising and re-educating its people, Ireland would be transformed into a society where economic wealth, political power and cultural leadership were correlatives; and its metamorphosis into a model English community would be complete' (p. 103).

A useful overview of the history of biblical commentary and translation across Europe in the fifteenth and sixteenth centuries is provided in a collection of essays edited by Richard Griffiths, *The Bible in the Renaissance*. This book is a salutary reminder of the 'blurred edges' in Renaissance reformation politics. In particular, the chapter by Ceri Davies, 'The Welsh Bible and Renaissance Learning', on William Morgan, translator of the first bible in Welsh (1588), is written with enthusiasm and also demonstrates the contradictions thrown up by the practicalities of colonialism. While the secular arm of Elizabethan government required the suppression of the Welsh language in the operation of the law, the politics of the Reformation pulled in exactly the opposite direction. It was clearly a denial of the tenets of the English Church to impose an English-language bible and prayer book on monoglot Welsh speakers. Morgan's bible not only kept the Welsh language alive but, like Tyndale's English bible, on which so much of King James's authorized version was based, was also instrumental in developing Welsh as a written, literary language.

Jennifer and Richard Britnell, eds., *Vernacular Literature and Current Affairs in the Early Sixteenth Century*, is another collection of essays that takes an interdisciplinary perspective, exploring the relationship between courts, poets and print cultures in French, English and Scottish contexts. Greg Walker, in 'John Skelton and the Royal Court', sees the early Tudor court as a 'complex and amorphous phenomenon: a mansion of many rooms' with a multitude of subcultures. He argues that 'the notion of "court" or "courtly" poetry therefore needs to be treated with care' (p. 1) and demonstrates that the inconsistencies in Skelton's work are the result often of 'simultaneously addressing more than one audience in a single text' (p. 13). Sarah Carpenter, in 'David Lindsay and James V', is interested in the way in which court literature does not necessarily simply reflect events but may seek to influence them. This is a period 'where the possessing of certain books, especially in the vernacular, might itself constitute a political act; and where literature was generally regarded as a natural form in which current affairs might be debated or even conducted' (pp. 136–7). With a slightly different emphasis, Julia Boffey, in 'Wynkyn de Worde, Richard Pynson, and the English Printing of Texts Translated from French', scrupulously demonstrates the various ways in which 'English printers could turn to French texts in their search for copy' (p. 182).

Ian Green, *Print and Protestantism in Early Modern England*, surveys the complete run of Protestant titles published in England from the 1530s to the 1720s, from bibles to chapbooks, ballads and cautionary murder tales. Green focuses this extensive, detailed study of an extremely long 'Long Reformation' period by adopting a statistical approach wherever possible, concentrating on those works which sold well over an extended period, although balancing this by also looking at those titles which were evidently influential but which did not sell in huge numbers because of their size (such as Foxe's *Actes and Monuments*), and others, such as the ballads and murder tales, which, if not individual bestsellers, were part of an ubiquitous popular genre. This analysis further contributes to the idea that there was more than one Protestantism on offer in the sixteenth century, and tells a rich story of the interplay between religious convictions and the search for commercial profit.

John N. King, '"The Light of Printing": William Tyndale, John Foxe, John Day and Early Modern Print Culture' (*RQ* 54[2001] 52–85), re-emphasizes the importance of the printing press as an agent of religious change, deepens our understanding of the literary influence of Tyndale's biblical translation and continues recent re-evaluation of the work of Eamon Duffy: 'In focusing on the smashing of saints' images, shattering of stained-glass windows, dismantling of altars, and despoliation of shrines, these scholars maintain an embarrassing silence about the emergence of a richly diverse and powerful literature grounded upon Tyndale's scriptural translations' (p. 53).

Sharon Achinstein, 'John Foxe and the Jews' (*RQ* 54[2001] 86–120), argues that the earliest edition of Foxe's *Book of Martyrs* [1563] takes an 'ecumenical or even anthropological' approach to the Jews, but that later editions emphasized the 'danger Jews posed to Christian society', reorganizing the material so that 'positive' approaches to the Jews 'indexed in the 1563 edition dropped out of the guide to the reader, *though they did not drop out of the text of the work*' (p. 111). Foxe can therefore be seen calling 'upon age-old stereotypes in order to construct a new relation to Jews for reforming purposes' that is tied to Elizabethan foreign policy. Foxe's true church is a universal one: 'the calling upon the name of the Lorde, is not unseparably bound to place, tyme, or persones: but that the largesse of his mercie is extended also upon all people, nations, and tongues, whether they be Jewes, or Gentiles, Scythians or Indians' (sig. K3r; p. 114).

Arnold Hunt, in 'Licensing and Religious Censorship in Early Modern England' (in Hadfield, ed., *Literature and Censorship*, pp. 127–46), makes a similar point about the extent to which nonconformists were initially accommodated within the established Church of England even though by the end of the sixteenth century it had become more difficult to ignore such differences in belief. In another essay in the same volume, '"Right puisante and terrible priests": The Role of the Anglican Church in Elizabethan State Censorship' (pp. 75–94), Richard McCabe makes a powerful argument that the objective of the 'Bishops' Ban' of 1599, which has been the subject of a great deal of recent interest, was political rather than moral control. This collection, which also includes essays by Janet Clare, Richard Dutton, Cyndia Clegg, David Loades, Annabel Patterson and Hadfield himself, among others, brings into close proximity a number of opposing interpretations of the effects of the various organs and decrees of censorship during the Elizabethan and Stuart periods, and the interrelationship between the demands of the state and the needs of the Stationers' Company to regulate its own business. The effect of the essays, taken together, is to deepen and complicate understanding, and remind us that in this difficult and sometimes dangerous area things are rarely straightforward or consistent.

Anthony Miller's *Roman Triumphs and Early Modern English Culture* is a subtle and detailed study of the military aspects of triumph in Renaissance literature and culture. Miller appropriately criticizes Roy Strong's 'triumphalist' and royalist approach to the subject, which has led to the neglect, for example, of the use of triumph in republican Venice, and refutes 'the similar acceptance' of triumphalist royal hegemony that 'has tended to mark "new historicist" work in this field' (p. 13). But his aim to 'give a new historical location to canonical literary texts that include triumphs, and to elucidate the ways in which triumphal discourse contributes to their literary interest' cannot be fully achieved by simply deciding not to treat the non-militaristic versions of Renaissance triumphs. So many of these later uses of the form consciously play with the tension between the display of personal power that is the military triumph and the celebration of the rise of the rational soul that was the common interpretation of Petrarch's allegorical *Trionfi*—a sequence of poems describing the successive triumphs of Love, Chastity, Death, Fame, Time and Eternity. These, and their derivatives, therefore furnished an ideal form for celebrating the Elizabethan and Jacobean imperial projects—power through peace—while, more or less, containing those who more openly sought war. Petrarch's sequence of poems was hugely influential in all forms of Renaissance art and celebratory ritual, and was translated into English by Lord Morley (probably published between 1553 and 1556). A direct comparison between these two strands of triumph in Miller's book would have been immensely helpful since those many studies of civic triumphs have equally neglected the military form.

The ceremonial progress of Anne of Cleves and the thirteen trumpeters loaned to her by her brother-in-law, the Duke Elector of Saxony, that announced her arrival in the towns along her route to England and marriage to Henry VIII occupies only a comparatively short section of Retha M. Warnicke's *The Marrying of Anne of Cleves: Royal Protocol in Tudor England*. In fact even its subtitle does not do full justice to the scope of this book, which in effect is a history of diplomatic and familial relationships between the princes of Renaissance Europe, with fascinating accounts of the types of ceremonial in which these were conducted. When Anne finally arrived in England after several weeks of delay caused by bad weather, she was visited in her rooms at Rochester by Henry VIII in disguise. She was watching a bull-baiting from the window and gave him scant attention. Henry was much given to disguising and the incident has normally been regarded as an example of his idiosyncratic behaviour, but here, as elsewhere in the book, Warnicke demonstrates that both he and indeed Anne, in affecting not to know who it was who had burst in upon her, were acting according to established protocol, a time-honoured ceremony for the greeting of foreign-born wives in order to 'nourish love'. She also shows that Henry's subsequent distaste for Anne probably derives not so much from a dislike for her appearance in the flesh, as an anxiety about a marriage with Francis of Lorraine to whom she had been contracted in her youth. There was a real question about her freedom to wed, which raised old ghosts, although politically at that time Henry had no option but to go through with the marriage. The book, indeed, casts a new light on Henry's actions with regard to his six marriages. It seems that he chose Anne as his bride 'in response to the Franco-Imperial alliance. When he was unable to consummate the union, he sought the reasons for his incapacity in the religious and scientific knowledge and lore of his day' (p. 262). Warnicke concludes that Henry's behaviour following Jane's death in childbed 'compared favourably with that of other bereaved rulers who sought to remarry for the purpose of begetting legitimate children to secure their dynasty's future' (p. 263).

The striking point about the collection that goes under the title *Allegory in the Theatre* (in the Theta series on Tudor theatre) is that the essays it contains deny their collective subject. In one sense, as the editor Peter Happé points out, virtually *all* sixteenth-century drama is allegorical, either because it makes use of personifications of virtues and vices as characters or because of what a contemporary audience was likely to read into it. Some of the essays therefore have a hard time of it, just rising above the enumeration of instances: 'It would be tedious to quote all the passages in Wager's play which pick up these ideas' (Francis Guinle, '"Where angels fear to tread": Allegory and Protestant Ideology', p. 146). On the other hand, as Greg Walker astutely points out, 'when allegory is presented as drama, the result is *always* concrete. The theatre abhors abstraction, its common currency is the human form, and when thus *embodied* allegory is inevitably solidified, personalised, and dis-abstracted' ('The State's Two Bodies: *Respublica* and the Allegory of Governance', p. 119). Bob Godfrey, however, seeks to provide an actantial methodology for distinguishing between different types of construction in early Tudor plays that are normally lumped together as moralities, while, in 'Representing Spiritual Truth in *Mankind* and *Ane Satyre of the Thrie Estaitis*', Amanda Piesse, who regards the agendas of her two chosen plays as 'clearly different', draws on her involvement with students in a production of *Mankind* at Trinity College, Dublin. 'We wondered how to communicate the sense we had of knowing contradictory truths simultaneously, of the audience being aware that there is a desired spiritual narrative (what the audience knows to be "right") which runs at times consistently with and at time diametrically opposed to the physical narrative taking place on stage' (p. 135). The solution was to incorporate the skills of a gifted student shadow puppeteer. Piesse describes and defends this decision, but—perhaps understandably, since she was involved—does not fully analyse its effect. With the exception of Jean-Paul Debax's valiant analysis of a neglected sermon play, 'The Use of Allegory in the Interlude: *St John the Evangelist*', what is missing from the collection is much sense of the plays as entertainment, and in particular the dislocation that comes from comedy. I would suggest that, at least in a theatrical context, it is comedy rather than allegory that enables us 'to think more than one thing at the same time'. Debax echoes Piesse in concluding that the 'characters are what they *say*, more than what their names would suggest according to a mysterious transmutation'. Like Walker, he denies the usefulness in this context of the term 'allegorical' and prefers instead to think of the characters as 'bearers of a collective discourse, partly orthodox, partly popular, i.e. unconventional or critical, in which the audience found a reflection of their own vision of the world' (p. 101).

Darryll Grantley, in *Wit's Pilgrimage: Drama and the Social Impact of Education in Early Modern England*, makes a compendious study of the influence of education on the playwrights and audiences of the sixteenth century, the uses of drama as an educational tool, and the instances of education within the drama. It is well researched, but he too neglects the importance of comedy and betrays little sense of the political, emotional or affective impact of this material in performance.

It is the desire to redraw our modern vision of the Renaissance world that lies behind Lisa Jardine's and Jerry Brotton's *Global Interests: Renaissance between East and West*. This is a handsomely produced volume, its 185 pages of argument comprising approximately sixty-six pages of illustrations, many of them in colour. The text itself is, by the authors' own admission, a 'broad-brush argument' liberally scattered with 'we are persuaded' and 'we feel'— 'Sometimes, we are persuaded that ours is a new kind of "cultural history", unrestricted by nation or moment' (p. 7). It consists of swingeing condemnation of the work of iconographical art critics such as Ernst Gombrich and some uneasy negotiation of Greenblatt's 'Renaissance self-fashioning', all interspersed with extended passages giving sometimes academic, sometimes elementary information about the nature or production of the commodities discussed—medals, tapestries, horses, etc. This is not always accurate—for example alum is a corrosive, a mordant used to intensify colour, not a dye (p. 72)—and sometimes the desire to make a particular point overwhelms the authors' reading of the evidence they adduce. The interesting letter to Queen Elizabeth from Johannes Sturm arguing for the secret importation of German equine bloodstock in order to strengthen English horse production (and of course also urging his own suitability as a projector) is predicated on a sentence pointing out the evident risks and expense of relying on foreign, mercenary cavalry, or 'reiters', and their horses. Sturm is saying that the importation of a few German stallions and skilled grooms, who as underlings could be persuaded to keep quiet, would obviate the danger by strengthening English bloodlines and increasing horse production at minimum cost. The authors, however, transform the *opening* sentence of what is a straightforwardly underhand business manifesto for an aspect of the arms trade into a *conclusion* with disturbing racial overtones: 'Somewhat surprisingly, perhaps, crossbreeding of this kind was regarded as strengthening the bloodline. Yet at the same time, there is a clear implication that an influx of foreign matter polluted and weakened: "There is nothing which more weakens the strength of a kingdom than forces of foreign soldiers and especially horse", wrote Sturm' (p. 159).

2. Sidney

A number of pieces focusing on Philip Sidney's *Arcadia* appeared in 2001. In an original and absorbing essay Gavin Alexander, 'Sidney's Interruptions' (*SP* 98[2001] 184–204), attends to the notion of completion and incompletion in responses to Sidney's life, death, and works after 1586. Drawing on various genres, including elegies, biographies, editions, and imitations, he considers the fascination surrounding Sidney's death and the incomplete nature of his works in relation to classical rhetorical theory, especially the figure of *aposiopesis*, not finishing what you have started. Biographies which consider Sidney's death either draw upon the *ars moriendi* tradition, which emphasizes the good death, and completion, or focus on the untimely nature of his death, and incompletion. The rhetoric of both is evident in Thomas Moffett's *Nobilis*, a Latin biography in manuscript commissioned by Sidney's sister for her son William. There were also two ways of talking about Sidney's works, one emphasizing the perfect planning of them, so that despite their unfinished state they were seen as somehow complete, and the other seeing them as fragments which could be ended by another author. Sidney's sister, Mary Sidney, countess of Pembroke, is particularly attentive to what Alexander calls 'Sidney's interruptions': she fills in all the blanks in her 1593 edition of his *Arcadia* and produces a work 'augmented and ended' (p. 191) where Greville's 1590 edition stressed incompletion. Alexander is not impressed by her efforts to complete works by Sidney and others, demonstrating how, in her translation of Garnier's *Marc Antoine*, the addition of two lines ruins the sense of the original. Pembroke's 'mania for ending' (p. 196) and its interference with the original sense of a piece can also be seen in her completion of Sidney's *Psalmes*: where Sidney employed stanzaic deviation Pembroke opted for stanzaic regularity, not understanding 'that asymmetry can give greater poetic closure' (p. 197). Alexander notes that Sidney based his new version of the *Arcadia* on 'a structure of interruptions' (p. 199) and a range of examples from the poem is considered in order to show that Sidney's use of *aposiopesis* is quite deliberate and expressive rather than accidental.

In a lengthy and detailed essay Kristin Hanson, 'Quantitative Meter in English: The Lesson of Sir Philip Sidney' (*EL&L* 5[2001] 41–91), considers Sidney's experiments in writing classical quantitative verse. Hanson notes that, although poets have been interested in the possibility of quantitative metre in English for centuries, experimentation with the form has not resulted in any real tradition. There was considerable interest in the form during the Renaissance, with most poets trying to write such verse and many discussing its principles, but most rejected it in favour of a stress-based metre, and there is disagreement amongst critics as to why they reached this conclusion. Sidney's quantitative experiments belong to his earliest verse, and his abandonment of them demonstrates his dissatisfaction with quantitative metre in English, but Hanson questions the plausibility of the theory put forward by some that he was 'incapable of apprehending a significant aspect of English phonology' (p. 42). D. Attridge credited Sidney with discoveries about the length of English vowels, the distinction between weight and stress, and innovations in the disposition of stress, but considered Sidney guilty of 'arbitrariness, inconsistency, and dependency on spelling' (p. 43), believing that such verse was admired because the Renaissance valued artifice and written language over spoken. Hanson's view is that Attridge does little justice to Sidney's phonological discoveries about quantitative metre in English, a view based on new developments in phonological theory. Of particular interest to Sidney specialists is section 4 (pp. 61–85), which provides a detailed analysis of Sidney's practice in the *Old Arcadia* and how it relates to his earlier poems. Hanson concludes that Sidney's practice is 'much more phonologically well-founded that it has been held to be' (p. 85) and that he and subsequent poets abandoned the project of quantitative metre in English not because it was too hard, as some critics have claimed, but because it did not suit their purposes.

Kathryn DeZur, in 'Defending the Castle: The Political Problem of Rhetorical Seduction and Good Huswifery in Sidney's *Old Arcadia*' (*SP* 98[2001] 93–113), reads Sidney's *Old Arcadia* in the context of sixteenth-century opinions concerning the effect of rhetoric upon women. While humanists regarded rhetoric as empowering for men, there was concern that women were more susceptible, and that rhetoric's power effected in them a loss of critical reasoning, thus reducing their ability to function as good wives. Sidney's *Arcadia* suggests that if women are not good huswives, of either the household or state, then political anarchy is likely. For Sidney good huswifery involves female chastity, since sexual passion clouds the judgement, and throughout the *Arcadia* he uses the metaphor of the castle to indicate the household, female body, and polis, which women must defend. DeZur usefully traces the relationship between chastity and rhetoric in guidebooks on female education in the early modern period, where some writers indicate that women are so susceptible to persuasive fictions that they should be prevented from reading certain materials, and others argued that learned women make better wives since they are intellectual companions for their husbands and more able to defend their chastity. As DeZur rightly points out, the debate surrounding the pros and cons of female education as a defence against rhetorical seduction became more crucial when governance of the state was at stake. Close attention is paid to three key female characters from the *Arcadia*—Gynecia, Philoclea, and Pamela—as examples of appropriate and inappropriate education for rulers. Sidney's most explicit linking of household and state is in the third eclogue, where a link is made between the good wife who rules a household and the good queen who rules the state, both of which depend on a balance of command and obedience. Of the three royal female characters in *Arcadia* only one, Pamela, is a good huswife and ruler, since both Gynecia and Philoclea give in to Pyrocles' rhetoric, but even here Sidney leaves his readers in doubt as to her judgement of rhetoric since she is prone to mistakes.

Two excellent collections of essays, Pincombe, ed., *The Anatomy of Tudor Literature*, and Robertson and Rose, eds., *Representing Rape in Medieval and Early Modern Literature*, contain notable chapters on Sidney. Regina Schneider, 'Late Tudor Narrative Voice(s): Philip Sidney and Barnaby Rich' (in Pincombe, ed., pp. 90–7), traces the parallel literary development of Philip Sidney and Barnaby Rich, usually considered to be two very different writers. Schneider notes that, in both Rich's *Pleasant Dialogue* and Sidney's 'Eclogues', the genre of philosophical dialogue is combined with anthology. At the same time both writers had started to use verse and prose together in their work, and in both cases the narrator's voice became less central, thus increasing the fictional nature of the writing. When Sidney's *New Arcadia* and Rich's *Brusanus* were written in the mid-1580s the distance between author and story had increased, with characters becoming more central to informing the reader about gaps in the plot. Schneider claims that it is 'this new and more sophisticated understanding of narrative structures that sets Sidney and Rich apart from their contemporaries' (p. 95). In their prose fiction Sidney and Rich were interested in a plurality of voices, something Schneider connects with their Protestantism, and they developed a new and more sophisticated understanding of narrative structures not evident in the work of their contemporaries.

Sidney's *Old Arcadia* and *Apology for Poetry* are the focus of Amy Greenstadt's essay '"Rapt from himself": Rape and the Poetics of Corporeality in Sidney's *Old Arcadia*' (in Robertson and Rose, eds., pp. 31–49), and both texts are carefully considered in the context of the ambiguity surrounding the definition of rape in early modern culture. In this period female beauty was identified as a primary agent of rapture, 'a ravishing power that seduced men's senses and overturned their higher mental faculties of reason and will' (p. 311). Ravishing effects were also ascribed to literary works, which suggests a connection between the aesthetic meaning of 'ravishment' and its use in English law, where it was a synonym for rape. In the *Old Arcadia* and the *Apology* Sidney 'attempts to reconceive the relationship between author and reader by investigating and questioning the concept of ravishment' (p. 312). Greenstadt considers 'the models of subjectivity that Early Modern rape law both reflected and enforced' (pp. 312–13) and how in the *Old Arcadia* Sidney's depiction of the crimes of ravishment negotiates complex and interrelated sexual and textual issues. In the *Apology* Sidney 'attempts to envision new models of textual production by portraying the paradoxical figures of the cross-dressed man and the desiring yet virtuous woman' (p. 313), who seem to transcend forces of textual and sexual violation but are limited by depictions of gender relations elsewhere in his work.

3. Spenser

Two important books on Spenser appeared: a monograph and a collection of essays. Jon A. Quitslund's solid and scholarly *Spenser's Supreme Fiction: Platonic Natural Philosophy and 'The Faerie Queene'* traces the Platonic philosophical tradition in Spenser's fiction. Quitslund believes that Spenser is more indebted than has been hitherto acknowledged to the writings of Marsilio Ficino, in particular his commentary on the *Symposium* and the *De Amore* or *On Love*. In part 1, 'The Maker's Mind', Quitslund announces that his study is 'author-centred, rather than reader- or character- or genre-centred' (p. 19), and chapter 1 is particularly focused on Spenser's careful development of a poetic persona, especially the dangers he encountered in striking the difficult balance between imitation and creation. Throughout his study Quitslund considers a range of episodes from *The Faerie Queene*, but there is particular focus on the Garden of Adonis in Book III and how its themes relate to Platonic philosophical concerns. Quitslund shows himself to be especially adept at thematic analysis and the close reading of particular episodes, but his study is not under-theorized since it is also informed by new historicism and other modern theoretical concerns. This book is broad in scope, but a usefully detailed general index and an index of names and places in *The Faerie Queene* help the reader who is attracted to the analysis of particular episodes.

Hadfield, ed., *The Cambridge Companion to Spenser*, is a collection of thirteen specially commissioned essays by prominent Spenserians in which a wide range of subjects is considered, as might be expected from a writer as eclectic and complex as Spenser. The book is divided into sections, with chapters on Spenser's literary work, the contexts within which he wrote, and his literary influences. That *The Faerie Queene* does not dominate is welcome—Spenser's pastoral poetry and minor poems are considered—but one would have thought that his prose tract *A View of the Present State of Ireland* would merit individual consideration. This objection might be countered by the fact that the *View* is discussed in particular essays, and indeed Richard A. McCabe's treatment of the text in his essay, 'Ireland: Policy, Poetics and Parody', is particularly good. Other subjects considered include Spenser's biography, his classical influences, his position on religious matters, and his attitude to gender politics, including his negotiations with Petrarchanism. Each essay contains a useful 'further reading' section and a very usable index, and the collection is an important addition to the field of Spenser studies.

Two essays from a publication of conference proceedings considered Spenser's *Faerie Queene* in the context of *A View of the Present State of Ireland*. Swen Voekel's offering, 'Fashioning a Tudor Body: Civility and State-Formation in *The Faerie Queene* and *A View of the Present State of Ireland*' (in Pincombe, ed., pp. 142–53), is a clever reading of *The Faerie Queene* in the light of early modern efforts by the state to absorb or eliminate aristocratic and religious rivals in the peripheral location of Ireland. Civil servants such as Sir John Davies were worried by the delegation of authority in Ireland, since local magnates held power that was unique to the state in England. Davies thought that incivility in Ireland and a lack of agrarian improvement were the consequences of forms of lordship where the individual is tied to the clan. In *The Faerie Queene* the situation in Ireland is represented in gigantic and monstrous figures whose primitive relationship to the earth is related to an inherent rebelliousness against civility and political order. These monstrous figures threaten the bodily integrity of the armoured knight and the body politic. Voekel focuses particularly on Arthur's defence of Alma's castle, the allegorical civilized and temperate body, against the siege of Maleger, who is associated with primitiveness and the earth 'and more precisely with a non-productive and unnatural (or, paradoxically, too natural) relationship to the land' (p. 149). The creation of proper divisions was considered necessary to occupy virgin land, and these are violated by Maleger, who is strengthened by a primitive bond with the earth. For the New English, effective occupation must be preceded by effective cultivation of the land, and in *The Faerie Queene* and the *View* that cultivation is shown to be 'the product of cuttings (metaphorical and quite literal) of the sword of state' (p. 151). In both texts the message is that civil society in Ireland would come about by planting New English tenants on Irish land, but violence was necessary 'to carve out the civil space of the English property-owning individual on the margins of the emerging British empire' (p. 152). This is a thoughtful and persuasive essay which is alert to the Irish context of the growth of state power in the early modern period and Spenser's role in the process.

Efterpi Mitsi's 'Veiling Medusa: Arthur's Shield in *The Fairy Queen*' (in Pincombe, ed., pp. 130–41) is a study of Spenser's iconoclastic treatment of ekphrasis in *The Faerie Queene*, where the poet juxtaposes descriptions of dangerous works of art with an undecorated shield that destroys idols and counterfeits. Arthur's supernatural shield evokes both the shield of Perseus and the gaze of Medusa, with the artifice of his armour recalling images of falsehood, pride and brightness in the poem, thus illustrating 'the ambiguity not only of art, artifice … but also of the significance of brightness, the quality which in *The Faerie Queene* characterizes both hero and villain, both truth and counterfeit' (p. 131). The ekphrasis of Arthur's armour stretches over eight stanzas and interrupts the narrative in the same way that ekphrases, especially of armour, interrupt the narrative of the *Iliad* and the *Aeneid*. Arthur's armour is similar to that of epic heroes, and it is the shield's mythic origin and romantic ancestry which invest it with a spiritual and national significance. Britomart, Arthur's historical counterpart, sees the future in another artefact created by Merlin, his enchanted mirror, and her focus on Artegall's face evokes idolatry which is only dispelled by her chastity and quest. Merlin's mirror, which creates idols, and Arthur's shield, which breaks them, are linked through a mistrust of images, and Spenser uses the myth of Medusa to cast doubt on the ability of pictures to recount history. The shield is of great significance from a providential, nationalistic, and iconoclastic point of view, and it is fitting that it should dominate Book V, which deals with contemporary history, particularly English antagonism toward Spain. In *The Faerie Queene*, as in the *Aeneid*, the shield is associated with the quest for national identity but also unease with a ruler's mode of governance. The *View*'s overt criticism of Elizabeth's policies is veiled in *The Faerie Queene*, for although the shield can destroy monsters it cannot protect heroes or poets from criticism. Allegory is an important form of protection and can be considered in the context of iconoclasm and Arthur's shield as a destroyer of counterfeits and idols: in his iconography of Elizabeth, Spenser decides to veil and shadow her so that there can be no danger of creating an idol.

Two essays from another collection explored Spenser's debt to Ovid. In an excellent piece by Michael Pincombe, 'The Ovidian Hermaphrodite: Moralizations By Peend and Spenser' (in Stanivukovic, ed., *Ovid and the Renaissance Body*, pp. 155–70), Jonathan Bate is taken to task for imposing 'a modern "romantic" fantasy' (p. 168) on Ovid's fable of Hermaphroditus and Salmacis in his *Shakespeare and Ovid*. Pincombe draws attention to the sinister side of the legend told by Ovid and considers the satirical treatment of the figure of the hermaphrodite in a poem by Thomas Peend, the *Pleasant Fable of Hermaphroditus and Salmacis* [1565], and Spenser's episode featuring Amoret and Scudamour at the end of the 1590 *Faerie Queene*. Bate emphasized the mutuality and sexual equality evoked by the figure, but Pincombe points out that Jonathan Crewe's reading of the union, in his *Trials of Authorship*, is less anachronistic. Crewe thought that Hermaphroditus represented 'immobility, bondage, repetition, and pain', an interpretation similar to Peend's, who thought the figure 'an allegory of enslavement' (p. 156). In the Amoret and Scudamour episode Spenser refers his readers, not to Ovid's treatment of the tale, but rather to an obscure Roman hermaphroditic statue which, Pincombe argues, he intended as an image of decadence and thus sexual concupiscence. According to Pincombe, Peend sees the story of Hermaphroditus as 'an allegory of the lapse into "our beastly nature" which awaits the sexually innocent' (p. 164) and the pool of Salmacis, in which the transformation takes place, as a type of hell. For Pincombe the embrace between Scudamour and Amoret can be read in similar terms: Scudamour can be compared to Red Cross in the presence of Duessa since, although Amoret's sprite is released in lawful love, Scudamour is guilty of carnal concupiscence.

Judith Deitch, 'The Girl He Left Behind: Ovidian *Imitatio* and the Body of Echo in Spenser's "Epithalamion"' (in Stanivukovic, ed., pp. 224–38), complains that criticism on the figure of Echo from Ovid's myth is usually concerned with 'abstractions of echo and echoing—as intertextuality, resonance, imitation, or belatedness' but that there is insufficient focus on the myth itself. Echo's passive repetition of other voices 'embodies classical imitation at its most facile and fragmented, as an icon of failed poetic descendance' (p. 224), but in Spenser's *Epithalamion* the invocation of Echo close to a female body 'cancels any figuration of the poet as epigone by transferring the ineffectual image onto the available woman' (p. 224). By ensuring that the bride is the focus of creation Spenser asserts the dominant role of the masculine poet. In Ovid's myth Echo's story is a sad one and a curious choice for a wedding song, but in Spenser's poem 'the threat of Echo as doomed repetition is evoked in order to be revoked, rejected, and transcended' (p. 225). Deitch asserts that there is no anxiety in Spenser's use of Echo as poetic imitation, but rather that he demonstrates that he is a poet very much in control of his sources.

In a collection focusing on war, Joan Curbet, 'Repressing the Amazon: Cross-Dressing and Militarism in Edmund Spenser's *The Faerie Queene*' (in Usandizaga and Monnickendam, eds., *Dressing Up For War: Transformations of Gender and Genre in the Discourse and Literature of War*, pp. 157–72), points out that the concerted effort by Elizabeth I and her administration to avoid the classical topos of the Amazon had important implications for Spenser's depiction of Britomart, the female martial heroine of Book III of *The Faerie Queene*. Instead of utilizing the figure of the Amazon, which was thought to challenge sexual hierarchies, Elizabeth focused on her own divinely ordained extraordinariness and androgyny: the queen's private body might be female, but as head of state and army she was always male. At the beginning of Book III Spenser blames classical male poets for restricting heroism to men, and notes that female heroism has not been excluded from historical records. Britomart's credibility, like Elizabeth's, relies on her being convincing as a man: the female warrior is transformed by transvestism into a male soldier and so patriarchal order is maintained. Britomart embodies the ideals of Christian knighthood and is exceptional, in contrast to Radigund, who destabilizes sexual hierarchies. Spenser's critique of the politics of romance echoes that made by Margaret Tyler twelve years earlier in *The Mirrour of Knighthood* [1586], but it is surprising that Spenser rather than Tyler should launch a critique of the epic genre's exclusion of women and that he, the courtly poet rather than the lower-class female writer, should vindicate female heroism.

A number of articles on *The Faerie Queene* appeared this year. According to Sarah J. Plant, 'Spenser's Praise of English Rites for the Sick and Dying' (*SCJ* 32 [2001] 403–20), various episodes from *The Faerie Queene* criticize the Catholic sacrament of extreme unction, while others praise the sacrament as redefined by the Church of England. Although retained in both the Edwardian and the Elizabethan Book of Common Prayer as 'The Order for the Visitation of the Sick', the sacrament had been altered, with a shift from anointing the sick with a mystical substance to spiritual education. Plant argues that the episode featuring Night's visit to the healer Aesculapius in Hades in Book I of *The Faerie Queene* is a parody of the Catholic sacrament since the efficacy of Aesculapius's treatment is denied and his failure to raise Sansjoy indicates that no sinner may return from hell without heavenly grace. The language in the episode further parodies the Catholic sacrament by associating it with witchcraft, something underlined by the presence of Duessa. In Book I of *The Faerie Queene* Red Cross is anointed with oil in the House of Pride after his battle with Sansjoy, where again the efficacy of the Catholic sacrament is denied. According to Plant, the negative healing in the House of Pride and Hades contrasts with the successful healing of Serena and Timias in Book VI, where the hermit, who follows a life of prayer and grace, treats their wounds by attending to both body and mind, recalling the healers in the House of Holiness where Red Cross receives instruction in the true religion, the rite of confession, and absolution for his sins. Another positive healer is Arthur, who saves Red Cross from the power of Orgoglio when he brings God's grace in the form of a precious box containing healing liquor; communion was an essential element of the redefined sacrament and Arthur's liquor represents the healing power of the eucharist rather than the oil of unction. This is a well-researched and engaging essay which adds to our understanding of religious allegory in *The Faerie Queene*.

In a scholarly piece which engages with recent criticism and early modern debates, John D. Staines, 'Elizabeth, Mercilla, and the Rhetoric of Propaganda in Spenser's *Faerie Queene*' (*JMEMS* 31[2001] 283–312), considers the Mercilla episode in Book V of *The Faerie Queene*, noting that it offers an examination of political rhetoric and propaganda. He identifies a shift in Spenser's writing away from a project of producing encomium, evident in the 1590 edition, and towards the 1596 edition's analysis of the state's use of praise and blame to its own advantage. Book V explores the tensions inherent in certain abstract terms central to Elizabethan political debates, and especially those surrounding the trial of Mary Queen of Scots: guile, treason, mercy, clemency, pity, zeal, grief, and justice. Spenser's depiction of the events surrounding Mary's execution is neither 'passive official propaganda' nor 'a vision of transcendent justice' (p. 304), as some critics have claimed, but rather an exploration of the rhetoric of the Elizabethan court. Spenser shows Elizabeth's government to be 'a model of effective politics' (p. 304) which controlled Mary's execution so that Elizabeth's treatment of the matter was viewed in the best possible light.

Staying with Book V, Jeff Dolven, 'Spenser's Sense of Poetic Justice' (*Raritan* 21[2001] 127–40), suggests that Spenser's scenes of symbolic punishment in *The Faerie Queene* were influenced by the public scenes of discipline witnessed by the poet in London. Via reference to emblems and typical early modern forms of punishment, Dolven notes that, unlike the modern practice of serving time, the Elizabethan justice system emphasized the public and physical nature of punishment. Dolven considers punishment in *The Faerie Queene* to be a form of allegory-making where the force of allegory is to provide a lesson for the spectator rather than the transgressor. In Book V the punishment of Sanglier seems to be a straightforward piece of poetic justice, but the next episode featuring Munera 'unsettles this sense that justice and allegory-making can so readily collaborate' (p. 137). Munera's punishment seems appropriate on the face of it, but raises certain questions, for example the reference to her 'sclendar wast' provides an 'unallegorical middle' between her allegorical hands and feet and constitutes a 'brief, humane rupture' to the allegory's 'prosecutorial rigor' (p. 138).

In a thoughtful and nicely nuanced piece Kate Wheeler, '"They heard a ruefull voice": Guyon's Agency and the Gloriana Framework in Book II of *The Faerie Queene*' (in De Smith, ed., *Proceedings of the Eighth Annual Northern Plains Conference on Earlier British Literature*, pp. 7–14), considers the tension between the origins of knightly action in Book II and the framework claimed in the *Letter to Raleigh* in which Gloriana assigns quests at her annual feast. That Guyon's main quest is to capture Acrasia and remove her power over knights means that temperance is 'defined as strongly in terms of the protection of knightly agency as with the control of knightly aggressions' (p. 8). In the *Letter to Raleigh* Guyon is assigned his quest by Gloriana, yet it seems clear that this quest is generated by his meeting Mordant and Amavia in canto 1. For Wheeler this 'narrative discontinuity' is crucial since it has the effect of 'distancing Guyon's knightly motivation and agency from the controlling rubric of Gloriana's assignment of quests' and the 'confusion surrounding the inception of Guyon's quest' is the key to Book II's meaning (p. 9). Acrasia's victims, Mordant and Amavia, represent the vulnerability of human agency, and Acrasia is responsible for destroying their will. Guyon's reaction to their predicament emphasizes 'knightly agency based on a kind of visceral sympathy, rather than the service of an ideal or of a sovereign', yet when relating the story of Mordant and Amavia in Medina's castle the knight is represented as an agent of the sovereign who employs him and his virtue is 'effaced by subjecthood' (p. 13). Wheeler regards this 'striking metafictional articulation of allegiance' to be one of the poem's many 'provocative and unresolved tensions' and evidence of how Spenser's desire to explore human truths comes into conflict with desire to revere Elizabeth.

Andrew King, '"Well grounded, finely framed, and strongly trussed up together": The "Medieval" Structure of *The Faerie Queene*' (*RES* 52[2001] 22–58), provides an overview of evidence for Spenser's interest in Middle English literature and historical writings throughout *The Faerie Queene*. King is particularly concerned with how *The Faerie Queene* conforms to the medieval conception of structure and offers a range of texts as models for the structure of Spenser's poem: medieval story collections, *The Canterbury Tales*, *Le Morte Darthur*, and manuscript anthologies of Romance. King comes to the conclusion that the poem's medieval structure should affect our response to it and we should see the poem in relation to the practice of compilation rather than as a linear structure. He also thinks that the poem's medieval structure should encourage a different methodology of reading, with a focus on dipping into specific parts rather than a cover-to-cover reading. He maintains that the structure outlined in *The Letter to Raleigh* differs from that of the poem in order to suggest that the poem is a product of the collective cultural memory, a memory which is real and therefore imperfectly recalled. This essay is subdivided into sections which can make King's analysis seem rather list-like, and the exclusive focus on structure without reference to thematic links between Middle English literature and Spenser's poem tends towards the mechanical.

This year's *Spenser Studies* was particularly comprehensive. Susanne Woods, 'Making Free with Poetry: Spenser and the Rhetoric of Choice' (*SSt* 15[2001] 1–16), points out that Milton, although usually thought of as the poet of individual liberty, was indebted to Spenser who, throughout his writings, was preoccupied with poetry as 'an exercise in freedom' (p. 1). Woods argues that, despite modelling himself on Virgil and his adherence to the imperial ideal, Spenser also challenged Elizabethan culture, and that ideas of freedom are central to his work. According to Woods, *The Mirror for Magistrates* influenced Spenser's thoughts on poetry and freedom, particularly the story of the poet Collingbourne, who claimed that free speech was an ancient privilege of poets and that riddles and metaphors could protect and thus liberate the poet. In *The Faerie Queene* and *Paradise Lost* virtue is depicted as right choice, and that choice depends not only on sovereignty over the self but also knowledge, which allows more freedom than high birth alone. The humanist meritocracy reinforced the notion of freedom as informed choice and a condition for virtue, but Reformation debates over freedom of the will complicated the issue, since Erasmus thought free will a condition for human choice and salvation but Luther said that man had no free will and that only God's grace offered salvation. Spenser adhered to the assumptions outlined by William Perkins, a Protestant apologist, who believed that man can do nothing to bring about his own salvation. In Book I of *The Faerie Queene* Red Cross cannot bring about his own salvation, and each of his testing moments requires divine intercession. In his poetry Spenser negotiates two paradoxes to develop his idea of freedom: the first is to reveal by hiding (under the cover of pastoral, fable, allegory, or simple metaphor), and the second is to call upon the reader's interpretation, or judgement, thus freeing the reader from accepting the poet's, or anyone else's, direction. The conclusion, that 'Spenser's poetry is his freedom' (p. 15), raises pertinent questions. Although Woods acknowledges that Spenser is working within a sixteenth-century definition of freedom and that political freedom in the modern sense was an alien concept, we might expect some analysis of Spenser's enthusiastic advocacy of autocratic control in Book V of *The Faerie Queene* and *A View of the Present State of Ireland*. Admittedly Woods's focus is on the poetry, but the exclusion of Spenser's prose text leaves the reader desiring a closer engagement with his notion of freedom and his adherence to the imperial ideal.

In a brilliantly argued and erudite essay Kenneth Borris, 'Flesh, Spirit, and the Glorified Body: Spenser's Anthropomorphic Houses of Pride, Holiness, and Temperance' (*SSt* 15 [2001] 17–52), challenges A.S.P. Woodhouse's assertion that Book I of *The Faerie Queene* is preoccupied with grace and all the subsequent books with nature, arguing rather that grace and nature interact in all parts of Spenser's poem. Like Caelia's household in Book I, the house of Alma in Book II focuses on subduing the flesh and privileging the mind, unlike Lucifera's House of Pride in Book I, which is associated with basic bodily functions and spiritual death. The Alma episode draws upon a range of interrelated religious, moral, and medical ideas outlined in detail by Borris: while some religious writings emphasized the notion that well-tempered bodies are divine works, so medical treatises focused on the physical illness caused by intemperance. Previous critics have not emphasized that Spenser 'integrates Alma into a pattern of symbolism initiated in Book 1, based mostly on the sartorial imagery of Christian redemption in the Book of Revelation' (p. 37). Some Reformers thought that the soul could sanctify the body, and Spenser's depiction of Alma seems to allow for sanctification of the body in earthly life. The main achievement of this essay is to take issue with the critical tendency to dichotomize what is a very complex poem, and Borris presents his nuanced reading in the context of fascinating writings, both theological and medical, which throw light on Spenser's attitude to the spirit and the body, and their relation to each other.

In another well-argued and scholarly piece Joseph D. Parry, 'Phaedria and Guyon: Traveling Alone in *The Faerie Queene*' (*SSt* 15[2001] 53–77), points out that Guyon's forward motion in Book II, especially in canto 12, is an important feature of the allegory on his moral progress. Guyon must negotiate various temptations before encountering Acrasia, but Phaedria is not one of these, functioning rather as 'an image of the persistently unstable, mobile, shapeshifting character of the knowledge that Guyon seeks on his journey' (p. 54). Phaedria is not a static figure whom Guyon can simply pass by since, unlike the other malevolent female characters in poem, she has agency. Although Acrasia is characterized by her own stillness and the immobilization she effects in others, Phaedria can 'move freely and unpredictably in Faeryland' (p. 56). Disagreeing with Sheila Cavanagh, Parry contends that the threat from Phaedria is textual rather than sexual: she poses a threat of interpretation and prevents Guyon from making a controlled and careful progress. The quick motions of Phaedria and her boat signify moral instability, but she may not be entirely malevolent. Parry borrows Derrida's term *pharmakon* to describe her: she is 'poison and/or medicine' (p. 67), that is, her effect is generally poisonous but she can occasionally be medicinal, something that becomes apparent when she stops the fight between Guyon and Cymochles. Additionally, her laughter need not necessarily denote moral degeneracy but may signify unruly youth or the foolishness of the court, or may even function as a check to Guyon's seriousness. Unlike Acrasia, Phaedria is not destructive nor does she invite desire; rather, she inhabits 'the textual space of the erratic, the unpredictable, and the not clearly discernible' (p. 73) and for Guyon the straying which she encourages may be part of the course he must follow towards righteousness.

Kyong-Hahn Kim, 'The Nationalist Drive of Spenserian Hermaphrodism in *The Faerie Queene*' (*SSt* 15[2001] 79–93), identifies a range of critical opinions on the significance of hermaphroditic images in *The Faerie Queene* and concludes that the image of the hermaphrodite is primarily a symbol of succession. When it became clear that Elizabeth would not marry there was a shift away from writing which encouraged her marriage towards that in praise of unmarried chastity and, in accordance with this, Spenser does not advise on love and marriage in *The Faerie Queene* but, rather, presents 'the androgynous form of a mythical union of the queen with the nation' (p. 85). The theme of androgynous marriage between the queen and the nation is established by genealogical method in the promised union of Gloriana with Arthur and in particular of Britomart and Artegall. Merlin's prophecy, which completes the British chronicle, confirms that the Tudors were descendants of Arthur and predicts that from Britomart will descend Briton kings down to Elizabeth. Britomart's union with Artegall is not realized, but is suggested by her androgynous vision in the temple of Isis which is an allegory of dynasty. For Kim, Spenser seems also to foresee 'the nation's future in permanence' through the hermaphroditic figure of Nature, who is entirely self-sufficient, in the Mutabilitie Cantos. Like other androgynous figures in the poem, Nature reveals her dynastic significance and, like the visionary son of Artegall and Britomart, looks like a lion, a consistent image of British ancestry in the poem. Kim is keen to assert that Spenser is not arguing for feminism or any kind of role reversal but rather that the queen is 'an exception to men's rule because she is ordained by divine law' (p. 89).

Donald Stump, 'Fashioning Gender: Cross-Dressing in Spenser's Legend of Britomart and Artegall' (*SSt* 15[2001] 95–119), points out that, despite the recent focus on gender in *The Faerie Queene*, little attention has been paid to 'the delicate interplay between episodes of crossdressing' which Stump believes has a special value in the education of Britomart and Artegall. The initial disposition of Britomart is a tendency to frowardness, while Artegall is inclined to be forward but, as their romance progresses, these extremes of temperament are moderated. The final stage in Britomart's transformation is her confrontation with Radigund, when she acts with masculine aggression, but it is odd that she should revert to her former tendency to withdraw by subordinating herself and the women of Radegone to Artegall. Similarly Artegall learns to modify his initial tendency towards aggression but again the process of tempering excess ends with a surprising reversal when, after restoring Irena, he shows no clemency towards her rebellious subjects. Stump thinks that Spenser may have been influenced by Aristotle's theory of temperance in the *Nicomachean Ethics*, which stated that we should move towards the opposite of our vice in order to arrive at the mean. Spenser may also be informed by Thomas Elyot, who in *The Governour* claimed that the midpoint between extremes of masculinity and femininity was the ideal for virtuous nobility. In Spenser's poem frowardness and forwardness are gendered, something which can be noted in other pairs of lovers in the poem, and although Britomart and Artegall may moderate their behavioural extremes they retain some of these original tendencies, which may explain the curious reversal to type mentioned above. For Stump, Spenser's attitude to gender is 'unusually rich and complex': while he believed that ethical dispositions could be 'fashioned', he also maintained that there is a difference between the sexes, although the ideal noble man or woman should moderate their natural inclinations in order to move closer to the other sex.

Moving away from the usual tendency to focus on *The Faerie Queene*, James Fleming, in '*A View* from the Bridge: Ireland and Violence in Spenser's *Amoretti*' (*SSt* 15[2001] 135–64), claims an important and hitherto overlooked connection between Spenser's sonnet sequence, the *Amoretti*, and his political prose tract, *A View of the Present State of Ireland*. In a persuasively argued piece Fleming notes that critics have tended either to avoid the violent poems in the sequence or explain them as 'parodies or travesties of Petrarchan violence' (p. 137), a reading which he considers unconvincing, noting that 'the violent patterns of *Amoretti* are noticeably congruent to those of the *View*, characterized by eruption, imprisonment, insurgency, and slaughter' (p. 138). Fleming provides a detailed analysis of several poems and relates their images of captivity and enclosure to the desire to contain Irish rebellion that prevails throughout the *View*. Irenius suggests famine as a final solution since exclusion from English mercy and enclosure within certain areas will effectively destroy the rebels. There is a structural connection between the sonnet sequence and the prose text, since both regard the final result to be external: the solution to the poet's imperfect life lies outside the sonnet sequence, in the *Epithalamion*, and an effective military solution lies outside current thinking about the containment of rebellion. Fleming notes a contradiction of attitude between the *Amoretti* and the *View*: in the former the lady's crime is to slaughter those who have yielded to her power, but in the *View* Irenius remembers Grey's slaughter of those who yielded as 'necessary and honourable' (p. 158). Fleming explains this contradiction by noting that the poet 'does not actually urge his lady not to kill her captives', but rather 'assumes that she tortures and kills them as a matter of course' (p. 158). Spenser does not express concern about the morality of slaughtering prisoners in either text, but is concerned with 'the public opprobrium' that can follow such conduct. The lady enjoys her bloody deeds, unlike Grey, who acted because of extreme provocation, and Fleming concludes that the aim of the poem is 'to slander the lady' (p. 159). Although the sequence was addressed to Elizabeth Boyle, critics have noted that the lady in question is Queen Elizabeth, and Fleming believes that the sequence, read in the context of Spenser's defence of Grey, thus constitutes a 'rhetorical revenge on the queen by fixing Grey's unique disgrace on her' (p. 159).

Joseph Black, '"Pan is hee"': Commending *The Faerie Queene*' (*SSt* 15[2001] 121–34), considers the possibility that Thomas Watson is the author of a manuscript poem held by Edinburgh University Library. The anonymous poem, dated 1588 and here reproduced and transcribed by Black, does not mention Spenser by name but is undoubtedly about *The Faerie Queene* and may have been written in the hope that it would be included as a commendatory verse in the 1590 edition of the poem. Watson is a strong candidate for authorship for various reasons: he was the first author to praise *The Faerie Queene* in print and, as a literary insider, he knew the people who had access to Spenser's texts in manuscript (the poem is written in Spenserian stanzas, only available before 1590 in manuscript form). Additionally, Watson knew Spenser and Spenser appears to have known Watson's work, apparently complementing him in *The Faerie Queene* and *The Ruines of Time*. The manuscript, which is heavily though not professionally decorated, appears to identify the writer's name via the Renaissance practice of naming through images: the visual representation of toes representing 'Thos', an abbreviation for Thomas, and the picture of a hare alluding to 'Wat', a common name for the animal in the period and hinting at 'Watson'. It may be that Watson's poem was excluded from the 1590 commendations because he was imprisoned in September 1589 for defending Christopher Marlowe in a street fight. The poem mentions being imprisoned during composition, and though the date of Watson's imprisonment is at least six months too late to correspond with the manuscript's date of 1588, Black thinks that, given that Watson is the most likely candidate for authorship, it is 'tempting' to consider the poem's date an error (p. 128). As Black points out, whether or not the manuscript poem is by Watson it is a valuable text since it appears to be the earliest extant poetic praise of *The Faerie Queene* and perhaps the earliest attempt to exchange praise for favour within the patronage system, reminding us also of the social and literary networks that contributed to literary production of the period.

In the first essay in a section on Spenser and Ralegh, William A. Oram, 'What Did Spenser Really Think of Sir Walter Ralegh when he Published his First Installment of *The Faerie Queene?*' (*SSt* 15[2001] 165–74), builds upon an earlier publication in which he considered Spenser's 'friendly but critical' (p. 165) attitude towards Ralegh. Although in the 1590s Ralegh was a more powerful man than Spenser as a result of his success at court, their early relationship was fairly mutual, a fact which presumably encouraged Spenser's independence from his old companion-turned-patron. In *Colin Clouts Come Home Againe*, which presents an account of their meeting in 1589, Spenser stresses their likeness, the only distinction being that the Shepherd of the Ocean is Cynthia's shepherd. Evidence for Spenser's independence from Ralegh can be found in the fact that Spenser did not allow Ralegh's competition with Essex to influence his opinion of the latter. Spenser's dedicatory poem to Ralegh in the 1590 *Faerie Queene* is more ambiguous than the other dedicatory poems, and Oram's detailed analysis of it detects criticism of Ralegh, with Spenser expressing the belief that it is better to have written *The Faerie Queene* than Ralegh's kind of poetry; Ralegh possesses a high mind, but he has given way to pleasure and his poetry has been led by his courtly ambitions. Ralegh thus conforms to Richard Helgerson's definition of an amateur poet whereas Spenser is keen to assert the importance of poetry.

In the second essay from the Spenser and Ralegh section Wayne Erickson, in 'Spenser Reads Ralegh's Poetry In(to) the 1590 *Faerie Queene*' (*SSt* 15[2001] 175–84), calls recent critics, including Oram, to account for taking Spenser's critique of Ralegh's poetry too seriously. Erickson detects 'sophisticated ironic play' (p. 176) in the literary dialogue between Spenser and Ralegh and asserts that 'they were probably teasing each other' (p. 177) while at the same time 'engaging in some serious play concerning competitive analyses of their careers' (p. 177). The playfulness, argues Erickson, is located in Spenser's discussion of genre and his assertion that Ralegh is the superior poet when it comes to praising Elizabeth. Although Spenser may be advising Ralegh on the limitations of his 'amateur, amatory lyric' (p. 177), he characterizes himself as a rude poet and praises Ralegh's superior verse, even adopting 'Ralegh's courtly language of erotic lyric to flesh out some of his representations of the queen' (p. 178).

The third paper in the section is Jerome S. Dees's 'Colin Clout and the Shepherd of the Ocean' (*SSt* 15[2001] 185–96). Dees argues that critics have been too one-sided in their discussion of the political and literary relations between Spenser and Ralegh, giving little attention to 'Ralegh's side of the picture' or 'the still muddy question' of textual links between *Colin Clout* and *The 11th: and last booke of the Ocean to Cynthia* (p. 186). Critics usually characterize the relationship between Spenser and Ralegh as one of a 'morally superior' Spenser correcting or controlling the consequences of his patron's '"private" politics of love' (p. 188), but Dees provides a much called for corrective to the dichotomizing by emphasizing the dialogue between their poems and Ralegh's engagement with and challenges to Spenser's ideas. In both poems there are passages which rely on Neoplatonic ideas of love and beauty, yet while Spenser affirms these ideas Ralegh subjects them to sceptical scrutiny.

The fourth piece in the section is Michael Rudick's 'Three Views on Ralegh and Spenser: A Comment' (*SSt* 15[2001] 197–203), a short comment on the three preceding papers which usefully summarizes the views presented by Oram, Erickson and Dees and offers some critical analysis of their opinions. On the whole, the comment calls for a less dichotomized approach to the relationship between

Spenser and Ralegh, always bearing in mind that they share common ground in their praise of Queen Elizabeth.

In the gleanings section of *Spenser Studies* Richard F. Hardin, 'Spenser's Aesculapius Episode and the English Mummers' Play' (*SSt* 15[2001] 251–3), detects a parallel between the mummers' play, also known as the St George play, and the episode from Book I of *The Faerie Queene* where Duessa tries to resurrect Sansjoy in the underworld. According to Hardin, several details from each episode correspond, with both featuring a 'combat, damsel, old woman, physician, and cure' (p. 251). There is no evidence of the play's performance until the early 1700s, but the *Faerie Queene* episode appears to suggest that the mummers' play was well known at least a century earlier, and Spenser adapted what was 'a remnant of paganism' to the theme of spiritual restoration that is central to Book I.

Andrew Hadfield, in 'Spenser and Chaucer: *The Knight's Tale* and Artegall's Response to the Giant with Scales (*Faerie Queene*, V. Ii. 41–42)' (*SSt* 15[2001] 245–9), contends that although critics, particularly Judith Anderson, have noted Spenser's indebtedness to Chaucer in his poetry, one example may have been overlooked because the parallels are thematic rather than verbal. He notes that, in the episode from Book V featuring the Giant with the Scales, Artegall's words before Talus throws the Giant into the sea echo passages in Chaucer's *Knight's Tale*, in particular Theseus' 'First Moevere' speech at the end (ll. 2987–3074) and Saturn's description of the effects of his rule over the universe (ll. 2453–78). The arguments put forward by Artegall and Theseus are, claims Hadfield, 'almost identical' (p. 247), both making a strong case against complaining about the will of the gods. Hadfield usefully compares sentences from each text in order to demonstrate that each speech contains 'verbal and syntactic parallels between sentences and phrases' (p. 246). He also contends that Spenser may have gone back to Chaucer's translation of Boethius' *Consolation of Philosophy*, a source text when composing the Knight's Tale. Chaucer's tale emphasizes the influence of Saturn and Jupiter, and in later books of *The Faerie Queene* the struggle between these gods and the Titans is paramount. The episode featuring Artegall and the Giant is part of this contest, since Artegall possesses powers from Jove via his sword Chrysaor, and the Giant is a Titan.

In an article that does not pull any punches, Lydia M. McGrew, 'A Neglected Gauntlet: J.W. Bennett and the Date of *Amoretti*' (*SSt* 15[2001] 257–72), questions the uncritical acceptance of Alexander Dunlop's Lenten interpretation of the *Amoretti*, despite a challenge to Dunlop's reading of the sequence by Josephine Waters Bennett. Dunlop argued that the sonnet sequence represents the period of time between Ash Wednesday and Easter in the year 1594, and that the forty-seven poems correspond to the number of days in the Lenten period. According to Dunlop, sonnet 22 is about Ash Wednesday and sonnet 62 about 25 March, also known as Lady Day, one of the days from which a new calendar year could be marked. Bennett disagreed, claiming that sonnet 62 refers to 1 January, New Year's Day, because there are references in the sequence to customs specifically associated with that day, which means that sonnet 22 cannot be about Ash Wednesday and that there is therefore no Lenten sequence. Carol Kaske, although apparently unaware of Bennett's article, elaborates upon points made by Bennett which undermine Dunlop's thesis. McGrew's language is strong: she claims that 'It is something of a scholarly disgrace that Bennett's gauntlet has remained so long neglected by those she challenged' (p. 269), but her point that Dunlop's reading of the sequence should be re-examined in the light of Bennett's article, especially given Dunlop's influence on other numerological interpreters, is entirely valid.

It is difficult to believe Alexander Dunlop's claim, in 'Sonnet LXII and Beyond' (*SSt* 15[2001] 273–7), that he found Lydia M. McGrew's scathing indictment of his failure to engage with Bennett's criticism gratifying (p. 273). Dunlop's defence for ignoring Bennett's arguments is not particularly convincing either: the fact that his prepared 'correction' was refused by *Renaissance Quarterly* (the journal which published Bennett's piece) did not prevent him from publishing elsewhere, nor should Bennett's death in 1975 have prevented his engagement with the objections she raised. It is disingenuous to claim that, because no one published work on Bennett's article between 1973, when it first appeared, and his 1989 edition of the *Shorter Poems*, he need not mention her argument in that edition (even though he summarizes his own). To characterize her argument as 'unessential quibbles' appears to be wishful thinking on the part of Dunlop, and his long overdue response to points raised in Bennett's article and revived by McGrew is not entirely convincing. Whether or not one is persuaded by Bennett or Dunlop, however, is not really the point since McGrew's complaint, that Bennett's argument has been unfairly ignored for years, is irrefutable.

This year's *Notes and Queries* saw a focus on Spenser and Ireland. Raymond Gillespie and Andrew Hadfield, 'Two References to Edmund Spenser in Chancery Disputes' (*N&Q* 48[2001] 249–51), consider two references to Spenser in the Irish Chancery recognisances (British Library Add. MS 19837), one of which appears to prove that the common interest of landowners in Ireland could take precedence over colonial politics. The first entry, dated 10 June 1589, notes Edmund Spenser gent. and Richard Roche of Kinsale entering a bond for a case in Chancery between Edmund Spenser and Hugh Strawbridge, but no further details are provided. The second entry, dated 18 June 1589, notes that Edmund Spenser of Cork was to provide security of delivery of James Shropp to Newgate in Dublin. Although no record of Shropp survives, it is clear that he was connected with Spenser, perhaps as a servant on his estate or via Spenser's civil service duties. The first entry is of particular interest to Spenserians because, although it might refer to undischarged debts, it probably relates to a dispute over land rights and titles. Hugh Strawbridge (or Strowbridge) was a servant of Sir William Fitzwilliam, then Lord Deputy, of whom Spenser was highly critical in his *View of the Present State of Ireland*. Spenser's co-operation with Roche, whose name suggests he was Old English and possibly related to Spenser's Munster enemies, 'suggests that alliances between New and Old English settlers were not polarized at this point' (p. 251). That Roche and Spenser 'could clearly combine against a well-connected crown servant when their self-interest and rights to land were threatened' (p. 251) strengthens Patricia Coughlan's claim that land and property disputes form an important subtext of Spenser's literary writing.

Andrew Hadfield, 'Spenser's *View* and Leicester's Commonwealth' (*N&Q* 48[2001] 256–9), also considers an anonymous text which may have influenced Spenser when composing the *View* and *The Faerie Queene. Leicester's Commonwealth: The Copy of a letter Written by a Master of Art at Cambridge* [1584], an influential and widely read text despite efforts to suppress it, would probably have been of interest to Spenser given its connections with Philip Sidney, who answered the attack on his uncle, and Lord Grey de Wilton, another object of its attack. The author of the text claims to be a scholar who has recorded the comments of a learned Catholic lawyer, a man both moderate and loyal to the Crown. The text consists of two main arguments: that Leicester, not the queen, governs England and his tyranny will force moderate Catholics to rebel, thus pushing England into a state of civil war; and that Mary Queen of Scots has the best claim to the throne of England and her line should succeed when Elizabeth dies. As Hadfield rightly notes, Spenser would have been interested in this subject matter since he showed himself to be anti-Stuart in the second edition of *The Faerie Queene*, where Mary Stuart is represented as the villainous Duessa. Spenser may also have had *Leicester's Commonwealth* in mind when composing a particular passage about Grey in the *View* which refers to a conspiracy against the Crown led by Thomas FitzGerald during Grey's deputyship. Whereas Grey is denounced as a traitorous commander in *Leicester's Commonwealth*, he is praised as a loyal and capable captain in the *View*. Although Ireland is characterized as a paradise in *Leicester's Commonwealth*, Spenser's *View* characterizes it as a dangerous land which requires a strong military leader. *Leicester's Commonwealth* considers the dangers of intolerance in England which may force moderate Catholics to revolt, but the *View* indicates the dangers of tolerance in Ireland, where disloyal Irish Catholics threaten English government. Another point of influence may be that *Leicester's Commonwealth* makes a connection between Leicester's treason, Ireland, and Ovid's story of Diana and Actaeon. Spenser may have remembered the connection between Ireland and this myth when writing *The Faerie Queene* since Ireland is the place where Actaeon sees the queen naked.

In a persuasive piece Thomas Herron, 'A Source for Edmund Spenser's "Blandina" in Holinshed's Irish Chronicle (1587)' (*N&Q* 48[2001] 254–6), identifies a hitherto overlooked source for the name 'Blandina', a character who appears in Book VI of Spenser's *Faerie Queene*. Although Blandina initially admonishes her villainous husband, she later protects him, and her words are judged by the narrator to be 'false and fayned' (VI. xlii–xliii). John W. Draper claimed that her name derived from the diminutive of the Latin *blandus*, 'enticing, tempting', which A.C. Hamilton translated as 'soothing' in reference to her speech, remarking that her name also derived from the Latin *blandiri*, 'to flatter'. Herron notes that the name also appears in the second edition of Holinshed's *Chronicles* [1587], a work with which Spenser was familiar since he used it as a source for Book III of *The Faerie Queene* in allegorizing Sir Walter Ralegh's military exploits in Ireland during the Desmond rebellion. In Holinshed 'Blandina' is the name of a mountain, and Herron claims that Spenser's character 'fit[s] into a pattern of peaceful but occasionally mischievous female characters named after Irish topography', among them the nymph Molanna of the Mutabilitie Cantos and the river nymph Mulla from *Colin Clouts Come Home Againe*, both of whom undermine figures of authority. In an effort to escape from Arthur, Blandina hides her husband beneath her garment, an action which Herron compares to Spenser's description in the *View* of 'the secretive uses, by rebels and loose women, of the trademark Irish garment, the mantle' (p. 256). Spenser's *View* also refers to the rebellious Irish hiding out in the mountains, and Herron concludes that in the episode from *The Faerie Queene* Turpine figuratively hides in the hills from British justice, allegorized in the shape of Prince Arthur.

Religion is central to a solid and thoughtful piece by Kathryn Walls, 'Archbishop Cranmer's "Poor Box" Injunction and *The Faerie Queene*, I. iii. 16–18' (*N&Q* 48[2001] 251–4), which considers Spenser's Kirkrapine episode in the context of Thomas Cranmer's injunctions, first issued in 1547 and reissued under Elizabeth. Although Kirkrapine is a villain in a work that is generally Protestant and iconoclastic, his theft of certain items 'is strongly reminiscent of the iconoclastic expeditions of Edward VI's commissioners' (p. 251). Kirkrapine's theft of 'poore mens boxes' is a reference to Cranmer's twenty-ninth injunction, in which he ordered churches to keep a box for the poor; this was a Reformation invention and so Kirkrapine is undermining a specifically Protestant institution. Kirkrapine also steals vestments and 'habiliments' from 'saints' and 'priests', which might suggest that his victims are Catholic, but, claims Walls, Spenser is here invoking two important Reformation doctrines: Calvin's claim that all Christians may be described as saints and Luther's doctrine of 'the priesthood of all believers'. These thefts thus expand upon his stealing of alms and thus all of Kirkrapine's thefts represent the same sin of refusing charity to fellow Christians. Further evidence that Kirkrapine is not an iconoclast is his idolatry of Abessa, feeding her with his offerings and paying her with gold.

Moving away from issues surrounding the colonization of Ireland and religious matters, Bart Van Es, 'The Life of John Dixon, *The Faerie Queene*'s First Annotator' (*N&Q* 48[2001] 259–61), provides new information on the biography of John Dixon, the earliest and most prolific early modern annotator of Spenser's poetry. In a private publication of 1964 Graham Hough analysed and transcribed Dixon's marginalia in a copy of the 1590 *Faerie Queene*, but he provided only a cursory biography of Dixon and, more recently, in *The Spenser Encyclopaedia* [1990], Michael O'Connell claimed that, besides a date for the annotations and the likelihood that Dixon lived in Kent, 'nothing is known of him'. Drawing upon a number of facts, presented here with an admirable attention to detail, Van Es concludes that it is possible to know more about Dixon than hitherto acknowledged. A historical and topographical survey of Kent, a publication featuring the Dixon family tree, and the register of the school attended by Dixon's brothers allow Van Es to establish that Dixon was at least 37 when he made the annotations. Furthermore, his father's will, which provides details about property and land bequeathed to family members, indicates that by the time he annotated *The Faerie Queene* Dixon 'probably possessed considerable wealth and property' (p. 260). Although little is known of Dixon's education it is clear that he was of a higher social status than imagined by Hough, who referred to him as a 'Puritan parson of moderately scholarly tastes'. Two further points, raised by Hough, are rectified by Van Es: Letters of Administration of Dixon's estate were granted in the Prerogative Court of Canterbury in February 1627/8, which Hough considered to be an indication that Dixon died at that time, but Van Es contends that the document concerns a different branch of the family and so tell us nothing about Dixon's date of death. Also, the copy of *The Faerie Queene* containing Dixon's annotations is no longer owned by Lord Bessborough but is in the care of the Stansted Park Foundation and kept at Stansted Park, Rowlands Castle, Hampshire.

Books Reviewed

Britnell, Jennifer, and Richard Britnell. *Vernacular Literature and Current Affairs in the Early Sixteenth Century: France, England and Scotland*. Ashgate. [2000] pp. xxv + 211. £45 ISBN 0 7546 0093 9.

De Smith, Robert J., ed. *Proceedings of the Eighth Annual Northern Plains Conference on Earlier British Literature*. Sioux Center, Iowa: Dordt College Press. [2001] pp. 98.

Grantley, Darryll. *Wit's Pilgrimage: Drama and the Social Impact of Education in Early Modern England*. Ashgate. [2000] pp. 278. £42.50 ISBN 0 7546 0167 6.

Green, Ian. *Print and Protestantism in Early Modern England*. OUP. [2000] pp. xxiii + 691. £70 ISBN 0 1982 0860 X.

Griffths, Richard, ed. *The Bible in the Renaissance: Essays on Biblical Commentary and Translation in the Fifteenth and Sixteenth Centuries*. Ashgate. [2001] pp. 222. £47.50 ISBN 0 7546 0394 6.

Hadfield, Andrew, ed. *The Cambridge Companion to Spenser*. CUP. [2001] pp. 298. £40 ISBN 0 5216 4199 3.

Hadfield, Andrew, ed. *Literature and Censorship in Renaissance England*. Palgrave. [2001] pp. xii + 256. £42.50 ISBN 0 3337 9410 9.

Happé, Peter, ed. *Allegory in the Theatre: Tudor Theatre*, vol. 5. Lang. [2000] pp. xx + 258. £28 ISBN 3 9067 6008 1.

Jardine, Lisa, and Jerry Brotton. *Global Interests: Renaissance Art between East and West*. Reaktion. [2000] pp. 224. £25 ISBN 1 8618 9079 6.

Khanna, Lee Cullen, ed. *Early Tudor Translators: Margaret Beaufort, Margaret More Roper and Mary Basset*. The Early Modern Englishwoman. A Facsimile Library of Essential Works: Printed Writings, 1500–1640; series I, part 2, vol. 4. Ashgate. [2001] pp. 464. £70 ISBN 1 8401 4217 0.

Miller, Anthony. *Roman Triumphs and Early Modern Culture*. Palgrave. [2001] pp. vii + 223. £47.50 ISBN 0 3337 1472 5.

Piesse, A.J., ed. *Sixteenth-Century Identities*. ManUP. [2001] pp. 192. £40 ISBN 0 7190 5383 8.

Pigman, G.W. III. *A Hundreth Sundrie Flowres*, by George Gascoigne. OUP. [2000] pp. lxv + 751. £110 ISBN 0 1981 1779 5.

Pincombe, Mike, ed. *The Anatomy of Tudor Literature*. Ashgate. [2001] pp. ix + 235. £45 ISBN 0 7546 0243 5.

Prescott, Anne Lake, ed. *Elizabeth and Mary Tudor*. The Early Modern Englishwoman. A Facsimile Library of Essential Works: Printed Writings, 1500–1640; series I, part 2, vol. 5. Ashgate. [2001] pp. 390. £55 ISBN 1 8401 4218 9.

Quitslund, Jon A. *Spenser's Supreme Fiction: Platonic Natural Philosophy and 'The Faerie Queene'*. UTorP. [2001] pp. xi + 373. $70 ISBN 0 8020 3505 1.

Robertson, Elizabeth, and Christine Rose, eds. *Representing Rape in Medieval and Early Modern Literature*. Palgrave. [2001] pp. ix + 453. £37.50 ISBN 0 3122 3648 4.

Stanivukovic, Goran V., ed. *Ovid and the Renaissance Body*. UTorP. [2001] pp. vi + 281. £45 ISBN 0 8020 3515 9.

Usandizaga, Aranzazu, and Andrew Monnickendam, eds. *Dressing Up for War: Transformations of Gender and Genre in the Discourse and Literature of War*.

Rodopi. [2001] pp. xix + 292. hb $70 ISBN 9 0420 1367 2, pb $30 ISBN 9 0420 1357 5.

Warnicke, Retha M. *The Marrying of Anne of Cleves: Royal Protocol in Tudor England*. CUP. [2000] pp. xv + 343. £22.50 ISBN 0 5217 7037 8.

Wayne, Valerie, ed. *Anne Cooke Bacon*. The Early Modern Englishwoman. A Facsimile Library of Essential Works: Printed Writings, 1500–1640; series I, part 2, vol. 1. Ashgate. [2000] pp. 474. £49.95 ISBN 1 8401 4214 6.

VI

Shakespeare

GABRIEL EGAN, PETER J. SMITH, LUCY MUNRO, DONALD
WATSON, JAMES PURKIS, ANNALIESE CONNOLLY, ANDREW
HISCOCK, STEPHEN LONGSTAFFE, JON ORTEN AND CLARE
MCMANUS

This chapter has four sections: 1. Editions and Textual Matters; 2. Shakespeare in
the Theatre; 3. Shakespeare on Screen; 4. Criticism. Section 1 is by Gabriel Egan;
section 2 is by Peter J. Smith; section 3 is by Lucy Munro; section 4(a) is by Donald
Watson, section 4(b) is by James Purkis, section 4(c) is by Annaliese Connolly,
section 4(d) is by Andrew Hiscock, section 4(e) is by Stephen Longstaffe, section
4(f) is by Jon Orten, and section 4(g) is by Clare McManus.

1. Editions and Textual Matters

The current crises in theories of editing Shakespeare pivot on a single question: can
we determine with tolerable certainty the kind of manuscript used as printer's copy
for each of the early printings? Editors who think that we can tend to use this
'knowledge' to discriminate between multiple early printings to find the one they
want to base their modern text upon and they conjecturally emend it by reference to
their theories of how its errors came about, while editors who think that we cannot
so discriminate tend to be more cautious, stressing the arbitrariness of their choices
about base text and emendation. This year two major critical editions of the same
play appeared, *3 Henry VI*, one for the Oxford Shakespeare—Martin, ed., *Henry IV,
Part Three*—and one for the Arden Shakespeare—Cox and Rasmussen, eds., *King
Henry VI Part Three*. The differences between them usefully illustrate the
consequences of differing answers to *the* central question.

Randall Martin's introduction to the Oxford Shakespeare *3 Henry VI* runs to 132
pages and is organized under eight heads that move from 'Rediscovery and
Reception' through analyses of particular characters (Richard of Gloucester,
Edward IV, Queen Margaret, but not Henry VI himself), to Martin's view of the
origins of, and relationships between, the early printings. The first edition was an
octavo of 1595 (O) called *The True Tragedy of Richard Duke of York*, which Martin
abbreviates to *True Tragedy* (the 1986 Oxford *Complete Works* chose *Richard Duke*

of York), followed by quartos in 1600 (Q2) and 1619 (Q3), and the Folio text of 1623 bearing the familiar name of *The Third Part of King Henry VI*. Martin takes the now common view that *True Tragedy* was the second part of a two-part play, the beginning of which is represented in the 1594 quarto called *The First Part of the Contention of the Two Houses of York and Lancaster*, and that the play we know as *1 Henry VI* was a prequel written later to tell the pre-history to the two-parter. It is worth distinguishing *True Tragedy* as represented by O and the quartos from *3 Henry VI* as represented by the Folio because Martin thinks that substantial authorial revision separates them; they are not merely different names for the same thing. Changing titles are revealing, and *True Tragedy*'s gives attention to York even though he dies in Act I while Henry lasts to almost the end. Martin thinks that *True Tragedy* was Shakespeare's first version of the play, written in 1591, that the 1595 octavo is an imperfect report of it, and that Shakespeare's longer version of the play was written 1594–6 and this is essentially what got into the Folio as *3 Henry VI*. Martin's edition is based on the Folio.

The Folio title is probably not authorial and it gives priority to Henry VI without, however, mentioning his life or death, and moreover it 'avoids the *contemptus mundi* associations hinted at by York's "true tragedy"' (p. 20). *3 Henry VI* does indeed deepen the character of Henry. The play would have reminded people of the danger of two monarchs claiming one kingdom when Mary Queen of Scots arrived in England in 1568, a situation which ended only with her execution in 1587. Sackville and Norton's *Gorboduc*, written early in Elizabeth's reign, was printed in 1590, the year before Shakespeare began on *True Tragedy*, and its representation of civil strife in a divided kingdom is alluded to in Shakespeare's play. An early performance of *Gorboduc* appears to have used a real company of soldiers in a formalized battle scene, showing the stage/reality crossover of 'drill as theatrical rehearsal and combat as performance' (p. 23). Neoclassicism demanded that violence be reported, not shown, and *Gorboduc* breaks this rule and had to be excused for it in Sidney's *Defence of Poetry*. Sidney and Jonson tried to distinguish 'low' from 'high' dramatic art, a distinction that rather misrepresents Elizabethan drama's mingling of 'official' and 'popular' culture. Popular civic dramas such as those performed at Coventry would have large, well-choreographed battles including female warrior characters (but not female actors), and Martin notes that victory over the Armada in 1588 did not bring an end to military preparations; just the opposite: there was increasingly conscription by the government as well as the older kind of feudal conscription by lords raising troops from amongst their tenants. Hence the play's son (conscripted in London) who kills his father (conscripted in Warwickshire), and the wider theme of the 'broken connection with local history' and the 'uncertain embrace of metropolitan culture' (p. 32). The first London playhouse, the Theatre in Shoreditch, was near the muster ground of Finsbury Fields, and the audiences may be expected to have appreciated (indeed, have experience of) drills being done well. On the stage weapons were 'not simulated period props but actual contemporary equipment' (p. 33). Martin offers no evidence for this last alarming claim, and one assumes that weapons were blunted to prevent accidental slaughter in performance. As usual with the Oxford Shakespeare, footnotes are used to reference supporting materials, which makes for convenience of use at the cost of limiting space. Martin elects to give what is known as a 'deep' link to an article in the online journal *Early Modern Literary Studies* (p. 33 n. 1)—

meaning that the internet address is specified right down to the particular document to be accessed—which is a practice to be deprecated because it wastes space and because the smallest error makes the link unusable. In this case there are several small errors and the link as printed does not work.

Continuing his exploration of contemporary contexts, Martin argues that history plays could be defended as tools for teaching military strategy and that where *True Tragedy* is overt and showy in its militarism, *3 Henry VI* is somewhat restrained, even pacifist. The opening stage direction of *True Tragedy* calls for the men to be wearing white roses, while *3 Henry VI* does not, and the latter increases the sense of confusion (who is who?) and makes the story more easily applicable to other conflicts (p. 26). Of course, Martin accepts that some differences between the *True Tragedy* and *3 Henry VI* might be due to the latter deriving from an authorial manuscript (so Shakespeare had not yet thought to add the detail about the roses) or indeed to editing in the printing house. But Martin detects in other differences, such as Margaret and Prince Edward being captured separately in *3 Henry VI*, the signs of subsequent authorial revision 'toning down the sound and fury' and making the play's attitude towards war 'more rueful'. In short, *3 Henry VI* has been distanced from 'official Elizabethan wartime and political contexts' (p. 37). Likewise *True Tragedy* lacks *3 Henry VI*'s imagery of war being like a sea (the water caught between the forces of the moon and the wind) that makes conflict seem like a natural condition rather than human sin.

Martin ties his introductory sections on particular characters to the stage history, and under the Brechtian heading 'The (Resistible?) Rise of Richard of Gloucester' he observes that one reason for the relative neglect of *3 Henry VI* was the success of Colley Cibber's adaptation of *Richard III* that held the stage between 1700 and 1821 and contained large sections of *3 Henry VI* (p. 46). Also, it is common to tack the beginning of *Richard III* onto the end of *3 Henry VI* by having Richard give his 'Now is the winter of our discontent' speech, which gratifies audiences by linking the obscure play to the well-known one and gives a teleological reading: it was all leading up to the evil reign of Richard and then the good reign of Henry VII. But Martin thinks that *3 Henry VI* actually has a weak sense of historical causality and there is little justification of present actions by past ones; indeed, Shakespeare is less teleological than his sources (pp. 49–50). Political motives for action quickly give way to blood-feud and competitive savagery, and then even familial ties cease to be a motive to action and all becomes 'expedient violence' for 'seizure of power' (p. 54). Under 'Edward IV' Martin notes that Henry VI's entailing of the crown removed the 'transgenerational continuity' that makes it 'an abiding authoritative symbol'; instead it is just a property. Hence Edward IV is not even given a coronation. Here Martin gives the substance of his illuminating note reviewed last year ('Rehabilitating John Somerville in *3 Henry VI*', *SQ* 51[2000] 332–40) on the regional and topical allusions of V.i, which features places near to Shakespeare's home town and a 'John Somerville' whose namesake was probably his disgraced relative. Indicating just how far Shakespeare's play has influenced modern attitudes, Martin notes that Shakespeare downplays to the point of extinction the historical Warwick's reputation as one of the old class of martial aristocrats, loved for his courtesy and hospitality, and makes him more a self-serving setter-up and plucker-down of others; we think of him as the 'kingmaker' largely because of this play (p. 79). In telling 'Margaret's story: a "new" play' (pp. 82–96), Martin records that for most of the stage history of the play—until the mid-twentieth century, in fact—Margaret lost out in cutting and adaptation, yet now the part is frequently compared to that of Lear. There was a distinct trend to liken Margaret to Britain's prime minister Margaret Thatcher in productions by the English Shakespeare Company and the Royal Shakespeare Company in the 1980s, combined with a noticeable anti-feminist backsliding from the progressive mid-century work; this tended to 'rehabilitate patriarchal biases against an outspoken non-domestic woman' (p. 94).

Martin's section on 'The Original Texts: Their History and Relationship' is of greatest concern to this review. Martin claims that the copy for F is 'generally agreed to be Shakespeare's manuscript', although there is debate about 'its state' and whether other hands annotated it 'in anticipation of use in the playhouse as a promptbook or script' (p. 96). It is hard to see what Martin means by 'or' in that last phrase: 'script' is certainly a less contentious term than the wildly anachronistic 'promptbook' favoured by new bibliography, but naming both does not make the claim any more tentative. Martin gives the standard new bibliographical reason for thinking that F is based on authorial papers: some of its stage directions are 'indefinite or vague', which suggests 'pre-performance' status, and others are authorially descriptive rather than practically prescriptive (p. 97). As if to soften his line, Martin footnotes the work of Paul Werstine and William B. Long that showed that vague and indefinite stage directions were not necessarily absent from 'playhouse copy', conjoining it to his own assertions with 'however'. But if one accepts the validity of Werstine and Long's scholarship, one simply cannot use the evidence of 'permissive' stage directions to determine printer's copy; it will not do to simply name-check them and move on without stating where one stands on the matter. The problem recurs with other evidence for authorial copy, 'Changes in speech prefixes [that] seem also to reveal subtle shifts in a character's function or status' (the indicator first seized on by R. B. McKerrow ('A Suggestion Regarding Shakespeare's Manuscripts', *RES* 11[1935] 459–65), and again Werstine's demonstration that these can be found in theatrical (as opposed to authorial) manuscripts is acknowledged but not refuted. On the matter of actors' names ('Gabriel', 'Sinklo', and 'Humfrey') occurring in the Folio text, Martin tangles with W.W. Greg much as Cox and Rasmussen do in the Arden version, as we shall see. Martin thinks that these names show that Shakespeare had specific people in mind for certain parts as he wrote, and in a footnote writes that 'The names are unlikely to derive from a prompter annotating the play, since this kind of annotation typically takes the form of extra information or duplicate directions in extant playhouse manuscripts of the period. See Greg, *Folio*, pp. 114–15' (p. 98 n. 5). It is worth remembering that Greg's view was that where an actor's name glosses a character's name, we are seeing signs of a prompter reminding himself who was playing a minor part. Where, as here, we find the actor's name instead of the character, Greg thought that this was typically authorial but should only occur where it would matter to the dramatist who played the part, since minor parts that anybody could take would not concern the dramatist during composition (*The Shakespeare First Folio: Its Bibliographical and Textual History*, pp. 117, 142). The problem here is that the actors' names are instead of character names (so, consistent with authorial copy), but the roles are minor ones that anyone could play (something about which the author should not care), and Martin cites Greg's firm view that in the present case the names could not have come from Shakespeare's pen (p. 99). In this Martin stands against Greg, whom he sees contradicted by the fact that actors' names in 'extant dramatic manuscripts' and early printings of Shakespeare 'are overwhelmingly hired men rather than sharers', in support of which assertion he cites a page of John Dover Wilson's 1952 Cambridge edition of the play. Wilson does indeed discuss the matter of actors' names, and disagrees with Greg about what they tell us, but he makes no such claim about 'extant dramatic manuscripts' generally, confining himself to Shakespeare alone.

The new bibliographical mast is broad enough to accommodate disagreements between Wilson and Greg, yet having pinned his colours to it Martin remains tentative: 'If these traces and anomalies point to F being Shakespeare's working papers' then we should consider whether they were annotated in the theatre. Departing from Greg and previous editors of this play in thinking that they were not, Martin follows William B. Long's lead ('"A Bed | for Woodstock": A Warning for the Unwary', *MRDE* 2[1985] 91–118) in deciding that unannotated papers could have been used in the playhouse 'as an acceptable, "finished" script' (p. 100). One is entitled to ask if Martin means by 'script' what he earlier meant by 'promptbook'—he uses the word 'prompter' on the previous page—and one detects here a trend. As reviewed here last year, Gordon McMullan's Arden Shakespeare edition of *Henry VIII* used the expression 'a score for a stage play' to avoid the problematic word 'promptbook'. Martin notes that F has none of the features that McKerrow claimed book-keepers added to their manuscripts—anticipatory calls for actors and properties, stage directions naming properties needed later in a scene, names assigned to character roles, and anticipatory entry stage direction ('The Elizabethan Printer and Dramatic Manuscripts', *Library* 12[1931] 253–73), but in the same footnote (p. 100 n. 2) Martin admits that Werstine ('Narratives About Printed Shakespeare Texts: "Foul Papers" and "Bad" Quartos', *SQ* 41[1990] 65–86) has 'questioned' the application of these criteria and advised taking each document individually. This is hardly an adequate description of Werstine's critique of new bibliography: if Werstine is even just mostly right, we have precisely nothing to tell us what copy underlay a given printing assessed solely on internal evidence. For Martin the most economical explanation is that F represents 'Shakespeare's draft papers' and that a fair copy of these was sent off to get the Master of the Revels's licence and become the 'official promptbook'. Little tweaks that seem un-Shakespearian (such as 'Speaking to Bona', 'Speaks to Warwick' in III.iii) might have been added by the Folio editors for readerly clarity (p. 101).

In his narrative of *True Tragedy*'s text, Martin records that O was reissued in 1600 to make Q2 and then in 1602 Thomas Millington (publisher of *The Contention of York and Lancaster* and *True Tragedy*) transferred his rights to Thomas Pavier, who in 1619 had William Jaggard (later publisher of F) print both plays together as *The Whole Contention betweene the two famous houses, Lancaster and Yorke* (Q3). The copy for our play in this composite Q3 was 'an edited copy of O' (about this Cox and Rasmussen disagree, as we shall see) with just one passage possibly altered with authority and the other changes occurring in the printing house (p. 104). O is about 1,000 lines shorter than F, needs the same number of actors, has some dramatic alternatives that are arguably preferable to F, and some verbal 'anomalies' that are hard to explain by revision or printing error. Edmond Malone thought O an earlier, non-Shakespearian, version of the play but in the twentieth century it was mostly held a report of the play better represented by F. The latter view has recently come in for criticism, and Martin thinks there is compelling evidence to support revision *and* reporting: '*True Tragedy* is a memorially reported early version of the play that Shakespeare substantially revised as *3 Henry 6*' (p. 105). What has traditionally been thought to clinch the argument for memorial reconstruction being the source for O is Peter Alexander's observation that it has a corrupted version of the row between King Edward and his brothers Gloucester and Clarence about the daughter-heiresses of lords Hungerford, Scales, and Bonville being married (with King Edward's consent) to Hastings, the Queen's brother, and the Queen's son respectively, rather than to Gloucester or Clarence, who, as the king's brothers, should come first. *3 Henry VI* gets it right, and followed the sources, while *True Tragedy* omits the important fact that it is the Queen's relatives being preferred that irks Gloucester and Clarence, and *True Tragedy* names Scales (rather than his daughter) and has him married to the daughter of 'Lord Bonfield'. This looks like the kind of error someone might make in dim recollection, although Steven Urkowitz claimed that *True Tragedy* makes good enough sense on its own; that the details are not historically correct does not make it a bad text. For Martin the important point is this name 'Lord Bonfield', which appears in no sources but does appear in Robert Greene's *George a Greene* which was published in 1599 with a title page claiming that it was performed by Sussex's men. We know from its 1594 title page that *Titus Andronicus* was owned by Derby's (also known as Strange's), Pembroke's, and Sussex's men, so this is a link to *True Tragedy* since the 1595 title page claims it was performed by Pembroke's. Thus 'Bonfield' appears in two plays with no historical connections but both performed 'by companies [Sussex's and Pembroke's] who shared scripts and personnel', something we know from the evidence of the *Titus Andronicus* title page and other company history. Hence the name Bonfield 'is a non-authorial interpolation by players', which supports Alexander's theory of memorial reconstruction, although there is nothing necessarily surreptitious about this (pp. 108–9). Also, *True Tragedy* has 'Edward, rhou [*sic*] shalt to *Edmund Brooke* Lord *Cobham*' (A7^r) where F has 'You *Edward* shall vnto my Lord *Cobham*' (TLN 353, I.ii.40). The sources do not give this man a personal name, only a title, and it is hard to imagine that F represents something removed from the play, for if the motive was to not offend the Cobhams the name could have been taken out altogether. Moreover, *True Tragedy* is incorrect: the man's name was Edmund not Edward Brooke, so the likeliest explanation (as Hattaway suggested in the New Cambridge Shakespeare edition) is that the personal name was added by an actor, perhaps to allude to the Lord Cobham of Shakespeare's time, William Brooke (p. 110).

Further, albeit weaker, evidence for memorial reconstruction is the phenomenon of characters betraying knowledge they could not yet have at a given point in the play. An example happens near the end of II.v in *True Tragedy* (C3^v) when Exeter enters in the middle of a battle and says 'Awaie my Lord for vengance comes along with *him*' (my emphasis), which word 'him' has no antecedent. In F, however, this line appears slightly differently ('Away: for vengeance comes along with *them*'; my emphasis, TLN 1275) and continues an ongoing onstage conversation. Martin's explanation of what happened is unfortunately foggy: 'O's entry was apparently changed so that Prince Edward preceded Exeter on stage' (p. 111). This is a badly worded ambiguity and might mean that the printed text O was changed in some way or that something was changed to make the printed text O; John Jowett's notational shorthand (MSO meaning 'the manuscript underlying O', MSF meaning 'the manuscript underlying F') is ideal for dispelling such confusion. Martin's suggestion seems to be that the reporters making O failed to have the Queen, Prince Edward, and Exeter enter as a group and instead had them enter successively, and then in response to this change the reporter(s) adjusted 'them' to 'him' because Exeter's line now responded only to what the Prince has just said, which would be about just one man, Warwick ('him'), whereas previously Exeter was responding to what the Prince had just said about Warwick and what the Queen said about Edward and Richard (thus 'them'). The reporters then omitted Prince Edward's comment on Warwick so that Exeter's comment has no antecedent. I find this inherently implausible: the reporters change a line of dialogue ('them' to 'him') to suit a change in stage direction, which is fairly fussy of them, and then they fail to notice that they have produced nonsense because another line of dialogue has been omitted. Alternatively, suggests Martin, F simply revises O, and then we have still the problem of Exeter's gibberish in O. Of the same kind of weak evidence for memorial reconstruction is the moment in O's V.i when Richard of Gloucester advises against entering the gates of Coventry in pursuit of Oxford's troops ('Weele staie till all be entered', E1^v) in language that suggests that he knows that more (making up 'all') are coming, which is in fact foreknowledge of the ensuing actions of Montague and Somerset. In F, by contrast, Edward simply cautions against going in because 'other foes' (TLN 2741) may turn up, which phrasing Martin calls 'strategically hypothetical' (p. 112). Finally, Martin observes that *True Tragedy* lacks the classical allusions that Shakespeare put in his other early plays, although of course one might argue that they were simply added to F as part of a process of authorial revision.

The relationship between O and F is so complex, Martin argues, that it cannot be explained solely by memorial reconstruction or revision; rather, both must be operating. Twentieth-century scholars who went beyond the theory of simple piracy as the reason for memorial reconstruction argued that O represents an abridgement for touring with fewer players, but they never quite agreed on how to do the calculations of doubling. Martin's calculation of the doubling shows that O and F need the same personnel: thirteen men and four boys, plus a couple of non-speaking walk-ons. Thus a rationale for abridgement (to save parts) falls, although one might still argue that O represents abridgement for shortened playing time. But O does not do its cutting simply; rather, it is full of 'complex rearrangement of scenes and lines' that seems oddly roundabout if the desire was just to save time. In some respects O actually expands on F (including having stage directions derived from the sources), so we cannot just say that O represents a badly remembered F, nor that O represents a heavily censored text since it retains surely the most censorable event, the disinheriting of Henry's son. Martin supports Malone's conjecture that Shakespeare went back to the play that we know from *True Tragedy* and amplified it to make the play we know as *3 Henry VI* (p. 115). In this he follows other twentieth-century critics, but where they merely applied subjective criteria—*True Tragedy* being good enough to stand on its own and not merely a bad report—or were simply expressing post-structuralist dissatisfaction with new bibliography, Martin thinks he has something more tangible to base his argument upon. By comparing O and F's dependence on Holinshed and Hall he attempts to show a pattern of authorial revision (p. 117). For this he uses three examples and promises more in a forthcoming essay called 'Reconsidering the texts of *The True Tragedy of Richard*

Duke of York and *3 Henry VI*'. Since publication of Martin's edition the essay has appeared, although under the more definite title of '*The True Tragedy of Richard Duke of York* and *3 Henry VI*: Report and revision' (*RES* 53[2002] 8–30) and it will be reviewed here next year. Martin's first example is in II.i where, between the towns of Wakefield and Towton, Warwick sizes the opposing Yorkist and Lancastrian forces: in O it is 50,000 Lancastrians versus 48,000 Yorkists, while in F it is 30,000 Lancastrians versus 25,000 Yorkists. Martin compares these numbers to those given in the sources. For the battle of Towton, Holinshed and Hall agree on 60,000 Lancastrians versus 48,660 Yorkists while for the second battle of St Albans Holinshed says 20,000 Lancastrians versus 23,000 Yorkists, while Hall mentions only the 23,000 Yorkists. Thus for II.i, O seems to be getting its numbers from the battle of Towton while F gets its from the second battle of St Albans. So much seems clear, but Martin goes on 'Thus it seems that O, with its figures linked to Towton, followed Hall, whereas F followed Holinshed' (p. 118), which is a claim I cannot fathom since both sources report on both battles. In any case, the numerical correspondences do not seem close enough to posit definite use of the sources and since an educated person would know something of the scale of the Wars of the Roses anyone might pick appropriate numbers unaided. Unfortunately, Martin's explanation of all this is tortuous.

More clearly, Martin's second illustration from source use is that, for the battle of Tewkesbury, O follows Hall in having Margaret and Prince Edward captured together, while F follows Holinshed in having Prince Edward captured separately. There are also in F a couple of pious lines from Margaret that might reflect Holinshed's unique report that she fled to a religious house. During the revision of the O version to make the F version, Shakespeare apparently turned from Hall to Holinshed, as he generally did with his history plays. Martin's final example is Clarence's return to the Yorkist side after supporting the Lancastrians for a while. Hall and Holinshed report that this was motivated by a 'damsel, belonging to the Duchess of Clarence' persuading him of the unnaturalness of his actions, while Hall alone also reports Richard's agency in bringing his brother back over to the Yorkists' side, with whispered words, but reminds the reader of the damsel's prior work. O dramatizes Richard's agency ($E1^v$–$E2^r$) and gives him alone the credit for bringing Clarence back, whereas Holinshed stresses instead Clarence's internal turmoil and his pretence to Warwick that he is still on the Lancastrian side, which is what F dramatizes. In F Clarence apologizes to his singular 'brother' (that is, Edward) for his betrayal, whereas in O he refers to his 'brothers' (Edward and Richard), thereby again stressing Richard's role as Hall does. In all, O seems influenced by reading Hall and F by reading Holinshed (pp. 119–21).

At this point Martin summarizes where we are ('Having established that O is a memorial report of an earlier version of the play which Shakespeare revised as F') and turns to F's use of O (or its derivatives) as printer's copy. McKerrow thought that the opening stage direction and first eighteen lines of IV.ii in F were set directly from O or Q3, and Martin rightly comments that 'none of the variants McKerrow cites is indubitably an error' (p. 122), although of course they are not 'variants' but invariants, places where F follows what McKerrow thought was an error in O, for that is how you prove the dependence of one text upon another. For the Arden 2 edition, Andrew Cairncross went further and claimed that much of F was set from O. The 1986 Oxford *Complete Works* editors were sceptical of the McKerrow/

Cairncross view but accepted that the F compositor might intermittently have glanced at Q3 and perhaps took a whole passage from it if his copy was not good. Martin, on the other hand, finds no evidence of Q3 being used in the printing of F and argues that one can explain the agreement of Q3/F against O/Q2 by 'acceptable metrical variation, different chronicle details, and rewriting'. Martin gives the example of George of Clarence saying in the Folio that Henry has passed a law 'To blot out me, and put his owne Sonne in' to which Clifford replies 'And reason too, I Who should succeede the Father, but the Sonne' (TLN 967–9). George's speech should, of course, be given to Edward (the son who has been blotted out) and Cairncross thought that it was the compositor following O (at least for the speech prefix) that caused the problem, for O has a different speech that does suit George of Clarence ('blot our brother out', B7ᵛ). In support of this view one can observe that at this point Q3 and F agree on some incidentals against O: the spelling 'Parliament' (Q2/Q3/F) against 'Parlement' (O) and the dividing of Clifford's next line ('And reason ... the son') into two verse lines (Q3/F) rather than being a single long overlapped line (O/Q2). But Martin observes that F has a pleasing literary opposition of sons/fathers that O/Q3 spoils with its 'blot our brother out' and that O/Q2/Q3 have Clifford say 'And reason George' where F has 'And reason too'. If the F compositor was following Q3 at this point (rather than his manuscript copy), why did he change 'George' to 'too' if his Q3 copy showed that George had indeed just spoken and hence 'And reason George' (the Q3 reading) would be correct? No, Martin concludes, more likely F is a revised version of O and O's problems are those of 'faulty reporting' (pp. 122–3).

In seeking the dates of original composition and staging, of the reporting to make *True Tragedy*, and of Shakespeare's revision to make what got into F, Martin notes some fixed points (pp. 123–5). The play's composition cannot precede publication of Holinshed's *Chronicles* in 1587 nor be later than Robert Greene's death on 2 September 1592, since Greene famously alluded to a line from *True Tragedy* ('Tiger's heart wrapped in a player's hide'). The significance of three other dates are debatable: Henslowe's record of 'harey the vj' being 'ne[w]' on 3 March 1592, the plague closure starting 23 June 1592 (and lasting until 1594), and Thomas Nashe's allusion in *Pierce Penniless* to a performance of *1 Henry VI* by August 1592 ('brave Talbot ... fresh bleeding'). We cannot be sure that Henslowe's 'harey the vj' is *1 Henry VI* (as opposed to parts 2 or 3), but Roslyn Knutson showed that, for multi-part plays, Henslowe consistently recorded if something were 'part 2', so probably 'harey the vj' is part 1; Henslowe often neglected to state the first part number for a multi-part play. If *True Tragedy* was written after *1 Henry VI*, then *Contention of York and Lancaster* and *True Tragedy* must have been written and performed between March 1592 ('harey the vj' being 'ne[w]') and June 1592 (the theatre closure), which does not seem enough time. Just possibly, Greene got the 'tiger's heart' line from a manuscript of the play, not from performance, so the plague closure is not relevant. Most likely is E.K. Chambers's explanation that *Contention of York and Lancaster* and *True Tragedy* formed a two-parter written before *1 Henry VI* (the prequel), but then the ownership of the different parts gets tricky. *1 Henry VI* we know was performed by Strange's men led by Edward Alleyn at the Rose (as Henslowe's Diary indicates) and *True Tragedy*'s title page says it was performed by Pembroke's men. Martin claims that *Contention of York and Lancaster* was definitely a Pembroke's men's play too even though its title page is silent on the matter, and does not indicate why he thinks so (p. 126). Andrew Gurr showed that Pembroke's company was created to fill the Theatre when Edward Alleyn rowed with James Burbage in May 1591 and took his company of Strange's men away. Initially Pembroke's were successful, playing at court over Christmas in 1592 and 1593, but they failed in their provincial tour of summer 1593 and pawned their apparel and playbooks. Shakespeare seems to have retained control of his plays, since they ended up with the Chamberlain's men, as did he. So, who reconstructed *True Tragedy* from memory? It could have been Pembroke's men, if Shakespeare had the play in his possession and did not go on their provincial tour of 1592–3. The *Titus Andronicus* title page suggests a traffic in playbooks and personnel from Strange's to Pembroke's to Sussex's, so alternatively those of Pembroke's company who did not move on to another one after its collapse in August 1593 might have tried touring, perhaps joining up with 'a downsized Strange's' and/or Sussex's. Martin claims that the fact of the *True Tragedy* title page mentioning only Pembroke's (not Strange's or Sussex's) suggests that a hard-up regrouping of Pembroke's 'made the report sometime after August 1593, which they subsequently published in early 1595' (p. 127). Again, Martin's logic defeats me: why does mentioning only Pembroke's on the *True Tragedy* title page suggest this? If they were poor in August 1593 and recollected *True Tragedy* to make some money from a printer, why wait until 1595 to get it printed? The argument here is too compressed even for a specialist to follow.

At all events, *True Tragedy* was written before *1 Henry VI* opened in March 1592 and if written before May 1591 (the creation date of Pembroke's men) then it was most likely written for Strange's, with Edward Alleyn as 'bigboond' Warwick (O, E3^r), or if after then for Pembroke's. That *True Tragedy* was in performance by 1591 is suggested by its being echoed in *The Troublesome Reign* (published 1591) and by its echoing of Spenser's *The Faerie Queene* (published 1590). But what of the objection that *1 Henry VI* just feels like his early, less accomplished, work, too 'rough' to be a later-written prequel to *Contention of York and Lancaster* and *True Tragedy*? We can get around that by saying that *1 Henry VI* is not all by Shakespeare, and multiple authorship would also explain its link with Strange's (the 'harey the vj' is definitely for Strange's at the Rose) but not Pembroke's; Martin gives the analogue of the multi-authored *Sir Thomas More* which belonged to Strange's (pp. 128–9). The final remaining question is 'when did Shakespeare revise the play to make the F text?' (pp. 130–2). The names of actors in the Folio texts of *2 Henry VI* and *3 Henry VI* help: John Holland and George Bevis appear in the former—although, as reviewed last year, Roger Warren, 'The Quarto and Folio Texts of *2 Henry VI*: A Reconsideration' (*RES* 51[2000] 193–207), believes that Holland is a name from the sources, not an actor, and Bevis is the mythical figure— and 'more certainly' (presumably a nervous glance at Warren's view, although his article is not cited) there are Gabriel Spencer, John Sinclo, and Humphrey Jeffes in *3 Henry VI* (p. 130). Spencer's death on 22 September 1598 gives us a *terminus ad quem* for the manuscript underlying Folio *3 Henry VI*. From the minor parts played by Spencer and especially Jeffes (whom we know of as an Admiral's men sharer later) we may guess that the manuscript is relatively early, else they would have bigger parts. Holland and Sincklo are in the plot of *2 Seven Deadly Sins* 'which was performed by Strange's Men at the Curtain around 1590, and certainly before 1592', for which claim Martin cites work by Greg, Gurr, and Scott McMillin and Sally-

Beth MacLean. Actually, this is not certain and McMillin seriously entertained the possibility that *2 Seven Deadly Sins* might be as late as 1594 ('Building Stories: Greg, Fleay, and the Plot of *2 Seven Deadly Sins*', *MRDE* 3[1988] 53–62) and in a forthcoming paper David Kathman dates it to 1597–8 on the basis of biographical knowledge about the actors named in the plot. Spencer, Sinclo, and Jeffes came together in the Chamberlain's men in 1594, so that is the earliest date of the revision that made the version of the play we know from the Folio, and the *terminus ad quem* is provided by the uncensored reference to Lord Cobham (discussed above), which must precede the controversy over *1 Henry IV* in 1596. There is also some evidence in the expansion of Margaret's oration in V.iv that Shakespeare was reading Arthur Brooke's *The Tragical History of Romeus and Juliet* as he revised the play, which would make it roughly contemporary with *Romeo and Juliet* written in 1595 and a hint of *Richard II* confirms 1595 as the likeliest year.

Having described precisely what he thinks of the materials he is working from, Martin is able is give a pleasingly crisp description of his editorial procedures: his edition is based on F, the expansion and revision of the play reported in O. F's variant passages are followed except in a few cases of 'error, omission, or indispensable clarification', and where O's stage directions are simply significantly different but not essential they are merely recorded in the collation (p. 133). (Being post-theatrical, O's stage directions perhaps offer insights about how particular matters were settled in the theatre, but the revision to make F diminishes this value.) Martin's edition uses the Oxford Shakespeare's broken brackets for 'plausible but debatable or ambiguous' stage directions and follows Stanley Wells's well-known rules on modernizing spelling. Because Martin thinks the Folio text substantially different from the O text, he 'reluctantly' uses the Folio's title. I defer an examination of Martin's choices regarding particular textual cruxes until the introduction to the Arden Shakespeare edition has been described so that the differing choices of the two editions can be compared directly. To conclude on Martin's Oxford edition it remains only to note his appendices. Appendix A, 'Commentary on Historical Sources' (pp. 327–56), is a study of how the play relates to what is described in Hall and in Holinshed keyed to the line-numbers in Martin's text, so it is a set of commentary notes, more full than could be got onto the pages of the main text. Martin's comments are about the differences in the narratives as well as the literary qualities of what Shakespeare does with his source material. Appendix B, 'Montague' (pp. 357–60), is about how this character relates to two historical figures, Warwick's father and Warwick's brother, and to the character of Salisbury in *2 Henry VI*. In Appendix C, 'Casting Analysis of "True Tragedy" and "3 Henry VI"' (pp. 361–78), Martin builds on David Bradley's *From Text to Performance in the Elizabethan Theatre* and T.J. King's *Casting Shakespeare's Plays: London Actors and their Roles, 1590–1642*, but he disagrees with their view that older boys could not double in non-speaking roles such as drummers, flag-carriers, and soldiers. Martin's view that they did perform such 'hack work' (as Greg called it) comes from the plots of *The Battle of Alcazar* and *Orlando Furioso*. Martin reckons that O needs fifteen men and four boys, while F needs thirteen men and four boys, but in fact this is effectively the same thing because the two extras in O could be just walk-ons. In Appendix D, 'Queen Margaret's Tewkesbury Oration' (p. 379), Martin reprints the bit of Brooke's *Romeus and Juliet* from which Shakespeare took this speech, and Appendix E, 'Alterations to Lineation' (pp. 380–2), needs no explanation.

The division of labour in John D. Cox's and Eric Rasmussen's Arden Shakespeare edition of *3 Henry VI* is made explicit: Cox thanks Rasmussen for editing the text and writing the textual introduction and textual notes (p. xv) and Rasmussen thanks Cox for 'overturning centuries of editorial tradition by pointing to overlooked analogues that render emendation unnecessary and the Folio eminently defensible' (p. xvii). The style of Cox and Rasmussen's long introduction (176 pages) is quite unlike Martin's for the Oxford Shakespeare and unlike other Arden Shakespeare editions, for they set out to tell the story of 'written engagement with the play (at least in English) from the earliest comment to the latest' (p. 4), surveying the reception rather than giving a reading of the play. Theirs is a huge undertaking, and some aspects of the reception (such as feminist criticism) are only sketched in. On the matters of Henslowe's receiving £3. 16s. 8d. for 'harey the vi' which was 'ne[w]' on 3 March 1592 and Nashe's *Piers Penniless* being entered in the Stationers' Register on 8 August 1592, with its reference to 'brave Talbot' bleeding again the English stage, and on Greene's *Groatsworth* being entered on 22 September 1592 with its allusion to *True Tragedy*, Cox and Rasmussen are on familiar ground surveyed above (pp. 5–6). O's stage directions are fuller than F's, although it is a third shorter overall, and call for use of the stage balcony ('on the walles' E1^r). Cox and Rasmussen are unaccountably confident that the play was first performed at Henslowe's Rose and for details of its design they rely on Christine Eccles's flawed book *The Rose Theatre*. Cox and Rasmussen reproduce a picture (p. 8) of Jon Greenfield's model of the first Rose [1587], which shows the theatre having no stage cover, but, as discussed in last year's review, an erosion line one foot in front of the foundations of the Rose's stage (uncovered in 1989) clearly indicates water running off a roof over the stage. Like Randall Martin for the Oxford Shakespeare, Cox and Rasmussen think that Jonson's mockery of 'York and Lancaster's long jars' being staged with 'three rusty swords' is, like Sidney's criticism, a misapplication of Italian neoclassicism to the English stage (pp. 9–10), but oddly they cite Jonson in original spelling ('iarres') although they modernized Henslowe's 'harey the vj' to 'harey the vi' on p. 5.

Cox and Rasmussen chart the stage history of the play from its first performances to the present, in particular via John Crowne's Restoration adaptation *The Miseries of Civil War* (pp. 12–14) and then nineteenth- and twentieth-century revivals that returned more or less to Shakespeare. Like Martin for the Oxford Shakespeare, Cox and Rasmussen reproduce photographs from notable twentieth-century productions, but they also devote nearly half a page to the picture of a horribly injured skull recovered from the site of the battle of Towton (p. 24), rather tenuously linked to Clifford's death from an arrow in his neck. Cox and Rasmussen report on the 1999–2001 Royal Shakespeare Company production of *3 Henry VI* in its *This England* cycle, but neglect to use that label, so adding to the difficulties of future theatre historians. This production ended with the Yorkists in the final scene walking over a stage covered with Henry VI's blood, and Cox and Rasmussen comment that 'Shakespeare's occasional pun on "guilt" and "gilt" has never been rendered more graphically' (p. 32). Without further explanation this remark is cryptic: what is the link between blood and gold-plating? Over-egging their critical pudding, Cox and Rasmussen claim that an amateur production of *3 Henry VI* by slave descendants on the Honduran island of Roatan in 1950, reported by Louise Wright George, 'undoubtedly staged the most radical version' of the play, in blissful ignorance of Bertolt Brecht and Jan Kott (p. 40).

Cox and Rasmussen are careful to separate the question of whether Shakespeare alone wrote *3 Henry VI* from the question of O representing a memorially reconstructed version. Edmond Malone took the view that Greene's charge against Shakespeare ('beautified with our feathers') was one of plagiarism, and hence that Shakespeare had rewritten an existing play by George Peele, and that this is why the first printings of *Contention of York and Lancaster* [1594] and *True Tragedy* [1595] name Pembroke's men rather than the Shakespearian company of Chamberlain's/ King's men. The memorial reconstruction hypothesis of Peter Alexander and Madeleine Doran provided a different way to explain *True Tragedy*'s inferiority to *3 Henry VI*, but it does not directly bear on the matter of authorship. Cox and Rasmussen think that the authorship question might be insoluble since even style detection by computer analysis is thrown off by 'variations in orthography and typography and poor proofreading of early printed texts' (p. 47); they might have added also the problem of one writer imitating another's style. On the matter of computerized stylometry, Cox and Rasmussen report as though factual Don Foster's objections to the work of the Shakespeare Authorship Clinic at Claremont McKenna College, specifically the failure to 'commonize' (regularize in matters of incidentals) the electronic texts used, and they give an over-generalized explanation of this procedure: 'As a basis for accurate computer analysis, texts need to be "commonized", i.e. rendered identical in textual accidentals such as spelling, punctuation and word breaks' (p. 47 n. 2). This may be true for some of the linguistic tests one may want to apply, but clearly not for tests that rely on idiosyncrasies of spelling, punctuation, and word breaks.

As part of their survey of the play's reception, Cox and Rasmussen offer potted histories of a number of 'criticisms': 'Moral' (pp. 49–64), 'Character' (pp. 64–81), 'Historical' (pp. 81–113), 'Psychoanalytic' (pp. 113–17), 'New' (pp. 117–35), 'Performance' (pp. 135–40), and 'Feminist' (pp. 140–8). Several of these sections are too brief to be of use, but in the first the editors offer something of their own reading: sidestepping Tillyardism, they claim that *3 Henry VI* exhibits '"magical" thinking', a belief in the power of 'spells, incantations, curses and blessings', in 'prophecies, omens, "prodigies", oaths and swearing'. About this the play is deeply ambivalent, and although such 'oppositional thinking' (God/Devil, good/evil) was not done away with until the Enlightenment, it could in Shakespeare's time be challenged by scepticism. This challenge was always ultimately futile since there was nothing to replace 'magical' thinking (pp. 57–9). Binary oppositions fused magical and moral thinking and were in the service of monarchial dynasties, but more than anything else Protestantism undermined 'magical' thinking from within by its 'miracles are ceased' principle, manifested in rejection of transubstantiation and exorcism (p. 60). This is a kind of deconstructivist reading, although the editors do not openly identify the self-destructing binary opposition in structural terms even after using the expression 'complementary oppositions' (p. 59). The history plays articulate the crisis in 'magical' thinking, Cox and Rasmussen claim, and although there is some providentialism in the Henry VI plays, much is not providential but man-made. The section on 'Historical Criticism' opens with the surprising claim that 'A "turn to history" marked criticism and critical theory since the 1980s, as a reaction against the "linguistic turn" of deconstruction' (p. 81). Deconstruction is as much a philosophical as a linguistic practice and one more properly seen in alliance with new historicist and cultural materialist thinking than against it. Cox and Rasmussen use the notion of intertextuality to argue that establishing biblical allusions and sources for Shakespeare is a fraught business since his culture was 'saturated with the Bible' and we might easily mistake him getting something directly from there that actually came from another area of contemporary culture such as other plays or prose writings (pp. 88–90). Thus they do not emend the Folio's 'Let me embrace the sower Aduersaries, I For Wise men say, it is the wisest course' (TLN 1422–3) because there is a biblical analogue for it as it stands, 'Agre with thine aduersarie quickely' (Matthew 5:25), which appears in the Geneva Bible and the Book of Common Prayer; Henry, we know, is carrying a prayer book (p. 91). It is this sort of supporting evidence enabling retention of Folio readings that Rasmussen thanks Cox for (p. xvii), although one must observe that the claimed analogy is not close.

Establishing the play within the context of Shakespeare's early career, Cox and Rasmussen point out that it is 'second only to *Titus Andronicus* in the number of words with the root "venge"', which is 'probably' a sign of Seneca's influence (p. 96). Such claims should always be accompanied by a statement of which texts were used to do the word-counting (or which concordance, if that is the source), and moreover rank order is not always as revealing as the raw data it conceals. Using the electronic edition of the Oxford *Complete Works*, I count *Titus Andronicus* having, at 43, nearly twice as many words based on 'venge' as *3 Henry VI*, which has 23. The third place goes to *Richard III* at 20, as one might expect, but in fourth place is *Cymbeline* at 19, ahead of fifth-placed *Hamlet* at 18. The link between frequency of 'venge' words and Senecan influence does not seem quite as clear in the light of this evidence. Stylistically the joining of the separate labours of Cox and Rasmussen is largely seamless, but because their introduction is written to be readable as discrete sections there is necessarily repetition between them, and a point about critical prejudice against Tudor morality plays is made several times. Indeed, an entire inset quotation from Philip Brockbank's seminal essay 'The Frame of Disorder' is produced on pp. 64 and 124. This militates against a 'through-line' of argument, and it is disconcerting to be told that Richard of Gloucester 'is based on the morality play figure called the Vice' on p. 106 of an introduction that has been referring to the Vice figure since p. 78. Congruent with the editors' slightly shaky comments on recent literary and philosophical theory is their misuse of the word 'over-determined' to mean 'trying too hard' or 'forced' ('[Richard] Simpson's reading [that *3 Henry VI* is about 1580s politics] seems arbitrary and over-determined', p. 110) rather than in its proper sense of 'having more determining factors than the minimum necessary'. Especially weak is the section on 'Psychoanalytic Criticism', which claims that Freudianism 'has strong affinities with the inclination to see the human psyche as transcendent and homogeneous across cultures' (p. 113). This does Freud an injustice, since he was much concerned with how specific cultural forms make us unwell, and his theory of the conscious/unconscious split is precisely the opposite of a homogeneous human psyche. Much better is the section on 'New Criticism' that Cox and Rasmussen convincingly claim incorporates the 'metatheatrical' criticism of Anne Righter, James Calderwood, and John Blanpied in which the 'governing theme' (what new critics look for) is always the same:

artistic creation itself. They approvingly cite, with a few reservations, Richard Levin's critique of this approach which pointed out that, if every play is about artistic creation, we might as well all pack up and go home for the critics' work is done (pp. 130–4).

Cox and Rasmussen begin their section on 'The Texts of *The True Tragedy* and *3 Henry VI*' (pp. 148–77) with a couple of useful summaries: a list of all the places where in editing F they have made 'judicious use' of O, and the information that, although it is not conclusive, they intend to present evidence against the view that O is based on a memorial reconstruction and that F was printed from authorial papers (pp. 148–9). As is usual with this third Arden series, the text not used as the basis for the edition is quite superbly reproduced in facsimile at the back of edition. Cox and Rasmussen's departures from the editorial tradition begin with their assertion that Q2 [1600] is not an exact reprint of O: dozens of irregularly divided verse lines in O are relined, properly put back into verse in Q2 (p. 151). Likewise, Q3 (1619, the 'Whole Contention' edition of *Contention of York and Lancaster* and *True Tragedy*) was identified as a reprint of O by Greg, but Cox and Rasmussen have found thirty-two places where Q3 follows Q2's lineation rather than O's. This could happen by independent relineation—after all, the verse was there to be recovered—but 'the simpler explanation' is that Q3 was reprinted from Q2 (p. 153). As the Q3 title page claims, it is indeed 'newly corrected' (there are nearly 300 substantive variants from O/Q2) and 'enlarged' (*Contention of York and Lancaster* gains eleven new lines, *True Tragedy* gains one), although the authority for these changes and additions is disputable. Cox and Rasmussen dispute a claim about space-wasting in Q3 made by the editors of the Oxford *Complete Works* of 1986 (*William Shakespeare: A Textual Companion*, p. 205): signature Q3v does have a couple of extra lines of dialogue, but Cox and Rasmussen wonder why, if these were compositorial padding (as the Oxford editors have it), the man did not just wait until finishing the next page (Q4r), which completed the inner forme, and then see what needed to be done (p. 155). One answer might be that he feared cumulative error making the situation even worse by then. More clear is the case of putative expansion on Q4r that Cox and Rasmussen rightly observe makes no new lines so 'can have nothing to do with problems of casting off' (p. 156). The agency and authority of Q3's variants are important in connection with the link between Q3 and F, and Cox and Rasmussen give the Hinman/Blayney compositor attributions for F, divided between compositor A and B, for whom they conveniently list the respective Folio signatures, Folio page numbers, and corresponding act, scene, and line numbers in their edition. F and Q3 were printed in the shop of William Jaggard and Folio compositor B worked on both. As Cairncross pointed out, there are frequent F/Q3 agreements against O/Q2, one of which (O: 'Henry and his sonne are gone, thou *Clarence* next' sig. E7r; Q3: 'King *Henry*, and the Prince his sonne are gone' sig. Q3v; F1: 'King *Henry*, and the Prince his Son are gone' TLN 3165) shows such strong F1/Q3 linkage that we should think that 'Q3 may have been used in some way by the Folio compositors' (p. 157). To be convincing, a claim of dependence should ideally rest on agreement in error, and since all three versions of the line are acceptable it is possible that each printing represents the reading of its underlying manuscript, which manuscripts differed for some reason.

Cox and Rasmussen agree with the editors of the Oxford *Complete Works* that there is evidence for no more than the occasional consultation of Q3 in the setting of

F, yet they offer a most surprising summary of the bibliographical stemma of textual descent: 'the first edition of 1595 (O) was reprinted with some minor changes in 1600; the second edition (Q2) was then reprinted with further revisions in 1619; this third edition (Q3) was then reprinted in a substantially revised form in 1623 (F1)' (p. 158). This stemma ignores the manuscript(s) entirely and describes only how the printed texts are related, and having just announced that 'Q3 was probably consulted only occasionally by the F compositors' it is bizarre to then use the phrase 'was reprinted ... in' to describe the Q3/F relationship. The hypothesis that O was printed from a memorial reconstruction of the play is based 'rather precariously' on a single variant passage (IV.i.47–57) about the matching of the heiresses of Hungerford, Scales, and Bonville to Hastings, the Queen's brother and the Queen's son. This is mangled in O, but accurately follows Hall's *Chronicle* in F, which fact is the 'linch-pin' of Alexander's argument that Cox and Rasmussen attempt to remove (pp. 161–3). There are, in fact, 'significant orthographic correspondences' between *True Tragedy* and Hall's *Chronicle* in the spellings of Penbrooke, Norffolke, Fawconbridge, and Excester, whereas F has Pembrooke, Norfolke, Falconbridge, and Exeter, and other O/Hall agreements against F include Warwick saying his men number '48. thousand' (O), '48,600' (Hall), but 'fiue and twenty thousand' (F TLN 839, II.i.180), Henry's having reigned for thirty-eight years (O and Hall) rather than thirty-six years (F TLN 1831, III.iii.96), York retreating to Sandall Castle in Wakefield (O and Hall) which is not unspecified in F (TLN 235, I.i.206), and his recollection of battles in Normandy (O and Hall) but in France (F TLN 395, I.ii.72). Less convincingly, there is a link between the phrasing of Hall's account of Warwick's landing in 1470 ('crying "King Henry! King Henry! A Warwick! A Warwick!"') and O ('*All. A Warwicke, a Warwicke*') against F ('*They all cry, Henry*', TLN 2216, IV.ii.27) and O's order of scenes Iv.iv and IV.v is historically correct while F has the chronology reversed. In short, there is much in O that 'could not have been derived from the version of the play preserved in the Folio text' (p. 163), and hence the hypothesis of memorial reconstruction receives another blow; Cox and Rasmussen do not entertain the possibility that simple revision might also separate O and F to account for these differences.

The idea that memorial reconstruction might be done because the authorized book was left behind when a company toured was 'effectively undermined' (p. 163) by Werstine's pointing out the entry in the Hall Book of Leicester dated 3 March 1583/4, which reads 'No Play is to bee played, but such as is allowed by the sayd Edmund [Tilney], & his hand at the latter end of the said booke they doe play'. One might respond that this evidence is open to the usual law of ambiguity in historiography: does a prohibition show that a thing never happened, because it was not allowed, or that it did happen, else why would anyone ban it? Formerly 'bad' quartos are indeed being critically rehabilitated as authorial first drafts, although the 1608 quarto of *King Lear* is a surprising example for Cox and Rasmussen to mention (p. 164) since no one has ever claimed it is 'bad'. The editors acknowledge Steven Urkowitz's argument that O is an original authorial version that was later revised to make the play represented by F, but 'are cautious about advancing this conclusion since other explanations are certainly possible' and they include amongst the other explanations the use of Hall by those making the memorial reconstruction. Laurie Maguire has 'puckishly' pointed out that the repetition of essentially the same lines in O ('For strokes receiude ... I rest my selfe', C1^r; 'For manie wounds receiu'd ... I yeeld to death', E2v) is traditionally attributed to memorial reconstruction (the reporter unintentionally anticipating himself), while the same phenomenon in Q2 *Romeo and Juliet* ('O true Appothecary ... with a kisse I die', L3r) is attributed to authorial false start, and Cox and Rasmussen agree that neither 'proves' anything (p. 165). Actually, these are not the same thing at all since the repetition in O occurs across a gap of about 1,800 lines while in Q2 *Romeo and Juliet* the repetition is on the same page. The former could have got into print without anyone failing to delete anything, since the 'error' is not easily noticed, while the latter must involve someone's failure to delete the repetition since no one produces such a thing intentionally. To put it another way, it is exceedingly difficult to make a single hypothesis that covers both cases: a false start followed by failed deletion works, for instance, in *Romeo and Juliet* but not *True Tragedy*; anticipation by a reporter is good for *True Tragedy* but not *Romeo and Juliet*. Contrary to Maguire and Cox and Rasmussen, Greg did not claim that these things 'prove' (Maguire's scare quotes) what kind of copy was used in the printings, only that they were 'characteristic' of different kinds of copy. Cox and Rasmussen admit the evidence of memory in O's apparent aural garbling of words that F seems to have got right: 'Wrath makes him death' (O B1r), 'Wrath makes him deafe' (F TLN 513, I.iv.53); 'his adopted aire' (O B2r), 'his adopted Heire' (F TLN 561, I.iv.98); 'Tygers of *Arcadia*' (O B3r), 'Tygers of Hyrcania' (F TLN 622, I.iv.155); 'Sore spent with toile as runners' (O C1r), 'Fore-spent with Toile, as Runners' (F TLN 1057, II.iii.1); 'the litnes of this railer' (O E5r), 'the likeness of this Rayler' (F TLN 3013, V.v.38); '*Cyssels*' (O E7v), 'Sicils' (F TLN 3210, V.vii.39) (p. 165). Hence Cox and Rasmussen, although 'dubious about the theory of memorial reconstruction by touring actors', do not think anyone can explain these homonymic errors saying that O was printed from authorial copy. Instead, they find 'more plausible' the view put forward by Blayney with support from Humphrey Moseley's preface to the Beaumont and Fletcher Folio of 1647 that memorial reconstruction was done by actors to give private transcripts to their friends (p. 166).

Like Martin editing the Oxford Shakespeare edition of *3 Henry VI*, Cox and Rasmussen think they have caught Greg in a contradiction in *The Shakespeare First Folio*: '[occasionally] the substitution of the name of an actor, when the part is written with a particular performer in view' shows that the copy was foul papers, and yet of the names of Gabriel Spencer, John Sincler, and Humphrey Jeffes appearing in F *3 Henry VI* Greg writes: '[In no case is it of the least consequence who took these minor parts, and their assignment] cannot possibly be attributed to the author' (p. 167). This does indeed look like an 'internal contradiction' in Greg's writing if one omits, as Cox and Rasmussen do, the words I have placed in square brackets. By selective quotation (dropping the qualification) Cox and Rasmussen make Greg definite where he was tentative ('occasionally') and they ignore his earlier explicit claim that there 'are *two ways* in which actors' names may find their way into dramatic manuscripts' (*The Shakespeare First Folio*, p. 120, my emphasis), from the author's pen and from the prompter's. What matters, Greg claims, is how important it is that a *particular* man plays the part and how big the part is, for an author will care (and write about it) if it does matter dramatically, while a prompter will want to know who is doing it either way, especially if it is a minor part he might otherwise forget the casting of. Here it does not seem to matter if the particular named men are used (Sincler's famous thinness, for example, is not exploited in the scene) so it would seem to be a matter for the prompter, not the author. After tracking the genesis of explanations about actors' names in printed plays for several pages (pp. 167–71) Cox and Rasmussen declare that the whole question has 'little relevance to the editing process' (p. 172) and speculate whether they are not actors' names after all. Gabriel would be a good name for the divine messenger of I.ii, and Humphrey too might be fictional name, although they concede that 'Sinklo' is a harder case to argue. (An obvious retort to this speculation is that even if these are fictional names, no one utters them in performance so any aptness would be lost on an audience.) Cox and Rasmussen support the recent rejection of McKerrow's 'suggestion' in 'Speech Prefixes in Some Shakespearean Quartos' (*PBSA* 92[1998] 177–209) that variant names in speech prefixes and stage directions show authorial copy, citing the usual work by Werstine and Long and also Richard Kennedy. Generally, modernized editions regularize speech prefixes, but there are special cases— aristocratic and monarchial titles get lost and won in the plays—and Cox and Rasmussen think that Lady Grey's speech prefix 'Wid[ow]' in III.ii is such a case: she is known to the audience only as a widow at this point and her widowhood is what makes Edward interested in her. Thus they break with 'three centuries of editorial tradition by retaining the WIDOW SPs in 3.2' (p. 175). This smacks of caprice, and taken further the same logic could change dozens of speech prefixes in modern editions bringing no great advantage and much confusion; a *Hamlet* without Claudius (just 'King') would be the next step, one supposes. Cox and Rasmussen conclude with their view that the compositional priority of *True Tragedy* and *3 Henry VI* is unknown, as are the natures of the underlying manuscripts (pp. 175–6), but one is then left wanting to know how they came to decide on the latter as their base text, even if it was only the tossing of a coin. After their text, Cox and Rasmussen provide four appendices. The first is a facsimile of the 1595 octavo keyed to the line-numbers of their modernized text and to the through line-numbering of Charlton Hinman's facsimile of the Folio. Appendix 2 is a doubling chart in which Cox and Rasmussen reckon that the play's sixty-seven roles require twenty-one men and four boys, which is eight more than Martin calculates in the Oxford Shakespeare. One reason for the difference is that Martin allows boys to double as soldiers and watchmen while Cox and Rasmussen have eight men do nothing but silent soldiering with drums, trumpet, or colours. The third appendix lists the names of the battles depicted in the play, together with their dates, their outcomes, and where they appear in the play, and the fourth gives genealogical tables for the houses of Lancaster, York, and Mortimer.

Regarding particular editorial choices, Martin's Oxford Shakespeare *3 Henry VI* and Cox and Rasmussen's Arden Shakespeare *3 Henry VI* are here considered together. The play begins with a stage direction that brings on the Yorkist party, and for the Arden Cox and Rasmussen import to F the additional information provided by O that they have 'white roses in their hats', and there is a similar detail for the entrance of the Lancastrians at I.i.49.2. Despite a long description of their views about the early texts, Cox and Rasmussen provide no rationale for borrowing stage directions from O, and since F makes sense on its own, it is hard to see this other than as old-fashioned textual conflation; this borrowing recurs throughout the text and only interesting cases will be noted. Martin, on the other hand, declares his intention to ignore O and use only F except where his hand is forced by 'error, omission, or indispensable clarification' (p. 133), so quite understandably he leaves

O's detail about roses out of the opening stage direction and the subsequent one for the Lancastrians. At I.i.19 Norfolk, observing the lopped-off head of Somerset, says 'Such hope have all the line of John of Gaunt' and both editions take this from F without worrying as their predecessors have done that Shakespeare might have meant 'Such hap' but 'hope' got picked up from Richard of Gloucester's next line, 'Thus do I hope to shake King Henry's head'. Richard of Gloucester's encouragement to his brother Edward to live up to the family tradition of slaughtering for power is given in F as 'For Chaire and Dukedome, Throne and Kingdome say' (TLN 749, II.i.93), which makes reasonable sense (with 'say' meaning 'declare yourself ambitious') and thus Martin uses it, whereas Cox and Rasmussen have the benefit of Richard Proudfoot's new and ingenious emendation to ''ssay' meaning 'make a successful attempt to gain'. Both editions use O's 'idle thresher' where F has Warwick say 'Or like a lazie Thresher with a Flaile' (TLN 789, II.i.130), although only Cox and Rasmussen explain that 'lazie' appears in the previous line too and must have been repeated by compositorial accident. Arden notes discussing 'editorial emendations or variant readings' are supposed to be 'preceded by *' (General Editors' Preface, p. xiii) but this one and many more in Cox and Rasmussen's editions lack the asterisk; I can detect no pattern in the few that do receive the mark. F's repetition of 'lazy' makes sense and is defensible as the kind of imperfect language that suits the moment and the speaker (as Frank Kermode explored in *Shakespeare's Language*), so it is surprising that this should be thought a clear error needing emendation.

Alone in the midst of battle, King Henry reflects on the quiet life: 'So Minutes, Houres, Dayes, Monthes, and Yeares | Past ouer to the end they were created' (TLN 1172–3, II.v.37–8). Cox and Rasmussen follow Rowe in inserting 'weeks' between 'days' and 'months' because the preceding speech considers in turn the passing of minutes, hours, days, weeks, and years and because it fills out the metre, whereas Martin passes over the matter in silence. At II.v.119 both editions use Dyce's 'E'en for the loss of thee' instead of F's obviously faulty 'Men for the losse of thee' (TLN 1257), and observe that the box holding types of the letter M lay directly below the one for letter E in the upper case used by compositors, so either the printer's hand went to M box by mistake or someone accidentally put an M in the E box. For Clifford's entrance, wounded, at the start of II.vi, Cox and Rasmussen borrow O's colourful stage direction 'with an arrow in his neck' that follows Hall, while Martin eschews it as 'perhaps faintly ludicrous', not quite what Hall has ('striken in the throte'), and unsuited to the action of the scene. It is worth observing that Cox and Rasmussen's long expression of the uncertainty regarding the nature and origin of the printers' copy for O and F gives them greater freedom to emend and conflate than Martin's more definite account of the textual situation permits him. Before Clifford's line 'And whither fly the gnats but to the sun?' (II.vi.9) Cox and Rasmussen insert from O the line 'The common people swarm like summer flies' that F omits, presumably thinking that the sense requires it. Martin lets F stand, points out that 'summer flies' and 'gnats' do not seem to be the same thing to Shakespeare (the former conjure up heat, the latter light), and persuasively argues that because 'summer flies' are mentioned by Clifford eight lines later in F, conflating O and F (as Cox and Rasmussen do) produces 'lame repetition' not present in either early printing. The moment when the Yorkists find dying Clifford is almost the same on both editions. Martin follows F exactly in having '*Clifford groans | Richard*. Whose soul is that which takes her heavy leave? | A deadly groan, like life and death's departing. | See who it is. | *Edward*. And now the battle's ended, | If friend or foe, let him be gently used. | *Richard*. Revoke that doom of mercy, for 'tis Clifford' (II.vi.41–5), while Cox and Rasmussen move Edward's speech prefix back three words to give him the command 'See who it is'. Both editors resist arguments by C.J. Sisson, among others, that O's distribution of these lines gives markedly superior staging, and both think that O's '*Clifford*. grones and then dies' would rob the scene of the horrible abuse of a dying man by the Yorkists. Martin observes that, although there is some difficulty in Richard answering his own interrogatory command ('See who it is … 'tis Clifford'), his giving orders in the presence of his brother (F's version) hints at his future ambition.

Just before he is captured by the gamekeepers, F has King Henry say 'Let me embrace the sower Aduersaries' (TLN 1422, III.i.24). Martin points out that the stress falling on 'ver' sounds wrong (it should fall on the first syllable), and although 'sweet adversity' is proverbial he follows Sisson (*New Readings in Shakespeare*, p. 84) in rejecting as unlikely a misreading of 'aduersitie' as 'aduersaries' and instead favours Pope's emendation to 'adversities'. Once the plural 'adversities' is accepted, there is no reason to suppose that F's 'the' is a form of the personal pronoun 'thee' and so no need to put a comma before it. Cox and Rasmussen make no emendation to F and rightly point out that 'polysyllabic words often vary in emphasis in Shakespeare'; moreover, they have what they believe to be a biblical analogue for the line as it stands (Matthew, 5:25 as discussed above). Another of Richard Proudfoot's happy suggestions appears in Cox and Rasmussen's alteration of F's 'Whom thou obeyd'st thirtie and six yeeres' (TLN 1831, III.iii.96) to 'six and thirty years' on the grounds that it scans properly and the underlying manuscript might well have had a numerical '36' that was badly expanded by the compositor. Martin follows F here, as he does for Rivers's question to Queen Elizabeth 'Madam, what makes you in this sudden change' (IV.iv.1), for which Cox and Rasmussen follow Collier's alteration of 'you in' to 'in you'. Yet again we see the new bibliographical Oxford Shakespeare editor being reluctant to emend if there is any hope of making sense of the base text, while the Arden Shakespeare editors, who offered lengthy reasons to be editorially cautious (since we do not really know much about the origins of O and F) and are scathing about new bibliography, are in practice more cavalier in their interventions. Both editions reluctantly let stand F's version of the proclamation at 4.769–75, which rather awkwardly uses a common soldier to do the public reading, rather than following O which has Montgomery do it, and both reject out of hand the complicated theory offered by the editors of the Oxford *Complete Works* in which the soldier was invented by a compositor trying to make sense of Hastings's phrase 'fellow soldier'. There remains the problem that the proclamation ends awkwardly ('Edward the Fourth, by the grace of God, King of England and France, and Lord of Ireland, etc'), which neither edition can explain and which both think might indicate that the actor playing the soldier could be relied upon to fill in the rest, whether from a property document or common knowledge.

Neither edition starts a new scene with the Folio's '*Exeunt*' of Henry's supporters at IV.viii.32, Martin adding '*all but Henry*' and then bringing on Exeter to talk to him, while Cox and Rasmussen add '*all but King Henry and Exeter*', the latter already on since the beginning of the scene because they followed Capell in replacing Somerset (who has nothing to do or say in this scene) with Exeter in the opening stage direction. Before the Yorkists burst in on Henry there is in F a '*Shout within, A Lancaster, A Lancaster*' (TLN 2653, IV.viii.50) that both editions retain, explaining that perhaps it is a Yorkist plot to confuse the Lancastrian guards or else the cry of the guards when they realize what is afoot. For the scene in which George of Clarence switches allegiance back to his Yorkist family, both editions have him accompany his line 'Father of Warwick, know you what this means?' (V.i.81) with some business with a red rose: showing it to Warwick in Martin's edition, taking it out of his hat and throwing it at Warwick in Cox and Rasmussen's edition, taking its stage directions from O, which has a quite different version on the scene. In O (as in Hall), a parley with his brother Richard of Gloucester persuades Clarence to change sides, while in F Clarence enters having already made this decision. Martin makes a case for F's version being superior because it focuses on the Clarence–Warwick relationship without the distraction of 'whispering Vice' Richard, while Cox and Rasmussen think O's version 'more dramatic' in its portrayal of 'Richard's rhetoric affecting a reconciliation'. Finally, F has Somerset speak of Montague's dying voice 'Which sounded like a Cannon in a Vault' (TLN 2846, V.ii.44) and both editions keep 'cannon' in preference to O's 'clamor', Cox and Rasmussen silently ignoring the common emendation while Martin alone goes to the trouble of refuting McKerrow's somewhat wild suggestion (actioned by the Oxford *Complete Works*) that the word should be the musical term 'canon'.

Only one monograph of relevance appeared this year, David Scott Kastan's *Shakespeare and the Book*. Kastan begins with a conviction that stage and page are incommensurable, that performance makes a new thing rather than enacting an existing one: '*Hamlet* is not a pre-existent entity that the text and performance each *contain*, but the name that each calls what it brings into being' (p. 9). Thus we should not always think in a stage-centred way, for the stage tends to dehistoricize, making him our Shakespeare, everybody's Shakespeare, while print conserves him. Because Shakespeare clearly intended his work to be seen in performance and seems to have had no concern for his books in print, a recurrent theme in Kastan's book is the ontological and epistemological status of extant early texts of Shakespeare, and although he never quite settles these matters Kastan is sure of the falsity of G. Thomas Tanselle's distinction that the 'work' is the set of unrealized intentions that the 'text' only approximates. Rather, it is the materialization that makes the 'work' possible in the first place (p. 4). Kastan sets out to chart the entire history of Shakespeare in print, beginning with the seldom-noted facts that Shakespeare was a best-selling published author in his own lifetime and that as early as 1638 a Folio of Shakespeare was represented in an oil painting (Van Dyck's painting of Sir John Suckling); already his prestige was a matter of print, not performance (pp. 10–11). Necessarily in a short book (136 pages of text), Kastan's narrative moves at a breathless pace and tends towards generalization, but for the sixteenth and seventeenth centuries in particular there is a wealth of information newly synthesized into a compelling argument. Citing the famous Q1 *Hamlet* line 'To be, or not to be, I there's the point' (D4v), Kastan points out that this seems like textual corruption only if one is expecting to find 'that is the question' and that 'I there's the point' is perfectly good language, indeed it provides a 'moment of unmistakably Shakespearean power along the tragic trajectory of the play' when it occurs in the Folio text of *Othello* (TLN 1855, III.iii.232) (pp. 26–7). From the evidence of early dramatic play texts Kastan constructs a convincing case for thinking that the market for printed plays was the playgoing audience and that only gradually during the period did the name of Shakespeare as author come to be as important as (and eventually more important than) the name of the performing company. The defining event, of course, was the publication of the 1623 Folio, to which Kastan devotes a central chapter, displaying great breadth of historical knowledge and a virtuosity of compression. Just one slip: Kastan gives the wrong date, March 1597 (p. 54), for Lord Hunsdon's promotion to Lord Chamberlain, which changed the name of Shakespeare's company back to the Chamberlain's men; it was in fact 17 April 1597, as Chiaki Hanabusa recently pointed out in 'A Neglected Misdate and *Romeo and Juliet* Q1 (1597)' (*N&Q* 46[1999] 229–30).

Repeating an argument he made in *Shakespeare After Theory* [1999], Kastan argues against one of the one founding principles of new bibliography, A.W. Pollard's distinction of the 'stolne and surreptitious copies' mentioned in the Folio preliminaries from the 'all the rest' in order to form two categories of pre-Folio publication of Shakespeare: the 'bad' quartos and the good. In a footnote to p. 73 Kastan assigns this distinction to Pollard's *Shakespeare's Fight with the Pirates* [1920], but in fact it appeared eleven years earlier in Pollard's *Shakespeare Folios and Quartos* (p. 4). Kastan thinks that, as actors used to textual instability, Heminges and Condell would not have made such a strong distinction between the existing quartos, but since Kastan earlier argues that good editions were produced to replace ones perceived to be 'bad', this appeal to casual theatrical sensibilities seems weak (p. 74). In an article to be reviewed next year ('Shakespeare and the Publication of his Plays', *SQ* 53[2002] 1–20), Lukas Erne argues that Shakespeare's fellow actors actively supported the publication of his plays, in which case there is little reason to suppose with Kastan that the Folio preliminaries dismiss all previously published Shakespeare as 'maimed and deformed'. After a tour of Shakespeare publishing from the seventeenth to the nineteenth centuries (pp. 79–110), Kastan returns to matters philosophical in his final chapter on the impact of electronic text (pp. 111–36), which Kastan values most of all because it defamiliarizes the textual medium, the codex having become so familiar to us that we easily overlook its conventions. Although he thinks recovery of authorial intentions is laudable, Kastan aligns himself with Jerome McGann's view that texts do not exist independently of the media that carry them, rather than Tanselle's Platonic view that textualizations are imperfect representations of unembodiable work, and Kastan's position is implicitly nominalist: '*Hamlet* is perhaps best considered not as something in itself at all but, rather, the name for what allows us comfortably to consider as some metaphysical unity the various instantiations of the play' (p. 133). Kastan's excitement over the possibilities of electronic text is leavened with a caution about the shift of power that the world-wide web brings as readers become 'dependent upon technologies ... [over which they have] distressingly little control' (p. 130–1). They cannot take away our books, he observes, but they can shut down the websites we use; true, but they cannot take our CD-ROMs either. Kastan gets a little carried away on the euphoria of textual copiousness of polymorphously self-connected hypertext, and takes up George Landow's argument that it realizes the textual *jouissance* promised by post-structuralism (pp. 125–7), but in fact in the case of Shakespeare all you need is a collection of about eighty electronic texts to encompass the entire pre-Commonwealth cache of printings. Kastan imagines a huge hyperlinked archive including the early printings, theatre reviews, film versions, etc., but one might argue that we already have such a thing: it is called a library. Marvelling at the possibilities raised by such projects as Peter Donaldson's Shakespeare Electronic Archive at Massachusetts Institute of Technology, Kastan wonders if they take away the need to edit at all, for unedited early editions 'are the most compelling witnesses to the complex conditions of their production' (p. 123). The economics of the print medium have denied readers cheap versions of the early printings in facsimile and Kastan, modestly omitting to mention that he is a general editor of the Arden Shakespeare, complains that today's editions of Shakespeare are too much alike and engender 'wasteful duplication of scholarly energy' (p. 124). Kastan's optimism that electronic text might offer new potentialities unavailable in the print medium is properly guarded, and amidst ever-changing technology he ruefully asks how many of us cannot open electronic documents of our own that we made more than ten years ago (p. 131). (To be fair, this is a matter of individual failing since the computer support departments of universities around the world have always provided the right advice about keeping one's personal archive in a machine-readable form; they report that academics in the humanities tend to ignore the advice which those in the sciences follow.) A tiny flaw that indicates the electronic origins of Kastan's book itself is the persistent use of the wrong kind of apostrophe (a right-facing instead of a left-facing one) at the start of words that begin with elision, as in ''em' (p. 85) and ''s' (meaning 'us', p. 109); Microsoft Word bossily enforces this change to prevent 'error'.

The Review of English Studies contained three articles of interest to this review, and they will be taken in order of appearance. In a companion piece to a previous article, 'Rhymes and Shakespeare's *Sonnets*: Evidence of Date of Composition' (*N&Q* 46[1999] 213–19), MacDonald P. Jackson, in 'Vocabulary and Chronology: The Case of Shakespeare's Sonnets' (*RES* 52[2001] 59–75), reaches the same conclusion by different means, namely that sonnets 104–26 are Jacobean while the rest date from the 1590s. Jackson's evidence for this is Shakespeare's use of particular words at particular times in his career, for example the almost total absence of 'goodness' and 'particular' from the early works can help date sonnets that contain these words. Eliot Slater showed that Shakespearian rare words (ones used more than once but fewer than eleven times overall in the canon) cluster in time and that the sonnets are lexically linked to the plays *Love's Labour's Lost*, *Romeo and Juliet*, *Richard 2*, *Midsummer Night's Dream*, *Much Ado About Nothing*, and *Henry V* (that is, to the period 1595–9), and Gregor Sarrazin's much earlier work found the sonnets to be linked to the period 1593–8 (p. 60). Slater and Sarrazin took the sonnets as a whole, and Jackson thinks it much better to follow A. Kent Hieatt, Charles W. Hieatt, and Anne Lake Prescott, whose work on the occurrence of early (pre-1599) and late (post-1599) Shakespearian rare words in the sonnets showed them that he was working on the sonnets after 1598 and so caused them to divide the sonnets into four zones: sonnets 1–60, sonnets 61–103, sonnets 104–26, and sonnets 127–54. Hieatt, Hieatt, and Prescott decided that zones 1, 2, and 4 were written in 1590–5, while zone 3 was about 1600, and zone 1 was revised in the seventeenth century, but their analyses were not finely grained: rare words were for them just 'early', 'late', or 'both periods', and they did not provide enough information about the distribution of different kinds of rare-words in their control texts for comparison with the distributions in the sonnets (p. 62). For Jackson, an important category of rare words is 'middle'—say, from *King John* [1595–6] to *Macbeth* [1606]—and although Hieatt, Hieatt, and Prescott do not use this category, Jackson manages to extract data about it from their tables. Jackson's table 1 shows the occurrences of 'early', 'middle', and 'late' rare words for the sonnets zones 1–4, although it has a line-wrapping problem that makes it unnecessarily hard to read and its own footnote ends mid-sentence: "'Early" means found in' (p. 63).

This refinement broadly supports Hieatt, Hieatt, and Prescott's earlier conclusions about the zones, but Jackson observes that very rare words tend to cluster more than averagely rare words, so that Sarrazin's category of words that occur only twice or thrice in the canon ought to be a highly sensitive indicator of chronology. Indeed it is: if one divides the canon into four chronological periods, the 'Sarrazin links' mostly confirm that the plays in each group belong together, as Jackson showed in his book *Studies in Attribution: Middleton and Shakespeare* [1979]. Jackson's groups are:

(1) *Titus Andronicus, 1 Henry VI, Comedy of Errors, 2 Henry VI, 3 Henry VI, Taming of the Shrew, Richard III, Two Gentlemen of Verona, Love's Labour's Lost, Midsummer Night's Dream*

(2) *Romeo and Juliet, Richard II, King John, Merchant of Venice, 1 Henry IV, 2 Henry IV, Merry Wives of Windsor, Much Ado About Nothing, Henry V, Julius Caesar*

(3) *As You Like It, Twelfth Night, Hamlet, Troilus and Cressida, Measure for Measure, Othello, All's Well That Ends Well, Timon of Athens*

(4) *King Lear, Macbeth, Antony and Cleopatra, Pericles* (Acts III–V only), *Coriolanus, Cymbeline, Winter's Tale, Tempest, Henry VIII* (excluding the Fletcher parts).

Jackson combines categories 3 and 4 to get a general index of 'lateness': calculate how many 'Sarrazin links' a given play has with this 'late' category (as a percentage of how many links it has to all the categories) and one should get a simple indication of how 'late' it is. If one puts all the plays in order of this ratio they come out pretty much in the chronology we know from Karl Wentersdorf's work. Jackson's explanation of his interpretation of the plays' ordering is somewhat compressed (he calls it 'reading their position on the vocabulary order as a position on Wentersdorf's chronological order'), and I presume his procedure is as follows: one notes that play A occupies position B on the vocabulary list (the plays in order of their 'lateness' index), one looks to Wentersdorf's list for the play occupying position B, which we may call play C, and look to the date, D, assigned to it by Wentersdorf. The question Jackson appears to ask is 'how close to D is the true date of play A?', and he reports that for thirty-one of the thirty-seven plays the answer is not more than three years out, and for half it is correct to within a year (p. 65). This provides a benchmark for an undated work, since one can calculate its 'lateness' index (from its 'Sarrazin links') and then read off the date from the known chronology of the plays. By this method *Venus and Adonis* comes out at 1592–3 and *The Rape of Lucrece* as 1593–4, as we would expect, and *A Lover's Complaint* comes out with such a high 'lateness' index that it has to be seventeenth-century. Thus Jackson's new method confirms results found by other methods, and should be reliable.

What of the sonnets? Jackson shows the 'Sarrazin links' tests for the four-zoned sonnets against the four-grouped plays as his table 2, and the most important thing is that zone 3 shows lots of links with groups 3 and 4, while for the other sonnet zones links with the first two play groups predominate. The pattern of 'Sarrazin links' for the 'Marriage' sonnets (1–17) is 3, 5, 2, 2, showing a bulge of links with the second group of plays and hence suggesting that these were written after rather than before 1595. Jackson does some other tentative reading of the detail, but has little confidence in it; the important thing is that zone 3 sonnets are most likely Jacobean not Elizabethan, and the others were probably written between 1595 and 1599 (p. 66). Having done this analysis for Sarrazin's twice- or thrice-used words, Jackson does it again with the Hieatt–Hieatt–Prescott rare words, which are not nearly so rare and hence not such a good indicator of date. Jackson counts how many sonnets in each zone have their highest number of links with play groups 1, 2, 3, and 4; in other words, for each sonnet he records which of the four play groups it has most links with, and then assigns the sonnet to that group. The results are as follows, with the four numbers for each zone showing how many sonnets in that zone are most strongly connected with play groups:

(1) *Titus Andronicus* to *A Midsummer Night's Dream*

(2) *Romeo and Juliet* to *Julius Caesar*

(3) *As You Like It* to *Timon of Athens*

(4) *King Lear* to *Henry VIII*

Respectively: zone 1 is 9, 12, 10, 7; zone 2 is 14, 9, 7, 1; zone 3 is 4, 4, 4, 3; zone 4 is 8, 4, 3, 3.

This confirms that the sonnets in zone 1 and probably also zone 3 are later than those in zones 2 and 4, for the latter profiles are front-loaded with links to the play groups 1 and 2 (the early plays). Jackson repeats the analysis using the Hieatt–Hieatt–Prescott word links between the sonnets and the poems *Venus and Adonis*, *The Rape of Lucrece*, and *A Lover's Complaint*, and gets the following profiles for links to the poems in that order: zone 1: 12, 33, 7; zone 2: 16, 28, 3; zone 3: 7, 17, 7; zone 4: 10, 12, 1.

Of course, the three poems are different lengths whereas the plays are roughly of equal length, and the specific ratios of length are 33.5:56.5:9.9 for *Venus and Adonis*, *The Rape of Lucrece*, and *A Lover's Complaint* respectively. (Something must be slightly adrift here, as the ratios sum to 99.9 instead of 100.) Thus 22.6 per cent (7 out of 31) of the sonnets in zone 3 have most links with *A Lover's Complaint*, a poem that occupies only 10 per cent of the total size of the three poems taken together, which difference (22.6 per cent being more than double 10 per cent) is caused by the chronological factor that Jackson is attempting to isolate. Since we now think that *A Lover's Complaint* is from the seventeenth century, this suggests that zone 3 (sonnets 104–26) and perhaps also zone 1 (sonnets 1–60) 'are later, or contain more late writing' than the other sonnets (p. 68).

In pursuit of a still more finely grained approach, Jackson counts the Hieatt–Hieatt–Prescott links between the sonnet zones and each individual play in the Shakespeare canon (rather than using four chronological groups as before), checking the observed frequency of the rare words against the background of each play's vocabulary, so that if a play contains 5 per cent of the total number of different words in the canon, it should have 5 per cent of the rare words found in a sonnet; any more than 5 per cent suggests a chronological link. Taken together sonnet zones 1 and 2 have unexpected links with *A Midsummer Night's Dream*, *Henry V*, and *King John*, and although the first of these might be explained by the shared genre of love, the last two cannot. This suggests composition of the 'Young Man' sonnets (1–103) in 1596–9, and that these sonnets have fewer than expected links with the last eleven plays (*All's Well That Ends Well* to *Henry VIII*) confirms this view. The 'Dark Lady' sonnets (127–52) have links with *2 Henry VI*, *The Comedy of Errors*, and *Richard II*, thus the zone 4 sonnets are early. Jackson breaks the sonnets down into still smaller collections (p. 69), although he is cautious with his conclusions because cognizant of the problem that small data sets are subject to distortion by random fluctuation. The case of *The Phoenix and Turtle* Jackson offers as a warning: by the linguistic link analyses described above it would seem to have been written or revised after the few first years of the seventeenth century, but in fact we know it was printed in 1601. Thus we should not rely on the evidence here to say that Shakespeare definitely was involved with the sonnets up to (and including participation in) the publication of the 1609 quarto (p. 73). But if Jackson is right that the 'Marriage' sonnets (1–17) were written after 1595, they cannot have been written to encourage Henry Wriothesley to marry, since from 1589 (his sixteenth birthday) to 1594 Wriothesley was being pressured by William Cecil, Lord Burghley, to marry Burghley's eldest granddaughter Elizabeth Vere, with the threat of a large fine when he was 21. Had Shakespeare written the 'Marriage' sonnets then, Wriothesley would have thought him Burghley's stooge. In 1594, when Wriothesley became 21, this fine was exacted, so addressing the 'Marriage' sonnets to Wriothesley then, when Wriothesley was impoverished and could not afford to marry, would be insulting. No, Jackson concludes, the 'Marriage' sonnets cannot have been addressed to Wriothesley at all; they were to Henry Herbert. Likewise, the 'Rival Poet' sonnets, if written 1596–1604, cannot be about Marlowe since he died in 1593 (p. 74). Conveniently, Jackson ends by restating his main conclusion: 'the majority, if not all, of the last twenty-odd of the sonnets to the Friend [numbers 104–26, in zone 3] were written in the seventeenth century. A few other sonnets, in both the Friend and the Dark Lady series, may have been written equally late, but the bulk of them belong to the 1590s' (p. 75).

Next from *RES* is Charles Cathcart's attempt, in '*Hamlet*: Date and Early Afterlife' (*RES* 52[2001] 341–59), to demonstrate that *Hamlet* must have been written in 1599 because it is echoed in Marston's *Antonio and Mellida* and the anonymous *Lust's Dominion*, both written in the winter of 1599/1600. *Antonio and Mellida* features a portrait inscribed 'Anno Domini 1599' and 'Aetatis suae twenty-four', suggesting composition in 1599 since Marston's twenty-fourth birthday fell in early October 1599 (p. 342) A reference to 'the new Poet *Mellidus*' in *Jack Drum's Entertainment* (late spring/early summer 1600) is the *terminus ad quem* of *Antonio and Mellida* and *Lust's Dominion* is 'widely accepted' to be 'the *spaneshe mores tragedie*' that Henslowe paid Dekker, Haughton, and Day for on 13 February 1600, and the view that Marston too wrote *Lust's Dominion*, for which he was loaned £2 on 28 September 1589, is strengthened in this article. Cathcart admits that the dating of *Antonio and Mellida* from the portrait is not entirely secure since it might be supposed to represent Marston's father and the date the year of his death, but Reavley Gair has argued that Marston's poor relationship with his father at the end makes this unlikely (p. 343). Michael Neill and MacDonald P. Jackson date *Antonio and Mellida* on a collocation of 'morphews' and 'Cousin german' (IV.i.25–6), which also collocate in Philemon Holland's translation of Pliny, published in 1601, but Cathcart points out that Jonson's *Poetaster* clearly satirizes both *Antonio* plays and was in performance by autumn 1601 (according to Tom Cain; earlier according to others), which does not leave enough time for the first *Antonio* play to be in performance by mid-1601, especially as the failure of *Antonio's Revenge* to fulfil the promise of *Antonio and Mellida*'s induction has suggested to several commentators that the second part did not follow hard upon the first. Thus Cathcart rejects the 'morphew … Cousin german' evidence as a piece of later revision not affecting the date of composition of *Antonio and Mellida* (p. 345). In *Antonio and Mellida* there is a ghost that Antonio can, and Mellida cannot, see, just like the closet scene in *Hamlet* except that in *Antonio and Mellida* it 'has no significance beyond the merely local' and hence the influence runs from Shakespeare to Marston and not the other way (p. 346). This logic is faulty, since one might by the same thinking argue that Martin Amis's *Time's Arrow* must be the source for Kurt Vonnegut's *Slaughterhouse Five* because Vonnegut does not make much of the 'time in reverse' idea, using it in just one paragraph. But in fact we know that Amis took this paragraph in Vonnegut's book and expanded it to make his novel. Having established the direction of influence, Cathcart sets out to marshal indisputable evidence of a *Hamlet–Antonio and Mellida* connection by numerous verbal parallels (pp. 346–8), such as 'this distracted globe' (*Hamlet* I.v.97) with 'your distracted eyes' (*Antonio* II.i.267); 'soul … hoops … steel' (*Hamlet* I.iii.63) with 'hooped … steel … soul' (*Antonio* V.ii.210–12); 'sliver' (*Hamlet* IV.vii.145) with 'sliftered' (*Antonio* I.i.219); 'plausive' (*Hamlet* I.iv.29) with 'applausive' (*Antonio* II.i.111); and 'chop-fallen' (*Hamlet* V.i.188) with 'chap-fall'n' (*Antonio* IV.ii.1), this last example being a late 1590s coinage, so unlikely to be due to shared descent from the ur-*Hamlet*.

The most thorough parallel is in Hamlet Senior's battlement speech to Hamlet (I.v) and Andrugio's speech to Antonio (IV.ii): 'thy fathers spirit' (*Hamlet* I.v.9) with 'Thy fathers spirit' (*Antonio* IV.ii.21); 'hold my heart' (*Hamlet* I.v.93) with 'my panting heart' (*Antonio* IV.ii.12); 'freeze thy young blood' (*Hamlet* I.v.16) with 'heat thy blood; be not froze' (*Antonio* IV.ii.18). There are reports of drownings in both plays, with the sinking thing buoyed up and making noise (singing in *Hamlet*, sighing in *Antonio and Mellida*), and the prologue of *Antonio and Mellida* refers to pouring 'pur'st elixed juice' of art into the audience's ears, just as distilled juice is poured in Hamlet Senior's ear. Indeed, both plays use imagery of damaged ears: 'assail your ears' (*Hamlet* I.i.29), 'do mine ear that violence' (*Hamlet* I.ii.170), 'the whole ear of Denmark … abused' (*Hamlet* I.v.36–8), 'cleave the general ear' (*Hamlet* II.ii.565), 'daggers enter in mine ears' (*Hamlet* III.iv.85), 'infect his ear' (*Hamlet* IV.v.88), 'ravished the ear' (*Antonio* II.i.116), and 'taint not they sweet ear' (*Antonio* II.i.193). Cathcart argues that Shakespeare's use is the more thoroughgoing—and there are previous examples in 'Piercing the night's dull ear' (*Henry V* IV.0.11) and 'bite thee by the ear' (*Romeo and Juliet* II.iii.72)—and hence the earlier. Cathcart offers a number of verbal similarities in common words between *Antonio and Mellida* V.ii and the Ghost-on-battlements scene (I.v) in *Hamlet*, as well as the thematic links of feverish sons deprived of their kingdoms, fathers in full armour exhorting sons to resist, and imagery of a poisonous snake. In Shakespeare the snake imagery follows from what precedes it (the story given out of Hamlet Senior's death by a snakebite), whereas in Marston it does not fit well, which tells Cathcart that Marston is the borrower; likewise Balurdo and Ophelia sing different lines from the same song and the same line from another song, but whereas Ophelia's song has thematic links with the rest of the play, Balurdo's does not. There are verbal parallels between the description of the ship headed for

England in *Hamlet* and *Antonio and Mellida*, but in the latter it is not integrated with the plot but rather 'unanticipated and undeveloped' (p. 350). Cathcart uses the same logic for the many echoes of *Hamlet* that occur in *Lust's Dominion* (pp. 351–3) and observes that if the borrowings are accepted we would have to dislodge at least two other datings (*Antonio and Mellida* by internal evidence, *Lust's Dominion* by external evidence) to avoid the conclusion that *Hamlet* was ready by the end of 1599. That particular year might seem already crowded with Shakespeare plays, but then the Chamberlain's men had the Globe to launch and, as Leeds Barroll has shown, Shakespeare wrote not at a steady rate but in bursts of high activity separated by lulls.

If *Hamlet* is as early as Cathcart suspects, we might find other early echoes of it, and Cathcart offers 'retrograde to our desire', with the word 'retrograde' being mocked in Jonson's *Cynthia's Revels* which he thinks was performed in 1600, as the Jonson Folio claims. In fact, the Jonson Folio dates must be March–March not January–December since *Volpone* alludes to the sighting of a whale in the Thames that Stow's *Annals* dates to 19 January 1606, yet the Folio insists it was acted in 1605. Greg made an uncharacteristic slip in this regard ('The Riddle of Jonson's Chronology', *Library* 6[1926] 340–7), thinking the verbal parallel inconclusive because he overlooked a marginal note in Stow that used precisely the words ('as high as Woolwich') found in the play and presumably circulated by word-of-mouth transmission. Thus *Hamlet* could be opened in the first three months of 1601 and yet be echoed by *Cynthia's Revels*, which by Jonson's March–March reckoning was performed in 1600, and Cathcart is wrong to claim that 'A debt to *Hamlet* in *Cynthia's Revels* would exclude 1601 as a possible date for *Hamlet*' (p. 355). Cathcart concludes with a consideration of the interpretative implications for a 1599 rather than 1600–1 date for *Hamlet*, such as bringing Hamlet's use of, and comments upon, satire closer to the Bishops' Ban of 1599, that 'arbitrary and petty ruling' (p. 359)

Finally from *RES* is Katherine Duncan-Jones's argument, in 'Ravished and Revised: The 1616 *Lucrece*' (*RES* 52[2001] 516–23), that the 1616 printing of *The Rape of Lucrece* was a clumsy attempt to make it look more accessible than it is. Many readers have agreed with Gabriel Harvey that *The Rape of Lucrece* is like *Hamlet* in being too long and too difficult. Despite the word 'rape' in the title, there is no titillation, no comedy, no farce, and none of Venus's sweaty physicality in 'bloodless and bodiless' Lucrece; instead, Shakespeare takes us (and his original, predominantly male, readers) into her mind. There is no real narrative in *The Rape of Lucrece* (except the Argument's summary); all is introspection and dialogue. *Venus and Adonis* was printed at least ten times by 1617, *The Rape of Lucrece* just six, and the format of the 1616 edition suggests that it was thought to be in need of editorial intervention to increase its attractiveness to readers. The final line is often mispunctuated as 'Tarquin's everlasting banishment' but Duncan-Jones points out that the Argument makes clear that the entire dynasty is meant (so it should be 'Tarquins'') and thus it should have been a warning to the earl of Southampton about his desires causing revolution, but the poem fails to make the point clear. A mark of the poem's reception in its own time is that Thomas Heywood, Shakespeare's admirer, copied *Venus and Adonis* in his *Oenone and Paris* in 1594, but took at least a decade to copy *The Rape of Lucrece* in his *The Rape of Lucrece: A Roman Tragedy*, which did try to inject the necessary storyline and humour. In

1614 John Harrison sold his rights in *The Rape of Lucrece* to Roger Jackson, who presumably knew that the reprinting of Heywood's bawdy play on the subject (also in 1614) would probably boost interest (p. 519). (Actually, Duncan-Jones writes that it was Nicholas Okes, not John Harrison, but this is merely a slip, as is a slight mixing of January–January and March–March dating schemes.) Jackson was an old hand at reprinting others' works from the past, but in this case he waited a couple of years, perhaps until Shakespeare died, so that his changes (advertised on the title pages as 'Newly revised') might pass as authorial, or perhaps this ruse simply occurred to him once Shakespeare had died. Either way, later seventeenth-century editors did act as though the changes were authorial, and respected them (p. 520). What are the changes? One was to change the title from *Lucrece* to *The Rape of Lucrece*, and another was to break the indigestible work into twelve numbered sections, each prefaced with a summary. But these are misleading, and the crucial moment when Lucrece is comforted by a painting about the sack of Troy and Hecuba's woes (a strong parallel with *Hamlet*) is not indicated. Overall, the section divisions look like an effort to make the work appear less hard going to prospective buyers (p. 521). Duncan-Jones surveys the variants between Q6 [1616] and the earlier printings and concludes that they are mostly silly slips with no overall intention. The most obvious 'revision' is a extensive use of italics: this does not make the thing easier to read, but it might well make the casual peruser *think* that it does, that these are signposts in a renownedly difficult work. By then Shakespeare was already 'dead' in the modern sense regarding an author's loss of control over his writing, as well as in the standard sense (pp. 522–3).

The journal *Analytical and Enumerative Bibliography* folded at the end of 2001 with a bumper double issue on 'Shakespeare's Stationers'. Paul Menzer, '"Tis Heere, Tis Here, Tis Gone": Q1 *Hamlet* and Degenerative Texts' (*AEB* 12[2001] 30–49), makes a rather slight argument that Q1 *Hamlet* needs fewer properties than Q2 or F, so it might reflect a touring text. Menzer's style is irritating in its jokiness and he is poorly served by the quality of typesetting, which renders parts of his own body text as inset quotations. In matters of substance that are slips and ambiguities, such as calling Q1 'a version of F1' (p. 31) which is, of course, impossible since Q1 was printed two decades earlier; he means that the underlying manuscripts might be so related; as ever, Jowett's terminology (MSQ1, MSF) is what is needed. At the end of Q1 Horatio calls for a stage to be erected in the marketplace for him to tell the tragic story of what has happened, whereas in F he says the bodies should be set up on a stage and he will speak the events over them, which sounds to me much the same thing, but for Menzer Q1 is metatheatrical, reflecting its own 'transient' conditions of performance. Menzer characterizes Q1 as 'built for speed' (p. 32) without saying why he thinks touring performances were faster; if he means they were shorter he should at least address recent scholarship showing that shortened plays typically need more actors because doubling opportunities are lost. Colloquialism gives the wrong impression when Menzer calls Philip Henslowe a 'clotheshorse' (p. 33) as though he thinks that the theatrical impresario's costume purchases were all for himself, and Menzer's analysis of the properties called for in different versions of the play is contestable. In what way is the 'Arbor' in which the victim lies in the Q1 dumbshow to *The Mousetrap* 'less specific than F1's "Banke of Flowers"' (p. 35)? I would have thought it equally specific and possibly calling for a more bulky property. Using the REED volume for the town of Cambridge,

Menzer attempts to work out the features of the stage at Queens' College Cambridge, one of the universities that Q1's title page claims hosted a performance, and to relate these to the phrasing of stage directions in Q1. Unfortunately, Menzer does not cite REED page numbers, or even which volume he is using (there are two for Cambridge), and my check of the index entries failed to turn up any evidence of the 17 ft width of the stage claimed by Menzer. Menzer uses the occurrence of 'gallery' in Jonson's *Epicoene* ('do you observe this gallery ... with a study at each end?', IV.v) to argue that the two projecting tiring houses at Cambridge (known from REED) effectively made a 'gallery' between them, hence Q1's stage-direction reference to a 'gallery'. But this overlooks the fact that *Epicoene* was written for the indoor Blackfriars playhouse where there was a flat *frons scenae*, not projecting booths, and in any case his 17 ft stage hardly has the room for what Menzer imagines to be staging. Assuming the two tiring houses were a minimum of 4 ft wide, there would be just 9 ft remaining for a 'gallery', so Hamlet's characteristic claustrophobia is more than adequately justified if, as Corambis says, 'The Princes walke is here in the galery' (pp. 36–8). Menzer's errors come thick and fast in the final pages, including his claim that, in the play's opening moment, 'the wrong guard issue[s] the challenge' (p. 43)—a contemporary military manual shows the pre-emptive challenge to be quite normal (see Charles Edelman, 'Hamlet, Soldier Manqué' (*Around the Globe* 21[2002] 44–5))—and Menzer thinks that Hamlet's 'shall I couple hell?' puns on 'shall I have sex with hell' and he cites the *OED* entry for 'couple' meaning 'come together sexually' without noticing that this entry is specifically intransitive (for reflexive) and Hamlet's usage is definitely transitive (p. 45). A choice ambiguity comes near the end: 'As the first quarto is nearly 1,600 lines briefer than F1 *Hamlet*, there is scant material unique to that text' (p. 46); who can tell which text he means? In the citations of authority, Robert E. Burkhart's book loses part of its title ('designed for') and R.A. Foakes is wrongly credited with sole editorship of the standard edition of Henslowe's Diary (R.T. Rickert was of course co-editor).

Jean R. Brink, 'William Ponsonby's Rival Publisher' (*AEB* 12[2001] 185–205), adds to our knowledge of the stationers William Ponsonby and Robert Waldegrave (not actually 'Shakespeare's Stationers', of course) and their rivalry in printing the works of Philip Sidney. Terri Bourus, 'Shakespeare and the London Publishing Environment: The Publisher and Printers of Q1 and Q2 *Hamlet*' (*AEB* 12[2001] 206–28), argues that Q1 *Hamlet* is not a piracy because the men involved in printing it would not do that, and we can account for the printing of Q1 and Q2 with simple bibliographical knowledge of Nicholas Ling, Valentine Simmes, and James Roberts. Bourus's knowledge of the printing industry is not always perfect: she claims that the Stationers' Company charter 'confined printing, though not bookselling, to the City of London with the exception of the university cities of Oxford and Cambridge' (p. 206). In fact it was not the cities of Oxford and Cambridge that were allowed to have printing presses, it was just the university presses that were allowed, and more importantly this was not in the company charter of 1557 but the Star Chamber Act of 1586, which also tightened up licensing. Bourus has considerable biographical knowledge about particular stationers, but is not always able to marshal it into an argument and has not avoided some egregious errors, such as claiming that puritans did not go to the theatre (p. 210). Bourus thinks that plague closure of the theatres in 1603 probably hurt sales of Q1 *Hamlet* (p. 216), but one might just as easily argue that serious addicts of drama would buy plays to get their fix, and she speculates that during plague closure from March 1603 until April 1604 Shakespeare revised *Hamlet* into something that was unperformable (p. 217), as I suppose he might were he thinking of a readerly market. Shakespeare might have offered this long version to Roberts, who would again have approached Ling, and the readerly potential of this version would have been apparent to them, but they would have worried about hurting sales of Q1 which still had not sold out (p. 218) At this point Bourus argues that the theatres being closed would have stimulated the demand for printed plays, but earlier she has argued the opposite: 'It seems reasonable to speculate that sales of this book [Q1 *Hamlet*] would have been below average, since Q1's release date coincided with the outbreak of the great plague of 1603' (p. 216). Bourus thinks that Roberts and Ling would have destroyed unsold Q1s (to help sales of Q2), which is why there is only one extant. Roberts gave Ling's compositor the new Shakespeare manuscript, plus a copy of Q1 to help where the manuscript was hard to read, which is why, as we know, Q2 follows Q1 in some accidentals in the first act. The compositorial errors in Q2 (by a man who did not make many errors in other work) probably show that the work was hurried, as we might suspect because, with Q1 suppressed, Ling needed the money (p. 220). This is an inherently implausible conjecture: Ling suppresses his own text to increase the market for a new version, which is then mangled because he is in a hurry because he has lost the income from the first one. Bourus concludes that Ling and Roberts were respectable men with professional relations to the playing companies, and they would not have got involved in piracy, and Simmes, although he got in trouble, did high-standard work so it is unlikely he would have done Q1 if it were mangled text; Q1 and Q2 are just different versions of Shakespeare's play. This is reasonable enough as a conclusion, but since the claim that 'bad' quartos are piracies is no longer commonly made, it is somewhat unnecessary.

The final piece in *AEB* is 'Notes on Shakespeare's *Henry V*' (*AEB* 12[2001] 264–87), a sequence of explanatory and emendatory notes on the Folio *Henry V* by Thomas L. Berger and George Walton Williams. The Prologue says 'O pardon: since a crooked Figure may I Attest in little place a Million, I And let vs, Cyphers to this great Accompt, I On your imaginarie Forces worke' (TLN 16–19, I, Prologue, 15–18). A 'crooked Figure' is usually taken to mean zero (the cipher), but as Gary Taylor notes in his Oxford Shakespeare edition of the play, the word 'crooked' nowhere else means a full circle. Some critics have argued that the 'crooked Figure' is a number one, which did have some finishing dashes that made it not a simple downstroke but a zig-zag. In *The Winter's Tale* Polixenes says 'And therefore, like a cipher, I Yet standing in rich place, I multiply I With one "We thank you" many thousands more' (I.ii.6–8): since a zero cannot go at the left end of a number, Shakespeare must think of the 'rich place' as the right-hand end of a number, and hence the 'little place' of *Henry V* must be the left-hand side. In *King Lear*, the Fool's 'Now thou art an 0 without a figure. I am better than thou art, now. I am a fool; thou art nothing' (I.iv.174–6) distinguishes the 'figure' from the zero, and *Henry V* does so too ('*And* let us' not '*So* let us'); there was indeed a 'learned tradition' that zero is not a number, and elsewhere in Shakespeare 'figure' and 'cipher' are contrasted. In all this, Berger and Williams are reading 'O pardon' as an exclamation, not as a form of 'Pardon the O' as Humphrey Tonkin did ('Wooden O': Letter to the Editor, *TLS* 14 Apr.[2000]), and they do not consider the force of Ernst

Gombrich's suggestion that 'wooden O' means 'wooden zero' ('Wooden O': Letter to the Editor, *TLS* 10 Mar.[2000]). In the Prologue's 'For 'tis your thoughts that now must deck our Kings, I Carry them here and there: Iumping o're Times' (TLN 29–30, I, Prologue, 28–9) the audience might be said to carry its thoughts (imperative) or perhaps the thoughts are said to carry the kings (indicative). Berger and Williams decide that it is perhaps better for line 29 to be, like line 28, indicative and thus for both to contrast with lines 1–27 where the principal verbs are imperative. In ''Gainst him whose wrongs gives edge unto the Swords. I That makes such waste in briefe mortalitie' (TLN, 174–5, I.ii.27–8), it is the swords that make waste, not the wrongs. The problem is 'whose wrongs gives' and the most likely explanation is that the repeated '-s' in 'whose wrongs' made the compositor add one to 'give' too, and perhaps also to 'Sword'. In 'for God before. I Wee'le chide this *Dolphin* at his fathers doore' (TLN 458–9, I.ii.307–8), 'God before' could be a prayer ('God going before') or an oath ('I swear before God'), and Berger and Williams advise that a prayer better suits the tone of the passage. The Act II chorus ends with two rhyming couplets (TLN 501–4), violating the pattern of the other choruses, although the first chorus might have a rhyme on its penultimate pairing of 'supply ... history' and might be allowed to be anomalous. But the other three choruses end on a personal note, with the chorus referring directly to the audience rather than the story. The penultimate couplet of the Act II chorus does this, and its final couplet does not, so Berger and Williams reckon this final couplet is a non-Shakespearian addition. For 'No, to the spittle goe' (TLN 575, II.i.71) the usual emendation to 'spital', short for 'hospital', makes it a place free of disease (as in *Love's Labour's Lost* V.ii.857), whereas the meaning each of the three times it is used in this spelling in Folio *Henry V* is the opposite, a place of disease, so Berger and Williams think we should retain F's 'spittle' as Shakespeare seems to mean something different from hospital by it. It is odd that Berger and Williams should think of the hospital referred to in *Love's Labour's Lost* as a place free of disease, since it contains 'the speechless sick' and 'groaning wretches' (V.ii.837–8), just as modern ones do.

For 'feare attends her not' (TLN 917, II.iv.29) Berger and Williams supply the somewhat obvious gloss that England is unfearful because she (in the form of her king) is giddy and vain. Emending '*Dolph.* For the Dolphin ... what to him from England? I *Exe*. Scorne and defiance, sleight regard, contempt, I And any thing that may not mis-become I The mightie Sender, doth he prize you at' (TLN 1010–14, II.iv.117–19) Capell put a semi-colon after 'defiance' since only up to there is Exeter answering the Dauphin's question; the rest is a sentence, with 'prize' its main verb. Taylor, on the other hand, put the semi-colon after 'contempt' because 'Scorne ... contempt' is the answer. Berger and Williams distinguish the 'externally directed' challenge of 'Scorne and defiance' that cannot be the objects of 'prize you at' from the 'internally conceived' words that follow ('slight regard' and 'contempt') that can be the objects of 'prize you at'. I would have thought that if you can prize someone at 'slight regard' you can prize them at 'scorn', and the waters are muddied here by a spurious negative in Berger and Williams's prose: '"he does *not* prize you at scorn and defiance" is not idiomatic'. To Berger and Williams the obvious break is after 'defiance' and Capell's semi-colon is right. Also, Exeter answers like this (a few syllables in direct response, then a longer comment) elsewhere in the play (TLN 970, 991). The end of the second act and the beginning of third go like this: 'To answer matters of this consequence. *Exeunt*. I *Actus*

Secundus. | Flourish. Enter Chorus'. Here and at TLN 462 (wrongly given as TLN 1462 on p. 268 where it appears in through-the-play sequence, as befits a glossarial note), a flourish accompanies the chorus's entrance, but probably only because elsewhere in the manuscript a flourish seems to float between the end of one scene (a king's exit) and the beginning of the next (the chorus's entrance) and the compositor wrongly attached it to the latter. The flourish should, of course, always be moved to the king's exit. This third act chorus says 'With silken Streamers, the young *Phebus* fayning' (TLN 1050, III, Chorus, 6), which last word is commonly emended to 'fanning', but 'fayning' meaning feigning also appears in F and the sense is appropriate, the streamers producing a false illusion of the rising sun. There is also a parallel moment in *3 Henry VI*: 'See how the morning opes her golden gates | And takes her farewell of the glorious sun. | How well resembles it the prime of youth, | Trimmed like a younker prancing to his love!' (II.i.21–4). Fluellen's speech prefix at *'Flu*. Up to the breach, you Dogges; auaunt you Cullions | *Pist*. Be mercifull great Duke to men of Mould' (TLN 1137–9, III.ii.21–3) is suspicious; should it not in fact be one of the great dukes that enters and rouses them? Fluellen later describes Pistol as brave; furthermore, this would be the first time we see Fluellen, and people are usually identified at their first appearance in a play. Fluellen becomes just 'Welch' in his speech prefixes fifty lines later, suggesting that at this point in the play some revision has occurred; Fluellen was originally not individuated and then became so.

There's a false exeunt in *'Erping*. The Lord in Heaven blesse thee, Noble | *Harry. Exeunt. | King*. God a mercy old Heart, thou speak'st cheare- | fully. *Enter Pistoll'* (TLN 1879–82, IV.i.33–IV.i.36) since the king remains and speaks, and even if only Erpingham leaves there is still the problem of his being addressed after he has gone. Presumably, the exit for Erpingham was on the same line as Pistol's entrance, and the compositor, short of space and unused to such a collocation, moved Erpingham's exit up two lines. Taylor reassigns the speech beginning *'Will*. 'Tis certaine' (TLN 2034 (not '12034' as given here), IV.i.197) from Williams to Bates, but there is no need since it makes perfect sense as it is and leads smoothly enough to Williams's quarrel with Henry. At TLN 2157–63 (IV.i.321–6) there are several short lines that editors have tried to force into a metrical scheme, but Berger and Williams think it hopeless and that we should just leave them as unmetrical. The king says 'My brother *Gloucesters* voyce? I: | I know thy errand' and T. W. Craik for Arden 3 deleted the first "I" on the grounds (explained in private correspondence to Berger and Williams) that it was Shakespeare's false start for 'I know thy errand' and that the compositor took it as an interjection and added the colon himself. Berger and Williams prefer to see 'I:' as an interjection, and note that the question mark after 'voyce' might indicate not interrogation but emphasis. The dialogue can stand as it is, no emendation necessary. Berger and Williams note that the preceding speech, an audible prayer by Henry, could become a silent prayer, hence the half-line 'Imploring pardon'. Like the end of Claudius's prayer, the half-line might indicate that the person praying continues to do so silently, and Berger and Williams think that rather than have Gloucester burst in and interrupt Henry's devotion, it is better if his call 'My liege' is made off stage, answered by Henry speaking to himself ('My brother's voice? Ay. | *Enter Gloucester*. | [*Rises*] I know thy errand') or perhaps a fraction earlier so that Henry's 'Ay' is addressed to him. There's a logical problem in *'Dolph*. Mount them, and make incision in their Hides. | That their hot blood may spin in English eyes' (TLN 2178–9, IV.ii.9–10) since blood does not spin, but it does 'spit' several times in Shakespeare, so that is the best emendation. Of course, the blood would have to spit itself for this emendation, and Craik (in private correspondence to Berger and Williams) points out that fire does that in 'Spit, fire! Spout, rain!' (*King Lear* III.ii.14). Presumably what happened was compositorial error: the word 'in' drove out the '-it' of 'spit' to make 'spin'. Accent perhaps obscures meaning in '*French. O perdonne moy.* | *Pist.* Say'st thou me so? is that a Tonne of Moyes?' (TLN 2403–4, IV.iv.22–3) and 'Tonne' could be 'tun' (a container) or a 'ton' (unit of weight). In private correspondence Craik argued that since 'tun' was spelt 'tun' earlier, it is unlikely to be spelt 'tonne' here, but perhaps, say Berger and Williams, the previous line's '-donne' was supposed to be echoed in a disyllabic 'Tonne'. Also, the compositor might have changed the spelling to fill out his prose line and also to distinguish the English word from the French pronoun 'ton' five lines earlier. It makes thematic sense of Henry to get a 'tun' from a Frenchman earlier and for swaggering Pistol to get a 'tun' from a Frenchman here too, so Berger and Williams favour reading 'tun'. There is un-Shakespearian repetition (of 'throngs') in '*Orl.* We are enow yet liuing in the Field, | To smother up the English in our throngs, | If any order might be thought vpon. | *Bur.* The diuell take Order now, Ile to the throng; | Let life be short, else shame will be too long' (TLN 2478–82, IV.v.20–4). The gap is a little too large for compositorial anticipation or recollection, and Berger and Williams think the second instance more right than the first since a throng generally has a purpose, so 'our throngs' seems the problem. Since the nobles have left the field, there is no need for the first word to respect the ranks of those on the field, so the Berger and Williams suggest emending the first 'throngs' to 'swarms' and wonder if the 'th-r' sound of 'smother' is what caused 'swarms' to get turned into 'throngs'.

There is an erroneous '*Actus Quartus*' at TLN 2524 (IV.vii.0.1), but something like '*Alarums. Excursions*' is needed to pass the time during which the English kill their prisoners and then the French attack the boys and the luggage. One cannot have Henry give the order to kill prisoners at TLN 2522 ('euery souldiour kill his Prisoners') and it be executed, together with the killing of the boys, by TLN 2526 when Fluellen reports it ('Kill the poyes'). The word 'law' (TLN 2673, IV.vii.150) is an Irish interjection, according to Berger and Williams, and is used several times by MacMorris, so its use here by Fluellen suggests that it was reassigned from MacMorris (given as 'WacMorris' here) for casting reasons. For '*Will.* Sir, know you this Gloue? | *Flu.* Know the Gloue? I know the Gloue is a Gloue. | *Will.* I know this, and thus I challenge it. | *Strikes him*' (TLN 2720–3, IV.viii.5–8) Berger and Williams sort out the exchanging of gloves and their passing between caps and hands. They reject Andrew Gurr's suggestion that Williams strikes the glove hanging from Fluellen's cap (a literal reading of 'has struck the glove' twenty lines later) because it is unchivalric and does not mean the same as a 'box o' the ear', as the blow is repeatedly called. Taylor's stage direction '*plucking the glove from Fluellen's cap*' has the advantage also of getting the gloves back into their rightful owners' hands. Just how much time is indicated by 'S. *Dauies* day is past' (TLN 2899 (not '12899' as given here), V.i.2)? The battle of Agincourt was on 25 October 1415 and the next St David's day after that was 1 March 1416. Historically, ten days after that St David's day (that is, on 11 March 1416) Henry's advance party of troops heading for Troyes arrived in France. In *A Midsummer Night's Dream* 'St. Valentine is past' is said well after 14 February, so there is no problem with thinking that Shakespeare used 'past' here to mean ten or more days past and that the scene is set before Troyes where Henry's men are awaiting his arrival. In 'The euen Meade ... | Wanting the Sythe, withall vncorrected, ranke; | Conceiues by idlenesse, and nothing teemes, | But hatefull Docks, rough Thistles, Keksyes, Burres, | Loosing both beautie, and utilitie' (TLN 3035–40, V.ii.48–53), is 'nothing' the subject of the verb 'teemes' or its object? Where 'teem' is used elsewhere in the canon it is transitive, so presumably it needs an object here and the only thing available is 'nothing'. The sense is thus: 'the mead conceives by idleness and teems [produces] nothing but'. At TLN 3041–4 (V.ii.54–8) Henry lists the domestic matters that have been neglected because of the war ('for want of time'), but Berger and Williams think that the fighting has not made less time available, so perhaps 'time' is a misprint for 'care'. (Personally, I would have thought it acceptable to say that people preoccupied with one thing would have less time for others.) Finally, just before the epilogue there is a flourish at the king's exit that the compositor might have misunderstood as accompanying the chorus's entrance after it (TLN 3366–7, but wrongly given as 3266–7 here.)

Three relevant articles appeared in *Papers of the Bibliographical Society of America* this year. Eric Rasmussen, 'The Date of Q4 *Hamlet*' (*PBSA* 95[2001] 21–9), argues from the evidence of a printer's device deteriorating that the undated Q4 *Hamlet* was printed 1619–23, probably within 1619–21, and was thus available to be the quarto used to help in the printing of the Folio text, as has been suspected from other evidence. On 19 November 1607 Nicholas Ling transferred his right to print *Hamlet* to John Smethwick, who published Q3 in 1611 and then at some point Q4 with an ornament on the title page (McKerrow's device number 376). Rasmussen sent out a team of researchers to find all the books Smethwick published between 1599 and 1640 and (for books in Bodleian and Huntington) to get colour slides of each title page on which this device appeared, which slides were electronically scanned at high resolution. The resulting images were taken on a laptop computer to the British Library to compare with its copies of Smethwick's book bearing the device. McKerrow reported no noticeable deterioration in the block in the books he saw it used in, but from their multiple copies of twenty-eight extant books bearing it Rasmussen's team found progressive deterioration in two areas. One is the bit of drapery hanging from the dog's mouth in the upper right-hand corner, which was attached to the scroll of the frame in every example up to and including STC 3670 [printed 1621] but is detached from STC 16672 [1623] and onwards. On the Bodleian, British Library, and Huntington Q4 *Hamlet*s it is attached, so 1623 is the *terminus ad quem*. (In an article on deteriorating printers' device reviewed below, Lynette Hunter cautions against mistaking insufficient or excessive inking for a break or non-break in a device, but Rasmussen's use of so many printings of the device should guard against that.) Similarly, the central forelock of the cherub's hair (at the top of the device) was still attached to the brow in STC 7222 [1619] but had broken free, leaving an 'island' of hair fragment floating unaided, in STC 3670 [1621]. This island is still visible in just one copy of STC 16672 [1623]. Q4 *Hamlet* has the forelock detached from the brow so the *terminus a quo* is 1619, but the 'island' is not yet visible and there seems to be more of the forelock present than in STC 3670 [1621] so this is the probable *terminus ad quem* (1623 is the certain *terminus ad quem*, as already established).

Rasmussen refers to the 'elegant progression of damage' (p. 27) in his illustration 6, but makes no mention of the obvious digital enhancement of the images from these books, for not only has he used enlargement (which is entirely reasonable), but clearly he has had his Adobe PhotoShop software (mentioned as doing the 1,200 times enlargement, p. 24 n. 4) perform line-edge detection which 'draws around' the inside and outside edge of a shape and then subtracts the shape, thus turning a filled circle, say, into pair of unfilled concentric circles. According to how sensitive a setting one uses for this feature, it will find edges to artefacts that are merely 'noise' such as dirt (not ink) on the paper, and this has clearly happened to some of the images in illustration 6, most clearly the one of the Bodleian Q4 *Hamlet* copy in his illustration 6 on p. 28. Arguably, the 'island' of cherub's hair that Rasmussen refers to has been created by this electronic processing, for clearly in the case of the Bodleian copy of STC 16672 the software has found a whole archipelago of islands far off the coast of the cherub's head that are in fact merely dirty marks on the paper, not inkings. With no discussion of the use of the software's 'edge-detection' feature, and no assurance that the same 'sensitivity' and 'discrimination' settings were used for each image, the results of this analysis are entirely suspect. Particularly peculiar is the fact that the 'edge-detected' Huntington STC 16672 image is free from the falsely identified islands yet its unprocessed source image suggests that this book is if anything more smudgy and dirty than the Bodleian STC 16672. With digital enhancement it is all too easy to make 'noisy' data seem more meaningful than they really are, and the variabilities of inking and of dirty paper are extremely loud 'noises' in this context. Rasmussen continues with the observation that some quarto has long been suspected of influencing the Folio, and the pattern of F/Q4 agreement against Q1/3 has made editors suspect it was Q4, if only we could be sure it was available. Now, claims Rasmussen, we *do* know that it was printed in time. This is not quite what Rasmussen has shown, however, for even if accepted in full his study indicates that Q4 *Hamlet* was printed before STC 16672 (Lodge's *Euphues Golden Legacy*) in 1623, for that is the certain *terminus ad quem* Rasmussen announced on p. 25; he attached an evasive 'probably' to the *terminus ad quem* of 1621 derived from the evidence of the cherub's forelock on p. 27. Moreover, we do not know when in 1623 Lodge's *Euphues Golden Legacy* was printed, and we know that F *Hamlet* was set in type beginning in the late spring of 1623, so Q4 might still not have been printed by then. The slippage in Rasmussen's prose is palpable: Q4 *Hamlet* was printed 'certainly before *Euphues* in 1623' (p. 27) transforms into 'published before 1623' (p. 29). Those are not the same things at all.

The most important and impressive of articles this year is Paul Werstine's demonstration, in 'Scribe or Compositor: Ralph Crane, Compositors D and F, and the First Four Plays in the Shakespeare First Folio' (*PBSA* 95[2001] 315–39), that the alleged differences of habit between Folio compositors D and F do not stand up to an analysis of the influence of copy; when one takes Ralph Crane's spellings into account, it is impossible to tell them apart. It has long been suspected that the first four Folio plays, *The Tempest*, *Two Gentlemen of Verona*, *Merry Wives of Windsor*, and *Measure for Measure* (occupying quires A–G), were printed from Crane transcripts, on the evidence of punctuation, spelling, elision and other features that match those in extant Crane dramatic manuscripts. Thus the compositors who set these plays cannot have been so fixed in their habits as to 'escape the influence of manuscript copy'. Hinman called them compositors A, B, C, and D, but Howard-

Hill showed that this A could not be the same A that Hinman found working on *The Winter's Tale* and the histories and tragedies, so he called the four men B, C, D, and F. John O'Connor showed that there was not much evidence to distinguish this new man F from D (perhaps he really was D?) so he tried to find some evidence from spelling. Howard-Hill discriminated between D and F by the habit of indenting the second line of an overflowing line, and thought the absence of this phenomenon from quires A to E showed D's absence, but Werstine counters that this proves nothing since there is no consistent idiosyncratic pattern, only collective ones: when D set indented flow-overs, so did others, and apparently when he refrained so did others. Moreover, D seems influenced by use of indented flow-overs in his copy, but again not consistently. This negative evidence is not convincing, but positive evidence is: the only use of flow-overs in quires A–G comes in D's stints, so the single one on G5v is probably his (p. 318). O'Connor too rested his argument on weak negative evidence: the absence of other compositors' habits. Four comedies were set from printed copy—*Much Ado About Nothing*, *Love's Labour's Lost*, *Midsummer Night's Dream*, and *Merchant of Venice*—and from D's habits in his stints (since source could be compared with results) O'Connor worked out D's spelling habits, although he admitted that D followed copy spelling so often that it is hard to tell just what his preferences are. O'Connor nonetheless came up with some preferences (setting *-ie* endings where his copy has *-y* endings, and also preferring the unusual spellings *sweete*, *meete*, *maide*, *eie*, and *praier*), and, because these are almost entirely absent from pages of quires A–G not set by B or C, O'Connor deduced that D worked on none of these quires except F. It is not hard to tell other compositors' habits if they are setting from printed copy still extant, but where the copy is a lost manuscript it is usually impossible. Quires A–G were set from manuscript copy that is now lost, but we have the advantage of knowing that this manuscript was in Crane's hand, and we know his spelling habits from other extant manuscripts (p. 319).

In *Ralph Crane and Some Shakespeare First Folio Comedies* [1972] Howard-Hill summarized Crane's spelling habits, so we can reliably guess at the spelling in the copy for quires A–G and see how far compositor D was influenced by copy in his spelling of words that we know his personal preferences about from those F passages we know were set from extant printed copy. Werstine's table 1 records what compositors B, C, D, and F did with seventeen words—*any*, *beautie*, *body*, *company*, *deny*, *happie*, *heavy*, *pittie/pitty*, *presently*, *try*, *very*, *euery*, *Lady*, *many*, *carry*, *marry*, *weary*—that Connor thought compositor D liked to end in *-ie*, starting with the Crane spelling (the one presumed to have stood in the lost manuscript copy for quires A–G), and then showing how often this word was made to end *-y* and how often *-ie* by each of the four compositors in Crane manuscript copy plays (*The Tempest*, *Two Gentlemen of Verona*, *Merry Wives of Windsor*, and *Measure for Measure*), in the Q copy plays (*Much Ado About Nothing*, *Love's Labour's Lost*, *Midsummer Night's Dream*, and *Merchant of Venice*), and in four other comedies (*Comedy of Errors*, *As You Like It*, *Taming of the Shrew*, and *All's Well That Ends Well*) that we know were set from lost manuscript copy. For each group Werstine's table shows how often each man set *-y* and *-ie* endings for the given word, taking care to separate out occasions when this was done in long lines, whose spelling might have been changed to achieve justification. (Werstine agrees with O'Connor that such cases tell us nothing about real spelling habits, for justification needs might well have taken precedence over personal preference.) Werstine summarizes from his own table: for twelve of the words (the first eleven plus the last one), compositor D showed a marked tendency to prefer -*ie* endings even where his printed copy had -*y*. For the same twelve words, where compositor F was working from Crane manuscript he only once set -*ie* (for *companie*) and eleven times set -*y*. However, for some words (*euerie*/*euery*, *Ladie*/*Lady*, *manie*/*many*) compositor D was inconsistent in his habits when setting from Q copy, sometimes changing the -*ie* ending to -*y* and sometimes vice versa, even in short lines where justification could not have been forcing his hand (p. 324). There are two occurrences of *euerie* in the Q copy, one of which compositor D changed to *euery*. Looking only at short F lines, there are six occurrences of *euery* in Q and of these compositor D left five alone and turned one into *euerie*. Again, looking only at short F lines, there are fourteen occurrences of *Lady* in the Q copy, five of which compositor D changed into *Ladie*. There are twelve occurrences of *Ladie* in the Q copy, nine of which D changed into *Lady*. (Actually, these changes are wrongly given in Werstine's prose, which states the *Ladie*-to-*Lady* figure as 14/5 and the *Lady*-to-*Ladie* as 12/9; in private communication Werstine has confirmed that the table is right and the prose is wrong.) Werstine goes on in his prose to describe in like manner what compositor D did with *manie*-to-*many* and *many*-to-*manie*, but it is impossible to check because for the word 'many' in his table 1 there is no row for compositor D at all. So, compositor D's preference for *euery*, *Lady*, and *many* seems stronger than the previous examples, but since D's preference is not clear we cannot make much use of this; indeed for the words *carry* and *marry* compositor D actually changed -*ie* endings in his Q copy to -*y* endings, just as compositor F does. For twelve words compositor D behaves in a way that distinguishes him from compositor F, but for three words he is inconsistent, and for a further two words he behaves like (and therefore could be) compositor F (p. 324).

Of those crucial twelve words for which compositor F distinctively uses -*y* and compositor D distinctively uses -*ie*, ten are spelt -*y* by Crane, so perhaps all compositor F is doing is following his scribal copy. There are some minor problems with Werstine's reporting of Howard-Hill's discovery of Crane preferences. Howard-Hill gives *heauy*, not *heavy* as Werstine has it, which cannot be simple modernization since Werstine preserves *euery*. Howard-Hill has not got *presently* (as Werstine has), and Howard-Hill gives both *very* and *verie* whereas Werstine just has *very*, although it is not clear why Howard-Hill does not report this as *very/ie* as he does for other words that Crane is inconsistent about. Werstine provisionally concludes that the lack of compositor D's -*ie* spellings in quires A–G does not prove D did not set the parts of quires A–G usually attributed to F since he might simply have tolerated the -*y* endings (Crane's preference) in his manuscript copy and set them even though his own preference when setting from printed copy was to use -*ie* endings. Certainly, in the part of quire F (from Crane manuscript copy) that compositor D did set, he used eighteen -*y* endings in short lines, to just one -*ie* ending. (This is not verifiable from Werstine's table 1 because it does not break quires A–G down into compositor D and compositor F parts.) O'Connor's observation that from quire F the number of -*ie* endings rises—and hence compositor D started there—is invalid because compositors B and C also demonstrably increased their usage of -*ie* endings from quire F onwards, and looking at their spelling habits when setting from quarto copy, compositor B and C also seem to have been strongly influenced by Crane's preferences when setting from manuscript copy in his hand (p. 325). Thus O'Connor's spelling tests that contain compositor D's work to just quire F amongst quires A–G would also deny compositors' B and C hands in quires A–G too. There were a further five spellings that O'Connor thought were distinctive of compositor D—*eie, maide, meete, praier, sweete*—but Werstine excludes *praier* and *meete* on the grounds that compositor D showed no preferences regarding these outside of long lines, and he tabulates the other three in his table 2. O'Connor's reliance on Compositor D's alleged preference for *eie* is mistaken: he did change some *eye* spellings in his Q copy to *eie* spelling, but then not only did he set *eye* twenty-seven times where his Q copy had that spelling, but three times he set *eye* even though his Q copy had *eie*, so if his Crane manuscript copy had a mix of *eie* and *eye* spellings, as seems likely, then compositor D might (like compositor F) have set only *eye* (p. 326). Regarding the *maid/maide* preference, we know that compositor B frequently used *maide* in setting from manuscript copy later in the comedies, and that compositor C showed his 'tolerance of *maide* spellings' when setting from Q copy (following his copy's *maide* spelling six times), so the fact that these two men (B + C) set only *maid* (never *maide*) in quires A–G probably means that they were following Crane's spelling in their copy, for he spells it *maid*, never *maide*, in a number of manuscripts that Werstine has checked electronic versions of (it is not in Howard-Hill's list of Crane spellings). Therefore, the two times that *maide* does turn up in the parts of A–G assigned to compositor F might instead be where compositor D is setting, because compositor D only ever set *maide* in his Q copy work, even where the Q copy had *maid*. Regarding the *sweet/sweete* preference, O'Connor observed that compositor F used only the short form *sweet* while compositor D used both *sweet* and *sweete*, but in fact looking at compositor D's work from Q copy we can see that he never changed *sweet* to *sweete* (as always, we are concerned only with short lines) and mostly what he did was follow his copy. So, since we know that Crane used the spelling *sweet*, the assignment of pages in quires A–G to compositor F on the grounds that they contain the spelling *sweet* is faulty: compositor D would have set *sweet* every time given that Crane copy, or in other words perhaps he only flitted between *sweet* and *sweete* when his copy had *sweete* (p. 328).

Another type of available evidence is elision of future tenses of the kind *he'll*. O'Connor argued that compositor D characteristically used *-le* (so, *heele*), changing Q copy spellings of *'ll* to *-le*, while compositor F favoured *'ll*. Werstine tabulates the behaviour of all the compositors of the first twelve Folio plays (B, C, D, F). This table is badly presented: there are lines of data for someone whose identificatory letter is not given (there is just a blank cell) and some cells are blank while others are filled with a hyphen, and nowhere does Werstine explain the difference between these two. Also, confusingly, Werstine refers to what happens in 'the bottom half' of the table, but he means the rows of data for quires H1–Y1^V, and because the whole table has been wrapped to fit the journal's printed page, those rows are not simply 'the bottom half' but rather occur twice in the table. Moreover, the labels seem to have gone wrong, for the first time the quires are called '*Hl–Yl^V*' (both alphabetic 'el' not numeric 1) and the second time '*Hl–Y1^V*' (one 'el', one 1). Nonetheless, correctly interpreted the table shows that from knowledge of Crane's habitual spellings we can say that compositor D never changed a quarto copy spelling of a future tense elision in a short line (p. 328). What of compositor D's practice in the manuscript copy plays? In those compositors B and C used -*le* against their usual practices ('*l* and '*ll* respectively), so perhaps they were just following copy, in which case compositor D's setting of -*le* in the same plays was just a matter of his following copy too. Elsewhere compositor D used -*le* and '*ll* in work for which we do not know what the copy was, but he might still have been simply following copy in each case, and indeed in this he would (if it were true) be like compositor F setting quires A–G, who used Crane's preference ('*ll*). Crucially, then, Howard-Hill's and O'Connor's work in distinguishing compositors D and F failed to take into account how copy might have influenced the spacing and spelling evidence they were using. What we need is positive evidence for F's habits not influenced by copy, but it is not available because, apart from the evidence adduced by Werstine so far, the working habits of D and F appear to have been the same or were inconsistent (so not distinguishing ones) or the influence of copy obscures the evidence (p. 330).

To attempt to distinguish compositor D and compositor F, Werstine repeated O'Connor's collation of D's setting from Q copy with those quartos, excluding changes due to eye-rhymes and excluding long lines. In order not to be fooled by ignorance of spellings drawn straight from copy, Werstine excluded words where we do not know Crane's spelling, and this left sixty words charted in the appendix to the article. We should be able to see compositor F's distinctiveness in spellings he prefers in quires A–G that are not Crane's nor compositor D's, but of the 322 times compositor F set one of these sixty test-words in short lines, 317 times he chose a spelling that was either the same as Crane's or the same as compositor D's, or the same as both of them. Five distinct spellings in 322 spellings is 1/64 (p. 331). For compositor B and compositor C's stints in quires A–G, the same 'distinctiveness' ratio, how many times in short lines they used a distinct (not Crane, not D) spelling out of how many times they set the word at all, is 1/14 for compositor B and 1/9 for compositor C. Of course, Werstine is not claiming that compositor D *is* compositor F, rather, he has most convincingly shown that we cannot tell them apart by their spellings. On a range of words they do not distinguish themselves by their spelling, and on specific words they actually do exactly the same things: both were weak about *been*, *deare*, and *sense* and would sometimes follow copy and sometimes apply their own spellings. Yet both were strong (to the point of absolutism in some cases) about *heart*, *diuell*, *grieue*, *answere*, and *indeede*, and overruled their copy on these spellings (p. 332). As Werstine observes, two men might share some preferences, but it is hardly likely that they 'would maintain these preferences with equal strength' (by being weak on the same three words and strong on the same five words). But what if we are being fooled by dependence on the incomplete list of Crane spellings found by Howard-Hill and there are other distinguishing words we could turn to? To discount this possibility, and to see if there is another way to distinguish compositor D from compositor F, Werstine has looked in compositor F's pages in quires A–G for spellings that we know—from his overruling of Q copy in quires H–V—compositor D did not share, and he compared them with spellings that compositor D actually used in quire F, the result being Werstine's table 4. The results are inconclusive, with compositor D never showing strong preferences that can be contrasted with compositor F's preferences; indeed we cannot be sure that we are rightly distinguishing by this means which pages of quires A–G compositor F set and which pages compositor D set, for they share spellings in those quires (*adieu*, *already*, *lyon*). Comparing compositor F's spellings in quires A–G with compositor

D's spellings in quires H–V there is some variation, but it is no greater than one man might show in his habits; indeed, it is no greater than the variation compositor D certainly *did* show, given current attribution of pages, between his work on quire F and his work on quires H–V. In short, Werstine is able to announce that 'Exhaustive analysis of Compositor D's habits thus produces almost no evidence to distinguish him from Compositor F, and much to associate him with Compositor F' (pp. 333–4). The main Folio compositors (A, B, C, E) are still in place, but the 'peripheral' ones (definitely, since this article, F, and most probably H, I, and J too) are not solidly grounded in evidence. As Werstine rightly concludes, this casts yet more gloom on new bibliography's dream of recovering what Shakespeare himself wrote.

William Searle, '"By foule authority": Miscorrection in the Folio Text of Shakespeare's *Troilus and Cressida*' (*PBSA* 95[2001] 503–19), argues that, contrary to Taylor, the manuscript used to annotate a copy of Q *Troilus and Cressida* to make the Folio text was not necessarily scribal, for the phenomena displayed in the Folio could be created by compositorial error (specifically the misunderstanding of an annotator's instructions about placement and substitutions) and subsequent miscorrection of these errors. Phillip Williams showed that F *Troilus and Cressida* was printed from an annotated copy of Q and Taylor attempted to show that the annotation was probably by reference to a scribal transcript of authorial papers. There are errors in F that Taylor claimed could only come from 'clearly legible misreadings' in the manuscript used to annotate Q (hence it was not an authorial manuscript), and this Searle sets out to disprove: they are in fact much more likely to be errors by one the compositors of F, for they all fall in one man's stint (p. 503). Alice Walker, who would not accept the idea of authorial revision, blamed compositor B for F *Troilus and Cressida*'s deficiencies, but Werstine has shown that B was a careful man. Compositor H, hired at the last minute as *Troilus and Cressida* was finally squeezed into F, worked only on this play so we cannot test his care in other plays in F, as we can for B. Taylor listed a number of miscorrections in F— things that Q got right that F got wrong—and Searle reprints it. Taylor has us imagine the work of the person who annotated Q by reference to an unknown manuscript. If that manuscript was hard-to-read foul papers, would he really have preferred his own stab at what it said over what Q said? For that is the phenomenon we're dealing with, the preference for wrong words over perfectly good ones in Q. Surely, Taylor argued, the annotator would have preferred his (wrong) manuscript only if that were a clearly written manuscript, the clarity of the writing giving it a spurious authority. Of course, this argument depends on Q being right in the first place (else F's reading is not a 'miscorrection'), and F being definitely wrong, and at least one of Taylor's claimed miscorrections is not right in Q to begin with. Also, Taylor did not consider the possibility that the error in F came not from the annotator but from the compositor misreading the annotator's handwriting. Also, we should not count cases where the apparent F error appears in a section for which the annotator did nothing to Q, and Taylor found four sections where F was printed directly from (unannotated) Q, some of which might be because the manuscript used to annotate Q lacked some sheets (p. 505). Any reprint will necessarily introduce new errors, and Searle's argument is essentially that the list of F miscorrections used by Taylor is really a list of random errors introduced in a reprinting of Q. It is noticeable that three of Taylor's twenty-eight examples were set by compositor B and twenty-four by compositor H (one Searle rejects as not being right in Q in the first place), and even allowing for H setting more than B did, that makes H's work much more frequently in error (p. 506). Worse for Taylor's theory, several of the Folio 'errors' on his list have recently been accepted into modernized editions of *Troilus and Cressida*, so they are not clearly errors in F at all; leaving them out changes the tally to just one 'error' in compositor B's stint, and twenty-one in compositor H's, so it really looks like the phenomenon is compositorial, not manuscriptural.

First Searle sets out to suggest that three of the items on Taylor's list are in fact 'faulty substitutions' (p. 508), not misreadings, and to these Searle adds four more of his own not on Taylor's list and then proceeds through these seven cases. The first, and one not discussed by Taylor, is 'He sate our messengers and we lay by. | Our appertainings, visiting of him | Let him be told so, least perchance he thinke, | We dare not moue the question of our place' (Q E1^r) versus 'He sent our messengers and we lay by. | Our appertainments, visiting of him | Let him be told of so perchance he thinke, | We dare not moue the question of our place' (F ¶4^r). Searle suggests that the annotation was supposed to make Q read 'He sent our messengers off, so we lay by' and the 'sent' made it, but the 'off' did not, and the 'off, so' of this correction got put in two lines further down, turning Q's 'so, least' into F's 'of so'. The extra word 'off' need not be extra-metrical, for 'messengers' could be two, not three, syllables. Searle's second example, Taylor's number 8, is 'To subtill, potent, tun'd to sharp in sweetnesse' (Q F1^v) versus 'To subtill, potent, and too sharp in sweetnesse' (F ¶5^v). Searle suggests that the annotation was supposed to make Q read 'Too subtle-potent, and tuned too sharp in sweetness' (that is, the intention was simply to get an 'and' in before 'tuned' but instead the 'and' replaced the 'tuned'). Searle admits that this involves an extra-metrical 'and', but the play has plenty of those. Searle's third example is Taylor's number 11, 'And violenteth in a sence as strong | As that which causeth it' (Q H3^r) versus 'And no lesse in a sence as strong | As that which causeth it' (F ¶¶2^v). Searle suggests that the annotation was supposed to make Q read 'And violenteth in a sense no less | Than', which is to say 'no less' was supposed to replace 'as strong' but instead was taken as a substitution for 'violenteth', and 'Than' was supposed to replace 'As' in the next line but was omitted. Taylor's claim is that the scribe reading the authorial manuscript (to make the scribal transcript that was used to annotate Q to make the copy for F) read 'no lesse' where the Q compositor (reading the same authorial manuscript) saw 'violenteth', but Searle objects that these two things are not graphically close (p. 511). Why should the same word get set properly by the Q compositor (for 'violenteth' is undoubtedly right) yet totally confuse the scribe, causing him to write nonsense? Searle invokes the same 'What's likelier?' principle as Taylor (that if the annotator had Q and an illegible authorial manuscript why would he allow his uncertain reading of the latter to overrule the possibility of what was in Q?—no, he must rather have had a fair copy manuscript and trusted it), but asks this of the scribe making the transcript from foul papers to fair copy rather than the annotator using the fair copy to mark up Q. After all, why would this scribe misread in the authorial foul papers a word that the printers of Q, using the same authorial foul papers, got right? Taylor sought a reason for the seemingly illogical behaviour of the annotator (the overruling of Q) and found it in a fair copy manuscript being used to make the annotations, but we do not have to accept this illogical behaviour on the part of the annotator since the Folio compositor misreading the annotative markings on the Q used as F's copy is the likelier source of the error.

Searle's fourth example, not discussed by Taylor, is 'To shame the seale of my petition to thee:' (Q H4^v) versus 'To shame the seale of my petition towards' (F ¶¶3^r). Searle suggests that the annotation was supposed to make Q read 'To shame the zeal of my petition towards thee' (that is, to change 'to' into 'towards', which could be monosyllabic), but the Folio compositor might have thought it had to be disyllabic and hence cut 'thee'. Searle's fifth example, not discussed by Taylor, is 'Astronomers foretell it, it is prodigious' (Q K2^r) versus 'Astronomers foretell it, that it is prodigious' (F ¶¶4^v). Searle suggests that the annotation was supposed to make Q read 'Astronomers foretell it, that is prodigious' (that is, to change the second 'it' to 'that', but instead the 'that' was put between the two 'it's. Searle's sixth example is a combination of Taylor's eighteenth and nineteenth, '*Vlis*. Shee will sing any man at first sight. | *Ther*. And any man may sing her, if hee can take her Cliff, | She's noted' (Q K2^r) versus '*Vlis*. She will sing any man at first sight. | *Ther*. And any man may finde her, if he can take her life: she's noted' (F ¶¶4^v). Searle suggests that the annotation was supposed to make Q read 'And any man may sing her if he can find her cliff: she's noted', that is to change 'take' to 'find', but instead the word 'sing' was changed to 'find'. Taylor claimed that both variants (sing/finde and Cliff/life) are misreadings, but Searle points out that a man who could read 'sing' in 'Shee will sing' should be able to read it in the next line also, and if he could not he must have been a dunce not to read around for context to make sense of the tricky word. The King's men would not have used a dunce for a scribe. Of the second change ('Cliff' to 'life') Searle does not give his view, but since 'take her Cliff' does not make sense, presumably compositor H altered it to 'take her life'; or perhaps the cliff/clef/cleft bawdy pun works as well with 'take' as 'find'. Searle's seventh example, not discussed by Taylor, is 'Bid me do any thing but that sweete Greeke' (Q K2^v) versus 'Bid me doe not any thing but that sweete Greeke' (F ¶¶4^v). Searle suggests that the annotation was supposed to make Q read 'Bid me do anything but not that, sweet Greek', that is the word 'not' was supposed to go between 'but' and 'that' but instead it got placed between 'do' and 'any', making a double negative (so, positive) that Cressida does not mean. Searle concludes this section by observing that errors like these are what we would expect 'a not-very-bright compositor' to do when confronted with 'the annotated text of a difficult Shakespearean play', so the problem resides in the compositor's mistaken interpretations of the interlineations, deletions, and other marks on the annotated Q he was given, whereas Taylor thought that the manuscript used to annotate Q had the errors because the scribe of this manuscript misread the authorial papers (p. 512).

The foregoing reduces Taylor's list of what he thought were graphic errors in the making of the fair copy later used to annotate Q to form copy for F, but under what circumstances would a compositor make mistakes that someone like Taylor could misunderstand as graphic errors? Searle answers: when his sheets are not getting proof-correction, or are miscorrected without reference to copy, and in these cases if the error generates a word—or what resembles a word and gets altered to one by press correction—we cannot see what went wrong and are likely permitting these interlopers in our editions (p. 513). Having revised downwards the number of graphic errors that happen to fall in compositor H's stints (by instead calling them compositorial error), we can recalculate the average number of times we should expect graphic error to hit compositor H's stints, and the answer is 1 line in 103 (down from 1 line in 82 calculated on p. 507). But are they spread evenly? No, on quire ¶ he sets three putative graphic errors (just one graphic error for every 208 lines), but everywhere else he sets one for every eighty-four lines. Of those three on quire ¶, one of them (Taylor's number 7) is 'greater hulkes' (Q) versus 'greater bulkes draw deepe' (F) and so arguably not an error at all since a bigger ship is elsewhere in the play called a 'bulk' (pp. 514–15). Likewise, of the other two putative graphic errors (in the transcript used to annotate Q) set by compositor H on quire ¶, Taylor's number 5 ('flexure' in Q to 'flight' in F) is an example of a common word replacing an unusual one and hence 'may readily enough have resulted from somebody's ignorant attempt at improvement'. The last one of these three on quire ¶, 'Fam'd' in Q to 'Fame' in F, might well be the compositor's 'insecurity—typical in the period—in the handling of terminal *d*' (p. 515), which is an explanation I do not understand. It is surely unlikely that compositor H read the quarto word 'Fam'd', thought it must be wrong, and so changed it to 'Fame'. From Hinman's analysis we know that compositor B and compositor H worked together on quire ¶, the first for Folio *Troilus and Cressida*, and they continued working together until the middle sheet of the second quire, ¶¶3–4, where compositor A set nearly 200 lines. Then compositor B was called away and compositor H had to work alone, and thus he did his own proof-reading, which is why his error rate dramatically rises. Looking at different states of the Folio separated by press correction, we can see what errors presumably made by H were caught by B's proof-reading, including a couple that cannot be explained by misreading but only 'the compositor's insecurity in the handling of dramatic materials'. One is the failure to give a speech prefix for Pandarus's 'In good troth it begins so' (TLN 1587) in the uncorrected state of F (¶5^v) so that it looks like the continuation of Paris's preceding speech. Presumably the whole line ('*Pan*. In good troth it begins so'), absent from Q (F1^r), was added as a marginal annotation to the copy of Q used to set F, and compositor H—not good with drama—missed out the speech prefix. Likewise in the uncorrected state of F (¶5^v) there is an obviously wrong '*Exeunt Pandarus*' that in the corrected state becomes '*Exit Pandarus*', so presumably the annotation to Q, which lacks this direction entirely (F1^v), was something like '*ex. Pan.*' and compositor H did not know enough about drama to expand this correctly, but the proof-corrector did (p. 516). Likewise setting the last line of the play, compositor H gives Pandarus an '*Exeunt*' which was allowed to stand because no one checked it. Compositor H made five errors of simple repetition of words, all in quire ¶¶, against compositor B's total of one in all, and one of them seems to have got miscorrected: Q has 'And like dew drop from the lions mane, I He shooke to ayre' (G3^r), and Folio has 'And like a dew drop from the Lyons mane, I Be shooke to ayrie ayre' (¶¶1r), so presumably in F 'ayre' got repeated by dittography and then the 'ayre ayre' mistake was sophisticated into 'ayrie ayre'. There are two items remaining on Taylor's list that are similar compound errors: Q's 'He that takes that doth take my heart withall' (K3^r), which becomes in the Folio 'He that takes that, rakes my heart withall' (¶¶5r), of which the *take/rakes* error might simply be a compositor misreading of his Q copy (p. 517).

Taylor's error number 18 is 'With the rude breuity, and discharge of one' (Q H3^v) versus 'With the rude breuity and discharge of our' (F ¶¶2^v). Searle suspects that compositor H, reading his own proof, found he had a turned letter making 'one' into 'oue' and realizing that 'oue' is nonsense changed it to 'our'. All the rest of the items in Taylor's list could be caused by misreading of printed copy, or are single-letter errors ('literals') that any compositor can make, or miscorrected literals. The problem has been that compositor H's incompetence was covered up by the good proof-reading of compositor B who checked his work, and in any case his incompetence only shows up when he has annotated Q for copy. When he is working from clean Q, compositor H is mostly fine, although when he has not got compositor B reading his proofs he again fails, setting 'yong *Diomed*' for 'yond *Diomed*' at TLN 2563. Three currently available editions of *Troilus and Cressida* (Taylor's, Foakes's, and Bevington's) accept Taylor's view that the manuscript used to annotate Q to make copy for F was a scribal manuscript, and hence although they prefer F for substantive variants (because it is a revised version), they prefer Q for indifferent ones on the grounds that its stemma is shorter and thus less likely to have 'merely casual or accidental error'. But Searle has shown by overwhelming evidence that there is no reason to suppose that the manuscript was scribal rather than authorial (p. 519).

Studies in Philology contains two articles of interest. Kenji Go, 'Unemending the Emendation of "Still" in Shakespeare's Sonnet 106' (*SP* 98[2001] 114–42), argues for the acceptance of a reading from the 1609 quarto of the sonnets. The quarto version of sonnet 106 reads 'So all their praises are but prophesies I Of this our time, all you prefiguring, I And for they look'd but with deuining eyes, I They had not still enough your worth to sing', and usually 'still enough' is emended to 'skill enough'. Go defends 'still' as an adverbial use (meaning 'nevertheless') that pre-dates the *OED*'s first example by a century. But 'enough' of what? Go thinks the referent is either all the descriptions that the sonnet mentions, or 'praises' earlier in the same sentence. Indeed, 'praises' is the key idea of the sonnet, but Go admits that the two words are quite far apart. On the other hand, they are in the same quatrain and sentence, the conceit is 'not *praises* enough to sing your *worth*', that praise–worth link runs throughout the sonnets to the fair youth, and Go traces it in seven other sonnets, *The Two Gentlemen of Verona* and the Shakespearian part of *Edward III* (pp. 118–21). Go explores why previous defenders of 'still', George Wyndham and C.J. Sisson, failed: they did not spot 'praises' as the implied complement of 'enough' and they saw a sharp antithesis in the sonnet between the talents ('tongues' or skills) of the old poets and the talents of the modern ones. But for Go the real antithesis is between those being praised in the past and the impossibly perfect boy being praised in the present, and this also deals with the objection that the word 'For' beginning the final couplet makes it a non sequitur (since it really needs 'But'), since the final couplet repeats the excuse of lines 11–12 that the youth is too perfect to be praised according to his worth (pp. 122–5). There remains the objection that 'still' wasn't used to mean 'as yet' before 1632 or to mean 'nevertheless' or 'however' until 1722, but there was 'as formerly' which would roughly do here, although it would be more likely if the word order were 'They still had not enough' rather than 'They had not still enough' as Q has it (p. 127). Go, however, has clinching evidence from *Cymbeline*: '[*Innogen*] The thanks I give I Is telling you that I am poor of thanks, I And scarce can spare them. *Cloten.* Still I swear I love you. I *Innogen.* If you but said so, 'twere as deep with me. I If you swear still, your recompense is still I That I regard it not. *Cloten.* This is no answer' (II.iii.86–91). This first of these uses of 'still' is obviously in the sense of 'nevertheless', which is why editors since the eighteenth century have put a comma after it, and Innogen's answer is not very witty unless 'still' carries the senses of 'nevertheless' *and* 'always' and she is quibbling (pp. 133–4). Go explores the less than compelling arguments against reading 'skill' in sonnet 106 and decides that the best reason to keep 'still' is the 'inexpressibility topos' that runs through quite a few sonnets, contrasting the dumb I-poet of the sonnets with other loquacious poets, of which 106 is the last and culmination (pp. 137–40). Since the point of the sonnet is the lack of praise of the youth, the ellipsis ('still enough' meaning 'still enough praises') is entirely appropriate as another example of the I-poet being dumb (p. 141). In an appendix Go considers that fact that two early manuscripts read 'skill', but they are not of value, being from the 1630s or later and possessing obvious errors.

John Klause, 'New Sources for Shakespeare's *King John*: The Writings of Robert Southwell' (*SP* 98 [2001] 401–27), argues that *King John* was influenced by a number of works by the Jesuit Robert Southwell.. Klause finds verbal parallels between Louis the Dauphin's language about loving Lady Blanche because he is reflected in her eyes and Southwell's poem *Saint Peters Complaint* on Christ's eye, and perhaps the Bastard's mocking of it with images of hanging, drawing, and quartering (I.ii.497–510) draws on Shakespeare's knowledge that Southwell himself was hanged, drawn, and quartered in 1595 (pp. 404–5). Klause lists a collection of collocations linking *Saint Peter's Complaint* and *King John* (pp. 406–7) and argues that the latter also owes something to Southwell's *Epistle of Comfort*, since *King John*'s use of a couple of biblical quotations (from Psalms and Galatians) is odd until we realize that Southwell too put them together. Likewise the language of the scene in front of the walls of Angiers follows *Epistle of Comfort*'s description of the destruction of Jerusalem, and there are some looser connections too (pp. 408–17). Cardinal Pandulph's speech to the French king in III.i about which of several obligations in an oath must be kept comes from the *Epistle of Comfort*, and Shakespeare's writing just after John's defiance of Pandulph (III.i) borrows a lot of words and phrases from *Epistle of Comfort*, none of which matches what is in *Troublesome Reign*, although for the actual defiance *Troublesome Reign* matches *King John* closely. Klause explores some phrases that *Epistle of Comfort*, *Troublesome Reign*, and *King John* have in common and observes that *Epistle of Comfort* 'shares nothing of significance with *TR* except what *King John* has in common with both works', so there's no possibility of descent by *Epistle of Comfort* to *Troublesome Reign* to *King John*, but there might be linear descent by *Epistle of Comfort* to *King John* to *Troublesome Reign* or else *Epistle of Comfort* to *King John* and *Troublesome Reign* to *King John* (p. 417 n. 21). Another Southwell work, *An Humble Supplication*, circulating in manuscript, also 'scatters its language throughout Shakespeare's play' and it was written in response to a government proclamation against Catholics of November 1591, and Klause lists the (rather weak) verbal parallels (pp. 419–22). Klause suspects that the putting out of Arthur's eyes (as a means to kill him) with hot irons came from Southwell too. In *Troublesome Reign* Pandulph says that whoever kills the king will be forgiven the sin, but that is doctrinally flawed from a Catholic point of view since forgiveness requires contrition of the sinner (religious authority is not enough), and it certainly cannot operate before the fact; thus Shakespeare (presumably informed by Southwell) changed this so that killing the king is a virtue and not a sin at all (p. 424). If these borrowings are accepted, the earliest date for *King John* is whenever

An Humble Supplication was written, and since *An Humble Supplication* was a response to a proclamation of November 1591, *King John* cannot be earlier than, say, December 1591. Just possibly, *King John* was written early in 1592 (counting January–December) and was imitated in *Troublesome Reign*, which got into performance and print before 25 March 1592, in which case its title page dating of 1591 is counting March–March (p. 425 n. 34). For Klause, the most important conclusion of all this is that Shakespeare 'welcomed a Jesuit into his mind' (p. 426).

This reviewer's stint began with work done in 1999, and it has been until now impossible to obtain volumes 12 [1999] and 13 [2000] of the journal *TEXT*, so relevant essays in those volumes will be reviewed here. Volume 12 contained nothing of interest to this section, but volume 13 had three articles. Volume 14 [2001] would normally be reviewed here, but because it was unavailable at the time this review was written it will be noticed next year.

W. Speed Hill, 'Where Would Anglo-American Textual Criticism be if Shakespeare had Died of the Plague in 1593?' (*TEXT* 13[2000] 1–7), considers the impact Shakespeare has had upon editing. If there were only the pre-1593 Shakespeare plays in existence, he presumably would not have become the national poet, and Hill thinks that the works of Spenser, Sidney, Jonson, Beaumont and Fletcher, and Middleton would not have generated the textual theory we have, either because until recently they were not thought to be important enough, or the early texts are just not difficult enough to edit. Indeed it is unlikely that Shakespeare's contemporaries would have been edited in the monumental editions we have of them, for this was in many cases preparatory work for doing Shakespeare himself. Other candidates for 'national poet' in Shakespeare's absence, such as Milton and Wordsworth, do not need much work to establish the text; rather, the energy goes into the glossing and commentary. Donne left us mostly manuscripts (whereas Shakespeare left us primarily books), but the importance of books in Shakespeare studies made editors of Donne prefer his 1633 and 1635 printings even though they knew that the lost manuscripts used as copy for printing them were further down the stemma than some surviving manuscripts. This is an important effect the editing of Shakespeare has had on the editing of others (pp. 6–7). Looking to earlier writings, Tim William Machan, '"I endowed thy purposes": Shakespeare, Editing, and Middle English Literature' (*TEXT* 13[2000] 9–25), argues that the Shakespeare editing tradition has imposed an inappropriate notion of authorship upon medieval literature. For seventeenth- and eighteenth-century readers, Shakespeare was more easily made the father of English poetry than his medieval forebears since he was not tainted by coming before the Reformation and he also, conveniently, wears his learning more lightly. Shakespeare was valued for creating 'cultural empathy', what Johnson called the 'faithful mirrour of manners and life', while medieval literature apart from Chaucer was virtually apologized for (in phrases about rustic charm and simplicity) when published (pp. 12–14). For medieval literature the problem was straightforwardly and narrowly how to make the difficult language accessible without losing accuracy, whereas the editorial problem in Shakespeare was beginning to span many cultural domains, including conceptualizations of the author, reader, and critic (pp. 16–17). Because of the textual-critical tradition, Shakespeare comes down to us 'in a resolutely unilinear fashion, monogenetically descending from either the first folio or one of the early quartos', which leads to an irony. Early editors of Shakespeare began by treating the Folios like classical manuscripts with independent authority (as Mowat also observes in a chapter reviewed below), and only later did editors fully realize the fact of monogenetic descent that made this invalid. Then, when later editors approached medieval works, they wrongly treated them as monogenetic when in fact they are more like classical works in their polygenesis (p. 19 n. 23). Despite their polygenesis, in the nineteenth century medieval works were edited like Shakespeare's works; multiple readings in manuscripts of equal authority have been reduced to single readings, and the singular author was invented as the source of authenticity (p. 20). Without Shakespeare we would now understand medieval literature via multiple manuscript descendance and with the originating agency of not one but a collection of voices (p. 22). Rather than focusing on the print culture that produced Shakespeare, we would be thinking about manuscript culture and its relation to 'late-medieval England's diglossia' of the simultaneously existing low English oral tradition and high Latin literary tradition. When we retrospectively apply our notion of authorial paternity to Chaucer and Langland and treat their agency as a given, we obscure the fact that Chaucer and Langland were insisting on the validity of their authorial consciousness precisely *in opposition to* a medieval culture that denied this to vernacular writers. Of course, authors do not alone create the idea of authorial agency (whole cultures do that), and the sense of relatively stable agency that we take back with us to Chaucer is 'more the creation of a Shakespearian-focused textual criticism than a historical medieval reality' (p. 23). This anachronism is being addressed in medieval textual studies, and the conception of authorship used by editors is rightly being historicized; this reorganization is not mere relativism or decadent postmodernism, but good historicism (pp. 24–5).

In a major work on the history of twentieth-century Shakespeare editing, Paul Werstine, 'Editing Shakespeare and Editing Without Shakespeare: Wilson, McKerrow, Greg, Bowers, Tanselle, and Copy-Text Editing' (*TEXT* 13[2000] 27–53), shows that new bibliography was never a matter of consensus and that McKerrow in particular rejected Greg's theory of copy-text; thus the 'new textualists' (not Werstine's term) are squarely within rather than without new bibliography's diverse field. In the matter of 'accidentals' (by which he meant spelling, punctuation, word-division, and so forth) Greg, in 'The Rationale of Copy-Text', advised ignoring your copy-text and following whichever text you think best represents the author's habits, for there were no standard habits for the sixteenth and seventeenth centuries and Greg denied competence outside this period. Yet Fredson Bowers promoted Greg's 'Rationale' principles for editors of nineteenth-century works and thus a Shakespeare-centred way of thinking dominated other periods, even though Greg's ideas did not even get realized in a Shakespeare edition, the closest thing to a realization of them being Bowers's edition of Dekker. Rather, Shakespeare continued to be presented in modernized spelling and punctuation rather than with the 'accidentals' of early printing as Greg advocated (pp. 27–8). Greg's ideas generally, and in particular his confident distinction between printings made from foul papers and those made from promptbooks, continue to inform modern Shakespeare editions. Recently the editing of Shakespeare has been decentred, starting with the Oxford *Complete Works*, which was 'edited without reference to poststructuralism' and yet was a decentring project nonetheless (p. 29). (Actually, I would argue that Wells and Taylor got to post-structuralism by a relentless pursuit of the empirical, as Derrida's ideas would indeed predict.) Wells and Taylor largely followed Greg, but crucially they admitted all readings that might have got onto the stage, not merely the authorial ones; in this they were effectively following Jerome McGann's *A Critique of Modern Textual Criticism* [1983] in their conception of the socialized text. Since McGann was actually concerned with the Romantic poets in this book, we might say that Shakespeare was thus edited by reference to Byron (p. 30). Greg got his confident, author-centred editorial principles from his belief that he could see authorial foul papers in Hand D of *Sir Thomas More*, and although he occasionally mentioned the possibility of scribal transcripts, he suppressed this possibility until he had formed his model of textual transmission based on the binarism of foul papers and promptbooks, the former too untidy to use directly but kept in the playhouse (and maybe annotated lightly), where they were transcribed to make the latter. Although in discursive writing Greg would admit that the binary was not terribly stable (since promptbooks might contain foul-paperish features), in practice, when determining underlying copy for particular printings, he discounted this possibility (pp. 31–2). Thus Greg would argue that the absence of evidence for promptbook copy means that the copy must have been foul papers, and since a company would guard its promptbook (which 'may have been' the one containing the censor's licence), Greg assumed that what went to the printers must have been foul papers, which therefore take us close to the Shakespearian manuscripts. Bowers, on the other hand, argued that nothing in Henslowe's Diary showed a dramatist handing over his foul papers; rather, he probably handed over a fair copy and kept the foul papers for himself. Bower suggested that there were more than two types of possible copy for printers, and Orgel has since argued that dramatic collaboration does not even locate the author at its centre: the text is just a 'working model' of the play (p. 33).

The expression 'foul papers' could mean specifically those that were incomplete, so Greg's sense of them as 'a complete authorial manuscript' is quite wrong (p. 34). This is not quite fair, for there is only Knight's transcript of Fletcher's *Bonduca* standing as an example of 'foul paper' incompleteness. Greg's term 'promptbook' was anachronistic and not analogous to 'book' in the period (as he claimed); indeed the entire binary classification Greg erected has been shown to be invalid, for manuscripts he called promptbooks have features that he claimed were unique to foul papers. Werstine thinks that there is 'no consensus' now about whether Hand D of *Sir Thomas More* is Shakespeare, and he cites Howard-Hill's tentative summary of the situation: 'none of them [the contributors to this collection of essays] believes that the case for Shakespeare's presence in the *More* manuscript is less strong than that which could be made to deny it or to identify another playwright'. This is not a fair quotation of Howard-Hill's view about the consensus of opinion, for he goes on to say that the hypothesis of Shakespeare's authorship and ownership of Hand D is supported by 'separate but convergent lines of enquiry conducted by scholars of pre-eminent skills and authority' and 'cannot be met by simple denial or doubts as to its adequacy', which is precisely what Werstine is doing (p. 34). Some modern editors have, then, abandoned Greg's narrative and his hope of determining underlying copy for printings, and of determining the relationship of that copy to Shakespeare's manuscripts. Werstine quotes Henry Woudhuysen's Arden 3 *Love's Labour's Lost* on the uncertainty about theatrical manuscripts generally and how, if the 'foul paper' features could get past the printers and into print (as new bibliography insists) then equally they could be transmitted into scribal copies. This is true, but the argument is usually run in the opposite direction: scribal transcripts contain noticeable things that would not be in authorial or theatrical copy, such as act intervals and Latinate labels. Werstine lists some recent editions that show the influence of his type of uncertainty, which leads to giving the reader more than one early text (as with Jill Levenson's Oxford Shakespeare *Romeo and Juliet* reviewed here last year) or to conflation with clear markers to show provenance and to show editorial construction work, as with R.A. Foakes's Arden 3 *King Lear* and Mowat and Werstine's New Folger Shakespeare series. Thus, claims Werstine, editing Shakespeare has become usefully decentred from the man and recentred on the early printed texts themselves (p. 36). Is this lack of an editorial consensus a new or old condition? Tanselle says it is new, but Werstine shows that it is old. Tanselle represents new bibliography as an evolution: McKerrow was opposed to eclecticism but in his *Prolegomena for the Oxford Shakespeare* he showed that he would be willing to emend an early text with variants from a later one if the variants were accepted as a unit, and then Greg (in *The Editorial Problem* and later 'Rationale') went the next step and argued for allowing editorial judgement to choose on each variant individually. But this is merely to repeat Greg's version of the story, and he understated the extent to which he and McKerrow disagreed; the divergences are all the more apparent if one brings in John Dover Wilson (p. 37). Although McKerrow often left implicit whom he was disagreeing with, we can reconstruct the ongoing progression of the arguments.

McKerrow in *Prolegomena* disagreed with Greg's notion of foul papers (holograph copy of a play in its final form) for he thought that if the players had it, they would write on it. McKerrow was not convinced Hand D was Shakespeare, so unlike Greg he did not think that he knew what a Shakespeare holograph would look like, and hence he did not think we could know Shakespeare's habits in spelling, capitalization, italicization and pointing (pp. 38–9). McKerrow also distanced himself from John Dover Wilson and Arthur Quiller-Couch's idea that many surviving printings of Shakespeare's plays incorporated parts of lost plays, and from Wilson's view that for some plays one person copied the text and another the stage directions. Wilson developed his elaborate model of repeated interference in the text of Folio *Hamlet* via scribe P, who made Shakespeare's manuscript (which underlies Q2) into a promptbook, and scribe C, who subsequently revised this promptbook to make the text that underlies F1; Greg wholeheartedly embraced his narrative. Overall, in *Prolegomena* McKerrow put as much distance as he could between himself and Wilson and himself and Greg about the possibility of inferring copy from printed text: to McKerrow it was hopeless (pp. 40–2). McKerrow alluded to a careless playwright sending individual sheets to the theatre as he wrote them, which must be Robert Daborne's letter to Henslowe ('J send you the foule sheet & ye fayr I was wrighting as your man can testify'), which Werstine interprets as showing how unusual it is to be giving Henslowe a foul sheet and 'how he feels obligated to provide better copy' (p. 43). I cannot see these things in the letter, only the sense that Daborne had to be pressed for it. Another cause of non-authorial (and hard to remove) errors and inconsistencies in a play imagined by McKerrow was incomplete revision, and Werstine says that *Sir Thomas More* and *Sir John van Olden Barnavelt* are the most famous examples of 'incompletely revised manuscripts' (p. 44). It would be fairer to call these 'allegedly' incomplete, since Werstine himself has long insisted on the impossibility of our knowing just what it took for a manuscript to be considered ready for the theatre. McKerrow, having no confidence in our ability to determine the underlying manuscripts of the early printings, felt that copy-text should be chosen on the basis of the overt qualities of the extant printings themselves, specifically 'carefulness and freedom from errors' rather than covert features of them informing a doubtful theory about their provenance. Thus, 'McKerrow's understanding of authority is documentary rather than metaphysical' (p. 46), which is an odd opposition; has 'metaphysical' become again an abusive epithet to throw at people whom you think are being unreasonably idealistic? Unlike Greg, McKerrow thought it impossible to tell if revision apparent in a later reprinting was authorial or not, and overall his advice to editors was surprisingly close to modern new textualism: one should determine 'the most authoritative text' that we have, and 'reprint this as exactly as possible save for manifest and indubitable errors' (*Prolegomena*, p. 7). After a year of claiming that new bibliography is self-deluding, Werstine now appears to think that McKerrow was a new textualist, but only by splitting McKerrow from Greg and Dover Wilson; I suspect if he looked closely at the latter pair he would find something of the new textualist acceptance of indeterminacy in their work. To be fair, Werstine explicitly denies that he thinks of McKerrow as a proto-new textualist, and he turns to McKerrow's inconsistencies.

Greg and Bowers pointed out that McKerrow's claim that we cannot really know what the copy-text of a printing was is in contradiction to his 'suggestion' ('A Suggestion Regarding Shakespeare's Manuscripts', *RES* 11[1935]), alluded to in *Prolegomena*, where he repeats its principle. They were right, but Greg was inconsistent too: in *The Editorial Problem in Shakespeare* he claimed that for *Hamlet* we can know that Q2 was printed from foul papers and F from promptbook and that this can be known for other works too, yet elsewhere in the same book he says that we do not know this for any other play. In the case of *Hamlet* Greg dithered between accepting Wilson's certainty (Q2 is from foul papers, F is from promptbook) and remarking on the problem that Q2 has signs of the prompter: 'Drum, trumpets, and shot. Flourish, a piece goes off' in Q2 looks like theatrical annotation creating repetition, while in F there are stage directions not easily derived from Q2 (which they should be for Wilson's theory), and moreover the stage directions are indeterminate in a way a promptbook's should not be (pp. 48–50). Greg's analysis showed that Wilson's categorization of Q2 *Hamlet* being printed from foul papers and F *Hamlet* being printed from promptbook was deeply problematic, yet this was the only example Greg could offer of our being able to tell underlying copy for two substantive versions of a Shakespeare play. Bowers strongly attacked Wilson's methods, and also attacked McKerrow for overreacting to Wilson and being too conservative, but Bowers too seems to flit between demolishing Wilson's edifice about *Hamlet* and adopting it. Twentieth-century editors are really back where McKerrow was in having to reject Greg's theory of the copy-text and falling back on the pragmatism that McKerrow shows in his *Prolegomena* (pp. 51–2). Thus, we should reject Tanselle's narrative of early twentieth-century new bibliography being a consensus that spread beyond Shakespeare editing and see it as a conflictual field from the start. Otherwise, those who reject Greg's theory (new textualists) seem cut off from the new bibliography tradition, whereas in fact they are within its diverse field (p. 53)

Werstine's narrative of new bibliography's capacity to incorporate the new textualism is markedly at odds with that in Barbara Mowat's 'The Reproduction of

Shakespeare's Texts' (in De Grazia and Wells, eds., *The Cambridge Companion to Shakespeare*), a survey of editorial thinking from the sixteenth century to the present day. Mowat begins by insisting on the consensus Werstine denies: 'For much of the twentieth century ... editors and textual critics accepted and depended upon a single larger story' (p. 13), and she turns to Thomas Kuhn's model of 'paradigm shifts' to distinguish the pre-twentieth-century pessimism regarding our ability to determine the underlying copy for printed texts from the new bibliographical confidence about this (p. 18). Yet the new bibliographical paradigm 'maintains its hold on the reproduction of Shakespeare's text' (p. 24) which can only be explained, Mowat claims, by the absence of a new paradigm to take its place. Where Werstine hopes to show that new bibliography can accommodate the disagreements that he and others have with Greg's binary thinking—which is admittedly a surprising position for Werstine to adopt after years of apparently self-imposed exile from the tradition—Mowat looks to the new textualists for 'a future in which a new paradigm may be established' (p. 26). If there has to be accommodation, it is new bibliography that must give ground and 'find a way to explain and absorb the factual and theoretical challenges to its hegemony', or else 'editing may flourish in the absence of any accepted paradigm' (p. 26), which last comment rather suggests that she does not fully accept the implications of what Kuhn meant by a 'paradigm', which was something we cannot do without.

Jeffrey Masten, 'More or Less: Editing the Collaborative' (*ShakS* 29[2001] 109–31), argues that the binarism of author's hand and alien hand is deconstructed in *Sir Thomas More* and was not at all stable in Shakespeare's time. Like Werstine, Masten notes that the rising importance attached to the manuscript of *Sir Thomas More* was closely related to new bibliography's category distinctions of good and bad quartos and foul papers versus promptbooks, and he thinks that we seek in this manuscript an authorial integrity witnessed in a hand that in fact the document denies in its dispersal of authority (p. 112). The problem is our failure to think up new ways to deal with editing collaborative works (as most plays of the period are): we continue to edit the person (Shakespeare) not the work, and we think of that person as singular (p. 113). Attribution studies, which takes identity as a fact, does not take seriously enough the ways in which habits are emulated, adopted, adapted, and thrown off; 'hands' in writing should not be understood as synecdoche for persons but as metonymy for writing (the process, not the person) (p. 115). We are still treating collaboration in an old historicist way: if only to keep the unity of the persons, we carve up the play, we disintegrate it to differentiate them. Rather, Masten exhorts, we should be new historicist in historicizing not only the text but also 'our models of agency, individuality, style, corporate effort, contention, influence, and so forth' to put those 'within the realm of the discursively social', and we might have to invent new editorial apparatuses and practices to do this. This would be to get back some of the sense of 'individual' that Raymond Williams drew our attention to in *Keywords*, that of indivisibility from the group, and would concentrate on the social whirl of interpenetrating texts and practices (as the new historicists have insisted on) that not only made texts but also made text-makers (p. 116). These are undoubtedly laudable aims, but while Masten gives a brilliant reading of the play *Sir Thomas More* (which will be only briefly noted here) he signally fails to invent new editorial apparatuses and practices that might achieve the desired ends.

Sir Thomas More begins with a scene about distinguishing English property (women, food) from foreigners' property, and in the quelling scene More does a 'radical denaturalization' that 'places its hearers (onstage and off) in a position of cross-identification that resonates throughout the play' (p. 117). As Masten admits, this might in fact seem 'a simple and transparently conservative move', and I would agree; conservatives know the power of the injunction to 'do unto others'. But the particular reversal of places entails a breaking of sumptuary laws ('you in ruff of your opinions clothed') since commoners were not supposed to wear ruffs (p. 118). Masten is wrong: law limited the size of ruffs, not who could wear them. The 'cross-class-dressed "ruff" comes back to redress itself' when More argues that other '*ruff*ians' will 'shark on' the rebels if the topsy-turvydom of rebellion is allowed to succeed. Of course, More himself does cross-dressing and shape-shifting (in the play within the play), and finally becomes a 'stranger' on the scaffold. Stripped of his titles, he becomes 'only More', a name that 'signifies a cross-identification between lack and excess' and all the more so pronounced, as it was then, 'one-ly More' (p. 119). The point of this reading is that traditional scholarship, which divides the text into 'hands', 'has stopped us from reading its continuities and theirs' (for the themes run throughout the play), but I would counter that Masten undoubtedly did his sparkling reading on the basis of existing editions—which served him well—and indeed that he could not assert that the continuities were continuities had not previous editors divided up the hands in the first place. In this period before coherent national identity, the various terms for otherness (alien, denizen, foreigner) were vague and overlapped, and foreigner could mean just 'not from this parish', or 'recently arrived in town from the countryside', as indeed Shakespeare was (pp. 120–1). A particularly fraught notion was the 'denizen', which meant a 'native' and also someone who lived 'within' (dans) and had certain limited rights to work; geographically as well as in the play, the boundaries of strangeness are not clear and Tilney's efforts in rewriting the play are at least partly to make it specific (he alters 'stranger' to 'Lombard') and yet also general ('English' to 'man'). Masten ends with a series of summarizing bullet points (pp. 122–3): there are native Secretary hands and foreign Italian hands in the manuscript and indeed literate men learned to write either and might mix them up (as Greg complains Hand S does), so in form too it encodes the deconstructive stranger/native theme. (Masten does not call it deconstructive, but that is the essence of what he argues.) The word 'stranger' was itself an only partly assimilated foreigner at this time, having come from France in the late fourteenth century, and Hand D's spelling of it as 'strainger' was a strange Scottish spelling used by James I, the foreigner monarch possibly on the English throne by the time of the play's revision. Such an interpenetration of the play and its linguistic and political contexts is, for Masten, what we should be concentrating on instead of parcelling up work into originating author(s) and 'alien hands' as though these were stable terms.

N.W. Bawcutt, 'Renaissance Dramatists and the Texts of their Plays' (*RORD* 40[2001] 1–24), argues against the wrong-headed and anachronistic sense of the 'socialized' text posited by Stephen Orgel, David Scott Kastan, W. Speed Hill, and Paul Werstine (he might have include Jeffrey Masten too), pointing out that the modern idea that theatre men had no literary ambitions is contrary to the evidence. In fact, dramatists did want their plays printed and without the actors' cuts, as shown by the title page of *Every Man Out of His Humour* [1600], which claims that the contents show the play 'As It Was First Composed by the Author B.I. Containing more than hath been Publickly Spoken or Acted', the title page of *The Duchess of Malfi* [1623], which claims that it contains 'diuerse things Printed, that the length of the Play would not beare in the Presentment', and the title page of Barnes's *Devil's Charter* [1607], which claims that the contents were 'more exactly reuewed, corrected, and augmented since [performance] by the Author, for the more pleasure and profit of the Reader'. Jonson, Webster, and Barnes might be dismissed as bookish and literary, but Brome cannot, and his *The Antipodes* [1640] ends with a note to the reader saying that the printing included all the things left out of performance, 'inserted according to the allowed *Original*'. To be fair, all these examples are discussed in David Scott Kastan's book reviewed above, and he holds his views in spite of them. Orgel claims that 'If the play is a book, it's not a play', but that is not so, and indeed in *The White Devil* [1612] Webster praised the performers while condemning the ignorant audience, and in *The Devil's Law Case* [1623] he asserts the mutual dependency of writer and performers (p. 5). Likewise Marston, in his preface to *The Fawn* [1606], insisted that, while comedy did not read well, his tragedy would withstand 'the most curious perusall'. This interest in printing is common in the period, Fletcher and Shakespeare being the exceptions to the rule: Brome, Heywood, and Shirley wrote about printing as a natural succession to performance, the classical drama was known only because it could be read, and a number of dramatists referred to their plays as poems, a genre that was normally published (pp. 6–7). Commendatory poems by fellow playwrights preceding the 1623 text call it 'his Dutchesse of *Malfy*' (Webster's, not the company's), and treat the printing of it as an appropriate monument to secure Webster's posterity (p. 11).

So much for ownership, what of fidelity? Jasper Heywood's preface to his translation of Seneca's *Thyestes* [1560] complains that an early work of his was 'corrupted' in the printing house, so accuracy is not a recent concern being foisted onto the period; it was already there, and Bawcutt cites complaints by Jonson, Chapman, and Heywood about bad printing (pp. 12–13). True, printers mixed corrected and uncorrected sheets, but this was due to thrift and inefficiency, not a post-structuralist concern for fluidity, and the address of 'The Printers to the Reader' of Thomas Urquhart's *Epigrams Divine and Moral* [1641] shows that, contrary to Orgel, the printers did idealize the final, perfected text even if they could not, for reasons of economy, make one. The printers explain that they include a full list of errata even though (because of the press correction) not every copy will have all the errors, for they are 'willing rather to insert the totall, where the parts are wanting in their distinguish't places, then by omitting any thing of the due count, to let an errour slip uncorrected'. Equally aimed at perfection were the requests in many books that the reader should go through and make the necessary corrections in pen (pp. 14–15). There was a tradition of authors going through and making corrections in copies of their books they wanted to present to someone, as Massinger did for *The Duke of Milan*, given to his patron Sir Francis Foljambe. We can summarize that plays were considered by their writers as their own intellectual property, that they were not always happy with what the players did to them, that they frequently arranged to publish them, and that they would be amazed at our modern veneration of printing errors (pp. 16–17). The new notions of the socialized text overthrow 'two centuries of patient and disinterested efforts to purify and clarify texts' that the Renaissance authors would have thanked us for (p. 20).

John Jowett, 'The Audacity of *Measure for Measure* in 1621' (*BJJ* 8[2001] 229–47), argues that the discussion about foreign war news in *Measure for Measure* I.ii would have been highly topical in 1621, which is when Middleton added it to Shakespeare's old play for revival. By 1621 the play's disguised-ruler topicality—arising from the accession of the unknown quantity James I in 1603—would have been decidedly old-fashioned. Middleton's addition of the material at the beginning of I.ii about the king of Hungary's peace alludes to Protestant resistance to Counter-Reformation Catholicism in Europe, the Thirty Years War, and the Palatinate wars, and Middleton did this sort of thing to other works at the time (p. 230). Vienna was ruled by the Catholic Habsburg emperor Ferdinand II, but in 1621 it was under attack from the Protestant king of Hungary (Bethlen Gabor), who wanted to free it from the Catholic Habsburg empire; Middleton changed the location from Ferrara to Vienna to take advantage of these events. James I's son-in-law Frederick, the Elector Palatine, was proclaimed king of Bohemia in 1620 and formed a league with Bethlen, king of Hungary (p. 231). So the politics of this Austrian war were topical in London, and what seems to have been of special interest was detail of the accords between princes, hence Lucio's reference to the dukes coming to 'composition with the King of Hungary' (p. 232). But the alliance of Bethlen Gabor with Frederick the Elector Palatine was not viewed with complete equanimity in England, because Bethlen was Turkish. James I asked Frederick to break off the alliance, and his hostility to Bethlen lies behind 'the tension surrounding Lucio's allusion to a truce between Vienna and the King of Hungary' (p. 233). Negotiations to end the conflict were reported as in process in a news-sheet of 6 October 1621, and presumably it was just after this that Middleton wrote the words 'If the Duke with the other dukes comes not to composition', since if the audience knew the outcome of the real negotiations the allusion would 'fall flat'. Ordinarily the delays of scripting, licensing, and rehearsal make such topicality hard to achieve in a play, but in the case of a revival of *Measure for Measure* these delays did not apply (p. 234). The location of the stage is both London and Vienna, for 'Heaven grant us its peace, but not the King of Hungary's' can be read from the Protestant English point of view (an ally of England making an unwanted unilateral peace with the enemy) and from the Catholic Austrian point of view (Bethlen's offer of peace is not to be trusted). Thus the stage is metaphoric, representing what is happening, and metonymic, partaking in the events depicted (pp. 236–7). The freedom to debate the matter of possible war with Spain was a prerogative that parliament was insisting upon and James was resisting as an encroachment on his power to make foreign policy, and indeed James tried to suppress corantos. Middleton's adaptation of *Measure for Measure* defies his efforts to control public discussion of the matters, and the old play presumably appealed because it relates sexual freedom with freedom of speech (pp. 238–9). In an appendix (p. 240), Jowett conveniently summarizes his previously published work on Middleton's hand in *Measure for Measure*, which showed that the un-Shakespearian oaths and the act divisions must post-date original composition (being later than 1606 and 1609 respectively), that the song 'Take oh take those lips away' originated in *Rollo, Duke of Normandy* written in 1617–20 and was apparently imported to the play with localized revisions to 'lock it into the dramatic action', that the 'news' passage in I.ii has Middletonian preferences (*has* instead of *hath*, *whilst* instead of *while*, *ay* instead of *yes*, *between* instead of *betwixt*), and that the idea of razing 'Thou shalt not steal' from the Ten Commandments occurs nowhere else in Shakespeare or any other dramatist, but crops up thrice in two other Middleton plays. The Middleton parallels come from works written before *and* after *Measure for Measure*, so it cannot be that *Measure for Measure* influenced Middleton to write like this.

Arthur Ing Freeman and Janet Ing Freeman, 'Did Halliwell Steal and Mutilate the First Quarto of *Hamlet*?' (*Library* 2[2001] 349–63), set out to dispel the myth that James Orchard stole and mutilated a Q1 *Hamlet* belonging to his father-in-law. The first Q1 was found in 1823, lacking its final leaf, and was reprinted in 1825 in 'quasi-facsimile', and the second (presumably recognized for what it was because of the facsimile) turned up in 1856, with its final leaf but not the title page. Halliwell bought this complete copy at an inflated price through an intermediary, having originally turned down the seller in person (pp. 350–1). Because *Catalogue of Printed Books at Middle Hall* by Sir Thomas Phillipps (Halliwell's future father-in-law) names a 1603 *Hamlet* quarto and yet none was known, William Alexander Jackson supposed that this was the one Halliwell later owned, that he stole it from Phillipps, and that he cut out its title page to conceal the Middle Hall stamp on it. Since Halliwell was barred from his father-in-law's house after he married Henrietta Phillipps, he would have to have pocketed the Q1 *Hamlet* fourteen years [1842–56] before he first showed it to anyone. Moreover, Halliwell's copy had a distinguishing feature, the interleaving of blank pages on which someone had written some notes from Theobald's edition; if he removed the title page to disguise his theft, Halliwell would surely have removed these too. Also, since Phillipps was always accusing Halliwell of dishonourable deeds, he would hardly have put up with the loss of his Q1 *Hamlet* without blaming his son-in-law, especially once that son-in-law publicly announced he had one (pp. 354–7). In fact, Phillipps did not have a Q1 *Hamlet* even if Halliwell had wanted to steal it: the catalogue entry is almost certainly for the quasi-facsimile reprint (pp. 358–9). Whoever interleaved the pages in the first complete Q1 *Hamlet* used an existing printed edition of the 'good' text and indicated that he sometimes preferred a Q1 reading over others (p. 360). He seems to have worked out, without a title page to guide him, that what he had preceded the 1605 and 1611 editions—presumably because their title pages claim they are enlarged texts—so he must have been quite knowledgeable about Shakespeare texts; the annotating is from the period 1726–33 (p. 362).

In the first of two essays reviewed here, Lynette Hunter, 'The Dating of Q4 *Romeo and Juliet* Revisited' (*Library* 2[2001] 281–5), argues that the date of Q4 *Romeo and Juliet* cannot be precisely determined from deterioration of its tailpiece device (as George Walton Williams claimed) and it could lie anywhere within the period 1616–28, although probably between 1618 and 28. In 1965 George Walton Williams suggested that the anonymous and undated Q4a *Romeo and Juliet* was printed in 1622 by William Stansby (for John Smethwick, as the title page says), but since Smethwick was involved in the Folio, Hunter thinks this would be odd. After all, the Pavier quartos were stopped to remove competition for the Folio, so why would Smethwick be doing something to hurt his own bigger project? (The rather obvious answer is that Smethwick was invited to join the Folio project late in its development, once it was clear that he already had the rights to a number of the plays.) The dating of Q4 to 1622 was done by looking at the degradation of the tailpiece device on L4^v and comparing it to other Stansby books from 1615 to 1623, but Hunter has had several Q4s looked at and 'the endpieces are not uniform in appearance in respect of these breaks', nor are they in other books that use the device. As such, we can only say from the tailpiece that Q4 is not earlier than 1616 (when one certain break does first appear in other books using the device) and not later than 1628 when Stansby stopped using the device, something we know because in 1629 he used another one of his favourite devices in the reprinting of a work that had previously used this one (p. 282). Hunter and her Arden 3 co-editor on the play, Peter Lichtenfels, together with their team, have found in Q4s only the consistent presence of Williams's break number 1 and the inconsistent presence of the other breaks. Although the evidence is not as clear as Williams first claimed, a cluster of his breaks (numbers 1, 2, and 4) does seem to emerge in 1618 and is present in a few Q4 copies, so that is the earliest *likely* date for Q4 (p. 283). Watermark evidence is inconclusive, and now that the date of Q4 is up for grabs (anywhere within 1618–1628) the relationship to the Folio is anybody's guess; where we previously thought it was printed around the same time as F, Q4 *Romeo and Juliet* might in fact have been printed four years earlier or five years later and had nothing to do with it (p. 284). Now that we do not know whether Q4 was printed before or after F, the possibilities about how their underlying copies are related, and what this tells us about printing house practices, are all up in the air. There are no parts of Q4 that seem dependent on F as their copy; there are parts of F that might be influenced by Q4, but if so we have to explain the absence from F of corrections that Q4 makes to Q3 (p. 285). At this point Hunter misuses the expression 'begs the question' to mean 'invites the question' and the reader is pointed to her second paper, about Q4 *Romeo and Juliet* itself.

Having claimed that we cannot know what was the copy for Q4 *Romeo and Juliet*, Hunter contradicts this assertion in 'Why has Q4 *Romeo and Juliet* such an Intelligent Editor?' (in Bell, Chew, Eliot, Hunter, and West, eds., *Re-constructing the Book: Literary Texts in Transmission*), an essay regarding the variants between Q1, Q2, Q3, and Q4 *Romeo and Juliet* that is by turns vague, ambiguous, and apparently ignorant of how variation and corruption can occur (as by compositorial slip), and puts everything down to the putative 'intelligence' of a supposed editor of Q4. Editors of the play, Hunter notes, usually adopt Q2 but then go on to edit it in ways that make it like Q4 or Q3, so why not use Q3 as copy-text for modern editions? Perhaps, she wonders, because it is merely a reprint of Q2 (indeed); nonetheless Q4 has been intelligently edited and should at least be collated in modern editions (p. 9). The signs of intelligent editing are, as we might expect, that it makes the changes modern editors make. There are points where Q4 agrees with Q2 against Q1/Q3, but not enough to suppose that the editor of Q4 had a copy of Q2 in front of him: Q4 is essentially an intelligent reprint of Q3, and it almost always follows Q3 where Q3 has already changed something from Q2. That is to say, where there is a problem that a smart person might try to fix, Q4 uses Q3's fix. Perhaps that is because the theatre people told the editor to trust Q3, or else because the editor of Q4 *was* the editor of Q3, Hunter speculates. Q3 was printed from Q2, but with a number of changes that suggest that an 'editor' marked up the copy of Q2 first, and this man was not from the playhouse (since speech prefixes and stage directions retain their errors) nor a compositor (since layout and catchword errors get through). As well as these errors there are intelligent changes, some showing access to Q1. At this point Hunter's essay becomes hard to read because she uses line-number references adjectivally, producing such gibberish as 'For example, at 5.2 Q2 mistakenly prints 5.2.23 (Exit. when Friar John leaves. Q3 slavishly reproduces this clear error, even adding a bracket to Friar Lawrence's 5.2.30 Exit. (2) (Exit. (3)' (p. 12). I cannot tell which words in those sentences are quotations nor which edition the line-numbers refer to; possibly these sentences have been mangled in their printing. In the next paragraph quotations from quartos are represented by a tiny change in the size of typeface and no quotation marks at all, so it is virtually impossible to see where the quotations of clauses start and finish. There is also fatal vagueness, as in 'Approximately 75 per cent of Q1 covers the same ground as Q2, and over half the lines in that 75 per cent are the same if not very similar (Irace)'; what does 'covers the same ground mean' if, as seems implied, the lines are not 'very similar'? Perhaps this is meant to imply a paraphrasal relationship, or merely the conveying of the same events of the plot. The Q2/Q3 variants are categorized by Hunter under three heads: (a) those occurring in the 25 per cent of Q2 which 'has no counterpart' in Q1; (b) those which follow Q1; and (c) those for which Q1 is different again from Q2 and Q3. This last category Hunter confusingly describes as 'those which occur where Q1 makes a change', but here the tense and agency are wrong: Q1, being the earliest text, did not change, or disagree with, anything that we know of.

Of the Q3/Q2 variants for which we have Q1 text also, nearly half are at places where Q1 has something different again, which statistically is an unlikely coincidence unless the person making Q3 had access to Q1; in other words were the locations of Q3/Q2 variants picked at random, they would not half the time turn out to be places where there are also Q2/Q1 variants. (Actually, one cannot be sure this is significant until one has determined the influence of Q1 on Q2—something Hunter has not done—because if Q1 heavily influenced Q2 then Q1/Q2/Q3 variants might merely be examples of repeated attempts to correct error in a single line of linear descent.) More significantly, of the hundred or so differences between Q3 and Q2, nearly half occur in the quarter of Q2 for which there is no corresponding section in Q1, so 'Q3 will change Q2 twice as many times where Q1 is not there to corroborate as when it is'. This does seem significant evidence for consultation of Q1 during the making of Q3, since were Q1 not used we would expect only a quarter of the changes to fall in places for which it lacks lines, and the chance of half the changes randomly falling in these places is extremely small. Yet, despite respecting Q1 (in the sense of emending more ambitiously when it is not there to contradict him) the editor of Q3 is not afraid to overrule it even where Q1 and Q2 agree (p. 14). From this, however, Hunter leaps to the assertion that Q4 seems to 'recognize the authority of the skill involved in editing Q3', following it rather than Q2 for nearly all Q3/Q2 variants. This is a mistake since Hunter has not shown that 'skill', only confidence in and respect for Q1, which is not the same thing. One would have to argue that a number of changes are intelligent improvements over previous printings to establish skill, and Hunter has not engaged in any serious debate of the value of particular Q3 variants. Hunter categorizes the 'decisions' of Q4 with respect to variants and agreements between the three preceding quartos and constructs a shaping intelligence at work. For example, she thinks that where Q3 shows a change from Q2, Q4 respects this change and follows it, and only very seldom does it overrule a Q3/Q1 agreement. Looking at occasions when Q4 agrees with Q1 against Q3/Q2, Hunter thinks the policy is one of 'allowing Q1 to advise but not dictate', which is pretty woolly, but worse is to come: there are occasions when Q1 differs from Q3, and although Q4 does not abandon Q3 to follow Q1, it 'moves in the direction of the spirit of Q1' (p. 15). In all this there is much counting of variation but little effort to *account* for it other than by a shaping intelligence, yet without detailed consideration of the particular changes the reader has no reason to suppose that the changes are improvements rather than merely errors in transmission.

Hunter attempts to show that the 'editor' of Q4 might have had some theatrical experience by the variant at II.i.10: 'dove' (Q1), 'day' (Q2 and Q3), 'die' (Q4). Hunter discusses the Great Vowel Shift, but without using the International Phonetic Alphabet so it is hard to know just what sounds she is trying to indicate, and she argues that Q4's not following Q3 and Q2's 'day' but instead putting 'die' would not have happened 'if the editor had not "heard" something different' (p. 16). Of course, this could easily have happened by any one of the many ways that error can creep into a text, including compositorial slip, something that Hunter does not mention as a source of variants. The 'most radical changes in Q4' (by which she means the most radical of Q4 departures from its copy Q3) occur in the quarter of the text for which there is no corresponding part in Q1 (just as was the pattern with Q3), but some of the changes 'make only a little difference to significance, for example 5.3.8 something (3/4) some thing (4)'. I am not sure that that makes any difference to the meaning in early modern English. Hunter lists changes (such as 'murd'red [2/3] murdered [4]') that one might expect a compositor to make in justifying a line, but without letting the reader know whether the line in question is full, and she sees 'an exceptionally attentive mind' making 'subtle adjustments to punctuation that radically affect or effect significance'. This insistence on a shaping mind reaches absurd heights with the attribution to 'the Q4 editor' of the mistake of turning at Q2/3's correct 'mouth of outrage' (V.iii.215) into Q4's 'moneth of outrage' and then claiming that it might be a variant spelling of 'moans' because 'mones' appears in Q4 (p. 17). Hunter overlooks the possibility of imperfect press correction: perhaps during proofing it was spotted that 'month' had been set, and since (as *OED* month[1] confirms) the spelling 'moneth' was almost universal in this period, it was wrongly changed to that. Hunter sets out to sketch the biography of her 'intelligent' editor of Q4, who 'seems to have had knowledge of the play in performance' because speeches are correctly reassigned against the advice of earlier printings (p. 17). There is an obvious objection to this line of reasoning: Hunter's own knowledge that Q4 is right is not based on seeing the original performances, so if she can work it out from the surviving printings then her imagined Q4 editor could have. Hunter thinks that Q4's making clear that Balthazar returns with Romeo from Mantua is also a sign of the theatre, but again one could 'fix' that from reading the play. Where Q3 names 'Will Kemp', Q4 has the character name 'Peter', and Hunter thinks that 'Q4 firmly deletes the actor's name presumably because it is no longer a selling point, Kemp must have faded from people's minds'. Would a name buried within a book ever have been a selling point in the first place? A final error: Hunter notes that F lacks oaths that would violate the 1606 Act to Restrain Abuses of Players whereas Q1, Q2, Q3, and Q4 retain them, and wonders if that is because 'they are less formal texts that [*sic*] F?' It is well known that the Act did not cover printing at all, and the Folio has other plays containing oaths that could not be said on stage after 1606. Hunter begins to recognize the image 'of an editor working just like a modern editor on the text itself, with the addition of a theatrical understanding' and concludes that the 'good practice' of her kind of theatre-centred editing 'goes back a long way' (p. 20).

Carl James Grindley, 'The Story of King Lear in John Hardyng's *Chronicle*' (*CahiersE* 59[2001] 77–80), provides a facsimile and transcript of an under-examined version of the *King Lear* story. It appears in John Hardyng's *Chronicle*, a work written between 1450 and 1470 and surviving in eleven complete manuscripts and many fragments, and two printings in 1543 (not based on one of the extant manuscripts) and a bad edition of 1812. Because of the variation between manuscripts, there is no establishable stable text. Tapan Kumar Mukherjee, 'The Sixth of July: *Much Ado About Nothing*: I.i.274' (*ELN* 38:iv[2001] 16–18) aims to clear up a calendrical obscurity when friends mock Benedick by seeming to complete an aural 'letter' of his with '*Claudio* To the tuition of God, from my house if I had it— I *Don Pedro* The sixth of July, I Your loving friend, I Benedick' (*Much Ado* I.i.265–7). Phillip Clayton-Gore argued that this referred to the quarter-days— 25 March (Lady Day), 24 June (Midsummer Day), 29 September (Michaelmas), and 25 December (Christmas Day)—or rather the variant used by the Crown Estate Commission in which Midsummer Quarter-day falls on 5 July. This would make Don Pedro's 'sixth of July' the start of a new quarter and hence an occasion of merriment with no rent to worry about for three months. Mukherjee reckons we need the Julian system of counting days before the Kalends (the first day of the month), the Nones (the seventh day of March, May, July, and October, the fifth of other months), and the Ides (the fifteenth day of March, May, July, and October, the thirteenth of other months). By this system, he claims, 24 June (Midsummer Day) is 'the sixth day of the Kalends of July', and hence the reference is to midsummer. Unfortunately he must have miscounted, for having already insisted that the days are counted inclusively, 24 June must be the eighth day of the Kalends of July (24th, 25th, 26th, 27th, 28th, 29th, 30th, 1st).

This year's *Notes and Queries* is much better printed than the last and it contains the typical crop of about two dozen pieces on matters textual. Geoff Wilkes, 'A Textual Problem in *Macbeth*, I.ii' (*N&Q* 48[2001] 293–5), considers the problem in *Macbeth* of 'As whence the Sunne 'gins his reflection, I Shipwracking Stormes, and direfull Thunders: I So from that Spring, whence comfort seem'd to come, I Discomfort swells' (TLN 44–7, I.ii.25–8). The sense has to be that the same place that gives hope brings discomfort, but how does the sun do reflecting? Perhaps by reaching the equinox or solstice and turning back again, but that is strained and the *OED* does not support the use of 'reflect' (turn back) until 1662. Wilkes thinks that the moon is where the sun ''gins his reflection', thereby giving comfort but also causing shipwrecking storms.

David Lake and Brian Vickers, 'Scribal Copy for Q1 of *Othello*: A Reconsideration' (*N&Q* 48[2001] 284–7), decide that the 1622 quarto of *Othello* was set from a transcript made by two scribes. E.A.J. Honigmann argued that Q was probably printed from a scribal transcript on the basis of some hypothesized contractions that caused misreadings ('ha' for 'have', and 'tho' for 'though'), and they are typical late Jacobean contractions, so non-authorial. Had Honigmann counted the contractions he would have found that Q has many more occurrences of 'ha'' and ''em' than we would expect from Shakespeare's habit around 1602 (the date accepted by Lake and Vickers), and none of his usual uses of ''a' meaning 'he'. So Q is almost certainly set from scribal copy, not authorial papers, and the likely explanation is that the scribe, working around 1621, consciously or unconsciously made the play 'sound more contemporary, more Jacobean' (p. 286). In *The Stability of Shakespeare's Texts* [1965] Honigmann showed evidence that two scribes did the work that made the copy of Q 1622, on the evidence of spellings that seem to follow a preference for either marginal or centred entrance stage directions, although Honigmann makes little of this in his more recent book *Texts of 'Othello'* [1996]. Reviewing the latter for *Shakespeare Survey*, MacDonald P. Jackson pointed out that the spelling switches that Honigmann noted in 1965 (*though/tho, bin/beene,* and use of *ha'* and *'em*) are so clustered that statistically they are unlikely to be produced by randomness. So, the two-scribe hypothesis for the copy underlying the 1622 quarto should again be taken seriously.

Continuing his excavation of Nashe in Shakespeare, J.J.M. Tobin, 'Nashe and a Crux in *Measure for Measure*' (*N&Q* 48[2001] 262–4), argues that there are borrowings from *Christ's Tears Over Jerusalem* in *Measure for Measure*. There Shakespeare would have found 'the hoode makes not the Moncke' that Lucio says in Latin at V.i.260, although Tobin does not observe that Shakespeare had already used *cucullus non facit monachum* in *Twelfth Night* two years earlier. Also, Angelo's 'The tempter or the tempted, who sins most, ha?' (II.ii.169) comes from Nashe's 'both the person of the tempted and the tempter', and so does the play's collocation of 'preserved' and 'temptation' (II.ii.157, 164). Tobin has even more tenuous *Measure for Measure* links to *Christ's Tears Over Jerusalem* via syntactical structure ('One thing ... another thing') and more distant collocations. Escalus's 'Some run from brakes of ice' (Riverside text) Tobin explains as 'an abbreviated reference' to a usurer's trick that Nashe describes, in which having 'broke the Ise' of borrowing once, the young gentleman victim will repeatedly borrow on increasingly unfavourable terms, which links with the Duke's reference to Nature's good usury at the beginning of the play ('nature never lends ... thanks and use', I.i.36–40). G. Blakemore Evans, 'An Echo of the *Ur-Hamlet*?' (*N&Q* 48[2001] 266), notices that, in the sources of *Hamlet* (Saxo Grammaticus, Belleforest, and *The Hystorie of Hamblet*), the letter that condemns Hamlet is cut on a wooden board, but in Robert Parry's 1595 chivalric romance *Moderatus* there is a scene of a letter being opened and then resealed using a copy of the signet that originally sealed it. Maybe Shakespeare knew *Moderatus*, but Blakemore Evans thinks it more likely that Parry ('who had visited London several times before 1595') recalled something he had seen in the ur-*Hamlet*. Eric Sams, '*King Leir* and *Edmond Ironside*' (*N&Q* 48[2001] 266–70), finds the anonymous plays *The Chronicle History of King Leir* and *Edmund Ironside* so full of verbal correspondences that they must be by the same person. Sams shows that there are over 140 verbal parallels between them, but many are too common to be significant—'be advised' might be shared by any two works, and so might 'Enter ... disguised' and 'fountain[s] ... spring'—and it is hard to know why he goes further and claims they were written 'at about the same time' (p. 266). Sams claims that he omitted some additional examples because 'they resist tabulation', such as the archaisms 'quondam' and 'whilom' (why those, especially?), and some links he does list are just silly, such as 'my gracious lord' used when addressing a king. Likewise Sams finds a parallel in the plays having 'antithesis ... references to the law ... proverbs, puns and word-play ... and usages antedating *OED* citations', which surely must be true of much literature of the period. There are technical problems with the note too, for Sams uses an 'author-date' style of citation but nowhere are the full bibliographical details provided, and the Oxford Shakespeare's *Textual Companion* is misdated to 1988. Sams ends with a complaint that all his evidence has never 'convinced anyone'.

Paul Vincent, 'Unsolved Mysteries in *Henry the Sixth, Part Two*' (*N&Q* 48[2001] 270–4), thinks that *2 Henry VI* was written by Shakespeare and person(s) unknown, since it is not all of a piece in spelling or in classical knowledge. Gary Taylor showed that *1 Henry VI* probably was written by four or more hands, and this note tries to show that likewise *2 Henry VI* is probably the work of at least two dramatists. Where a play is set 'directly from authorial papers' (decided on the basis of variability in speech prefixes and imprecision or faulty stage directions) as Folio *2 Henry VI* seems to be, the spelling choice O/Oh can tell us a lot. (No mention here of the suspicion recently cast on the new bibliographical idea that variability and imperfection in speech prefixes and stage directions indicate authorial copy, nor does Vincent mention the role of Q3, a Q1 reprint, in the printing of Folio *2 Henry VI*.) Vincent tabulates O/Oh preference in Folio *2 Henry VI* and it is pretty clear: apart from III.ii and III.iii, 'O' predominates (twenty-six 'O's to five 'Oh's). In III.ii and III.iii it is the other way round: twelve 'Oh's to one 'O'. III.i has no 'O's or 'Oh's, which is odd because it is tense stuff plot-wise, but it does have seven 'Ah's, something Shakespeare rarely used. (Vincent does not mention it, but Shakespeare's preference was 'O', of course.) The abnormally high occurrence of 'ye' (something Shakespeare avoided) over 'you' in the play points away from it being all by Shakespeare, and if we look at one type of compound adjective—the highly original and Shakespearian 'conjunction of a noun, adjective, or preposition with a present participle'—then we find them clustering in III.i and III.ii, suggesting these were written by someone who did not write the rest of the play. (Placed together with the previous evidence this is problematic: there are un-Shakespearian 'Ah's in III.i and un-Shakespearian 'Oh's in III.ii, yet these are the places Vincent finds Shakespearian compound adjectives; Vincent does not juxtapose the evidence in a way that would make this problem readily apparent.) The level of learning that we can infer from classical allusions also varies noticeably. In III.ii there are two errors of classical mythology known to educated men from the *Aeneid*: Aeolus keeping his winds in 'brazen caves' (III.ii.89), a faulty adjective, and Ascanius 'witch[ing]' Dido and telling her about the fall of Troy (III.ii.116–18) when it should be Cupid-as-Ascanius doing the witching and Aeneas, Ascanius's father, relating the fall of Troy. These could not have been made by Green, Nashe, Peele, or Marlowe, and again, Act III marks itself out as different. (But since this act contains the un-Shakespearian preference for 'Oh', it is not his either; we are running out of candidates.)

Being led off to execution, Suffolk comments on some famous deaths: 'A Roman sworder and banditto slave | Murdered sweet Tully; Brutus' bastard hand | Stabbed Julius Caesar; savage islanders | Pompey the Great; and Suffolk dies by pirates'(IV.i.137–40) which is wrong on all counts, and the idea of Brutus being a bastard son of Caesar is especially interesting as Shakespeare makes nothing of it in *Julius Caesar*, although he presumably knew of it because it is in Plutarch and was notorious. The implication—and here Vincent is following and quotes J.A.K. Thomson (misspelled Thompson, p. 273 n. 22)—is that Shakespeare knew the claim, but chose not to use it in *Julius Caesar* and therefore probably did not use it in *2 Henry VI* either, so this part is someone else's writing. There are plenty of correctly made classical allusions in *2 Henry VI*, so presumably the faulty ones are by someone who did not write the good ones. An example of a good one is a correct distinction of the famous Ajax from the lesser Locrian Ajax (son of Telamon, called Telamonius Ajax): 'like Ajax Telamonius, | On sheep or oxen could I spend my fury' (*2 Henry VI* V.i.26–7). Vincent thinks that Shakespeare elsewhere distorts the story of Telamonius Ajax in 'he's more mad | Than Telamon for his shield' (*Antony and Cleopatra* IV.xiv.1–2) since it was Telamonius Ajax (son of Telamon) and not Telamon himself who ran mad after failing to win the shield of dead Achilles. (Actually, the latest Oxford Shakespeare and Arden Shakespeare editors of *Antony and Cleopatra* agree to let 'Telamon' mean 'Telamonius Ajax' and do not treat this as an error.) Thus Vincent concludes that the classical allusions in *2 Henry VI* do not all come from the same hand.

Anthony Mortimer, '"Crimson liveries" and "their verdour": *Venus and Adonis*, 505–8' (*N&Q* 48[2001] 274–5), wonders about the following lines in *Venus and Adonis*: 'Long may they kiss each other, for this cure! | O, never let their crimson liveries wear, | And as they last, their verdure still endure | To drive infection from the dangerous year' (ll. 505–8). If the lips are 'crimson', how do they also have 'verdure', greenness? Answer: 'crimson' (or at least the related French word *cramoisi*), like 'scarlet', might mean bright colours other than red (although red was the dominant meaning), so these marginal senses come into play in Shakespeare's shift from red lips to green herbs used to ward off the plague. John M. Rollett, 'The Compositor's Reader: Shakespeare's Sonnet 146 Revisited' (*N&Q* 48[2001] 275–6), has more evidence to add to his theory that part of the 1609 sonnets quarto was set by someone reading the manuscript to the compositor. Two years ago Rollett argued, in '"Repel these rebel powers": Shakespeare's Sonnet 146 Emended' (*N&Q* 46[1999] 228), that sonnet 146 shows what can happen by aural transmission, and now he cites Hardy M. Cook's work on the sonnets for Ian Lancashire's Renaissance English Texts (RET) project. (Actually, Rollett does not mention Lancashire or RET, and he wrongly gives the url, which should be <http://www.library.utoronto.ca/utel/ret/shakespeare/1609int3.html>. Cook thinks that at times only one of the two compositors was setting type, and Rollett thinks the other might have been free to do the copy-reading. Rollett claims that 'Cook states that the only other serious error in Q occurs in line 6 of sonnet 144', whereas in fact Cook wrote that 'the only emendation of a substantive universally followed by modern editors is Malone's "{{s}i}de" for "{{s}i}ght" in line six of Sonnet 144', which is not the same thing. (Cook's curly braces represent the long 's' and ligatures, but most readers will not in any case find the reference since Rollett gives it as 'Hardy M. Cook, ibid., 1, 1' whereas in fact one has to load a different file into one's web-browser—it is at <http://www.library.utoronto.ca/utel/ret/shakespeare/1609int1.html>—and look for its first paragraph.) Rollett points out that 'side' to 'sight' is more likely to be a hearing error than a reading one, and that the errors in sonnets 144 and 146 occur on signature I3^r and were made by compositor Eld A, who together with the person reading (perhaps Eld B) just had a bad day.

A.D. Nuttall, 'Bottom's Dream' (*N&Q* 48[2001] 276), observes that there is an old chestnut of inverse nomenclature in *lucus a non lucendo* (it is called a wood [*lucus*] because there is no light [*lux*] there) written about by many ancient grammarians. This is what Bottom's 'It shall be called "Bottom's Dream", because it hath no bottom' (*Midsummer Night's Dream* IV.i.212–13) alludes to, appropriately because the play's wood is dark. Deanne Williams, 'Herod's Cities:

Cesarea and Sebaste in *Twelfth Night*' (*N&Q* 48[2001] 276–8), thinks that from John Lydgate's *The Fall of Princes*, where Herod's cities of similar names are mentioned, Shakespeare got the names Sebastian and Cesario in *Twelfth Night*, and also got the play's relationship between gloom and celebration. The twin cities of Sebaste and Cesarea were built by Herod, whose Massacre of the Innocents is commemorated eight days before Twelfth Night, the celebration of the arrival of the Magi. Orsino's court is like Herod's (as represented in 'medieval Christmas plays', none of which Williams cites) in its 'exotic-erotic luxuria', and Malvolio's outburst is like Herod's rage; his failure is also like Herod's. The city of Cesarea was situated most unfavourably for ships, hence the shipwreck. Shakespeare probably got the names from John Lydgate's *Fall of Princes* [1431–8], where 'Cesaria' and 'Sebasten' are described as 'tweyne' (which Williams thinks 'hints at their status as twins' although it really just means two) and are named there alongside 'Antipadra', which Williams thinks gave Shakespeare the idea of 'after' (anti) 'Father' (padra): their father is dead. From *The Fall of Princes*, which is about Petrarch cheering up gloomy and lethargic Bochas, Shakespeare got Viola's cheering up melancholic Illyria, manifested in Orsino's moping, Olivia's mourning, and Feste's 'the rain it raineth every day'. The dichotomy of the Feast of the Holy Innocents (a celebration despite the slaughter) was about getting on with things despite disaster, and this is the dichotomy of *Twelfth Night*: Viola shows how to carry on despite losing a brother and a father. The Feast of the Holy Innocents was a Christian version of the Roman Saturnalia, with inversions like that of the play, which of course ends with a gloomy song (the point is to accept life *and* death).

In the first of two pieces, Thomas Merriam, 'Feminine Endings and *More*' (*N&Q* 48[2001] 278–80), argues that all of *Sir Thomas More* is by Shakespeare and not Antony Munday, who used feminine endings and deviant lines much less often. Contrary to Philip W. Timberlake's assertion that Munday's use of feminine endings rose during the 1590s, it fell. Timberlake found that on average Munday used feminine endings in 13.7 per cent of his lines (the minimum in some scenes being 7.8 per cent and the maximum 24 per cent), and *Sir Thomas More* comes out at 20.7 per cent. There is not agreement on how to define feminine endings, and Merriam chooses 'the notion of deviant lines which accommodates 8, 9, 11, 12, and 13 syllables per line, irrespective of final stress', which is much more broad than the usual identification by an additional unnecessary and unaccented syllable. Even with this wider net Merriam cannot get Munday's percentage of 'deviant lines' up to *Sir Thomas More*'s level. Here the article becomes a compressed and incomprehensible argument, not least because Merriam omits 'Koenig's first name and draws upon data in Halliday's *Shakespeare Companion* and Chambers's *WS: Study of Facts and Problems* without explaining how those data were compiled or for what purpose. The data should really be the texts we now have, in named editions, something Merriam omits even for *Sir Thomas More*, where choice of edition makes a huge difference. Merriam names the percentages that other people have given for feminine endings in Shakespeare plays, and then reports that he did some 'extrapolating from the figures given by Chambers' without saying what he means by extrapolating or how it was done, other than a formula with two detailed constants that he does not explain the derivation of. I presume he compared all the Timberlake figures with all the Chambers figures, and derived a formula for converting one into the other, and then fed Chambers's count for *Merry Wives of*

Windsor into it to get a figure that Timberlake would have got had he analysed that play.

Merriam offers a table comparing the proportion of feminine endings in *The Two Gentlemen of Verona*, Munday's *John a Kent and John a Cumber*, *Sir Thomas More*, *The Merry Wives of Windsor*, and an average for three Munday texts: *Downfall of Robert Earl of Huntingdon*, *Death of Robert Earl of Huntingdon*, and the Munday parts of *1 Sir John Oldcastle*. From comparing *John a Kent* (early 1590s) at 13.8 per cent with the composite Munday figure for the late 1590s, 10.8 per cent, Merriam observes that his proportion of feminine endings/deviant lines did not rise in the 1590s, but we should note that the latter is the average of three widely different tallies of 8.1, 10.7, and 13.2 per cent, and that incidentally these average to 10.7 per cent not 10.8 per cent as given in Merriam's table. Merriam also notices that *Sir Thomas More* and *The Merry Wives of Windsor* are alike in their high proportion of 'feminine endings' (20.7 and 21.8 per cent). He plots how Shakespeare's plays increasingly used feminine endings through his career, using Chambers's data adjusted to make them nearer to what Timberlake would have counted had he been looking at them, compared to other plays looked at by Timberlake (who stopped at 1595), and concludes that *Sir Thomas More* has far too much metrical deviancy (20.7 per cent of lines) to be by anyone but Shakespeare. However, Merriam's data exclude everyone after 1595 except Shakespeare and Munday, and even then Munday is not terribly far off at 13.8 per cent in *John a Kent*. Perhaps everyone started being more deviant towards the end of the 1590s, when Timberlake's data stop. All this is unpersuasive since Merriam says nothing about the revisions in *Sir Thomas More* (which could well date from the 1600s) nor about which edition he used, which matters because different editors incorporate the revisions in different ways.

In his second article, 'A Simple Discriminator of Shakespeare and Fletcher' (*N&Q* 48[2001] 306–9), Merriam counts uses of the word 'hath' to distinguish Shakespeare's work from Fletcher's. He begins by quoting Stanley Wells on the problem that authorship attribution studies use tricky mathematics, which Merriam thinks untrue. I disagree: Merriam's own explanation of 'principal component analysis' of data about 'logometric habits' last year was a model of obscurity in advanced mathematics, as when he wrote that 'the eigenvalues and eigenvectors of the characteristic equation of the correlation matrix are derived by an algorithm' ('An Unwarranted Assumption', *N&Q* 47[2000] 438–41). To show how easy it all is, Merriam here patiently explains that 'relative word frequency' means the number of times a word occurs divided by the total number of words in the text, as though that were the sort of thing that stumps the non-specialist. The substance of this piece is that the frequency of 'hath' in the Shakespeare Folio is stable across the plays, and likewise in thirteen of fourteen Fletcher plays, and these frequencies are different so it is a good discriminator. Merriam gives a table of 'hath'-counts for Shakespeare's 'First Folio plays' and many Fletcher ones, but does not indicate the precise provenance of the electronic texts other than 'the Oxford Text Archive and/or Professor Ward Elliott' and the Chadwyck-Healey English Verse Drama database. The obvious questions that Merriam leaves unanswered are whether they are in original spelling and what has been done to represent the long 's' and ligatures, these things being widely known only for the Chadwyck-Healey texts, which have original spelling, do not attempt to represent ligatures, and modernize the long 's'.

Most surprisingly, for the plays from Chadwyck-Healey's database 'no total word count was established' so a single figure of 22,264 was used, it being the average word-count for the Fletcher plays taken from the Oxford Text Archive. It is a trivial matter to do total word-counts from the Chadwyck-Healey texts, so I have made my own. I agree with Merriam's counts for occurrences of 'hath', but we can discard his assumption of a single figure for total word-counts for the plays and supply the actual figures in each case. Here are the counts for each play, followed by the relative frequency of 'hath' in round brackets, correcting Merriam's where necessary: *A Wife for a Month* 23,335 (0); *Wild Goose Chase* 23,150 (0); *Women Pleased* 22,005 (0.000136 not 0.000135); *Wit Without Money* 23,204 (0.000215 not 0.000225); *Love's Pilgrimage* 24,858 (0.000443 not 0.00049); *Elder Brother* 22,521 (0.000533 not 0.00043); *Beggar's Bush* 20,586 (0.000729 not 0.00067); *Fair Maid of the Inn* 22,580 (0.000797 not 0.00081); *Queen of Corinth* 21,825 (0.001054 not 0.00103); *Noble Gentleman* 20,355 (0.001916 not 0.00175); *Faithful Shepherdess* 21,616 (0.002174 not 0.002111). The only difference these revised figures make is to push *Noble Gentleman* down Merriam's list into a slot in between Shakespeare's *Julius Caesar* and *Coriolanus*; Merriam would doubtless explain this as being due to its being a collaboration. But Merriam says nothing about the textual provenance, which matters because if all his group A plays were printed (or indeed transcribed) by one person and all of group B by another, it would be entirely possible that the differences between them on a matter like 'hath' reflect the printers' or scribes' habits, not the authors'. Merriam turns to the outlying anomaly, *Faithful Shepherdess* (a Fletcher-only play that appears right in the middle of the Shakespeare's in his table), and offers another table that merely shows its outlyingness in a different way; it is much more like Shakespeare than Fletcher according to his test. Having taxed the intelligent reader's patience with a description of how to calculate relative frequency, which is trivial, Merriam suddenly assumes the background knowledge needed to make sense of 'the middle two quartiles or central half of each distribution of relative frequency values' and indeed this second table is bewildering for a number of reasons. Not least of these is its vertical scale being labelled –0.0005 (at the origin) and then 0.0004, 0.0013, 0.0022, 0.0031, 0.0040, or intervals of 0.0009. Starting with a negative origin point is absurd since there can never be a negative number of *hath*s in a play (nought is the minimum) and the true origin is the bottom of the Fletcher group since two of his plays never used the word. Merriam ends with a dig at 'traditionalist literary scholars' who posit a wide gulf between themselves and the number-crunchers; on this evidence they are quite right.

Roger Stritmatter, 'The Biblical Source of Harry of Cornwall's Theological Doctrine' (*N&Q* 48[2001] 280–2), argues that Henry V's speech about the king not being responsible for the souls of his men comes from the Geneva Bible, Ezekiel 18:20. Stritmatter begins by declaring his hand with an announcement that the notes he has published in *Notes and Queries* over the last five years about Shakespeare's knowledge of the Bible came from his Ph.D. thesis on a 1568–70 Geneva bible owned by Edward de Vere, seventeenth earl of Oxford, in which these passages are underlined. Ezekiel 18:20 is the hitherto unknown biblical source for Henry V's theological lecture at IV.i.146–84, which Stritmatter gives as IV.i.130–305, much too long a stretch, and he does not state which edition he is using. Stritmatter claims that, because Ezekiel 18 is about 'the heritability of sin', its lines 'the same soule

that sinneth, shal dye: the sonne shal not beare the iniquity of the father' are alluded
to in Macduff's 'Sinful Macduff, I They were all struck for thee. Naught that I am, I
Not for their own demerits but for mine I Fell slaughter on their souls' (*Macbeth*
IV.iii.226–9) and again in 'Let sin alone committed light alone I Upon his head that
hath transgressèd so; I Let guiltless souls be freed from guilty woe. I For one's
offence why should so many fall, I To plague a private sin in general?' (*Rape of
Lucrece* 1480–4). The latter is slightly more plausible than the former, being at least
about punishing only the sinner. There are two further references to parental sin
alighting on the child: '*Launcelot*. Yes, truly; for look you, the sins of the father I are
to be laid upon the children' and '*Jessica*. So the sins of my mother should be visited
upon me' (*Merchant of Venice* III.v.1–2, 11–12). Stritmatter says that these express
'the opposite moral, that the sins of the parents *should be* visited on the children' (his
emphasis), but surely Jessica means 'should not'. The two-way detachment of 'the
sonne shal not beare the iniquity of the father, nether shal the father beare the
iniquitie of the sonne' (Ezekiel 18:20) is used by Henry to absolve himself for the
state of the souls of his men who die in battle, and he uses the word 'iniquities' too.
Stritmatter neglects to mention that, if the parallel is right, Henry's argument is not
merely derived from Scripture but is a perversion of it. The initial question is
whether doing the sinful bidding of a king ('if the cause be not good', IV.i.133)
attracts eternal damnation, whereas Ezekiel is about whether being merely related to
a sinner (although free from sin oneself) is enough. Henry elides this distinction and
brings in the obfuscation that many soldiers have serious previous sins to their
names. I would say that the difference between Henry and Ezekiel is so great that it
is more likely to be theological commonplace than allusion.

Howard Jacobson, '*Julius Caesar*, I.ii.39–40' (*N&Q* 48[2001] 282), observes that
Cassius' 'The fault, dear Brutus, is not in our stars, I But in ourselves, that we are
underlings' (*Julius Caesar* I.ii.141–2) is close to Seneca's *non locorum vitium esse
quo laboramus sed nostrum* (*De tranquillitate* 2.15), and even if Shakespeare did
not get it from Seneca directly, the latter appeared in a collection of Senecan
sententiae that came out in 1597. MacDonald P. Jackson, '"But with Just Cause":
Julius Caesar, III.i.47' (*N&Q* 48[2001] 282–4) finds a way in which *Julius Caesar*
can be emended to take account of Jonson's mockery about Caesar wronging with
'just cause' without having Caesar make the absurdly megalomaniacal claim that his
'wrong' is 'right'. The Folio reads '[*Caesar*] Thy Brother by decree is banished: I If
thou doest bend, and pray, and fawne for him, I I spurne thee like a Curre out of my
way: I Know, *Caesar* doth not wrong, nor without cause, I Will not be satisfied'
(TLN 1251–5), and in the posthumously published *Discoveries* Jonson mocked
Shakespeare's 'Caesar did never wrong but with just cause' as a response to 'Caesar,
thou dost me wrong'; the latter line is not in F. John Dover Wilson argued for
emending F to 'Caesar did never wrong but with just cause' as typically dictatorial
and (on the evidence of Jonson's comment) as probably what Shakespeare wrote,
but which was changed by the actors after Jonson's mockery. But this still leaves the
problem that Caesar's comment is not prompted by anything and does not really
mean anything: what is the 'cause', what might make him 'satisfied', and of what?
Jackson suggests that Metellus Cimber throws himself at Caesar's feet and gets
kicked, and complains 'Caesar, thou dost me wrong', so that the exchange goes like
this: '[*Caesar*] Thy brother by decree is banished. I If thou dost bend, and pray, and
fawn for him, I I spurn thee like a Cur out of my way. I *Metellus Cimber*. Caesar,

thou dost me wrong. I *Caesar*. Know, Caesar doth not wrong, I But with just cause
will he be satisfied'. In this suggestion 'But with' means 'Only with', as it is used in
Hamlet ('But with the whiff and wind of his fell sword I Th' unnerved father falls',
II.ii.476–7). This emendation has the advantage of making Caesar speak sense and
not megalomaniacally (as 'Caesar did never wrong but with just cause' would) since
nothing else in the play makes him megalomaniacal. An actor speaking Jackson's
version and wrongly pausing after 'just cause' would make the gaffe that Jonson
seized upon, and in altering the script to deflect Jonson's mockery they changed
'But with just' into 'Nor without' and accidentally omitted Metellus's interjection.
(Actually, they must also have changed 'will he be satisfied' into 'will not be
satisfied', so turning 'But with just' into 'Nor without' is not 'the sole change', as
Jackson claims.)

Steven Doloff, 'Shakespeare's *Othello* and Circe's Italian Court in Ascham's *The
Scholemaster* (1570)' (*N&Q* 48[2001] 287–9), points out that Elizabethans would
have had a sense of Italian, and especially Venetian, life as corruptly bestial from
(amongst others) Roger Ascham's *The Scholemaster* [1570], which refers to
'Circe's Court'. There is a distinct Circean motif (from men to beasts) in *Othello*,
with its endless animal imagery, so there is Italian beastly otherness as well as
Moorish racial otherness in the play, and indeed it makes the former more dangerous
(via Iago) than the latter. In a second note, 'Lear's Howl and "Diogenes the Doggue"
(*N&Q* 48[2001] 292–3), Doloff argues that Lear's 'Howl, howl, howl, howl!' while
carrying dead Cordelia (V.iii.232) is not only (as W.R. Elton has it) a rejection of
Stoic philosophy but also an allusion to Diogenes the dog-like Cynic. Edgar-as-Tom
calls himself a 'dog in madness' (III.iv.87–8), the usual Cynic–Dog association, and
Lear calls him a 'philosopher' (III.iv.144) and identifies with him to the extent of
wanting to disrobe too ('unbutton here', III.iv.103), but only at the end of the play,
stripped of everything (not just clothes) does Lear truly become like Diogenes and
howl like a dog. Roger Prior, 'Shakespeare's Debt to Aristo' (*N&Q* 48[2001] 289–
92), thinks that for *Othello* and *Love's Labour's Lost* Shakespeare borrowed from
Ariosto's Italian poem *Orlando Furioso* and not Sir John Harington's English
translation of it. We can surmise that Shakespeare read Italian, for he seems to have
read *Othello*'s source, Giraldi Cinthio's *Hecatommithi*, in the original, and he also
seems to have read Ariosto's *Orlando Furioso* in Italian, since Cassandra's 'furor
profetico' is echoed in Othello's 'A sibyl ... In her prophetic fury sewed the work'
(III.iv.70–2), which was already known but can now be confirmed by further
borrowings from Ariosto that Priors describes. The handkerchief in Cinthio does not
have the 'supernatural qualities' that Shakespeare wanted, so he instead took these
from the tent that in Ariosto Cassandra makes for Hector (a soldier), which passes to
Menelaus (a soldier-cuckold), and which much later is owned by another sorceress,
Melissa, and given away by her as a wedding present. Likewise the handkerchief in
Othello is made by a 'sybil' and is later given by an 'Egyptian ... charmer'
(III.iv.56–7) to Othello's mother and given by Othello as a wedding present.
Shakespeare could have got these narrative details from Harington's 1591
translation of *Orlando*, but there are many verbal parallels that suggest that he used
the Italian text. For example, 'fece un bel don di quello' ('she made a fine gift of it',
canto 46, stanza 80) became 'made a gift of it' (III.iv.61), and in stanza 82 there is
'poi che ... ebbe la morte' (on Hector's death) the cloth passed 'in sorte' ('by fate')
to Menelaus, who had an unfaithful wife, Helen ('la moglie'), which becomes

Othello's mother passing on the handkerchief on her deathbed (III.iv.63) with the instruction that 'when my [Othello's] fate would have me wived, | To give it her' (III.iv.64–5), which he does and later thinks the wife, Desdemona, unfaithful. Prior gives some lesser examples of Shakespeare's verbal borrowing from Ariosto, and admits that they might just have come from Harington instead. Shakespeare had already used Ariosto in Armado's speech as Hector in *Love's Labour's Lost* ('Mars ... gift ... of Ilion ... pavilion ... flower', V.ii.644–8), which comes from canto 46, stanza 80 of *Orlando Furioso*: 'padiglion' ('pavilion'), 'un bel don' ('a splendid gift'), 'd'Ilia' ('of Ilion'), and stanza 85: 'Marte ... fiori' ('Mars ... flower'). Ariosto wrote his poem for Hippolytus of Este, who claimed descent from Hector, so Ariosto has his Cassandra prophesy the appearance of his descendant and work his image into the cloth of the tent that she makes, so 'Hippolytus, Hector's heir, thus becomes part of the gift' and likewise Armado's line means the same: 'Gave Hector a gift, the heir of Ilion'. Again, Prior shows some lesser links that might have come via Harington, but also some verse-structure parallels which cannot have: Armado's eleven- or twelve-syllable lines, as in Ariosto, their similar trochaic endings, and their rhyming abab like the beginning of one of Ariosto's stanzas. Coincidentally, Robert Tofte, who we know saw *Love's Labour's Lost*, was a translator of Ariosto.

Catherine Loomis, '"What bloody man is that?" Sir Robert Carey and Shakespeare's Bloody Sergeant' (*N&Q* 48[2001] 296–8), finds a contemporary historical analogue for the transmission of news in *Macbeth*. Sir Robert Carey carried the news of Elizabeth I's death to King James, and a brief account of this journey was published in 1603, his full memoirs being published in 1759. The news of Elizabeth's death, like that of Lady Macbeth, is conveyed first by crying women. Carey got a bloodied head from a kick from his horse on the long journey to Scotland, and the detail appeared in the 1603 pamphlet. Thus an audience hearing Duncan's opening line 'What bloody man is that?' (I.ii.1) would think of Carey's story of a king of Scotland receiving news of a death from a bloodied man, and Carey's story also had belligerent porters and a knocking at a gate (James's) presaging death. (George Steevens's name is misspelled 'Steven's' here, and not in a possessive context, p. 297 n. 4). MacDonald P. Jackson, 'Spurio and the Date of *All's Well That Ends Well*' (*N&Q* 48[2001] 298–9), dates *All's Well That Ends Well* to before mid-1606 by Parolles's use of the name Spurio. Only two other plays use this name: one is Middleton's *The Revenger's Tragedy* and the other is Thomas Nabbes's *The Unfortunate Mother*. Nabbes is much too late, but Middleton's play was printed in 1607–8 and all its names are appropriate to their characters; Middleton's Spurio is important, while in *All's Well That Ends Well* it is just a casual reference. Jackson thinks that for this reason 'Shakespeare must surely be the debtor'. (I do not think this follows at all; Middleton could have heard the name as used in *All's Well That Ends Well* and added it to his list of suitable names to be used in the composition of *The Revenger's Tragedy*.) Around this time Middleton and Shakespeare worked together on *Timon of Athens*. Jackson is editing *The Revenger's Tragedy* for the Oxford Complete Middleton, and thinks the date of composition is early spring 1606 since it is indebted to *Volpone* (which was written in the first few months of 1606) and *King Lear* (not completed before the autumn of 1605). (Again, these give *termini a quo* but not *termini ad quem*; *The Revenger's Tragedy* could have been written any time after these and before its Stationers' Register entry on 7 October 1607.) So, if (Jackson is careful to place this 'if') *The

Revenger's Tragedy was first performed in early 1606, *All's Well That Ends Well* cannot have been composed before mid-1606.

David George, 'Hector's Bleeding Forehead: *Coriolanus*, I.iii.34–9' (*N&Q* 48[2001] 299–302), thinks that Caxton's *The Recuyell of the Historyes of Troye* (reissued in a new version in 1607) is the source of Volumnia's image of Hector's bleeding forehead in *Coriolanus*. Volumnia pictures her son's bloody brow like "Hector's forehead when it spit forth blood | At Grecian sword, contemning" (I.iii.44–5), which is not from Homer's *Iliad* since there Hector's fight with Grecian Achilles is not with swords when he contemns him, and his face does not bleed. In any case, there was no complete English *Iliad* for Shakespeare to read until 1611, and although George Chapman's partial version was out, the only part that seems even close to Volumnia's allusion is in book 12, which Chapman probably did not publish until 1609, which is probably too late to influence *Coriolanus*. The likeliest source is Caxton's *The Recuyell of the Historyes of Troye*, which Shakespeare used for *Troilus and Cressida*, and which was published in a new version amended by William Fiston in 1607; this has a fight between Achilles and Hector (who uses a sword), with Hector contemning and with his face bleeding. On the other hand, 'contemning' might not be the correct emendation of the Folio's 'Contenning', and we can wonder what is doing the contemning and at what is it directed; F2's 'contending' is also possible. George discusses the relative merits of these and does not recommend one over the other. David Roberts, '*Henry VIII* and *The True Chronicle History of King Leir*' (*N&Q* 48[2001] 302–3), notes that in *King Leir* Ragan reads a letter and 'bytes her lip, | And stamps' which is similar to the way in which Wolsey receives bad news in a letter in *Henry VIII* ('bites his lip, and starts', III.ii.114), although he admits that this is a pretty tenuous link, and it is hardly unusual to bite one's lip.

Rodney Stenning Edgecombe, 'Southwell's "burning babe" and the "naked new-born babe" in *Macbeth*' (*N&Q* 48[2001] 295–6), notes that *Macbeth* has a difficult image in 'pity, like a naked new-born babe, | Striding the blast' (I.vii.21–2), which is virtually oxymoronic is its soft limbs striding. There is the same paradoxical mixture of weakness and strength as the baby Jesus has in Robert Southwell's *Epistle of Comfort*, so that is a source of the image. In *As You Like It* I.ii Le Beau picks out Celia by saying 'the taller is his daughter' (TLN 440), but later it is clear that she is shorter than Rosalind; in preference to such emendations as 'shorter' and 'lower' (which are not graphically close), Edgecombe, in '"The taller is his daughter" in *As You Like It*' (*UCrow* 20[2000] 153), proposes 'tawnier' since later Celia-as-Aliena is called 'browner'. (The obvious objection, and the reason no one has suggested it before, is the unlikelihood of 'wni' being mistaken for 'll'; in combination 'w' and 'ni' might pass for each other, but all three letters lack the top loop that characterizes 'l' in Secretary and Italic handwriting.) Later Celia says that Orlando has 'bought a paire of cast lips of *Diana*' (TLN 1725, III.iv.14) and the problem is 'cast'. Edgecombe, in 'Cast Lips of Diana in *As You Like It* III.iv' (*ShN* 51[2001] 63), thinks that it is a spelling of 'cased', that the lips are enclosed like a relic; the context supports this being a reference to Catholic relic worship. (He might, but does not, point out that the spelling 'cast' for 'cased' occurs in the first quarto of *Pericles*, sig. H4[r].)

2. Shakespeare in the Theatre

Michael Pennington's *Twelfth Night: A User's Guide* [2000] is written by a practitioner who thankfully avoids the all too frequent sentimentality of the thespian overawed by the Bard's genius. Pennington's precise and eloquent account derives from his experience as a three-time director of *Twelfth Night*: for the touring English Shakespeare Company [1991]; the Haiyuza Company in Tokyo [1993]; and the Chicago Shakespeare Theatre [1995]. Detailed examination of the play, scene by scene, is punctuated by reflective discussion of the rehearsal processes of each of these productions. In the case of the Chicago version, Pennington reproduces not only his thoughts on and reactions to rehearsals but his letters to the designer, the company's artistic director and other interested parties. Pennington is refreshingly uncowed by the play and only very occasionally lapses into luvvie-speak such as when, in a moment of carelessness, he opines that Shakespeare 'wrote from the heart' (p. 10). But this is a rare blunder; more usually the tone is incisive and attentive to both the text's lyrical beauty and its theatrical problems. For example, Pennington speaks of the play's 'deluded eroticism, its profound sense of fugue' (p. 32). He notes how Fabian's mention of a bear-baiting 'plunges us straight into the feculent heart of London in 1600 and far away from Illyria' (p. 100). Of Orsino's 'Oh thou dissembling cub!', Pennington remarks, 'Regret has soaked into his rage … and his malediction of Cesario has a semblance of dignity' (p. 205). Toby's stern warnings to Cesario ('Dismount thy tuck, be yare in thy preparation') are described as 'military buckshot' (p. 173) while Malvolio's (self-)deception is all too comparable with that of the similarly aspiring Macbeth, 'Like Macbeth's dagger, the letter marshals him the way that he was going' (p. 106). But as well as his capacity for the *mot juste*, Pennington is a confident dissenter when the play or its author is found wanting. Too often the problem with Shakespeare's Act IVs is that 'this is the moment when, with all due respect, you begin to want to go home' (p. 181), or, apropos Feste's exchange with Cesario on living 'by the church' and the Gravedigger's quibbles in *Hamlet*, 'Shakespeare's one-liners are fine but then he will pull the stuffing out of them' (p. 145). Pennington has an acute eye, noticing details which have hitherto escaped this reviewer for one—for instance that the play's 'midsummer madness' or its 'more matter for a May morning' belie its wintry title (p. 7); that 'Fabian saves [Maria] from disgrace by pretending that the joke against Malvolio was his and Toby's idea, not hers' (p. 5); or that at his moment of triumph, Feste quotes back part of the letter to Malvolio 'which in fact he has never seen' (p. 219)—the letter is given to Fabian to read before Feste gets as far as 'some are born great …'. Pennington rightly asserts that the unique musical epilogue is entirely fitting 'since *Twelfth Night* declared its business with its very first line, and has been punctuated throughout with songs' (p. 221). The volume ends with a forlorn letter to Barbara Gaines (artistic director of the Chicago Shakespeare) which regretfully and politely refuses her invitation to direct Shakespeare's contemporary tragedy: 'The fact is that *Hamlet* has died on me, and *Twelfth Night*'s not far behind … at the moment I feel like one of Shakespeare's old mistresses—an old limp rag after thirty-five years in the service' (p. 255). Within four pages, however, the opal-minded Pennington is declaring the need for Shakespeare, especially in relation to young people, 'to maintain a vital restraint, to qualify selfish violence with a little mutual attentiveness. That's where their hope lies. Ours too' (p. 259). With such a confident motivation and such an accomplished knowledge of the play under his belt, it is hoped that Michael Pennington and *Twelfth Night* will not remain dead to each other for too long. (The publisher should seriously consider the addition of production shots if and when this book goes to a second edition.)

Pennington's Tokyo *Twelfth Night* is mentioned along with a number of other productions by visiting directors in Ted Motohashi's 'Directing "Japanese Shakespeare" Locally and Universally: An Interview with Gerard Murphy' (in Minami, Carruthers, and Gillies, eds., *Performing Shakespeare in Japan*, pp. 172–9: 172). The author collaborated with Murphy on productions of *The Merchant of Venice* [1993 and 1996] and *As You Like It* [1994] as interpreter. He was also involved in shortening the script, which amounted to the 'excision of rhetorical bits' (p. 174). The essay concludes by noting the 'huge imbalance of power and knowledge' (p. 179) between Europe and Asia with regard to Shakespeare, which results in the not infrequent visits of Western directors (Pennington and Murphy among them) to Japan 'while no English theatre companies would yet dream of inviting a Japanese director to do a Shakespeare with English actors' (p. 179). The obvious exception is Suzuki Tadashi, who offers an interview elsewhere in the same volume (pp. 196–207). Here he sets out his prioritization of consciousness, 'the inner world of a character' (p. 199), over narrative. He also, towards the end of his interview, accuses Peter Brook of 'look[ing] down on Japan artistically. There are many things that we have to fight as Japanese' (p. 206). Yet if Japanese Shakespeare still causes consternation in the West, there is little doubt of the security of its cultural footing. As the editors point out in their introduction, 'anywhere between fifty to one hundred productions of Shakespeare can be seen in Tokyo every year' (p. 1). Moreover, this volume acknowledges and situates itself as a continuation of Sasayama Takashi, J.R. Mulryne and Margaret Shewring, eds., *Shakespeare and the Japanese Stage* [1998] (*YWES* 80[2001] 264–6). Japanese Shakespeare, epitomized by the opening of Tokyo's Globe in 1988, is here to stay. Nonetheless, the question 'What do we mean by "Japanese" Shakespeare?' (pp. 17–20) is still a legitimate one. Anzai Tetsuo asserts that it is 'not necessarily an exotic, eccentric, exceptional case; rather, it forms an integral part of the worldwide process of realizing the inexhaustible potentialities latent in Shakespeare' (p. 19), but, as he explains, it does this from within a theatrical tradition which acknowledges historical forms 'from ancient folk rituals to postmodern theatres' (p. 19) as alive and well. In England, by contrast, Elizabethan theatre only exists in experiments, like those of William Poel, or the 'reproduction' of the Southwark Globe; furthermore, as Anzai points out, 'Each generation of English directors has endeavoured to destroy the previous style and to create their own new, innovative approach' (p. 19). Yoshihara Yukari identifies 1854 as the year in which Japan was opened up 'under pressure from the United States navy' (p. 23). His 'Japan as "Half-Civilized"' (pp. 21–32) explores the ideological weight of English literature 'as introduced to, consumed and appropriated by Japan in the age of the construction of its "national" culture' (p. 21). According to this reading, Shakespeare has been a foundation stone of Japanese culture since the middle of the nineteenth century.

Matsumoto Shinko attests to this in his account of 'Osanai Kaoru's version of *Romeo and Juliet*, 1904' (in Minami, Carruthers, and Gillies, eds., pp. 54–66), which he considers to be 'Japan's first conscientious Shakespearean production' (p. 63). Ueda Munakata Kuniyoshi considers 'Some Noh Adaptations of Shakespeare in English and Japanese' (pp. 67–75) and points out that, while Kabuki versions have been widespread, 'no Shakespearean Noh play was seen until the 1980s' (p. 68). Ueda founded the Noh Shakespeare Group in 1981, which premiered *Noh Hamlet* the following year. This play was especially apt since 'Noh is distinctively a theatre of ghosts, or of the subconscious world of dreams. In its world the living and the dead exist together' (p. 69). Since then Ueda has composed *Noh Othello*, *Noh Macbeth* and *Noh King Lear*, while the company has toured the United States. Alongside Noh developed a lighter mode called Kyogen, which provided 'scenes of comic relief within Noh plays or as comic interludes between Noh works' (p. 77). Michael Shapiro details '*The Braggart Samurai*: a Kyogen adaptation of Shakespeare's *The Merry Wives of Windsor*' (pp. 76–84) which was written by Takahashi Yasunari and performed at the Tokyo Globe in 1991. Kyogen's 'comically realistic' style and its traditional exploration of 'relations between husbands and wives, or masters and servants' (p. 78) suited it eminently to the antics of Falstaff but, as Shapiro insists, Takahashi's version spared Sir Jack's humiliation and so became a 'sharp critique of Shakespeare's moral didacticism' (p. 82). In 'Innovation and Continuity: Two Decades of Deguchi Norio's Shakespeare Theatre Company' (pp. 101–11), Suematsu Michiko identifies as characteristic of the company a lack of 'nuance in delivery, amateurish acting, and bold but naïve interpretations of text' (p. 104). However, this Shakespeare 'in jeans on an empty set' (p. 102) was also hallmarked with 'emotional and physical intensity [and] contemporaneity' (p. 103). In 'Tragedy with Laughter' (pp. 112–20) Takahashi Yasunari discusses Suzuki Tadashi's *The Tale of Lear*, first performed in 1984, in which a hospitalized old man takes himself for Shakespeare's ruined monarch while a nurse figure reads the play and occasionally provides a 'raucous cackle' (p. 113). This is one of the volume's less successful pieces and prone to mystification: 'From time to time, the structure is turned inside out, and parallelism becomes intersection' (p. 113), or 'What he does is to keep de-creating the stylized beauty that he has just come closest to creating' (p. 116). Ian Carruthers, in '*The Chronicle of Macbeth*: Suzuki Method Acting in Australia, 1992' (pp. 121–32), charts the staging of this adaptation, set in 'an institutional space that could be seen as the meeting hall of a New Age religious cult, a prison, or an infirmary' (p. 122). This contribution also contains some infelicitous material: 'Shakespeare's *Macbeth* is used as the ladle with which to stir the institutional soup of history' (p. 130) or '[the Australian audiences] were close enough to feel the electrical energy pouring off actors' bodies and glistening on their skin as sweat' (p. 123). 'The Rose and the Bamboo: Noda Hideki's *Sandaime Richâdo*' (pp. 133–45), by Suzuki Masae, is odder still. There is something distinctly off-target about referring to the deeds of Richard III as 'merry pranks' (p. 134), though some of this peculiarity might derive from the adaptation itself which was set in a 'prestigious flower arrangement school' (p. 137). The inclusion of 'wild flower arrangements titled "Dammit! I'll Kick Your Ass!" or "Mind Your Own Fucking Business!"' (p. 139) or the trial of Richard in which Shakespeare and Shylock also appear suggests the distance we have come from Shakespeare's play. Minami Ryuta is unembarrassed about this, insisting that 'Shakespeare's oeuvre only supplies [Japanese] playwrights with a framework for their own plays … They use Shakespeare as a source material' (p. 156). The title of his essay makes this artistic freedom explicit: 'Shakespeare Reinvented on the Contemporary Japanese Stage' (pp. 146–58). Here he describes Noda Hideki's

Twelfth Night [1986], 'a play that starts with the arrival of an androgynous Venus dividing into two bodies and ends with Venus's departure as a complete androgyne' (p. 148). Hideki's *Much Ado* [1990], set in the world of sumo wrestling, or his *Midsummer Night's Dream* [1992], set in a restaurant and including Mephistopheles from *Faust* along with elements of *Alice in Wonderland*, are further examples of this artistic licence, which allows 'Japanese writers and directors to write new meanings into Shakespeare' (p. 157). Ohtani Tomoko's 'Juliet's Girlfriends: The Takarazuka Revue Company and the *Shôjo* Culture' describes this 1950 version of *Romeo and Juliet* in the context of *Shôjo* culture of 'young girls or adolescent women' (p. 160). The company was set up by Kobayashi Ichizô, 'a Hankyû railway and department store tycoon, in 1913 ... The characteristics of youthfulness, virginity, and unmarried status were required, probably because Kobayashi attempted to promote the ideals of the "good wife" and "wise mother"' (p. 160). This distinctly dodgy-sounding project actually turns out, argues Ohtani, to be 'a counterattack on the ideology of the patriarchy' (p. 164). But the exact process of this subversion is not adequately explained and these kinds of sentences do little to help: 'In such a transcultural encounter between the occidental presence and its oriental semblance, Takarazuka's simulacrum as the metonymy of presence is an aberrant, eccentric strategy of authority in transcultural discourse' (p. 169).

The next section of the book comprises five interviews with Japanese actors and directors whose work has formed the subject of the critical discussions. Deguchi Norio is refreshingly acidic, stating of the RSC, 'They do not make much progress in real terms, I think. ... they are stagnating' (p. 188) or, describing the translations he uses, 'when I read *Hamlet* in Odashima's version, I thought it was very weak: in fact, it was terrible!' (p. 185). Perhaps that explains why 'Odashima did not come to our studio. We did thirty-seven works, and he never came once ... There was absolutely no relationship between the director and the translator. When we saw each other on opening night, we just got drunk together!' (p. 185). Even when describing his own company, Deguchi is withering: 'I thought that the actors had uninteresting faces, that their noses didn't look right and so on' (p. 186). Ninagawa Yukio is similarly bracing about the realities of the theatre. When directing *Romeo and Juliet* he discovered that his actors could not remember their lines: 'The lines just didn't mean anything. So I though I should submerge them under Elton John's music. Then you wouldn't hear anything when the play started, only sound' (p. 210). Ninagawa's visual solutions seem as radical as his aural ones: 'on a more practical level, there was the problem of how shabby the actors looked in tights! So I made the theatre really dark' (p. 211). This blunt pragmatism is a salutary corrective to the more theoretically dense contributions above. Finally, John Gillies contributes an afterword to the volume. In 'Shakespeare Removed: Some Reflections on the Localization of Shakespeare in Japan' (pp. 236–48) he sets out with the question: 'What does the assimilation of an imperial cultural icon amount to?' (p. 236). This eloquent and elegant essay is sensitive to the cultural authority of 'Shakespeare' as well as appreciating the achievements of Japanese artists in aesthetic terms. Perhaps most significantly, Gillies insists on the diversity of ways in which Shakespeare is appropriated in Japan's culture, talking about a 'pluralism of localism' (p. 246). He also insists on the vitality of Japanese Shakespeare in spite of its occasional eccentricities, 'Shakespeare is spoken back to as well as heard' (p. 240); this vitality is central to this vigorous and entertaining collection.

Golder and Madelaine, eds., *O Brave New World: Two Centuries of Shakespeare on the Australian Stage*, sets out to redress the critical erasure of antipodean Shakespeare: 'Australian appropriations of Shakespeare have seldom been acknowledged in their own right' (p. 1). Thirteen essays follow on Shakespeare down under which testify to its vigour and its regional variety. As a result essays deal with both different historical periods, from the first Australian performance in 1800 (of *Henry IV*) up to 2000, and various regions. In 'High and Low Culture: The Changing Role of Shakespeare, 1833–2000' (pp. 17–39), Richard Waterhouse traces Shakespeare's cultural elevation to the second half of the nineteenth century. In the 1830s and 1840s 'the quality of performance was usually appalling' (p. 20). He cites the case of Harry Kemble who, on one occasion, 'when he came to Hamlet's line in the soliloquy, "Oh what an ass am I", the audience voiced its agreement with shouts of "Bravo Kemble!" On another they reacted by letting off fireworks and throwing eggs, candlesticks and tobacco-pipes at the stage' (p. 22). The sacralizing of Shakespeare and 'his separation from everyday culture' (p. 29) led to a decline in the number of performances after the 1860s. Following the Second World War a number of English touring companies put Shakespeare back on the scene, and the Australian Elizabethan Theatre Trust was founded in 1954. The centrality of Shakespeare on the syllabus led to the foundation of the Young Elizabethan Players in 1958. The essay concludes by coming up to date with a section on 'Shakespeare and Australia post-high culture'. This is a broad and well-written piece (though something seems to have gone wrong with the numbering of the endnotes). Elizabeth Webby examines the early part of the period in greater depth. Her 'Shakespeare in Australia: The Early Years, *c*.1830–50' (pp. 40–55) considers 'the fondness for the portmanteau evening' (p. 48) as well as the significance of burlesques and parodies such as the eminently Australian, 'Get thee to a grog-shop' from 1829! In '"Sir, I am a Tragedian": The Male Superstars of the Melbourne Stage, 1850–70' (pp. 56–71), Harold Love considers the impact of William Charles Macready on 'the line of male Shakespeareans who dominated the Australian stage from the late 1850s to the mid-1870s—G. V. Brooke, Barry Sullivan, Charles Kean, Walter Montgomery, James Anderson and William Creswick' (p. 56). As well as describing the variety of each, the essay argues that the tragedian 'embodied notions of patriotism and imperial ardour, while at the same time projecting a vision of life as a serious, heroic matter. This was particularly appropriate to audiences engaged in the earnest, though often far-from-heroic, business of subjugating new territories of the world in the name of civilisation' (p. 67). Interestingly Love suggests that the tragedian's transcendental status was notably successful in a culture riven by religious diversity and that, in this sense, 'the cult of Shakespeare might be regarded as a secular religion' (p. 70). Janette Gordon-Clark offers a parallel essay, 'From Leading Lady to Female Star: Women and Shakespeare, 1855–88' (pp. 72–86). This was always a secondary role. Occasionally hired 'by the male star to travel with him, she was expected to act in whatever plays he chose, whether the female role suited her or not' (p. 72). Her essay includes accounts of Fanny Cathcart, who arrived in Melbourne in 1855 and built up 'a Shakespearean repertoire of twenty leading roles in eighteen plays, something unlikely to be achieved by an actress today' (p. 76); Louisa Cleveland, whose most important role was as Cleopatra in October 1867; and the Australian-born Essie (Esther) Jenyns, who emerged in the 1880s and was highly praised.

Douglas McDermott's essay, '"This isle is full of noises": American Players of Shakespeare in Australia, 1879–89' (pp. 87–102), contains accounts of the mediocre William H. Leake and the equally old-fashioned George Crichton Miln (both of whom were English born). William E. Sheridan, on the other hand, was deemed to be 'the most reputable American actor to play in Australia during the period' (p. 95). Louise Pomeroy was castigated for her obtrusive American accent, though she was also 'the only American actress to attempt the role [of Hamlet] in Australia, and while the critics were unanimous that a woman could never succeed in the part, they gave her credit for the care and intelligence with which she tried' (p. 101). The work of the Australian-born theatrical virtuoso is the subject of 'Substantial Pageant: Oscar Asche, Latter-Day Pictorialism and Australian Audiences, 1909–24' (pp. 103–20), in which Richard Madelaine considers Asche to have been 'the last major actor-manager in the final flowering of the pictorial mode of Shakespearean production' (p. 103). It examines Asche's three Australian tours, in 1909–10, 1912–13 and 1922–4. Asche's most significant production seems to have been of *Antony and Cleopatra* [1912]. Madelaine considers the third tour to have been an artistic and commercial failure, while the success of the first two tours 'demonstrates that Australian middle-class audiences still wanted large-scale spectacular Shakespeare' (p. 119). Pictorialism is also the theme of 'A Cultural Missionary On Tour: Allan Wilkie's Shakespearean Company, 1920–30' (pp. 121–42), in which John Golder asserts that after 1926 a 'new pictorialism' (p. 125) arose to keep pace with the popularity of the cinema. Wilkie's company was founded in Melbourne in September 1920 along pro-empire lines, and Wilkie received a CBE in June 1925. For Golder, the actor becomes a 'cultural missionary' (p. 142).

There follow a number of essays on the regions of Australia. Alan Brissenden covers 'Shakespeare in Adelaide: Professionals and Progressive Amateurs' (pp. 143–62). He stresses the importance of the amateur scene: 'The Adelaide Repertory Theatre, formed in 1908, still continues and is the oldest such theatre group in Australia' (pp. 144–5). Brissenden finds in Adelaide a long tradition of intellectual endeavour 'stemming from the founding of South Australia' (p. 160), but which, he argues, continues today partly as the result of the city's physical size and plan, with its 'cultural boulevard' (p. 161) of state library, museum, art gallery, and the universities of Adelaide and of South Australia. Bill Dunstone moves us to Western Australia in 'Dinkum Shakespeare? Perth, Empire and the Bard' (pp. 163–79). He devotes special attention to the productions of *Hamlet* and *Othello* staged in 1898 by Wilson Barrett. Dunstone asserts that these performances 'embodied paradigms of race and masculinity that were strong features of late-Victorian imperialism and colonial nativist sentiment alike' (p. 165). Wilkie, as we have already seen, continued this traditionalism throughout the 1920s, but this brought his work into tension with 'the emerging modernist orientation in Australian nationalism' (p. 171). This national identity came to be voiced through the productions of Perth's many amateur companies (a feature it shared with Adelaide). The essay ends with an account of Jeana Bradley's not entirely successful 1964 production of *Hamlet* on the outdoor stage of the New Fortune Theatre, built 'closely to the dimensions in the London Fortune contract of 1599' (p. 178) at the University of Western Australia. In 'International Glamour or Home-Grown Entertainment? 1948–1964', Penny Gay considers the tensions between Shakespeare as represented by the British tour, especially that of the Old Vic, headed by Laurence Olivier and Vivien Leigh [1948] and domestic Shakespeare. The need for an Australian national theatre was first perceived by Tyrone Guthrie, who spent a fortnight in the country in 1949. His report was rejected by the then Australian prime minister, Robert Menzies, but not without raising the temperature of the debate. The John Alden Company had toured Shakespeare in every state by 1952 and this provided the impetus for the creation of the Australian Elizabethan Theatre Trust shortly afterwards. This in turn led to the subsequent founding of the National Institute for Dramatic Arts in Sydney in 1958.

A couple of essays follow which consider 'Experiments in Shakespeare'. Mark Minchinton examines the contribution of 'Rex Cramphorn and *Measure for Measure*, 1973–88' (pp. 200–8). Cramphorn directed the play four times, exploring the relationship between movement and position. He also 'refused psychological and naturalistic approaches to character' (p. 202), believing rather that character is built up throughout a play rather than existing independently or in advance of it. Finally he placed (misplaced?) a good deal of faith in the accuracy of the original punctuation, often working directly from facsimiles of the Folios and Quartos. John Senczuk, 'The DSI Elizabethan Experiments, 1986–93' (pp. 209–17), reflects on the work of Philip Parsons and Wayne Harrison, who founded Dramaturgical Services Inc. in 1987. Its small tours and all-male casts marked it out, but eventually the findings of the company became assimilated by the mainstream. Up until his death in 1993, Parsons believed that 'Australian writers could benefit from the imaginative freedom that the Elizabethan tradition and theatrical conventions could provide' (p. 217). In 'Shakespeare in Queensland: A Cultural-Economic Approach' (pp. 218–35), Richard Fotheringham examines the complicated interrelationship of cultural and economic pressures. Culturally the promotion of Shakespeare in Australia relates both to a left perspective (a redistribution of cultural capital) and a more class-centred perspective, with its 'beliefs in the value of elocution, deportment, and high-cultural art forms' (p. 224). Educational demands led to the expansion of Shakespeare in performance and the Queensland Theatre Company was founded in 1969–70 with state subsidy. Its productions seem not to have been successful either artistically or economically: in 1998 audiences so loathed Barrie Kosky's *King Lear* 'that the ushers were issued with cards to give patrons bearing a disclaimer from the venue management and including a number to ring to complain' (p. 231)! Unsurprisingly, funding policy has shifted 'away from Shakespeare and towards supporting new Australian work' (p. 234).

Adrian Kiernander counters this tale of woe with his account of 'John Bell and a Post-Colonial Australian Shakespeare, 1963–2000' (pp. 236–55). Bell co-founded, with Ken and Lilian Horler, the Nimrod Theatre Company, which operated in Sydney between 1970 and 1987. Since 1990 he has been artistic director of the Bell Shakespeare Company. Despite his English residence of five years working alongside Peter Hall, Peter Brook, and Michel St Denis (mainly with the Royal Shakespeare Company), Bell was determined to pioneer an Australian Shakespeare: 'There would be no attempt to emulate a traditionalist or British approach to the canon' (p. 239). Kiernander discusses Bell's radical stagings at a time when there was a 'very real struggle taking place between the temporarily ascendant forces of a distinctively Australian culture and those wishing to return to traditional British values' (p. 244). John Golder and Richard Madelaine round off the volume with 'Australian Shakespearean Premieres, and Other Curiosities: A Chronology' (pp. 256–63), which contains the surprising facts that *Titus*, *Pericles*, and *Troilus* did not reach 'the professional Australian stage in any form until 1958, 1971 and 1989 respectively' (p. 256), while the 1980s saw the first performances of the three parts of *Henry VI*.

In her short study, *Shakespeare and Feminist Performance: Ideology on Stage*, Sarah Werner attempts both an exploration of the sexism which resides within the theatre industry and an examination of ways forward for 'dissident [here, feminist] readings of the plays' (p. 19). She is much more successful in the former than the latter, giving a sprightly and incisive history of the RSC Women's Group (set up in 1985), which aimed to challenge the company's masculinist bias: Werner notes that women 'had been almost completely absent from directorial posts since the formation of the RSC in 1961' (p. 52). Further, there is a revealing analysis of the 'fetishized notion of primitivism' (p. 25) and the naturalizing assumption of psychological authenticity in the voice work of Cicely Berry and Patsy Rodenberg which submerge interpretations 'grounded in an historicist or materialist framework' (p. 28). In an exposition of Gale Edwards's 1995 RSC *Taming of the Shrew* and the reviews it prompted, Werner interrogates the supremacy of the notion of fixed or consistent characterization which, she alleges, militates against 'a political engagement with the play' (p. 79). Too frequently, however, Werner indulges in the kind of theatrical vagueness which she is attacking: 'we discover that we are Shakespeare' (p. 104); 'the role of the personal is crucial when working with performed Shakespeare' (p. 70). Her praise for Cary Mazer's *Two Gentlemen of Verona* [1999], in which 'Water bottles represented letters, and drinking from the bottle meant reading' (p. 99), forces one to question her outright rejection of the RSC's 'transparent theatrical language' (p. 96)—patriarchal it may be but it is, at least, comprehensible.

Cartmell and Scott, eds., *Talking Shakespeare*, contains five essays of relevance to this section. In 'Shakespeare and the Elizabethan Stage: Touring Practice in Shakespeare's Day' (pp. 39–54), Peter Davison considers the problem of 'diverse, partial and conflicting evidence' (p. 40) surrounding the circumstances of touring— size of company, itinerary, modes of transport, and destinations. He is confident of a high level of touring activity operating in addition to the officially sanctioned companies: 'there was a host of other licensed dramatic companies crisscrossing the country, as well as individual entertainers such as rope-dancers [really?] and musicians, not to mention unlicensed vagrant performers' (p. 43). The latter part of the essay is an attempt to explain the mystery of 'why so many companies visited Marlborough' (p. 49). The answer seems to be that the proximity of the estates of the Pembrokes and the earl of Hertford may have afforded the players the opportunity to mount private performances. (Much of the latter half of this essay overlaps with Davison's own 'Commerce and Patronage: The Lord Chamberlain's Men's Tour of 1597' (in Grace Ioppolo, ed., *Shakespeare Performed: Essays in Honour of R.A. Foakes* [2000], pp. 56–71), reviewed in *YWES* 81[2002] 356. In 'Shakespeare and History' (pp. 70–82), Dermot Cavanagh eloquently challenges the new historicist assumption that 'Shakespeare's plays reinforce distinctions between social ranks and are preoccupied with the consolidation and maintenance of royal power' (p. 75). Focusing on the gardeners' scene in *Richard II*, Cavanagh deftly draws out the ambiguities surrounding the play's analysis of political authority and demonstrates the theatre's capacity to 'provoke awareness of contrary viewpoints as well as disclosing similarities between apparent opposites' (p. 80). He concludes by advocating a return to the theoretical models of the Frankfurt school, with their attention to the workings of ideology, linked to a heightened awareness of 'the complexity of rhetorical form in the plays' (p. 81). Cavanagh's is a fluent and engaging essay.

In '"Home, Sweet Home": Stratford-upon-Avon and the Making of the Royal Shakespeare Company as a National Institution' (in Cartmell and Scott, eds., pp. 85–101), Colin Chambers turns from the plays to the institutions which realize them, focusing on the 'symbiotic rivalry' (p. 88) between the National Theatre and the RSC. Chambers charts the difficulties the RSC experienced over funding, but suggests that this was partly its own fault for conceding so readily to the inequities of its cultural situation: 'As an organisation, it was certainly reflecting—if not representing—the nation insofar as it embraced a post-Thatcher, top-heavy management model and in being overwhelmingly white, middle-class and male-led' (p. 89). In spite of this, or perhaps because of it, the RSC along with the NT, English National Opera and Royal Opera House secured a public grant from central government which Chambers rightly points out 'means it is necessarily of national concern' (p. 91). Under the directorship of Peter Hall the RSC evolved a house style which concentrated on verse-speaking as well as a politically sceptical orientation. This was dissipated in 1991 when the incoming artistic director, Adrian Noble, 'removed the associated directors from the payroll and went over to a freelance system' (p. 94) which precipitated, according to Chambers, the company's 'free-fall into a market-driven ideology' (p. 95). As a result, experimental work was confined to the smaller performance spaces while the move to the Barbican necessitated the courting of private sponsors so that 'experiment with the Bard faded. Innovation was left to groups outside the RSC, inspired by new performance cultures and theatre practices abroad' (p. 100). Following Noble's recent resignation, the next chapter of the RSC story is about to begin. Janice Wardle offers a comparison of two RSC productions including, as it happens, one by Noble. Her '*Twelfth Night*: "One face, one voice, one habit and two persons!"' (pp. 105–22) begins where Chambers left off in its attention to the RSC's 'ongoing corporate theatrical discourse' (p. 106). Within this broad church, Wardle compares and contrasts John Barton's 1969 and Noble's 1997 productions of *Twelfth Night*. Barton, influenced by Northrop Frye and C.L. Barber, redefined the play's festive elements to encapsulate 'a heightened mood and emotion in which the behaviour of individuals could be explored' (p. 110). But in the wake of Stanislavsky, the production focused on personal awareness rather than a carnival solidarity, on 'ageing individuals trapped in an artificial festive world' (p. 114). Feste, in particular, was used to expose 'the artificiality of Illyria and its romantic inhabitants' (p. 113) rather than as a spokesman for collective comic revelry. By contrast, Noble's 1997 version (the one with the giant fridge) was 'exaggerated, comic and non-realistic [and the design was] bold, brash and cartoon-like' (pp. 117–18). The broad festive atmosphere of Noble's production, its 'playful postmodern pastiche of styles … challenged the Bartonian "psychological" frame of reference and released some of the inherent comic energy of *Twelfth Night*' (p. 122).

In 'Shakespeare and the Homoerotic' (in Cartmell and Scott, eds., pp. 123–37), Miles Thompson and Imelda Whelehan concisely rehearse the salient material on this topic. They note the fact that the children's companies 'came under the protection of the Church [and so] were not subject to sudden closure by the Lord Mayor' (p. 124). They go on to hypothesize that the parts given to boys in the public, purpose-built theatres were 'markedly advanced [with roles which] included demonstrations of female emotion and sexuality' (p. 125). Shakespeare's boy player then was both more vulnerable and skating on thinner theatrical ice than his indoor contemporary (though the authors need to provide more evidence of the latter). Thompson and Whelehan cite the bile of the anti-theatricalists as testament to the concerns incited by the boy player, before suggesting that Rosalind's epilogue 'knowingly awakens all those anxieties' (p. 134). This competent essay ends with an intriguing attack on *Shakespeare in Love* on the grounds that it 'obscures the homoerotic potential of performance [and] enables a purely heterosexist reading of *Romeo and Juliet*' (p. 136) though I can't help thinking that such an attack on a frivolous comic vehicle is a little dourly over-earnest.

Much more engaging is the discussion of the shifts in masculinity between the early modern and the modern periods discussed in Rebecca Ann Bach's 'Tennis Balls: *Henry V* and Testicular Masculinity, or, According to the *OED* Shakespeare Doesn't Have Any Balls' (*RenD* 30[1999–2001] 3–23). Having noted that *OED* cites *Lady Chatterley's Lover* as the first source of the word *balls* meaning '(manly) power or strength', she argues for an antecedent in Shakespeare's *Henry V*, 'a play that repeatedly shows its audience an embodied English masculinity' (p. 5). She defines 'testicular masculinity' as 'a notion of male bodily power that values breeding for itself and not for the sexual act' (p. 5). In contrast to the effete Dauphin and the uxorious Pistol (all mouth and no trousers in terms of martial masculinity), Henry represents a manliness concerned to conquer and *reproduce*. Bach suggests that the 'French castrate themselves in the first act in their gift of the "Paris-Balls" … With the gift of the balls the French have lost their masculine heat: both their courage and their power to breed' (p. 10). Bach cites a number of early modern medical authorities such as John Banister, Helkiah Crooke, Alexander Read and Ambrose Paré to illustrate the importance of testicular potency and temperature to the begetting of male progeny—essential in a patriarchal society founded on martial authority and primogeniture (and particularly under scrutiny in a campaign justified by Salic law). She argues that heterosexual desire is actually irrelevant in terms of this testicular masculinity, which prioritizes homosociality in the solidarity of the fighting force—the band of brothers—as well as valuing dynasty rather than a plurality of female partners. This contrasts, she concludes, with the ideology of manhood fostered by late capitalism, where earning rather than fighting is prized. Consequently the ideal of manhood has shifted from the potent soldier to the 'male executive with a body pumped only in and for gym display and a "trophy wife" to demonstrate his heterosexual vigor' (p. 20).

Ruth Lunney provides a challenging piece on the fraught business of subjectivity and character. In 'Rewriting the Narrative of Dramatic Character, or, Not "Shakespearean" but "Debatable"' (*MRDE* 14[2001] 66–85) she challenges the critical orthodoxy that, because Marlowe's characters are 'larger-than-life' (p. 66), they do not contribute to the emergence of subjectivity in the theatre of the 1590s. She coins the term '"debatable" character' which finds its 'first full expression' (p. 67) in *Dr Faustus*. Lunney suggests that the technique of psychomachia had always, long before the 1590s, allowed audiences some glimpse into a character's interiority, but what happens in Marlowe's play is that Faustus responds to the angels in a 'fluctuating and erratic' (p. 72) way which intensifies a shift from situation to psychology. Faustus's 'defective awareness' (p. 76) means that the character 'does not perceive as the spectators perceive' (p. 76), which signals 'a realignment of the way that the audience relates to the character' (p. 77). Moreover, this partial attention is not a simple character flaw (as it is usually taken to be in critical accounts) but rather needs to be 'considered in the context of early performances and the past experience of early audiences' (p. 73). Lunney sees the influence of Marlowe's 'debatable character' on Shakespeare's Richard II: 'Richard, like Faustus, detaches from conventional frames, sees separately, and struggles to make sense of his situation' (p. 79). Lunney concludes that the 'debatable character' 'signals an epistemological shift in popular theatrical experience' (p. 82).

3. Shakespeare on Screen

No monographs were published on the subject of Shakespeare on film in 2001. The year's essays cover a wide range of subjects: 'straight' interpretations (Kenneth Branagh's *Hamlet*, Julie Taymor's *Titus*, Baz Lurhmann's *William Shakespeare's Romeo + Juliet*), films based more loosely on Shakespeare's plays (Akira Kurosawa's *Ran* and *Throne of Blood*, Gus Van Sant's *My Own Private Idaho*), sustained Shakespearian allusions or plays-within-films (such as Branagh's 'little Hamlet film' *In the Bleak Midwinter*), studies of 'Shakespearian' actors (John Barrymore, Vincent Price), and the cinematic representation of Shakespeare himself in John Madden's *Shakespeare in Love*. An abiding concern is the question of what constitutes—or should constitute—'Shakespeare on film' studies. Most impressive are the articles that move away from merely reviewing a particular film or group of films, particularly when they focus on the institutional or cultural contexts within which any given film (or indeed actor) might function. Such contexts might be broadly political or ideological, but might also encompass the film's relationship with early modern culture, its place in the 'Shakespeare-on-film' canon, or its situation in a wider cinematic milieu (generic, temporal or technical).

First, some general articles and overviews. In 'Shakespeare and the Cinema' (in De Grazia and Wells, eds., *The Cambridge Companion to Shakespeare*, pp. 217–33), Russell Jackson offers an evaluative survey of a hundred years of Shakespearian films, from the brief glimpse of Herbert Beerbohm Tree's *King John* [1899] to the late 1990s; although he concentrates on the Anglo-American tradition, he includes films by prominent non-Anglophone directors such as Kurosawa and Grigori Kozintsev. He argues that Shakespearian films are best assessed on their own terms, but that on the other hand these films are often provoked by a director's interest in the 'original' plays and his or her desire to do them justice on screen.

The character of 'Shakespeare-on-film' criticism also concerns Kenneth S. Rothwell's 'How the Twentieth Century Saw the Shakespeare Film: "Is it Shakespeare?"' (*LFQ* 29[2001] 82–95), an introduction to a special issue of *Literature Film Quarterly* entitled 'Shakespeare Century'. Rothwell surveys the history of scholarly writing on the 'Shakespeare film' in the twentieth century, arguing that we have gradually 'ceased to ask "Is it Shakespeare?" but instead "Is Shakespeare in it?"'. On a more practical level, in her introduction to a special issue of *Colby Library Quarterly*, Laurie Osborne, 'Screening Shakespeare' (*CLQ* 37[2001] 5–15) calls for studies which are alert to 'the cinematic contexts of film editing, star production, or the specific distribution and marketing situations that affect filming'. Further comment on Shakespearian film and the state of the 'industry' can be found in Jim Welsh, 'Shakespeare Boom or Bust' (*WVUPP* 47[2001] 150–4).

The most impressive general essays are Denise Albanese, 'The Shakespeare Film and the Americanization of Culture' (in Howard and Shershow, eds., *Marxist Shakespeares*, pp. 206–26), Gabriel Egan, 'Showing Versus Telling: Shakespeare's *Ekphraseis*, Visual Absences, and the Cinema' (in Cartmell and Scott, eds., pp. 168–86), and Celia R. Daileader, 'Nude Shakespeare in Film and Nineties Popular Feminism' (in Wells and Alexander, eds., *Shakespeare and Sexuality*, pp. 183–200). Albanese analyses the economic and ideological conditions involved in the production of Shakespeare as a 'cinematic commodity', contrasting Branagh's *Hamlet* with Luhrmann's *William Shakespeare's Romeo + Juliet*. 'In each case', she argues, 'a proposal about Shakespeare, either as burnished (and imported) cultural good, or else as locus of excitement and irony already naturalized to the United States, informs and is subtended by the test of the market'. She also usefully notes that critics tend to downplay the complicated nature of cinematic Shakespeare: 'the false genre called "the Shakespeare film" seems to insist on the stability of Shakespeare as a sign, and on the transparency of the film industry as a screen upon which Shakespeare is projected'. Egan's essay profitably explores the potential gap between the mediums of the early modern theatre and the postmodern film, analysing the cinematic interpretation of those scenes in which Shakespeare chooses to show rather than tell. Examples are drawn from Branagh's *Hamlet* and *Much Ado About Nothing*, Franco Zeffirelli's *Hamlet*, Peter Brook's *King Lear*, Derek Jarman's *Tempest*, and Peter Greenaway's *Prospero's Books*. Daileader examines the influence on filmic interpretation of Shakespeare of 1990s 'popular feminism', comparing the courting of the 'hetero female gaze' in films such as Luhrmann's *William Shakespeare's Romeo + Juliet*, Oliver Parker's *Othello*, and Michael Hoffman's *A Midsummer Night's Dream* with the more male-orientated *Shakespeare in Love*. She concludes that 'Shakespeare needed feminism in 1611, when John Fletcher pleased audiences with the first *Shrew* rebuttal, *The Tamer Tamed*, and Shakespeare needs feminism today.'

More modest in scope are Yong Li Lan, 'Returning to Naples: Seeing the End in Shakespeare Film Adaptation' (*LFQ* 29[2001] 128–34)—a study of the closing shots of four Shakespearian films: Greenaway's *Prospero's Books*, Branagh's *Hamlet*, Luhrmann's *Romeo + Juliet* and *Shakespeare in Love*—and John C. Tibbetts, 'Backstage with the Bard: or, Building a Better Mousetrap' (*LFQ* 29[2001] 290–6), a collection and analysis of Shakespearian allusions.

The most popular individual play is *Hamlet*, aided by the publication of *Enter Text*'s special supplement on 'Hamlet on Film', a collection of essays deriving from a conference held at Shakespeare's Globe in April 2001 and introduced by conference organizer Gabriel Egan (*Enter Text* 1[2001] 171–9). Subjects range from the influence of film tradition on the editorial rehabilitation of the first quarto of *Hamlet*: Terri Bourus, 'The First Quarto of *Hamlet* in Film: The Revenge Tragedies of Tony Richardson and Franco Zeffirelli' (*Enter Text* 1[2001] 180–91), to the mediation of high and low culture in Italian parodies of *Hamlet*'s 'To be or not to be': Mariangela Tempera, 'To Laugh or not to Laugh: Italian Parodies of *Hamlet*' (*Enter Text* 1[2001] 289–301). In 'To Take Arms Against a Sea of Anomalies:

Laurence Olivier's Film Adaptation of Act Three, Scene One of *Hamlet*' (*Enter Text* 1[2001] 192–203), James Hirsh argues that Hamlet's speech was originally intended as a 'feigned soliloquy' meant to be overheard, a fact that has been obscured by post-Renaissance interpretation and performance tradition. He concludes by describing how Olivier re-sequences the scenes in order to justify this mistaken interpretation of the speech as an outpouring of personal feeling. In another close 'reading', Lisa Hopkins, 'Denmark's a Prison: Branagh's *Hamlet* and the Paradoxes of Intimacy' (*Enter Text* 1[2001] 226–46), examines various aspects of Branagh's *Hamlet*— including casting, visual tropes, lighting, camera technique and the central performance—in order to argue that the film remains a theatrical rather than a cinematic experience, lacking the intimacy that a fully filmic interpretation might provide. Two essays focus on the potential tension between the visual and the verbal in film adaptations of *Hamlet*. In '"The Beached Verge": On Filming the Unfilmable in Grigori Kozintsev's *Hamlet*' (*Enter Text* 1[2001] 302–16), Saviour Catania explores the 'complex problem' of filming Shakespearian monologues and the means by which Kozintsev 'makes Shakespeare's "head play" think in predominantly visual images'. Elsie Walker's 'A "Harsh World" of Soundbite Shakespeare: Michael Almereyda's *Hamlet* (2000)' (*Enter Text* 1[2001] 317–41) analyses the tension in Almereyda's film between postmodernism and the idealistic attraction of Shakespeare's verse: 'paradoxically, the director both seems to confirm and critique the notion that film itself is antagonistic to the rhythm and subject matter of Shakespeare's verse'.

The most ambitious essays take more oblique views, either in the choice of material or approach. In 'Yorick's Skull: Hamlet's Improper Property' (*Enter Text* 1[2001] 206–25), Pascale Aebischer examines the 'unruliness or impropriety of Yorick's skull as a property', drawing on Olivier's *Hamlet*, Branagh's *In the Bleak Midwinter* and *Hamlet*, and Almereyda's *Hamlet*. She also provides us with the memorable story of a pianist, André Tchaikovsky, who by leaving his skull to the RSC hoped eventually to play Yorick, and was foiled only by the more tender desires of the actors not to dishonour the dead. Mark Robson's '"Trying to pick a lock with a wet herring": *Hamlet*, Film, and Spectres of Psychoanalysis' (*Enter Text* 1[2001] 247–63) poses the question, 'Why are there so many versions of *Hamlet*?' and offers a series of explorations of issues connected with the subject of repetition, specifically as it pertains to psychoanalytic interpretations of *Hamlet*: 'writing, film, ghosts, tragedy, Branagh's film, monuments, trauma, technology, the end of history, and inheritance'. In '*Hamlet* in Warsaw: The Antic Disposition of Ernst Lubitsch' (*Enter Text* 1[2001] 264–88), Nicholas Jones examines Lubitsch's *Hamlet* comedy *To Be or Not To Be* in its political context, arguing that the play is poised between rival pre- and post-war interpretations of Shakespeare.

Three essays in Kliman, ed., *Approaches to Teaching Shakespeare's Hamlet*, focus on *Hamlet* on film. Kenneth S. Rothwell's 'An Annotated and Chronological Screenography: Major Hamlet Adaptations and Selected Derivatives' (pp. 14–27) offers an evaluative survey of *Hamlet* films, including 'major' adaptations and some derivatives, such as Claude Chabrol's *Ophelia*. The other two essays, Rob Kirkpatrick's 'Two Ways to Use Film for Student Writing' (pp. 219–21) and Stephen M. Buhler's 'To Challenge Ghostly Fathers: Teaching *Hamlet* and its Interpretations through Film and Video' (pp. 77–80), focus on the place of *Hamlet* films in the classroom.

Kliman's own 'The Unkindest Cuts: Flashcut Excess in Kenneth Branagh's *Hamlet*', (in Cartmell and Scott, eds., pp. 151–67) attempts to decide what should be retained in a two-hour version of Branagh's *Hamlet* in order to make a better 'Branagh film'. Her targets include the 'flashcuts' or brief inset scenes, which, she argues, distort the play's tempo, and Branagh's interpolation of second-quarto lines into the Folio text. Finally, in 'The Castle of Elsinore: Gothic Aspects of Kenneth Branagh's *Hamlet*' (*ShakB* 19[2001] 36–9), Philippa Shepherd compares Branagh's stylistic choices with Gothic novels such as Horace Walpole's *The Castle of Otranto* and Ann Radcliffe's *The Mysteries of Udolpho*.

Branagh's 'little' *Hamlet* film, *In the Bleak Midwinter* (known to American audiences as *A Midwinter's Tale*), is the subject of Courtney Lehmann's 'Shakespeare the Savior or Phantom Menace? Kenneth Branagh's *A Midwinter's Tale* and the Critique of Cynical Reason' (*CLQ* 37[2001] 54–77). Drawing on Peter Sloterdijk's *Critique of Cynical Reason*, Lehmann analyses the connection between *In the Bleak Midwinter* and Branagh's 'big' *Hamlet*, produced a year later, arguing that 'returning to the primal, small-scale, and often thankless scene of regional theater, *A Midwinter's Tale* positions itself in the breach where "affect" seems to have lost its connection to "art" and seeks to restore belief in the cultural value of Shakespeare'.

Two essays focus on the intersection of race and gender in film adaptations of *Othello*. Pascale Aebischer's 'Black Rams Tupping White Ewes: Race vs. Gender in the Final Scene of Six *Othellos*' (in Cartmell, Hunter, and Whelehan, eds., *Retrovisions: Reinventing the Past in Film and Fiction*, pp. 59–73) focuses on cinematic interpretation of the tragic conclusion, noting that it is 'sobering to see' that these adaptations have found it hard to move beyond the 'racist and misogynist heritage' of the stage tradition. 'Directorial decisions', she argues, 'force audiences to see the killing of Desdemona as either a murder or a sacrifice, to condemn Othello or to excuse him'. In '"Othello/Me": Racial Drag and the Pleasures of Boundary-Crossing with *Othello*' (*CompD* 35[2001] 101–23), Elise Marks looks at stage and film interpretations, notably Fishbone's Othello, and asks whether an Othello played by a black actor can ever live up to the expectations of (white) audiences. She concludes that 'only a non-African knows how to be the perfect African, at least for the emotional fantasy-use of a thrill-seeking white audience. A real black actor, like a real woman, has too much independent selfhood getting in the way.' Two essays, David G. Hale's 'Order and Disorder in *Macbeth*, Act V: Film and Television' (*LFQ* 29[2001] 101–6) and Arthur Lindley's 'Scotland Saved from History: Welles's *Macbeth* and the Ahistoricism of Medieval Film' (*LFQ* 29[2001] 96–100) focus on the mediation of history in filmic *Macbeth*s. The interaction between Shakespearian adaptation and historical reality is also examined in James Forse's 'Staging (on Film) *Richard III* to Reflect the Present' (*PCRev* 12[2001] 33–9).

Baz Luhrmann's *William Shakespeare's Romeo + Juliet* received less attention than in recent years, but Courtney Lehmann's 'Strictly Shakespeare? Dead Letters, Ghostly Fathers, and the Cultural Pathology of Authorship in Baz Luhrmann's *William Shakespeare's Romeo + Juliet*' (*SQ* 52[2001] 189–221) was one of 2001's highlights, a sophisticated analysis of the relationship between early modern and postmodern conceptions of authorship and authority. Lehmann analyses the relationship between Luhrmann's film and Shakespeare's play, but also that between Shakespeare's play and its own source, Arthur Brooke's *Tragicall Historye of Romeus and Juliet*. Lurhmann's film, she argues, 'really does live up to its title as "*William Shakespeare's*" *Romeo* + *Juliet*, uniquely transmitting both the authorial audacity *and* anxiety embedded in Shakespeare's own attempt to cheat the *auctoritas* of the legend'.

In another outstanding essay, 'Shakespeare and the Holocaust: Julie Taymor's *Titus* is Beautiful, or Shakespeare Meets (the) Camp' (*CLQ* 37[2001] 78–106), Richard Burt offers a multi-layered and hugely detailed analysis of the problematic debt that Taymor's *Titus* owes to the 'Holocaust industry', and of the film's interaction with the 'schlock' Shakespeare exemplified by the more obviously exploitative adaptations of Lorn Richey, Christopher Dunne and Richard Griffin. He suggests that 'it is in the crosscurrents of schlock ... that Shakespeare films (and Holocaust memorials as well) must now necessarily be read if we are to grasp fully both their strengths and their limitations'. In a rather less complex analysis of the same film, Mary Lindroth's '"Some device of further misery": Taymor's *Titus* Brings Shakespeare to Film Audiences with a Twist' (*LFQ* 29[2001] 107–15) asserts that Taymor moves away from the Elizabethan play by adding 'hope and compassion' to the tragedy, but that this addition paradoxically 'brings audiences closer to Shakespeare'.

A group of neglected television adaptations of *Henry VI* is collected by Patricia Lennox in '*Henry VI*: A Television History in Four Parts' (in Pendleton, ed., *Henry VI: Critical Essays*, pp. 235–52). Two adaptations were made specifically for television: Peter Dew's series of fifteen one-hour dramas based on Shakespeare's histories, entitled *An Age of Kings*, and Jane Howell's BBC/Time-Life *Henry VI*. The other two were adapted from stage productions: Peter Hall and John Barton's RSC *Wars of the Roses* and Peter Bogdanov and Michael Pennington's English Shakespeare Company *Wars of the Roses*. Lennox pays close attention to issues such as adaptation, casting, original broadcast contexts and audience reaction, and concludes with a call for the BBC to make its three versions more widely available.

Two substantial essays focus on Trevor Nunn's *Twelfth Night*. In '"What's to come is still unsure": Madness and Deferral in Nunn's *Twelfth Night*' (*CLQ* 37.15–29), Eric C. Brown argues that the film spins on the tension between mirth and madness, and between past, present and future. 'In its production of visual imagery that adopts and enlivens ideas already available in this play', he writes, 'this film refashions early modern notions of time, hope, and madness into a vibrant exploration of the power and impotency of love, desire, and identity.' Maria F. Magro and Mark Douglas's 'Reflections on Sex, Shakespeare and Nostalgia in Trevor Nunn's *Twelfth Night*' (in Cartmell, Hunter and Whelehan, eds., pp. 41–58) looks at the way in which the film naturalizes heterosexual relations through its rehearsal of homosexual desire but simultaneously undoes its own ideological constructions. Although Nunn's *Twelfth Night* 'may sound the trumpet of nostalgia for a heterosexual historical past that never was, this representation is always equivocal and will always attempt to cover its tracks. It is in these ghostly footprints that we can find the evidence for a counter-reading that suggests that maybe there is something queer about Shakespeare after all'.

Tempest adaptations also attracted some solid work. In 'Conjuring *The Tempest*: Derek Jarman and the Spectacle of Redemption' (*GLQ* 7[2001] 265–84), Jim Ellis analyses the intersection between class and race in Jarman's *The Tempest*. He focuses in particular on Jarman's adaptation of the masque element, arguing that

'Jarman's most radical intervention into the masque form is to make the antimasque into the masque'. In 'Prospero in Cyberspace' (in Bell, Chew, Eliot, Hunter and West, eds., pp. 184–96), Martin Butler focuses on the nature of texts and textuality in Greenaway's *Prospero's Books*. Placing the film in the context of emergent technologies in the early 1990s, Butler argues that even as it upholds the authority of the written word—Prospero's and Shakespeare's—Greenaway's film undermines it, notably during its ambivalent conclusion. He concludes: 'Hesitating between an all-powerful centralizing technology where everything is known, and a decentred consumerism where anything is possible, the unresolved tensions of *Prospero's Books* bespeak the opportunities and anxieties of the new electronic age.' Another essay on *Prospero's Books*, Stephen Marx's 'Greenaway's Books' (*EMLS* 7:ii[2001]), also focuses on texts, arguing that, although the Bible is not among Prospero's books, its in-the-film presence is pervasive, particularly in allusions to the Revelation of St John: '*The Tempest* alludes to Revelation ... but Greenaway's adaptation makes the connection unmistakable'.

More thorough reworkings of Shakespeare's plays receive attention elsewhere. In 'Weaving the Spider's Web: Interpretation of Character in Akira Kurosawa's *Throne of Blood (Kumonosu-jô)*' (in Ryuta, Carruthers and Gilles, eds., *Performing Shakespeare in Japan*, pp. 87–100) Paula Von Loewenfeldt argues that, in addition to approaching it as an instance of the 'Japanization' of Shakespeare, we also need to acknowledge Kurosawa's film as the intensely personal engagement of an individual film director with *Macbeth*. Another Kurosawa film, *Ran*, is the subject of Zvika Serper's 'Lady Kaede in Kurosawa's *Ran*: Verbal and Visual Characterisations through Animal Traditions' (*Japan Forum* 13[2001] 145–58). Serper asserts that the character of Lady Kaede is 'sought and crystallised' through Kurosawa's allusions to Japanese theatrical traditions surrounding the fox and the serpent. Returning to the Anglo-American tradition, in '"Shakespeare, he's in the alley": *My Own Private Idaho* and Shakespeare in the Streets' (*LFQ* 29[2001] 116–21), Hugh H. Davis argues that *My Own Private Idaho* is an 'intertextual mosaic blending serious Shakespeare with popular culture references'. In '*Forbidden Planet* and the Retrospective Attribution of Intentions' (in Cartmell, Hunter, and Whelehan, eds., pp. 148–62), Judith Buchanan questions the very basis upon which we study 'Shakespeare on film', comparing the critical reception of *Forbidden Planet* with that of *The Island of Lost Souls*, a film which 'despite its considerable Shakespearean parallels, has no history of being discussed in these terms'. What do we invest in films when we treat them as Shakespearian adaptations, and what are our motives in doing so?

Looking at the 'Shakespearian' from another angle, two articles emphasize the interpretative importance of star actors. In 'What[?] Price[?] Shakespeare[?]' (*LFQ* 29[2001] 135–41), Thomas A. Pendleton surveys the Shakespearian allusions surrounding Vincent Price in three films: *Tower of London* [1939], *Tower of London* [1962] and *Theater of Blood*. Douglas Lanier offers a more fully developed example of this approach in 'The Idea of John Barrymore' (*CLQ* 37[2001] 30–53). Seeking to explore the '*idea* of a John Barrymore', Lanier draws on film theory's 'star studies', arguing that stars can be more important 'principles of meaning' than more familiar figures such as directors or authors. Concluding, he suggests that this approach 'invites speculation about the ideological function of other Shakespearean stars ... whose status as "popular" Shakespeareans shaped perceptions of Shakespeare in their own historical moments'.

Finally, interest in *Shakespeare in Love* remains high. Kim Fedderson and J.M. Richardson's '"Love like there has never been in a play": *Shakespeare in Love* as Bardspawn' (*WVUPP* 47[2001] 145–9), draws on the sonnets in order to question whether *Shakespeare in Love* is 'authentically Shakespearean'. A more sophisticated examination of the film's authorial persona can be found Elizabeth Klett's 'Shakespeare in Love and the End(s) of History' (in Cartmell, Hunter and Whelehan, eds., pp. 25–40). Klett argues that there is a tension between different kinds of universalization in *Shakespeare in Love*. While the film 'aims to divest the Bard of his intimidating iconic status and make him readily understandable to everyone, it simultaneously endorses his work as a bearer of universal values couched in the greatest poetry ever written'. Ultimately, the film works to depicts Shakespeare as 'authentic, heterosexual, passionate, sexy, and funny', ensuring his appeal to the widest possible audience. Similar emphasis on the heterosexism of the film can be found in Sujata Iyengar, 'Shakespeare in Heterolove' (*LFQ* 29[2001] 122–7) and in Daileader (discussed above). In the introduction to *Shakespeare and Feminist Performance* (pp. 1–20), however, Sarah Werner contends that the film portrays Shakespeare as androgynous at crucial points in its narrative: it is only by 'opening himself to femininity' that Shakespeare can regain his masculine inspiration.

4. Criticism

(a) General

Dobson and Wells, eds., *The Oxford Companion to Shakespeare*, embraces all things Shakespearian and greatly deserves its jacket's billing as 'the most comprehensive reference book' on his life and times and his presence through the centuries not only on stage but in ballet, opera, music, film, television, and even in novels and comic strips. A magnificently produced volume of 541 oversized pages, it contains thousands of entries from A to Z in three-column format on Shakespeare's family, theatrical colleagues, literary and political contemporaries, and playing companies. Each of the plays' dramatis personae receives an entry, usually a line to several sentences, though some—Ophelia, Cordelia, Caliban, Hotspur—get several hundred words. One might think other non-title characters—Falstaff, Desdemona—equally deserving, but the reader is referred to the larger entries on their plays. More than a hundred illustrations—from paintings to advertisements—are strategically placed throughout this well-designed book. Rhetorical and literary terms receive entries, as do works and authors Shakespeare used in composing the plays. The major actors and actresses, productions, theatres, adaptations, editors, critics, illustrators, painters, writers, all are identified in helpful and mostly unpretentious and jargon-free language by more than a hundred international scholars.

Editors Michael Dobson and Stanley Wells key this encyclopedia to *The Oxford Shakespeare* [1986] so the individual plays, which receive three or four full pages each, appear under the titles used in that edition (*All Is True*, for example, for *Henry VIII*) and with its editors' textual preferences (for example, the division of *King Lear* into twenty-four scenes). These longer entries place the play within a chronology of composition, discuss its textual history and sources, provide an adequately detailed synopsis, describe the play's 'artistic features', summarize its critical, stage, film, and television histories, list recent single editions, and provide six to ten 'representative' critical books and articles. Though these lists can be idiosyncratic sometimes, the intention is to include some up-to-date scholarship along with the notable reference points: Bradley, Eliot, Tillyard, Wilson Knight, Dover Wilson, and so on. In their introduction the editors explain their design as the best for providing information rather than interpretation, so the lively style and accurate summary in these pages are directed at a general reader rather than an advanced scholar.

Opinion and preference, of course, will necessarily be involved in the process of selecting and summarizing, and the overt or the subtle remark will occasionally point to the excesses of appropriating Shakespeare to popular taste, current fashion, or the director's or critic's ideology. But unlike the 'companions' from Cambridge, the *Oxford Companion* eschews the wide-ranging interpretative synthesis and the 'chapter-length meditations on large topics' (Dobson and Wells's phrase). Rather than being rivals, the two complement each other, and some booksellers offer them together as a discounted package deal. The real problem with the *Oxford Companion* is its alphabetical design: inevitably, one will have questions for which the entries do have answers, but one may not easily find them. Who was the vicar of Holy Trinity when Shakespeare was baptized? What's the name of that rhetorical figure for repeating a phrase at the beginning of successive clauses? In the early eighteenth century what play was adapted to feature Falstaff? Who wrote it and what was its title? For this kind of minor detail, the editors offer a 'thematic listing of entries' which may provide clues and definitely will help locate scattered entries. A genealogy of the Yorks and Lancasters and a geographical map follow the Z entries to help readers locate the characters and places of the dramatic world of the English histories and *Macbeth*. A partial chronology [1564–1999] and several pages of even 'further' reading complete the volume.

There's much else Shakespearian here. Worth singling out, however, are the substantial entries on Shakespeare's afterlives in the cultures of twenty-six nations and six 'regions' (the Arab world, Latin America, and Scandinavia, for example). Together they underline Shakespeare's global influence and continued presence, a topic that has been on the front burner for many recently. The institutional and cultural prestige of Shakespeare has presented a problem for the Royal Shakespeare Company from its inception, according to Colin Chambers in *Talking Shakespeare*, a collection of new essays edited by Deborah Cartmell and Michael Scott. Chambers offers a balanced view of the origins of the RSC, its first directors, its claims for Shakespeare and the Elizabethan theatre as 'unequalled in any other epoch or language', and its 'special place' at the centre of Shakespeare's 'contemporary presence'. The RSC has struggled to navigate the challenges of conflicting expectations: the pressure of a nationally subsidized institution to present conservative 'English' values, the academic demands to present an uncut text free from ideological 'relevance', the artistic imperative to innovate, and the economic necessity to attract audiences, especially to make the plays 'fresh' for a new generation of theatregoers. He concludes with a rather pessimistic view of the RSC's future in a financially troubled England with a conservative politics in control.

Crystal Bartolovich's 'Shakespeare's Globe?' (in Howard and Shershow, eds., *Marxist Shakespeares*, a collection of new essays) provides a complementary perspective on the Globe Trust and the Third Globe. She examines the genesis of the Globe Trust in the 1970s, the opening of the reconstructed Globe under the partial sponsorship of transnational corporations, its choice of *Henry V* as its initial production, and its 'playnotes' which fashion a hero and a play to celebrate the language, culture and unity of England. But, she argues, the play as much represents a fractured nation of many tongues and cultures, and beyond the confines of the new playhouse lies an English economy which has long since lost its competitiveness in the globalized, corporatized world in which Shakespeare's plays are circulated, performed, appropriated and adapted. The Bard can no longer belong to Stratford and London, the RSC and the Globe. Several other essays take on the process of globalization. Denise Albanese uses a comparison of Kenneth Branagh's 'reverential' Hamlet and Buzz Luhrmann's *Romeo + Juliet* to assert that the global circulation of the film as commodity undermines any alternative cultural logics.

In the introduction to a 'casebook' of previously published essays, *Shakespeare, Feminism and Gender*, Kate Chedgzoy also writes of a recent controversy in which Shakespeare became the 'site' of the contested values of high culture and English privilege versus the 'anti-English multiculturalism' of an underclass of economically disadvantaged, ethnically diverse and mostly immigrant school children. The cultural icon at the centre of local politics provides another version of Shakespeare's ambivalent presence in English ideology, but his centrality in educational and cultural systems also suggests to Chedgzoy the main rationale for why literary studies of the kind she has collected really do matter, and the essays in the volume mostly reflect the feminist political self-consciousness and commitment of the 1990s.

Beehler and Klein, eds., *Shakespeare and Higher Education: A Global Perspective*, provides another perspective on the globe's Shakespeare. The emphasis here on teaching Shakespeare takes us through a dozen countries—from Brazil to China to South Africa—as the essayists find themselves relearning the plays while encountering cultural differences. Other instructors relate their experiences teaching the plays to engineering students, to the easily distracted, to heterogeneous populations, to prisoners in solitary confinement. Classroom practices offer another focus and involve innovations from new technologies, traditional approaches, and all kinds of successes (and a few instructive failures) in teaching the plays, as well as the frequent self-discoveries by the teachers themselves. A few essays also examine Shakespeare's own openness to diversity and his dramatic representations of other cultures: his four African plays, for example, are discussed by James Andreas as historically part of Shakespeare's own expanding global map and as valuable in presenting a forum for engaging students with contemporary issues of race. Shakespeare clearly is no longer an English export nor the possession of an elite, privileged western European educational and cultural system. The fifty very dense pages of Christopher Morrow's bibliography of 'Shakespeare and Pedagogy' are also very international in scope.

Much of the year's 'historical' criticism also involves Shakespeare in conversations with the present or very recent past. Walter Cohen's long and very detailed explanation (in Howard and Shershow, eds., *Marxist Shakespeares*), of Shakespeare's own 'globalism' under the influence of the expanding English international trade to the further reaches of exotic geographies is framed by references to the transformation of our own international capitalist and consumer culture. Though Cohen does not 'read' the mercantilism of the early 1600s through contemporary lenses, his concerns are influenced by our own economic issues.

Carol Chillington Rutter examines some of the distortions and appropriations of Shakespeare in both the criticism and the theatrical productions of relatively recent years. In the introduction to her *Enter the Body: Women and Representation on Shakespeare's Stage*, Rutter argues against recent scholars' creation of an 'eroticized, historicized playhouse' in which the cross-dressing of Shakespeare's boy actors heightened the 'sodomitical desire' and explored the 'transgressive erotic impulses' of his audiences. As a 'corrective' to feminist criticism's emphasis on 'discursive bodies', Rutter reads Shakespeare's words as a 'playtext', as incomplete without performance, as offering many possibilities, and also as limiting both critical interpretation and theatre practice. This approach forms the core of 'performance studies' of Shakespeare, and Rutter sees how productions both succeed and fail to embody the 'script'. By concentrating on women's bodies, the male 'gaze' and other elements of costuming, design, body language and movement, she pursues a constant conversation with the representation of the body on stage (and screen), current fashion, and alternative possibilities. For example, productions of *Troilus and Cressida* provide her with an analysis of how contemporary culture influences theatrical decision-making; 'peplum' B films from Italy, the sensational success of Ken Tynan's *Oh! Calcutta*, and unisex and other fashion trends of the 1960s and 1970s are convincingly introduced as influential in the costuming and design of various productions of the play, as well as responsible for the play's emergence from a dark, neglected corner of the canon to the forefront of directors' interests. Frequently Rutter also explores the context of performance before the original audience: for example, she discusses sixteenth- and early seventeenth-century works which all suggest that Shakespeare wrote Cleopatra as 'black' . The 'recovery' of the 'performativity' within the Jacobean context of the several plays she examines works well with the analysis of recent productions to demonstrate the insight and complexity which this kind of critical approach can attain. Though often the fashionable dress, events, or ideologies which influence what gets put on stage show the blindness or indifference of film or theatre directors and actors to what Shakespeare wrote, Rutter knows that, at the same time, performance also can reveal previously neglected aspects of Shakespeare's genius in developing the representation of women in his plays.

Several chapters in Cartmell and Scott, eds., *Talking Shakespeare*, illustrate the same ambivalence towards 'our Shakespeare'. Very near the beginning of the collection, Michael Scott asks: 'Does Shakespeare, through his plays, talk to us, or do we, through reading and performing Shakespeare, merely talk to ourselves?' Nigel Wood offers a good example of this scepticism by arguing that any attempt to impose an interpretation on the last fifteen or so lines of *Hamlet* must grapple with the possibilities offered within even one version of the text, whether that of the quartos or that of the First Folio. Other essays make this collection hard to categorize. Peter Davidson struggles with the scanty evidence to speculate, often persuasively, about the touring practices and economics of theatrical companies in Elizabethan times, and Emma Smith pairs three of Shakespeare's plays with three of his contemporaries to 'identify a Shakespeare in dialogue with other theatrical writers on an equal basis, assuming audience knowledge of previous plays, struggling with the burden of dramatic tradition, borrowing snippets or topics, or himself providing the basis of other drama'. Dermot Cavanagh assesses the contributions of 'new historicism' and 'cultural materialism' in creating a new interest in the ideology of the plays and suggests that the Frankfurt school of criticism (Adorno and Benjamin) could provide a better framework than that of the post-structuralist French theorists by offering an approach that considers the 'capacity of art to be both constituted by ideologies, but also to be able to achieve a critical perspective upon these'. Kiernan Ryan reminds us again that Shakespeare is reinvented by each age according to its contemporary concerns, and Michael Collins's essay just might summarize the collection: 'all of Shakespeare's plays ... do magnificently what all literature seeks to do: to create a richly patterned, resonant, engaging structure of words that evokes, for reader and audience alike, an experience that, while true to the complexity of the world it reflects, seems at once greatly significant and profoundly satisfying'. In an appendix, Josephine Wells provides an up-to-date descriptive bibliography of electronic resources which focus upon Shakespeare, the Renaissance and early modern culture.

Another set of instances of how Shakespeare continues to talk to us is the extraordinary influence of plays such as *The Tempest* and *King Lear* upon new literary creations. In *Novel Shakespeares: Twentieth-Century Women Novelists and Appropriation*, Julie Sanders examines the novels of several dozen writers who use Shakespeare to various extents in creating their characters, plots, and the texture of their fiction. The best known of these are Iris Murdoch, Gloria Naylor and Jane Smiley, but Sanders is informative and convincing about lesser-known writers and produces a discussion of truly international scope—another version of 'global Shakespeare'. The influence of *The Tempest* and *King Lear* revolves around postcolonial politics and family dysfunction as well as a few other themes important to these novelists and feminist critics; her analysis combines some impressive close readings with a balanced view of 'appropriation' and makes persuasive cases for the merits of novelists such as Leslie Forbes, Barbara Trapido, and others.

Several monographs under review present new approaches without involving 'Shakespeare' in the present or recent past. For Jack D'Amico in *Shakespeare and Italy: The City and the Stage*, 'Shakespeare's Italy was a society uniquely open to exchange and transformation, a distant place that was, at the same time, a variation on the urban world of London', therefore a valuable setting for eleven of his plays and a useful focus for representation of 'urban geography' and theatricality of city life. The opening chapter explores the diverse perceptions of the Italian city-state available in the literary and popular imagination: its urbanity, courtliness, civic humanism, arts and education; its violence and amorality, sexuality and raucous revelry; its international trade, materialism, conspicuous consumption; Castiglione and Machiavelli; comedy and tragedy. Along with the emphasis on 'openness', the survey provides threads of analysis woven into later discussions. The next chapters take on, one by one, how Shakespeare exploited the theatricality of urban spaces: piazzas, streets, interiors, court, garden, temple, city walls. D'Amico apologizes that his 'fresh perspective' necessarily 'breaks up the treatment of individual plays', but it does allow valuable examinations of familiar themes—indoor and outdoor, private and public—and new connections: the great hall as an extension of the openness of the piazza, the garden as 'mediator' between house and street, the walls of the family home and the city walls as analogous fortresses against the lawlessness outside. Yet this arrangement limits the pursuit of larger segments of interpretation and downplays other influences, such as Plautus's comedic dramaturgy, upon the dramatic structuring of Shakespeare's scenes.

Kenneth Gross's title, *Shakespeare's Noise*, refers to violent and disorderly language: slander, defamation, rumour, curse. The work of these aggressive words enables Shakespeare to explore 'ways of creating a world as well as ways of creating a character'. Violent speech 'opens up a realm of fantasy otherwise unavailable to the hero', a 'revelatory' and 'liberating' energy which leads to 'privileged, if tragic, forms of knowledge'. *Shakespeare's Noise* pursues this line of analysis in *Hamlet*, *Othello*, *Measure for Measure*, *Coriolanus*, and *King Lear*. An extensive chapter on the way contemporary writers and legal folk regarded slander anchors the monograph historically, but Gross only sporadically applies his scholarship to interpreting the plays. It is difficult to identify a consistent thread of discussion or argument in his chapters, though often his close readings of large segments of these plays are dazzlingly impressive. Gross's fondness for his own wordplay and some wildly speculative or meditative digressions are sometimes irritating, and his sense of the 'desolation' of these plays needs to be clearer.

In *Playing Companies and Commerce in Shakespeare's Time*, Roslyn Lander Knutson challenges several well-established views of the relationships among the theatrical companies in Shakespeare's time. The 'War of the Theatres', she argues, is based upon misconceptions about the business practices of the 'playing companies' and a misreading of the animosities between Jonson, Marston, and Dekker in their exchanges around 1599 to 1601. The 'little eyases' passage in *Hamlet* has been read as implicating Shakespeare in the hostility between the open-air and indoor playhouses, the professionals and the child actors. But, for Knutson, considering the world of London theatre as one of a dog-eat-dog, angry and bitter rivalry and one-upmanship has questionable documentable basis; instead, by looking closely at wills, marriages, and other public records, she shows that there was easy mobility from one company to another, that there were marriages that involved families from supposedly competitive companies, that there were wills that left property or money to players from other companies than the deceased's. She sees the 'playing companies' as involved in cooperative and sophisticated business strategies designed to nurture and expand the theatre 'industry'. Certainly, this is what happened during Shakespeare's career in the theatre, as the sites for theatrical performance around London increased almost exponentially. She compares the relationships between theatre professionals to a kind of fellowship like a guild, sharing in the success of their craft and developing marketing practices, one of which may have involved staging public quarrels to attract attention and good publicity for all, including the book trade. As for Shakespeare's involvement, Knutson argues that the 'little eyases' passage refers to a problem raised by the children's companies much later than 1600–1, as the 'fickle' theatregoers in 1606–8 were patronizing the Children of Blackfriars and placing the cooperative nature of the theatre industry at risk. The research into primary documents, the implications drawn from dramatic texts and known detail about the theatres, printers, and players make this book one of the year's most anchored in the fabric of Shakespeare's professional life, and provide a model of commerce with which future theatre historians will have to contend.

The ambitious project announced by Michael Taylor's title, *Shakespeare Criticism in the Twentieth Century*, might suggest the undertaking of another Oxford Companion. Taylor writes so well, however, that anyone expecting this impossible endeavour will probably be disarmed by his wit, humour, not a little sarcasm, and judiciousness in selecting just the right phrase, detail, or passage to bring out the critics' strengths or, more often, weaknesses. An introduction traces the beginnings of what we today call 'criticism' to the nineteenth-century scholars' investment in Shakespeare: an 'age of grammar and lexicography', of compiling and editing, of philology and the 'science' of R.G. Moulton. In a short space, we are led through the embattled twentieth century to our own, in which 'If the world is now a global village, then Shakespeare is arguably its headman.' The following four chapters are organized around approaches to interpreting the plays—through characterization, dramatic form and theme, the theatre and staging, and historical contexts—and a final chapter groups various strands of feminist, gender, postcolonial, archetypal and myth, and religious criticism. With A.C. Bradley's *Shakespearean Tragedy* [1904] as a starting point, Taylor explores the assumptions behind unravelling responses to the texts' dramatic representations; for example, Bradley's own fondness for identifying his readers' responses with his own through the recurrent 'we' know or 'we' understand, or his 'tyrannical' inclusion of his readers in a sort of 'exclusive club' whose members are 'determined by taste' and so agree with his 'moral certainty'. But with Bradley, as with those whom he influenced or those who followed different approaches to characterization, Taylor seldom neglects to point up the strength and value of the critical works under scrutiny.

He traces the direct routes of influence and connection where he can, but they are sometimes few, as critical fashions flourish, decline, disappear, and resurface in new guises. What keeps these chapters going is often Taylor's style and willingness to encapsulate his analysis in a short phrase: for example, calling the monographs of Wilson Knight, whose long engagement with Shakespeare he praises for 'its persistence, conviction and affection', 'ho-hum', 'less than gripping' and irresponsibly obsessed with characters who somehow turn themselves into 'themes'. Northrop Frye's total indifference to performance is matched by the total indifference to literary form of the 'new historicists'. Some of the groupings, such as the formalists around F.R. Leavis at Cambridge in the 1940s, help to organize his chapters, but when fewer connections seem natural Taylor forges ahead, and one follows, knowing he will not hold back, even if (and perhaps because) his scrutiny will yield another succinct, well-turned, perhaps merciless phrase. This very self-confident survey will repay close reading, an impressive response to the daunting undertaking of gathering a century of criticism within 225 pages.

(b) Comedies
This year's criticism saw a number of different approaches to the study of *Twelfth Night*. David Carnegie's '"*Malvolio within*": Performance Perspectives on the Dark House' (*SQ* 52[2001] 393–414) traces the stage history of Malvolio's incarceration in IV.ii and considers its implications for our understanding of the play. Pointing out that it is not until the nineteenth century that an incarcerated Malvolio was visible on stage, the article considers different possibilities and problems for the staging of the direction '*Malvolio within*' on the early modern stage if he is hidden from sight.

Referring to past performances, Carnegie also explores some of the dramatic possibilities opened up or excluded by different ways of staging the scene, with Malvolio visible or hidden. In '"Here I am ... yet cannot hold this visible shape": The Music of Gender in Shakespeare's *Twelfth Night*' (*Comitatus* 32[2001] 99–125), Marcus Cheng Chye Tan discusses the manner in which music contributes to, and even exemplifies, the play's elusive balance between comedy and melancholy. In particular, Tan argues that the 'problematics of androgyny' are pivotal to the play's 'double tonality' (p. 106), and then discusses how different musical properties in *Twelfth Night*'s songs accentuate or mediate this gender uncertainty. Paul Dean's '"Comfortable doctrine": *Twelfth Night* and the Trinity' (*RES* 52[2001] 500–515) explores the appearance of triads in the play—particularly that of Viola, Sebastian, and Cesario—by reading Shakespeare's work in relation to early modern Neoplatonism and Augustinian thought on the Trinity, and, finally, more recent theological study. Deanne Williams's note entitled 'Herod's Cities: Cesarea and Sebaste in *Twelfth Night*' (*N&Q* 48[2001] 276–278), also discussed in section 1 above, asserts that the names Cesario and Sebastian refer to twin cities built by King Herod, and argues that the shadow of Herod, as well as of the feast of the Holy Innocents, may be discerned in many aspects of the play.

A similar diversity marked critical responses to *As You Like It*. Martha Ronk's 'Locating the Visual in *As You Like It*' (*SQ* 52[2001] 255–77) interrogates the interaction of verbal and visual representation in the play by calling upon the concepts of allegory, emblem, and most notably ekphrasis (a category which, the essay claims, reproduces post-Reformation cultural anxieties over the nature of the visual). Through discussion of different representations of Rosalind and of the pastoral, and referring to the original performance conditions of the play, Ronk argues that verbal pictures frequently compete with, and even overwhelm, what is seen on stage, revealing the instability of representation itself. Robert Leach's '*As You Like It*—A "Robin Hood" Play' (*ES* 82[2001] 393–400) seeks to place Shakespeare's comedy in relation to the tradition of the Robin Hood May games. Leach maintains that the play shares basic structural elements with the traditional games, as well as reproducing a number of other facets associated with the festivities, such as a sense of timelessness, role reversal, and the (at least symbolic) re-creation of the greenwood. In 'Horns, the Dream-Work, and Female Potency in *As You Like It*' (*SoAR* 66:iv[2001] 45–69), Cynthia Lewis concentrates upon the play's often displaced or concealed concern with the male fear of cuckoldry. Lewis argues that by exploiting patriarchal structures and expectations to incite a fear of betrayal in Orlando, Rosalind finds a form of potency to achieve a balance of power with her future husband. Yet the play resists falling into misogyny directed at the woman taking control, and instead probes the psychological process by which such anxieties are worked through, most notably in Oliver's recounting of Orlando's defeat of the lioness in IV.iii. Nathaniel Strout explores the senses of mutuality which pervade the play in '*As You Like It*, *Rosalynde*, and Mutuality' (*SEL* 41[2001] 277–95). Strout contrasts the male-centred aspects of Thomas Lodge's *Rosalynde*, such as its exclusive address to male readers and its focus upon male concerns, with the more inclusive, mutual nature of Shakespeare's transformation of the tale. But while Shakespeare presents characters acting and choosing together, Strout insists that the play's mutuality is not that of equals, but to be understood within early modern patriarchal hierarchies. Finally, Dorothea Kehler's 'Shakespeare's

Recollections of Marlowe's *Dido, Queen of Carthage*: Two Notes' (*ANQ* 14[2001] 5–10) proposes that Phoebe's praise for Ganymede in *As You Like It* (III.v.127–8), and Adriana's laments in II.i and II.ii of *The Comedy of Errors*, allude to Marlowe's *Dido*.

Drawing upon Slavoj Žižek's theory that the written rules of the law are always supplemented by clandestine forms of trangression and enjoyment, John Nickel's 'Shylock in Washington: The Clinton Crisis, *The Merchant of Venice*, and Enjoyment of the Law' (*TPr* 15[2001] 317–35) juxtaposes the Republicans' attempts to remove President Clinton from office with Shylock's appeal to the court. Tracing some of the issues of enjoyment and recognition which animate the unwritten aspect of rule in the play, Nickel argues that Shylock epitomizes taking the law too literally, and by ignoring its unwritten codes, he threatens to expose both the underside of Christian life and legal artificiality. Peter Holland's '*The Merchant of Venice* and the Value of Money' (*CahiersE* 60[2001] 13–30) explores the 'strangely creative' (p. 14) force of money in the play by relating its precise and consistent circulation of ducats to social economies of masculinity and morality. Considering performance perspectives, and focusing in particular upon Jessica's exchange of Leah's ring, the essay ends with speculation upon that which is emotionally and personally precious. Sharing some concerns evident in Holland's essay, Jacques Derrida's 'What is a "Relevant" Translation?' (*CritI* 27[2001] 175–200) contains a detailed discussion of the court scene (IV.i) which draws upon senses of conversion, translation, exchange-value and indebtedness. Perhaps most notably, Derrida probes some of the interrelations between gratitude, pardon and mercy in what he sees as a staging of 'all the great motives of Christian anti-Judaism' (p. 191). Unfortunately, Jason Gleckman's 'The Merchant of Venice: Laws Written and Unwritten in Venice' (*CR* 41[2001] 81–93) was unavailable for review.

From Venice we move to England with Leo Salingar's 'The Englishness of *The Merry Wives of Windsor*' (*CahiersE* 59[2001] 9–25), which interprets the play as a comedy of social pretensions, arguing that Windsor is 'a bourgeois society marked by aristocratic inclinations' (p. 11). The essay examines how the characters' pretensions and attendant self-deception are supplemented by their verbal peculiarities, which appear most frequently in the form of blunders and affectation. In 'The "ill kill'd" Deer: Poaching and Social Order in *The Merry Wives of Windsor*' (*TSLL* 43[2001] 46–73), Jeffrey Theis analyses the pervasive references to literal and metaphorical poaching in the play by reading them in relation to early modern forest laws, particularly as they are expressed in John Manwood's treatise. By evoking the challenge to property, linguistic and spatial boundaries, and hierarchies of social order that poaching represents, Shakespeare's play constantly destabilizes authority, ownership and propriety, and instead presents in Windsor a fluid and continually, communally revised organization of space and social relations. A similar historicist emphasis is evident in 'Why Does Puck Sweep? Fairylore, Merry Wives, and Social Struggle' (*SQ* 52[2001] 67–106), where Wendy Wall explores the significance of both real and imaginary fairies in *A Midsummer Night's Dream* and *The Merry Wives of Windsor* by examining the interrelation of fairy lore with early modern England's contested discourses of domesticity and the household, and emerging notions of nationalism. Wall argues that, whereas *Dream* presents a gentrified notion of popular ritual related to 'an elite humanist male fantasy of returning to domesticity' (p. 106), *Merry Wives* presents a more sceptical and workaday domestic realm.

A Midsummer Night's Dream also attracted attention in three note-length publications. A.D. Nuttall, in 'Bottom's Dream' (*N&Q* 48[2001] 276), comments that the acknowledged allusion in the weaver's pronouncement 'It shall be call'd "Bottom's Dream", because it hath no bottom' (IV.i.212–13) to the familiar expression *lucus a non lucendo* ('It is called a wood [*lucus*] because there is no light [*lux*] there') seems far from casual and evokes the 'darkened pastoral excursion' of the play. In 'Shakespeare's *A Midsummer Night's Dream*' (*Expl* 59[2001] 176–8), Rodney Stenning Edgecombe, pointing out other references to sex and offspring in the passage, recommends that 'increase' (I.ii.114) in Titania's speech on the effects of the fairy quarrel should be read as 'progeny'. And Samuel Schuman's 'Sprites' (*ANQ* 14[2001] 44–6) posits an allusion to *A Midsummer Night's Dream*'s Puck in Vladimir Nabokov's earliest published story, 'The Wood Sprite'.

Wynne-Davies, ed., *Much Ado About Nothing* and *The Taming of the Shrew*, in the New Casebooks series, brings together five previously published articles on each play. Wynne-Davies's introduction discusses the manner in which the featured articles, predominantly written from feminist and historicist perspectives, reflect the transformation in critical approaches to, and appreciation of, the plays over the past two decades. New critical work on these two plays was limited this year to a couple of articles and a note. In the light of the 'creative imitation' (p. 188) of the character in the play's sequel, and the resonances of epic tradition which both plays exhibit, Margaret Maurer's 'Constering Bianca: *The Taming of the Shrew* and *The Woman's Prize, or The Tamer Tamed*' (*MRDE* 14[2001] 186–206) argues that we should reconsider traditional views of Shakespeare's Bianca that place her in simple opposition to her sister. Maurer claims that, consistent with both the epic allusions and sequel, but obscured beneath a mass of now unquestioned emendations, the First Folio text of the play presents an ambivalent, witty and saucy Bianca. 'Controlling Clothes, Manipulating Mates: Petruchio's Griselda' (*ShakS* 29[2001] 93–108) sees Margaret Rose Jaster turn to the Griselda story to analyse Petruchio's control of Katherina's apparel in the tailor scene (IV.iii). Jaster explores the relation between identity and apparel, arguing that Petruchio's choice of his wife's clothing is an emblem of his control over Katherina's identity and will, as well as embodying his estate to the world. In 'Shakespeare's *Much Ado About Nothing* 5.4.109–118' (*Expl* 59[2001] 115–17), Katherine Jacobs discusses why it might be that Claudio predicts that Benedick will be unfaithful to Beatrice within the context of the play's homosocial exchanges.

Finally, in 'Shakespeare's *The Two Gentlemen of Verona*' (*Expl* 59[2001] 68–71) David Thatcher reflects upon Proteus's allusion: 'For Orpheus' lute string was strung with poets' sinews' (III.ii.77). Considering a number of glosses and sources, he concludes that this is an expression of the mutually enhancing relation between verse and music.

(c) Problem Plays

In 'Spurio and the Date for *All's Well that Ends Well*' (*N&Q* 48[2001] 298–9), MacDonald P. Jackson makes a case for a later date for the play of early 1606. Jackson's claim is based on his use of the Chadwyck-Healey database to research Parolles's reference to 'One Captaine Spurio' (II.i.41). The name Spurio only occurs in one other play contemporaneous with *All's Well*, which is *The Revenger's Tragedy*, first performed in 1606, and Jackson, an editor of the forthcoming Oxford edition of Middleton's collected works, has concluded that Shakespeare borrowed the name from Middleton. Jackson's argument rests on the assertion that 'If one dramatist was influenced by another's introduction of the name Spurio to the English stage Shakespeare must surely have been the debtor' (p. 299). The argument concludes that since *The Revenger's Tragedy* was performed early in 1606 *All's Well* cannot have been written earlier than this. Jackson's article is pertinent in that it not only highlights the use of electronic databases as one of the current trends in academic research, but also underlines both the pitfalls and the benefits of their use. The evidence that Shakespeare was necessarily influenced by Middleton's use of the name is suggestive, but cannot stand on its own as a convincing argument for dating the play as late as 1606.

The only other piece on *All's Well* was Henry D. Janowitz's 'Helena's Medicine in *All's Well That Ends Well*: Paracelsian or Hermetical in Origin?' (*CaudaP* 20[2001] 20–2), which argues that Helena is in fact a hermetical healer, with Shakespeare drawing on influential texts by Cornelius Agrippa and the figure of John Dee. While providing some useful insights into the origins of the hermetic tradition, the scope of the article would have been better suited and more fully developed within the format of a book. As it is, the argument fails to really persuade the reader that there were specifically hermetic influences at work within the play.

The year 2001 yielded only a handful of individual publications on *Measure for Measure*. In 'Nashe and a Crux in *Measure for Measure*' (*N&Q* 48[2001] 262–4), J.J.M. Tobin outlines Shakespeare's borrowings from Nashe's *Christ's Tears Over Jerusalem*. Tobin's suggestion sheds light on Escalus's lines in Act II, scene i, 'Some rise by sin, and some by virtue fall, | Some run from brakes of ice and answer none, | And some condemned for a fault alone' (II.i.38–40), which have been subject to various readings concerning injustice and the punishment of crime. Tobin argues that these lines can be read against Nashe's account of a trick in *Christ's Tears*, employed by usurers to secure their social advancement, whilst avoiding condemnation for their practices. Tobin suggests that 'Escalus's statement of the unjust nature of human success looks as if it is an abbreviated reference to the specific trick Nashe describes' (p. 263).

John Jowett's 'The Audacity of *Measure for Measure* in 1621' (*BJJ* 8[2001] 229–47) develops the claims put forward by Jowett and Taylor in *Shakespeare Reshaped 1603–1623*, in which they argued that *Measure* had been adapted in 1621 by Middleton for a revival that year. Jowett presents a persuasive localized reading of I.ii to argue that Licio's discussion of the king of Hungary is Middleton's addition and refers to events of 1621. The article locates the play within the context of the print industry and the interest in foreign affairs to describe how the play, like news pamphlets, was in fact in breach of a recent proclamation issued to restrict freedom of speech on foreign matters. Jowett argues that '*Measure* does not simply allude to events in the news; it thematizes the public reception of foreign news, staging its transmission as urbane but licentious conversation' (p. 245).

Finally for *Measure for Measure* was George L. Geckle's *Measure for Measure* in the Shakespeare: The Critical Tradition series. The volume contains a range of material on the play from the period 1780–1920, and is meticulously catalogued, with each extract accompanied by brief notes on its critical history and a biography of its author. The volume enables the reader to utilize the entries through several introductory essays by Geckle and the series editor Brian Vickers, who usefully locates and discusses each entry in relation to key developments in critical attitudes towards the play. The volume also provides exemplary notes, bibliography and index system, and will no doubt be invaluable to future editors and mined by academics as a source of teaching material.

Troilus and Cressida continues this year to be the problem play that stimulated the most critical interest. In 'Ethics and Anxiety in Shakespeare's *Troilus and Cressida*' (*C&L* 50[2001] 225–45) Michael G. Bielmeier presents an existentialist reading of the play focusing on the work of the Danish theologian Søren Kierkegaard to offer insights into the character development of the lovers and the play's world-view. In his note 'The Title Page of Troilus Q1b: A New Reading' (*ANQ* 14[2001] 10–11) Jeffrey Kahan counters Kenneth Muir's assertion that the text of Q1b's title page misleads the reader by placing undue emphasis on Pandar's role as go-between for the lovers. Kahan argues that the text in fact refers to Pandar's relationship with each of the lovers, as he himself is wooed by each of them in order to prolong their own courtship. The title page's focus upon wooing, Kahan concludes, draws attention to its pivotal role in both the play and the subplot as Cressida feigns disinterest in Troilus's suit to secure his attention, mirroring the way in which the Greeks, keen to win over Achilles, do so similarly by feigning disinterest.

In contrast, the focus of Ronald St Pierre's article 'The Forked One: *Troilus and Cressida*' (*ShLR* 34[2001] 1–14) is the theme of cuckoldry. A close reading of Troilus's discussion with Helen in I.i, of the forked hair on his chin, is used to examine the roles of cuckold and cuckold-maker in the triangular relationships between Menelaus, Paris and Helen and Troilus, Diomed and Cressida. However the article, like its title, fails to indicate the overall aim of the detail it provides, concluding with general comparisons of *Troilus* with *All's Well*.

Daniel Juan Gil's 'At the Limits of the Social World: Fear and Pride in *Troilus and Cressida*' (*SQ* 52[2001] 336–59) offers an extremely erudite discussion of social and sexual relationships in the play in which Gil reassesses the model of homosociality in the light of modern theories of sexuality and emerging early modern theories on the formation of social relations. Another publication of note for *Troilus* this year was James P. Bednarz's *Shakespeare and the Poets' War* in which he re-evaluates the so-called rivalry between Jonson and Shakespeare during the War of the Theatres. In the opening chapter, 'Shakespeare's Purge of Jonson: The Theatrical Context of *Troilus and Cressida*' Bednarz, through the distillation of earlier critical works, makes the claim that Shakespeare's Ajax is in fact a portrait of Jonson and is the Bard's attempt to 'purge' his rival. Bednarz's argument has attracted a range of critical responses, and no doubt the evidence concerning Shakespeare's role in the War of the Theatres will continue to generate academic dialogue. Finally, an article I have been unable to obtain is William Searle's '"By foule authority": Miscorrections in the Folio Text of Shakespeare's *Troilus and Cressida*' (*PBSA* 95[2001] 503–19).

(d) Poetry

In 'Shakespeare's Poems' (in De Grazia and Wells, eds., *The Cambridge Companion to Shakespeare*, pp. 65–81), John Kerrigan gives a lively overview, underlining that for contemporary audiences Shakespeare 'seems to have been almost as well known for his narrative and lyrical poems' as for his dramatic works. Interestingly, Kerrigan pauses to review the difficulties of establishing the Shakespeare poetic canon, especially when considering the attribution of a very short texts, and clearly remains unconvinced about the Shakespearian attribution of 'The Funeral Elegy in Memory of the Late Virtuous Master William Peter'. His accounts of the narrative poems are of an introductory nature in keeping with the overall expectations of the volume. Discussion of the sonnets concentrates principally upon the organization of the collection, themes and critical responses. On the whole, this chapter presents a clear and concise introduction to the subject in hand.

Declaring her work on the sonnet sequence complete in 'Shakespeare's Other Sonnets' (in Moisan and Bruster, eds., *In the Company of Shakespeare: Essays on English Renaissance Literature in Honor of G. Blakemore Evans*, pp. 161–76), Helen Vendler turns her attention to the sonnets embedded within the dramatic works which, she believes, suggest 'that not all sonnets by Shakespeare were thought by him to belong to his sequence (if it were he, as seems probable, who assembled the sequence)'. These 'extrasequential experiments' are probed by Vendler for the insights they may shed upon the more famous collection. The consequent journeys to *Love's Labours Lost* (various) *Troilus and Cressida* (I.ii.289–302), *All's Well That Ends Well* (I.i.217–30) and 'the perfect pas de deux' sonnet in *Romeo and Juliet* (I.v.95–112) certainly open up an interesting vista for future study. The subsequent essay in this volume, Jonathan Hart's 'Conflicting Monuments: Time, Beyond Time, and the Poetics of Shakespeare's Dramatic and Nondramatic Sonnets' (pp. 177–205), also, as its title suggests, takes an interest in sonnets in the dramatic works. However, here the discussion of textual monuments against time and time as a rival poet pursues a familiar path and is largely summative in nature. Patrick Cheney's '"O, let my books be ... dumb presagers": Poetry and Theater in Shakespeare's Sonnets' (*SQ* 52[2001] 222–54) focuses on the extraordinariness of Shakespeare among his fellow writers in being both a prolific playwright and the composer of a sonnet collection. Rather than divorcing the two aspects of his career, Cheney insists that they form an organic whole and analyses the theatrical metaphors in the sonnets: 'Shakespeare does not use his poetry to erase his role in the theater but rather makes his shameful theatrical profession a part of his self-presentation.'

In *Hearing the Measures: Shakespeare and Other Inflections*, George T. Wright devotes a chapter to 'The Silent Speech of Shakespeare's Sonnets', proposing that it may be more 'accurate' to see the collection as 'the language of silent thought, unvoiced, unsounded, unperformed, the words of a consciousness' contrasting them with the 'sounded and public' thoughtful speech in his drama. In 'Pretended Speech Acts in Shakespeare's Sonnets' (*EIC* 51[2001] 283–307), Peter Robinson concentrates initially upon the significance of the relations between 'the fictional and the real' and how these must affect the reader's engagement with Shakespeare's collection: 'we can't help asking who is saying the lines, who are they being said to, when is it happening, and what are the dramatic consequences of these speeches'. Robinson pays welcome attention to John R. Searle's *Speech Acts* [1969] for definition of terms of reference, but spends most of the essay highlighting Vendler's unhelpful usage of the term rather than prosecuting his own case. Despite having acknowledged the insightfulness of Vendler's volume (reviewed in *YWES* 76[1997]), Robinson argues that it returns to an 'older formalism' and pays too little attention to 'cultural knowledge and circumstantial realities'. In *Reading Shakespeare's Will: The Theology of the Figure from Augustine to the Sonnets*, Emily Freinkel ponders the theological and textual commitments of Augustine, Petrarch and Luther before concentrating a chapter each on the sonnets and on *The Merchant of Venice*. With regard to the sonnets, Freinkel launches her argument with Luther's contention that the human spirit can neither be reconciled to nor divorced from the body. From this premise of interminable struggle, Freinkel proceeds to identify a Lutheran universe at work in Shakespeare's collection (she underlines that this does not require Shakespeare to have read the works of the Reformist). Freinkel is illuminating throughout her discussion in her exposure of critical appetites which still desire details of the collection's paternity: 'Even after the Death of the Author, we cannot seem to let daddy go.' In addition, this discussion is particularly persuasive in its emphasis that critics may need documentary lacunae as well as historical records in order to flesh out the writer they seek. Subsequently much care and attention is devoted to summarizing recent, theorized criticism of the sonnets (most especially that of Fineman), but rather too often Freinkel's voice appears to be squeezed out in the process. In general, Freinkel is attracted to the indeterminacy of meaning in the sonnets ('For all we can tell, both canker and rose smell equally sweet—and equally sour, for that matter, for both, in their life, yield no essence at all. And yet, the difference between the two flowers— is, precisely, *essential*'), and pursues this theme in details of textual transmission and in analyses of the poems themselves. As well as being Lutheran, it seems that the universe of the sonnets may be Lacanian ('a world continually telling loss: a world of repetition without sameness, reproduction without succession'), though rather too often Freinkel's delving into the collection's aporia may emerge for the reader as her 'fatal Cleopatra'.

In Brown and Johnson, *Shakespeare 1609: Cymbeline and the Sonnets*, Richard Danson Brown offers a critical study of the evolution of the sonnet form, an overview of succeeding critical interpretations of the collection, and finally a consideration of the representation of desire in Shakespeare's collection. This study is intended to be introductory, and generally maps out a more familiar narrative of critical responses adopted across the centuries than is the case in David Johnson's preceding appreciation of *Cymbeline*, which draws together material from diverse areas which is much less readily available in one volume for the late play. Brown concludes his section with some brief analyses of individual sonnets. The volume is particularly helpful in compiling a varied collection of source and critical material to assist undergraduate study of these texts.

In 'Vocabulary and Chronology: The Case of Shakespeare's Sonnets' (*RES* 52[2001] 59–75), MacDonald P. Jackson focuses upon the statistical analysis of rare words in the Shakespeare canon in order to facilitate the dating of the sonnets. Jackson turns to Gregor Sarrazin's work in lexical organization at the end of the nineteenth century and to Hieatt, Hieatt and Prescott's more recent lexical study of the collection. In the final stages of the discussion, Jackson insists that we 'must beware, however, of exaggerating the efficacy of the vocabulary evidence adduced so far' and concedes that 'the vocabulary evidence put forward in this article supports and clarifies some of the Hieatt–Prescott findings and muddies others'. In general, Jackson argues that the bulk of the writing for the sonnets would seem to be concentrated in the pre-seventeenth-century period; however, Shakespeare may have been revising and reordering the collection as late as 1603–4. Ulrich Busse's 'The Use of Address Pronouns in Shakespeare's Plays and Sonnets' (in Andersen, ed., *Actualization: Linguistic Change in Progress*, pp. 119–42) reconsiders the usage of alternatives such as *thou/you*, *you/ye*, *-th/-s*, *will/shall*, *which/the which*, use or non-use of *do* and so on, and revisits statistical analyses of Shakespearian writing from earlier studies. Busse underlines that the end of the sixteenth century was a period of sociolinguistic change, and apart from pointing up the predominance of 'thou' forms in Shakespeare's poetry as opposed to the higher incidence of 'ye' forms in the drama, he also stresses that, in the 'Dark Lady' sonnets, for example, the lady is never addressed as 'you' and that, in comparison with seventeen other contemporary sonnet collections, Shakespeare is 'much more careful to avoid pronominal inconsistency in one poem'.

In *Sexual Shakespeare: Forgery, Authorship, Portraiture*, Michael Keevak devotes his first chapter to 'Queer Sonnets and the Forgeries of William Henry Ireland'. Keevak's interest in biographical mythologies and fictional identities attributed to Shakespeare since the beginning of the seventeenth century leads him initially to consider documents and poetic works forged by Ireland at the end of the eighteenth century to draw attention to himself as 'a new young bard'. With reference to the sonnets, Keevak concentrates on a forged letter penned by a rather unlikely correspondent: 'Wee didde receive youre prettye Verses goode Masterre William through the hands off oure Lorde Chamberlayne, and wee doe Complemente thee onne theyre greate excellence. ... Wee shalle departe fromme Londonne toe Hamptowne forre the holydayes where wee Shalle expecte thee withe thye beste Actorres thatte thou mayste playe before oureselfe toe amuse usse bee notte slowwe butte comme toe usse bye Tuesdaye nexte asse the lorde Leycesterre will bee withe usse.' Keevak is particularly persuasive in unmasking the scholarly penchant for different Shakespeares down the centuries. Like a number of recent critics, he also draws attention to the anxiety which the sexual personae deployed in the sonnets have caused to successive generations of readers. E.K. Chambers's insistence upon the heterosexuality of the Bard, for example, in his consideration of the sonnets is studied in some detail. After having given some contextual discussion of early modern discourses of sodomy, Keevak nonetheless arrives at the conclusion that 'it really makes little difference if the sonnets "really are" "gay" poems, since modern culture continues to respond to them—or apologize for them—as if they were'. In *Writing Prejudices: The Psychoanalysis and Pedagogy of Discrimination from Shakespeare to Toni Morrison*, Robert Samuels also devotes a chapter of his study to 'The Cycle of Prejudice in Shakespeare's Miscegenating Sonnets'. He raises the interesting point that 'critics have often assumed that if one reveals the presence of prejudice in cultural texts, one has contributed to the fight for social justice and the undermining of different forms of social oppression. I will argue that this assumption is misguided.' Pursuing this premise, Samuels reflects initially upon the interpellation of various reader personae generally in textual engagements and insists that 'cultural critics need to attach the discovery of prejudices in texts to the prejudices that dominate our own culture and subjectivity'. However, it rapidly becomes apparent that Samuels is much more interested in engaging with issues of ethnocentrism and homosociality than with historicizing any discussion of the sonnets. He mostly refers to the sonnets in very general terms, and thus produces a rather uniform narrative of the triangulation of desire and sexual/racial Othering between three clearly delineated 'characters'. In privileging his account of contemporary cultural and critical theory, Samuels forces Shakespeare's collection to shed many of its nuances, ambiguities and resistances to narrativization.

In 'The Compositor's Reader: Shakespeare's Sonnet 146 Revisited' (*N&Q* 48[2001] 275–6), John M. Rollett returns to query in the opening two lines of sonnet 146 (see YWES 78[1999]) and finds another fault in the same quarto page for Sonnet 144 ('sight' instead of 'side'): he concludes that these errors stand as 'a monument to a bad day in the printing house'. Tom D'Evelyn's article 'The More in the Less: Notes on Shakespeare's Sonnet 116' (*Providence* 6:ii[2001] 42–9) engages predominantly with John Kerrigan's criticism of the poem in his edition of the collection, but also refers to other accounts offered elsewhere by Vendler and Booth, for example. Much of the discussion is summative in nature. However, instead of adhering to Kerrigan's reading of the impossibility of desire's fulfilment in this sonnet, D'Evelyn prefers to place a 'rhetorical self' at the heart of the poem which is participating in a developing analysis of the nature of desire itself. Kenji Go's 'Unemending the Emendation of "still" in Shakespeare's Sonnet 106' (*SP* 98[2001] 114–42) concentrates on line 12 of the chosen sonnet and shows how successive recent editions have accepted the conjectured reading of 'skill' for 'still'. However, Go argues that 'still enough' in this line should be read as an ellipsis of 'still enough praises'. Stephen Orgel's edition of the sonnets was not available for review at the time of publication.

Ralph Berry turns his attentions to *Venus and Adonis*, amongst other texts, in *Shakespeare and the Hunt*, exploring the cultural paradox of the female hunter for early modern culture, hunting rites of initiation relating to the poem, and the symbolism of hunting associated with both protagonists and the boar in Shakespeare's narrative poem. Berry feeds his debate by drawing upon a wide range of early modern contexts for understanding Shakespeare's representation of hunting. His study casts a refreshing new light on the narrative poem and on a number of the dramatic works such as *Julius Caesar*, *Merry Wives of Windsor* and *As You Like It*. In '"crimson liveries" and "their verdour": *Venus and Adonis*, 505–8' (*N&Q* 48[2001] 274–5), Anthony Mortimer returns to Shakespeare's narrative poem and most especially to its colour symbolism to tease out the wordplay involving the movement from 'crimson' to 'verdour' in the chosen lines: Mortimer chooses to link the 'crimson' here with *cramoisi*, a material dyed in 'any intense colour'. In 'A Bloody Question: The Politics of *Venus and Adonis*' (*Religion and the Arts* 5[2001] 297–316), Richard Wilson presents a revised version of his discussion reviewed in YWES 78[1999]. He again places the narrative poem in a context of Catholic cultural expectations and most particularly refers to the proposed disappointment of Southwell at Shakespeare's misuse of his talents in this poem. Wilson gives great emphasis to the contention that 'the Dedication "To the Right Honourable Henry Wriothesley" ... places the poem firmly at the heart of recusant England' and the belief that 'from its opening lines, the politics of *Venus and Adonis* are expressed in the oppositional terms of recusant culture that promoted the poet from the heartland of the Old Religion, in Warwickshire, to feudal Lancashire, and then to the clan around the Earl of Southampton, in the other bulwark of Catholic resistance'. In 'Shakespeare and Religion' (*TPr* 15:i[2001] 1–4), Dympna Callaghan fears that the critical preoccupation with the possible Catholicism of Shakespeare the poet (and playwright) may be seeking to occlude the theoretical debates which have unfolded over recent decades and hark back to a strain of antiquarianism and/or old historicism. Callaghan urges that these questions of religious affiliation should be firmly linked by early modern scholars to current critical debates concerning Otherness and religious and sexual identities: thus we should consider 'How does the production of otherness operate in a culture where others are essentially invisible (unmarked, hidden) and alarmingly proximate? (Your neighbour/brother/ friend might be a Catholic?)'.

Margo Hendricks's '"A word, sweet Lucrece": Confession, Feminism and *The Rape of Lucrece*' (in Callaghan, ed., *A Feminist Companion to Shakespeare*, pp. 103–18) reviews in its initial stages some significant approaches to the poem adopted by feminist critics. Hendricks then goes on to focus upon Christian discourses of confession in the early modern period and finally considers the importance of early modern ideologies of race (in terms of lineage) in Shakespeare's poem. The discussion is wide-ranging, looking at the doctrine of Augustine and turning to Althusser's theory of interpellation and Foucault's political emphasis on the importance of confession. Despite the brevity of the discussion, the linking of theological debate with textual analysis is lively and persuasive; the discussion of racial identities, however, unfolds along more familiar terms.

In 'Ravished and Revised: The 1616 *Lucrece*' (*RES* 52[2001] 516–24), Katherine Duncan-Jones outlines the faint praise and anxieties that have surrounded Shakespeare's poem in recent criticism, claiming it to be the 'only joke-free zone in the entire corpus of Shakespeare's works'. The discrepancy in popularity between *Venus and Adonis* (at least ten reprintings before 1617) and *Lucrece* (only six up to 1616) in the early modern period is also stressed. Duncan-Jones speculates that, when Roger Jackson purchased publication rights (including those relating to Shakespeare's poem) in 1614, he may have wished to exploit the popularity of Heywood's 1608 drama (*The Rape of Lucrece: A True Roman Tragedie*) with a republication of Shakespeare's poem in more 'saleable' format: numbering of sections prefaced with short summaries and italicization of some nouns and proper nouns. In 'Tarquin Dispossessed: Expropriation and Consent in *The Rape of Lucrece*' (*SQ* 52[2001] 315–35), Catherine Belsey worries away at the question of 'possession' (in terms of ownership, appropriation and mental disturbance) in Shakespeare's poem. She reviews prominent feminist analyses of the poem, invites her reader to consider Tarquin briefly as a version of Lacan's 'doomed, desiring subject, in command of everything but its own desire (and thus, paradoxically, in true control of nothing whatever)' and then more centrally turns her attentions to the status of Lucrece in Augustinian appreciations of the narrative outlined by Roman historians and the status of a victim such as Lucrece under early modern law.

In 'The Phoenix and Turtle in its Time' (in Moisan and Bruster, eds., pp. 206–30), John Klause turns refreshingly to take a detailed look at the *Love's Martyr* collection in order to map out the textual environment of Shakespeare's poem. Shakespeare is compared and contrasted with other contributors to the volume such as Jonson, Chapman, Marston, and one Ignoto, and Klause makes the telling point that, unlike the other contributors, 'Shakespeare makes clear that his birds are "dead" and have left "no posterity"'. Unlike some recent scholars working on the poem, Klause inscribes the poems firmly within the narrative of the lives of Sir John and Ursula

Salusbury (Sir John Salusbury of Llewenni was the dedicatee of the volume), linking the volume to the celebration of his knighthood in 1601. Klause makes a case for the influence of Chaucer's *Parliament of Fowles* and/or Skelton's *Phyllyp Sparowe* upon Shakespeare's poem. However, the latter half of the article turns upon the familiar topic of Shakespeare's poem's affinities with Catholic ritual and doctrine and the fact that Salusbury's elder brother had been involved in the Babington plot. The discussion concludes with an emphasis upon the inability of Shakespeare to refuse a request to contribute to the volume given the fact that his own credentials were in question in the aftermath of Essex rebellion: Salusbury's star was rising and Elizabeth would not have knighted him personally in 1601 'had he not persuaded her of his hostility to Essex, executed after his failed uprising five months later'. In 'Set Upon a Golden Bough to Sing: Shakespeare's Debt to Sidney' (*TLS* 16 Feb.[2001] 13–15), Barbara Everett celebrates *The Phoenix and the Turtle* as 'brilliant and beautiful', but acknowledges that 'its extravagant rhetorics and unusual formality bring about a real opacity'. Unconvinced by Salusbury, Catholic or Lancastrian links for the poem ('historical contexts give no purchase on the poem') or by broader philosophical analysis of the poem's abstractions ('Any extractable belief is too commonplace'), Everett concentrates upon prosody, and links Shakespeare's poem to the eighth song in Sidney's *Astrophil and Stella*. In 'A Phoenix for Palm Sunday: Was Shakespeare's Poem a Requiem for Catholic Martyrs?' (*TLS* 13 Apr.[2001] 14–15), Clare Asquith crosses swords with Everett and pursues material published in the previous year and reviewed in *YWES* 79[2000]. Asquith links the distinctive metre of Shakespeare's poem once again with the trochaic metre of Thomas Aquinas's 'Lauda Sion', a text which was being set to music by Byrd and translated by Southwell apparently in the same period in which Shakespeare is imagined composing this tricky lyric. Southwell and his fellow Jesuit, poet, and martyr Henry Walpole are brought into the frame as the chaste couple imagined in Shakespeare's text, and Asquith concludes that this poem not only stands as evidence of Shakespeare's religious persuasions but was written, she believes, 'to be recited at a secret Palm Sunday requiem over the ashes of the two martyrs'.

(e) Histories

Benjamin Griffin's *Playing the Past: Approaches to English Historical Drama, 1385–1600* is a book not to be missed by anyone with an interest in the history play, though (or perhaps, because) its treatment of Shakespeare is relatively sparse. Griffin revisits questions of generic boundaries, the question of 'formlessness', the 'master narratives' of Ribner and Helgerson, the origins of the genre in saints' plays, and its decline in the Jacobean period. His chapter on 1590s histories situates Shakespearian plays within a revitalized sense of these and other issues, suggestively indicating where Shakespeare (and, he is careful to add, Marlowe) differs from historical drama up to that point. This is wide-ranging, lucid and scholarly work, and should be read by everyone who has ever been impressed by the Shakespeare-centred generalizations of Tennenhouse or Rackin on what could or couldn't be done with historical drama in the period.

Shakespeare's histories have attracted the attention of quite a few non-specialists of late. This year's contribution is Tim Spiekerman's *Shakespeare's Political Realism: The English History Plays*. Spiekerman's thesis is that 'Shakespeare is an author from whom we can learn something significant about politics' (p. 4). Unfortunately for his potential readership within English studies, he hasn't read much recent criticism on the histories, and dislikes what he has read ('for the new historicists, a literary text is a historical document, a reliable reflection of the social and political views that dominated at the time', p. 10). The text thus feels like it comes from a parallel universe, one in which one can still find 'respectable critics' (p. 64), and where knowledge of 'the large body of critical opinion about Shakespeare's treatment of divine right in *Richard II*' (p. 72) is to be found in the New Variorum edition dated towards the end of *the century before last*. Unlike the recent work of Theodore Meron or Ian Ward reviewed in these pages, Spiekerman's book brings little from his own discipline: Irving Ribner is preferred to Quentin Skinner as a guide to early modern political thought, for example. A book of stunning pointlessness for anyone who has bothered to read post-1975 criticism at all, and of banal statement of the obvious for anyone who has bothered to read pre-1975 criticism carefully.

Prince Hal and King Henry continued to engage. R.V. Young, in another piece at some distance from contemporary critical concerns, revisits the question of Hal's/Henry's Machiavellianism in 'Shakespeare's History Plays and the Erasmian Catholic Prince' (*BJJ* 7[2000] 89–114), offering 'a "no" and a qualified "yes"' to the question of whether Henry V lives up to Erasmian ideals. The piece concludes that 'the nagging questions about the triumphant King's character and methods are evidence of the residual influence of Catholic humanism in the national consciousness' (p. 111). Rebecca Ann Bach, in 'Tennis Balls: *Henry V* and Testicular Masculinity, or, According to the *OED*, Shakespeare Doesn't Have Any Balls' (*RenD* 30[1999–2000] 3–23), begins from the 'coyness' of the *OED* regarding the Shakespearian usage of 'balls' before going on to defend Gary Taylor's 1982 discussion of the testicular punning in the second scene of *Henry V*. Arguing that the pun is a 'key lexical moment in a play that repeatedly shows its audience an embodied English masculinity' (p. 5), Bach argues that the play here produces the castration of the French to cope with the gendered weakness of an English claim through the female line. Pistol likewise serves to show the distance between Henry's hyperbolic English masculinity and 'parody and disempowering bluster' (p. 15). The article also explores differences between early modern and contemporary masculinity, particularly the ways in which the period's, and the play's, English masculinity conjoin 'male martial power and the ability to produce potent seed' (p. 10). It is the Dauphin's 'wasteful' sexual activity which marks him as effeminate in early modern terms; in contrast, York and Suffolk's 'potent homoerotic death' is 'the picture of virility in the play' (p. 12).

Carol Banks, in 'Shakespeare's *Henry V*: Tudor or Jacobean?' (in Pincombe, ed., *The Anatomy of Tudor Literature*, pp. 174–88), begins from the contrasts between the Tudor and Jacobean texts of the play, before reading the 'Tudorness' of the earlier text's 'more considerate attitude to women' (p. 176). Banks shows how, for example, the quarto's omission of Henry's rape threats to Harfleur, and the Chorus's references to his rejection of Katherine, places the language lesson in a rather more benign context than it has in the Folio text. Without the 'Jacobean' Folio choruses, which Banks suggests can be read as a 'historicizing' tribute to Essex, the play's first scene centres round the issue of female inheritance rather than the 'masculine, military' scene set in the Folio.

Alison A. Chapman's 'Whose Saint Crispin's Day Is It? Shoemaking, Holiday Making, and the Politics of Memory in Early Modern England' (*RenQ* 54[2001] 1467–94) revisits the St Crispin's Day speech in *Henry V* through a discussion of the representation of shoemakers in the period. Chapman claims they were depicted as 'calendar-makers', able to fashion new holidays for themselves, and explores the resonances of the brothers Crispin and Crispianus, princes who worked as shoemakers. Thus in *Henry V* 'by linking Saint Crispin's Day to a rhetoric of obedience, martial solidarity, and loyalty to the king, the play counters image [*sic*] of the shoemaker who fashions subversive holidays to celebrate his own material advancement' (p. 1482). Henry's speech also appropriates the brotherhood associated with the saints, who were martyred together. Chapman reads the play alongside *The Shoemaker's Holiday*, and makes some interesting points about the two plays' divergent representations of 'gentling'.

Jennifer Low explores '"Those proud titles thou hast won": Sovereignty, Power, and Combat in Shakespeare's Second Tetralogy' (*CompD* 34[2000] 269–90), pointing out that the political tensions issuing in civil war in the first tetralogy are to be read through individual challenges and combats in its successor. Low shows the duel, in particular, to be positioned at the intersection of various kinds of power, royal, aristocratic, and divine. Lorna Hutson's 'Not the King's Two Bodies: Reading the "Body Politic" in Shakespeare's *Henry IV*, Parts 1 and 2' (in Kahn and Hutson, eds., *Rhetoric and Law in Early Modern Europe*, pp. 166–98) argues, through a rereading of Edmund Plowden, that the late Elizabethan reach of the doctrine of the monarch's two bodies has been exaggerated, and that a conception of the commonweal existed which did not depend upon the indispensability of the monarch's body. She then argues for the presence of such a civic conception of the body politic in the *Henry IV* plays, with representation of justice, as embodied both in Hal's intentions and the judiciary itself, signalling the limits of monarchical power. Hutson also points out some intriguing similarities between the world of Eastcheap and that of the anonymous pamphlet *The Discoverie of the Knights of the Poste* [1597].

Hugh Grady addresses the persistence of Falstaff in theatrical and critical memory in 'Falstaff: Subjectivity between the Carnival and the Aesthetic' (*MLR* 96[2001] 609–23). He sees the two *Henry IV* plays addressing the crisis of Machiavellianism in *Richard II* through a turn to subjectivity, with Falstaff a thought-experiment in 'imagined autonomous autotelic subjectivity' (p. 610). He embodies both playfulness-as-resistance and destructive egoism, attempting to inhabit a 'counter-factual carnival' (p. 615). Falstaff's metadramatic function is a key to understanding both his appeal to audiences and readers and this contradictory embodiment. His carnival is poised between a communal medieval world and an 'atomistic and egotistical' modernity. In that sense, Falstaff the character's appeal is to be understood as a function of his liminal historical positioning: 'two quite different conceptual contexts can be constructed for him, one, however, for which he is too late (the carnival), the other for which he is too early (the aesthetic)' (p. 621).

James Biester's 'Shaming the Fool: Jack and anti-Jack' (*ELR* 31[2001] 230–9) strengthens the thesis, advanced by Richard Helgerson and David Wiles among others, that Shakespeare rejected William Kempe as incompatible with his social and theatrical ambitions at the end of *2 Henry IV* by considering a parallel case. He shows that Thomas Deloney had a similarly antagonistic relationship with Kempe, for much the same reasons. Deloney's *Jack of Newbury* features the shaming of the fool Will Sommers, who, Biester argues, resembles Kempe; Deloney's bourgeois hero John (Jack) Winchcombe shares many characteristics with Shakespeare's Hal. Both writers banish 'festive clowning' from their texts.

The first issue of the online journal *Early Modern Culture: An Electronic Seminar* [2000] contained an article by Carol Banks and Graham Holderness on gender and history plays, along with a response from Phyllis Rackin. Banks and Holderness argue in '"Effeminate Dayes"' that at least some of the audience for 1590s histories would have brought a gendered critical perspective to them formed in the 'effeminate dayes' of the late Elizabethan regime, and that in writing women's parts dramatists catered for an expanded sense of historical action. The scene at Mortimer's court in *1 Henry IV*, for example, 'counteracts the grotesque impression of women in the official record of events, an "effeminate" implant within the historical drama'. Rackin responds that there are very definite limits to the scope of such implants: 'The female characters can be either womanly or warlike. They can be either virtuous or powerful. But never both.' *Edward III*, by contrast, presents a pregnant warrior queen of England. Stefani Brusberg-Kiermeier, in 'The Role of Body Images in the Tudor Myth and its Subversion in Shakespeare's History Plays' (in Pincombe, ed., pp. 189–94) revisits Tillyard's Tudor Myth via a brief consideration of some aspects of the staging of *Richard III*, *Henry VIII* and *Henry V*.

Thomas Pendleton, ed., *Henry VI: Critical Essays*, supplies fourteen mostly short essays on the plays, plus an introduction. Pieces on TV versions, theme and design in recent productions, illustration, and an interview with an actor from a 1996 New York production lie outside the remit of this section. Steven Urkowitz, in 'Texts with Two Faces: Noticing Theatrical Revisions in *Henry VI, Parts 2* and *3*', considers how Folio and quarto texts provide distinct and theatrically viable patterns of language and gesture before critiquing the memorial reconstruction thesis informing editions of the plays pre-Arden 3. J.J.M. Tobin argues, in 'A Touch of Greene, Much Nashe, and All Shakespeare', that the Nashean elements in *1 Henry VI* show his influence on Shakespeare rather than his hand in the play, before going on to consider similar influences in *Julius Caesar*, *Macbeth* and other texts. Harry Keyishan's 'The Progress of Revenge in the First Henriad' discusses the ways in which the psychology of revenge drives the action. Naomi C. Liebler and Lisa Scancella Shea focus on a single character in 'Shakespeare's Queen Margaret: Unruly or Unruled?', arguing that Margaret's 'amazing endurance despite the pervasive corruption, duplicity, and political intrigue of which she is sometimes the agent and at other times the intended victim' has been underrated by critics. They point out how Margaret's differing roles in the plays are set off by other female characters acting as foil—Joan the maid, Eleanor Cobham the ambitious wife, Lady Grey the mother of the heir, and the Duchess of York, the 'cursing crone'. Yoshio Arai provides a brief history of '*Henry VI* in Japan'.

Nina da Vinci Nichols, in 'The Paper Trail to the Throne', traces the plays' use of paper and writing, examining the emblematic significance of key props, and of related issues of signification more widely considered. The piece also includes a consideration of the Corpus Christi elements within *3 Henry VI*. Frances K. Barasch reads Joan's and the Duchess's witchcraft scenes in 'Folk Magic in *Henry VI*, Parts 1 and 2', presenting them as microcosms of the whole in their themes of 'dangerous women, English heroics, and political treacheries'. James J. Paxson's

'Shakespeare's Medieval Devils and Joan La Pucelle in *1 Henry VI*' begins with the presence of devils onstage with Joan, pointing out that 'to imagine a devil in the fifteenth or sixteenth centuries meant to envisage a thing with a face on its crotch as readily as it meant envisioning a devil's horns, scales, and saucerlike eyes' (p. 128) before using the gendered iconography of the demonic to supplement, and challenge, recent feminist approaches to Joan. This is a fascinating essay, breaking new ground in a much worked over and important area.

Maurice Hunt's 'Climbing for Place in Shakespeare's *2 Henry VI*' considers the motif of social climbing, concluding that the pervasiveness of the theme 'reflects its author's generally conservative political assumptions' (p. 173). M. Rick Smith writes on 'sources' in '*2 Henry VI*: Commodifying and Recommodifying the Past in Late-Medieval and Early-Modern England'. Smith situates the theatre as 'recommodifying' a past already 'commodified' between 1450 and 1550, drawing parallels between early modern and postmodern cultural production, particularly in the use of pastiche. He then reads Duke Humphrey and the Cade rising, positing an audience experience akin to Jameson's postmodern 'virtual delirium' as already commodified narratives are commodified once more as theatre.

Another perspective on the plays is supplied in Gregory M. Colon Semenza's 'Sport, War and Contest in Shakespeare's *Henry VI*' (*RenQ* 54[2001] 1251–72). Sport's early modern figuration was contradictory: as a preparation for war (archery, riding, wrestling), or as effete leisure (hawking, bowls). During the sixteenth century, as a consequence of the development of gunpowder, the latter became more dominant; sport was less easy to read as utilitarian. War itself came to be seen as less heroic, and the essay proposes that war and sport are collapsed in the *Henry VI* plays, for example via hunting or trapping imagery. It concludes by suggesting that these uses of language serve to devalue the ideological grounds for conflict, serving 'to expose the military and political conflicts as little more than empty contests between noblemen' (p. 1270). Lisa Dickson writes on 'the political, historical and epistemological implications of a visible economy without a defining centre' (p. 144) in 'No Rainbow Without the Sun: Visibility and Embodiment in *1 Henry VI*' (*MLS* 30[2000] 137–56). *1 Henry VI*'s world, in which the monarch speaks only 6 per cent of the lines and does not appear at all until the third act, is 'a world evacuated of its panoptic vantage'. The various indeterminacies and contradictions of the play are thoroughly explored within a psychoanalytic framework.

James P. Saegar's 'Illegitimate Subjects: Performing Bastardy in *King John*' (*JEGP* 100[2001] 1–21) argues that, although the play is concerned like Shakespeare's other histories with the relationship between personal identity and political legitimacy, it splits its focus between John's political legitimacy and the Bastard's personal legitimacy. The latter's self is based upon action, performance, and presence, and thus requires constant re-enactment. Saegar reads the contradictions in the Bastard's 'character' as indicating a contemporary collision between emergent and other conceptions of identity. John Klause, in 'New Sources for Shakespeare's *King John*: The Writings of Robert Southwell' (*SP* 98[2001] 401–27), challenges the widely held view that Shakespeare's *John* play avoids the 'special pleading' of other sixteenth-century representations of John while attending only to Protestant sources. He claims Southwell's influence on language, images and arguments within the play, though he stops short of using these parallels to read the play towards a 'Catholic Shakespeare'. The essay would have been more persuasive if it had sought to show that such parallels as it adduces between the two writers (some of which strike this writer as tenuous) could not be produced from any other texts.

Emrys Jones, in 'Reclaiming Early Shakespeare' (*EIC* 51[2001] 35–50), reviews the twentieth century's academic and theatrical rediscovery of *Titus*, *King John* and the *Henry VI* plays before using examples of the 'bone structure' of *1 Henry VI* to argue that it is 'more "Shakespearian" than often supposed' (p. 42). The examples given include the pattern of defeat-victory-defeat in *Antony and Cleopatra*, which Jones assumes is recalling *1 Henry VI*, the 'preoccupation with fame' and use of death scenes in both plays, and the parallels between the time-scheme of the play and *The Winter's Tale*. Though elegantly written, this piece is curiously detached from current critical debate, and ends with a rather old-fashioned appreciation of the 'complex, sophisticated, and achieved' nature of *1 Henry VI*.

(f) Tragedies

Many scholars have written on some aspect of Shakespeare's tragedies in the year 2001. The following tries to give an overview of publications within the field. Volumes dealing with more than one tragedy have been placed before studies focusing on one specific play. Early tragedies will be discussed before the later ones. Obviously, some tragedies, not least *Hamlet* but also *Othello*, have received more attention than others. The approaches represented are multifarious, reflecting a broad field including feminism, psychoanalysis, new historicism and cultural materialism, as well as critical directions partly opposed to them. Furthermore, a greater emphasis on 'global' Shakespeare has been noted. As Ruth Morse points out (*TLS* 20 Apr.[2001]), the field of Shakespeare scholarship is 'fissiparous', making it virtually impossible to deal with more than a fraction of it. Still, different approaches and directions in the scholarship commented on below will hopefully help in whetting the reader's appetite for the further study of Shakespearian tragedy.

De Grazia and Wells, eds., *The Cambridge Companion to Shakespeare*, is the fourth Shakespeare companion published by CUP, the first having appeared in 1934, the second in 1971, and the third in 1986. The present volume is made up of entirely new essays. It attempts to reflect changes in emphasis in Shakespeare studies. Thus the present volume is influenced by new historicism and cultural materialism, while the mainly formalist approach of former companions has been left behind. For example, an interest in textual studies, questions of gender and sexuality, in other cultures, and in Shakespearian performance on stage and film are reflected in the book. The editors' aim is 'to offer readers an expansive historical, cultural, and global context which will enhance the enduring but ever-changing value and force of Shakespeare's works'. Therefore context comes first, and discussions of plays (and poems) are secondary concerns.

However, within the larger area of context, the volume contains many excellent essays by some of the most established academics in the field, including Anne Barton, Ernst Honigmann, Peter Holland, and Lois Potter. We find no in-depth study of any of the plays, but the reader wanting to increase his knowledge within the general field of Shakespeare studies will find several pertinent references to the tragedies. For example, Susan Snyder's chapter on 'The genres of Shakespeare's plays' (pp. 83–97) makes some brief but striking observations on changing concerns in Shakespeare from the early tragedies to the later plays, while Margreta De Grazia illustrates her chapter on 'Shakespeare and the Craft of Language' (pp. 49–64) with multiple examples from the major tragedies.

The Oxford Companion to Shakespeare is edited by Michael Dobson, with the assistance of Stanley Wells. This is in several respects an impressive book with a wealth of material about Shakespeare and his plays. It is produced with the objective of contributing to a better understanding of the place occupied by Shakespeare's writings and is intended as 'an aid to the enjoyment of the plays and poems'. Further, the volume is designed with a view to informing readers about Shakespeare's works, his times, lives, and afterlives rather than interpreting the works. The editors have therefore favoured short, informative entries rather than chapter-length coverage of specific topics. Areas covered include biography, criticism, theatre history, translation, printing and publishing. Literary features and terms are also included, as well as Elizabethan and Jacobean literary contexts. Surveying such a vast field is, admittedly, a hazardous task. Difficult decisions have to be made concerning the relative space to be apportioned between different areas. However, in their selections the editors have managed to reflect something of the breadth of Shakespearian studies, in that the volume includes a diversity of opinions. Each play receives a general introduction. For the tragedies this typically contains a comment on the text and on sources, then gives a fairly full synopsis. The remainder will include a commentary on artistic features, critical history, stage history, and finally comments on film and television productions of the play in question. Finally recent major editions are covered and some representative criticism is given. A special feature is the thematic listing of entries, which is a guide to short treatments of special features within Shakespeare studies. In the case of the tragedies there are listings of entries on the principal characters. The listings of songs and song fragments contain references to *Antony and Cleopatra, Hamlet, King Lear, Othello,* and *Romeo and Juliet*. A special treat is a map of the British Isles and France in the English Histories and *Macbeth* (pp. 530–1), including geographical locations with corresponding references to scenes in the play. *The Oxford Companion to Shakespeare* is in many respects an impressive undertaking. It is richly illustrated and presents a wealth of information on different aspects of Shakespeare study, including the tragedies. As such it appears a great resource to the general reader.

W.H. Auden's views on Shakespeare are interesting partly because of his insight into literature, and partly because they contribute to our understanding of Auden. Although in some ways reflecting views now considered dated, Auden's lectures, as they appear in Kirsch, ed., *Lectures on Shakespeare*, reveal a thoughtful and intelligent mind. Strictly speaking, this is not Auden's lectures for the course on Shakespeare conducted at the New School for Social Research in New York in 1946–7, but a version largely based on notes taken by Auden's friend Alan Ansen. Arthur Kirsch's editing organizes and amplifies Ansen's material. Auden himself lectured impromptu from aide-memoires, which are no longer extant. In these lectures on Shakespeare's plays and sonnets, Auden makes use of multifarious references to authors from Homer and Augustine to Kierkegaard and T.S. Eliot, as well as to various art forms such as movies and cartoons, and to newspapers and magazines. The lectures contain comments on most of Shakespeare's tragedies, including *Romeo and Juliet, Julius Caesar, Hamlet, Othello, Macbeth, King Lear, Antony and Cleopatra, Timon of Athens,* and *Coriolanus*. His discussion of *Hamlet* includes a consideration of Hamlet's self-absorption and of seeing him in

Machiavellian terms, while his views on *Julius Caesar* link Brutus to Stoicism and Cassius to Epicureanism. Auden believed criticism to be 'live conversation', and the book might be viewed as an extended instance of such conversation. His interpretations show the pervasive influence of Freud, but, above all, the book testifies to Auden's wide reading and intelligent appreciation of Shakespeare's texts. If the book is outdated in some respects, for example its indifference to feminism, it may have been ahead of its time in its interest in dramatic and theatrical readings and interpretations.

Pilar Hidalgo's *Paradigms Found: Feminist, Gay, and New Historicist Readings of Shakespeare* traces the paradigm shift in Shakespeare studies beginning in the 1970s. It concentrates on feminism and new historicism, viewed as the two critical schools that have brought about significant changes in Shakespeare studies. One chapter is devoted to issues in early modern culture and drama highlighted by gay scholars. The chapter 'Reading Shakespeare as Women' surveys some of the studies of gender relations in the 1970s and 1980s. It includes references to Neely's essay on *Othello* in *Woman's Part* [1980], which notes a pervading contrast between men and women in the tragedy, and striking similarities between *Othello* and the comedies. Of special interest in the same chapter is the reference to Richard Levin's article 'Feminist Thematics and Shakespearean Tragedy', giving the feminist objection that Levin concentrates on early feminist works and deals exclusively with tragedy, while feminist scholars reject traditional genre hierarchies. Hidalgo's chapter on 'Material Subtexts' contains discussions of *King Lear*, *Hamlet*, and *Antony and Cleopatra*, partly in the light of earlier studies influenced by psychoanalysis. Greenblatt's work is frequently referred to, including his reading of *King Lear* in 'Fiction and Friction' (from *Shakespearean Negotiations* [1988]), to the effect that the play is pervaded by the feeling that rituals and beliefs have no effect any more—they have been 'emptied out'. By referring to and discussing relevant books and articles, Hidalgo tracks the shifting interests of feminist, gay, and new historicist critics from the 1970s on. It is a useful book to readers who want to be informed about the views of critics that have significantly contributed to changes in Shakespeare studies.

Dympna Callaghan's *Shakespeare Without Women: Representing Gender and Race on the Renaissance Stage*, in the Accent on Shakespeare series, is a challenging book that seeks to determine what the absence of women and racial others meant in their historical context and why they matter today. Callaghan focuses on three categories of people who were not present on Shakespeare's stage: women, Africans, and the Irish. To Callaghan, the Irish are the primary subjects of racist discourse in early modern England. These three categories, she argues, pose quite distinct problems in relation to representation. To take an example, female impersonators on the stage served to figure whiteness as a racial category as much as they signified gender difference. In her discussion Callaghan notes that there is no record of *Antony and Cleopatra* ever having been performed during Shakespeare's lifetime. She observes that the fact that Cleopatra is so compelling a *female* character role written for a male actor indicates the impossibility of pure sexual or gender categories. Of specific interest to readers of *Othello* is chapter 3, which deals with racial impersonation in the play. Callaghan argues that 'women in the play serve to mark whiteness against Othello's negritude, and that the play of race and gender needs to be read, first of all, in terms of theatrical integument'. She notes that very little attention has been paid to the fact that both black Othello and Desdemona were played by white males. Callaghan further finds 'the advent of the commodity and the system of representation required by it' to be one of the reasons it is difficult to discern the play of difference on the Renaissance stage.

Adamson et al., eds., *Reading Shakespeare's Dramatic Language*, is an interdisciplinary collection of essays divided into two main parts: 'The Language of Shakespeare's Plays' and 'Reading Shakespeare's English'. The first part covers a wide selection of topics, including metre, style, puns and parody, narrative and persuasion, body language, and Shakespeare's language in the theatre. Part two focuses on Shakespeare's grammar and sounds, his new words, and his language in relation to 'Standard' English and social variation. The book has short or more developed references to all the tragedies. Of special interest for the student of Shakespearian tragedy is Pamela Mason's 'Characters in Order of Appearance', which discusses *King Lear*, *Othello*, and *Antony and Cleopatra*, Peter Lichtenfels's 'Shakespeare's Language in the Theatre', which considers *Romeo and Juliet* and *Hamlet* (V.i), and Keir Elam's 'Language and the Body', which mainly focuses on *Hamlet*. Rooted in practical examples, these and other essays help increase the reader's awareness of different aspects of dramatic language. A special feature of the book is an A–Z of common Renaissance literary and language terms.

In the Oxford Shakespeare Topics series, Russ McDonald is the author of *Shakespeare and the Arts of Language*. While primarily giving an overview of the 'arts' of Shakespeare's language, especially as it is used in his verse drama, it is a book that offers practical help with linguistic obstacles. Written in a non-technical style, it illuminates Shakespeare's artistic tools, such as imagery and wordplay and rhetorical features of his text. The examples used include references to the language of the different tragedies. Interestingly, McDonald finds that it is in *Romeo and Juliet* that Shakespeare explicitly confronts the problem of language. The discussion triggered by Juliet's 'What's in a name?' (II.ii) is most illuminating. McDonald further notes a change in Shakespeare's attitude to equivocation as he moves from the Henry plays to representing the world through tragedy. Gradually serious wordplay becomes one of the chief elements in the speech of such figures as Iago, Macbeth, Timon, and Cleopatra. Much of the wordplay becomes assimilated into the protagonists' and antagonists' roles, so that Hamlet, to take the most obvious example, is his own clown. According to McDonald, this theatrical shift shows Shakespeare's increased concentration on the tragic ambiguities of human experience. Containing a great many pertinent observations on Shakespeare's language, McDonald's book helps deepen our insight into the playwright's texts.

Shakespeare's Reading by Robert S. Miola, published in the same series, explores Shakespeare's reshaping of sources in his work by looking at specific texts such as Holinshed's *Chronicles*, Plutarch's *Lives*, and Chaucer's *Canterbury Tales*. Miola's discussion of poetry shows that Italian love poetry, especially Petrarch's, helped shape *Romeo and Juliet* as well as the sonnets. The chapter on tragedies considers Plutarch's *Lives* in relation to *Julius Caesar*, *The True Chronicle History of King Leir* in connection with *King Lear*, and Senecan revenge in relation to *Titus Andronicus* and *Hamlet*. In discussing Shakespeare's sources throughout his career in the light of intertextuality as well as more traditional methods, Miola's book is a valuable contribution to the field.

Lawrence Danson's *Shakespeare's Dramatic Genres*, in the same series, points out that the divisions established by the original edition of *Mr. William Shakespeare's Comedies, Histories, and Tragedies* (the First Folio) have been very influential. But, as Danson notes in this short book, such a tripartite division is not inevitable. His guide to the types of Shakespearian drama gives an account of genre theory at the time of Shakespeare, demonstrates how the different genres were staged, and devotes different chapters to Shakespeare's comedies, histories, and tragedies. The definition of Shakespeare's tragic canon has never been stable, Danson notes, because the definition of tragedy as a genre has not been stable. Danson's own interest in discussing tragedy does not lie in distinguishing between 'pure' and 'impure' tragedy, but in discussing the generative combinations that make up the range of Shakespeare's practice. Although in principle favouring the Folio's division of plays, Danson suggests that the line between tragedy and history plays is sometimes worth crossing, that for some purposes we can distinguish the 'Roman plays' as a group, that for other purposes we can pair *Titus Andronicus* and *Hamlet* as 'revenge tragedies', and that at other times we can group both plays, along with *King Lear* and *Macbeth*, as plays about dynastic succession. In casting the net widely, Danson even on occasion takes in the final romances, which he assumes Shakespeare might have called tragicomedies, in order to demonstrate the variety of Shakespeare's experimentation with the tragic genre. The ensuing discussion of tragic characters is quite illuminating, and so is the passage on gender and genre. Few would disagree with Danson's observation that 'Shakespeare's tragic protagonists make great demands upon their worlds, and eventually those worlds refuse to sustain the demand'. This is a thought-provoking book that makes the reader rethink Shakespeare's use of genres.

Shakespeare Criticism in the Twentieth Century by Michael Taylor, also in the Oxford Shakespeare Topics series, is an overview of Shakespeare's critical reception from the end of the Victorian era to the present day. Its aim is to describe the place of the major Shakespeare critics in the different schools and movements. The book begins with a survey of the chief trends in Shakespeare criticism in the twentieth century, and succeeding chapters deal with the various aspects of this criticism in a more elaborate manner. Taylor sees the different strands within criticism as coming from differences of principle and methodology and distinguishes parallels and connections among various approaches. The book has a wide range and does not limit itself to the plays. Because of the enormous proliferation of studies on Shakespeare, such a survey must necessarily be selective. The first chapter contains a broad introduction to the twentieth century, revealing how much of today's criticism relies on the work of the Victorians and Edwardians. Taylor shows, however, that the earlier obsession with the discovery of verifiable facts led into a century of criticism marked by scepticism. Chapter 2 focuses on the first decades of the twentieth century, dominated by A.C. Bradley's approach through an in-depth study of Shakespeare's characters. According to Taylor, this approach met with severe criticism until it was partly re-accepted in the 1980s and 1990s. Chapter 3 considers criticism representing an adverse reaction to Bradleyism, in that the study of the formal arrangements of language is mostly separated from a concern for the character of the speaker. Chapter 4 deals, among other things, with the plays' life in the theatre of Shakespeare's time and that of the twentieth century. Chapter 5 returns Shakespeare's works to the world, focusing on his history plays. The final chapter deals with a number of different approaches to Shakespeare, including feminist, ethnic, and religious criticism. While Taylor's book contains a great many interesting observations on the tragedies, it also reveals twentieth-century critics' efforts at finding new and invigorating subdivisions of the canon.

John Sutherland and Cedric Watts were obviously intrigued by the loose threads in Shakespeare's plays when writing *Henry V, War Criminal? And Other Shakespeare Puzzles*. The book consists of a great many short chapters on specific puzzles. All the tragedies, except *Macbeth*, are among the plays dealt with. In the authors' view, Shakespeare loves loose ends and red herrings, and he sometimes seems to court confusion deliberately. As Stephen Orgel notes in the introduction, implausibilities or impossibilities abound in Shakespeare's plays. For example, at the beginning of *Hamlet*, when Horatio identifies the ghost as the dead King Hamlet by his armour and his frown, he refers to events to which he could hardly have been a witness. As for *Othello*, it does not allow enough time for the action it contains. Discussing 'Cleopatra—deadbeat nun', Sutherland asks how we should take Cleopatra's indifference to the fate of her children and contrasts this with Lear's love of his daughter Cordelia. Turning to the *mise-en-scène* in *Hamlet*, Sutherland comments on the sudden change of seasons between summer and arctic winter. He finds that as a writer Shakespeare can create whatever climatic conditions that suit him at any moment. However, the effect in *Hamlet*, according to Sutherland, is not one of artistic arbitrariness but the creation of the disturbing feeling that time is out of joint. With similar critical eyes Watts considers *Hamlet*, asking 'Where is the Ghost from? Is he stupid?'. Looking at *Titus Andronicus*, Watts asks 'How many Shakespearian cannibals?'. His answer is that, at the literal level, there is only one cannibal on stage in Shakespeare: the Empress Tamora. At the metaphysical level, however, there are scores, for example in the mutually lethal schemings found in *Hamlet*, *Macbeth*, and *King Lear*.

Alison Thorne's richly illustrated *Vision and Rhetoric in Shakespeare: Looking through Language* includes chapters on '*Hamlet* and the Art of Looking Diversely on the Self' (pp.104–33) and '*Antony and Cleopatra* and the Art of Dislimning' (pp. 166–97).

The book sets out to examine how visual and verbal modes of figuring the world, 'ways of seeing and ways of talking', are brought into productive relationship in Shakespeare's work. It has thus a double emphasis on vision and rhetoric and engages with comparative criticism of the arts as well as studies of dramatic viewpoint.

As Thorne notes in her interesting chapter on *Hamlet*, Shakespeare's introspective prince has been taken to symbolize the shift towards an interiorized model of subjectivity that is associated with the inception of the modern age. The main purpose of Thorne's chapter is to re-examine Hamlet's claim to possess 'that within which passes show'. The devices that facilitate Hamlet's participation in the activity of introspection are visual as well as verbal, drawing upon different modes of self-imaging as well as rhetorical strategies, Thorne observes. Pointing out that Hamlet's interest in the theatre provides a useful place of convergence for these different media, Thorne argues that his methods of representing himself to himself can be analysed no less productively by reference to the trope of self-portraiture, as it was deployed by both Renaissance painters and writers. She further argues that the techniques Hamlet uses to dramatize the self 'serve to establish *ut pictura poesis* as one of the main discursive contexts within which the play's concern with subjectivity is worked out'.

Thorne's chapter on '*Antony and Cleopatra* and the Art of Dislimning' initially notes Cleopatra's extraordinary effect on others, the fact that initial distrust gives way to undisguised admiration. She wants to show how the manner in which the imagination is conceived as operating in the play is conditioned by contemporary discourses of this faculty and its role in artistic production. The ongoing cultural debate over the value of the *fantasia* provides an important forum for the conflict at the heart of *Antony and Cleopatra* for, in Thorne's view, the power struggle between Rome and Egypt is waged through their opposed representations of themselves and each other, and the rival aesthetics that underpin these images. In accordance with its dialectical mode of presentation, Thorne argues, the play offers a 'double take' on the lovers' policy of enlisting the *fantasia* as a powerful weapon in their conflict with Caesar. While Antony's death puts a severe strain on Cleopatra's mythologizing ambitions, Cleopatra's policy of refashioning Antony as a figure not subject to rational criteria or human limitations culminates in her dream-vision of V.ii, representing a virtual manifesto for the creative powers of the *fantasia*. Cleopatra meets the challenge implicit in the Roman representation of events by staging herself on a higher plane, according to Thorne. To create the eikastic fiction, Cleopatra uses both visual spectacle and figurative language. Finally she employs the moment of transition from life to death to bring about the most startling metamorphosis, according to Thorne. By turning herself from a 'breather' into a figure of marble constancy, she confers upon the fluid products of her *fantasia* the permanence of art.

In *Medieval and Renaissance Drama in England* 14[2001], which has an emphasis on Elizabethan and Jacobean drama, Ruth Lunney has an article on 'Rewriting the Narrative of Dramatic Character, or, not "Shakespearean" but "Debatable"' (*MRDE* 14[2001] 66–85). She points out that the traditional narrative of dramatic character tells of the advent of a new kind of character in the 1590s, usually labelled 'Shakespearian', which is considered to be quite different from the limited figures of earlier plays. The new character is defined in terms of its essential nature, as being 'individual', 'complex', more 'real', having achieved 'self-expressiveness' and 'interiority' and 'subjectivity'. She points out that this traditional view has been under siege for many years, first because of the problems of defining 'the real', but more recently because of revisionist challenges to the timing, and even the fact, of change. Her essay proposes that the narrative of dramatic character should be rewritten, and shifts the focus of discussion from essential nature to performance, from the labels appropriate to the figure on stage to the rhetoric that shapes the relationship between figure and spectators, leading them to observe and interpret in particular ways. According to Lunney, Marlowe's place in the narrative should be seen not as marginal but as seminal. While her discussion includes comment on *Titus*, Shakespeare's earliest tragedy, Lunney's attention is mainly directed towards dramatic character from the 1580s on, with a special focus on the importance of Faustus. As such the essay may be viewed as a reappraisal of Marlowe's contribution.

One essay that refers to several of the tragedies is Heather James's discussion of 'Dido's Ear: Tragedy and the Politics of Response' (*SQ* 52[2001] 360–82).

Although primarily a discussion of *The Tempest* in the light of the 'dangerous' fascinations of Shakespearian scenes of sympathy or pity, James observes that at the end of *Titus Andronicus* an allusion to Dido's longing unexpectedly surfaces in the context of political tumult in V.iii.79–86. The reference to 'lovesick Dido's sad-attending ear' in line 81 is most evocative, since Aeneas's tale becomes important only if it is granted close attention by the listener. Furthermore, James finds Aeneas's tale to Dido an unlikely classical precedent to substitute for a rebel cry. Commenting on the 'greedy ear' that 'Devour[s]' Othello's 'discourse' (*Othello* I.iii.149–50), she points out that, compared with *Titus Andronicus* V.iii, Othello's speech in I.iii 'more intensively examines pity's uncertain origins and unlimited potential for transformation'. Explaining the 'metacritical' character of Othello's tale, James finds that it estranges pity and foregrounds its status as an object of semantic study. The article also comments on the Player's speech in *Hamlet*, noting that the revolutionary potential of pity suggests why Hamlet feels at once drawn to and scandalized by the actor's power to transform his audience.

Shakespeare Survey 54[2001] is devoted to 'Shakespeare and Religions', which contains Robert S. Miola's '"An alien people clutching their gods"? Shakespeare's Ancient Religions' (*ShS* 54[2001] 31–45). Miola comments on *Titus Andronicus*, observing that this play 'represents Shakespeare's most sensational depiction of Roman violence'. In his view, the spectacle of human sacrifice, mutilation, murder, and the Thyestean banquet defines the Romans as an 'Alien people clutching their gods'. The line between antiquity and modernity fluctuates throughout the play, making ancient Rome metamorphose into familiar landscapes of contemporary England. The barbarous action of *Titus Andronicus* evokes several contemporary paradigms, such as the question of martyrdom. But as Miola points out, in any sixteenth-century sense, neither Lavinia, as a pathetic victim, nor her tormentors Chiron and Demetrius suffer martyrdom, for a martyr must suffer *for* something and give witness to a higher truth, to Christ. According to Miola, the martyrological discourse in this play questions the cultural practice of making martyrs. Detached from its theological basis, such practice devolves to mere bloodsport and propaganda. Instead of encouraging the oppressed and celebrating God's victory, 'it turns the individual tragedy into a titillating spectacle that merely justifies hatred and more violence'. To Miola, Shakespeare exposes the dark side of the Elizabethan martyrdom industry, demonstrated by Titus martyring Chiron and Demetrius by slitting their throats on stage and by, finally, plunging the knife into Lavinia. Another area within the religious domain, the controversy over relics, is evoked in the display of *disjecta membra*, the cut-off tongue, heads, hands. While relics in Catholicism meant bringing believers into contact with the saints, no Catholic practice ever incited as much Protestant ridicule. Miola shows how Aaron in III.i plays contemptuous reformer in demythologizing relics to gullible Catholics. But while the bereaved Andronici family pledge future action and take up the hand and heads as signs of their belief and love, their sanctification leads only to more brutality and revenge.

In a well-documented article on 'The Need for Lavinia's Voice: *Titus Andronicus* and the Telling of Rape' (*ShakS* 29[2001] 75–92), Emily Detmer-Goebel initially reports on Act II of *Titus Andronicus*, where Lavinia refuses to name rape, referring to an impending sexual assault as that which 'womanhood denies my tongue to tell' and as a 'worse-than-killing lust' (II.iii.174, 175). She finds rape the centrepiece of

Shakespeare's fictional history of Rome. While in the world of the play the woman is denied the 'tongue' to talk of rape, the play, in Detmer-Goebel's opinion, also feeds on the unrest that such silence creates. While the mutilation of Lavinia is brutally oppressive, her silence is troubling. Revealing the rape is dangerous for the rapists but necessary for the family of the victim. Thus *Andronicus* illustrates the cultural need for both a raped woman's silence and her testimony. Noting a change in statutory law during the sixteenth century to the effect that the definition of rape came to exclude abduction, Detmer-Goebel explores the relationship between statutory law and the play, arguing that '*Titus Andronicus* dramatically registers the culture's anxiety over men's increased dependence on women's voices and, in doing so, shapes and sustains early modern England's contradictory attitude toward a woman's accusation of rape'.

In *English Studies*, David Lucking considers 'Uncomfortable Time in *Romeo and Juliet*' (*ES* 82[2001] 115–26), pointing out that, as the play dramatizes the apparent power of love to release the individual from the trammels of human concerns, it is also inevitably about time. This is evidenced on the level of the plot by the way incidents are coordinated so as to create the familiar outcome. Attempts to make time subservient to human volition necessarily turn out to be futile. What gives the situation of the two lovers a genuinely tragic dimension and makes their fate ironic, according to Lucking, is less the fact that they are defeated by external time than that their ways of thinking are fatally conditioned by the very time they strive to escape. They paradoxically participate in those areas that they try to see their own reality in opposition to. The fault lies in themselves rather than their stars, because they do not take into account the fact that they are enslaved by the tyranny of time, which they reject. The only alternative to what sonnet 115 describes as 'time's tyranny' is to find posthumous continuance in art, signalled by the erection of gold statues to commemorate the lovers. As Lucking reasons, the society that used to conspire with time to frustrate the lovers now seems to work with them in their aspiration to transcend time.

Howard Jacobson (*N&Q* 48[2001] 282) argues that the phrasing in *Julius Caesar*, I.ii.139–40 ('The fault, dear Brutus, is not in our stars | But in ourselves') is so close to a passage in Seneca that it is hard to see pure coincidence. Speaking of geographical location rather than fate, Seneca observes, *non locorum vitium esse quo laboramus sed nostrum* (*De tranquillitate* 2.15). If Seneca had *astrorum* rather than *locorum*, there would undoubtedly be direct influence in this case. In Jacobson's opinion, there still is; Shakespeare has made the change to fit the context. As Jacobson points out, a small collection of *sententiae* from Seneca's work was published in 1597. Among these was the quoted sentence from *De tranquillitate*.

In '"But with just cause": *Julius Caesar*, III.i.47' (*N&Q* 48[2001] 282–4), MacD. P. Jackson remarks that Ben Jonson recalled the lines in which the protest 'Caesar, thou dost me wrong' elicited the response, 'Caesar did never wrong but with just cause', a reply Jonson found 'ridiculous'. However, this quote does not appear within the First Folio [1623], upon which modern editions of *Julius Caesar* are based. Pointing out the discrepancy between Jonson's quotation and the Folio text, Jackson suggests that what Shakespeare wrote (modernized) was: '[*Caesar*] Thy brother by decree is banished. | If thou dost bend and pray and fawn for him, | I spurn thee like a cur out of my way. | *Metellus*. Caesar, thou dost me wrong. | *Caesar*. Know, Caesar doth not wrong. | But with just cause will he be satisfied.' According to Jackson, this reconstruction makes it clear that Caesar's scornful dismissal of Metellus' humble entreaties is perfectly proper: 'submissiveness and flattery cannot divert the fixed course of his imperial justice; the nature of the case is the sole consideration'.

Tetsuo Kishi's article 'When Suicide Becomes an Act of Honour': *Julius Caesar* in Late Nineteenth-Century Japan' (*ShS* 54[2001] 108–14) points out that, of all Shakespearian characters who either kill themselves or think of killing themselves, relatively few seem conscious of the sinfulness of the act. For example, Romeo and Juliet appear almost jubilant when they end their lives, and the same is true of Pyramus and Thisbe. As for Gloucester in *King Lear*, Kishi finds his affliction when he tries suicide to be too great to consider the religious implications of the act, and in the case of Lady Macbeth and Goneril (although their deaths are not enacted on stage), it may be assumed that their guilt is more overwhelming than their scruples. Discussing *Hamlet*, Kishi finds a curious coexistence of two kinds of codes of behaviour, one Christian (for example represented by the priest talking about Ophelia's death) and one Roman or pre-Christian (exemplified by Horatio, claiming to be more an antique Roman than a Dane). In Roman plays the situation seems simpler, according to Kishi. To Antony and Cleopatra, who admittedly are dejected, suicide is in no way religiously unacceptable, and in *Julius Caesar* killing oneself is almost obligatory in order to avoid humiliation. Kishi finds this surprising, since Shakespeare was writing for a Christian audience. Shakespeare seems to have changed his standards depending on which historical period he was dealing with. According to Kishi, it follows that Shakespearian plays with suicidal characters are understood quite differently in a non-Christian culture. This is exactly what happened when his plays were introduced to the late nineteenth-century Japanese audience. Kishi maintains, for example, that adaptations of *Julius Caesar* and *Hamlet* aimed at Japanese readers seem to share a great deal with their European counterparts, suggesting that Shakespeare's tragedies without religious overtones are easier to understand, less unfathomable, and less tragic.

Stephen Greenblatt's *Hamlet in Purgatory* provides a fascinating contribution to *Hamlet* studies. This interesting and original study traces the traditions concerning purgatory, with a focus on the Ghost of Hamlet's father. In the play the Ghost appears in three scenes and speaks in only two, but is central to the tragedy's magical intensity. In Greenblatt's words 'it is amazingly disturbing and vivid'. This leads him to a broad enquiry into the 'poetics' of purgatory in England. Being primarily concerned with what Shakespeare inherited and transformed, he traces purgatory as a belief and institution, trying to show the way in which it was conceived in English texts of the later Middle Ages and then attacked by English Protestants in the sixteenth and seventeenth centuries. The first three chapters, on the history of purgatory as a 'poet's fable', as Tyndale called it, and on remembering and encountering the dead, seem preliminary to the chief concerns of the book. They provide background material that may seem unduly lengthy and detailed, but which nevertheless deepen our knowledge concerning purgatory and the system of indulgences and pardons that went with it. Greenblatt shows his independence here in establishing a rather broad historical and contextual background including, for example, references to *The Gast of Gy*, St Patrick's Purgatory, and the *Supplication of Souls*, as well as indulgences, trentals, chantries, and requiem masses. To many students of Shakespeare the most interesting parts of the book will be the framing sections, the illuminating footnotes, and chapters 4 and 5, 'Staging Ghosts' and 'Remember Me', which demonstrate that Greenblatt values literary power, that he has an eye for Shakespeare's capacity to 'invent the human', and that he has a lively sense of the importance of theatricality. Greenblatt communicates clearly, and often brilliantly, his fascination with *Hamlet*, his attraction to its compelling ghost, and the powerful claim that Shakespeare's imaginary characters can make on modern readers. The reader can therefore condone what appears to be the main deficiency of the book, its virtual neglect of Dante, Chaucer, and the Book of Common Prayer.

Kliman, ed., *Approaches to Teaching Shakespeare's 'Hamlet'*, contains a great many stimulating essays as a means of providing different points of view on teaching this tragedy. Like others in the MLA's Approaches to Teaching World Literature series, this volume is divided into two parts. While the first part, 'Materials', selects from thousands of works on *Hamlet* editions, anthologies, web notes, reference materials and films that are thought to be of greatest help to teachers, the second part, 'Approaches', contains a wide variety of techniques for presenting the play to students. These include textual approaches, comparative studies, performance strategies, and postmodern methodologies. The volume also contains twenty 'short takes', in the form of syllabus additions, tips, and exercises for teaching *Hamlet*. Of the many insightful essays on some aspect of *Hamlet* one could mention George T. Wright's concise introduction to Shakespeare's metre and Ellen J. O'Brien's view of metre as a dance. T.H. Howard-Hill approaches the multiple-text *Hamlet* from the viewpoint that Shakespeare's plays are constructed. Using the 'Mousetrap' scene, he suggests collating different editions to call attention to factors that influence editorial choices. Several performance approaches focus on individual scenes, such as the nunnery and play scenes. Essays on narrative, character, and theme concentrate on a variety of aspects. For example, Arthur F. Kinney's '*Hamlet*'s Narratives' instructively tests the relationship between drama and narrative, while Roy Battenhouse's contribution has a special focus on the Ghost. Under the section 'Focus on Scenes', John Drakakis focuses on 'Language, Structure, and Ideology' in IV.v. Comparative approaches to the play include views on teaching *Hamlet* in a Western civilization course and in a global literature survey. In an essay on the Pyrrhus speech, Lisa Hopkins queries the uses of the Troy story. A section on modern and postmodern strategies contains views as different as teaching Shakespeare with Freud, Eliot, and Lacan and approaching *Hamlet* through comic books. A separate section gives illuminating approaches to specific scenes. In addition, the volume considers the possibilities of verbal and dramatic exchanges in cyberspace. The 'short takes' are succinct comments on limited aspects of the play. In sum, this exciting sourcebook is a stimulating study of different strategies employed in teaching *Hamlet*. Although primarily written for the teacher who has undergraduates in mind, this book will no doubt be a valuable source of inspiration for specialists as well as non-specialists approaching the play.

Richard C. McCoy writes on 'A Wedding and Four Funerals: Conjunction and Commemoration in *Hamlet*' (*ShS* 54[2001] 122–39). The article comments on the funerals in *Hamlet*, which number four if we count the first for Hamlet's father. From beginning to end this is a play obsessed with getting a decent burial, according to McCoy. He finds that what constituted a decent burial in Shakespeare's time is not clear, because the Elizabethan settlement was so ambiguous on this point. A growing belief in predestination, the subordination of human works to faith alone, and the abolition of purgatory and indulgences made traditional Catholic practices unnecessary. In an apparent concession to conservative feelings, Elizabeth in 1560 authorized publication of a Latin prayer book that included a requiem communion service. McCoy calls this 'liturgical double-bookkeeping' and considers it a classic Elizabethan compromise. As McCoy sees it, *Hamlet* can be regarded as a textbook demonstration of the theological irresolution and liturgical failure of the Elizabethan compromise. The ghost haunting it comes from an old religious world, claiming to return from a suppressed Catholic purgatory. Later in the play, the consolation of a requiem is invoked and then withdrawn, leaving mourners with a sense of 'maimèd rites' (V.i.214). McCoy draws parallels between events during Queen Elizabeth's life and *Hamlet*, reminding us that the tragedy first appeared during the troubled final years of her reign, when people feared her imminent death. But Shakespeare's own attitude towards the cult of Elizabeth and the mystique of sacred kingship is ambiguous. Maintaining that memorial objects permit a sustained if tenuous connection between the living and the dead, McCoy finds that the image of Hamlet has maintained a much stronger hold on our imagination than that of Queen Elizabeth. Hamlet overwhelms all his rivals, including those claiming their own rights of memory.

Theatre Journal 53[2001] 119–44 has an article by Alan L. Ackerman Jr., who observes that since plays have always represented a reality that is invisible, a key problem for the drama since Shakespeare has been to represent or express human interiority on the stage. The premise of Ackerman's essay is that a widespread reimagining of the subject in the early decades of the nineteenth century is fundamental to what we think of today as 'modern' drama. *Hamlet*, with its emphasis on the Ghost and on Hamlet's imagination, becomes a central Romantic text. In *Hamlet*, Shakespeare is faced with the problem of theatre, of literally making visible subjects and objects of knowledge. The Ghost's appearances across the boundaries of the stage are emblematic of that problem. This essay traces a genealogy that begins with Romantic interpretations of *Hamlet* and debates dramatic structures and terms, images and characters taken from *Hamlet* and represented in turn by artists such as Goethe, Ibsen, and Wilde.

Margreta De Grazia's article '*Hamlet* Before its Time' (*MLQ* 62[2001] 355–75) observes that no work in the English literary canon has been so closely identified with the beginning of the modern age as *Hamlet*. The protagonist is *timeless* in value, De Grazia maintains, precisely because he is found *timely* by each successive age. But it is a strange prolepsis that a work is anachronous with its own time and contemporaneous with one several centuries later. The essay demonstrates that *Hamlet* acquires its precocious modernity only with the arrival of the modern period itself. The focal period is between 1600 and 1800. Early allusions to the play suggest that it was regarded as behind the times. This attitude continued after 1660, and well into the eighteenth century it was considered 'antiquated', 'old', 'barbarous', and even 'Gothic'. It has been noted before that Hamlet was not seen as a character of psychological depth and complexity until the end of the eighteenth century. To this De Grazia remarks the degree to which Hamlet's problematic interiority depends on the shift of delay from plot to character. By internalizing plot, *Hamlet* overturned the classical definition of tragedy. It is from the construal of *Hamlet* as a tragedy disembedded from plot and residing in the character Hamlet that the play acquires its anticipatory outreach.

In 'Hamlet: Date and Early Afterlife' (RES 52[2001] 341–59) Charles Cathcart observes that Shakespeare's Hamlet was repeatedly echoed in two plays of winter 1599/1600: Antonio and Mellida and Lust's Dominion. According to Cathcart, correspondences between Hamlet and each of these plays are too strong to be coincidental. The comic genre of Antonio and Mellida and the existence of distinctive material shared by Hamlet and both Antonio plays make the prospect of a common source for these plays (such as the lost ur-Hamlet) highly unlikely. Furthermore, the evidence for the dates of the debtor plays is powerful. On this basis it is Cathcart's claim that Hamlet must have been composed by the end of 1599. This is right at the edge of the generally accepted range for the play.

Recognizing a probable borrowing from Marlowe's Dido, Queen of Carthage in Hamlet, where the First Player, as Aeneas, recounts for Dido the slaying of Priam (II.ii.468–518), Dorothea Kehler (ANQ 14[2001] 5–10) argues that Marlowe appears to be using 'adulteress' in a now obsolete sense, the OED's second definition of adulterer: 'one who adulterates, corrupts, or debases'. Applied to Hamlet, Kehler feels that by 'adulterate', Shakespeare may have had in mind something similar to Marlowe's broader usage. If 'adulterate' in Hamlet is taken to mean 'corrupted' or 'debased', 'unchaste' or 'lewd', the case for an adulterous affair motivating King Hamlet's murder is definitely weakened. Gertrude would be guilty of no more than insensitivity to Hamlet's feelings and an 'o'erhasty marriage' (II.ii.57).

In another study of Hamlet, '"Let me not burst in ignorance": Skepticism and Anxiety in Hamlet' (ES 82[2001] 218–30), Aaron Landau observes that the humanist revival of Academic and Pyrrhonian scepticism in the late Renaissance is explained by historians of philosophy as being primarily a response to 'the 16th century schism in the Church and the subsequent contention of ultimate religious legitimacy between the different factions into which Christianity had disintegrated'. Noting that this historical connection is often ignored by Shakespearians, Landau wants it to bear on a possible understanding of Hamlet. Referring to Mark Matheson's statement in SQ 46[1995] 383, that 'Religious discourse is integral to Hamlet, but Shakespeare's representation of religion in the play is oblique and inconsistent', Landau remarks that Matheson, although perceptively analysing the dramatic roles played by Roman Catholicism, Protestantism, and neo-Stoicism, does not mention scepticism as a working factor in the play. Landau suggests that critical interest in the play's religious inconsistency will benefit by examining the play in the context of early modern scepticism. That context accounts for the comprehensiveness and instability of ideological systems in the play and allows critics to come to different conclusions about Hamlet's religious content. In Landau's opinion, Hamlet should not be conceived as a statement about positive religious knowledge that 'continuously undoes various claims on knowledge with a scepticism of palpable religious resonance'.

Othello has also received much attention. David Lake and Brian Vickers, in 'Scribal copy for Q1 of Othello: A Reconsideration' (N&Q 48[2001] 284–7), discuss aspects of Ernst Honigmann's views on the text of Othello as they appear in the monograph The Texts of 'Othello' and Shakespearian Revision [1996]. Acknowledging Honigmann's observation that the scribe who made this transcript divided the play into acts, used a heavier punctuation than in other 'good quartos', was guilty of many misreadings of Shakespeare's foul papers, and relined prose as verse, Lake and Vickers add to this that, knowingly or unknowingly, the scribe made the play's language far more colloquial. In their view, he might have tried to update it, make it sound more contemporary, more Jacobean, 'or perhaps he was unaware that his idiolect was more up-to-date than Shakespeare's'. Finding support in MacDonald Jackson's independent analysis, Lake and Vickers contend that scribal influence on the 1622 quarto of *Othello* was greater than has been thought. The scribe(s) of the copy-text had a peculiar taste for colloquialisms that Shakespeare did not share.

Michael John DiSanto, in 'Nothing if Not Critical: Stanley Cavell's Skepticism and Shakespeare's *Othello*' (*DR* 81[2001] 359–82), considers Stanley Cavell's essay 'Othello and the Stake of the Other' from his book *Disowning Knowledge in Six Plays of Shakespeare* (CUP [1987]), which DiSanto finds unsettling, creating a dual response of familiarity and strangeness. DiSanto attempts to redirect Cavell's approach, which is based on the notion of the 'sceptical problematic'. In Cavell's reading, Othello is the sceptic; it is his mind that suffers from the tortures of doubt. DiSanto counters that it is not Othello that is the voice of doubt in the play but Iago, who is also the voice of scepticism. Furthermore, he finds that Cavell misses the powerful insistence of Desdemona's belief and misreads the importance of perfection and virginity in *Othello*. The essay deals instructively with the role of Othello, Iago, and Desdemona. It illuminates two entirely different readings of the tragedy, and DiSanto's is by far the more conventional of the two.

While Shakespeare's principal source for *Othello* was the story of the Moor in Giraldi Cinthio's *Hecatommithi*, Roger Prior points out, in 'Shakespeare's Debt to Ariosto' (*N&Q* 48[2001] 289–92), that the play contains convincing indications that he read Cinthio in the original Italian. It has also long been supposed that Shakespeare had read canto 46, stanza 80 of Ariosto's *Orlando Furioso*. According to Prior, Shakespeare's description of the episode of the handkerchief is much more elaborate than in Cinthio. Prior suggests that Shakespeare used Ariosto's description in *Orlando* of the wedding present in the form of a tent, which Cassandra made for Hector and which the sorceress Melissa later contributed as a wedding gift. To Shakespeare Ariosto's description of this wedding tent would fill out the bare outlines that Cinthio had provided. In his short article, Prior points to further evidence of Shakespeare's indebtedness to Ariosto, both in *Othello* and in *Love's Labour's Lost*.

According to Steven Doloff, Iago's description of the adulterous practices of Venetian wives, as part of his scheme to drive Othello mad with jealousy, would not have surprised many in Shakespeare's audience (III.iii.204–7). In 'Shakespeare's *Othello* and Circe's Italian Court in Ascham's *The Scholemaster* (1570)' (*N&Q* 48[2001] 287–9) Doloff points out that sixteenth-century English travel writers had already popularized Italian stereotypes of tragedy and sensuality. Roger Ascham's *The Scholemaster* contains one of the most well-known indictments of Italian vices, including an extended reference to 'Circe's court' in the tenth book of Homer's *Odyssey*, Circe being the sorceress who turns men into beasts. The resulting disparaging view of Italian society, Doloff suggests, may have provided Shakespeare with the idea for a similar Circian motif in *Othello*. The relative prominence of animal metaphors and epithets in *Othello* is well known among scholars. Doloff finds it fitting with a Circian motif that it is Iago, 'the most sorcererlike of the play's Italians', who 'rhetorically performs the majority of such verbal "transformations" upon the characters'. Recognizing a Circian motif in the play, Doloff suggests, may reveal something about the relative significance of Othello's perceived racial 'otherness' as a factor in the play.

Carl James Grindley (*CahiersE* 59[2001] 77–80) suggests that, of the many sources for Shakespeare's *King Lear*, one of the least familiar is the version of the story found in John Hardynge's *Chronicle*. This work survives in eleven manuscripts and a great many fragments and extracts, but still no modern edition is available. The *Chronicle*, written between 1450 and 1470, exists in two printings by Richard Grafton in 1543. These editions are, however, very rare and, according to Grindley, they seem to be taken from a lost manuscript. A post-Renaissance rather inferior edition of the text, based on Grafton, was made in 1812 by Henry Ellis. Although Hardyng's *Chronicle* does not exist in a 'stable' form, Grindley finds that it presents an interesting version of the Lear story. The article includes the entire version of the verse story of King Lear as found in Hardyng's *Chronicle*. The text is taken from the University of Glasgow's Hunterian Library MS 400.

Gary Taylor's 'Divine [ ]sences' (*ShS* 54[2001] 13–30) discusses representations of the divine in Shakespeare. Taylor refers to Stephen Greenblatt's influential account, in *Shakespearean Negotiations* [1988], of the relationship between Shakespeare's *King Lear* and Harsnett's *Declaration of Egregious Popish Impostures*. While calling Greenblatt's essay 'our most sophisticated critical account of the relationship between early modern religion and theatre', Taylor says it fits Middleton well, but questions whether it fits Shakespeare. He comments on Greenblatt's observation that in *King Lear* 'there are no ghosts, as there are in *Richard III*, *Julius Caesar*, or *Hamlet*; no witches, as in *Macbeth*; no mysterious music of departing demons, as in *Antony and Cleopatra*'. The absence of such effects may distinguish *King Lear* from these other plays, Taylor admits, but it does not demonstrate that it is more typical of its author, or more typical of institutional exchanges between church and state. Taylor also questions Greenblatt's claim that '*King Lear* is haunted by a sense of rituals and beliefs that are no longer efficacious, that have been *emptied out*. The characters appeal again and again to the pagan gods, but the gods remain utterly silent'. To this Taylor counters that this is exactly what a Christian audience would expect to happen, namely that appeals to non-existent gods would remain unanswered. Observing that Greenblatt's essay is devoted not to the divine, but to the demonic, Taylor argues that 'the absence from *King Lear* of real demonic possession, or real devils, does not prove that the essence of the divine has been emptied out of Shakespeare's theatre'. For, as he makes clear, the gods do not remain silent in Shakespeare's other plays written between 1605 and 1613. Taylor's main contention is that Greenblatt generalizes about the relationship between religion and 'Shakespeare's theatre' on the basis of *King Lear* alone, attributing this to the fact that new historicism is synchronic, so that 'chronological changes within one writer's oeuvre become irrelevant'. Another criticism advanced by Taylor is of what he calls Greenblatt's 'slippage', namely that in his account 'Shakespeare's theatre' becomes synonymous with 'the Elizabethan theatre' or even 'the theatre'.

In 'Lear's Howl and "Diogenes the Doggue"' (*N&Q* 48[2001] 292–3) Steven Doloff comments on W.R. Elton's proposal that Lear's heart-rending cry 'Howl, howl, howl, howl! O! you are men of stones ...' (V.iii.257) as he holds Cordelia's body at play's end is part of the tragedy's pointed rejection of Stoic impassivity in the face of ill fortune. According to Doloff, Shakespeare may have intended to provoke another classical association with Lear's howl, namely Diogenes the Cynic philosopher (c.412–323 bc). Shakespeare explicitly refers to the Cynics in *Julius Caesar* (IV.iii.132) and, as Doloff argues, seems to parody in Lear's encounter with the disguised Edgar many aspects of Renaissance accounts of the Cynic Diogenes' famous meeting with Alexander the Great. As Doloff sees it, it is not until the play's end, with Cordelia dead in his arms, that Lear fully becomes Shakespeare's new Diogenes. What the tragedy represents at that point is a bleak vision of basic man, stripped of all redemptive faith in natural or heavenly order.

A brief article by Geoff Wilkes, 'A Textual Problem in *Macbeth*, I.ii' (*N&Q* 48[2001] 293–5), comments on earlier interpretations of this passage that are summarized in J.C. Eade's *The Forgotten Sky*. One interpretation takes 'reflection' to mean 'shining'; another argues that the sun 'reflexes as it approaches the vernal equinox, while a third reading is based on the view that the sun does reflex when it turns back from the Tropic of Capricorn at the winter solstice'. Wilkes suggests a new interpretation, believing that the *Captain* refers primarily to the moon, rather than to the sun. As the moon reflects sunlight, it is the place 'whence the Sunne 'gins his reflection', and is therefore arguably a source of 'comfort'. And as the moon also governs the tides, it is also the place 'whence ... Shipwrecking Stormes, and direfull Thunders' come, and therefore equally a source of 'discomfort'. This interpretation, according to Wilkes, is more plausible than the three discussed by Eade.

Ken Jackson writes on '"One Wish" or the Possibility of the Impossible: Derrida, the Gift, and God in *Timon of Athens*' (*SQ* 52[2001] 34–66). The essay is in great part an attempt to use Derrida's recent work on the gift (*Given Time: 1. Counterfeit Money*) and the gift's relationship to religion (in *The Gift of Death*) to illuminate what Jackson sees as Shakespeare's profound exploration of religion in *Timon of Athens*. He argues that Timon seeks what Derrida calls 'the gift, the impossible' and that a religious passion motivates the search. This passionate religious search for the gift, Jackson maintains, produces the crux that both fascinated and tortured critics of the play: Timon's sudden shift from generous noble to mad misanthrope. In his discussion Jackson frequently refers to G. Wilson Knight's treatment of the play in *The Wheel of Fire*.

Kenneth Parker's 'brief chronicle' of *Antony and Cleopatra*, in the Writers and their Work series, is a historical and critical exposition of commentaries of the play. In Parker's view, *Antony and Cleopatra*, perhaps more than any other Shakespeare play, challenges certainties about ways of seeing the very moment of their enactment. In line with this, Parker attempts to uncover influential competing readings of the play in their specific contexts. Dominant interpretations of, for example, 'Rome' or 'Egypt', or seeing Antony as a 'deserter' and Cleopatra as a 'gypsy' or 'whore', are debated, and alternative readings are offered. Discussing the humanist inheritance, Parker notes that while several characters in the play, including the protagonists, commit suicide, only one critic since Dryden, namely Irving Ribner, has argued that the play should be interpreted in terms of Christianity's absolute injunction against self-slaughter in Christian theology. In Parker's opinion, the 'monstrous regiment' of women critics has helped transform the reading of the play. For example, he quotes Linda Fitz's remarks that the reduction of the play's action to 'the fall of a great general' and the definition of the play's major interest as 'transcendental love' make impossible a fair assessment of the character of Cleopatra. Parker notes a critical engagement with the play by critics of the 1950s, 1960s, and 1970s, but finds it noteworthy that there is very little consideration of the play—and especially of Cleopatra—in many texts of great distinction that appeared in the 1980s, especially those that have to do with feminist theory and with history. What needs to be added to reappraisals of Cleopatra, according to Parker, is the realization that she is constructed as Other, not simply because she is female, but above all because she is 'Oriental'. Commenting on sources, Parker points out that Shakespeare's Octavius invariably tends to come out less favourably than he appears in the translations of the classics, while the reverse is true with regard to Antony. Parker's concluding argument is that, of all Shakespeare's plays, *Antony and Cleopatra* is a text for our times that is 'past the size of dreaming'. To sum up, this small monograph gives a useful introduction to various commentaries on the play under the competent guidance of Kenneth Parker, whose own responses seem mostly influenced by postcolonial and feminist theories.

(g) Late Plays

In his Oxford edition of *The Tempest*, Stephen Orgel lists some of the many and varied interpretations of the play and asserts that 'The question of correctness is not the issue in these readings; the play will provide at least some evidence for all of them, and its critical history is a good index to the ambivalences and ambiguities of the text' (p. 11). It is easy to see why this play in particular and the criticism which surrounds it would elicit such a response. Having read through critic after critic discussing almost precisely the same sections of text (the most popular moments are the opening tempest, the exposition scene (I.ii), the masque, and Prospero's epilogue), to arrive at conflicting and often opposed interpretations, it is tempting to wonder at the inventiveness and specificity of the arguments. However, a more measured response will see such abundance as a testament to the power and resonance of *The Tempest*; it has to a great extent become a battlefield of sorts for the working out of important cultural, political and aesthetic ideas. These ideas and the critical approaches to this most discussed of plays have moved forward in important ways during this year.

As far as this play is concerned, the work of 2001 falls broadly into two camps. One body of work offers an overview of historical and current responses to the play and of possible interpretative positions; another group of research, although admittedly at times seeming to circle obsessively around the same textual and theatrical moments and their interpretation, moves the arguments forward into new terrain. As with all such cases, this is a blunt categorization, and very often these approaches overlap. It is also important to say that, in many ways, the anthologies and essays which fall into the first category allow the work of the second to take place. Perhaps the most constructive way in which new directions have emerged has been in the synthesis of critical and creative responses to the play.

A fine example of this turn towards the creative in *Tempest* studies is Peter Hulme and William H. Sherman, eds., *'The Tempest' and its Travels*. This impressive book of specially commissioned essays does not confine itself to criticism, but calls upon the history of creative responses to the play, with poems by Merle Collins, David Dabydeen and Robin Kirkpatrick, visual materials by Jimmie Durham and a section on appropriations of the play called 'On the World Stage'. These materials are also interspersed with introductory pieces from the editors, and primary materials—

visual and otherwise—for reading the play. This creates a collection which lives both in and beyond itself, and which vitally reinstates the act of criticism with the act of creation. Cross-disciplinary in the sense of involving poets and performers, it brings together, as the editors claim, 'voices that are too rarely heard in dialogue' (p. xii) and offers the reader a wonderful chance to see the impact of this particular play on other works of art, and to hear creative voices within a critical text. This is a collection which is intelligently, originally and vitally put together, and which takes an engaged and open-eyed stance towards its object of study. As well as revitalizing the format of the essay collection, this imaginative and fresh book has found a way to allow work on *The Tempest* to move forward, allowing the play a continued life after the hard-fought critical debates of recent years.

The editors themselves are very much alive to the multiplicitous nature of *The Tempest* and its criticism. As they point out, this play has 'emerged as one of the most contested texts in the critical sphere. It has been classified as every genre and no genre, located in every place and no place, and enlisted in support of colonial, anti-colonial and apolitical views' (p. xi). To this end they offer a wide variety of critical, poetic, theatrical and visual responses to the play. The book is divided into three sections. 'Local Knowledge' deals with the historical circumstances of the seventeenth-century writing and performance of the play. 'European and Mediterranean Crossroads' answers Jerry Brotton's 1998 appeal for the Mediterranean's, and hence Africa's, reinstatement into *Tempest* studies. Brotton returns to this argument in his own very short piece, and Barbara Mowat's sophisticated essay modifies that appeal. 'On the World Stage' takes a subsidiary position between this and the following section, 'Transatlantic Routes', which deals with that most critically debated trajectory to the Americas. Such a structure admits to the variety of critical responses created by the play and puts those competing voices in dialogue, bringing together arguments from one of the most contentious of Renaissance play texts and successfully introducing both a student and an advanced readership to the issues involved.

The theatre productions examined are, in line with the focus on critical and creative responses to the play, adaptations of the play rather than 'straight' performances. The multi-media performance of *Tempest(s)* at the Terra Nova Theatre Institute, Copenhagen [1999] is discussed; through the use of multimedia, this production examined ideas of exile, displacement and asylum in contemporary Europe, and highlighted the displacement of both Caliban and Miranda. Teatro Buendía's *Otra Tempestad* at the Globe in London [1998] and the production of Aimé Césaire's *Une tempête* at the Gate Theatre (Notting Hill, London) in the same year are the other two productions under discussion. Alongside this interest in adaptations of the play, it is also interesting, if perhaps inevitable, that the bulk of creative responses (whether theatrical, visual or poetic) are made from the subject position of, or simply concerning, the colonized.

Some of the essays are quite short, shorter than one might expect in such a collection. This is by no means an introductory text, however, as the chapters consider single issues briefly, but in complex and revealing ways. For instance, Joseph Roach's discussion of the commodification of experience through vicarious tourism is marvellous. Certain essays, such as Christy Anderson's short historicized piece on waterworks and hydraulics or Alden T. Vaughan's thorough essay on the presence of American natives in seventeenth-century London, offer information,

and gesture towards its impact upon the play, leaving the reader to analyse the text and the effect of this information upon its interpretation. By way of contrast in approach, Roland Greene's 'Island Logic' is perhaps the most subtle and persuasive of the shorter pieces and, tellingly, it is the one that most opens the play up to scrutiny. Strangely, for a collection that focuses on a single play, one can at times feel somewhat at a distance from the play text itself. To a certain extent, this book seems to dance around *The Tempest*; rather than engaging directly with it, the collection's function seems to be to provide a layered system to enable others to get to grips with the play. This, however, is a very small quibble. This is an important new kind of book which is both a valuable source of information and a framework for future study and research. It will stimulate students and scholars alike to further work in the area and encourage creative thinking on the play.

A collection of a rather different kind, although of equal use to students of Shakespeare's late plays, is Patrick M. Murphy, ed., *The Tempest: Critical Essays*. Once again, we can see the wealth of comment which the play has provoked, this time on display in a historical overview of theatrical and critical responses complemented by a section of newly commissioned essays. Indeed, as M.C. Bradbrook puts it in her 'Romance, Farewell! *The Tempest*', included in this collection, 'the whole play is like a great chamber, full of echoes. Many writers have been caught up to develop it' (p. 195). Murphy's anthology proves that this has been the case from the word go. Alongside an introduction which runs the gamut of critiques of the play, from the earliest commentaries through the particularly convoluted history of its criticism in the twentieth century, Murphy draws on important theatrical responses to *The Tempest* as well as critical ones, dealing with Jonson's *Bartholomew Fair* and Fletcher's *Sea Voyage* among others. This collection, refreshingly, puts its money where its mouth is in recognizing the importance of performance and creative responses to the play in addition to more mainstream critical interventions, and in doing so it removes some of the artificial boundaries between those categories. Again, the inclusion of early commentaries gives readers easy access to the forceful voices of theatrical and textual critics who may otherwise be neglected by students.

Murphy's selections move from historical interpretations and commentaries to the present day. The stated aim of the general editor of the Garland Critical Essays series, Philip C. Kolin, is 'to provide the most influential historical criticism, the most significant contemporary interpretations, and reviews of the most influential productions' (p. xi) from the seventeenth century to the present day, and this allows readers to see how responses and interpretations of a single play have altered over the centuries. One extremely valuable aspect of this and the other collections in the series is that, as Kolin makes clear, essays are in the main reproduced in their entirety rather than edited into smaller sections. This admirable project makes for a long and weighty book, and it provides the reader with an invaluable trajectory of *Tempest* criticism should one choose to read it from cover to cover, or an essential source of information should one choose simply to dip in and out.

The book is divided into sections of existing essays, a consideration of *The Tempest* in performance, and a concluding section of new essays. The new writings on the play demonstrate the extent to which current concerns are consistently projected onto it. For instance, Geraldo U. de Sousa's historicized ecological reading, and Barbara Ann Sebek's clear-sighted interpretation of the idea of pleasure and its effects on the gendered discourses of the play (and the models used to interpret gender roles more generally) are good examples, while Alan de Gooyer reconsiders the relationship between Shakespeare's play and one of its best-known source texts, Montaigne's essays and in particular 'Of the Cannibals' and 'Of Cruelty'. The ongoing life of the play and its openness to revision and to creative responses, witnessed in other books reviewed here, is again attested to in Edward O'Shea's consideration of 'Modernist Versions of *The Tempest*: Auden, Woolf, Tippett'.

The performance section of the volume works through contemporary accounts and later reconstructions of theatrical productions, mainly European and American. The main exception is an account of the production in Bali by an Australian company, the Murdoch Performing Group. The section includes the writings of those who have directed or acted in the play and of commentators on performance, such as Virginia Mason Vaughan and Alden T. Vaughan, whose review of Bob Carlton's *Return to the Forbidden Planet*, Peter Greenaway's *Prospero's Books* and Aimé Césaire's *Une tempête* covers most of the usual ground in a single article. Meanwhile, following the theory that we can learn a lot about a play from what fails in performance as well as from what works well, Randall Louis Anderson writes on the partially successful 1991 production at the Guthrie Theater in Minneapolis. As the above suggests, there are quite a few North American productions included in this section. This may be because the collection is aimed at a North American readership or perhaps a result of the consideration of the play from a North American perspective in recent criticism, but, as I will suggest, this emphasis seems oddly weighted.

This North American slant has an impact on the development of the collection. For one thing, the issue of Ireland's relationship to the play is almost entirely ignored. Regardless of how contentious such readings might be felt to be, they have been the focus of important criticism in recent years and as such deserve rather more of a showing than they get here. The only representation of this particular slant is Claudia W. Harris's 'The Tempest as Political Allegory', which includes a consideration of—among others—the 1993 production of the play in Dublin's Kilmainham Gaol (where the leaders of the 1916 Easter Rising were executed) by the Island Theatre Company. This is revealed as a remarkable piece of theatre, and its resonances with the Irish situation are profound. However, it seems unwise to ask one essay to bear the weight of the critical interest in Ireland in *The Tempest* in this manner and, in so doing, to ignore the connections between early modern England and Ireland by focusing on the twentieth century in this way.

As this last section suggests, there are, as in any collection of this kind, some absences. In this case, the absences at first seem surprising but in fact suggest an engaging and revealing editorial trajectory. Of the usual suspects from late twentieth-century materialist or historicist criticism, most are simply mentioned in the introduction rather than included in the body of the anthology. While Orgel's 'Prospero's Wife' is rightly here, much seminal but oft-reprinted work by critics such as Paul Brown is noticeably absent. Although the inclusion of such pieces would be predictable, they do nevertheless represent defining moments in *Tempest* criticism. However, this aside, the approach that Murphy has chosen shows a lively and various history of approaches to the play which is valuable in itself. Essays include Ernest Law's 'Shakespeare's *Tempest* as Originally Produced at Court',

Michael Dobson's work on later appropriations of Shakespeare—which seems to fit perfectly with the remit of this collection and for which a context is established early on with the preface from Dryden's adaptation, *The Tempest or the Enchanted Island*—and Douglas Bruster's work on the 'Local *Tempest*'. This said, the collection seems rather light in terms of its engagement with issues of feminism, gender or colonialism. Of the 'older' pieces included, only Lorie Jerrell Leininger's vivid writing on and rewriting of Shakespeare explicitly takes a feminist approach, and Orgel's and Sebek's pieces also engage with issues of gender. As far as colonialist readings are concerned, it seems that the editor means the reader to do the work, providing him or her with the necessary information to trace the emerging racial and colonialist consciousness of readings of Caliban and Sycorax. Let me say that this approach is entirely appropriate and works extremely well. My one misgiving, though, is that the result of leaving such a narrative implicit rather than making it explicit is to slightly misrepresent recent decades of critical interest.

Misgivings aside, this collection, perhaps working around inclusions made in other recent anthologies (for example, R.S. White's New Casebook [1999], which includes much of the kind of criticism absent here) offers a different view of *Tempest* criticism than is sometimes seen. Although I feel that there should be more work included on the interpretations of the racial, colonial and gendered discourses of the play, there are undeniable benefits from the editorial decisions. While not diminishing the undoubted and critically enshrined importance of the debates over the geographical location of the play and its dealing with colonialism, the chronology and trajectory of this collection—and its underlying admission that the things that we care about as critics, performers, directors, readers, and audience change over time—put these debates, vital as they are and all-absorbing as they have been, into perspective.

So, with some reservations about the selections made in Murphy's anthology, his collection presents a richer vision of the history of *Tempest* criticism, and a context for these later statements, than might otherwise be seen. Also, it is worth noting that, as with so many books of this kind, this collection is a great resource. At a time when university libraries often have to cut back on their holdings, this kind of anthology becomes increasingly important to students in allowing them access to seminal comments on Shakespeare's play.

Another book on *The Tempest* which deals with it from a North American angle is Heidi Hutner's *Colonial Women: Race and Culture in Stuart Drama*. Indeed, this book is so invested in an exploration of the 'American' *Tempest* that the assumption of the play's location is never questioned and the debates over its geography never raised. Hutner's book offers a further renewed vision of *The Tempest*, this time through a new chronology which reconnects the play with its later seventeenth-century counterparts. Importantly, the book explores the figure of the colonized woman in Stuart drama, taking off from a consideration of *The Tempest* alongside John Fletcher's less-studied *Sea Voyage* and against the Pocahontas myth to consider the roles of race, gender and colonialism in post-Restoration drama. Using Shakespeare's play as a starting point, the author assesses the representation of European and non-European women in the theatre of the seventeenth century, moving through Restoration adaptations of *The Tempest*, Dryden and Howard's *Indian Queen*, and Dryden's *Indian Emperour*, and concluding with a chapter on the work of Aphra Behn.

The scope and focus of the book are apparent from this brief summary. The chronology is a strong and sensitive one, wisely chosen and capable of discerning shifts in the culture of English colonialism and its theatrical treatment, including issues of casting, transvestism and women actors. What is more, this monograph brings several less canonical plays into contact with Shakespeare's work and exposes them to scrutiny. One noticeable absence, however, is a consideration of John Fletcher's *The Island Princess* [1621], which would have stood allusively alongside his *Sea Voyage* and Shakespeare's *Tempest*. However, the main thrust of the book is its focus on issues of gender and colonialism.

In carrying out this analysis, Hutner brings important information concerning the Spanish colonization of the Americas and the history of the lives of native American, particularly Algonquian, women and the gynocentric social order in which they lived to bear on readings of English plays with colonialist themes and concerns. She explores the myths of Pocahontas and Malinche who, she writes, 'both figure as symbols of the native woman who is willingly conquered and exploited by the European lover/colonizer' (p. 7), discussing the relationship of each with John Smith and John Rolfe, and Cortes respectively. This is valuable, as it goes beyond the sometimes vague considerations of native American cultures used in readings of the drama. At times, however, the introduction's analysis seems slightly clumsy, and some of Hutner's conclusions seem rather less exciting than her material would suggest. Added to this, there are worrying inaccuracies, such as a description, in her discussion of Dryden and Davenant's *Enchanted Island*, of Sycorax as a 'freckled hag-born [whelp] ... not honoured with a human shape' (p. 53). This is problematic because those lines refer firstly to Caliban and secondly (in the Oxford edition at least) to the island, and they do so too (with appropriate alterations to include Caliban's sister, Sycorax) in the Restoration adaptation. Most limiting, though, is the reading of the play and its intersections of gender and race solely through its American context. Hutner's project, and her focus on the women of the Americas, is extremely valuable, but it would be better served were the other possibilities of this allusive and resonant play, as instanced in Murphy's anthology, also admitted and considered.

An article which deals with the American history of *The Tempest* rather more successfully is Coppélia Kahn's 'Caliban at the Stadium: Shakespeare and the Making of Americans' (*MR* 41[2000] 256–84). Analysing accounts of the 1916 performance in New York of an adaptation of the play called *Caliban by the Yellow Sands*, Kahn considers the place of Shakespeare in the forging of a modern American identity at the point of entry for many of the country's immigrants. Interestingly, this is an updating of the place of Caliban in relation to American readings of *The Tempest* and it argues strongly for a vision of Shakespeare as a means to unite an English-speaking America in the face of ongoing immigration. By way of contrast, and as an example of some of the debates which Hutner's book might acknowledge, Rowland Wymer's '*The Tempest* and the Origins of Britain' (*CS* 11[1999] 3–14), reinserts 'Britain' into the play as itself a construct and site of colonization. Set out as a response to American-centred readings, Wymer's article successfully historicizes writings on the play within a discourse of 'Britishness'. Gabriel Egan's 'Ariel's Costume in the Original Staging of *The Tempest*' (*TN* 52[1997] 63–72) is another historicized piece, focusing intently on the moment surrounding the play's initial performances to discuss possibilities for the costuming of the actor playing Ariel, and challenging the theories of Saenger and Gurr on the matter. Steven Marx, 'Greenaway's Books' (*EMLS* 7:ii[2001]), analyses Peter Greenaway's *Prospero's Books* and *The Tempest* through the book of Revelation.

Two articles which take explicit issue with the ways in which *Tempest* criticism has recently been conducted are Tom McAlindon's 'The Discourse of Prayer in *The Tempest*' (*SEL* 41[2001] 335–55), and Jessica Slights's 'Rape and the Romanticization of Shakespeare's Miranda' (*SEL* 41[2001] 357–79). McAlindon deals with the language of prayer in *The Tempest*, setting it against imperialist interpretations of Caliban's famous outburst that he has learnt to curse to offer a new view of language in the play than that of postcolonialist critics. In what he admits is a controversial move, he sets out to show that language does not function only as a colonialist tool on the island of *The Tempest*, and to challenge the idea of a 'tyrannical Prospero and a finally unreconciled Caliban' (p. 336). Equally controversially, he sees a play which does not legitimize an oppressive hierarchical order but which 'advances a levelling, horizontal ethic of interdependence and reciprocity' (p. 336). Particularly persuasive is his point that Prospero's plan throughout (and indeed for) the play is to safeguard Miranda after his death, rather than leave her to life with Caliban on the island. While he does not touch on the colonial dynamics of this observation, which might well be explored, this is an astute remark which alters the whole thrust of the play, redirecting it away from Prospero's relationship with Alonso and the need for reconciliation and towards the need to secure Miranda's marriage and future off the island.

Slight's discussion of Miranda stands interestingly next to McAlindon's arguments, and also has much in common with Barbara Ann Sebek's analysis in Patrick M. Murphy's anthology on *The Tempest* of the role of female agency (see above). While Slights and Sebek argue from a rather different standpoint as far as feminist readings of this character are concerned, both argue for the reconsideration of Miranda as an agent. Slights takes on what she regards as the exclusion of Miranda from critical discourse (certainly something which Murphy's anthology seems to bear out) in favour of the female characters—Claribel and Sycorax (and, I would add, Medea)—who are not on stage. She does this through a reconsideration of the idea of 'character criticism', going back through the work of Christy Desmet, Michael D. Bristol and Harry Berger Jr. to Alan Sinfield's *Faultlines* to discuss a reinvigorated interest in the construction of character. Slights criticizes the representation of Miranda in contemporary criticism as nothing more than an 'unwitting object of exchange in a matrix of colonial and nuptial economies' (p. 359), or 'a cipher, a figure important only for her unwitting role in helping to realize her father's political aspirations' (p. 361). Slights takes particular issue with the treatment of the threatened rape of Miranda by Caliban as a purely colonialist event and as somehow beyond the realm of feminist criticism. She convincingly argues against the binary (and implicitly colonialist) thinking which proposes that either Miranda or Caliban, but not both, can act morally.

One other book dealing with *The Tempest* this year is Mary Ann McGrail's *Tyranny in Shakespeare*. In two chapters, one dealing with *The Tempest* and one with *The Winter's Tale*, McGrail applies early modern political theory to these texts and argues for 'a more extreme subversion' than previously recognized in the plays as far as the idea of tyranny is concerned. Indeed, she sets up *The Tempest* as a marker for this exploration and for the other plays (*Macbeth* and *Richard II*) which she discusses. McGrail sees the two late plays under consideration here as centrally concerned with the idea of tyranny through the prism of 'a world influenced or ruled by art' (p. 79). After laying out several early modern definitions of tyranny in the introduction, and applying them to the plays in question, she draws the very natural conclusion, after recent years of criticism which has obsessively unravelled the relationship of the plays to the politics of the early modern and the present-day world, that, rather than withdrawing from it, the late plays are thoroughly engaged in the political realm.

The Winter's Tale crops up again as a subject of interest in the 2001 edition of Renaissance Drama, edited by Jeffrey Masten and Wendy Wall. This particular issue deals with the theme 'Institutions of the Text', and explores early modern theatre in relation to the printing industry, the marketplace, ideas of authorship and of family, theatre companies and manuscript circulation. The diverse range of material includes two articles on The Winter's Tale, Aaron Kitch's 'Bastards and Broadsides in The Winter's Tale' (RenD 30[2001] 43–71), and Steven R. Mentz's 'Wearing Greene: Autolycus, Robert Greene, and the Structure of Romance in The Winter's Tale' (RenD 30[2001] 73–92), and ends with Kate McLuskie's reconsideration of the commodification of Shakespeare in the era of late capitalism. Kitch's essay explores the language of printing, and the press in particular, and of bastardy in Paulina's appeal to Leontes for Perdita's life in II.iii, developing a materialist argument concerning the 'imprinting' or 'stamping' of the image of paternity on the child, to focus specifically on the image of the printing press. This is later related to Autolycus's role in the play and to the London broadside industry. Mentz examines the haunting of Shakespeare's play by the textual influence of Robert Greene, centring on the subplots of cony-catching and repentance in The Winter's Tale as they relate to or develop from Greene's work. He concludes that Shakespeare reconciled himself both to Greene's life and literary career and to his fiction and pamphleteering through a play which comes to stand for the all-encompassing world of romance.

Other explorations of The Winter's Tale include Walter S. Lim's 'Knowledge and Belief in The Winter's Tale' (SEL 41[2001] 317–34). Starting, as so much work does, with the reanimation of Hermione's statue, this essay considers the theme of religious belief and the scriptural and religious antecedents of this bringing back to life. As the author says, 'The Winter's Tale tantalizes its audience by finally raising the question of how one can know with absolute certainty and total conviction that the faith to which one adheres is indeed valid and true' (p. 319). Frederick Keifer's 'The Iconography of Time in The Winter's Tale' (Ren&R 23[1999] 49–64), offers a thorough exploration of the iconography and emblems of Time in Renaissance culture.

Shakespeare's Cymbeline attracted rather less attention than other of Shakespeare's late plays, but there were two interesting pieces. Eve Rachele Sanders offers an interpretation of gender and the reading of the letter on the early modern stage in 'Interiority and the Letter in Cymbeline' (CS 12[2000] 49–70); J. Clinton Crumley reconsiders the generic form of the play, seeing a dynamic relationship between history and romance, in 'Questioning History in Cymbeline' (SEL 41[2001] 297–315).

Books Reviewed

Adamson, Sylvia, Lynette Hunter, Lynne Magnusson, Ann Thompson, and Katie Wales, eds. *Reading Shakespeare's Dramatic Language: A Guide*. ArdenSh. [2001] pp. 321. £12.99 ISBN 1 9034 3629 X.

Andersen, Henning, ed. *Actualization: Linguistic Change in Progress*. Papers from a Workshop Held at the 14th International Conference on Historical Linguistics, Vancouver, 14 August 1999. CILT 219 ser., vol. 219. Benjamins. [2001] pp. viii + 250. $77 ISBN 1 5881 1081 8.

Bednarz, James P. *Shakespeare and the Poets' War*. ColUP. [2001] pp. x + 334. $51.50 ISBN 0 2311 2243 8.

Beehler, Sharon A., and Holger Klein, eds. *Shakespeare and Higher Education: A Global Perspective*. Mellen. [2001] pp. 476. £79.95 ISBN 0 7734 7262 2.

Bell, Maureen, Shirley Chew, Simon Eliot, Lynette Hunter, and James L. W. West III, eds. *Re-Constructing the Book: Literary Texts in Transmission*. Ashgate. [2001] pp. xi + 231. £37.50 ($59.95) ISBN 0 7546 0360 1.

Berry, Ralph. *Shakespeare and the Hunt*. CUP. [2001] pp. 266. £40.79 ISBN 0 5218 0070 6.

Brown, Richard Danson, and David Johnson. *Shakespeare 1609: Cymbeline and the Sonnets*. Macmillan. [2001] pp. 189. hb £47.50 ($59.95) ISBN 0 3339 1318 3, pb £15.50 ($24.95) ISBN 0 3339 1322 1.

Callaghan, Dympna, ed. *A Feminist Companion to Shakespeare*. Blackwell. [2001] pp. 416. hb £60 ISBN 0 6312 0806 2, pb £ 16.99 ISBN 0 6312 0807 0.

Callaghan, Dympna. *Shakespeare Without Women: Representing Gender and Race on the Renaissance Stage*. Routledge. [2000] pp. 160. hb £60 ISBN 0 4152 0231 0, pb £18.50 ISBN 0 4152 0232 9.

Cartmell, Deborah, I.Q. Hunter, and Imelda Whelehan, eds. *Retrovisions: Reinventing the Past in Film and Fiction*. Pluto. [2001] pp. viii + 168. hb £45 ($60) ISBN 0 7453 1583 6, pb £14.99 ($19.95) ISBN 0 7453 1578 X.

Cartmell, Deborah, and Michael Scott, eds. *Talking Shakespeare: Shakespeare into the Millennium*. Palgrave. [2001] pp. ix + 253. £15.50 ISBN 0 3337 7773 5.

Chedgzoy, Kate, ed. *Shakespeare, Feminism and Gender*. Palgrave. [2001] pp. ix + 269. £13.99 ISBN 0 3337 1652 3.

Cox, John D., and Eric Rasmussen, eds. *King Henry VI Part Three*. ArdenSh. [2001] pp. xvii + 460. £7.99 ISBN 1 9034 3631 1.

D'Amico, Jack. *Shakespeare and Italy: The City and the Stage*. Florida. [2001] pp. 198. $55 ISBN 0 8130 1878 1.

Danson, Lawrence. *Shakespeare's Dramatic Genres*. OUP. [2000] pp. 160. hb £27.50 ISBN 0 1987 1173 5, pb £12.99 ISBN 0 1987 1172 7.

De Grazia, Margreta, and Stanley Wells, eds. *The Cambridge Companion to Shakespeare*. CUP. [2001] pp. xx + 328. hb $60 ISBN 0 5216 5094 1, pb $22 ISBN 0 5216 5881 0.

Dobson, Michael, and Stanley Wells, eds. *The Oxford Companion to Shakespeare*. OUP. [2001] pp. xxix + 541. $45 ISBN 0 1981 1735 3.

Freinkel, Emily. *Reading Shakespeare's Will: The Theology of the Figure from Augustine to the Sonnets*. ColUP. [2001] pp. 416. hb $ 52.50 ISBN 0 2311 2324 8, pb $ 19.50 ISBN 0 2311 2325 6.

Geckle, George L., ed. *Shakespeare: The Critical Tradition. Measure for Measure.* Athlone. [2001] pp. xxxvi + 382. £95 ISBN 0 4858 1004 2.

Golder, John, and Richard Madelaine, eds. *O Brave New World: Two Centuries of Shakespeare on the Australian Stage.* Currency. [2001] pp. xiii + 306 + 61 b/w figs. $A39.95 ISBN 0 8681 9613 4.

Greenblatt, Stephen. *Hamlet in Purgatory.* PrincetonUP. [2001] pp. 322. £19.95 ISBN 0 6910 5873 3.

Griffin, Benjamin. *Playing the Past: Approaches to English Historical Drama, 1385–1600.* Brewer. [2001] pp. xiii + 193. £40 ISBN 0 8599 1615 4.

Gross, Kenneth. *Shakespeare's Noise.* Chicago. [2001] pp. 304. hb $42 ISBN 0 2263 0988 6, pb $17 ISBN 0 2263 0989 4.

Hidalgo, Pilar. *Paradigms Found: Feminist, Gay, and New Historicist Readings of Shakespeare.* Rodopi. [2001] pp. 162. $32 ISBN 9 0420 1235 8.

Howard, Jean E., and Scott Cutler Shershow, eds. *Marxist Shakespeares.* Routledge. [2001] pp. xii + 304. hb £60 ($90) ISBN 0 4152 0233 7, pb £17.99 ($29.99) ISBN 0 4152 0234 5.

Hulme, Peter, and William H. Sherman, eds. *'The Tempest' and its Travels.* Reaktion. [2000] pp. xiv + 319. pb £14.95 ISBN 1 8618 9066 4.

Hutner, Heidi. *Colonial Women: Race and Culture in Stuart Drama.* OUP. [2001] pp. ix + 141. £25 ISBN 0 1951 4188 1.

Kahn, Victoria, and Lorna Hutson, eds. *Rhetoric and Law in Early Modern Europe.* YaleUP. [2001] pp. 355. £30 ISBN 0 3000 8485 4.

Kastan, David Scott. *Shakespeare and the Book.* CUP. [2001] pp. xiii + 167. £10.95 ISBN 0 5217 8651 7.

Keevak, Michael. *Sexual Shakespeare: Forgery, Authorship, Portraiture.* WSUP. [2001] pp. 175. hb £ 31.50 ($ 39.95) ISBN 0 8143 2953 5, pb. £ 15.95 ($19.95) 0 8143 2975 6.

Kirsch, A., ed. *Lectures on Shakespeare* by W.H. Auden. Faber. [2001] pp. 398. £30 ISBN 0 5712 0712 X.

Kliman, Bernice W., ed. *Approaches to Teaching Shakespeare's Hamlet.* MLA. [2001] pp. xiv + 291. hb $37.50 ISBN 0 8735 2767 4, pb $18 ISBN 0 8735 2768 2.

Knutson, Roslyn Lander. *Playing Companies and Commerce in Shakespeare's Time.* CUP. [2001] pp. x + 198. $55 ISBN 0 5217 7242 7.

McGrail, Mary Ann. *Tyranny in Shakespeare.* Lexington Books. [2001] pp. ix + 181. £46 ISBN 0 7391 0082 3.

Martin, Randall, ed. *Henry IV, Part Three.* The Oxford Shakespeare. OUP. [2001] pp. x + 392. £7.99 ISBN 0 1928 3141 0.

McDonald, Russ. *Shakespeare and the Arts of Language.* OUP. [2001] pp. 222. hb £25 ISBN 0 1987 1170 0, pb £12.99 ISBN 0 1987 1171 9.

Miola, Robert. *Shakespeare's Reading.* OUP. [2000] pp. 211. hb £25 ISBN 0 1987 1168 9, pb £12.99 0 1987 1169 7.

Moisan, Thomas, and Douglas Bruster, eds. *In the Company of Shakespeare: Essays on English Renaissance Literature in Honor of G. Blakemore Evans.* FDUP. [2001] pp. 357. £44 ($55) ISBN 0 8386 3902 X.

Murphy, Patrick M, ed. *The Tempest: Critical Essays.* Routledge. [2001] pp. xiv + 586. £60 ISBN 0 8153 2471 5.

Parker, Kenneth. *Antony and Cleopatra*. WTW. Northcote. [2000] pp. 104. £8.99 ISBN 0 7463 0825 6.

Pendleton, Thomas A., ed. *Henry VI: Critical Essays*. Garland. [2001] pp. xii + 302. £60 ($95) ISBN 0 8153 3301 3.

Pennington, Michael. *Twelfth Night: A User's Guide*. Hern. [2000] pp. 259. £12.99 ISBN 1 8545 9475 3.

Pincombe, Mike, ed. *The Anatomy of Tudor Literature*. Ashgate. [2001] pp. x + 235. £42.50 ISBN 0 7546 0243 5.

Ryuta, Minami, Ian Carruthers, and John Gillies, eds. *Performing Shakespeare in Japan*. CUP. [2001] pp. xiii + 259; 8 colour plates + 16 b/w figs. £45 ISBN 0 5217 8244 9.

Rutter, Carol Chillington. *Enter the Body: Women and Representation on Shakespeare's Stage*. Routledge [2001] pp. xxi + 218. £18.27 ISBN 0 4151 4164 8.

Samuels, Robert. *Writing Prejudices: The Psychoanalysis and Pedagogy of Discrimination from Shakespeare to Toni Morrison*. SUNYP. [2001] pp. 224. £14.25 ISBN 0 7914 4876 2.

Sanders, Julie. *Novel Shakespeares: Twentieth-Century Women Novelists and Appropriation*. Manchester. [2001] pp. xi + 258. hb £45 ISBN 0 7190 5815 5, pb £24.95 ISBN 0 7190 5816 3.

Spiekerman, Tim. *Shakespeare's Political Realism: The English History Plays*. SUNYP. [2001] pp. 208. hb £50 ISBN 0 7914 4867 3, pb £14.50 ISBN 0 7914 4868 1.

Sutherland, John, and Cedric Watts. *Henry V, War Criminal? And Other Shakespeare Puzzles*. OUP. [2000] pp. 238. pb £4.99 ISBN 0 1928 3879 2.

Taylor, Michael. *Shakespeare Criticism in the Twentieth Century*. OUP. [2001] pp. vii + 278. hb £25 ISBN 0 1987 1185 9, pb £12.99 ISBN 0 1987 1184 0.

Thorne, Alison. *Vision and Rhetoric in Shakespeare: Looking through Language*. Palgrave. [2000] pp. 290. £47.50 ISBN 0 3122 2657 8.

Wells, Stanley, and Catherine Alexander, eds., *Shakespeare and Sexuality*. CUP. [2001] pp. ix + 207. hb £40 ($55) ISBN 0 5218 0031 5, pb £13.95 ($20) ISBN 0 5218 0475 2.

Werner, Sarah. *Shakespeare and Feminist Performance: Ideology on Stage*. Routledge. [2001] pp. 132. £16.99 ISBN 0 4152 2730 5.

Wright, George T. *Hearing the Measures: Shakespearean and Other Inflections*. UWiscP. [2001] pp. xiv + 327. hb £50.50 ($60) ISBN 0 2991 7190 6, pb £20.95 ($24.95) ISBN 0 2991 7194 9.

Wynne-Davies, Marion, ed. *Much Ado About Nothing and The Taming of the Shrew*. New Casebooks. Palgrave. [2001] pp. 272. hb £45 ISBN 0 3336 5790 X, pb £14.50 ISBN 0 3336 5791 8.

VII

Renaissance Drama: Excluding Shakespeare

SARAH POYNTING, PETER J. SMITH, MATTHEW STEGGLE
AND DARRYLL GRANTLEY

This chapter has three sections: 1. Editions and Textual Scholarship; 2. Theatre History; 3. Criticism. Section 1 is by Sarah Poynting; section 2 is by Peter J. Smith; sections 3(a) and (c) are by Matthew Steggle; and section 3(b) is by Darryll Grantley.

1. Editions and Textual Scholarship

There has been a considerable reduction in editorial productivity this year, with even the usual steady flow of student editions almost drying up. However, there was one outstanding single edition in the Revels series from Manchester University Press: complementing Robert Miola's edition of Ben Jonson's *Every Man In* (reviewed last year), we have Helen Ostovich's *Every Man Out of His Humour*. She uses Q1 (1600) as copy-text, collated against Q2 and Q3 (both also 1600) and the 1616 Folio, and makes a very strong case for having done so, arguing that 'it is this text which first made Jonson's literary reputation' and 'vehemently represents Jonson's intention in 1600' (p. 8). Her discussion of the revisions made by Jonson for the Folio is not only clear, but, more unusually, entertaining. She has given priority to Jonson's original ending for the play, with the revised versions (from Q1 and the Folio) printed in an appendix, along with his 'Apology for the Original Catastrophe'. I would have appreciated a more extended discussion of the revisions to the denouement in the critical introduction, which is substantial enough to have accommodated it. Once the choice of copy-text and ending has been made, the text itself presents few problems. A small number of variants have been accepted from F1, as well as its supplements to Q's stage directions, but otherwise the text has been subject only to the normal Revels modernization, with Jonson's punctuation and sentence length apparently quite extensively updated. The critical annotation is very thorough indeed; it seems unlikely that any questions readers may have are not answered here, and there is a generous amount of absorbing contextual information. The lengthy and at times densely argued introduction focuses first on genre, with a consideration of comical satire, humours plays and farce leading to a discussion of Aristophanic influences in Jonson's work, including the use of the chorus, comic invective and dramatic structure. The milieu and revels of the Inns of Court are explored, followed by a siting of *Every Man Out* in the context of the theatre—of its theatrical potential in general, and its staging at the Globe in particular. Ostovich believes that dramatic developments in the twentieth century, from Brecht to *Monty Python*, would make modern audiences receptive to Jonson's comedy, not performed since 1675: as I so often have reason to say at this point, perhaps we can hope for a revival. The relationship the play creates with the audience, especially through the medium of its chorus, the Grex, is analysed, as well as the interplay between the characters, and the effect that both of these have on the audience's perception of levels of illusion and reality. The 'dance of observers and participants' in the paradigmatic setting of Paul's Walk, viewed as both 'Arid circularity' and 'a celebratory ballet', epitomizes for Ostovich in its complexities and contradictions the polysemousness that Jonson wishes to evoke (pp. 62, 64, 68). While I was not always convinced by some of her arguments (in her discussion of the female characters, Jonson emerges as something of a proto-feminist) this introduction gives its readers a great deal to ponder.

The year's Malone Society volume was a near-diplomatic transcription by Elizabeth Baldwin of a hitherto unpublished and untitled play, *The Wisest have their Fools about Them*, from a manuscript among the Crewe family papers in the Cheshire and Chester archives. Earlier articles written by Baldwin about the play have given it the title *Musophilus*, but as this was found to cause confusion with Samuel Daniel's poem of the same name, a new editorial title has been assigned on the basis of the use of the proverbial phrase in the play, and its emphasis on the role of the fool. The usual scrupulously detailed physical description of the manuscript is followed by a consideration of the date of the play, which Baldwin places as likely to be in the late 1620s on the grounds of topical references, its vocabulary (which includes a number of words cited by the *OED* as first used in the 1620s and 1630s), and events in the life of its possible first owner, Sir Ranulph Crewe. She finds no evidence of identifiable direct borrowings from other dramatic texts in the play, although the playwright was evidently familiar with a common stock of characters and situations. Jonson is proposed as an influence, and examples of phrases with echoes of his plays and masques are provided. On the basis of its careful stage directions, Baldwin suggests that the play may have been prepared for performance, perhaps at the Inns of Court, although there is no evidence as to whether one ever took place. Its production by a professional company was feasible, with twenty-seven parts to be played by eight or nine actors, and limited requirements for scenery, costumes and props, all of which Baldwin outlines. This is a very welcome edition of a play that will be new to most of us.

The other two volumes this year are both collections. Oxford University Press have added to their World's Classics Oxford English Drama series with *The Roaring Girl and other City Comedies*, edited and introduced by James Knowles, with explanatory notes and a glossary by Eugene Giddens. The title play is actually the final one in the collection, preceded (chronologically by performance) by Dekker's *The Shoemaker's Holiday*, Chapman, Jonson and Marston's *Eastward Ho!* and Jonson's *Every Man In His Humour*. The first three have all been re-edited from their respective first quartos, the last from the rewritten Folio version of 1616. The textual introduction briefly discusses problems specific to each play, including the censorship (but not the shared authorship) of *Eastward Ho!* and the revision of *Every Man In*, but in general usually accepted emendations are silently adopted with a few exceptions recorded in the introduction. Giddens's notes succinctly explain problematic words and phrases, topical allusions, proverbial utterances and literary references; there is a short but useful critical bibliography. As with other volumes in this series, Knowles succeeds in supplying the target readership (presumably of undergraduates) with a critical introduction that covers a good deal of essential ground in a limited space. The unique nature of London as an English city in the early seventeenth century is addressed, as well as the way in which its size and heterogeneity gave rise to 'distinct sub-cultural groups', creating mass theatre audiences of unprecedented social variety whose experience of the structure of the city's economy made the plays' use of metaphors of exchange and the market immediately appropriate. He considers the contemporary performance history both of the plays in this volume and of others drawing on popular ballads, newsworthy events, or 'underworld chic', to challenge the belief that the existence of popular and elite theatres can be 'translated straightforwardly into taste and repertoire differences' (p. xv). The linguistic forms—music, moral tags, canting, fashionable affectations, catchphrases—of the four plays are briefly examined in relation to their audiences, as are the popular traditions and aspirations concerning London that inform their narratives. The differences in the dramatists' depiction of the city, from the romance of *The Shoemaker's Holiday* to the disgusted satire of *Eastward Ho!*, are clearly delineated, with the portrayal of female characters shown to be of particular significance in this respect. The dangers and pleasures of urban life all find a place in these plays, and in Knowles's introduction to them.

Jonson makes his third appearance of the year in the second edition of the Norton Critical Edition of *Ben Jonson's Plays and Masques*, edited by Richard Harp. This inevitably has a considerable overlap with the 1979 first edition: *Volpone, Epicoene, The Alchemist, Mercury Vindicated from the Alchemists at Court* and *Pleasure Reconciled to Virtue* have all survived, but *The Sad Shepherd, The Masque of Queens* and *Oberon* have all been dropped in favour of *The Masque of Blackness* (which does not feel entirely like a fair exchange). The textual information on them is even more minimal than in most student editions; all have helpful, if limited, explanatory notes. The same material as previously is presented in the section 'Jonson on his Work', with the addition of the Epistle Dedicatory to *Volpone*; Godolphin, Waller, Mayne and Carew on Jonson remain in place, as do essays by Jonas Barish, John Dryden and Edward B. Partridge. Different pieces by Ian Donaldson ('Jonson's Magic Houses') and Stephen Orgel ('*The Masque of Blackness*') are included, while articles by Anne Barton on names, Robert C. Evans ('Thomas Sutton: Jonson's Volpone?'), Robert Watson ('*Epicoene*'), Richard Harp ('Ben Jonson's Comic Apocalypse'), D.J. Gordon ('The Imagery of *The Masque of Blackness*'), John Mulryan ('Mythic Interpretations of Ideas in Jonson's *Pleasure Reconciled to Virtue*') and Leah Marcus ('*Pleasure and Virtue Reconciled*') take the place of those by Harry Levin, William Blissett, Swinburne, Robert M. Adams and T.S. Eliot. A shortened version of Robert M. Adams's introductory piece, 'The Staging of Jonson's Plays and Masques', is also printed, while a Jonson chronology has been added, and the bibliography updated. The major departure from the first edition, though, is the addition of a 'Backgrounds and Sources' section, which includes four beast fables, Horace's satire on legacy-hunting, 'The Alchemy Swindle' from the *Colloquia* of Erasmus, and sections from Stanton J. Linden's *Darke Hierogliphicks: Alchemy in English Literature from Chaucer to the*

Restoration [1996]. I was unconvinced by the usefulness of this section, which is unavoidably very short and which feels rather arbitrary, especially as the remaining plays and masques receive no similar attention. However, it is a reasonable way of obtaining a substantial amount of useful material.

There were at least rather more articles than editions, and I suspect that the one which may attract most attention is N.W. Bawcutt's polemical piece with the innocent title 'Renaissance Dramatists and the Texts of their Plays' (*RORD* 40[2001] 1–24). He takes issue in particular with the conclusions of the forum on the editing of early modern texts recorded in *Shakespeare Studies* 24 (1996), which considered the impact of post-structuralism on textual and bibliographical studies, and in general with current editing theories which insist on the primacy of textual instability and the 'social text', and which challenge the validity of editorial emendation: 'the death of the author is followed by the death of the editor'. He argues that the concept of the Renaissance dramatist as author is not an anachronism, citing evidence of playwrights' resentment at interference with their work by actors, and of their engagement in the printing of their plays, the shoddy printing of which they also resented; the concept of textual 'corruption' was current by the mid-sixteenth century. A necessary questioning of the Greg–Bowers school, he suggests, has hardened into a dominant orthodoxy which appears to wish to jettison more than two centuries of disinterested efforts to clarify texts in a way that would have delighted their authors.

Richard Levin has a rather less contentious, if sometimes speculative, article in the same volume: '*Friar Bacon and Friar Bungay, John of Bordeaux*, and the 1683 Edition of *The History of Friar Bacon*' (*RORD* 40[2001] 55–66). He examines the relationship between the two plays and the 1683 pamphlet (a revised version of *The Famous History of Friar Bacon* adapted almost a century before by Greene), looking in detail at the new chapters in the *History*, some of which derive from *Friar Bacon*, and others apparently from *John of Bordeaux*, which, though normally attributed also to Greene, survives only in an anonymous damaged manuscript. In discussing how the *History* deviates from scenes in *John of Bordeaux*, Levin considers the possible light thrown on the play's corrupt text, and especially its curtailed conclusion, and speculates on what access the author of the pamphlet might have had to a full version of it, suggesting that it might have been printed or performed under another title. The article raises some very interesting questions without always providing wholly persuasive answers to them.

The relationship between prose work and play is also considered in 'A Pre-1592 English Faust Book and the Date of Marlowe's *Doctor Faustus*' by R.J. Fehrenbach (*Library* 2[2001] 327–35). Fehrenbach suggests that the recently discovered inventory of books belonging to an Oxford student who died in 1589 provides evidence for the argument that there was an edition of the English Faust Book earlier than that published in 1592. The article lays out in detail the reasons for believing the inventory entry 'Doctor faustus' to refer to the English Faust Book rather than any other text, and for its having been made no later than December 1589. Fehrenbach recognizes that while this provides no proof that Marlowe's play was written earlier rather than later in his career, it strengthens the possibility that he did so.

Pre-post-structuralist editing theory makes a comeback in *Studies in Bibliography*, which for the first time prints R.B. McKerrow's three 1928 Sandars lectures, 'The Relationship of English Printed Books to Authors' Manuscripts during the Sixteenth and Seventeenth Centuries', edited by Carlo M. Bajetta (*SB* 53[2000/2] 1–65). Bajetta presents the texts as revised slightly by McKerrow on the typescripts presented to Cambridge University Library with a proviso that they were unsuitable for publication. This, Bajetta suggests, is because McKerrow used the lectures to launch his own polemic on contemporary editing theory, and in particular on Pollard and Dover Wilson. The lectures develop the ideas posited first in the 1927 *Introduction to Bibliography*, exploring at length the textual questions sketched out in the book, and doing much to overturn existing dogma.

Bibliographical description of the most detailed kind is considered in G. Thomas Tanselle's article in the same volume, 'The Concept of Format' (*SB* 53[2000/2] 67–115), in which he examines the problems inherent in the correct description of paper sizes and formats, and proposes methods of rectifying the current muddle. He focuses particularly on issues like that delineated by Ostovich in her textual introduction to *Every Man Out*, the first quarto of which has a mixture of genuine quarto gatherings, and pages which are the size and shape of quartos but have the watermark and chain-line arrangement of octavos (termed 'bastard quartos' by Greg). While Tanselle's article goes well beyond the early modern period, and therefore deals with problems unlikely to be found within its printing and manuscript history, as well as proposing solutions that may not always be appropriate to it, it is relevant to anyone with an interest in the bibliographical description of paper.

Questions of attribution arise in two articles this year. The first is '*Lust's Dominion; or The Lascivious Queen*: Authorship, Date and Revision' by Charles Cathcart (*RES* 52[2001] 360–75). Cathcart agrees with earlier arguments that Marston had a hand in the play, and that it is the same play as *The Spanish Moor's Tragedy*, payments for which were listed by Henslowe. However, he argues against its being an adaptation of a 1590s play, suggesting that it was started by Marston in 1599, completed by Dekker, Haughton and Day in 1600, and revised about 1606. He proposes *The Lascivious Queen* as the most likely authorial and performance title. The article includes a table of linguistic preferences of its putative authors, which seems a little inconclusive, and about the weaknesses of which Cathcart is entirely honest. Thomas Merriam, in 'A Simple Discriminator of Shakespeare and Fletcher' (*N&Q* 48[2001] 306–9), is more convinced by the merits of stylometric analysis, which he defends with some passion against Stanley Wells's lack of enthusiasm for it (on the grounds of incomprehensibility). He illustrates his point by showing that the plays of Shakespeare and Fletcher can be easily distinguished by a relative frequency analysis of the word 'hath', although *The Faithful Shepherdess* presents 'a known anomaly' which can be disregarded. His argument that the gulf between traditional and non-traditional methods of attribution can be bridged if the desire on the part of the traditionalists exists to do so is rather undermined by a diagram involving torsos and whiskers.

The problem of how a playwright might have been familiar with rare source material, raised by Levin in relation to *Friar Bacon*, is returned to by Patrick Kincaid in 'John Marston's *The Dutch Courtesan* and William Percy's *The Cuck-Queanes and Cuckolds Errants*' (*N&Q* 48[2001] 309–11). Kincaid suggests that, while the ultimate source for the subplot of both plays is Painter's *Palace of Pleasure*, Marston may have also drawn on Percy's play, which exists only in manuscript, and was apparently never performed. He proposes that Marston may have seen a transcription of *The Cuck-Queanes* made for the St Paul's theatre, in the reopening of which he was involved. Gabriel Heaton makes a further contribution to the study of drama in manuscript in 'The Copyist of a Ben Jonson Manuscript Identified' (*N&Q* 48[2001] 385–8). By a comparison with papers in the Brotherton Library, he shows that the copyist and original owner of Folger Shakespeare Library MS X. d. 475, which includes Jonson's *Entertainment of the King and Queen at Theobalds* of 1607, was John Kaye (Kay/Keye) of the Middle Temple, a member of an obscure Yorkshire gentry family. Heaton successfully traces the auction route by which the manuscript arrived at the Folger, but admits to being less certain as to how Kaye came to have it the first place, since, *pace* Cokayne and *Alumni Cantabrigienses*, he does not seem to have been the John Keyes knighted at Whitehall five days after the performance of the *Entertainment*. As he says, Kaye's ownership illustrates both the extent and haphazardness of manuscript circulation.

Useful editorial footnotes are supplied in the two remaining articles. William M. Hamlin draws attention to a possible source used by Chapman in 'A Borrowing from Nashe in Chapman's *Bussy d'Ambois*' (*N&Q* 48[2001] 264–5). He notes that the conjunction of 'lion' and 'dunghill cock' in Barrisor's speech (I.ii.149–50)—'Why here's the Lion, scared with the threat of a dunghill cock'—has gone 'virtually unremarked' by editors, and suggests that Chapman borrowed the image from Nashe's *Unfortunate Traveller*, in which Jack Wilton describes a knight's shield as depicting 'a lion driuen from his praie by a dunghill cock'. In 'The Challenge to Duel in Jonson's *The Magnetic Lady*' (*N&Q* 48[2001] 314–15), Eugene Giddens offers an amendment to a footnote in Happé's recent edition of the play. In relation to III.vi.3–22, and particularly lines 68–72, he argues that Jonson is making a reference to James I's edict of 1613, in which the same punishment was laid on the seconds to a duel as on the principals. Under this reading, when Ironside speaks of saving 'the law a labour' (l. 72), it is not because of his agreement to a duel, but because he has forestalled the delivery of a challenge, in itself a crime.

2. Theatre History

Before the rise of the modern director at the end of the nineteenth century, 'performances were readied in another way' (p. 10). While Tiffany Stern's *Rehearsal from Shakespeare to Sheridan* approves of the increased focus given by literary criticism to plays in performance, it is keenly alert to the ways in which the rise of the director has led to the unwitting imposition of 'present theatrical practice onto the past ... Nowhere is the tendency to conflate modern and past theatrical practice more marked than in the field of the rehearsal' (pp. 2–3). In her introduction Stern defines three kinds of rehearsal: 'private rehearsal', in which the individual actor studies his or her part with or without instruction; 'partial rehearsal', which involves a small group of actors, usually those who share scenes; and 'ensemble rehearsal', which involves the whole company who, when they are not actually performing, watch those who are in an effort to form an overall picture of the play and to bond the actors together. While the modern theatre tends always towards the last (with some use of the other two forms), individual study was almost exclusively used until surprisingly recently. The key difference, which both encouraged and was encouraged by this focus on private rehearsal, was the use of 'parts', which 'consisted of the individual actor's lines only, each speech preceded by a short "watchword" or "cue" of the last one to four words of the previous speaker's lines' (p. 10). The advantages of such a system were obvious in Renaissance theatre, which enjoyed such a rapidly revolving repertoire: 'The cueing system allowed players to act a play with knowledge only of their own parts, and therefore made it possible to put on productions with the minimum of preparation' (p. 66). This rapidity was aided by typecasting as well as allowing the prompter a much greater degree of responsibility during the running of the show (rather in the manner of the conductor of an orchestra): 'much of what was necessary for performance [including decisions about blocking, for instance] would be prompted within performance itself' (p. 97). Rehearsals, where they occurred, were more likely to comprise the private recital of the play in front of the Master of the Revels or the mayor of a town to which the players were touring, in an effort to secure official approval rather than additional practice—in other words it was the play rather than the players that was being rehearsed and so these were textual rather than theatrical affairs.

This lack of a company ethos extended to the realization of the play in front of an audience. Right through the Restoration actors seemed to have dropped out of role when they were not speaking. Stern includes examples of players who chatted to one another or to members of the audience despite the action continuing beside them: 'the fact was that actors, trained to be successful in their parts, had often been encouraged only to be good in their roles, not to make the full play a success: the play as a unity and the actor as a player of parts were naturally opposed' (p. 182). Moreover the fragmentation of the play into individual roles meant that the overall view of the play was not visible to any of the actors within it: Hannah Pritchard, 'famous for her Lady Macbeth' (p. 254), had, according to both Samuel Johnson and Thomas Davies, never read the whole play! Elsewhere the prompter's safeguarding of the manuscript of the full play meant that, while it was secure, it was also unavailable to be read by any of the company.

What might strike us as ill prepared in a modern production was more readily accepted by earlier audiences. Since a new play might easily fail on its first night, the actors held off learning their parts thoroughly; after all the play might not survive or might not survive in its present form: 'a play on its opening was offered to the audience as a mutable text ready for improvement' (p. 118). Rewrites occurred rapidly, even overnight, and the figure of the pensive playwright pondering composition or revisions is certainly a recent invention; Sheridan's *Pizarro* [1779] 'was still unfinished as its first performance started; the last act was delivered to the actors during the production, and learnt between scene-breaks' (p. 241).

Stern charts the changes that occurred in the theatre following the Restoration: the influence of the French theatre 'that had so entertained the exiled court' (p. 124), the longer runs for plays, the use of female actors (though more detail is needed here), and the emergence of the actor-manager and his authority over the entire process from choosing the play right through to its performance. The key figure here is Garrick, though even he continued to focus primarily on individual rather than ensemble rehearsal. 'Almost no play seems to have passed through Garrick's hands without serious revision' (p. 251), and this is indicative of the eclipsing of authorial control by that of the actor-manager. Garrick's own performances were of course those of a star: 'the audience was frequently watching the actor first and the play second' (p. 280); "*hush* men" kept spectators quiet whenever Garrick played, but did not stop chatter during any other actor's performance' (p. 285).

Stern concludes that 'Theatrical preparation did not fundamentally alter between the sixteenth and eighteenth centuries, though its emphases changed' (p. 290). This consistency means that the book is sometimes repetitive—for instance on the implications of plays being divided into separate parts or the provisional nature of the first night's script. Its scholarship is thorough though conspicuous, with many long, dense footnotes and a bibliography of over thirty pages (the book began life as a Ph.D. thesis). Glaringly, the greatest questions remain unanswered: if individual study was so consistently used from the time of Shakespeare to that of Sheridan, whence does our modern predilection for ensemble preparation derive? What brought about such a dramatic change and what were the processes whereby the actor-manager was himself eclipsed by the modern director?

In 'The Patronage Network of Philip Henslowe and Edward Alleyn' (*MRDE* 13[2001] 82–92), S.P. Cerasano demonstrates that, contrary to popular belief, these showbiz stars were 'patrician and politically conservative' (p. 82) and 'implicated with the nobility' (p. 89). Both their fathers were armigerous, with Edmund Hensley (Philip's father) appointed 'as Master of the Game by Henry VIII' (p. 83) and Edward Alleyn Sr. holding 'a position at court, serving as porter to the queen' (p. 85). Cerasano further demonstrates their contacts with powerful members of the aristocracy, especially the Howards of Sussex, the Earl of Nottingham (later Lord Admiral) and Thomas Sackville (Lord Buckhurst). Cerasano urges that we explore beyond the patronage alluded to in the names of the playing companies since these 'ignore the larger patronage networks implied' (p. 89). Finally, she asserts that we need to 'look instead to the complicated social picture generated by the interaction between ancient privilege and new money' (p. 89). Cerasano's second contribution to the same volume is also on Edward Alleyn. In 'Edward Alleyn: His Brothel's Keeper?' (*MRDE* 13[2001] 93–100), she takes issue with E.J. Burford who, in *The Bishop's Brothel* (first published in 1976), accused both Alleyn and his wife Joan of running prostitutes in Southwark. His allegation rested on the documents linking Alleyn to four tenements: the Barge, the Bell, the Unicorn and the (suitably named) Cock. These buildings had been used as 'stews'—though, as Cerasano points out, the term may have been used to describe 'public bathing houses' (p. 97). Essentially her defence of Alleyn rests on the difficulty of proving 'that because some of Alleyn's properties were once houses of prostitution they must have remained so under his ownership' (pp. 96–7). For obvious reasons pimping and procuring aren't the kinds of professions to boast of, and this (as well as the evasively itinerant nature of the prostitutes themselves) makes researching prostitution 'a slippery business' (p. 97)!

Herbert Berry attempts to answer the question 'Which was the Playhouse in which the Boy Choristers of St Paul's Cathedral Performed Plays?' (*MRDE* 13[2001] 101–16). The evidence is confusing, not least because Berry's arguments are based on the archival work of J.P. Malcolm, who was working on the cathedral documents at the beginning of the nineteenth century. At that time 'the muniments belonging to the cathedral were in various places, some not even in the cathedral proper' (p. 106). Moreover, the document which Malcolm claims to have seen has since disappeared: 'Though nobody else has reported seeing it, and apparently it does not exist now, it probably did exist, and, in any event, the building in which the playhouse should have been was certainly where Malcolm's remarks put the playhouse' (p. 113). This building was the almonry on the south side of the cathedral and on the middle storey, since the ground floor was used for other things. 'The site of the almonry now is partly in Sir Christopher Wren's new cathedral, partly south of it. The middle of the north wall would have been on the north side of the south aisle, some 80 feet from the top of the famous stairs at the west front. The place is worth noting, for in the playhouse plays by, among others, Lyly, Marston, Middleton, Webster, Chapman, Dekker, Jonson, and Beaumont had their first performances' (p. 113).

The dichotomy between theatrical and fictional stage directions is challenged by Michela Calore in '*Enter out*: Perplexing Signals in Some Elizabethan Stage Directions' (*MRDE* 13[2001] 117–35). Conventionally the former are directed to an actor while the latter refer 'to what is happening in the narrative' (p. 118). However, with reference to some of the Queen's Men's playtexts, Calore demonstrates that this polarity is too simple and that 'fictional terms coexist with theatrical ones' (p. 119). The ambiguities found in the stage directions are the product of collaborative playwriting, indeterminacy surrounding the theatrical practices of the day, as well as an inbuilt adaptability designed to serve the variety of spaces within which the play might be staged. Calore argues that what strikes us as ambivalence may in fact have been an enabling device to facilitate this theatrical versatility, and should be viewed in this positive light 'rather than being dismissed as the result of more or less voluntary manipulations in the process of textual transmission' (p. 131).

Ronda A. Arab's 'Work, Bodies, and Gender in *The Shoemaker's Holiday*' (*MRDE* 13[2001] 182–212) is a compelling and thorough treatment of the issues of class and gender in Dekker's ostensibly innocuous comedy. The author argues that situated at the play's centre is 'the adulation of the male artisan body' (p. 185), and through this adulation, as well as the fraternity of the guild of the Gentle Craft, the play offers 'a nostalgic, idealized picture of the late sixteenth-century work world that masks the considerably grimmer reality' (p. 186). Arab has rather a rose-tinted view of Eyre's mastership—after all he skimps on his round, fails to save Ralph from conscription, is unable to cater for Jane, listens to his workers (over the recruitment of Hans for instance) only after they threaten industrial action, and fails to protect the mutilated Ralph (following his return from the French wars) from the gibes of his workmates. However, she writes well on the treatment of women in the play, noting of Margery that she 'desires to join the realm of power on its existing hierarchical, paternalistic terms' (p. 198). Bakhtinian theory is also used to good effect here as Arab explains how *The Shoemaker's Holiday* denigrates its female characters: 'Artisan woman are associated with the bodily orifices of the grotesque body—the mouth, the anus—and the processes of digestion; their bodies are represented as open in the most repulsive of ways' (p. 199). This vilification comes about because the women are perceived to be 'a threat to the idea of a male-dominated society based on the power and authority of the distinctly masculine artisan body' (p. 201). It thus becomes a strategy 'for dealing with women in the workplace' (p. 201) at the level of ideology and 'helps to ensure that [women] remain on the margins of the increasingly important work world' (p. 201). Despite occasional, local, disagreements with this essay, I consider it to be a fine piece of work.

Two more articles occur on the staging of *The Shoemaker's Holiday* in the following number of *MRDE* (which oddly has the same year of publication). The battle between city authorities and the theatre is examined by Charles Whitney in 'The Devil his Due: Mayor John Spencer, Elizabethan Antitheatricalism, and *The Shoemaker's Holiday*' (*MRDE* 14[2001] 168–85). Spencer, Mayor of London between 1594 and 1595, opposed the playhouse and called for a complete and final ban in the wake of the riots of that year. 'His reputation for avarice, his alleged sale of offices, his lack of concern for enforcing the fixed prices of food staples in a famine year, his failure to consult colleagues during the crisis period—all suggest a remote and selfish member of an emerging super-rich class' (p. 179). Whitney suggests that Dekker draws an analogy between Oatley and the spendthrift Lacy of the play with Spencer and William, Lord Compton, who, despite being heavily indebted, married Spencer's daughter Elizabeth (much to Spencer's annoyance). In this way, argues Whitney, 'the play manages indirectly to take a good-natured poke at Spencer the anti-theatricalist' (p. 180). Moreover, he goes on, 'In contrast to Spencer's civic pugnacity, which encouraged the Privy Council to take over regulation of the theater, the play depicts city and court in harmony' (p. 182). In 'Hans and Hammon: Dekker's Use of Hans Sachs and *Purim* in *The Shoemaker's Holiday*' (*MRDE* 14[2001] 144–67), Frank Ardolino describes the *Fasnachtspiele* written by Sachs (a German Protestant shoemaker, 1494–1576): 'carnival plays [which] promoted Lutheran reforms in their attack on the greed and hypocrisy of the Catholic Church' (p. 147), which were performed by craft guilds of Nuremberg. The second dramatic tradition is that of *Purimspiele*—'plays that depict the Jewish victory over their enemy Haman, who planned to exterminate them' (p. 148). Ardolino suggests that Dekker's use of the name Hammon provides 'a comic parallel to Haman and ... signal[s] his debt to *purimspiele*' (p. 148). Throughout Ardolino suggests some powerful correspondences, but never quite manages to convince his reader that Dekker was using either tradition as a model.

William Ingram examines the archival material pertaining to the life of 'Laurence Dutton, Stage Player: Missing and Presumed Lost' (*MRDE* 14[2001] 122–43). Dutton and his brother John both seem to have been players as well as silk-weavers. In 1583 'John Dutton, but not Laurence, was chosen by Edmund Tilney as one of the twelve founding members of the Queen's company of players' (p. 124). Laurence had joined the company subsequently (and no later than 1588). From then on, Laurence's affairs are beset by debt and litigation and, despite a series of broken bonds, and the general penury exacerbated by the plague years, 'both brothers—perhaps intermittently, perhaps regularly—seem to have been touring in the provinces with the Queen's players' (p. 127). The latter end of the 1590s finds Laurence in Ludgate prison before escaping and leaving his bad debts in the charge of a number of acquaintances as well as his brother. Thereafter he turns up again in the Privy Council registers of 1597, which suggests that 'Laurence Dutton—stage player, silkweaver, prison escapee, fifty years old if not more, brother of John who with good cause was probably quite angry at him—was still in London, still at large, still evading creditors, still trying to find ways to make some money, and (presumably) still not finding the secret, as the 1590s came to a close' (p. 140).

3. Criticism

(a) General

Luke Wilson's *Theaters of Intention: Drama and the Law in Early Modern England* ranges through Shakespeare, Jonson, and Marlowe, but also gives attention to a number of lesser-known playwrights and plays from the early modern period. The book's theme is the impact of law and legal thinking on early modern constructions of the self, and plays such as the anonymous *Nobody and Somebody* provide it with plenty of ammunition. Even wider in coverage is Chris Meads's monograph *Banquets Set Forth: Banqueting in English Renaissance Drama*, which synthesizes evidence from the ninety-nine plays from the years 1585–1642 that feature banquets. Bare summary does not do justice to the richness of the evidence Meads accumulates for the cultural baggage associated with different sorts of banquet, for the practical considerations of staging a banquet, and for the sense of the banquet as an evolving dramaturgical technique.

Next comes a group of articles, each of which considers stage treatment of a given social issue in a wide range of pre-1642 drama. What social issue links Kyd's *The Spanish Tragedy*, Marston's *The Dutch Courtesan*, Chapman's *The Widow's Tears*, Webster's *The Duchess of Malfi*, and *Arden of Faversham*? It is a situation which is also common in Shakespeare, in plays including *Twelfth Night*, *Othello*, and *The Merchant of Venice*. What they all have in common is that they depict or discuss an aristocratic woman marrying someone of lower social rank than herself. In 'Marrying Down: Negotiating a More Equal Marriage on the English Renaissance Stage' (*MRDE* 14[2001] 227–55), Marliss C. Desens looks at the practicalities of these marriages in the context of Renaissance opinion and practice more widely, and argues that such marriage was one of the favourite subjects of the Renaissance stage, marking conflict between gender and class hierarchy.

Desens's article goes well with one by Ira Clark, 'The Widow Hunt on the Tudor–Stuart Stage' (*SEL* 41[2001] 399–416). Clark details Renaissance attitudes towards this form of marriage, and accompanies the discussion with a series of examples, mostly from city comedy. Particular attention is paid to Heywood, *The Second Part of If You Know Not Me, You Know No Body*; Cooke, Greene's *Tu Quoque*; Brome's *A Mad Couple Well Matched* and *The Northern Lass*; Rowley's *A New Wonder*; and plays by Lording Barry, Thomas Middleton, and Ben Jonson. Clark is particularly interested in the ways in which the stage's widow hunt reflects a 'masculine fantasy' of social achievement which is in fact at odds with demographic data from the period.

In turn, a third article dovetails well with Clark's: Martin Bainton, '"Good tricks of youth": Renaissance Comedy, New Comedy and the Prodigal Son Paradigm' (*Renfor* 5:ii[2001]). Bainton's survey of attitudes to disaffected youth is once again grounded in Renaissance social theory and practice, with particular references to apprentices. He examines comedies including Middleton's *The Phoenix* and *Michaelmas Term*, Chapman's *All Fools*, and the Jonson–Chapman–Marston collaboration *Eastward Ho!*, to build his argument that Renaissance comedy often complicates the traditional prodigal son paradigm with a Terentian idea of resourceful but amoral youth. Again and again in these plays, he argues, it is the older generation whose morals are held up to the most searching and critical scrutiny.

Now to cover various generally applicable books and articles. In 'Early Modern Collaboration and Theories of Authorship' (*PMLA* 116[2001] 609–27), Heather Hirschfeld reviews the current critical terminologies used to describe multiple-authored plays, arguing that if anyone connected with a playtext in any way is a collaborator in it, then we need a new word to describe what 'collaboration' used to mean. 'Censorship' is another term with a long and contested history, as recent critical work has revealed, and *Licensing, Censorship and Authorship in Early Modern England: Buggeswords* is the latest of Richard Dutton's distinguished contributions to this field of enquiry. The main thrust of his argument is that in early modern reading practices it was the norm, not the exception, to look to make topical application of what one was reading. Hence, argues Dutton, surviving evidence concerning early modern censorship often reflects not so much the activities of a thought police, as moments when the usual social structures that could accommodate such politicized readings without undue offence broke down. He pursues this argument through a number of plays and playwrights, including Marlowe, Sir Henry Herbert's 1632–4 difficulties with the players, Jonson's Epistle to *Volpone*, and Middleton's *A Game at Chess*. Anyone working on early modern censorship will also be glad of Dorothy Auchter's *Dictionary of Literary and Dramatic Censorship in Tudor and Stuart England*. The main contents of the book are ninety-two long entries, each offering in effect a case study of a particular act of censorship from the period. Each entry is structured into historical context, synopsis of the work involved, censorship, and further reading. Numerous plays are covered, including *A Game at Chess*, *Eastward Ho!*, *The Isle of Dogs*, Chapman's *Byron*, Tailor's *The Hog Hath Lost his Pearl*, and the Massinger–Fletcher collaboration *The Tragedy of Sir John Van Olden Barnavelt*. The book is also furnished with various other useful illustrative materials, and a good index.

Gabriel Egan's long note, 'Hearing or Seeing a Play? Evidence of Early Modern Theatrical Terminology' (*BJJ* 8[2001] 327–48), checks the basis of a widely held belief. The statement that early modern discussions of theatre tended to privilege the auditory rather than the visual—literally, terminology of auditors rather than spectators—is so widespread that it would seem churlish to examine the evidence for the proposition. But Egan does so, using Chadwyck-Healey's *Literature Online*, and shows that in fact 'plays were much more commonly thought of as visual rather than aural experiences in the literary and dramatic writing of the period' (p. 332). Another cherished belief about Renaissance drama bites the dust.

In chronological terms, work on specific plays this year starts with two articles on Bale. Dermot Cavanagh considers 'The Paradox of Sedition in John Bale's *King Johan*' (*ELR* 31[2001] 171–91), arguing that the personified Sedition is a profoundly uncomfortable and destabilizing figure encapsulating contemporary political and religious uncertainty, as well as the subversive potential of the very drama in which he is condemned. Peter Happé, in 'John Bale's Lost Mystery Cycle' (*CahiersE* 60[2001] 1–12), explores the surviving evidence concerning Bale's lost cycle, of which only three of the projected fourteen parts survive. Happé discusses the paradoxes involved in Protestant mystery plays, and the question of whether and how Bale used the cyclic form.

This year work on Lyly has focused on *Gallathea*, with two articles both looking, in different ways, to treat the play as a whole rather than just the interesting lesbian motifs. Christopher Wixson, 'Cross-Dressing and John Lyly's *Gallathea*' (*SEL*

41[2001] 241–56), notes the play's socially conservative elements, especially its stress on class and order. An article by Kate D. Levin, 'Playing with Lyly: Theatrical Criticism and Non-Shakespearean Drama' (*RORD* 40[2001] 25–54), reports on her experiences in directing a college production of *Gallathea*, and on the 'supple and vivid theatricality' revealed in the process (p. 47). Also on Lyly, Derek B. Alwes's article '"I would faine serve": John Lyly's Career at Court' (*CompD* 34[2001] 399–422) argues that the traditional view of the plays as centred entirely on the presentation of the queen could usefully be modified. Lyly, he argues, is also using characters in the plays—the scholars, philosophers, and especially the servants—to advertise the possible roles for which the queen could reward him, including 'panegyrist, advisor, courtier, censor, or Master of the Revels' (p. 400). Alwes reviews Lyly's plays from this perspective.

Robert Greene again receives the attention of Richard Levin in '*Friar Bacon and Friar Bungay, John of Bordeaux*, and the 1683 edition of *The History of Friar Bacon*' (*RORD* 40[2001] 55–66). Levin explores the complex textual history of the prose narrative, which appears to represent a source for the two Elizabethan plays, as well as having been influenced by them in its 1683 version. On the basis of this, Levin also offers a more extensive reconstruction of the original ending of *John of Bordeaux*, suggesting that we can expect it to have featured a magic duel between Bacon and Vandermast and a scene in which Bacon renounces magic.

Eric Griffin's 'Ethos, Empire, and the Valiant Acts of Thomas Kyd's Tragedy of "the Spains"' (*ELR* 31[2001] 172–92), represents the year's work on Kyd. Discussion of the political import of *The Spanish Tragedy* has in recent years tended to focus on historically specific detail, such as Spanish–Portugese relations in the 1580s, the presence in England of the pretender Dom Antonio, and the vexed question of the play's relationship to the Armada crisis. But Griffin argues that the play should be seen in terms of a more 'global cultural watershed' (p. 193), the changing Renaissance dynamic between church, state, and empire. According to Griffin, Bel-Imperia, with her awkwardly multivalent name, personifies the tensions involved in *translatio imperii*.

Still in the area of Elizabethan drama is an article by Randall Martin, '"Arden winketh at his wife's lewdness, & why!": A Patrilineal Crisis in *Arden of Faversham*' (*Early Theatre* 4[2001] 13–33). The answer Martin suggests is that Arden desires a male heir, putting him in a position not unlike that of Henry VIII, from whose activities Arden has profited.

MacDonald P. Jackson revisits an Elizabethan history play best known for being a source for *Richard II*, and argues that it is neither a source for *Richard II*, nor indeed Elizabethan. In 'Shakespeare's *Richard II* and the Anonymous *Thomas of Woodstock*' (*MRDE* 14[2001] 17–65), Jackson enlists Chadwyck-Healey's *Literature Online* as part of his assertion that, metrically and in terms of vocabulary, this is an early Jacobean drama. In this case, it would be an imitation of, not a source for, Shakespeare: and if we were looking for an author for the text Samuel Rowley would be a strong suspect, since the play's linguistic forms are strikingly similar to those of *When You See Me You Know Me*. Also on attribution, Eric Sams, in '*King Leir* and *Edmund Ironside*' (*N&Q* 48[2001] 266–70), argues that both items from the Shakespeare apocrypha are written by one author. Sams does not name his favoured candidate, but gives enough hints to suggest who that candidate might be.

The most discussed Dekker play of the year is, rather surprisingly, *The Shoemaker's Holiday*. An article by Frank Ardolino (also discussed in section 2 above) considers 'Hans and Hammon: Dekker's Use of *Hans Sachs* and *Purim* in *The Shoemaker's Holiday*' (*MRDE* 14[2001] 144–67). Hans Sachs (1494–1576), a German shoemaker, wrote pro-Lutheran dialogues and plays including the splendidly titled *The Inquisitor and all his Soup Cauldrons* (1553). Ardolino argues that Dekker's militant Protestant play has Sachs's style of *Fastnachtspiel* as an important point of reference. Furthermore, he looks to link the play to the German Jewish tradition of *Purimspiele*. Certainly, Ardolino convincingly demonstrates that Dekker's villain Hammon resembles the biblical Haman, but it is unclear whether this necessarily invokes German Jewish drama. The article looks set to generate further debate. Alison Chapman has another surprising argument about the play in 'Whose Saint Crispin's Day is it? Shoemaking, Holiday Making and the Politics of Memory in Early Modern England' (*RQ* 54[2001] 1467–94). She considers it alongside other texts that feature cobblers—Thomas Deloney's *The Gentle Craft*, Rowley's *A Shoemaker a Gentleman*, and two Shakespeare plays, *Julius Caesar* and *Henry V*. Her argument is that in such texts shoemakers are surprisingly and consistently depicted as calendar-makers: a profession with an unusual freedom to declare holiday periods. Other texts which support this argument include the anonymous plays *Locrine* and *George a Greene*. Hence incidents in the two Shakespeare plays, in which shoemakers do *not* get to determine what is a holiday period, have an unexpected significance. Thirdly, and finally, Charles Whitney (also discussed in section 2 above) gives 'The Devil His Due: Mayor John Spencer, Elizabethan Civic Antitheatricalism, and *The Shoemaker's Holiday*' (*MRDE* 14[2001] 168–85). John Spencer was mayor of London in 1594–5, and one of the most dangerous opponents of the professional theatre. Whitney reconstructs the career of this charmless and tireless antitheatrical warrior, in an article with important implications for our understanding of how and why civic authorities in the 1590s sought to control the theatre. Dekker's Mayor Oatley, Whitney argues, bears a striking resemblance to Spencer, and hence the play can be seen as to some extent a commentary on Spencer's antitheatrical activities.

Dekker also looms large in an article by Katherine Acheson, '"Satiate yet unsatisfi'd": Desire, Commodification and the Sublimity of the Early Modern English Playwright' (*PsyArt* 5[2001]). Acheson's theme is the presentation of the early modern playwright in paratexts to dramas ranging from *Gorboduc* up to the mid-1630s. It is, she suggests, useful to employ the terminology of Slavoj Žižek, and trace a progression in the status of playtext over the period from perfect commodity to sublime body. Dekker's prefaces provide many of Acheson's examples.

Dekker and Middleton's *The Roaring Girl* is a play very interested in the forging of money. In 'Marked Angels: Counterfeits, Commodities, and *The Roaring Girl*' (*RQ* 54[2001] 1531–60), Valerie Forman contextualizes this in terms of early modern discourses of coinage and currency. She suggests that this interest reflects a growing concern in the nature of the market. In a world where anything seems to be for sale as a commodity, it seems hard to find anything entirely authentic. Such contradictions become embodied in the body of Moll herself. The play is pushed by such contradictions into redefining the generic expectations of comedy: *The Roaring Girl* is a form of marriage comedy in which the heroine, very emphatically, does not get married.

Dekker and Marston are both subjects of James P. Bednarz's *Shakespeare and the Poets' War* (reviewed in 3(*c*) below). However, one of the cornerstones of the usual accounts of the war is attacked in Roslyn L. Knutson's '*Histrio-Mastix*: Not By John Marston' (*SP* 98[2001] 359–77), which does exactly what it says on the tin. The attribution of *Histriomastix* to Marston is conjectural, and it was never made before 1878. It has depended on the play's style and vocabulary, both allegedly distinctively Marstonian, and on its supposed implication in the War of the Theatres. Knutson goes back to first principles, and shows that the evidence from style and vocabulary is worse than flimsy. Furthermore, whereas Marston's work is usually very 'trendy' in terms of its allusions to current events and fads, *Histriomastix* certainly is not. Likewise, the play is shown to be very weakly connected to the theatrical dispute which it allegedly ignited. Debate about Knutson's claims is certain to continue, but this article is a provocative and scholarly piece of work.

Although Marston may be losing *Histriomastix*, he may be gaining another play. In '*Lust's Dominion; or, the Lascivious Queen*: Authorship, Date, and Revision' (*RES* 52[2001] 360–75), Charles Cathcart reviews the evidence concerning this play, first published in 1657 and misattributed then to Marlowe. This play can be tentatively identified with the lost *The Spanish Moor's Tragedy* written in 1600 by Dekker, Haughton, and Day. However, Marston's involvement in the writing has long been suspected, and Cathcart uses quantitative and qualitative evidence to build up the case for this. He also notes evidence of a limited revision of the play, probably datable to around 1606. A related article, also by Cathcart, is '*Hamlet*: Date and Early Afterlife' (*RES* 52[2001] 341–59). Of particular interest for the task at hand is its discussion of echoes of *Hamlet* in *Antonio and Mellida* and in *Lust's Dominion*. Also on sources is Patrick Kincaid's note, 'John Marston's *The Dutch Courtesan* and William Percy's *The Cuckqueanes and Cuckolds Errants*' (*N&Q* 48[2001] 309–11). The current consensus has been that the similarities between these two plays are due to their common sources in the sixty-sixth novel in Painter's *Palace of Pleasure*. But Kincaid shows that the plays share similarities not in Painter, notably in the episodes in which their respective dupes are arrested. He suggests, then, that Marston knew Percy's unperformed play—probably from when he was working as, in effect, a theatre manager for Paul's Boys—and that he used material from it in preparing his own comedy. In the interests of completeness, it should also be mentioned that *The Dutch Courtesan* and *Eastward Ho!* do feature in the articles discussed above by, respectively, Desens, and Bainton.

Mention of *Eastward Ho!* brings up Chapman, whose *The Widow's Tears* is also discussed by Desens. *Byron* and *Caesar and Pompey* both receive the attention of Nina Taunton in *1590s Drama and Militarism*, reviewed more fully in section 3(*b*) below. Taunton relates the two plays, as well as plays by Marlowe and Shakespeare, to late Elizabethan theories of war, warfare, and tactics. Chapman also gets one note to himself: William H. Hamlin, 'A Borrowing from Nashe in Chapman's *Bussy D'Ambois*' (*N&Q* 48[2001] 264–5). Hamlin explicates the play's description of the Duke of Guise as a lion 'scared with the throat of a dunghill cock', by referring back to *The Unfortunate Traveller* and beyond that to Pyrrhonist philosophy.

There is one more article to be considered which features an Elizabethan playwright—of a sort. Richard Vennar's entertainment, *England's Joy*, was performed on 6 November 1602, or at least the first six lines were, proceedings then being halted when Vennar was hauled off stage by bailiffs and imprisoned for debt.

The audience was thus deprived of the proposed entertainment, which had been advertised as containing fireworks, music, twelve gentlemen fighting at barriers, and a representation of the apotheosis of Queen Elizabeth. In 'Richard Vennar, England's Joy' (*ELR* 31[2001] 240–65), Herbert Berry combs archival sources to reconstruct the interesting and rather sad career of this poet, debtor, and conman.

Later drama has, on the whole, had a quieter year. Ian Munro's 'Making Publics: Secrecy and Publication in *A Game at Chess*' (*MRDE* 14[2001] 207–26) is a subtle meditation on Middleton's play's interest in publication, publicity, and the public. The central question, for Munro, is 'how can we connect the physical space of the public theater with the conceptual space of the public sphere?' (p. 212), and he explores the various ways in which *A Game at Chess* and its paratexts negotiate these relations. The article makes an interesting comparison with Dutton's discussion of the play mentioned above. Mathew R. Martin's *Between Theater and Philosophy*, a discussion of Middleton and Jonson, is postponed to section 3(*c*) below. Although John Jowett's 'The Audacity of *Measure for Measure* in 1621' (*BJJ* 8[2001] 229–47), does not on the face of it sound like an article about Middleton, it should be mentioned here as it is based on the argument that *Measure for Measure* I.ii survives in a form heavily adapted by Middleton for performance in 1621. The rest of the article explores the topical implications of the scene in the context of 1621, arguing that its discussion of foreign news and newsbooks can be linked closely to contemporary events and can also be linked forward in Middleton's own writing to *A Game at Chess*.

John Fletcher's *The Woman's Prize* is studied by Margaret Maurer in 'Constering Bianca: *The Taming of the Shrew* and *The Woman's Prize, or The Tamer Tamed*' (*MRDE* 14[2001] 186–206). This is in the context of the textual problems surrounding Bianca in the Shakespeare play, and Maurer's contention that the Folio preserves a more interesting and complex version of Bianca which subsequent editorial interventions have regularized away. Maurer argues that Fletcher's Byancha is distinctively an imitation of Shakespeare's original Penelope-like Bianca, and not of the simplified version produced by later editors.

Work on Webster is represented by one discussion of *A Cure for a Cuckold*, and two discussions of *The Duchess of Malfi*. The first is 'Action and Confession, Fate and Despair in the Violent Conclusion of *The Duchess of Malfi*', by John C. Kerrigan (*BJJ* 8[2001] 249–58). Kerrigan puts the play in the context of contemporary Anglican uncertainties about confession, forgiveness, and free will, arguing that in spite of the nominally Catholic setting the play is rooted in these Protestant theological anxieties. He notes that it is full of the language of confession, and that the violence it contains is linked to 'the frustration resulting from the lack of an outlet for expressing guilt and the inability to confess' (p. 251). The second discussion of the play is by Richard Levin, in '*The Duchess of Malfi*: What's to come is still unsure' (in his *Shakespeare's Secret Schemers: The Study of an Early Modern Dramatic Device*, pp. 109–26). Levin's book as a whole is devoted to the phenomenon of characters in Renaissance drama who appear to be pursuing secret plots, even though no one in the play comments upon these plots, and although most of the examples he chooses are Shakespearean, it makes an interesting tool with which to examine Webster's play. What exactly are Delio and Pescara up to, and where does their true loyalty lie? The true allegiance of these minor characters does matter a great deal, as more or less only they are left at the end to usher in the new regime, but it remains vague: in this respect, Levin argues, the play reflects not merely Websterian uncertainty about divine providence, but a Renaissance unease about the ethics of 'enlightened Machiavellianism' (p. 37). On a lighter note, the comedy *A Cure for a Cuckold* is the play that Webster co-wrote with Rowley and perhaps Heywood at some point in the 1620s, and it is reconsidered in David Carnegie and MacDonald P. Jackson, 'The Crux in *A Cure for A Cuckold*: A Cryptic Message, a Doubtful Intention, and Two Dearest Friends' (*MLR* 96[2001] 14–20). The article reviews the murderous riddling letter sent by Clare, on which hinges the whole question of her motivation through the play. Their conclusion, that her actions are more psychologically consistent and plausible than has previously been thought, has implications for our understanding of the whole play.

Richard Brome is also the subject of two articles, both by Matthew Steggle. In '*The New Academy* and the New Exchange' (*RORD* 40[2001] 67–82), Steggle suggests that Brome's comedy is strongly inflected by its setting in London's premier shopping centre, and that the whole play is permeated by the language of exchange. 'Brome, Covent Garden, and 1641' (*Renfor* 5.ii[2001]), argues that the revival of *The Weeding of Covent Garden* can be dated to summer 1641, on the basis of echoes of its catchphrases in contemporary pamphlet literature. Furthermore, this revival may well have had a topical application to the downfall of Suckling and Davenant after the Army Plot in May 1641.

Two articles, too, are devoted this year to Renaissance drama by women. *The Tragedy of Antonie* by Mary Sidney Herbert, *The Tragedy of Mariam* by Elizabeth Cary, and *Love's Victory* by Mary Wroth, are studied by Irene Burgess in '"The wreck of order" in Early Modern Women's Drama' (*EMLS* 6:iii[2001] 1–24). Burgess's particular focus is on the three central characters, which as she notes are all iconic figures of 'bad' womanhood. All three are presented with particular emphasis on their corrupt and corrupting bodies, and are associated with the breaking of all societal norms. Cary's Mariam and Herbert's Cleopatra feature again in an article by Kathy Acheson, '"Outrage your face": Anti-Theatricality and Gender in Early Modern Closet Drama by Women' (*EMLS* 6:iii[2001] 1–16). Like Burgess, Acheson ponders the paradox that these female-authored plays represent heroines in such a destructive way. Both Mariam and Cleopatra are famously beautiful, and yet within the plays they deface themselves: Acheson classifies this strategy as the 'refusal of the gaze' (p. 3), using both historicist and psychoanalytic approaches in her reading of the plays' difficult relation to theatricality itself.

(b) Marlowe

After the very substantial body of work that appeared in 2000, 2001 produced a relatively meagre yield of Marlowe scholarship, though this observation refers to the quantity rather than the quality of material. There were no book-length studies wholly devoted to Marlowe, and several of the items are merely brief notes. *Doctor Faustus* enjoyed the greatest amount of attention, with four other plays being the subject of one article each.

Religion in *Doctor Faustus* is examined in two essays, William Hamlin's 'Casting Doubt in Marlowe's *Doctor Faustus*' (*SEL* 41[2001] 257–75) and Adrian Streete's '"*Consummatum Est*": Calvinist Exegesis, Mimesis and *Doctor Faustus*', (*L&T* 15[2001] 140–58). Hamlin seeks to argue that *Doctor Faustus* is a play offering a viewpoint of religious scepticism, his argument being grounded in an exploration of the Pyrrhonist ideas in the sixteenth and early seventeenth centuries. After an extended discussion of the potential for religious scepticism made available by these ideas, as well as the attendant problems, he moves to a brief discussion of the play itself. He suggests that, in contrast to the detachment advocated by Pyrrhonism, the play's religious scepticism resides in its dramatization of Faustus's passionate attachment to belief, with its disastrous consequences. Conversely Adrian Streete reads *Doctor Faustus* in the light of sixteenth-century Calvinist Christology, seeing Faustus as a parodic imitation of Christ. He emphasizes relationality in the subjectivity of Marlowe's tragic figure, looking at this especially in the context of early modern Calvinist ideas and particularly in terms of the inscribed violence present in the conception of Christ as a masochistic paradigm. He concludes by suggesting that the play offers a paradox of Faustus's being most unlike Christ at the moment when he most closely symbolically represents him.

The other essays on *Doctor Faustus* range widely in their focus. In '"Be silent then, for danger is in words": The Wonders of Reading and the Duties of Criticism' (*ES* 82[2001] 106–14), Jürgen Pieters makes some tentative inroads into an examination of the relationship between power and words, with a focus on the early modern period. He proceeds from the quotation in his title taken from *Doctor Faustus*, and argues that words destroy the immediacy of visual experience which produces wonder. Ranging over the fact of the marvellous sights and cultural alterity that the new world offered to early explorers, and to the effects of the emergence of print culture, he makes a brief comparison between *Doctor Faustus* and *The Tempest* before touching on the work of several modern theorists in respect of the sublime in literature. Christopher Wessman, in '"I'll play Diana": Christopher Marlowe's *Doctor Faustus* and the "Actaeon Complex"' (*ES* 82[2001] 401–19), sees Marlowe as an 'overpeerer' in contradistinction to the now more established idea of an overreacher, his writing revealing an interest in voyeuristic sexual spying, and regards this as relevant to his supposed role in espionage. He suggests that the Actaeon myth has an important role to play in *Doctor Faustus* and argues for its presence largely through an examination of imagery, but also with reference to some narrative details. He concentrates principally on the Benvolio episode, but Faustus is also contended to have a fascination with illicit visual pleasure, and to show considerable correspondences with Actaeon at the end of the play when he faces being torn to pieces by demons. Ruth Lunney focuses on dramatic character in 'Rewriting the Narrative of Dramatic Character, or, Not "Shakespearean" but "Debatable"' (*MRDE* 14[2001] 66–85), discussing the new type of character endowed with interiority to emerge on the stage in the 1590s. While arguing that there was no sudden shift from the type of externalized conflict of mind represented in the morality plays to the internalized conflict of the Shakespearean soliloquy, she considers Marlowe as centrally instrumental in developing a new rhetoric of character in his construction of Faustus. Focusing mainly on the psychomachia scene, she suggests that Faustus is a figure not only separate from the conflicting good and bad angels, but also 'separate-seeing' in that he gives them a different level of attention to that available to the play's audiences. Furthermore, he is a character who is 'debatable'—a term she uses in preference to 'realism', 'individuality' or 'complexity' in that it involves multiple perspective frames—exemplifying detachment and dislocation, and is perhaps a form of anticipatory Cartesian character.

The remaining *Doctor Faustus* items are rather briefer, either only partly focusing on the play or being just notes. Modern production is the subject of Kim Axline's 'A "New Deal" and a New Direction: Welles' and Houseman's Depression-Era Productions of *Macbeth, Doctor Faustus*, and *Julius Caesar*' (*TheatreS* 45[2001] 16–49), in which she discusses Orson Welles's and John Houseman's productions of these plays in the context of the work of the Federal Theatre Project, that of *Doctor Faustus* featuring Orson Welles in the starring role and being remarkable for its innovative approach to the use of lighting, lack of traditional scenery and its overwhelming popular success. Robert Fehrenbach (also discussed in section 1 above) makes a contribution to the discussion surrounding the dating of *Doctor Faustus* in 'A Pre-1592 English Faust Book and the Date of Marlowe's *Doctor Faustus*' (*Library* 2[2001] 327–35), suggesting that there may have been an earlier English translation of the German Faust book, potentially a source for the play. He cites an entry on 'Doctor faustus' in the 1589 inventory of a young Oxford scholar's library and advances various arguments as to why this is likely to have been an English-language text, other than the play itself. Finally, a note by Robert Coogan, 'The Four and Twenty Years of Marlowe's Faustus' (*N&Q* 48[2001] 265–6), points to an iconic and ironic significance in the number 24, being that of the years in Faustus's contract with Lucifer, and links its significance to the writings of Cornelius Agrippa, and to the book of Revelation.

Of the studies on the other plays, the most substantial is Nina Taunton's *1590s Drama and Militarism: Portrayals of War in Marlowe, Chapman and Shakespeare's 'Henry V'*. Taunton argues that *Tamburlaine I* and *II*, as well as plays by Chapman and Shakespeare, crystallize into a debate around problems of space, order, command, national boundaries and defence as responses to specific personalities and events of the decade under discussion. In the first section of the book she reads Tamburlaine's generalship (alongside that of various of Chapman's and Shakespeare's characters) against not only the plethora of military manuals on the market in the period, but also the actions of certain prominent contemporary military figures, such as the earl of Essex. In part 2 she focuses the same comparative approach on strategies, military tactics, size of armies, arms, and rhetoric, especially in terms of the notion of threatened manhood. The final part argues that Foucault's theories about surveillance are in evidence in this period too, antedating his identification of the appearance of the phenomenon, and offers the organization of military camps as evidence of this. In the case of the Tamburlaine plays, it is specifically the issue of gender in respect of the masculine space of the military camp that is considered. In a coda she emphasizes that her project is both to demonstrate the discursive and ideological nature of war and to show the appearance of the host of strategy manuals as constituting a response to the anxieties generated by the political and military situation in Europe in the 1590s.

Edward II is the only other of Marlowe's plays to be the subject of a full critical essay, Ronald Knowles's 'The Political Contexts of Deposition and Election in *Edward II*' (*MRDE* 14[2001] 105–21). Noting that modern scholarship has tended to see *Edward II* in terms of a personal play, Knowles chooses instead to focus on its engagement with royal deposition and election as issues of intense interest in the period. He argues that, despite its ostensibly impeccable political orthodoxy, the play opens up an engagement with resistance theory and ideas of the legitimacy of royal deposition, a history of which he briefly outlines. Knowles suggests that

Marlowe avoids coming into conflict with censoring authorities by balancing the dangerous ideas in the representation of royal tyranny and corruption in the earlier sections of *Edward II* with doctrinal orthodoxy in the second half. The remaining two items are short notes: Ceri Sullivan, 'Silver in *The Jew of Malta*' (*N&Q* 48[2001] 265) relates the disdain shown by Bellamira for silver coin to the debasement of silver coinage in the late sixteenth century, and Dorothea Kehler, 'Shakespeare's Recollections of Marlowe's *Dido, Queen of Carthage*: Two Notes' (*ANQ* 14:i[2001] 5–10) suggests a verbal echo of *Dido, Queen of Carthage* in *As You Like It*, and possible Marlovian influence on Shakespeare's understanding of the term 'adultery' in *Hamlet*.

Constance Kuriyama writes a biographical essay in 'Second Selves: Marlowe's Cambridge and London Friendships' (*MRDE* 14[2001] 86–104), briefly discussing the sources of information about Marlowe's life and the problems associated with these, before going on to note the evidence for his friendships with various men— including university friends later to be executed for their religious beliefs—and the poet and playwright Thomas Watson. She attempts to offer some redress to a biographical image of Marlowe based on points of conflict in his life and problems with the authorities, by suggesting a capacity for enduring friendships. Kuriyama then turns to the representation of friendship in the plays, suggesting that these are frequently based on intense intellectual affinities.

Three items from 2000 that were not covered in the entry for that year should be mentioned here. Noting in 'Marlowe's Literary Double Agency: *Doctor Faustus* as a Subversive Comedy of Error' (*Ren&R* 24:i[2000] 23–44) that the comic elements in *Doctor Faustus* are often seen as a problematic element, Suzan Last suggests that the real source of difficulty is the imposition of a generically consistent tragic or moral reading of the play. Focusing on the B-text, with its greater comic content, she argues that the play parodically travesties belief in and fear of the supernatural through a strong element of burlesque, and that the comic passages work against the tendency to accept orthodoxy. George Geckle, in '*Edward II* and *Richard II*' (*RenP* [2000] 99–117), sees *Edward II* as the first great English history play because of its structural coherence, complex themes, development of character, and narrativity, and maintains that Shakespeare exhibits different strengths in *Richard II*. Looking at the way in which Marlowe compresses, conflates and develops the material from his sources, he contends that the playwright both gives tragic structure to otherwise formless narrative and creates a fast-moving drama. Geckle then goes on to discuss Shakespeare's play and examines ways in which it diverges from the approach in Marlowe's. Finally, Pam Whitfield argues in '"Divine Zenocrate", "Wretched Zenocrate": Female Speech and Disempowerment in *Tamburlaine I*' (*RenP* [2000] 87–97) that no Renaissance drama embodies the contradictions of the masculine and suppression of the feminine more than *Tamburlaine I*. The play has, for Marlowe's work, an extensive range of female characters, and Zenocrate shows some eloquence in providing an alternative point of view to that of her husband. Nevertheless, the futility of her utterances and Tamburlaine's constant thwarting of her speech acts result in her disempowerment as a woman being embodied in language and speech.

(c) Jonson

This has been a relatively lean year for studies specifically of Jonson's drama, although various items listed in section 3(*a*) above—including the articles of Desens, Clark, and Bainton—discuss Jonson sometimes quite extensively in terms of early modern drama as a whole. A similar tendency to compare Jonson is present in a number of the items listed in this section, starting with William F. Blissett's "'The strangest pageant, fashion'd like a court": John Donne and Ben Jonson to 1600—Parallel Lives' (*EMLS* special issue 7[2001] 1–51). Blissett explores biographical links between Donne and Jonson, with particular reference to *Cynthia's Revels*.

James P. Bednarz's *Shakespeare, Jonson, and the Poets' War* compares Jonson to Dekker and Marston. For Bednarz, the Poets' War is an important arena for early modern argument about the nature of subjectivity and the role of the poet. In this light, Bednarz develops interesting readings of *Histriomastix, Jack Drum's Entertainment, What You Will,* and *Satiromastix,* as well as of Jonson's three early comical satires, *Every Man Out of His Humour, Cynthia's Revels,* and *Poetaster.* More controversial will be his argument that Shakespeare is deeply implicated in the War of the Theatres, as victim and as writer of personally satirical plays (*Troilus and Cressida* being, allegedly, a prime example). Like Blissett and Bednarz, Ian Donaldson discusses the early Jonson's relations with other writers. In 'Looking Sideways: Jonson, Shakespeare, and the Myths of Envy' (*BJJ* 8[2001] 1–22), he shows that the Renaissance tradition of Envy—an emaciated figure, forever looking sideways—functions as something of a master-trope for early critical discussions of the relationship between Jonson and Shakespeare. Without discarding this idea entirely, Donaldson weaves possible variations on it. This throws up many intriguing insights, for instance on the sequential relationship between *Every Man In His Humour, Othello,* and *Volpone.*

An adaptation of *Volpone,* in turn, is studied by Hanna Scolnicov. The play was adapted for film in 1941, fortified, appropriately enough, with elements of *The Merchant of Venice.* The film forms the subject of her article, 'The Merchant in *Volpone*: Narrative and Conceptual Montage in Maurice Tourneur's Film' (*BJJ* 8[2001] 133–46). Scolnicov draws attention to the important intermediate stage, Stefan Zweig's free adaptation of *Volpone* into German in 1926, itself perhaps influenced by earlier German adaptations. This fascinating 'chain of transformations' (p. 143) culminated in a screenplay by Jules Romains which took three directors and three sets of funding to film in stages over three years. Scolnicov draws attention to the collage-like nature of the resulting film, and offers a remarkable sense of a modern, internationally European reception of Jonson and Shakespeare. Also on *Volpone* is an article by Jonathan Gil Harris, '"I am sailing to my port, Uh! Uh! Uh! Uh!": The Pathologies of Transmigration in *Volpone*' (*L&M* 20[2001] 109–32), which I have not seen. *Volpone* is also the starting point for Mathew R. Martin, *Between Theater and Philosophy: Skepticism in the Major City Comedies of Ben Jonson and Thomas Middleton.* Martin's subject is the philosophical scepticism which is more usually studied with relation to the tragedies of the era. But in a series of close readings setting Jonson's four major city comedies against three Middleton plays—*Michaelmas Term, A Trick to Catch the Old One,* and *A Chaste Maid in Cheapside*—Martin argues that these plays set the idea of the self in problematic relation with, in particular, the locations and the market forces of the early modern city. Whereas, Martin argues, Middleton's scepticism is 'primarily social', Jonson is a Pyrrhonist who addresses the philosophical and aesthetic dimensions of the sceptical world-view. The monograph culminates in an excellent reading of *Bartholomew Fair* in terms of the 'aesthetics of carnivalesque travesty' (p. 134), as a deeply sceptical piece of theatre which creates the fair as a heterocosm resistant to all attempts to contain, map and appropriate it.

Bartholomew Fair, indeed, has received the most attention of any Jonson play this year, including Noel Blincoe's '*Bartholomew Fayre*: A Celebration of English Folk Festivals' (*BJJ* 8[2001] 65–84). Blincoe sees the play in terms of the carnivalesque, as a Saturnalian celebration of laughter with echoes of fertility rites. He draws attention to several parallels with the fertility rites of ancient Greece, arguing that in celebrating native English traditions Jonson is making a political intervention arguing for their wholesomeness. In this account the raucous energies of the fair are mimetic of, not opposed to, the theatre itself. David Weil Baker, in '"Master of the monuments": Memory and Erasure in Jonson's *Bartholomew Fair*' (*ELR* 31[2001] 266–87) also considers *Bartholomew Fair* relative to the texts and customs of the past. For Baker the play 'targets the deceptive vanity of poetic monuments' (p. 268), in a wide range of forms from Overdo's classical learning, through the highly erasable written documents, to the stage-keeper's nostalgia and the parodies of the final puppet-show. He concludes that in this play 'the desire to keep the past simply as it was, sealed off from the present, is doomed to failure' (p. 287).

Meanwhile Paul Cantor, 'In Defense of the Marketplace: Spontaneous Order in Jonson's *Bartholomew Fair*' (*BJJ* 8[2001] 23–64), argues, like Blincoe, that the fair is mimetic of the theatre, but for him this holds true in that the economic system of the fair is mimetic of the market conditions of theatre itself as an institution. Cantor sees the play as a celebration of self-regulation, of the beneficial effects of market forces. Whereas previous readings of *Bartholomew Fair* in terms of market forces have tended to use Marxist economics as their reference point, Cantor develops his reading in terms of Friedrich Hayek's theory of spontaneous ordering within economic systems. Finally, in *Theaters of Intention* (reviewed in section 3(*a*) above), Luke Wilson draws attention to the complications of the contracts that run through the play from the Induction to the end, relating them to contemporary legal issues.

Similar issues are studied in relation to Jonson's next play by Barbara Irene Kreps in 'Contract and Property Law in *The Devil is An Ass*' (*BJJ* 8[2001] 85–122). She notes that the play is structured by a series of contracts and promises, crucially the instrument of enfeoffment signed by Fitzdottrell in Act IV. She reads these situations in terms of contemporary property law, arguing that Fitzdottrell's enfeoffment, for instance, has a moot-like complexity which tests weaknesses in contemporary legal theory. Furthermore, she traces legal language bleeding out into other parts of the play's dialogue, inflecting, for instance, its language of clothing. She concludes by arguing that, while the conclusion of the play obeys the logic of property law, it still offers a critique of the inadequacy of that law, particularly for Frances.

Eugene Giddens discusses 'The Challenge to Duel in Jonson's *The Magnetic Lady*, III.vi' (*N&Q* 48[2001] 314–15). He shows that Bias is reluctant to carry Silkworm's challenge to Ironside because such an act was illegal under legislation passed in 1613, a fact which in turn makes the dialogue of the scene a little clearer.

There is also a thoughtful review of both the play and a recent production of it in an article by Peter Happé, 'The Magnetic Lady Seen Again' (*BJJ* 8[2001] 369–74).

Jean E. Graham studies 'The Performing Heir in Jonson's Jacobean Masques' (*SEL* 41[2001] 381–98). The heir in question is the heir to James's throne, first Prince Henry, and then after his death Prince Charles, and the recurring question is how to celebrate a figure whose main function at the time is to wait for his time to come. Graham's close analysis of the treatment of Henry and then Charles in Jonson's Jacobean masques observes that the masques surprisingly and consistently omit 'the language of paternal love', concentrating instead on the dutifulness of the heir apparent, and the formality of his relationship with his father. Teresa Grant addresses a detail concerning one of these masques in 'White Bears in *Mucedorus, The Winter's Tale*, and *Oberon, the Fairy Prince*' (*N&Q* 246[2001] 311–13). Was Prince Henry on stage with a men in bear suits, with real white polar bears, or merely with ordinary bears covered in whitening powder? To answer this question Grant reviews what is known about polar bears in the Renaissance.

Also on Jonson's masques, *The Masque of Beauty, Pleasure Reconciled to Virtue*, and *Love's Triumph through Callipolis* are all considered in Thomas M. Greene's learned article, 'Labyrinth Dances in the French and English Renaissance' (*RQ* 54[2001] 1403–66). Greene traces occurrences of the labyrinth dance from Virgil to *Paradise Lost*, arguing that it possesses a significance in terms of Orphic cosmogony. Jonson's masques are thus drawing on a deep well of almost ritual significance, although each deploys the symbolism of the maze in different ways.

Books Reviewed

Auchter, Dorothy. *Dictionary of Literary and Dramatic Censorship in Tudor and Stuart England*. Greenwood. [2001] pp. 440. $94.95 ISBN 0 3133 1114 5.

Baldwin, Elizabeth, ed. *The Wisest Have their Fools about Them*. Malone 164. OUP. [2001] pp. xxvi + 43. £25 ISBN 0 1972 9040 X.

Bednarz, James P. *Shakespeare and the Poets' War*. ColUP. [2001] pp. 334. $51.50 ISBN 0 2311 2243 8.

Dutton, Richard. *Licensing, Censorship, and Authorship in Early Modern England: Buggeswords*. Palgrave. [2000] pp. 256. $59.95 ISBN 0 3122 3624 7.

Harp, Richard, ed. *Ben Jonson's Plays and Masques*. Norton. [2001] pp. xix + 513. pb £8.99 ISBN 0 3939 7638 6.

Knowles, James, ed. *The Roaring Girl and Other City Comedies*. World's Classics. OUP. [2001] pp. lx + 414. pb £8.99 ISBN 0 1928 2800 2.

Levin, Richard A. *Shakespeare's Secret Schemers: The Study of an Early Modern Dramatic Device*. UDelP. [2001] pp. 172. $35 ISBN 0 8741 3737 3.

Martin, Mathew R. *Between Theater and Philosophy: Skepticism in the Major City Comedies of Ben Jonson and Thomas Middleton*. UDelP. [2001] pp. 191. $35 ISBN 0 8741 3739 X.

Meads, Chris. *Banquets Set Forth: Banqueting in English Renaissance Drama*. ManUP. [2001] pp. 257. £45 ISBN 0 7190 5567 9.

Ostovich, Helen, ed. *Every Man Out of His Humour*, by Ben Jonson. Revels. ManUP. [2001] pp. xvi + 400. £47.50 ISBN 0 7190 1558 8.

Stern, Tiffany. *Rehearsal from Shakespeare to Sheridan*. OUP. [2000] pp. xii + 337. £45 ISBN 0 1981 8681 9.

Taunton, Nina. *1590s Drama and Militarism: Portrayals of War in Marlowe, Chapman and Shakespeare's 'Henry V'*. Ashgate. [2001] pp. 239. £42.50 ISBN 0 7546 0274 5.

Wilson, Luke. *Theaters of Intention: Drama and the Law in Early Modern England*. StanfordUP. [2000] pp. 367. $55 ISBN 0 8047 3414 3.

VIII

The Earlier Seventeenth Century: General and Prose

JAMES DOELMAN

This chapter has two sections: 1. General; 2. Prose.

1. General

It might seem odd to begin a review of 2001 scholarship with two books of
republished material, but David Norbrook's *Poetry and Politics in the English
Renaissance* [2002] and Kevin Sharpe's *Remapping Early Modern England* [2000]
are significant works, both for their republished material (which has already been so
influential) and their overviews of the state of the discipline. While Norbrook (a
literary scholar) takes his bearings from the Whig/Marxist approach to history and
Sharpe has been among the leading historians questioning that approach, the two
share a commitment to a bringing together of history and literary studies.

Norbrook's 1984 book is not completely rewritten, but does offer revised sections
rich in updated footnotes. The 'Afterword 2002' begins with a neat reading of his
original book's context in an early 1980s Britain marked by fierce strife between
socialist tradition and Thatcherism, set in the broader sphere of the Cold War. He
also situates *Poetry and Politics* in the turmoil of British historiography provoked by
revisionism and the theoretical turn in literary studies as new criticism and
traditional historicism were pushed to the side. Norbrook is careful in his
distinctions, noting the varying views of the value of literary evidence among
historians, and distinguishing between the British and North American
developments in literary studies. He notes the affinities between revisionism and
new historicism in their focus on *moments* and suspicion of grand narratives. He
quietly challenges that dimension of 'new historicism' that has turned away from
empirically based argument to embrace Foucault as an 'auctoritas' (p. 280). While
he questions many of the revisionists' conclusions, he notes how their work has
opened up archival possibilities for literary scholars (unlike Northrop Frye, many
now *can* find their way to the Public Record Office). The second half of the
Afterword presents a survey of recent scholarship in the field: it is a model of clarity
and fairness, fully up on the most significant scholarship. He notes promising signs:

'tendencies to synthesis' between formerly opposed camps, for example, as cultural materialists and traditional bibliographers find common ground in the history of the physical book. He provides significant overviews of the work on the court, imperialism, and censorship. He also points out areas for further exploration (for example, a consideration of not just ethnic 'otherness' but political otherness), and editions and anthologies needed. While fair and balanced, his commitment to empirical scholarship and his belief in the effect of language and literature are clear. He calls for an engagement with the past: 'We can never speak with the dead as we can with the living; but with patience, much is possible.'

The essays in Sharpe's *Remapping Early Modern England* are republished from a variety of journals and collections ranging from 1989 to 1998. As in his introduction to last year's *Reading Revolution* [2000] Sharpe devotes his opening chapter here to urge a transformed approach to history that considers 'the broader politics of discourse and symbols, anxieties and aspirations, myths and memories'. He begins the essay with an overview of Whig history that goes back to the 1688 revolution, and which he argues is tightly bound up with both American and English identity. He makes the bold charge that Whig history is in fact 'ahistorical' in approach, concerned with explaining the present not the past. Sharpe suggests that the early 'revisionists' all challenged the Whig model from different vantage points, and affirms the post-revisionist re-emphasis on ideology practised by Peter Lake, Ann Hughes and Richard Cust.

Sharpe acknowledges the influence of new historicism (in spite of its anti-revisionist tendencies), and the 'linguistic turn' of Pocock and Skinner, upon his own work, and how his study of Charles in the 1630s (*The Personal Rule* [1992]) ultimately came to find many of its sources in literature and culture. Through his career Sharpe has come to an increased appreciation of the role of rhetoric, of what texts do to readers, and what readers do to texts, and the fact that everything, from financial documents to masques, is engaged in rhetorical performance. (He acknowledges Blair Worden as another historian who has attempted something analogous to his own approach.) Ultimately, Sharpe calls for an interdisciplinary approach: a revisionist emphasis on the moment and event informed by 'new historicism, the linguistic turn and Geertzian anthropology'.

In the second half of this opening essay, Sharpe considers how societal divisions and differences that were veiled and contained in the rituals of Elizabeth's reign became manifest as James 'rationalized the political culture' and through his own use of words opened up the possibility of debate and discord. Charles attempted to reinstitute a ritual power, and Cromwell failed to develop a 'culture of authority'. This is a broad outline for work that Sharpe anticipates, which will include a study of royal writings from Henry VIII to William III. Taking a different vantage point, he will also examine the 'reading of authority' in the period, what readers did to texts. A major instance of this has already been published in *Reading Revolutions*. Finally, Sharpe projects a study of the representation (in both texts and art) of authority from the Reformation to 1688, and shows here already the significance of the often overlooked engraving trades as a means of disseminating political images. Much of the last part of the essay consists of a series of questions awaiting answers: if Sharpe doesn't get to these, I certainly hope that other scholars will. Some of the republished essays that follow this opening essay already touch on these issues: we can look forward to the fuller studies that Sharpe is engaged in.

As with the Norbrook and Sharpe volumes, the introduction to Wells, Burgess and Wymer, eds., *Neo-Historicism: Studies in Renaissance Literature, History and Politics* [2000], is a very important work of historicist literary scholarship. More combative in tone than Sharpe or Norbrook, this volume challenges some of the scholarship that goes under the name of 'new historicism'. While the individual essays, by solid scholars such as Blair Worden, Andrew Gurr, Heather Dubrow and Katharine Eisaman Maus, are worthwhile in themselves, the introduction (by the editors) and opening essays by Glenn Burgess and Stanley Stewart present a forceful critique of much new historicist and cultural materialist practice. They take issue with the frequent dismissal of earlier historicist practices (and point out that Tillyard, the usual straw man, was challenged from the beginning), and attempt to reassert a distinct aesthetic realm which can nevertheless be approached in a historically grounded way. Ultimately, the opening chapter leads to a distinction, not between old and new historicists, but between historicists and presentists (into which category some 'new historicists' fall). This is something of a manifesto, ending with an injunction to recognize 'the otherness of the past'.

Burgess' essay, 'The "Historical Turn" and the Political Culture of Early Modern England: Towards a Postmodern History?' explores the inconsistencies in many 'new historicist' and revisionist challenges of metanarratives, and then shows how the widespread 'metanarrative' of royal absolutism, as used by Patterson, Dollimore and Goldberg, is far too simplistic as the context for the literature of the time. Reflecting on Jonson's *Sejanus* as his example, he argues that 'the play cannot be read as either an absolutist ideology or its opposite', and is ethically rather than constitutionally concerned. Stanley Stewart's essay returns to the well-known Tuve–Empson debate over Herbert's 'The Sacrifice' as a starting point for his reflections on old and new historicism. He notes the irony of the new historicists' embracing of the new-critical Empson over the historicist Tuve.

Further chapters are divided into three sections: 'The Politics of Theatre', 'Making History' and 'Shakespeare in Context'; the middle section is of chief concern here. Graham Parry traces how Jacobean writers used the legacy of the ancient Britons: the sceptical and empirical Camden and the mythological Geoffrey of Monmouth frequently appeared 'side by side in Jacobean writing'. Jonson, for example, had been educated by Camden, and his influence is evident in the playwright's scholarly notes, but for the central myth of Brutus ('whether fabulous or true') Jonson turned to Monmouth on the occasion of James's 1604 entry. Similarly Daniel, Drayton and Milton were influenced by Camden but 'found Brutus irresistible': Monmouth presents 'history for the benefit of poets'. Less-discussed writers are also examined by Parry: John Selden on ancient British law, William Browne's use of Brutus in *Britannia's Pastorals* [1616], John Fletcher's treatment of the Druids in *Bonduca* [1619], and Edmund Bolton's historical research in *Nero Caesar* [1624]. Parry notes how the ancient British period offered a moment of conflict between the native British and imperial Roman legacies. In spite of the tension, however, both 'led to a vision of a classical destiny for Britain'.

In the same volume, R. Malcolm Smuts, 'Occasional Events, Literary Texts and Historical Interpretations', begins by considering the problem of using texts to recreate a non-textual past, and asks some pertinent questions about what 'literary' documents survive and why. After this theoretical opening he argues that the 'theatricality of Renaissance monarchy' greatly pre-dates the surviving printed texts that scholars frequently turn to. He traces the developing practice of printed progress entertainments from the 1570s on (which was much later than on the continent), and argues that the dynamics of the printed accounts are very different because of the audience they were meant to reach. They are not to be trusted as reliable accounts of the queen's public appearances or the entertainments performed for her. The article culminates in a look at competing accounts of James's March 1604 royal entry.

As in recent years the English royal family and court received extensive discussion: King James's own writings are the subject of Fischlin and Fortier, eds., *Royal Subjects: Essays on the Writings of James VI and I*, a large collection of essays, written from a variety of critical perspectives, on the king's political, religious and poetic works. As many of the contributors note, James's position as royal author changed the dynamics of text and audience, and put the vexing question of authority on a new level. He could claim an authority denied to all others, whether writing on religion, politics or poetry. As a king who not only wrote, but relentlessly published his work, James holds an exceptional place among early modern monarchs. While James's writings, especially his political ones such as *Basilikon Doron*, have attracted increased scholarly attention of late, no other work has covered the range of his writing as this has done. Fischlin and Fortier were especially concerned to include discussion of the relatively neglected poetry of the king. To this end, Peter Herman frames James's poetry by considering it in the context of other verse by early modern English monarchs. Two essays, by Morna Fleming and Sarah Dunnigan, consider *Amatoria*, James's poems dealing with Queen Anne: the first shows James's rejection of a Petrarchan approach, and the latter probes the problems raised by a royal voicing of desire. Simon Wortham examines James's tragic poem *Phoenix* within the context of royal gift-giving and patronage. Other notable contributions include Curtis Perry on the late manuscript poetry, Johann Sommerville on constitutional matters, Malcolm Smuts on James and peace-making, and John King on the iconography of King David applied to James. The writers here largely agree that, whatever the subject, this was first of all 'monarchic writing', a conclusion also reached by Herman in 'Authorship and the Royal "I": King James VI/I and the Politics of Monarchic Verse' (*RQ* 54[2001] 1495–1530), an article which focuses on the political dimension of James's Lepanto, his sonnet to Elizabeth and his elegy on Sidney.

Leeds Barroll, *Anna of Denmark, Queen of England: A Cultural Biography*, successfully challenges the idea, most fully articulated by Roy Strong, that the Jacobean period saw cultural power centred exclusively in James's own court and that Queen Anne (or Anna, as Barroll argues) was a mere 'royal idler'. Rather, he presents her as a significant political figure and patron of the arts. The book does not attempt a full biography of Anna (a need which still stands), but rather a cultural biography that focuses on the early years of James's reign. Barroll argues that the masques of her court did not simply gesture towards James's power, but were 'a series of self-conscious presentations by the queen of herself'. The opening chapters, where Barroll traces Anna's political involvement in Scotland, and the make-up of her court in the early English years, will prove valuable as a resource for future scholars. Anna deliberately chose the members of her English court, typically young, like-minded women (many of the Essex circle), who were separate from the families that dominated the king's court. Barroll posits that Anna and her circle significantly shaped the culture of Prince Henry's court, and that she continued after his death as the 'center of an extended anti-Howard circle'. The final chapters explore a number of specific individual masques, shifting attention away from the poets involved to the royal and noble participants and audience. In a corresponding article, 'Assessing "Cultural Influence": James I as Patron of the Arts' (*ShakS* 29[2001] 132–62), Barroll challenges two frequent assumptions: that James was incompetent as king in political matters, and that he was of significant artistic influence. As with his book on Queen Anne, the focus here is on the first decade of the English reign.

A number of essays in Cruikshanks, ed., *The Stuart Courts*, which began life as 1994 conference papers, will prove valuable to literary scholars exploring the cultural world of the Stuart court. 'The court' has become a standard part of the vocabulary of literary history, but has frequently been used with an imprecision that Neil Cuddy's article might do much to correct. We have often confused the abstract with the concrete and projected on to the early Stuart court that which was only typical of later ones. Cuddy asserts a plain and clear definition: '"the Court" was where the king was'. Cuddy is especially good at noting how the court changed through the period: James *came* to embrace the 'magnificence' of court dinners, even as Cecil and others pressed for their abolition. James was readopting a more medieval approach that also involved compelling the nobility to offer similar hospitality. Cuddy makes a similar point in regard to the Privy Chamber, suggesting that James and Charles were reviving earlier practices that had fallen out of use. The tilts of Elizabeth's reign have been much analysed; Arthur MacGregor's essay, 'The Household out of Doors: The Stuart Court and the Animal Kingdom' attempts to redirect attention to those performed under James. The royal princes were themselves involved in these, and as all the Stuarts were noted horsemen the functioning of the royal stables was an important matter. McGregor's essay moves beyond iconographic readings to a straightforward account of royal horsemanship, hunting and menageries, with a particular focus on King James. Other relevant chapters include Murray Pittock on Scottish court culture both before and after the pivotal date of 1603, Nick Myers comparing the mythology applied to James and to France's Henri IV, and Jeremy Wood on Inigo Jones and Giulio Romano. The essays in the second half of the volume concern the court culture of Charles II and James II.

The deluge of books on 'Otherness' pouring from American university presses continues, and always, very predictably, these Said-inspired books argue that the construction or representation of 'otherness' is needed to establish the host people's identity and superiority. Shankar Raman, *Framing 'India': The Colonial Imaginary in Early Modern Culture*, which emerged from his doctoral thesis, examines the imaginative framing of 'India' in a series of early modern literary works. Raman considers cartographical as well as literary analysis, and argues quite convincingly that through the period 'voyage' replaced 'cosmos' as a way of understanding the human encounter with the world. The second section of the book examines more specifically the English experience of the East, and traces the creation of a colonial identity on the stage, which was more ideal than real at first. In the process he provides some welcome analysis of such relatively ignored works as John Fletcher's *The Island Princess* and Dryden's *Amboyna*. The final part of the book is a self-conscious attempt at a psychoanalytic reading of the Indian Boy in *Midsummer Night's Dream*, with the aim of showing how 'psychoanalytic readings potentially rehearse' the typical treatment of India in the colonialist works under examination. The writing is rendered rather turgid at times by the heavily worn theoretical framework (Marxist, materialist and metaphorological), which is unfortunate as there is some solid historical and literary investigation here.

Linda E. Merians, *Envisioning the Worst: Representations of 'Hottentots' in Early Modern England*, differs from Raman in her focus on travel writing rather than literary works, but like him moves away from the focus on the Americas as the site of European encounters with 'Otherness'. Merians helpfully establishes her project in the first sentence: 'This study examines how and why the early-modern English constructed "Hottentots" as the world's most beastly people.' What distinguishes the 'Hottentots' (a term which Merians always uses with quotation marks) is that they were not in a colonial relationship with England through the early modern period. Since the term only appeared in English for the first time in 1670, after what Merians (and others) identify as a new epistemology based on skin colour arose, the book's treatment of the earlier seventeenth century is mostly preliminary to the larger project, which concerns the period 1670–1800. However, Merians also traces depictions of the Khoikhoi people of the Cape area pre-1670, beginning with the first Portuguese contact in 1488; limited English contact dated from the 1590s. These early travellers, stopping at the Cape after suffering a long sea voyage, celebrated the land as a paradise, but one strangely populated by what they presented as beastly inhabitants. In Merian's view this confirmed in a 'precolonialist' way an English right to use the land better, to restore paradise. The Cape peoples were described as unclothed and dirty eaters of repulsive animal parts, and even at times as beings without language.

It was with the English entry into the slave trade in the 1660s that a new rhetoric of black Africans developed: the 'emerging constructions of "Hottentots" played a unique role in arguments for and against slavery'. Early English descriptions of the Cape people had described them as black-skinned, but in the Restoration it was increasingly suggested that 'Hottentots' were fairer than other sub-Saharan Africans, and in fact were born white-skinned, a classification that also excluded them from slavery. Merians shows how encounters with other indigenous peoples (the Irish and Native Americans) shaped later English depictions of the 'Hottentots', an argument similar to that made by Nabil Matar in *Turks, Moors and Englishmen in the Age of Discovery* [1999].

Merians argues that, in depicting Native Americans, English writers were colonialist: they were forced to learn from and hence acknowledge Native expertise in certain areas, and worked a progress motif into their depiction of Native Americans. However, with the peoples of southern Africa they had no such relation or need (p. 23). The first chapter considers English descriptions up to 1634, mostly those of East India Company men. Chapter 2 turns to the emerging concept of 'Hottentots', and its circulation through geography texts. In chapter 3 Merians presents the fascinating narrative of 'Cory', a native of the Cape brought to England in 1614, a story which was widely and significantly retold in later periods. The later chapters examine eighteenth-century representations.

Merians' approach is open to challenge: while she questions every comment of the English writers which offers an explained intention on the part of the Cape people, she herself repeatedly articulates a complete knowledge of the English writers' intentions: 'The strategies employed here show the author wanted his readers ... '; 'The concluding paragraph shows how keen this anonymous author was to present the English in a positive light'. Merians claims to know their intentions, to see through their rhetoric and their corporate psychological drives, and in doing so goes beyond the claims of Empson to know Herbert's mind, and perhaps confirms some of Stewart's charges.

Burgess and Wells urged a recognition of the 'otherness' of the past, but what Merians slips into is the simplistic binary 'Otherness' that typifies most Saidian colonial analysis: the western European past is 'constructed' as an 'Other' in order to establish the present writer's own non-racist, non-hierarchical, enlightened credentials. What is lacking is a sense that writers of the past might have been far more complex, both rhetorically and psychologically, in their 'otherness'. But perhaps I've reduced her, made her an other to consolidate my own position as *laudator temporis acti*. I have carped at Merians as representative of a certain approach to early modern literary studies, but her book must be credited with presenting in a well-written fashion a great deal of information about a little known aspect of English travel writing.

Herbert Grabes, ed., *Writing the Early Modern English Nation*, is a collection of papers largely republished from Continental books and journals, many originally in German. They range in coverage from the reign of Henry VIII to the 1689 revolution, but exclude the Civil War, which Grabes suggests needs a volume of its own. Most significant are the essays by Grabes himself, which follow up ideas first presented in his *Das englische Pamphlet I: Politische und religiose Polemik am Beginn der Neuzeit* [1990]. Unlike the broad cultural phenomena that are the subject of Merians' and Raman's books, Grabes considers the higher politics of an emerging national identity. He also looks homeward to the effect that printing (especially of pamphlets) and the Reformation had on this growing national sensibility, one that divided the geographic nation from the monarchic dynasty. Grabes argues that the political pamphlet, anonymous and often printed on the Continent, could evade the control to which sermons were subject. The Reformation had its effect in making possible the idea of England as the 'Elect Nation', which Grabes calls 'the most potent myth of national identity and excellence'. Claus Uhlig's essay examines the histories of England that began to appear in the sixteenth century; he helpfully considers these within the broader context of European historiography, especially that of Jean Bodin. Martina Mittag traces the use of anti-Spanish rhetoric from Elizabeth's accession to the attempted Spanish Match of 1623, a subject also addressed by Roberta Anderson in '"Well disposed to the affairs of Spain?" James VI and I and the Propagandists: 1618–1624' (*RH* 25[2001] 613–35), with a focus on the work of Thomas Scot and Thomas Middleton.

While largely non-literary in focus, David Armitage, *The Ideological Origins of the British Empire*, offers a solid historical study of the ideas of state and empire from the sixteenth to nineteenth centuries that will be useful for scholars examining the literary reflections of the Atlantic empire. By taking a long run at the topic (beginning with its roots in Rome), Armitage achieves a far more credible reading than most of the seventeenth-century situation of England, Scotland and Ireland. He challenges the common interpretation of Ireland as the first step in westward empire-building, and situates the roots of British empire-building in 'the problematics of composite monarchy'. He also presents an analysis of Hakluyt and Purchas's reflections on travel and the New World, and in the process identifies problems with seeing Protestantism at the root of British imperial ideology. Hakluyt was much more informed by Aristotle's *Politics* than Protestant eschatology, and even Purchas, while stridently anti-Catholic, drew on a variety of justifications for English exploration and settlement, working from the vantage point of international Calvinism rather than any sense of England as an elect nation.

Kamps and Singh, eds., *Travel Knowledge: European 'Discoveries' in the Early Modern Period* was not available from the publisher.

The culture of collecting and curiosities in early modern Europe has received considerable scholarly attention lately. In addition to such recent general studies as Philipp Blom, *To Have and to Hold: An Intimate History of Collectors and Collecting* [2002], is Marjorie Swann's *Curiosities and Texts: The Culture of Collecting in Early Modern England*, which examines a range of collecting activities in seventeenth-century England, and Barbara Benedict's somewhat broader *Curiosity: A Cultural History of Early Modern Inquiry*. A good portion of Swann's book is devoted to the subject of collecting natural artefacts, where a major shift in approach took place in the later seventeenth century. New World plants and animals presented a challenge to the long-standing philological approach, and the medicinal and emblematic emphases of medieval natural history was largely replaced by something closer to empiricism. Swann argues that Bacon validated the collection of natural artefacts as part of a new approach to natural history, where a massive collation of material would precede systematic theorizing; to accomplish this, however, he needed first to collect men who would serve as a hierarchical collecting community, with Bacon himself as the 'governor' of knowledge. This vision was never realized, and ultimately it was his theoretical works that influenced subsequent natural history, as Bacon was used to authorize the activities of the gentleman collectors of the Royal Society. These men were not the factors imagined by Bacon, but virtuosi who, paradoxically, collected the curious and unique to enhance both their genteel independence and their status as part of the collecting community. All this Swann perceptively describes as a 'shared participation in virtuoso activities'. This section of the book could have been strengthened by a closer attention to the effects of the Civil War and Interregnum, and this is reflective of a broader neglect of historical specificity in the book: to collapse the era of John Hoskins and Robert Burton with that of Shadwell and *The Tatler*, as Swann does at one point, is to miss out on significant shifts within the period. That she frequently quotes primary sources not directly but as used in other secondary works would seem to be part of this problem.

Swann's chapter on Browne attempts the ambitious thesis that there was a massive social shift in the understanding of landownership through the period, a thesis that would require much more than the examples and argumentation presented here. She sees in Browne more than just a conservative; he was one who found a new role as a collector of antiquities as he established a new power and place to speak from. As with Bacon, she finds in Browne a collector of men, who notes the illustrious owners and sources of artefacts in *Urn-burial*. Swann notes a gradual shift later in the century towards a focus on things, whether houses or natural artefacts, and a movement away from the connection of these to illustrious families. She profitably uses the activities and writings of Robert Plot to illustrate how collecting became an alternative lineage as a means to status.

Swann's final chapter uses Jonson and Herrick to examine 'practices of collecting to create new modes of authorship'. Both poets 'collected' their own texts, Jonson in his *Works* [1616] and Herrick in *Hesperides*, in a way that constructed their autobiographical selves or situations, ones closely connected to the other individuals collected in the works. This chapter covers material that has already been well served by scholars such as Richard Dutton and Ann Baynes Coiro, and there is only limited value added here in framing it within the larger study of collections. The book ends with an epilogue on Hans Sloane as a collector of collections, whose Restoration activities eventually led to the 'ornament to the nation', the British Museum and British Library. The interesting range of material brought together in this book could have been presented much more briefly, and the book is rife with phrases such as 'potentially, at least' and 'tempting to view', which indicate the speculative nature of much of the argumentation. The book is most compelling when discussing the collection of artefacts: the collection of texts and people is a more nebulous concept.

Benedict's *Curiosity* is a much more broad-ranging and engaging work than Swann's: while it focuses on the period 1660–1800, Marlowe's *Faustus* and late twentieth-century detective fiction also come within its scope. Benedict is concerned with literary representations of the curious, both as subject and object, and argues that, in early modern England, curiosity is typically perceived as presumption (especially when engaged in by women), a manifestation of threatening ambition, and individualism. Also considered is the attendant issue of fraud, where discerning is the business of the reader's curiosity. Benedict convincingly argues that through the seventeenth and eighteenth centuries there was a transformation of curiosity from an intellectual desire to an empirically based visual one, an argument that confirms Swann's emphasis on collections of artefacts. Most significant for seventeenth-century studies is Benedict's first chapter on the Royal Society, which she sees as the domain of 'new men' who through subversive enquiry present the 'new worlds' found through the telescope and microscope. This book is very much a 'world of wonders' itself, with many illustrations for the curious.

Ann Jones and Peter Stallybrass, *Renaissance Clothing and the Materials of Memory*, impressively explores the manufacturing and wearing of clothing in the English Renaissance: they argue convincingly that 'fabrics were central both to the economic and social fabrication of Renaissance Europe and to the making and unmaking of Renaissance subjects' (p. 14). This rich study begins with a discussion of the terms 'habit', 'fetish' and 'fashion' in the late sixteenth century, the last of which was shifting from its etymological meaning of 'a thing made' to that which was constantly changing. Jones and Stallybrass consistently move beyond the simple surface-versus-substance model, which does do not do justice to the reality of the period; the outer aspect of clothing was seen to affect the inner: for a courtier to dress as Frenchman was to take some of his nature; for a priest to don the liturgical robes associated with Rome was to absorb Catholic ideology, in the eyes of his Puritan opponents.

Clear from this book is the dominance of fabric and the making of clothing in the economy of the period. Spinning was a nearly all-pervasive part of women's work, and the clothing trade exploded through the Jacobean period. Clothing was not only a source of wealth for those employed in its manufacture and sale; it was a significant way of storing and displaying wealth, and a means of payment to one's employees, especially servants. Jones and Stallybrass argue that the period saw a significant shift in the meaning of clothing, from livery, which identified wearers in terms of their social relationships, to the individual self-fashioning allowed by a more independent clothing market.

The individual chapters are fairly independent. Chapter 2 explores the fashioning of identity through clothing in portraiture, and the expense-based significance of the different pigments used; this leads to an especially impressive reading of Holbein's *Ambassadors*. Chapter 3 traces the fashion for yellow starch in the 1610s and 1620s and shows how this style played a role in the Overbury murder scandal. The following chapters, impressive for their understanding of the classical tradition and Renaissance uses of it, are important in establishing the centrality of spinning in the economy and women's lives, both as an actual and as a symbolic task. While the Renaissance saw a decline in spinning among high-born women, it was still maintained as 'an ideal of female diligence'. Chapter 6, on needlework, shows Renaissance women drawing on emblem books and other illustrated volumes for the sources of their craft, which might involve classical as well as biblical material (Esther was a favourite); frequently the arts of writing and needlework were conflated, or the latter used to justify the former. The authors also show how at times, most notably in the case of Mary Queen of Scots, these works could become political texts, the domestic practice thus becoming a public act. Often the book shows the centrality of Ovidian tales as informing myths for women and cloth: Arachne, the Fates, and Philomela all figure prominently.

Chapter 7, 'The Circulation of Clothes', builds upon the earlier discussion of the clothing trade to show how the theatre was in fact shaped by it. Costumes were a continuing dimension of the theatrical company, mended and reused, whereas plays would come and go. Henslowe's role in the used clothing trade and the provision of costumes to companies are closely examined. Audiences also competed to don impressive clothing, often wearing rented apparel. Thus, clothes from court, church and city ultimately ended up in the theatre, and this circulation was often reflected in the plots of the plays themselves. Jones and Stallybrass posit the centrality of clothing to identity, and the subsequent malleability of identity in the theatre. On the stage, the hood does make the monk, or at least provides the material memory of him. Clothes 'both *are* material presences and they *absorb* other material and immaterial presences' (p. 204). Beginning with a history of the clothing of Hamlet's ghost, chapter 10 considers the problem of the materiality of ghosts on stage: 'The most prominent feature of Renaissance ghosts is precisely their gross materiality' (p. 248). Once again the costume made the ghost, establishing its identity as a particular dead person; stage directions for ghosts were more explicit about costumes than others. However, since the mid-nineteenth century directors have opted for ways to efface the material costume. This chapter establishes the significance of the ghost appearing in armour, for this is what young Hamlet should have inherited. It notes also the irony of armour, both longer-lasting than clothing, and thus frequently an inheritance, but also subject to fashion and outmoded by the late sixteenth century. Jones and Stallybrass's conclusion turns to biblical stories of clothing, especially that of Adam and Eve, and what Renaissance commentators did with these, and then to Richardson's Pamela and her revolutionary rejection of clothing not her own. Clothing embodies or materializes memory, but is also transformative, allowing for a mutability of identity as different garbs are donned.

Striking in the way it comfortably moves between the material reality and its artistic and literary representation, this volume succeeds by keeping its focus on its subject, not the authors' cleverness. They avoid reductive readings, and in the process raise significant questions about 'materialism' and our tendency to see the present as materialist in contrast to the anti-materialist past. My only quibble with this book is the authors' occasional collapsing of a long, complex period into a single, static whole. They explicitly challenge and reject this approach, but in listing examples sometimes slip into it.

Another work in the cultural materialist vein, Juliet Fleming, *Graffiti and the Writing Arts of Early Modern England*, considers the widespread use of non-paper writing surfaces in the early modern period. Beginning with the question 'What is writing?', Fleming presents a Derridean exploration of graffiti, tattoos and inscriptions on utensils, all of which she calls 'Posies', a term borrowed from Puttenham's *Arte of English Poesie*. While later twentieth-century theory underlies the work, Fleming also draws significantly on Puttenham in other ways, for example by using his sections on physical proportion in poetry. The book argues that the physicality of much writing was significant, and that scholars have often overlooked this in their concern with a 'text' that lies beyond any particular physical inscription. A second major point is that graffiti was not perceived as transgressive in the period (although it is difficult for us to empty the term of this connotation, and I fear the word may have been insisted on for the 'hipness' it brings to the book's title). This is clearly an area ripe for exploration, and the book frequently presents new information and insight. However, Adam Fox's study of wall-writing in *Orality and Literacy* [2000] presents a more thorough and clear guide to the subject. Unlike Fox, most of Fleming's evidence is material: surviving wall-writing in various English homes is described, and in some cases presented in photograph. And Fleming is certainly helpful with her descriptions of the whitewashing process, a common form of erasure in the period which was not complete, as the inscription at times survives to be recovered. The relating of this to Freud's 'Mystic Writing Pad' may be helpful to some.

Fleming's section on 'Tattoo' is primarily concerned with early antiquarians' description of the practice among the ancient British and the peoples of the New World . However, towards the end she considers the rarer instances of tattooing in Christendom, much of which in the fifteenth to seventeenth centuries was of holy names or symbols inscribed at Jerusalem or Bethlehem. The most extensive instance involves William Lithgow, a courtier of King James and King Charles, who claimed to have not only a Jerusalem cross, but the crowns of Scotland and England, and a poem celebrating James, all engraved on his right arm. Fleming certainly puts paid to the insistence of Camden and Speed that the British of the early modern era were beyond the barbaric practice. Fleming's final chapter is on inscriptions or 'devices' on rings, pots and other household objects.

Joshua Scodel's *Excess and the Mean in Early Modern English Literature* is a worthy contribution to the ongoing study of the mentality of the early modern period and its relationship with the classical and Christian heritage. While the significance of the classical virtue of temperance for the period has often been noted, Scodel's study fully explores the competing understandings of the concept in both classical and early modern times. While nearly all extolled the virtue of the mean, its fuzziness meant that there were widely varying ideas of how it might be put into practice. Focusing primarily on the Stuart period, Scodel considers a range of writers, and his close readings of individual texts, fully informed by an understanding of the classical legacy, prove to be very rich. Even such much-discussed works as Donne's 'Satire 3', which Scodel sees as using 'the mean to enlarge the sphere of individual freedom', are illuminated by being considered in this context. Scodel also examines Spenser's *Faerie Queene* II as a Georgic work that explores the values and dangers of the temperate realm, usually associated with Italy but here translated to England. Similarly, Milton's 'L'Allegro' and 'Il Penseroso' present an Anglicized Virgilian Georgic, in which the heat and passion of the Italian rural scene are tempered.

A solid contribution to scholarship on the writings on the Civil War period is offered in Bradstock, ed., *Winstanley and the Diggers, 1649–1999*, a collection of essays that emerged from a conference marking the 350th anniversary of the Diggers' occupation of St George's Hill. It is stronger than most collections of conference proceedings, largely due to the calibre of scholars, both literary and historical, contributing. Gerald Aylmer examines the social, economic and physical circumstances that prevented a full Digger revolution, and his blunt assessment of why they failed is refreshing. Resisting the biographer's bane, 'must have', James Alsop outlines what can and cannot be known of Winstanley's life. Warren Chernaik argues that Winstanley, like Milton and other radicals, contributed to the emergence of a public sphere in the 1640s and 1650s, with the attendant possibility of advising those in power. Nigel Smith explores the self-conscious tension between 'digging' and 'writing': the former was central to the identity of the movement, but ultimately Winstanley was led to 'digging on the page'. Other essays explore the topics of Winstanley and women, the Diggers and their opponents, representations of the Jews in Digger writings, and the relationship between the Digger movement and Marxism and liberation theology. Altogether the book presents a more solid overview of the Digger movement and Winstanley's writings than has hitherto been available.

The essays in Coleman, Lewis and Kowalik, eds., *Representations of the Self from the Renaissance to Romanticism*, range in coverage from Descartes to Sir Joshua Reynolds; the most significant for this survey is that by Debora Shuger, 'Life-Writing in Seventeenth-Century England'. She argues that identity in the period was based on speech, not an inner emotional life. Her emphasis then is on 'rhetorical performance' in life-writing, where the spoken (and hence public) word is what typifies the life.

Aughterson, ed., *The English Renaissance: An Anthology of Sources and Documents*, is a paperback reprint of a wildly expensive 1998 publication. It offers short excerpts from primary sources divided into eight categories: religion, politics, society and social life, education, literary and cultural theories, science and magic, gender and sexuality, and exploration and travel. Texts are presented in modernized spelling, and Aughterson provides short introductions to the eight major sections, as well as paragraph-length introductions to the individual excerpts. The volume seems to be geared to a student audience, but the cryptic and very meagre annotations will limit its classroom usefulness. I suspect that it might be most useful to the teaching scholar, looking for a convenient place to find Montaigne's essay 'Of Cannibals', or Chamberlain's letters on the Overbury affair, or bits from Henry Peacham's *Complete Gentleman* for classroom quotation.

While print offerings of primary material were meagre this year, it saw an internet release which constitutes the most significant development since the University of Michigan's commencement of the microfilming of the *Short-Title Catalogue* material. I speak of *Early English Books Online* <http://www.lib.umi.com/eebo>, which offers access to facsimiles of printed books from 1475 to 1700 in PDF format. At times the downloading of the images may be slow, but that the full range of printed primary sources might now be available to scholars regardless of their proximity to a major research library is a development with far-reaching implications.

2. Prose

The year offered only two book-length single-author studies: on Izaak Walton and Richard Baxter. Jessica Martin's *Walton's Lives: Conformist Commemorations and the Rise of Biography* is the first study of Walton's *Lives* since David Novarr's *The Making of Walton's Lives* [1958]. Unlike Novarr, Martin is not concerned with the reliability of the *Lives*, nor the process of emendation. Instead, she examines its roots in other forms of life-writing: Plutarch's *Lives*, funeral sermons, and biographical prefaces to collected writings. The first half of Martin's book examines genres and conventions; the second half turns to the *Lives* themselves. Her main thesis is that the life-writings that influenced Walton saw themselves as presenting exemplary accounts for imitation, and that this impulse was central to Walton's own work. Martin surveys a wide range of sixteenth- and seventeenth-century funeral sermons; while Protestantism hesitated to engage in praise of the dead, funeral sermons would include biographical detail to achieve the goals of the edification of the listeners and the praise of God. Martin argues that ecclesiastical biography arose partly because of the limits imposed by the funeral sermon. As Walton was unlike most church biographers of his age in his limited education and lay status, Martin suggests that he saw himself as a humble medium between his subjects and his audience, and that the true commemoration of the worthy dead took place in the act of reading. Plutarch's model provided Walton with the understanding that constancy was a prime virtue in a commemorated life. The biographer's task, then, is how to show that which is innate throughout the life becoming manifest, a task more challenging in the case of Donne than Herbert. Through her long third chapter on 'Godly Prototypes', Martin recognizes a number of commonplaces in the writing of godly lives: scriptural prototypes, the life as a 'living sermon', faith manifest in facial appearance and gesture, and the importance of dying well. It concludes with a thorough discussion of John Harris's life of Bishop Arthur Lake [1629].

In considering the *Lives* themselves, Martin focuses first on those of Donne and Herbert, written out of Walton's own affections, and then the commissioned lives of Hooker and Sanderson. In the *Lives* of Donne and Herbert, Walton figures prominently, working from a position of the 'truth of love' rather than a more objective one. Walton's ideal is autobiography, and hence his *Lives* approximate this ideal through a heavy use (and conflation) of the subject's own words and an exclusion of that which the subject himself would omit. Hence, much of this chapter is devoted to showing how Walton reshapes and uses the words of Donne and Herbert. In the *Lives* of Hooker and Sanderson Martin sees an attempt to come to terms with the Civil War from a Restoration perspective. The initial publication of the *Life of Hooker* as part of the first complete edition of *The Lawes of Ecclesiastical Polity* (replacing that of Gauden) is significant in Martin's view, and much of this chapter discusses this context. The late *Life of Sanderson* is presented as an argument for 'the necessity of obedience in questions of ceremony and church-government', but Sanderson was a difficult subject, both because of his Calvinism and because of his resistance to the idea that conduct was a reliable guide to inner virtue. *The Life of Wotton*, as it treats a secular rather than a clerical life, is not part of this study. The book concludes with a study of the subsequent influence of the *Lives*.

Through a close consideration of Baxter's letters, Tim Cooper, in *Fear and Polemic in 17th-Century England: Richard Baxter and Antinomianism*, argues that the preacher's shift away from his earlier support for Antinomianism was a matter of both personality and the political situation of the 1640s. While focused on a particular theological issue, Cooper suggests that the rhetoric surrounding it was typical of the ruthless and extreme nature of seventeenth-century polemic. Clear is Baxter's use of Antinomianism as the other pole in a binary opposition, which meant 'not so much to destroy an opponent's position as to reinforce and conserve one's own values'. In his methodology Cooper builds upon that used by J.C. Davis in *Fear, Myth, and History: The Ranters and the Historians* [1986] and Conal Condren in *The Language of Politics in Seventeenth-Century England* [1994]. Thus, his concern is with what fears in Baxter and others compelled them to render the 'Antinomians' as they did, and his discussion supports the conclusion of Leo Solt that the Antinomians were relatively conservative and authoritarian in political matters. This will prove a useful work for all those interested in language and rhetoric in the Civil Wars period.

Graham Parry, 'The Devotional Flames of William Austin' (*EMLS* special issue 7[2001] 1–30) provides an overview of the little-known Austin's life and writings, and suggests that the meditations of his *Devotionis Augustinianae Flamma* [1635] show the influence of the High Church emphases of Andrewes and Laud even on the laymen of the age.

Surprisingly, two separate articles address the metaphoric use of Proteus in seventeenth-century natural philosophy. William Burns, '"A proverb of versatile mutability": Proteus and Natural Knowledge in Early Modern Britain' (*SCJ* 4[2001] 969–80), convincingly challenges the oft-repeated idea that Nature in classical and Renaissance writing was invariably depicted as female. He notes the frequency with which Bacon and alchemical writers use Proteus as a figure of both changeable primeval nature itself, and of the investigator of that nature. The interrogation of Nature was presented in the figure of the bound Proteus, compelled to reveal himself. Peter Pesic, 'Proteus Unbound: Francis Bacon's Successors and the Defense of Experiment' (*SP* 98[2001] 428–56), nicely picks up where Burns leaves off. He challenges the commonplace that Bacon advocated the torture of Nature to reveal her secrets, a caricature which he lays at the feet of Goethe. Neither did such followers of Bacon as Samuel Hartlib, Thomas Sprat or Robert Boyle use violent metaphor to describe the interrogation of Proteus. Abraham Cowley, the sole poet discussed, made a strikingly renegade use of the image by transforming Proteus into a female figure. Both Burns and Pesic note that this metaphoric use of Proteus declined in the later seventeenth century as writers adopted a more detached and empirical approach.

In 'Rhetorical Structure and Function in *The Anatomy of Melancholy*' (*Rhetorica* 19[2001] 1–48), Angus Gowland provides a close and careful anatomy of Burton's overarching rhetorical structures. Encouraging us to see a scepticism in the narrator's explicit stylistic claims, he sees in the work an exercise in epideictic rhetoric. In 'Disfiguring the Body of Knowledge: Anatomical Discourse and Robert Burton's *The Anatomy of Melancholy*' (*ELH* 68[2001] 593–613), Grant Williams explores 'how disfiguration produces the epistemological aberration known as *The Anatomy*'. Completed this year was the Oxford edition of *The Anatomy of Melancholy*, edited by J.B. Bamborough and Martin Dodsworth, with volumes 5 and 6. These continue the commentary, provide a full bibliography of authors and works cited by Burton, and conclude with a helpful topical index to the full edition. These are up to the high standards set in the earlier volumes: annotations are clear and direct, not overwhelming. Burton's major work is finally available in a scholarly and accessible edition.

Editor's Note: The women's writing section will be resumed next year.

Books Reviewed

Armitage, David. *The Ideological Origins of the British Empire*. CUP. [2000] pp. 258. pb £14.95 ISBN 0 5217 8978 8.

Aughterson, Kate, ed. *The English Renaissance: An Anthology of Sources and Documents*. Routledge. [2002] pp. xiii + 608. pb $28.95 ISBN 0 4152 7115 0.

Bamborough, J.B., and Martin Dodsworth, eds. *The Anatomy of Melancholy* by Robert Burton, vols. 5 and 6. OUP. [2000] pp. 1392. £20 ISBN 0 9403 2266 8.

Barroll, Leeds. *Anna of Denmark, Queen of England: A Cultural Biography*. UPennP. [2001] pp. 256. $36.50 ISBN 0 8122 3574 6.

Benedict, Barbara M. *Curiosity: A Cultural History of Early Modern Inquiry*. UChicP. [2001] pp. 321. $25 ISBN 0 2260 4263 4.

Blom, Philipp. *To Have and to Hold: An Intimate History of Collectors and Collecting*. Overlook. [2002] pp. 274 $27.95 ISBN 1 5856 7377 3.

Bradstock, Andrew, ed. *Winstanley and the Diggers, 1649–1999*. Frank Cass. [2000] pp. 167. hb $59.50 ISBN 0 7146 5105 2, pb $24.50 ISBN 0 7146 8157 1.

Coleman, Patrick, Jayne Lewis and Jill Kowalik, eds. *Representations of the Self from the Renaissance to Romanticism*. CUP. [2000] pp. xii + 284. $65 ISBN 0 5216 6146 3.

Cooper, Tim. *Fear and Polemic in 17th-century England: Richard Baxter and Antinomianism*. Ashgate. [2001] pp. 238. $79.95 ISBN 0 7546 0301 6.

Cruikshanks, Eveline, ed. *The Stuart Courts*. Sutton. [2000] pp. xv + 288. £30 ISBN 0 7509 2264 8.

Fischlin, Daniel, and Mark Fortier, eds. *Royal Subjects: Essays on the Writings of James VI and I*. WSUP. [2002] pp. 521. $39.95 ISBN 0 8143 2877 6.

Fleming, Juliet. *Graffiti and the Writing Arts of Early Modern England*. UPennP. [2001] pp. 224. $35 ISBN 0 8122 3629 7.

Grabes, Herbert, ed. *Writing the Early Modern English Nation*. Rodopi. [2001] pp. xv + 199. $34 ISBN 9 0420 1525 X.

Jones, Ann Rosalind, and Peter Stallbyrass. *Renaissance Clothing and the Materials of Memory*. CUP. [2000] pp. xiii + 368. pb $28 ISBN 0 5217 8663 0.

Kamps, Ivo, and J.G. Singh, eds. *Travel Knowledge: European 'Discoveries' in the Early Modern Period*. Palgrave. [2001] pp. 368. $19.95 ISBN 0 3212 2299 8.

Martin, Jessica. *Walton's Lives: Conformist Commemorations and the Rise of Biography*. OUP. [2002] pp. 320. $80 ISBN 0 1982 7015 1.

Merians, Linda E. *Envisioning the Worst: Representations of 'Hottentots' in Early Modern England*. UDelP. [2001] pp. 289. $46.50 ISBN 0 8741 3738 1.

Norbrook, David. *Poetry and Politics in the English Renaissance*, rev. edn. OUP. [2002] pp. xix + 327. hb $72 ISBN 0 1992 4718 8, pb $22 ISBN 0 1992 4719 6.

Raman, Shankar. *Framing 'India': The Colonial Imaginary in Early Modern Culture*. StanfordUP. [2002] pp. 391. $60 ISBN 0 8047 3970 6.

Scodel, Joshua. *Excess and the Mean in Early Modern English Literature*. PrincetonUP. [2002] pp. viii + 367. $55 ISBN 0 6910 9028 9.

Sharpe, Kevin, *Remapping Early Modern England*. CUP. [2000] pp. 493. pb £19.95 ISBN 0 5216 6409 8.

Swann, Marjorie. *Curiosities and Texts: The Culture of Collecting in Early Modern England*. UPennP. [2001] pp. 280. $49.95 ISBN 0 8122 3610 6.

Wells, Robin Headlam, Glenn Burgess and Rowland Wymer, eds. *Neo-Historicism: Studies in Renaissance Literature, History and Politics*. B&B. [2000] pp. 256. $75 ISBN 0 8599 1581 6.

IX

Milton and Poetry, 1603–1660

KEN SIMPSON, MARGARET KEAN, PAUL STANWOOD, PAUL DYCK AND JOAD RAYMOND

This chapter has five sections: 1. General; 2. Milton; 3. Donne; 4. Herbert; 5. Marvell. Section 1 is by Ken Simpson; section 2 is by Margaret Kean; section 3 is by Paul Stanwood; section 4 is by Paul Dyck; section 5 is by Joad Raymond.

1. General

A broad critical spectrum is represented in studies of early seventeenth-century poetry this year: rhetorical, archetypal, gender studies, cultural materialist, new historicist, textual/editorial and biographical approaches all make their presence felt. Implied in most of these studies, however, is the importance of reading early modern works in their historical and material contexts for the purpose of recovering ideological nuances and tensions. The ongoing project of exposing the myth of royalist hegemony and of exploring the political varieties of retirement continues in a number of works, especially those devoted to Henry Vaughan, whose responses to political defeat and personal grief are shown to be subtle and varied. Although the advantages of historicism—old, new and revised—are obvious, the disadvantages are equally glaring: references to versification and the art of poetry are few and far between.

Tom Cain's scholarly edition, *The Poetry of Mildmay Fane, Second Earl of Westmorland, from the Fulbeck, Harvard and Westmorland Manuscripts*, will be invaluable to scholars of royalist poetry and politics since over 500 poems in English are published, most for the first time, and the Latin poems, although not included, are indexed. The provenance of the manuscripts is clearly explained, the notes provide essential literary and historical background, and editorial decisions are defended with care. The editor notes, for example, that this is not a transcription, but, since print alters our perceptions of the texts, the typographical conventions of Richard Coates, the printer of Fane's *Otia Sacra* [1648], are followed. He also resists the temptation to modernize the author's spelling and idiosyncratic punctuation, and reproduces Fane's marginalia and emblems. As Cain acknowledges in the introduction, Fane is a minor poet, but 'he is nearly always interesting because of the context in which he is writing' (p. 3). A powerful landowner and senior peer with an unassuming poetic persona; a staunch monarchist and opponent of the king; a man of Presbyterian sympathies who commemorated feast-days of the Church calendar, Fane defies easy categorization. During the time of Charles I's personal rule, through a productive period of 'uneasy neutrality' following the battle of Edgehill until the Restoration, and continuing until his death in 1666, Fane responded to seventeenth-century politics in a variety of genres, from translations, acrostics, and Herrick-like epigrams, to satires, country house poems, and lyrics celebrating hunting, fishing, friendship and the value of *otium*. Cain's impressive edition will encourage interest in this fascinating poet, who counted Herrick among his friends, and who probably influenced Marvell.

An important contribution to manuscript and textual studies of seventeenth-century poetry is also made by Scott Nixon in 'Henry Lawes's Hand in the Bridgewater Collection: New Light on Composer and Patron' (*HLQ* 62[2001] 232–72). Nixon has discovered and identified Henry Lawes's hand in an emendation of Thomas Carew's translation of Psalm 104, a work completed in the 1620s but set to music by Lawes, performed with four other psalm settings on 22 November 1655, and included in a pamphlet probably presented to the second earl of Bridgewater. In his thorough and conclusive study, the author sheds light on Lawes's insistence on accurate poetic texts for his songs and on the continued patronage of the Egerton family, but the wider political and cultural implications of this rare pamphlet are addressed as well. The psalms are royalist in theme and their elaborate performance on a national day of fasting—also, perhaps not coincidentally, the feast day of St Cecilia—is evidence of 'unrepentant Anglicanism' (p. 251) and the 'continuity of Caroline court culture' (p. 233) during the Interregnum. It should be noted in this context that a new edition of works by Edmund Waller, another intriguing royalist poet who, like Fane, is hard to pin down, is being prepared by Timothy Raylor and Michael P. Parker. In his article, 'Moseley, Walkley, and the 1645 Editions of Waller' (*Library* 2[2001] 236–65), Raylor distinguishes between the issues, editions and variant states of Waller's *Poems* and concludes that the second edition, printed by John Norton for Humphrey Moseley, is probably, although not yet certainly, the best copy-text for a new edition. For Raylor, Moseley successfully combined 'political nostalgia and the profit motive' (p. 257). He shrewdly gained the rights to royalist texts, manipulated dates to suit political circumstances, and did everything he could to control his corner of the market. Political opportunism is also the subject of Gerald W. Morton's 'A Note on Waller's "To My Lady Morton, On New Year's Day, 1650"' (*N&Q* 48[2001] 18–19). Waller added eight lines praising the royal family before publishing the poem in 1661. The lines are not included in an earlier manuscript version found in one of Mildmay Fane's collections and, given Waller's track record and the timing, were probably added to gain royal favour.

Studies of the ideological implications of book production and print culture, authorship and self-fashioning, book-collecting and poetry anthologies all reinforce the emphasis on the historical and material matrix of early modern poetry. Marjorie Swann's chapter on Jonson's *Works* [1616] and Herrick's *Hesperides* [1648] in *Curiosities and Texts: the Culture of Collecting in Early Modern England* is part of a new historicist examination of collecting as a material practice in which new modes of self and subjectivity are constituted. The early modern self is defined by owning and collecting objects, and this parallels the emergence of new markets and new commodities for a nascent consumer culture. Swann looks at the Tradescant collection acquired by Elias Ashmole, the curiosities gathered by natural historians, the landscapes shaped by collecting practices, and the textual self-fashioning of Jonson and Herrick, tracing her theme with compelling wit through these disparate activities. Jonson used the humanist 'notebook method' to gather and fashion himself, but as a proprietary author in print he monumentalized himself too soon, leading to a premature, textual death of the author. For Herrick, on the other hand, *Hesperides* is an anthology of royalist life experiences gathered to survive the flood of puritanism. The aesthetics and politics of discrete objects reinforce each other since Herrick fashions himself as a collector of things and experiences worth remembering from a better time before the civil war. Anne Ferry also scrutinizes anthologizing in *Tradition and the Individual Poem: An Inquiry into Anthologies*, but she is interested in canon formation and, more importantly, how the material book affects interpretation. As the title suggests, T.S. Eliot is a touchstone. Ferry argues that Eliot used his review of Grierson's anthology, *Metaphysical Lyrics and Poems* [1921], to promote his own poetics and to include himself in the 'imaginary library' of the literary canon. This insight underlies the author's unpacking of the ideological and aesthetic assumptions behind a variety of anthologies, including Tottel's *Songes and Sonettes* [1557] and Palgrave's *Golden Treasury of Songs and Lyrics* [1861], but not the Norton. Ferry's analysis is especially strong when she explains how the material features of a specific anthology can shape the reception of a poem: prefaces, titles, notes, and headings; chronological, thematic and stylistic groupings of works; font size and the disposition of space around the poem can all influence how it is experienced. In Palgrave's *Golden Treasury*, for example, Carew's 'Disdaine returned', entitled 'The True Beauty', is paired with an excerpt from Jonson's 'To the Immortal Memory, and Friendship of That Noble Paire, Sir Lucius Cary, and Sir H. Morison', but we are not told that it is an excerpt and the editor assigns it his own title. The pairing also downplays the bitterness at the end of Carew's poem (pp. 94–6). Early seventeenth-century poets also figure importantly in Ferry's attempt to sketch the characteristics of the most common anthology pieces. Examining Jonson's 'Queen and Huntress', Herbert's 'Virtue', Carew's 'Song' ('Ask me no more'), Waller's 'Song' ('Go, lovely rose'), and Herrick's 'To Daffodils', she concludes that spatial and temporal length, stanzaic patterns, song rhythm structures, and intertextual echoes predispose anthologists to include these works, ensuring their place in literary history.

Turning from the material to the social and political contexts of seventeenth-century verse, in *Country House Discourse in Early Modern England: A Cultural Study of Landscape and Legitimacy* Kari Boyd McBride explores country house poetry as part of a 'discourse field' which registers shifts in the legitimation crisis that pervaded England from the dissolution of the monasteries until the Restoration. During this period, the country house became a symbol designed to mediate the socio-economic change from a rural, moral economy to one in which capital was sovereign. Residual forms of authority based on lineage, land and royal patronage competed, often in the same work, with emergent forms of legitimacy based on humanist ideals of virtue and merit and, by mid-century, the accumulation of wealth. McBride begins by showing that sixteenth-century country house discourse both acknowledged and assimilated protests based on nostalgia for the pre-Reformation, pre-dissolution past, portraying the lord and his house as a source of moral virtue and economic order at a time when new agricultural methods developed which began to displace that order. In the third chapter, she argues that the architecture of the country house displayed the legitimacy of the nobility, but alterations to country houses by two exceptional women, Elizabeth of Shrewsbury (1527–1608) and Anne Clifford (1590–1676), also depict women struggling for their own space within a male-dominant household and culture. McBride then turns to country house poetry of the early seventeenth century. The landed legitimacy, *sponte sua* (by their own will), *dapes inemptae* (unbought goods), and hospitality motifs are compared and contrasted in poems by Lanyer, Jonson, Carew, and Herrick, revealing the specific cultural work performed by each author's use of country house discourse. Absent from these poems, however, are references to the economic revolution occurring in the countryside or to the growing importance of world trade and the accumulation of capital. These later developments are taken up in the final chapter in which the country house, as well as country house poems and paintings, are described as signs rather than sources of legitimacy; the land, the house, and its furnishings become objectified signs of wealth circulating in a capitalist economy. Surveying works by Fane, Lovelace, Denham, Marvell, Finch, Waller and Philips, McBride finds two important patterns: the use of objects and furnishings, not the house or land, to symbolize the legitimacy of wealth rather than the authority of lineage or virtue; and the reappearance of the ruins motif, popular in the sixteenth century, to question the notion of legitimacy itself, an important concern during the civil war. Even though the trajectory of McBride's analysis has been traced before by Raymond Williams and others, and even though the sections on architecture and painting are largely derived from secondary sources and add little to country house discourse as a whole, McBride does contribute to our understanding of the poetry of the period. Her analysis of legitimacy and its representation uncovers layers of race, gender and class that haven't been noticed before, and this gives a well-worn topic a new appeal.

The contrast between old and new is especially clear in two books devoted to metaphysical literature in 2001. George Williamson's *Six Metaphysical Poets: A Reader's Guide* [1967] has been reprinted without new prefatory material or modifications. In a sense, why should it be modified? We might argue about who should be called 'metaphysical' or whether 'metaphysical' is a useful term at all, but Williamson has made his decisions and his rationale is implicit in those choices and in the readings he offers. A starker contrast would be hard to imagine when we turn to Michael Morgan Holmes's *Early Modern Metaphysical Literature: Nature, Custom and Strange Desires*. Taking his cue from the 'denaturalizing interests' of cultural materialist, lesbian, gay, and queer theorists, Holmes argues that metaphysical literature should be defined by the strangeness, unnaturalness and wonder evoked when early seventeenth-century literature challenges seemingly 'natural' systems of knowledge, perception and gender formation. By showing these systems to be conventional and contingent rather than essential and natural, metaphysical literature does not subvert existing power structures, but it does create new possibilities for opposition, dissidence and desire. The theme is developed in some detail through chapters on Lord Herbert of Cherbury's epistemology, Marvell and Donne's depictions of female homoeroticism, Lanyer's conflation of 'religious devotion and homoeroticism' (p. 5), and Crashaw, Donne and Milton's discourses of hagiology and martyrdom. The argument is somewhat strained, dependent as it is on an ahistorical and abstract dichotomy between nature and custom and on its exclusive focus on 'metaphysical secularity', but, seen beside Williamson's book, Holmes does offer one way of breathing new life into a contentious term and of charting the course of the discipline through our responses to what 'metaphysical' happens to mean at different times.

A historicist and intentionalist rather than cultural materialist approach to early modern literature and history is taken by Robert Wilcher in *The Writing of Royalism, 1628–1660*. Wilcher presents a chronological survey of works, ranging from masques and prose satires to propaganda, news reports and non-dramatic poetry written by those loyal to the king and/or the monarchy (both absolute and constitutional) and the Church of England. Although more attention to prose romances would have been helpful, this is a perceptive, carefully researched and thorough study that builds on earlier work by Potter, Sharpe, Loxley and others. Wilcher is especially skilful in tracing the subtle changes that occur in genres and tropes as royalist authors respond to changing political circumstances. Cleveland's combativeness, Lovelace and Fane's different versions of cultivated retirement, Vaughan's movement from inwardness to resolution and Cowley's resignation are all explored with careful attention to historical context. The strength of Wilcher's approach, however, can also be a weakness. The analysis of *Cooper's Hill*, for example, shows how Denham responded to different events in the 1640s and 1650s as he revised drafts and printed versions of the poem, but because of the chronological arrangement the discussions of the poem are separated from one another.

The two poets who benefit most from Wilcher's approach are Cowley and Vaughan, while Herrick could have been considered in more detail. Cowley, a complex figure deeply sympathetic with the aesthetic culture of the Caroline court and the rationalist humanism of Falkland and the Great Tew circle, manifests more than any other poet the 'strain exerted by a changing world upon traditional modes of poetic discourse' (p. 99). In panegyrics he maintained the values of the court even as civil war approached; he turned to satire as the war began, but he was out of his element; perhaps most successfully, he charted a course from despair to deliverance in his odes, but he was eventually overtaken by history; in *The Civil War* he hoped to celebrate royalism but was thwarted by the victorious puritans; in his religious epic *Davideis* he fails to find a convincing religious voice for a political and religious vision dangerously close to extinction and suffocated by censorship and fear of reprisal. Although Wilcher is not specific about why Cowley's most ambitious poems were left incomplete, leaving this complex question open is prudent. On the other hand, Stephen Guy-Bray, basing his thesis on a variety of textual silences, concludes in 'Cowley's Latin Lovers: Nisus and Euryalus in the "Davideis"' (*CML* 21[2001] 25–42) that Cowley failed to finish the *Davideis* because of anxieties about the homoeroticism of his Virgilian models for the friendship of Jonathan and David.

The tragic trajectory of Cowley's career, however, should be compared to Vaughan's more triumphant one. For Wilcher, Vaughan, once read as a figure of inwardness and mysticism, is now a battle-tried veteran of culture wars who 'plays a prominent role in the literary resistance to the new Commonwealth of the 1650s' (p. 243). The book becomes the way the exiled royalist community remembers, consoles and constitutes itself. Vaughan began his career writing cavalier lyrics and royalist complimentary verse, but turned to religious poetry in the first edition of

Silex Scintillans [1650], hoping for divine release from personal catastrophe and the corruption and sinfulness of human history. Wilcher argues that this mood of despair turns to patient expectation and, at times, passionate resolve when we look carefully at some of the poems added to the 1655 edition of the collection. According to Wilcher, Vaughan expresses a renewed faith that the ancient way of the Church, the guidance of Scripture and the order of nature will sustain the faithful until their time comes, a message conveyed vigorously, even aggressively in poems like 'The Proffer' (p. 325).

Wilcher's view of Vaughan as a committed royalist and Anglican is complemented by Philip West's excellent study of the poet's use of the Bible in *Henry Vaughan's 'Silex Scintillans': Scripture Uses*. As the title suggests, this is more than an account of Vaughan's biblical allusions; the author shows what such allusions do, what work they perform, for the writer and his biblical readers. Each chapter explores how Vaughan uses Scripture to make sense of events such as his illness, his conversion (assumed rather than demonstrated to be in 1648/9), the defeat of royalism, the regicide, and the eviction of Anglican ministers due to the Act for the Better Propagation and Preaching of the Gospel in Wales (February 1650). In chapter 2 West shows how Vaughan uses the story of Jacob in 'Regeneration' as a type of console Anglicans, but he also shows how Vaughan refers to the patriarch in 'Jacob's Pillow, and Pillar' to condemn the puritan myth of return to apostolic purity. Chapter 3 turns to the prophetic books and King Hezekiah for a model of sickness, recovery and praise that Vaughan used, in the 1655 preface to *Silex Scintillans*, to suggest how he overcame his illness and his doubts about his religious and poetic vocation. In chapter 4 West argues that Scripture is used in *The Mount of Olives* [1652] and in several poems in *Silex Scintillans* to teach Anglicans 'how to live well in hard times' by following a disciplined, orderly devotional regimen. In the absence of the liturgy, prayer is linked through Scripture to the hours of the day and the natural world. The last two chapters, the strongest in the book, examine Vaughan's use of apocalyptic texts to counter radical millennarians' claims of imminent apocalypse and personal possession of the Spirit with patient waiting for the Last Days, the acceptance of affliction as a providential trial, the denial of false prophets, and the rejection of human perfectibility. According to West, 'the keynote of all Vaughan's uses is affliction' (p. 21) and although he demonstrates that even this has a political context, it implies a passivity that is not consistent with a number of the poems included in the second edition of *Silex Scintillans*. As Milton demonstrates in *Paradise Regained*, patient fortitude and activism are not necessarily mutually exclusive.

Vaughan is also well represented in the group of short essays written on early seventeenth-century poetry in 2001. Alan Rudrum published three essays in which Vaughan is prominent. 'Royalist Lyric' (in Keeble, ed., *The Cambridge Companion to Writing of the English Revolution*, pp. 181–97), presents a short survey, suitable for undergraduates, of works by authors who 'responded to the Civil War itself' (p. 181). The politics of retirement and the continued political engagement of royalist poets are emphasized in the brief sketches of Herrick, Cleveland, Lovelace, Cowley and Vaughan. In 'Paradoxical Persona: Henry Vaughan's Self-Fashioning' (*HLQ* 62[2001] 351–67), Rudrum argues that Vaughan's authorial persona changes in response to social, political and religious developments. Carefully and subtly unfolding the nuances of Vaughan's self-references, Rudrum ultimately finds tension between Vaughan the gentleman and Vaughan the Christian and 'a paradox in Vaughan's situation': theologically Arminian, he was, nevertheless, led by class consciousness and political circumstances to emphasize the corruption of humanity and 'the sense that he was part of a righteous, beleaguered, minority' (p. 367), two views associated with the kind of puritanism he steadfastly opposed. In 'Henry Vaughan and Roland Watkyns, Neighbors but not Friends' (*Scintilla* 5[2001] 61–71), Rudrum looks at the relationship between two neighbours who had much in common (both were poets, doctors and royalists), but who apparently never responded to each other's work. The 'apparently' must be seriously questioned after this article, however, because although Vaughan doesn't refer to Watkyns, Rudrum shows that, in verbal parallels, Watkyns refers to Vaughan defensively and critically.

Other essays devoted to Vaughan in *Scintilla* demonstrate the variety of useful approaches that continue to be taken to the poet and his work. Geoffrey Palmer offers a musical setting of 'Awake, Glad Heart' (*Scintilla* 5[2001] 23–6), and three essays take a comparative, archetypal path to Vaughan. David Annwn's '"Deep Hymns": "Holy" Orpheus in the Poetry of Henry Vaughan, John Milton and Ronald Johnson' (*Scintilla* 5[2001] 7–21), links Vaughan to the Orpheus archetype through water images and the emphasis on the oneness of creation. In 'Henry Vaughan and Sufism' (*Scintilla* 5[2001] 37–49), Parvin Loloi shows that Vaughan's light, dark and bird images are similar to those used by Sufi poets, while Hilary Llewellyn-Williams traces the underworld journey in 'Land of Darkness: The Poet in the Underworld' (*Scintilla* 5[2001] 171–8), revealing in Vaughan's positive references to darkness images of the creative process itself. Roland Mathias's biographical essay, 'The Midlands: Introductions and Identifications' (*Scintilla* 5[2001] 93–103) continues the important work of establishing Vaughan's royalist cultural milieu between 1642 and 1653. Here Mathias suggests that Vaughan had important connections with the Digbys of Coleshill, Warwickshire, where he probably first met his wife Catherine, and Sir Charles Egerton of Newborough Hall, his wife's uncle, to whom he dedicated *The Mount of Olives* and *Flores Solitudinis* [1654]. Glyn Pursglove's '"Bright Shadows": The Religious Wit of Henry Vaughan' (*Scintilla* 5[2001] 117–38), and June Sturrock's 'Cock-crowing' (*Scintilla* 5[2001] 152–8), present sensitive and careful readings of specific features of Vaughan's lyrics. Pursglove unfolds Vaughan's inventive use of accumulated metaphors in 'Son-days' and silent puns in the son/sun/sin pattern, revealing a side of Vaughan's sophisticated theological wit that is usually overlooked. Sturrock's close reading of 'Cock-crowing' emphasizes the universal interanimation of bird, sun and God, but also underlines parallels between the poet and bird: the poet sings to his God, waiting and longing for light and unity just as the bird sings and longs for the dawn.

As Pursglove's and Sturrock's essays indicate, studies of poetic texture and influence, although clearly in the minority this year, have not disappeared altogether. Robert W. Halli, Jr. argues, in 'Versifying the Metaphor: Ben Jonson's "Song. That Women are but Mens shaddowes"' (*BJJ* 8[2001] 123–31), that Jonson attempts to distract the attention of the countess of Pembroke, the principal audience of the poem, from the lyric's sexism by creating clever, witty verbal parallels and contrasts which shadow each other. David Reid's 'Lord Herbert of Cherbury's "Elegy Over a Tomb" and Carew's "Aske me no more"' (*N&Q* 48[2001] 388–90) makes a strong case for ascribing 'Aske me no more' to Carew despite Scott Nixon's arguments to the contrary. Reid shows that, even if we acknowledge the uncertain provenance of the poem, verbal echoes and inversions as well as thematic similarities and socio-political contexts make it likely that the poem is Carew's graceful response to Lord Herbert. Finally, Thomas Kaminski claims, in 'Edmund Waller, English *Précieux*' (*PQ* 79[2000] 19–43), that if we read Waller's poetry within the context of Continental *précieux* poetics and manners, we can better understand why he was lauded in his own time but virtually ignored since. Waller's use of plural nouns, double entendre and conventional Petrarchan images were all aspects of the *précieux* mode encouraged by Henrietta Maria and her retinue, but his characteristic delicacy of sound, gallant restraint, and skilful adaptations of *précieux* tropes make Waller a unique figure in this misunderstood style, even if it quickly fell out of favour.

As I have shown in my review of books, the historical approach to early seventeenth-century poetry in 2001 is varied: intentionalist historicism, the history of ideas, cultural materialism, revised new historicism, textual criticism, and the history of the book are all noteworthy. The same range can be found in the short essays for review, some of which have been mentioned already. Examining physical and metaphorical maps and their influence on literary works, the contributors to Gordon and Klein, eds., *Literature, Mapping, and the Politics of Space in Early Modern Britain*, explore the material and historical conditions of the conceptualization of space. Andrew McRae's essay, '"On the famous voyage": Ben Jonson and Civic Space' (pp. 181–203) offers a Bakhtinian reading of Jonson's poem, suggesting that Jonson imagines an 'alternative spatiality' that undermines official, sanitized descriptions of London. Images of urination, filth, defecation and the grotesque body reveal Jonson's moral disgust, but the exuberance and vitality of the city are registered as well. In the same collection, Bernhard Klein's 'Imaginary Journeys: Spenser, Drayton, and the Poetics of National Space' proposes that each poet constructs space and national identity in contrasting ways. In *Poly-Olbion* [1612/22], Drayton inscribes the totalizing and static sense of geography and social order embodied in Camden's *Britannia* [1586], while in *The Faerie Queene* [1590/ 6], Spenser is more dynamic and progressive in his construction of landscape and nationality. Spenser's allegory, like Harrison's *Historicall Description of the Islande of Britayne* [1577], invites individuals to participate in the making and mapping of the nation, a notion that resists absolutist impulses in cartography and politics. Although quite different in emphasis, Peter Herman's 'Authorship and the Royal "I": King James VI/I and the Poetics of Monarchic Verse' (*RQ* 54[2001] 1495–1530) also considers the interpretative dimensions of material and textual production. Examining the title pages, organization, layout, fonts, and running heads of successive editions of James's *Lepanto* [1585, 1591, 1603], Herman observes that not only does the king's presentation of himself as a royal author perform different political work in each edition, but the penultimate edition of 1603 is a specifically 'monarchic performance' as the king claims 'poetic authorship's cultural empowerment upon his ascension to the English throne' (p. 1523). Rather than the king conferring authority upon authorship, authorship confers authority on the king (p. 1518).

The ideological and political nuances of seventeenth-century writing are treated throughout the works reviewed this year, but the remaining essays focus on these concerns exclusively. In '"Thomas Traherne: A Critique of Political Economy'

(*HLQ* 62[2001] 369–88), David Hawkes argues that Traherne's critique of political economy is based on Aristotle's distinction between nature and custom, natural value and exchange value. For Traherne, alienated perception, distorted ontology and idolatrous fetishism result when the value of things is determined not by their original, God-given, 'inherent qualities' but by their 'exchangeability in the market' (p. 370). According to Alan De Gooyer, in *Essays in Verse and Prose* [1668] Cowley anticipates later thinkers such as Locke in his construction of a self that is anterior to and independent of social and political obligations. 'Sensibility and Solitude in Cowley's Familiar Essay' (*Restoration* 25[2001] 369–88) suggests that, in the process of defending his retirement, Cowley emphasizes the importance of solitude and the emotions in the retrieval of his authentic self from society's corrupting influence, introducing more informality and immediacy into the essay and contributing to new modes of interiority which make the market economy possible. Pamela Coren's 'In the Person of Womankind: Female Persona Poems by Campion, Donne, Jonson' (*SP* 98[2001] 225–50) examines the subtleties of gender politics in Renaissance lyrics which feature disguised female voices, a topic familiar to scholars of Renaissance drama. Male hierarchy is reinforced in Campion's song, 'A secret love or two, I must confesse', Donne's manuscript performance, 'Confined Love', and Jonson's folio text, 'In Defence of their Inconstancy. A Song', when male desire is associated with the female persona, especially when the poem is spoken or sung by a man. The possibility of subversive female performances of male, female persona poems remains intriguing, but more research is needed to see how women actually received the Renaissance lyric. Clifford Davidson challenges the narrow definition of 'Protestant' implied in Barbara Lewalski's exclusion of Richard Crashaw from the canon of Protestant poets. 'The Anglican Setting of Richard Crashaw's Devotional Verse' (*BJJ* 8[2001] 259–76) shows the poet to be profoundly biblical, and, more importantly, deeply immersed in Anglican ritual, especially as it was practised at Peterhouse, Cambridge. The Anglican Church, Davidson reminds us, is both Protestant and Catholic, but he begs the question of Crashaw's Protestantism when he associates him mainly with the Catholic side of the equation. Nevertheless, as Davidson argues, Crashaw's relationship to the tradition of Cosin and to the context of Anglican worship are important to remember, especially when reading the poems written before his conversion.

2. Milton

Stanley Fish, *How Milton Works*, is according to Harvard University Press, a 'definitive statement on Milton for our time'. The volume incorporates many of Fish's earlier essays on the prose and shorter poems and seems determined to construct a unified concept of both Milton as writer and Fish as critic. The encompassing thesis is that Milton has always worked 'from the inside out' (p. 23), finding value in the inner integrity of the individual rather than in external proofs or public recognition. There is much to recommend such an argument, particularly from such a renowned critic, and Fish's reading of *Paradise Regained* seems especially sensitive. However, many will balk at the determined nature of the overall approach. All of Milton has to be fitted to a single model or dropped. The ahistorical and apolitical tendencies are particularly unfortunate when Fish comes to consider the (mainly early) prose, and some rather partial quotation of Milton takes place. This is certainly a major critical publication. It would convince us of a single truth, but it seems more likely to prompt much critical debate and dissent. The cat has been set amongst the pigeons.

The intellectual contexts for discussion of Milton's work are reshaped by four excellent monographs this year. Matthew Jordan, *Milton and Modernity: Politics, Masculinity and 'Paradise Lost'*, charts the emergence of the autonomous masculine subject within the epic's discussions of work, love and self-mastery. Jordan carefully positions Milton's ideal of individual moral freedom within the context of the fundamental changes in conceptions of society and state taking place in the early modern period and further juxtaposes our understanding of 'modernity' as a story of nostalgia and loss against the context of *Paradise Lost*. A different slant on the public sphere is taken by Richard J. Du Rocher, *Milton among the Romans: The Pedagogy and Influence of Milton's Latin Curriculum*. Du Rocher has taken Edward Phillips's account of his education under John Milton in the 1640s seriously and has undertaken a scholarly examination of the set texts—Lucretius, Pliny, Virgil; Vitruvius on architecture; Cornelius Celius on medicine; Cato Varro, Columella and Palladius on agriculture; Marcus Manilius on astrology. Du Rocher is interested in the curriculum itself as a means of preparing students for public service but also in how these chosen texts intersect with Milton's own writings. This is a worthy endeavour that results in many fresh contexts for understanding Miltonic cruces. Equally fresh are the insights to be gleaned from two monographs dealing with religious themes. Jameela Lares, *Milton and the Preaching Arts*, offers a fascinating explanation of the rhetoric of Reformed preaching. She is clearly right to presume that Milton's education and intended vocation would suggest a formative debt to such preaching arts. In pursuing this case, Lares not only makes available a good deal of background information on the alternative methods available to the preacher but traces a specific Christ's College tradition. Intriguingly, she argues that William Chappell, tutor at Christ's and advocate of a preaching model of correction linked to consolation, may have been of more long-standing influence on Milton than we commonly allow. Lares looks at Milton's anti-episcopal tracts and the closing two books of *Paradise Lost* in detail. One wishes that she had had time to consider more of Milton's work. An expanded analysis of *Paradise Regained*, which as she so rightly says 'richly deserves to be investigated in terms of the preaching arts' (p. 169), would have been particularly beneficial, but perhaps we can hope for that in the near future. Jeffrey S. Shoulson, *Milton and the Rabbis: Hebraism, Hellenism, and Christianity*, is a confident and scholarly reconsideration of the influence of rabbinical writings upon Christian thought, and specifically Milton's *Paradise Lost*. Shoulson premises his approach on the fluid interaction of Hebraic, Hellenist and Christian traditions over the centuries and is more interested in the concept of midrash than the identification of specific sources. He is to be congratulated both for the balance of his approach and the clarity with which he handles such complicated materials.

There are two book-length studies of *Samson Agonistes* for review this year. Both are highly readable, mature critical responses to the hermeneutical difficulties of the text. For John T. Shawcross in *The Uncertain World of 'Samson Agonistes'* the many uncertainties of the text and its interpretation are to be acknowledged rather than elided. However, ultimately, he does not see such difficulties as overriding a positive belief system that promises salvation for God's true servants. Derek N.C. Wood, in *Exiled from Light: Divine Law, Morality, and Violence in Milton's 'Samson Agonistes'*, is more of a doubter. He is not convinced of Samson's status as a hero or as a true servant of God. The treatment of Dalila is brutal and callous, and in Wood's view we must turn to the mercy of Christ and *Paradise Regained* for an ethical hero and an example worth imitating.

Kenneth Borris's *Allegory and Epic in English Renaissance Literature: Heroic Form in Sidney, Spenser, and Milton* is a wide-ranging discussion of the relation between heroic poetry and allegory in the English Renaissance period. Borris devotes a substantial section of his argument to Milton's *Paradise Lost*, showing persuasively that a reformulated allegorical mode underpins the Christian heroism of the poem and its *ex Deo* metaphysics.

Corns, ed., *A Companion to Milton*, was published this year in the series Blackwell Companions to Literature and Culture. This is a first-class collection of twenty-nine commissioned essays that together offer a vigorous and stimulating response to all major aspects of Milton studies. Diversity and debate are the volume's watchwords, making this a very readable collection. Soon to be available in paperback, this Companion looks set for a long shelf-life as a standard critical volume. It contains the following chapter-length essays: Thomas N. Corns on the Nativity Ode; Leah S. Marcus on *Comus*; Stella P. Revard on 'Lycidas'; Sharon Achinstein on *Samson Agonistes*; Margaret Kean on *Paradise Regained*; Elizabeth Skerpan Wheeler on the early political prose; Annabel Patterson on the divorce tracts; Laura Lunger Knoppers on the later political prose. Five chapters are devoted to aspects of *Paradise Lost*: Stephen M. Fallon, '*Paradise Lost* in Intellectual History'; David Loewenstein, 'The Radical Religious Politics of *Paradise Lost*'; Michael Schoenfeldt, 'Obedience and Autonomy in *Paradise Lost*'; Amy Boesky, '*Paradise Lost* and the Multiplicity of Time'; John Leonard, 'Self-Contradicting Puns in *Paradise Lost*'. In addition, the following themed chapters were commissioned. Barbara K. Lewalski, 'Genre'; John K. Hale, 'The Classical Literary Tradition'; Regina M. Schwartz, 'Milton on the Bible'; Graham Parry, 'Literary Baroque and Literary Neoclassicism'; Achsah Guibbory, 'Milton and English Poetry'; Thomas N. Corns, 'Milton's English'; Cedric C. Brown, 'The Legacy of the Late Jacobean Period'; N.H. Keeble, 'Milton and Puritanism'; John Rumrich, 'Radical Heterodoxy and Heresy'; Diane Kelsey McColley, 'Milton and Ecology'; Andrew Hadfield, 'The English and Other Peoples'; Joad Raymond, 'The Literature of Controversy'; Martin Dzelzainis, 'Republicanism'; Kay Gilliland Stevenson, 'Reading Milton, 1674–1800'; Peter J. Kitson, 'Milton: The Romantics and After'; and Gordon Campbell, 'The Life Records'.

Amongst the essays for review this year no single theme dominates, and there is less work on the political prose than one might expect. One can, however, identify a continued debate over Milton's subordination of women and two important discussions of Milton's theory of love by Luxon (*MiltonS* 40[2001] 38–60) and Chaplin (*MP* 99[2001] 266–92).

The essays in this year's *Milton Studies* cover a variety of texts and theoretical positions. In '"The melting voice through mazes running": The Dissolution of Borders in *L'Allegro* and *Il Penseroso*', (*MiltonS* 40[2001] 1–18) Eric C. Brown responds to the concern with borders and boundaries in these companion poems. He both conscientiously reviews the critical tradition and has much to add to our understanding of Milton's nuanced use of light imagery and Ovidian myths. George F. Butler, 'Spenser, Milton, and the Renaissance Campe: Monsters and Myths in *The Faerie Queene* and *Paradise Lost*' (*MiltonS* 40[2001] 19–37) suggests that the figuration of Campe in Nonnos of Panopolis' *Dionysiaca* has influenced both Spenser's Errour and Milton's depictions of Sin and Death, either directly or through the Renaissance mythographies. Thomas H. Luxon, in 'Milton's Wedded Love: Not about Sex (As We Know It)' (*MiltonS* 40[2001] 38–60), sends a clarion call for more self-discipline in our reading of edenic love. Modern concepts of sexuality are fuelling a critical obsession with the human body and physical desire that Milton may not share, according to Luxon. Instead, he identifies a Platonic slant to Milton's use of the term 'wedded love', arguing that it refers to the procreation of the soul. The argument proceeds by close textual work focused on Book IV of *Paradise Lost*, but its ramifications are wide-reaching, re-centring Milton as a poet of purity and a Platonist. Ken Hiltner's 'The Portrayal of Eve in *Paradise Lost*: Genius at Work' (*MiltonS* 40[2001] 61–80) is a clever piece aligning Milton and Luther with Nietzsche and Heidegger as proponents of 'deconstruction'. Milton's depiction of Eve's fall in *Paradise Lost* is, it is argued, a deconstruction of medieval theology's dualistic representations of Christianity. Juliet Lucy Cummins, 'Milton's Gods and the Matter of Creation' (*MiltonS* 40[2001] 81–105) works through the tensions inherent in depicting God as male but prime matter as female within the epic. She writes well on the competing strands of the argument, but ultimately uncovers a masculinist bias. Michael Fixler, 'Milton's Passionate Poetics, or Paradigms Lost and Regained' (*MiltonS* 40[2001] 106–49), is intrigued by the integrity of Renaissance poetry, the energy and impulse that give internal shape to the text. The immediacy of this aesthetic moves beyond structural theory to what he calls 'passionate poetics'. His discursive essay centres on 'At a Solemn Music' but also considers both the formal qualities and the experiential frames adopted in the late poems. Susannah B. Mintz, 'Dalila's Touch: Disability and Recognition in *Samson Agonistes*' (*MiltonS* 40[2001] 150–80) engages with the multiple interpretative perspectives admitted within the reading experience of *Samson Agonistes*. She suggests that to take Dalila's hand would be to counter cultural prejudice and intransigence. It would allow change to take place and sensitize Samson to alternative positions. The rejection of Dalila can therefore be interpreted by the modern reader as a tragic inability on Samson's part to break through his ideological conditioning. Paula Loscocco, '"Not les renown'd than Jael": Heroic Chastity in *Samson Agonistes*' (*MiltonS* 40[2001] 181–200), accepts a more standard view of Dalila, but explores the ramifications of Dalila's surprising introduction of the model of Jael. Dalila's status as unfaithful wife makes it impossible for her to retain control over this model of heroic virtue of chastity within this text, but equally she must be scapegoated in order to make it possible for Samson as recuperated spouse to be reinvested with Hebraic and Miltonic chaste heroism. In a carefully argued piece Eric Nelson, '"True Liberty": Isocrates and Milton's *Areopagitica*' (*MiltonS* 40[2001] 201–21), looks at how Isocrates was actually edited, published and read in the early modern period. He points out that Isocrates' *To Nicoles* was taken to be his 'monarchical' text and *Areopagiticus* his 'republican' text. From this base Nelson argues strongly that Milton's *Areopagitica* is not likely to be intended solely as an attack on censorship but aims to be a broad account of liberty and republican government. David Loewenstein, 'Milton among the Religious Radicals and Sects: Polemical Engagements and Silences' (*MiltonS* 40[2001] 222–47), is intrigued by Milton's lack of vocal support for radical sectarian groups during the 1650s. He suggests a sympathetic silence on Milton's part, but considers his priority to lie in the construction of his own distinct and independent polemical voice.

Issue three of *Milton Quarterly* 35[2001] was a special issue, comprising a photographic reproduction of the volume *Justa Edovardo King* [1638], with an introduction, full translations and notes by Edward Le Comte. The other issues included the following essays. Catherine Gimelli Martin, 'The Sources of Milton's Sin Reconsidered' (*MiltonQ* 35[2001] 1–8), foregrounds Francis Bacon's application of the Scylla myth in the *Advancement of Learning* and the *Novum Organum* to represent an idolatrous amassing of knowledge for its own sake. She cogently suggests that Milton may have intended us to link the description of Sin to Baconian thought. Mandy Green, 'Softening the Stony; Deucalion, Pyrrha, and the Process of Regeneration in *Paradise Lost*' (*MiltonQ* 35[2001] 9–21), neatly employs the Deucalion simile as a springboard into a wider discussion of the dynamic of reconciliation and regeneration within Books X and XI of the epic, identifying a repeated motif based on the relenting (softening) of obdurate positions. In 'Gender and Spiritual Equality in Marriage: A Dialogic Reading of Rachel Speght and John Milton' (*MiltonQ* 35[2001] 22–32), Desma Polydorou compares Milton's view of female subordination with Rachel Speght's arguments in defence of woman's spiritual equality. She finds it telling that a near contemporary such as Speght should have found so many exemplars of deserving women, and concludes that Milton chose to leave such exemplars out. William Shullenberger, 'Into the Woods: The Lady's Soliloquy in *Comus*' (*MiltonQ* 35[2001] 33–43), reads the masque as a rite of passage for the Lady and sees the section surrounding the echo song as the Lady's first steps to mature ethical reflection and adult affirmation of faith. Maria Magro, 'Milton's Sexualized Woman and the Creation of a Gendered Public Sphere' (*MiltonQ* 35[2001] 98–112), employs the divorce tracts and the epic to investigate the ways in which Milton's concept of male civil liberty relies on a domesticated construct of femininity. Having argued this through interestingly, Magro then goes on to consider the implications of this for the (female) writer in the public sphere. Ken Hiltner, 'Place, Body and Spirit Joined: The Earth–Human Wound in *Paradise Lost*' (*MiltonQ* 35[2001] 113–17), is interested in the typology that might connect Earth's wound at the Fall to the creation of Eve and the origin of the Church.

Paul R. Sellin, 'Some Musings on Alexander Morus and the Authorship of *De Doctrina Christiana*' (*MiltonQ* 35[2001] 63–71), tests our tools for determining authorship (including stylistic statistical analysis) against the possibility that Alexander Morus might be the author of *De Doctrina Christiana*. The results make him seem a likely candidate. Sellin's point is that we simply cannot prove 'authorship' in this case and that it would be better not to fight quite so adamantly for our hunches. Kent R. Lehnhof, 'Deity and Creation in the *Christian Doctrine*' (*MiltonQ* 35[2001] 232–44), uses *De Doctrina Christiana* to prove that for Milton the act of creating defines the deity. From that theological premise Lehnhof can justify the centrality of the creative process within Milton's thought processes and poetry. J. Allan Mitchell, 'Reading God Reading "Man": Hereditary Sin and the Narrativization of Deity' (*MiltonQ* 35[2001] 72–86), questions our standard reading of God's justice in Book III. Mitchell finds that the presentation of God the Father as a persona disturbs the abstract theology. He finds particular difficulty with the division of justice and mercy, arguing that the Son equates the two values and that the dichotomy enforced by the Father is both false and unjust. John K. Hale, 'The 1668 Argument to *Paradise Lost*' (*MiltonQ* 35[2001] 87–97), gives a fresh response to the 'Argument' added to *Paradise Lost* in 1668 by Milton at the request of the printer Samuel Simmons. He considers the text to provide evidence of Milton's own interpretation of his poem, noting for example the relative length of the argument for Book III, the grouping of ideas within sentence divisions and the emphasis on consolation. Geoffrey F. Nuttall, 'Milton's Churchmanship in 1659: His Letter to Jean de Labadie' (*MiltonQ* 35[2001] 227–31), turns his attention to whether Milton was ever a Congregationalist. Milton wrote a letter in April 1659 on behalf of a French church in London to a French minister in Orange, Jean de Labadie, inviting him to be their minister. Nuttall explores the fascinating background to this congregation and finds it tantalizing that we should have this one piece of extant evidence showing Milton's involvement with a gathered church.

Margaret O. Thickstun, 'Raphael and the Challenge of Evangelical Education' (*MiltonQ* 35[2000] 245–57), uses the figure of Raphael in *Paradise Lost* to muse more widely on the role of the educator. She sees Raphael as conscious of his teaching role and as an inspiration to all teachers in fulfilling their challenging task. Verne M. Underwood, 'Feigned Praise: Authorship Problems in the Extant Poems of John Milton, Sr.' (*MiltonQ* 35[2001] 44–9), is rightly cynical about the authorship of two commendatory verses for John Lane thought to have been composed by Milton's father. Underwood does not think it beyond the bounds of consideration that Lane penned the verses himself. Derek N.C. Wood, 'Milton and Galileo' (*MiltonQ* 35[2001] 50–2), surveys the critical controversy over whether Milton did or did not visit Galileo in Florence. He notes a number of connections between the Diodati family and Galileo, not least the fact that Charles Diodati had been a student of Galileo and was a friend of his son. Based on such important personal connections, Wood thinks it likely not only that Milton would have been invited to visit Galileo, but that he would have acted as intermediary and messenger for both families. Finally, Wendy Furman-Adams and Virginia J. Tufte, 'Anticipating Empson: Henry Fuseli's Re-Vision of Milton's God' (*MiltonQ* 35[2001] 258–74), offer a richly illustrated comparison of Blake's and Fuseli's responses to Milton's epic. Placed alongside Blake's redemptive, Christocentric, vision, Henry Fuseli's compositions appear stark and lacking in consolation. Furman-Adams and Tufte read Fuseli as, in effect, 'Milton's first anti-theistic interpreter' (p. 259), and suggest that his work is akin to the critical indictment of Milton's God undertaken by William Empson.

Modern Philology devoted an issue to Milton studies in November 2001. The four essays here span a diverse range of Miltonic texts and topics and each is well argued and thought-provoking. Bruce Boehrer, 'The Rejection of Pastoral in Milton's *Elegia Prima*' (*MP* 99[2001] 181–200), gives his attention to genre with a clear reading of Milton's *Elegia Prima*. This under-valued text he takes to be a complex and controlled piece which shows the young poet to be in conscious dialogue with the neo-Latin tradition of pastoral, and aware of his own ability to manipulate the tensions inherent in that choice of genre. William Walker challenges the new orthodoxy of monism amongst Milton critics in 'Milton's Dualistic Theory of

Religious Toleration in *A Treatise of Civil Power, Of Christian Doctrine*, and *Paradise Lost*' (*MP* 99[2001] 201–30). This is an important, cautionary, essay that exposes the flaws in critical presumptions of a consistent monist ontology throughout Milton's later works. Catherine Gimelli Martin, '"What if the sun be centre to the world?"': Milton's Epistemology, Cosmology, and Paradise of Fools Reconsidered' (*MP* 99[2001] 231–65), provides an ambitious reassessment of Milton's cosmology and, through a comparison with Bacon, his place in the scientific revolution. Gregory Chaplin, '"One flesh, one heart, one soul": Renaissance Friendship and Miltonic Marriage' (*MP* 99[2001] 266–92), sees *amicitia* as having precedence over heterosexual bonds throughout Milton's work. The divorce tracts make the friendship model clear and this sets the scene for the dialogue of love between Adam and Raphael in Book VIII of *Paradise Lost*.

Of the diverse essays to be found in other journals, four are particularly stimulating. In '"Through Mazes Running": Rhythmic Verve in Milton's *L'Allegro* and *Il Penseroso*' (*RES* 52[2001] 376–410), John Creaser shows that the young poet developed a distinct versification for these companion poems. He shows how these poems can be read as both technical metrical exercises and virtuoso rhythmical pieces. Each reader must in effect choose how to read, and the choice made will give a distinct flavour to their reading experience. The skill and playfulness of the poet in maintaining such a charged composition should not be underestimated, but it takes work of this calibre to bring the formal qualities of the text to the attention of many critics and most students. Meanwhile, Neil D. Graves, 'Milton and the Theory of Accommodation' (*SP* 98[2001] 251–72), sees Milton's theory of divine accommodation as based on synecdoche. Basing his argument on a reading of Book I, chapter 2, of *De Doctrina Christiana*, 'Of God', Graves encourages us to take on board the full implications of Miltonic thought, whereby the accommodated image of God is the truth but not the whole truth. Dennis Kezar, 'Milton's "Lazar-House"' (*ELN* 38[2001] 52–6), suggests a link between the disturbing passage in Book XI of *Paradise Lost* and Jeremy Taylor's *The Rule and Exercises of Holy Dying* [1651]. He finds direct links in the detail of the two texts, but also quite correctly suggests that the wider tradition of *ars moriendi* (the art of dying) is important within Milton's epic. David Hawkes, 'The Politics of Character in John Milton's Divorce Tracts' (*JHI* 62[2001] 141–60), offers an intriguing exploration of the divorce tracts as a sustained ethical analysis of personal character based on the conjunction of Aristotelian political tenets with Pauline doctrine. The emphasis is on judging the character of the individual, with the servile or 'fleshly' mind being found to be unfit. Hawkes considers this analytical approach to have implications for Milton's later political prose and its further consideration of the basic question of who is best fitted for governance.

Lee Morrissey, 'Eve's Otherness and the New Ethical Criticism' (*NLH* 32[2001] 327–45), finds a postmodern *via media* for discussions of Eve's 'otherness'. Rather than defending Milton's subordination of women or proscribing his anti-feminist bias, Morrissey suggests that we take Eve's response to being positioned as secondary and 'other' as the topic for critical consideration. He reads the relationship of Adam and Eve through the theory of Emmanuel Levinas with an emphasis on the need to 'respect the other as what it is'. Kari Boyd McBride and John C. Ulreich, 'Answerable Styles: Biblical Poetics and Biblical Politics in the Poetry of Lanyer and Milton' (*JEGP* 100[2001] 333–54), already show respect for the individual approach to biblical narratives and the psalms adopted by Aemilia Lanyer and Milton. Their comparison of these authors shows how both manage to embrace the prophetic mode and extract a radical principle of liberty from their appropriation of biblical texts. Linking the prophetic to the political, Paul Stevens, 'Milton's Janus-faced Nationalism: Soliloquy, Subject, and the Modern Nation State' (*JEGP* 100[2001] 247–68), finds Milton's self-revelatory moments to be linked to his articulation of Protestant nationalism. He looks at Milton's subjective rhetoric in announcing the awakening nation in *Reason of Church Government*, *Areopagitica*, the *First Defence* and *Samson Agonistes* and suggests that ironically it is the king's success in providing similarly affective subjective discourse that Milton reacts to so strongly in his condemnation of *Eikon Basilike*. In a separate essay published this year, Stevens again identifies Milton's Protestant nationalism as key to his politics in the 1650s. Paul Stevens, 'Milton's "Renunciation" of Cromwell: The Problem of Raleigh's *Cabinet-Council*' (*MP* 98[2001] 363–92), reconsiders the likely contemporary view of Raleigh's work and takes his reputation as a Protestant writer to be sufficient for Milton's publication of *Cabinet-Council* at a time when England feared Spanish invasion. Unlike Dzelzainis, Stevens remains convinced that Milton remained supportive of Cromwell and would have defended liberty of conscience over republican values.

Articles on *Samson Agonistes* have already been reviewed *en passant*. Two essays on *Paradise Regained* remain. David Gay, 'Astrology and Iconoclasm in Milton's *Paradise Regained*' (*SEL* 41[2001] 175–90), focuses on *Paradise Regained* IV.382–93 in considering astrology and its 'starry rubric' as a locus of opposition between Satan's idolatrous methodology and the Son's iconoclasm. Marjorie O'Rourke Boyle, 'Home to Mother: Regaining Milton's Paradise' (*MP* 97[2001] 499–527), makes the somewhat shocking suggestion that one possible source for the homecoming in the last line of *Paradise Regained* may be the medieval *Meditationes vitae Christi*. This text specifies that, following the temptation in the wilderness, Jesus returned home to be welcomed and embraced by his mother. Boyle draws attention to the medieval emphasis on the Saviour's humility and meekness and suggest that this may have influenced Milton's composition. She further proposes that the victory related here looks forward to Christ's resurrection and mentions the medieval tradition that the risen Christ appeared first to his mother on Easter Sunday.

Finally, *Notes and Queries* includes a number of Miltonic notes. M.J. Edwards, 'A Rebirth of Images: Milton on the Massacre in Piedmont' (*N&Q* 48[2001] 391–2), finds an analogy between Tertullian's *Apology*, where the blood of the martyrs is termed 'seed', and the imagery of martyrdom in Milton's fifteenth sonnet. He traces a further link to Cyprian, bishop of Carthage, and suggests that Milton might have been interested in Cyprian as an advocate of episcopal consensus rather than papal supremacy. William Poole, 'Milton, Ausonius, and Denham: Two Reworkings' (*N&Q* 48[2001] 23–5), returns to Eve's encounter with her reflection and identifies two teasing analogies. First, in Ausonius' *Mosella*, boys play at the river bank, but girls admire themselves in mirrors, which may have offered Milton a suggestive approach to the well-known Narcissus myth. Secondly, in the contemporary poem *Coopers Hill*, John Denham idealizes the landscape as one where 'no threatening heights | Access deny' (p. 58). Milton echoes that phrase, but denies access at *PL* IV.317, perhaps intending actively to counter the royalist poetics of Denham.

Michele Valerie Ronnick offers two notes on Milton. In 'Cimex, Tinea, and Blatta: Insect Imagery in Milton's *Pro Populo Anglicano Defensio Secunda*' (*N&Q* 48[2001] 20–1), she enjoys explaining the abusive insect imagery used by Milton in the *Second Defence* and his splicing of contexts from Martial and Horace, while in 'From Remigio Pedum to "Oary Feet": Statius' *Thebaid* IX.250 and Milton's *Paradise Lost* VII.340' (*N&Q* 48[2001] 25–6), she proposes that the 'oary feet' of the newly created swan are coined more directly from Milton's knowledge of Statius than Virgil (as John K. Hale has previously argued). Lastly, John Talbot, 'A Horatian Pun in *Paradise Lost*' (*N&Q* 48[2001] 21–3), reads the phrase 'horrid arms' (*PL* II.63) against 'horrida bracchiis' in Horace, *Odes* III.iv, teasing out the full connections between diabolic bombast, indecorous punning and a classical context of imperial compliment.

3. Donne

This has been a busy year in Donne studies, with a new edition, as well as other books and articles to record. Anthony Raspa has added *Essayes in Divinity* to his other scrupulously edited and annotated editions of Donne's prose work. This very welcome work, the first since E. M. Simpson's edition fifty years ago, follows his previous editions of *Devotions Upon Emergent Occasions* [1987] and *Pseudo-Martyr* [1993]. Scholars and students of Donne will be indebted to Raspa's extensive study of sources in the *Essayes*, which greatly expands the Simpson edition, for Raspa has patiently and conscientiously tracked down Donne's often very elusive references to numerous exegetical works. He provides also a detailed and helpful introduction to the cultural context and the argument of *Essayes*, as well as a thorough account of his textual research and practice.

David L. Edwards, one-time dean of King's College, Cambridge, and provost of Southwark Cathedral, draws upon his long experience as pastor and preacher and his fascination with Donne to write a 'popular' life that he hopes will reach a broad audience of non-specialists and specialists alike. The result is *John Donne: Man of Flesh and Spirit*, a literary biography that reviews the life and works in a highly readable fashion. But Edwards, who seems to have read all of Donne's writing and that of many of those who have written about him, has his own critical presuppositions. He is surprisingly tendentious on Donne's sexuality, and really not obviously alert to the literature and culture in which Donne flourished; he is frequently as speculative, especially about Donne's love life, as some of the critics he most dislikes—notably John Carey, whose *Life* [1981] prompts Edwards to write a chapter of dismissal.

Maria Salenius has written of *The Dean and his God: John Donne's Concept of the Divine*, a sensitive thematic study that considers Donne's concern with 'light'. She relates this theme to medieval and later mystical theology, which points her towards six sermons by Donne that see God through this light. Most of Salenius's thoughtful work focuses on the three sermons on John 1:8 (including the Christmas sermon of 1621); the Easter sermon of 1628; Easter Monday 1622; and Candlemas Day, perhaps of 1624. Salenius reads these sermons with close concern for their metaphorical complexity and their elaborate development.

Since so many discussions of Donne, and notably of his life, invoke Izaak Walton, mention should be made here of an important book by Jessica Martin: *Walton's 'Lives': Conformist Commemorations and the Rise of Biography* deals at large with issues of 'life writing' and the tradition that Walton inherited and put to use in his celebrated *Life of Dr. John Donne* [1640; revised 1658, 1670]. Martin writes with cogency and fresh insight of 'Walton as Donne's Author' (pp. 168–203). Another recent and more general study of Walton, but with a chapter devoted to the construction of his portrait of Donne, is by P.G. Stanwood, a volume simply called *Izaak Walton,* in the Twayne English Authors series.

Finally, notice should be made of H.L. Meakin's *John Donne's Articulations of the Feminine* [1998], an important theoretical study that owes much to Luce Irigaray. The book may be seen as a further exploration of gender and feminist approaches to Donne, such as that by Maureen Sabine, *Feminine Engendered Faith: The Poetry of John Donne and Richard Crashaw* [1992] and Elizabeth M.A. Hodgson, *Gender and the Sacred Self in John Donne* [1999]; reviewed in *YWES* 81[2002]. An essay closely related to many of the concerns of these studies is Susannah B. Mintz's '"Forget the hee and shee": Gender and Play in John Donne' (*MP* 98[2001] 577–603). Mintz, who frequently refers to Meakin, argues that Donne commonly depicts male–female roles with blurred boundaries, and that his playful wittiness allows him to rework 'the possibilities of gender and erotic connection' (p. 583).

The *John Donne Journal,* which now appears annually, again includes a number of notable articles. Volume 20[2001] opens with the first of a two-part essay by Richard S. Peterson, 'New Evidence on Donne's Monument' (*JDJ* 20[2001] 1–51), a literary and artistic description of this remarkable sculpture. Peterson describes, with the help of twenty-four excellent illustrations, the vicissitudes of Donne's effigy from its first erection in about 1632. In a subsequent essay, Peterson will discuss the relationship of the monument to Donne's thought and writings. These essays are surely likely to tell us all that we know or need to know about this famous sculpture.

Paul Stevens writes convincingly of 'Donne's Catholicism and the Innovation of the Modern Nation State' (*JDJ* 20[2001] 53–70), juxtaposing Carey's *Life* and Dennis Flynn's *John Donne and the Ancient Catholic Nobility* [1995]. Donne is caught, says Stevens, between the cultural changes that were to produce the modern nation-state, and he is pulled towards an aristocratic Catholic background on the one hand, and an emerging modern state on the other. Thomas Fulton also seeks to settle Donne within a context of belief and culture. In his essay on 'Hamlet's Cloak and Donne's *Satyres*' (*JDJ* 20[2001] 71–106), Fulton demonstrates the unity of the five Satyres, studying particularly numbers III and IV, arguing that they (and above all Satyre III) are part of a kind of courtly debate, anticipating Hamlet's disenchantment, which has often been declared the very embodiment of the Elizabethan satiric mentality. The next essay is also concerned with the Satyres: Dennis Flynn's 'Donne's Most Daring *Satyre*: Richly for Service Paid, Authoriz'd' (*JDJ* 20[2001] 107–20) is a fascinating historical study that clearly presents Satyre V in context. In this poem, Donne is in fact addressing his new relationship as assistant to Lord Keeper of the Great Seal Thomas Egerton, and ultimately to the queen herself. Basing his analysis of the Tudor court on Juvenal's thirteenth satire,

Donne is rebuking corruption and hoping for general reform of the patronage system.

Barry Spurr examines Donne's only sonnet sequence in 'The Theology of *La Corona*' (*JDJ* 20[2001] 121–39). Spurr suggests that this Marian crown of devotion, Italian in form, reveals Donne in the midst of balancing public and private prayer. There is in these seven linked sonnets an obvious veneration for Mary, but Donne 'rectifies' his devotion, expressing divided theological allegiance to his Catholic heritage and to his English Protestantism. He displays, according to Spurr, doctrinal and liturgical diversity. Theresa M. DiPasquale continues her study of sacramental theology in the somewhat awkwardly entitled '"To good ends": The Final Cause of Sacramental Womanhood in *The First Anniversarie*' (*JDJ* 20[2001] 141–50) (cf. her *Literature and Sacrament: The Sacred and the Secular in John Donne* [1999, 2001], reviewed in *YWES* 80[2001]). DiPasquale argues that Donne portrays mankind's alienation from the sacraments, not only baptism and the eucharist, but also 'the Sacrament of Woman'; for Donne is representing women as 'conduits of grace ... whose final cause is the good of man' (p. 141). In 'Phonological Analysis and Donne's "Nocturnall"' (*JDJ* 20[2001] 151–60), Sara Anderson studies 'A Nocturnall Upon St. Lucies Day' through the details of its sounds. Anderson is convinced that the poem provides incontrovertible phonetic signs (or symbols) of the speaker's desolation. Whatever he may believe *intellectually*, he utterly disbelieves *emotionally*.

Other articles in this issue of the *John Donne Journal* take up issues of bibliography and textual criticism. Nathanial B. Smith writes of 'The Apparition of a Seventeenth-Century Donne Reader: A Hand-Written Index to *Poems, By J.D.* (1633)' (*JDJ* 20[2001] 161–218), a study which offers fascinating insight into the methods of early modern reading habits. Richard Todd, in 'Donne's "Goodfriday, 1613. Riding Westward.": The Extant Manuscripts and the Group 1 Stemma' (*JDJ* 20[2001] 201–18), demonstrates the difficulties inherent in editing this poem, with its numerous verbal variants. Donald W. Rude's 'Some Unreported Seventeenth- and Eighteenth-Century Allusions to John Donne' (*JDJ* 20[2001] 219–28) points to the need for further investigation into Donne's reception in the Restoration and eighteenth century—the poet may have enjoyed a much greater reputation than has been commonly assumed. Finally, there is a concluding section, or 'Colloquium', of three essays on 'The Sunne Rising'. Ernest W. Sullivan II and Robert Shawn Boles contribute 'The Textual History of and Interpretively Significant Variants in Donne's "The Sunne Rising"' (*JDJ* 20[2001] 275–80); Dayton Haskin writes 'Impudently Donne' (*JDJ* 20[2001] 281–7); and Meg Lota Brown offers 'Absorbing Difference in Donne's Malediction Forbidding Morning' (*JDJ* 20[2001] 289–92)—these last two articles are aimed principally at teachers and general students of 'The Sunne Rising'.

The Southeastern Renaissance Conference (North Carolina State University, USA) has for a number of years published its annual proceedings as *Renaissance Papers*, and one or more essays on Donne usually appears in each of the volumes. Andrew Shifflet writes on 'Sexual Calvinism in Donne's "Communitie"' (*RenP* [1998] 53–67), in which he ingeniously urges that this poem—much disliked by many readers—needs to be read not as an unpleasantly cynical poem, but one that satirically treats 'things indifferent'. Donne is playfully treating the doctrine of *adiaphora*, which is easily adaptable to the sexual relationships of men and women in a fallen world. M. Thomas Hester looks appreciatively at Ovid and Donne in his elusive '"Over reconing" the "Undertones": A Preface to "Some Elegies" by John Donne' (*RenP* [2000] 137–53), while Jay Stubblefield turns to Donne's 1628 sermon in his '"I have taken a contrary way": Identity and Ambiguity in John Donne's Sermon to the Virginia Company' (*RenP* [2001] 87–106). Stubblefield is concerned with the kinds of illustration that Donne uses that show the Thomistic elements of his preaching; the effect is to arouse the moral consciousness of his hearers—no wonder the Virginia Company officials rushed this sermon into print.

Donne's life and career, especially his alleged 'conversion', continue to fascinate and trouble his readers. One of the most original works in this vein is by Gregory Kneidel, on 'John Donne's *Via Pauli*' (*JEGP* 100[2001] 224–46). Kneidel writes about Donne's four sermons on the Feast of the Conversion of St Paul (1625, 1628, 1629, and 1630), showing how, through these sermons, Donne is identifying with the apostle and describing a *via Pauli*. Donne harmonizes or melds Paul's pastoralism with his own and affirms 'the communal and ecclesiastical basis for all Christian assurance' (p. 246); like Paul, Donne speaks to a varied audience that needs instruction and consolation. It must be seen that Donne is no careerist, but rather a deeply concerned preacher and pastor anxious to display various paths to truth. In a similar way, Lukas Erne, 'Donne and Christ's Spouse' (*EIC* 51[2001] 208–29), reads the famous Holy Sonnet 18, 'Show me, deare Christ, thy spouse so bright and clear', presumably written sometime in the years of Donne's ordained ministry, as the preacher's anxious and vexing concern to discern the True Church— the object of all individuals' 'earthly quest for the transcendent' (p. 220)—a desire that surpasses denominational allegiance.

Likewise, Dennis Flynn has more to say about Donne's 'ambition' in his splendid historical and biographical essay on 'Donne's Politics, "Desperate Ambition", and Meeting Paolo Sarpi in Venice' (*JEGP* 99[2000] 334–55). In his subtle and complex argument, Flynn urges that Donne, far from being concerned for advancement, had no special political ambition, even resisting opportunities. The seven or so years after 1601, the year of his marriage, which have long been the subject of biographical speculation, thus need re-examination in light of Donne's burst of literary activity around 1608 with the composition of *Biathanatos, Pseudo-Martyr* and *Ignatius his Conclave*. Flynn writes of Donne's possible visit to Venice in 1605–6 in company with his friend Sir Henry Wotton. There he met Sarpi, who was a principal amongst those who declared that the Venetian state was independent of Rome, a view that Donne shared and likely reflected in his *Pseudo-Martyr*.

Donne's little-read casuistical work receives major attention from Olga Valbuena, in 'Casuistry, Martyrdom, and the Allegiance Controversy in Donne's *Pseudo-Martyr*' (*R&L* 32[2000] 49–80). Valbuena explores Donne's desire 'to mediate between the state's rigor and the obstinacy of papists' (p. 51), and between enforcement and external compliance. His conscience is divided in *Pseudo-Martyr*; he remembers his own Catholic inheritance, but he sees the usefulness of submission to the state religion. Thus Donne 'negotiates' between belief and coercion by providing Romanist dissenters with a casuistical programme, not by offering submission but by 'encoding' advice on how to circumvent James's appeal to his subjects for fidelity. Another of Donne's prose works to receive particular attention is *Ignatius his Conclave*, whose publication history is complex. In a very ably presented analysis based on many copies of the earliest editions, Willem Heijting and Paul R. Sellin reach a number of far-reaching conclusions in their 'John Donne's *Conclave Ignati*: The Continental Quarto and its Printing' (*HLQ* 62[1999/ 2000] 401–21). The Latin edition of Donne's work, they believe, was first printed by Thomas Villerianus at Hanau, in a quarto version, and the book seems to have been in circulation in Germany before it reached publication in England. This fact may suggest the internationalism of Donne's work and reputation, a point that might well be emphasized.

A general, but pleasing and appreciative, essay is Barbara Everett's 'Donne and Secrecy' (*EIC* 51[2001] 51–67). Everett regards Donne as a poet of the contemplative life who is also a highly public figure, and who conveys a strong sense of social involvement while also being elusive and complex. Donne is a 'secret' poet, speaking privately to each of his readers, and who, in his best poems, poses a hypothetical 'if'—the word is important to the interior experience that he elicits. Following her essay in the same issue of *Essays in Criticism*, Ian Donaldson writes comparatively of Donne and Ben Jonson. In 'Perishing and Surviving' (*EIC* 51[2001] 68–85), he notes that the two poets, whose careers intersect at many points, are very close in style and subject matter, much closer, indeed, than has traditionally been recognized; and like Donne, Jonson, in fact, reserved most of his poems for private readership. Another study that sees Donne in company with others is Michael Schoenfeldt's fascinating essay, '"That spectacle of too much weight": The Poetics of Sacrifice in Donne, Herbert, and Milton' (*JMEMS* 31[2001] 561–84). Schoenfeldt asks why the Passion, so important and central to medieval devotional writing, becomes in the seventeenth century a comparatively marginal subject. 'Sacrifice', Schoenfeldt argues, is for Donne and the poets that follow him not so much 'a ritual action as a devotional state achieved in the temple that is the heart of the devout' (p. 561). Reformed religion must in part be responsible for this movement from the exterior observation of Christ's sacrifice to its interiorization in the poet's own blood.

Donne's metrical ingenuity has received regular attention, even in his own lifetime, when Ben Jonson is reported to have said that the poet 'for not keeping of accent deserved hanging'. Most recently, Henri Suhamy writes of Donne's frequently difficult versification in 'Un cas pendable? La versification de John Donne' (*EA* 54[2001] 401–13). Suhamy draws a distinction between Donne's metre and rhythm, his various stanza designs, and his rhyme and enjambments, with many examples from the Satyres and Elegies. While Donne may seem difficult, he is also ingenious, inventive, and original, and very much in control of his effects. Another sort of analysis of Donne's Elegies, especially of 'Loves Progresse' is provided in Shankar Raman, 'Can't Buy Me Love: Money, Gender, and Colonialism in Donne's Erotic Verse' (*Criticism* 43[2001] 135–68). This long, highly theoretical essay takes up and interrelates money, colonial voyaging, and sexuality, and tries to show that the Elegies generally, and this poem particularly, investigate valuation itself as 'problematic' (p. 162). Economic metaphors form the subject of yet another essay on Donne's Elegies by Barbara Correll, 'Chiasmus and *Commodificatio*: Crossing Tropes and Conditions in Donne's Elegy 11, "The Bracelet"' (*Exemplaria* 11[1999] 141–65). Correll reads this poem as exemplary of her theme of 'erotic economy' in Donne's canon, in which the trope of 'commodificatio' (Correll's neologism) connects 'commodity, chiasmus, poetic production, and rhetoric as fundamentally economic sites of subjective loss and poetic gain' (p. 143). So Donne is seen to bring together the language of love and money.

A somewhat different approach to Donne's Elegies considers them in relation to court and sexual politics in the late Elizabethan period. Daniella E. Singer, in 'Despair and Subjectivity in the Erotic Verse of Sidney and of Donne' (*Neophil* 80[1996] 493–500), studies 'Oh let not me serve so', 'Natures Lay Ideott', and 'Allthough thy hand, and fayth and good works too' (commonly called 'Change'); she sets these poems alongside Sir Philip Sidney's sonnet sequence *Astrophil and Stella*. The unifying point is despair, whose presence, Singer suggests, signals in both poets 'the realization of a perceived or actual threat to the self-definition of identity' (p. 499). Gregory Machacek gives a more limited but certainly useful view of 'The Comparison' ('As the sweet sweate of roses in a still') by examining Donne's use of pronouns in the poem. Machacek's brief article (*Expl* 59[2001] 71–3) demonstrates that the poem is really addressed to a single woman, with a clever 'punch line' at the end that suggests the elegy is much more than an exercise in exaggerated contrasts, for it is also 'a psychological study of the effects of faithfulness on desirability' (p. 73). In another brief but helpful article, Rodney Stenning Edgecombe is concerned with 'The Meaning of "Rage" in "The Canonization"' (*ANQ* 14[2001] 3–5). 'Rage' most appropriately refers to the world that the lovers, now sainted, have left—our world, not theirs: 'a future anger and heatedness, not a sublime version of the terrestrial love ... already experienced' (p. 5).

Perhaps an unexpected place to find a study of Donne's 'Valediction: Forbidding Mourning' might be in *Cardozo Studies in Law and Literature* (Yeshiva University) 13[2001] 271–98. But Alyson Sprafkin, in commenting on a judicial opinion concerning a Connecticut statute, discerns a number of language and discourse similarities with Donne, strategies that also employ certain visual effects like those in Wallace Stevens's 'Thirteen Ways of Looking at a Blackbird'. 'When reading either a judicial opinion or a poem', Sprafkin writes, 'one must yield to the power of its language because that language is the reader's only tool to decipher meaning' (p. 272). The legal and poetic language is parallel and comparatively or mutually instructive. Such broad reflections on Donne lead one to conclude this survey with the most pleasing and genial essay of the year—Judith Scherer Herz writes 'Under the Sign of Donne' (*Criticism* 43[2001] 29–58), an amusing influence study that begins with a description (and the first of a number of illustrations) of Stanley Spencer's painting, *John Donne Arriving in Heaven*. Herz invokes a number of other figures—mostly of the last hundred years—artists, poets, and essayists, all of whom work 'under the sign': Lytton Strachey, Hart Crane, Herbert Read, T.S. Eliot, William Empson, and more. Emily Dickinson, Herz notes, along with Donne, is the most notable poet of death in English, which leads Herz to comment on Marsden Hartley, a mid-twentieth-century American poet and painter whose 'Last Look of John Donne' portrays the familiar image of Donne in his shroud. Yet Herz wisely remarks at the conclusion of her essay that 'as the allusions accumulate, there is always another sighting to record or encounter to assess' (p. 54). Donne's stock is evidently rising.

A handsome volume of general interest to students of the seventeenth-century, especially of John Donne, appeared as a Festschrift to honour Paul Grant Stanwood, *Wrestling with God: Literature and Theology in the English Renaissance*, edited by

Mary Ellen Henley and W. Speed Hill with the assistance of R.G. Siemens, published both in hard copy and online in *EMLS* special issue 7[2001]. There is an introduction by Henley, with a sonnet prelude by the American poet X.J. Kennedy followed by fifteen essays, all contributions from friends and others associated with Stanwood's long career, so largely occupied with devotional literature. The first of these essays is by the late Louis L. Martz (who died in December 2001, shortly after the appearance of the book), 'Donne, Herbert, and the Worm of Controversy' (pp. 11–25), which thoughtfully defines the role of sacramental grace in the thought of Herbert and Donne, with the gradual passing away of the dominant Calvinism of the age. John T. Shawcross, in '"The virtue and discipline" of Wrestling with God' (pp. 27–43) analyses two poems by Edward Herbert, Lord Cherbury, and two by Henry Vaughan, which unexpectedly display the quality of 'wrestling'. John E. Booty writes of the sense of community and participation that defines 'The Core of Elizabethan Religion', most ably espoused by Richard Hooker (pp. 45–51). In a fascinating comparison, Claude J. Summers considers the putative Shakespearean 'A Funeral Elegy' alongside Donne's Epicedes and Obsequies, especially the Anniversaries (including the 'Funeral Elegy for Elizabeth Drury'), in 'W[illiam S[hakespeare]'s *A Funeral Elegy* and the Donnean Moment' (pp. 53–65). The 'Shakespeare' elegy misses the expression of grief that characterizes Donne's poems, for 'W.S.' is 'neither symbolic nor philosophical nor witty nor hyperbolic nor remote' (p. 65).

Graham Parry writes of a little-known contemporary of Donne, a devotional poet called William Austin (1587–1634), whose posthumous publication appeared with the title *Devotionis Augustinianae Flamma* [1635], or 'The Flame of Austin's Devotions' (with an obviously intended allusion to St Augustine). In his 'The Devotional Flames of William Austin' (pp. 67–83), Parry convincingly demonstrates that Austin's contemplative prose merits 'an honourable place in the repertory of early Stuart devotional writings' (p. 67). Other devotional works are the subject of Ted-Larry Pebworth's 'John Donne's "Lamentations" and Christopher Fetherstone's *Lamentations … in prose and meeter* (1587)' (pp. 85–98, with an appendix of comparative passages), in which Pebworth reveals Donne's indebtedness not only to Tremelius's translation of Lamentations, but also the helpfulness (with occasional adaptation) of Fetherstone.

William Blissett, in '"The strangest pageant, fashion'd like a court": John Donne and Ben Jonson to 1600—Parallel Lives' (pp. 99–121), presents Donne's Satyre IV and Jonson's *Cynthia's Revels: or the Fountain of Self-Love* in order to show each author's concern with the decline of morals in the court. Jonson would seem to portray the courtiers as full of self-love, who are unmasked, but Donne delights in drawing attention to court degeneracy without being nearly so 'preachy'. Another of Donne's satiric poems is discussed by Wyman H. Herendeen, '"I launch at paradise, and saile toward home': *The Progresse of the Soule* as Palinode' (pp. 123–38), an ingenious, persuasive and subtle study. Herendeen shows how *The Progresse* is related to *La Corona*, and finally to the Holy Sonnets. Herendeen sees firm textual links and thematic parallels which give coherence to the satire as preparation for these two poetic groups. Two kinds of progress are at work here, one secular, the other sacred, and their sequential status in the first printed edition reinforces and justifies this point.

R.G. Siemens turns to one of Donne's often neglected prose works in his essay, '"I haue often such a sickly inclination": Biography and the Critical Interpretation of Donne's Suicide Tract, *Biathanatos*' (pp. 139–53). The work is not necessarily autobiographical, though it may contain some personal features, and these combine with Donne's casuistical rhetoric and parodic engagement. In a somewhat similar fashion, Diana Treviño Benet urges a reading of the Holy Sonnets 'as emblems of the author', in her cogent re-examination of these poems, '"This booke, (thy emblem)": Donne's *Holy Sonnets* and Biography' (pp. 155–73). The Holy Sonnets are a model of effort, energy, and determination; they show spiritual development which any of his contemporaries would have appreciated both for the biblical persona and for Donne's own affirmation of faith. In 'Trumpet Vibrations: Theological Reflections on Donne's Doomsday Sonnet' (pp. 175–92), G. Richmond Bridge thoughtfully examines 'At the round earths imagin'd corners'. Bridge urges readers to recognize that in this sonnet, as in so much of Donne's work (especially the sermons), the doctrine of the atonement is absolutely fundamental. 'If one drop of Christ's blood can redeem the "numberlesse infinities of soules" who will be aroused by Doomsday trumpeters', Bridge writes, 'one drop could surely seal John Donne's pardon' (p. 192).

A further essay on the Holy Sonnets is a unique and important contribution to their study. Trained as both a musicologist and a literary critic, Bryan N.S. Gooch turns his attention to 'Britten and Donne: *Holy Sonnets* Set to Music' (pp. 193–212). His illuminating essay shows how a great twentieth-century composer successfully interpreted several of the Holy Sonnets: Benjamin Britten rises to Donne's challenge; 'his wrestle, like Donne's, is with the problem of faith in a tortured world with its death and misery, and in *The Holy Sonnets* both musician and poet find their resolution' (p. 204). Gooch illustrates his essay with twenty-one examples from Britten's composition.

One essay in this volume treats Milton. Ken Simpson, in 'The Rituals of Presence in *Paradise Regained*' (pp. 213–32), writes splendidly of this difficult poem. He shows how Milton has made his brief epic into a model of worship according to the Holy Spirit, a form that is appropriate for isolated nonconformists like himself. Yet *Paradise Regained* has a liturgical form enacted through good works, free choice, and reason guided by the Scriptures and the Spirit; for external worship accomplishes little without the action of inner worship. *Wrestling with God* concludes with two essays that extend the essential concerns of the book; Lee M. Johnson, in 'Renaissance Copresences in Romantic Verse' (pp. 233–51), approaches the seventeenth century above all through the poetry of Wordsworth. The great Intimations Ode and *The Prelude* speak to and with Milton, as Milton spoke with Virgil, or T.S. Eliot with Dante, in an archetypal language 'of incarnational forms in literary copresences' (p. 251). Finally, Kathleen Grant Jaeger looks back from mid-Victorian Protestantism through John Lingard (1771–1851) and James A. Froude (1818–94), though the two held quite different aims as they recalled the reign of Elizabeth. Jaeger's 'Martyrs or Malignants? Some Nineteenth-Century Portrayals of Elizabethan Catholics' (pp. 253–74) seems an unusual but fit conclusion for this major volume (there are also bibliographical notes and a list of Stanwood's publications at the end). By anyone's standards, this book is filled with first-rate writing by many notable scholar-critics working at the top of their form.

4. Herbert

Publications on Herbert this year primarily examine poetics and doctrine. Kenneth J.E. Graham's 'George Herbert and the "Discipline of History"' (*JMEMS* 31[2001] 349–77) reads in the poem 'Discipline' an outstanding example of 'good' discipline. Graham notes the tendency in Foucauldian readings to suspect all discipline of being coercive and repressive, especially that discipline that presents itself as humane and enlightened. Whether discipline is repressive or humane, though, can only be seen by examining its historical moment, its practice along with its theoretical claims. Graham finds in the poem's bold speaking and in its desire for a gentle discipline not only an articulation of a Reformation theology that emphasizes the voluntary obedience of the believer, but also resistance to an increasingly authoritarian Caroline church government, one which was at odds with such voluntarism. The poem's claim to a loving discipline bears itself out by intervening not only spiritually between the individual and God, but also politically, between the individual and the Church hierarchy.

Robert Whalen, in 'George Herbert's Sacramental Puritanism' (*RQ* 54[2001] 1273–1307), argues that Herbert's *Temple* successfully brought together the sacramental and sacerdotal practices of the eucharist and the reformed emphasis on the centrality of the inner life of the spirit, but that this success happens largely in the drama of the conflict between these doctrinal positions. Poems such as 'Divinitie', 'H. Communion', 'The Agony', and 'Love Unknown' bear witness to both the Real Presence of Christ in the external elements of the eucharist and to the transforming work of Christ in the individual believer. While the former's emphasis on the institution and the latter's limiting of institutional power are most easily seen as mutually exclusive, Herbert's engagement of both produces an inward devotional enthusiasm that is cultivated through a fully sacramental and sacerdotal apparatus. Whalen examines theologies of eucharist from Tridentine transubstantiation to Calvinist virtualism, ultimately asserting that, for Herbert, only a Real Presence can adequately testify to the incarnation and the gift which that mystery brings to the individual.

Michael Schoenfeldt, in '"That Spectacle of too much weight": The Poetics of Sacrifice in Donne, Herbert, and Milton' (*JMEMS* 31[2001] 561–84), asks why the Passion became a relatively marginal subject for seventeenth-century devotional poets. He argues that this is chiefly because, in Reformed theology, sacrifice is not so much a ritual action tied to corporeal suffering as an inner devotional state. For Donne, Herbert, and Milton, the most fitting object of sacrifice is 'the tacitly arrogant self that would claim to be able to respond appropriately' to the Passion (p. 564). Poems on the topic, then, express best its inexpressibility. Schoenfeldt reads the sequence of Herbert's poems from 'The Altar' to 'Good Friday' as dramatizing first the desire to express, then the humility of stammering, and finally the sacrificial invitation for God to write on the speaker's own heart.

Ceri Sullivan, in '"Shooters" in Herbert's "Artillerie"' (*N&Q* 48[2001] 15), notes the importance of the image of God as an archer. She uses the analogue of John Marbeck's 1581 gloss of Psalm 7:12–13 to highlight a sense of a punishing God in the Herbert poem. William Donaghue, in 'A Curious Tenant in George Herbert's *Temple*' (*N&Q* 47[200] 179–80), inadequately supposes that 'The British Church' is the middle poem of the book, and then notes that its middle stanza describes the

Roman Church as the Whore of Babylon. Donaghue assumes that Herbert meant something by this central position of a 'curious tenant', but he does not say what.

5. Marvell

There was, strangely, little to be found on Marvell's prose this year. As for his verse, readings tended towards the political. Sidney Gottlieb's '"The Nymph Complaining for the Death of her Faun": Marvell's Ovidian Study in Hysteria' (*HLQ* 62[2001] 273–94) traces the modulation of the lyric voice, suggesting that the poet diligently represents a hysterical response to loss; the essay concludes with a meditation on the indebtedness of Marvell's 'Nymph Complaining', and the female complaint more generally, to Ovid's *Heroides*. With a very different impetus, Chris Fitter, in 'The Slain Deer and Political *Imperium*: *As You Like It* and Andrew Marvell's "Nymph Complaining for the Death of her Faun"' (*JEGP* 98[1999] 193–218), focuses on the political connotations of hunting motifs. While Shakespeare may reflect upon Nashe's maltreatment in *As You Like It* II.i, and celebrate popular poaching in IV.ii, Marvell's 'Nymph Complaining' is a pre-eminently political poem that deliberates upon the recent political 'brutality' of the regicide, and the sentimental responses to the death of the king who had, ironically, further restricted hunting, making it a powerful symbol of royal prerogative.

For Victoria Silver, as for Fitter, the regicide looms large in Marvell's imagination. Silver offers, in 'The Obscure Script of Regicide: Ambivalence and Little Girls in Marvell's Pastorals' (*ELH* 68[2001] 29–55), a series of meditations on Marvell's pastoral poetry that reads nature as a transposition of perverse and excessive emotion that irrupts into the lyric present, including sexuality and recollections of regicide. Silver contends that this is evidence of the erotic and authoritarian nature of Marvell's politics, royalist and Cromwellian. Joad Raymond (the present author) adopts more or less the opposite position in 'Framing Liberty: Marvell's *First Anniversary* and the Instrument of Government' (*HLQ* 62[2001] 313–50), arguing that the poem engages intimately with the language used in debates over the short-lived constitution by which Cromwell was made Lord Protector. Marvell subordinates man and office to the republican constitution, while acknowledging their fraught relationship, expressing an active commitment to the Protectorate. The fifth chapter of David Loewenstein's excellent *Representing Revolution in Milton and his Contemporaries: Religion, Politics and Polemics in Radical Puritanism* also uses detailed and well-documented political contextualization to present Marvell's 'First Anniversary' in its historical and polemical moment. Loewenstein finds in its powerfully anti-sectarian passages evidence of the anxiety the Cromwellian felt about radical millenarianism; Marvell emerges supporting a moderate constitutionalism.

Several other essays undertake cultural contextualization. In a sophisticated and involved essay, 'The Politics of Garden Spaces: Andrew Marvell and the Anxieties of Public Speech' (*SP* 97[2000] 331–61), Andrew Barnaby reads Marvell's style, in particular in 'The Garden', as a response to the dissipation of a unified voice of authority that followed the expansion of the reading public in the 1640s, and to Restoration fantasies of a universal language. Marvell's pastoral retreat imagines an ideal world of unhindered communication and reflects sceptically upon these ambitions (there are specific implications here for the uncertain date of this poem). Christine Rees, in '"*Atlantick* and *Eutopian* Polities" in Andrew Marvell's Poetry' (*FMLS* 37[2001] 241–51), finds in Marvell's poetry an exploration—and ultimately a rejection—of the utopian ideas of the mid-seventeenth century. Defining utopianism broadly—more as an impulse than as a literary genre—she interprets the utopian in 'Upon Appleton House', 'The First Anniversary' and 'Bermudas' as testing utopian ideals without conviction. In 'Andrew Marvell's Garden-Variety Debates' (*HLQ* 62[2001] 297–311), Curtis Whitaker finds in Marvell's poetic aesthetic, and in his ruminations on the role of art in shaping nature, as response to, and rejection of, England mannerist garden design. For Daniel Jaeckle, in 'Bilingual Dialogues: Marvell's Paired Latin and English Poems' (*SP* 98[2001] 378–400), a close textual analysis of the paired Latin–English poems ('On a Drop of Dew', 'Ros', 'The Garden' and 'Hortus') reveals that linguistic difference enables a dialogue: the Latin poems being embedded in Roman culture and its ideological connotations, whereas their English partners address a Christian context in more flexible, less culturally bound (and thus aesthetically superior) forms.

More briefly, Lisa Hopkins, in 'A Possible Source for "An Horatian Ode Upon Cromwell's Return From Ireland"' (*N&Q* 48[2001] 19–30), identifies a series of echoes of Charles Aleyn's poem *The Historie of that Wise and Fortunate Prince, Henrie of that Name the Seventh* [1638] in Marvell's poem, most notably in the concluding couplet. John Richardson, 'Marvell's "Fleckno" and Melchisadech' (*N&Q* 48[2001] 392–4), detects in the opening lines of Marvell's poem an echo of the Catholic mass, and suggests that the structure of the mass may be 'a faint presence' (p. 393) in Marvell's anti-Catholic satire. Takashi Yoshinaka's 'Religio-Political Associations of "The Orange" in Marvell's "Bermudas"' (*N&Q* 48[2001] 394–5) suggests that 'the orange bright' in 'Bermudas' may allude to the Prince of Orange, and that in the context of the (alleged) change in Cromwellian/republican attitudes to the Dutch prince, Marvell represents his religious enthusiasts ironically; it is a tenuous argument that may understate the complexity of Anglo-Dutch relations in the 1650s. More persuasively, E.E. Duncan-Jones, writing with Helen Wilcox on 'Marvell's "Holt-Felster"' (*N&Q* 48[2001] 395–7), contends that Marvell's peculiar collocation derives from the Dutch '*holt-vester*, meaning an overseer or keeper of the woods' (p. 396), an observation that enriches this passage from 'Upon Appleton House'.

Books Reviewed

Borris, Kenneth. *Allegory and Epic in English Renaissance Literature: Heroic Form in Sidney, Spenser, and Milton*. CUP. [2000] pp. xii + 320. £45 ISBN 0 5217 8129 9.

Cain, Tom, ed. *The Poetry of Mildmay Fane, Second Earl of Westmorland, from the Fulbeck, Harvard and Westmorland Manuscripts*. ManUP. [2001] pp. xii + 415. £75 ISBN 0 7190 5984 4.

Corns, Thomas N. *A Companion to Milton*. Blackwell. [2001] pp. xvi + 528. £80 ISBN 0 6312 1408 9.

Du Rocher, Richard J. *Milton among the Romans: The Pedagogy and Influence of Milton's Latin Curriculum*. Duquesne. [2001] pp. 224. $58 ISBN 0 8207 0328 1.

Edwards, David L. *John Donne: Man of Flesh and Spirit.* Continuum. [2001] Eerdmans. [2002] pp. xiv + 368. $25 ISBN 0 8028 0522 1.

Ferry, Anne. *Tradition and the Individual Poem: An Inquiry into Anthologies.* StanfordUP. [2001] pp. 289. $45 ISBN 0 8047 4235 9.

Fish, Stanley. *How Milton Works.* HarvardUP. [2001] pp. vii + 616. £23.50 ISBN 0 6740 0465 5.

Gordon, Andrew and Bernhard Klein, eds. *Literature, Mapping and the Politics of Space in Early Modern Britain.* CUP. [2001] pp. xiv + 276. £40 ISBN 0 5218 0377 2.

Henley, Mary Ellen and W. Speed Hill, eds. *Wrestling with God: Literature and Theology in the English Renaissance.* M.E. Henley. [2001] pp. vi + 336. $50 ISBN 0 9687 1950 3.

Holmes, Michael Morgan. *Early Modern Metaphysical Literature: Nature, Custom and Strange Desires.* Palgrave. [2001] pp. x + 204. £45 ISBN 0 3337 6021 2.

Jordan, Matthew, *Milton and Modernity: Politics, Masculinity and 'Paradise Lost'.* Palgrave. [2001] pp. ix + 228. £47.50 ISBN 0 3337 4675 9.

Keeble, N.H., ed. *The Cambridge Companion to Writing of the English Revolution.* CUP. [2001] pp. xxii + 296. £14.95 ISBN 0 5216 4522 0.

Lares, Jameela. *Milton and the Preaching Arts.* Clarke. [2001] pp. 368. £ 40 ISBN 0 2276 7964 4.

Loewenstein, David. *Representing Revolution in Milton and his Contemporaries: Religion, Politics, and Polemics in Radical Puritanism.* CUP. [2001] pp. xiv + 414. £40 ISBN 0 5217 7032 7.

Martin, Jessica. *Walton's 'Lives': Conformist Commemorations and Rise of Biography.* OUP. [2001] pp. xxii + 353. £50 ISBN 0 1982 7015 1.

McBride, Kari Boyd. *Country House Discourse in Early Modern England: A Cultural Study of Landscape and Legitimacy.* Ashgate. [2001] pp. viii + 191. $59.95 ISBN 0 7546 0381 4.

Raspa, Anthony, ed. *Essayes in Divinity*, by John Donne. McG-QUP. [2001] pp. lxxx + 209. $75 ISBN 0 7735 2300 6.

Salenius, Maria. *The Dean and his God: John Donne's Concept of the Divine.* Société Néophilologique (Helsinki). [1998] pp. vi + 208. $40 ISBN 9 5196 0307 7.

Shawcross, John T. *The Uncertain World of 'Samson Agonistes'.* Brewer. [2001] pp. ix + 158. £45. $75 ISBN 0 8599 1609 X.

Shoulson, Jeffrey S. *Milton and the Rabbis: Hebraism, Hellenism, and Christianity.* ColUP. [2001] pp. xv + 340. hb $52.50 ISBN 0 2311 2329 9, pb $22.50 ISBN 0 2311 2328 0.

Stanwood, P.G. *Izaak Walton.* Twayne. [1998] pp. xviii + 126. $34 ISBN 0 8057 7052 6.

Swann, Marjorie. *Curiosities and Texts: The Culture of Collecting in Early Modern England.* UPennP. [2001] pp. viii + 280. $49.95 ISBN 0 8122 3610 6.

West, Philip. *Henry Vaughan's 'Silex Scintillans': Scripture Uses.* OUP. [2001] pp. xii + 271. £45 ISBN 0 1981 8756 4.

Wilcher, Robert. *The Writing of Royalism, 1628–1660.* CUP. [2001] pp. xii + 403. $64.95 ISBN 0 5216 6183 8.

Williamson, George. *Six Metaphysical Poets: A Reader's Guide.* SyracuseUP. [1967; repr. 2001] pp. 274. pb $17.95 ISBN 0 8156 0698 2.

Wood, Derek N.C . *Exiled from Light : Divine Law, Morality, and Violence in Milton's 'Samson Agonistes'.* UTorP. [2001] pp. xxii + 247. £35 ISBN 0 8020 4848 X.

X

The Later Seventeenth Century

CLAIRE PICKARD, LESLEY COOTE, JANE MILLING AND JAMES OGDEN

This chapter has three sections: 1. Poetry; 2. Prose; 3. Drama. Section 1 is by Claire Pickard, section 2 is by Lesley Coote, section 3(a) is by Jane Milling, and section 3(b) is by James Ogden.

1. Poetry

Richard Terry's *Poetry and the Making of the English Literary Past, 1660–1781* explores the development of 'literary history' and its changing scope and purpose over the course of the seventeenth and eighteenth centuries. Terry's range is broad. He opens by considering the way in which the category of 'literature', defined as purely imaginative writing, was distilled from the broader, more inclusive, field of *belles lettres*. Terry then moves on to discuss the creation of a canon of literary texts in English and argues that this process began earlier than is usually acknowledged, in the post-Restoration period. By charting the emergence of such a canon, Terry shows how attitudes towards the literary past changed from the belief that 'it was incumbent upon an ethically mature society to exercise charge over, to tend and nurture, the fames of its reputable dead', to more selective modes of remembrance.

While much of this volume is concerned with the eighteenth century, the significance of the later seventeenth century is emphasized throughout. Of particular interest is the lively and informative chapter that places the Battle of the Books within the context of wider debates about the possibility of a native literary tradition. Terry's chapter on Dryden emphasizes the writer's centrality to such a tradition, a centrality bolstered by the fact that 'Dryden was probably the earliest major English writer to be capably versed in the writings of an antecedent vernacular tradition'. The chapter that deals with canonical women writers includes much material on the posthumous reputations of late seventeenth-century female authors. Terry argues that such writers were not overlooked entirely, but he also acknowledges that they tended not to be incorporated into the developing canon of male writers. Rather, they were placed within a separate female canon that was concerned as much with their moral as their literary qualities.

Whereas Terry investigates the connections between English literature and ideas of English history, Donna Landry's *The Invention of the Countryside: Hunting, Walking, and Ecology in English Literature, 1671–1831* explores the links between literature, history and the physical landscape. The scope of Landry's work extends from the passing of the Game Act in 1671 to its repeal in 1831. She argues that this period witnessed the birth of 'the countryside', a concept which refers not to specific geographical areas but rather to 'an idea, and a way of giving an imaginary, yet material, form to a unified, homogeneous vision of the nation'. The potency of this idea meant that it 'became a symbolic repository of all that was and is most cherished about being English'.

Landry has two parallel objectives in this work. She explores the historical impact of hunting and walking on the land of England while also examining the ways in which literary representations of hunting and walking influenced attitudes towards that same land. Although much of Landry's focus is upon the literature of the Romantic period, she also draws heavily on the poetry of the second half of the seventeenth century. *Cooper's Hill* is used as a recurrent example and there is a brief but informative section entitled 'Women, Hunting and Poetry in the Seventeenth-Century'.

Constructions of the literary and cultural past also form the basis of Kay Gilliland Stevenson's *Milton to Pope, 1650–1720*. This volume is part of the Transitions series from Palgrave, which 'seeks to examine the ways in which the very idea of transition affects the reader's sense of period so as to address anew questions of literary history and periodization'. The works in this series combine readings of individual texts with historical context and theoretical discussion. The second chapter of Stevenson's volume, entitled 'Poems and Occasions', includes sections on Milton and *Paradise Lost*, generic developments and debates in the second half of the seventeenth century, a consideration of 'Poetic Topics and Poetic Diction', information about the publication and dissemination of poetry in this period, and a survey of individual poetic reputations. The volume concludes with a consideration of contemporary and late twentieth-century attitudes to the concept of literary periods, including an introduction to the Battle of the Books controversy.

T.R. Langley's *Image Government: Monarchical Metamorphoses in English Literature and Art, 1649–1702* is also dominated by ideas of 'transition'. Langley uses a vast array of late seventeenth-century sources, particularly the poetry of Waller, Marvell and Dryden, and the artist Antonio Verrio's decoration of Wren's King's Staircase at Hampton Court, to examine the imagery of monarchy in the late seventeenth century and the ways in which such imagery encapsulates changing conceptions of sovereignty and political authority.

This year saw the publication of several works devoted to women writers of the period. Female poets of the later seventeenth century are well represented in Jane Stevenson and Peter Davidson's excellent *Early Modern Women Poets (1520–1700): An Anthology*. As well as familiar names such as Aphra Behn, Anne Finch and Mary Astell, the volume contains a broad selection of less well-known figures, including a sample of women who wrote in the Celtic languages. The superb introduction provides sufficient historical context to enable readers to contemplate the various frameworks—religious, political, and linguistic—in which the poems might be read. The fact that this introduction provides a survey of the current state of scholarship on early modern women's writing while also seeking to emphasize new directions which it might take, combined with the impressive selection of poets, will make this volume of interest to both the general reader and the specialist.

Ann Messenger's *Pastoral Tradition and the Female Talent: Studies in Augustan Poetry* examines the use of pastoral by women writers over the course of the long eighteenth century. Messenger believes that 'it is possible to explore the autobiographical element in women's pastoral poetry, and to see it as a significant, gender-related difference from men's poetry'. She does not seek to provide a unified reading of the relationship between women writers and pastoral poetry, but rather to investigate the work of individual female poets in this genre. Despite this, she does cite one central aim of her volume, which is 'to make more familiar these insufficiently known women poets, to tell something of *what* they wrote as well as to say something about it, to encourage readers of poetry to read them and take them seriously'. Although much of the volume inevitably focuses upon writing in the eighteenth century, chapters on Behn, Finch, and Mary, Lady Chudleigh, as well as general and thematic chapters, explore the writing of pastoral verse by women in the late seventeenth century.

Harriette Andreadis's *Sappho in Early Modern England: Female Same-Sex Literary Erotics, 1550–1714* seeks to describe 'the historical process in which an eroticized discourse of intimate relations evolved among literate women, most often in the guise of patronage or friendship poetry'. Opening chapters explore the language associated with female homosexuality and the difficulties of applying concepts such as 'lesbian history' and 'lesbian identity' to the early modern period, while also analysing representations of Sappho in sixteenth- and seventeenth-century texts. Andreadis contends that 'as sexual acts between women began to be identified as transgressive by public discourse in the vernacular, "respectable" women ... developed a second, more sexually evasive yet erotically charged language of female friendship to describe female same-sex intimacy'. The mid-seventeenth century is identified as the historical moment when this development occurred. Thus, while some women, such as Margaret Cavendish, Aphra Behn and Delarivière Manley, were prepared to be seen as openly 'transgressive', others developed more oblique and concealing discourses. Katherine Philips is seen as central to this tradition of 'erotic ellipsis', which also includes poetry by Ephelia, Mary, Lady Chudleigh, Anne Finch and Jane Barker. An interesting section on the work of Anne Killigrew explores how this neglected poet complicates the divisions between transgression and ellipsis. In her final chapter, Andreadis provides a reading of John Crowne's masque *Calisto* (1674/5), a work which simultaneously prefigures 'the complex erotic dynamics that later informed the court of Queen Anne' and provides an illuminating example of a male author's perspective on female homosexuality in the late seventeenth century.

Male perspectives form the basis of Linda Zionkowski's *Men's Work: Gender, Class, and the Professionalization of Poetry, 1660–1784*. Zionkowski explores the ways in which changing constructions of both masculinity and authorship in the long eighteenth century led to the emergence of a new 'professional identity for poets'. She argues that many Restoration authors viewed print as a medium that rendered them 'a vehicle for the reader's pleasure', thus robbing them of 'their autonomy and integrity as masculine subjects'. Tracing the transformation of such negative attitudes towards print publication, Zionkowski illustrates the ways in which poetry's association with aristocratic cultural hegemony was eroded. Samuel

Johnson's 'success at characterizing poetry as an occupation suited to bourgeois men' is presented as the epitome of this transformation.

In her opening chapter, Zionkowski argues that Rochester saw the coterie exchange of manuscript texts as a means of 'creating a kind of exclusive homoerotic tie among aristocratic male poets and their male audiences'. Oldham, however, is seen to contest this perspective and to aver that print 'is the medium appropriate for men of all ranks because printed texts are subject to forms of public scrutiny that enforce normative sexual behaviour'. Chapter 2 suggests that Dryden viewed the need to please theatre audiences as a form of emasculation, and preferred to see his plays appreciated in print by private readers capable of respecting the integrity of both play and playwright. However, Zionkowski also argues that Dryden's translation of Virgil, while it enabled the author to 'distinguish model readers', also led to public praise which linked mental and physical prowess and which thus negated 'the dissociation between physicality and literary talent' which Dryden had sought to maintain. Later chapters shift the focus to eighteenth-century writers such as Pope, Gray and Johnson and extend the consideration of the developing connections between the commodification of literature and changing conceptions of masculinity.

Rochester's place in the cultural landscape of the late seventeenth century is less significant than the poet's personality in Cephas Goldsworthy's *The Satyr: An Account of the Life and Work, Death and Salvation of John Wilmot, Second Earl of Rochester*. Goldsworthy's volume is essentially a biography of Rochester as legendary Restoration libertine rather than a critical study of the poet. There are no footnotes, and many reviewers have complained about the essentially speculative nature of much of the text. However, the author, a QC who died before his book was published, makes no claims for academic status and, taken on its own terms, *The Satyr* is an entertaining read full of colourful information about life in Restoration England.

Events in 1690s London form the backdrop to Patrick J. Daly Jr.'s Fourth Parliament's 'Monarchy, the Disbanding Crisis, and Samuel Garth's *Dispensary*' (*Restoration* 25[2001] 35–52). Daly argues that the 'widespread structural confusion' and abrupt change of tone in *The Dispensary* results from Garth's response to the fourth parliament's attempts to reduce King William's standing army.

This year Thomas Traherne receives consideration in terms of both his religious and his linguistic practice. In 'Felicity Incarnate: Rediscovering Thomas Traherne' (in Cunnar and Johnson, eds., *Discovering and (Re)Covering the Seventeenth-Century Religious Lyric*, pp. 273–89), Barry Spurr suggests that an informed awareness of Traherne's Anglo-Catholicism is essential to an understanding of his poetry. Arguing that his attitude towards the Incarnation led Traherne to hold a positive view of the human body, Spurr claims this 'celebration of carnality' was 'unique in the explicitly religious poetry of the period'. Carol Ann Johnston's 'Heavenly Perspectives, Mirrors of Eternity: Thomas Traherne's Yearning Subject' (*Criticism* 43[2001] 377–405), explores Traherne's interest in Petrarchan conceptions of metaphor and Renaissance theories of perspective in painting and the influence these interests had on the poet's approach to questions of subjectivity and objectivity. Johnston argues that such influences led to Traherne 'forging a unique poetic language, one predicated upon the non-representational metaphor'.

Continuing the spate of publications inspired by last year's tercentenary of Dryden's death, this year saw much critical interest in the author. Steven Zwicker and David Bywaters published *John Dryden: Selected Poems*. The editors state that they were guided in their selection of texts by the desire 'to represent the arc of an entire career' and also to do justice to the sheer diversity of Dryden's poetic writings. This is clearly a mammoth task, but Zwicker and Bywaters have succeeded in producing a volume that does indeed provide a useful and informative introduction to Dryden's complex body of work. In addition to the poems, significant prologues and epilogues are included to illustrate the quality of both Dryden's prose style and his literary criticism. The edition includes a brief critical biography and a select bibliography. Headnotes to individual works seek to elucidate and contextualize them, and the substantial annotations provide clear and instructive explications of textual difficulties. As a result of its accessibility, this edition serves as a useful and informative introduction to the poet.

Two articles use Dryden's work as starting points for the exploration of very specific historical and political contexts. D. Christopher Gabbard's '"The She-Tyrant Reigns": Mary II and the Tullia Poems' (*Restoration* 25[2001] 103–16) examines representations of Mary II as Tullia, the notorious Roman parricide, in Jacobite poetry and propaganda after the Revolution of 1688. In particular, Gabbard focuses upon the 'ranting queen' passage in Dryden's translation of Juvenal's Sixth Satire. In his 'The "All-Atoning Name": The Word *Patriot* in Seventeenth-Century England' (*MLR* 96[2001] 624–43), Ronald Knowles provides a summary of the use of the word 'patriot' in the English language. He draws upon this historical context in order to examine Dryden's use of the word, and hence to shed light on its relevance to late seventeenth-century political and religious discourse.

A pronounced interest in Dryden's translations, particularly his adaptations of Virgil, was evident in the year's work. Richard F. Thomas's chapter 'Dryden's Virgil and the Politics of Translation' in his *Virgil and the Augustan Reception* illustrates how Dryden's concept of 'paraphrase, or translation with latitude' led him to create a version of the *Aeneid* which reflected the circumstances of its production. Thomas's emphasis is not upon whether Dryden's Virgil was Jacobite or Williamite, but rather upon the actual process by which he transformed his works 'to match his own political horizons'. Of particular interest is Thomas's examination of the influence of French critics Ruaeus, Segrais and le Bossu upon Dryden and their role in his 'domestication and appropriation of Aeneas as seventeenth-century prince'. By contrast, Michael Harbinson looks, not at influences on Dryden, but at the poet's influence upon a later writer, in his 'Keats and Dryden: Source or Analogue?' (*N&Q* 48[2001] 138–40), which traces possible sources for Keats's poems in Dryden's translations of Virgil.

The year also sees the dedication of an entire volume of *Translation and Literature* to Dryden's work in this area. The eight articles in 'John Dryden, Classicist and Translator' (*T&L* 10[2001] 1) focus on different aspects of Dryden's theory and practice as a translator. Charles Tomlinson's 'Why Dryden's Translations Matter' (*T&L* 10[2001] 3–20) places Dryden's translations in the context of debate about translation and poetry earlier in the seventeenth century by poets such as Denham, Cowley and Fanshawe and charts Dryden's influence on the poet-translators who followed him, most notably Pope. Felicity Rosslyn's 'Dryden: Poet or Translator?' (*T&L* 10[2001] 21–32), considers how we should approach

Dryden's translations in view of the larger debate about his inconsistencies and apparent self-contradictions. Jan Parker, in 'Teaching Troubling Texts: Virgil, Dryden, and Exemplary Translation' (*T&L* 10[2001] 33–50), argues the case for studying classical texts in conjunction with both 'classic translations' and 'literal, pedestrian versions' in order to lead students to more 'multi-voiced, multi-layered' readings.

Robin Sowerby's 'Augustan Dryden' (*T&L* 10[2001] 51–66) argues that Dryden's much-remarked 'refinement' results from the 'systematic application of artistic principles and techniques supremely embodied in the poetry of Virgil'. In 'Dryden: Classical or Neoclassical?' (*T&L* 10[2001] 67–77), Kenneth Haynes refutes C.S. Lewis's accusations that Dryden's translations of Virgil possessed a 'false classicism' and argues instead that Dryden's deployment of diverse registers enables him to do justice to 'the complex interplay of voices in Virgil'. Philip Smallwood's 'Dryden's Criticism as Transfusion' (*T&L* 10[2001] 78–88) examines Dryden's critical writing in the context of the history of criticism, and parallels our relationship to Dryden as a literary-historical figure to Dryden's relationship with the source-texts of his classical translations. In '"Et versus digitos habet": Dryden, Montaigne, Lucretius, Virgil, and Boccaccio in Praise of Venus' (*T&L* 10[2001] 89–109), Tom Mason traces the impact of Montaigne's essay 'Upon Some Verses of Virgil' on Dryden and concludes that 'Dryden's reading of Lucretius through the eyes of Montaigne seems to have produced or encouraged a continuing meditation on the sexual relations between men and women, and the relationship between sexual desire and the poetic impulse'. The final article in the volume, Paul Davis's '"But slaves we are": Dryden and Virgil, Translation and the "Gyant Race"' (*T&L* 10[2001] 110–27), explores possible links between Dryden's translations of the 1680s and the poet's 'desire for self-abnegation', and connects both to Dryden's belief that English poets in the later seventeenth century needed to 'atone' for the 'imaginative profligacy' of their predecessors. The volume also includes review essays by Paul Davis and Tom Mason.

Other articles explore Dryden's connections with music and the visual arts. Martin Holmes's 'A Song Attributed to Dryden: A Postscript' (*Library* 2:i[2001] 65–8) is a response to Paul Hammond's 1999 article. Holmes reveals that the song 'Whilst Europe is allarm'd by warrs' appears in 'the unpublished first-line index to songs in the Harding Collection at the Bodleian Library'. Holmes provides biographical information about Robert King, who composed the song's musical setting, and confirms that the song was composed in 1689. Anne Barbeau Gardiner's 'Dryden, Bower, Castlemaine, and the Imagery of Revolution, 1682–1687' (*ECLife* 25[2001] 135–46) examines the classical and Christian symbolism which links two medals produced by George Bower, Dryden's poetry of the 1680s and the engraving *The King's Arms* commissioned by Lord Castlemaine. The relationship between this imagery and the political unrest of the 1680s is explored.

Robert E. Stillman considers Dryden's connection, not to other arts, but to science. In 'The State (Out) of Language: Dryden's *Annus Mirabilis* as a Restoration Paradigm for Scientific Revolution' (*Soundings* 84[2001] 201–27), Stillman argues that *Annus Mirabilis* provides a vision of a future in which an ideal state is influenced by Restoration developments in science, particularly the search for a universal language.

Dryden's critical reputation is also subjected to analysis. In 'The Type of a Kind; or, The Lives of Dryden' (*ECLife* 25[2001] 3–18), Jayne Lewis uses nineteenth-century biographies of Dryden, particularly those by Walter Scott and Edmund Malone, to examine the ways in which Dryden's posthumous reputation has been influenced by the fact that he is seen as profoundly representative of the age in which he wrote. Barbara Everett's 'Unwritten Masterpiece' (*LRB* 23:i[2001] 29–32) also focuses on Dryden's posthumous status, and asks 'where ... do we look for Dryden's *Hamlet*, the focal and representative work that can still command our attention?' Concluding that there is no single definitive Dryden text, Everett argues that Dryden's masterpiece is his own understanding of 'what was possible and impossible for himself in his own time'.

2. Prose

Given the large amount of surviving material, there are relatively few books and articles concerned with prose writing from the civil war to the eighteenth century. Most of the books reviewed are either only partly concerned with the period, or only partly concerned with prose writing. These have been reviewed here from the perspective of their importance to later seventeenth-century prose studies only. Most of the books and articles reviewed concentrate on philosophy and ideology, but a few offer assessments of language, or of prose as a construction. There is some evidence of interdisciplinary work, and one book offers analysis of visual art alongside literary texts.

The introduction to Keeble, ed., *Cambridge Companion to Writing of the English Revolution* states that it is a 'collection of fifteen essays by leading scholars' examining the 'extraordinary diversity and richness of the writing produced in response to, and as part of' the English Revolution. In this collection only a few (such as Loewenstein on Milton's prose, Patterson on Marvell, Norbrook on historiography, and Smith on *Paradise Lost*) actually stand alone as contributions to a literary debate. This is a textbook, and a superior one.

The book is divided into five parts: contextualization, radical Protestant literature, women's writing, royalist literature and the rationalization of the war after the Restoration. Interestingly—and refreshingly—the contents offer an introduction to an entire spectrum of the period's literature, most of which (a student may be surprised to discover) is prose. The placing of historical writing, such as Clarendon's *History of the Great Rebellion*, alongside 'royalist' epics and romance, Harrington's *Oceana*, and the post-1660 writing of Hobbes, Marvell and Milton is particularly useful, as are the reminders that the Book of Common Prayer, along with devotional diaries and manuals, also qualifies as 'literature'. As Elaine Hobby notes in her essay on 'Prophecy, Enthusiasm and Female Pamphleteers', the need to cover as much ground as possible detracts from the contributors' ability to write anything in real depth. However, as an introduction to the period, and to the traumatic and all-pervasive influence of the events of 1638–67, the format works extremely well.

The introductory section is especially effective, providing a very valuable context for the literary studies. It deals with important elements of the historical background, such as the 'Britishness' of the civil wars and the way in which they seem to have caught the British population unawares. An important study of the printing press, readership and circulation, and the nature and breakdown of government censorship provides invaluable background information without sacrificing scholarship.

One problem is that the use of different writers for each section causes some repetition and/or overlap, but this is minimal. The category of 'women's writing' is annoying, as it implies that all the rest is 'men's writing'. However, David Norbrook has included Lucy Hutchinson as a historiographer alongside May, Harrington, Ludlow, Milton and Clarendon. The way in which it is arranged enhances the book's value as a teaching tool. It begins with a chronology, giving dates for both historical and literary 'events'. Endnotes appear at the end of each chapter rather than at the end of the book, avoiding the truly annoying necessity to struggle to turn to the back of the volume each time one wants to look up a reference. In addition, each chapter has its own bibliography, again at the end of the chapter, enabling readers to find key works specific to each topic quickly, and without any prior bibliographical knowledge.

This is an extremely useful basic introduction to the literature of the period, giving a significant amount of space to prose writing. The wide variety of literary output covered, or simply mentioned, by the contributors conveys some idea of the importance of this under-researched subject to readers in revolutionary Britain.

My reason for reviewing a book ostensibly about John Milton, David Loewenstein's *Representing Revolution in Milton and his Contemporaries: Religion, Politics and Polemics in Radical Puritanism*, in this section is that half of it is not, in fact, a book about Milton, but about the 'contemporaries' of the title, writers of radical prose such as John Lilburne, Gerard Winstanley, Abiezer Coppe, Anna Trapnel and George Fox. From the point of view of students of radical prose, it is a shame that the second half of the book has to deal with *Paradise Lost* and *Samson Agonistes*; this could (and, I feel, should) really be the subject of a second volume. The first half locates Milton where he belongs, as a dynamic writer of prose polemics during the civil war and Commonwealth periods. This was the lifetime occupation, that of national prophet, to which Milton himself felt that God had called him, but which for modern readers has been overshadowed by his great epic poetry. In seeking to demonstrate that these poems are intimately connected to Milton's revolutionary prose, Loewenstein embarks on a close examination of the prose writing of some of Milton's contemporaries in the late 1640s and 1650s.

Beginning with an examination of Leveller writing (not simply that of John Lilburne), Loewenstein goes on to discuss both the social and the religious writings of the Digger Winstanley, noting the similarities between them, and the writings of Quakers and Ranters. What is striking about his method is his interest in form and language, and how this relates to historical and ideological context. In this sense, the study is a truly interdisciplinary one, opening up fresh insights and possibilities. As an examination of radical writing of the period *c*.1640–60, the first section of this book is excellent.

The aim of T.R. Langley's *Image Government*, to explore aspects of sovereignty and underlying principles of political cohesion as represented in literature and art, is an interesting one. There are some areas, in particular those examining the work of Thomas Hobbes and Edmund Waller, which present some very interesting new ideas about the relationships between their ideologies in the political context of the Commonwealth and Protectorate. The literary and visual imagery surrounding

Oliver Cromwell is of extreme interest; however, no *visual* art is mentioned in the study for this period. The imagery of Antonio Verrio's work on the ceremonial staircase at Hampton Court is discussed in relation to contemporary literary ideologies, in particular those of churchmen such as Gilbert Burnet. One of the shortcomings of the book as a whole is its general lack of visual images, or discussion thereof, which is disappointing given that the word 'art' appears in the book's title. There are also interesting insights into the work of Dryden, particularly the chapters dealing with *Absalom and Achitophel*, and Dryden's ideology is related to those of Hobbes and Waller.

The greatest problem with *Image Government* is its style: this is not very accessible, and it can be difficult to follow what point exactly is being made, although the effort is worth while. Having said this, it is a very valuable piece of scholarship. It obviously represents a stunning research achievement, and its greatest strength is its bibliography, especially the section of primary sources, which is an absolute goldmine for researchers of all levels. Likewise, Langley's knowledge of secondary sources is extremely wide-ranging. There is treasure hidden in this book, but the reader may need to dig for it.

In *The Luxury of Skepticism: Politics, Philosophy and Dialogue in the English Public Sphere, 1660–1740*, Timothy Dykstal uses as his starting-point Habermas's theory of the public and the private spheres, although, as he himself notes, this model sometimes proves inadequate to describing the actual nature of the society he discusses. Using this idea of the public sphere as the arena in which differences are negotiated and consensus is formed, Dykstal examines attitudes towards diversity, beginning with the political theories of Thomas Hobbes. He approaches this, interestingly, through the study of a genre, the political dialogue, from Hobbes's *Dialogue Between a Philosopher and a Student of the Common Laws of England* [1681] and the much better known *Behemoth* [1682], to George Berkeley's *Alciphron* [1732]. He also examines James Harrington's *Valerius and Publicola* [1659], Henry Neville's *Plato Redivivus* [1681], the third earl of Shaftesbury's *Characteristicks of Men, Manners, Opinions, and Times* [1711], and *The Fable of the Bees* [1714–29] by Bernard Mandeville. Using these sources, the dialogue is presented in its relationship to the public sphere. Hobbes sees oratory as related to the forces of social disorder, but admits of teaching, which is based upon evidence rather than opinion, and counsel, which is authoritative teaching, and which admits of disagreement. However, all must ultimately submit to the will of the sovereign, who guarantees the people's safety. Harrington and Neville put forward the idea of a 'debating few' and a 'resolving many', while Shaftesbury removes the idea of political dialogue from the public sphere altogether, confining it to a privileged, discerning elite. Berkeley, like Hobbes, presents diversity as a social problem, but he does not advocate political dialogue. Instead, he advocates that the vulgar masses should be allowed their prejudices, as this holds the political community together. Only those who are confirmed in the right religious faith (Anglican Christians, in this case) should debate, and the rest of society should accept what it is told.

While relating the 'story' of political dialogue in this way Dykstal also examines the texts, teasing out the sometimes contradictory meanings they contain, to give as balanced a view as possible of each. The method and aims of the study are clearly stated in the introduction, and the threads are very ably drawn together in the conclusion. The introduction states that this book is concerned with 'the long eighteenth century', but Dykstal himself seems aware that he is actually describing 'the extended Civil War and Commonwealth'. Once again, the notes and bibliography are very useful, the primary sources in particular.

Linda C. Mitchell's *Grammar Wars: Language as a Cultural Battlefield in 17th- and 18th-Century England*, based on a dissertation, is dynamic, exciting and full of potential. Mitchell begins by stating her case, that grammar texts represent attempts to grapple with controversial issues within society as a whole. By changing language paradigms one changes society, and this is addressed by attempting to change ideas about grammar. Mitchell defines her subject very well, setting out her arguments and giving a full and respectful account of previous scholarship, which is extremely useful from a researcher's point of view. She gives a brief survey of the history of the grammar text from the end of the fifteenth century, then examines the five areas of standardization, pedagogy, writing instruction, universal language and social position in relation to grammar texts of the seventeenth and eighteenth centuries.

It would not be possible, given the restrictions of space, to detail the many different aspects of literature and society touched upon by this study, but they include issues of nationalism and colonialism, the superiority (or otherwise) of the vernacular, social change, education and the Enlightenment, the relationship between education and scientific investigation, religious faith and difference, the position of women, children and other marginalized groups within English society, the relationship between rhetoric and grammar, educational philosophy, the spread of literacy, and, of course, the relationship between what was taught and learned, and what was subsequently written—that is, literature itself.

The subject is set out with great clarity, and illustrations are provided where necessary. In addition, the bibliography is full of interesting primary sources, many of which are unedited. This is a really useful book, and a good example of why 'the book of the thesis' should continue to be published.

As far as articles are concerned, there were three on Locke and two on Hobbes; the rest have varied subjects, although two are concerned with scientific discourse.

Paul Schuurman, in 'Locke's Way of Ideas as Context for his Theory of Education in *Of the Conduct of the Understanding*' (*HEI* 27[2001] 45–59), seeks to distance this text from its association with Locke's educational theory, and to re-establish its (intended) links with *An Essay Concerning Human Understanding*. Locke states the liability of human understanding to error, and tells us how to correct this. There are two kinds of error: accepting confused or obscure ideas as bases for argument, and defects in reason itself. We err by reason of outside factors, such as the passions, or the desire for our own opinion to be the true one, or because of defects in our own understanding. Locke's preferred remedies for error are mental exercise or practice, which can be applied to education. This is a development of the ideas presented by Locke in the *Essay*, demonstrating how to prevent and correct errors as well as how to understand them.

The *International Journal of Political Philosophy* features an ongoing debate between Michael P. Zuckert and Samuel Zinaich, Jr. (*IJPP* 29[2001] 55–73, 75–89), on whether Locke contradicts himself concerning ideas about natural law in his *Questions Concerning the Law of Nature*. Zuckert argues that Locke contradicts himself in several important sections of the text; Zinaich argues that either these are not contradictions, or that they are based on misunderstandings of the book itself, particularly the part which Locke himself wished to delete. Zinaich proposes a future comparison with Hobbes's *Leviathan*, on the basis that Locke was attempting to answer a similar question, 'Does the private interest of each individual constitute the foundation of the law of nature?'

'Hobbes on Explanation and Understanding', by Ioli Patellis (*JHI* 62[2001] 445–62), is really an essay in philosophy, but merits a place here because of its possible relevance for Hobbes's other writings. Patellis is attempting to find and assemble a Hobbesian theory of explanation as understanding, using his opposition to scholastic understanding as her starting point. Her thesis is that Hobbes does believe that science has theoretical as well as practical value. Science is not simply practical, but provides explanations of phenomena, which yield understanding. Humans are motivated by both admiration and curiosity, and a mixture of language, reason and curiosity makes scientific knowledge possible. This is to be distinguished from curiosity in general (without reason), which leads only to superstitious ideas such as that of God as the Prime Mover. Science, in which all is causally related, yields infallible knowledge, but prudence, relying on the relationship between consequent and antecedent, is conjectural. However, evidence shows that Hobbes did not always distinguish between these two types of knowledge. It is the people's need to seek causes, but yet their inability to gain scientific knowledge, which enables their manipulation by seekers after power. Reason must be used to determine whether factors are relevant causal ones, or not.

A different perspective on Hobbes is offered by Simon Kow, in 'Maistre and Hobbes on Providential History' (*Clio* 30[2001] 267–88). The object of this article is to re-examine the ideas and proto-fascist reputation of Joseph de Maistre (1753–1821), in the light of the connection made by Maistre between the French Revolution and the English civil war. Hobbes's *Behemoth* is the basis for the investigation. The two writers have similar attitudes to the supremacy of royal authority, but any association breaks down on the subject of religion. This is demonstrated in the case of original sin, but chiefly on the relationship of religion to authority. Hobbes believes that religion is the chief cause of social unrest and war, and that religious authority should be concentrated in the hands of the sovereign. Maistre argues for papal authority on the same basis, but says that the Pope should have superior authority to the civil ruler. This is good, as religion keeps the people quiescent in the face of authority. The Pope is the instrument of divine justice, which is responsible for the continuation of the 'blood sacrifice', of which war and the suffering of the innocent is an inevitable part. As is often the case with unusual pairings of subjects, this is an interesting reassessment of Hobbes.

On the subject of scientific discourse, Peter Pesic, in 'Proteus Unbound: Francis Bacon's Successors and the Defense of Experiment' (*SP* 98[2001] 428–56), examines the meaning of Bacon's idea of 'vexing' Nature by the performance of experiments, and traces the history of both the term and the meaning through the scientific writings of Bacon's successors. Samuel Hartlib and John Dury advocated the 'ripping up' of Nature, but this is to be understood in the old sense of 'opening up', or 'discovering'. John Evelyn and Joseph Glanvill used the term 'evisceration', but this means penetrative insight, not violent disembowelment. Thomas Sprat spoke of the uselessness of 'torturing' Nature on one's own in order to prove one's own theories: he saw this as a perversion of science. Abraham Cowley compared experiment to a female Proteus offering up her virtues to the pursuer like a willing Daphne, a theme compared with Milton's views in Book III of *Paradise Lost*.

Robert Hooke did not mention the terms at all, and Robert Boyle avoided figurative language altogether, balancing the cruelty of vivisection against the need to understand. Isaac Newton simply used mathematical language, a form of anti-rhetoric. The apparent lack of care for the torments of experimental subjects is balanced against accounts of actual experiments, and the origins of the idea of 'torture' are examined, with particular reference to Leibniz. Bernadette Baker, 'Moving On (Part One): The Physics of Power and Curriculum History' (*Journal of Curriculum Studies* 33[2001] 157–77), defines Aristotelian interpretations of power, space, and change. She goes on to examine how these were challenged and changed by the theories of Isaac Newton. This is the first of a two-part article on power, the child and the curriculum, but its value for non-educationalists lies in its very clear explanation of these two sets of theories. The second part of the article promises a similar examination of the biological and physical nature of humanness, especially the knowledge acquired from human dissection.

The context and meaning of the word 'patriot' is examined by Ronald Knowles in 'The All-Atoning Name': The Word *Patriot* in Seventeenth-Century England' (*MLR* 96[2001] 624–43). Knowles traces the history of this word from its use in the 1590s to *c*.1711. He notes the humanist, Ciceronian, understanding of 'patriot' to mean 'fatherland' and 'citizenship', and the localized meaning of 'benefactor'. This changed during the 1640s, when support of Parliament came to be equated with 'patriotism', a term which was also used by royalists of their supporters. In fact, all manner of participants in the public affairs of the time (John Lilburne is given as an example) used it in order to differentiate themselves and their supporters from others. The word was used by both Whigs and Tories during and after the Exclusion Crisis, while retaining its other meanings.

Naomi Baker, 'Men of Our Own Nation: Gender, Race and the Other in Early Modern Quaker Writing' (*L&H* 10[2001] 1–25), is concerned with the missionary and travel writings of male Quakers during the later seventeenth and early eighteenth centuries. In terms of Orientalism and colonialism during this period, the Turks are seen as the antithesis of the dominant paradigm of English Christian masculinity, but Baker notes that this is problematized in the writings of Quaker missionaries and travellers. She uses the writings of Thomas Lurting [1710], Daniel Baker [1662], John Taylor [1710] and James Dickinson [1745] to demonstrate how these men position themselves both as the dominant Christian male and as 'other' than this. They demonstrate a degree (different in each case) of identification with the marginalized and feminized Turks, and identify their Christian persecutors with Jews, Catholics and heathens, even with women. As the conclusion to the article states, 'the life writing of early male Friends illuminates in new and different ways the working of gender, colonialism and identity in the early modern period'.

Finally, an article on preaching: Jameela Lares, '*Officium concionatoris* [1676] and the Survival of Doctrines-and-Uses Preaching' (*Cithara* 40[2001] 37–49). Why, she asks, was the *Officium concionatoris*, a manual for preachers first published in 1655, republished in a cheaper form in 1676? This question is examined in view of the changing attitudes to preaching which prevailed in the work of post-Restoration manual writers, such as Isaac Barrow, John Wilkins and Robert South. Lares notes the similarities between the *Officium* and the 'doctrines and uses' principles of writers such as William Perkins [d. 1602]. Late seventeenth-century critics were chiefly concerned with new ideas on matters of style and delivery of sermons, rather than the gathering and ordering of material, on which they accepted older models. An examination of the circumstances of production reveals that the book was probably printed in Cambridge for an alumnus, or member/s of the scholarly community. Lares concludes that, despite new models for Anglican preaching, the older one persisted.

3. Drama

(a) General

This year saw the publication of two studies of the representation of English expansion and colonization on the Restoration stage. Heidi Hutner's *Colonial Women: Race and Culture in Stuart Drama* offers a detailed reading of plays set in the New World, through the lens of gender. Her careful dissections of Restoration versions of *The Tempest* from Dryden, Davenant, Duffet and Durfey, alongside *The Indian Emperour*, *The Indian Queen*, and *The Widdow Ranter*, are contextualized by contemporary stories and documents of colonialization. By concentrating on the representation of the female figures in the plays, Hutner explores the ways in which anxieties about colonial contact are played out through the role of the native woman, or the European woman 'gone native'. She briefly connects the English political context with each play to make sense of the diversity of responses to the 'other' women. For example, she shows how the relatively stable colonial worlds of Shakespeare's *Tempest* or Fletcher's *Sea Voyage* become the site of battles for fatherly authority and control over native female bodies in Restoration redactions. In Dryden and Davenant's *Enchanted Island* Prospero's difficult daughter Dorinda and Caliban's black sister Sycorax trouble both family and island orders at a point when English political discourse was becoming increasingly divided. Dorinda is redeemed through marriage, Sycorax left to people the island with a profitable under-class. In Dryden's later 'Indian' plays assimilation and acculturation through intermarriage are no longer possible, but, Hutner argues, 'the playing of Indian women, nonetheless, reflects the ambivalent and disturbing bond between English women and Indian women, and the (feared) potential for the blurring of English self and racial other in the performance of inter-cultural colonial exchange'.

Bridget Orr's excellent *Empire on the English Stage, 1660–1714* also takes up the idea of the stage as 'a crucial location for debates over England's contemporaneous colonial expansion'. A central thesis of the study is that critics have too often read plays set in 'exotic' locations simply as parallels for English political history, rather than for what they reveal about the development of English imperial ideology. Her thorough survey of English drama from 1660 to 1714 looks at many modes of imperial expansion from the Romans to the Ottomans, and locations from Mexico to Morocco. This yields a carefully nuanced picture of the complexity of the colonial project. The main focus of her study is the serious drama of the period, which returned again and again to the histories of competing empires. These histories are mostly stories of decline and fall, and they form a contrast to the rise of England's maritime empire as represented on the stage. The crises that cripple other imperial states are explored in the drama as the debate about colonialization itself and its flaws—the attendant threat of luxury, over-expansion and rival states—is pursued. Attitudes and representations of different empires over time are contextualized against Britain's relations in war or trade with those empires. For example, Orr's detailed readings of a number of 'Great Turk' plays during the 1660s to the 1680s show how the Turkish empire was broadly represented as an absolutist imperial model, unbounded by law, and was used in different ways to reflect positively on England's religious tolerance, political balance and sexual continence. At the same time, the plays also presented the Turkish world as a parallel, and occasionally bound Turk and Christian characters in love and honour plots. As the active threat of Turkish expansion in Europe declined over the period, so too did the wilder portraits of the aggressive expansionism of the sultanate. Orr charts the way in which, in the later part of her period, the stage began to represent England's uniquely mercantile empire, delighting its audiences with new commodities, but replacing fears of despotic absolutist monarchy with fears of luxury and the social consequences of colonial wealth. She urges readers to consider the characters of comedies during this period, not just in terms of sexual mores and social standing, but also in terms of geography, and she studies the mockery of new social types, such as East Indies merchants, colonial planters and sea-captains. Overall, Orr's study emphasizes theatre's role in staging the debates surrounding the emergence of the first English empire.

In *Women, Writing and the Theater in the Early Modern Period: The Plays of Aphra Behn and Susanne Centlivre*, Annette Kreis-Schinck sets out to 'investigate the distribution of sexualized theatrical space by female dramatists' (p. 31). Robert Gould's satiric quip equating the poetess and punk is a headnote for her study and stands for her sense of the prevailing contemporary discourse regarding women's participation in the arts. Her focus is on the different phases of domestic or personal female experience: marriage, divorce, widowhood, and affairs or abstinence. For her, the concentration on the private, domestic arena in comedies and tragedies during this period is a product of theatrical scenic innovation in indoor houses, and accounts for the appearance of the actress and the woman dramatist. She sees the investigation of the proto-bourgeois drawing-room on stage as allowing women more freedom to be seen and heard, and yet she acknowledges that the drama also helped to contain and transform, through moral compulsion and etiquette, a dominant construction of gender boundaries. The writings of Behn and Centlivre are on the cusp on this translation. She categorizes Behn's work as battling with social and moral strictures for women, dramatizing the multiple potential meanings of 'wife', 'widow', 'mistress' and 'courtesan'. Centlivre's work, she argues, was transitional, part of a culture that was on its way to equate femininity with domesticity and sentiment. Kreis-Schincke finds it impossible to identify a stable point of view on gender issues from Centlivre, and suggests some of her work is 'easily dismissible as an ugly, misogynistic farce'. Centlivre's interest in political liberty does not offer new possibilities for female liberty, she asserts, whereas Behn explores the glorious possibilities and contradictions of divorce, widowhood and amoral sexual activity for her female characters. The work of these dramatists is discussed alongside that of male contemporaries, and in the light of a post-structuralist feminism.

Derek Hughes's refreshing and lively look at *The Theatre of Aphra Behn* is also concerned to identify Behn's feminism. He too explores Robert Gould's satiric quip, but is at great pains to set limits on Gould's significance; as he points out, Gould elsewhere 'bestowed warm praise on Katherine Philips and Anne Wharton'. Rather than see Behn as a lonely, embattled woman working out of her sphere, Hughes charts her interaction with theatrical culture, championing her emergence, with Dryden and Shadwell, as one of the most successful professional playwrights to emerge after the Restoration. He takes a careful and theatrically alert look at all of the plays in the Behn canon and envisages them as staged documents, yielding as much through their staged picture of 'spaces, bodies, objects and actors' as through detailed literary criticism. This leads him to some interesting new conclusions, for example challenging an easy equation of the character of Angellica Bianca with the female writer, despite Behn's reference to her 'sign of Angellica' in a forced postscript to the printed text, in defence of Langbaine's plagiarism charge. Hughes's detailed study of the stage signs of *The Rover*, from the mislabelled masquers to the increasingly illegible signs of the carnival, the unnamed bodies under threat and the rare occasions when women control the outdoor space, lead him to a reading of Angellica as tragic figure, 'inexpert at signification'. He charts a careful path through the burgeoning industry in Behn studies, which has attempted to adopt her for a variety of causes. His analysis of her feminism is closely contextualized alongside that of her male counterparts, who also produced proto-feminist work at the same time. In this study Behn is a professional writer, attuned to her marketplace, experimenting with new forms when the old certainties and regimes changed. Her concerns with social transformation, economics, militarism, and a developing party politics are teased out in this thought-provoking study.

Behn's play *The Younger Brother* is studied alongside Mary Pix's *The Beau Defeated: or, The Lucky Younger Brother* by Michael Austin in 'Aphra Behn, Mary Pix, and the Sexual Politics of Primogeniture' (*RECTR* 16[2001] 13–23). Austin outlines the way in which these female playwrights parallel the fate of the younger brother within family economic structures with that of women, and argues that both Behn and Pix represent the virtue of all family members, even if economic distribution was not to follow this more egalitarian model. Another female dramatist, Katherine Philips, is discussed by Sophie Tomlinson in her study 'Harking Back to Henrietta: The Sources of Female Greatness in Katherine Philips's *Pompey*' (in Wallwork and Salzman, eds., *Women Writing, 1550–1750*). Her work argues for an acknowledgement of the influence on Restoration women writers and performers of their forebears, notably women such as Queen Henrietta-Maria.

Janet Clare has edited five plays and entertainments of the English republic, *The Tragedy of Cicero*, Shirley's *Cupid and Death*, and Davenant's three experimental 'semi-operas' *The Siege of Rhodes*, *Cruelty of the Spaniards in Peru* and *The History of Sir Francis Drake*. Clare's excellent introduction outlines the interaction of politics and dramatic aesthetics during the Commonwealth period. Her survey of theatre's many reassertions in the form of pamphlet play, closet drama, interludes, drolls and the very rhetoric of the period sets the scene for the appearance, with official sanction, of the novel hybrid forms of the plays she edits. The introduction persuasively builds the evidence of surreptitious performance of old plays and the performative potential of many newly written pamphlet plays and closet dramas into an argument for an enduring, essentially royalist, theatrical subculture throughout the period. There is a careful reassessment of the performative undercurrents of republican culture itself, as Flecknoe and Davenant offer the regime 'a reformed stage, officially revived, and ... governed by a new theatrical aesthetics'. Contextualized in this way, the dramas that follow become easier to read as a record of entertaining performance and political display, celebrating in diverse forms 'victorious England'.

Gillian Manning's *Libertine Plays of the Restoration* also offers an unusual selection of plays: Dryden's *Marriage-à-la-Mode* and *The Kind Keeper*, Shadwell's *Libertine*, Otway's tragic *Orphan*, Southerne's *Wives' Excuse* and both parts of Behn's *Rover*. Manning's introduction helpfully charts the presentation of rake figures in their variety and the range of genres they inhabit. She notes the rise and decline in the popularity of libertine plays and surveys the main critical commentary on the 'rake' phenomenon. The collection of plays allows a reader to examine the range of libertines created from the 1670s to the early 1690s, and the transition from the homosocial bonds of the relatively sedate Rhodophil and Palamede to the cataclysmic incestuous libertinism of Polydore and Castalio in Otway's tragedy. The inclusion of *The Wives' Excuse* gives readers a chance to see how libertine ideology is affected by gender in the female libertine, Mrs Witwoud. Individual introductions to each play outline the main themes in their political context and comment briefly on the casting and performance of the play and its reception. This user-friendly volume has a helpful historical and dramatic chronology, plot summaries, advice for further reading, and thorough and interesting notes. The reproduction of dedications, prologues and epilogues where included in the first printed edition helps in viewing the texts in their theatrical context. A related article is M.L. Stapleton's 'Ovid the Rakehell: The Case of Wycherley' (*Restoration* 25[2001] 85–102), which examines rakish behaviour in *The Country Wife*. This follows Stapleton's extensive study of the libertine figure and its sources in, and adaptation from, Ovid's *Ars amatoria* in the work of a variety of writers. A third contribution to the libertine debate comes in Holger Hanowell's old-spelling critical edition of Sir Charles Sedley's *The Mulberry Garden* [1668] and *Bellamira* [1687]. Hanowell makes the case for regarding Sedley as an important theatrical satirist alongside Etherege and Shadwell, and as more than just a court wit. Sedley brings a unique set of theatrical and satirical strategies to his sexual predators and stages a biting satire of materialistic society of the Restoration years.

Canfield and Von Sneidern, eds., *The Broadview Anthology of Restoration and Early Eighteenth-Century Drama*, collects an impressive range of plays, across genres. Most satisfyingly, women dramatists are well represented, with work from Aphra Behn, Delarivière Manley, Mary Pix, Catherine Trotter, Susanna Centlivre and Hannah Cowley. Nor have lesser-known male writers who had a highly successful hit in their day, as with John Tatham's *Rump* and John Lacy's *Old Troop*, gone unnoticed. The editorial policy allows for easy reading, with modernized spelling and minimal footnotes. Each editor provides a very brief introduction that touches on the play's significant themes and gives some sense of its first performance. No doubt on the basis of space, prologues, epilogues and cast lists, which would have added another layer to understanding both the political placement of the plays and their theatrical interpretation, are absent. The overarching introduction to the volume sets out a highly readable political context for the drama presented and gives a brief orientation to the physical space of the theatre and composition of the theatre companies. With the inclusion of Goldsmith, Sheridan and Cowley, the volume offers even more than it promises, although the leap to the end of the eighteenth century rehearses a traditional and unhealthy blindness to mid-century stage practice, nor can the late plays be as effectively contextualized. Overall, the range of the collection makes this an excellent resource.

Paul D. Cannan's study of '*A Short View of Tragedy* and Rymer's Proposals for Regulating the English Stage' (*RES* 52[2001] 207–26), attempts to relocate this benighted text in a more thoughtful context. Rymer drew vilification from many contemporaries, such as Dryden, Dennis and Gildon, for some of the more outlandish suggestions of his work. Cannan carefully works through the entirety of Rymer's thesis to reveal a plea for government support and sponsorship for the stage. He also contributes a chapter on dramatic theory to Owen, ed., *Blackwell Companion to Restoration Drama*. This very useful collection gathers twenty-five original essays from a wide range of scholars on the pragmatic and political context of Restoration drama, on genres, types and shifts in dramaturgy, and on the dramatists themselves. It aims to offer consideration not only of the old chestnuts of Restoration drama, but also of figures such as Thomas Durfey, whose contribution to the genre of musical comedy has frequently been overlooked. To find a chapter on theatre music by Todd Gilman is equally refreshing, and most contributors attempt to provide the reader with a sense of the theatrical and spectacular delights of the drama, as well as its literary or political significance. The grouping of essays leads the reader towards cumulative insights: for example, the placing of a study of libertine ideology alongside a debate on the representational complexity of the Restoration actress and a chapter on the staged investigation of masculinity allows ideas about the political and social construction of sexuality and identity in Restoration drama to be interrogated more fully. Each chapter is accompanied by advice on further reading. This volume manages both to be readable and accessible for the student reader and to offer new and stimulating ideas for scholars.

(b) Dryden

Two books placed Dryden's plays in new perspectives. Bridget Orr's *Empire on the English Stage, 1660–1714* argues convincingly that the Restoration theatre regularly staged debates on colonialism, national identity, and ethnicity. Hence *Aureng-Zebe* appears in a chapter on 'The Most Famous Monarchs of the East'; *The Indian Queen*, *The Indian Emperor*, *Amboyna*, *The Conquest of Granada* and *Don Sebastian* appear in one on 'Spain's Grand Project of a Universal Empire'; and *The Tempest* appears in one on 'Utopian Plays of the Restoration'. Dryden and other dramatists, despite the mockery of their critics and their own awareness of imperial corruption, saw themselves as 'celebrants of heroic greatness'. The project of a Christian empire, improving on previous models, is viewed enthusiastically in *The Conquest of Granada* but despairingly in *Don Sebastian*. Such conclusions are not surprising, but on the way to them Dryden's plays are perceptively analysed. John Michael Archer's *Old Worlds* explores early modern English writing on Egypt, south-west Asia, India and Russia. Here *Aureng-Zebe* appears as the conclusion to which earlier accounts of India had tended, admiration for the country's ancient civilization giving way to horror at its barbaric customs. Dryden's theatrical evocation of suttee 'makes it the mark of a heroic, barbaric, but inevitably self-consuming world'. Orr's discussion of this play is more straightforward and sympathetic, and it appears rather as a source of later attitudes to India. *Aureng-Zebe* held the stage till well into the eighteenth century and, it could be added, deserves revival today.

Some relevant essays were published in *Huntington Library Quarterly*'s splendid 'Tercentenary Miscellany' (*HLQ* 63:i–ii[2000]). In his introduction Steven N. Zwicker claims that Dryden rightly saw his plays, as well as his other works, as 'the best preservation of fame', so I was disappointed that no contributor emphasized their literary merits or theatrical possibilities. Gavin Foster's 'Ignoring *The Tempest*: Pepys, Dryden, and the Politics of Spectating in 1667' (*HLQ* 63:i–ii[2000] 5–22) argues that, although he saw this play eight times without noting any political parallels, 'Pepys's deep-seated fears for the kingdom, for his job, and for his sex life are crystallized by the play and collective play-going'. This speculative and interesting essay is in the end more about Pepys and other playgoers than about Dryden. Ann A. Huse's 'Cleopatra, Queen of the Seine: The Politics of Eroticism in Dryden's *All for Love*' (*HLQ* 63:i–ii[2000] 23–46) suggests that, by representing Antony's love for Cleopatra as 'an appreciation for a foreign culture and religion', like Charles II's love for Louise de Kéroualle, and by dedicating the play to the king's chief minister Lord Danby, Dryden was advising against a Francophobic and anti-Catholic policy. Richard Kroll's 'The Double Logic of *Don Sebastian*' (*HLQ* 63:i–ii[2000] 47–69) discerns in this play, and incidentally in *Amphitryon*, 'a double thesis about monarchy at the end of the seventeenth century': as actual kings are problematic if not self-destructive, the ideal king is absent or 'virtually dead', and 'acts as the transcendental signifier for the system, securing but not disrupting it'. Some of Kroll's own signifiers—'there is an experiential disequilibrium that catapults one historical moment into the next, so weaving the web by which we recognize "history" at all'—might have been banished too. Bridget Orr's 'Poetic Plate-Fleets and Universal Monarchy' (*HLQ* 63:i–ii[2000] 71–97) refers to Dryden among others in showing, as in her book, that the heroic plays were often about ancient and modern versions of the imperial dream. Finally, David Bywaters's 'Historicism Gone Awry: Recent Work on John Dryden' (*HLQ* 63:i–ii[2000] 245–55) finds that historicism is now producing a dozen bad essays and books for every two good ones: 'Why can't we do better?' An answer is implied by his comment on a good essay, which has 'a rare sensitivity to the nuances of Dryden's poetry'.

A 'tercentenary John Dryden number' of *Aligarh Critical Miscellany* (*ACM* 13:i[2000]) made a belated but welcome appearance. The editor, A.A. Ansari, surprisingly reprints F.R. Leavis's '*Antony and Cleopatra* and *All for Love*'(*ACM* 13:i[2000]13–25), which found that Shakespeare has vitality where Dryden has only eloquence. Paul Hammond's 'Redescription in *All for Love*' (*ACM* 13:i[2000] 26–43) emphasizes Dryden's frequent use of this rhetorical figure, whereby characters and actions are reconsidered. Hammond does not redescribe Leavis's adverse critique, but reaffirms the play's intrinsic merit 'as a series of questions about who Antony and Cleopatra are, what words now describe them'.

Books Reviewed

Andreadis, Harriette. *Sappho in Early Modern England: Female Same-Sex Literary Erotics, 1550–1714*. UChicP. [2001] pp. xiii + 254. hb £31.50 ($45) ISBN 0 2260 2008 8, pb £12 ($17), ISBN 0 2260 2009 6.

Archer, John Michael. *Old Worlds: Egypt, Southwest Asia, India and Russia in Early Modern English Writing.* StanfordUP. [2001] pp. ix + 241. $49.50 ISBN 0 8047 4337 1.

Canfield, J. Douglas, and Maja-Lisa Von Sneidern, eds. *The* Broadview *Anthology of Restoration and Early Eighteenth-Century English Drama.* Broadview. [2001] pp. xxi + 1977. £34.99 ISBN 1 5511 1270 1.

Clare, Janet, ed. *Drama of the English Republic, 1649–1660.* ManUP. [2002] pp. xiii + 311. £45 ISBN 0 7190 4482 0.

Cunnar, Eugene R., and Jeffrey Johnson, eds. *Discovering and (Re)Covering the Seventeenth-Century Religious Lyric.* Duquesne. [2001] pp. viii + 408. £57 ($59) ISBN 0 8207 0317 6.

Dykstal, Timothy. *The Luxury of Skepticism: Politics, Philosophy and Dialogue in the English Public Sphere, 1660–1740.* UPVirginia. [2001] pp. 222. $39.50 ISBN 0 8139 2003 5.

Goldsworthy, Cephas. *The Satyr: An Account of the Life and Work, Death and Salvation of John Wilmot, Second Earl of Rochester.* W&N. [2001] pp. vii + 295. £25 ($40) ISBN 0 2976 4319 3.

Hanowell, Holger, ed. *Sir Charles Sedley's The Mulberry Garden* [1688] and *Bellamira: or, The Mistress* [1687]. Lang. [2001] pp. 314. £37 ISBN 3 6313 7700 2.

Hughes, Derek. *The Theatre of Aphra Behn.* Palgrave. [2001] pp. viii + 230. £50 ISBN 0 3337 6030 1.

Hutner, Heidi. *Colonial Women: Race and Culture in Stuart Drama.* OUP. [2001] pp. ix + 141. £25 ISBN 0 1951 4188 1.

Keeble, N.H. ed. *Cambridge Companion to Writing of the English Revolution.* CUP. [2001] pp. xxii + 296 . hb £42.50 ISBN 0 5216 4252 3, pb £15.95 ISBN 0 5216 4522 0.

Kreis-Schinck, Annette. *Women, Writing, and the Theater in the Early Modern Period: The Plays of Aphra Behn and Susanne [Susanna] Centlivre.* AUP. [2001] pp. 273. $46.50 ISBN 0 8386 3861 9.

Landry, Donna. *The Invention of the Countryside: Hunting, Walking, and Ecology in English Literature, 1671–1831.* Palgrave. pp. xx + 306. £ 45 ($65) ISBN 0 3339 6154 4.

Langley, T.R. *Image Government: Monarchical Metamorphoses in English Literature and Art, 1649–1702.* Clarke. [2001] pp. 256. £45 ($60) ISBN 0 2276 7963 6.

Loewenstein, David. *Representing Revolution in Milton and his Contemporaries: Religion, Politics and Polemics in Radical Puritanism.* CUP. [2001] pp. xiii + 413. £42.50 ISBN 0 5217 7032 7.

Manning, Gillian. *Libertine Plays of the Restoration.* Dent. [2001] pp. lxiii + 787. pb £9.99 ISBN 0 4608 7745 3.

Messenger, Ann. *Pastoral Tradition and the Female Talent: Studies in Augustan Poetry.* AMS. [2001] pp. ix + 248. £74.50 ($62.95) ISBN 0 4046 3525 3.

Mitchell, Linda C. *Grammar Wars: Language as a Cultural Battlefield in 17th- and 18th-Century England.* Ashgate. [2001] pp. viii + 218. £42.50 ISBN 0 7546 0272 9.

Orr, Bridget. *Empire on the English Stage, 1660–1714.* CUP. [2001] pp. x + 350. £40 ISBN 0 5217 7350 4.

Owen, Susan J., ed. *A Companion to Restoration Drama*. Blackwell. [2001] pp. xvi + 456. £65 ISBN 0 6312 1923 4.

Stevenson, Jane, and Peter Davidson, eds. *Early Modern Women Poets (1520–1700): An Anthology*. OUP. [2001] pp. lii + 585. hb £70 ($110) ISBN 0 1981 8426 3, pb £27.50 ($29.95), ISBN 0 1992 4257 7.

Stevenson, Kay Gilliland. *Milton to Pope, 1650–1720*. Transitions. Palgrave. [2001] pp. x + 292. hb £45 ($55) ISBN 0 3336 9612 3, pb £14.99 ($19.95) ISBN 0 3336 9613 1.

Terry, Richard. *Poetry and the Making of the English Literary Past, 1660–1781*. OUP. [2001] pp. vii + 354. £45 ($72) ISBN 0 1981 8623 1.

Thomas, Richard F. *Virgil and the Augustan Reception*. CUP. [2001] pp. xx + 324. £40 ($60) ISBN 0 5217 8288 0.

Wallwork, John, and Paul Salzman, eds. *Women Writing, 1550–1750*. Meridian. [2001] pp. 256. £14.50 ISBN 0 9578 9710 3.

Zionkowski, Linda. *Men's Work: Gender, Class, and the Professionalization of Poetry, 1660–1784*. Palgrave. [2001] pp. viii + 279. £40 ($49.95) ISBN 0 3122 3758 8.

Zwicker, Steven N., and David Bywaters, eds. *John Dryden: Selected Poems*. Penguin. [2001] pp. xxiv + 582. pb £10.99 ($14) ISBN 0 1404 3914 5.

XI

The Eighteenth Century

ADAM ROUNCE AND FREYA JOHNSTON

This chapter has two sections: 1. Poetry; 2. Novel. Section 1 is by Adam Rounce; section 2 is by Freya Johnston.

1. Poetry

It has become something of an annual litany for this section to note that, for all the widening of interest in neglected eighteenth-century poets in recent times, the dictates of publishing are evidently more conservative. What emerges, as usual, is a great deal of criticism on Pope, some general surveys with a lot of Scriblerian emphasis, and a sprinkling of works on other figures. The general quantity and proportions of the material remain constant.

In terms of quality, of course, there are highlights. James McLaverty's *Pope, Print and Meaning* is one of the most enjoyable works on Pope to appear for some time. Taking as its thesis Pope's constant interaction with print culture, both in the presentation and editing of his work and in the subject of the poetry itself, McLaverty offers a series of readings that start from bibliographical issues (whether book presentation, editing, annotation, or revision) but move outwards to encompass a great deal of matter indeed, so much so as to be very much reduced by summary. The changes from the 1712 *Miscellanies* two-canto *Rape of the Lock* to its now familiar version are sifted for evidence of court and sexual politics, amongst other things, as part of Pope's endless self-fashioning; the grandeur and ambition of the *Works* of 1717 evince the potential modernity of Pope's authorship, and its relationship with the public sphere. In the prefatory material, the ordering of the poems, and their level of annotation, Pope manages to create a monumental public persona and a sense of personal responsibility. With the *Dunciad Variorum*, the very idea of the persona is deliberately disordered within what McLaverty describes as a qualified Bakhtinian heteroglossia. The voices of the work are not dialogic so much as 'double-printed' (p. 87), and the notes are brilliantly described as a 'talking bibliography' (p. 95). Importantly, McLaverty uses the presentation of the poem to take issue with the influential post-1945 idea of Scriblerus representing Pope, arguing that to do so reduces (and misreads) the level of Pope's parody.

The *Essay on Man* is read alongside a work that Pope seems willing to have been wrongly identified as his own, Walter Harte's *Essay on Reason*. Indeed, it is possible that Pope wanted Harte's poem to seem a companion (as indeed it does, from its appearance and the details of its presentation), not least, McLaverty thinks, because of Harte's notably different scheme of reason as the path to revelation (in contrast to the limited powers of reason in the *Essay on Man*). The endless arguments over Pope's deistic implications are thus potentially negated by the contemporary comparison (even though Harte, ironically, would later change his theological tune). The parallel texts of the first Horatian imitations are discussed in terms of Pope's design to be seen as the modern Horace, and as an important part of Pope's self-presentation after the 'Timon' controversy over the *Epistle to Burlington*. The uses of the Latin and English parallels to emphasize Pope's inherent virtue are not always to his advantage, for McLaverty, in that egotism is not always sufficiently controlled. Pope's war with the many egotists of his time comes to the fore in the chapter on the *Epistle to Arbuthnot*, and its revisions and variants. Most notable are the related claims that the poem responds to Montagu and Hervey's *Verses Addressed to the Imitator of Horace*; that Pope probably helped to publish that poem in a desire to combat public calumny rather than private gossip; and that *Sober Advice from Horace* carries the offensive upon Hervey further, with Pope attacking his bisexuality through a contrast with his own sense of 'independent masculinity' (p. 205), akin to a more abstract classical idea of homosexuality.

The final chapter looks at the *Works* of 1735–6, and the contrast between the quarto and folio subscriber-led edition and the octavo, aimed at a wider reading public. Pope's changing sense of his audience is of a piece with his consistent negotiation with the past that McLaverty details throughout this excellent book. Its bibliographical point of entry allows it to contain and summarize every significant area of Pope scholarship, and to do so in an informed, direct, authoritative and congenial style that is at times Empsonian. Bibliography and the 'history of the book' have rarely been so effective in illuminating poetic content.

Elsewhere Pope dominates James Noggle's *The Skeptical Sublime: Aesthetic Ideology in Pope and the Tory Satirists*, a work not, despite its subtitle, as interested in politics as in aesthetics. A chapter on Pope's Horatian works was discussed previously in these pages (see *YWES* 81[2002] 556), and if the thesis at length is sometimes so remorseless as to seem oppressively schematic, it certainly has a rounded solidity. For Noggle, radical scepticism after the Restoration is related to discourses on the sublime because both exist at the limits of rationality. Scepticism as a modern version of Pyrrhonism (Montaigne is a latent presence throughout), is a way of noting the sublime folly of satiric targets, from the degraded seekers after supposed reason of Rochester's *Satire Against Mankind* to Pope's Dunces. Such a blunt summary does not do justice to the weighty philosophical questions that Noggle is aiming at, with examples from *The State of Innocence* to *A Tale of a Tub*, but it is the half of the book devoted to Pope that offers the most cogent progression of his thesis. Noggle's Pope necessarily makes the *Essay on Man* contradictory, in its simultaneous sense of human limitation and transcendence, out of a distrust of the sublime (debased in the works of Blackmore, amongst others) which is both conservative and liberal in its humility and scepticism. The integrity of the speaker of the Horatian poems and *Moral Essays* is a result of (what else but) self-fashioning, an adoption of scepticism that makes Pope unable to resolve the social instabilities of his time, yet also distanced from them, with the proviso that he is not immune to the larger human weaknesses that his satiric targets reflect. The most practical benefits of this come in Noggle's reading of the *Epistle to a Lady*, where Pope is also defined by the inconstancy he diagnoses. The concluding reading of the 1743 *Dunciad* builds upon the rest of the book, seeing Pope's final vision as a logical end of post-Restoration scepticism, which has inculcated doubt of the possibilities of rationality to such a degree that it overpowers and speaks through the unwilling Pope in a sort of sublime experience, as he prophesies the inevitable triumph of Dulness.

As such a précis indicates, there are many parts of Noggle's thesis that will strike some readers as somewhat over-sophisticated, though those interested in the ideological workings of the sublime will find much of interest here, not least in the many supporting discussions of more directly philosophical material. The author is polite enough to constantly recapitulate his argument, which is a great help, as there are many fine-grained distinctions that are introduced and repeatedly worked around throughout. Yet this is nevertheless a dense read. While it may seem carping to complain about a lack of stylistic character in a work concerned with epistemological problems, for all that he is writing about four of the funniest satirists in the language, Noggle's book is ultimately as solemn as Foxe's *Acts and Monuments*.

In journals, John Richardson (*ECS* 35[2000] 1–17) looks at Pope's attitude to slavery in *Windsor Forest*, the subject of wildly different arguments by Laura Brown and Howard Erskine-Hill, and finds Pope disguising the geography of Africa from the regions in which slavery will be no more, partly from knowledge of the Asiento contract of the treaty of Utrecht (guaranteeing a British monopoly on slave-trading to South America) and also because of his unease over Tory support of his sentiments (which nevertheless makes him suggest an anti-slavery position as a distancing tactic). Pope's burgeoning poetic career is marked by careful political positioning. Given the complicated political and literary machinations that much modern criticism assigns to him, it is surprising Pope found time to write so much verse. A more traditional argument is found in 'Wordsworth, Pope, and the Alps' (*RoN* 7[2001] 58–72), where Grevel Lindop traces Wordsworth's remembrance in *The Prelude* of the anti-climax of crossing the Alps to its literary source: Pope's warning to the poetically ambitious in the *Essay on Criticism* that '*Alps* on *Alps* arise' to humble their efforts. Pope's reminder of the dangers of pride is then compared to Wordsworth's boat-stealing scene (between Wordsworth and Pope the metaphor was used by Grainger and Darwin, amongst others), and followed back to its own likely source, Juvenal's dismissal of the doomed, hubristic Hannibal in his tenth satire. Wordsworth's memory of his crossing is therefore, for Lindop, a metaphor for his quiet, modest overthrow of literary tradition. In a discussion of no little detail, Valerie Rumbold (*RES* 52[2001] 524–39) looks at a manuscript revision from Book II of *The Dunciad*, where Pope took out an episode of female caterwauling originally intended to complement the male noisemaking contests. Tracing the history of one of Pope's targets in the scene, the playwright Mary Pix, Rumbold suggests that the omission points to a larger absence in the poem of female creativity as a target for satire; even the well-known attack on Eliza Haywood is more personally motivated than an assault upon women's writing *per se*. By denying women writers the sort of criticism directed towards Blackmore *et al.*, Pope refuses to take them seriously; subsequent feminist criticism of the poem has thus concentrated on the Goddess Dulness as a familiar type of sexual excess, and female creativity is marginalized.

Pope inevitably plays a large part in the most significant survey of the year, Richard Terry's *Poetry and the Making of the English Literary Past, 1660–1781*. This heroically inclusive book fits in so much information that it becomes not so much a single thesis as a series of discussions of the background to canon-formation, and is all the better for it. It refuses (refreshingly) to make the literary past fit into one schema, all the while straining to overlook the inevitable exceptions. Instead, Terry offers up a number of debates, starting with the evolution of the idea of 'literature' as an evaluative rather than a descriptive term, and moving onto the (unrealized) schemes of poetic history of Pope, Spence and Gray, and the contributions towards canon-formation in the 'progress' poems of Samuel Cobb, Judith Madan, Gray, Collins, and others. A significant support to the overall discussion is an exploration of the ethical necessity for many seventeenth-century biographers and historians in memorializing the fame of writers (a necessity that would be erased in the next century by largely commercial forces). The odd, yet crucial, influence of Chaucer as a figure of canonical origin is then compared with the partial rediscovery of Anglo-Saxon poetry, and competing myths of British poetic origin concerning the Druids, and other forms of primitivism. Here, as elsewhere, Terry resists the idea of a uniform canon emerging: the supposed need for linguistic purity in poetry (often tagged onto a line of poets from Waller to Pope via Dryden), is contradicted by the polyvalence of the competing origins of such verse. Furthermore, a canon has its own momentum. Dryden is then examined as the first important employer of poetic relationships as a tradition, in both a familial sense and as part of his interest in Pythagorean notions of metempsychosis, a metaphor of rebirth that Terry finds artistically suggestive. A different tradition is then explored (somewhat digressively), in a long look at pedagogy, and the introduction of English poetry into education as part of the formation of taste, and elocutionary skills, though its often overlooked practical benefits get due attention. Another old canard, Johnson as the evil genius of poetic canon-formation, is attacked, thankfully, in an excellent chapter on the *Lives of the Poets*, in which Johnson's use of an earlier biographical tradition and his own methods are accurately described. Terry is good on the contradictions of many readings of the *Lives*: if they really enshrined conservative taste, why did so many people attack them so vociferously? Johnson emerges, ironically, as the defender of neglected poets, the role ostensibly played by many of his more superficial modern critics. The book is equally even-handed on the problems of a female canon, pointing out the surprising amount of biographical space given to women writers from early in the eighteenth century, but also showing how the acceptance of women poets was concomitant with patronizing notions of inherent artistic difference.

The book ends with a reading of Spenser and the historical enterprise of his ephebe Thomas Warton, placing the 'Gothic' against (but dependent upon), the 'Classical', and touching upon many other avenues, needless to say. This packed book is admirably accessible; its sheer weight of information goes some way to explaining the numerous and otherwise inexplicable examples of mistaken dating that litter it (from Dryden's *Fables* to poor Percival Stockdale, who is given the wrong years for both of his major works; a right one then becomes wrong again in the bibliography). The reader may also take issue with some of Terry's passing comments: is the inscription 'O *Rare* Ben Jonson' 'flatly uninspired'? Does Gray's nervous and ambiguous self-address at the end of *The Progress of Poesy* seem like 'self-congratulating egotism'? Terry often works better at assimilating enormously valuable information than at analysing its details, but no matter; here is critical plenty, both for affirmation and argument.

In a more narrow chronological survey, *Transforming the Word: Prophecy, Poetry and Politics in England, 1650–1742*, Margery Kingsley explores the ways in which the rhetoric of civil war prophecy is negotiated in later poetry, from *Hudibras* and *Mac Flecknoe* to *The Dunciad*. What this means in practice is the adaptation of millenarial language to the evolving political and economic situation, such as the reading of Butler's great satire as an avoidance of the extremist absolutism of monarchist or puritan discourse, in favour of progressive economic debate. Dryden provides social cohesion through the (hyperbolic) descriptions of the providential resolution of the Fire of London in *Annus Mirabilis*; the theatrical surrealism of *Mac Flecknoe*, on the other hand, is an attack on the cultural politics of disorder that Shadwell represents, a threat to the stability of negotiated social order that Dryden desires in the potentially tumultuous early 1680s. For Kingsley, Dryden has to acknowledge that instability undermines his attempts to control chaos through the text, just as the unstable forces of the artistic and political market undermine the cultural and social order of the nation. The most successful part of the book is a section on the *Fable of the Bees*, where Mandeville's bald satire shows that the presentation of economic forces, in their mixture of arbitrary power and supposedly unchecked freedom, is the most telling and objective way of describing contemporary social representation. It matters not that the supposed relation of this to the Whiggish renegotiation of discourse after 1689 is not made evident. Less convincing is the concluding description of *The Dunciad* as an admission of the failure of the kind of wider cultural judgement it ostensibly makes, partly as this has all been said before many times (in less gnomic form), and also because the argument creates more strands than it can follow through with authority. It is not disparaging to remark that Kingsley's readings are of more interest than the general thesis, which disappears into the background at the best moments, or surfaces obtrusively at the weakest, when more obscure prophetic texts (usually of interest in their own right) are brought into often uneasy juxtaposition with the main subjects. The prose, filled with new historicist inflections of the paradoxes of power, often doubles back on itself in a fashion not dissimilar to some of the enthusiastic prophecies of the Interregnum.

On a more directly pedagogic note, the essays collected in Sitter, ed., *The Cambridge Companion to Eighteenth Century Poetry* are (inevitably) something of a mixed bag, though on the whole, this will probably become a library standard for undergraduates. J. Paul Hunter offers a very readable, pleasant and inclusive introduction to the intrinsic relationship between couplets and the social world (pp. 11–35); Christine Gerrard traces the shifting political momentum of poetry from 1710 to the Wilkesian protests of Churchill (pp. 37–62). Barbara Benedict analyses the development of the publishing industry and its effect on writers and audience (pp. 63–82); Brean Hammond's examination of the city ranges from standards such as *Trivia* and Blake's 'London' to Anstey, Chandler and Fergusson's Edinburgh (pp. 83–107). Tim Fulford looks at 'Nature' poetry, in a wide-ranging tour that ends on

Darwin and William Jones (pp. 109–31). A key essay is Sitter's discussion and defence of poetics from Addison to Wordsworth, which is an intricate and welcome corrective to many a tired description, pointing out the flexibility of eighteenth-century poetry, its refusal to see poetic theory as restraining, and the wrong-headedness of most of the generalizations brought against it in the past two centuries (pp. 133–56). Claudia Thomas Kairoff's survey of women poets (pp. 157–76) addresses the ambivalent role of Pope as a poetic model, and the routes taken after his death by women, among other matters. David Fairer (pp. 177–201) delivers an account of Miltonic and Spenserian influence in the century, placing the post-1740 uses of them against the Popean line supported by Johnson (who comes in for some barbed remarks). Ralph Cohen's discussion of the ode (pp. 203–24) gives a taxonomy whereby the ballad and sonnet revival are versions of the 'lesser' ode, though the argument suffers from not explicating the 'greater' ode, and its debt to the seventeenth century, sufficiently. David Morris's somewhat diffuse look at poetic 'absence' (pp. 225–48) takes in enthusiasm, melancholy, dreams and (generally) desire and its lack. Patricia Spacks's reading of sensibility attempts to give flesh to the often vague term by looking at its social functions and very real effects, not least in the ever-present debates around sympathy (pp. 249–68). Finally, Jennifer Keith rejects the old canard of 'pre-Romanticism', positing instead a poetic from 1770 to 1800 in Cowper, Smith, and others that is marked (perhaps too insistently) by its alienation in a series of rather enclosed readings, though the premise of freeing space from the weight of Romanticism is sound.

This thematic collection is often enlightening, though it can produce a lot of repetition, not least because the same examples are frequently used to illustrate a (supposedly) different topic. The reader of these essays is told too regularly that Joseph Warton more or less 'proclaimed Pope a second-rate poet' (which is anyway a very crude simplification of Warton's arguments, even when paraphrased more diplomatically elsewhere), or that Cowper was a 'stricken deer' who perished beneath a 'rougher' sea; Gray's bard falls into 'endless night' in three different essays. Still, at least a student could hardly fail to grasp some of the key poetic moments of the century, when presented with them so often.

Due attention was given to many other poets, from the more renowned to the very obscure. Changing the perceived view of a writer is never an easy task. Chris Mounsey's *Christopher Smart: Clown of God* is a critical biography concerned, primarily, with the evolution of the cliché of 'poor Kit Smart', the 'mad' poet. As with Thomas Chatterton, it needs countering, in that such myth proves a stumbling-block to real appreciation of the poetry and Smart's many other writings. Mounsey's principal revisionist argument is that Smart was not mad at all. His thesis is acknowledged as speculative at many points, though it is backed up by a vast amount of potential evidence. The structure of the biography even allows for a final chapter that posits the various reasons why the idea of 'mad' Smart has proved so congenial. In bald outline, Mounsey argues that Smart's incarceration was a result of political pressure resulting from his inflammatory journalism in the early 1750s, or a consequence of the Machiavellian dealings of his publisher and father-in-law John Newberry, with whom he had fallen out. These two possibilities are not exclusive: Newberry could have been the agent of political pressure, or the embarrassment of Smart's bohemian behaviour and reputed compulsive worship could have made his incarceration helpful to many.

I am all for attacking misleading romanticized stereotypes, and Mounsey marshals a formidable body of publishing details and apparent coincidences to back his case (although the idea that Smart was asthmatic, valuable in itself, is overplayed in partially explaining away the compulsion to prayer). On the other hand, speculative argument can easily assume its own tenets too readily: the descriptions of the villainous Newberry persecuting Smart through (sometimes very tenuous) implications in assorted publications are occasionally reminiscent of the pursuit of Caleb Williams. What is lost, or distorted, is proportion, and the energy with which Smart is thrown into a ceaseless set of conflicts (with, amongst others, an unusually active Thomas Gray) prevents a rounded, settled picture of the author from emerging. As a discussion of the breadth of Smart's work, Mounsey's book is more winning. The value of his extensive reading of Smart's prodigious journalism (most notably in *The Midwife*) and its theatrical offshoots goes beyond his interpretations of Smart's politics. The disparate strands of Smart's religious thought are related to William Stukeley (the two might have known each other, though our old friend 'could have' becomes more certain too quickly on some occasions), in a provocative assimilation that takes in the *Jubilate*; the unique qualities of this and *A Song to David* are well (if relatively briefly) described. The real regret is that more time is not spent on the post-incarceration poems of the 1760s: by then, the heroic Smart is too busy fighting off his enemies for Mounsey to do justice to this part of his achievement. The reader does not have to accept the book's central argument to find much of use here; it is a controversial corrective to previous works, and (more particularly and more usefully) a store of knowledge of the less illumined corners of Smart's output.

There were some very interesting editions of works neglected for a variety of reasons. Bill Overton's *A Letter to My Love* presents a fascinating series of poems first published in the *Barbados Gazette* in the 1730s (but presumed to have been written earlier). A sequence of twenty-six anonymous love poems by the so-called 'Amorous Lady' (a sobriquet rejected by Overton, who prefers the more neutral 'Anonymous Lady') are followed by fifteen other poems by women also included in the magazine (and reprinted in *Caribbeana* in 1741), included partly to allow comparison with the first poems, and to foster potential future research into the detective story of their authorship. To support his claim that the original sequence can stand beside the most celebrated love poems in English, Overton offers a thorough introduction, copious notes, prefatory material from *Caribbeana* with hints about possible authorship, and an afterword describing the poetic context of the poems, their originality and achievement, and noting potential thematic and metrical similarities. He does not follow Phyllis Guskin's attribution of authorship of the entirety of the poems to Martha Fawke Sansom, in an article summarized in these pages (*YWES* 81[2002] 557), and makes some significant points against the details of her argument. Until more evidence is unearthed, for Overton the issue of authorship remains unclear, and this edition seems likely to encourage further investigation and debate. It is also very good to see evaluative questions addressed directly, rather than covered over with more nebulous issues, in the motives behind republication; Overton claims a lot for these poems, and gives the reader all the necessary material to join the debate.

Other than his cameo roles in survey literature, Thomas Gray's appearance this year was limited to a publication of his prose. The journal he kept during his tour of the Lake District in 1769 has previously only been available as part of the Toynbee and Whibley *Correspondence*. It took two forms: a series of letters to his friend Thomas Wharton, and two incomplete notebooks. William Roberts has put together a composite edition, complete with commentary on each day of following in Gray's footsteps, drawings (by Gray's admirer Joseph Farington), notes, maps and daily endpieces of Gray's lists and recipes. This is intended to be both a scholarly edition of an important piece of travel writing and a good read and travelling companion: the introduction and commentary are aimed at the comprehension of any reader, and like much modern travel writing it includes Roberts's contemporary anecdotes, and a description of the many subsequent developments in the Lakes. Gray was never a dull observer, and his own descriptions of a Lake District very remote from the modern tourist conception of it are well complemented by Roberts's own exegesis, which contains much never noted before; it is a mine of curious information.

Given its subject, it would be somewhat tasteless, though accurate, to call John Gilmore, ed., *The Poetics of Empire* a mine of information. The book is perhaps misleadingly entitled, as it is not so much a study of James Grainger's Caribbean georgic *The Sugar-Cane* [1764], as the first full edition of it since 1836. Grainger's poem celebrating the major product of West Indian slavery was for a long time unread, and known by Johnson and Boswell only as an object of ridicule; more recently it has attracted opprobrium as the epitome of thoughtless and offensive British imperialism, the ideology of its author at best ignorant and at worst disgusting. Gilmore is not an apologist for Grainger, but in his excellent introduction he does point out the folly of expecting ideologically suspect works to be otherwise; Grainger, a Scot living in St Kitts (who had been at Culloden), was not likely to write against slavery. None of his contemporaries wrote anti-slavery poetry until the 1780s, and it was entirely possible to use the celebratory georgic form for a subject that was not unequivocally approved of by many. For all that his poem is an acceptance of slavery, Gilmore argues that Grainger's introduction of the Caribbean into the poetic subjects of the empire was a bold move in itself, however unpalatable its details undoubtedly remain. This strange poem with its Eurocentric perspective is a mixture of the earnest, the enraptured, the cumbersome, the offensive and the grotesque; as well as Grainger's own notes, Gilmore adds a hundred pages of additional explanation. This is necessary, given the poem's propensity to jump from highfalutin didacticism to minute local detail. This edition does great credit to the oddities and contradictions of the eighteenth century, and the necessity of facing up to them.

To adapt a popular comment on public transport, there have been no works on Grainger for ages, and then two come along at once. Shaun Irlam's '"Wish you were here": Exporting England in James Grainger's *The Sugar-Cane*' (*ELH* 68[2001] 377–96), finds Grainger guilty of failing to domesticate the West Indies and of encouraging the pre-eminence of empire at the end of the Seven Years War. For Irlam, the poem's pastoral is fenced in and constrained by its ideological impossibilities, and the resulting tension reveals the crude exploitation that is always latent in the poem. The cruelty of this, together with its unintended bathos, ensured its harsh reception from Johnson and others (though Gilmore would argue that the success of the poem was more widespread than Irlam allows).

Post-Scriblerian satire makes a rare critical appearance in Donald Nichol's discussion of the *New Foundling Hospital for Wit* (*SLI* 34[2001] 101–19), an entertaining trip through the often scurrilous forbear of the modern satirical magazine. Nichol dwells mostly on the attacks of John Wilkes and Charles Churchill upon William Warburton through illustrations and squibs, the *Essay on Woman*, Churchill's poems, including his masterpiece, the 'Dedication to the *Sermons*', and Wilkes's subsequent annotations of it. Nichol's own sense of humour allows him to see when the pair overstepped the bounds of taste, particularly when the feud extended to Warburton's son; the eminent divine got the enemies he deserved, in this reviewer's opinion. This is an excellent introduction to the tangled quarrels of the 1760s. In a bibliographical account of an earlier poet, James Sambrook surveys James Thomson's relationships with publishers and patrons (*SLI* 34[2001] 137–53), from initial dedications to famous folk personally unknown to the poet, to his lasting relationship with Lyttelton, for whom Thomson was the model of a patriot bard. That Thomson survived and prospered owed not a little to his combining patronage from the likes of Lyttelton with peddling his poetic and dramatic wares in the marketplace to booksellers: though hardly riveting today in totality, all his plays were performed, and his poems read, to some extent. As Sambrook says, enlightened and high-minded patronage might, in Thomson's view, be a better artistic guarantee than the whims of publishers, but few were in the position to reject the money that the latter provided; Thomson managed to retain more independence than most, and his dealings with patrons and booksellers place him exactly in the middle of the changing world of publishing.

Stephen Duck, a poet with more ambivalent experiences of patronage, gets attention from Bridget Keegan (*SEL* 41[2001] 545–62), who offers a corrective to readings of *The Thresher's Labour* as merely a realistic representation. Looking at the poem as part of a continual dialogue on georgic, Keegan sees Duck responding to the contradiction of Addison's notion of the form's poetic representation of real work; Duck's polyvalent poem is a knowing recognition and description of this distance between creative and physical labour, and its contesting voices show the inability of georgic to proceed in line with its classical precepts, not least in its silencing of the first person singular as the poem progresses (an anticipation, for Keegan, of Duck's own turning away from the theme).

Of almost opposite intention and tone to most criticism published this year, the lectures collected in *Saving from the Wreck* by the poet Peter Porter have many relevant moments for the eighteenth century: Porter discusses Smart and Cowper in a look at poetry and madness (pp. 1–22), Pope is the subject of an enthusiastic chapter (pp. 100–18), and his Homer is part of an introductory tour of translation (pp. 23–48). George Crabbe's couplet poetics are also given rare attention (pp. 82–99). These lectures by a practising poet are not directed at an academic audience, and have a winning accessibility, seeking, as they do, the source of poetic pleasure as their starting point. Students needing reasons for reading important texts could do a lot worse.

As the century ends with the demise of William Cowper, it seems fitting to conclude with the mixture of works concerning him this year. Julie Ellison (*MLQ* 62[2001] 219–37) looks at the importance of newspapers to Cowper's world, with a glance at that of Crabbe as well, arguing that Cowper's relationship with the daily papers was a necessary way of participating in metropolitan life, while negotiating his distance from it. The most famous example, the reading of the newspaper at the beginning of Book IV of *The Task*, is read as an emblem of provincial domesticity, with the consuming characters turning into citizens of the world while avoiding any of the harshness of its events. By 1793 Charlotte Smith's dedication of *The Emigrants* to Cowper compares his poetic effect upon her with that of the political orators he had admired in the newspapers, thus showing his ironic assimilation into the public world of news he had read about so earnestly from a distance (though Ellison does not follow the story to the end of the decade, when Cowper would increasingly be confronted with disturbing implications from the most incidental reading material, as his last two poems show). Ken Smith's *William Cowper: A Reappraisal* is an introductory survey of extended pamphlet length, published by the Cowper and Newton Museum with the purpose of introducing readers to the poet, and aiming to draw together the threads of Cowper scholarship from the last twenty or so years in an accessible fashion. Thus, the old (and largely sentimentalized) 'stricken deer' is challenged by nods to recent views of the changing political landscape that he inhabited and, more consistently, by discussion of the evangelical tradition which caused the poet so much trouble or liberated him from otherwise greater burdens, depending on your point of view; Smith wisely declines to adjudicate in this perennial critical debate, holding instead Cowper's own sense of damnation in equipoise with the undoubted relief that the quotidian aspects of Calvinism brought him. The intellectual possibility of salvation was present for Cowper even after his final sense of reprobation became fixed in 1773, as Smith argues, yet the evidence for his being able to consistently rationalize the issue in this fashion is the problem. The result is an ever-shifting scale of alleviation of potential torment, and his greatest poetry. What is important, as Smith stresses, is the affirmative sense of much of Cowper's life and work, for all his suffering: the values of trust, companionship and compassion are present, though sometimes all but obscured, even in the last, darkest years. For Smith, no mean part of the achievement of *The Task* is its apparently mundane but vital ability to find the providential in nature, and to show the necessity of one to the other in Cowper's version of pastoral. Similarly, it is Cowper's charming sense of Homer as a venerable old gentleman, and the dignity given to ideas of friendship and fellowship in his poetry, that attracted Cowper's blank verse translations, despite his apparent antipathy to the many scenes of blood and gore in the epics. The idea that Cowper was not always as sensitive and fastidious as has been assumed is also significant in asserting the intellectual independence of his work, for all his sporadic protestations presenting himself as religious victim. There are points where, even in this brief critical biography, Smith is contentious (the end of 'Yardley Oak' refers not to Jesus but to Adam, surely), and there are moments of typographical error, but these are forgivable in this sort of modest yet encouraging publication, which fulfils its task with a clarity and enthusiasm appropriate to its subject.

The Cowper Museum also helped with the publication of Malpas, ed., *The Centenary Letters*, put together with the express intent of offering an affordable selection of Cowper's correspondence to a general audience. The principles of inclusion are based on representing every chronological stage of Cowper's adult life, and on displaying the widely varying range of tones and themes upon which he touched. From Cowper's many letters, criticism often quotes those directly germane to its purposes, which usually involve religion as the fixed point around which his relatively narrow existence moved, displaying at best temporary consolation, and more often fear and utter hopelessness. It is good to find him here often confronted by doubt but equally often comforted by the everyday and the wonder of the intangible. The result, linked by Malpas's explanatory headnotes, is a kind of epistolary autobiography, showing the many sides of a figure who was regularly tortured into being 'a forlorn and miserable being' (p. 155), as the penultimate letter has it (the recipient Lady Hesketh received some of the most chillingly forlorn letters in the language), yet could also show qualities of wit, verve, humour and spleen far removed from the picture of the reprobate obsessed with 'dismal doctrines' noted by Boswell. He was also a discriminating (and often acerbic) literary critic—his description of contemporary criticism evaluating poetry 'as a cook serves a dead turkey' (p. 84) is part of a brief discussion of versification that suggests the complexity of Cowper's supposedly hostile view of Pope, and his not inconsiderable relish for bathos. It also challenges what Malpas, in his introduction, describes perhaps too readily as his 'neo-classical aesthetic' (p. ix).

The critical offerings of the last bounteous year cannot, thankfully, be described as dead turkeys, despite a few token fashionable critical gestures, and the revisiting of some old themes in a not always progressive manner; most encouragingly, despite the amount of criticism in the period staying fixed, the ambition of the best work is suggestive of new avenues.

2. The Novel

Two hundred and sixty-one years after her first appearance in print, Pamela Andrews had even more reason to feel smug: the richest and most illuminating resource for students of the eighteenth-century novel to appear in 2001 was Thomas Keymer and Peter Sabor's six-volume compendium *The Pamela Controversy: Criticisms and Adaptations of Samuel Richardson's 'Pamela', 1740–1750*. The editors broaden their remit beyond the apparently principal documents, embracing pre-publication newspaper puffs and notices as well as spurious continuations, operas, dramas, novellas, poems and illustrations. Most of the key British and Irish sources are here reproduced; some have already appeared in Augustan Reprint Society facsimiles and the Garland series 'Richardsoniana' (1974–5). Keymer and Sabor acknowledge that the European response to *Pamela*—scarcely touched upon here—would require as many volumes again, as would the torrent of American reactions. Volume 1 contains various ancillary writings by Richardson himself, Fielding's *Shamela* and a number of verse responses. Volume 2 reprints a series of prose criticisms, paintings and engravings. Volume 3 houses two fictional offshoots, Eliza Haywood's *Anti-Pamela* and the anonymous *Memoirs of the Life of Lady H—*. The most prominent of the unauthorized sequels, John Kelly's *Pamela's Conduct in High Life*, occupies volumes 4 and 5, while volume 6 showcases five dramatic and operatic adaptations. The opportunity to compare a range of visual with written representations is welcome, but the best feature of *The Pamela Controversy* is its editorial apparatus. Each volume is prefaced with a generous scholarly introduction, based on new research, which outlines the critical and historical context of the ensuing material. A chronology, meticulously plotting the stampede into print, and a select bibliography of secondary sources are equally indispensable. The editors' background in book history helps them explain the importance of Richardson's role not only as author (and purported editor), but also as printer and advertiser. They convincingly assert that *Pamela*'s brilliance 'lay as much in commercial strategy as in literary achievement' (vol. i, p. xv) and that the received interpretation (dating back to 1744) of a two-sided debate between rival camps of 'Pamelists' and 'Anti-pamelists' will no longer hold. As these volumes triumphantly demonstrate, *Pamela*'s 'vogue' is more properly styled a 'controversy' that swiftly outgrew its immediate source, 'a multi-voiced dispute, beginning with matters of local interpretation but typically extending much further' (vol. i, p. xvii).

Six volumes of parody, imitation, burlesque and moral rejoinder might be produced to document eighteenth-century reactions to *Tristram Shandy*; Ian Campbell Ross, *Laurence Sterne: A Life*, similarly accents entrepreneurial adroitness alongside literary brilliance. Ross deftly charts his subject's transition from 'client of the aristocracy' to 'one of modernity's first respectable and respected commercial writers', largely thanks to Sterne's collaboration with the publisher Robert Dodsley, who successfully urged him to excise the novel's more pointed satire and obtrusive provincialisms (pp. ix, 431, 203–4). At the heart of this *Life* is the contention that, although *Tristram Shandy* was 'the triumph of the writer in the marketplace' (p. 11), Sterne never relinquished aspirations to gentility or promoted the view that he wrote out of financial necessity. His career thus embodies the complex evolutionary shift from patronage to print culture that has informed much recent criticism. The biography is enlivened by piquant anecdotes which at once underline Ross's point and are diverting in their own right: it says a great deal for the stir caused by the novel that—in allusion to Mrs Shandy's celebrated question—London prostitutes soon took to asking potential customers, 'Sir, will you have your clock wound up?' (p. 18). The misfortunes to which Sterne's agricultural venture was subject have a surprisingly modern and cautionary ring: his livestock perished in an outbreak of cattle plague, which the government had thirty years previously attempted to eradicate by 'a programme of slaughtering' and 'compensation of the farmers affected' (p. 145). 'Curse on farming', as Sterne later exclaimed (p. 147). Ross makes frequent use of parish records, often to poignant effect: he notes, for instance, that of the twelve babies Sterne christened in Sutton between April 1745 and May 1746 four died young (including his own daughter, Lydia). Much of this material sheds light on the tender reverence for the little in *Tristram Shandy* and *A Sentimental Journey*. Another great strength of the biography is its informed discussion of Sterne's reluctant and disastrous career as a political journalist, which does not shy away from his distasteful anti-Catholic prejudice (pp. 136–7). Behind this career lurks the malign presence of Sterne's uncle Jacques, archdeacon of Cleveland, whose Machiavellian equivocations and unwillingness to relinquish 'the Uses of such a Handle' as Sterne caused much suffering (p. 164). The intersections between art and life are treated delicately and suggestively; having outlined the sad estrangement of Sterne from his mother, Agnes, Ross observes that 'Elizabeth Shandy never addresses a word to her son, nor he to her' (p. 168). In view of the dearth of firm evidence, he deals as expertly with the eclectic mix of books to which the 'English Rabelais' is likely to have had access (p. 116). Ross's conjectures about the possible influence of diverse ancient and contemporary works (ranging from Josephus' *De Bello* to Edward Young's *Night Thoughts*) on Sterne's literary development will prove invaluable to students getting to grips with the multiply allusive nature of *Tristram Shandy*.

Jonathan Laidlow and Stuart Sim are two such students. In 'A Compendium of Shandys: Methods of Organizing Knowledge in Sterne's *Tristram Shandy*' (in Spencer, ed., *The Eighteenth-Century Novel*, pp. 181–200), Laidlow convincingly demonstrates that Walter Shandy's preoccupation with digesting, categorizing and applying knowledge springs from concerns manifested in the Ancients versus Moderns debate, and in a host of serious and parodic codifying enterprises pre-dating Sterne. Claiming *Shandy* as a descendant of Renaissance Menippean satire pitched at 'universalizing scholars' and their 'tendency towards totalizing', rather than as a precursor of twentieth-century modernism, Laidlow concludes: 'If it is possible to suggest that Sterne was a self-conscious, metafictional writer, then let us at least say that he was self-conscious about eighteenth-century learning and scholarship' (pp. 189, 197–8). In 'Sterne—Chaos—Complexity' (in Spencer, ed., pp. 201–15), Stuart Sim probes the connections between science, metaphysics, philosophy and literary practice in *Shandy*. Pursuing the 'butterfly effect' of complexity theory, whereby small triggers may prompt gargantuan consequences, Sim discerns in Tristram and his family 'a chaotic life, lacking in any apparent design or sense of linear progression; a life beset by chance, fate, and endless digressions … a non-linear system obsessively trying to construct a linear route through life' (p. 209). Following Laidlow's method, Sim might fruitfully have traced the progress from minute cues to disproportionate effects, or the combination of disordered events with a linear structure, via mock-heroic verse rather than twentieth-century physics. The usefulness of invoking a modern or postmodern category in order to interpret eighteenth-century literary procedures is equally questionable in James How, 'Clarissa's Cyberspace: The Development of Epistolary Space in Richardson's *Clarissa*' (in Spencer, ed., pp. 37–69). How emphasizes 'the inherent instabilities' of a 'state of almost perpetual communication' (p. 38). So far, we are on familiar ground. Yet it adds little to our understanding of the novel to assert that Clarissa achieves a 'tip in the balance of power' comparable to the internet's purported gifts of individual freedom and self-enhancement, or that Richardson's 'band of dwellers in the cities of London and epistolary space come together as a result of the same conditions that allow cyberspace to contribute towards the "forming [of] communities of interest that are not bound by the accidents of geography"' (p. 64).

Carol Houlihan Flynn, 'Richardson and his Readers', introducing Flynn and Copeland, eds., *Clarissa and her Readers: New Essays for the Clarissa Project* (pp. 1–17; published by AMS in 1999 but not reviewed in *YWES* two years ago), is as concerned as Keymer and Sabor to emphasize varieties of 'engagement and resistance' among Richardson's readers, who continue to 'perform acts of cultural revision and reform' on his later novel (pp. 1, 17). Contributors variously locate the origins of this impulse in the authority of an emerging middle-class or female audience, in *Clarissa*'s refinements on literary tradition, appropriations of space and the human body. Rachel Trickett, 'Dryden's Part in *Clarissa*' (Flynn and Copeland, eds., pp. 175–87), elegantly and perceptively identifies the 'interior world' of the novel with that of Restoration drama, casting Richardson's Dryden as 'the laureate of a corrupt society' whose tone of easy, rakish familiarity Lovelace finally rejects (justly or not) for its lack of spiritual vision (p. 177). To enter into Lovelace's allusive world entails familiarity with the exuberance and versatility of Dryden's verse: Richardson's 'artistic imagination responded to the skill and force of

Dryden's poetry; his conscience repudiated what Dryden seemed to him to stand for' (p. 186). Jayne Elizabeth Lewis, '*Clarissa*'s Cruelty: Modern Fables of Moral Authority in *The History of a Young Lady*' (Flynn and Copeland, eds., pp. 45–67), also attends to the libertine mercilessness of Lovelace's interior life, persuasively linking it to the suffering experienced by his readers: 'as cruelty informs the inner world of Richardson's novel, so historically the language of cruelty mediated between that world and the outer one inhabited by readers who felt that they suffered too' (p. 48). Associating Richardson's novel with the techniques of Lockean fable, Lewis argues that both forms enforced their morals through instantaneous sense impressions which seemed to emanate from within the reader, so that an agonized response became tantamount to didactic efficacy: 'The reader's pain verifies the "justice" of (Richardson's) representations. It proves them grounded in material reality for, as her own body testifies, that is the realm of their effects. Pain induces credibility, narratable correspondence with the sensible world, aesthetic "Justice"' (p. 50).

Two contextual studies of the relationship between *Clarissa* and eighteenth-century abduction law appeared in 1999 and 2001: Joan I. Schwarz, 'Eighteenth-Century Abduction Law and *Clarissa*' (in Flynn and Copeland, eds., pp. 269–308), and Beth Swan, 'Clarissa Harlowe, Pleasant Rawlins, and Eighteenth-Century Discourses of Law' (in Spencer, ed., pp. 38–71). Both authors conclude that Lovelace could have been prosecuted for a statutory felonious abduction in the light of the trial narrative of Haagen Swendsen, indicted in 1701 for duping, removing and forcibly marrying a young heiress. Richardson, as the printer of *A Complete Collection of State Trials*, was familiar with abduction law; Schwarz and Swan argue that *Clarissa* sought expansively to complicate and humanize the criminal acts of seduction, kidnapping and rape. Their work on the dramatically intrusive courtroom procedures that Clarissa, as her father's legal property, might have encountered—had she prosecuted Lovelace for her abduction from Harlowe Place and/or Hampstead—is a congenial supplement to April London, *Women and Property in the Eighteenth-Century Novel* (CUP, 1999).

In Blewett, ed., *Passion and Virtue: Essays on the Novels of Samuel Richardson*, fourteen contributors (whose essays originally appeared in *Eighteenth-Century Fiction*) discuss the causes and effects of amorous suffering. Two authors chart *Pamela*'s relationship to print culture. Through an analysis of the novel's claims to historical and emotional truth and the moral authenticity created by allusions to the Bible and to Aesop's *Fables*, John B. Pierce, 'Pamela's Textual Authority' (Blewett, ed., pp. 8–26) describes the heroine's progress as reader and writer. John A. Dussinger, '"Ciceronian Eloquence": The Politics of Virtue in Richardson's *Pamela*' (Blewett, ed., pp. 27–51) examines the period in which Richardson's printing house issued the *Daily Gazetteer*, 'the chief organ of propaganda for the Walpole government'. Arguing for the novel's 'significance in the history of the printing press as a paradoxical and dialogical rendering of the conflict between private expression and public authority', Dussinger forges connections between the 'power of the written word' in Richardson's profession and Pamela's story: virtue is ultimately profitable for heroine and author (pp. 27, 35, 51). Albert J. Rivero, 'The Place of Sally Godfrey in Richardson's *Pamela*' (Blewett, ed., pp. 52–72), revisits the 'poor Sally Godfrey' episode, reading *Pamela*'s conclusion in terms opposed to the solution Richardson auspiciously provides—the transparent lessons of Sally's errors and a speedy resolution of the plot through her appropriate disposal—preferring to be 'suspicious' of its providential ending (p. 55). Betty Schellenberg, 'Enclosing the Immovable: Structuring Social Authority in *Pamela 2*' (Blewett, ed., pp. 73–91), attempts to recover Richardson's sequel from critical disdain, arguing that what may seem to be a lack of vitality is, in fact, a formal attempt to stabilize and relocate *Pamela*'s 'comic plot' in 'an exemplary model of social authority ... an alternative to the fictional structure patterned upon opposition between the individual and the group' (p. 75). Margaret Anne Doody, 'The Gnostic *Clarissa*' (Blewett, ed., pp. 210–45), claims that the incorporation of occult material allows Richardson to 'resist the pressure of what convention and custom had made of Christianity as a set of rules making the poor and women know their place' (p. 224). Doody's inventive reading seeks to counter the assumption that the novel is an unambiguous replication of the conduct manual. Similarly, Lois A. Chaber, '"Sufficient to the day": Anxiety in *Sir Charles Grandison*' (Blewett, ed., pp. 268–94), endeavouring to redeem *Grandison* from the charge of psychological shallowness, emphasizes the novel's sharp concern about 'the precariousness of human fate' and likens it to aspects of eighteenth-century Anglican homiletic literature (p. 279). George E. Haggerty, '*Sir Charles Grandison* and the "Language of Nature"' (Blewett, ed., pp. 317–31), asserts that passion becomes a virtue when characters acknowledge, understand and communicate their emotions. Comparing Richardson to Johnson in his concern to limit the dangerous prevalence of fancy, Haggerty concludes that the former is 'inspired at least in part by a fear that imagination is a threat to social stability'. By acquiring 'the language of nature', his protagonists successfully redirect the private agony of their inner lives outwards: 'If the dangers of the public world are legion, they are less detrimental than the kinds of debility that imaginative isolation suggests' (p. 331).

Victor J. Lams' structural and psychoanalytic study, *Clarissa's Narrators*, proposes that the novel contains five act-like movements which depend on a 'round robin' transfer of narrative dominance (p. x), from the interiorizing drama performed on the epistolary stage first by Clarissa's and subsequently by Lovelace's ruminations on events of the immediate past, to Belford's more conventionally novelistic 'reportage' (p. 3) and summation that closes the history. Belford, unlike Lovelace and Clarissa, lacks a 'self-project' that would concentrate and determine his conduct, 'and in that sense he is a neutral narrator' (p. 3). The conduct of the novel is determined by three correspondents who serially forward the narrative and displace one another. Lams, considering *Clarissa* as a 'speech action' rather than 'event novel' (p. 2), contrasts the heroine's use of soliloquy to achieve self-understanding with the villainous Lovelace's employment of dramatic monologue to facilitate self-deception. While Clarissa wishes to confront reality, Lovelace practises 'energetic imposture' and 'introjection', a process whereby he 'shapes fantasies out of realities to transform reality into something which can help him maintain cohesiveness' (pp. 113, 126). His recovery, Lams argues, takes the form of an opposite psychological process of 'extrojection'; for Lovelace, 'the alteration of reality into fantasy' is finally 'reversed' (p. 139). Lams's argument at this point resembles George Haggerty's claim that *Sir Charles Grandison* reorientates the private imagination towards the realm of the public.

Henry Austen wrote after his sister Jane's death that, in spite of her admiration for Richardson's last novel, taste had secured her from lapsing into his prolixity. That judicious avoidance of tediousness is evident in the young Austen's compressed family playlet, *Sir Charles Grandison, or The Happy Man*, which is the prompt to a slightly enlarged reissue of Brian Southam, *Jane Austen's Literary Manuscripts: A Study of the Novelist's Development through the Surviving Papers*, which originally appeared in 1964. The 2001 edition incorporates a new, summary account of Austen's manuscript alongside a transcript and the story of its discovery and attribution (the last two items have already been published, however, in Southam, ed., *Sir Charles Grandison* [Clarendon, 1981]). A more sustained investigation of *Grandison*'s impact on Austen, Joe Bray, 'The Source of "Dramatized Consciousness": Richardson, Austen, and Stylistic Influence' (*Style* 35[2001] 18–34), compares the way in which first-person narrators re-enact past thoughts in the epistolary novel with the stylistic procedures third-person speakers employ to represent character in *Pride and Prejudice* and *Emma*.

Gloria Sybil Gross, 'In a Fast Coach with a Pretty Woman: Jane Austen and Samuel Johnson' (*AgeJ* 12[2001] 199–246), and John Wiltshire, *Jane Austen's 'Dear Dr. Johnson': The David Fleeman Memorial Lecture, 2001* also reconstruct a dexterous novelist exercised by her response to the eighteenth century (Gross's article is a foretaste of her monograph of the same title [AMS, 2002]). Gross's and Wiltshire's studies in the psychology of imitation usefully supplement earlier criticism on the grave and public Johnson's presence in Austen. Wiltshire argues that the private, unbuttoned sage of Boswell's and Piozzi's commemorations 'may have given Austen confidence in her presentation of a particular style of conversational interaction', and that 'it was this figure, superimposed upon the Johnson of the writings, who inhabited Austen's imagination' (pp. 10, 51). Gross is interested in 'the *process* rather than the product of Johnson's influence' (p. 204). Building on her *This Invisible Riot of the Mind: Samuel Johnson's Psychological Theory* [UPennP, 1992], she discerns in Austen a Johnsonian disquiet and subdued emotional chaos: 'Thus the novels close with barely the standard distributions of reward and punishment, triumph and failures, but with frustration and wistful hints at what was not' (p. 246). Finally, Li-Ping Geng, '*The Loiterer* and Jane Austen's Literary Identity' (*ECF* 13[2001] 579–92), examines the Austen brothers' bi-weekly undergraduate newsletter and review, whose title nicely mediates between those of Johnson's *Rambler* and *Idler*.

Alison Conway, *Private Interests: Women, Portraiture, and the Visual Culture of the English Novel, 1709–1791* is a rangy interdisciplinary study which formulates a new and persuasive definition of the eighteenth-century novel's investment in 'the act of beholding and of being beheld' (p. 211). In 1761 Rousseau repeated a standard complaint of the period about the eviscerating influence of private interests on public life. Yet in England, at least, an alternative argument—one that emphasized a connection between private interests and the development of community—was already competing with this refrain. The debate often centred on two sorts of objects, English portraits and English novels. In bringing the forms together, Conway attempts to establish the principal tenets of art criticism's understanding of the portrait, and to read the novel's reception history in terms of its close proximity to that of portraiture. She documents the parallel emergence of fiction and of the equally contentious and lowly genre of the portrait, especially as represented in the novel itself. Both forms were subject to connotations of sexual misconduct, commentators alternately praising and upbraiding the affective powers of each:

'Critics hostile to the novel viewed the intimate world it created as a breeding ground for illicit behaviour, while the portrait's detractors pointed to its relationship to solipsistic states of vanity and narcissism; advocates for the novel praised its ability to inculcate principles of morality and sympathy in its readers, and supporters of the portrait celebrated its role in establishing affective relationships between individuals' (p. 14).

Focusing on the prose fiction of Richardson, Fielding, Haywood, Manley, Sterne, Wollstonecraft and Inchbald, and the portraits of Hogarth, Reynolds, Gainsborough, Highmore and Hudson (among others), *Private Interests* discovers intimate relations between literature and painting, between female sitters, readers and literary heroines. Arguing, in a series of pertinent and enjoyable close readings, that the novel's representation of the portrait exhibits a tension between opposing conceptions of the self, Conway claims that private interests are depicted as simultaneously decorous and illicit: the portrait is at once an instrument of propriety and of scandal.

P.N. Furbank and W.R. Owens, 'Defoe's "South-Sea" and "North-Sea" Schemes: A Footnote to *A New Voyage Round the World*' (*ECF* 13[2001] 502–8), and 'Defoe and King William: A Sceptical Enquiry' (*RES* 52[2001] 227–32), investigate the possibility that Defoe constructed an imaginary intimacy between himself and William III on the basis of his friend William Paterson's genuine letters of advice to his monarch: 'If so, it would constitute one of the more amazing facts about this extraordinary man and prove, once again, the soundness of William Minto's admiring remark: "He was a great, a truly great liar, perhaps the greatest liar that ever lived"' ('Defoe and King William', p. 232). Fittingly, in a year that saw the publication of Beryl Bainbridge's fictionalized treatment of Johnson and his circle, *According to Queeney*, the complex relationship between fact and the eighteenth-century novel informs two critical enquiries. G.S. Rousseau, '*Ingenious Pain*: Fiction, History, Biography, and the Miraculous Eighteenth Century' (*ECLife* 25[2001] 47–62), surveys the persistence into our own time of a Georgian 'crossover of history and literature, biography and autobiography, and all four in every direction (especially the idea that fiction is history, biography autobiography, and vice versa)' (p. 48). Lisa Zunshine, 'Eighteenth-Century Print Culture and the "Truth" of Fictional Narrative' (*P&L* 25[2001] 215–32), interrogates Defoe's and Richardson's experiments with the truth-value of their writing as 'a case study for hypothesizing a conceptual framework sensitive to the ways in which the functioning of our evolved cognitive architecture *both* informs and is informed by specific cultural circumstances' (p. 217).

Two articles consider the folkloric origins of the eighteenth-century novel. Arlene Fish Wilner, '"Thou hast made a rake a preacher": Beauty and the Beast in Richardson's *Pamela*' (*ECF* 13[2001] 529–60), argues that 'Richardson is reworking themes popularized in seventeenth- and eighteenth-century adaptations of an ancient folklore, Cupid and Psyche, the source of the literary versions of *Beauty and the Beast*', in order to address tensions between older social hierarchies and the upwardly mobile middle classes (pp. 531–2). Patrick Parrinder, 'Highway Robbery and Property Circulation in Eighteenth-Century English Narratives' (*ECF* 13[2001] 509–28), discerns three kinds of highwayman in fiction, the aristocratic, the bourgeois and the benevolent rogue, the last of which is rooted in oral tradition, but turns out to be unsustainable even in radical or Jacobin prose: 'What the novel offers, instead, is the figure of a benefactor who radiates benevolence and patronage and yet ultimately reveals certain affinities with the robber' (p. 511).

John Skinner, *An Introduction to Eighteenth-Century Fiction: Raising the Novel*, begins with the disheartening acknowledgement that fewer and fewer people now read eighteenth-century novels. His select review of the last fifty years of criticism on the subject opposes 'universalist' to 'historicist' approaches, opening with feminist revisions to the canon in the 1980s before turning its attention to the seminal accounts of Ian Watt and Michael McKeon. The ensuing chapters continue to mediate between critics and theorists, seeking to forge an approach 'neither traditionally historical nor fashionably historicist' (p. x). Skinner's account is dogged by anomalies resulting from an attempt to make the evidence fit his binary conceptual model (which is strained to the point of collapse), rather than allowing his conclusions to evolve from the texts themselves. He tries to 'group eighteenth-century novels around "literary" (elitist male) and "non-literary" or "documentary" (female or *demotic*) poles' (p. 15). Readers might reasonably object that the 'literary' is not to be automatically equated either with the elitist or the male (is Daniel Defoe, a 'canonical' male novelist, in any sense an 'elitist'?). From these tendentious elisions within purportedly tough polarities, we proceed to 'a whole series of broadly analogous divisions' (p. 15) on which the subsequent paired readings (juxtaposing texts by Behn and Defoe, Sterne and Smollett, Lennox and Burney, Radcliffe and Godwin, and Austen) rely. Perhaps the most bewildering of these multiply qualified, obscurely gendered oppositions is that of the '*hieratic* (or esoteric and also, by association, elitist)' to 'the *demotic* (or popular)' (p. 15). As if this weren't enough to swallow, we are also asked to relish the 'amusing' quirk whereby 'the word *demotic*—once the s-for-sex letter has been removed—is a perfect anagram of *domestic*' (pp. 15–16). Would this donnish frisson (does 's' always stand for 'sex'?) have meant anything to the novelists concerned, especially as 'demotic' is not a 'perfect anagram' of 'domestic'? On such shaky foundations are the links between the popular and the feminine allowed to rest. Skinner is himself forced to admit, on several occasions, that his polarizations will not hold: Richardson must undergo 'a suitable sex-change'; Austen, although female, is 'hardly ... demotic', and each of the writers he considers as inhabiting one camp has a disconcerting tendency 'to gravitate towards the opposite' (pp. 26–7). A rule is only as good as the instances it covers: there are so many exceptions to the model presented by this book that Skinner inadvertently demonstrates 'the exhilarating variety' (p. 28)—and, happily, the conceptually resistant verve and mobility—of eighteenth-century novels.

Books Reviewed

Blewett, David, ed. *Passion and Virtue: Essays on the Novels of Samuel Richardson*. UTorP. [2001] pp. 312. $CAN55 (£30) ISBN 0 8020 3503 5.

Conway, Alison. *Private Interests: Women, Portraiture, and the Visual Culture of the English Novel, 1709–1791*. UTorP. [2001] pp. 328. $CAN65 (£40) ISBN 0 8020 3526 4.

Flynn, Carol Houlihan and Edward Copeland, eds. *Clarissa and her Readers: New Essays for the Clarissa Project*. AMS Studies in the Eighteenth Century 31. AMS. [1999] pp. 319. $84.50 ISBN 0 4046 3531 4.

Gilmore, John, ed. *The Poetics of Empire: A Study of James Grainger's 'The Sugar-Cane'*. Athlone. [2000] pp. x + 342. £16.99 ISBN 0 4851 2148 4.

Keymer, Thomas, and Peter Sabor, eds. *The Pamela Controversy: Criticisms and Adaptations of Samuel Richardson's 'Pamela', 1740–1750*, 6 vols. P&C. [2001] pp. 2,100. £495 ($795) ISBN 1 8519 6615 3.

Kingsley, Margery A. *Transforming the Word: Prophecy, Poetry and Politics in England, 1650–1742*. AUP. [2001] pp. 223. £32 ISBN 0 8741 3749 7.

Lams, Victor J. *Clarissa's Narrators*. American University Studies Series 4: English Language and Literature 194. Lang. [2001] pp. x + 172. $45.95 (£29) ISBN 0 8204 5162 2.

Malpas, Simon, ed. *William Cowper: The Centenary Letters*. Carcanet. [2000] xxii + 162. pb £12.95 ISBN 1 8575 4463 3.

McLaverty, James. *Pope, Print and Meaning*. OUP. [2001] pp. iv + 257. £50 ISBN 0 1981 8497 2.

Mounsey, Chris. *Christopher Smart: Clown of God*. AUP. [2001] pp. 342. £40 ISBN 0 8387 5483 X.

Noggle, James. *The Skeptical Sublime: Aesthetic Ideology in Pope and the Tory Satirists*. OUP. [2001] pp. xi + 269. £48 ISBN 0 1951 4245 4.

Overton, Bill, ed. *A Letter to My Love: Love Poems by Women First Published in the 'Barbados Gazette', 1731–1737*. AUP. [2001] pp.155. £27 ISBN 0 8741 3746 2.

Porter, Peter. *Saving from the Wreck*. Trent. [2001] pp. xvi + 202. pb £8.99 ISBN 1 8423 3055 1.

Roberts, William, ed. *Thomas Gray's Journal of his Visit to the Lake District in October 1769*. LiverUP [2001] pp. 160. pb £11.95 ISBN 0 8532 3667 4.

Ross, Ian Campbell. *Laurence Sterne: A Life*. OUP. [2001] pp. xi + 512. £25 ($40) ISBN 0 1921 2235 5.

Sitter, John, ed. *The Cambridge Companion to Eighteenth Century Poetry*. CUP. [2001] pp. xix + 298. pb £13.95 ISBN 0 5216 5885 3.

Skinner, John. *An Introduction to Eighteenth-Century Fiction: Raising the Novel*. Palgrave. [2001] pp. xi + 317. hb $65 ISBN 0 3337 7624 0, pb $24.50 ISBN 0 3337 7625 9.

Smith, Ken. *William Cowper: A Reappraisal*. Cowper and Newton Museum. [2001] pp. 91. pb £5.99 ISBN 0 9514 5701 2.

Southam, Brian. *Jane Austen's Literary Manuscripts: A Study of the Novelist's Development through the Surviving Papers*. Rev. edn. Athlone. [2001] pp. xvi + 159. pb £18.99 ($29.95) ISBN 0 4851 2143 3.

Spencer, Susan, ed. *The Eighteenth-Century Novel*, vol. 1. AMS. [2001] pp. 343. $89.50 ISBN 0 4046 4651 4.

Terry, Richard. *Poetry and the Making of the English Literary Past, 1660–1781*. OUP. [2001] pp. xi + 354. £45 ISBN 0 1981 8623 1.

Wiltshire, John. *Jane Austen's 'Dear Dr. Johnson': The David Fleeman Memorial Lecture, 2001*. Vagabond. [2001] pp. 58. $A20 ISBN 0 9578 3787 9.

XII

The Nineteenth Century: The Romantic Period

CARL THOMPSON, DANIEL SANJIV ROBERTS, SARAH WOOTTON, JASON WHITTAKER, EMMA MASON AND AMY MUSE

This chapter has six sections: 1. General; 2. Non-Fictional Prose; 3. Poetry; 4. Blake; 5. Women Romantic Poets; 6. Drama. Section 1 is by Carl Thompson; section 2 is by Daniel Sanjiv Roberts; section 3 is by Sarah Wootton; section 4 is by Jason Whittaker; section 5 is by Emma Mason; section 6 is by Amy Muse.

1. General

Amongst works falling under the category 'General Romanticism', perhaps the most impressive monograph published this year was Alan Richardson's *British Romanticism and the Science of the Mind*. A work of broad and insightful scholarship, this study takes as its starting point the pioneering brain science carried out by figures such as Erasmus Darwin, Charles Bell, Sir William Lawrence, the Frenchman P.J.-G. Cabanis, and the Austrians F.J. Gall and J.G. Spurzheim. In various ways, these researchers all advanced the biological science of mind—that is to say, an understanding of the mind as an embodied entity, its operations intimately connected to the workings of the brain and the nervous system. 'Only in the Romantic era,' Richardson points out, 'was the brain definitively established as the organ of thought.' The implications of this were far from trivial. The new science brought into question some profound intellectual and religious orthodoxies—including, *inter alia*, 'the existence of the soul, the necessity of God and the integrity of the self'—and as a consequence became strongly, although not exclusively, associated with avant-gardism and political radicalism. Inevitably, moreover, the shock waves of what Richardson here dubs 'neural romanticism' were felt in Romantic-era literary productions. A chapter on 'Kubla Khan' accordingly situates that poem in the context of Coleridge's lifelong preoccupation with emerging theories of the unconscious mind—theories which Coleridge was eager to explore yet which he was also, increasingly, concerned to reject, as he became ever more committed to a transcendent theory of mind. The new awareness of the role played by the body and the nervous system in organizing perception and shaping feelings, without any intervention from the conscious mind, is the subject of the next chapter; here the new science is shown as underpinning Wordsworth's commitment to the idea of 'organic sensibility', which in turn provides the basis for the Wordsworthian attempt to return poetry to a condition of 'natural language'. Chapters 4 and 5 focus on Austen and Keats respectively: *Persuasion* is discussed in relation to the growing contemporary conviction, soon to become a Victorian article of faith, that mind and character are shaped as much by innate, biological predispositions as by experience, while Keats's hospital training, which brought him into contact with some of the cutting-edge neural science of his day, is seen as giving rise to 'an unprecedented poetics of embodied cognition'. And in a final, wide-ranging chapter, Richardson argues that the new science underwrote an all-too-brief moment of 'embodied universalism'. Although this aspect of 'neural romanticism' was soon to modulate into more dubious racial and physiological theories, for a short period it enabled a remarkable empathy towards individuals and peoples that Western science had previously regarded as less than fully human: idiots, feral children, 'savages' and the like. Here as elsewhere, Richardson marshals successfully a daunting mass of contextual material, and then applies that material fruitfully to canonical literary texts; the result is a hugely stimulating volume that makes a significant contribution to Romantic studies.

Also impressive—and demanding—in its scholarly range was Philip Connell's *Romanticism, Economics and the Question of 'Culture'*. This study seeks to complicate our understanding of the relationship between Romanticism and those contemporary political, economic and social theories that literary critics generally lump together under the term 'political economy'. Connell's agenda is twofold. On the one hand, he aims to promote a better sense of what political economy actually was, in the period (roughly, the first half of the nineteenth century) in which it constituted '*the* dominant mode of social analysis'; on the other hand, he seeks to explore literary responses to, and representations of, political economy. These representations typically caricatured political economy so as to fashion a binary opposition between a hard-headed, and hard-hearted, 'scientific' attitude to social issues, and a more affective 'aesthetic' attitude, mindful not just of material things but also of larger human values. For Connell, this over-schematic division—to which most modern historiography continues to subscribe—obscures the subtlety and complexity of a wide variety of Romantic-era debates, and simplifies unduly the relationship between Romantic 'literary' writers and their supposed antagonists, the political economists. To redress this state of affairs, Connell offers some meticulous and finely nuanced contextualizations of Romantic literary texts. The first chapter explores the 'close, complex and often ambivalent relationship' between Malthus and the Lake school in the late 1790s and early 1800s. Thereafter, two long, painstaking chapters are dedicated to early nineteenth-century educational theories, and to Wordsworth and Coleridge's response to them (in *The Excursion* and *The Constitution of Church and State* respectively): Connell argues persuasively that what distinguishes the Lake school from other literary conservatives of the age is 'the depth of their commitment to the cause of popular education'. Chapter 4 explores the Cockney school's engagement with Malthus and Bentham, while chapter 5 situates Southey's *Colloquies on the Progress and Prospects of Society* in the context of contemporary debates about Catholic emancipation and the growing commercialization of society. The volume as a whole succeeds admirably in narrating the emergence of 'a rapidly widening fault line within British intellectual life', as political economy and literature are set against each other, while simultaneously demonstrating the extent to which this apparent division was actually an illusion conjured by literary writers.

If British Romanticism took shape partly in reaction to political economy, it also defined itself in opposition to new forms of mass entertainment. These are the subject of Gillen D'Arcy Wood's *The Shock of the Real: Romanticism and Visual Culture, 1760–1860*, which explores the emergence, in the later eighteenth century, of a recognizably modern visual culture. Adopting a critical perspective derived to a considerable extent from Theodor Adorno and Walter Benjamin, Wood argues persuasively that we need to extend some aspects of the Frankfurt school's critique of the modern 'culture industry' back into the Romantic era. For it was this period that first witnessed the widespread diffusion of visual images through British culture, brought about by a combination of new technologies, new marketing strategies by publishers, and a new mass audience in the form of the increasingly prosperous middle classes. The growing appetite for visual stimulation generated further phenomena that seem to us distinctively modern. A celebrity culture sprang up, as actors such as David Garrick and Frances Abington cashed in on their status as 'stars', cannily controlling and selling their images. Also emerging was a pronounced popular taste for 'the shock of the real': that is to say, for images which seem to offer an astonishingly direct, unmediated simulation of reality. And this tendency led in turn to ever more ambitious, large-scale visual spectacles: the special effects engineered by de Loutherbourg on the London stage, for example, and the total re-creation of reality seemingly provided by the huge panoramas and dioramas which came into vogue in this period.

Wood's main narrative, then, charts the progress of a culture taking its first steps towards the age of the Hollywood blockbuster. Closely interwoven with this main narrative are the horrified reactions of the highbrow cultural elite to this new cultural situation. Moving deftly between the visual and the literary, between high-, middle- and lowbrow forms, and between public and private modes of cultural consumption, successive chapters focus on Lamb's distress at 'the too close pressing semblance of reality' achieved by Garrick on the stage, Hazlitt and Reynolds's anxieties over the mass reproduction of paintings in the form of prints, and Wordsworth's attempt in *The Prelude* to elevate poetry over the new, highly popular panoramas. Chapter 4 then focuses on the Elgin marbles and Keats's reaction to them in his museum odes and 'The Fall of Hyperion': Wood's theme here is a different sort of 'shock of the real', the shock produced by the vigorous realism of the marbles, and their conspicuously dilapidated condition, which both served to confound established, idealistic notions of what Greek art should be. Finally, chapter 5 examines the use of illustrations in tourism and travel books, and brings Wood's narrative to a logical conclusion with the appearance of that quintessentially modern medium, photography.

It is partly in response to the new emphasis on a naive visual literalism, Wood suggests, that Coleridge insists so vehemently in his notebooks and lectures on the desynonymization of 'copy' and 'imitation'. Distinctions of this sort are central to Frederick Burwick's study of *Mimesis and its Romantic Reflections*. Here Burwick takes on the conventional wisdom, most famously expressed by M.H. Abrams in *The Mirror and the Lamp* [1953], that Romantic aesthetics are marked by a turn from mimetic theories of art (the mirror in Abrams's title) to expressive theories (Abrams's lamp). Burwick contests the traditional literary history by showing, first, that mimesis has always been a far more complex trope than is sometimes acknowledged, and secondly, that in its more complex and sophisticated aspects, mimesis remains a rhetorical strategy of central importance to Romantic writing. What changes, Burwick suggests, is not the principle of imitation *per se*, but rather the understanding of what it is, precisely, that imitation is supposed to imitate. Mimesis takes a self-reflexive turn as Coleridge, following Schelling, argues that what art imitates is not the world, but the mind beholding the world. To understand why it takes this turn, Burwick devotes the first half of his study to teasing out three key foundational principles that enable the Romantic reorientation of mimesis. The first of these, somewhat counter-intuitively, is 'art for art's sake', a slogan apparently coined in the 1800s: from one perspective a rebellion against the older, simplistic account of mimesis, this proclamation of art's autonomy is also, Burwick suggests, a vital first step towards a more subjectivist mimesis. Burwick then discusses the concept of *idem et alter*, identity and difference, from which proceeds an understanding of mimesis as 'a transformation in which an essential sameness is retained in spite of the otherness of its material mediation', before finally turning to the 'mimesis of the mind', in a chapter principally organized around that Coleridgean distinction between 'copy' and 'imitation'. In the second half of the book, Burwick expands on the literary enactment of this self-reflexive mimesis, focusing on tropes or topoi that enable the Romantic writer to hold up a mirror not to nature, but to other representations of nature. Thus chapter 4 considers the Romantic use of ecphrasis, with particular reference to De Quincey's *The English Mail Coach*, while chapter 5 considers the reflections and mirrorings that occur in the works of Coleridge and Wordsworth. Chapter 6 then examines fictions by Brockden Brown, Hoffman and Hogg in connection with the device of the 'twice-told tale'. Taken as a whole, Burwick's study is a work of somewhat daunting erudition. The first half especially makes few concessions to its reader: the narrative is heavily laden with technical terms, and perhaps wanders a little too freely between the Greek, German and British discussions of mimesis, with the result that the overall drift of the argument is hard to follow. Yet it is worth struggling with: it is ultimately a fastidious exposition of its subject, offering some finely nuanced insights into Romantic aesthetic theory.

Two useful studies published this year invited Romanticists to work with both children and animals, disregarding all injunctions to the contrary. The former were the subject of *Romanticism and the Vocation of Childhood*, in which Judith A. Plotz casts a productively suspicious eye over the Romantic and Victorian obsession with the figure of the child. Her subject more specifically is what she dubs the 'Romantic discourse of the essential child'. This discourse typically works to reify children into timeless, decontextualized and solitary figures—Lucy, the Boy of Winander and so forth—who are representative of an elemental, pre-cultural life, somehow simultaneously in touch with both nature and imagination. Understood in such powerfully honorific terms, childhood becomes a 'vocation' both for the child—who more often than not must be figured as dying before entering into adulthood—and for the adult writer, whose cultural authority resides in his ability to pass on to readers the wisdom and imaginative sustenance gleaned from his interaction with children. I use the masculine pronoun here advisedly: it is clear that Plotz considers the discourse of essential childhood to be very much a male invention, and a projection of various sorts of masculine fantasy and anxiety. It is accordingly a quartet of men—Wordsworth, Lamb, De Quincey and Hartley Coleridge—that Plotz discusses in four rich, if somewhat rambling, chapters. Each of these writers is impugned for an 'aesthetically embalmed apartheid'—one of the pleasures of this book is its vivid, punchy style—which allegedly traps real children in a dubious myth of childhood, with some highly detrimental results. Yet Plotz perhaps overstates her case here, through focusing too exclusively on this one particular mode of Romantic and post-Romantic response to children. Wordsworth in particular did not allow his fantasy boys and girls entirely to obscure his sense of the responsibilities owed to their living counterparts, taking a keen interest in contemporary educational debates and incorporating those debates into poems like *The Excursion* (as Philip Connell's study, reviewed earlier, makes clear). Yet with this proviso, this is a lively, stimulating study that interrogates profitably not only the Romantic construction of childhood, but also the extent to which we continue to subscribe unquestioningly to many Romantic attitudes towards children.

In *Kindred Brutes: Animals in Romantic-Period Writing*, Christine Kenyon-Jones offers a wide-ranging and enjoyable, if somewhat diffuse, survey of Romantic attitudes to, and representations of, animals. Diffuse, because Kenyon-Jones develops no particular thesis in relation to this topic. Rather, taking her cue from Lévi-Strauss's celebrated dictum that 'animals are good to think with', she pursues chapter by chapter—and even, to some extent, within each chapter—diverse lines of enquiry, reflective of the highly divergent uses to which animals were put in Romantic-era writing. Chapter 1 relates Byron's epitaph to his pet dog Boatswain to a tradition of 'theriophily', a sub-genre of satire in which animals are seen as morally superior to humans. Chapter 2 looks first at children's literature in the Romantic period, distinguishing between a Lockean and a Rousseauistic tradition in the genre's handling of animals, and then explores Coleridge's debt to this literature in poems such as 'To a Young Ass' and 'The Ancient Mariner'. Chapter 3 uses contemporary parliamentary debates about bull-baiting in Britain to shed light on the bull-fight stanzas in *Childe Harold* 1, and locates both in a larger framework of Burkean and anti-Burkean discourses. Chapter 4 considers animals as food, examining Shelley's vegetarianism and Byron's anxieties over meat-eating, while Chapter 5 ponders the relative infrequency with which animals appear as part of Wordsworth's conception of 'Nature'. Chapter 6, finally, explores how pre-Darwinian evolutionary ideas provided the writers of the period (and in particular Keats and Byron) with a rich stock of themes and images. Taken as a whole, the volume assembles a mass of fascinating material, and comments perceptively upon it: it will be especially useful to those concerned to trace the emergence in the Romantic period of modern ecological and conservationist attitudes.

John D. Morillo's *Uneasy Feelings: Literature, the Passions and Class from NeoClassicism to Romanticism* explores the close interdependence of the discourse of passion and the discourse of class in the eighteenth and early nineteenth centuries. Concerned to problematize the conventional periodization of literary history by finding discourses and structures of feeling which are common to both neoclassicism and Romanticism, this study is chiefly organized around the topics of enthusiasm and benevolence. Chapters on John Dennis's criticism and Wordsworth's *Prelude* address the first of these topics: both Dennis and

Wordsworth are shown as wanting to harness something of the sublimity and energy associated with enthusiasm, while simultaneously remaining wary of its taint of vulgarity, its association with political unruliness and, ultimately, its democratic tendency. A similar ambivalence towards benevolence is articulated in Alexander Pope's *Essay on Man*, the subject of Morillo's next chapter. On the one hand, Pope wants to insist that we have a natural desire to be charitable to each other and that this charity reflects the providential design of the cosmos; on the other hand, he must negotiate the awkward fact that this charity taken to an extreme would level all distinctions of wealth and rank. Such contradictions are energetically exposed by Byron: a chapter on *The Corsair* and *Lara* reads these poems as sceptical critiques of Pope, and also of Wordsworth, who in poems such as *Michael* exhibits an 'enthusiastic benevolence' that seeks 'to ground political action in fervent identification with the passions of others'. The final two chapters examine the ways in which the eighteenth-century debates on feeling underpin the political theories of Adam Smith and Karl Marx. Throughout his discussion, Morillo proves adept at probing the contradictions in both texts and ideologies; this is a wide-ranging, and frequently very thought-provoking study.

Three studies this year addressed the legacy of Romanticism, and the extent to which recognizably Romantic paradigms recur in twentieth- and twenty-first-century art, philosophy and politics. The most sophisticated of these studies was Richard Eldridge's *The Persistence of Romanticism: Essays in Philosophy and Literature*. This is a challenging, because genuinely interdisciplinary, collection of essays. Eldridge is a professional philosopher, and his work is an elegant attempt not only to use philosophy to shed light on literature, but also to use literature to interrogate philosophy. This is an endeavour underwritten by Eldridge's sense that a crucial feature of Romanticism is a cross-fertilization, or symbiosis, between these two areas of cultural activity. And this is just one of the dialectical, dynamic exchanges which for Eldridge constitute Romanticism. The Romantic attitude and the Romantic text as Eldridge understands them exhibit a constant, creative tension between a pull in one direction, towards transcendence, larger truths and grand totalizing statements, and a pull in the opposite direction, towards conjecture, inconclusiveness and what is here dubbed 'a lingering in process'. In substantiation of this view, Eldridge explores in the first section of his book a range of topics relating chiefly to the work of Kant, although there are also interesting discussions of the way in which Hölderlin's lyric writing constitutes a form of ethical thinking, and of Wordsworth's technique, in *The Prelude*, of simultaneously drawing conclusions from experience and allowing his poetry to constitute a test or critique of those conclusions. The second section, 'Twentieth-Century Philosophical Romanticisms: Wittgenstein, Cavell, and the Arts', explores analogous patterns of ethical thought and artistic expression in the work of more recent writers and philosophers, and by so doing seeks to demonstrate that recent claims regarding the death of Romanticism are much exaggerated. Throughout the volume, Eldridge's tendency to approach Romanticism through philosophical, rather than literary-critical, debates and discourses—his readiness, for example, to address problems in ethical as well as aesthetic theory—is both fascinating and refreshing: these essays offer a challenging yet invigorating perspective on a range of familiar authors and themes.

Christian Quendler's *From Romantic Irony to Postmodernist Metafiction* and David Beran's *Early British Romanticism, the Frankfurt School, and French Post-Structuralism: In the Wake of Failed Revolution* are also concerned to explore the legacy of Romanticism. Quendler's subject is literary self-reflexivity, and the use of metafictional devices to undermine the mimetic illusions created by literary texts. This has become almost the defining strategy of the postmodern novel, yet, as Quendler plausibly demonstrates here, it has a genealogy that takes us back to the theories of Romantic irony developed by Schlegel and Novalis. With commendable thoroughness and precision, although also in somewhat dry, over-technical prose, Quendler surveys these theories, and then explores how the romantic-ironic commitment to self-questioning, fragmentary texts finds expression in two novels of the period, Clemens Brentano's *Godwi* and Thomas Carlyle's *Sartor Resartus*. A bridging chapter focusing on the influence of Kierkegaard, Nietzsche and Derrida sketches the evolution from Romantic irony to postmodernism, and then postmodern inflections of self-reflexivity are explored in two further close readings of novels (namely, William H. Gass's *Willie Masters Lonesome Wife* and John Fowles's *Mantissa*). To his credit, Quendler is sensitive to the differences as well as to the similarities between the two aesthetics: romantic irony, he suggests, typically exhibits a joyous 'prospectivity', deploying self-reflexivity so as to gesture beyond itself towards possibilities of transcendence, while postmodernism is bleaker in tone, its self-reflexivity reflecting a mood of belatedness and a sense of the impossibility of transcendence. Yet the latter can arguably be regarded as an 'escalation' of the former, and Quendler's study, while containing little that is startlingly new, nonetheless constitutes a useful narrative of the stages by which this escalation proceeds.

Similarly useful, without being startlingly original, is David Beran's exploration of the theme of 'failed revolution' in Romantic and post-Romantic literature and philosophy. Beran's organizing principle is the fact that British Romantic poetry, the critical theory developed by the Frankfurt school in the 1930s and 1940s, and the post-structuralist thought emanating from France in the 1970s and 1980s, all seem to emerge out of a profound sense of political disillusionment. The apparent failure of the French Revolution to deliver all that it promised was a lifelong stimulus to Wordsworth and Coleridge; the fact that the Russian Revolution seemed to fail in similar ways was a vital spur to Max Horkheimer and Theodor Adorno; while Jacques Derrida and Michel Foucault evince repeatedly in their writings a frustration at the failure of the political radicalism of the 1960s to translate into any sort of revolution. This is hardly breaking news, and Beran acknowledges as much in his introduction. Yet the juxtaposition of these three cultural moments is a profitable exercise: there are some interesting continuities revealed as the Enlightenment attitudes inherent in the idea of revolution are revisited and revised by the three different generations, although the conclusions and insights Beran draws from his material are occasionally a little simplistic.

Four collections of articles were published this year. The most tightly focused of these, and the most innovative in its subject matter, was Russell and Tuite, eds., *Romantic Sociability: Social Networks and Literary Culture in Britain, 1770–1840*. Romanticism has traditionally been associated with the figure of the lone poet; from one perspective, it seems to reject an Enlightenment sociability, centred on the coffee-house and the club, in favour of retirement into a close-knit domestic circle.

The limitations of this view are amply demonstrated by the essays gathered here. Articles on the international republican community, Robert Merry and Della Cruscanism, romantic lecturing, and Hazlitt's theatre criticism (by Margaret C. Jacob, Jon Mee, Gillian Russell, and Julie A. Carlson respectively), explore the diverse ways in which sociability continued to be championed as, variously, a virtue, a right and a civic necessity. Jurgen Habermas's influential work on the eighteenth-century 'public sphere' underpins many of these pieces. Most of the contributors here are concerned to contest, or at least qualify, Habermas's account of the erosion of that public sphere in the latter part of the century; in cities and in radical circles especially, it is suggested, there persisted sites and modes of social interaction which enabled a significant degree of political critique and public expression. At the same time, a vivid picture is painted of an increasingly politicized culture, with many traditional modes of sociability increasingly coming under suspicion and, in some cases, state scrutiny: in this connection, a fascinating essay by James Epstein explores the changing protocols pertaining to social spaces such as the coffee-house and the London street. A secondary theme also fruitfully explored in this volume is the gendering of social networks, and the diverse ways in which women negotiated public and private spheres through their friendships and social circles. In this vein, Clara Tuite discusses Anne Lister's adoption of a scandalous Byronic persona, and Deirdre Shauna Lynch explores the extent to which shops constituted a female equivalent to the coffee-house and tavern. Issues pertaining to both radical culture and gender, meanwhile, are addressed in the two articles offered here on Anna Barbauld, by Anne Janowitz and Deirdre Coleman, and in Judith Barbour's article on William Godwin's fraught account of his relationship with Mary Wollstonecraft. Every one of the papers included here fully justifies the editors' bold claim that social networks need to be regarded as 'a kind of text in [their] own right, a form of cultural work ... which was a fundamental part of the self-definition of Romantic writers and artists': the collection as a whole opens up an exciting new area of Romantic studies.

Less coherent as a whole, but still containing a wealth of interesting material, is Kitson, ed., *Placing and Displacing Romanticism*. As the editor, Peter J. Kitson, discusses in his introduction, the contributors here understand 'placing' and 'displacing' in a variety of literal and figurative senses. The volume's rubric raises questions about the 'placing' of Romanticism in literary history, and about the placing of individual writers in (or out) of the Romantic canon; it raises questions equally about the strategies of 'displacement' and evasion that have recently come to be seen as so characteristic of Romantic literature. Finally, some contributors here also understand 'place' in a more straightforwardly geographical sense, and are concerned to trace the Romantic writer's engagement with his or her immediate environment, with the sites offered to them by the emerging tourist industry, and with more remote or exotic parts of the globe. Within this broad range of concerns, attention falls equally on major and minor, canonical and non-canonical, writers of the period. There are three papers on Wordsworth, two on Keats and one on Blake. Lucy Newlyn discusses Wordsworth's 'anxiety of reception' as he negotiates the problem of audience in a modern print culture, while Paul D. Sheats and Tim Fulford offer readings of, respectively, 'The Ruined Cottage' and 'The Haunted Tree', seeking in both cases to contest new historicist critiques which see these poems as evasive of socio-political realities. The pieces on Keats, by Michael

O'Neill and Thomas McFarland, are fascinating in their own right, but perhaps less obviously related to the volume's main themes: both discuss Keats as a 'Camelion' or mask-wearing poet, capable of great imaginative empathy. Angela Esterhammer's article on Blake, meanwhile, discusses *Jerusalem* in connection with a performative theory of language that sees utterance as creating place. Turning to more marginal figures in the Romantic canon, Philip W. Martin writes on John Clare, Michael Scrivener discusses John Thelwell's pedestrian writings, while John Williams discovers in an obscure literary dispute between Joseph Weston and Anna Seward an interesting anticipation of the critical controversy that will surround Wordsworth and Coleridge's *Lyrical Ballads*. Southey is the subject of two papers: Lynda Pratt reads *Joan of Arc* in the light of the other national epics being written in the 1790s while Philip Shaw discusses the poet's visit to Waterloo, making particular reference to the tourist industry which swiftly sprang up around the battlefield, and to the new forms of visual technology deployed by that industry. The latter aspect of Shaw's article is usefully complemented by Michael Charlesworth, who writes on panoramas, and the Romantic distaste for them. Finally, Mary Anne Perkins and Peter J. Kitson broaden the understanding of 'place' still further with an article apiece on cosmopolitan and nationalist tendencies in British Romanticism, and on Romantic representations of cannibalism.

Also wide-ranging in scope, and rich in its insights, is McDayter, Batten and Mulligan, eds., *Romantic Generations: Essays in Honour of Robert F. Gleckner*. Again, this is a very strong collection of essays containing work by some leading scholars in the field. The emphasis is principally on the major canonical figures, with Blake and Wordsworth especially prominent. R. Paul Yoder discovers in Blake a somewhat surprising respect for the poetry of Alexander Pope; Saree Makdisi offers a new reading of *America*; Glen Brewster draws out the political resonance of the images of composite bodies found in Blake's and Mary Shelley's work. With regard to Wordsworth, Matthew Biberman finds something new to say about that oft-visited topic, Wordsworth's relationship with Milton, while Scott McEathron excavates the different versions of *Michael* to show how Wordsworth developed a persona which would enable him to act as a conduit between rural and metropolitan society. Nigel Alderman looks at the problems besetting Wordsworth, Keats and Carlyle as they took on the role of professional 'man of letters', and Barry Milligan explores Byron's antipathy to Wordsworth and Castlereagh, paying particular attention to the treatment of sisters in Wordsworth's and Byron's poetry. A variety of more marginal texts and authors—all, interestingly, with an Irish connection—also come under scrutiny. Ghislaine McDayter offers a political reading of Caroline Lamb's *Glenarvon* that connects that novel to the Irish rising of 1798, Amanda Berry discusses the interplay of blindness and vision in Edmund Burke's work, John Waters recovers a tradition of Irish topographical poetry, and Guinn Batten explores the legacy of Romanticism in the work of W.B. Yeats and Paul Muldoon. Taken as a whole, this is an eclectic volume in terms of the critical methodologies adopted, yet it maintains throughout a consistently high standard of scholarship. It constitutes a worthy Festschrift to Robert Glecknor, and also provides a full bibliography of Glecknor's work.

While the three collections just discussed all focus exclusively on British Romanticism, Møller and Svane, eds., *Romanticism in Theory*, adopts a more global perspective, including articles on British, German, French, Scandinavian and

American writers. The articles are grouped under three headings. The first, 'Language and Semiotics', explores the diverse ways in which Romantic theories of language inform Romantic poetics. The Schlegel brothers are the primary focus of papers by Ernst Behler and Bengt Algot Sorenson, while Marie-Therese Federhofer discusses the semiotic implication of Novalis's mineralogical studies. Angela Esterhammer examines Coleridge and Wilhelm von Humboldt in connection with theories of linguistic performativity; Otto Fischer discusses the Swedish poet P.D.A. Atterbom in relation to changes that took place in this period in the teaching of reading and writing. The second section of the collection, 'Image, Imagery, Imagination', addresses visual aesthetics and 'the pictorial dimension of the creative imagination': there are articles here on Novalis and Tieck, Tieck and Hoffman, Turner and Wordsworth, Carl Gustav Carus, and Kierkegaard, by Alice Kuzniar, Andreas Bohn, Klaus P. Mortensen, Diana Behler and Isak Winkel Holm respectively. The final section, 'The Romantic Other', concerns itself with the Romantic fascination with the marginalized and repressed. Ib Johanson discusses Blake's *Tiriel* and *The French Revolution*; three essays in a Freudian-Lacanian vein, by Cecilia Sjöholm, Chenxi Tang and Ide Hejlskov Larsen respectively, explore Schelling's interest in the unconscious, Hoffman's depiction of male sexuality, and the representation of the split psyche in Walt Whitman and Emily Dickinson. Finally, Alain Montandon (writing in French) surveys a broad range of German, French and English Romantic writers so as to assert the paradigmatic role of the dream in Romantic conceptions of poetic language.

Turning to the individual articles, there were two explorations of the imbrication of Romanticism with the new intellectual disciplines taking shape in the period. W.J.T. Mitchell, 'Romanticism and the Life of Things' (*CritI* 28:i[2001] 167–84) focuses on natural history and anthropology, and explores how fossils and totems are both produced by, and help to produce, a distinctively 'Romantic' consciousness. Jennifer Wallace, 'Digging for Homer: Literary Authenticity and Romantic Archaeology' (*Romanticism* 7:i[2001] 73–87), uses the debate around the location of Homer's Troy as a lens through which to examine a formative stage in the disciplines of geography and archaeology, and at the same time probes the 'problematic relationship between imaginative writing and material culture' in this period. Two articles approached Romanticism from a Japanese perspective. Akiko Okada discussed 'The Reception of Romanticism in Japan before World War II' (*KSR* 15[2001] 88–106), while a line of influence flowing in the opposite direction was explored by Ciaran Murray in 'A Japanese Source of Romanticism' (*WC* 32:ii[2001] 106–8). Elsewhere in *The Wordsworth Circle*, John Beer offered an excellent overview of the various meanings and manifestations of apocalypse in Romantic writing in 'Romantic Apocalypses' (*WC* 32:iii[2001] 109–16).

There were also two issues of *The Wordsworth Circle* devoted to specific themes pertaining to Romanticism. In an issue on 'Transatlantic Romanticism', Joselyn Almeida's 'The Sight of a New World: Discovery and Romanticism' (*WC* 32:iii[2001] 148–51), an interesting survey of the trope of geographical discovery in Romantic poetry, emphasizes especially the many representations of Columbus. An issue on 'Romanticism and Interdisciplinarity: "Centres and Peripheries"' (*WC* 33:i[2001]), meanwhile, dealt chiefly with Victorian texts and themes. Of interest to Romanticists are pieces on Maria Edgeworth's *Harrington*, the native American missionary Samson Occam, Orientalist panoramas, Leigh Hunt and musical theatre, the literary representation of the smuggler, and the now largely forgotten poet Mary Howitt: Judith Page, 'Maria Edgeworth's *Harrington*: From Shylock to Shadowy Peddlers' (*WC* 33:i[2001] 9–13); Polly Fields, 'Samson Occam and/in the Missionary's Position: Consideration of a Native-American Preacher in 1770s Colonial America' (*WC* 33:i[2001] 14–20); Edward Ziter, 'Orientalist Panoramas and Disciplinary Society' (*WC* 33:i[2001] 21–4); Kathryn Pratt, 'Leigh Hunt's Melancholia and English Musical Theater' (*WC* 33:i[2001] 29–33); Elizabeth Teare, 'Smugglers' Daughters and Britain's Sons' (*WC* 33:i[2001] 33–5); Karen Karbiener, 'Scribbling Women into History: Reconsidering and Forgotten British Poetess from American Perspective' (*WC* 33:i[2001] 48–52).

Studies in Romanticism contained two articles that fall under the 'General Romanticism' rubric. In a paper which complements usefully Philip Connell's monograph (reviewed earlier), Tim Fulford, 'Apocalyptic Economies and Prophetic Politics: Radical and Romantic Responses to Malthus and Burke' (*SiR* 40[2001] 345–68), argues that the radical and Romantic response to Malthus is in part a matter of literary style, as writers were variously attracted and repulsed by the potent blend of sublimity and statistics that Malthus learnt from Burke. Andrew McCann, meanwhile, addresses the topic of 'Romantic Self-Fashioning: John Thelwell and the Science of Elocution' (*SiR* 40[2001] 215–32).

Two articles in *Eighteenth Century Life* will be of interest to Romanticists: Kim Wheatley discussed 'Comedies of Manners: British Romantic-Era Writers on America' (*ECLife* 25:ii[2001] 63–77), while David Duff wrote on 'Antididacticism as a Contested Principle in Romantic Aesthetics' (*ECLife* 25:ii[2001] 252–70). *Romanticism on the Net* ran two special themed issues, on 'Romanticism and Sexuality' and 'Romanticism and Science Fictions', the more generalist articles being: Richard C. Sha, 'Scientific Forms of Sexual Knowledge in Romanticism' (*RoN* 23[2001]); Bradford K. Mudge, 'Romanticism, Materialism and the Origins of Modern Pornography' (*RoN* 23[2001]); and Timothy Morton, 'Imperial Measures: *Dune*, Ecology and Romantic Consumerism' (*RoN* 21[2001]).

Finally, all Romanticists have a stake in the issues addressed in two eloquent essays by Susan J. Wolfson and Charles J. Rzepka. Wolfson, 'Our Puny Boundaries: Why the Craving for Carving Up the Nineteenth Century?' (*PMLA* 116:v[2001] 1432–41) ponders the present construction and periodization of the Romantic canon, while Rzepka, 'The Feel of Not to Feel It' (*PMLA* 116:v[2001] 1422–31), explores the extent to which Romanticism as a distinct area of academic study is in crisis, threatened on either side by the claims of a 'long eighteenth century' and a 'long nineteenth century'.

2. Non-Fictional Prose

In keeping with the massive historicization of literary studies over the last decade and more, recent years have seen the area of Romantic non-fictional prose expand its boundaries prodigiously. Where previously Romantic non-fictional prose typically referred centrally to the triad of personal essayists, Lamb, Hazlitt and De Quincey, and took in peripherally the writings of major political commentators such as Burke, Godwin, Paine or Cobbett mainly as a context for the supposedly 'literary' writers, the field has now expanded to include a range of writings across diverse disciplinary and topical areas, notably for this year (as indicated below), travel writing, political economy, political journalism, medical literature and Orientalist writings. Nor is this a matter of expanding 'contexts' for the study of literature: these writings have become an appropriate object of literary study in themselves, sometimes explicitly linked to issues of literary value, at other times implicitly treating value itself as a construct, and therefore open to revision. None of this is news to the literary scholar today; but the implications are immediately evident while reviewing the field.

The first task for many critics and scholars hoping to refine or even redefine Romantic studies (or, concomitantly, eighteenth-century or Victorian studies by extension or overlap) is often substantially a textual one. The urgency of placing texts at the disposal of a burgeoning scholarship already engaged with the writings in question, though necessarily only in rare editions or even manuscripts, is the motivation for four important editions reviewed here: *The Works of Thomas De Quincey*, edited by Grevel Lindop; Coleridge's *Marginalia*, edited by H. J. Jackson and George Whalley; *Travels, Explorations and Empires*, edited by Peter Kitson and Tim Fulford; and *The European Discovery of India: Key Indological Sources of Romanticism*, edited by Michael Franklin.

After the first seven volumes in 2000 (reviewed in *YWES* 81[2002]), *The Works of Thomas De Quincey* was augmented this year by a second series of seven volumes: volume 8, edited by Robert Morrison; volume 9, edited by Grevel Lindop, Robert Morrison and Barry Symonds; volume 12, edited by Grevel Lindop; volume 13, edited by Grevel Lindop and John Whale; volume 14, edited by John Whale; and volumes 17 and 18, edited by Edmund Baxter. This largely covers De Quincey's middle and later periods, when he was engaged in High Tory political journalism, political economy, fiction and criticism. His later pieces in volume 18 tend to turn towards an autobiographical and reminiscent mode, as De Quincey found himself at last lionized as a successful literary figure. Much of this writing, particularly the essays for *Blackwood's Edinburgh Magazine* in volumes 8, 9, 12, 13, and 14 as well as those for *Hogg's Instructor* in volumes 17 and 18, is here published for the first time outside magazine format, as these essays were uncollected in any of the several Victorian collective editions, both British and American, that established his literary reputation. De Quincey himself apparently regarded the bulk of his political writings as ephemeral or impossible to collect, but they are remarkable in indicating the extent to which his 'visionary' writing employs figurative language deployed in political commentary, and are thus interrelated. Each volume is annotated with headnotes, textual notes, explanatory notes and manuscript transcripts, making the series a major triumph of collaborative scholarship. The headnotes and explanatory notes are extremely helpful in recovering the immediate contexts of De Quincey's writings which have often been lost in the bland cohesive effect of the earlier collected editions, while the textual notes show how De Quincey often modified his texts substantially in response to his publishing environment. The manuscripts are also often interesting, for they show De Quincey at work, often tailoring his essays to the specifications and needs of his journal editors, and hence calling into question the issue of his agency as an author. When the edition is complete and indexed it will provide a monumental addition to Romantic prose studies, and will be of interest to a wide range of scholars on account of the extraordinary variety of topical issues and literary forms that De Quincey represents.

A timely accompaniment to the De Quincey edition is the critical monograph by Frederick Burwick, *Thomas De Quincey: Knowledge and Power*. Starting with De Quincey's famous distinction between the 'literature of knowledge' and the 'literature of power', Burwick seeks to apply this distinction to 'the many antagonisms and tensions he saw at work in society, in the arts, and in the individual mind' (p. xii). The argument focuses on a series of key texts and moments identified in each chapter. An amusing chapter on De Quincey's 'translation' into English of a hoax 'translation' of Walter Scott into German, exhibits De Quincey's playful sense of irony which Burwick contrasts effectively with the forger Willibald Alexis's more manipulative use of irony. The episode is highly indicative of the shaping influences of market forces in the production of authorial identity and fictional styles. Burwick's apparently throwaway suggestion to 'David Simpson, or Anne Mellor, or anyone else' (p. 65) that this may be seen as an appropriate case study for comparing English and German modes of Romantic irony might be developed further, if not itself intended perhaps ironically. Ranging through De Quincey's correspondence and manuscripts alongside texts in the new edition, as well as those in older editions (where not yet covered by the new one), this interesting book is an early indication of how the recent textual editing of De Quincey could transform critical study.

The extraordinarily difficult challenge of editing Coleridge's scattered marginalia has finally been brought to a close with the sixth volume of Jackson and Whalley, eds., *Marginalia*, over twenty years after the first volume appeared in 1980. The volume covers authors from Valckenaer to Zwick, including interesting and fairly extensive comments on Robert Vaughan's *Life and Opinions of Wycliffe* [1828], John Walsh's writings on reform in the 1830s, Daniel Waterland's *Doctrine of the Holy Trinity* [1734] and *A Vindication of Christ's Divinity* [1719], John Webster's *Displaying of Supposed Witchcraft* [1677], John Whitaker's *Origin of Arianism Disclosed* [1791], and William Wordsworth's *The Excursion* [1814], MS B of *The Prelude*, and *Translations of Aeneid*. Even a brief indication of titles suggests the range of theological, political and poetic concerns to which the marginalia testify. While Coleridge scholarship often seems to risk pursing ever more hypothetical sources that this famously omnivorous reader might or *must* have read, the marginalia provide precise and often datable evidence of Coleridge's engagement with other writers and are thus an excellent basis for intertextual study. Volume 6 also supplies the omissions of earlier volumes and an index, making the collection as complete as such a work can reasonably aspire to be.

Moving from author-based scholarly editions to critical editions offering to collect and anthologize thematic/generic concerns, we have, first, *Travels, Explorations and Empires: Writings from the Era of Imperial Expansion, 1770– 1835*, which addresses itself to the immensely diverse field of travel writing in the Romantic period. Following Edward Said's seminal *Orientalism* [1985], Romantic studies have been deeply preoccupied with the repercussions of his work for the period. The huge expansion of explorationist writings and the avidity with which these were read by the general public, as well as authors canonical and non-canonical, male and female, suggests the general complicity of readerly and writerly sensibilities in the imperialist project. Previously regarded as non- or sub-literary, these writings have been neglected until recently and are often difficult to find; the edition selects judiciously from the vast expanse of material available and offers itself to the general student of the period. Each of the volumes provides a helpful general introduction to the geographical area being covered and each of the individual selections is accompanied by brief biographical and explanatory notes. Some of the authors, such as William Bartram, James Cook, Constantin Volney, Karsten Niebuhr, and so on are well known; others are more likely to have been encountered by scholars interested in the more specific regions represented. The volumes are organized on the basis of geographical areas: volume 1, edited by Tim Fulford with Carol Bolton, covers North America; volume 2, edited by Tim Fulford and Peter Kitson, the Far East; volume 3, edited by Peter Kitson, the North and South Poles; and volume 4, edited by Tilar J. Mazzeo, the Middle East. A further set of four volumes will complete the set and cover Africa, India, South America and the Caribbean, and finally the South Seas and Australasia. Altogether this edition will be a very useful primary resource, especially for those working without the benefit of a major research library within constant reach.

Another editorial work citing itself in the area of post-Saidian Orientalist scholarship is the six-volume *European Discovery of India*. Franklin's selection includes several of the best-known 'translations' of Orientalist writings, such as those by William Jones, Charles Wilkins, and H.H. Wilson, as well as travel writing (represented by William Hodges's *Travels in India* [1793]) and critical writings on India and the East by the likes of Henry Thomas Colebrook and Carl Schlegel. His anthology is more diverse in generic scope than that of Kitson and Fulford and more basic in its apparatus, with a brief biocritical essay prefacing each of the selections and an index to each volume but no textual annotation. Franklin's selection emphasizes the favourable 'Orientalist' perspective (in its original eighteenth-century sense, rather than the Saidian one) on Indology, 'predicated upon respect for indigenous authority and resistance to missionary activity' (p. xvi), rather than the negative 'Anglicist' one, most famously exemplified by James Mill's *History of India* [1817], which mocked the pretensions of Indian culture and history. Other scholars may disagree with Franklin, arguing with Said that these oppositions, though real enough to the participants in such debates, were still deeply subsumed under imperialist ideology. In whichever way the case is argued, Franklin's edition will provide useful source material for readers interested in the outlines of Romantic Indology.

Philip Connell's complex and lucidly argued book *Romanticism, Economics and the Question of 'Culture'* examines the influence of political economy on a range of cultural issues marking the onset of economic modernity, such as the growth of literature, education and knowledge during the Romantic period. 'Culture' thus emerges from this study as a counterweight to the materialistic modes of economic discourse, a disjunction that has far-reaching effects on modernity. Although the topic of political economy is often seen today as technical and arcane, the very antithesis of poetry, Connell shows the extent to which public debates engendered by the writings of major political economists such as Malthus, Adam Smith, David Ricardo and others interact crucially with those of the more familiar Romantic literary figures and help to break down the rigid opposition between utilitarianism and Romanticism. A final chapter on 'The Politics of Romanticism' examines the results of the Victorian privileging of the Lake poets as central exponents of Romanticism and the modernist reactions of T.S. Eliot and F.R. Leavis. Despite the contentious nature of Romanticism for the twentieth century, Connell shows persuasively that the Victorians mediated it in a way that curiously homogenized Wordsworth and Shelley within the single construct of Romanticism. Also dealing with a major political economist, Tim Fulford's article, 'Apocalyptic Economics and Prophetic Politics: Radical and Romantic Responses to Malthus and Burke' (*SiR* 40[2001] 345–68), shows how Malthus's Miltonic and apocalyptic use of the sublime helped to shape the rhetoric of Romanticism. While Connell's approach to political economy is philosophical and argumentative, Fulford's is more linguistic and figurative, teasing out the rhetorical tropes that underlie the apocalyptic imaginings of figures such as Burke and Malthus, and arriving at similar conclusions regarding Wordsworth's and Coleridge's responses, through a very different route.

Two articles this year on John Thelwall suggest that his reputation as major radical but only a minor literary figure may be due for revision. Andrew McCann's 'Romantic Self-Fashioning: John Thelwall and the Science of Elocution' (*SiR* 40[2001] 215–32) looks at Thelwall's writings after 1800 when he emerged for the public as a teacher of elocution and the author of the first book that deals solely with speech impediments to be published in English, his *A Letter to Henry Cline* [1810]. McCann's argument is that Thelwall's theory of elocution may be seen as 'an everyday discursive practice ... implicated in a range of concerns that meld aesthetics with fields like anatomy, physiology, vocational training and liberal education' (p. 217). McCann shows how Thelwall's elocutionary practices were an extension of his more famous 1790s politics, though adopting a more conciliatory attitude, and turning his political fervour into a more acceptable cultural patriotism which views martial and elocutionary eminence as having the potential to unify national sentiment. Another essay dealing with Thelwall's apparent retreat from politics and arguing similarly for a more complex understanding of his position is Michael Scrivener's 'Jacobin Romanticism: John Thelwall's "Wye" Essay and "Pedestrian Excursion" (1797–1801)' (in Kitson, ed., *Placing and Displacing Romanticism*, pp. 73–87). Scrivener's article explores interestingly the politics of publication for a figure like Thelwall already marked by government for his suspiciously radical tendencies. Greater awareness of this fraught context allows for a more sensitive reading of Thelwall's carefully articulated politics in his comments on the rural economy and his descriptions of nature. Scrivener ends by arguing for the literary value of Thelwall's texts and places them with the canonical poetic texts of Wordsworth's 'Tintern Abbey' and Coleridge's 'Dejection' ode as equally to be regarded works of literature, sharing resonances of politics and nature.

James Mulvihill's essay on 'William Hazlitt on Dramatic Text and Performance' (*SEL* 41[2001] 695–709) looks at Hazlitt's drama criticism, particularly his theatre reviews, and other political and critical works, to argue for a reciprocity between Hazlitt's descriptions of theatrical display and of public life, particularly in the events of revolutionary France. This suggests his perception of a performative element in Regency cultural life. Hazlitt's despair at the drama of his own age reflects his view of the exceedingly dramatic nature of public and political life, which paradoxically rendered its (literary) drama inconsequential. In an interesting though slightly breathless essay, 'Leigh Hunt's Melancholia and English Musical Theatre' (*WC* 32[2001] 29–33), Kathryn Pratt also makes the link between the literary and public spheres occasioned by theatre criticism. In Pratt's view, Hunt's laments regarding the 'degraded condition of modern drama' are linked with his melancholia, which in turn is a symptom of a larger cultural depression from which he suffered from on account of the failure of political reform.

Michael J. Hofstetter's monograph, *The Romantic Idea of a University: England and Germany, 1770–1850*, tackles a promising topic somewhat disappointingly. Contrasting the conservative English system of university education with the intellectual ferment of German universities, Hofstetter provides a bland account of the university careers of several of the leading authors of both English and German Romanticism. Despite his treatment of Coleridge, for instance, Hofstetter's canonical and usually synchronic model does not allow him to stray into the more promising byways of literary history, such as the case of William Frend (Coleridge's tutor at Cambridge whose Unitarian beliefs resulted in his dismissal from the university while Coleridge was an undergraduate there) or to examine the development of Coleridge's thought on higher education from his early Pantisocratic days to his later position articulated in *The Constitution of Church and State* [1830]. A final monograph which I shall treat here in the context of non-fictional prose on account of its treatment of Coleridge, is Alan Richardson's elegantly argued *British Romanticism and the Science of Mind*. Linking literary Romanticism with the physiology of contemporary brain science, Richardson shows how the early establishment of this complex science during the Romantic period has certain precisely determined implications for the way in which we read the works of writers such as Wordsworth, Coleridge and Keats. Richardson's chapter on 'Coleridge and the New Unconscious' revisits the Preface to 'Kubla Khan' and the various comments on dream work and the unconscious that Coleridge penned in his *Letters* and *Notebooks* to reopen the problem of Coleridge's reluctance to publish one of his most celebrated poems. Richardson argues that Coleridge's late publication and hedging of the poem with defensive remarks indicates his reluctance to surrender his reputation as an idealist philosopher of *will*—not a new perspective by any means, but one that Richardson articulates with a degree of physiological detail that earlier accounts have lacked.

3. Poetry

A number of important publications on Keats appeared this year, including Richardson's *British Romanticism and the Science of the Mind*. The significance of neuroscience during the Romantic period is outlined, providing the context for an absorbing rereading of familiar authors, including Wordsworth and Coleridge— agreeing with Roe's approach in *Samuel Taylor Coleridge and the Sciences of Life*—while also focusing on Keats and Jane Austen. A revised version of 'Keats and the Glories of the Brain' (pp. 114–50), stressing the influence of Keats's training as an apothecary on his poetic conceptions of the mind and brain, is also included in Wolfson, ed., *The Cambridge Companion to Keats*. This is an indispensable guide, with essays covering Keats's poetry, language and letters alongside more recent concerns over politics and gender. Each contribution provides a condensed yet accessible survey of the subject, and the volume as a whole establishes the current position on Keats scholarship. All the essays are commendable, but worthy of particular note is Jack Stillinger's 'The "Story" of Keats'. To compress the poet's 'story' into one essay is impressive, but Stillinger also resists the temptation to give us a single history, attributing the longevity of Keats's poetry to the multiplicity of the self.

The issue of a 'multiple Keats'—the poet's 'unresolved imaginative dividedness'—was a popular topic of debate this year. Kitson, ed., *Placing and Displacing Romanticism*, is concerned with issues of place (in the literal sense of location), the place authors inhabit in relation to the canon and the context of their work. Reading historically is the governing remit of this collection, but two essays on Keats interrupt this trend. In 'Keats and the "Poetical Capability"', Michael O'Neill questions the applicability of this approach to an essentially ambivalent poet. Rather, our interest in Keats should be governed by the 'internal debate' within his aesthetic, the 'ability to inhabit contradictions'. Thomas McFarland's 'Masking in Keats' claims that the poet's authentic 'self' was a mask, successfully performed by the destruction of the primary self. McFarland demonstrates his argument through analysing the masks of Camelot and Hellas, but Keats's repertoire need not be limited to a double act. Jeffrey Wainwright contemplates both Keats's and Wordsworth's lack of fixity in 'The Uncertainty of the Poet' (*PNR* 140[2001] 9–14) and, in keeping with the topic, the critic declines to reach a conclusion. Irena Nikolova's *Complementary Modes of Representation in Keats, Novalis, and Shelley* also explores the indeterminacies that result from 'self-revisions and self-interpretations'. However, rather than suggesting an ultimate disunity in Romantic literature, Nikolova perceives a totality within corresponding modes of representation. On related themes and the issue of formalism were Hye-Young Park's 'Beyond Formalism: The Problem of Keatsian "Self"' (*KSR* 15[2001] 118–32), and Robert Kaufman's 'Negatively Capable Dialectics: Keats, Vendler, Adorno, and the Theory of the Avant-Garde' (*CritI* 27[2001] 354–84).

In 'Clouds, Sensation and the Infinite in the Poetry of John Keats' (*HudR* 53[2001] 599–606), Emily Grosholz explores the poet's use of clouds, mist and shadows to 'represent the indeterminacy of the immediate'. The senses are employed as a contrast to the specificity of vision, but the 'infinity of the immediate' can also be evoked through the expansion or extension of an image. Keats's aesthetic is also under scrutiny in 'Psyche's Progess: Soul- and Self-Making from Keats to Wilde' (*Intertexts* 5[2001] 7–22), in which Joel Black argues for consideration of the soul when discussing the self. The immediate association between Keats and the soul, and Wilde and self-making, is revised: Black outlines the latter's interest in the soul and the former's reliance on the self to create or achieve a soul. In 'The Endgame of Taste: Keats, Sartre, Beckett' (*RoN* 24[2001] 1–14), Denise Gigante marks Romanticism as the period in which 'taste as a means of aesthetic self-making begins to fail', and suggests that Keats's portrayal of nausea was essentially modernist. Gigante elaborates on this theme in 'Keats's Nausea' (*SiR* 40[2001] 481–510), in which taste, literal and figurative, relates both to the act of consumption and to Keats himself as a consumptive. The knight in 'La Belle Dame sans Merci' is *'too hungry to experience taste'* (original emphasis), while the poetical character of Hyperion suffers from nausea, induced by smell, indicating the poet's 'failures to allegorize, or sublimate, the material substance of the body'. Still on the issue of food, Michael Harbinson's 'Keats's "Roots of Relish Sweet"' (*N&Q* 48:ii[2001] 137–8) identifies the vegetable in 'La Belle Dame sans Merci' as a wild parsnip, known for its symbolic associations with love, serpents and hallucinations.

Ayumi Mizukoshi's *Keats, Hunt and the Aesthetics of Pleasure* challenges the notion of Keats's aesthetic separation from Hunt, arguing that 'the central link between Keats and Hunt—their appetite for leafy luxury—remained intact'. Mizukoshi demonstrates how Keats's poetry exemplified his mentor's principles, but the final stages of the book, in which Keats struggles with a Life of Thoughts, detracts from the overall argument. The primary recommendation of this book is the research into the 'bourgeois aesthetics of pleasure'. Context is equally important in 'John Keats, Barry Cornwall, and Leigh Hunt's Literary Pocket-Book' (*Romanticism* 7[2001] 163–76). Richard Marggraf Turley argues for the reinstatement of Cornwall into discussions of Cockney culture, largely as a result of a shared political dialogue with Keats which was grounded in seasonal imagery. Keats's political preoccupations are also the subject of 'Plebeian Gusto, Negative Capability, and the Low Company of "Mr Kean": Keats' Dramatic Review for the *Champion* (21 December 1817)' (*NCP* 28[2001] 130–41), in which John Kandl suggests that Keats consciously participated in 'the reformist challenge to Regency culture'.

A number of significant articles on Keats and gender were published this year. In '"Greater Love": Wilfred Owen, Keats, and a Tradition of Desire' (*TCL* 47[2001] 20–39), James Najarian notes how the representation of desire and suffering in the biographies of both poets suggests 'a closeted gay male', and argues that Owen's continued familiarity with Keats's poetry enabled him to 'create a homoerotic ethic'. Also on the theme of gender and literary inheritance is Margaret Homans's 'Amy Lowell's Keats: Reading Straight, Writing Lesbian' (*YJC* 14[2001] 319–51). Homans describes an odd coupling whereby Keats's sexual ambiguity and gender affinities enabled Lowell to express her same-sex tendencies. Moreover, Homans argues that their relationship was not one-dimensional, but provided Lowell with an 'endless variability' of gender roles. An aside on the issue of literary influence is Michael Harbinson's 'Keats and Dryden: Source or Analogue?' (*N&Q* 48:ii[2001] 138–40), while Ruth Richardson comments on the defamiliarizing effect of reading Keats's lecture notes in 'From the Medical Museum: Keats's Notebook' (*Lancet* 357[2001] 320).

Articles on individual poems included 'Keats's *Hyperion*: Time, Space, and the Long Poem' (*PoT* 22[2001] 89–127). Lilach Lachman discusses the conflict between space and poetic language, the estrangement between the world and the activity of writing, as a result of 'narrative experimentation' in the Romantic long poem. Mark Taylor's 'Marvell's Mower and Keats's Knight' (*LitI* 3[2001] 43–66) is a fascinating comparison of the two poems, highlighting the inertia of both protagonists; the mower is caught up in a positive cycle of renewal while the knight languishes in a negative degeneration. *The Explicator* featured a series of short articles on Keats's poems: Thomas C. Harrison's 'Keats's "To Autumn"' (*Expl* 59[2001] 125–8) focuses on onomatopoeia, Thomas Dilworth's 'Keats's "On First Looking into Chapman's Homer"' (*Expl* 59[2001] 124–5) discusses the change from metaphor to simile as the sonnet moves from octave to sestet, and Susan Parry's 'Keats's *Lamia*' (*Expl* 59[2001] 178–9) examines the symbolic significance of plants. In addition, Cook, ed., *John Keats: The Major Works*, is worthy of mention. By omitting *Otho the Great* and 'The Cap and Bells', this edition includes a good selection of letters, some prose, including the marginalia to Milton and

Shakespeare, and variant versions of 'La Belle Dame sans Merci' and 'The Eve of St Agnes'.

The issue of Shelley and politics proved to be as lively as usual this year. In a special edition of *Romantic Circles Praxis Series* entitled 'Reading Shelley's Interventionist Poetry, 1819–1820', Mark Kipperman queries the dismissal of Shelley's politics in *Mask of Anarchy*. Controversial in both form and content, associating Promethean virtue with the outcasts of society, 'Shelley, Adorno, and the Scandal of Committed Art' (*RCPS* May[2001]) asserts that 'Its utopianism is not a sign of political irrelevance'. In 'Shelley's Agenda Writ Large: Reconsidering Oedipus Tyrannus; or, Swellfoot the Tyrant' (*RCPS* May[2001]), Samuel Gladden is not such a devotee, commenting on the ease with which sexual transgression, part of Shelley's broader liberty-through-love agenda, can be appropriated by tyrants. Transgressive sexuality is also the subject of Barbara Judson's 'The Politics of the Medusa: Shelley's Physiognomy of Revolution' (*ELH* 68[2001] 135–54), in which the poet's employment of Medusa is seen to diverge from typical conservative representations. According to Judson, Medusa serves as an internal critique of Shelley's liberalism, reflecting both his desire and despair at the destructive prospect of libidinal excess. Reaching a similar conclusion, Christopher Hitt's 'A Sword of Lightening: Shelley's "Ode to Liberty" and the Politics of Despair' (*KSR* 15[2001] 64–85) examines not only Shelley's ineffective politics, but 'the limits and even perils of poetical idealism'—medium and message are doubly invalidating. By contrast, in 'Shelley and the Poetics of Political Indirection' (*PoT* 22[2001] 765–94) Andrew Franta argues that 'the indirection of poetic address is presented as a means by which to circumvent the impasse of contemporary political opposition'. In 'Flaming Robes: Keats, Shelley and the Metrical Clothes of Class Struggle' (*TPr* 15[2001] 101–22), Drew Milne questions our ability to discuss Shelley's politics at all. Echoing O'Neill, Milne points to the ahistorical, or autonomous, qualities of poetry such as 'rhythm, phonetic form and textual inscription'.

Stuart Peterfreund's *Shelley among Others: The Play of the Intertext and the Idea of Language* is a comprehensive study of Shelley's language and the issue of intertextuality from a perspective informed by Kristeva and Lacan. Contrasting Romantic poets is the subject of Alan Weinberg's '"Yet in its depth what treasures": Shelley's Transforming Intellect and the Paradoxical Example of Coleridge' (*RoN* 22[2001] 1–14), while Neil Arditi examines the privileged status accorded to Shelley's final fragment in 'T.S. Eliot and *The Triumph of Life*' (*KSJ* 51[2001] 124–43). Arditi focuses on the complex 'continuities and discontinuities between Eliot's modernism and Shelley's last poem', claiming that Shelley's darker view of sexuality, the shift away from a 'redemptive strain', appealed to Eliot's belief in the degradation of humanity. Robert Kaufman's 'Intervention and Commitment Forever! Shelley in 1819, Shelley in Brecht, Shelley in Adorno, Shelley in Benjamin' (*RCPS* May[2001]) explores the poet's influence on the left modernists and Frankfurt school, while William Stroup's 'Henry Salt on Shelley: Literary Criticism and Ecological Identity' (*RCPS* November[2001]) considers Salt's interest in Shelley's humanitarianism, and the possibility of employing the 'pre-professional cultural critic' as a model for contemporary ecocriticism. In '"Mont Blanc": Transcendence in Shelley's Relational System' (*L&T* 15[2001] 159–71), Fazel Abroon contributes to the subject of Shelley's Platonism.

Of the articles on particular poems, *The Cenci* attracted a good deal of interest. Kris Steyaert's meticulously researched 'A "Massive dramatic plum pudding": The Politics of Reception in the Early Antwerp Performance of Shelley's *The Cenci*' (*KSJ* 51[2001] 14–26) discusses performances of the play by the Royal Dutch Theatre in January 1929. Rather than reflecting a sanitized view of the poet, the reception of this production recalled the 'inflammatory power' of both Shelley and his play. On a more recent performance, Scott Masson's 'Review of *The Cenci*: Performed at the People's Theatre, Newcastle' (*KSR* 15[2001] 47–8) confirmed both the dramatic nature of the work and the deficiencies of the play in production. Mark J. Bruhn's '"Prodigious mixtures and confusions strange": The Self-Subverting Mixed Style of *The Cenci*' (*PoT* 22[2001] 713–64) argues that, in contrast to Shelley's aesthetic principles, his play can be seen as radically mixed and 'realistic'. Viewed in the light of Racinian tragedy or post-Restoration English drama, *The Cenci* represents a 'revolutionary anticipation' of twentieth-century approaches to mimesis. In 'Shelley Laughs: Comic Possibilities in *The Cenci*' (*KSR* 15[2001] 44–6), Christopher Goulding identifies 'some light relief' in one of Shelley's darkest works, whereas John Bleasdale's '"To Laughter": Shelley's Sonnet and Solitude' (*RoN* 22[2001] 1–16) perceives a more pessimistic and critical voice in the apparently jovial.

Other articles on individual poems included '"Here is thy fitting temple": Science, Technology and Fiction in Shelley's *Queen Mab*' (*RoN* 21[2001] 1–16). Robert Mitchell identifies how Shelley's annotations to this poem attempt to 'scientifically verify' his imagery. In turn, the 'various sciences are themselves unified by a vision that only poetry can provide'. Ross Woodman's 'Figuring Disfiguration: Reading Shelley after De Man (*SiR* 40[2001] 253–88) explores the legacy of De Man's readings, and also worthy of mention is Toby Venables's prizewinning essay on 'Ozymandias', 'The Lost Traveller' (*KSR* 15[2001] 15–21). Christopher Goulding also reproduced 'An Unpublished Shelley Letter' (*RES* 52[2001] 233–7), dated 27 August 1820, in which the poet discusses, amongst other topics, *A Philosophical View of Reform*, previously thought to have been finished before this time. For those interested in representations of the Romantic poets in literature, Alan Halsey's *The Text of Shelley's Death* consists of an imaginative reconstruction of the days before and after Shelley's death, and an original poem. Byron also makes an appearance in M.R. Lovric's *Carnevale*, which charts the heroine's fictional encounters with famous residents of Venice.

Following recent laments on the state of Byron studies, Brewer, ed., *Contemporary Studies on Lord Byron*, strikes an upbeat note. Brewer begins his introduction by proclaiming that 'As the new millennium begins, students of Byron's life, poetry, and prose have much to celebrate', and predicts that 'we can reasonably expect to see a host of scholarly re-examinations of this central Romantic figure during the twenty-first century'. If the current collection is an indicator of this trend, acknowledging the 'multi-faceted Byronic "self"' in essays on politics, literary influences and successors, sexuality and gender, and neglected poems and plays, expectations will be high. Karen McGuire's 'Byron Superstar: The Poet in Neverland' investigates the cult of celebrity, comparing the self-conscious performativity of the poet with the pop icon Michael Jackson. To give another example, Jonathan Gross's 'Epistolary Engagements: Byron, Annabella, and the Politics of 1813' traces the course of the poet's relationship with his wife from the rejection of his role as libertine to the homosocial transactions over an insignificant female.

From his wife to an infamous affair: Susan Normington's *Lady Caroline Lamb: This Infernal Woman* attempts to recover the life of an intelligent, wilful woman whose potential was thwarted by the time in which she lived. Normington's account of her relationship with Byron rehearses well-trodden ground, recording rather than enquiring about the story. Byron is reduced to the archetypal 'rake' while Lamb's conduct remains unaccountable. A more successful work on Byron's relationships is Jeffrey W. Vail's *The Literary Relationship of Lord Byron and Thomas Moore*, in which the author asserts that 'Thomas Moore was a larger presence in Byron's life and work than any other contemporary writer'. Vail reminds us of the strong affinities between these two men, particularly in terms of their popularity. Although neglected now, Moore's poetry, particularly his use of form, influenced Byron, and in turn Byron influenced, or was featured in, much of Moore's later work. Vail also argues for the continuing significance of Moore's biography, given his intimacy with the poet and understanding of Byron's theatrical guises. Byron's acquaintances also feature strongly in *The Byron Journal*, which includes articles on Thomas Taylor and Alexander Scott, alongside discussions of the poet's afterlife in biography, portraits and the multimedia.

Byron's relationships with men and women were not the only subjects of interest; Christine Kenyon-Jones's *Kindred Brutes: Animals in Romantic-Period Writing* explored man's kinship with animals. Kenyon-Jones discusses Shelley, Coleridge and Wordsworth—also the subject of Kurt Fosso's '"Sweet Influences": Human/Animal Difference and Social Cohesion in Wordsworth and Coleridge, 1794–1806' (*RCPS* November[2001])—but Byron remains the focus. This book ably fills the lacuna on the Romantic poets' interest in, depictions of and engagements with philosophical debates on animals in the age preceding Charles Darwin. The influence of evolutionary concepts and geological theories on Keats, Shelley and Byron is the subject of Kenyon-Jones's '"When this world shall be former": Catastrophism as Imaginative Theory for the Younger Romantics' (*RoN* 24[2001] 1–9). Kenyon-Jones's diversity and lucid style is also apparent in her contribution to a special edition of *European Romantic Review* entitled 'Byron and Disability', and edited by Andrew Elfenbein. This collection of essays is intended to rectify a noticeable gap in Byron studies, and, as Rosemarie Garland Thomson argues, provide a model for new disability studies. Through an analysis of *The Deformed Transformed*, an interpretation of disability as difference, and even distinction, becomes possible. Andrew Elfenbein, for example, argues against the myth that the disabled compensate for their 'supposed handicap', while Kenyon-Jones points to the degree of licence it offered Byron to 'express his antipathy towards many kinds of oppressive orthodoxy'.

As noted below in relation to Wordsworth, the significance of place received much critical attention. John Beckett's *Byron and Newstead: The Aristocrat and the Abbey* studies the poet's connection with his ancestral home, and attempts to overcome the bias towards viewing Byron as a poet rather than an aristocrat. Through a consideration of financial records, Beckett places Byron within his cultural context and emphasizes that for someone so conscious of his social position, 'by selling Newstead he failed his caste'. The significance of place is similarly stressed in Stephen Cheek's 'Being There: Byron and Hobhouse Seek the "Real"

Parnassus' (*Romanticism* 7[2001] 236–44), while Jennifer Wallace focuses on 'temporal and spatial poetics' in 'Digging for Homer: Literary Authenticity and Romantic Archeology' (*Romanticism* 7[2001] 73–85). William J.P. Neish's *The Speaking Eye: Byron's Aberdeen—People, Places and a Poem* provides a wealth of detail about the poet's early life in Aberdeen and the people he knew. One of the principal motivations behind Neish's book, however, is the search to authenticate a poem entitled 'Old Pupil', written to a former teacher of Byron. After engaging the quantitative methods of cusum plots, Neish is fairly convinced that Byron is the author, but of greater interest is his appendix listing the usage of a phrase that appears in the poem, 'speaking eye'.

Byron's use of language, or more specifically 'bad language', was the subject of a few articles, including Charles LaChance's 'Byron's Bad English' (*English* 50[2001] 111–25). According to LaChance, 'The bad English of *Don Juan* denotes the viciousness of existence', generating the pretence of honesty through dissonance. The subversiveness of Byron's language is also the subject of Gary Dyer's 'Thieves, Boxers, Sodomites, Poets: Being Flash in Byron's *Don Juan*' (*PMLA* 116[2001] 562–78). Dyer identifies a shared code of communication between sodomites, criminals and boxers that is apparent throughout Byron's epic poem. Rather than a sign of freedom, Dyer reads this language as the product of constraint.

Byron's influence is also discussed in Caroline Franklin's *Byron and Women Novelists*, the published text of a lecture given at the University of Nottingham in March 2001. Franklin argues that the image of Byron as a libertine enabled women writers, most notably Harriet Beecher Stowe, to critique his immorality, thus reaffirming their religious and feminist convictions, while also questioning Calvinism. Andrew Elfenbein's 'Paranoid Poetics: Byron, Schreber, Freud' (*RoN* 23[2001] 1–23) discusses Freud's admiration, via Schreber, for Byron, which is somewhat surprising given that 'Byron challenges the hegemony of psychiatry's internalization of the libido'. Ian Dennis examines the figure of the victim-hero in '"Making death a victory": Victimhood and Power in Byron's "Prometheus" and "The Prisoner of Chillon"' (*KSJ* 51[2001] 144–61), while in '"The gory head rolls down the giants' steps!": The Return of the Physical in Byron's *Marino Faliero*' (*ERR* 12[2001] 226–36), Melynda Nuss discusses Byron's critique of the stage, with *Marino Faliero* 'illustrating both the drama's ability to communicate and its failure'. Also worth mentioning is James Soderholm's 'Byron and Romanticism: An Interview with Jerome McGann' (*NLH* 32[2001] 47–66), in which McGann discusses a number of current issues relating to 'Cultural Studies legacies', teaching Byron and the poet as an unheroic figure. On the subject of Byron's politics, James Soderholm's 'A Tale of Two Citizens: Byron, Wordsworth, and Political Idealism' (*ByronJ* 29[2001] 72–8) contrasts the poets' 'ideals of citizenship' with regard to their respective treatments of Beaupuy and Rousseau. Gordon Spence wrote on 'Natural Law and the State in *The Two Foscari*' (*ByronJ* 29[2001] 27–35), while Andrea Casadio discussed Byron's increasing irritation with the local representatives of papal power in Ravenna (*ByronJ* 29[2001] 90–7). The *John Clare Society Journal* celebrated its twentieth birthday with Jonathan Bate rectifying a number of errors in biographies of Clare, Sara Lodge discussing 'The Mole Catcher', and numerous articles recovering or reconstructing the poet's work alongside original poems and eye-catching illustrations.

The main editorial Coleridge publication of 2001 was Mays, ed., *The Collected Works of Samuel Taylor Coleridge: Poetical Works*. *Poems* consists of four parts, two reading texts and two variorum texts, and is arranged chronologically from 1782 to 1834. Mays selection of reading text is admittedly subjective, the governing principle being to 'give the version of the poem which reflects Coleridge's concern, up to the time he lost interest'. While this raises immediate concerns, Mays reassures us that 'The text for each poem in all but a few cases selects itself', and defends his editorial approach by stating that 'consistency could become a self-denying ordinance'. The benefits of the 'variable copytext' are evident in the reading text of *The Rime of the Ancient Mariner* where the 1798 *Lyrical Ballads* version and the 1834 *Poetical Works* version are reproduced on facing pages. Annotations, which are kept to a minimum throughout this edition, only appear alongside the 1834 version, highlighting Coleridge's own editorial addition of the marginal glosses. Mays is keen, however, to move away from 'an essential poetic core of some dozen poems'; accordingly, more than 300 fragments and poems of dubious authenticity have been added since Ernest Hartley Coleridge's edition. The variorum text is intended as an indispensable companion to the reading text, but at first glance resembles what the editor himself describes as 'an algebraic nightmare'. Mays has adopted a European method of display, beginning with the earliest version of a poem and incorporating revisions vertically down the page. The scholarship and detailed research necessary to accumulate all these variants is almost bewildering. Mays modestly claims that he does not intend *Poetical Works* to be the definitive edition of Coleridge's poetry, but it certainly will be for the foreseeable future. Jackson and Whalley, eds., *Marginalia VI*—Valckenaer to Zwick—also appeared in 2001, including Coleridge's annotations on Wordsworth's poetry.

Another major publication was Roe, ed., *Samuel Taylor Coleridge and the Sciences of Life*. Roe's objective is to further erode the 'traditional views of Romantic transcendence [that] have continued to be prominent in studies of this author' by emphasizing the 'diversity of Coleridge's interests and achievements'. Roe and a number of contributors to this collection of essays stress Coleridge's interest in scientific discoveries and debates, 'notably optics, chemistry, geology, anatomy, and medicine', but the sciences of life are also interpreted more broadly. Essays engage with a range of discourses, from politics and theories of race to language. The author and his work are re-explored in context, but a voice of somewhat Coleridgean dissent emerges in Kelvin Everest's essay on the persistent problems of historical method, particularly in relation to electronic editions. Coleridge and science fiction is a prominent theme in Beth Lau's essay on '*The Rime of the Ancient Mariner* and *Frankenstein*' and Daniel Burgoyne's 'Coleridge's "Poetic Faith" and Poe's Scientific Hoax' (*RoN* 21[2001] 1–16). Burgoyne explores 'scientific and futuristic hoaxes in the early nineteenth century', and discusses how the hoax became a 'literary gesture' in the work of Poe and Coleridge. Focusing on the supernatural aspects of Coleridge's poetry, Burgoyne explores a character's suspension of disbelief and the reader's subsequent acceptance of the plausibility of an event, which, in turn, reinforces the boundaries of external reality.

From science to philosophy, David P. Haney's *The Challenge of Coleridge: Ethics and Interpretation in Romanticism and Modern Philosophy* examines the connections, or 'conversations', between Romantic theories of interpretation and ethics and those of modern philosophers on the same subject. Rather than applying contemporary philosophy to Coleridge's poetry, using the 'sophisticated' approaches of the present to comprehend the past, Haney engages Coleridge in a debate which both illuminates his own work and challenges that of others. The relationship between Coleridge and Emerson also featured heavily in articles published this year. In 'Self-Reliance: Individualism in Emerson and Coleridge' (*Symbiosis* 5[2001] 51–68), David Vallins re-examines Emerson's 'temporary renunciation of his enthusiasm for English Romanticism (and especially for Coleridge)'. Vallins observes Coleridge's influence on Emerson's most significant work, not only in terms of the democratization of genius, but on the issues of individual character and destiny. Eric Wilson's 'Coleridge, Emerson, and Electromagnetic Hermeticism', Joel Pace and Chris Koenig-Woodyard's 'Coleridge and Divine Providence: Charles King Newcomb, and Ralph Waldo Emerson', and J. Robert Barth and Elizabeth C. Nordbeck's 'Coleridge's Orthodoxy in Transcendentalist New England' all appeared in the *Wordsworth Circle* (*WC* 32[2001] 134–7, 138–41, 142–4). Another article that explores the issue of literary influence is Seamus Perry's 'Coleridge, Bunyan, and the Arts of Bafflement' (*WC* 32[2001] 89–95).

A number of articles focused on Coleridge's most prominent poems, particularly *Christabel*. J. Robert Barth's '"In the midnight wood": The Power and Limits of Prayer in *Christabel*' (*WC* 32[2001] 78–83) discusses the temptation to read Christabel and Geraldine as binary opposites, and structure the themes of order and disorder, spiritual and fleshly energies on this separation. Barth argues that these 'warring forces' are found in both characters, and a lack of reconciliation renders the completion of the poem impossible. Moving on to the theme of the title, Barth sees prayer as a redeeming factor, providing hope and vision in an otherwise fractured experience of humanity. Christian la Cassagnère's 'The Strangeness of *Christabel*' (*WC* 32[2001] 84–8) also explores dichotomies or, more specifically, 'the double'. Cassagnère views Christabel and Geraldine as mirror images, with the latter reflecting what the former has 'disowned or negated'; Geraldine is the 'alien within', the Other, with the poem staging an 'uncanny moment' of recognition. From this psychoanalytical perspective, the ethics of good and evil become irrelevant. In 'Making Christabel: Sexual Transgression and its Implications in Coleridge's "Christabel"' (*JH* 41[2001] 145–65), Benjamin Scott Grossberg argues for a reading of the poem in which the social and psychological consequences of lesbianism are prioritized above the demonization of Geraldine. The 'unnatural' nature of Christabel and Geraldine's courtship, highlighted by the gender role reversals, results in secrecy, guilt and disgrace; by reinventing herself as 'a passive tool of orthodoxy', Geraldine is able to reclaim some power within the patriarchy. The problem with Grossberg's approach is that he attempts to resolve 'the almost unanswerable ambiguities of this poem', overlooking, for example, the transgressive histories of both women prior to their first encounter.

By contrast, in 'The "Invention" of a Meter: "Christabel" Meter as Fact and Fiction' (*JEGP* 100[2001] 511–36) Brennan O'Donnell explores a heightening of ambiguity through the archaic use of syllable, stress and verse paragraphing. Anya Taylor's 'Coleridge and the Pleasures of Verse' (*SiR* 40[2001] 547–69) similarly focuses on metre and Coleridge's status as 'among the most purposeful practitioners of verse as verse in his era'. For Coleridge, 'musical perfection' could improve character, and, most importantly, generate pleasure. For example, in both *Christabel* and *The Rime of the Ancient Mariner* sounds generate a pitch of anxiety which can be enjoyed by the reader (although I am not convinced his 'supernatural poems frighten' or that Coleridge would have been happy with the label of 'zany' to describe some of his poems). Nicholas Reid's 'Coleridge, Language, and Imagination' (*RoN* 22[2001] 1–22) considers how the recent rise of linguistic theory has over-emphasized Coleridge's interest in this subject. Reid argues that the 'conventionality of language was a sign of its limitation' for the poet, rendering it of secondary importance to the concerns of form and the imagination.

Unsurprisingly, *The Rime of the Ancient Mariner* attracted much critical attention. Warren Stevenson's *A Study of Coleridge's Three Great Poems: Christabel, Kubla Khan, and The Rime of the Ancient Mariner* concentrates on the poet's 'inner canon', but is primarily concerned with *The Rime of the Ancient Mariner*. Consisting of revised essays from the last forty years, the book demonstrates a range of eclectic approaches, from biographical, cultural and geographical, to an interest in form, symbol and mythology. In 'Coleridge, Violence and *The Rime of the Ancient Mariner*' (*Romanticism* 7[2001] 41–57), R.A. Foakes also attempts to find 'another way of understanding' the poem by reading it in the light of the Cain and Abel story. This story, Foakes argues, has parallels with Coleridge's tale. Cain is regarded as amoral, yet, conversely, he is seen as in control of his destiny. Similarly, the Mariner is guilty of an arbitrary act of violence which can be seen as a way of defining the self. In Scott Hess's lucid article 'The Wedding Guest as Reader: "The Rime of the Ancyent Marinere" as a Dramatization of Print Circulation and the Construction of the Authorial Self' (*NCStud* 15[2001] 19–36), the relationship between the Mariner and the wedding guest parallels that of author and reader. Coleridge dramatizes the desire to dictate a reader's experience of his poem, and thereby lessen the anxiety of reception. Hess states that the poem can be read in terms of Romantic self-representation, while also examining the historical context of print circulation with the wedding guest representing one of the 'autonomous individuals' who share experiences through the text.

Coleridge's 'Hymn before Sun-rise' also attracted critical interest in Angela Esterhammer's 'Coleridge's "Hymn before Sun-rise" and the Voice Not Heard' (in Roe, ed., pp. 224–45) and Morton D. Paley's '"This valley of wonders": Coleridge's *Hymn before Sun-rise in the Vale of Chamouni*' (*ERR* 12[2001] 351–71). 'Hymn before Sun-rise' provides the focus for Matthew C. Brennan's 'Coleridge, Friedrich, and the "Hymn" to Mountain Glory' (*LJHum* 26[2001] 21–38). For both Coleridge and Friedrich, Nature evokes 'longings for God's presence' which is sometimes revealed in 'visions unifying perceiving artist and perceived landscape'. Poet and painter are alike in their ultimately frustrated desire for 'spiritual transcendence and unity'.

Two articles focused on Coleridge's relationship with James Mackintosh which, according to John Beer in 'Coleridge, Mackintosh and the Wedgwoods: A Reassessment, Including some Unpublished Records (*Romanticism* 7[2001] 16–40), ranged from 'bitter criticism, through cynical satire to expressions of high regard'. Both Beer's article and Edmund Garratt's '"Lime blossom, bees & flies": Three Unpublished Letters of Samuel Taylor Coleridge to Sir James Mackintosh' (*Romanticism* 7[2001] 1–15) rely on original archive material with, for example, one of Coleridge's previously unseen letters lamenting the practical consequences of his 'religious and political creeds'. An interesting aside is David Chandler's suggestion of 'A Source for Southey and Coleridge's 'Green Light ... in the West' (*N&Q* 48[2001] 128–9). Chandler proposes that both authors received their inspiration, for 'Dejection: An Ode' and *Madoc* respectively, from Jacques-Henri Bernardin de Saint-Pierre's *Études de la Nature*.

On the issue of religion, Mark Canuel's article on 'Coleridge's Polemic Divinity' (*ELH* 68[2001] 929–63) discusses the organized dissent of *The Watchman*. According to Canuel, 'Religious dissent acquires a positive value' for Coleridge because it challenges established opinions and encourages freedom of thought. In 'John Foster and Samuel Taylor Coleridge' (*C&L* 50[2001] 631–56), Timothy Whelan discusses the neglected Baptist essayist John Foster, and his sustained interest in Coleridge. Whelan identifies a number of affinities between the two men, with both 'advocating a distinctly intellectual Dissenting tradition in literature, politics, and culture' while also prioritizing a close relationship with Nature. Foster's reservations over Coleridge were based on the lack of a 'practical desire' to communicate his beliefs through evangelical religion. On a similar theme, Daniel E. White's '"Properer for a sermon": Particularities of Dissent and Coleridge's Conversational Mode' (*SiR* 40[2001] 175–98) examines the poet's 'vexed relationship to nonconformist religion during the 1790s'. White argues that Dissenters have been viewed as a homogenous group. Coleridge opposed middle-class Dissenters, and this rejection defined his own dissident Unitarian beliefs, shaping the 'Coleridgean language that became early romanticism'.

Coleridge's 'conversational mode' also figures in David Fairer's 'Texts in Conversation: Coleridge's *Sonnets from Various Authors* (1796)' (in Bell, Chew, Eliot, Hunter and West, eds., *Re-Constructing the Book: Literary Texts in Transmission*, pp. 71–83). Fairer observes how Coleridge's return to the sonnet in this 'modest little pamphlet' takes the form of a collaboration, generating dialogue between the contributors. In 'Secret(ing) Conversations: Coleridge and Wordsworth' (*NLH* 32[2001] 67–98), Bruce Lawder views Coleridge's conversational poems as mimetic, dramatizing the rivalry between Wordsworth and Coleridge. Also pairing the two poets, Francesca Cauchi's 'Mood and Metaphysics in Wordsworth and Coleridge' (*ERR* 12[2001] 328–43) discovers that 'Mood's nostalgia, engendered by loss' is endemic to both poets, but while Wordsworth 'worships the conceits of his own making, Coleridge flagellates himself with his'. In "Twinkle, Twinkle, Little Star" as an Ambient Poem; a Study of a Dialectical Image; with Some Remarks on Coleridge and Wordsworth' (*RCPS* November[2001]), Timothy Morton considers the advantages and disadvantages of focusing on ambience when thinking about 'Composed upon Westminster Bridge' and *The Rime of the Ancient Mariner*.

Collaboration between Wordsworth and Coleridge is naturally an issue when considering *Lyrical Ballads*. The most distinguished publication on this collection was Trott and Perry, eds., *1800: The New Lyrical Ballads*. This volume of essays commemorates the bicentenary of the second edition of *Lyrical Ballads*. The editors argue for, and the calibre of the contributions attests to, the re-evaluation of 1800 as 'one of the most famous dates in English literary history'. The introduction of the 'preface' was a defining moment for British Romanticism and for Wordsworth as a poet. Kenneth Johnston's essay discusses Wordsworth's self-invention, John Beer and Zachary Leader interrogate the notion of unity in the collection, Michael O'Neill and Nicola Trott highlight the unsettling aspects of the poems themselves, and Lucy Newlyn and Nicholas Roe explore the 'afterlife' of *Lyrical Ballads*. Other articles on *Lyrical Ballads* included Heidi Thomson's '"We are two": The Address to Dorothy in "Tintern Abbey"' (*SiR* 40[2001] 531–46). Thomson refutes the recent argument that Dorothy acts as a narcissistic projection by reading the poem in the context of *Lyrical Ballads*. Thomson sees 'Tintern Abbey' as part of a 'dialectical' on shared experience over isolation; Dorothy plays a crucial role in substantiating memory. However, Thomson's attempts to persuade frequently result in contradiction: 'Tintern Abbey' is subsequently set aside from the rest of *Lyrical Ballads* as a poem which prizes 'mutual protection', and autobiographical readings are rejected at the beginning of the article to later emphasize the intimacy between Wordsworth and his sister. Thomson's rejection of a gendered approach to the poem, on the basis that it results in a rather neat dichotomy, necessitates the unsexing of the female in a bid to avoid 'labelling Dorothy as a woman'.

In 'Wordsworth versus Malthus: The Political Context(s) of "The Old Cumberland Beggar"' (*ChLB* 115[2001] 72–85), David Chandler reconsiders the accepted view that Wordsworth's politics are self-evident in this poem. He examines 'The Old Cumberland Beggar' in the context of Malthus's view of poverty as 'an economic impracticality rather than an essentially moral problem'. Another article that seeks to contextualize Wordsworth is Victoria Myers's 'Justice and Indeterminacy: Wordsworth's *The Borderers* and the Trials of the 1790s' (*SiR* 40[2001] 427–57). Rather than discuss *The Borderers* in the light of the French Revolution and the political climate in England, Myers concerns herself with the influence of the 'notorious legal cases of the 1790s' on Wordsworth's play, and with tracing 'his transition from radical action to a state of radical indeterminacy'. Mark Keay's *William Wordsworth's Golden Age Theories during the Industrial Revolution in England* views Wordsworth, particularly his politics, as a product of 'a Golden Age ideal of social life and moral relations' which developed in response to the social changes he witnessed in the Lake District. As Keay states, his book has 'a revisionist aim', positioning Wordsworth within an anti-modernist tradition opposed to the fragmentation of society.

Extending the discussion of domestic politics, Tim Fulford's essay 'Primitive Poets and Dying Indians' (in Trott and Perry, eds., pp. 44–73) highlights the relationship between *Lyrical Ballads* and the contemporary trend for exotic travel literature featuring the 'primitive'. Fulford also discusses Wordsworth's conservative 'politicization of nature' in 'Wordsworth's "The Haunted Tree" and the Sexual Politics of Landscape' (*RCPS* November[2001]). In 'Dances with Daffodils: Wordsworth and the Postcolonial Canon' (in Gorak, ed., *Canon vs. Culture: Reflections on the Current Debate*, pp. 153–74), J. Edward Chamberlin suggests that by examining Wordsworth's position as a poet who wrote about marginal subjects, 'I wandered lonely as a cloud' can be reclaimed as an approach to post-colonial poetry. Demonized and caricatured during his lifetime, Wordsworth becomes a 'fellow traveller' who shares many affinities with West Indian poets. Considering Wordsworth in the light of harsh and misguided reviewers is the subject of Nicola Trott's 'Wordsworth in the Nursery: The Parodic School of Criticism' (*WC* 32[2001] 66–77).

A significant contribution to the review culture surrounding Wordsworth is Robert Woof's addition to the Critical Heritage series. This volume includes a vast amount of material, chronologically arranged and subdivided into reviews and opinions. Woof is careful to highlight the 'special vital audience which nurtured Wordsworth', and there are significant entries by family members, friends and contemporary poets. However, even though the significance of Coleridge's *Biographia Literaria* is stressed in the introduction, no extracts are included, and there is a notable absence of Wordsworth's own commentaries in a book that aims to elucidate his poetry (as Woof notes, in its entirety, such a project falls outside the remit of this book, but a selection would have added to the volume). The book finishes with responses to *The River Duddon* volume of 1820, but with regard to a second volume, Woof virtually dismisses the reception of Wordsworth's later poems: '*The Prelude* was largely mistaken for a repetition of *The Excursion*, and its appearance was muffled by the publication of *In Memoriam*'.

The importance of those closest to Wordsworth is demonstrated in Jonathan Roberts's 'Shared Grief in the Elegies on John Wordsworth: "Farewell the heart that lives alone"' (*WC* 32[2001] 155–61). Similarly concentrating on Wordsworth's immediate circle, John Powell Ward's article on 'Wordsworth, Friendship, and the Writing of Poetry' (*WC* 32[2001] 96–101) explores why, with a few exceptions, friendship is largely ignored in Wordsworth's poetry. Ward suggests a number of explanations, from anxiety of influence to the subtle prioritization of kinship above friendship and a distaste for direct addresses to intimate acquaintances. Friendship is certainly not an issue in Ken Parille's 'All the Rage: Wordsworth's Attack on Byron in *Lines Addressed to a Noble Lord*' (*PLL* 37[2001] 255–78). As Parille argues, 'Lines Addressed to a Noble Lord' represents one of the few occasions when Wordsworth directly expressed hostility towards Byron's poetry and jealousy over his commercial success. It is unfortunate that Parille feels compelled to demonstrate at length Wordsworth's input into the poem (Woof attributes it to Mary Barker). From contemporaries to successors, Anne Ferry's 'Revisions of Visions: Wordsworth and his Inheritors' (*Raritan* 21[2001] 67–93) traces the influence of Wordsworth's 'optical illusions' in the poetry of Eliot, Stevens, Frost, Merrill, Heaney and Bishop. In 'O "Shining in Modest Glory": Contemporary Northern Irish Poets and Romantic Poetry' (*WC* 32[2001] 59–65), Michael O'Neill detects the influence of Romantic poets, largely Wordsworth and Keats, on Northern Irish poets. Although this is seemingly incongruous, O'Neill reminds us that the Romantics were concerned with the common man, and argues convincingly that an intrinsic element of discord or disruption in Romantic poetry appeals to poets such as Heaney. David Towsey's 'Platonic Eros and Deconstructive Love' (*SiR* 40[2001] 511–30) explores Plato's influence on Wordsworth, while Deanne Westbrook's *Wordsworth's Biblical Ghosts* considers the poet's indebtedness to the New Testament in terms of narrative and linguistics.

One of the most significant publications of 2001 was L.J. Swingle's 'Our Will: A Presence that Disturbs' (*ANQ* 14:iv[2001] 4–15). Swingle takes exception to the trend for denigrating Wordsworth's poetry. By concentrating on what Wordsworth tries to achieve, Swingle argues that 'a picture of persistent artistic incompetence' is emerging, with serious consequences for generations of undergraduates. According to Swingle, the problem originates with critics who cannot understand Wordsworth properly and do not wish to admit their ignorance. Somewhat contentious given the critic's vehement hostility towards academics, Swingle's article is thought-provoking. An immediate example from this year's publications is Frank Kermode's article on 'Palaces of Memory' (*IoC* 30[2001] 87–96), in which he refers to *The*

Prelude as 'adequately inadequate'. The main problem with Swingle's notion of 'Attempt Criticism' is, of course, that it relies on a generalization. Scholarship is currently emerging that seeks to reaffirm Wordsworth's accomplishments. Sally Bushell's *Re-Reading The Excursion: Narrative, Response and the Wordsworthian dramatic voice* is an excellent example, in which the author reclaims a text that has been 'treated as a failed monologic utterance'. By researching the contemporary habit of rereading long poems such as *The Excursion*, Bushell foregrounds her discussion of the 'communicative structures' between author and reader. Leon Waldoff's *Wordsworth in his Major Lyrics: The Art and Psychology of Self-Representation* similarly focuses on the problematic position of the speaker. A noticeable tendency within Wordsworth studies is the revision or, as Soheil Ahmed suggests in 'Figures of Revision in Wordsworth's Critical Arguments' (*RoN* 24[2001] 1–9), 're-vision' of his poetry, a process to which Swingle's objections undoubtedly contribute.

Amongst those articles that focused on a single poem, Mary Wedd's 'The Leech Gatherer' (*ChLB* 115[2001] 86–104) refutes the notion that Wordsworth's melancholy borders on morbidity. On the contrary, Wedd sees 'The Leech Gatherer' as celebrating the 'courage and endurance of many faceless sufferers'. The poem is also referred to in Gabriel Josipovici's 'The Singer on the Shore' (*PNR* 138[2001] 16–20). In addition, *The Prelude* was the subject of several articles this year. Dewey W. Hall's 'Signs of the Dead: Epitaphs, Inscriptions, and the Discourse of the Self' (*ELH* 68[2001] 655–77) concentrates on the moment in the 1805 text when Wordsworth 'chanced' upon William Taylor's gravesite. The accidental nature of this event, Hall argues, suggests a conscious 'elision' and an attempt to stress spontaneity; Wordsworth negotiates signs of the dead to construct the self. Henry Weinfeld covers similar territory in '"Knowledge not purchased by the loss of power": Wordsworth's Meditation on Books and Death in Book 5 of *The Prelude*' (*TSLL* 43[2001] 334–63). Two very different approaches to this poem were Celeste Langan's 'Mobility Disability' (*PC* 13[2001] 459–84) and Willard B. Frick's 'Symbolic Latency: Images of Transformation Across Space and Time' (*JHuP* 41:iii[2001] 9–30). In Langan's article, Wordsworth's 'travelling cripple' is read alongside a range of contemporary films, including Jan De Bont's *Speed* [1994], to illustrate the class-based inequalities of transport. Frick develops his theory of symbolic latency in relation to 'spots of time'. A 'unity of experience' in which the past, present and the future are interconnected, albeit not yet fully understood, underpins the significance of these Wordsworthian moments. A crucial factor is anticipation, and a child can more readily discover these 'sustaining images'.

Childhood has been a topic of some critical interest this year. In Catherine Robson's *Men in Wonderland: The Lost Girlhood of the Victorian Gentleman* (pp. 16–45), Wordsworth sustains a 'vital boyish self' through killing off the innocent ideal of childhood as represented by girls. This vision of childhood is therefore preserved intact and no transition disturbs the boy's growth into adulthood. Marilyn Gaull's essay 'Wordsworth and the Six Arts of Childhood' (in Trott and Perry, eds., pp. 74–94), explores how the poet's interest in folklorists influenced his nonconformist depictions of wilful, and even savage, children. Ann Wierda Rowland also discusses Wordsworth's problematic association between childhood and revolutionary France in 'Wordsworth's Children of the Revolution' (*SEL* 41[2001] 677–94).

A significant topic of discussion this year was travel. In 'The Wages of Travel: Wordsworth and the Memorial Tour of 1820' (*SiR* 40[2001] 321–43), Robin Jarvis attempts to redress a lack of critical interest in the tours Wordsworth undertook in the latter part of his life. Focusing on the connection between writing and mobility (converging on Langan's approach), Jarvis reassesses the memorial tour sequence. Another article exploring the older Wordsworth's travels was Anthony John Harding's 'Wordsworth, Coleridge, Dora, and the Meuse–Rhine Tour of 1828' (*WC* 32[2001] 161–8). Grevel Lindop's 'Wordsworth, Pope and the Alps' (*Romanticism* 7[2001] 58–72) argues for the fortuitousness of Wordsworth mistakenly taking the 'road less travelled' in the Alps, and reads the Simplon Pass passage in *The Prelude* as a reply to Pope's *Essay of Criticism*. A more sombre reflection on this passage is 'Wordsworth's Gondo: Gone' (*WC* 32[2001] 117–200), in which Donald E. Hayden laments the devastation of the village in Switzerland where the poet stayed. Linda Brigham discusses the related subject of tourism in 'Beautiful Conceptions and Tourist Kitsch: Wordsworth's "Written with a Slate Pencil ... "' (*SiR* 40[2001] 199–214). Tomoya Oda's 'The "Minstrel" Episode in Book II of *The Prelude* and an Amusement of the Tourists to the Lakes' (*N&Q* 48[2001] 124–7) relates the scene when the Hawkshead boys listen to the minstrel playing his flute with a popular pastime for tourists visiting the Lake District. In 'Warner's Unrecognized Visit to Wordsworth in July 1801' (*N&Q* 48[2001] 123–4), Oda speculates that Warner visited Wordsworth around 10 July 1801, a time when little is known about the poet's life. Another significant contribution is the publication of 'An Unpublished Dorothy Wordsworth Letter of 20 March 1837' courtesy of Jiro Nagasawa (*N&Q* 48[2001] 121–3).

4. Blake

The starting point for any scholar conducting research into Blake remains, as has been noted before, G.E. Bentley's annual report in *Blake: An Illustrated Quarterly*. 'William Blake and his Circle: A Checklist of Publications and Discoveries in 2001' (*Blake* 36:i[2002] 4–37), conducted with the assistance of Keiko Aoyama for Japanese publications, draws together an extended list of Blake publications for 2001 as well as additions for earlier years that had not been recorded in previous lists.

Bentley is also significant, of course, for his monumental contributions to Blake's biography and bibliography in terms of *Blake Books* and *Blake Records*. Since publication of each of these at the end of the 1960s, supplements have appeared updating the information contained in each one, and a revised edition of *Blake Records* is to be published in 2002. In the meantime, Bentley has issued *The Stranger from Paradise: A Biography of William Blake*. Blake has not been badly served by biographers (there is a handy list at the back of *The Stranger from Paradise*), but most recent biographies, notably those by James King in 1991 and Peter Ackroyd in 1995, rely heavily on *Blake Records*. Bentley's biography, therefore, is an opportunity for him to put the record straight and place before a wider public some of the detailed and immensely important scholarship that he has been pursuing for the past half-century. As it is his intention to provide as much information as possible to enable the reader to judge his interpretations of Blake's life, this can be a difficult book to read, but Bentley realizes the dangers of omitting such detail. As he remarks in a rather savage footnote near the beginning of the book, 'Peter Ackroyd, *Blake* [1995], 20 says that Blake's maternal grandfather was a "hosier", but as he identifies Blake's mother as "Catherine Hermitage" rather than Catherine Wright (her maiden name) or Catherine Armitage (her first married name), we may wonder about the accuracy of the unidentified source of his information about her father.' Bentley is more generous in his appendix of principal biographies, listing Ackroyd's book as 'a careful and usually accurate biography with few pretensions to originality', but the casual reader has been warned! This book is not as easy to get to grips with as Ackroyd's (and King's) more derivative texts, but it is wonderful that so much information from *Blake Records* is available at a reasonable price to more readers than ever before.

Probably the other most important titles published in 2001 were Sheila Spector's two companion books on Blake and kabbalism, *'Wonders Divine'* and *'Glorious Incomprehensible'*. The first of these, *'Wonders Divine': The Development of Blake's Kabbalistic Myth* concentrates on the general mythopoetic structure of Blake's prophetic writing, beginning from the pertinent observation that in *Jerusalem* Blake draws deliberate attention to his use of kabbalistic mysticism to explain the fall and reintegration of the giant Albion. *'Wonders Divine'* begins with a thoughtful account of Blake's problems in using traditional Christian mythographic frameworks, ones that insisted on a conjunction between divine ideology and temporal demonstrations of power, before providing a brief but definitive history of the development of kabbalism. It is to Spector's credit that she does not attempt to read kabbalism as a chosen hobby-horse into every aspect of Blake's writing—indeed, her treatment of Blake's supposedly prophetic writings up until the time of *The Book of Urizen* indicate the ways in which Blake was struggling with his mythographic themes in a fashion that did not benefit, other than in a very superficial and occasional way, from kabbalistic doctrines. The problem that this occasionally raises for the reader is a sense of covering necessary but slightly tedious ground at times before settling on the real focus of this book.

That focus, as she announces in a chapter on 'The Transcendent Myth: Kabbalism', is to explain how, 'In the major prophecies, the various kabbalistic motifs Blake had been experimenting with evolve into a complex, multi-faceted myth whose archetypal structure provides the means of reconciling the two dilemmas he had been grappling with throughout the composite art: the function of Christ and the role of the prophet in the fallen world.' Intensive readings of Blake's often confusing mythology by means of another system such as kabbalism can often generate more heat than light, and at times it is tempting to ask why a certain reading of a neologism or name in Blake should be made according to one mystical tradition and not another (personally, I baulked at the reading of Albion as *al*, 'God', and *ben*, 'son'). Nonetheless, as an explanation of how the fall and regeneration of Albion can be mapped out against the Tree of the Sefirot and other notions from the kabbala, Spector's book is thorough and engaged. Particularly impressive is her understanding of how Blake only gradually came to see *himself* as a prophet in his own life, 'Culminating an intellectual quest Blake had initiated at the time he began working on the illuminated art' and which reached fruition with *Milton* and *Jerusalem*.

The second volume, *'Glorious Incomprehensible': The Development of Blake's Kabbalistic Language*, is less satisfactory. While Spector is a superb authority on the influence of kabbalism until the early nineteenth century, her account of linguistic theories that would have been significant for Blake is less compelling. In this regard, her chapter on 'The Languages of Eighteenth-Century Reading' suffers in comparison to Robert Essick's *William Blake and the Language of Adam* [1989], a title that remains authoritative not simply because it charts the (frequently bizarre) linguistic theories of Blake's contemporaries but also in so far as it critiques such theories in the light of twentieth-century linguistic and historicist frameworks, all the while navigating the dangerous straits of jargon that such theories of both the eighteenth and twentieth centuries present.

Spector's ambition, to demonstrate how intentionality could operate within the very language employed by Blake as well as the structures of his myths, enabling him to achieve the transcendental language of prophecy, appears more constrained by kabbalism in *'Glorious Incomprehensible'* than in *'Wonders Divine'*. As with the companion volume, Spector is exceptional in tracing the development of Blake's thought through a career spanning between thirty and forty years, how the Bard's Song in *Milton* finally enables Blake to conceive a mystical 'grammar of practice', which is then enacted in *Jerusalem*. Yet the general task of tracing the language of Blake's works through the kabbala is often unsatisfactory, not least because his experiments with grammar and mythopoetic language draw much more widely from contemporary linguistic frameworks, such as the bardic poetry of Ossian and Gray, Milton and Shakespeare and the more conventional forms of neoclassical pastoral. Spector admits each of these influences—and more—yet the imperative of her reading of the prophetic writings according to kabbalistic forms (which only works effectively with the later prophecies) often results in far too speculative word games. Both *'Wonders Divine'* and *'Glorious Incomprehensible'* represent the most comprehensive treatment of Blake and kabbalism yet written, and will probably dominate this area of Blake studies for many years to come. There is, unfortunately, a sense of some repetition in both volumes which, while extremely scholarly, would have benefited being published as a single, longer volume.

One other book dedicated to a study of Blake's work is A.A. Ansari's *William Blake's Minor Prophecies*. Ansari was responsible for *Arrows of Intellect* [1965], also on Blake, but there is not a great deal to recommend in this particular book, published by the Edwin Mellen Press. Where it may be useful is in terms of its comprehensive coverage of the poetic books published by Blake during the 1790s, and there is a short essay on 'Blake and the Kabbalah' that serves as a helpful introduction to Jewish mysticism; for the more serious student of Blake's kabbalism, however, Spector's two titles are much more definitive. The greatest problem with *William Blake's Minor Prophecies* is a sense of having missed most critical work that has taken place with regard to Blake over the past two decades: this book obviously owes a great debt to the important synthesizers of Blake's thought from the mid-twentieth century—Northrop Frye, David Erdman and Harold Bloom, with additional influences from Desiree Hirst, Joseph Bronowski and Kathleen Raine—but while there are passing glances towards the most important contemporary critics such as Morris Eaves, Robert Essick and Morton Paley, their interest in contemporary critical theory or the material culture of Blake's work is barely registered. I suspect as well that Ansari has simply never encountered the important work done by Joseph Viscomi on the production of Blake's books, or historicist contextualizations pioneered by figures such as David Worrall, Steve Clark and Jon Mee. *William Blake's Minor Prophecies* would perhaps be of some value to a reader new to Blake's poetry from this period, although I found it a difficult book to read precisely because so much of it was familiar as a style of criticism that has been unpopular in Blake studies at least since the 1970s. The best use of this title is for readers who have no or little idea of Blake's intentions in these early works, but even at this level it would be hard not to recommend (for all their faults) returning to Frye's *Fearful Symmetry* and Erdman's *Prophet Against Empire* as more useful starting points.

While not given over entirely to Blake's works, substantial Blakean criticism is included in McDayter, Batten, and Milligan, eds., *Romantic Generations: Essays in Honor of Robert F. Gleckner*. Gleckner was, of course, one of those significant twentieth-century American critics who helped to shape opinion of Blake, most notably as the author of *The Piper and the Bard*, as well as working on other Romantics such as Byron and Wordsworth. As such, three essays from this collection provide new perspectives on Blake. The first, 'Blake's Pope', by R. Paul Yoder, begins from the observation that although Blake was critical of the 'tamer of Homer's passion and imagination', he 'also knew [the translations of Homer] well, and borrowed from them for some of his best known lines'. Working from Robert Griffin's *Wordsworth's Pope* [1995], Yoder continues the recent restoration of Pope as intrinsic to the development of a Romantic sensibility, both the anxious Other of Romanticism and also the wit and satirist who best espoused many personal aspirations of Romantic poets such as Blake. Blake may have denounced Pope for being praised by Hayley, but Yoder finds considerable similarities between certain lines of Blake's verse and sections of Pope's Homer.

Glen Brewster, in 'From Albion to Frankenstein's Creature: The Disintegration of the Social Body in Blake and Mary Shelley', traces the critical visions of the social body offered by both of these writers, suggesting that 'Blake's later prophetic works envision an idealized absorption of male and female principles into the body of Albion', while 'Shelley's novel counters the myth of Albion, and thus serves as a model of the disintegration of social order in the late Romantic Period.' Working through late eighteenth- and early nineteenth-century political theory that discussed the body politic, or social body, Brewster suggests that the final formulation of works such as *Jerusalem* is typically read as subsuming both male and female into a potentially androgynous form that actually idealizes a divine brotherhood of masculinity as Romantic idealism. Instead, Brewster indicates that reading Blake against Shelley (*Jerusalem*, after all, is roughly contemporary with *Frankenstein*) indicates a common concern with the 'charnel house' of Albion after decades of war with France. By the end of his essay, Brewster has returned to a separation of these two writers as polar representations of the body of Albion, one idealized the other nightmarish, that is ultimately unsatisfactory (particularly to account sufficiently for recent work done by Helen Bruder and Christopher Hobson, amongst others, on Blake's readings of sexuality and gender), but his comparison of Blake and Shelley is both imaginative and, frequently, constructive.

Probably the best of the three chapters devoted to Blake in *Romantic Generations* is Saree Makdisi's 'Blake, America and the World', drawing on work that contributes to his forthcoming and much-anticipated book, *William Blake and the*

Impossible History of the 1790s. Makdisi's sophisticated reading of the three prophecies *America*, *Europe* and the *Song of Los* (the latter incorporating *Africa* and *Asia*) sees them less as a Eurocentric exposition of historical development from biblical Egypt and Arabia to revolutionary America and Europe, and more as a 'synchronic map of the world system within which Blake was working', one which treats history and geography as discursive formations rather than conventional maps of time and space. Offering a pertinent critique of those interpretations of *America* that have followed Erdman's optimistic interpretation of that poem far too uncritically, Makdisi suggests that the illustrator of Stedman's *Narrative of a Five Years' Expedition Against the Revolted Negroes of Surinam* [1796] would have found the Declaration of Independence full of 'cruel irony'. Some of Makdisi's observations are perhaps not entirely as new as he claims—similar points have been made recently in Linebaugh and Rediker's *The Many-Headed Hydra* [2000], while Julia Wright's essay, '"Empire is no more": Odin and Orc in *America*' [1992] goes even further in terms of representing the conflict of Orc and the American revolutionaries as no more than a struggle for colonial power rather than liberty versus tyranny. Nonetheless, this is a welcome preview of *Impossible History*.

A slightly odd title for inclusion in a review of English studies, Andrew Shanks's *What is Truth?*, will be interesting for those studying Blake because he uses the Romantic poet and artist as a case study, alongside Hölderlin and Nelly Sachs, to illustrate the subtitle of his book, *Towards a Theological Poetics*. Shanks views such a theological poetics as part of what he calls a 'pathos of shakenness', as opposed to the more typical pathos of glory that has motivated much art and poetry in celebration of the temporal status quo. Beginning with the prophet Amos, Shanks explores the lineage of prophetic writings which (in a fashion not dissimilar to the investigations undertaken by Robert Lowth in the eighteenth century) discovers the true value of Hebrew Scripture to lie in its poetry. For Shanks, Blake is an example of 'militant shakenness', the poet-prophet who refuses to countenance any value in the typical order of glorifying pathos that he associated with the classics, and which Shanks (following Kundera) identifies with kitsch, or that which 'excludes everything from its purview which is essentially unacceptable in human existence'. Blake, by contrast, expresses in a vivid form what Shanks sees as the essential features of a shaken theology, a radical unease with establishment-mindedness, against which is posited neither a complacent individual agnosticism nor regimented counter-dogma, but the real desire for 'fresh air' that also seeks solidarity even when it realizes such a desire will be frustrated. In a very interesting appendix, Shanks compares Blake's Albion as an example of this desire for solidarity with another national group, Hobbes's Leviathan, which, despite its apparent celebration of the pathos of glory has actually unnerved elites because it so clearly (even mischievously) lays bare the trappings of their power. While Shanks's reading of Blake makes the poet subservient to the theological poetics, *What is Truth?* is a worthwhile examination of reading the Bible as poetry in which the author has taken on more than a little of Blake's style and manner, as when he writes of contradictions to his notion of truth as pure honesty: 'There is however a rather widespread error, to the contrary, that religious faith is a form of metaphysical *opinion*.'

A text aimed at students (and teachers) is Nicholas Marsh's *William Blake: The Poems*, part of Palgrave's 'Analysing Texts' series. Despite the title, it is really concerned with *Songs of Innocence and of Experience* and, as a series of readings of individual poems, is useful insofar as it considers the relation of design and text. The second part of Marsh's book on Blake and critical contexts is, unfortunately, rather inadequate, failing to engage with the most important developments in recent Blake criticism. Despite the fact that it was published a decade before this particular text, serious students should read Andrew Lincoln's edited version of the *Songs* published as part of the Tate Gallery/Blake Trust illuminated works. Now available in paperback, it is only a few pounds more expensive than *William Blake: The Poems* and has the advantage of providing full-colour reproductions of all plates from the *Songs*.

One fascinating area where Blake has leapt over other Romantic poets and artists is in terms of his reception. Sometimes, the range of Blake's influence is extremely surprising: only a few years after his death accounts of him were being published in Russia, Germany and the United States, and Agnes Peter provides a brief history of Blake's reception in Hungary during the twentieth century in 'The Reception of Blake in Hungary' (*Blake* 34:iii[2001] 68–81). Thus, for example, Jószef Pati compiled an illustrative Bible in 1924 that used Blake's engravings of Job, while Antal Szerb, a modernist critic and author, published a Freudian and Jungian assessment of Blake in 1928, the conclusions of which 'strike the critic today as amazingly well informed and profound'. Most remarkable, however, is the work of Béla Kondor [1931–72], an artist and poet whose paintings, engravings and graphics (for example of a Printing House in Hell and, more tongue-in-cheek, a Pub in Hell) were quickly picked up on by his contemporaries as demonstrating the influence of Blake in addition to that of Bosch and Dürer.

The same issue of *Blake* that contains Peter's article also includes a short essay by Michael Ferber on 'Blake's "Jerusalem" as a Hymn' (*Blake* 34:iii[2001] 82–9). This is a useful introduction to the development of the stanzas from *Milton* into one of the primary national anthems of the last night of the Proms, particularly as it traces the history of Parry's arrangement and the first appearances of *Jerusalem* in hymnals. While there is more to be written on the life of *Jerusalem* in the twentieth century, Ferber concludes his piece with an account of its use by Billy Bragg as 'a left-wing anthem'.

The Spring 2001 edition of *Blake* (34:iv[2001] 100–58) was devoted to annual checklists of Blake sales and research compiled by Robert Essick and covering the year 2000, which he described as 'disappointing' for Blake collectors, the most exciting attempted sale being that of the painting *God Blessing the Seventh Day* (an export licence for which was turned down by the British government).

Andrew Stauffer provides a detailed reading of possible sources for 'Blake's Poison Trees' (*Blake* 35:ii[2001] 36–9), in which he argues that, while Blake knew of the legendary poisonous Upas tree of Java, he probably also drew on the legend of the Manchineal for 'A Poison Tree'. The Manchineal, as described by Erasmus Darwin, was 'comfortably shady, safe and inviting to the traveler, who is killed in his sleep by its secret poison', making it a more suitable symbol for false friendship. The same issue of *Blake* includes an extensive supplement to Donald Fitch's *Blake Set to Music* (35:ii[2001] 40–61), cataloguing additional Blakean texts set to music since 1990, when the original book was published, as well as discoveries made by Fitch that did not make it into print at that time.

Before moving on to Blake essays published in other journals in 2001, it is also worth remarking a short essay written by Michael Ferber in *Blake: An Illustrated Quarterly*, which is perhaps my personal favourite of the whole year. In 'Blake for Children' (*Blake* 35:i[2001] 22–4), Ferber outlines how he was commissioned by a popular children's publisher to edit a collection of Blake's poetry for children. After a long and slow process of attrition during which the majority of Blake's poems selected by Ferber were weeded out (the word 'harlot' in 'London' would offend Christians, 'The Little Black Boy' would anger the NAACP, 'The Divine Image' was too religious), Ferber withdrew from the project and, in his own words, wrote a self-righteous letter to the editor denouncing the timidity and conformity of children's publishing. This is not the final word, however (nor is the publisher's response that he would prefer an editor who understood the market), and Ferber's reflection on how best we can serve Blake in terms of extending his reputation as widely as possible—and whether he did, indeed, make the best decision in withdrawing from the task—is enlightened and humane.

Elsewhere, essays and articles on Blake included a detailed reading of an intriguing incident in *Milton* by Masashi Suzuki: '"Signal of solemn mourning": Los/Blake's Sandals and Ancient Israelite Custom' (*JEGP* 100[2001] 40–56) takes as its starting point the strange event in *Milton* when Los removes his sandal from his foot and places it on his head, which is in turn linked to the entry of Milton into Blake's left tarsus. Suzuki details traditional interpretations of this event, for example a reading from Ezekiel that relates the action of walking barefoot to mourning. More interesting, however, is his discussion of this motif from *Milton* in the light of the new biblical criticism that was being explored by theological writers such as Anthony Geddes at the end of the eighteenth century, in particular how sandals were used in the book of Ruth to express the symbolic practice of the *go'el*, or redeemer, who has the right to prevent family property from being alienated, rights to which could be symbolically transferred by this item of clothing. By giving his sandal to Blake, Los enacts a complex symbolic handover of his prophetic powers to the poet who, by joining with Milton and a new, dynamic Los, redeems vision by this imaginative act.

Tristanne J. Connolly, in an essay on 'Miscarriage Imagery in Blake' (*Romanticism* 7:ii[2001] 145–62), discusses whether the recurrence of such imagery in Blake's work has any basis in biographical fact, as well as examining how it could be used to explore themes on the precariousness of personal identity, bodily existence and the relationship between mortal and eternal life. Connolly observes that archival research that listed one 'Cath.e Blake' as a patient of the British Lying-In Hospital in Endell Street, Holborn, is inconclusive, and in any case Blake could have gleaned a great deal about childbirth from medical acquaintances. Connolly argues convincingly that *The Book of Thel* should be read as a compassionate reflection on eighteenth-century abortion (where mother as well as child could be killed by dangerous abortifacients). Likewise, Reuben in *Jerusalem* is depicted by Blake as 'a nexus of taboos', an unborn child who horrifies all who see him; as those who see him 'become what [they] behold', Reuben's state connects 'the condition of earthly life … to an abortive birth.'

As part of a collection of articles on 'The New International', Claire Colebrook considers the recent re-evaluation of Blake as an icon of national and post-Enlightenment identities in her essay 'The New Jerusalem and the New

International' (*Parallax* 7:iii[2001] 17–28). Colebrook is concerned with the double irony of 'professional' readers who may take issue with the ways in which the original fidelity to Blake's apocalyptic meaning is transformed by jingoistic interpretation, while neglecting that Blake is part of a post-Enlightenment practice of reading that undermines their own cultural confidence. While the Enlightenment attempts to remove the illusions and spectres of our thinking, Blake's work 'is a performance, rehearsal and working through of spectres'. As such, the notion that we can conjure up a pure Blake, one free from the depredations of popular culture and the Blake industry, is severely criticized by Colebrook.

Issue 6 of *The Journal of the Blake Society at St James* includes a number of essays on Blake worthy of note. Peter Cochran, editor of the Byron Society newsletter, traces some of the similarities between Blake and Byron's ideas on politics and religion in 'Blake, Byron and the Blushing Archangels' (*JBSSJ* 6[2001] 5–17), concentrating in particular on Blake's final illuminated work, *The Ghost of Abel*, as a sequel to Byron's *Cain*. In 'Apocatastasis Now: A Very Condensed Reading of William Blake's *Jerusalem*' (*JBSSJ* 6[2001] 18–25), Susanne Sklar argues that Blake is not apocalyptic but apocatastatic, that is (following a doctrine of Origen and Gregory of Nyssa) he believes that all free creatures will be redeemed by God's universal love. A rather charming paper is Tim Heath's 'The Botanic Blake' (*JBSSJ* 6[2001] 26–37), tracing the influence on Blake's art and writing of contemporary writers such as Erasmus Darwin and events such as the importation of the Dahlia into eighteenth-century Europe; particularly interesting is the way that Heath traces the publication of a book on the brown-tail moth in 1782 to Blake via Curtis's publisher, Joseph Johnson, indicating the ways in which Blake drew on writers such as Curtis when he came later to illustrate *The Songs of Innocence*.

In 'Words and Acton in Blake's *Songs*' (*JBSSJ* 6[2001] 38–47), Angela Esterhammer discusses some of the implications for *Songs of Innocence and of Experience* of communication theory, something she has explored in books such as *Creating States: Studies in the Performative Language of John Milton and William Blake* [1994]. Arguing that echoes, responses and repetitions effect a 'dialogic relationship between Piper and Child' in the *Songs of Innocence*, Esterhammer finds that 'Experience, by contrast, is a state of failed speech acts'. Jay Beichman offers a fairly descriptive account of '*The Marriage of Heaven & Hell*: Notions of Good & Evil in William Blake' (*JBSSJ* 6[2001] 62–73), but Dee Drake's 'Blake's *Hecate*: A Tribute to Infernal Female Desire' (*JBSSJ* 6[2001] 51–9) is a playful and fascinating reading of the illustration typically known as 'Hecate' in the light of Apuleius's *The Golden Ass*. As part of a longer doctoral dissertation on Blake's 'infernal females', Drake reads the dark female in the painting as the Sibyl practising a diabolic method of writing that the male, represented as an ass (that is Bottom, in *A Midsummer Nights Dream*, or Aeneas—Any Ass—in Virgil's *Aeneid*) refuses to countenance.

Of essays published in 2001, finally, there is Hikari Sato's 'The Devil's Progress: Blake, Bunyan, and *The Marriage of Heaven and Hell*' (*SEL* 41:ii[2001] 121–46). Part of a doctoral dissertation concerned with Blake's reception and rewriting of other writers, Sato argues that Blake's reading of *The Pilgrim's Progress* is highly oppositional, resisting the ways in which Bunyan attempts to restrict readerly interpretation to certain, predetermined outcomes, constructing an alternative priesthood to attack the Anglican hierarchy rather than encouraging each individual to discover their own spiritual enlightenment.

The year 2001 also saw some important developments on the Blake archive (<www.blakearchive.org>), not least of which was the establishment of a mirror site hosted by the Humanities Computing Unit at Oxford University (<www.blakearchive.org.uk>). By the end of 2001, the archive contained forty-five copies of eighteen of Blake's nineteen illuminated books, as well as the full electronic edition of David Erdman's *Complete Poetry and Prose of William Blake*. Important additions of the year included editions of copy G of *The Marriage of Heaven and Hell* and copy P of *Visions of the Daughters of Albion*, both originally printed in 1818. These represent the first reproduction of this particular copy of *The Marriage*, and the first colour reproduction of *Visions* copy P since a microfilm version in the 1970s. The copy of *The Marriage* is significant, as Viscomi, Essick and Eaves point out, because it is the only copy with a variant plate order that can be traced directly to Blake; in addition, the copy also shows original designs of cave and rock forms that were wiped from plates in early printings, and represent— alongside *The Book of Thel*, with which they were bound until 1890— 'extraordinarily beautiful copies' in Blake's late style.

As with other electronic editions published in the archive, the copies of *The Marriage* and *Visions* have been colour-corrected to represent the originals as closely as possible, with accompanying SGML-encoded texts. The year 2001 also saw the introduction of a comparison feature, enabling users to juxtapose plates from different copies of the illuminated books. With more recent additions from Blake's non-illuminated work, as well as the forthcoming publication of *Jerusalem*, the Blake archive remains—as the most comprehensive collection of his works—a vital resource for all Blake scholars.

5. Women Romantic Poets

'Why Hemans now?' asks Marlon B. Ross in his foreword (pp. x–xxvi) to Nanora Sweet and Julie Melnyk's sparkling collection of essays, *Felicia Hemans: Reimagining Poetry in the Nineteenth Century*. The most important contribution to this area of research this year, not least because of the superb line-up of contributors, Sweet and Melnyk's grouping of essays reveals as much about the state of enquiry regarding women's Romantic poetry as Hemans herself. As Ross argues, Hemans's emotive verse opens up a series of questions concerning modern attitudes towards uncurbable feeling, sentiment, domesticity and community, and provides a brave counter to the current obsession with reason, rationality and enlightenment. For Ross such debate is founded on issues of 'taste', Hemans's work defining the national taste of Britain and Anglophone America during the nineteenth century and then falling out of favour with the onset of high modernism and its avant-garde aesthetic. She is almost 'too human' for the twenty-first century and has created a 'crisis in taste' within the academy, betraying the 'arbitrariness of value' within literary criticism and testing our capacity to analyse or break down her glassy style. Where criticism is possible, its focus has often stopped with 'Casabianca', a poem learned by heart in many schools during the mid-twentieth century and representing for many a warmongering patriotism. Far from asserting such views, the poem, once placed in the context of Hemans's excessive sentimentality, advances a profound alarm at the notion of conflict. Such readings, which demand a more subtle analysis of emotion and feeling, have been dismissed because of modern allergies to the kind of religious or spiritual passion Hemans advocates. As Ross intimates, we might need to fix our thoughts on 'something higher but less tangible' if Hemans, as well as poets like Charlotte Smith or Letitia Landon, are to be considered seriously, a task this excellent volume addresses directly. Sweet and Melnyk's introduction (pp. 1–15) refocuses these concerns in terms of 'history, gender and critical method', discussing Hemans's position as 'the last Romantic and the first Victorian', an ambivalent status that has produced distinctly contrasting readings of her work. Detailing previous studies of Hemans and drawing on her biography, Sweet and Melnyk provide an excellent preface to the poet's career, which is usefully considered in terms of the early and occasional poetry, the middle-period lyric poems and late, experimentally scriptural verse.

The remaining twelve essays address each phase, grouped in three parts which focus first on readings of Hemans's poetry; second on her reception and establishment as a 'woman poet'; and finally on the historical and literary contexts which frame her work. As the editors note, much ink has been spilled regarding Hemans's worth as a poet, and the first section moves on from such deliberation to provide the reader with specific evaluations of her elegiac, narrative and religious poetry. Michael T. Williamson's 'Impure Affections: Felicia Hemans's Elegiac Poetry and Contaminated Grief' (pp. 19–35) explores Hemans's role as a self-conscious elegist of national mourning, rethinking misguided notions of her as a familial patriot. 'Survival, restitution and repentance' mark these dramas rather than consolation, Williamson suggests, eloquently illustrating, with reference to *Lays of Many Lands*, *Records of Woman* and *Songs of the Affections*, that 'the living, not the dead, are the true subjects of elegy'. Like her elegies, Hemans's ekphrastic poetry also struggles against the hegemony, and visual dominance, of masculine poetics, Grant F. Scott contends, in 'The Fragile Image: Felicia Hemans and Romantic Ekphrasis' (pp. 36–54). For Scott, Hemans replaces visual, immortal artistry with aural, tactile and temporal imagery, 'Properzia Rossi', for example, shifting the focus away from the 'material condition of the artefact' to the 'emotional reception of the artwork'. The emotional and non-material power of Hemans's literary articulation is also apparent in John M. Anderson's 'The Triumph of Voice in Felicia Hemans's *The Forest Sanctuary*' (pp. 55–73). Using Dale Bauer's feminist dialogics to read Hemans's epic poem, Anderson suggests that the speaking voices within are dematerialized into cogent psychological and religious presences, coming to resemble Echo-like instruments of power. Anderson's recognition of Hemans's characteristically biblical style and religious concerns finds a complement in Melnyk's important essay, 'Hemans's Later Poetry: Religion and the Vatic Poet' (pp. 74–92). A deeply Christian writer, Hemans's religious aspect has been shockingly underplayed in criticism, and Melnyk astutely connects her 'Romantic' visionary powers to her holier mission as evinced through her Wordsworthian hymns.

Representing piety and feeling, then, Hemans was predictably feminized in the nineteenth century, although, as Stephen C. Behrendt's '"Certainly not a female pen": Felicia Hemans's Early Public Reception' (pp. 95–114) illustrates, this was not always the case. With reference to reviews of the poet's work appearing in the periodical press from 1808 to 1820, Behrendt conveys how Hemans was fashioned as an academic and masculine writer in her early career, an image she countered by developing her 'feminine' themes to secure commercial and aesthetic success. Certainly she gained new markets for her work, while also finding a platform on which to enter public debates of the day, winning the Royal Society of Literature's poetry contest in 1821 with 'Dartmoor', an event explored by Barbara D. Taylor in 'The Search for a Space: A Note on Felicia Hemans and the Royal Society of Literature' (pp. 115–23). The commercial viability of her work also preoccupies Chad Edgar's 'Felicia Hemans and the Shifting Field of Romanticism' (pp. 124–34), in which he suggests that Hemans collaborated with her readers by swiftly responding to their demands. Edgar suggests that in her contributions to the annuals and lighter periodicals, Hemans joined a discursive space in which women poets wrote about female subjectivities for their female readership, and in doing so began to 'feminize' Romanticism. Frauke Lenckos's '"The spells of home": Hemans, "Heimat" and the Cult of the Dead Poetess in Nineteenth-Century Germany' (pp. 135–51) relates such feminization of literature to a specifically German context, showing how the poet came to influence a generation of nineteenth-century German poetesses such as Annette von Droste-Hülshoff. Hemans's devoted study of figures such as Goethe and Schiller, Lenckos illustrates, helped to forge her own notion of home, one also developed through her reading of Byron. As Susan J. Wolfson argues in 'Hemans and the Romance of Byron' (pp. 155–80), she replaced her predecessor's 'lurid eroticizing' with 'domestic affection', thus gendering his simultaneously impassioned and dangerous strains.

Wolfson's stimulating essay opens the final section of the volume, comprising four distinguished critics' evaluations of Hemans's cultural significance within both the current moment and the nineteenth century. For Wolfson, Hemans's youthful adoration of Byron had a marked effect upon her depiction of heroines within 'scenes of the heart's desolation', one that effected a 'feminized Byronism' which substituted 'his recurring drama of the alienated soul'. Such a reshaping of Byron's voice also denotes a sensitivity towards the question of conveying masculine emotion within language, a theme Nanora Sweet turns to in 'Gender and Modernity in *The Abencerrage*: Hemans, Rushdie, and "The Moor's Last Sigh"' (pp. 181–95). In this remarkable piece Sweet suggests that the figure of the 'sentimental Moor' is for Hemans radically unstable, both Muslim and Christian, rational and emotional, masculine and feminine and so subversive of Rushdie's, and Byron's, less enlightened presentations of gender and feeling. Hemans's blurring of gender roles in her strong female narrators and feminized men is also central to Gary Kelly's 'Death and the Matron: Felicia Hemans, Romantic Death, and the Founding of the Modern Liberal State' (pp. 196–211). Exploring, like Williamson, Hemans's representation of death as meaningful and individual, rather than senseless and depersonalized, Kelly argues that the poet skilfully renders mourning as a communal and national form of stimulation, rather than of solace. The feminized male narrator of *The Forest Sanctuary*, divided from his wife by religious difference and at last by death, is exiled from Spain only to find comfort in the absent ideal of home, Kelly intimates, one that enables human bonding free from the fetters of any physical land. Sweet and Melynk's volume closes with a wonderfully lucid piece by Isobel Armstrong, 'Natural and National Monuments—Felicia Hemans's "The Image in Lava": A Note' (pp. 212–30). Unlike Shelley's 'Ozymandias', to which Armstrong compares 'The Image in Lava', Hemans's poem presents a radical sublime dissociated from violence and so privileging the love between the volcanically cast mother and child. This love, intersubjective and social, excludes the force of masculine feeling to induce a feminine language, ephemeral and so exempt from commodification. Locating the poem within both contemporary reports on discoveries at Pompeii and Hemans's earlier poems on national monuments and tombs, notably *The Restoration of the Works of Art to Italy* and *Modern Greece*, the essay delicately confirms Hemans's ability to celebrate all that is fleeting, intangible and emotive through the material and political events of her day.

Two further collections including essays on women's Romantic poetry appeared this year: Shattock, ed., *Women and Literature in Britain, 1800–1900* and Craciun and Lokke, eds., *Rebellious Hearts: British Women Writers and the French Revolution*. Joanne Shattock's volume offers critical assessments of women's feminism, journalism, drama, autobiography and children's literature from the wider nineteenth century, but there is much here in contextual terms for the reader of women's Romantic poetry. As the editor claims in the introduction (pp. 1–7), the period produced 'a heightened awareness, even a sense of excitement about women's increased presence on the literary scene', and 'women poets were singled out for special treatment'. Noting the fascination with the 'poetess' in works by Alexander Dye, Leigh Hunt, George W. Bethune and Frederick Rowton, Shattock also considers how the press contributed to both the construction and the reception of the woman poet. Joanne Wilkes's 'Remaking the Canon' (pp. 35–54) focuses on the impact 'the legend of the Brontës' had on the canon, Romantic Emily in particular prey to accusations of wild, literary genius which 'bewildered, even horrified' reviewers unable to ignore the 'sheer power' of her writing. The Brontës also appear in Elisabeth Jay's 'Women Writers and Religion' (pp. 251–74), which, while primarily concerned with the novel, raises the question of why nineteenth-century religious verse by women is often ignored. Its very reputation, Jay suggests, is threatened by both its volume, 'which makes it a laborious exercise to winnow the wheat from the chaff', and its tendency to 'narrow the Romantic sensibility into piously sentimental versifying'. The most significant essay in the volume in relation to women's Romantic poetry, however, is Virginia Blain's important piece, 'Women Poets and the Challenge of Genre' (pp. 162–88). Mapping the period through Mary Tighe, Caroline Bowles, Emily Brontë, Dorothy Wordsworth, Eliza Hamilton, Hemans and Landon, before moving on to Victorian and *fin-de-siècle* women poets, Blain points to many key poetical shifts during the period. The 'romantic glorification of abandonment in love', for example, is dropped for an interest in the 'psychology of couples', just as conflicts such as that between faith and fame were subsumed by a turn to domestic loneliness and science.

Blain's essay is also crucial because it challenges two key hypotheses that currently dominate the field. First, she dismantles Anne Mellor's distinction between 'politically engaged "female poets"' and more conventionally feminized "poetesses"', suggesting that such a 'rigid divide' encourages a 'kind of post-feminist sexism'. Many serious poets, notably Barrett Browning, dealt with the issue of romantic love, Blain argues, just as sentimentality had a forceful political power, as it did in the poetry of Hemans, a figure whose popularity and significance are attested to throughout the essay. Second, Blain rethinks Daniel Karlin's assumption that women poets bypassed the Wordsworthian 'pleasure principle' of poetry, increasingly taking the art form too seriously. The difficulties women experienced in attempting to write from a 'motive of pleasure' are deftly highlighted here, and Karlin's surmise is insightfully compared to 'early (male) reactions to women as undergraduates in the universities, where they were constantly ridiculed for taking their studies too seriously'. While much of the essay concentrates on privileged poets who were able to write for pleasure, Blain is careful to note the major working-class poets of the period, Mary Colling, Janet Hamilton and Ellen Johnston, although Ann Yearsley, perhaps a little late for this piece, is not referred to. Yearsley does, however, warrant a fleeting mention in Adriana Craciun and Kari Lokke's volume, notably in Angela Keane's 'The Anxiety of (Feminine) Influence: Hannah More and Counterrevolution' (pp. 109–34). Keane departs from the patronage controversy, however, to address More's counter-revolutionary politics, rooted in her vision of a virtuous femininity which she believed would both financially and morally ground Britain's economy during the 1790s. Welcoming the destruction of the Bastille but troubled by the transfer of power in France, More pitied the monarchy, whose members she regarded as victims of mob rule, itself produced by secular values her evangelicalism and Sunday School movement sought to prevent in Britain. As Craciun and Lokke show in their introduction (pp. 3–30), many women, French and British alike, commented on the French Revolution in a public and authorial manner often respected, as well as critiqued, by their male contemporaries. Acknowledging women's responses to this public and political debate, *Rebellious Hearts* balances prevailing conceptions of literary interactions with the Revolution, founded as they are on both Wordsworth and Coleridge's desertion of its cause and Blake, Hazlitt and Shelley's continued enthusiasm.

Moreover, Craciun and Lokke contend, women writers often asserted themselves in the name of religious truth, suggesting that old conceptions of the Habermasian public sphere must be broadened to include prophecies, as in the case of Joanna Southcott, or evangelical effusion, such as that voiced by More. Underlining the limitations of understanding the revolution in purely secular terms, then, the study includes three essays on women's poetry, one of which directly addresses the relevance of religion in this period. Ann Frank Wake's 'Indirect Dissent: "Landscaping" Female Agency in Amelia Alderson Opie's Poems of the 1790s' (pp. 261–89) reveals the tension between retaining a sense of feminine propriety while expressing dissenting views on political subjects such as slavery. For Frank Wake, Opie implemented landscape imagery to 'paint' her response to the revolution within poetry, strategically implying her views rather than directly declaring them, like Barbauld or Charlotte Smith. Despairing that the landscape of spring will fail to bring liberty, for example, Opie's narrator in 'Ode on the Present Times' can only long for freedom's 'form sublime', unable to 'join I The song of triumph!' (ll. 35–8). Smith, however, envisages spring as a prospect producing a more straightforward sense of despondency, openly attacking war in *The Emigrants* as that which stains the land 'with blood', annihilating 'The hope of cultivation' (ll. 71–4). Both Opie and Smith ultimately pull back from politics, however, and Lokke's contribution to the book, '"The mild dominion of the moon": Charlotte Smith and the Politics of Transcendence' (pp. 85–106), explores Smith further by discussing the cover she used to articulate radical views. For Lokke, Smith employed 'images of transcendence and sublimity' in her poetry to represent an 'emancipatory distance and detachment' from the political struggles of the age. Such a perspective achieves a clear and compassionate picture of the revolution, Lokke argues, the bright moon envisioned in so many of Smith's *Elegiac Sonnets* benevolently illuminating the landscape to project upon it a peaceful and feminine consciousness, rather than the hostility of war.

Single-author studies are still rare in this field, and Dick Wakefield's *Anna Laetitia Barbauld* is a welcome contribution. Wakefield, 'a computer systems designer by profession' and 'historian by temperament', claims to have stumbled across Barbauld while researching eighteenth- and nineteenth-century merchants in Liverpool. Despite this rather dubious preface, the study is the first published book to be wholly devoted to the poet since Betsy Rodgers's *Georgian Chronicle*, and gives the reader a solid biographical introduction. Five chapters covering Barbauld's numerous geographical shifts trace her development from the precocious 'Nancy Aikin' to the matured 'Mrs Barbauld', presenting her throughout as an at once rational and whimsical thinker. Her intellect and 'firmness of belief' are also central for Wakefield, who focuses on the influence of Dissent upon her and her family as that which motivated their unusual appreciation of education for all. The book opens at Kibworth Harcourt, and carefully catalogues the poet's genealogy from her great-grandfather, John Jennings, a Dissenting minister during the seventeenth century. One of his students, Philip Doddridge, would later establish a Dissenting academy at Northampton, in which poetry was privileged as the vehicle of learning. This, and the Dissenting congregation at Kibworth, where Barbauld's father was pastor, became the basis for the Warrington Academy, to which the Barbaulds moved in 1758. Wakefield continues to emphasize the importance of poetry in Dissenting education in his second chapter on Warrington, and debates the pedagogical techniques developed at the academy by Barbauld's father, the Priestleys and Gilbert Wakefield. The liberal, religiously tolerant and public-spirited philosophy promoted by the school touched Barbauld, although she is pictured here as someone who 'rebelled against the seriousness' of its project. Experimenting with poetry and prose while under the sway of numerous figures, the handsome Rigbys, gentle-spirited Kinders and later Joseph Johnson, Barbauld embraced the critical reason encouraged by her education, Wakefield shows, while absorbing the vibrancy of society.

As Wakefield shows, however, the vitality Barbauld found in social interaction was lost when she moved to Palgrave as Rochemont Barbauld's wife. Oddly, no mention is made of their troubled relationship, and his later violence towards her, and the study sometimes becomes problematically linear, offering little commentary on Barbauld's actions or opinions. Yet Wakefield's constant reminders regarding Barbauld's at once religious and emotional temperament are useful in light of previous portrayals of her as a woman of reason and good taste alone. This latter image of Barbauld is borne out here too, but the reader is always aware of her interest in feeling as the conductor of devotion, especially when communicated through poetry. Despite the publication of her literature for children, which Samuel Johnson notoriously attacked as trivial and foolish, and her role as a political commentator, editor and essayist, Barbauld the poet shines out here. While it is perhaps disappointing that Wakefield draws on little of her poetry, his manuscript sources, consisting mainly of letters, tell us much about Barbauld's attitudes towards fame, celebrity, contemporary drama and poetical taste. His chapter on Hampstead is particularly focused on the Joseph Johnson circle and her acquaintances within it, Mary Wollstonecraft, Elizabeth Inchbald, Sarah Siddons, Thomas Holcroft and the

Opies among them. Stressing again the 'sustained power of feeling' that comes forth in Barbauld's *Civic Sermons to the People* [1792] and *Sins of the Government; Sins of the Nations* [1793], Wakefield draws a link between this work and her later editions of Mark Akenside and William Collins's poetry. The final part, on Stoke Newington, addresses Henry Crabb Robinson's friendship with the poet, and her correspondence with Wordsworth (who preferred Barbauld 'as poet rather than critic'); Hannah More and Maria Edgeworth are also cited. The public furore over the publication of *Eighteen Hundred and Eleven*, and her work on the *British Novelists* project are also filled out here, and yet we are left with a slightly idealized portrait of a fun-loving elderly sage, whose youth never left her.

Such a short study may have been restricted from offering a more comprehensive picture, perhaps, but any scholar hoping to find bibliographic or manuscript detail will be disappointed, Wakefield failing to provide any footnoted citation. Archival records are noted, however, and the book does cover many pivotal moments in Barbauld's career, including her depiction in Richard Samuel's *Nine Living Muses of Great Britain* [1775]. A more erudite analysis of the portrait is offered by Elizabeth Eger this year, in her essay 'Representing Culture: *The Nine Living Muses of Great Britain* (1779)' (in Eger *et al.*, eds., *Women, Writing and the Public Sphere, 1700–1830*, pp. 104–32). For Eger, Barbauld's representation in the picture, along with her fellow models, is an 'act of embodiment' which 'suggests in itself the rise of the woman writer's professional activity during the eighteenth century'. The allegorical piece, Eger argues, works through contemporary links between culture, commerce and women, recognizing women's cultural capital in the period and so challenging John Barrell's influential notion of the history painting as a vehicle for upholding a public and masculine ideal of virtue. Barbauld herself, Susan Rosenbaum argues in '"A thing unknown, without a name": Anna Laetitia Barbauld and the Illegible Signature' (*SiR* 40[2001] 369–99), also complicated the notion of the woman writer in her poetry, the utterance of a gendered and restrained lyrical voice critiquing political and economic shapings of the private sphere. Rosenbaum's fascinating piece identifies a 'miniaturist aesthetic' in Barbauld's poetry, taking as it does miniature objects as a focus, the tininess of which opposes notions of 'capitalist expansion' and the 'expansive romantic self'. In doing so, her poetry charts a response to the marketing of 'poetic sincerity and the culture of literary celebrity', immersed at once in the world of Romantic fame and the small, local audiences through which Barbauld's work was circulated. David Chandler's 'Barbauld's "To Mr. S.T. Coleridge": A Possible Source' (*N&Q* 48:ii[2000] 129–31) traces her famous poem on Coleridge back to the anonymously published, 'The Temple of Wealth: A Vision' [1792]. The essay, included in the Unitarian periodical *Christian Miscellany*, is attributed by Chandler to Charles Marsh, a pupil at Barbauld's Palgrave school, who may have read, and been influenced by, her 'The Hill of Science: A Vision' [1773].

Two articles return to Barbauld's controversial epic. The first, Karen Hadley's '"The Wealth of Nations" or "The Happiness of Nations"? Barbauld's Malthusian Critique in *Eighteen Hundred and Eleven*' (*CLAJ* 45:i[2000] 87–96), suggests that the poem's critique of imperialism is specifically gendered. For Hadley, *Eighteen Hundred and Eleven* explores the British empire's origins in 'enlightenment culture and free-market capitalism' while subverting its 'gendered logic', thus questioning the masculine foundations of 'genius', 'science', 'freedom' and 'power'.

Responding to William Godwin, Thomas Malthus and Adam Smith, Hadley contends, Barbauld encouraged her readers to see beyond Enlightenment rationality and the 'materialist desire for wealth and conquest' to which it is yoked. The second, Penny Bradshaw's 'Dystopian Futures: Time-Travel and Millenarian Visions in the Poetry of Anna Barbauld and Charlotte Smith' (*RoN* 21[2001]), puts forward the idea that Barbauld, like Smith, appropriated the 'fantastic device of time-travel' in her poetry to provide a 'vision of the ruins of British and European civilisation'. Drawing on Rosemary Jackson's socially produced notion of fantasy, Bradshaw suggests that Barbauld and Smith complicate the conventional male-authored visionary epic by envisioning what is to come through past events and so producing a dystopian, rather than utopian, future. *Eighteen Hundred and Eleven*, like Smith's 'Beachy Head', are regarded here as offering a radical commentary on society through a feminized figure of Fancy as 'time-traveller', moving freely in time and space to challenge 'nineteenth-century restrictions on the female body and mind'. Smith is also discussed by Kathryn Pratt in 'Charlotte Smith's Melancholia on the Page and Stage' (*SEL* 41[2001] 563–81), a paper which traces the melancholia of the *Elegiac Sonnets* back to a theatrical persona that serves to expose conventional poetic productions of sorrow. In doing so, Smith insists on her own sorrow as a sign of authentic literary power, constructing a stage from her verses on which to scrutinize the relationship between 'feeling spectator' and 'pitiable spectacle'. Diane E. Boyd also turns to Smith in her '"Professing drudge": Charlotte Smith's Negotiation of a Mother-Writer Author Function' (*SoAR* 66:i[2001] 145–66), an exploration of the poet's conception of motherhood as a way to understand the role and make-up of the woman author.

Robinson and Landon, like Hemans, continue to be central within this area, as three excellent essays portray this year: Myra Cottingham's 'Felicia Hemans's Dead and Dying Bodies' (*WW* 8:ii[2001] 275–94); Ashley Cross's 'From *Lyrical Ballads* to *Lyrical Tales*: Mary Robinson's Reputation and the Problem of Literary Debt', (*SiR* 40[2001] 571–605); and Valerie Sanders's '"Meteor wreaths": Harriet Martineau, L.E.L.: Fame and *Fraser's Magazine*' (*CS* 13:ii[2001] 42–60). Cottingham traces the numerous dead and dying warriors that litter Hemans's *Records of Woman* to show how they forge a coded critique of warfare, and, notably, its effects on women. By privileging the expression of pain and loss, Hemans removes male presences from her poetry in order to both force and free women to adopt traditionally masculine roles of protection, vengeance and sometimes warfare itself, as in her powerful depiction of Joan of Arc. Cottingham also focuses on the poet's presentation of young women who, despairing of the potential loss of their lovers, question the value of marriage and assume a sense of independence, albeit one that is uneasy and troubled. Such trepidation, however, is overcome by the notion of female friendship, the article shows, the closing poem of *Records* prefaced with an epigraph from Madame de Staël and dedicated to Mary Tighe. Cross returns to the subject of fame and reputation in her discussion of Robinson, who linked her own status to that of Wordsworth and Coleridge in *Lyrical Tales* [1800], read here as a revisionary response to the *Lyrical Ballads* [1798]. Far more famous than her male colleagues at the turn of the century, Robinson responded to the *Ballads* not to enhance her celebrity, but instead to remind her readers of the radical politics at the core of her poetic project. This, Cross argues, enabled Robinson to recast herself as more than a performative and sexualized actress, regarded, as Coleridge declared, as much as 'sister whore' as 'undoubted Genius'. Sanders is also concerned with the question of fame, expressly in the 1830s, reflecting on Landon's treatment by critics and comparing it to that endured by Martineau. Both, she claims, considered the attentions of a male literary establishment 'upsetting and intrusive', represented here by *Fraser's Magazine*'s William Maginn. Maginn's tendency to be overly chivalrous in addressing Landon pushed her into a position of disillusionment and despair regarding women's vulnerability in the literary market, one which she worked through, Sanders illustrates, in her reviews of Bulwer Lytton's novels and Hemans's life for the *New Monthly Magazine*, and in her poem 'Erinna'.

Joanna Baillie is increasingly considered in print, and, in addition to Broadview's outstanding edition of *Plays on the Passions*, reviewed in section 6 below, Natasha Aleksiuk and Judith Slagle's short articles attest to such interest. Aleksiuk's excellent 'Joanna Baillie's "Thunder" in 1790 and 1840' (*N&Q* 48:ii[2001] 132–6) argues that the poet reshaped the volatile 1790 poem into a more subdued form palatable to Victorian tastes before reprinting it in 1840. In discussing the revisions, Aleksiuk shows that both versions of the poem end on a religious note which invokes a divinely sent storm, an equalizing force which causes both rich and poor, women and men, to search for shelter. Slagle's 'A Note on Joanna Baillie's Addresses: Corrections to Published Historical Records' (*N&Q* 48:ii[2001] 131–2) emerges from her forthcoming biography of the poet, which suggests that she had completed *Poems* [1790] and the first volume of *A Series of Plays* [1798] before moving to London. This is an important discovery because it reveals that both volumes could not have been influenced by the Hampstead circle, although Slagle admits that Baillie may have had previous contact with Barbauld through church connections.

Hannah More also continues to engage critics, Mona Scheuermann's 'Hannah More and the English Poor' (*ECL* 25:ii[2001] 237–51) contextualizing her poetry and other writing by examining its connections with eighteenth-century Poor Law. Scheuermann declares, in perhaps overly simplistic terms, that More was the 'opposite of a revolutionary' and the 'standard-bearer' of the status quo, directly challenging those who render her a feminist pioneer. *Village Politics* thus becomes little more than a disapproving reaction against Paine's *Rights of Man* in the article, More deemed one who considered the raising of 'the poor from their poverty' counter to 'God's plan'. In 'A Moral Purchase: Femininity, Commerce and Abolition, 1788–1792' (in Eger *et al.*, eds., pp. 133–59), Kate Davies constructs More as a self-appointed overseer of a 'global softening process' in which the poor are refined and humanity 'assimilated into a commercial brotherhood'. Davies is specifically concerned with abolitionism here, and the manner in which it positioned femininity and sympathy in a moral space beyond politics and commerce, a division which More helped to dissolve by positing women as the regulators of an 'international market of peace and plenty'.

Finally, Harriet Kramer Linkin's 'How It Is: Teaching Women's Poetry in British Romanticism Classes' (*Pedagogy* 1:i[2001] 91–115) provides a forum in which several critics comment on the state of teaching poetry in this field, extending the work previously accomplished in Linkin's earlier book, *Approaches to Teaching British Women Poets of the Romantic Period* (see *YWES* 79[2000] 241). For Linkin, quoting Nanora Sweet, the infusion of Romantic-era women poets into the canon, classroom and conference arena has helped to reshape the study of Romantic literature into 'a conversation again and not an exercise in worshipful piety'. Yet questions remain regarding the inclusion of such new material, and Linkin's choice of contributors reflects a variety of reactions to such query, exploring student responses (Stephen C. Behrendt, Alan Richardson); personal processes of discovery (Elizabeth Fay, Carol Shiner Wilson, Mary A. Favret); teaching techniques (Jerome McGann, Catherine Burroughs, Anne K. Mellor, Marjean Purinton, Nanora Sweet); and considerations of 'what else needs to get done' (Jeanne Moskal, Judith Pascoe, Harriet Kramer Linkin). Much of the commentary is insightful, clarifying the strengths of an at once emotional and political poetics which demands that we reread men's poetry in new ways, recognizing their investment in domestic issues previously considered the sole domain of women. Yet Linkin's conjecture that the field offers untold opportunities to graduate students in search of projects 'not yet researched to death' is unfortunate, commodifying women's poetry as that which can simply 'produce publishable research in a semester'. Those working in this field might be wary of both pushing out research on women's Romantic poetry and assuming that there is little left to be said on already much-contemplated poets. Without a gradual build-up of careful and meditated criticism on Romantic women, scholarship will render their poetry a commercial platform on which professional careers are made, instead of securing the place of such work within the intellectual sphere and thus protecting it from future dismissal.

6. Drama

Genre, gender, and nation intersecting with the theatrical is the subject of Betsy Bolton's *Women, Nationalism and the Romantic Stage: Theatre and Politics in Britain, 1780–1800*, but could also be said to be the focal point of current Romantic drama studies. Bolton examines these mutual influences, ultimately building an argument about the nation of Britain developing its image through a lens of sexual difference. Noting that it is a commonplace now to see the British nation viewed as a stage on which the public drama is enacted, and to consider politicians and other public figures as performers, Bolton conceives of the theatre as an 'intermediate public sphere' between the public press, Parliament, and coffee-houses, on the one hand, and the private, domestic novel on the other. Her monograph is a richly illustrated, densely layered study that makes good use of the cartoons and caricatures that theatricalized public figures and events. The book is organized in three parts: the first examines the interpenetrations of genre, gender, and nation in the political performances (onstage and off) that range from heartfelt sentiment to flamboyant spectacle; the second looks at the figures of Emma Hamilton and Mary 'Perdita' Robinson, who become publicly characterized in accordance with the conventions of dramatic romance; and the third studies 'mixed-genre' plays of Hannah Cowley (*A Day in Turkey*) and Elizabeth Inchbald (*A Mogul Tale, Such Things Are, Wives as They Were, Maids as They Are*), which use mimicry and farce in order to comment on England's growing imperialism and involvement in war. Bolton's study further develops our knowledge of the political and cultural contexts in which the drama performed its work, but she does so in the service of setting the stage for examining Romantic drama's aesthetic contributions, observing that 'Romantic drama makes aesthetic sense as well as political sense only when seen in its large cultural context'. While Bolton seems to feel the need to apologize for choosing to focus on minor genres—farce and dramatic romance and well as the 'mixed-genre' plays of Cowley and Inchbald—the most valuable contributions to this book include her analyses of these genres, especially her observations on the ways in which their conventions can be used to convey (and hide behind) political messages. Considering that it was a time of such vigorous experimentation with dramatic genre—revealing dramatists' desire to create forms that could represent the culture in flux—this aspect deserves even more study.

Perhaps the most useful publication of the year is Peter Duthie's edition of Joanna Baillie's *Plays on the Passions*, a fully annotated and contextualized reprint of the 1798 first volume of *A Series of Plays* that is sure to become a standard text in literature and theatre courses and to encourage the reading of more Romantic plays as well as to ensure Baillie's canonical status. This volume features what are already the most often taught and currently discussed plays in Baillie studies: the tragedy *De Montfort*, and the comedy *The Tryal* with its tragic counterpart *Count Basil*, along with Baillie's theoretical 'Introductory Discourse', the prologue and epilogue from the Larpent version of *De Montfort*, and well-chosen contextual pieces ranging from Wollstonecraft's *Vindication* to Locke, Hume, Burke, Smith and Stewart on the passions and moral sentiments, to Wordsworth's Preface to *Lyrical Ballads* and contemporary reviews of the plays. Duthie's excellent critical introduction provides biographical detail and a portrait of the London theatre of Baillie's day, and makes a strong case for the *Series of Plays* as a text of social reform. Its greatest strength, though, lies in Duthie's explanation of Baillie's theories in comparison with those of the other moral philosophers of the day, thus situating her within the era's broader philosophical discourses on the head and heart, reason and passion, and helping us understand more rigorously the *science* in her work on the passions and moral enquiry. As Duthie writes, 'here in one volume is an opportunity to re-think the character of the eighteenth century in all its dynamic diversity, to reconsider the role women played in the artistic communities of those times, and to review our place at the end of over two hundred years of profound change'.

Marjean D. Purinton's new research into Baillie and Romantic studies is her conceptualization of the 'techno-Gothic', an 'ideologically charged and melodramatic structure' in which the supernatural experiences of the Gothic become recontextualized by modern science and technology. In 'Science Fiction and Techno-Gothic Drama: Romantic Playwrights Joanna Baillie and Jane Scott' (*RoN* 21[2001]), Purinton argues that techno-Gothic works such as Baillie's drama *Orra* and Scott's comedy *The Old Oak Chest* allowed a venue for women to participate in scientific discourse as creators, not objects, of experiments; she also postulates that the roots of science fiction may lie in the techno-Gothic drama written by women before 1818, rather than in *Frankenstein*. Baillie biographer Judith Bailey Slagle provides a concise introduction to the author in 'Joanna Baillie: Synthesis of Romanticism, Nationalism, and Feminism' (in Behrendt and Kushigian, eds., *Scottish Women Poets of the Romantic Period*).

Since the publication of Michael Simpson's *Closet Performances: Political Exhibition and Prohibition in the Dramas of Byron and Shelley* [1998] and Gleckner and Beatty, eds., *The Plays of Lord Byron: Critical Essays* [1997], Byron's dramatic corpus has received a deserved renewal of attention as work with much to say to us today about the desires for and frustrations of attempting political action. The new collection, *Contemporary Studies on Lord Byron*, edited by William D. Brewer and Marjean D. Purinton (Mellen [2001]), not received in time for review, includes several essays that address Byron's drama, including Alan Rawes, 'Beyond the Fitting Medium of Desire: Lord Byron and D.H. Lawrence' (pp. 121–39), and, especially, Thomas Crochunis, 'Byronic Heroes and Acting: The Embodiment of Mental Theater' (pp. 73–94) on Edmund Kean's acting and *The Two Foscari*, *Marino Faliero*, and *Sardanapalus*. Melynda Nuss, in '"The gory head rolls down the giants' steps!": The Return of the Physical in Byron's *Marino Faliero*' (*ERR* 12:ii[2001] 226–36), presents a sceptical Byron whose *Marino Faliero* exemplifies 'both the drama's ability to connect and its failure'. Byron's desire to reform the stage, Nuss argues, was in truth a desire to return to the earlier stages where the public mingled and the drama served to connect them, for in the giant houses of the early nineteenth century audiences were rendered passive observers. In these massive spaces only the grossly physical, not the subtly verbal, would communicate; the play's gory head is one of the few physical signs that conveys meaning, but, Nuss sagely notes, as the rolling of this head would inevitably be comic, not scary, onstage, Byron negates the possibility of positive (political) action. Gordon Spence, in 'Natural Law and the State in *The Two Foscari*' (*BJ* 29[2001] 27–35), calls *The Two Foscari* 'the most modern of the plays of the Romantic period' because it puts the audience in the position of confronting the mysteries of the state, filled with secret trials, tortures, executions of political prisoners. In an Antigone-like move, the play pits appeals to natural law (humanity) against the Doge's law (the state), with the key debate between Marina and the Doge speaking to us today 'with a voice of prophecy'. Peter Cochran's '*Manfred* and Thomas Taylor' (*BJ* 29[2001] 62–71) uses close reading of the manuscripts of *Manfred* with Byron's notes to posit that classicist Thomas Taylor's translation of Pausanias is the famous 'something else' that influenced the writing of *Manfred*.

'Byron and Disability' is the title of a special collection of essays in *European Romantic Review* (*ERR* 12:iii[2001]), edited and introduced by Andrew Elfenbein, three of which concern Byron's curious autobiographical dramatic fragment *The Deformed Transformed*. Elfenbein leads off with 'Byron and the Fantasy of Compensation' (*ERR* 12:iii[2001] 267–83), in which he argues that Byron rebels against the 'narrative of compensation' found in Milton's response to his own blindness or in Wordsworth's 'Tintern Abbey', where the spirit must overcome the body's deficiencies. *The Deformed Transformed* is decidedly not a compensation narrative, as the deformed is *not* transformed, but the argument holds true not only in cases where characters have physical disability, as Elfenbein shows in his reading of *Manfred*, at the moment where Manfred wants to commit suicide and is held back in his body's desires by the Chamois Hunter. Stuart Peterfreund, in 'Byron, *The Deformed Transformed*, and the Problematic of Embodiment' (*ERR* 12:iii[2001] 284–300), takes a Lacanian view of Byron's play. Both linguistically and psychically Byron is unable to 'symbolize difference', and as a result associates embodiment itself with being disabled: since all humanity, being embodied, has fallen from grace and is imperfect, it is already disabled. Marjean D. Purinton continues to develop her concept of the techno-Gothic in 'Byron's Disability and the Techno-Gothic Grotesque in *The Deformed Transformed*' (*ERR* 12:iii[2001] 301–20). Analysing Byron's obsession with his own body, his own grotesqueness, Purinton reads the grotesqueness that informs identity not only in the individual, but in the cultural body of Rome, and, metadramatically, the fragmented, incomplete play itself. Rosemarie Garland Thomson follows with 'Byron and the New Disability Studies: A Response' (*ERR* 12:iii[2001] 321–27), in which she describes the new disability studies as a category of critical analysis.

One of the most extensively researched and impressive pieces of scholarship this year was Victoria Myers's 'Justice and Indeterminacy: Wordsworth's *The Borderers* and the Trials of the 1790s' (*SiR* 40[2001] 427–57). Instead of a work of introduction or recovery, Myers's essay feels like a certain completion of a conversation. She carefully constructs her argument upon details from several legal cases of the 1790s to reveal how Wordsworth works them into his play in order to convey, both rhetorically and dramaturgically, the crises of political justice that cause 'mental transition', or a change in character. This action by Wordsworth allows him—and us—to theorize history both as custom and as trauma. As seen in book X of *The Prelude*, disturbing public events, such as notorious trials or wars, caused Wordsworth to lose trust in institutions, particularly the justice system, and turn to trust in Nature. While such a mental transition is extraordinarily difficult to show onstage, Wordsworth writes *The Borderers* as a drama in order to highlight discrepancies between appearance and reality, to which a theatre audience is always attuned. The audience, then, is thrust into a state of indeterminacy—much as Wordsworth himself felt, in his own move from 'radical action to a state of radical indeterminacy'.

In *Prism(s)* (9[2001]) Franca Barricelli continues her research on late eighteenth-century civic theatre in Venice with 'The Tears and Terror of Foscolo's Trieste: Theatre and Politics in Republican Venice' (*Prism(s)* 9[2001] 31–49) and Marjean D. Purinton her research into science and medicine in Romantic drama in 'Socialized and Medicalized Hysteria in Joanna Baillie's *Witchcraft*' (*Prism(s)* 9[2001] 139–56). Interest in Scottish Romantic drama outside Baillie is found in the special edition of *Studies in Romanticism* (40:i[2001]), which includes Cairns Craig's 'Scott's Staging of the Nation' (*SiR* 40[2001] 13–28), which discusses in part Scott's 'manipulation of history into national theater', and Yoon Sun Lee's 'Giants in the North: *Douglas*, the Scottish Enlightenment, and Scott's *Redgauntlet*' (*SiR* 40[2001] 109–21), which gives much-deserved attention to John Home's moving tragedy *Douglas* as a nationalist drama.

Historical scholarship on performance gives us a more complex understanding of the cultural work of actors as well as playwrights, as seen in several articles this year. Catherine Burroughs, in 'British Women Playwrights and the Staging of Female Sexual Initiation: Sophia Lee's *The Chapter of Accidents* (1780)' (*RoN* 23[2001]) explores the use in Lee's dramaturgy of 'pornographic patterns' such as the re-enactment of the loss of virginity. Lee offers two 'non-virgins' as heroines of the comedy and makes the assumption of their innocence a matter of comic and erotic effect throughout the play. Burroughs argues that Lee's staging of a 'performative chastity'—a virginity that can be re-enacted and put on—explores sexual fantasies while also exploring cultural fantasies of a sexual relationship in which both men and women take responsibility and derive pleasure. Jim Davis's '"They shew me off in every form and way": The Iconography of English Comic Acting in the Late Eighteenth and Early Nineteenth Centuries' (*TRI* 26:iii[2001] 243–56) presents an abundantly illustrated study of comic actors John Liston and Joseph Munden in order to demonstrate how prints educated audiences (then and now) in reading the iconography of actors' expressions. Kathryn Pratt's 'Leigh Hunt's Melancholia and English Musical Theater' (*WC* 32:i[2001] 29–33) argues that Hunt, while he was often critical of the drama, desired the social interaction of theatre and an English national theatre that would unify people and lighten them from depression, both individually and culturally; we can see his plans in his 1815 masque *The Descent of Liberty*, which brings down the 'Enchanter', Napoleon, and his unfinished *Musical Evenings*, a 'sing-along primer' for middle-class home enjoyment. And Kris Steyaert, in 'A "Massive dramatic plum pudding": The Politics of Reception in the Early Antwerp Performance of Shelley's *The Cenci*' (*KSJ* 51[2001] 14–26), challenges Stuart Curran's assertion that *The Cenci* grew in popularity in the 1920s because the era was less conservative and became enamoured of Shelley's fame as a lyric poet. Even though *The Cenci*'s Dutch translator 'politically sanitized' the play so that it expressed a concern for the underprivileged more than a fight against tyrannical autocracy, the six performances in Antwerp in January 1929 were a financial flop because of conservative critics, who warned viewers to avoid the seditious nature of the play and the disreputable Shelley himself.

Adding actual performances to our repertoire of research methods is the most recent innovation in Romantic drama studies. At the 2000 conference of the North American Society for the Study of Romanticism (NASSR), the members were treated to an unusual plenary session: a production of John Fawcett's melodrama about slavery, *Obi; or, Three Finger'd Jack* [1800], punctuated by a panel of critical respondents. Catherine Burroughs recounts the evening in *European Romantic Review* (12:iii[2001] 381–9) and articulates the advantages of incorporating live performance into our research and analysis. In conjunction, the always impressive hypertext *Romantic Circles Praxis Series* includes a special volume on *Obi; or, Three-Finger'd Jack*. The edition includes the complete text of the melodrama and modern video reproductions of both the melodrama and original pantomime versions of this work, along with an introduction by Charles Rzepka and six critical essays. Jeffrey Cox's 'Theatrical Forms, Ideological Conflicts, and the Staging of *Obi*' analyses generic differences between melodrama and pantomime in terms of releasing or containing radical messages. Peter Buckley, in '*Obi* in New York' presents the early history of the play, while Jerrold Hogle, in 'Directing *Obi* in 2000' explains rationales of the two contemporary stagings at the NASSR conference and in Boston. Robert Hoskins's 'Savage Boundaries: Reading Samuel Arnold's Score' examines the score for the pantomime version, and Debbie Lee's 'Grave Dirt, Dried Toads, and the Blood of a Black Cat: How Aldridge Worked his Charms' spotlights the actor Ira Aldridge (the first internationally renowned African American actor, sometimes called the 'nineteenth-century Paul Robeson'), who played Jack, to show how his onstage rituals of obi-death made obi a cure for the disease of slavery.

Our scholarship continues to be aided by more access to primary texts themselves, and the website British Women Playwrights Around 1800 continues its excellent and important work of recovering, editing, and publishing dramas with the new additions of the full texts of Elizabeth Berkeley Craven, the Margravine of Anspach's 'spectacular operatic fairy tale' *The Georgian Princess* [1798], with an introduction by John Franceschina; and Mary Russell Mitford's *Charles the First* [1834], edited by Thomas Crochunis.

Books Reviewed

Ansari, Asloob Ahmad. *William Blake's Minor Prophecies*. Mellen. [2001] pp. xvi + 139. £64.95 ISBN 0 7734 7432 3.

Beckett, John. *Byron and Newstead: The Aristocrat and the Abbey*. UDelP. [2001] pp. 347. £42 ISBN 0 8741 3751 9.

Behrendt, Stephen, and Nancy Kushigian, eds. *Scottish Women Poets of the Romantic Period*. Alexander Street Press electronic publishers. [2001] <http://www.alexanderstreetpress.com>.

Bell, Maureen, Shirley Chew, Simon Eliot, Lynette Hunter and James L.W. West III, eds. *Re-Constructing the Book: Literary Texts in Transmission*. Ashgate. [2001] pp. 252. £37.50 ISBN 0 7546 0360 1.

Bentley, G.E. Jr. *The Stranger from Paradise: A Biography of William Blake*. YaleUP. [2001] pp. xxvii + 532. £25 ISBN 0 3000 8939 2.

Beran, David. *Early British Romanticism, the Frankfurt School and French Post-Structuralism: In the Wake of Failed Revolution. Studies on Themes and Motifs in Literature*. Lang. [2001] pp. 207. $53.95 ISBN 0 8204 4530 4.

Bolton, Betsy. *Women, Nationalism and the Romantic Stage: Theatre and Politics in Britain, 1780–1800*. CUP. [2001] pp. xi + 272. $60 ISBN 0 5217 7116 1.

Brewer, William D. *Contemporary Studies on Lord Byron*. Mellen. [2001] pp. 184. £64.95 ISBN 0 7734 7537 0.

Burwick, Frederick. *Mimesis and its Romantic Reflections*. PSUP. [2001] pp. ix + 203. £29.50 ISBN 0 2710 2037 7.

Burwick, Frederick. *Thomas De Quincey: Knowledge and Power*. Palgrave. [2001] pp. xiii + 192. £47.50 ($59.95) ISBN 0 3337 7403 5.

Bushell, Sally. *Re-Reading The Excursion: Narrative, Response and the Wordsworthian Dramatic Voice*. Ashgate. [2001] pp. x + 272. £45 ISBN 0 7546 0576 0.

Connell, Philip. *Romanticism, Economics and the Question of 'Culture'*. OUP. [2001] pp. xiii + 338. £45 ($60) ISBN 0 1981 8505 7.

Cook, Elizabeth, ed. *John Keats: The Major Works*. OUP. [2001] pp. xxxvi + 667. £9.99 ISBN 0 1928 4063 0.

Craciun, Adriana, and Kari E. Lokke, eds. *Rebellious Hearts: British Women Writers and the French Revolution*. SUNY. [2001] pp. xiii + 395. hb £45 ($63.50) ISBN 0 7914 4969 6, pb £15 ($20.95) ISBN 0 7914 4970 X.

De Quincey, Thomas. *Works*. P&C. [2001]. vol. 8: *Articles from Blackwood's Edinburgh Magazine and 'The Gallery of Portraits; Klosterheim: or, the Masque', 1831–2*, ed. Robert Morrison. pp. xii + 485. ISBN 1 8519 6519 X. vol. 9: *Articles from Blackwood's Edinburgh Magazine and Tait's Edinburgh Magazine, 1832–8*, ed. Grevel Lindop *et al*. pp. xi + 633. ISBN 1 8519 6519 X. vol. 12: *Articles from Blackwood's Edinburgh Magazine, 1840–1*, ed. Grevel Lindop. pp. ix + 376. ISBN 1 8519 6519 X. vol. 13: *Articles from Blackwood's Edinburgh Magazine and the Encyclopaedia Britannica, 1841–2*, ed. Grevel Lindop and John Whale. pp. x + 437. ISBN 1 8519 6519 X. vol. 14: *Articles from Blackwood's Edinburgh Magazine, 1842–3*, ed. John Whale. pp. x + 352. ISBN 1 8519 6519 X. vol. 17: *Articles from 'Hogg's Instructor' and 'Tait's Edinburgh Magazine', 1850–2*, ed. Edmund Baxter. pp. xii + 382. ISBN 1 8519 6519 X. vol.

18: *1853–8*, ed. Edmund Baxter. pp. ix + 248. ISBN 1 8519 6519 X. Set: £550 ($825).

Duthie, Peter, ed. *Plays on the Passions* by Joanna Baillie. Broadview. [2001] pp. 469. $15.95 ISBN 1 5511 1185 3.

Eger, Elizabeth, Charlotte Grant, Clíona Ó Gallchoir, and Penny Warburton, eds. *Women, Writing and the Public Sphere, 1700–1800.* CUP. [2001] pp. xi + 320. £40 ($60) ISBN 0 5217 7106 4.

Eldridge, Richard. *The Persistence of Romanticism: Essays in Philosophy and Literature.* Modern European Philosophy. CUP. [2001] pp. xii + 249. hb £37.50 ISBN 0 5218 0046 3, pb £13.95 ISBN 0 5218 0481 7.

Franklin, Caroline. *Byron and Women Novelists.* UNott. [2001] pp. 55. £3 ISBN 0 8535 8103 7.

Franklin, Michael, ed. *The European Discovery of India: Key Indological Sources of Romanticism*, 6 vols. Ganesha. [2001] pp. 2,600. £495 ($795) ISBN 1 8621 0016 0.

Fulford, Tim and Peter J. Kitson, eds. *Travels, Explorations and Empires: Writings from the Era of Imperial Expansion, 1770–1835.* P&C. [2001]. vol. 1: *North America*, ed. Tim Fulford, with Carol Bolton. pp. xlii + 405. ISBN 1 8519 6720 6. vol. 2: *Southeast Asia*, ed. Tim Fulford and Peter J. Kitson. pp. xxiii + 389. ISBN 1 8519 6720 6. vol. 3: *North and South Poles*, ed. Peter J. Kitson. pp. xxii + 401. ISBN 1 8519 6720 6. vol. 4: *Middle East*, ed. Tilar J. Mazzeo. pp. xxviii + 368. ISBN 1 8519 6720 6. Set: £350 ($570).

Gorak, Jan, ed. *Canon vs. Culture: Reflections on the Current Debate.* Garland. [2001] pp. 304. £60 ISBN 0 8153 0889 2.

Halsey, Alan. *The Text of Shelley's Death.* WHB. [2001] pp. 84. £8.95 ISBN 1 9040 5200 2.

Haney, David P. *The Challenge of Coleridge: Ethics and Interpretation in Romanticism and Modern Philosophy.* UPennP. [2001] pp. xviii + 309. £46.50 ISBN 0 2710 2051 2.

Hofstetter, Michael. J. *The Romantic Idea of a University: England and Germany, 1770–1850.* Palgrave. [2001] pp. xiv + 162. £47.50 ($58) ISBN 0 3337 1888 7.

Jackson, H.J., and George Whalley, eds. *The Collected Works of Samuel Taylor Coleridge*, vol. 12: *Marginalia VI.* Bollingen series LXXV. PrincetonUP. [2001] pp. xxxv + 715. £105 ($187.50) ISBN 0 6910 0495 1.

Keay, Mark. *William Wordsworth's Golden Age Theories during the Industrial Revolution in England, 1750–1850.* Palgrave. [2001] pp. ix + 295. £52.50 ISBN 0 3337 9436 2.

Kenyon-Jones, Christine. *Kindred Brutes: Animals in Romantic-Period Writing.* The Nineteenth Century. Ashgate. [2001] pp. viii + 229. £45 ISBN 0 7546 0332 6.

Kitson, Peter J., ed. *Placing and Displacing Romanticism.* The Nineteenth Century. Ashgate. [2001] pp. xv + 232. £45 ($79.95) ISBN 0 7546 0602 3.

Lovric, M.R. *Carnevale.* Virago. [2001] pp. 634. pb £7.99 ISBN 1 8604 9866 3.

Marsh, Nicholas. *William Blake: The Poems.* Palgrave. [2001] pp. xi + 253. £11.99 ISBN 0 3339 1467 8.

Mays, J.C.C., ed. *The Collected Works of Samuel Taylor Coleridge: Poetical Works*, vol. 1: *Poems (Reading Text).* PrincetonUP. [2001] pp. clxxviii + xxiii + 1,403. £135 ISBN 0 6910 0483 8.

Mays, J.C.C., ed. *The Collected Works of Samuel Taylor Coleridge: Poetical Works*, vol. 2: *Poems (Variorum Text)*. PrincetonUP. [2001] pp. li + xxv + 1,439. £135 ISBN 0 6910 0484 6.

McDayter, Ghislaine, Guinn Batten, and Barry Milligan, eds. *Romantic Generations: Essays in Honour of Robert F. Gleckner*. BuckUP. [2001] pp. 299. £38 ISBN 0 8387 5470 8.

Mizukoshi, Ayumi. *Keats, Hunt and the Aesthetics of Pleasure*. Palgrave. [2001] pp. vii + 228. £45 ISBN 0 3339 2958 6.

Møller, Lis, and Marie-Louise Svane, eds. *Romanticism in Theory*. AarhusUP. [2001] pp. 272. £19.95 ISBN 8 7728 8786 9.

Morillo, John D. *Uneasy Feelings: Literature, the Passions and Class from NeoClassicism to Romanticism*. AMS. [2001] pp. viii + 313. £58.50 ISBN 0 4046 3537 7.

Neish, William J.P., *The Speaking Eye: Byron's Aberdeen—People, Places and a Poem*. Book Guild. [2001] pp. xviii + 312. £10.50 ISBN 1 8577 6593 1.

Nikolova, Irena. *Complementary Modes of Representation in Keats, Novalis, and Shelley*. Lang. [2001] pp. xiii + 209. £35 ISBN 0 8204 5239 4.

Normington, Susan. *Lady Caroline Lamb: This Infernal Woman*. Stratus. [2001] pp. xv + 323. £18.99 ISBN 0 7551 1348 9.

Peterfreund, Stuart. *Shelley among Others: The Play of the Intertext and the Idea of Language*. JHUP. [2001] pp. xiii + 406. £38.50 ISBN 0 8018 6751 7.

Plotz, Judith. *Romanticism and the Vocation of Childhood*. Palgrave. [2001] pp. xvi + 304. £35 ISBN 0 3339 1535 6.

Quendler, Christian. *From Romantic Irony to Postmodernist Fiction: A Contribution to the History of Literary Self-Reflexivity in its Philosophical Context*. European University Studies. Peter Lang. [2001] pp. 182. $34.95 ISBN 3 6313 6718 X.

Richardson, Alan. *British Romanticism and the Science of the Mind*. Cambridge Studies in Romanticism. CUP. [2001] pp. xx + 243. £37.50 ($55) ISBN 0 5217 8191 4.

Robson, Catherine. *Men in Wonderland: The Lost Girlhood of the Victorian Gentleman*. PrincetonUP. [2001] pp. 262. £19.95 ISBN 0 6910 0422 6.

Roe, Nicholas, ed. *Samuel Taylor Coleridge and the Sciences of Life*. OUP. [2001] pp. xvi + 364. £55 ISBN 0 1981 8723 8.

Russell, Gillian, and Clara Tuite, eds. *Romantic Sociability: Social Networks and Literary Culture in Britain, 1770–1840*. CUP. [2001] pp. 280. $60 ISBN 0 5217 7068 8.

Shanks, Andrew. *What is Truth? Towards a Theological Poetics*. Routledge. [2001] pp. xii + 195. £19.99 ISBN 0 4152 5326 8.

Shattock, Joanne, ed. *Women and Literature in Britain, 1800–1900*. CUP. [2001] pp. xxii + 311. hb £40 ($60) ISBN 0 5216 5055 0, pb £14.95 ($22) ISBN 0 5216 5957 4.

Spector, Sheila. *'Glorious Incomprehensible': The Development of Blake's Kabbalistic Language*. BuckUP. [2001] pp. 201. $59.50 ISBN 0 8387 5469 4.

Spector, Sheila. *'Wonders Divine': The Development of Blake's Kabbalistic Myth*. BuckUP. [2001] pp. 213. $59.50 ISBN 0 8387 5468 6.

Stevenson, Warren. *A Study of Coleridge's Three Great Poems: Christabel, Kubla Khan, and The Rime of the Ancient Mariner.* Mellen. [2001] pp. v + 136. $99.95 ISBN 0 7734 7496 X.

Sweet, Nanora, and Julie Melnyk, eds. *Felicia Hemans: Reimagining Poetry in the Nineteenth Century.* Palgrave. [2001] pp. xxix + 242. £47.50 ($59.95) ISBN 0 3338 0109 1.

Trott, Nicola, and Seamus Perry, eds. *1800: The New Lyrical Ballads.* Palgrave. [2001] pp. x + 245. £45 ISBN 0 3337 7398 5.

Vail, Jeffrey W. *The Literary Relationship of Lord Byron and Thomas Moore.* JHUP. [2001] pp. xi + 251. £33.50 ISBN 0 8018 6500 X.

Wakefield, Dick. *Anna Laetitia Barbauld.* Centaur Press. [2001] pp. 113. £10.99 ($17.95) ISBN 0 9000 0145 3.

Waldoff, Leon. *Wordsworth in his Major Lyrics: The Art and Psychology of Self-Representation.* UMissP. [2001] pp. ix + 180. £23.50 ISBN 0 8262 1329 4.

Westbrook, Deanne, *Wordsworth's Biblical Ghosts.* Palgrave. [2001] pp. xi + 244. £32.50 ISBN 0 3122 4014 7.

Wolfson, Susan J., ed. *The Cambridge Companion to Keats.* CUP. [2001] pp. xliii + 272. hb £40 ISBN 0 5216 5126 3, pb £14.95 ISBN 0 5216 5839 X.

Wood, Gillen D'Arcy. *The Shock of the Real: Romanticism and Visual Culture, 1760–1860.* Palgrave. [2001] pp. xiv + 273. £37.50 ISBN 0 3122 2654 3.

Woof, Robert, ed. *William Wordsworth: The Critical Heritage,* vol. 1: *1793–1820.* Routledge. [2001] pp. xx + 1092. £150 ISBN 0 4150 3441 8.

XIII

The Nineteenth Century: The Victorian Period

WILLIAM BAKER, HALIE A. CROCKER, KIRSTIE BLAIR, JIM DAVIS AND DAVID FINKELSTEIN

This chapter has five sections: 1. Cultural Studies and Prose; 2. The Novel; 3. Poetry; 4. Drama and Theatre; 5. Periodicals and Publishing History. Sections 1 and 2 are by William Baker and Halie A. Crocker; section 3 is by Kirstie Blair; section 4 is by Jim Davis; section 5 is by David Finkelstein.

1. Cultural Studies and Prose

(a) General

An important contribution to cultural studies for the year 2001 is MacKenzie, ed., *The Victorian Vision: Inventing New Britain*, a survey of Victorian culture published to coincide with the exhibition at the Victoria and Albert Museum in London. *The Victorian Vision* challenges the stereotype of Victorians as repressed and repressive, arguing instead that the Victorian world was one on the verge of modernity—new, ambitious, outward-looking, and intent upon improvement and change. This comprehensive and well-illustrated survey includes a wide range of topics: photography, art, science, gender roles, education, transportation, health, religion, the home, leisure, and everyday life. It also includes a thoughtful examination of the Far East, India, and Africa's influence on art and design, as well as a final chapter contrasting the early years of Queen Victoria's reign to the culmination of its achievements in the later years. It is divided into three sections: 'Society', 'Technology', and 'The World', each with contributions from noted experts and scholars in the field.

Matthew Sweet, *Inventing the Victorians: What We Think We Know about Them and Why We're Wrong*, also challenges popular assumptions about the Victorian period, arguing that contemporary society has invented the stereotype of the repressed, humourless, and stern Victorian in order to make today's culture seem more enlightened by contrast. Covering a wide range of topics from poverty, capitalism, and religion to sex scandals, serial killers, and freak shows, Sweet argues that our 'twenty-first-century smugness' is misguided since the Victorian period was less violent, less racist, and less intolerant. Sweet's coverage of important issues such as sexuality, racism, and intolerance is especially noteworthy, as is his coverage of topics such as pleasure-seeking in opium dens, motion pictures, and even pornography. Also of interest is his discussion of media and advertising in the Victorian period.

John and Jenkins, eds., *Rethinking Victorian Culture*, brings together several essays from the 'Victorian Studies: Into the Twenty-First Century' conference at the University of Liverpool [1996]. The essays, by Kate Flint, Regenia Gagnier, and editors Juliet John and Alice Jenkins among others, provide reassessments of Victorian culture and literature, and are 'predicated on the view that the histories of Victorian and modern culture form a continuous narrative'. Andrew Horrall, *Popular Culture in London c.1890–1918: The Transformation of Entertainment*, discusses the fads and public crazes creating foundations for the modern 'celebrity' culture. Covering from the end of the Victorian period to the end of the First World War, Horrall explores interactions between performers and audiences in various arenas—on stage, in music halls, and in sport and cinema—to show how popular culture was continuously 'updated' by public crazes such as cycling, flying, and football, for example, by performers who incorporated them into their routines. Horrall's fascinating study challenges conceptions of popular culture as means of social control and cultural hegemony, arguing that authentic culture was not, as some historians have argued, transformed into a 'sanitized, morally acceptable professional industry voicing conservative nationalism, jingoism and a complacent acceptance of class distinctions'.

Another important contribution is Alan Rauch's *Useful Knowledge: The Victorians, Morality, and the March of Intellect*, an examination of how the unprecedented increase in encyclopedias, periodicals, lending libraries, and various other means by which knowledge was disseminated affected how Victorians thought about knowledge. Rauch first examines the growth and development of the knowledge industry, and then demonstrates how this knowledge industry was eventually confronted with Darwin's *Origin of Species*. *Useful Knowledge* includes especially interesting commentary on the increase in scientific writing and how it helped shape Victorian culture and consciousness. It also includes some discussion of nineteenth-century literature, such as Charlotte Brontë's *The Professor*, Charles Kingsley's *Alton Locke*, and George Eliot's *The Mill on the Floss*.

Jonathan Rose's mammoth and significant *The Intellectual Life of the British Working Classes* is a thoughtful consideration of perceptions of two centuries of working-class life and thought—from pre-industrial to twentieth-century Britain. Rose's study seeks to show how the working classes read and responded to the works of canonical writers, classical music, Shakespeare, Marx, penny dreadfuls, and the Bible. He explores the working class's responses to and understanding of a variety of subjects, including science, history, sexuality, politics, and philosophy, drawing on a wide range of sources in memoirs, opinion polls, newspapers, and other personal accounts. Most of his illustrative material is drawn from 'the reading experience of professional intellectuals', from those who in some cases did, and in others failed, to write themselves out of the British working classes! His time-frame is largely the nineteenth century with special emphasis on the late Victorians and Edwardians through to the Labour party victory of 1945. Thereafter Rose perceives a decline in the working-class movement of self-education. This impressive 'history of audience' contains surprising omissions, such as Harold Pinter. It is a work which will be discussed for a long time to come. In *Pedagogical Economies: The*

Examination and the Victorian Literary Man, Cathy Shuman looks at the arbitrary and biased nature of examinations in British and American educational systems.

The year's work in Victorian studies is also marked by a continued growing interest in the history of books and publishing. Daniel Berkeley Updike's *Printing Types: Their History, Forms and Use*, is an important survey of the art of typography, which traces the development of type design from the beginnings of print to the present day. In 'Never Mind the Value, what about the Price? Or, How Much Did *Marmion* Cost St. John Rivers?' (*NCL* 56:ii[2001] 160–97), Simon Eliot looks at the ways in which price, inflation, disinflation, and other notable occurrences such as the failure of the three-decker novel, determined who read what. John Sutherland, 'Michael Sadleir and his Collection of Nineteenth-Century Fiction' (*NCL* 56:ii[2001] 145–59), examines the career of Michael Sadleir primarily as a book collector and founder of the discipline of publishing history, but also as a publisher, novelist, and biographer. Somewhat disappointing is Peter Newbolt's book on *William Tinsley (1831–1902): 'Speculative Publisher'*. Referred to as 'A Commentary' the work contains a checklist of books published by Tinsley Brothers from 1854 to 1888. Tinsley published, amongst other authors, William Harrison Ainsworth, Wilkie Collins's great novel *The Moonstone* [1868], Richard Jefferies, George Meredith's *Rhoda Fleming* [1865] and early Thomas Hardy, including *Under the Greenwood Tree* [1872], *Desperate Remedies* [1871], and *A Pair of Blue Eyes* [1873]. Newbolt's 'Commentary' relies far too heavily on Tinsley's *Random Recollections of an Old Publisher* [1900] and insufficiently on primary materials.

James A. Secord's *Victorian Sensation: The Extraordinary Publication, Reception, and Secret Authorship of 'Vestiges of the Natural History of Creation'* is a carefully researched study considering the anonymously published Victorian bestseller mentioned in the title. The widely read and often discussed *Vestiges* offers a mystical account of the origins of planets and stars. Secord includes numerous excerpts from letters, diaries, reviews, journals, and newspaper articles to examine the cultural history of reading in civic life and the role of reading in the development of the first mass industrial society. He also explores the topic of evolution and its place in public discourse, arguing that the debate over evolution is important in understanding not only the Victorian debate over science, but also the conflicts of class, religion, and gender that characterized the era. Along with an explanation of how and by whom *Vestiges* was written, Secord also provides a rich account of the burgeoning world of publishers, printers, and booksellers.

The subject of Pamela Thurschwell's fascinating book *Literature, Technology and Magical Thinking, 1880–1920* is the 'intersection of literary culture, the occult and new technology at the fin-de-siècle'. Using the works of such writers as George du Maurier and Oscar Wilde, Thurschwell argues that the suffusion of technologies such as the telephone and telegraph in the public imagination helped support the claims of spiritualist mediums. Thurschwell compares talking to the dead to talking on the phone in order to illustrate the type of 'magical thinking' necessary for two people to communicate in ways that were previously unimaginable. She includes discussion of the beginnings of psychoanalysis, as well as the scientific study of the occult as reflected in the works of du Maurier and Wilde.

There are fewer Victorian reference items of interest this year. New from OUP is Cox, ed., *A Dictionary of Writers and their Works*, a quick reference guide to British titles, authors, and characters from the fifteenth century to the present with some coverage of American and European writings. The three sections (title index, author index, and character index) are carefully cross-referenced, and the title index covers drama, poetry, short stories, and novels, as well as some non-fiction such as biography, memoirs, and science. The late Norman W. Schur's *British English A to Zed*, revised by Eugene Ehrlich for the second edition, is a collection of definitions for over 5,000 colourful and entertaining British expressions along with comparisons of British to American pronunciation and word use. The book contains five sections: 'Syntax', 'Punctuation', 'Spoken Usage and Figures of Speech', 'Punctuation and Style', and 'Spelling'. Appendix 1 provides a general account of differences between British and American English.

Quite a few works this year deal with issues related to poverty and the urban landscape. The second edition of William J. Fishman's *East End 1888: A Year in a London Borough among the Labouring Poor* provides a thorough account of working-class life in the Tower Hamlets borough of London and an analysis of the growing disparity between rich and poor in late nineteenth-century London. Fishman includes a range of topics, from social unrest, unemployment, and poverty to leisure and entertainment. Of particular interest is his discussion of the widespread fear and loathing of the hospitals and the workhouse. Tina Young Choi, 'Writing the Victorian City: Discourses of Risk, Connection, and Inevitability' (*VS* 43:iv[2001] 561–90), examines the emergence of two new types of non-fiction prose during the Victorian period—literatures of urban exploration and social statistics—and how these influenced conceptions of inevitability, disease, mortality, and risk during the period. M.E. Goodlad, '"Making the working man like me": Charity, Pastorship, and Middle-Class Identity in Nineteenth-Century Britain. Thomas Chalmers and Dr. James Phillips Kay' (*VS* 43:iv[2001] 591–618), examines the writings and careers of two pioneers in social work, Thomas Chalmers and Dr James Phillips Kay, with the aim of analysing Victorian attitudes about social welfare. Goodlad focuses on charity and poor laws to show the preoccupation with middle-class morality and the mission of many middle-class Britons at that time to 'civilize' the urban working class.

In *British Opinion and Irish Self-Government, 1865–1925: From Unionism to Liberal Commonwealth*, G.K. Peatling investigates the acceptance of Irish self-government in British public opinion, focusing on international developments as they influenced ideological movements as well as on British attitudes towards Ireland. Peatling's analysis revolves around three case studies: Comptean positivism and how it helped promote the acceptance of Irish self-government; new liberalism as it supported Irish independence; and advocates of imperial consolidation, who regarded Irish independence as inevitable in the early twentieth century. There is also a new edition of Joseph Sheridan Le Fanu's historical novel set in Ireland, *The Cock and Anchor: Being a Chronicle of Old Dublin City*, edited by Jan Jedrzejewski. First published in 1845, *The Cock and Anchor* presents a colourful and detailed account of Dublin, along with an exciting story of crime and manners. Jedrzejewski includes contemporary reviews published in Ireland, England, and Scotland.

In *Rapt in Plaid: Canadian Literature and Scottish Tradition*, Elizabeth Waterston explores the connection between Scottish and Canadian literary traditions in order to show how Scottish ideas and values are still prevalent in Canadian politics, education, economics, and social mores. *Rapt in Plaid* draws from a range of sources such as biography, memoir, and several genres of fiction. Passages from writers such as Robert Louis Stevenson, J.M. Barrie, and Thomas Carlyle are analysed in the context of multicultural, narrative, and postcolonial theories. Also of interest is a new edition of the classic *Glasgow in 1901* by James Hamilton Muir (a pseudonym for James Bone, Hamilton Charteris, and Muirhead Bone) with illustrations by Muirhead Bone. This vivid account details a faithful description of the city along with sixty-eight black and white illustrations. The new edition comes with an introduction by Perilla Kinchin, an index to the text, and a simplified version of the fold-out map by Sylvester Bone, Muirhead's grandson.

Hospitals and medicine are the subject of a few works this year. First, ed., *Medical Progress and Social Reality: A Reader in Nineteenth-Century Medicine and Literature*, is an anthology of nineteenth-century literature on medicine, medical progress, and other medical issues, covering mostly fictional accounts from British, American, French, and Russian writers of the changing social realities of medicine during the period. Female doctors, the role of the hospital, and the use of new instruments are just a few of the topics covered. The anthology includes a concise overview of important aspects of medical progress during the period. The subject of Jenny Bourne Taylor's '"Received, a blank child": John Brownlow, Charles Dickens, and the London Foundling Hospital—Archives and Fictions' (*NCL* 56:iii[2001] 293–365), is the London Foundling Hospital's place in nineteenth-century English culture and how self-representation, along with other shifting circumstances, helped shape its significance. Taylor's discussion includes analysis of how writers like Brownlow (in *Memoranda; or, Chronicles of the Foundling Hospital* and *Hans Sloane, a Tale Illustrating the History of the Foundling Hospital in London*) and Dickens (in *Oliver Twist, Little Dorrit*, and the 1867 Christmas story 'No Thoroughfare') articulate changing perceptions of the hospital as its policies for admittance began to involve examination of the mother's sexual history.

Not surprisingly, numerous works explore the subject of women, gender, and feminism. Shattock, ed., *Women and Literature in Britain, 1800–1900*, brings together a collection of new articles by leading critics on a variety of topics about women and literature in order to examine women's participation in literary culture as interpreters, consumers, and practitioners. The book covers a wide range of female writing: poetry, novels, biography, journalism, autobiography, drama, and children's books, as well as historical and scientific writing. The essays are as follows: 'The Construction of the Woman Writer', by Joanne Shattock (pp. 8–34); 'Remaking the Canon', by Joanne Wilkes (pp. 35–54); 'Women and the Consumption of Print', by Margaret Beetham (pp. 55–77); 'Women Writing Woman: Nineteenth-Century Representations of Gender and Sexuality', by Lyn Pykett (pp. 78–98); 'Feminism, Journalism and Public Debate', by Barbara Caine (pp. 99–118); 'Women, Fiction and the Marketplace', by Valerie Sanders (pp. 142–61); 'Women Poets and the Challenge of Genre', by Virginia Blain (pp. 162–88); 'Women and the Theatre', by Katherine Newey (pp. 189–208); 'Women Writers and Self-Writing', by Linda Peterson (pp. 209–30); 'The Professionalization of Women's Writing: Extending the Canon', by Judith Johnston and Hilary Fraser (pp. 231–50); 'Women Writers and Religion', by Elisabeth Jay (pp. 251–74); and 'Women Writing for Children', by Lynn Vallone (pp. 275–300).

Kathryn Gleadle's well-written and highly readable *British Women in the Nineteenth Century* provides a reassessment of the 'separate spheres' ideology in order to argue that a more holistic and diverse approach to women's own subjectivities is necessary to understand how factors such as law, family, consumerism, and literary discourse, impacted women's identities. Providing comprehensive analysis of women's experiences in the home, at work, in politics, and in the community, Gleadle also emphasizes the importance of regional differences in the development of women's identities. Thus her analysis includes commentary on Irish, Scottish, and Welsh, as well as English, women. Gleadle's introduction provides an interesting overview of some recent trends in feminist theory and criticism, such as the 'new revisionism' in feminist studies. The study is divided into three parts: 'Working Class Women, 1800–1860'; 'Middle-Class and Upper-Class Women, 1800–1860'; and 'Middle-Class and Upper-Class Women, 1860–1900'. Each section includes the following subdivisions: 'Work'; 'Politics, Community, and Protest'; and 'Families, Relationships and Home Life'.

Suzanne Fagence Cooper, *The Victorian Woman*, challenges the stereotype of the passive Victorian woman, highlighting instead her resilience and resourcefulness. Cooper's well-illustrated study incorporates photography and images of women from magazines and advertisements, along with a diverse range of women's stories, from educators to artists to factory workers. Helen Rogers, *Women and the People: Authority, Authorship and the Radical Tradition in Nineteenth-Century England*, examines radical traditions in the women's movement and women's involvement in politics in Victorian England, exploring connections between and among populism, feminism, and liberalism. Arguing that the forms adopted by radicals were important in shaping the reception of their ideas as well as their own self-perception, Rogers examines a variety of forms such as fiction, poetry, autobiography, political writing, speeches, and journalism in order to analyse the ways in which women adopted and changed genre conventions to develop a unique voice in writing about reform.

Laura Morgan Green's *Educating Women: Cultural Conflict and Victorian Literature* examines the trend of universities becoming more open to women and authors beginning to include intellectual and ambitious heroines at the centre of their plots. Green argues that, while women in university settings were becoming more valued for their intellectual achievements, fictional women were still valued more highly for their emotional goals. Green's study focuses on works by Charlotte Brontë, George Eliot, Anna Leonowens, and Thomas Hardy.

The subject of Susan Torrey Barstow's '"Hedda is all of us": Late-Victorian Women at the Matinee' (*VS* 43:iii[2001] 387–412), is how women's domination of both popular and independent theatrical matinees provided a space for watching and critiquing staged femininity, which in turn allowed for the development of a new feminist self-consciousness. Barstow focuses on female protagonists, the middle-class heroines in Ibsen performance matinees, along with the female spectators who helped shape turn-of-the-century feminism. Yaffa Claire Draznin's *Victorian London's Middle-Class Housewife: What She Did All Day* explores the many roles of middle-class women integral to the Victorian household—from consumer to financial manager to moral arbiter. Draznin discusses the impact women had in creating a modern consumer culture as they sought increasingly to buy manufactured products and labour-saving devices.

There are also several contributions about family life. Thad Logan's thoughtful *The Victorian Parlour: A Cultural Study* builds on the growing body of feminist scholarship about the private sphere and domesticity. Logan examines the domestic interior as a place where many aspects of Victorian culture can be read. In Logan's words, 'the Victorian parlour—extraordinarily rich in detail, situated in a central position within the theory and practice of Victorian culture—can be taken as a kind of synecdoche for that culture itself, a microcosm of the middle-class Victorian world, miniaturized, as if under glass'. The book includes illustrations and chapters on various subjects: decorative arrangement and aesthetics in the parlour, the parlour as an artefact and its objects of empire, and literary and artistic representations of the Victorian parlour. Karen Chase and Michael Levenson's *The Spectacle of Intimacy: A Public Life for the Victorian Family* explores the idea of domestic space as a place for spectacle, arguing that romanticized expectations of home life caused a paradoxical craving for public scandal. Levenson and Chase show how families perfected various forms of private pleasure as they were exposed to public view. Included in this discussion is coverage of a wide range of public scandals, such as the public trials of Caroline Norton and Lord Melbourne, young Queen Victoria's bedchamber crisis, and the Bloomer craze. Also discussed are the Deceased Wife's Sister Bill 1848 and the controversies over divorce in the 1850s, as well as representations of domesticity and household life in the works of Dickens, Eliot, Tennyson, and Oliphant, among others.

The purpose of Craig Randall's *Promising Language: Betrothal in Victorian Law and Fiction* is to explore the linguistic dimensions and implications of the practice of promising, specifically in marriage. Randall looks at the emergence of several nineteenth-century discourses—the science of language, utilitarian social theory and jurisprudence, and the language of realism, for example—to show the practice of promising at the intersection of said discourses: 'as speech act, as social practice and legal contract, and as structural principle and topos'. The introduction centres on a discussion of nineteenth-century thought about the nature of language in general and the British tradition of relativism, focusing in particular on the works of important writers such as John Locke and John Stuart Mill. Randall then moves to critical analyses of novels by Charlotte Brontë, George Eliot, Anthony Trollope, George Meredith, and Henry James.

Leila Silvana May's *Disorderly Sisters: Sibling Relations and Sororal Resistance in Nineteenth-Century British Literature* has as its theme the family, and in particular the sibling bond. Silvana argues that the figure of the sister is at the centre of nineteenth-century domestic ideology. She writes that the '"angel of the house" required by the logic of Victorian Moral Discourse was not, as is usually supposed, the figure of the mother/wife, but ... her sexually and economically uncontaminated shadow-surrogate, the daughter/sister, particularly in her role as sister'. May's study includes examinations of law and philosophy, domestic tracts, and novels by writers such as Eliot, Dickens, Collins, Mary Shelley, Charlotte Brontë, and Poe. Finally, Valerie Sanders's *Records of Girlhood: An Anthology of Nineteenth-Century Women's Childhoods* is a fascinating collection of autobiographical accounts by prominent nineteenth-century women writers about their childhoods and early family lives.

A few works this year address the subject of madness. Thomas Cooley's fascinating study *The Ivory Leg in the Ebony Cabinet: Madness, Race, and Gender in Victorian America* looks at cultural 'artefacts' that represented Victorian thinking and conceptions of madness. Cooley examines an array of these cultural fragments, from Samuel Morton's collection of Native American skulls to William James's writings on the consciousness of lost limbs, arguing that they are connected by the new model of psychology just beginning to emerge before the influence of Freud. Cooley describes this new theory of the mind, showing how madness was thought to be the result of the separate chambers of the mind being cut off from one another. He then demonstrates how this theory of the individual was also applied to the group: happy marriages and strong nations 'all drew their legitimacy from the same essentially racist and sexist model, one that posited a union of parts arrayed in an ostensibly natural hierarchy of authority'.

The subject of David Wright's thoughtful and well-researched book *Mental Disability in Victorian England: The Earlswood Asylum, 1847–1901* is the social history of institutionalization. Wright argues that an understanding of family and community is necessary to understanding the institutionalized confinement of the disabled and mentally ill. He looks at the 'networks of care and control that operated outside the walls of the asylum', and in particular the family's role in identification and medical treatment of mental disability, as well as its role in facilitating discharge. He takes the Earlswood asylum, the National Asylum for Idiots, as a case study, focusing also on John Langdon Down's identification there of 'mongolism', the disability now known as Down's Syndrome.

Also of interest are examinations of infamous unsolved crimes during the Victorian period. Michael R. Gordon, *Alias Jack the Ripper: Beyond the Usual Whitechapel Suspects*, provides a comprehensive overview of the crimes and evidence linked to Jack the Ripper, as well as discussion of the man thought to have been the killer. Gordon's study includes an analysis of the five periods of Jack the Ripper's career, his American connection, the Thames torso murders, his use of poison on some of his later victims, and step-by-step descriptions of many of his crimes. James Ruddick's intriguing new study *Death at the Priory: Sex, Love, and Murder in Victorian England* examines the unsolved case of the Charles Bravo murder, a story that generated great public attention in Victorian England. Ruddick recounts the events surrounding Bravo's murder, with special emphasis on Charles and Florence's troubled marriage in order to unmask the real murderer in the unsolved case. *Death at the Priory* reads like an exciting detective story while also offering insightful cultural and social analysis.

John M. Picker, 'The Victorian Aura of the Recorded Voice' (*NLH* 32[2001] 769–86), provides an interesting assessment of various Victorian perceptions and receptions of the phonograph machine and its recording of the human voice. Meirion Hughes and Robert Stradling present a second edition of *The English Musical Renaissance, 1840–1940: Constructing a National Music*, a well-written study of how music helped shape England's national identity, beginning in the early nineteenth century and ending in the 1940s. There is a second edition of Denis Wright's *The English amongst the Persians: Imperial Lives in Nineteenth-Century Iran*, originally published in 1977. Wright examines the difficult relations between Iran and Britain in the nineteenth century, focusing on topics such as British interests in Persia, diplomacy, business relations, and missionaries in Iran.

Victorian Periodicals Review 34:ii[2001] includes the following reviews: *Kegan Paul—A Victorian Imprint: Publishers, Books, and Cultural History*, by Leslie

Howsam, reviewed by Linda E. Connors (*VPR* 34:ii[2001] 185–6); *The Quest for the Grail: Arthurian Legend in British Art, 1840–1920*, by Christine Poulson, reviewed by Kristine Ottesen Garrigan (*VPR* 34:ii[2001] 190–1); *Gender, Race, and the Writing of Empire: Public Discourse and the Boer War*, by Paula M. Krebs, reviewed by Jane Marcellus (*VPR* 34:ii[2001] 192–3); and *A Companion to Victorian Literature and Culture*, ed. Herbert F. Tucker, reviewed by Brian McCuskey (*VPR* 34:ii[2001] 194–5).

VPR 34:iii[2001] includes the following reviews: When Art Historians Use Periodicals: Methodology and Meaning, a review essay by Julie F. Codell (*VPR* 34:iii[2001] 284–9); *Down with the Old Canoe: A Cultural History of the Titanic Disaster*, by Steven Biel, reviewed by Peter C. Grosvenor (*VPR* 34:iii[2001] 294–5); *Ruskin's Mythic Queen: Gender Subversion in Victorian Culture*, by Sharon Aronofsky Weltman, reviewed by Vincent A. Lankewish (*VPR* 34:iii[2001] 295–7); *Cause Book: The Opium-Eater, the Magazine Wars, and the London Literary Scene in 1821*, by Richard Woodhouse, reviewed by Daniel Sanjiv Roberts (*VPR* 34:iii[2001] 298–9); *Women and British Aestheticism*, ed. Talia Schaffer and Kathy Alexis Psomiades, reviewed by Solveig C. Robinson (*VPR* 34:iii[2001] 300–1); and *Victorian Travelers and the Opening of China, 1842–1907*, by Susan Schoenbauer Thurin, reviewed by Anne M. Windholz (*VPR* 34:iii[2001] 302–3).

VPR 34:iv[2001] includes the following reviews: *Essays and Reviews: The 1860 Text and its Reading*, ed. Victor Shea and William Whit, reviewed by Josef L. Altholz (*VPR* 34:iv[2001] 387); *The Forgotten Female Aesthetes: Literary Culture in Late-Victorian England*, by Talia Schaffer, reviewed by Stephen Arata (*VPR* 34:iv[2001] 388); *Plotting Women: Gender and Narration in the Eighteenth- and Nineteenth-Century British Novel*, by Alison A. Case, reviewed by Elizabeth M. Archer (*VPR* 34:iv[2001] 390); *Amy Levy: Her Life and Letters*, by Linda Hunt Beckman, reviewed by Clare Cotugno (*VPR* 34:iv[2001] 394); *'Struggle and Storm' The Life and Death of Francis Adams*, by Meg Tasker, reviewed by Richard Duvall (*VPR* 34:iv[2001] 395–6); *American Slaves in Victorian England: Abolitionist Politics in Popular Literature*, by Audrey Fisch, reviewed by Richard D. Fulton (*VPR* 34:iv[2001] 397–9); and *Rereading Victorian Fiction*, ed. Alice Jenkins and Juliet John, reviewed by Pamela K. Gilbert (*VPR* 34:iv[2001] 400); *After the Pre-Raphaelites: Art and Aestheticism in Victorian England*, ed. Elizabeth Prettejohn, *The Pre-Raphaelite Body: Fear and Desire in Painting, Poetry, and Criticism*, by J.B. Bullen, and *Reading the Pre-Raphaelites*, by Tim Barringer, reviewed by Beth Harris (*VPR* 34:iv[2001] 401–3); *Contest for Cultural Authority: Hazlitt, Coleridge, and the Distresses of the Regency*, by Robert Keith Lapp, reviewed by Victoria Myers (*VPR* 34:iv[2001] 404–5); *Nineteenth-Century British Women Writers: A Bio-Biographical Critical Sourcebook*, ed. Abigail Burnham Bloom, reviewed by Solveig C. Robinson (*VPR* 34:iv[2001] 406); *Trollope and the Magazines: Gendered Issues in Mid-Victorian Britain*, by Mark W. Turner, reviewed by that fine critic and scholar, the late Barbara Quinn Schmidt (*VPR* 34:iv[2001] 407–8); *Dialogues in the Margin: A Study of the Dublin University Magazine*, by Wayne E. Hall, reviewed by Elizabeth Tilley (*VPR* 34:iv[2001] 409–10); *Tales of Terror from 'Blackwood's Magazine'*, ed. Robert Morrison and Chris Baldick, and *John Polidori: 'The Vampyre' and Other Tales of the Macabre*, ed. Robert Morrison and Chris Baldick, reviewed by Nicola Trott (*VPR* 34:iv[2001] 411–12); and *Oscar

Wilde's Decorated Books, by Nicholas Frankel, reviewed by Linda Gertner Zatlin (*VPR* 34:iv[2001] 413–15).

Victorian Studies 43:i[2001] includes the following reviews: *Reproductive Urges: Popular Novel Reading, Sexuality, and the English Nation*, by Anita Levy, reviewed by Athena Vrettos (*VS* 43:i[2001] 105–7); *J.M. Robertson: Rationalist and Literary Critic*, by Odin Dekkers, reviewed by Edward Royle (*VS* 43:i[2001] 107–8); *Secret Selves: Confession and Same-Sex Desire in Victorian Autobiography*, by Oliver S. Buckton, reviewed by Vincent A. Lankewish (*VS* 43:i[2001] 114–15); *The Self-Fashioning of Disraeli, 1818–1851*, ed. Charles Richmond and Paul Smith, reviewed by Stanley Weintraub (*VS* 43:i[2001] 128–31); *The Letters of Matthew Arnold*, volume 3: *1866–1870*, ed. Cecil Y. Lang, reviewed by John P. Farrell (*VS* 43:i[2001] 131–2); and *Matthew Arnold: A Literary Life*, by Clinton Machann, reviewed by Francis Golffing (*VS* 43:i[2001] 133–4). There is also *British Imperial Literature, 1870–1940*, by Daniel Bivona, reviewed by Deirdre David (*VS* 43:i[2001] 142–4), and *The Regional Novel in Britain and Ireland, 1800–1990*, ed. K.D.M. Snell, reviewed by Ian Duncan (*VS* 43:i[2001] 153–5).

VS 43:ii[2001] includes the following reviews: *Writing Under the Raj: Gender, Race, and Rape in the British Colonial Imagination, 1830–1947*, by Philippa Levine reviewed by Nancy L. Paxton (*VS* 43:ii[2001] 293–4); *Out of Place: Englishness, Empire and the Location of Identity*, by Ian Baucom, a detailed review article by James R. Buzzard (*VS* 43:ii[2001] 294–8); *From Nineveh to New York: The Strange Story of the Assyrian Reliefs in the Metropolitan Museum and the Hidden Masterpiece at Canford School*, by John Malcolm Russell [1997], and *Nineteenth-Century Collecting and the British Museum*, by A.W. Frank, reviewed by Frederick N. Bohrer (*VS* 43:ii[2001] 298–301) are not without interest to students of Victorian antiquarianism and collecting. Also of note are *Religion in Victorian Britain*, volume 5: *Culture and Empire*, ed. John Wolf, reviewed by Gilley Sheridan (*VS* 43:ii[2001] 301–3); *Victorian Pulpit: Spoken and Written Sermons in Nineteenth-Century Britain*, by Robert H. Ellison, reviewed by Mary Wilson Carpenter (*VS* 43:ii[2001] 305–6); *Names and Stories: Emilia Dilke and Victorian Culture*, by Kali Israel, reviewed by Elizabeth Mansfield (*VS* 43:ii[2001] 307–9); *Smile of Discontent: Humor, Gender and Nineteenth-Century British Fiction*, by Eileen Gillooly, reviewed by Dianne F. Sadoff (*VS* 43:ii[2001] 309–11); *Serious Play: The Cultural Form of the Nineteenth-Century Realist Novel*, by J. Jeffrey Franklin [1999], reviewed by Elizabeth Rosdeitcher (*VS* 43:ii[2001] 317–19); *Victorian Culture and the Idea of the Grotesque*, ed. Colin Trodd, Paul Barlos and David Armigoni [1999], reviewed by J.R. Reed (*VS* 43:ii[2001] 319–21); and *Victorian Journalism. Exotic and Domestic: Essays in Honor of P.D. Edwards*, ed. Barbara Garlick [1998], reviewed by Joseph O. Baylen (*VS* 43:ii[2001] 321–4).

VS 43:iii[2001] includes the following reviews: *A Companion to Victorian Literature and Culture*, ed. Herbert F. Tucker, reviewed by Alexander Welsh (*VS* 43:iii[2001] 461–2); *Gender, Genre, and Victorian Historical Writing*, by Rohan Amanda Maitzen, reviewed by Clare A. Simmons (*VS* 43:iii[2001] 469); *Kegan Paul: A Victorian Imprint: Publishers, Books and Cultural History*, by Leslie Howsam, reviewed by Bradley Deane (*VS* 43:iii[2001] 471–2); *Strange and Secret Peoples: Fairies and Victorian Consciousness*, by Carole G. Silver, reviewed by Christine Wiesenthal (*VS* 43:iii[2001] 475–7); *William Rossetti's Art Criticism: The Search for Truth in Victorian Art*, by Julie L'Enfant, reviewed by Susan P. Casteras

(*VS* 43:iii[2001] 480); *Victorian Painting*, by Lionel Lambourne, reviewed by Susan P. Casteras (*VS* 43:iii[2001] 481); *After the Pre-Raphaelites: Art and Aestheticism in Victorian England*, ed. Elizabeth Prettejohn, reviewed by Susan P. Casteras (*VS* 43:iii[2001] 482); *Popular Culture and Performance in the Victorian City*, by Peter Bailey, reviewed by Keith Wilson (*VS* 43:iii[2001] 490–1); *The Quest for the Grail: Arthurian Legend in British Art, 1840–1920*, by Christine Poulson, reviewed by Debra N. Mancoff (*VS* 43:iii[2001] 497–8); *The Science of Energy: A Cultural History of Energy Physics in Victorian England*, by Crosbie Smith, reviewed by De Witt Douglas Kilgore (*VS* 43:iii[2001] 504–5); *Mansex Fine: Religion, Manliness and Imperialism in Nineteenth-Century British Culture*, by David Alderson, reviewed by Ross G. Forman (*VS* 43:iii[2001] 507–8); *Victorian Sexual Dissidence*, ed. Richard Dellamora, reviewed by Andrew Elfenbein (*VS* 43:iii[2001] 509–10); *Crimes of Passion: Sex, Violence and Victorian Working Women*, by Shani D'Cruze, reviewed by Gail Savage (*VS* 43:iii[2001] 511–12); *Journeys in Ireland: Literary Travellers, Rural Landscapes, Cultural Relations*, by Martin Ryle, reviewed by Robert Tracy (*VS* 43:iii[2001] 526–7); and *Homes and Homelessness in the Victorian Imagination*, ed. Murray Baumgarten and H.M. Daleski, reviewed by Elaine Hadley (*VS* 43:iii[2001] 533–4).

VS 43:iv[2001] includes the following reviews: *Liberalism and Empire: A Study in Nineteenth-Century Political Thought and Practice*, by Uday Singh Mehta, reviewed by Michael Bentley (*VS* 43:iv[2001] 619); *The Great Exhibition of 1851: A Nation on Display*, by Jeffrey A. Auerbach, and *The Great Exhibition*, by John R. Davis, both reviewed by James Buzzard (*VS* 43:iv[2001] 620–2); *Place in Literature: Regions, Cultures, Communities*, by Roberto M. Dainotto, reviewed by Donald Ulin (*VS* 43:iv[2001] 637–8); *The Gothic Family Romance: Heterosexuality, Child Sacrifice, and the Anglo-Irish Colonial Order*, by Margot Gayle Backus, reviewed by Vera Kreilkamp (*VS* 43:iv[2001] 646–8); and *Ventures into Childland: Victorians, Fairy Tales, and Femininity*, by U.C. Knoepflmacher, reviewed by Jeffrey L. Spear (*VS* 43:iv[2001] 648–9).

Nineteenth-Century Literature 56:i[2001] includes the following reviews: *Romanticism and the Gothic: Genre, Reception, and Canon Formation*, by Michael Gamer, reviewed by Chris Baldick (*NCL* 56:i[2001] 105–6); *Allegories of Union in Irish and English Writing, 1790–1870*, by Mary Jean Corbett, reviewed by Terry Eagleton (*NCL* 56:i[2001] 107–9); *Detective Fiction and the Rise of Forensic Science*, by Ronald R. Thomas, reviewed by Lawrence Frank (*NCL* 56:i[2001] 117–20); and *The Forgotten Female Aesthetes: Literary Culture in Late-Victorian England*, by Talia Schaffer and *Women and British Aestheticism*, ed. Talia Schaffer and Kathy Alexis Psomiades, both reviewed by Meri-Jane Rochelson (*NCL* 56:i[2001] 121–5).

NCL 56:ii[2001] includes the following reviews: *The Representation of Bodily Pain in Late Nineteenth-Century English Culture*, by Lucy Bending, reviewed by Allison Pease (*NCL* 56:ii[2001] 260–2); *Desire and Excess: The Nineteenth-Century Culture of Art*, by Johan Siegel, reviewed by Hilary Fraser (*NCL* 56:ii[2001] 263–4); *Victorian Writing about Risk: Imagining a Safe England in a Dangerous World*, by Elaine Freedgood, reviewed by Eleanor Courtemanche (*NCL* 56:ii[2001] 265–8); and *The Victorians and the Visual Imagination*, by Kate Flint, reviewed by Dianne Sachko Macleod (*NCL* 56:ii[2001] 268–79). There is also a review by Frances Austin of Manfred Görlach's *An Annotated Bibliography of Nineteenth-Century Grammars in English* (*ES* 82:i[2001] 94–6).

Some of the most interesting contributions of the year to our knowledge of Victorian culture we found in *Victorians Institute Journal* 29[2001]. F.S. Schwarzbach's 'Twelve Ways of Looking at a Staffordshire Figurine: An Essay in Cultural Studies' (*VIJ* 29[2001] 7–60) is an extensive and fascinating account. Schwarzbach wisely concludes: 'no analysis can fully account for the richness of cultural values, symbols, allusions, and resonances that surround even a single commonplace object such as … [the] figurine'. Watercolour painting is the interest of Elizabeth Howells's 'On the Commodification of Eastern Art: John Frederick Lewis' *The Hareem of 1850*' (*VIJ* 29[2001] 61–84), which focuses on Lewis's perceptions of the East and his audience. A popular art form, the music hall, provides the context for Martin Danahay's 'Sexuality and the Working-Class Child's Body in Music Hall' (*VIJ* 29[2001] 102–31). Danahay's canvas ranges from Sickert's paintings, through James R. Kincaid's *Child-Loving: The Erotic Child and Victorian Culture*, to Marie Lloyd, Henry Mayhew and others, to illuminate the context of Sickert's representation of sexuality in music hall. Architecture and design is the focus of a detailed review essay by Charles Brownell focusing on two books by Susan Weber Soros on E.W. Godwin (*VIJ* 29[2001] 133–40). Other review essays include *The Victorians and the Visual Imagination*, by Kate Flint, reviewed by Srdjan Smarjić (*VIJ* 29[2001] 140–2); *Caverns of Night: Coal Mines in Art, Literature, and Film*, ed. William B. Thesing, reviewed by Jonathan Silverman (*VIJ* 29[2001] 142–5); and *The Shock of the Real: Romanticism and Visual Culture, 1760–1860*, by Gillen d'Arcy Wood, reviewed by Victoria Olsen (*VIJ* 29[2001] 145–7). There are also shorter reviews of interest in *VIJ* 29[2001] written by Meri-Jane Rochelson, Ellen Bayuk Rosenman, Nicholas Frankel, Pamela K. Gilbert, Susan Walsh, and Mary Ellis Gibson, amongst others.

(b) Prose

Several general prose listings include books and articles written by and about women. Kimberly VanEsveld Adams's *Our Lady of Victorian Feminism: The Madonna in the Work of Anna Jameson, Margaret Fuller, and George Eliot* looks at these three writers' reassessments and new interpretations of the Madonna in Christian belief and art. Richardson and Willis, eds., *The New Woman in Fiction and in Fact: Fin-de-Siècle Feminisms*, is a collection of essays about the Victorian debate over motherhood, gender, class, and race as they relate to popular conceptions of feminism and the New Woman.

Susan Hamilton, 'Making History with Frances Power Cobbe: Victorian Feminism, Domestic Violence, and the Language of Imperialism' (*VS* 43:iii[2001] 437–60), looks at connections between established mainstream periodicals and the 'Victorian feminisms' of special-interest periodicals, and how the complex interactions between the two help inform our understanding of Victorian feminisms themselves. Hamilton focuses on Frances Power Cobbe's 'Wife Torture in England' and her controversial use of imperialist rhetoric.

Lila Marz Harper's insightful study of women's travel and natural history writing, *Solitary Travelers: Nineteenth-Century Women's Travel Narratives and the Scientific Vocation*, examines the lives and natural history and travel-writing works of Mary Wollstonecraft, Harriet Martineau, Isabella Bird Bishop, and Mary

Kingsley. Harper looks at new opportunities for, as well as cultural constraints on, solitary women explorers as they fought for the freedom to pursue their interests in science and the natural world. Cheryl McEwan's study *Gender, Geography and Empire: Victorian Women Travelers in West Africa* describes and analyses accounts of British women travelling in West Africa from 1840 to 1915.

Several works reflect a growing interest in women's autobiography. Carol Hanbery MacKay's critically imaginative study *Creative Negativity: Four Victorian Exemplars of the Female Quest* looks at what she calls creative negativity in the Work of four covert female revolutionaries who wrote 'reflected or refracted autobiography' as a means of exploring the repressed self, the female quest of 'interdependent self-construction'. According to MacKay, this quest (a counterpart to the male *Bildungsroman*, or novel of maturation) is a manifestation of 'fluid and reinventive' redefinition of self and a means of voicing multiple lives and selves. MacKay's interdisciplinary study contains the following chapters: 'Creative Negativity and the Female Quest'; 'The Singular Double Vision of Julia Margaret Cameron'; 'Self-Erasure and Self-Creation in Anne Thackeray Ritchie'; 'The Multiple Deconversions of Annie Wood Besant'; and 'Elizabeth Robins Outperforms the New Woman'.

Linda H. Peterson's *Traditions of Victorian Women's Autobiography; The Poetics and Politics of Life Writing* is another contribution to the growing body of critical appraisal of women's autobiography. Emphasizing the diversity of approaches and purposes found in various forms of women's life writings, Peterson examines Victorian women's experimentation with the various forms of autobiography available to them, from spiritual autobiography to the *chroniques scandaleuses* of the eighteenth century. In the first chapter, Peterson provides a useful reconstruction of the generic traditions of women's autobiography as interpreted by nineteenth-century critics and editors; she then gives analyses of Charlotte Elizabeth Tonna's *Personal Recollections*, Harriet Martineau's *Autobiography*, and Margaret Oliphant's *Autobiography*, among others.

Anne H. Lundin's *Victorian Horizons: The Reception of the Picture Books of Walter Crane, Randolph Caldecott, and Kate Greenaway* looks at the critical reception of said children's authors, as well as their careers, reputations, and reviews of their works. Lundin uses reader-response theory to examine the reader's role in the process of signification and what she calls the '"horizons of expectations " that characterized the historical intersection of contemporary Victorian audiences with children's books'.

Dennis Denisoff's thought-provoking study *Aestheticism and Sexual Parody, 1840–1940* examines interactions between various forms of sexual parody in the works of Beerbohm, du Maurier, and Isherwood as well as those of canonical writers such as Pater, Swinburne, and Tennyson. Denisoff argues that the aestheticism movement's depiction of non-normative sexuality came to be accepted 'through works of parody and self-parody'. Mancoff, ed., *John Everett Millais: Beyond the Pre-Raphaelite Brotherhood*, is a collection of new essays re-examining Millais, the leading figure at the Royal Academy, and his association with the Pre-Raphaelites. This study includes essays on Millais's interests in literature, theatre, science, and nature, and his position among and relationship to contemporary artists. Editor Anna Gruetzner Robins offers a comprehensive collection (over 400 entries) of the writings of the artist and art critic Walter Richard Sickert (1860–1942) in the well-produced *Walter Sickert: The Complete Writings on Art.* 'C.B. Fry: The Sportsman-Editor' (*VPR* 34:ii[2001] 165–84), by Kate Jackson, describes Fry's popular sports magazine, its illustrations and articles covering a wide range of sports.

There are a number of new biographical studies for 2001. Andrew Roberts's *Salisbury: Victorian Titan* is a biography of Robert Cecil, marquess of Salisbury. Drawing on papers from the Salisbury archive and those of numerous contemporaries, this carefully researched study encompasses Salisbury's complete life and career. Michael Bentley's *Lord Salisbury's World: Conservative Environments in Late-Victorian Britain* is a biography examining Salisbury's political, religious, and intellectual ideas within the context of a conservative world-view 'coming under severe strain'. Bentley's coverage is not merely biographical; he also examines conservative politics, the church, state, empire, and society of the late Victorian period. W.J. McCormack draws on previously unpublished materials for *Fool of the Family: A Life of J.M. Synge*, a carefully researched biography of Synge's life and works, as well as portrait of turn-of-the-century Ireland.

John Stokes, ed., *Eleanor Marx (1855–1898): Life, Work, Contacts*, comprises new articles about Karl Marx's youngest daughter. Eleanor Marx was a journalist and translator who made important contributions to the critical study of Flaubert, Ibsen, and Shakespeare, and the essays vary in subject, treating her involvement in politics, her career as an actress and her work as a translator. Carolyn Burdett offers an intriguing look at South African politics in her book *Olive Schreiner and the Progress of Feminism: Evolution, Gender, and Empire*. Burdett focuses on Schreiner's opposition to imperialism in South Africa, as well as Schreiner's interest in social activism and women's rights. Burdett discusses Schreiner's life in terms of modernity, progress, and the New Woman. It also includes biographical information and readings of Schreiner's fiction and non-fiction.

An intriguing biography is *Hans Christian Andersen: The Life of a Storyteller*, by Jackie Wullschlager. With its Dickensian connections, this biography emphasizes the darkness of Andersen's work, which Wullschlager connects to the driving ambition, hypochondria, and sexual confusion in his own life. There is also Mike Ashley's *Algernon Blackwood: An Extraordinary Life*, a full account of his life and supernatural tales. Brian Thompson's *The Disastrous Life of Mrs. Georgina Weldon: The Lifes, Loves, and Lawsuits of a Legendary Victorian* looks at Georgina's marriage to Harry Weldon, the *ménage à trois* between them and the French composer Gounod, Harry's attempt to have Georgina committed for lunacy, and Georgina's ill-fated involvement with two crooks called Menier. Marvin Spevack's *James Orchard Halliwell-Phillipps: The Life and Works of the Shakespearean Scholar and Bookman* will be of great interest to students of the history of the book trade and collecting. Spevack highlights Halliwell's immense contribution to our understanding of Shakespeare's life and times, and his affiliation with numerous literary, antiquary, and other scholarly societies. This carefully researched study provides a vivid portrait of an important Victorian figure, as well as a detailed account of everyday Victorian domestic life. Jenny McMorris's *The Warden of English: The Life of H.W. Fowler*, is a fascinating biography of the life, career, and writings of Henry Watson Fowler, author of *Modern English Usage* and editor of the *Concise Oxford Dictionary* and *Pocket Oxford Dictionary*. Meg Tasker's biography of Francis William Lauderdale Adams, *Struggle and Storm: The Life and Death of Francis Adams*, explores his life and career as a poet, social analyst, journalist, and writer of the *fin de siècle*. Finally, Patrick Waddington, *A Modest Little Banquet at the Arts Club; or, How William Ralston Shedden-Ralston Gave a Grand Dinner Party for Sixteen Literary Men in London on 22 October 1881 to Honour Ivan Sergeyevich Turgenev*, includes interesting information concerning Turgenev's English translator, the man who did much to popularize Turgenev in England, William Ralston Shedden-Ralston.

Editor Ann Brown (with Keith Bennett) brings together the Cretan diaries of the famed excavator of Knossos in *Arthur Evans's Travels in Crete, 1894–1899*. The diaries shed light on sites Evans visited, some of which have yet to be investigated. Margaret Belcher, ed., *The Collected Letters of A.W.N. Pugin*, volume 1: *1830–1842* collects the letters of designer, architect, and ecclesiologist A.W.N Pugin to a variety of correspondents, from bishops to tradesmen. As well as being valuable to the study of architecture, religious history, and the Gothic revival, Pugin's letters highlight important public events of the time. Joukovsky, ed., *The Letters of Thomas Love Peacock*, volume 2: *1828–1866*, brings together the correspondence of Peacock, a prolific letter-writer who rose to the position of Examiner in the East India Company's service. Peacock corresponded with Shelley, along with other nineteenth-century radicals.

Editor David Lisle Crane's fascinating well-illustrated and nicely bound *Letters Between a Victorian Schoolboy and his Family, 1892–1895* is a collection of about 300 letters from a young boy at Clifton College to his parents and family. The introduction is informative and the letters provide a detailed account of the daily life, emotions, and experiences of one Tankred Tunstall-Behrens while he attended a Victorian public school between the ages of 14 and 17. The letters also provide an intriguing portrait of a well-off middle-class Victorian family.

Jonathan Fryer's biography *Robbie Ross: Oscar Wilde's Devoted Friend* examines Ross's friendship and romantic involvement with Wilde, as well as his ability to maintain his position in the literary establishment while living an openly homosexual life. Fryer's study also provides a good overall portrait of the 1890s London literary scene. Ann Blainey's biography *Fanny and Adelaide: The Lives of the Remarkable Kemble Sisters* will be of special interest to students of theatre and women's studies. Blainey examines the theatrical world in which the sisters were immersed early in their lives, Adelaide's reputation as an opera singer, Fanny's acting career, and the two sisters' complex relationship. There is also coverage of Fanny's *Journal of a Residence on a Georgian Plantation in 1838–1839, 1863* and her troubled marriage to plantation-owner Pierce Butler. Blainey's biography is more comprehensive than previous biographies since it includes recently uncovered letters written by the Kemble sisters.

In *Comedy after Postmodernism: Rereading Comedy from Edward Lear to Charles Willeford*, Kirby Olson discusses how laughter 'has escaped every means of rational description by philosophers and other writers during the whole history of our civilization, despite thousands of valiant tries, from Cicero to Hobbes to Freud'. Kirby's study looks at humour in the works of Kant, Ruskin, André Breton, Philippe Soupault, P.G. Wodehouse, Peter Kropotkin, and Charles Fourier. In *The Search for Selfhood in Modern Literature*, Murray Roston includes a section evaluating the influence of Darwin and Freud on the value of individuality. Schad, ed., *Writing the Bodies of Christ: The Church from Carlyle to Derrida*, is a collection of essays about the way in which the church has been spoken and written of by important figures, including Carlyle and Darwin. In *T.H. Green's Moral and Political Philosophy: A Phenomenological Perspective*, Maria Dimova-Cookson offers a dense and detailed analysis, throwing much light on late Victorian philosophical and phenomenological interpretation of Green's political and ethical philosophy. Frederick S. Roden, 'Medieval Religion, Victorian Homosexualities' *(PSt* 23:ii[2000] 115–30), shows how medieval writings facilitated the formation of homosexual communities in the nineteenth century and made space for the expression of same-sex desire in the Victorian age.

New from Victorian Fiction Research Guides is Graham Law's *Indexes to Fiction*, a useful index of over 3,000 fiction numbers of *The Illustrated London News* from 1842 to 1901 and over 1,500 numbers of *The Graphic* from 1869 to 1901. The book includes author and chronological indexes to fiction, detailed publishing information, six full-page illustrations, and summaries of each periodical's importance. *Victorian Periodicals Review* 34:iv[2001], devoted to recent corrections and additions to the *Wellesley Index to Victorian Periodicals*, includes the following articles and notes: '2001 RSVP New York City Conference', by William H. Scheuerle *(VPR* 34:iv[2001] 314–20); 'More *Wellesley*: Curran and Ford', by Robert Colby *(VPR* 34:iv[2001] 321–3); 'The *Wellesley Index*: Additions and Corrections', by Eileen M. Curran *(VPR* 34:iv[2001] 324–58); 'The *Wellesley Index*: *Bentley's Miscellany* Additions and Corrections', by Richard Ford *(VPR* 34:iv[2001] 359–80); 'Eileen M. Curran's Queries on Richard Ford's #1913, #2223, and #2362', by Eileen M. Curran *(VPR* 34:iv[2001] 381–2); and '"Fanny Power Cobbe": A Case of Slightly Borrowed Identity and Two Misattributions in the *Wellesley Index*', by Sally Mitchell *(VPR* 34:iv[2001] 383–6).

Frederick Burkhardt et al., eds., *The Correspondence of Charles Darwin*, vol. 12: *1864*, covers Darwin's recovery from an extended illness and his continued work on hybridizing experiments for the book *The Variation of Animals and Plants Under Domestication* (the sequel to *On the Origin of Species*). The volume also covers his work studying barnacle structures and his search worldwide for specimens, and his interest in microscopic investigations and zoological terms. This extensively annotated and erudite volume also includes letters reflecting his international network of sources and connections. Norton Critical Editions presents a third edition of *Darwin*, edited by Philip Appleman. It includes excerpts from Darwin's own writing, current analysis, and criticism from Darwin's contemporaries. This edition is divided into nine sections: an updated introduction; 'Darwin's Life'; 'Scientific Thought: Just before Darwin'; excerpts from other of Darwin's works; 'Darwin's Influence on Science'; 'Darwinian Patterns in Social Thought'; 'Darwinian Influences in Philosophy and Ethics'; 'Evolutionary Theory and Religious Theory'; and 'Darwin and Literature'. In a special edition of *Philosophy and Literature* devoted to the relationship between evolution and literature, Joseph Carroll, 'The Ecology of Victorian Fiction' *(P&L* 25[2001] 295–313), argues that 'responsiveness to the sense of place is an elemental component of the evolved human psyche and that it thus can and should be integrated into a Darwinian literary theory'. Rebecca Steinitz is concerned with royal prose in her 'Travel Domesticity and Genre in Queen Victoria's *Journal of Our Life in the Highlands*' *(VIJ* 29[2001] 149–68). Its publication in 1868 is seen as a tactical manoeuvre to gain the sympathy of her subjects.

The subject of K.C. O'Rourke's *Stuart Mill and Freedom of Expression: The Genesis of a Theory* is Mill's philosophy of intellectual liberty and freedom beyond what is set forth in the second chapter of *On Liberty*. O'Rourke provides a clear and more comprehensive than usual examination of the evolution of and influences on Mill's principles of freedom. Bruce L. Kinzer's *England's Disgrace? J.S. Mill and the Irish Question* is a comprehensive investigation of Mill's fairly Anglocentric perspective on Irish politics over a period of four decades, with special emphasis on issues fundamental to Ireland's relationship with England, such as the Irish famine, land reform, and higher education. George Levine, 'Two Ways Not To Be a Solipsist: Art and Science, Pater and Pearson' (*VS* 43:i[2000] 7–41), looks at shifting oppositions throughout history, arguing that the alignment of science against culture is anything but inevitable. Levine's discussion centres on Walter Pater's modernist aestheticism and Karl Pearson's positivist science, and how the two are not antithetical, as is normally assumed, since they are both rooted in empiricism. Helena Michie's 'Victorian Honeymoons: Social Reorientation and the "Sights" of Europe' (*VS* 42:ii[2001] 229–51) focuses on John Addington Symonds's *Memoirs*, Matthew Arnold and Flu Wightman Arnold, Leslie Stephen, and the fictional Dorothea, to consider the representations of European honeymoons.

In exploring the legacy of Romanticism, Kenneth Daley, *The Rescue of Romanticism: Walter Pater and John Ruskin*, examines Pater's and Ruskin's ideas about the Renaissance and Michelangelo, their divergent views of Romanticism, their complicated intellectual relationship, and joint work in defining the concept of Romanticism. Daley shows how Pater was influenced by Ruskin's Oxford lectures, and also how Pater's conceptualizations of Romanticism were drawn from Ruskin's more conservative distrust of art and Romanticism, and his ideas about pathetic fallacy. Most interesting is a discussion about their opposing views of Wordsworth, whom Ruskin considered a false seer. Daley relates these differences to modern artistic, cultural, and political concerns and includes some interesting analysis of the Victorian reception of Romanticism.

Francis O'Gorman's *Late Ruskin: New Contexts* is a study of Ruskin's later works from 1860 to 1889, and includes discussions of *Unto This Last*, the *Lectures on Art*, *Fors Clavigera*, *The Bible of Amiens,* and *Sesame and Lilies*. O'Gorman's book includes discussion of unpublished materials. There is also Cianci and Nicholls, eds., *Ruskin and Modernism*, published a hundred years after Ruskin's death, which focuses on Ruskin's impact on the development of Anglo-American modernity. *Victorian Studies* 43:iii[2001] includes the following reviews of critical work on Ruskin: *Ruskin and the Dawn of the Modern*, ed. Dinah Birch, reviewed by Kristine Ottesen Garrigan (*VS* 43:iii[2001] 486); *Ruskin's Culture Wars: Fors Clavigera and the Crisis of Victorian Liberalism*, by Judith Stoddart, reviewed by Kristine Ottesen Garrigan (*VS* 43:iii[2001] 487–8); and *Ruskin's Mythic Queen: Gender Subversion in Victorian Culture*, by Sharon Aronofsky Weltman, reviewed by Kristine Ottesen Garrigan (*VS* 43:iii[2001] 488–9). Judith Stoddart reviews *Ruskin's God* by Michael Wheeler (*NCL* 56:i[2001] 114–16).

Melissa Knox's source book, *Oscar Wilde in the 1900s: The Critic as Creator,* examines and assesses a wide range of recent Wilde criticism with the idea that criticism cannot be objective as Matthew Arnold claimed it could be. Knox also explores Wilde's claim that a critic can interpret the works of others only by 'intensifying his own personality'. The book is divided into seven sections: 'Close

Readings'; 'Theater History and Criticism'; 'New Historicism'; 'Gay, Queer, and Gender Criticism'; 'Reader Response Criticism'; 'Irish Ethnic Studies and Cultural Criticism'; 'Biographic Studies'; and 'Summary and Future Trends'. *Oscar Wilde's Decorated Books*, by Nicholas Frankel, is reviewed by Catherine J. Golden (*VS* 43:i[2001] 140–1); *Oscar Wilde: The Critic as Humanist*, by Bruce Bashford is reviewed by Ian Small (*VS* 43:i[2001] 142–3); and *Oscar Wilde: Recent Research: A Supplement to 'Oscar Wilde Revalued'*, by Ian Small, is reviewed by Regenia Gagnier (*NCL* 56:ii[2001] 276–9).

This review of studies in Victorian prose should not ignore Rick Rylance's important and detailed *Victorian Psychology and British Culture, 1850–1880*. Rylance offers 'a systematic overview of the development of mid-Victorian psychological theory in a way that pays attention to its diverse traditions'. There are clearly expounded sections on the writings of Alexander Bain (1818–1903) the pioneering student in the field of psychology, 'Herbert Spencer and the beginnings of Evolutionary Psychology' and 'G.H. Lewes: History, Mind and Language'. In the first part of his book Rylance writes in detail on various types of nineteenth-century psychological theory. This monograph will prove to be a seminal work on the history of ideas and Victorian prose.

In *George Borrow the Dingle Chapters, with Biographical and Critical Commentary*, Richard Shepheard and Barrie Mencher introduce George Borrow to a new generation of readers through their carefully selected sections of Borrow's two largely autobiographical novels *Lavengro* and *The Romany Rye*. Divided into three sections, the first contains an introduction by Mencher, the second contains extracts from *Lavengro* and *The Romany Rye*, and the third, which is the largest, contains 'The Dingle Chapters' by Shepheard and numerous maps and illustrations dealing with all manner of things Borrowesque. The *George Borrow Bulletin* 22[2001] is devoted to the memory of the late great scholar and Borrovian, Sir George Fraser, and includes many tributes to him. The bulletin also contains: Clive Wilkins-Jones, 'Norwich Central Library Rises from the Ashes, a Note' (*GBB* 22[2001] 12–13); Richard Shepheard, 'Lavengro the Boxer, Part 1' (*GBB* 22[2001] 13–24); Peter Missler, 'Benedict Mol: The Fabrication of a Treasure-Hunt, Part 2: Warp of Truth, Woof of Fiction' (*GBB* 22[2001] 25–38). There is a note from the editor Ann Ridler on 'Harald Harfagr' (*GBB* 22[2001] 39), and Kedrun Laurie writes on 'Testing Borrow's Truthfulness: From the Quakers to the Bohemians, Part 1' (*GBB* 22[2001] 40–64). Containing, as always, items of interest, this issue also offers 'An Address on George Borrow by Ian Maxwell, Contributed by Angus Fraser' (*GBB* 22[2001] 76–80) and four notes and queries: David Chandler, 'Borrow and Taylor on Language and Human Diversity' (*GBB* 22[2001] 65–7); Andrew Dakyns, 'George Burrow and the Manx Poet T.E. Brown (1830–1897)' (*GBB* 22[2001] 68–73); Juan Campos, 'El Valiente de Finisterre Gets Closer to H.M.S. Victory' (*GBB* 22[2001] 74–5); and Grahame Watson, 'The Aqueduct Near Stockport' (*GBB* 22[2001] 76).

One of the most important prose contributions of the year, *Serializing Fiction in the Victorian Press*, Graham Law provides an empirically based study on the role of provincial newspaper fiction syndicates during mid- to late nineteenth-century England, and how they were eventually supplanted by weekly publications headquartered in London. In doing so, Law relies on previously published materials and examines unpublished materials, but also breaks new ground on a previously neglected topic and provides a firm foundation for further research efforts in this neglected area.

2. The Novel

(a) General

In another of the Cambridge Companions to Literature series, David, ed., *The Cambridge Companion to the Victorian Novel*, includes: Kate Flint, 'The Victorian Novel and its Readers'; Simon Eliot, 'The Business of Victorian Publishing'; Linda M. Shires, 'The Aesthetics of the Victorian Novel: Form, Subjectivity, Ideology'; Joseph W. Childers, 'Industrial Culture and the Victorian Novel'; Nancy Armstrong, 'Gender and the Victorian Novel'; Jeff Nunokawa, 'Sexuality in the Victorian Novel'; Patrick Brantlinger, 'Race and the Victorian Novel'; Ronald R. Thomas, 'Detection in the Victorian Novel'; Lyn Pykett, 'Sensation and the Fantastic in the Victorian Novel'; John Kucich, 'Intellectual Debate in the Victorian Novel: Religion, Science, and the Professional'; and Robert Weisbuch, 'Dickens, Melville, and a Tale of Two Countries'. The volume also contains a useful guide to further reading and an index.

Regan, ed., *The Nineteenth Century Novel: A Critical Reader*, provides a selection of essays and reviews from the nineteenth century, placed alongside modern critical essays, on twelve novels. The essays deal with elements of realism and the changing reception of realist fiction, focusing on a variety of British, American, and French novels. Among them are the following: *Northanger Abbey, Jane Eyre, Dombey and Son, Middlemarch, Far from the Madding Crowd, The Woman in White*, and *Dracula*. Another contribution is Jenkins and John, eds., *Rereading Victorian Fiction*, a reassessment of primarily canonical works with some coverage of lesser-known Victorian works. The essays present a wide range of critical and theoretical approaches to fiction, emphasizing 'the ideological, aesthetic, intellectual and moral diversity of both Victorian fiction and its critical reception'.

Gravil, ed., *Master Narratives: Tellers and Telling in the English Novel*, is a compilation of essays covering mostly canonical works of the 'long' nineteenth century, including writers such as Sterne, Fielding, Austen, Emily Brontë, Gaskell, Dickens, and Eliot. Each essay examines an aspect of narrative technique in a single work, focusing on the 'objective' structures of particular texts. Of interest to scholars of the Victorian period are the following articles: '*Wuthering Heights* as Bifurcated Novel', by Frederick Burwick (pp. 69–86); 'Negotiating *Mary Barton*', by Richard Gravil (pp. 87–100); 'The Androgyny of *Bleak House*', by Richard Gravil (pp. 123–38); and '*Middlemarch* and "the Home Epic"', by Nicola Trott (pp. 139–58). The overarching theme of Walder, ed., *The Nineteenth-Century Novel: Identities* is how conventions of realism were affected by new philosophies of race and gender, and fiction's role in constructing gender identity. *Identities* includes the following chapters on nineteenth-century novels, all by Valerie Pedlar: '*The Woman in White*: Sensationalism, Secrets and Spying' (pp. 48–68); 'Drawing a Blank: The Construction of Identity in *The Woman in White*' (pp. 69–94); '*Dracula*: A Fin-de-Siècle Fantasy' (pp. 196–216); and '*Dracula*: Narrative Strategies and Nineteenth-Century Fears' (pp. 217–41).

Drawing on the work of scholars such as Martha Nussbaum and Paul Ricoeur, *Ethics and Narrative in the English Novel, 1880–1914*, by Jill Larson, looks at ethical concepts in Victorian and turn-of-the-century narratives and literary theory. Larson's study includes thoughtful discussion of ethical concepts in the novels of Thomas Hardy, Sarah Grand, Olive Schreiner, Oscar Wilde, and Henry James. She writes that the book's two functions are 'to read ethics through narrative by reflecting on ethical concepts or problems as they take shape in the telling of a story' and 'to further an argument about late Victorian aesthetics and ethics'. In the chapter about Wilde and James, Larson examines the 'aestheticist desire to refashion the world'. Her study also includes a particularly compelling discussion of Hardy and the concept of 'moral luck', in which she argues that his belief in moral luck confounds his interest in Kantian ethics.

Andrew Dowling's *Manliness and the Male Novelist in Victorian Literature* explores such topics as constructions of male identity in the Victorian novel, male deviance and fear of effeminacy in Victorian culture and literature, and the way in which manliness is often defined by what it is not. Dowling's thoughtful study includes the following chapters: 'Victorian Metaphors of Manliness'; 'Dickens, Manliness, and the Myth of the Romantic Artist'; 'Masculinity and its Discontents in Dickens's *David Copperfield*'; 'Homosocial Bohemia in Thackeray's *Pendennis*'; 'Masculinity and Work in Trollope's *An Autobiography*'; and 'Masculine Failure in Gissing's *New Grub Street*'. Another important contribution to studies in the novel is Catherine Robson's *Men in Wonderland: The Lost Girlhood of the Victorian Gentlemen*, which examines the era's obsession with the figure of the little girl. Robson looks at constructions of girlhood in the fictional representations of important male writers such as Lewis Carroll, Ruskin, Wordsworth, and De Quincey. She argues that girlhood mirrors an early stage of the fantasy of male development, providing opportunities for men to reconnect with their own lost selves.

Patricia E. Johnson's *Hidden Hands: Working-Class Women and Victorian Social-Problem Fiction* is concerned with the myth of 'the male breadwinner' who was long thought to have fuelled the Industrial Revolution. Since women made up to 80 per cent of the workforce in light industries, Johnson questions their gradual disappearance from Victorian 'social problem' fiction. She argues that this disappearance was caused by a threat posed by the figure of the working woman in Victorian fiction, who was even more dangerous to Victorian sexual and gender politics than the figure of the prostitute. In *Women and Domestic Experience in Victorian Political Fiction*, Susan Johnston argues that political representations in Victorian fiction serve important political functions by offering a means of evading politics. Susan E. Schaper, 'Victorian Ghostbusting: Gendered Authority in the Middle-Class Home' (*VN* 100[2001] 6–13), argues that gender roles and gender spheres are complicated by 'the very aristocratic ideals they profess to reject', showing how representations of haunted houses in Victorian fiction offer a glimpse into gender constructions of power in the home.

Liggins and Duffy, eds., *Feminist Readings of Victorian Popular Texts: Divergent Femininities*, is a collection of essays by various contributors on the subject of the 'apparent endorsement and subversion of class and gender norms in Victorian popular fiction, poetry, periodicals and modes of theatrical entertainment'. A variety of types of fiction are examined, such as sensation fiction, ghost stories, women's annuals, and stage comedy. The first section, on short stories, poetry and periodicals, includes the following contributions: '"The False Prudery of Public Taste': Scandalous Women and the Annuals, 1820–1850', by Harriet Devine Jump; '"Too Boldly" for a Woman: Text, Identity and the Working-Class Woman Poet', by Margaret Forsyth; and 'Every Girl's Best Friend? The *Girl's Own Paper* and its Readers', by Hilary Skelding. The second section, on popular fiction, includes the following contributions: 'Good Housekeeping? Domestic Economy and Suffering Wives in Mrs. Henry Wood's Early Fiction', by Emma Liggins; 'After Lady Audley: M.E. Braddon, the Actress and the Act of Writing in *Hostages to Fortune*', by Kate Mattacks; 'See What a Big Wide Bed It Is! Mrs. Henry Wood and the Philistine Imagination', by Deborah Wynne; '"Weird Fascination": The Response to Victorian Women's Ghost Stories', by Clare Stewart; 'The Popular Stage: Feminist Discourse in Popular Drama of the Early and Mid- Victorian Era', by Daniel Duffy; and 'Women's Playwriting and the Popular Theatre in the Late Victorian Era, 1870–1900', by Kate Newey.

Adding to the growing body of research about serial sensation novels is a valuable contribution by Deborah Wynne, *The Sensation Novel and the Victorian Family Magazine*. Wynne looks at the connection between bestselling serial novels and their host magazines, the process of serialization, and sensation- novel formulas and readerships. Her study includes sections on the following works and magazines: Wilkie Collins's *The Woman in White* (*All the Year Round*); Ellen Wood's *East of Lynne* (*New Monthly Magazine*); Charles Dickens's *Great Expectations* (*All the Year Round*); Wilkie Collins's *No Name* (*All The Year Round*); Mary Elizabeth Braddon's *Eleanor's Victory* (*Once a Week*); Charles Reade's *Very Hard Cash* (*All the Year Round*); and Wilkie Collins's *Armadale* (*The Cornhill Magazine*).

In a detailed and extensive scholarly study drawing upon primary as well as neglected secondary sources, Jane Wood's *Passion and Pathology in Victorian Fiction* looks at neurological theories and writings alongside the fiction of writers such as Charlotte Brontë, Wilkie Collins, Thomas Hardy, George Gissing, George Eliot, and George MacDonald. Wood explores the interest shared by medical and fiction writers in the mysterious connection of and interactions between the mind and body, psychological and physical states. In *Amnesiac Selves: Nostalgia, Forgetting, and British Fiction, 1810–1870*, Nicholas Dames looks at the threatening nature of memory and the repression of painful memories in the fiction of novelists such as Austen, Trollope, Thackeray, Eliot, and Collins. Dames shows how these writers attempt to eliminate detailed memories in favour of nostalgic amnesia. He also examines popular Victorian theories of the mind such as physiognomy and associationism, exploring the ways in which such writings attempt to create and define a new concept of memory. John Peck's *Maritime Fiction: Sailors and the Sea in British and American Novels, 1719–1917* explores the cultural significance of sea novels, and the historical, social, and cultural influences that shape them, to show how the often masculine brutality of the ship contrasts to the civility of the shore. Peck includes analysis of fiction by Austen, Marryat, Cooper, Dickens, and Stevenson, among others.

Phyllis Weliver, *Women Musicians in Victorian Fiction, 1860–1900: Representations of Music, Science and Gender in the Leisured Home*, looks at scenes in Victorian fiction from 1860 to 1900, when female musicians used music as a way to display their personality, gentility, and education. Weliver looks at the shift from musical 'angel' to musical 'demon', from satirical portrayals of female musicians by writers such as Charlotte Brontë and Jane Austen to portrayals of female musicians 'who were to be feared' in works such as George du Maurier's *Trilby*. This fascinating study includes examinations of *The Mystery of Edwin Drood*, *The Mill on the Floss*, *Middlemarch*, *Daniel Deronda*, *The Woman in White*, *Lady Audley's Secret*, and *Trilby*. Weliver also examines the ways in which novelists use the language of science to describe women making music. According to Weliver, science and music meet in the relationship between music and mesmerism, hypnotism, and other psychological theories pertaining to personality and identity.

Essaka Joshua, *Pygmalion and Galatea: The History of Narrative in English Literature*, examines the history of the Pygmalion tale in print, focusing on changes in the story's reception from the early to late Victorian period. Joshua argues that, by the end of the nineteenth century, the patriarchal framework of Pygmalion is challenged by the 'emasculation of the artist'. Appendix 2 provides a useful bibliography of Pygmalion references. Novy, ed., *Imagining Adoption: Essays on Literature and Culture*, is a collection of essays examining portrayals of adoption and the importance of heredity in literary works. It includes analysis of the works of George Eliot and Anthony Trollope. Pollard, ed., *The Representation of Business in English Literature*, includes an article entitled 'The High Victorian Period (1850–1900): "The Worship of Mammon"' by Angus Easson (pp. 65–98). There is a new edition of the late Ian Watt's *The Rise of the Novel*, which includes a new afterword by W.B. Carnochan in praise of Watt's seminal study of the social and historical conditions that gave rise to the novel as a dominant literary form.

Victorian Studies 43:iii[2001] includes the following reviews of critical work on the novel: *Narrative Reality: Austen, Scott, Eliot*, by Harry E. Shaw, reviewed by Andrew H. Miller (*VS* 43:iii[2001] 467–9); and *Professional Domesticity in the Victorian Novel: Women, Work and Home*, by Monica F. Cohen, reviewed by Tim Dolin (*VS* 43:iii[2001] 517–18). Also reviewed in *VS* are *Plotting Women: Gender and Narration in the Eighteenth-and Nineteenth-Century British Novel*, by Alison A. Case, reviewed by Lynne Vallone (*VS* 43:iv[2001] 659–60), and *Scenes of Sympathy: Identity and Representation in Victorian Fiction*, by Audrey Jaffe, reviewed by Andrew H. Miller (*VS* 43:iv[2001] 667–8). *VS* 43:i[2001] includes the following reviews of critical works on the novel: *The Haunted Mind: The Supernatural in Victorian Literature*, ed. Elton E. Smith and Robert Haas, reviewed by William Hughes (*VS* 43:i[2001] 131–2); *Cooking with Mud: The Idea of Mess in Nineteenth-Century Art and Fiction*, by David Trotter, reviewed by John Marx (*VS* 43:i[2001] 133–5); and *The Foreign Woman in British Literature: Exotics, Aliens, and Outsiders*, ed. Marilyn Demarest Button and Toni Reed, reviewed by Meri-Jane Rochelson (*VS* 43:i[2001] 157–8). Judith Wilt reviews *The Anthology and the Rise of the Novel: From Richardson to George Eliot*, by Leah Price (*NCL* 56:iii[2001] 411–13).

(b) Individual Authors

There are several listings for those interested in the writings of Mary Elizabeth Braddon. Patricia Marks, 'Seeing into "the life of things": Nature and Commodification in *Phantom Fortune*' (*SNNTS* 33:iii[2001] 285–305), argues that the polarity of styles in Braddon's *Phantom Fortune* is an expression of the social and political reformism in this novel, the Wordsworthian sublime juxtaposed to societal materialism. New from Sensation Press is Malcolm, ed., *Circe*, the heretofore difficult-to-obtain novel by Mary Elizabeth Braddon reprinted and unabridged from the Ward, Lock & Tyler edition [1867]. This new edition includes excerpts from contemporary articles concerning the controversy surrounding *Circe*'s publication amidst accusations of literary theft. Also included are three of Braddon's uncollected poems and an essay entitled 'The Woman I Remember'.

Also new from the enterprising, and worthy of support, Sensation Press are several most welcome and useful reissues of Braddon's works: *Dead Love Has Chains*; *Cut By the County*; *His Darling Sin*; and *Dross; or, the Root of Evil and Marjorie Daw*. There is also *One Fatal Moment and Other Stories* and *At the Shrine of Jane Eyre* edited and with an introduction by Jennifer Carnell. *One Fatal Moment* is the last collection of stories Braddon published in book form. Initially published in 1893 in *All Along the River* (in the third volume of the first edition), these stories were omitted in subsequent editions. The stories are as follows: 'One Fatal Moment'; 'It is Easier for a Camel'; 'The Ghost's Name'; 'Stapylton's Plot'; 'His Oldest Friends'; 'If There Be Any of You'; 'The Island of Old Faces'; and 'My Dream'. The final selection, 'At the Shrine of Jane Eyre', is an essay Braddon published in 1906 in *Pall Mall Magazine*. Mattacks, ed., *The Christmas Hirelings* and *Fifty Years of Novel Writing: Miss Braddon at Home*, reprints the first edition published in 1894. The rare interview with Braddon, 'Fifty Years of Novel Writing: Miss Braddon' [1911], is also reprinted and unabridged from its first appearance in *Pall Mall Magazine*.

New in Brontë studies is *The Brontë Myth*, a thoughtful and well-written book in which Lucasta Miller looks at the ways in which the Brontë reputation has been manipulated to reflect changing cultural attitudes. It includes examinations of numerous Brontë biographies and their misleading portrayals of each of the sisters at various times in history. Nash and Suess, eds., *New Approaches to the Literary Art of Anne Brontë,* is a collection of essays by leading Brontë scholars assessing Anne's literary achievements. It includes the following essays: 'Contextualizing Anne Brontë's Bible', by Maria Frawley (pp. 1–14); 'The First Chapter of *Agnes Grey*: An Analysis of the Sympathetic Narrator', by Larry H. Peer (pp. 15–24); 'Class, Matriarchy, and Power: Contextualizing the Governess in *Agnes Grey*', by James R. Simmons, Jr. (pp. 25–44); '"The food of my life": Agnes Grey at Wellwood House', by Marilyn Sheridan Gardner (pp. 45–62); 'Anne Brontë's *Agnes Grey*: The Feminist; "I must stand alone"', by Bettina L. Knapp (pp. 63–74); 'Narrative Economies in *The Tenant of Wildfell Hall*', by Garrett Stewart (pp. 75–102); '"I speak of those I do not know": Witnessing as Radical Gesture in *The Tenant of Wildfell Hall*', by Deborah Denenholz Morse (pp. 103–26); 'Anne Brontë's Method of Social Protest in *The Tenant of Wildfell Hall*', by Lee A. Talley (pp. 127–52); 'Aspects of Love in *The Tenant of Wildfell Hall*', by Marianne Thormählen (pp. 153–72); '*Wildfell Hall* as Satire: Brontë's Domestic Vanity Fair', by Andrés G. López (pp. 173–94); 'Helen's Diary and the Method(ism) of Character Formation in *The Tenant of Wildfell Hall*', by Melody J. Kemp (pp. 195–212); and 'A Matter of Strong Prejudice: Gilbert Markham's Self Portrait', by Andrea Westcott (pp. 213–26).

Debra Teachman's *Understanding Jane Eyre: A Student Casebook to Issues, Sources, and Historical Documents* is a student casebook which includes literary analysis, discussion of important historical contexts, and primary documents such as excerpts from legal and medical writings, articles, letters, and first-hand accounts. There is a reissue by Norton Critical Editions of their third edition of *Jane Eyre: An Authoritative Text, Contexts, Criticisms* edited by Richard J. Dunn. This includes fully revised explanatory notes, expanded contextual materials and footnotes, a select bibliography, a chronology of Charlotte Brontë's life and works, and new discussion of *Jane Eyre* films. Included are criticism from, among others, Adrienne Rich, Sandra M. Gilbert, Jerome Beaty, Lisa Sternlieb, Jeffrey Sconce, and Donna Marie Nudd. The text is based on the third edition published in 1848, with minor changes. Deborah Lutz provides new notes for *Villette* from the Modern Library Classics. The text, which is based on the 1853 edition, is accompanied by an introduction by A.S. Byatt and I. Sodré. Edward Chitham, *The Birth of Wuthering Heights: Emily Brontë at Work*, argues that *Wuthering Heights* was expanded and recast between the time it was first sent to a publisher in 1846 and its acceptance for publication in 1847. Chitham suggests that the carefully plotted chronologies of the book were innovations of this second version. His carefully researched study also includes, among other topics, analysis of physical conditions of work and the drafting and correcting Emily did while in Brussels.

The Brontë Society Transactions: The Journal of Brontë Studies 26:i[2001] includes the following articles, notes, and reviews: 'A Fresh Look at Patrick Branwell Brontë: The Prose', by James C. Reaney (*BST* 26:i[2001] 1–9); 'Workers, Gentlemen and Landowners: Identifying Social Class in *The Professor* and *Wuthering Heights*', by Neville F. Newman (*BST* 26:i[2001] 10–18); 'Charlotte Brontë's Art of Sensation', by John Hughes (*BST* 26:i[2001] 19–26); '"Miss Temple" and the Connors', by Margaret Connor (*BST* 26:i[2001] 27–45); 'Anne Lister and Emily Brontë 1838–39: Landscape with Figures', by Jill Liddington (*BST* 26:i[2001] 46–67); '"Often rebuked, yet always back returning": The Poem Itself', by Ian M. Emberson (*BST* 26:i[2001] 68–70); 'Robert Taylor: A Portrait by Branwell Brontë', by Rachel Terry (*BST* 26:i[2001] 71–2); 'Two Letters: Transcripts of Letters', by Patrick Brontë and Arthur Bell Nicholls (*BST* 26:i[2001] 73–6); 'Branwell Brontë and the Robison–Merrall Link', by Humphrey Gawthrop (*BST* 26:i[2001] 77–83); 'The Haworth Parish Registers, Trade Directories and Tithe Awards', by Steven C. Wood (*BST* 26:i[2001] 84); 'Cesare Brontë', by Maddalena De Leo (*BST* 26:i[2001] 85); '*Wuthering Heights*: An Oddity', by Humphrey Gawthrop (*BST* 26:i[2001] 85–6); *The Letters of Charlotte Brontë*, volume 2: *1848–1851*, reviewed by Edward Chitham (*BST* 26:i[2001] 87–8); *Jane Eyre* and *Villette*, by Charlotte Brontë, New Oxford Word Classics editions, reviewed by Joan Bellamy (*BST* 26:i[2001] 89–90); *Emily Brontë*, by Robert Barnard, reviewed by Luke Spencer (*BST* 26:i[2001] 91–2); *Charlotte Brontë's Promised Land: The Pensionnat Heger and Other Brontë Places in Brussels*, by Eric Ruijssenaars, reviewed by Dudley Green (*BST* 26:i[2001] 92–3); *Reading the Brontës*, by Charmian Knight and Luke Spencer, reviewed by Gina Bridgeland (*BST* 26:i[2001] 94–5); *A Stranger within the Gates: Charlotte Brontë and Victorian Irishness*, by Kathleen Constable, reviewed by Amber M. Adams (*BST* 26:i[2001] 95–6); *Jane Eyre. An Opera* by Michael Berkeley, reviewed by Patsy Stoneman (*BST* 26:i[2001] 97–8); *Mad woman in the attic*, reviewed by Bob Duckett (*BST* 26:i[2001] 99); and *Haworth Churchyard: Who Were They?* by Ann Dinsdale, reviewed by Bob Duckett (*BST* 26:i[2001] 99–100).

In *Nonsense Against Sorrow; A Phenomenological Study of Lewis Carroll's 'Alice' Books*, David Holbrook provides a thorough description of the analytical and phenomenological approach he uses to examine *Alice's Adventures in Wonderland*, *Through the Looking-Glass*, 'The Wasp in a Wig', and 'Jabberwocky'. Other work on Carroll includes a review by Morton N. Cohen of *The Annotated Alice: The Definitive Edition, Introduction and Notes*, by Martin Gardner (*VS* 43:iii[2001] 473–4); a review by Donald Rackin of *In the Shadow of the Dreamchild: A New Understanding of Lewis Carroll*, by Karoline Leach (*VS* 43:iv[2001] 650–2), and a review by Donald Gray of *The Making of the Alice Books: Lewis Carroll's Use of Earlier Children's Literature*, by Ronald Reichertz (*VS* 43:iv[2001] 653–4).

David Trotter's *Paranoid Modernism: Literary Experiment, Psychosis, and the Professionalization of English Society* looks at modernism in England and what he calls the 'will-to-experiment' or to 'make it new'. Trotter's study includes a chapter on Wilkie Collins and William Godwin entitled 'Career Development: William Godwin, Wilkie Collins, and the Psychopathies of Expertise', in which he argues that Collins's *The Woman in White* 'can be taken to demonstrate the durability of the (paranoid) fantasy of social recognition through expertise which had animated Godwin's *Caleb Williams*'. Tom Pocock's thoughtful biography *Captain Marryat: Seaman, Writer and Adventurer* traces Marryat's life, from his experiences in the Royal Navy and Napoleonic Wars, through his travels in the United States, to his ties with important literary figures such as Charles Dickens. Pocock also examines Marryat's creation of a new literary genre, popularized by his stories of the sea, *Frank Mildmay* and *Mr. Midshipman Easy*.

The subject of Anthea Trodd's 'Messages in Bottles and Collins's Seafaring Man' (*SEL* 41[2001] 751–65), is the collaboration of Wilkie Collins and Charles Dickens on the story *A Message from the Sea*, in particular the fourth chapter, 'The Seafaring Man'. Trodd shows how working within the strict limits of Dickens's theories of storytelling eventually helped Collins develop his own unique narrative technique using eyewitness accounts and first-person testimonies. Carolyn Oulten, 'A Vindication of Religion: Wilkie Collins, Dickens and *The Frozen Deep*' (*Dickensian* 97:ii[2001] 154–8), looks at origins of the play *The Frozen Deep* in order to show how Dickens's conception of 'manliness' is reflected in the play's conflict between the hostile elements of the North Pole and the stranded voyagers. *No Thoroughfare*, the mystery story Wilkie Collins wrote in collaboration with Charles Dickens and originally published in *All the Year Round*, 12 December 1867, and in *Every Saturday* (Boston) in December 1867, is the subject of a new edition. This is published by the Christchurch (New Zealand) branch of the Dickens Fellowships, and provides a useful short introduction and commentary on editorial procedures.

The *Wilkie Collins Society Journal* 4[2000], edited by Lillian Nayder and Graham Law, contains three articles. Emma Liggins's 'Her Resolution to Die: "Wayward Women" and Constructions of Suicide in Wilkie Collins' Crime Fiction' (*WCSJ* 4[2000] 5–17) focuses on Rosanna Spearman in *The Moonstone* [1868], and similar cases as reported in the *Illustrated Police News*, 19 February 1870 and 30 May 1874. She also discusses interesting episodes in *Armadale* [1866] and *The Law and the Lady* [1875]: 'Collins focuses on suicides which elude easy interpretation in terms of class or sanity, highlighting the ways in which women's violence exposes their dissatisfaction with middle class marriage as well as their unacknowledged sexual desires' (p. 9). Natalie Kapetanios, 'Hunger for Closure in *Lady Audley's Secret* and *Armadale*' (*WCSJ* 4[2000] 18–37), uses the two novels as a means of demonstrating 'that the eating tropes that recur in Victorian criticism of the sensation novel were more than merely a convenient means for critics to express the sensation novel's moral shortcomings'. She suggests 'that the language of hunger captures a subtlety of the way in which sensation novels were written' (p. 18). Mary Elizabeth Braddon's sensation novel is also the subject of Richard S. Albright's '"A twisted piece of paper ... half-burned upon the hearthrug": Depictions of Writing in *Lady Audley's Secret*'. Albright argues in a persuasive manner that, by 'exploring the limitations, not just of genre, but of language itself', Braddon 'like her mercurial heroine [Lady Audley] is also able to transform herself' from being a mere sensational novelist. The issue of the *Wilkie Society Journal* concludes with four reviews: Lyn Pykett on Deborah Wynne, *The Sensational Novel and the Victorian Family Magazine* (*WCSJ* 4[2000] 50–2); Steve Dillon on Christopher GoGwilt's *The Fiction of Geopolitics Afterimages of Culture, from Wilkie Collins to Alfred Hitchcock* (*WCSJ* 4[2000] 52–4; Michael Lund on Graham Law's *Serializing Fiction in the Victorian Press* (*WCSJ* 4[2000] 55–7); and Martha Stoddard Holmes on Marlene Tromp's *The Private Rod: Marital Violence, Sensation and the Law in Victorian Britain* (*WCSJ* 4[2000] 58–61). In the final review of the issue, Graham Law writes on Ronald's R. Thomas's *Detective Fiction and the Rise of Forensic Science* [1999] (*WCSJ* 4[2000] 62–4).

Ira B. Nadel reviews *The Letters of Wilkie Collins*, volume 1: *1838–1865* and *The Letters of Wilkie Collins*, volume 2: *1874–1881*, both edited by William Baker and William M. Clarke (*VS* 43:i[2001] 148–50). Lillian Nayder reviews *Wilkie Collins: An Illustrated Guide*, by Andrew Gasson and the two-volume *Letters of Wilkie Collins*, edited by William Baker and William M. Clarke (*VPR* 34:ii[2001]) 199–201).

Also of interest to Wilkie Collins scholars, and students of Victorian literature in general, is the *Newsletter of the Wilkie Collins Society*, produced by Andrew Gasson and Paul Lewis (email: paul@paullewis.co.uk). The Spring 2001 and Winter 2001 issues include information on London screenings of the 1982 BBC television version of *The Woman in White*, the 1917 film version of the novel called 'The Dream Woman' and details of the French translation of *The Lighthouse* (5). Paul Lewis has an interesting note on 'Wilkie in Italy' stimulated by the sale of a painting belonging to Wilkie's father, William Collins, RA, *The Caves of Ulysses at Sorrento*, at the Phillips Knowle sale, in Solihull (West Midlands) on 10 January 2001, for £144,000 (plus premium and taxes). Among items of interest in the Winter 2001 *Newsletter* are notes on 'The Society of Authors', 'Wilkie in the Press' (largely British-orientated), 'Charles Collins' Grave', and recent auction sales of William Collins's paintings. In addition an occasional paper is separately issued by the Wilkie Collins Society with its *Newsletter*. The 2001 paper is by Paul Lewis, on 'Wilkie Collins: Lunacy on the Isle of Man', describing in some detail Collins's August 1863 visit to the Isle of Man, his transformation of his visit in *Armadale*, and facts about the state of lunatics on the island. Finally, Susan R. Hanes's most useful privately printed *The Persistent Phantom: Wilkie Collins and Dorothy Sayers* should not be ignored. Hanes, the former librarian at Wheaton College, carefully produces an 'Examination and Transcription of an Unpublished Lecture by Dorothy L. Sayers Held at the Marion Wade Center, Wheaton College, Wheaton, Illinois'. A well-written scholarly introduction is followed by information on the provenance of Dorothy Sayers's Wilkie Collins lecture, a physical and textual description, dating (probably 1930), an explanation of the methodology of transcription, and a transcription (pp. 12–51). Hanes concludes her introduction with the observation that Sayers's 'enthusiasm for [Collins] is affirming and infectious, and her understanding of Collins' genius and his shortcomings is revealing of them both' (p. 11).

A valuable contribution to Dickens studies is Jordan, ed., *The Cambridge Companion to Dickens*. It provides a valuable introduction to Dickens on a variety of topics, as well as current critical theory by noted Dickens scholars. The study includes chapters on individual texts (from *Sketches by Boz* to *The Mystery of Edwin Drood*), as well as chapters treating thematic issues such as portrayals of the city, theatre and film, childhood, gender, and family. In *Dickens's Villains: Melodrama, Character, Popular Culture*, Juliet John argues that Dickens's villains embody 'the crucial fusion between the deviant and theatrical aspects of his writing'. John suggests that Dickens's preference for melodrama stems from a desire for cultural and social inclusiveness.

New from Greenwood Press's excellent Dickens Companions series is Metz, ed., *The Companion to Martin Chuzzlewit*, a collection of critical readings by various scholars along with appendices, select bibliography, and notes that 'revise and expand the conventional wisdom regarding the sources for the American chapters, demonstrating that Dickens drew on a much wider field of writings about America than has been traditionally acknowledged'. Jeremy Tambling, *Becoming Posthumous; Life and Death in Literary Cultural Studies*, makes an interesting argument about the idea of 'the posthumous' as a valuable means of looking at history and the past. Tambling's study includes a chapter on Dickens entitled 'Without Origins: *David Copperfield*' (pp. 59–87), in which he argues that *David Copperfield* is a text concerned with the many ways a psyche can understand or know the past and present when both can be known only in a textual sense. Tambling also includes chapters with discussion of works by Shakespeare, Nietzsche, and Walter Benjamin. In 'Curiosity as Didacticism in *The Old Curiosity Shop*' (*Novel* 34:i[2001] 28–55), Sarah Winters argues that 'Dickens's novels seek not only to persuade but also to provide the patterns of logic and emotion through which readers form their judgments of society'. Curiosity, according to Winters, provides the impetus for 'the kind of questioning that readers of Dickens's novels are taught to engage in as a means of overcoming habitual prejudices, including those they have acquired at school'. Krista Lysack, 'Imperial Addictions: West End Shopping and East End Opium' (*VN* 100[2001] 17–21), examines the addictive pleasures of opium and shopping in *The Mystery of Edwin Drood* in order to explore its colonial subtexts. Lysack shows how the disruptive presence of women in both these spaces reflects anxieties concerning women, their spending habits, and their shifting roles in public spaces.

Pam Morris, '*Bleak House* and the Struggle for the State Domain' (*ELH* 68:iii[2001] 679–98), provides readings of *Bleak House* using the ideas of Foucault and Bentham as a means to analyse systems of control in the novel. Peter M. Stokes, 'Bentham, Dickens, and the Uses of the Workhouse' (*SEL* 41[2001] 711–27), examines differences in Bentham's and Dickens's views of the workhouse, as well as some illuminating similarities. Susan Ferguson, 'Dickens's Public Readings and the Victorian Author' (*SEL* 41[2001] 729–49), looks at eyewitness accounts of Dickens's public readings of his own novels, as well as his own remarks about them in order to understand how these performances inform our understanding of Dickens as a writer, novelist, and performer. Josef L. Altholz, 'Oliver Twist's Workhouse' (*Dickensian* 97:ii[2001] 137–43), contrasts Dickens's usual highly specific place descriptions of London to the unnamed city in which Oliver Twist's workhouse is located.

In 'Trauma, Memory, and Railway Disaster: The Dickensian Connection' (VS 43:iii[2001] 413–36), Jill L. Matus looks at connections between the trauma Dickens experienced in the nearly fatal train accident of 1865 (an account of which is included in the postscript of *Our Mutual Friend*) and his ghost story 'The Signalman'. Matus argues that the story provides a link between discourse of shock trauma and Victorian conceptions of the unconscious. She focuses on the symptoms Dickens experienced afterwards (for example, loss of his voice and the 'shakes') and the various discourses of trauma in the 1860s that might have provided him with a means by which to respond to the experience. Alexander Welsh's *Hamlet and his Modern Guises*, a study of Hamlet's influence on the novel as a literary form, includes a discussion of *Great Expectations*. Two chapters in Roger D. Sell's *Mediating Criticism: Literary Education Humanized* are relevant to Dickens studies: 'Decorum versus indecorum in *Dombey and Son*' (pp. 165–94) and 'The Pains and Pleasures of David Copperfield' (pp. 263–90). In 'David Copperfield and *The Stranger*: "A Doctors' Commons sort of play"?' (*Dickensian* 97:iii[2001] 235–41), John Russell Stephens examines David's third visit to the London theatre to see *The Stranger*, arguing that he sees the performance as an important marker of initiation into his new professional life. Stephens also discusses the nature of the play and the identity of its adapter and translator.

Elaine Ostry, '"Social wonders": Fancy, Science, and Technology in Dickens's Periodicals' (*VPR* 34:i[2001] 54–78), examines Dickens's use of 'fanciful rhetoric' in *All the Year Round* and *Household Words* as he used it to make science more appealing to his readers. Ostry looks at the cultural anxieties revealed by these allusions to scientific writings, arguing that they helped teach readers about science in a non-threatening way at a time when adjusting to scientific development was difficult. Shu-Fang Lai, 'Fact or Fancy: What Can We Learn about Dickens from his Periodicals *Household Words* and *All the Year Round*?' (*VPR* 34:i[2001] 41–53), challenges the notion that the ideas in *Household Words* and *All the Year Round* necessarily represent the views of the editor, Dickens. Emphasizing Dickens's reliance on his sub-editor William Henry Wills, Lai suggests that Dickens was not as much a hands-on presence at the two journals as has been presumed. According to Lai, recent criticism has overestimated the extent to which articles not written by Dickens represent his own views. Deborah Wynne, 'Responses to the 1851 Great Exhibition in *Household Words*' (*Dickensian* 97:iii[2001] 228–34), discusses how Dickens felt pressured as the editor of *Household Words* to include coverage of the Great Exhibition, even though he was personally uninterested in it. Another problem for the magazine, according to Wynne, was that it was unable to present exciting visual illustrations and images like the ones in rival magazines.

The *Dickens Studies Annual: Essays on Victorian Fiction* 30[2001] includes eighteen essays on Dickens: 'Styles of Stillness and Motion: Market Culture and Narrative Form in *Sketches by Boz*', by Amanpal Garcha (*DSA* 30[2001] 1–22);

'Clock Work: *The Old Curiosity Shop* and *Barnaby Rudge*', by Robert Tracy (*DSA* 30[2001] 23–44); 'Executing Beauty: Dickens and the Aesthetics of Death', by Goldie Morgentaler (*DSA* 30[2001] 45–58); 'Did Dickens have a Philosophy of History? The Case of *Barnaby Rudge*', by Patrick Brantlinger (*DSA* 30[2001] 59–76); 'Masques of the English in *Barnaby Rudge*', by Judith Wilt (*DSA* 30[2001] 75–94); 'Politics and *Barnaby Rudge*: Surrogation, Restoration, and Revival', by John Glavin (*DSA* 30[2001] 95–112); 'Demons on the Rooftops, Gypsies in the Street: The "Secret Intelligence" of *Dombey and Son*', by Michelle Mancini (*DSA* 30[2001] 113–40); '"More like than life": Painting, Photography, and Dickens's *Bleak House*', by Regina B. Oost (*DSA* 30[2001] 141–58); 'Wax-Work, Clock-Work, and Puppet Shews: *Bleak House* and the Uncanny', by Robyn L. Schiffman (*DSA* 30[2001] 159–72); 'Towards a Dickens Poetics: Indexical and Iconic Language in *Bleak House*', by James E. Marlow (*DSA* 30[2001] 173–92); '*Hard Times*: The Disciplinary City', by Barry Stiltner (*DSA* 30[2001] 193–216); '"Like or no like": Figuring the Scapegoat in *A Tale of Two Cities*', by Mark M. Hennelly Jr. (*DSA* 30[2001] 217–42); 'Monstrous Displacements: Anxieties of Exchange in *Great Expectations*', by Clare Pettitt (*DSA* 30[2001] 243–62); 'Servants' Logic and Analytical Chemistry: George Eliot, Dickens, and Servants', by Jonathan Taylor (*DSA* 30[2001] 263–84); 'Hetty and History: The Political Consciousness of *Adam Bede*', by Eleni Coundouriotis (*DSA* 30[2001] 285–308); '"The good angel of our lives": Subversive Religion in *The Woman in White*', by Carolyn Oulton (*DSA* 30[2001] 309–20); 'A Forgotten Collaboration of the Late 1860s: Charles Reade, Robert Barnes, and the Illustrations for *Put Yourself in his Place*', by Simon Cooke (*DSA* 30[2001] 321–42); and 'Recent Dickens Studies: 1999', by Michael Lund (*DSA* 30[2001] 343–72).

Also included in *The Dickensian* 97:ii[2001], edited by Malcolm Andrews, are the following articles: 'Silent Film Adaptations of Dickens, Part II: 1912–1919', by Graham Petrie (*Dickensian* 97:ii[2001] 101–15); '"He do the police in different voices": *Our Mutual Friend* and *The Waste Land*', by Allyson Booth (*Dickensian* 97:ii[2001] 116–22); 'The 'Paradox of Acting' in *A Tale of Two Cities*', by Anny Sadrin (*Dickensian* 97:ii[2001] 123–36); 'Edmund Wilson on Orwell on Dickens: A Note', by Edgar Rosenberg (*Dickensian* 97:ii[2001] 144–5); 'Dickens and the Forty Thieves', by Charles Forsyte (*Dickensian* 97:ii[2001] 146–53); and 'Woodbine Cottage, Petersham', by John Beardmore and David Parker (*Dickensian* 97:ii[2001] 159–61). Also included in *The Dickensian*, 97:iii[2001], edited by Malcolm Andrews, are 'Silent Film Adaptations of Dickens: Part III—1920–1927', by Graham Petrie (*Dickensian*, 97:iii[2001] 197–214) and 'Cavalletto, The Italian Patriot?' by Trey Philpotts (*Dickensian*, 97:iii[2001] 215–20). John O. Jordan reviews *Dickens and the Spirit of the Age*, by Andrew Sanders, and *Other Dickens: Pickwick to Chuzzlewit*, by John Bowen (*VS* 43:i[2001] 126–8). Rhoda L. Flaxman reviews Baruch Hochman and Ilja Wachs's *Dickens: The Orphan Condition* [1999] (*VS* 43:ii[2001] 311–13).

Norton Critical Editions have published an edition of the 1854 first-edition text for a third edition of *Hard Times*, edited by Fred Kaplan and Sylvere Monod, with revised annotations and new criticism based on recent scholarly findings. The new edition also includes background, sources, appendices about the author's working notes, reprints of contemporary reactions and reviews, chronology, and bibliography. There are new notes by James Danly and a new introduction by Jane

Jacobs for the Modern Library Classics edition of Dickens's *Hard Times*. New from Penguin is a reissue of *The Old Curiosity Shop*, edited by Norman Page and based on the first edition in volume form [1841]. This edition includes an introduction, chronology, explanatory notes, and original illustrations by George Cattermole, Hablot K. Browne, Daniel Maclise, and Samuel Williams. There is also a revised edition of the Oxford World's Classics *Dombey and Son*, edited by Alan Horsman, which includes a new introduction and notes by Dennis Walder. The Modern Library Classics' edition of *Oliver Twist* includes a new introduction by Philip Pullman, along with original illustrations by George Cruikshank and notes and appendix by James Danly. Haywood, ed., *Chartist Fiction: 'The Political Pilgrim's Progress', Thomas Doubleday; 'Sunshine and Shadow', Thomas Martin*, reprints these two radical narratives for the first time since their appearance in Chartist newspapers. The third and final volume of Chartist fiction in the series is Haywood, ed., *Chartist Fiction: 'Woman's Wrongs', Ernest Jones*.

Arthur Conan Doyle and the Meaning of Masculinity by Diana Barsham looks at Doyle's biography and literary career, comparing representations of masculinity in the Sherlock Holmes stories to Doyle's histories of the Boer War and the First World War. Drawing on a comprehensive range of Doyle's work, including his novels and stories as well as his historical, legal and religious works, Barsham explores numerous representations of masculinity, and the way Doyle offered himself and his writings as models for masculinity. This study also includes a useful survey of Doyle biographies and a good bibliography. Tony Earnshaw's *An Actor and a Rare One: Peter Cushing as Sherlock Holmes* examines Peter Cushing's portrayal of Sherlock Holmes and provides commentary about Cushing's interpretation of the character.

The Modern Library Classics' edition of *The Adventures and Memoirs of Sherlock Holmes* brings together all twenty-four Sherlock Holmes stories, the first twelve of which were first published in book form in *The Adventures of Sherlock Holmes* [1891], and eleven of which (not including 'The Cardboard Box') were first published in book form in *The Memoirs of Sherlock Holmes* [1893]. All of the stories in this collection are based on the initial book publications, with the exception of 'The Cardboard Box' and 'The Resident Patient', which are based on their first publication in *Strand Magazine*. This edition includes an introduction by John Berendt and newly commissioned notes by James Danly. Penguin's *The Lost World and Other Thrilling Tales* is edited and with an introduction and notes by Philip Gooden, and includes a chronology of Doyle's life. Along with *The Lost World* are the following stories: 'The Poison Belt'; 'The Terror of Blue John Gap'; and 'The Horror of the Heights'. All are based on their original publication in book form.

A most important publication this year for George Eliot studies is the new Clarendon edition of *Adam Bede*, edited by Carol A. Martin. From among eleven British typesettings of the work issued during its author's lifetime, Martin chooses the corrected eighth edition [1861]. Her 158-page introduction is replete with erudition, and concludes with a descriptive listing of editions of *Adam Bede*. Martin's discussion ranges from a detailed analysis of the genesis, composition, and publication of the novel, consideration of its differing editions in relation to the manuscript, now in the British Library, the dialect of the novel, and treatment of copy-text. Informative textual notes at the foot of the page accompany the text of the novel itself, and twenty-four pages of explanatory notes follow the text. In short, this is a magisterial edition which will stand the test of time.

Levine, ed., *The Cambridge Companion to George Eliot*, is a comprehensive study of Eliot's fiction, and her scientific, philosophical, religious and political views, including eleven specially commissioned essays about numerous aspects of her writing. The essays are as follows: 'Introduction: George Eliot and the Art of Realism', by George Levine (pp. 1–19); 'A Woman of Many Names', by Rosemarie Bodenheimer (pp. 20–37); 'The Early Novels', by Josephine McDonagh (pp. 38–56); 'The Later Novels', by Alexander Welsh (pp. 57–75); 'George Eliot and Philosophy', by Suzy Anger (pp. 76–97); 'George Eliot and Science', by Diana Postlethwaite (pp. 98–118); 'George Eliot and Religion', by Barry Qualls (pp. 119–37); 'George Eliot and Politics', by Nancy Henry (pp. 138–58); 'George Eliot and Gender', by Kate Flint (pp. 159–80); 'George Eliot and her Publishers', by Donald Gray (pp. 181–201); 'George Eliot: The Critical Heritage', by Kathleen Blake (pp. 202–25); and 'Works Cited and Further Reading', by Tanya Agathocleous (pp. 226–43).

Heather V. Armstrong, *Character and Ethical Development in the Three Novels of George Eliot: Middlemarch, Romola, Daniel Deronda*, provides readings of the three novels using the ethical philosophies of Emmanuel Levinas and Martin Buber. Armstrong also explores Eliot's views on duty, morality, sympathy, and imagination. Kimberly Van Esveld Adams, *Our Lady of Victorian Feminism: The Madonna in the Work of Anna Jameson, Margaret Fuller, and George Eliot* examines how images of the Madonna are used by each of the nineteenth-century women mentioned in the subtitle in arguments designed to promote the empowerment of women. The discussion of Eliot centres on the representations of Dinah Morris in *Adam Bede*. Adams focuses on the inability of the woman to be simultaneously virgin and mother, arguing that 'the mother could not escape the impediment imposed by the social construction of the female body'. In this sense, Adams argues, Eliot endorses the 'benefits of sexual and psychic virginity: a woman could enjoy freedom and empowerment only in a virgin's state of physical and emotional self-denial'.

Linda S. Raphael's *Narrative Skepticism: Moral Agency and Representations of Consciousness in Fiction* traces the growth of scepticism in narrative, beginning with an examination of *Middlemarch*. Raphael explores what she calls Eliot's representation of 'the nexus of moral agency, responsibility, and psychological depth in fiction'. Penelope LeFew-Blake, *Schopenhauer, Women's Literature, and the Legacy of Pessimism in the Novels of George Eliot, Olive Schreiner, Virginia Woolf, and Doris Lessing*, argues that Schopenhauer may have had more influence during his lifetime on literature and literary figures (such as George Eliot) than he did on actual academic philosophy. LeFew-Blake looks at how characters in the works of Eliot, Schreiner, Woolf, and Lessing 'devour themselves in an effort to renew themselves' and the various ways in which they 'reflect the struggles of Schopenhauer's artistic outsiders'. Two chapters of particular interest to George Eliot scholars are 'George Eliot's *Middlemarch*: A Schopenhauerian Shadowplay' (pp. 13–34) and 'George Eliot's *Daniel Deronda*: A Study in Schopenhauerian Morality' (pp. 35–48).

Peter Hodgson, *Theology in the Fiction of George Eliot*, looks at religious aspects of Eliot's life and works. After a chapter describing Eliot's religious pilgrimage,

Hodgson devotes chapters to religious themes and figures in the following individual works: *Scenes from Clerical Life*, *Adam Bede*, *The Mill on the Floss*, *Silas Marner*, *Romola*, *Felix Holt*, *Middlemarch*, and *Daniel Deronda*. His concise study concludes with a chapter about Eliot and postmodern theology. Laura Fasick, 'No Higher Love: Clerical Domesticity in Kingsley and Eliot' *(VN* 100[2001] 1–5), examines the Victorian debate over the origins and scope of priestly authority in literary representations of clergymen, arguing that in fictional representations (Kingsley's *Two Years Ago* and Eliot's *Scenes from Clerical Life* and *Adam Bede*), the priest's effectiveness runs 'parallel to the current of his erotic and domestic life'.

Stefanie Markovits, 'George Eliot's Problem with Action' *(SEL* 41[2001] 785–803), examines the nature of the action happening inside Eliot's characters (for example, 'willing, judging, desiring, feeling') versus agency, or the external outward expression of characters' inner actions. Focusing on *Daniel Deronda*, *Adam Bede*, and *Felix Holt*, Markovits looks at Eliot's theories of political action, progress, and reform. Sarah Gates provides an interesting analysis of *Daniel Deronda* and genre in '"A difference of native language": Gender, Genre, and Realism in *Daniel Deronda*' *(ELH* 68:iii[2001] 699–724). Claudia L. Johnson, 'F.R. Leavis: *The Great Tradition* of the English Novel and the Jewish Part' *(NCL* 56:ii[2001] 198–227), re-examines Leavis's call for an excision of the 'Jewish part' of *Daniel Deronda* in order to argue that 'deracination and dispossession, rather than parochial English and possession, condition Leavis's great tradition'.

John R. Reed, 'Soldier Boy: Forming Masculinity in *Adam Bede*' *(SNNTS* 33:iii[2001] 268–84), persuasively argues that the figure of the soldier in *Adam Bede* serves as a kind of role model for mid-Victorian masculinity and morality. Josephine McDonagh, 'Child Murder Narratives in George Eliot's *Adam Bede*: Embedded Histories and Fictional Representation' *(NCL* 56:ii[2001] 228–59), argues that the various uses of the child murder in *Adam Bede* by historicist literary critics, literary critics, and historians have failed to take into account its operation as a 'nodal point' or a kind of repository for associations and ideas from several historical and political contexts. McDonagh argues that Eliot attempts to construct child-murder narratives (dating from the 1624 statute) into a narrative of the English past, but that other associations in the novel interfere. Sheila Stern, 'Truth So Difficult: George Eliot and Georg Büchner, A Shared Theme' *(MLR* 96:i[2001] 2–13), looks at similarities between chapter 17 of *Adam Bede* and Georg Büchner's *Lenz* in order to argue that Büchner's story may have helped inform Eliot's ideas about truth in art.

The subject of Aeron Haymie's 'The Illegitimacy of the Colonial Entrepreneur in George Eliot's *Felix Holt*' *(VN* 100[2001] 26–31), is the effect on national consciousness of the 1857 uprisings in northern India. Haymie shows how 'the male colonial project is appropriated and used as a metaphor to express issues of feminine agency in George Eliot's *Felix Holt*', and discusses the role of rumour in creating the figure of 'the violated Englishwoman' in fictional representations. In '"Influencing the moral taste": Literary Work and the Aesthetics of Social Change in *Felix Holt, the Radical*' *(NCL* 56:i[2001] 52–75), Elizabeth Starr looks at Eliot's ambivalence about the business aspect of writing and the tension between commercial enterprise and idealism, using Esther and Felix to 'embody and engender cultural hierarchies that were of direct concern' for Eliot, who was a 'commercially successful woman writer'. In 'George Eliot and the Precious Mettle of Trust' *(VS* 44:i[2001] 41–76), Richard D. Mallen looks at Eliot's representations of bureaucratic regulation of money. Hilda Hollis, 'The Other Side of Carnival: *Romola* and Bakhtin' (*PLL* 37:iii[2001] 227–54), looks at elements of Bakhtinian carnival in Eliot's *Romola*. There is also Bachmann Günter's *Philosophische Bewußtseinsformen in George Eliot's Middlemarch*, which contains a detailed discussion in German of critical reactions to the novel.

There are several new editions of Eliot works. The Penguin edition of *The Lifted Veil* and *Brother Jacob* is edited, with notes and an introduction, by Sally Shuttleworth. The text for both is based on the revised Cabinet editions, along with notes indicating major alterations. Modern Library Classics presents *Silas Marner: The Weaver of Raveloe* with a new introduction and notes by Chris Bohjalian. The text of this edition is based on the Cabinet edition [1878], the last edition reviewed and corrected by Eliot. Also new from Modern Library Classics is *The Mill on the Floss*, which reproduces the text of the third edition [1878], the last for which Eliot made revisions, and includes newly commissioned explanatory notes by Hugh Osborne and an introduction by Margot Livesey.

George Eliot–George Henry Lewes Studies, 40–1[Sept. 2001] includes two obituary notices, four articles, Donald Hawes's indispensable annual review 'George Eliot and George Henry Lewes: Selected Articles 2000' (*GEGHLS* 40–1[2000] 68–75), and nine reviews. There are obituaries of Professor Thomas F. Deegan (1934–2001), whose most important edition of George Eliot's translation of Spinoza's *Ethics* [1981] was published in the Salzburg Studies in English Literature series. Professor Kathleen Tillotson (1906–2001) was, to use the words of Donald Hawes's obituary, 'one of the most distinguished literary scholars of our time'. Articles include Kirstie Blair's well-written and argued 'A Change in the Units: *Middlemarch*, G.H. Lewes and Rudolf Virchow' (*GEGHLS* 40–1[2000] 9–24). Oskar Wellens considers 'The Contemporary Dutch Reception of George Eliot' (*GEGHLS* 40–1[2000] 25–33). This article provides a supplement to Diederick L. van Werven's detailed and very important illustrated *Dutch Readings of George Eliot 1856–1885*, a most informative illustrated study which assesses the impact of Eliot in Holland, including a lengthy description of the various Dutch translations of her work. Three indispensable appendices contain the tabulated dates of translation 'in Holland, France and Germany, up to 1885', a 'Documented Reception in Dutch, 1860–1885' and a 'Bibliographical Description of Dutch Translations of George Eliot's Works in Chronological Order'.

To return to *GEGHLS*, David L. Smith's laboured '*Middlemarch*: Eliot's Tender Subversion' (*GEGHLS* 40–1[2000] 34–46) treads some familiar territory relating to Dorothea and restrictions on the education of Victorian women. On the other hand, less familiar territory is tackled in Andrew Lynn's 'Schleirmacher, Spinoza, and Eliot: Hermeneutics and Biblical Criticism in *Adam Bede*' (*GEGHLS* 40–1[2000] 47–64). In a 'Note', Donald Hawes provides a succinct review of the BBC Radio 4 version of *Adam Bede*. Reviews include A.G. van den Broek on three recent editions of *Felix Holt, the Radical* (*GEGHLS* 40–1[2000] 76–9); Michelle L. Goins on James Secord's *Victorian Sensation* (*GEGHLS* 40–1[2000] 79–82); William R. McKelvy on John Rignall's *Oxford Reader's Companion to George Eliot* (*GEGHLS* 40–1[2000] 82–5); Nicole Clifton on Andrew Wawn's *The Vikings and the Victorians* (*GEGHLS* 40–1[2000] 86–8); and Andrew Thompson on Carole Levine and Mark W. Turner's *From Author to Text* (*GEGHLS* 40–1[2000] 88–93). Lucy Armitt reviews Kathryn Hughes's *George Eliot: The Last Victorian* (*GEGHLS* 40–1[2000]

94–7), Laura Vorachek assesses the second edition Elizabeth Deeds Ermarth's *Realism and Consensus in the English Novel* (*GEGHLS* 40–1[2000] 97–9), and Sophia Andres reviews Lawrence J. Starzyk's *If Mine had been the Painter's Hand: The Indeterminate in Nineteenth-Century Poetry and Painting* (*GEGHLS* 40–1[2000] 100–3). Finally, Linda K. Robertson assesses Kathleen McCormack's *George Eliot and Intoxication: Dangerous Drugs for the Condition of England* (*GEGHLS* 40–1[2000] 103–6).

   The George Eliot Review: Journal of the George Eliot Fellowship 32[2001], in addition to publishing Viscount Daventry's speech 'At the Wreath-Laying in the George Eliot Memorial Gardens, 18 June 2000' (*GER* 32[2001] 7–8), Jonathan G. Ouvry's 'Address at the Wreath-Laying in Poets' Corner, Westminster Abbey, 21 June 2000', at the twentieth anniversary of the unveiling of the George Eliot memorial stone (*GER* 32[2001] 9–10), and Serena Evans's speech at the 'Opening of the Garden at the George Eliot Hospital, Nuneaton, 9 July 2000' (*GER* 32[2001] 11–12), contains Barbara Hardy's moving and insightful 'George Eliot for the Twenty-First Century: *Middlemarch* and the Poetry of Prosaic Conditions' (*GER* 32[2001] 13–22), the twenty-ninth George Eliot Memorial Lecture [2000], which was to have been given by the late Jerome Beaty. In 'The Toast to the Immortal Memory', Kathleen Adams's speech at the George Eliot birthday luncheon on 19 November 2000, she reflects upon her own childhood contact with Eliot's writings (*GER* 32[2001] 23–7). Articles include June Skye Szirotny's 'Edward Casaubon and Herbert Spencer' (*GER* 32[2001] 29–43), a contribution replete with fifty-one footnotes. Kirstie Blair's 'Priest and Nun? *Daniel Deronda*, Anti-Catholicism and the Confessional' (*GER* 32[2001] 45–50) brilliantly demonstrates the manner in which 'expectations that the novel would end with Deronda's and Gwendolen's marriage ... are thwarted' by the writer's 'clever, gradual transformation of one meaning of a set of religious signifiers into another'. Beryl Gray's 'Nobody's Daughters: Dickens' Tatty Coram and George Eliot's Caterina Sarti' (*GER* 32[2001] 51–62) discourses intertextually on *Little Dorrit*, 'Mr. Gilfil's Love Story' and *The Natural History of German Life*. Graham Handley as usual writes insightfully, bringing a lifetime of reading experience to bear upon '*Middlemarch* and *Belinda*' (*GER* 32[2001] 63–7), Rhoda Broughton's novel [1883].

   A poem by Edwin J. Milliken first published in *Punch* on 8 January 1881, written seventeen days after George Eliot's death, appears (*GER* 32[2001] 68), accompanied by an illustration of the grave in the Highgate Cemetery (p. 69). *George Eliot Review* also contains a brief letter from Barbara Hardy on the purchases by the British Library of the George Eliot–Jane Senior letters (p. 70). There are several reviews: Carol A. Martin reviews John Rignall's *Oxford Reader's Companion to George Eliot* (*GER* 32[2001] 71–4); Nancy Henry treats Neil McCaw's *George Eliot and Victorian Historiography* and Hao Li's *Memory and History in George Eliot*, both published in 2000 (*GER* 32[2001] 75–8). Mary Wilson Carpenter also reviews two recent works, Audrey Jaffe's *Scenes of Sympathy: Identity and Representation in Victorian Fiction* and Ellen Argyros's '*Without Any Check of Proud Reserve': Sympathy and its Limits in George Eliot's Novels* (*GER* 32[2001] 79–82). Angelique Richardson assesses the second edition of a seminal work: Gillian Beer's *Darwin's Plots* (*GER* 32[2001] 83–7). First published in 1983, the new edition [2000] contains a foreword by George Levine and a new preface by Beer. Three other reviews of works published in 2000 include:

Joanne Shattock writing on Barbara Onslow's *Women of the Press in Nineteenth-Century Britain* (*GER* 32[2001] 88–90); Regula Hohl Trillini on Phyllis Weliver's *Women Musicians in Victorian Fiction, 1860–1900*; and Margaret Wolfit on Kathleen Adams's detailed *A Community of Interest: The Story of the George Eliot Fellowship 1930–2000*. One other George Eliot item of interest is Céline Trautmann-Waller's 'La Science du judaïsme au risque du roman: Heinrich Heine et George Eliot' (*Romantisme* 114:iv[2001] 61–9), in which she discusses in some detail the influence of Heine on Eliot's thought, and that of others.

A new edition of *Ruth* by Elizabeth Gaskell from the Everyman Library is edited and introduced by Nancy Henry, who writes a detailed introduction and provides most useful annotation. This edition is based on the first single-volume Cheap Edition [1855]. Two items of particular interest to students of Mrs Gaskell appear in *Victorian Studies*: Lynette Felber, 'Victorian Publishing and Mrs. Gaskell's Work' (*VS* 43:ii[2001] 324–6), is a review of Linda K. Hughes and Michael Lund's *Victorian Publishing and Mrs. Gaskell's Work* [1999], and Tamar Heller reviews Deirdre d'Albertis, *Dissembling Fiction: Elizabeth Gaskell and the Victorian Social Text* [1997] (*VS* 43:iii[2001] 515–16). The treatment of death, burial and their relationship to customs of social class concerns Mary Elizabeth Hotz in 'A Grave with No Name: Representation of Death in Elizabeth Gaskell's *Mary Barton*' (*NCStud* 15[2001] 37–61). Unpublished letters to John M.F. Ludlow from Elizabeth Gaskell are drawn upon in Frances E. Twinn's 'Unpublished Letters and Geographical Errors in *Sylvia's Lovers*' (*N&Q* 48[2001] 37–61) to illuminate 'apparent errors' in Mrs Gaskell's fifth novel. The *Gaskell Society Journal* 15[2001] contains the following articles: Kay Millard's 'The Religion of Elizabeth Gaskell' (*GSJ* 15[2001] 1–13); Tatsuhiro Onho's 'Is *Mary Barton* an Industrial Novel?' (*GSJ* 15[2001] 14–29); Larry K. Uffelman's 'From Serial to Novel: Elizabeth Gaskell Assembles *Round the Sofa*' (*GSJ* 15[2001] 30–7); Frances Twinn's 'Navigational Pitfalls and Topographical Constraints in *Sylvia's Lovers*' (*GSJ* 15[2001] 38–52); and Alan Shelton's 'Alligators Infesting the Stream: Elizabeth Gaskell and the USA' (*GSJ* 15[2001] 53–63). There are two notes: Jo Pryke on 'Gaskell Scholars Re-discovered: (1) Annette B. Hopkins' (*GSJ* 15[2001] 64–7) and Philip Yarrow on 'Mrs. Gaskell and France: A Postscript' (*GSJ* 15[2001] 68–70). The journal contains extensive reviews of books of Elizabeth Gaskell interest: the reviewers are Margaret Smith, Alan Shelston, Margaret Darby, Renzo d'Agnillo, Tatsuhiro Uhno, Siv Janssen, Rosemary Marshall, Elizabeth Williams and Jo Pryke. In '"What a certainty of instinctive faith I have in heaven, and in the Mama's living on": Unpublished letters of Mrs. Gaskell and Unpublished Gaskell Family Letters' (*VIJ* 29[2001] 185–206), William Baker transcribes and comments on four previously unpublished letters of Mrs Gaskell, new letters from her daughter Margaret Emily ('Meta') Gaskell (1837–1913), two letters from Henry Crompton (1836–1904), and a letter from Charles Gaskell Higginson to Mrs Henry Crompton.

Stephen P. Haddelsey's critical study of Irish novelist Charles Lever in *Charles Lever: The Lost Victorian* takes a look at a writer who, after immense popularity and success, fell into obscurity not long after his death. Margot Stafford 'Keeping One's Own Counsel: Authorship, Literary Advice and *New Grub Street*' (*GissingJ* 37:ii[2001] 1–18), examines advice about the literary scene in *New Grub Street*, the possible effect of such advice on a writer's career, and the effectiveness (or ineffectiveness) of such advice. Stafford draws comparisons of advice given in *New*

Grub Street to literary advice given by George Lewes, Anthony Trollope, and Wilfred Meynell, all of whom provide very different models of literary success based on artistry, artisanship, or commercial or economic profit. Christine DeVine, 'Two Classes of Story: Literature and Class in Gissing's *Demos*' *(GissingJ* 37:iii[2001] 24–9), argues that Gissing's depictions of the working class attempt to 'avoid the middle-class myths that he sees as dangerous because of the ideological work they perform'. Arlene Young, 'Money and Manhood: Gissing's Redefinition of Lower-Middle-Class Man' *(GissingJ* 37:iii[2001] 16–23), shows how Gissing challenges condescending portrayals of lower-middle-class male characters who were comic, domestic, and ineffectual. While in most Victorian novels a man's economic impotence parallels his intellectual, physical, and sexual impotence, Gissing manipulates tradition to avoid lower-middle-class myths such as the rags-to-riches storyline in which the deserving poor inevitably rise to the middle class. Young's discussion centres on Edmund Widdowson in *The Odd Women* and Maurice Hilliard in *Eve's Ransom*. Diana Maltz's, 'Bohemia's Bo(a)rders: Queer-Friendly Gissing' *(GissingJ* 37:iv[2001] 7–27), looks at Gissing's conflicting depictions of homosexuals, arguing that he views 'queerness' not as a same-sex preference, but as a way of describing a more indeterminate kind of relationship. In 'An Upstart Odd Woman: A Daughter of the Lodge' *(GissingJ* 37:ii[2001] 19–23), Robert L. Selig contrasts May Rockett (the daughter of the lodge) with Rhoda Nunn (the odd woman).

The *Gissing Journal* 37:i[2001] includes the following articles: '"A hell constructed by man": Depictions of the Poor in *The Nether World*' *(GissingJ* 37:i[2001] 1–16), a detailed and perceptive analysis by Christine DeVine, and 'The Dispossessed: A Consideration of George Gissing', by the late Walter Allen, with an introduction by Anthony Curtis *(GissingJ* 37:i[2001] 17–35). Issue 37:ii[2001] also includes: 'Of Ethics and Mess: Two Contributions to Gissing Studies', by Jacob Korg *(GissingJ* 37:ii[2001] 24–6); '"The most delicately sensitive face I have ever seen": Coulson Kernahan's Reminiscences of Gissing', by Pierre Coustillas *(GissingJ* 37:ii[2001] 27–9); and a report on the 'MLA Special Session on Gissing', by Christine DeVine *(GissingJ* 37:ii[2001] 30–4). *Gissing Journal* 37:iii[2001] includes: 'Gissing's Triumphant Return to the Reading Room', by Bouwe Postmus *(GissingJ* 37:iii[2001] 1–2); 'Gissing and the Theatre: A Lucid Outlook on "The Drama in the Doldrums"', by Pierre Coustillas *(GissingJ* 37:iii[2001] 3–15); and book reviews by Pierre Coustillas *(GissingJ* 37:iii[2001] 30–7). Issue 37:iv[2001] includes: '"At cemetery found a delightful guardian": The Crotone Gardener Identified', by Teresa Liguori and Pierre Coustillas *(GissingJ* 37:iv[2001] 1–6); 'Gissing and Railways', by Sydney Lott *(GissingJ* 37:iv[2001] 28–31); and 'More on Gissing and the Theatre', by Jacob Korg *(GissingJ* 37:iv[2001] 32–3). There is also Simon J. James's '"The truth about Gissing": Reassessing the Literary Friendship of George Gissing and H.G. Wells' *(Wellsian* 24[2001] 2–21). Finally, of interest to students of Gissing, is Giulio Grilletta's 'Da Norman Douglas a George Gissing un rinnovato interesse culturale: Quei viaggiatori inglesi affascinati dalla Calabria' *(La Provincia* 3[2001] 14–25).

Lindy Stiebel, *Imagining Africa: Landscape in H. Rider Haggard's African Romances*, draws on postcolonial theory to show how Haggard's formulaic African topographies function to express desire and cultural anxieties. Stiebel's study explores Haggard's representations of Africa as Eden, as a dream world, as a sexualized bodyscape, and as home of ancient white civilizations. An important new addition to H. Rider Haggard studies is *Diary of an African Journey, 1914*, edited by Stephen Coan. The hitherto unpublished manuscript chronicles Haggard's journey back to South Africa for the first time in over twenty-five years. Haggard, once an unyielding imperialist, describes his reactions to the political and cultural changes in South Africa in the aftermath of the Anglo-Boer War. This well-documented edition, an important addition to Haggard and postcolonial studies, also includes an introduction, notes, and a useful bibliography. H. Rider Haggard's *She: A History of Adventure*, edited and with an introduction by Patrick Brantlinger in a new Penguin edition, reproduces the first edition [1887], the revised version of the original serial in the *Graphic*. The Modern Library Classics' edition of *She* includes a new introduction by Margaret Atwood. Illustrations are by Maurice Greiffenhagen and Charles H.M. Kerr, and notes are by James Danly.

Millgate, ed., *Thomas Hardy's Public Voice: The Essays, Speeches, and Miscellaneous Prose* is an important contribution to Hardy studies. Edited by the doyen of Hardy scholars, Michael Millgate, this useful volume includes a variety of contributions by Hardy to public discourse: acknowledged essays and letters, formal speeches, and even anonymous excerpts from gossip columns. The well-annotated collection includes several pieces that have only recently been attributed to Hardy, providing greater understanding of him through his public utterances about a wide variety of social, literary, and political issues. Millgate challenges the idea that Hardy, a man usually considered very private, was cautious and conservative, and includes unsigned items 'from obituaries to clandestine contributions to literary gossip-columns that have now been securely or tentatively identified'. In *Ecstatic Sound: Music and Individuality in the Works of Thomas Hardy*, John Hughes argues that study of Hardy's references to music facilitates a fuller understanding of the affective qualities of his poetry and fiction. Hughes examines musical representations in moments of individual expression, inspiration and memory, and unconscious and bodily experience. In *Haunted Hardy: Poetry, History, Memory*, Tim Armstrong explores 'the way in which the self is constituted by and writes itself into history', comparing the theoretical underpinnings of Hardy's work with the ideas of Derrida, Abraham, and Torok. Norman Page's *Thomas Hardy: The Novels* is a close analysis of Hardy's novels, beginning with explorations in six chapters of the following thematic issues: 'Writer and Reader'; 'Beginnings and Endings'; 'Nature and Humanity'; 'Individuals and Communities'; 'Tradition and Change'; and 'Men and Women'. Part 2 provides the biographical and historical context for Hardy and his novels. Andrew Radford, 'The Unmanned Fertility Figure in Hardy's *The Woodlanders* (1887)' (*VN* 99[2001] 24–32), explores the male figures Edred Fitzpiers and Giles Winterborne, and how they embody oppositional perceptions of 'power at play'. There is also Andrew Nash's 'The Serialization and Publication of *The Return of the Native*: A New Thomas Hardy Letter' (*Library* 2:i[2001] 53–9). Patricia O'Hara reviews *The Cambridge Companion to Thomas Hardy*, edited by Dale Kramer (*VS* 43:iv[2001] 639–40); Angelique Richardson reviews *Ambivalence in Hardy: A Study of his Attitude to Women*, by Shanta Dutta (*VS* 43:i[2001] 155–6).

Norton Critical Editions presents a second edition of *The Mayor of Casterbridge: An Authoritative Text, Backgrounds and Contexts, Criticism*, edited by Phillip Mallett. This edition includes more of Hardy's non-fiction, along with criticism written since the first edition, including contributions by Elaine Showalter, George

Levine, William Greenslade, Suzanne Keen, H.M. Daleski, and Michael Millgate. Like the first Norton edition, the text is based on the Macmillan Wessex edition of 1912, the last major revision for which was done by Hardy. Oxford World's Classics reissue, of the 1987 edition of *The Mayor of Casterbridge*, edited by Dale Kramer, includes an introduction by Rick Moody. Modern Library Classics presents a reissue of its 1994 edition of *Jude the Obscure* with a new introduction by Rosselen Brown and notes by Julie Grossman. The text is based on the second impression of the 1912 Wessex edition. Talia Schaffer reviews *The Cambridge Companion to Thomas Hardy*, ed. Dale Kramer (*VPR* 34:ii[2001] 196–7). *Tess of the d'Urbervilles* is one of several texts in Joseph Carroll's biopoetical exploration 'Human Universals and Literary Meaning: A Sociobiological Critique of *Pride and Prejudice*, *Villette*, *O Pioneers!*, *Anna of the Five Towns*, and *Tess of the d'Urbervilles*', in *Interdisciplinary Literary Studies* (2:ii[2001] 9–27). Elaine Freedgood reviews Sophie Gilmartin's *Ancestry and Narrative in Nineteenth-Century British Literature: Blood Relations from Edgeworth to Hardy* [1998] (*VS* 43:ii[2001] 314–15). Laura Green assesses Jane Thomas's *Thomas Hardy, Femininity and Dissent: Reassessing the Minor Novels* [1999] (*VS* 43:ii[2001] 315–17). John R. Reed, in the detailed clearly written 'Jude's Music: Music as Theme and Structure in Hardy's *Jude the Obscure*' (*VIJ* 29[2001] 85–101), convincingly demonstrates that, 'in uniting the qualities of music and literature', Hardy shows that 'only in art can ideality, intellectuality, emotionality, and materialism cooperate harmoniously'.

The late Noel Annan, in 'Kipling's View of "Society"' (*KJ* 75:297[2001] 28–30), examines Kipling's ideas about social control. In 'Recovering an Image from Dead Eyes' (*KJ* 75:297[2001] 43–4), George Engle looks at possible sources for Kipling's portrayal of the death of the railway engineer in the story 'At the End of the Passage', and Kipling's idea of 'recovering an image from dead eyes'. Bard C. Cosman compares 'Rikki-Tikki-Tavi' to the Beowulf saga in 'Rikki-Tikki-Tavi as Beowulf' (*KJ* 75:300[2001] 16–27). In 'More Foxhunting with Kipling', F.A. Underwood describes letters about foxhunting written by Kipling found in a rare book entitled *Letters from Rudyard Kipling to Guy Piaget, 1919–1936* (*KJ* 75:300[2001] 28–34). Hugh Brogan, 'A Question of Art: Kipling's Narrator' (*KJ* 75:300[2001] 35–45), examines narrators in the works of Kipling who are readily recognizable to readers. Adam Nicholson's *The Hated Wife: Carrie Kipling, 1862– 1939* is an interesting and succinct reassessment of Kipling's wife Carrie, a woman often criticized by her contemporaries as well as by Kipling biographers. Focusing on the Kiplings' dysfunctional marriage, Nicholson paints a more sympathetic portrait of Carrie, despite the fact that she has long been portrayed as controlling, argumentative, and suspicious. *The Kipling Journal* 76:302[2002] includes the following essays: 'Kipling's Burma: A Literary and Historical Review [Part II]', by George Webb (*KJ* 76:302[2002] 10–19); 'The Spirit of the Land: Puck of Pook's Hill', by Peter Bramwell (*KJ* 76:302[2002] 20–7); 'Blue Roses and Green Carnations: Correspondences in the Works of Rudyard Kipling and Oscar Wilde', by D.C. Rose (*KJ* 76:302[2002] 28–38); and 'Imperialism, Racism and "The God of Small Things"', by Shamsul Islam (*KJ* 76:302[2002] 40–7). *Essays in Criticism* includes T.S. Eliot's Harvard essay 'The Defects of Kipling' (*EIC* 51[2001] 1–7) printed in its entirety for the first time. Eliot was in his junior year when he wrote the essay for the Harvard course English 12. Eliot criticizes Kipling's 'restless and straining immaturity', and argues that Kipling's popularity was due more to the 'unfamiliarity and picturesqueness of his backgrounds' than to any technical merit or style. New from Oxford World's Classics is a reissue of their 1987 edition of *Plain Tales from the Hills*, edited and with an introduction by the late Andrew Rutherford, and including a chronology of Kipling's life, explanatory notes, and a select bibliography.

Lindskoog, ed., *Surprised by C.S. Lewis, George MacDonald, and Dante: An Array of Original Discoveries*, is a collection of twenty-three essays exploring various interesting and sometimes surprising connections between and among the lives, works, and beliefs of the three writers. Of special interest to George MacDonald scholars are two essays in the collection: 'Roots and Fruits of *The Secret Garden*: George MacDonald, Frances Hodgson Burnett, Willa Cather, and D.H. Lawrence' (pp. 98–103) and 'The Salty and the Sweet: Mark Twain, George MacDonald, and C.S. Lewis' (pp. 104–17). In the former, Lindskoog explores the links between characters named Colin in MacDonald's 'The Carasoyn', Frances Hodgson Burnett's *The Secret Garden*, Willa Cather's *My Ántonia*, and D.H. Lawrence's *Lady Chatterley's Lover*. In the latter essay, Lindskoog argues convincingly that Twain bought and read MacDonald's *Sir Gibbie* while writing *Huckleberry Finn*, and that Twain's children urged their father to create stories modelled on that of Diamond, the hero of MacDonald's *At the Back of the North Wind*. Also relevant to those interested in George MacDonald are 'Links in a Gold Chain: C.S. Lewis, George MacDonald, and Sadhu Sundar Singh' (pp. 63–74) and 'Plan for the Curing: George MacDonald and Modern Child-Training Methods' (pp. 82–8).

In 'Colonial Male Authority in George Meredith's *Lord Ormont and his Aminta*' (*SEL* 41[2001] 805–20), Timothy L. Clarens argues that Meredith does not accord complete independence to Aminta, 'restricting her agency through a pattern of figures comparing her to India'. Republished for the first time in over a century is popular sensation novelist David Pae's *Lucy, the Factory Girl; or, The Secrets of the Tontine Close*, edited by Graham Law. Pae, who was also founding editor of the *People's Friend*, published his most popular work *Lucy* in the Edinburgh newspaper *The North Britain* [1858–9]. Margaret Oliphant's novella, *The Doctor's Family* [1863] is placed in the context of 'representation of colonialism and imperialism' in Aeron Haynie's 'A Colonial Woman in the Literature of Empire: Margaret Oliphant's *The Doctor's Family*' (*VIJ* 29[2001] 169–83). Penelope LeFew-Blake's *Schopenhauer, Women's Literature, and the Legacy of Pessimism* includes a useful chapter about Olive Schreiner entitled '"A striving and a striving": Schopenhauerian Pessimism in Olive Schreiner's *The Story of an African Farm* and *From Man to Man*' (pp. 49–68). Mark Sanders looks at male feminism in 'Towards a Genealogy of Intellectual Life: Olive Schreiner's *The Story of An African Farm*' (*Novel* 34:i[200] 77–97).

Philip Callow examines Robert Louis Stevenson's passionate temperament and impulsive lifestyle in *Louis: A Life of Robert Louis Stevenson*. Callow's engaging biography focuses on the 'mass of contradictions' in Stevenson's life, tracing his growth from sickly child to bohemian dandy to nomadic seafarer. In 'Melancholy Magic: Masochism, Stevenson, Anti-Imperialism' (*NCL* 56:iii[2001] 293–365), John Kucich looks at doubling devices and psychological economies, arguing that Stevenson 'experiments with masochistic psychological economies in various ways, and he succeeds in harnessing masochistic psychological power to an evangelically inflected anti-imperialist crusade, thus harnessing the respectability of a bourgeois masochistic style for oppositional political purposes'. Kucich also suggests that the 'political valence of masochistic psychic economies ... remains unstable'. The subject of Gordon Hirsch's 'The Travels of RLS as a Young Man' (*VN* 99[2001] 1–7), are Stevenson's travels in Scotland, England, and France, and how these journeys facilitated self-discovery while also providing material for his writings. New from Modern Library Classics is *Kidnapped, or The Lad with the Silver Button*, edited and with a preface and notes by Barry Menikoff along with an introduction by Margot Livesey. Most of the text for this edition is based on the autograph manuscript in the Huntington Library, but since that holograph is incomplete, the last three chapters are based on the *Young Folks Paper* serial.

Peter Shillingsburg's *William Makepeace Thackeray: A Literary Life* is, not unsurprisingly, a well-researched, well-written biography, focusing on the influence of Thackeray's experiments with narrative strategy. It is the highlight of a rather thin year for Thackeray studies, and includes a particularly interesting discussion of Thackeray's commentary on women and his readers' responses to this commentary. Nicholas Dames, 'Brushes with Fame: Thackeray and the Work of Celebrity' (*NCL* 56:i[2001] 23–51), looks at journalism and the growth of celebrity culture by examining moments in two of Thackeray's novels (*Pendennis* and *The Newcomes*) when a character suddenly collides with a famous person. In 'Thackeray's Letters to Hobhouse' (*RES* 52[2001] 540–2), Nicholas A. Joukovsky sheds light on Thackeray's relationship to Sir John Cam Hobhouse (later Baron Broughton), drawing on eleven previously unpublished letters—ten to Hobhouse himself and one to his half-brother Thomas Benjamin Hobhouse. Joanna Trollope provides a new introduction for the Modern Library Classics edition of *Vanity Fair*, the text of which is accompanied by commentary by George Henry Lewes, Anthony Trollope, and Robert Louis Stevenson. Judith L. Fisher reviews Thackeray's *Catherine: A Story*, ed. Sheldon F. Goldfarb (*VPR* 34:ii[2001] 187–8). There are also two reviews by Robert A. Colby: of *Thackeray*, by D.J. Taylor (*VPR* 34:iii[2001] 290–1) and of *W.M. Thackeray and the Mediated Text*, by Richard Pearson (*VPR* 34:iv[2001] 391–3).

Trollope studies also had, in terms of actual publication, a lean year. Elsie B. Michie, 'Buying Brains: Trollope, Oliphant, and Vulgar Victorian Commerce' (*VS* 44:i[2001] 77–98), explores connections between Anthony Trollope's *The Last Chronicle of Barset* and Margaret Oliphant's *Phoebe Junior: A Last Chronicle of Carlingford*. Michie focuses on the emphasis on money in both novels in order to show how characters dramatize the culture's anxieties about and responses to a changing economy—one that shifted emphasis from production and saving to consumption and pleasure. Richard Dellamora, 'Stupid Trollope' (*VN* 100[2001] 22–6), draws on early traumatic experience in Trollope's childhood in order to focus on the metadiscursive issue of what politics are referred to by use of the term and to show how cultural politics motivates the representation of a variety of politics in Trollope, including the Parliamentary sort'. Judith Knelman reviews *Trollope and the Magazines: Gendered Issues in Mid-Victorian Britain*, by Mark W. Turner (*VS* 43:i[2001] 113–14). There is also 'Anthony Trollope's Marginalia in Macaulay's *Critical and Historical Essays*' by G.P. Landow and E. Chew (*N&Q* 48:ii[2001] 152–5). New from Oxford World's Classics is Trollope's *Orley Farm*, edited and with an introduction and notes by David Skilton. Finally, David Brooks provides a new introduction for the Modern Library Classics edition of *The Way We Live Now*, which is accompanied by notes by Hugh Osborne.

The seventh available work in the Annotated H.G. Wells series is *The Sea Lady: A Tissue of Moonshine: A Critical Text of the 1902 London First Edition, with an Introduction and Appendices*, edited by Leon Stover. Stover provides an extensive introduction along with the text, a select bibliography, and three useful appendices, 'A Moonlight Fable', 'After Year of Journalism: Outbreak of Auto-Obituary', and 'The Great Outside and Plato', all by H.G. Wells. Annotations by H.G. Wells are also included, along with *The Sea Lady* text. Also from the series and edited by Leon Stover is *The War of the Worlds: A Critical Text of the 1898 London First Edition, with an Introduction, Illustrations, and Appendices*.

Lucy McDiarmid's articulate article, 'Oscar Wilde's Speech from the Dock' (*TPr* 15:iii[2001] 447–88), looks at the genealogy of Wilde's speech, arguing against the commonly held belief that he was an eager martyr for the cause of homosexuality when he made it. According to McDiarmid, Wilde had not at this time formulated his notions of sexuality as a political issue; rather, she says, he was an 'oppositional celebrity, for whom politics was a continuing public performance that, with luck, led in the long run to some kind of interesting immortality'. The article further looks at the framing of Wilde's sexuality, in personal letters written after he had served time and in 'The Ballad of Reading Gaol'.

To conclude, Jerusha Hull McCormack's *The Man Who Was Dorian Gray* is a creative compilation of fact and fiction, blending the true life of Gray with that of his fictive counterpart. Piotr Sadowski's *Gender and Literature: A Systems Study* includes a chapter on Oscar Wilde entitled '"A delicate bubble of fancy": Oscar Wilde's *The Importance of Being Earnest*', in which Sadowski examines gender role reversals and satiric representations of sentimentalized stereotypes of femininity. *Notes and Queries* 48:ii[2001] includes the following two articles: 'Wilde's *The Picture of Dorian Gray*' by D. Richards (*N&Q* 48:ii[2001] 158) and 'The Farquhar and Arbuthnot Connection in Oscar Wilde's *A Woman of No Importance*' by C.S. Nassaar (*N&Q* 48:ii[2001] 158–62).

3. Poetry

One of the most significant events in Victorian poetry this year, it may prove, was the publication of a special double issue of *VP* 39:ii[2001] on 'The Poetics of the Working Classes', edited by Florence S. Boos. This issue might stand as indicative of the continuing interest in politicizing Victorian poetry (something which a number of this year's publications seek to do) and in rediscovering 'marginal' or forgotten poets, particularly from the traditions of working-class writing or women's writing. Boos's introduction (*VP* 39[2001] 103–9) argues strongly that 'nineteenth century working-class poetry blended protest, reformist politics, self assertion and moral reflection in complex and deeply interesting ways' (p. 105). She notes the fragmented and flawed nature of the canon, given that much working-class poetry has not survived, and remarks that the poetry which did tended to owe its survival to the intervention of middle-class patrons, editors and publishers. Boos suggests that this patronage, while a mixed blessing, should therefore be recognized for its part in preserving many of these dissident voices. The introduction also provides a short and helpful critical overview of previous work in the field.

The volume is divided into three sections—'The Poetics of Chartism', 'Women and Working-Class Poetics' and 'Language, Criminality and Gender'—titles which themselves make the link between gender studies and class studies explicit. In the first section, Michael Sanders writes on 'Poetic Agency: Metonymy and Metaphor in Chartist Poetry, 1838–1852' (VP 39[2001] 111–36). He posits two poetic strategies for representing Chartist agency: the first invokes and evokes agency through metaphor and metonymy, and the second discusses particular groups in the hope of inciting them to become agents of change. The first part of the article then examines poetic figures, and the second discusses poems which abandon metaphor to some extent in favour of identifying and addressing actual or imagined social groups, whether within or without the Chartist camp. These are persuasive readings of the ways in which poetry operates to achieve specific political ends. The next essay on Chartism, Kelly J. Mays, 'Slaves in Heaven, Laborers in Hell: Chartist Poets' Ambivalent Identification with the (Black) Slave' (VP 39[2001] 137–64), has some similarities to Sanders's essay in discussing the tension between metaphorical references to slavery and the actual historical phenomenon of black slavery in the United States. Mays concludes that the language of Chartist poetry builds on such inherent contradictions, offering readers the opportunity to see themselves either as part of a transcendent humanity, or as a particular national and racial community.

Stephanie Kuduk's 'Sedition, Criticism and Epic poetry in Thomas Cooper's The Purgatory of Suicides' (VP 39[2001] 165–88) turns to the most 'canonical' of Chartist poets. She describes the ways in which Cooper appropriated poetic forms and techniques in converting his political speeches into epic verse or Spenserian stanzas. The final article on Chartism, Ronald Paul's '"In louring Hindostan": Chartism and Empire in Ernest Jones's The New World' (VP 39[2001] 189–206), again discusses how metaphor functions, in this case to convey an anti-colonial perspective in Jones's work. Paul makes a strong case for Jones (often excluded from the working-class tradition because of his upper-class origins) as one of the most significant—if not the most significant—poets of Chartism, who moved Chartist writing towards a more international perspective in The New World and provided 'one of the most remarkable and elaborate examples of a poetic critique of imperialism' (p. 202) in the period.

The first two articles in the section on working-class women deal with two of the better-known women poets: Ellen Johnston and Eliza Cook. Judith Rosen, in 'Class and Poetic Communities in the Works of Ellen Johnston, "The Factory Girl"' (VP 39[2001] 207–28), sees Johnston as triumphant in her ability to negotiate class, gender and writing and to discuss both private and public concerns in her poems. Rosen discusses editorial and readerly interventions in Johnston's verse, and describes (and supports) her claim to be the 'public voice of labour' (p. 217). She also looks at the unconventional aspects of Johnston's autobiography. Solveig Robinson's 'Of "Haymakers" and "City Artisans": The Chartist poetics of Eliza Cook's Songs of Labor' (VP 39[2001] 229–54) discusses, from a similar perspective to that of Paul's article on Jones, how Cook has failed to be recognized as a radical working-class poet, despite her constant use of the language and tropes of Chartist poetry. Robinson traces Chartist traditions in Cook's writing and identifies her with the project of 'levelling up' the workers. The concluding article in this section,

Florence Boos's 'Working-Class Women Poets and the Periodical Press: "Marie", Janet Hamilton and Fanny Forrester' (VP 39[2001] 255–86; note that the title in the text, 'The "Homely Muse" in her Diurnal Setting: The Periodical Poems of "Marie", Janet Hamilton and Fanny Forrester', differs from that in the index), considers the publication history of several female poets, their contacts with editors and readers, and the contexts in which they were read.

The last section of this volume, which is considerably less unified than the preceding two, opens with a significant reading of dialect poetry by Larry McCauley, 'Language, Class and English Identity in Victorian Dialect Poetry' (VP 39[2001] 287–302). McCauley concentrates on Lancashire dialect poems and suggests that they should be considered in terms of 'the signifying force of dialect itself' (p. 289), rather than being read simply in terms of the ideologies they express, or fail to express. His readings conclude that dialect is primarily concerned with wider notions of Englishness and English identity rather than with class identity. Alexis Easley's essay on 'Ebenezer Elliott and the Reconstruction of Working-Class Masculinity' (VP 39[2001] 303–18) also considers poetry which seems to support middle-class beliefs, describing how Elliott's promotion of domesticity and traditional gender roles in the working-class home fitted into a programme of reform. Elliott both advocates Christian manliness, Easley argues, and was held up as an exemplar of it himself. This article therefore seeks to contribute to the growing literature on masculinity in the early Victorian period as well as to criticism of working-class poetry. Last in the volume comes Ellen O'Brien's '"Every man who is hanged leaves a poem": Criminal Poets in Victorian Street Ballads' (VP 39[2001] 319–42). This study of an important and little-discussed genre of literature assesses the transgressive power of ballads narrated by condemned criminals and their potential for social commentary. As in many of these articles, O'Brien situates her work as the start of an ongoing effort of reconstruction and suggests that much remains to be done on this subject. This collection is less a definitive account of Victorian working-class poets than a determined effort to introduce their names and their works to a wider audience and to suggest fruitful avenues for exploration. As such, it will be invaluable to those working in the field.

A very different perspective on some similar themes—the ability of poetry to participate in social and political commentary, the role of poetics in national and international ideologies—was provided by Matthew Reynolds's The Realms of Verse: English Poetry in a Time of Nation-Building, the only major account of general importance in the field published in 2001. Reynolds notes that: 'The poems with which I will be engaging characteristically maintain a generic distance from their immediate historical surroundings. Yet they did not thereby turn their back on politics, for by abstracting themselves from the present, so as to open up a longer timescale for the imagination, they brought themselves into proximity with perhaps the most momentous political concept in the nineteenth century: "nation"' (p. 16).

As this makes clear, Reynolds's scope is ambitious, and his aim is not only to describe the relations between nationality and poetry in the nineteenth century, but also to formulate ways of thinking about the links between poetry and politics more generally. Outside Britain, the nation that this book is most concerned with is Italy, seen as the site of poetic negotiations over questions of nationhood and liberty. Whereas the first section, 'Orientations', ranges widely in discussing types of national unity imagined by poetry (whether in terms of marriage, language and aesthetics, or political sympathies), the second part is directly concerned with 'The Inspiration of Italy'. This includes an excellent reading of how Barrett Browning's *Casa Guidi Windows* forms a 'new style' (p. 89) in which to present Italy, and how *Aurora Leigh* also imaginatively elaborates questions related to the cause of Italian liberty. Reynolds then reads Arthur Hugh Clough's poetry, particularly *Amours de Voyage*, as a 'force of repulsion' (p. 156) against sympathetic association and community, and concludes by discussing Robert Browning's attitudes towards Italy, particularly as shown in *The Ring and the Book*. The final section of *The Realms of Verse*, 'Tennyson's Britain', turns towards home. Returning to the metaphor of marriage—which runs throughout this book—Reynolds considers how *The Princess* and *Idylls of the King* negotiate Britain's relations with other countries and with the empire through images of assimilation and communication between different peoples and classes. As in earlier chapters, the argument here progresses through detailed and often brilliant close readings of the verse. Indeed, this book is particularly strong in its attention to language and form, especially in discussing how the latter operates in shaping an argument.

Reynolds focuses primarily on several 'major' Victorian poets—Browning, Barrett Browning, Clough and Tennyson—which does give the impression that they were the writers most important in forming an imaginative ideal of the nation for the nation. Other poets tend to be introduced simply to provide contrast and context. Indeed, Daniel Karlin criticized Reynolds in the *TLS* precisely for failing to include working-class and Chartist poetry in his account. While praising *The Realms of Verse* for its close readings, he suggested in his review (*TLS* 5135:xxiii[2001]) that it is socially and politically exclusive in concentrating on canonical, well-educated, middle-class writers, and hence that it ends up supporting the kinds of generalizations about poetry and politics which it objects to. To some extent, this is a valid objection. Reynolds's book is very ambitious, and at points it seems that his intentions are not quite carried out. Yet as a work discussing England and Italy, and as a very timely contribution to discussions of Browning, Tennyson, Clough and Barrett Browning in relation to nation and empire, *The Realms of Verse* is a deserved success. It does not offer any definitive answers to the vexed issue of the links between poetry and politics, or poetry and nationhood—Seamus Perry acutely comments in another review (*TRB* 7[2001] 278–80) that the book's stance is 'more like an avoidance of error than a statement of a position' (p. 278)—but at least, as he notes, it worries over the right questions. In conjunction with the *VP* special issue, this book also shows that such questions are very much alive in work on Victorian poetry and poetics.

Minor or neglected Victorian poets, particularly women poets, attracted critical interest elsewhere. The major addition to this field is volume 240 of Thesing, ed., *Dictionary of Literary Biography, Late Nineteenth- and Early Twentieth-Century Women Poets*. This is an invaluable guide not simply to women's poetry in this period, but also to women's writing in general, given that many writers who were not primarily known as poets are included. Helen Waddell is here, for instance, and Rosa Newmarch, famous for her writings on classical music—though it is worth noting that George Eliot provides one counter-example of a writer whose poetry does not entitle her to inclusion here nor in other volumes. The forty-five poets described in this volume include many now decidedly obscure authors, as well as the usual suspects: Christina Rossetti, Amy Levy and Augusta Webster, for example.

Entries vary according to contributor, but most give a brief description of the writer's life and works, sometimes venturing into detailed literary criticism, and often recounting the reception history of her poetry. The volume has a lavish number of photographs, facsimile pages and so forth. Each entry also has a helpful bibliography of sources and criticism, though such is the current interest in women poets that some of these are already outdated. If there is a problem with this fascinating book, it lies simply in the range of the period covered. Any volume which includes poets born in 1812 with those born in the 1880s and 1890s is bound to cover a lot of historical ground, and it is a slightly uneasy reading experience to move from Camilla Crosland, who began publishing in the 1840s, to Nancy Cunard; or from Rossetti to Margaret Sackville (1881–1963). More so than the decades covered by the preceding volume, the years 1860–1930 surely saw a vast change in the position of the woman writer, and indeed, as Thesing notes in his introduction, in the position of women in general. In some ways this volume would read better chronologically than alphabetically, so that the sense of the relations between women poets, and the networks of support they formed, would be more easily conveyed. That said, this still remains one of the most valuable publications on women's poetry likely to appear for some time.

Women poets were also discussed in various articles. In *Studies in Scottish Literature*, A.A. Markley, 'Eliza Ogilvy, Highland Minstrelsy, and the Perils of Victorian Motherhood' (*SSL* 32[2001] 180–94), assesses the significance of Eliza Ogilvy's *A Book of Highland Minstrels* [1846], reading her poems for evidence of attitudes towards gender and motherhood in the mid nineteenth century. He finds that she uses Scotch myth and legend to express anxieties about the death of children, often staging her poems as laments for a lost child. On the evidence of this reading, it certainly seems that Ogilvy deserves attention, and that her relations with her contemporaries (notably her close friend Barrett Browning) would merit further discussion. Two essays on nineteenth-century women's poetry are included in Liggins and Duffy, eds., *Feminist Readings of Victorian Popular Texts*. In the first, '"The false prudery of public taste": Scandalous Women and the Annuals, 1820–1850' (pp. 1–17), Harriet Devine Jump discusses the association between Caroline Norton, Marguerite Gardiner (the Countess of Blessington), and L.E.L. and the popular annuals of the period. She finds that the ideals of womanhood promoted by the annuals, which were to some extent intended as educational for their readers, contrasted with the scandalous gossip surrounding the careers of these three women writers and editors. Jump then examines several instances in the annuals where these writers seem to display willingness to parody conventions. Although these parodies are rare among the masses of conventional verse and narrative produced and published by women poets, Jump's essay is useful in calling attention to them. The second chapter on women poets, Margaret Forsyth's '"Too boldly" for a Woman: Text, Identity and the Working-Class Woman Poet' (pp. 18–34) deals with similar material to Florence Boos's article (described above). Forsyth deals with Ellen Johnston, Janet Hamilton and Fanny Forrester. Again, Johnston is the key writer, and Forsyth spends much of the chapter examining how Johnston positioned and marketed herself within discourses about female factory workers. She also examines the role of local magazines and autobiography in creating a culture where these poets could flourish, and notes the instances in which they became involved in dialogue with their readers through the press. While neither chapter presents a novel argument, they are useful contributions to the growing body of literature on women and print culture in the nineteenth century.

The continuing interest in this subject is additionally shown by Valerie Sanders's essay in *Critical Survey* 13[2001], a special issue on 'Literature, Fame and Notoriety in the Nineteenth Century', entitled '"Meteor wreaths": Harriet Martineau, L.E.L., Fame and *Fraser's Magazine*' (*CS* 13[2001] 42–60). The ground covered here is akin to that of Jump's essay, as Sanders also considers the press interest in the scandalous lives of female authors. She sets L.E.L. and Martineau in the context of an increase in literary 'lionism' in the 1830s, but shows how their portrayal in *Fraser's Magazine*, and in particular their appearance in the 'Gallery of Illustrious Literary Characters', both feted and criticized them. The article concludes by arguing that a number of L.E.L.'s works display a certain ambiguity towards her fame. This edition of *CS* also contains an article on Christina Rossetti's publishing practices, which is reviewed below.

With regard to women poets, it should additionally be noted that Felicia Hemans was the subject of a major revisionary study this year: Sweet and Melnyk, eds., *Felicia Hemans: Reimagining Poetry in the Nineteenth Century*. This collection of essays, by a number of distinguished contributors including Isobel Armstrong, Susan Wolfson and Stephen Behrendt, seeks to answer the question raised in the introduction, 'Why Hemans Now?', by highlighting Hemans's relevance to her culture and society, her influence on other poets and on the poetry and poetics of her period. Sweet and Melnyk's introduction argues that studying Hemans involves necessary engagement with vexed questions of history, gender and critical method. She is in this way a peculiarly contemporary poet for today's critics, in the sense that her poetry provides a model for critical re-evaluation of how to read and criticize both Romantic and Victorian poems. This volume is an important contribution to such re-evaluation, one likely to be of interest to anyone working on poetry in the long nineteenth century. The individual essays in this volume will be discussed in detail elsewhere. Hemans is also the subject of an article by Myra Cottingham, 'Felicia Hemans's Dead and Dying Bodies' (*WW* 8[2001] 275–94), in which she examines Hemans's conflicting attitudes towards war in *Records of Women*. She remarks the constant presence of bleeding male bodies in Hemans's poetry, and reads this as a 'feminization of the defeated male warrior' (p. 284), noting that women take on powerful roles in terms of nurturing helpless men and anticipating their defeat and return. The article, like many in Sweet and Melnyk's book, thus provides a valuable countercharge to discussions of Hemans's nationalistic and imperialistic views.

Another contribution to recent studies of war and nationalism in nineteenth-century culture is Natalie Houston's 'Reading the Victorian Souvenir: Sonnets and Photographs of the Crimean War' (*YJC* 14[2001] 353–84). She reads the sonnet as a commemorative form, which describes and preserves a particular moment. This essay sets out to position sonnets and photographs as analogous 'technologies of representation' in the Victorian period, using the example of the Crimean War sonnets by Alexander Smith and Sydney Dobell, and the photographs of Roger Fenton. Houston makes a convincing argument for the significance of Smith and Dobell's volume—too often overshadowed by their earlier spasmodic efforts—in terms of its effort to 'explore and record a self-consciously important moment of national history' (p. 381). This is a notable contribution both to criticism on these writers, and to accounts of the cultural and poetic significance of the Crimean War. In *VP* Kerry McSweeney briefly discusses another prospective member of the 'spasmodic' school, J. Stanyan Bigg, and gives a straightforward critical commentary on one of his poems: 'J. Stanyan Bigg's "An Irish Picture"' (*VP* 39[2001] 407–12).

There were few general accounts of Pre-Raphaelite poetry this year, although the *Journal of Pre-Raphaelite and Aesthetic Studies* celebrated its twenty-fifth anniversary, and to commemorate the occasion republished two early essays on Pre-Raphaelitism: Laurence Housman's 1929 essay on 'Pre-Raphaelitism in Art and Poetry' (*JPRAS* 10[2001] 9–26), and Stephen Spender's 1945 critique of 'The Pre-Raphaelite Literary Painters' (*JPRAS* 10[2001] 27–34). Both these are interesting critical responses to the movement from different historical perspectives. The journal also includes a hitherto unpublished conversation between Northrop Frye and Christopher Lowry on William Morris, primarily concentrating on his social and political ideals (*JPRAS* 10[2001] 35–42). Other general accounts of Victorian poetry worth mentioning include Isobel Armstrong's review essay 'When is a Victorian Poet Not a Victorian Poet? Poetry and the Politics of Subjectivity in the Long Nineteenth Century' (*VS* 43[2001] 279–92), in which she considers five books published in the field in 1998 and 1999. She suggests that what these studies share is a theoretical awareness and an ability to 'open out the politics of the subject' (p. 291), rejecting notions of a unified Victorianism.

While Arnold received surprisingly little critical attention in 2001, the year was still marked by a major event in Arnold studies: the completion of Cecil Lang's edition of the *Letters*. Volume 6 covers Arnold's last years, 1885–8. It follows him through inspection visits to Germany, France and Switzerland, his second trip to America, his retirement, the birth of a grandchild, and the publication of *Discourses in America* and (posthumously) *Essay in Criticism: Second Series*. The bulk of the letters are to his close family, and particularly to his daughter Lucy, now married and living in America; but this volume also includes such additional interests as his letters to Humphrey Ward about the possibility of standing again as Oxford Professor of Poetry, his two letters to the *Times* on Home Rule (the subject of his fiercest rhetoric in this volume), and correspondence with Edmund Gosse, Charles Eliot Norton, Andrew Carnegie and Alfred Austin, to name a few. As in earlier volumes, Lang's notes are scholarly and meticulously detailed. This volume also includes two appendices, the first containing several letters unpublished in previous volumes, and the second an address by Arnold on Chicago republished in the *New York Tribune* [1884]. With the completion of Lang's edition, an extremely important scholarly resource is available for Arnold critics and for all those interested in the period. This monumental edition is unlikely to be superseded for many years.

Further work on Arnold was restricted to two brief articles. In *Symbiosis*, Ian McGuire picks up on connections between Arnold's writing and the literature of the United States (a topic also raised in the final volume of the letters), and discusses the relation between Walt Whitman's *Democratic Vistas* [1871], Emerson's 'Culture' and Arnold's *Essays in Criticism* (*Symbiosis* 5[2001] 77–84). He notes that Arnold, not Emerson, appears to be Whitman's chief opponent, and examines differences in the definition of 'culture' in these three writers. Christopher Ricks describes Arnold's failure to appreciate the novel as a high form of art in a talk published by *Salmagrundi*: 'Matthew Arnold and the Novel' (*Sal* 132[2001] 76–95).

Martin Garrett's latest contribution to the British Library Writers' Lives series, *Elizabeth Barrett Browning and Robert Browning*, provides an informative and well-balanced account of the Brownings' lives and works. His narrative, like many, focuses primarily on the period before Barrett Browning's death, and devotes little attention to Browning's later poems. This series is clearly aimed more at the general reader than the scholar, yet although Garrett adds little to the wealth of biographical material already available on the Brownings, he provides a clear introduction to both poets, and his book would be useful for undergraduates—although the lack of references is slightly frustrating. The many illustrations and photographs reproduced here are perhaps the most attractive aspect of the book for the specialist.

This year's *Studies in Browning and his Circle* contains seven essays on the Brownings. John Woolford, 'The Romantic Brownings' (*SBHC* 24[2001] 7–30) considers the Brownings' writings of the 1830s and notes their closeness to 'Romantic' rather than 'Victorian' interests and ideas, particularly the concept of the sublime. He traces this engagement with the sublime through to poems from the 1850s, and ends with a good discussion of the differences between *Aurora Leigh* and *The Prelude*. The next article deals chiefly with Barrett Browning: 'Entombing the Woman Poet: Tributes to Elizabeth Barrett Browning' (*SBHC* 24[2001] 31–53), by Samantha Matthews. Matthews considers the iconography of Barrett Browning's tomb, and the significance of the tribute poems and commemorations written after her death. In the next article, 'Tipping the Scales: Contextual Clues in "Bishop Blougram's Apology"' (*SBHC* 24[2001] 54–67), Peter Epps examines the biblical contexts of the 'Apology', and argues that close examination of these contexts 'indicates that Blougram's self-justification ultimately condemns him, while Gigadibs' rejection of the casuistry is redemptive' (p. 54). This volume also contains four shorter essays by Browning scholars from non-English-speaking backgrounds. In '"A scorpion ringed with fire" and "A rose for the breast of God": *The Cenci* and *The Ring and the Book*' (*SBHC* 24[2001] 68–77), Shigeko Kurobane briefly discusses comparisons between Shelley's and Browning's uses of historical sources from Italy, and their transformation of these sources into poetry. Piergiacomo Petrioli, 'The Brownings and their Sienese Circle' (*SBHC* 24[2001] 78–109) describes the Brownings' stays near Siena and sets them in the context of the artists and intellectuals who also lived there for a time. Rodica Sylvia Stan, in 'The Confessional Mode of Robert Browning's Dramatic Monologues' (*SBHC* 24[2001] 110–15), briefly discusses 'confessional moments' in several of Browning's more famous poems, without adding a great deal to the body of criticism already existing on these works. In the last article of this volume, Dmitry Usenko, 'Dramatic Temptation in "Ivàn Ivànovitch"' (*SBHC* 24[2001] 116–28), provides a helpful and informative reading of a poem from *Dramatic Idylls*.

Barrett Browning was additionally the subject of two articles in *VP*. Steve Dillon's 'Barrett Browning's Poetic Vocation: Crying, Singing, Breathing' (*VP* 39[2001] 509–32) focuses on imagery associated with poetic articulation. This article is a nice reading of moments where the voice breaks into a cry, or breaks down into breathlessness, in Barrett Browning's poetry, and is particularly good on changes in her imagery between early poems such as 'The Seraphim' and the more ambiguous *Aurora Leigh*. In the succeeding essay, '"In silence like to death": Elizabeth Barrett's Sonnet Turn' (*VP* 39[2001] 533–50), Amy Billone argues that the turn to the sonnet in Barrett's poetics reflects her growing investment in silence as inhibitor and sustainer of art, her questioning of the model of lyric as redemptive. Like John Woolford, Billone sets up a dialogue between Barrett and Wordsworth, and suggests that Barrett is deliberately re-evaluating the Wordsworthian poetics of the sublime. Finally, in *N&Q* Alison Chapman, 'Elizabeth Barrett Browning and Sophia Eckley: A Note on the End of the Affair' (*N&Q* 48:ii[2001] 144–5), publishes parts of two letters by Barrett Browning from the Fitzwilliam Museum, Cambridge, which shed new light on the end of her friendship with Sophia Eckley by demonstrating her strong disillusion with Eckley's character, probably influenced by Browning's suspicions of her. The most valuable contribution to studies of Barrett Browning this year, however, is probably that made by Reynolds, especially in his discussion of the relatively neglected *Casa Guidi Windows*.

The two editions of Robert Browning's works continue apace: 2001 saw the publication of *Aristophanes' Apology*, volume 12 in the Ohio University Press series, and of *The Ring and the Book*, books V–VIII, in the Oxford edition. *Aristophanes' Apology; Including a Transcript from Euripides: Being the Last Adventure of Balaustion*, is edited by Rita Patteson and Paul Turner. The edition used, as with all volumes in this series, is that of the *Poetical Works* [1889]. Notes are given at the end of the volume, with textual variations at the foot of each page. Patteson's collation of variant editions offers some helpful insights into Browning's changes and revisions, mostly on the small scale. In lines 3142–4, to give one characteristic example, Browning's manuscript read: 'He ruled his life long and, when time was ripe, | Died fighting for amusement,—well done he!' Both published editions alter the last three lines to 'good tough hide!'—a change which converts a weak conclusion into a trenchant and sarcastic reference to the narrator's comment, several lines earlier, which advocated cutting Kleon into 'shoe-sole-shreds'. Similar revisions occur throughout. Paul Turner's notes identify the numerous classical allusions in the poem and also provide helpful glosses on Browning's vocabulary. His introduction to the poem, however, seems slightly too abrupt. It is certainly a tricky proposition to elucidate even the plot of *Aristophanes' Apology*, one of Browning's more difficult poems, and one likely to be more alien to the modern reader because of its assumption of classical knowledge. For these reasons, however, a lengthier discussion should perhaps have been included, and it would be preferable to have the introduction before the poem rather than at the end of the volume. The comments on sources and on poetic form, at about one and a half pages each, feel unsatisfactorily abrupt, and Turner's conclusion that the main 'emotional pressure' behind Browning's composition of the poem was the resemblance between Balaustion and Barrett Browning may be true but seems reductive. The reader (particularly the student reader) unfamiliar with this poem or the earlier *Balaustion's Adventure* is unlikely to find clarification and explanation here, though for the scholar or expert it will undoubtedly be a welcome addition to this series.

The Ring and the Book, books V–VIII, edited by Stefan Hawlin and Tim Burnett, takes us to the heart of Browning's poem, with Guido's first monologue, those of Pompilia and Caponsacchi, and the first lawyer's monologue, Dominus Hyacinthus de Archangelis. As in *Aristophanes' Apology*, the textual notes here show how Browning's revisions for the most part serve to 'tighten up the sense, or make the language more vivid' (p. ix). The copy-text is that of the *Poetical Works* [1888–9], incorporating changes made by Browning to the second impression of 1889. Both variants and notes to the text are helpfully given at the bottom of each page, making for an easier read. The notes are clear, extensive and detailed, carefully explaining the context of Browning's historical references and the sense behind his characters' speech. The brief introductions to each book are also excellent: explaining the narrative, suggesting potential readings and summarizing critical opinion. Without directing the reader towards any one interpretation, these whet the appetite for the book to come. This volume also has useful appendices on Molinism, Caponsacchi's ancestry, and the torture of the vigil, which assess Browning's research into historical practices, and a list of variants in the Yale manuscript. This edition would be invaluable for student readers, and it is a pity it should be outside the price range of most individuals. More accessible to the common reader is the reprint of Richard Altick and Thomas Collins's Penguin edition of *The Ring and the Book* by Broadview [1971]. This edition has been the standard critical one since its first publication, and the fact that it is now available again is cause for celebration. This reissued edition retains all of Altick's fine commentary and notes (the latter less extensive than in the Oxford edition), and adds a chronology of real historical events to enable the reader to follow the story and identify Browning's alterations. It contains two appendices: one giving a variety of contemporary responses to the poem, the other listing the revisions Browning made. In addition, it has a valuable select bibliography of criticism. Danny Karlin discusses both editions of *The Ring and the Book* in a review article, 'Resurrection Man' (*LRB* 24:xiii[2001] 13–16), in which he argues that the poem should be read as a 'rescue mission' for Browning's poetic career, characterized by its self-awareness about literary production. With regard to these editions, Karlin points out that even since their publication new historical material relevant to the poem, mainly relating to Pompilia and Caponsacchi, has come to light in the Arezzo archives. Clearly there is more to the story, and in this sense neither edition can be regarded as complete.

Sarah Wood's *Robert Browning: A Literary Life* was the only full-length study of Browning this year. Wood's biography is eclectic and wide-ranging. She is also interested in Browning's self-consciousness about literary production and reception, and much of this book explores his interest in reading and being read: 'His worldly decisions and dealings with theatres and publishers, critics and audiences, were often affected by too powerful a propensity to imagine and invent the genesis and reception of his poetry' (p. 17). Thus each chapter sets Browning firmly in the context of his contemporary readers and writers. The first deals with John Stuart Mill and *Pauline*, the second with *Sordello* and its reviewers, the third with Browning's writings for the stage, the fourth with Carlyle and history, the next two with Ruskin's theories of art and with Arnold's poetry and comments on translation, and the final chapter with publishing history. Barrett Browning also haunts Browning's texts throughout, in Wood's assessment, as his primary reader and influence. This interest in Browning's contexts is both a strength and a weakness of Wood's book, at times producing valuable intertextual readings, but also creating what sometimes seem like arbitrary relations between a particular Browning poem and a particular contemporary. Wood's readings of the poems are insightful and well judged, with close attention paid to language, although less to poetic form. It is refreshing to see how much attention she pays to less well-known Browning poems, such as *Paracelsus* and *Sordello*, and she argues convincingly for their significance. Yet whether this is a deliberate effort to move discussion of Browning away from familiar texts or not, it seems slightly odd that this study, positioned as a general account of Browning's life and work, largely stays away from those poems most often studied and taught. It is noticeable, for example, that *Men and Women* receives relatively little attention (although poems such as 'One Word More' would surely be crucial to Wood's line of argument), and that there is no entry in the index for 'dramatic monologue'. As a biography, this book is also chronologically unusual. Each chapter moves fluently between texts from different periods in Browning's career, so that *Paracelsus*, for instance, is extensively discussed in the final chapter, and Ezra Pound's reading of *Sordello* creeps into chapter 4. This means that it is hard to gain a sense of Browning's development as a writer throughout his life, or to keep in mind how responses to his writing changed as the century progressed. A conclusion summing up these points, or some concluding comments in the final chapter, would have been a good addition. Overall, *Robert Browning: A Literary Life* works less well as an introductory biography, or a 'literary life', than as a general work of Browning criticism.

Besides these editions and Reynolds's discussion of Browning in *The Realms of Verse*, Charles Laporte also wrote on *The Ring and the Book*: 'Sacred and Legendary Artists: Anna Jameson and Barrett Browning in the Hagiography of *Pompilia*' (*VP* 39[2001] 551–72). He argues that the use of virgin martyr hagiography in Browning's poem owes a great deal to Jameson's work on saints' legends, and that *Pompilia* is carefully constructed (by Pompilia herself, at many points) to exploit this tradition. Additional work on Browning includes a short article by A.D. Nuttall, 'Browning's Grammarian: Accents Uncertain?' (*EIC* 51[2001] 86–100), in which he defends 'A Grammarian's Funeral' against charges of ambiguity or confusion. Donald S. Hair discusses the ways in which meaning and metrical form are aligned in *Fifine at the Fair*, in 'A Note on Meter, Music and Meaning in Robert Browning's *Fifine at the Fair*' (*VP* 39[2001] 25–35). This admirable reading of one of Browning's more difficult poems shows that revelation lies in form as much as content, and that the metre and music are the physical embodiment of the spirit which animates the poem, even of the 'rhythms of creation itself' (p. 34).

The slightly sensational title of Rupert Christiansen's brief biography of Clough, *Arthur Hugh Clough, 1819–1861: The Voice of Victorian Sex*, does the book no favours. This is a well-balanced, witty and entertaining account of Clough's life and career, and the predominant interest in Clough's relations with women (which Christiansen reads as 'more problematic' than his relations with Christianity) contributes to rather than detracts from the worth of the book. There are also some engaging asides on Clough's relations with men: Arnold, of course, but new light is also shed on characters such as W.G. Ward. Christiansen argues that Clough should be regarded as the most modern of Victorian poets: 'His verse does not sing or soar or rhapsodise: it is prosy, anxious, witty, multivalent, and it delves into matters of sexual instinct with a startling frankness and sensuality' (p. 10). The readings of Clough's poetry in this book are necessarily limited by space, but Christiansen's comments are generally acute. He manages to temper evident admiration for Clough's writing, and sympathy with him, with an awareness of how exasperating he could seem in his vacillations and indecisions. This biography is aimed rather at the general reader than the specialist. The lack of footnotes is problematic for scholars—the 'newly emerged documents' mentioned on the cover are never identified, for instance—although undergraduates and those seeking an introduction to Clough's work will find this book very helpful. Given that, as Christiansen points out, no full-length biography of Clough has been published in over thirty years, it seems a shame that this book should not have been one. In addition, one article was published on Clough's poetry: 'Arthur Hugh Clough, *Amours de Voyage*, and the Victorian Crisis of Action' (*NCL* 55[2001] 445–78), by Stefanie Markovits. Markovits treads a fairly familiar path in identifying this 'crisis of action' in Clough's life and poetry. She notes that hexameters are a traditionally active form, subverted in *Amours de Voyage*, and also links the lack of action in that poem with a shift towards the novelistic in Clough's work. As mentioned above, there is also an important discussion of Clough in *The Realms of Verse*.

Michael Field's drama *The Tragic Mary* was the subject of an article by Vickie L. Taft in a special issue of *Nineteenth-Century Contexts* on 'Women's Friendships and Lesbian Sexuality': '*The Tragic Mary*: A Case Study in Michael Field's Understanding of Sexual Politics' (*NCC* 23[2001] 265–96). This piece treads familiar ground by analysing the ways in which same-sex desire is represented in Field's work, and notes, interestingly, how Field's play on Mary Queen of Scots differs from earlier representations in emphasizing the queen's attraction for women as well as men. This is another good contribution to literature on Field and gender studies, particularly valuable in concentrating on Field's neglected drama.

Edward FitzGerald was the subject of a fine essay by Erik Gray, 'Forgetting FitzGerald's Rubaiyat' (*SEL* 41[2001] 765–84). Starting with a discussion of *In Memoriam*, Gray argues that much Victorian poetry is predicated on the contradictory wishes to remember and to forget. He reads forgetfulness into the form, language and publication history of FitzGerald's poem, suggesting that not only does FitzGerald constantly misremember Khayyam's words, but also that the reader him- or herself is seduced into forgetting the poem by the existence of numerous different versions. Gray's reading of the text is playful, rich in significance and has intriguing links to other Victorian poems.

Thomas Hardy's poetry was the subject of one full-length book this year: Sven Bäckman's *The Manners of Ghosts: A Study of the Supernatural in Thomas Hardy's Short Poems*. This is a considerably less theoretically charged volume than Tom Armstrong's recent book on a similar theme (*Haunted Hardy*; reviewed elsewhere, and Bäckman's method is straightforwardly to identify references to the supernatural in Hardy's poems, and to associate these both with Hardy's personal interest in folklore and superstition, stemming from his childhood, and with cultural interest in the supernatural in the late nineteenth century. *The Manners of Ghosts* is in a sense a historical or biographical study of Hardy's obsession with 'spectres, mysterious voices, intuitions, omens, dreams, haunted places' (p. 53) rather than primarily a work of literary criticism. The book contains chapters on ballads, ghosts, haunted lovers, and omens and signs. It is a useful contribution to literature on Hardy and the supernatural, but is perhaps less helpful as a general work on Hardy's poetry, given that Bäckman devotes little time to discussing how the formal elements of poetry might interact with or inform the supernatural elements. The question of why poetry in particular should be associated with such hauntings is one that begs an answer—and it is worth noting here that such an answer has been at least partially supplied by two books published in 2002: Robert Douglas-Fairhurst's *Victorian Afterlives*, and Julian Wolfreys' *Victorian Hauntings*, both of which will be reviewed next year.

John Hughes devotes two chapters of his book on music in Hardy's work, *'Ecstatic Sound': Music and Individuality in the Work of Thomas Hardy*, to Hardy's poetry. Hughes argues that music matters in Hardy not because of 'what the song means for the poet so much as what it *does* to him' (p. 5). Music is in this reading a means of creating empathy and a sense of solidarity through emotional communication, yet it is inevitably, in Hardy's writing, perceived as transient and associated with loss and regret. In terms of poetry, Hughes suggests that music is significant for several reasons. It sets up scenes of identification, it is associated with eroticism and romantic love, it provides a means of representing aesthetic inspiration, and it highlights Hardy's relation to the poetic tradition. Music is also, of course, significant in its links to rhythm, and while Hughes does not significantly advance our understanding of Hardy's metrics from Dennis Taylor's definitive *Hardy's Metres and Victorian Prosody*, he provides a helpful theoretical reading of rhythm through the work of Gilles Deleuze. This account of how music functions in Hardy is well worth reading, and contains many persuasive suggestions as to how music negotiates the constant shift between community, solidarity and fellow-feeling, as opposed to individuality, alienation and loss, in Hardy's poems.

The *Thomas Hardy Journal* contains the second part of Dennis Taylor's article on 'The Chronology of Hardy's Poetry', in which he continues his argument that Hardy's chronology is not muddled but carefully ordered, and shows that with careful attention to Hardy's writings the vast majority of his poems can be dated. This article will be concluded in the 2002 edition. This year's volume also includes a brief piece by Eric Christen, entitled, 'Proud Poets Transformed: Hardy and Lucretius' (*THJ* 17[2001] 64–7), which stresses the importance of Hardy's interest (one shared with many other Victorian poets) in the writings of Lucretius. The *Thomas Hardy Yearbook* contains one bibliographical piece on Hardy's poetry: Brigitte Brauch-Velhorn, 'Bibliographies and Secondary Literature on the Language/Vocabulary in Hardy's Poetry (*Forschungsbericht*)' (*THY* 30[2001] 37–55). The Thomas Hardy Society this year published an engaging volume in its occasional series, *Thomas Hardy's Emma Poems*, edited by Rosemarie Morgan and William Morgan, which comprises the 'extended conversation' (p. x) on these poems from contributors to the society's website. Responses range from the personal to detailed critical analysis: many of the poems are assessed in terms of Hardy's biography, but there are also examinations of their formal aspects, including some fine attention to metre and syntax. For those who have not already followed the discussion on the web, this volume is a lively introduction to such critical work. *Hardy Review* contains a similar discussion of thirteen of Hardy's nature poems, grouped under the heading 'Hardy and the Nature of Nature' (*HardyR* 4[2001] 38–90). This issue also publishes a useful checklist, by Martin Ray, of the considerable differences between James Gibson's New Wessex edition of Hardy's poems [1976] and Samuel Hynes's Clarendon edition [1982–5]: 'A Collation of the Gibson and Hynes Editions of Hardy's Poems' (*HardyR* 4[2001] 127–40).

This year's work on Hopkins includes the publication of Plowman, ed., *G.M. Hopkins: An Inventory of the Anthony Bischoff Research Collection at Gonzaga University*, in the *ELS* monograph series. This valuable catalogue lists all the materials collected by Fr. Bischoff over the course of nearly fifty years, including original Hopkins poetic fragments and sketches, some unpublished letters by Hopkins and his contemporaries—Robert Bridges, John Henry Newman and

Richard Dixon, among others—research material on Hopkins, sound recordings, photographs and more. The inventory is divided into clear sections and an extensive index makes it relatively easy to use, although the fact that some items are not listed in consecutive order by box number is slightly confusing. The catalogue will, however, undoubtedly be of considerable use to Hopkins scholars.

The spring 2001 edition of *VP* contains three essays on Hopkins and religion. In '"To prove him with hard questions": Answerability in Hopkins' Writings' (*VP* 39[2001] 37–68), Lesley Higgins discusses the importance of questions in Hopkins's work, and the significance these have both within the context of his theological learning and within a theoretical reading of the poems. Higgins associates questions with 'being called to answerability by God, and accepting the unanswerability of God' (p. 60), so that questioning functions as an allegory of understanding. James Finn Cotter's article on 'Hopkins and Augustine' (*VP* 39[2001] 69–82) continues his earlier work on Augustine and *The Wreck of the Deutschland* by widening Augustine's influence to encompass many of Hopkins's major Christian themes and concerns. This is a short article for such a large topic, but manages to convey a sense of the powerful effect of Augustine's writings on Hopkins throughout his career. Finally, Michael Lackey argues, in '"God's Grandeur": Gerard Manley Hopkins' Reply to the Speculative Atheist' (*VP* 39[2001] 83–90), that 'God's Grandeur' responds to the growing movement towards atheism in Hopkins's day, which, he suggests, largely rested on naturalists' arguments, by admitting the problems in seeing God in a violent and cruel nature yet positing a view which might include moments of amorality or natural suffering in God's plan for resurrection.

Four more articles on Hopkins can be found in the *Hopkins Quarterly* double issue for Summer/Fall. Kunio Shimane, in 'The Power of Trenching Sounds in "The Sea and the Skylark"' (*HQ* 28[2001] 89–103), discusses Hopkins's interest in phonetics and the sound of words, arguing that his linguistic training is clear from his diaries and journals. Shimane then provides a detailed reading of how sound operates with sense in 'The Sea and the Skylark'. This is an engaging account, if slightly marred by awkward use of English. In 'A More Rational Hope: The Influence of George MacDonald's *Phantastes* on Hopkins' Short Story "The Dolphin"' (*HQ* 28[2001] 103–13), Nathan Elliott finds convincing parallels between Hopkins's unfinished story and MacDonald's popular tales, and suggests that this shows the wider influence of Pre-Raphaelitism on young writers in the 1860s. It might also indicate, as he suggests, that both Hopkins and MacDonald aimed to reach a similar audience of Pre-Raphaelite readers. In a contribution to criticism on Hopkins's views on nature and the changing environment of mid- to late Victorian Britain, Mariaconcetta Costantini, '"The city tires to death": Images of Urbanization and Natural Corruption in Hopkins' Work' (*HQ* 28[2001] 114–29), discusses Hopkins's anxiety about the corruption of nature by urban and industrial development, in terms of his writings on and images of pollution and contagion. In the last essay in this volume, Eynel Wardi writes on 'Gravity and Grace in the Poetry of Gerard Manley Hopkins' (*HQ* 28[2001] 130–61). Drawing on object-relations theory, Wardi argues that the tension between 'doing' and 'being' lies at the heart of Hopkins's poetic. His detailed readings draw out the ambiguities in Hopkins's poems from a loosely psychoanalytic perspective.

There were several articles on Hopkins in other journals. Maureen Moran contributes to the recent upsurge of literature on Victorian masculinity in '"Lovely manly mould": Hopkins and the Christian Body' (*JVC* 6[2001] 61–88). She argues that the Roman Catholic perception of manliness and the male body still needs to be explored, and suggests that Hopkins attributes value to the male body as part of a reinterpretation of this discourse: he recasts 'notionally perverse or effeminate pleasures of the body' in religious language (p. 67). Peter Whiteford published 'A Note on Hopkins' Plough in "The Windhover"' (*VP* 39[2001] 617–20), in which he points out an unnoticed source for Hopkins's image of the plough in George Herbert's *A Priest to the Temple*. Three brief notes on Hopkins's poems were also published elsewhere. Neville F. Newman, 'Hopkins's "The Times Are Nightfall"' (*Expl* 59[2001] 86–7), discusses the tension between confusion and resolution in the alternative lines of the fragment 'The Times Are Nightfall'. Kevin Heller, 'Hopkins's "Pied Beauty"' (*Expl* 59.190) comments on how Hopkins creates pied words and sounds which combine to form beauty and order, and Nathan Cervo, 'Hopkins's "The Windhover"' (*Expl* 59[2001] 189), traces 'bow-bend' and 'buckle' in Hopkins's poem to a passage from Francis Bacon's *The Advancement of Learning*, which he was reading at the time.

Only one article was published on William Morris this year: Florence Boos, 'Ten Journeys to the Hill of Venusberg: Morris's Drafts for "The Hill of Venus"' (*VP* 39[2001] 597–615). She suggests that Morris's indecision over this particular poem mirrors events in his personal life, and echoes the narrative's theme of elusiveness and deferral. She also describes the significant variations in the many drafts Morris produced, and provides a useful checklist of versions.

One of the most important events in Victorian poetry this year was the publication of a complete annotated edition of Christina Rossetti's poetry by Penguin, using Rebecca Crump's text from her three-volume variorum edition of Rossetti's poems, with added notes and introduction by Betty Flowers. The volume thus includes all Rossetti's privately printed and unpublished poems, as well as her published volumes. The decision to publish the complete poems in one paperback edition makes this a lengthy and densely packed book, but also one readily accessible to all readers: this long-overdue text is likely to do more than anything else to cement Rossetti's reputation as one of the major Victorian poets and to encourage study of her work. Flowers's brief introduction is primarily biographical in content, yet she also provides an excellent argument for the value of Rossetti's religious poems, pointing out that her constant biblical allusions 'create a virtual chorus of voices within Rossetti's own and turn what secular readers might experience as a flat piety into a richly shaded emotional journey' (p. xl). As we might surmise from this, the notes, given at the end of the volume, are particularly good at picking up Rossetti's religious allusions—not only to the Bible but to Milton, Dante and a wide range of nineteenth-century texts. Secular references are also carefully annotated, so that with regard to the riddling children's verse 'A city plum is not a plum' we learn that a 'plum' was slang for someone who possessed £100,000, and that a 'sailor's cat' was part of the mechanism by which an anchor was raised (p. 948). Such details are both essential for the understanding of the poem and interesting in the light of nineteenth-century studies in general. Flowers's notes also indicate her own sources of information and thus supply a guide to Rossetti studies. In Tom Paulin's review of this edition, 'The Cadence in the Song: George Herbert and the Greatness of

Christina Rossetti' (*TLS* 5155[2001] 3–4), he makes a strong case for Rossetti's importance as a poet in a wide-ranging discussion of her practice, concluding that 'to read her is to participate in the exercise of pure style' (p. 4). He particularly remarks upon the importance of her Anglican beliefs and her reading of Herbert in forming her verse.

'Goblin Market' continues to attract new readings. Sarah Fiona Winters, in 'Questioning Milton, Questioning God: Christina Rossetti's Challenges to Authority in "Goblin Market" and "The Prince's Progress" (*JPRAS* 10[2001] 14–26), returns to the idea that Rossetti's poem reworks earlier Christian narratives, particularly *Paradise Lost*, and suggests that Lizzie in 'Goblin Market' represents not Christ but Milton's Adam. When Lizzie redeems Laura, therefore, she demonstrates that humanity can save itself and thus rewrites the Fall. Winters additionally reads 'The Prince's Progress' as a similar challenge to God's authority. *JPRAS* contains Diane d'Amico's 'Lisa Wilson: "A Friend of Christina Rossetti"' (*JPRAS* 10[2001] 109–29) in which she explores the life of one of Rossetti's intimate friends, and through Wilson comments on the importance of female friendship and love in Rossetti's life and work. Also in this volume, Allen J. Salerno's 'Reappraisals of the Flesh: Christina Rossetti and the Revision of Pre-Raphaelite Aesthetics' (*JPRAS* 10[2001] 70–89) moves from reading Charles Dodgson's photographs of the Rossetti family to a general discussion of how Pre-Raphaelitism sought and failed to contain women. Christina therefore, Salerno suggests, 'at once embodies, even upholds, the Pre-Raphaelite aesthetic code while simultaneously undercutting it' (p. 73).

In 'Regarding Christina Rossetti's "Reflection"' (*VP* 39[2001] 389–406), Christine Wiesenthal follows a somewhat similar line of thought. She offers a Lacanian reading of 'Reflection' as a poem in which Rossetti reframes important questions of 'subjectivity, gender ideology and epistemology raised by the gaze of the "framed" woman' (p. 389). Gendered revisions of poetry are also key to Alexis Easby's argument about Rossetti's relationship with her brother's magazine, *The Germ*, in 'Gender and the Politics of Literary Fame: Christina Rossetti and *The Germ*' (*CS* 13[2001] 61–77). Easby investigates the extent to which Rossetti was involved in editing *The Germ*, and explores how the magazine and its editors helped to construct her image, finding that her contributions are formed by 'conflicts between her desire for authorial fame and her fear of self-display' (p. 62). Kevin Mills, 'Pearl-Divers of the Apocalypse: Christina Rossetti's *The Face of the Deep*' (*L&T* 15[2001] 25–39), provides an interesting contribution to the literature on Rossetti's late theological text. He explores the rhetoric of surface and depths found in *The Face of the Deep*, and argues that, through a series of rhetorical strategies, Rossetti positions herself as a 'shallow' interpreter—which of course serves to highlight the apparent depths of meaning found in the apocalyptic text. Mills also usefully locates his discussion in the context of critical comment on masks, veils and hidden depths in Rossetti's poetry.

VP contains the only article on Dante Gabriel Rossetti published this year, Joseph Bristow's 'Rossetti's Other Man' (*VP* 39[2001] 365–88). Bristow considers how Rossetti's 'He and I' confuses the paradigms of heterosexuality in *The House of Life* by introducing dialogue between men. He claims that moments of same-sex intimacy are important in Rossetti's sonnets because they are associated with loss, melancholia, and fears about masculine authority, whether of Love or God. This is an excellent essay, both in terms of Rossetti and of queer studies in the nineteenth century.

Swinburne attracted little attention this year, with the exception of Stephanie Kuduk's article, "'A Sword of a Song": Swinburne's Republican Aesthetics in *Songs Before Sunrise*' (*VS* 43[2001] 253–78). Kuduk locates Swinburne within a radical tradition which envisaged poetry as an agent of social and political change and attempted to translate republican ideals into poetic form. She explores *William Blake* and several poems from *Songs Before Sunrise* in order to show the influence of Swinburne's republican ideals on his work. Given the prevalence of studies on poetry and politics this year, this is a timely contribution to Swinburne scholarship. Further material on Swinburne consists of Catherine Maxwell's note on 'Swinburne and Sappho' (*N&Q* 48:ii[2001] 155–8), in which she argues that Swinburne's interest in Sappho was more extensive than has been suggested and discusses an unnoticed allusion in his early poem 'August'; and a brief note by Nathan Cervo, 'A Note on "Swallow" in Swinburne's "Itylus"' (*VN* 99[2001] 15–16), considering the role of the speaker (identified as Philomela) in 'Itylus' and assessing Swinburne's possible puns in the poem on the word 'swallow'.

There were no full-length studies of Tennyson in 2001, though again Reynolds devotes considerable space to his work. This year did, however, see a major conference hosted by the Tennyson Society at Lincoln, and several of the papers given have been published in the *Tennyson Research Bulletin*. Of particular note is Angela Leighton's plenary address 'Touching Forms: Tennyson and Aestheticism' (*TRB* 7[2001] 223–38) (a version of which has also been published in *EIC* 52 [2002]). Leighton argues that, while Tennyson was never fully engaged with the Victorian aesthetic movement, his work none the less made him 'perhaps the most powerful, undeclared voice of English aestheticism' (p. 224). She notes how Tennyson's reviewers—notably Hallam and George Brimley—constructed him as a poet of 'pure aestheticism', despite the troubled relationship his poems have with the aesthetic. This volume also contains John Crompton, '"His wife his wife no more": Films and the Sexual Politics of *Enoch Arden*' (*TRB* 7[2001] 239–45), which discusses the various filmic renderings of *Enoch Arden* and their take on the gender issues in the story and Kirstie Blair, '"Touching hearts": Queen Victoria and the Curative Properties of *In Memoriam*' (*TRB* 7[2001] 245–54), which argues that *In Memoriam* was read after Albert's death as a poem which could literally heal and soothe Victoria's heart, and through her the nation's grief, and considers how elegies for Albert rewrote Tennyson's poem. Richard Whittern, 'Tennyson's Visual Sources' (*TRB* 7[2001] 261–3) provides a short article on Tennyson's visual knowledge and on the relation of his poetic descriptions to the discourse of the picturesque, and Gerhard Joseph introduces Mary Ann Caws's translation of Stephane Mallarmé's '"*Tennyson, vu d'ici*": "Tennyson, seen from here"' (p. 255), an 1892 eulogy (*TRB* 7[2001] 256–8). Christopher Ricks also contributes a short note correcting a misattribution in his edition of Tennyson: the fragment listed in Appendix B of that edition, beginning 'Oh but alas for the smile of smiles that never but one face wore' is not, as assumed, by Tennyson, but by Cosmo Monkhouse, from his volume *Corn and Poppies* [1880] (*TRB* 7[2001] 260).

Daniel Denecke, in 'The Motivation of Tennyson's Reader: Privacy and the Politics of Literary Ambiguity in *The Princess*' (*VS* 43[2001] 201–28), argues along somewhat similar lines to Reynolds in suggesting that in this poem Tennyson 'developed an argument about the political effects of poetry with a degree of sophistication not recognized by either fans of his fine ear or critics of his social agenda' (p. 201). Denecke suggests that *The Princess* is both a conversion narrative (specifically linked to similar narratives about Jews and about women) and a critique of such narratives, which engages with the crucial contemporary issue of 'the political coordination of personal beliefs' (p. 204). In 'Identifying Men at Ida's University: Education, Gender, and Male/Male Identification in Tennyson's *The Princess*' (*NCC* 23[2001] 121–48), William Weaver considers *The Princess* in the light of developments in schooling and educational debates, suggesting that these to some extent encouraged same-sex identification between friends. He also discusses the 'Apostolic subtext' (p. 141) of the poem, and concludes that Tennyson both supports and destabilizes contemporary notions of masculinity. *VP* contains another article on *The Princess*: Lindal Buchanan's '"Doing battle with forgotten ghosts": Carnival, Discourse and Degradation in Tennyson's *The Princess*' (*VP* 39[2001] 573–96). Buchanan suggests that the poem does not, as others have claimed, re-establish a stable patriarchy, but rather uses techniques of carnival and language of disruption and inversion to show the continued 'vibrancy and disruptive force of the feminine word' (p. 574).

Michael Hancock turns to *Idylls of the King* in 'The Stones in the Sword: Tennyson's Crown Jewels' (*VP* 39[2001] 1–24). He notes that jewels 'become part of the king's commerce with his wife and knights' (p. 1) in *Idylls*, and that, after the Grail, they are the most sought-after of objects. Jewels are identified with women, and are metaphorically associated with Victoria's extensive collection of foreign gems and hence with the prizes and dangers of empire. This is an excellent essay which deftly adds new evidence to the links between *Idylls of the King* and the imperialist enterprise. Matthew Bevis, 'Tennyson, Ireland and "The Powers of Speech"' (*VP* 39[2001] 345–64), also produces a convincing account of another Tennysonian engagement with politics—in this case Irish politics in the last decades of the nineteenth century. Bevis sets Tennyson in the context of political debates on the Irish Question and reads 'The Voyage of Maeldune' and 'Locksley Hall Sixty Years After' as contributions to or comments on these debates. He also illuminates the relationship between Gladstone and Tennyson.

Two more general works of criticism included chapters on Tennyson. The first chapter of Dennis Denisoff's *Aestheticism and Sexual Parody, 1840–1940* is entitled 'Alfred Tennyson and the Critical Sexualization of Aestheticism'. Denisoff uses Tennyson as an example in a persuasive discussion of how critical ideas about poetry changed in the course of the century, and how critical terminology exploited associations of effeminacy and sexual subversion. Tennyson, he argues, became caught up in 'critical efforts to define an immoral aestheticist community' (p. 17): a community that would eventually be located in the 1880s and 1890s. Julian Wolfreys provides a Derridean reading of *In Memoriam* and its relation to Christ's presence in 'The Matter of Faith: Incarnation and Incorporation in Tennyson's *In Memoriam*' (in Schad, ed., *Writing the Bodies of Christ: The Church from Carlyle to Derrida* pp. 59–74). The doublings, hauntings and ambiguities Wolfreys describes here are discussed at more length in his *Victorian Hauntings* [2002], which will be reviewed next year.

James Thomson received some attention this year with the publication of *Secret City: The Emotional Life of Victorian Poet James Thomson (B.V.)*, by Richard

Pawley. Thomson remains a relatively neglected Victorian poet (although Tom Leonard's biography, *Places of the Mind* [1993], went some way towards rehabilitating his reputation) and his masterpiece, *The City of Dreadful Night*, has rarely received the attention it might merit. Unfortunately, Pawley's book does little to contribute to our understanding of Thomson's poetry, as it uses the poems solely as source material for a Freudian reading of Thomson's life. In critical terms, *Secret City* is a strangely old-fashioned book. Freud is cited throughout, wholly uncritically, as evidence that Thomson's poems reveal underlying neuroses stemming from childhood, which led to the alleged impotence, anxiety and alcoholism of his adult life. Though Pawley does illuminate some fascinating facts about the poet's life and his circle of friends and acquaintances, little is done to set the poems themselves in the literary and cultural context of the time, and the assumption that every poem is wholly autobiographical in content leads to an apparent misrecognition of Thomson's manipulation of common literary tropes and symbols. The book is divided into chapters roughly corresponding to the different aspects of Thomson's life at different times, e.g. 'Journalist', 'Friend', 'Home', which leads to some confusing overlap. In sum, *Secret City* may be a helpful contribution to biographical material on Thomson, and the chapters on Thomson's loss of faith and on his journalism would, for instance, be worth reading for those studying Victorian secularism or print culture, but in terms of Victorian poetry and poetics it is unlikely to be of interest to any but the most diehard psychoanalytical critics.

The poems of Francis Thompson, largely out of print since the 1913 edition of his *Works*, were published this year in a collected edition, edited by Thompson's most recent biographer, Brigid Boardman. The first part of the book consists of Thompson's three published volumes, *Poems* [1893] (which includes his best-known poem, 'The Hound of Heaven'), *Sister Songs* [1895] and *New Poems* [1897]. The second part reprints poems published in journals and other publications, the third consists of his unpublished verse, and the final part contains his juvenilia. Boardman's introduction places Thompson in the context of the contemporary poets he knew or admired, in particular Coventry Patmore, Gerard Manley Hopkins, Dante Gabriel Rossetti, and Alice Meynell. She argues that, in his own century, 'Shelley is the only comparable figure' to Thompson (p. xxvii), and sets out those aspects of his biography which undoubtedly influenced his poetry: his training for the priesthood, followed by disillusion and the pursuit of a medical career, and his later experience of homelessness and opium addiction. On the evidence of the poems printed here, which are meticulously annotated by Boardman, 'The Hound of Heaven' still stands out as the most original and interesting of Thompson's works. Yet there is also much here of interest to scholars of late nineteenth-century poetry. Thompson's fervid religious poems should be given their rightful place as part of the Catholic tradition stretching from Newman to Hopkins and beyond. His occasional foray into nationalism—the poem 'To England' [1898] is an excellent late Victorian example of patriotic fervour combined with anxiety about the imperialistic enterprise—is also worthy of comment, and his surprising and entertaining light verse (including his 'Cricket Poems') comes as an additional bonus at the end of the volume. This is a good scholarly edition of Thompson's work which should deservedly introduce his poetry to a wider audience.

4. Drama and Theatre

Audiences, the politicization and representation of women theatrically, the impact of ethnography on racial stereotypes in melodrama and the actor-manager are among the subjects of the somewhat miscellaneous range of publications offered in this area. In *Reflecting the Audience: London Theatre Audiences, 1840–1880* Jim Davis and Victor Emeljanow provide the first full-length study of theatre audiences in nineteenth-century England. While a considerable body of material has been published on music-hall audiences, there has been an absence of systematic work on London theatre audiences, especially after the deregulation of London theatres in 1843. Moreover, many twentieth-century studies of nineteenth-century London theatre have leant very heavily on the impressionist accounts of Victorian journalists without investigating their reliability. This study sets out to test such accounts against other available data. The outcome is a book about London theatre audiences, drawing on parliamentary papers, census returns, transport timetables, maps, police reports, local newspapers and other data. Many previously held assumptions are questioned, while the study casts new light on the composition of the audiences at south and east London theatres, reveals the social manipulation of audiences by the authorities, and exposes the myth-making of nineteenth-century journalists.

The book is divided into four sections. The first section considers two London theatres south of the Thames, the Victoria and the Surrey. While these theatres clearly shared a local audience at times, for they were only a ten-minute walk apart, the Surrey's repertoire generally attracted a more affluent and educated audience, both locally and from further afield. While its reputation for nautical melodrama is not in dispute, local demographics show that there was not a maritime audience in the theatre's neighbourhood, unlike the theatres situated in London's East End. While the derisory term 'surrey-side' was justified to some extent, the history of the Surrey Theatre belies the assumption that transpontine audiences were the rowdy working classes described by Dickens, Sala and others. The East End theatres also demonstrate the dangers of simplistic categorization. The East End is regularly set up as the 'other', as in Dickens's accounts of the Britannia Theatre, but theatres in the East End catered to a diverse audience and, in the case of the Whitechapel Pavilion, seriously attempted to attract a wide social range of spectators. The mythic construction of the East End audience by West End journalists is discussed with reference to Said's theories of orientalism, demonstrating the manifestation of the 'other' in specifically local terms.

Myth-making is the theme of the section on the Prince of Wales's and Sadler's Wells theatres. Demographic shifts are used to suggest that Sadler's Wells's success under Samuel Phelps owed more to changes in the population of Islington and Pentonville than to a missionary zeal to bring Shakespeare to a popular audience. The overnight transformation of the Queen's into the Prince of Wales's theatre by Marie Wilton, and the assumed revolution in theatre-going that this created, is also shown to be open to question. The condition of the Queen's had already been improving prior to Marie Wilton's arrival; moreover, it was not until Wilton's venture had proved a success that she began consciously to encourage only the middle and upper echelons of society to her theatre. In the concluding chapters on the West End itself, which partly focus on the quest to turn Drury Lane into a national theatre, it becomes clear that West End theatre-going developed largely as a tourist attraction in an area which the authors describe as a gigantic 'theme park'.

The purpose of *Reflecting the Audience* is to provide a portrait of London theatre-going during the mid-nineteenth century, in an informed but speculative, way. Two additional studies of theatre-going in the mid- and late nineteenth century look specifically at female audiences. In 'The Invisible Spectatrice: Gender, Geography and Theatrical Space' (in Gale and Gardner, eds., *Women, Theatre and Performance: New Histories, New Historiographies*) Viv Gardner discusses the problems of gender and movement in the city, with specific reference to the female spectator in the second half of the nineteenth century. Using Virginia Woolf's 'Pargiter girl' as her model spectator and a typically respectable matinée girl, Gardner looks at the restrictions on female movement in nineteenth-century London and argues that, despite increased access to public spaces, the female spectator remained relatively invisible in the West End theatre. In '"Hedda is all of us": Late-Victorian Women at the Matinee' (*VS* 43:iii[2001] 387–411) Susan Torrey Barstow takes a more radical view of the impact of the matinée on female spectators and the politicization of such spectators through performances of Ibsen. Although the matinée may have arisen initially as an economic speculation by theatre managers, its impact on women is of particular significance. Barstow believes that the prevalence of women at matinées of the plays of Ibsen and of other new works contributed to the development of a 'new feminist self-consciousness' (p. 387) and encouraged experimental theatre. These women identified with the new heroines, within the public space of the theatre, an experience which was 'collectively transformative' (p. 389). In particular, Barstow shows how *Hedda Gabler* functioned in precisely this way so that the matinée became 'a space in which middle-class women not only confirmed but also threatened the hegemony of middle-class men' (p. 391). The shock of recognition, accentuated by the realistic, fourth-wall staging of Ibsen, enabled female matinée audiences to re-evaluate their own lives. The hostility of many male reviewers, not only to the plays themselves but also to the female spectators' responses, suggests that quite alternative readings of the plays occurred during the matinée performances. For women 'theatrical identification ceased to be a passive, private experience and became the active matrix around which women built a collective identity' (p. 405).

The first English performance of *Hedda Gabler* is also the starting point for Joanna Townsend's essay 'Elizabeth Robins: Hysteria, Politics and Performance' (in Gale and Gardner, eds.). Reviewing Robins's performance of Hedda in 1891, her jointly authored play *Alan's Wife* [1903] and her performance in and authorship of *Votes for Women* [1907], Townsend traces Robins's journey towards 'the ability to articulate her own desires, and desires of the women in the society in which she lived, through her work as an actress, playwright and suffragette' (p. 103). Robins's increasing politicization is attributed to her ability to understand the relationship between speech and silence and between knowledge and its repression and to transcend these divisions through performance. In *Hedda Gabler* the use of 'hysterical gesture' is cited as one of the means through which she articulated Hedda's intentions and motives. The silence of Alan's wife, who has killed her deformed child as a means of protecting it from the cruelty of society, shows gesture used as a political rather than a hysterical medium. In *Votes for Women* the power of the female body is put to political use: despite moments of hysterical revelation, the body and the word are combined to achieve political action on women's behalf.

One early influence on the changing perceptions of women on and off the stage, according to Robin A. Werner in 'The Angel in the Theatre: Marie Wilton, the Performance of Femininity and Intertheatrical Playwrighting' (*THS* 21[2001] 43–59), may have been Marie Wilton, who arguably created 'an alternative, respectable Victorian femininity ... a kind of subversive performance, which not only empowered Marie Wilton the individual but also helped to reveal the ruptures in nineteenth-century hegemonic codes of gender' (p. 43). Drawing on recent essays by Jane Moody and J.S. Bratton, Werner shows how Wilton's collaboration with T.W. Robertson creatively developed a new sort of heroine, whose independence was not openly rebellious, yet capable of gaining greater freedom within the restrictions of Victorian society and of marriage. This is hinted at in her role of Maud in *Society*, but has a far stronger presence in the part of Mary Netley in *Ours*, in which Wilton 'subversively undermines Victorian concepts of fixed, natural and innate gender' (p. 54). The performance of an alternative model of respectable, yet independent, femininity is also apparent in Wilton's autobiographical writing, suggests Werner, although her reading of Wilton's marriage to Squire Bancroft as a reflection of her Robertsonian roles is open to question.

Autobiographical issues are a central issue in Jim Davis's and Victor Emeljanow's '"Wistful Remembrancer": The Historiographical Question of Macqueen-Popery' (*NTQ* 17:iv[2001] 299–309). W. Macqueen-Pope has long been considered less than reliable as a source for theatre historians, but his nostalgia for past theatrical eras, particularly the Edwardian theatre of his youth, suffuses his work. Davis and Emeljanow discuss the possible significance of his recollections and the historiographical problems that memory and nostalgia create in shaping our sense of the theatrical past. Macqueen-Pope's books regularly contain diatribes in which an imperfect theatrical present is compared with an ideal theatrical past. For historians these may be among the most significant aspects of his work, since they have inevitably informed our own responses, even if only in reaction to their extremity. For Macqueen-Pope class, individualism and national superiority were important factors in English life, embodied, as he saw it, in the Edwardian theatre of his youth. His nostalgia for this era is of course little more than a narrative construction; however, it is significant, contend the authors, 'in any investigation of a theatrical past that must always be a melting-pot of "imperfect recognitions" and unattainable desires' (p. 309).

Contending ideologies underlie all the works discussed so far and have long been acknowledged as a factor in nineteenth-century melodrama. A particularly incisive article by Scott Boltwood, '"The ineffaceable curse of Cain": Race, Miscegenation and the Victorian Staging of Irishness' (*VLC* 29[2001] 383–96) demonstrates the impact of contemporary ethnographic theory on the plays of Dion Boucicault. With particular reference to *The Colleen Bawn* and some of the later Irish plays, Boltwood shows how the ethnographical arguments for the subjection of the Irish on grounds of racial temperament surface, albeit unwittingly, in Boucicault's plays. *The Octoroon*, written immediately before *The Colleen Bawn*, is also relevant in that it anticipates the conflation of Irish and African which surfaces in the 1880s ethnographic theories of John Beddoe. The earlier work of Robert Knox and Goldwin Smith, which constructs the Irish as inferior, unbalanced, indolent, immature and compliant to external government, is also drawn on. The importance of racial purity, as signified in Boucicault's *Old Hearts and Young Heads* and *The Octoroon*, is subsequently evident in *The Colleen Bawn*, in its 'examination of the symbiotic relationship uniting the two strata of Irish society: the racially Celtic peasantry and the Anglo-Irish ascendancy' (p. 388). Boltwood reveals how the play's portrayal of the Irish peasantry resonates with 'the prejudicial stereotypes of Knox and Smith' (p. 388). In such a context the marriage of Eily O'Connor, the Irish peasant girl, to the Anglo-Irish but undisciplined Hardress can be see as an instance of his 'slide down the eugenic slope to racial dilution' (p. 392). In his remaining Irish plays Boucicault maintains 'a strict connubial segregation of Celts and Saxons' (p. 392), reflecting the contemporary ethnographic community in his opposition to miscegenation. 'Ultimately, throughout his Irish plays, the native Irish resemble the African-Americans of *The Octoroon* in their need for the love of their Saxon masters, while reflecting the common ethnographic verdict that the Saxons and Irish should remain separate races' (p. 393). According to Boltwood, in such a context the implicit unease that Eily O'Connor displays in the final moments of the play reflects an unease within the community at large.

A number of books and articles published in 2001 concern the nineteenth-century manager and actor-manager. Paul Ranger's *Under Two Managers: The Everyday Life of the Thornton–Barnett Theatre Company, 1785–1853* largely falls outside the period covered by this essay, but will be useful as a reference work for those who wish to explore the continuation of the old provincial circuits into the Victorian period. A substantial recovery of the career of one Victorian actor-manager occurs in Philip and Susan Taylor's *Jonathan Dewhurst: The Lancashire Tragedian, 1837–1913*. Dewhurst commenced his professional career in Charles Calvert's Manchester company and achieved a reputation as a leading tragedian in the provinces, particularly in his native Lancashire. He concluded his theatrical career as manager of the Theatre Royal, Leigh, but in the interim visited Australia and India in the early 1880s, in the Shakespearean and Bulwer Lytton roles that were his particular forte. The colonial exploits of British actors are also reflected in Rosemary Gaby's article, 'On the Edge of the Empire: Hobart Town Shakespeare, 1864' (*TN* 55:ii[2001] 83–91), on Charles Dillon's performance of Hamlet in Hobart, Tasmania. Gaby considers the cultural implications of the occasion, in so far as it was attended by several aboriginal spectators. Robert I. Lublin's 'Unpublished Letters from Charles and Ellen Kean's Final American Tour' (*TN* 55:ii[2001] 80–2) usefully supplements J.M.D. Hardwick's *Emigrant in Motley: The Journey of Charles and Ellen Kean in quest of a theatrical fortune in Australia and America, as told in their hitherto unpublished letters* [1954]. Lublin draws attention to a further collection of letters from the Keans to their daughter, covering the period from October 1864, when they arrived in San Francisco, to their arrival in Cuba in March 1865, just prior to their final New York and East Coast performances. There is little of literary or theatrical interest in the letters, although they include intriguing reference to the alcoholism of fellow-actor James Cathcart.

Until 1858 Charles Kean was responsible for the organization of royal Christmas command performances at Windsor, but may have resigned the office after a public dispute over his meagre payment of the actors involved on these occasions. Kean was replaced by W.B. Donne, then the Examiner of Plays, whose organization of the Windsor theatricals continued until their cessation on the death of the Prince

Consort in December 1861. Drawing on new evidence from the Royal Archives at Windsor, T. Hughie Jones, in 'The Censor Turns Manager: William Bodham Donne and the Windsor Theatricals' (*TN* 55:i[2001] 37–47), pieces together Donne's scrupulous management of these proceedings. Donne was concerned that all companies and actors should receive adequate payment and that there should be no appearance of partiality, inviting Samuel Phelps and the Sadler's Wells Company to perform at Windsor. His effective organization of these events, which included satisfying the royal request for specific performers and vetting scripts for their suitability, was highly acclaimed by the royal family.

5. Periodicals and Publishing History

The versatility and mobility of print in even the most extreme of climates is the subject of Elaine Hoag's fascinating piece 'Caxtons of the North: Mid-Nineteenth-Century Arctic Shipboard Printing' (*BoH* 4[2001] 81–114). Following the disappearance of Sir John Franklin's fourth Arctic expedition in 1847, dozens of rescue expeditions were launched over the ten following years in a fruitless effort to locate him and his men. Hoag chronicles the work, and the individuals responsible for manning the small presses carried on the rescue ships, used both in service of the rescue operation (printing off slips of rescue details, for example, for scattering across the Arctic) and for onboard entertainment and official purposes. The use of these presses on board Arctic-bound vessels, Hoag suggests, played a vital role in boosting morale and demonstrated the resourcefulness and resilience of on-board printers and the technology that made such activity possible.

Robert Darnton uses the metaphor of the literary policeman in 'Literary Surveillance in the British Raj: The Contradictions of Liberal Imperialism' (*BoH* 4[2001] 133–76) to uncover how textual exegesis became enmeshed in the policing of India by the British authorities following the Indian rebellion of 1857. Between 1868 and 1905, the Indian Civil Service monitored all publications in Bengal, creating a register in which details were kept of published work, and commentary made on their plots and narratives. The record was a partial attempt to monitor the use of print for seditious purposes: the surveillance of vernacular literature was to lead to criminal prosecution and court cases whose main arguments often turned on varying interpretations of 'seditious' poetic and prose passages. Darnton's piece convincingly demonstrates the social and political forces through which print culture in dominated states could be filtered and laden with conflicting meaning, creating 'hermeneutic battlefields' within the Indian legal system.

British representations of the Middle East, on the other hand, are the subject of Paul Auchterlonie's relevant survey and sampling of articles from the late century periodical press in 'From the Eastern Question to the Death of General Gordon: Representations of the Middle East in the Victorian Periodical Press, 1876–1885' (*British Journal of Middle Eastern Studies* 28:i[2001] 5–24). Drawing on over 400 articles from ten major journals of the period (*Blackwood's Magazine, Contemporary Review, Fortnightly Review, Nineteenth Century, Fraser's Magazine, Macmillan's Magazine, Edinburgh Review, National Review, Quarterly Review, Cornhill Magazine*), Auchterlonie illustrates how assessments of British strategic interests in the Middle East shaped periodical discourse on the subject

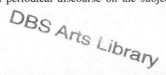

between 1876 and 1885. At the same time, while many journals drew on informed individuals well travelled through the areas in question, the general tone and language evident in these public pieces very much reflected home-based British concepts of racial superiority and of the 'civilizing mission' of imperial activity in the Middle East.

Politics and the periodical press are part of the subject of Michael J. Turner's 'Radical Opinion in an Age of Reform: Thomas Perronet Thompson and the *Westminster Review*' (*History* 86:281[2001] 18–40). Turner utilizes unpublished material from Thompson's papers at the University of Hull to offer a thorough and detailed history of his role as contributor, co-editor and co-owner of the *Westminster Review* from 1829 to 1836. Past studies have neglected or underplayed Thompson's role in shaping the early history of the *Westminster Review*, founded in 1824. His assumption of co-ownership and editorship of the journal in 1826 injected much-needed capital into the enterprise. In seeking to make the review a radical force for change, he encouraged the dissemination of its contents in as wide a form as possible, ranging from insertion of extracts in other journals and newspapers to separate publication as individual pamphlets. During his nine-year association with the review he ploughed over £10,000 into its production and personally contributed over 100 articles on topics ranging from politics and parliamentary reform, the Irish question, and religion to slavery, free trade and Corn Law repeal. Turner makes a convincing case for rethinking Thompson's place in the history of the political periodical press.

In the same issue of *History* there is a fascinating article by David Brown on politics, politicians and the manipulation of mid-century press reportage. 'Compelling but not Controlling? Palmerston and the Press, 1846–1855' (*History* 86:281[2001] 41–61) focuses on the manner in which Lord Palmerston, foreign secretary, home secretary and ultimately prime minister, created positive relations with editors and journalists in order to produce press reportage needed to gain support from the voting public in the run-up to his accession as minister in 1855. Faced throughout the 1840s with parliamentary hostility over his foreign policy decisions, his political career survived in large part thanks to his ability to successfully gain support beyond Westminster through media sources. This was done through careful manipulation of his public image in influential press outlets such as the *Times*, the *Morning Post* and the *Morning Chronicle*. Brown argues that Palmerston was one of the first British prime ministers to recognize and utilize the power of the press to influence and shape in positive fashion his public image.

Palmerston reappears late in Jeremy Black's survey work *The English Press, 1621–1861*, in his role first as opposer and then champion of William Gladstone's parliamentary bill to repeal tax and duty on paper in 1861. Black continues his prolific rate of publication with this latest work, a general history of the development of journalism and the press in England, focusing mainly on his period of special interest, the eighteenth century. He also notes in passing Palmerston's skill in media relations. The final two chapters of the work serve as useful sources on nineteenth-century press history, but the narrow focus on English press history obscures the place of Welsh, Irish and Scottish developments in the history of British press freedom and activity.

Equally relevant background information regarding late nineteenth-century magazine and literary periodical history can be found in Mark S. Morrison's *The*

Public Face of Modernism: Little Magazines, Audiences and Reception, 1905– 1920. Morrison uses Jurgen Habermas's concept of the public sphere to contextualize the preoccupations of such modernist editors and producers as Ford Madox Ford, T.S. Eliot, and Ezra Pound. In particular he draws attention, in an accessible yet theoretically informed manner, to the nineteenth-century periodical and print culture contexts which inform the founding and development of early twentieth-century journals such as the *English Review*, *Poetry and Drama*, the *Egoist* and the *Freewoman*.

Gerry Beegan uses the illustrated weekly *The Sketch* in 'The Up-to-Date Periodical: Subjectivity, Technology and Time in the Late Victorian Press' (*Time & Society* 10:i[2001] 113–34), to explore how late Victorian illustrated journals used new technology to tap into contemporary demand for novelty, leisure information and a desire to be kept 'abreast of the times'. When journalist Clement Shorter founded *The Sketch* in 1893 as a spin-off from the *Illustrated London News*, his ambition to 'hunt and illustrate that sudden and slippery worm, the popular whim in all its haunts' (p. 123) led him to make innovative use of photographic images and illustrations of popular entertainers and acts to attract a large paying audience. The 'wildly frivolous' and short texts that accompanied such visual material fitted in with the 'new journalism' style of reportage then making its presence felt in British media production. Beegan makes some interesting and relevant comparisons between contemporary activity and Shorter's editorial integration of new journalism techniques. In placing such activity within the context of theories on subjectivity, modernity and the metropolis produced by Shorter's contemporary, the German sociologist Georg Simmel (and subsequently developed by Simmel's student Walter Benjamin), Beegan falters slightly however, producing an uneven bolting together of what seem to be two separate essays.

Similar theorization of the periodical space can be found in Cynthia L. Bandish's 'Bakhtin's Dialogism and the Bohemian Meta-narrative of *Belgravia*: A Case Study for Analyzing Periodicals' (*VPR* 34:iii[2001] 239–62), and Kathryn Summers's 'Epideictic Rhetoric in the *Englishwoman's Review*' (*VPR* 34:iii[2001] 263–81). Both take mid-century periodical work (in Bandish's case, Mary Braddon's *Belgravia*, in Summers's case, the 1870s output of the *Englishwoman's Review*) to attempt close readings of the texts for insight into the cultural values embedded within their general prose and fiction narratives. They conclude that, in their own ways, the texts of both journals seek to guide and channel female readers to reconsider their values and positions, both through subversion of contemporary cultural norms regarding feminine values and women's position within society and through adherence to particular 'valued' aspects of the private sphere.

By far the best work this year covering new journalism is Kate Jackson's excellent study *George Newnes and the New Journalism in Britain, 1880–1910: Culture and Profit*. The work is part of the Nineteenth Century series for Ashgate Press, which has been developing a very strong list recently in nineteenth-century media history and periodical studies. Jackson's extremely well researched book is interdisciplinary in the best sense, linking history, literary criticism, cultural history and media studies in an attempt to contextualize George Newnes's role as founder and editor of the most distinctive and bestselling mass-market journals of the late nineteenth century. Jackson pays particular attention to Newnes's links with seven periodicals established between 1881 and 1899, namely *Tit-Bits* [1881], *The Strand*

Magazine [1891], *The Million* [1892], *The Westminster Gazette* [1893], *The Wide World Magazine* [1898], *The Ladies' Field* [1898] and *The Captain* [1899]. The range of sources used and the depth of analysis are admirable and the book is extremely accessible in tone.

In 'C.B. Fry: The Sportsman-Editor' (*VPR* 34:ii[2002] 165–84), Kate Jackson again turns her attention to a corner of Newnes's empire, in this case charting the career of C.B. Fry, author, amateur sportsman and editor of an illustrated literary sports monthly for Newnes (*C.B. Fry's Magazine*) that ran from 1904 to 1914 and attracted contributions from Rudyard Kipling, Edgar Wallace, Hilaire Belloc, P.G. Wodehouse and Jack London. Fry's late nineteenth-century experience in journalism with Newnes served him well in his role as editor, as Jackson aptly chronicles.

The refashioning of the New Woman for commercial purposes by the *fin-de-siècle* periodical press is the subject of Margaret Diane Stetz's 'The New Woman and the British Periodical Press of the 1890s' (*Journal of Victorian Culture* 6:ii[2001] 272–85). Stetz draws on examples from varied journals such as the *Bookman*, *Yellow Book*, and *Woman's World* to explore how the image of the New Woman, linked to modernity and originality, was exploited commercially to increase readership and interest in such publications. Oscar Wilde's repositioning of the *Lady's World*, which on assuming editorship he subsequently renamed the *Woman's World*, is one well-known example of the utilization of the New Woman as iconic representation of avant-garde and modernist interests. Stetz does not say anything in this piece that we haven't seen in previous work by her in this area; she does, however, draw on less-featured periodicals to make her point, which in the end adds value to the general argument.

In 'Reviewing New Woman Fiction in the Daily Press: The *Times*, the *Scotsman*, and the *Daily Telegraph*' (*VPR* 34:i[2001] 79–96), Constance Harsh examines reactions to New Woman fiction in the early 1890s in the columns of these particular establishment dailies. The results suggest a diversity of reaction that belies a stereotyped definition in such conservative sources, with dailies such as the *Scotsman* and *The Times* evaluating novels on individual merits rather than on the basis of conceived generalities.

The New Woman also features in an anthology of women's contributions to British Victorian periodicals, Beetham and Boardman, eds., *Victorian Women's Magazines*. Here you will find samples from various kinds of journals (the fashion magazine, the general illustrated magazine, the feminist magazine) as well as samples covering various elements within a magazine (from mastheads and covers to discursive prose, prose fiction and poetry). The result is a useful synchronic and diachronic overview of women's journalistic and literary activity in the nineteenth century that will prove useful in educating students interested in the area. The only thing one might have wished for to make the work complete is a more comprehensive introduction from the editors to situate the selections more firmly within relevant cultural contexts.

One of the most dynamic and significant figures in the nineteenth-century British feminist movement was Florence Fenwick Miller (1854–1936). Activist, politician, editor and for over thirty years a columnist for the *Illustrated London News*, Fenwick Miller was indefatigable in her activities on behalf of women's causes. Rosemary T. Van Arsdel chronicles her life in *Florence Fenwick Miller: Victorian*

Feminist, Journalist and Educator. This is a descriptive biography that will provide readers with useful background material on Miller's life.

Rosemary T. Van Arsdel also turns her attention to female contributions to the first fifteen years of *Macmillan's Magazine* in a two-part extended article '*Macmillan's Magazine* and the Fair Sex: 1859–1874 (Part One and Part Two)' (*VPR* 33:iv[2000] 374–96 and 34:i[2001] 2–15). Launched in a period of literary periodical expansion aimed at the middle class (the *Cornhill Magazine* and others of the same ilk followed suit in the same period), *Macmillan's* was to prove a reliable outlet for a core of significant literary women during the period: in its first fifteen years of existence, it would feature work from sixty-three women and include eleven serialized novels, sixty-one works of poetry and 120 prose articles. Notable contributors discussed in this piece include Dinah Maria Mulock Craik, Frances Julia Wedgwood, Caroline Norton, Christina Rossetti, Frances Power Cobbe, Eliza Lynn Linton, Harriet Martineau and Lucie Duff Gordon (who contributed significant prose articles chronicling her travels to Egypt later collected in her best-known work, *Letters from Egypt* [1865]). Van Arsdel provides a competent if rather descriptive account of much of this output. Her conclusions occasionally veer towards untheorized simplicity: given the amount of material produced in recent years on the use of anonymity amongst nineteenth-century women writers, for example, it seems rather slight to suggest that in much of their periodical production 'Women often preferred anonymity, not wishing to seem forward or pushy…' (pt. 1, p. 376). One could point out here how editorial stances and cultural circumstances, for example, might have dictated such anonymity amongst contributors.

This is one of the points made in *Their Fair Share: Women, Power and Criticism in the Athenaeum, from Millicent Garrett Fawcett to Katherine Mansfield, 1870– 1920*, Marysa DeMoor's in-depth and long-awaited study of women reviewers for that enduring weekly literary journal. The *Athenaeum*, founded in 1828 and in existence until 1921, was arguably one of the leading journals of the period, if not 'the single most important literary periodical of Victorian times' (p. 25). Reviews of contemporary work were published anonymously, but with access to marked archival files DeMoor has been able to identify significant trends and patterns relating to the use of women reviewers by the editors of the *Athenaeum*. She also tracks the shift in emphasis from the impartial and objective reviewing style of the early period to a deliberate and personalized critical engagement in the 1880s–1890s with the New Woman, and in the late 1910s–1920s with the modernist literary movement (the latter in particular due to the influence of Katherine Mansfield, main contributor and wife of *Athenaeum* editor and critic John Middleton Murry). The results revise some of the general conceptions of the range and extent of literary activity by women for this important periodical publication.

Going back to the early part of the century, Janis Dawson looks at gendered periodical constructions in 'Writing for the Young in the Age of Revolution and Reaction: William Fordyce Mavor and *The Young Gentleman's and Lady's Magazine (1799–1800)*' (*VPR* 34:i[2002] 16–40). Mavor (1758–1837), author of over forty books, including the bestselling *English Spelling Book* [1801], used his editorship of the short-lived *Young Gentleman's and Lady's Magazine* to enter into contemporary debate on women's education, the social order and women's place in society, engaging in particular with Rousseau's controversial educational treatise *Émile* to expound a conservative view of gender identity and activity.

Children's magazines are similarly singled out by Diana Dixon in 'Children's Magazines and Science in the Nineteenth Century' (*VPR* 34:iii[2001] 228–38), in this case for an intriguing but very generalized look at the popularization of science within representative journals of the period. Most children's journals until the late 1860s were bent on didactic exposition, and there was much practical science material featured in their pages. With the rise of more entertaining boys' and girls' weeklies such as the *Boy's Own Paper* and *Boy's World* from the 1870s onwards, such didactic material disappeared, to be replaced by more practical and less theoretically informed coverage.

Blackwood's Magazine's championing of Shelley in its early years has been the subject of some critical debate in the past. Robert Morrison, in '"Abuse wickedness, but acknowledge wit": *Blackwood's* and the Shelley Circle' (*VPR* 34:ii[2001] 147–64), argues convincingly that the positive reception accorded the works of Percy and Mary Shelley, her father William Godwin and her half-brother William had much to do with the Blackwood editorial circle's use of the flamboyance of the Shelley circle to berate their rivals the *Edinburgh* and the *Quarterly* for lack of spirit, as well as with their 'keen appreciation of the literary spirit of the age' (p. 160). This accounts for *Blackwood's Magazine* being among the first to defend and praise Percy Shelley for his literary talents in a perceptive and penetrating fashion that went against contemporary convention.

On a medical note, Mary Elizabeth Leighton's prizewinning article '"Hypnosis Redivivus": Ernest Hart, the *British Medical Journal*, and the Hypnotism Controversy' (*VPR* 34:ii[2001] 104–27) examines the phenomenon of hypnosis, both as debated in the late nineteenth-century pages of the *BMJ* and as articulated in popular culture in such textual productions as George du Maurier's *Trilby* [1894]. Although ultimately deemed illegitimate by the *BMJ* as a therapeutic medical tool, hypnosis gained much credence through its representation in popular culture. The two intersections are neatly explored in this succinctly argued piece.

Similarly strong in content is another prizewinner, Russell M. Wyland's 'The Attic Society's "Oxford Review": Idealism, Failure, and Early Nineteenth-Century Periodical Culture at the University of Oxford' (*VPR* 34:ii[2001] 128–46). His piece enquires into the Oxford circle led by Augustus Hare, Thomas Arnold, John Keble and J.T. Coleridge, who, inspired by literary ambitions and contemporary literary periodical productions, planned but ultimately failed to start an 'Oxford Review'. Their experiences in pursuit of this failed goal, Wyland argues, were put to good use in their subsequent literary careers.

The Irish Literary Revival of the late nineteenth century forms the context for Clare Hutton's study of the publication in 1893 of Douglas Hyde's popular *The Love Songs of Connacht*. 'Reading *The Love Songs of Connacht*: Douglas Hyde and the Exigencies of Publication' (*The Library*, 7th ser. 2:iv[2001] 364–93) uses Don McKenzie's approach to the 'sociology of texts' to demonstrate how Hyde's bilingual collection of Irish folk songs and stories, though written as the result of a long-term interest and commitment to recording and reviving the Irish language, was, through publication with the London-based T. Fisher Unwin, ironically to create an unanticipated and larger readership across the UK and the US for his work and, as others have suggested, lay the seeds for the emergence of new literature in modern Irish.

Several recent publications make good use of archival material to offer useful information about turn-of-the-century British publishing and copyright practices. Julian Pooley tracks the fate of the papers of the Nichols family and press (London-based printers and publishers active 1766–1873) in 'The Papers of the Nichols Family and Business: New Discoveries and the Work of the Nichols Archive Project' (*The Library*, 7th ser. 2:i[2001] 10–52). Much work has already been done on the early years of the firm and the family's editing and printing of the *Gentleman's Magazine* between 1776 and 1865, principally by Keith Maslen in his monumental study of the Bowyer ledgers, published in microfiche [1991]. Pooley sketches in details of the nineteenth-century activities of the firm's directors, and describes a currently ongoing project to create a searchable, analytical database guide to the private and public collections of Nichols papers. An appendix provides a useful supplementary checklist of the locations of significant holdings of Nichols papers.

In 'J.W. Arrowsmith's Royalty Ledger' (*PubH* 48[2000] 85–110), John R. Turner analyses material from a royalty ledger at the Bristol Record Office relating to the Bristol publisher J.W. Arrowsmith, covering agreements made with various authors between 1884 and 1923. Among the facts uncovered include details of Arrowsmith's sales of their general texts, and negotiations with other publishers of general Continental rights, serial rights, American rights, and, finally, colonial rights (for Arrowsmith texts issued in India, Australia and other British colonies).

Brendan Fleming uses unpublished archival material to discuss unknown links between George Moore, Émile Zola and the British publisher Vizetelly & Co. in 'The First English Translation of *La Terre* (1888): An Assessment of the letters from Vizetelly and Co. to Émile Zola' (*PubH* 50[2001] 47–59). The piece draws on unpublished letters between the Vizetelly & Co. and Zola from 1887 to 1888 concerning *The Soil*, the first English translation of Zola's *La Terre*. The British publication of this naturalist novel in 1888 led to prosecution for obscenity and eventual bankruptcy for the firm. The letters reveal the author George Moore's role in acquiring the rights in *La Terre* for the firm, suggest a hitherto unknown connection between the book and the Irish land struggles of 1887–8, and confirm the firm's attempt to consolidate its position as primary publisher of English translations of Zola's work.

Transatlantic connections are the focus of a substantial section of *George Palmer Putnam: Representative American Publisher*, Ezra Greenspan's magisterial biography of a significant and dynamic player in nineteenth-century US publishing circles. By the time of his death in 1872 at the age of 58, after a career in the book trade spanning forty years, Putnam had established G.P. Putnam as a leading publishing firm, with particular ties to the UK fostered during a ten-year sojourn in London between 1838 and 1848. Victorianists will find these chapters on Putnam's London career of great interest: during this period, Putnam negotiated important US retail rights to leading journals of the day (the *Quarterly Review*, *Blackwood's Magazine*, *Fraser's Magazine* and others), secured the works of George Borrow and Thomas Carlyle for his US lists, and played a leading role in contemporary debates on international copyright. Greenspan contextualizes and writes well on his subject—the work is a great pleasure to read.

Another publisher who is the focus of a full-length biography (or rather 'commentary', as the author labels it) is William Tinsley, subject of Peter Newbolt's

William Tinsley (1831–1902): 'Speculative Publisher'. Short chapters are dedicated to Tinsley's many links with important bestselling literary authors of the period, including Mrs Henry Wood, Ouida, Mary Elizabeth Braddon, George Meredith and Thomas Hardy. While competently managed, the work tends to rely heavily on Tinsley's autobiography for salient facts without adequate counterbalancing from more recent scholarship. Thus, for example, Tinsley's assessment of Mudie's Select Library, the leading retail outlet for novels of the day, as a triumphantly successful endeavour has been shown in research published in the last ten years to be inaccurate: at one point during the period discussed (the 1860s), Mudie faced bankruptcy and required a secret consortium of publishers to nurse the business back to health. Less concentration on the literary aspects of Tinsley's publishing career (his connections with famous and not-so-famous literary authors) and more about the publishing contexts and non-literary texts Tinsley was responsible for, would have also been of use here.

Bestsellers are the focus of Troy J. Bassett and Christina M. Walter's 'Booksellers and Bestsellers: British Book Sales as Documented by *The Bookman*, 1891–1906' (*BH* 4[2001] 205–36). The piece offers an analysis and full listing of the top five 'bestsellers' noted in specific columns on the topic in the *Bookman* in the two decades spanning the turn of the nineteenth century. Sales figures provided by regional bookshops in England, Scotland and Ireland were used by *Bookman* editors to create general listings for information purposes. The results offer insight into the contemporary popularity of texts and authors now long forgotten by the literary establishment.

Chris Baggs offers similar insight into popular reading habits in his piece on Welsh miners, 'How Well Read Was My Valley? Reading, Popular Fiction, and the Miners of South Wales, 1875–1939' (*BoH* 4[2001] 277–301). Primary material from library catalogues of institute and welfare hall libraries set up to service mining communities in South Wales, as well as secondary material from newspapers and other accounts, suggest that readers overwhelmingly favoured popular, light reading over the didactic material generally stocked in such institutions. The conclusion is similar to that reached by Jonathan Rose in his *The Intellectual Life of the British Working Classes* (reviewed in section 1(a) above).

Over the past five years, various initiatives to map national histories of the book and print culture have begun to release their findings to the wider world. Lyons and Arnold, eds., *A History of the Book in Australia, 1891–1945*, is the latest entrant, the second volume (but first to be published) of a planned three-volume set. One of the strengths of this work is the way the editors and contributors attempt to explicate in a clear and accessible manner various aspects of the history of the book in Australia, in both a material and a cultural sense. Threaded through the volume are two main themes, highlighted as key to understanding 'the golden era' of Australian print culture, namely the influence of imperial connections, in this case Britain, and Australian attempts to shape a national literary culture in response to this influence. Some of the best sections of the work cover the explicit intertwining of British publishing and the Australian book trade and culture, both through control of the export markets and through the control of opportunities offered (or denied) Australian writers. Of particular relevance to those studying nineteenth-century publishing trends are the first two sections by Richard Nile, David Walker and Martyn Lyons, which focus on the 'Paternoster Row Machine', as Henry Lawson called the British publishers whose clout and marketing strength Australian writers sought in order to sustain writing careers back in their native land. They argue convincingly that it was mainly British publishers who in effect directed and determined the general flow of texts in Australia between the 1890s and 1930s, both shaping and responding to Australian reading habits with the colonially aimed books they sought out for publication.

Some of this is repeated, as he freely admits, in Wallace Kirsop's 'From Colonialism to the Multinationals: The Fragile Growth of Australian Publishing and its Contribution to the Global Anglophone Reading Community' (in Michon and Mollier, eds., *Les Mutations du livre et de l'édition dans le monde du XVIIIe siècle à l'an 2000*, arising from an international colloquium on the history of the book held in May 2000 in Sherbrooke, Canada. Senior figures join new and emerging scholars in the field to compare methodologies and survey book-trade history as it is currently being practised in Europe, North America, Australasia, Scandinavia and the African subcontinent. The results, published in 2001 in a hefty paperback of almost 600 pages, is rich in material and repays investigation. While most pieces are written in French, there are a substantial number of English language pieces worth noting which deal specifically with British publishing history. Among these are 'British Publishing and Bookselling: Constraints and Developments', James Raven's overview of British book-trade developments from an economic historian's point of view. For him, the transformation of British publishing into a major business by the mid-nineteenth century can be traced directly not only to the successful adaptation of technological innovation to drive down the cost of production, but also to the establishment of a mercantilistic society and framework within which such developments were achieved. Such a mechanistic approach, however, needs to make room for the role of the individual entrepreneur and the place of social contexts in the general formula—what one might ask is: who bought the new texts produced, and why? Some answers are to be found in Leslie Howsam's well-argued piece on British religious publishing of the nineteenth century, 'Beliefs, Ideologies, Technologies: Locating Religion in the History of the Book'. Howsam argues convincingly for reviewing the place of religious publishing within the general matrix of book history studies, given that several recent studies have located religious publishers as pioneers of the economic practices subsequently taken up by the British industry as a whole. Howsam uses the moment to call for a shift in publishing history studies away from equating book production solely with the literary to allow the location of publishers and publishing within significant non-literary spheres such as devotional book production. Similar concerns with non-literary textual production drive Rimi B. Chatterjee's interesting piece 'How India Took to the Book: British Publishers at Work under the Raj', which surveys general activity in India throughout the second half of the nineteenth century by publishers such as Longman and Macmillan. Using statistics culled from a variety of Indian sources, Chatterjee demonstrates how the educational market in particular was an arena of negotiation between British publishing interests and Indian indigenous requirements that was not as one-sided in nature as past studies have suggested.

In summer 2001 John Barnard, Professor of English Literature at the University of Leeds, retired. To mark the occasion, Ashgate Press has published a Festchrift in his honour, Bell *et al.*, eds., *Re-constructing the Book: Literary Texts in Transmission*, which offers contributions on a wide range of topics from seventeenth-century poetry to nineteenth- and twentieth-century publishing and literary history. Two contributions cover areas specific to nineteenth-century publishing interests. First, Simon Eliot, in 'Sir Walter, Sex and the SoA', uses contrasting portions of Walter Besant's partially revised autobiography (published without alteration after Besant's death in 1901) to reveal Besant's youthful reactions to London and sexual temptation. Comparison of revised and unrevised material thus contributes to our understanding of the place of Victorian morality in the fashioning of such memoirs. Eliot's piece seems a bit unfinished, though, since the place of the Society of Authors (the SoA of the article title) is not fully made clear in this analysis. In 'Reading the Brontës Abroad: A Study in the Transmission of Victorian Novels in Continental Europe', Inga-Stina Ewbank moves us from internal readings to external marketing and distribution, following the twisting fate of foreign-language adaptations of *Jane Eyre* in the French and German markets from 1848 onwards. Ewbank competently, if rather briskly, notes the important role of particular early translators in refashioning such texts for the French and German markets—this is an area that deserves more enquiry, on which this piece makes a good start.

Typography and literary study, itself of some interest to John Barnard, is the subject of a richly illustrated if rather abstruse collection, Gutjahr and Benton, eds., *Illuminating Letters: Typography and Literary Interpretation*. To quote the editors, this collection aims to explore 'both the typographic strategies of those who produce books and the interpretive tactics of readers who make sense of a text's presentation' (p. 6). In other words, what a printer/publisher produces on paper, and how readers react to this. The focus is mainly on US typographical examples, from Walt Whitman and Edgar Allan Poe to studies of graphic novel fonts. Two pieces, however, are relevant to nineteenth-century studies, examining typographical activity in Victorian contexts. Sarah A. Kelen's *'Peirs Plouhman* [sic] and the "formidable array of blackletter" in the Early Nineteenth Century' examines the context of the edition of *Piers Plowman* issued by Thomas Dunham Whitaker [1813], to argue that his controversial use of dense and archaic blackletter typeface (not very popular with contemporary readers), was in fact an anti-Catholic act, an attempt to distance and antiquate the poem's Catholic origins, thus confining it to the status of a literary artefact irrelevant to modern English Protestantism. The argument is slightly stretched but plausible. Megan Benton moves us into the late nineteenth century with a brief mention of William Morris's typographical activity in 'Typography and Gender: Remasculating the Modern Book'. The piece focuses mainly, though, on US contemporaries and twentieth-century innovators in the area, and the manner in which their typographical work could be read as an attempt to narrow audiences and reject 'feminine' typefaces and return to pre-industrial forms associated with privileged, elite male book culture.

A review article worth studying for what it has to say about nomenclature and the intersecting position in Victorian studies of periodical literature, journalism, book history and publishing history is Laurel Brake's 'On Print Culture: The State We're In' (*Journal of Victorian Culture* 6:ii[2001] 125–36). Coming at a time when 'book history' is starting to emerge as a field of endeavour in its own right, this piece calls for a reorientation of the subject title to 'Print Culture'—a definition that allows inclusion of general work (journalism, prose periodical work, fiction, verse) and ephemeral work (chapbooks, advertisements, billboards) representing the whole gamut of textual production that historians and literary critics should draw on to inform their discussions. To do so, Brake argues, would 'interpellate, welcome into visibility a body of work which has been gestating for some time' (p. 136). Brake revisits this theme in 'Star Turn? Magazine, Part-Issue and Book Serialisation' (*VPR* 34:iii[2001] 208–27). This thoughtful general study of nineteenth-century magazine serialization draws our attention to the lost ephemeral material through which such texts were filtered for consumption—that is, the advertisement supplements and individual issue covers and wrappers that, so central to initial reception by contemporary audiences, have been stripped away to form the general bound library volumes that most current analysts of Victorian periodical production rely on for primary material. The 'privileging' in research libraries of the format of a book over the original, news-orientated format of the monthly, weekly or bi-weekly periodical echoes a similar privileging of the production of authors (fiction versus periodical prose contributions) that until recently was part and parcel of nineteenth-century studies. Examples from *Macmillan's Magazine*, *Blackwood's Magazine* and the *Fortnightly Review* are drawn on to make the important point that form as well as function is crucial to our understanding of the place of material print culture in the nineteenth century, and one that researchers would do well to explore further.

If you are unable to locate *Victorian Periodicals Review* to read Brake's article, then you can always turn to her essay collection *Print in Transition, 1850–1910: Studies in Media and Book History*, where you can find it reprinted, along with thirteen other pieces on Victorian media and cultural history (the acknowledgements, though, do not mention its original appearance in *VPR*). The collection also includes studies on serialization, gender and the publishing career of Walter Pater. Only one of these pieces is unpublished; the rest have appeared between 1995 and 2000 either in other essay collections or in academic journals. What is on offer is a thoughtful compilation of some of Brake's best work in recent years, useful for those who cannot access the originals via a library loan service. However, one must wonder what market there is for a book consisting almost entirely of material already in the public domain, and indeed including several pieces that have appeared in other essay collections recently edited by Brake under the same publishing imprint.

Books Reviewed

Adams, Kimberly Van Esveld. *Our Lady of Victorian Feminism: The Madonna in the Work of Anna Jameson, Margaret Fuller, and George Eliot*. OhioUP. [2001] pp. 300. hb $59.9 ISBN 0 8214 1361 9, pb $24.95 ISBN 0 8214 1362 7.

Altick, Richard D., and Thomas J. Collins, eds. *The Ring and the Book*. Broadview Literary Texts. Broadview. [2001] pp. xviii + 824. £12.99 ISBN 1 5511 1372 4.

Appleman, Philip, ed. *Darwin*. Norton. [2001] pp. xvii + 695. $19.20 ISBN 0 3939 5849 3.

Armstrong, Heather V. *Character and Ethical Development in the Three Novels of George Eliot: Middlemarch, Romola, Daniel Deronda*. Mellen. [2001] pp. v + 196. $89.95 ISBN 0 7734 7325 4.

Armstrong, Tim. *Haunted Hardy: Poetry, History, Memory.* Palgrave [2000] pp. 198. $59.95 ISBN 0 3335 9791 5.

Ashley, Mike. *Algernon Blackwood: An Extraordinary Life.* C&G. [2001] pp. 320. $28 ISBN 0 7867 0928 6.

Atkinson, Damian, ed. *The Selected Letters of W.E. Henley.* Ashgate. [2000] pp. xxv + 366. $94.95 ISBN 1 8401 4634 6.

Bäckman, Sven. *The Manners of Ghosts: A Study of the Supernatural in Thomas Hardy's Short Poems.* Gothenburg Studies in English 82. GothU. [2001] pp. 274. $57.50 ISBN 9 1734 6413 9.

Barsham, Diana. *Arthur Conan Doyle and the Meaning of Masculinity.* Ashgate. [2000] pp. 288. $84.95 ISBN 1 8592 8264 4.

Beetham, Margaret, and Kay Boardman, eds. *Victorian Women's Magazines: An Anthology.* ManUP. [2001] pp. 230. hb $74.95 ISBN 0 7190 5878 3, pb $29.95 ISBN 0 7190 5879 1.

Belcher, Margaret. *The Collected Letters of A.W.N. Pugin,* vol. 1: *1830–1842.* OUP. [2001] pp. 448. $125 ISBN 0 1981 7391 1.

Bell, Maureen, Shirley Chew, Simon Eliot, Lynette Hunter, and James L.W. West III, eds. *Re-constructing the Book: Literary Texts in Transmission.* Ashgate. [2001] pp. xi + 231. £35 ISBN 0 7546 0360 1.

Bentley, Michael. *Lord Salisbury's World: Conservative Environments in Late-Victorian Britain.* CUP. [2001] pp. viii + 334. £29.95 ISBN 0 5214 4506 X.

Black, Jeremy. *The English Press 1621–1861.* Sutton. [2001] pp. ix + 213. £20 ISBN 0 7509 2524 8

Blainey, Ann. *Fanny and Adelaide: The Lives of the Remarkable Kemble Sisters.* Dee. [2001] pp. x + 339. $27.50 ISBN 1 5666 3372 9.

Boardman, Brigid M. *The Poems of Francis Thompson.* Continuum. [2001] pp. xxxviii + 513. £40 ISBN 0 8264 5169 1.

Braddon, Mary Elizabeth. *Cut By the County.* Sensation Press. [2001] pp. 126. pb £15 ISBN 1 9025 8011 7.

Braddon, Mary Elizabeth. *Dead Love Has Chains.* Sensation Press. [2001] pp. 102. £15 ISBN 1 9025 8010 9.

Braddon, Mary Elizabeth. *Dross; or, The Root of Evil and Marjorie Daw.* Sensation Press. [2001] pp. 69. £12 ISBN 1 9025 8005 2.

Braddon, Mary Elizabeth. *His Darling Sin.* Sensation Press. [2001] pp. 128. £15 ISBN 1 9025 8012 5.

Brake, Laurel. *Print in Transition, 1850–1910: Studies in Media and Book History.* Palgrave. [2001] pp. xv + 341. $69.95 ISBN 0 3337 7047 1.

Brantlinger, Patrick, ed. *She: A History of Adventure* by H. Rider Haggard. Penguin. [2001] pp. xxxi + 325. $9 ISBN 0 1404 3763 0.

Brown, Ann, with Keith Brown, eds. *Arthur Evans's Travels in Crete, 1894–1899.* Ashmolean Museum Publications. [2001] pp. xxx + 509. £56 ISBN 1 8417 1281 7.

Burdett, Carolyn. *Olive Schreiner and the Progress of Feminism: Evolution, Gender, and Empire.* Palgrave. [2001] pp. ix + 232. $59.95 ISBN 0 3336 1532 8.

Burkhardt, Frederick, Sheila Ann Dean, Duncan Porter, Sarah Wilmot, and Paul S. White, eds. *The Correspondence of Charles Darwin,* vol. 12: *1864.* CUP. [2001] pp. xxvii + 694. $80 ISBN 0 5215 9034 5.

Callow, Philip. *Louis: A Life of Robert Louis Stevenson.* Dee. [2001] pp. xi + 336. $27.50 ISBN 1 5666 3343 5.

Carnell, Jennifer, ed. *One Fatal Moment and Other Stories* and *At the Shrine of Jane Eyre.* Sensation Press. [2001] pp. 132. £15 ISBN 1 9025 8014 1.

Chase, Karen, and Michael Levenson. *The Spectacle of Intimacy: A Public Life for the Victorian Family.* PrincetonUP. [2001] pp. 250. $39.95 ISBN 0 6910 0668 7.

Chesterton, G.K. *The Man Who Was Thursday: A Nightmare.* Modern Library Classics. [2001] pp. xvii + 198. $8.95 ISBN 0 3757 5791 0.

Chitham, Edward. *The Birth of Wuthering Heights: Emily Brontë at Work.* Palgrave. [2001] pp. 228. $18.95 ISBN 0 3339 4545 X.

Christiansen, Rupert. *Arthur Hugh Clough 1819–1861: The Voice of Victorian Sex.* Short Lives. Faber. [2001] pp. 96. £4.99 ISBN 0 5712 0815 0.

Cianci, Giovanni, and Peter Nicholls, eds. *Ruskin and Modernism.* Palgrave. [2001] pp. xvii + 219. £40 ISBN 0 3339 1560 7.

Coan, Stephen, ed. *Diary of an African Journey, 1914* by H. Rider Haggard. C. Hurst. [2001] pp. xiii + 345. £20 ISBN 1 8506 5468 9.

Collins, Wilkie, and Charles Dickens. *No Thoroughfare.* The Christchurch Dickens Fellowship, PO Box 21–392, Otautachi, New Zealand 8030. [2001]. $NZ20 inc. postage.

Cooley, Thomas. *The Ivory Leg in the Ebony Cabinet: Madness, Race, and Gender in Victorian America.* UMassP. [2001] pp. xxvi + 302. $34.95 ISBN 1 5584 9284 4.

Cooper, Suzanne Fagence. *The Victorian Woman.* V&A. [2001] pp. 95. $16.95 ISBN 0 8109 6580 1.

Cox, Michael, ed. *A Dictionary of Writers and their Works.* OUP. [2001] pp. x + 666. £25 ISBN 0 1986 6249 1.

Crane, David Lisle, ed. *Letters Between a Victorian Schoolboy and his Family, 1892–1895.* Wrangham. [1999] pp. lxi + 385. ISBN 0 9485 4511 9.

Crump, Rebecca, and Betty Flowers, eds. *Christina Rossetti: The Complete Poems.* Penguin. [2001] pp. lix + 1,221. pb £12.99 ($17) ISBN 0 1404 2366 4.

Daley, Kenneth. *The Rescue of Romanticism: Walter Pater and John Ruskin.* OhioUP. [2001] pp. 180. $39.95 ISBN 0 8214 1382 1.

Dames, Nicholas. *Amnesiac Selves: Nostalgia, Forgetting, and British Fiction, 1810–1870.* OUP. [2001] pp. viii + 298. £40 ISBN 0 1951 4357 4.

David, Deirdre, ed. *The Cambridge Companion to the Victorian Novel.* CUP. [2001] pp. xx + 267. hb £40 ISBN 0 5216 4150 0, pb £14.95 ISBN 1 5216 4619 7.

Davis, Jim, and Victor Emeljanow. *Reflecting the Audience: London Theatregoing, 1840–1880.* UIowaP. [2001] pp. xiv + 299. $45.95 ISBN 0 8774 5781 6

DeMoor, Marysa. *Their Fair Share: Women, Power and Criticism in the Athenaeum, from Millicent Garrett Fawcett to Katherine Mansfield, 1870–1920.* Ashgate. [2000] pp. x + 163. £42.50 ISBN 0 7546 0118 8.

Denisoff, Dennis. *Aestheticism and Sexual Parody, 1840–1940.* CUP. [2001] pp. xii + 191. £37.50 ISBN 0 5218 0039 0.

Dickens, Charles. *Hard Times.* Modern Library Classics. [2001] pp. xx + 338. $6.95 ISBN 0 6796 4217 X.

Dickens, Charles. *Oliver Twist.* Modern Library Classics. [2001] pp. xxxi + 442. $8.95 ISBN 0 3757 5791 0.

Dimova-Cookson, Maria. *T.H. Green's Moral and Political Philosophy: A Phenomenological Perspective*. Palgrave. [2001] pp. xiii + 175. $60 ISBN 0 3339 1445 7.

Dowling, Andrew. *Manliness and the Male Novelist in Victorian Literature.* Ashgate. [2001] pp. viii + 139. $69.95 ISBN 0 7546 0380 6.

Doyle, Arthur Conan. *The Adventures and Memoirs of Sherlock Holmes*. Modern Library Classics. [2001] pp. 501. $12.95 ISBN 0 3757 6002 4.

Draznin, Yaffa Claire. *Victorian London's Middle-Class Housewife: What She Did All Day*. Greenwood. [2000] pp. xvi + 227. $39.95 ISBN 0 3133 1399 7.

Duffy, Daniel, and Emma Liggins, eds. *Feminist Readings of Victorian Popular Texts: Divergent Femininities*. Ashgate. [2001] pp. 242. £46.50 ISBN 0 7546 0293 1.

Dunn, Richard J. *Jane Eyre by Charlotte Brontë: An Authoritative Text, Contexts, Criticism*. Norton. [2001] pp. ix + 534. $11.40 ISBN 0 3939 7542 8.

Earnshaw, Tony. *An Actor and a Rare One: Peter Cushing as Sherlock Holmes*. Scarecrow. [2001] pp. xiv + 146. $26.50 ISBN 0 8108 3874 5.

Ehrlich, Eugene, ed. *British English A to Zed* by Norman W. Schur. Checkmark. [2001] pp. 430. $18.95 ISBN 0 8160 4239 X.

Eliot, George. *The Mill on the Floss*. Modern Library Classics. [2001] pp. xviii + 627. $8.95 ISBN 0 3757 5783 X

Eliot, George. *Silas Marner: The Weaver of Raveloe*. Modern Library Classics. [2001] pp. xvii + 209. $6.95 ISBN 0 3757 5749 X.

Fishman, William J. *East End 1888: A Year in a London Borough among the Labouring Poor*. Hanbury. [2001] pp. xii + 343. £20 ISBN 0 9541 0590 7.

Fryer, Jonathan. *Robbie Ross: Oscar Wilde's Devoted Friend*. C&G. [2000] pp. ix + 278. $25 ISBN 0 7867 0781 X.

Furst, Lilian R., ed. *Medical Progress and Social Reality: A Reader in Nineteenth-Century Medicine and Literature*. SUNYP. [2000]. pp. xiv + 314. $66.50 ISBN 0 7914 4803 7.

Gale, Maggie B., and Viv Gardner, eds. *Women, Theatre and Performance: New Histories, New Historiographies*. ManUP. [2000] pp. xi + 243. £14.99 ISBN 0 7190 5713 2

Garrett, Martin. *Elizabeth Barrett Browning and Robert Browning*. Writers' Lives. BL. [2001] pp.128. £9.95 ISBN 0 7123 4715 1.

Gleadle, Kathryn. *British Women in the Nineteenth Century*. Palgrave. [2001] pp. vi + 250. hb £65 ISBN 0 3336 7629 7, pb £16.50 ISBN 0 3336 7630 0.

Gooden, Philip. *The Lost World and Other Thrilling Tales* by Arthur Conan Doyle. Penguin. [2001] pp. xxxiv + 348. pb $9 ISBN 0 1404 3765 7.

Gordon, Michael R. *Alias Jack the Ripper: Beyond the Usual Whitechapel Suspects*. McFarland. [2001] pp. x + 353. £31.50 ISBN 0 7864 0898 7.

Gravil, Richard, ed. *Master Narratives: Tellers and Telling in the English Novel*. Ashgate. [2001] pp. viii + 209. $74.95 ISBN 0 7546 0128 5.

Green, Laura Morgan. *Educating Women: Cultural Conflict and Victorian Literature*. OhioUP. [2001] pp. 178. $42.95 ISBN 0 8214 1402 X.

Greenspan, Ezra. *George Palmer Putnam: Representative American Publisher*. PSUP. [2000] pp. xvii + 510. £37.95 ISBN 0 2710 2005 9.

Günter, Bachmann. *Philosophische Bewuβtseinsformen in George Eliot's Middlemarch*. Lang. [2000] pp. 298. ISBN 3 6313 6985 9.

Gutjahr, Paul C., and Megan L. Benton, eds. *Illuminating Letters: Typography and Literary Interpretation.* UMassP. [2001] pp. ix + 198. £32 ISBN 1 5584 9288 7.

Haddelsey, Stephen P. *Charles Lever: The Lost Victorian.* Smythe. [2000] pp.170. £29 ISBN 0 8614 0420 3.

Haggard, H. Rider. *She: A History of Adventure.* Modern Library Classics. [2002] pp. xxiv + 334. $8.95 ISBN 0 3757 5905 0.

Hanes, Susan R. *The Persistent Phantom: Wilkie Collins and Dorothy Sayers.* Privately printed, River Forest, Illinois. [2000]. Copies available from the author: Director, River Forest Public Library, 735 Lathrop Avenue, Ill. 60305 USA.

Hardy, Thomas. *The Mayor of Casterbridge.* OUP. [2001] pp. xxiv + 335. $18 ISBN 0 1951 4810 X.

Harper, Lila Marz. *Solitary Travelers: Nineteenth-Century Women's Travel Narratives and the Scientific Vocation.* AUP [2001] pp. 277. $45 ISBN 0 8386 3860 0.

Hawlin, Stefan, and Tim Burnett, eds. *The Poetical Works of Robert Browning,* vol. 8: *The Ring and the Book, Books V–VIII.* Clarendon. [2001] pp. xvii + 401. £75 ISBN 0 1981 8647 9.

Haywood, Ian, ed. *Chartist Fiction: 'The Political Pilgrim's Progress',* Thomas Doubleday; *'Sunshine and Shadow',* Thomas Martin. Ashgate. [1999] pp. xv + 200. £45 ISBN 1 8401 4648 6.

Haywood, Ian, ed. *Chartist Fiction: 'Woman's Wrongs',* Ernest Jones. Ashgate [2001] pp. iii + 177. $79.95 ISBN 0 7546 0303 2.

Henry, Nancy, ed. *Ruth* by Elizabeth Gaskell. Dent. [2001] pp. xxxvii + 416. pb £5.99 ISBN 0 4608 7660 0.

Hodgson, Peter C. *Theology in the Fiction of George Eliot.* SCMPress [2001] pp. 244. £17.95 ISBN 0 3340 2827 2.

Holbrook, David. *Nonsense Against Sorrow; A Phenomenological Study of Lewis Carroll's 'Alice' Books.* Open Gate. [2001] pp. ix + 144. $20.95 ISBN 1 8718 7149 2.

Horrall, Andrew. *Popular Culture in London c.1890–1918: The Transformation of Entertainment.* Palgrave. [2001] pp. xiv + 267. hb £49.99 ISBN 0 7190 5782 5, pb £16.99 ISBN 0 7190 5783 3.

Horsman, Alan, ed. *Dombey and Son* by Charles Dickens. OUP. [2001] pp. 967. £5.99 ISBN 0 1928 3990 X.

Hughes, John. *'Ecstatic Sound': Music and Individuality in the Works of Thomas Hardy.* Ashgate. [2001] pp. 246. $69.95 ISBN 1 8401 4633 8.

Hughes, Meirion, and Robert Stradling. *The English Musical Renaissance, 1840–1940: Constructing a National Music.* Palgrave. [2001] pp. xxi + 330. $27.95 ISBN 0 7190 5830 9.

Jackson, Kate. *George Newnes and the New Journalism in Britain, 1880–1910: Culture and Profit.* Ashgate. [2001] pp. xi + 293. £45 ISBN 0 7546 0317 2.

Jedrzejewski, Jan, ed. *The Cock and Anchor: Being a Chronicle of Old Dublin City* by Joseph Sheridan Le Fanu. OUP. [2000] pp. xxviii + 489. £55 ISBN 0 8614 0423 8.

Jenkins, Alice, and Juliet John, eds. *Rereading Victorian Fiction.* Macmillan. [2000] pp. xxvi + 218. £50 ISBN 0 3337 1445 8.

John, Juliet. *Dickens's Villains: Melodrama, Character, Popular Culture.* OUP. [2001] pp. xiii + 258. £45 ISBN 0 1981 8461 1.

John, Juliet, and Alice Jenkins, eds. *Rethinking Victorian Culture*. Macmillan. [2000] pp. xvi + 244. £55 ISBN 0 3337 1446 6.

Johnson, Patricia E. *Hidden Hands: Working-Class Women and Victorian Social-Problem Fiction*. OhioUP. [2001] pp. ix + 224. hb $55 ISBN 0 8214 1388 2, pb $24.95 ISBN 0 8214 1389 9.

Johnston, Susan. *Women and Domestic Experience in Victorian Political Fiction*. Greenwood. [2001] pp. 181. $59.95 ISBN 0 3133 1634 1.

Jordan, John O., ed. *The Cambridge Companion to Dickens*. CUP. [2001] pp. xvii + 235. hb £40 ISBN 0 5216 6016 5, pb £14.95 ISBN 0 5216 6964 2.

Joshua, Essaka. *Pygmalion and Galatea: The History of Narrative in English Literature*. Ashgate. [2001] pp. xxi + 216. £45 ISBN 0 7546 0447 0.

Joukovsky, Nicholas A. *The Letters of Thomas Love Peacock*, vol. 2: *1828–1866*. Clarendon. [2001] pp. 340. $99 ISBN 0 1981 8633 9.

Kaplan, Fred, and Sylvere Monod, eds. *Hard Times* by Charles Dickens. Norton. [2001] pp. xi + 480. £12.76 ISBN 0 3939 7560 6.

Kinzer, Bruce L. *England's Disgrace? J.S. Mill and the Irish Question*. UTorP. [2001] pp. x + 292. $60 ISBN 0 8020 4862 5.

Knox, Melissa. *Oscar Wilde in the 1900s: The Critic as Creator*. Camden. [2001] pp. xxiv + 206. $65 ISBN 1 5711 3042 X.

Kramer, D., ed. *Jude the Obscure* by Thomas Hardy. Modern Library Classics. [2001] pp. xxix + 494. $7.95 ISBN 0 3757 5741 4.

Lang, Cecil Y., ed. *The Letters of Matthew Arnold*, vol. 5: *1879–1884*. UPVirginia. [2001] pp. xxiii + 500. $60 ISBN 0 8139 1999 1.

Lang, Cecil Y., ed. *The Letters of Matthew Arnold*, vol. 6: *1885–1888*. UPVirginia. [2001] pp. 416. $60 ISBN 0 8139 2028 0.

Larson, Jill. *Ethics and Narrative in the English Novel, 1880–1914*. CUP. [2001] pp. ix + 176. $49.95 ISBN 0 5217 9282 7.

Law, Graham. *Indexes to Fiction in 'The Illustrated London News' (1842–1901) and 'The Graphic' (1869–1901)*. UQP. [2001] pp. x + 91. $7.75 ISBN 1 8649 9565 3.

Law, Graham. *Serializing Fiction in the Victorian Press*. Palgrave/St Martins. [2000] pp. xx + 214. $59.95 ISBN 0 3122 3574 7.

Law, Graham, ed. *Lucy, the Factory Girl; Or, The Secrets of the Tontine Close* by David Pae. Sensation Press. [2001] pp. xx + 35. £25 ISBN 1 9025 8013 3.

LeFew-Blake, Penelope. *Schopenhauer, Women's Literature, and the Legacy of Pessimism in the Novels of George Eliot, Olive Schreiner, Virginia Woolf, and Doris Lessing*. Mellen. [2001] pp. vi + 134. $99.95 ISBN 0 7734 7437 4.

Levine, George, ed. *The Cambridge Companion to George Eliot*. CUP. [2001] pp. 241. hb $54.95 ISBN 0 5216 6267 2, pb $19.95 ISBN 0 5216 6473 X.

Liggins, Emma, and Daniel Duffy, eds. *Feminist Readings of Victorian Popular Texts: Divergent Femininities*. Ashgate.[2001] pp. xxix + 175. £46.50 ISBN 0 7546 0293 1.

Lindskoog, Kathryn. *Surprised by C.S. Lewis, George MacDonald, and Dante: An Array of Original Discoveries*. MercerUP. [2001] pp. 221. £25 ISBN 0 8655 4728 9.

Logan, Thad. *The Victorian Parlour: A Cultural Study*. CUP. [2001] pp. xviii + 282. £40 ISBN 0 5216 3182 3.

Lundin, Anne H. *Victorian Horizons: The Reception of the Picture Books of Walter Crane, Randolph Caldecott, and Kate Greenway*. Scarecrow. [2001] pp. xii + 266 $60 ISBN 0 8108 3739 0.

Lutz, Deborah, ed. *Villette* by Charlotte Brontë. Modern Library Classics. [2001] pp. lv + 590. $10.95 ISBN 0 3757 5850 X.

Lyons, Martyn and John Arnold, eds. *A History of the Book in Australia, 1891–1945*. UQDE. [2001] pp. xix + 444. hb $A50 ISBN 0 7022 3234 3.

MacKay, Carol Hanbery. *Creative Negativity: Four Victorian Exemplars of the Female Quest*. StanfordUP. [2001] pp. xix + 275. $60 ISBN 0 8047 3829 7.

MacKenzie, John M., ed. *The Victorian Vision: Inventing New Britain*. Abrams. [2001] pp. 360. $65 ISBN 0 8109 6579 8.

Malcolm, Gabrielle, ed. *Circe* by Mary Elizabeth Braddon. Sensation Press. [2001] pp. 214. £35 ISBN 1 9025 8008 7.

Mallett, Phillip, ed. *The Mayor of Casterbridge* by Thomas Hardy: *An Authoritative Text, Backgrounds and Contexts, Criticism*. Norton. [2001] pp. xvii + 461. $16.51 ISBN 0 3939 7498 7.

Mancoff, Debra N., ed. *John Everett Millais: Beyond the Pre-Raphaelite Brotherhood*. YaleUP. [2001] pp. vii + 233. £35 ISBN 0 3000 9119 2.

Martin, Carol A, ed. *Adam Bede*. OUP. [2001] pp. clviii + 526. $150 ISBN 0 1981 2595 X.

Martin, Ray. *Thomas Hardy: A Textual Study of the Short Stories*. Ashgate. [1997] xiv + 357. $89.95 ISBN 1 8592 8202 4.

Mattacks, Katherine, ed. *The Christmas Hirelings* and *Fifty Years of Novel Writing: Miss Braddon at Home* by Mary Elizabeth Braddon. Sensation Press. [2001] pp. 101. £15 ISBN 1 9025 8015 X.

May, Leila Silvana. *Disorderly Sisters: Sibling Relations and Sororal Resistance in Nineteenth-Century British Literature*. BuckUP. [2001] pp. 276. $46.50 ISBN 0 8387 5459 7.

McCormack, Jerusha Hull. *The Man Who Was Dorian Gray*. Palgrave. [2000] pp. 368. $24.95 ISBN 0 3122 3278 0.

McCormack, W.J. *Fool of the Family: A Life of J.M. Synge*. NYUP. [2000] pp. xii + 499. $40 ISBN 0 8147 5652 2.

McEwan, Cheryl. *Gender, Geography and Empire: Victorian Women Travelers in West Africa*. Ashgate. [2000] pp. 260. $74.95 ISBN 1 8401 4252 9.

McMorris, Jenny. *The Warden of English: The Life of H.W. Fowler*. OUP. [2001] pp. xix + 242. £19.99 ISBN 0 1986 6254 8.

Menikoff, Barry, ed. *Kidnapped, or The Lad with the Silver Button* by Robert Louis Stevenson. Modern Library Classics. [2001] pp. 240. $7.95 ISBN 0 3757 5725 2.

Metz, Nancy Aycock. *The Companion to Martin Chuzzlewit*. Greenwood. [2001] pp. xvi + 554. $84.95 (£50) ISBN 0 3133 2310 0.

Michon, Jacques, and Jean-Ives Mollier, eds. *Les Mutations du livre et de l'édition dans le monde du XVIIIe siècle à l'an 2000*. ULavalP. [2000] pp. 597. pb $CAN45 ISBN 2 7475 0813 7.

Miller, Lucasta. *The Brontë Myth*. RandomH. [2001] pp. xiv + 320. $26.24 (£18.99) ISBN 0 2240 3745 5.

Millgate, Michael, ed. *Thomas Hardy's Public Voice: The Essays, Speeches, and Miscellaneous Prose*. OUP. [2001] pp. xi + 500. £70 ISBN 0 1981 8526 X.

Morgan, Rosemarie, and William Morgan, eds. *Thomas Hardy's Emma Poems*. The Thomas Hardy Association Occasional Series vol.2. The Hardy Association Press. [2001] pp. x + 69. £15 ($20) ISBN 0 9669 1766 9.

Morrison, Mark S. *The Public Face of Modernism: Little Magazines, Audiences, and Reception, 1905–1920*. UWiscP. [2001] pp xiv + 279. hb £42.50 ISBN 0 2991 6920 0, pb £16.95 ISBN 0 2991 6924 3

Muir, James Hamilton. *Glasgow in 1901*. White Cockade. [2001] pp. xxxi + 255. $16.95 ISBN 1 8734 8709 6.

Nash, Julie, and Barbara A. Suess. *New Approaches to the Literary Art of Anne Brontë*. Ashgate. [2001] pp. xiii + 232. $69.95 ISBN 0 7546 0199 4.

Newbolt, Peter, comp. *William Tinsley (1831–1902): 'Speculative Publisher'*. OUP/ Ashgate [2001] pp. xv + 370. £59.95 ($104.95) ISBN 0 7546 0291 5.

Nicholson, Adam. *The Hated Wife: Carrie Kipling, 1862–1939*. Macmillan. [2001] pp. 96. $8.95 ISBN 0 5712 0835 5.

Novy, Marianne, ed. *Imagining Adoption: Essays on Literature and Culture* UMichP. [2001] pp. vii + 316. $47.50 ISBN 0 4721 1181 7.

O'Gorman, Francis. *Late Ruskin: New Contexts*. Ashgate. [2001] pp. xii + 180. $69.95 ISBN 1 8401 4629 X.

Olson, Kirby. *Comedy after Postmodernism: Rereading Comedy from Edward Lear to Charles Willeford*. TTUP.[2001] pp. vi + 184. $29.95 ISBN 0 8967 2440 9.

O'Rourke, K.C. *John Stuart Mill and Freedom of Expression: The Genesis of a Theory*. Routledge. [2001] pp. vi + 226. $90 ISBN 0 4152 5304 7.

Page, Norman. *Thomas Hardy: The Novels*. Palgrave. [2001] pp. viii + 199. £37.50 ISBN 0 3339 1436 8.

Page, Norman, ed. *The Old Curiosity Shop: A Tale* by Charles Dickens. Penguin. [2000] pp. xxxi + 575. $10 ISBN 0 1404 3742 8.

Patteson, Rita, and Paul Turner, eds. *The Complete Works of Robert Browning*, vol. 12. OhioUP. [2001] pp. xxv + 420. £54.95 ISBN 0 8214 1359 7.

Pawley, Richard. *Secret City: The Emotional Life of Victorian Poet James Thomson (B.V.)*. UPA. [2001] pp. xviii + 271. $67 ISBN 0 7618 2003 5.

Peatling, G.K. *British Opinion and Irish Self-Government, 1865–1925: From Unionism to Liberal Commonwealth*. IAP. [2001] pp. xvi + 316. £9.99 ISBN 0 7165 2661 1.

Peck, John. *Maritime Fiction: Sailors and the Sea in British and American Novels, 1719–1917*. Palgrave. [2001] pp. 214. $59.95 ISBN 0 3337 9357 9.

Peterson, Linda H. *Traditions of Victorian Women's Autobiography: The Poetics and Politics of Life Writing*. UPVirginia. [2001] pp. 272. $17.50 ISBN 0 8139 2060 4.

Plowman, Stephanie Edwards. *G.M. Hopkins: An Inventory of the Anthony Bischoff Research Collection at Gonzaga University*. ELS Monograph Series 86. UVict. [2001] pp.223. $A13 ISBN 0 9206 0479 X.

Pocock, Tom. *Captain Marryat: Seaman, Writer and Adventurer*. Stackpole. [2000] pp. 208. $26.95 (£19.95) ISBN 0 8117 0355 X.

Pollard, Arthur, ed. *The Representation of Business in English Literature*. IEA. [2000] pp. xv + 182. £12 ISBN 0 2553 6491 1.

Randall, Craig. *Promising Language: Betrothal in Victorian Law and Fiction*. SUNYP. [2000] pp. 352. hb $72 ISBN 0 7914 4425 2, pb $24.95 ISBN 0 7914 4426 0.

Ranger, Paul. *Under Two Managers: The Everyday Life of the Thornton–Barnett Theatre Company 1885–1853*. STR. [2001] pp. xiii + 245. £18 ISBN 0 8543 0069 4.

Raphael. Linda S. *Narrative Skepticism: Moral Agency and Representations of Consciousness in Fiction*. AUP. [2001] pp. 238. £30 ISBN 0 8386 3900 3.

Rauch, Alan. *Useful Knowledge: The Victorians, Morality, and the March of Intellect*. DukeUP. [2001] pp. 292. hb $59.95 ISBN 0 8223 2663 9, pb $19.95 ISBN 0 8223 2668 X.

Regan, Stephen, ed. *The Nineteenth Century Novel: A Critical Reader*. Routledge. [2001] pp. xii + 573. £16.99 ISBN 0 4152 3828 5.

Reynolds, Matthew. *The Realms of Verse: English Poetry in a Time of Nation-Building*. OUP. [2001] pp. xii + 300. £40 ISBN 0 1981 8712 2.

Richardson, Angelique, and Chris Willis. *The New Woman in Fiction and in Fact: Fin-de-Siècle Feminisms*. Palgrave. [2001] pp. xvi + 258. $59.95 ISBN 0 3122 3490 2.

Roberts, Andrew. *Salisbury: Victorian Titan*. W&N. [1999] pp. xxi + 938. £25 ISBN 0 2978 1713 2.

Robins, Anna Gruetzner, ed. *Walter Sickert: The Complete Writings on Art*. OUP. [2000] pp. xli + 699. £90 ISBN 0 1981 7225 7.

Robson, Catherine. *Men in Wonderland: The Lost Girlhood of the Victorian Gentlemen*. PrincetonUP. [2001] pp. xii + 250. $29.95 ISBN 0 6910 0422 6.

Rogers, Helen. *Women and the People: Authority, Authorship and the Radical Tradition in Nineteenth-Century England*. Ashgate. [2000] pp. 352. $74.95 ISBN 0 7546 0261 3.

Rose, Jonathan. *The Intellectual Life of the British Working Classes*. YaleUP. [2001] pp. ix + 534. $39.95 ISBN 0 3000 8886 8.

Roston, Murray. *The Search for Selfhood in Modern Literature*. Palgrave. [2001] pp. vi + 248. $62 ISBN 0 3337 6334 3.

Ruddick, James. *Death at the Priory: Sex, Love, and Murder in Victorian England*. Atlantic Monthly. [2001] pp. xii + 209. $24 ISBN 0 8711 3832 8.

Rutherford, Andrew, ed. *Plain Tales from the Hills* by Rudyard Kipling. OUP. [2000] pp. xxxvi + 279. £4.99 ISBN 0 1928 3571 8.

Rylance, Rick. *Victorian Psychology and British Culture, 1850–1880*. OUP. [2000] pp. x + 355. £58.50 ISBN 0 1981 2283 7.

Sadowski, Piotr. *Gender and Literature: A Systems Study*. UPA. [2001] pp. xxvi + 396. $60 ISBN 0 7618 2132 5.

Sanders, Valerie, ed. *Records of Girlhood: An Anthology of Nineteenth-Century Women's Childhoods*. Ashgate. [2000] pp. 248. $69.95 ISBN 0 7546 0148 X.

Schad, John, ed. *Writing the Bodies of Christ: The Church from Carlyle to Derrida*. Ashgate. [2001] pp. iii + 180. £37.50 ISBN 0 7546 0538 8.

Secord, James A. *Victorian Sensation: The Extraordinary Publication, Reception, and Secret Authorship of 'Vestiges of the Natural History of Creation'*. UChicP. [2001] pp. 624. $35 ISBN 0 2267 4410 8.

Sell, Roger D. *Mediating Criticism: Literary Education Humanized*. BenjaminsNA. [2001] pp. vii + 431. hb $92.25 ISBN 1 5881 1104 0, pb $41.76 ISBN 1 5881 1105 9.

Shattock, Joanne, ed. *Women and Literature in Britain, 1800–1900*. CUP. [2001] pp. x + 311. hb £40 ISBN 0 5216 5055 0, pb £14.95 ISBN 0 5216 5957 4.

Shepheard, Richard, and Barry Mencher. *George Borrow the Dingle Chapters, with Biographical and Critical Commentary*. Brynmill. [2001] pp. 133. £20 ISBN 0 9078 3963 0.

Shillingsburg, Peter. *William Makepeace Thackeray: A Literary Life*. Palgrave. [2001] pp. xi + 163. $49.95 ISBN 0 3336 5092 1.

Shuman, Cathy. *Pedagogical Economies: The Examination and the Victorian Literary Man*. StanfordUP. [2001] pp. 200. $49.50 ISBN 0 8047 3715 0.

Shuttleworth, Sally, ed. *'The Lifted Veil' and 'Brother Jacob'* by George Eliot. Penguin. [2001] pp. lv + 103. £5.99 ISBN 0 1404 3517 4.

Skilton, David, ed. *Orley Farm* by Anthony Trollope. OUP. [2000] xxix + 421. $10.95 ISBN 0 1928 3856 3.

Spevack, Marvin. *James Orchard Halliwell-Phillipps: The Life and Works of the Shakespearean Scholar and Bookman*. S-W. [2001] pp. xii + 612. £45 ISBN 0 8568 3193 X.

Stiebel, Lindy. *Imagining Africa: Landscape in H. Rider Haggard's African Romances*. Greenwood. [2001] pp. xv + 155. $59.95 ISBN 0 3133 1803 4.

Stokes, John, ed. *Eleanor Marx (1855–1898): Life, Work, Contacts*. Ashgate. [2000] xi + 196. £45 ISBN 0 7546 0113 7.

Stover, Leon, ed. *The Sea Lady: A Tissue of Moonshine* by H.G. Wells. Critical text of the 1902 1st edn. McFarland. [2001] pp. xi + 170. £49.50 ISBN 0 7864 0996 7.

Stover, Leon, ed. *The War of the Worlds* by H.G. Wells. Critical text of the 1898 1st edn. McFarland. [2001] pp. xi + 321. $55 ISBN 0 7864 0780 8.

Sweet, Matthew. *Inventing the Victorians: What We Think We Know about Them and Why We're Wrong*. St Martin's Press. [2001] pp. xxiii + 264. $23.95 ISBN 0 3122 8326 1.

Sweet, Nanora, and Julie Melnyk, eds. *Felicia Hemans: Reimagining Poetry in the Nineteenth Century*. Palgrave. [2001] pp. xxix + 242. £47.50 ISBN 0 3338 0109 1.

Tambling, Jeremy. *Becoming Posthumous: Life and Death in Literary Cultural Studies*. EdinUP. [2001] pp. ix + 158. £15.99 ISBN 0 7486 1477 X.

Tasker, Meg. *Struggle and Storm: The Life and Death of Francis Adams*. MelbourneUP. [2001] pp. xii + 259. $39.95 ISBN 0 5228 4946 6.

Taylor, Philip, and Susan Taylor. *Jonathan Dewhurst: The Lancashire Tragedian, 1837–1913*. Book Guild. [2001] pp. xvi + 240. £16.95 ISBN 0 8577 6524 9.

Teachman, Debra. *Understanding Jane Eyre: A Student Casebook to Issues, Sources, and Historical Documents*. Greenwood. [2001] pp. xvii + 212. $39.95 ISBN 0 3133 0939 6.

Thackeray, William Makepeace. *Vanity Fair: A Novel Without a Hero*. Modern Library Classics. [2001] pp. xvi + 746. $7.95 ISBN 0 3757 5726 0.

Thesing, William B., ed. *Late Nineteenth- and Early Twentieth-Century Women Poets*. Dictionary of Literary Biography 240. Gale. [2001] pp. xix + 436. $175 ISBN 0 7876 4657 1.

Thompson, Brian. *The Disastrous Life of Mrs. Georgina Weldon: The Lifes, Loves, and Lawsuits of a Legendary Victorian*. Doubleday. [2001] pp. 343. $26 ISBN 0 3855 0090 4.

Thurschwell, Pamela. *Literature, Technology and Magical Thinking, 1880–1920*. CUP. [2001] pp. x + 194. £35 ISBN 0 5218 0168 0.

Trollope, Anthony. *The Way We Live Now*. Modern Library Classics. [2001] pp. xx + 864. $11.95 ISBN 0 3757 5731 7.

Trotter, David. *Paranoid Modernism: Literary Experiment, Psychosis, and the Professionalization of English Society*. OUP. [2001] pp. 358. £35 ISBN 0 1981 8755 6.

Updike, Daniel Berkeley. *Printing Types: Their History, Forms and Use*. OakK. [2001] pp. xlvi + 329. $85 ISBN 1 5845 6056 8.

Van Arsdel, Rosemary T. *Florence Fenwick Miller: Victorian Feminist, Journalist and Educator*. Ashgate. [2001] pp. 316. £45 ISBN 0 7546 0331 8.

Waddington, Patrick. *A Modest Little Banquet at the Arts Club; or, How William Ralston Shedden-Ralston Gave a Grand Dinner Party for Sixteen Literary Men in London on 22 October 1881 to Honour Ivan Sergeyevich Turgenev*. Privately printed. [2001]. Available from the author c/o Department of English, University of Auckland, Auckland, New Zealand.

Walder, Dennis, ed. *The Nineteenth-Century Novel: Identities*. Routledge. [2001] pp. vii + 368. $29.95 ISBN 0 4152 3827 7.

Waterston, Elizabeth. *Rapt in Plaid: Canadian Literature and Scottish Tradition*. UTorP. [2001] pp. x + 344. $45 ISBN 0 8020 4785 8.

Watt, Ian. *The Rise of the Novel*. UCalP. [2001] pp. 339. $17.95 ISBN 0 5202 3069 8.

Weliver, Phyllis. *Women Musicians in Victorian Fiction, 1860–1900: Representations of Music, Science and Gender in the Leisured Home*. Music in 19th-Century Britain. Ashgate. [2000] x + 330. $79.95 ISBN 0 7546 0126 9.

Welsh, Alexander. *Hamlet and his Modern Guises*. PrincetonUP. [2001] pp. xii + 178. $32.50 ISBN 0 6910 5093 7.

Werven, Diederik Lüch van. *Dutch Readings of George Eliot, 1856–1885*. Typographical Academica Traiectina Utrecht. [2001] pp. 192. ISBN 9 0769 1215 7.

Wood, Jane. *Passion and Pathology in Victorian Fiction*. OUP [2001] pp. viii + 232. £45 ISBN 0 1981 8760 2.

Wood, Sarah, *Robert Browning: A Literary Life*. Literary Lives. Palgrave. [2001] pp. xvii + 232. £47.50 ISBN 0 3336 4337 2.

Wright, David. *Mental Disability in Victorian England: The Earlswood Asylum, 1847–1901*. OUP. [2001] pp. xii + 244. £40 ISBN 0 1992 4639 4.

Wright, Denis. *The English amongst the Persians: Imperial Lives in Nineteenth-Century Iran*. I.B. Tauris. [2001] pp. xv + 218. £14.99 ISBN 1 8606 4638 7.

Wullschlager, Jackie. *Hans Christian Andersen: The Life of a Storyteller*. Knopf. [2001] pp. vii + 489. $30 ISBN 0 6794 5508 6.

Wynne, Deborah. *The Sensation Novel and the Victorian Family Magazine*. Palgrave. [2001] pp. x + 202. $62 ISBN 0 3337 7666 6.

XIV

Modern Literature

JULIAN COWLEY, COLIN GRAHAM, CHRIS HOPKINS, DANIEL
LEA, PAUL POPLAWSKI, JOHN NASH, NANCY PAXTON, JOHN
BRANNIGAN, MAGGIE B. GALE, MALCOLM PAGE, JO GILL
AND FRAN BREARTON

This chapter has eight sections: 1. General; 2. Pre-1945 Fiction; 3. Post-1945 Fiction; 4. Pre-1950 Drama; 5. Post-1950 Drama; 6. Pre-1950 Poetry; 7. Post-1950 Poetry; 8. Irish Poetry. Section 1(a) is by Julian Cowley; section 1(b) is by Colin Graham; section 2(a) is by Chris Hopkins; sections 2(b–d) are by Daniel Lea; section 2(e) is by Paul Poplawski; section 2(f) is by John Nash; section 2(g) is by Nancy Paxton; section 3 is by John Brannigan; section 4 is by Maggie B. Gale; section 5 is by Malcolm Page; section 6 is by Jo Gill; section 7 is by John Brannigan; section 8 is by Fran Brearton. The section on the English novel 1900–1930, by Lynne Hapgood, has been omitted this year, but will cover 2001–2 publications in *YWES* 83.

1. General

(a) British
In *Literary Value/Cultural Power: Verbal Arts in the Twenty-First Century*, a series of brief probes into complex issues, Lynette Hunter continues her investigation of 'situated textuality', where 'common grounds for value cohere not only around similarity but around the recognition of the differences in which we participate' (p. x). Hunter starts from the question 'What is literary value?', looking into the terms under which certain contemporary writers have entered a canonical mainstream of English literature sustained within the matrix of publishing and educational institutions. She examines the fate of new writing from Canada and the Indian subcontinent, referring to work by Githa Hariharan, Salman Rushdie, Margaret Atwood, and Michael Ondaatje amongst others. The third chapter investigates oral performance techniques in texts by black writers, including Wilson Harris, Claire Harris, and E. Kamau Brathwaite. Communal authorship and ownership of stories is considered in relation to First Nation or aboriginal peoples in North America. Hunter evaluates the challenge posed by electronic communication to traditional

publishing values and ponders the aesthetic value of hypertext. Letters, diaries, and life-writing come under scrutiny. Finally, Hunter sketches textual communities within which value in verbal arts may be determined.

Paul Cobley begins *Narrative* by asserting that fundamentally narrative 'consists of signs' and is 'a sequence which starts and moves inexorably to its end'. He differentiates his key term from 'story' and 'plot'. Matters grow more intricate as Cobley elaborates theories of narrative space and time and outlines ontogenetic and phylogenetic positions on the origin of narrative practices. Subsequent chapters chart the development of narrative from pre-literacy to postmodernism, citing along the way texts that signalled the novel's rise and alluding to a wide range of secondary authorities, diverse in their views and modes of interpretation. Discussion of *Middlemarch* forms the heart of a chapter on realist representation. Moves beyond realism are sketched with reference to *Heart of Darkness*. Cobley takes *A Portrait of the Artist as a Young Man* as his starting point for commentary upon modernism in relation to the new narrative technologies and devices of cinema, and John Fowles's *The French Lieutenant's Woman* serves as his literary touchstone for an outline of postmodernism that also addresses the impact of television. The concluding chapter ventures into cyberspace, unpacking the narrative implications of computers, the internet and hypertext before returning to broader consideration of the issue of narrative signs. As an introductory guide, *Narrative* is dense but well organized and furnished with a helpful glossary and bibliography.

'Immersion' and 'interactivity' are often cited as defining qualities of computer-generated virtual reality. In *Narrative as Virtual Reality: Immersion and Interactivity in Literature and Electronic Media*, Marie-Laure Ryan transfers these qualities to the literary domain and installs them as cornerstones of a phenomenology of reading. Jean Baudrillard and Pierre Lévy are brought to bear on the optical and scholastic potential of virtuality. Maurice Merleau-Ponty is drawn upon for insights into 'the embodied nature of perception'; Gaston Bachelard for his concept of 'elemental imagination'. Literary engagement with 'artificial realities' is shown in texts by Baudelaire and Huysmans. The immersive character of textual worlds is explored in depth, with literary reference ranging from Emily Brontë to Italo Calvino. Interactivity is approached through ludic texts, with particular reference to the Oulipo group, and there are regular references to theorists and practitioners of literary hypertext, including Michael Joyce. Participatory interactivity in various media is considered as a reconciliation of immersive and interactive experiences. Ryan rethinks 'textuality, mimesis, narrative, literary theory, and the cognitive processing of texts' (p. 1) in the light of possibilities opened up by new electronic technologies, and her conclusion outlines a viable place for literature within the current media landscape.

'We have no more beginnings', declares George Steiner at the start of *Grammars of Creation*, his book of linked essays originating in the Gifford Lectures at the University of Glasgow [1990]. He proceeds to reflect upon origins and ends, being and nothingness, creation and destructiveness, invention and sterility at the close of a century of unprecedented public violence. Solitude, privacy, and exile are considered as conditions for creative action. Heidegger remains a touchstone for Steiner's pronouncements as he surveys productions in the arts from Dante and Cervantes to Dada and Celan.

Tim Woods has compiled a *Who's Who of Twentieth-Century Novelists*, a helpful reference guide to a selection of significant novelists from numerous countries. Woods, conscious of the pitfalls of the selection process, aims to present writers who have been shapers of genre, market, audience, form and perspective. He also seeks to retrieve neglected individuals and overlooked areas of fiction. Emphasis falls on the post-1945 period, recognizing that many pre-war authors have received extensive documentation elsewhere and acknowledging the multiplicity of literatures that emerged with national independence movements after 1945. The first entry is Ahmad Abbas, the Punjabi writer, followed by Kobe Abe from Japan, Austrian-born American Walter Abish, South African Peter Abrahams, Chinua Achebe from Nigeria, New Yorker Kathy Acker, and Londoner Peter Ackroyd. Such juxtapositions and clusters are stimulating, and Woods has been resourceful in the scope of his choices and the concision of his summaries. Popular writers such as Barbara Cartland and Douglas Adams find their way in, but few readers will fail to encounter some unfamiliar names. Many entries conclude with recommendation of a secondary text. An appendix lists winners of the Nobel, Pulitzer, and Booker McConnell literary prizes from their inception to 2000.

Susan Watkins's *Twentieth-Century Women Novelists: Feminist Theory into Practice* is an introduction to feminist critical theory, offering a series of readings in literary texts while suggesting possible underlying connections between theoretical positions and characteristics of the fiction. Watkins is cautious in establishing the necessarily provisional nature of her account. The opening chapter, 'First-Wave Feminism', touches on Woolf and de Beauvoir to find a route into a short story by Doris Lessing, which is then fed back to reflect upon theory. That effective feedback model is sustained throughout the study. 'Liberal Feminism' sets up interaction between Betty Friedan's writing and Alison Lurie's *The War between the Tates*; 'Marxist Feminism' between Sheila Rowbotham, Michèle Barrett, and Lessing's *The Golden Notebook*; 'Psychoanalytic Feminism' between Juliet Mitchell, Nancy Chodorow, and Margaret Atwood's *Lady Oracle*; 'Poststructuralist Feminism' between Hélène Cixous, Luce Irigaray, Julia Kristeva, and Woolf's *Orlando*; 'Postmodernism and Feminism' between Alice Jardine, Seyla Benhabib, and Angela Carter's *Nights at the Circus*; 'Lesbian Feminism and Queer Theory' between Adrienne Rich, Monique Wittig, Judith Butler, and Jeanette Winterson's *Sexing the Cherry*; 'Black Feminism and Post-Colonial Theory' between Barbara Smith, Gayatri Chakravorty Spivak, bell hooks, and Toni Morrison's *Sula*. Emphasis falls repeatedly upon the importance of storytelling as a means to cultivate and adapt identity.

Political and Social Issues in British Women's Fiction, 1928–1968 is a matter-of-fact title and Elizabeth Maslen is purposeful in her handling of neglected texts which she shows to address important and sensitive issues in complex and often indirect ways. Maslen is alert to authorial blind spots and to significant communication taking place through ostensibly lightweight fiction. She has chosen 1928 as the year of universal suffrage; 1968 as a year of political unrest that saw the emergence of new-wave feminism. This study restores to visibility figures such as Storm Jameson, Phyllis Bottome, Pamela Frankau, Clemence Dane, Edith Pargeter and Susan Ertz. The list of novels referred to is extensive and includes writers such as Naomi Mitchison and Sylvia Townsend Warner, who are currently receiving significant critical attention elsewhere. An initial consideration of viable modes of writing extends from varieties of realism to Christine Brooke-Rose's innovative departures. Literary responses to war are investigated, emphasis falling on shared concern to defend severely threatened democratic values, while a pacifist core is identified in women's writing of the 1950s and 1960s. Maslen indicates shifting margins within fictional framing of issues of class and race from 1920s novels such as Ellen Wilkinson's *Clash* to 1960s works by Lynne Reid Banks and Maureen Duffy. Issues of gender and sexual roles are surveyed, from contexts of domesticity through rebelliousness to progressive social change.

In *The Feminine Middlebrow Novel, 1920s to 1950s: Class, Domesticity and Bohemianism* Nicola Humble boldly shifts that contentious term 'middlebrow' to the critical foreground and announces her intention to rehabilitate it. The inter-war years, she points out, manifested a pronounced interest in the nature of popular reading habits, with cultural commentators such as Q.D. Leavis and Orwell offering an analysis of trends. Humble makes overt links between 'middlebrow' tastes and middle-class identities. Her approach is thematic, gathering together disparate fiction by authors including Angela Thirkell, Dodie Smith, Elizabeth Taylor, Ivy Compton-Burnett, E.M. Delafield, Rachel Ferguson and Nancy Mitford in order to examine representation of home, family, sexuality, gender and class identities and to displace monolithic conception, gravitating towards modernism, of the period's values. The 'middlebrow' novel, she argues, offers 'a shared cultural fantasy of a middle class freed to a degree from the restraints it had traditionally imposed upon itself' (p. 148).

In *Writing the Meal: Dinner in the Fiction of Early Twentieth-Century Women*, Diane McGee posits that 'individual perspectives on and responses to dinners can signify a more general attitude toward society: whether alienation, insecurity, rebellion, challenge, passivity, or complacency' (p. 6). She looks at meals in fiction by early twentieth-century women writers, in particular Edith Wharton, Katherine Mansfield, Virginia Woolf, and Kate Chopin. Her opening chapter draws on anthropological discourse to make a case for recognizing the meal as a communicative text. The second briefly surveys trends during that period in the conceptualization and organization of dining in England and America. Wharton's fiction is read for its depiction of manners, set to a standard agreed amongst a socially elite group and contributing to that group's self-definition. Dining arrangements in Mansfield's short stories are considered indicative of modern homelessness; depiction of meals aids disclosure of women caught between liberation and alienation. Woolf's hostesses Mrs Dalloway and Mrs Ramsay are regarded as part of the novelist's interrogation of the established ideological model of women's domestic work as a civilizing influence. Chopin's fictional dinners are seen to help chart the awakening of Edna Pontellier.

Susan Rowland's *From Agatha Christie to Ruth Rendell: British Women Writers in Detective and Crime Fiction* is, self-evidently, a study of crime fiction by women. In addition to Christie and Rendell, Rowland looks at Dorothy L. Sayers. Margery Allingham, Ngaio Marsh and P.D. James. In her preface she reveals that her book's real subject is readerly pleasure. Later that pleasure is placed under psychoanalytic scrutiny. After a series of biographical sketches of the writers plus speculation on the bearing such details might have had on their fiction, Rowland offers forty-two case studies of 'key texts' arranged thematically in groups. The genre is considered in terms of gender, and her chosen writers are defended against the charge of uncomplicated conservatism. Their overt and implied positions on English identity and issues of race and colonialism are examined. Detective fiction's inheritance of Gothic conventions is discussed and its metaphysical dimensions (with emphasis on the occult) are delineated. Finally, Rowland examines representations of women by these so-called queens of crime and discerns the ethics of a moderate feminism in the aesthetic of detective novels. The findings of her conversations with Rendell and James are reported in brief appendices.

The studies in media and book history that form Laurel Brake's *Print in Transition, 1850–1910: Studies in Media and Book History* have at their core findings from her sustained enquiry into 'the nature of serialization and serials'. Brake is especially interested in those instructive moments when 'there is a collapse of barriers between what is now the high culture of book history and what is deemed the popular culture of ephemera' (p. 33). At such points attention to late nineteenth-century material print culture discloses texts existing as commodities within an expanding market, charged with 'differing potentials for meaning' from those assigned within high-cultural perspectives. Brake investigates issues of gender in the *Westminster Review*, identifies visible gay discourse in *The Artist* prior to the Wilde trials, reads the *Yellow Book* in terms of gender and its participation in the new journalism, and looks into advertising in the *Savoy*. The concluding section of the book is an extended examination of Walter Pater's publishing career. An afterword testifies to the value of archival research amongst paper as well as electronically reproduced documents.

Quinn and Trout, eds., *The Literature of the Great War Reconsidered: Beyond Modern Memory* explores the impact of recent changes on our understanding of the First World War as 'a cultural event' and of our expanded conception of what constitutes 'war literature'. Chris Hopkins attends to narratives of the war, offering analysis of William Bishop's autobiographical account, *Winged Warfare of 1918*. Glenn R. Wilkinson sifts newspaper reports in search of imagery corresponding to attitudes that gave momentum to the breaking conflict. Debra Rae Cohen argues that the interplay of realism and fantasy in the wartime novels of Stella Benson sheds light on conflicting ideologies on the home front. Terry Phillips looks into May Sinclair's pro-war writing and finds a concern with identity, gender, and the transcendent rather than an uncomplicated response to propaganda. Deborah Tyler-Bennett examines poetry by women, including Edith Sitwell, Iris Tree, and 'the undeservedly obscure' Phyllis M'egroz. Allesandria Polizzi discloses an ignored version of history in the writings of catalytic modernist Harriet Monroe. Nancy Sloan Goldberg investigates how French women poets responded to the conflict. Donna Coates finds differing agendas in fiction by women from Australia, Canada, and New Zealand. Mary R. Ryder examines responses by American authors Edith Wharton and Dorothy Canfield Fisher. Milton A. Cohen identifies a symbiotic relationship between modernism and the war, in terms of language and disruptive action. He appends a catalogue of killed, wounded, and displaced artists. William Blazek focuses upon the primitivism of e.e. cummings's *The Enormous Room*. John Gibson addresses Owen's poetry and letters from the angle of social class; Malcolm Pittock offers a dissenting reappraisal of Owen's achievement. Patrick Campbell links Sassoon with psychoanalyst W.H.R. Rivers in a discussion of repression of war experience, and Patrick Quinn depicts Sassoon between the two world wars.

David Trotter's *Paranoid Modernism* is subtitled *Literary Experiment, Psychosis and the Professionalization of English Society*. The word 'paranoia' is taken to designate 'some aspects of masculinity's continual refurbishment' or, following Freud, reconstruction after breakdown (p. 11). Fantasizing 'the means to a place in the world', paranoia is shown to have become a focus for the modernist critique of social mimesis. Trotter offers a concise history of paranoia, then looks into Freud's analysis of the notorious case of Daniel Schreber, with a cursory glance at fantasy fiction by M.P. Shiel. Cultural deployment of paranoid fantasy in pursuit of professional status during the nineteenth century, in Rousseau's wake, is investigated with specific reference to William Godwin, Dickens and Wilkie Collins. The rise of 'professional society' in England between 1880 and the First World War is registered in work by Wells. Buchan is invoked to identify the structuring principle of 'paranoid symmetry' in Edwardian spy fiction. Trotter finds the structural break in Conrad's amalgam of modernist experiment and turn-of-the-century popular romance, *Lord Jim*, to be consistent with strategies of paranoid narrative. Turning attention to Conrad's impressionist ally, he asks 'What was the matter with Ford?' Prefaced by mention of T.E. Hulme, he investigates the 'will-to-abstraction' in writings by Wyndham Lewis, including his depiction of persecution mania in *Tarr*, and by D.H. Lawrence, including *Women in Love* and 'The Prussian Officer' considered as a case-study in insanity. Trotter concludes that for Ford, Lewis and Lawrence paranoia was a method and an imaginative resource.

Brad Bucknell's *Literary Modernism and Musical Aesthetics: Pater, Pound, Joyce and Stein* interrogates a widespread modernist belief that music possesses a special capacity for deep significance and a kind of higher coherence beyond the reach of words. He contrasts Wagner's faith in 'potential totality' with Mallarmé's 'notion of the mysterious fulfilment of meaning in deferment'. Bucknell is alert to the possibility that literature aspiring to the condition of music might consequently produce representations of a particular kind of inwardness. He scrutinizes Pater's assumption that music, although temporal in its nature, can serve as the paradigm for all arts. He identifies Joyce's 'amplification of the codes of hearing as these construct the multiple spaces of Dublin' (p. 223), outlines Pound's efforts to incorporate music into his 'practice of an aesthetics of absolute immanence' (p. 223), and suggests that Stein and composer Virgil Thomson, in their collaborative operas, succeeded in making music 'part of the articulation of the complexities of meaning and expression' rather than their resolution (p. 222). In conclusion, Bucknell offers the suggestion that music's real significance for modernist writers was 'the excess of time and history as they collide with and shape the composition … in ways unforeseen and uncontrollable by any aesthetic design', an anxious return of artistic production to history and the social realm.

Papers from the Second International Conference on Word and Music Studies held at Ann Arbor, Michigan in August 1999 form the basis for essays collected in Bernhart and Wolf, eds., *Words and Music Studies: Essays on the Song Cycle and on Defining the Field*. The section entitled 'Defining the Field' opens with John Neubauer's helpful critique of organicist aesthetics in modernist literature and music. Michael Halliwell looks at tensions between words and music in Richard Meale and David Malouf's operatic version of Patrick White's *Voss*. Mary Breatnach examines Baudelaire's response to Wagner. Peter Dayan probes Mallarmé's silence with respect to specific musical works. Frédérique Arroyas ponders terms of musico-literary analogy with especial reference to the 'blended space' of Roger Laporte's *nouveau roman*, *Fugue* [1970]. The second section of the book addresses issues in the analysis of song cycles, from Franz Schubert and Robert Schumann to Paul Simon.

Martin Halliwell's aim in *Modernism and Morality: Ethical Devices in European and American Fiction* is to shed light on the moral anxieties that pervade the pluralistic discourse of modernism, even as they are denied by its practitioners. Halliwell starts by reading decadent attitudes towards Victorian morality in texts by Huysmans, Wilde, and Proust. He then discusses responses to America's perceived moral inertia in naturalistic fiction by Wharton and Norris. He unpacks metaphors of illness in Gide's *The Immoralist* and Mann's *Death in Venice*, examines attempts to reinvent a moral trajectory through the extreme strategies of Dada and surrealism, and investigates the contrasting roles of idiocy in Conrad's *The Secret Agent* and Faulkner's *The Sound and the Fury*. American expatriates in Paris are shown deploying exile, literary experimentalism and an aesthetics of pleasure to explore alternative gender identities. Visions of America in works by Kafka and Lorca are assessed as recognitions of cultural and ethnic Otherness. Musil, Hesse, Hurston, and Henry Roth illustrate the moral consequences of 'adventure' in the modernist picaresque. Klaus Mann's 'magico-political tale' *Mephisto* is reviewed in the historical context of Nazi Germany. A concluding chapter looks to Christa Wolf and Paul Auster to register a preserved sense of moral agency in 'a world of diminished possibilities'.

The long opening chapter of Murray Roston's *The Search for Selfhood in Modern Literature* traces the malaise reflected by early twentieth-century writers such as D.H. Lawrence, Huxley, Yeats, Eliot and Kafka about the impact on moral judgement of Darwinian and Freudian models of human nature. Following this familiar analysis of a modernist 'crisis of identity', Roston addresses subsequent responses found in writing from the 1940s to the late 1960s. The allure of communism for intellectuals in search of a viable faith provides a context for reading Arthur Koestler's attack on Stalinism in *Darkness at Noon*. Greene's *The Power and the Glory* is identified as an early presentation of the anti-hero figure, soon to become widespread during a period when the human individual's reduced significance was strongly felt. A chapter traces loss of consolatory belief in uncorrupted childhood and emergence, in Salinger's Holden Caulfield and Philip Roth's Alexander Portnoy, of the adolescent rebel as a kind of compensatory type. Alienation and absurdity are found in obvious places in drama: Osborne, Beckett, Pinter, Albee. Rosten concludes his study of disparate indicative instances with scrutiny of John Barth's existentialist orientation, the despair of Plath at 'a merciless world', and Baldwin's depiction of human suffering in *Another Country*.

Smith and Wallace, eds., *Gothic Modernisms*, collects essays that aim to disclose subterranean connections between modernism's perceived elitism and the mass appeal of the Gothic. David Punter configures haunted tales by Bowen, Conrad and de la Mare. David Glover looks back from one of May Sinclair's *Uncanny Stories* to detect troubling textual spectres lurking in Conrad's *Heart of Darkness* and Ford's *The Inheritors*. David Seed couples Sinclair with Virginia Woolf in his study of transformations of the supernatural made in accordance with new models of mental life. Judith Wilt explores other aspects of Woolf's fascination with ghosts. Djuna Barnes's *Nightwood* lends itself readily to Avril Horner and Sue Zlosnik's analysis of waywardness and instability shared by modernist discourse and Gothic legacy. Deborah Tyler-Bennett identifies Gothic elements elsewhere in Barnes's writing. Jeff Wallace looks at 'living death' in Joyce's *Dubliners* as a manifestation of 'the generalised ghostliness of bourgeois societies'. Kelly Hurley attends to disjointed narratives and fragmented identities in William Hope Hodgson's monstrous fictions. Andrew Smith writes on D.H. Lawrence's use of images of vampirism to focus his ideas on degeneracy. Francesca Orestano addresses Wyndham Lewis's 'violent vitality' and 'subversive dynamism' and the Gothic vorticism of his *Self Condemned*. Essays on the films *Metropolis* and *Sunset Boulevard* are also included.

John Peck's *Maritime Fiction* is subtitled *Sailors and the Sea in British and American Novels, 1719–1917*. Its more weighty concern is with the fictional registration of the effects of a flourishing maritime economy upon 'the political, social and cultural character of the nation', and with the forms of injustice and curtailments of individual liberty that can underpin ostensible success. His survey harks back to Homer before steering a steady course towards Conrad by way of Defoe, Smollett, Austen, Marryat, Dickens, Cooper, Poe, Dana, Melville, Stevenson, and Kipling. Peck argues that the stature of Melville and Conrad as authors of maritime fiction corresponds to the decline of maritime influence within their respective nations. Their unrivalled achievement signals an imminent waning of the capacity of tales of the sea to sustain broad social analysis. With Conrad, he suggests, loss of confidence in the sea story as a literary form tallies with more general loss of confidence, the crumbling of generic conventions corresponding to the onset of a widespread state of collapse.

Felix Driver, historian of human geography, has written *Geography Militant: Cultures of Exploration and Empire*, an investigation of relations between geographical knowledge and cultures of exploration with their freight of contested meanings associated with science, literature, religion, commerce and empire. The title derives from a late essay by Conrad, where it signifies an epoch between 'Geography Fabulous' and 'Geography Triumphant', a phase of Western exploration when 'open spaces' on the globe were still available for 'heroic' enterprise. Driver locates the Royal Geographical Society within the histories of scientific exploration and of empire and examines the place of its manual *Hints to Travellers* within the discipline of observation in the field. He examines critically the contemporary reputations of David Livingstone, H.M. Stanley, and novelist, adventurer, and 'martyr' Winwood Reade. He scrutinizes Africa exhibited in London at the end of the nineteenth century, and 'darkest England', mapped by William Booth through his adoption of the language of social exploration. The afterlife of 'Geography Militant' is briefly delineated in discourses of tourism, advertising, popular magazines, fashion, and collections of memorabilia.

Jonathan Rose, in *The Intellectual Life of the British Working Classes*, argues against theoretically grounded analyses of canon formation and the cultural and political implications arising from it. He opts instead for an investigative method that tackles the pragmatics of working-class reading experiences, and concludes that, 'far from reinscribing traditional ideologies, canonical literature tended to ignite insurrections in the minds of workers' (p. 9). Observing that the doctrinal texts of the emerging Labour party were in effect the canon of classic literature, he contends that 'classic conservative texts could make plebeian readers militant and articulate' (p. 39). His study refers back to the sixteenth century, but focuses mainly on the industrial working classes of the nineteenth and twentieth centuries. He discusses the movement for mutual improvement and consequences of the 1870 Education Act. Literary figures including Flora Thompson, Catherine Cookson, Alison Uttley, and V.S. Pritchett are amongst those bearing witness to intellectual adventure they found in books and to the contribution it made to their personal growth. Rose writes about J.M. Dent's Everyman Library, the Welsh Miners' Libraries, Ruskin College, the Workers' Educational Association, and the BBC's Third Programme. He considers the failure of Marxism to become effectively established in Britain in relation to the challenging nature of its key texts. Following Orwell's lead in 'Boy's Weekly' Rose examines the impact of school yarns. He looks at responses to thrillers, American literature and Hollywood cinema. He outlines Charlie Chaplin's heuristic reading habits, considers Hugh MacDiarmid as a political radical and 'intellectual snob', and compares Forster's characterization of Leonard Bast with actual reading experience amongst clerical workers, including novelist Richard Church. The concluding chapter ventures into Bloomsbury and Bohemia in company with various working-class commentators, and Rose bemoans 'the withering away of the autodidact tradition' (p. 464).

In *Einstein's Wake: Relativity, Metaphor and Modernist Literature*, Michael H. Whitworth examines certain metaphors occurring in modernist literature and in contemporaneous scientific discourse. His focus falls largely upon periodical publications, which he takes to correspond in specific ways to those social networks that fostered modernist attitudes and beliefs. After sketching the significance of populist, generalist, and specialist positions for developments in science, Whitworth homes in upon Conrad's *The Secret Agent* as an instance of literary entropy. D.H. Lawrence, Woolf, T.S. Eliot and Huxley are touchstones elsewhere in this study. A chapter addresses 'descriptionism', which supported 'the idea that representations of reality were selective shorthands' (p. 110) and fed a new rapprochement between the literary and scientific domains. Changing conceptions of matter, conditions of simultaneity, and non-Euclidean geometries are discerned in both fields. Whitworth has tracked down occasional direct reference by modernist writers to scientific theory; elsewhere he speculates on the extent of their awareness of developments, but his main preoccupation is with the apparent concurrence of figurative language.

David L. Wilson and Zack Bowen's *Science and Literature: Bridging the Two Cultures* is conceived as a dialogue that aspires to form the bridge of the subtitle by uncovering similarities of motive and method. An overt dialogic format is observed: for example, Wilson's brief survey of scientific accounts of the origins of the universe is followed by Bowen's musings on the Genesis account, and that given in a short story by John Barth. Originating in an undergraduate course, the book is conversational in tone, pitched at a general yet relatively well-informed reader's assumed level of understanding. It works with specific and predictable examples while positing the existence of universal problems which science and the humanities can address in their own distinctive and sometimes complementary ways. Broad issues such as 'language and uncertainty' and 'ethics within science' are broached. Fowles's *The French Lieutenant's Woman* is read against the Darwinian paradigm; Pynchon's *The Crying of Lot 49* against thermodynamic and information theory. The dystopian vision of Huxley's *Brave New World* is re-evaluated, and revolutions in scientific thinking are contrasted with the cyclical version of history outlined by Yeats in *A Vision*.

Tilmann Vetter's introduction to Barfoot, ed., *Aldous Huxley: Between East and West*, offers a broad overview of Huxley's ideas about religion, and his shifting alignments with positions ranging from materialism to mysticism. Subsequent essays tap into his fiction, plays, poetry, and essays and bring contextual materials to bear to track key shifts: early exposure to the values of his family (especially his novelist aunt Mary Ward); early modernist cultural disorientation; deep personal concerns about uncontrolled science and over-regulated society; creative engagements with Utopian conceptions; encounters with Buddhism and Eastern spirituality, and experimentation with psychedelic drugs. In two concluding essays Albrecht Wezler and the late Wilhelm Halbfass correct erroneous claims that Indian philosophical tradition validates the attribution of religious significance to such drug experience.

In *Henry James and the Art of Dress*, Clair Hughes unpacks social and textual meanings encoded in James's fiction in the language of fashion: conspicuous consumption complicated within a transatlantic discourse in *Daisy Miller* and 'The Pension Beaurepas'; irony of dress in *Washington Square*; symbolic notations in *The Portrait of a Lady*; characterization through tell-tale attire in *The Wings of a Dove*; the importance of hats as 'odd but insistent grace-notes' in *The Princess Casamassima*; the implications of 'muffling' and 'uncovering' in *The Ambassadors*; the significance of overdressing and sensuous adornment in *The Golden Bowl*; the revelatory role of clothing in the ghost stories. Working largely with James's hints and nuances rather than such overt description as he both admired and mistrusted in Balzac, Hughes draws on 'the material evidence of contemporary dress to try to approximate the clothes James was likely to have in mind' (p. 3). That secondary evidence is utilized with apt discrimination and its effect is persuasive and illuminating. A discerning eye is also cast over cinematic interpretations of James's novels.

Nikki Gamble's introduction to Tucker and Gamble, *Family Fictions*, takes on the large task of tracing the development of changing representations of the family in children's fiction taking into account social, political, and economic influences. A single chapter is clearly inadequate for such an ambitious project, but in preparation for reading contemporary children's literature Gamble does offer glimpses of pertinent antecedents and a sense of the scope of current writing that may serve to unsettle naive assumptions. The focus narrows in the book's three other chapters, where Gamble investigates Morris Gleitzman, and her co-author Nicholas Tucker writes on Anna Fine and Jacqueline Wilson. The capacity of these novelists to sustain narrative interest while addressing with appropriate candour the serious problems faced by children as they grow up in a difficult world is this study's central concern.

Kate Agnew and Geoff Fox's *Children at War* is, in effect, an introductory guide to literature designed for or readily accessible to young readers that deals with the experience of warfare. Fox's opening essay charts a course, profusely illustrated with quotation and close reference, 'from the cultural certainties of 1914 to the pluralism and ambiguities of 2000', from the chirpy Tommy to Gulf War trauma, from John Buchan and W.E. Johns to Raymond Briggs and Robert Westall. Agnew contributes chapters on recent fiction about the First World War, and about the Second World War as experienced in the United Kingdom and North America. Fox's closing essay examines late twentieth-century fiction about the Second World

War set in mainland Europe. The authors extend their survey across a wide range of writing, disclosing numerous facets of that complexity of response, common to disparate texts, which forms the mainstay of their argument.

Kimberley Reynolds, Geraldine Brennan and Kevin McCarron have co-authored *Frightening Fiction*. Reynolds supplies an introductory chapter which addresses the broad issues arising from the publication of books for children, including *X-Files* narratives and *Buffy* texts, that might be taken to constitute a new genre of 'frightening fiction'. McCarron investigates the appeal of the popular 'Point Horror' series, paying particular attention to the thrillers of R.L. Stine and supernatural tales by Caroline B. Cooney. He also examines Robert Westall's novelistic manipulation of fear. In the closing chapter Brennan looks at sinister games played out in fiction written for young adolescents by David Almond, Philip Gross and Lesley Howarth.

Peter Hunt and Millicent Lenz share authorship of *Alternative Worlds in Fantasy Fiction*. Hunt's introduction considers evaluations of fantasy literature, ranging from its dismissal as childish, reactionary or inconsequential to enthusiastic endorsement of a serious and potentially subversive genre. Hunt efficiently surveys fantasy's history and conveys a sense of the range of alternative worlds it offers. Lenz then narrows the focus to sketch a map of Ursula Le Guin's 'Earthsea' cycle. In the following chapter Hunt addresses Terry Pratchett's 'Discworld' series, and, to conclude, Lenz investigates Philip Pullman's trilogy, *His Dark Materials*. An underlying concern throughout is how fantasy can gloss or intervene in the passage from childhood to maturity.

Roberts, ed., *A Companion to Twentieth-Century Poetry*, engages consciously with a 'vast, heterogeneous and paradoxical' field within literatures in English. Roberts notes at the start that the subject 'exists because of the successive historical phenomena of British imperialism and American cultural, economic and political dominance' (p. 1), yet registration of the erosion of those centre–periphery structures is a vital component of the book's organization. Hugh Witemeyer writes on modernist interaction of European and American energies. Peter Brooker and Simon Perril then unravel 'the text of modernism' knotted around Pound and Eliot by recalling precursors of its purported newness. Subsequent chapters survey non-modernist Edwardians and Georgians, imagism, the Harlem Renaissance, new critical verse, Black Mountain College and Olson's projective verse, the Beats, confessional writing, the Movement, mid-century interrupted monologue, and language poetry. Other essays examine intersections of poetry with politics, war, science and technologies, literary theory, and gender. There are summary views of poetry from the West Indies, Africa, the Indian subcontinent, Australia, New Zealand, Canada, Scotland, Wales, and Ireland. There are more detailed readings in selected canonical authors: Hardy, Frost, Eliot, Lawrence, Williams, Stevens, Moore, Yeats, Auden, Bishop, Pound, Lowell, MacNeice, Plath, Hughes, Heaney, Ashbery, and Walcott. A concluding section offers cursory overviews of contemporary American, British, Irish, and postcolonial poetries.

Chris Beyers's *A History of Free Verse* asks how we may best define and understand twentieth-century poetry's dominant form. The apologetics of modernist verse, he argues, involved 'aesthetic myths' that their proponents failed to recognize or acknowledge. His book surveys existing definitions of 'free verse' and scrutinizes enabling 'myths' concerning the nature of poetry, including various organicisms and adherence to 'poetic modality with prose virtues'. Beyers seeks to historicize the study of prosody. The 'loose tradition' running from Abraham Cowley's Pindaric adaptations to T.S. Eliot's work is examined. A chapter attends to ways in which traditional form haunts the poetry of Wallace Stevens; another shows the short line of imagism emerging from past poetics, placing H.D. in particular within a tradition of English poetry. Beyers identifies William Carlos Williams as the central spokesman for free verse, and investigates his creation of 'dynamic poems about still things' and his all-encompassing version of organic form. The discussion pays close attention to specific examples while analysing critically various explanations and aids to reading furnished by poets and commentators.

(b) Irish

'What difference has theory made to the study of Irish culture?' asks Claire Connolly at the beginning of her article 'Theorising Ireland' (*ISR* 9:iii[2001] 301–16). Since in this instance 'theory' in the context of Irish culture means 'theory' generated through Irish literary studies, Connolly's article is an immensely useful one. She steps back from the debates which have often haphazardly occurred in the last two decades or so and sees the rapid developments in Irish 'theory' primarily in terms of the integrity of the theoretical arguments at stake rather than reductively as a clash in which closet versions of old political debates get dressed up in the borrowed clothes of more glamorous French or postcolonial criticisms. Noting early on the kind of recalcitrance within Irish literary studies which has led to a belated theory skirmish, Connolly quotes W.J. McCormack's dislike of 'what he calls "Weetabix Theory"—"incredibly dense and regular in structure, but lighter than its box"' (p. 301). Connolly's story begins in earnest in 1983 and from an early stage, in the criticism of Seamus Deane, it is clear that the explosive and in many ways unlikely mixture of Yeats, Joyce and the Troubles in Northern Ireland will be the anachronistic cocktail of ingredients in this ongoing battle. Connolly's essay is important because, though not a blow-by-blow history of critical thought in the past twenty-odd years, it does begin to map out differences between critical alignments in more nuanced ways than has been done previously. Thus, for example, more sense is made than is usual in discussing the differences between the approaches of, say, Deane and that of the earlier work of Declan Kiberd. Often jointly glossed by their opponents' too easy label of nationalist, Kiberd's criticism of the 'callow amnesia' (p. 302) of the Irish state is shown to have a basis in a more materialist critique than Deane's. Connolly picks this up again later in implicitly countering criticisms of Kiberd's later *Inventing Ireland* by discussing Shaun Richards's reading of the book in the light of Frankfurt school thought. Connolly's wish that Richards had pursued this line further attests to an understandable impatience with the morbidly inert form of postcolonial criticism which has crept into Irish literary studies and is one way in which her essay also points towards future directions in which she, at least, might see Irish literary criticism progressing.

Future critical directions are also fascinatingly and promisingly set out in another essay published in *Irish Studies Review* in 2001. Margaret Kelleher's 'Writing Irish Women's Literary History' (*ISR* 9:i[2001] 5–14), like Connolly's article (which led to the publication of her anthology *Theorising Ireland* [2002]), is very much a report on work in progress, and its fascination lies in knowing that a major critic and scholar is working, both archivally and conceptually, in an area which has received little or no attention until now. Kelleher's article thinks very broadly about the politics of Irish women's writing and the attendant difficulties which the scholar will have in arguing for the status of this previously neglected area. Part of the subtlety of Kelleher's argument is its awareness that none of these issues is being discovered or worried over for the first time. She comments on the work of female critics such as Elizabeth Sharp, 'involved in works of retrieval a century or more ago', and others such as Elizabeth Owens Blackburne, Julia Kavanagh and Catherine Hamilton. Kelleher begins with the problems facing the recovery of these women's work, and the difficulties they faced in their own acts of recovery, but she then moves on to a discussion of how this act of scholarship (too often reduced to an act of scholarship *per se* and nothing else) can be understood through the prism of the most recent critical thinking on the place of gender in Irish criticism. Kelleher's intelligent discussion of David Lloyd's *Ireland After History*, and his Gramscian-postcolonial view of the 'subaltern', suggests that Kelleher's article here is the beginning of a project which will fill one of those genuine gaps in Irish literary studies—a theoretical analysis which is also able to carry a large and new weight of scholarship as part of its argument.

Connolly's and Kelleher's articles suggest an increasing sophistication in 'theoretical readings' of Irish literary studies (one which one hopes will eventually lead to the end of having to discuss 'theory' in scare quotes, and with the sense that its newness in Irish studies makes it the equivalent of, at best a tourist, at worst, a largely unwelcome immigrant). A special issue of the journal *Cultural Studies* (*CS* 15:i[2001]), edited by Spurgeon Thompson, on 'Irish Cultural Studies', also gives a sense of things on the move, though it is unfortunate that, as Thompson notes, most of the essays are versions of papers given at a conference in 1995, while others have obviously dated (or matured) somewhat while sitting in the press. Thompson's introduction (*CS* 15:i[2001] 1–11) is an intelligent assessment of the state of the art, while also being an argument for a particular kind of materialist Irish cultural studies which balances uneasily on an argument which both needs and excoriates the nation—Thompson admires both Luke Gibbons and David Lloyd in their reconfiguration of nationality as a necessity in need of critique 'from below'. His contributors largely bear out his ideas, though, as is typical of such ventures in Irish studies, some show themselves more comfortable with a cultural studies mode than others. Karen Steele's interesting essay, 'Biography as Promotional Discourse' (*CS* 15:i[2001] 138–60) has a title entirely fitting for *Cultural Studies*, but its content could as easily be in a more mainstream literary-critical journal. Equally 'Riverine Crossings: Gender, Identity and the Reconstruction of National Mythic Narrative in *The Crying Game*' (*CS* 15:i[2001] 173–91), by Margot Backus and James Doan (both distinguished literary critics), discusses a text which is now the exhausted and over-interpreted staple of those moving from Irish literary studies into Irish film, and which stretches the credibility of an interdisciplinary (as opposed to cultural studies) approach by seeing the film as a rerun of a Cuchulainn motif, and viewing the whole through the lens of queer theory. Some of the articles collected by Thompson do, however, point to the genuinely new. Diane Negra, for example, comes to the discipline without a literary studies background being immediately obvious, and her article 'Consuming Ireland: Lucky Charms Cereal, Irish Spring Soap and 1–800-SHAMROCK' (*CS* 15:i[2001] 76–97) is a more convincing model of what Irish cultural studies might eventually be. (Negra also published a linked article, 'The New Primitives: Irishness in Recent US Television' in *Irish Studies Review* (*ISR*

9:ii[2001] 229–39)). The lesson from this may be simply that Irish literary studies, theory, and Irish cultural studies are still something of strangers to each other's ways of thinking and speaking, and that, while it may be regrettable, theory, in the Irish case, will remain 'theory' for some time to come.

The year 2001 did see the beginning of another venture which suggests that these barriers between strictly literary studies and other disciplines will be under ever-increased pressure in the years to come. Cork University Press published the first three in a series of books entitled 'Ireland into Film' which, in the words of its own publicity, 'brings together writers and scholars from the fields of Film and Literary Studies to examine notable adaptations of Irish literary texts'. The first three books in the series are *The Dead* by Kevin Barry, *December Bride* by Lance Pettitt, and *This Other Eden* by Fidelma Farley. Kevin Barry's *The Dead* (also reviewed below in section 2(f)) is a perfect example of how the series might work: it combines excellent Joycean scholarship and a finely tuned understanding of Joyce's short story with a well-informed capacity to discuss film in specifically filmic ways; his chapter comparing Huston's *The Dead* to Rossellini's *Voyage to Italy* is excellent in illuminating Huston's technique and also has marvellously Joycean resonances.

Lance Pettitt's *December Bride* examines the film by Thaddeus O'Sullivan, adapted from Sam Hanna Bell's novel of the same title of 1951. Pettitt's book is highly researched and informative, both about O'Sullivan and Bell. He is strongest on the processes of adaptation, the necessary compromises of film-making, and in reading the thematics of film and text. In this Pettitt makes the most of his material; O'Sullivan's film is certainly, of the three discussed in first publications in the series, the most visually complex, and the film which is made furthest from the pressures of commerciality. In his chapter 'Movie Matters: Inter-Texts and Text' Pettitt sets the film in the context of the French *nouvelle vague*, Truffaut, Dreyer and Bergman, while his chapter on the production history of *December Bride* is an impressive reconstruction, using O'Sullivan's own film diaries and papers, of the practicalities of the film's making. Throughout the book Pettitt is alive to the contexts of both book and film, and is able to draw out the intimate ways in which both texts sit against the Ulster Presbyterian culture which is their cultural context. If it is characterized by a less agile critical perception than Barry's book, Pettitt's *December Bride* more than makes up for this through its understanding of film-making and its relationship to Irish and Ulster identity.

Fidelma Farley's *This Other Eden* has less substantial material to work on than either Barry or Pettitt are blessed with. The play on which the film was based, written by Louis D'Alton, a minor Abbey playwright, is, Farley argues, based on Shaw's *John Bull's Other Island*, but her arguments for the film's significance rest less on quality than, first, its importance as an Irish film directed by a woman, second, its status as the 'most accomplished' (p. 1) of the Abbey play adaptations made into film at Ardmore Studios, and third, the interest of its ways of negotiating Irish identity through what was effectively becoming a mode of cinema at the time (broadly the genre known as Ealing comedy). Farley struggles at times to make any of these arguments stick and this is, unfortunately, as much a problem with the sometimes rather leaden nature of her own criticism as it is with the passingly interesting but in the end slight sources. While the authors of these short monographs have undoubtedly been encouraged by the series editors to treat the material expansively, Farley never quite convincingly finds a generic context to enliven the reader's understanding of play or film. The Ireland into Film series, however, is a fascinating and welcome venture which will expand the canon of Irish studies texts, and certainly enable teachers and lecturers to confidently think about adding new texts to third-level courses, as well as appealing to the film buff in Ireland—a species so far badly catered for in print.

The year 2000 had seen the publication of the first volume of the New Voices in Irish Criticism series, the proceedings of an annual conference of the same title which caters for postgraduate students working in Irish studies, or more generally in literary studies in Ireland. Four Courts Press has taken on the role of publishing the proceedings of these conferences in a series of books, and the continuing success of the conferences has thus been ensured. In 2001 the second in the series was published and, like the previous volume, it gives an intriguing snapshot of the kind of doctoral work currently being undertaken in Irish literature. The second New Voices conference was held at Queen's University Belfast and, as with the first volume, those who organized it have the role of editing the proceedings. This year Alan A. Gillis and Aaron Kelly take the reins, under the title *Critical Ireland: New Essays in Literature and Culture*. Their editorial policy is to favour, frankly, the miscellaneity of what they call 'that indeterminate discipline: Irish literary criticism' (p. xii), and they do this by refusing to impose a false unity on the whole by ordering the essays alphabetically by the surnames of the contributors. This policy seems wise enough given the range of interests represented by the thirty-two essays which are published. As might be expected, Yeats, the Revival and Joyce figure large, with Nicholas Allen's essay on Æ, 'A Political Vision: George Russell and *The Interpreters*' (pp. 1–6) notably fitting the short format which the collection necessitates. Julie Anne Stevens's essay 'The Staging of Protestant Ireland in Somerville and Ross' *The Real Charlotte*' (pp. 188–95) is New Voices at its best— a too often ignored novel by neglected writers is discussed in a specific context (that of Gilbert and Sullivan operas) which is able to shed light on text, textual politics and the politics of identity in a brief space. The best pieces in these collections always hint at more argument and debate to come, and for that reason the showcase of New Voices will be a crucial part of the development of Irish criticism in the future. In *Critical Ireland* there is also a strand of writing which reveals young critics searching, with varying degrees of frustration, for a new mode or language with which to express themselves. This takes a variety of forms; Stephanie Bachorz's 'Postcolonial Theory and Ireland: Revising Postcolonialism' (pp. 6–13) is an excoriation of the poorly defined use of postcolonialism in Irish criticism (for which, according to Bachorz, the antidote is to be found in a synthesis of postcolonial theory with the kind of negative dialectic espoused by Adorno. It bears some similarities to Aaron Kelly's densely argued and at times brilliant contribution, 'Reproblematizing the Irish Text' (pp. 124–32), which also advocates a Marxian materialism to counter the phantasms which a criticism obsessed with national identity conjures for itself. Less theoretically minded, but nevertheless asking similarly searching questions about the very nature of Irish criticism is John Kenny, whose essay 'The Critic in Pieces: The Theory and Practice of Literary Reviewing' (pp. 132–41) argues that reviewing has a crucial part to play in keeping the academic world in touch with the general reader. Such self-consciousness about criticism is largely a good thing amongst those who make up each year's 'new voices', though even the more adventurously meta-critically minded may baulk at

David Cotter's 'Notes from the Rathmines Underground, or, The Spiders and the Bees' (pp. 37–41) which, when read several times, is apparently 'about' Joyce and masochism, but is in fact a long refusal to engage with academic writing because of the things it will not allow us to say. Cotter's anarchic version of deconstruction is amusing—it even has a point—but it in the end it is a self-defeating bout of self-pity. It is to the credit of Kelly, Gillis and the plurality of the New Voices project that it is included here at all.

Amongst the best of the essays in *Critical Ireland* is Paul Delaney's 'Becoming National: Daniel Corkery and the Reterritorialized Subject' (pp. 41–8). In examining Corkery, that often stereotyped originator of what seems like an unremittingly essentialist, nationalist and Catholic form of literary Irishness, or, as Delaney describes him, a 'cultural commissar' (p. 41) for de Valera's version of Irishness, Delaney argues that the typical view of Corkery assumes too easily that his work expresses an anti-colonial antagonism over which he has complete control. Instead, using the work of Homi Bhabha and Deleuze and Guattari, Delaney suggests that Corkery's work is symptomatic of more complex processes 'whereby the minor becomes major', and that 'his work might be taken as an example of the process whereby an inventive potential becomes swamped by the rhetoric of official nationalism'. As this final assessment reveals, Delaney is capable of seeing critical and cultural politics as a complex, varied process, and this marks out his work from some others in the volume. In 2001 Delaney also published 'Representations of the Travellers in the 1880s and 1900s' (*ISR* 9:i[2001] 53–68). Here Delaney, taking on an under-researched area, asks what reasons there might have been 'underlying the Literary Revival's interest in the representation of the Travellers' (p. 65). As with his work on Corkery, Delaney shows an ability to take an intelligent and forceful overview of his subject, here seeing the Revival's version of the 'tinker' in terms of literary aesthetics and cultural politics, both of which render the Traveller community in Ireland (then and now) as what Spivak calls the 'domesticated Other'. Delaney, particularly through his reading of Synge's plays (*The Tinker's Wedding* being the best-known work of the Revival explicitly about Travellers), manages to suggest that the figure of the 'tinker' is more fundamental to the definition of Irishness in the Revival than has previously been countenanced, and in a step which is typical of the convincingly bold stance he takes in both these essays, he goes on to hint that the exclusion of Travellers from Irish society is structurally replicated in Irish literature and criticism. Delaney's critical voice is one of the most sophisticated and promising to emerge (partly) through the New Voices project, and his work signals a turn towards a genuinely politically engaged 'subaltern' studies within Irish criticism, a turn often advocated but rarely given substance so far.

From the other Irish literary-critical journals published in 2001 a few contributions stand out. *Irish University Review* published 'History and Ellipsis in Elizabeth Bowen's *The Last September*' by Neil Corcoran (*IUR* 31:ii[2001] 315–33), a critic perhaps better known for his writing on poetry. Corcoran's reading of Bowen is littered with some questionably stereotypical assumptions about Irish Protestant identity, but he is on much more certain ground in interpreting the text, which he reads with an empathy that enhances the novel's status. Discussing the 'Gothic' nature of some elements of the novel (the symbolically vampiric moment of minor bloodletting at the mill, or the fleeting presence of the IRA man, for example), Corcoran is able to show both how *The Last September* is a kind of declension of other 'Anglo-Irish' novelistic traits (derived, for example, from Le Fanu's *Uncle Silas*) and, with even more force, how the novel 'courts deconstructive alternatives to, or remakings of, its own in any case attenuated plot' (p. 329). If the end of Corcoran's essay is a little disappointingly standard in its melancholic assumptions about Anglo-Irishness, this is more than made up for by the complexity of his reading of the plot of *The Last September* as a novel which willingly works against itself.

The Irish Review's Winter 2001 issue was guest-edited by Cairns Craig on the theme 'Ireland and Scotland: Colonial Legacies and National Identities', picking up on an increasingly active area of study in Irish criticism, and certainly one which, in the context of the British Isles strand to the Belfast agreement, looks like it will continue to attract academic interest and government funding. *Irish Review* 28 includes one literary-critical essay on Scottish–Irish connections, 'Waking Up in a Different Place: Contemporary Irish and Scottish Fiction' by Glenda Norquay and Gerry Smyth (*IR* 28[2001] 28–45). Norquay and Smyth start from the premise that 'we appear to have entered a period of history in which the spatial constructions of Scotland and Ireland are almost changing faster than cultural representations can cope with' (pp. 28–9). Norquay and Smyth are perhaps unusual in their take on the Scottish–Irish connection in that they do not see the pivot of this relationship as placed somewhere in Northern Ireland. Instead their beginning point is the continually shifting powerbase of Europe, and then the place of the cumbersomely named 'Atlantic archipelago' within the European formulation of what is in fact a wider globalization. Initially taking a broad sweep back to that well-rehearsed Scottish–Irish novelistic connection, Walter Scott's admiration for Maria Edgeworth, Norquay and Smyth then focus on contemporary fiction, ranging over the works of Roddy Doyle, Irvine Welsh, and Alasdair Gray, with mentions of Iain Banks, Dermot Healy and A.L. Kennedy, amongst many others. Norquay and Smyth are brave enough to come to the kind of conclusion which will undoubtedly be challenged by future critics, since it characterizes not one but two national fiction traditions still in the making (both of which, in true archipelagic style, are largely dependent on London publishers); so they write that 'in Irish fiction the past functions as a metaphor for the difficulty of coming to terms with conflicting national narratives', while 'the contemporary Scottish novel appears to be developing a concern with "personal" histories, moving from the past towards birth or rebirth' (p. 42). The conclusion is an uncomfortably predictable one, and seems, as Norquay and Smyth themselves more or less acknowledge at several points in the essay, to suggest that critical discourse (here bounded by the need to see nationality as the defining boundary of how literary change might be described) is having trouble keeping up with the world, events and texts which it is trying to describe.

Several important publications on Irish theatre appeared in 2001. Mary Trotter's *Ireland's National Theaters: Political Performance and the Origins of the Irish Dramatic Movement* is a welcome reassessment of theatre history in Ireland, revising our sense of the predominance of the Irish Literary Theatre, and then the Abbey, at the start of the century. Trotter's work looks like being one of a series of scholarly works which will re-examine this aspect of the story of Irish theatre in the next few years, and as a beginning this book is a solid enough basis, being both well written and gently yet polemically revisionist. Trotter goes back as far as Boucicault to trace a time-line of development, and this at least displaces the Yeatsian self-making which imagines the Literary Theatre producing drama in a cultural void. Trotter's chapters on the Irish Literary Theatre, and later on the Abbey, are given freshness by the other chapters around them—on the complex stage Irishness of the Queen's Royal Theatre, on the use of drama as political action by Inghinidhe na hEireann, and on the place which theatricals had at Patrick Pearse's school at St Enda's. The mixture here of 'literary theatre' with both popular and political dramas is an encouraging sign in theatre history in Ireland, and these strands have very recently been further amplified by books published in 2002 by Christopher Morash and Ben Levitas (to be reviewed in *YWES* 83[2004]). Along with these later publications, Trotter's *Ireland's National Theaters* will be an essential reference point in future histories of the origins of twentieth-century Irish drama.

Contemporary drama criticism in Ireland has long been hampered by the lack of indigenous publication outlets. We noted here last year the advent of Carysfort Press, and in 2001 it continued to build its list, adding, most importantly, Chambers, FitzGibbon and Jordan, eds., *Theatre Talk: Voices of Irish Theatre Practitioners*. *Theatre Talk* is not strictly literary criticism, but that is its strength, since its series of interviews with playwrights, actors, directors, producers and administrators gives one of the most comprehensive overviews ever of theatrical practice in Ireland. Throughout the interviews, no matter what the role of the interviewee, it becomes clear that Irish theatre is still predominantly conceived of as a writer's theatre and that this brings with it a reliance on a critical notion of what the canon and nature of Irish theatre is, even if many of the contributors rightly resent the dominance of the playwright over other theatre crafts. For example, in her interview, Olwen Fouéré, one of the best actresses currently working in Irish theatre, seems initially to reject the standard canon of Irish drama by talking about LePlage, Berkoff, Anne Bogart and Peter Brook, and yet she goes on to place herself and her own practice (which has been one of the most strongly individualistic of current Irish actresses) by citing Fintan O'Toole's theatre criticism as what Irish theatre criticism should be. Meanwhile O'Toole himself is interviewed in the book by Redmond O'Hanlon, and again the role of criticism within the production of theatre is examined. As Fouéré herself suggests, O'Toole is impressive because of the uncompromising way in which he sees theatre at work within a society. *Theatre Talk* is the kind of book which would never have appeared before the advent of Carysfort Press, and it is to be hoped that the Press can build on its continuing success.

Another Irish-produced theatre book in 2001 was *Druids, Dudes and Beauty Queens: The Changing Face of Irish Theatre*, edited by the dramatist and novelist Dermot Bolger. The book is a Festschrift for Phelim Donlon, who was Drama Officer for the Arts Council in Ireland from 1984 to 2001, and it features a series of articles by major critics and commentators. One of the most fascinating is a very tentative essay by John Waters, 'The Irish Mummy: The Plays and Purpose and Martin McDonagh' (pp. 30–54). Better known as a controversial journalist, Waters was asked to respond to Martin McDonagh's plays; his essay argues that these are best understood as the product of a second-generation British-Irishness which enters into dialogue with the 'home' culture in an irreverent way, made possible by the competing tensions of distance and attachment. Waters compares McDonagh's plays to the music of the Pogues, writing that their 'removal allowed them to participate in the organic growth of the culture in a more authentic manner than if they had fully "belonged" … So it is with Martin McDonagh' (p. 32). Among other contributions to the book, Vic Merriman's stands out in contrast to that of Waters, who, after one has read Merriman's piece, might be seen as beguiled by the 'newness' which McDonagh offers. Merriman espouses a radical theatre which is different because of dramatic practices and techniques, not 'literary' themes, and so he celebrates the drama of, for example, Donal O'Kelly, while scorning the idea that 'to be an Irish playwright is to be a dissenting voice, an outsider'. Here he particularly singles out McDonagh, whose reputation, he suggests, rests largely on 'the improbable proposition that mainstream theatre audiences are composed of courageous radicals' (p. 63). Merriman may have a point, and at least he has an opinion, though his views seem a little intemperately blind to the quality as well as the impact of McDonagh's writing. *Druids, Dudes and Beauty Queens* also includes a fine essay by Ronan McDonald, 'Between Hope and History: The Drama of the Troubles' (pp. 231–49), and as a collection it will repay a close reading, as it breaches the gap between practitioners and academics which *Theatre Talk* (discussed above) leaves open.

Two other slightly more idiosyncratic publications in 2001 are worth ending with. Mark Patrick Hederman has for some time been a major figure in Irish cultural commentary, most noted for his involvement in the journal *The Crane Bag*. In *The Haunted Inkwell: Art and our Future* he collects a series of his essays broadly on the theme of spirituality and literature. Hederman's voice is not that of the trained literary critic, but that far from invalidates his critique. He is a believer in the redemptive powers of art, in both an old-fashioned and a refreshingly enthusiastic way. Which is not to say that he is naive. His philosophical training, for example, comes into view in his analysis of Heaney, which at times is too celebratory, and is contained by Heaney's own sense of his poetry, but is still capable of seeing Heaney in Lacanian terms: 'Heaney is searching for "the Thing", as Lacan also calls it, which is the core of human activity in the midst of the forest of desires' (p. 190). As is clear even from this short quotation, Hederman is intent on 'translating' philosophical and conceptual complexities into a kind of discourse which also enables Heaney to be seen as a popular poet who retains a belief in the 'magic of poetry' (p. 198). Hederman is a different, non-institutional voice in Irish criticism, and *The Haunted Inkwell*, with its many good qualities, also functions as a reminder to academic criticism that accessibility is still a possibility in critical writing.

Finally a publication which is remarkable as a testimony to the power of criticism in what is probably its most accessible form—teaching. Brearton and Hughes, eds., *Last Before America: Irish and American Writing*, is a collection of essays brought together to honour Michael Allen, who taught English, American and Irish literature at Queen's University Belfast, and who retired in 2001. The list of contributors gives a sense of Allen's benign and quiet influence over the major writers to have come out of Northern Ireland in recent decades, including work by Paul Muldoon, Seamus Heaney, Michael Longley, Ciaran Carson, Medbh McGuckian and Bernard MacLaverty. Allen also 'trained' and influenced a distinguished list of Irish critics. These include Peter McDonald, who contributes 'Faiths and Fidelities: Heaney and Longley in Mid-Career' (pp. 3–15), which argues that Heaney has suffered through the years by being over-scrutinized, while Longley's verse has by comparison remained pristine. McDonald is typically hard on Heaney's 'inclination to congratulate himself' (p. 10) over his non-politics, and overall his essay forcefully argues that Heaney is largely responsible for his own poor criticism, while Longley is in need of better critics. *Last Before America* also has essays by Edna Longley ('Ulster Protestants and the Question of "Culture"', pp. 99–120), Richard Kirkland ('Ways of Saying/Ways of Reading: Materiality, Literary Criticism and the Poetry of Paul Muldoon', pp. 69–79), and Elmer Kennedy-Andrews ('Antic Dispositions in Some Recent Irish Fiction', pp. 121–41), who discusses the apparently postmodern take on madness which links Pat McCabe, Robert McLiam Wilson and Eoin MacNamee. That *Last Before America* is able to include such essays, along with distinguished poetry and fiction, attests to the power of criticism to intervene in cultural debate, to make aesthetics political, and to bring out the politics of aesthetics. It is to be hoped that the critical debates outlined by Claire Connolly, with which we began this section, do not force creative and critical acts into falsely opposing corners, and that a book such as *Last Before America* does not appear to be a curio in a few years' time.

2. Pre-1945 Fiction

(a) The English Novel 1930–1945
The year 2001 was a thin one for publication on the English novel from 1930 to 1945. Several works not discussed last year are covered in this section.

Jane Miller's article 'Re-Reading Elizabeth Bowen' (*Raritan* 20:i[2000] 17–31) takes the opportunity presented by the 1999 centenary of Bowen's birth to look back over her work and reputation. It notes that almost all her work is now in print again in the US, though in what Miller thinks 'an ugly paperback edition' (p. 17). The essay suggests that those who read Bowen's work when it first appeared may have underrated its complexity (though the examples are all of post-war reviewers), and that 'in most of her writing women speak and are spoken for in more depth and detail than men are' (p. 31).

John Boening's essay 'Into Thin Air: The Ocean Voyage in the Travel Writings of Graham Greene' was published in the bilingual collection, Seixo, ed., *Travel Writing and Cultural Memory / Écriture du voyage et mémoire culturelle* [2000]. Here he writes interestingly about Greene's comparison, in much of his travel and other writing, of the differing experiences and possibilities of flying to destinations and the older mode of travel offered by the ocean voyage. Boening remarks that Greene's interest in travel in its last, classic age (as opposed to the succeeding 'age of tourism' in Paul Fussell's taxonomy) makes his attitude to sea voyages an obvious focus, but then goes on to observe that 'it might be more interesting yet— and more revealing—to examine those voyages in the context of Greene's remarks on air travel as an alternative' (p. 209). Boening suggests that Greene repeatedly observes the difference between the real sense of distance travelled on board ship, and the dislocating sense of having arrived without having really travelled given by plane journeys. He traces Greene's discussion of the meaning of these differences in many of his works, including *England Made Me*, *Journey without Maps*, *Reflections*, *In Search of a Character* and *The Comedians*.

David Wykes's impressive *Evelyn Waugh: A Literary Life* [1999] shares the virtues of other volumes in the Macmillan Literary Lives series in formulating an approach which articulates what constituted the 'literary life' as compared to simply the life. Wykes outlines a particular problem in articulating this difference for

Waugh: 'His dependence on his own history was nearly total. Waugh was not very good at invention, but he was unsurpassed at embroidery. His experience appears transformed, imaginatively made over and artistically perfected in his fiction, but he denied his genius for embroidery' (p. 4). Wykes explores the patterns of the fictional embroidery of life which are at the heart of Waugh's writing (suggesting too that Waugh's autobiography *A Little Learning* is in fact best approached as an especially interesting example of his technique of fictionalizing his own life). He identifies the key variations as deriving from Waugh's initial desire not to be a 'man of letters' like his father and brother, from his liking for 'things going wrong' (p. 1), from a highly coherent religious conviction that all humans are not in their 'true home' in this world, but are 'exiles, outcasts, people with no valid landmarks' (p. 2), and from a lifelong and partially hostile engagement with the comic and autobiographical fictions of Dickens and the atheistical Enlightenment irony of Gibbon. Wykes argues interestingly that, in the second half of Waugh's writing career, his novels did something which the author could never do in life: they often rethought, apologized and explained (though here the most obviously autobiographical 'novel', *The Ordeal of Gilbert Pinfold*, is an exception). Wykes observes that Waugh's literary career contained some odd shifts in choice of genre and technique: 'his had been an unpredictable career, not at all easy for literary history to categorize even when it had come to a close' (p. 211). This literary life does a good deal to bring out some of the drives in this curious writer, whose approach to writing was itself based on a deeply held (if sometimes far from attractive) sense of division between the 'little systems of order' which writing could at least suggest and the essential meaninglessness of earthly life.

(b) Joseph Conrad

This year we have seen a considerable number of articles published outside the major Conrad journals, and the breadth and range of that material has been especially impressive. Indeed the diversity of critical perspectives employed this year makes it difficult to provide a cohesive overview of the current direction of Conrad studies. Analyses of the themes of exile and estrangement continue to figure strongly, as does the engagement with national self-fashioning, but it is interesting to see scholars exploring new avenues of interpretation such as Conrad and the abject and Conrad's influence on twentieth-century music. While the major novels are still the subject of considerable debate, it is pleasing to see critical attention being turned to the less familiar fictions and also to Conrad's work as an essayist and dramatist. On the whole contributions to the journals have been more impressive than the work produced in monograph form, with one exception.

Certainly the most interesting and innovative volume produced this year was John G. Peters's *Conrad and Impressionism*, a book that threatens a tired recapitulation of a well-worn theme, but in fact provides a fresh and challenging perspective on the philosophical credentials of Impressionism. The success of this approach depends upon Peters's re-examination of the aesthetic origins of Literary Impressionism, and in particular its focus on what he terms 'objects of consciousness' (p. 2). Impressionism, he contends, functions by filtering all phenomena through the human consciousness at a specific place and time, and, given that each individual consciousness will perceive the objective world differently, knowledge of that world must therefore be a subjective rather than a universal experience. The subjective nature of impressionistic perception, then, fundamentally destabilizes any solid conception of universal truth, rendering all epistemological structures relative rather than absolute. 'For Conrad', claims Peters, these questions 'lead to two unpleasant logical possibilities ... epistemological solipsism and ethical anarchy' (p. 5). The resolution of such unpalatable questions is Conrad's focus on subjectivity, which in its insubstantiality becomes a paradoxical symbol of certainty. Peters seeks to break away from the notion that Impressionism concerns itself purely with the visual, and broadens his focus to address the negotiated status of human subjectivity. Subjectivity is always under construction, he argues, in the interchange between Self and Other, an exchange that contains serious political ramifications in the colonial encounter. The absolutist philosophical values of Western civilization are at ideological odds with the principles of Impressionism and, so Peters claims, Conrad rejected the solidities offered by realism and science in favour of the impressionistic value of relative experience. *Conrad and Impressionism* is a consistently insightful volume that offers a valuable reading of its subject.

Daniel R. Schwarz's *Rereading Conrad* is a collection of previously published essays that range across Conrad's fiction but with an emphasis on the period of the major novels. The essays represent a cross-section of Schwarz's work in the area since the early 1980s, but he has updated his readings of Conrad as a response to the changing emphases of theoretical positioning. This critical self-consciousness is, in fact, one of the more interesting facets of this volume, for it indicates an increasingly prevalent tendency towards the history of personal engagement with theory, which it seems necessary to have put in place before any substantive comment can be made. Schwarz's collection constitutes an intriguing interaction between formalist and humanist analyses of Conrad and perspectives gained from postcolonial, feminist and ecological theories. Whether it is possible to integrate the localized political agendas of theory with the imperatives of humanism seems to be at the heart of Schwarz's approach and it is a valid and pertinent question, especially in debates on the post-theory landscape. Schwarz argues against the appropriation of Conrad for specific political ends, instead urging a holistic criticism that can incorporate the broader themes of metaphysical scepticism and exile with a sympathetic and inclusive politics. What undermines this rather utopian approach is the didactic quality of Schwarz's prose. Admittedly this is a book designed, at least partly, for a student market, but Schwarz's tendency towards explanation and reiteration can prove wearing, as can his desire to justify his own writing position at the margin as a result of his Jewishness. Identification with the exile is a common feature of Conradian criticism, and is perhaps also a cause of his continuing popularity in an increasingly attenuated cultural landscape, but I am not convinced that it leads to better criticism. Schwarz's collection makes a fine case for Conrad's contemporaneity, but would have made a finer one without the theoretical hand-wringing.

The major Conrad journals continue to produce work from a wide variety of established and emerging scholars and it is work of a consistently high quality, although there are possibly fewer contributions this year that stand out as startlingly original. *The Conradian* contains the customary mixture of bibliographical research, biographical insight and critical analysis, and as a whole the journal maintains an extremely creditable level of scholarship. In the first number Nic Panagopoulos follows up his monograph on the influence of Schopenhauer on Conrad, *The Fiction of Joseph Conrad* [1998], with an essay on the Schopenhauerian will-to-live as manifest in *Victory*. '"Will" and "Representation" in *Victory*' (*Conradian* 26:i[2001] 17–32) contends that the novel is founded upon Schopenhauer's theories of will but that Conrad rejects the philosopher's pessimistic outlook in favour of a more affirmative sense of the positive force of illusion. In 'Topography in "The Secret Sharer"' (*Conradian* 26:i[2001] 1–16) J.H. Stape explores the accuracy with which Conrad represents the topography of the Gulf of Siam. By tracing similarities between actual and fictionalized locations, Stape argues that the story's concern with freedom and entrapment is mirrored in its portrayal of a historically concrete topography. David Mulry's 'Patterns of Revision in *The Secret Agent*: Conrad as Anarchist' (*Conradian* 26:i[2001] 33–59) is a close textual examination of the revision process as *The Secret Agent* proceeded from holograph to final publication. The intricate analysis of these revisions is fascinating for what it shows of the maturing artist, but Mulry's contention that the revisions reveal the author's anarchistic politics is less convincing. The remaining two essays in this first number are Chris Fletcher's 'Kurtz, Marlow, Jameson and the Rearguard: A Few Further Observations' (*Conradian* 26:i[2001] 60–4) and Walter Putnam's 'The Ill-Fated French Translation of *Chance*: Philippe Neel, G. Jean-Aubry, André Gide' (*Conradian* 26:i[2001] 65–84). Fletcher's short but entertaining essay offers possible historical forebears for the figures of Marlow and Kurtz from the records of Stanley's Emin Pasha relief expedition. Putnam's commentary on the correspondence between Neel and Conrad has appeared previously in *The Conradian* (*Conradian* 24:i[1999] 59–91), and this essay provides an interesting account of further exchanges surrounding the translation of *Chance*.

The second number of this year's *Conradian* begins with Richard J. Hand's essay-cum-cultural history 'Conrad and the Reviewers: *The Secret Agent* on Stage' (*Conradian* 26:ii[2001] 1–67). Hand provides a short, prefatory commentary on the history of Conrad's dramatic career and on the problems he faced in translating the novel for stage performance. The remaining fifty-four pages of the article reproduce reviews, publicity material, photographs and ephemera concerned with the play's production. This is an admirable feat of collation and provides not only a fascinating slice of critical history, but also a wealth of contextual detail on the popular tastes of the early 1920s. On the shorter side, but equally compelling in a different way, is Andrea White's 'The "Planter of Malata" Fragment: A Twice-Lost Manuscript' (*Conradian* 26:ii[2001] 68–70). White details the history of disappearance, reappearance and ultimate disappearance of a fragment of Conrad's 1913 manuscript. In 'The "Unnatural Rigidity" of Almayer's Ethnocentrism' (*Conradian* 26:ii[2001] 71–8) A. James M. Johnson argues that Conrad's clustering of images of entrapment, enclosure and rigidity around the figure of Almayer reveals the mentality of racist self-isolation that characterized Western involvement in the East. By refusing to acknowledge the potential of the exotic, Johnson claims, Conrad shows how Almayer (and empire) denies the possibility of a fuller existence. The most unusual essay in this year's *Conradian* is Rolf Charlston's 'A Rhapsodic *Heart of Darkness*: John Powell's *Rhapsodie Nègre*' (*Conradian* 26:ii[2001] 79–90). This fascinating piece explores Powell's 'symphonic poem' of *Heart of Darkness*, contextualizing it within Powell's own politics of racial integrity, but also drawing attention to the presence of spiritual and ragtime motifs in its construction.

Conradiana also continues to spotlight innovative and provocative work in the field, and this year saw a bumper crop with no less than fourteen essays published. The first number saw a rather mixed bag, however, with the quirkily original but limited sitting alongside the stolidly meticulous. Among the former is Gerald Morgan's spikily idiosyncratic piece on one of Conrad's last essays in 'Yule and Then: Conrad's "Christmas Day at Sea"' (*Conradiana* 33:i[2001] 3–15). Also in the former category I would include Chaim Seymour's 'A Heart Still Beating: Conrad and the Israeli Reader' (*Conradiana* 33:i[2001] 16–23). Seymour observes the popularity of *Heart of Darkness* in Israel while commenting upon the difficulties and compromises involved in the translation of the text into Hebrew. One of the more innovative contributions to this number, though, is Catharine Rising's 'Raskolnikov and Razumov: From Passive to Active Subjectivity' (*Conradiana* 33:i[2001] 24–39). In this essay Rising contrasts Dostoevsky's anti-hero from *Crime and Punishment* with Razumov from *Under Western Eyes* and explores their constructed subjectivities through the lens of Lacanian psychoanalysis. Her contention that the subject's relationship with discourse is more constitutive than post-structuralists would argue is enlightening, as is her application of that theory to Conrad's ambivalent feelings about Polish independence.

Also in this number is James Morgan's essay 'Harlequin in Hell: Marlow and the Russian Sailor in Joseph Conrad's *Heart of Darkness*' (*Conradiana* 33:i[2001] 40–8). Morgan discusses the ambiguous figure of the Russian sailor in relation to the archetypal harlequin character. Marlow undergoes a journey of psychological deracination, but in the sailor (as harlequin) Conrad offers the possibility of a wholeness which is gained after the hellish ordeal. In 'Images of South America in Some Texts of Joseph Conrad' (*Conradiana* 33:i[2001] 49–58) Mariano Siskind explores representations of the continent in *Nostromo* and *Gaspar Ruiz*. Where Conrad attended to the topographical aspects of these novels, argues Siskind, he chose to focus on images of virgin nature and/or the notion of nature as an obstacle to modernization. The other most substantial contribution to this number is Sung Ryol Kim's interesting, but slightly unwieldy, essay 'Witness to Death: Marlow in *Heart of Darkness*' (*Conradiana* 33:i[2001] 59–77). The essay focuses on Marlow's various encounters with the death of others and relates individual fates to the grander scale of murder being perpetrated by imperial powers. Marlow's failure wholeheartedly to commit himself to the plights of the African people he meets, leads, it is argued, to the reader's questioning of his degree of complicity in their fate. The essay is consistently provoking without being entirely convincing.

'Lord Jim's Heroic Identity' (*Conradiana* 33:ii[2001] 83–106) is Sung Ryol Kim's second essay in this year's *Conradiana*, and like the first it makes a plausible case without ever being totally conclusive. Kim examines the relationship between death and the idea of self in *Lord Jim*, and in particular how Jim's fear of death acts as an imperative for moral action. Whether Jim's eventual death confers upon him a heroic identity is a valuable debate that Kim paraphrases rather than intervenes in. Brad Jackel's essay 'Re-Painting Hell: Conrad's Infernal Imagery' (*Conradiana* 33:ii[2001]) offers a reading of Conrad through patterns of Dantean allusion. Jackel draws attention to the imagery of the *Inferno* in 'Falk', *An Outcast of the Islands* and *Lord Jim*. The essay is most assured when discussing the last of these texts and the author makes a useful parallel between the infernal punishment of unbridled romance and Jim's own romantic misapprehensions. In a not dissimilarly macabre way, Monika Elbert considers Conrad's appropriation of the Gothic in 'The Return' and 'The Smile of Fortune'. In 'The Ligeia Syndrome, or Many "Happy Returns," in Conrad's Gothic' (*Conradiana* 33:ii[2001] 129–52) she produces a sustained argument for a reading of Poe's influence on Conrad, but more interestingly she also situates Gothic within the context of modernist notions of the dual self. Finally in this second number, the dialogue between Conrad and Achebe is given another airing, but Padmini Mongia's 'The Rescue: Conrad, Achebe and the Critics' (*Conradiana* 33:ii[2001] 153–64) at least manages to carve a new angle. She explores not the tired debate over racism but the need of Western critics repeatedly to refute Achebe's claims. What these renunciations articulate, she suggests, is a desire to rescue Conrad from the murky waters of ideological suspicion in order to reassert his position in the canon of high art.

The final number of *Conradiana* opens with Robert Hamner's thoughtful essay 'The Enigma of Arrival in "An Outpost of Progress"' (*Conradiana* 33:iii[2001] 171–88). Here Hamner explores the discomforting experience of arrival by contrasting Conrad's story with Giorgio de Chirico's *The Enigma of Arrival and the Afternoon*, a painting that parallels Conrad's portrayal of 'alienated men in an alienating landscape' (p. 177). William A. Martin's '"To grapple with another man's intimate need": Trauma–Shame Interdependency (Masochism) in Joseph Conrad's *Lord Jim* (1900)' (*Conradiana* 33:iii[2001] 231–50) continues the trend of reading Conrad in the light of psychoanalytical theories of trauma. Martin argues for the effective interdependence of shame and trauma, but his most interesting idea is that the fragmented confessions of Jim and Brown are therapeutically ordered by Marlow. There has certainly been a greater variety of Conradian texts addressed than in recent years and in G.W. Stephen Brodsky's '"What Manners!": Contra-Diction and Conrad's Use of History in "The Warrior's Soul"' (*Conradiana* 33:iii[2001] 189–230) we have an analysis of a rarely encountered story. Brodsky focuses upon the slippages in historical fact that Conrad perpetrates, and argues that such wide-ranging contra-diction cannot be unintentional. Instead, he argues, the construction of the warrior myth around Napoleon's Russian exploits threatens to be replicated on the battlefields of 1916 France. Coming full circle, Ray Stevens and Robert W. Trogdon contribute '"Christmas Day at Sea": A Whaler, a Bundle of Papers, Two Boxes of Figs, Bibliographical Completeness, Biographical and Textual Inaccuracies of Hemispheric Proportions' (*Conradiana* 33:iii[2001] 251–63). Sadly the essay only hints at the complexities of its title, but this is nevertheless an intriguing examination of the drafting emendations of one of Conrad's last essays.

There was also a healthy number of articles published outside the major Conrad journals. One particularly interesting contribution to *Modern Fiction Studies* this year is Peter Mallios's 'Undiscovering the Country: Conrad, Fitzgerald and Meta-National Form' (*MFS* 47:ii[2001] 356–90). Mallios explores the dynamics of national self-imagining in *The Great Gatsby* in the light of Fitzgerald's explicit identification with Conrad. Drawing on the trope of the absent centre in Fitzgerald's novel and in *Nostromo*, Mallios contends that the fashioning of a coherent national identity involves the fictive idealization of collective social will as a response to that blankness. Also in *Modern Fiction Studies* is David Adams's '"Remorse and Power": Conrad's Karain and the Queen' (*MFS* 47:iv[2001] 723–52). Here Adams argues that Conrad's story articulates domestic concerns about the weakening symbolic power of the British monarch through an analogy of the exotic East. Imperial culture, it is suggested, is burdened by a sense of remorse which is emphatically enhanced by the mournfulness of the ageing queen. Adams explores the symbolic connotations of the gilded Jubilee sixpence which stands both for the actualized power of empire and its suspect ideological presumptions.

Also of interest is Nigel Messenger's '"We did not want to lose him": Jimmy Wait as the Figure of Abjection in Conrad's "The Nigger of the Narcissus"' (CS 13:i[2001] 62–79). Messenger offers a reading of Conrad's notoriously elusive tale in terms of Kristevan abjection. Wait represents the 'unclean and improper' that threatens the integrity of the collective body on board ship. Interestingly Messenger goes on to argue that Wait symbolizes not just the unrepressed primitive but also the seductive threat of modernity and the degeneration that was seen to attend it. Wait's unstable subjectivity as the abject compromises the solidarity of the crew, but equally challenges the solidity of its individual selfhoods. In the *Slavic and East European Journal* Daniel C. Melnick contributes a well-argued piece on '*Under Western Eyes* and Silence' (*SEEJ* 45:ii[2001] 231–42). He argues that Conrad constructs images of East and West which 'participate in the opposition between silence and speech' (p. 231). He proceeds to explore the political contexts of the novel, in particular the silence of Polish culture enforced by a Russian regime, before going on to consider how British modernism depends upon the implicit opposition of speech and silence. Silence as the creation of meaning is fundamental to Conrad, he suggests, but also to our understanding of the fragmentariness and incoherence of modernism.

Under Western Eyes is also the subject of L.R. Leavis's article in *Neophilologus*: 'Guilt, Love and Extinction: *Born in Exile* and *Under Western Eyes*' (*Neophil* 85:i[2001] 153–62). Leavis draws a line between George Gissing's 1892 novel and Conrad's 1911 one, and suggests the influence of the former on the latter. Some of the parallels that are drawn between the novels are intriguing, but on the whole this essay proves too mechanical an exercise to be compelling. *Studies in the Novel* has Brian Richardson's essay 'Construing Conrad's "The Secret Sharer": Suppressed Narratives, Subaltern Reception, and the Art of Interpretation' (*SNNTS* 33:iii[2001] 306–21). In it he argues that Conrad's text presents significant problems of interpretation because it continually casts doubt upon the interpretative stances that it appears to privilege. That it offers contradictory readings which foreground the instability of the act of interpretation Richardson takes to be indicative of its high-modernist character. Wide-ranging and polemical in its argument, Geoffrey Galt Harpham's *Raritan* essay, 'Conrad's Global Homeland' (*Raritan* 21:i[2001] 20–33) explores the senses of national and post-national identity in readers' responses to *Lord Jim*. Harpham examines the implications of Jim's being 'one of us', and goes on interestingly to debate the political and ideological parameters that modify interpretations of 'us'.

(c) George Orwell

George Orwell continues to be one of the most contentious and debated of British writers, yet Orwell studies seems to have been caught in a critical stasis for too long. The work produced this year does offer fresh perspectives on his writing, but for a figure who instils polarized opinion very little in the way of critical material is being produced. This year has seen no monograph and only a handful of journal essays.

Nevertheless what has been published has been diligently researched and conscientiously written.

The Road from George Orwell: His Achievement and Legacy is edited by Alberto Lázaro from the proceedings of the University of Alcalá's eighth conference on English literature [2000]. The volume seeks to quantify Orwell's achievements by re-examining some of the major works in the light of fifty years of critical interpretation. It also seeks to explore the legacy of Orwell through an eclectic variety of late twentieth-century texts. The second aim is certainly the more successful. While there is nothing intrinsically at fault in the essays in the first half of the book, there is also very little that is substantially new about the material. Orwell studies have for many years now wallowed in the mire of readings that foreground his contradictoriness, his idealism or his patriotism. Many of these essays offer tired rereadings not of Orwell but of the Orwell mythology. I do not include Alberto Lázaro's essay 'George Orwell's *Homage to Catalonia*: A Politically Incorrect Story' in the above group: it offers an interesting textual study of Orwell's Spanish account from the perspective of the Franco government's censorship and bowdlerization of the text. The second half of the volume, entitled 'Orwell, History and Dystopia', examines the influence of Orwell on post-1950 writing. Some of these essays—Sonia Villegas's '"History is Not a Thing of the Past": The Theory and Practice of Historical Discourse in Alasdair Gray's *A History Maker*' and Ben Clarke's 'Orwell and the Evolution of Utopian Writing'—are interesting exercises in charting the notoriously insubstantial nature of influence. Others are less persuasive, and some appear to bear little relation to Orwell (one fails to mention him). Inevitably this impacts upon the collection. Instead of being an investigation of Orwell at the century's end this volume appears to be what it is: a patchy, ultimately unsatisfying set of conference proceedings.

Also published this year is Daniel Lea, ed., *George Orwell—Animal Farm/Nineteen Eighty-Four: A Reader's Guide to Essential Criticism*, published in Icon's Reader's Guide series, which provides detailed critical histories for significant literary texts. Here I must declare an interest, being the said Daniel Lea. The book charts the changing critical reactions to Orwell's most celebrated texts through extracts from the major interpretative sources, and these extracts are linked and qualified by the editor. The volume tries to show the ways in which Orwell's writings have been appropriated, not just by political factions but also by visual media seeking to annex their dystopian visions of the late twentieth century. The final chapter, for instance, explores the filmic histories of *Animal Farm* and *Nineteen Eighty-Four* and surveys the casual employment of Orwellian motifs in television events such as *Big Brother*. Elsewhere the book foregrounds the contest over Orwell's political afterlife, the persistence of psychobiographical criticism, and the emergence of feminist readings of Orwell. Vanity demands that I say more, but word limits thankfully prevent.

From the journals, one of the brighter moments of the year comes with Stephen Schwartz's vituperative condemnation of Peter Davison's editorial reconfiguration of *Homage to Catalonia*. 'Rewriting George Orwell' (*NewC* 20:i[2001] 63–5) dismisses as buffoonery Davison's decision to remove chapter 5 from the body of the text and to position it as an appendix. As Schwartz rightly, but perhaps too colourfully, claims, this fundamentally disturbs Orwell's own anti-Stalinist invective. Equally spirited is Gorman Beauchamp's essay in the *Partisan Review*.

'Orwell, the Lysenko Affair, and the Politics of Social Construction' (*PR* 68:ii[2001] 266–78) begins with an entertaining rant against the emperor's-new-clothes quality of postmodernism, but develops into a very interesting discussion of Soviet science's denial of objective truth. Using O'Brien's diktat that two plus two equals five as a fictional paradigm, Beauchamp explores the career of T.D. Lysenko and his fellow social constructionists who contended that genetic programming was fundamentally inimical to the core principles of Marxism and that it was therefore equally fundamentally false. Orwell is perhaps a side issue in this essay, but it is nonetheless engaging and enlightening. Mention should also be made of Phyllis Lassner's article 'A Bridge Too Close: Narrative Wars to End Fascism' (*JNT* 31:ii[2001] 131–54). Although not primarily concerned with Orwell, Lassner uses his essay 'Marrakech' as a comparative model for Phyllis Bottome's novel *Under the Skin*. Both texts, she argues, attack Western imperialism for its implicit models of racism which are only one step removed from the intolerance of fascism.

(d) Wyndham Lewis

Very little has been produced on Lewis this year, but of note are the following two articles. Francesca Ortesano's 'Arctic Masks in a Castle of Ice: Gothic Vorticism and Wyndham Lewis's *Self Condemned*' appears in Smith and Wallace, eds., *Gothic Modernisms*. In a wide-ranging and complex argument Orestano argues for a re-evaluation of the influence of the Gothic on Lewis's writing and, in particular, on his late novel *Self Condemned*. Orestano explores the employment of Gothic motifs and landscapes as aesthetic correlatives of Lewis's fascination with external style and the politics of surface. In her reading of *Self Condemned* she focuses on Lewis's condemnation of history, and suggests that the catalogue of horrors initiated by the Second World War questions the aesthetic politics of modernism. The Gothic as a genre becomes the most effective way of encapsulating the physical destruction of Europe and the moral relativism of post-war humankind.

In '"This implacable doctrine": Behaviorism in Wyndham Lewis's *Snooty Baronet*' (*TCL* 47:ii[2001] 241–67) Paul Scott Stanfield presents a case for the greater estimation of Lewis's much-overlooked novel of 1932. Stanfield argues that it has wrongly been dismissed as insubstantial and futile, for it reveals Lewis's serious engagement with behaviourist psychology, which, so Stansfield contends, was connected to a host of Lewis's other antipathies. The essay suggests that in behaviourism Lewis saw the reduction of the complex human mind to a delimited set of automated and involuntary actions, a passivity that contradicted all the violence that he believed to be at the core of identity. Stansfield chooses *Snooty Baronet* as it is a novel that seems to construct its characters exactly on the lines of a behaviourist paradigm. The novel is fundamental to our understanding of Lewis's loathings because it represents an attempt deliberately to work through those loathings in a fictional format. Conscious of the need to at least acknowledge popular taste, Stansfield suggests that the novel sees Lewis developing a style that could incorporate polemic within a digestible novelistic context. It stands as a watershed between the early experimental work and the later realistic material.

(e) D.H. Lawrence

In an introduction to a new edition of Lawrence's *The Fox* (Hesperus Press [2002]), Doris Lessing writes, 'Lawrence the man and D.H. Lawrence the writer: both provoked strong reactions in his lifetime, and it all still goes on.' Well, it certainly does, judging by the glut of Lawrence criticism produced in 2001: four monographs, four essay anthologies, a new and much-expanded edition of the primary bibliography of Lawrence, and, overall (counting those in the anthologies), in excess of a hundred essays and articles. As far as I am aware, there is no special anniversary to account for all this activity, but it clearly confirms the continuing fascination Lawrence holds for critics at the start of the new millennium, despite those premature rumours of his critical demise circulating in the 1980s and 1990s. The highly engaged and varied nature of the year's criticism also fully bears out Lessing's point that Lawrence does indeed continue to provoke strong and widely divergent reactions amongst his readers and critics, and it suggests that the apparently perennial need to revisit and re-evaluate his work will persist into the foreseeable future.

As in last year's review, moreover, I can note that the theoretical diversification within Lawrence criticism continues to show something of an exponential growth, to the extent that I cannot think of any major contemporary theory that is *not* applied to Lawrence within the work this year. Partly as a result of this, a welcome number of new 'Lawrences' are now coming more clearly into focus, while overall within the field it is indeed Lawrence's plural and protean nature which is increasingly being emphasized (or re-emphasized). To make use of a comment from one of this year's essays, 'One thinks of Lawrence's maxim about nailing down the novel and Catherine Carswell's reminder that Lawrence "is like Joey in the Punch and Judy Show. He will not 'stay put'" (*Savage Pilgrimage* [1932] vii)': Howard Mills, '*Sea and Sardinia*: If You Can Teach Only One Lawrence Text' (in Sargent and Watson, eds., *Approaches to Teaching the Works of D.H. Lawrence*, pp.164–71: 165).

Among the works under review, two titles stand out as broadly representative of themes and concerns common to many discussions this year. The first, from an essay by M. Elizabeth Sargent and Garry Watson, is 'D.H. Lawrence and the Dialogical Principle: "The Strange Reality of Otherness"' (*CE* 63:iv[2001] 409–36), and the second is Poplawski, ed., *Writing the Body in D.H. Lawrence: Essays on Language, Representation, and Sexuality*. Apart from being easily one of the best essays of the year in its own right for its deftly probing and nuanced exploration of Lawrence's 'ethics of alterity' (p. 421), Sargent and Watson's piece is important for giving sharp definition to the issues of otherness and dialogism in Lawrence (and in recent Lawrence criticism), as well as in contemporary cultural and critical debates more generally. As this suggests, the essay actually stages a complex critical dialogue on these issues between Lawrence and other thinkers and theorists such as Buber, Bakhtin, Kristeva, Irigaray, Levinas, Todorov, Dollimore and Mohanty; and, as this further suggests, the essay thus provides an authoritative point of reference for related discussions, helping to underwrite and link the wide range of other current work on Lawrence that is also largely preoccupied with these matters, albeit sometimes in broader contexts such as those of postcolonialism, gender studies, post-structuralism, or ecocriticism.

As with otherness and dialogism, questions of language, representation and sexuality may always have been with us in Lawrence studies, but the critical agendas of recent years have given them much sharper theoretical definition, and this is clearly reflected in the many works dealing with such questions this year. Not all of the thirteen essays in *Writing the Body in D.H. Lawrence* are radically theoretical, but they all draw, to a greater or lesser extent, on contemporary critical theory, and together they represent a varied cross-section of possible critical approaches to the complex of issues indicated in the book's title and subtitle. In the first essay, 'D.H. Lawrence and the Abject Body: A Postmodern History', Garry Watson is again exemplary in catching the pulse of current thought and theory—this time in relation to the 'abject' body—and setting it off in a carefully wrought and always illuminating dialogue with Lawrence's own thinking (principally, here, as demonstrated in his late essay 'Introduction to these Paintings'). At the end of the collection, Maria Aline Ferreira's essay, '"Glad Wombs" and "Friendly Tombs": Re-embodiments in D.H. Lawrence's Late Works', takes up some of Watson's concerns from a feminist-inflected psychoanalytical perspective; see also her 'Lawrence's "Fleurs du mal"': Abjection in *Women in Love*' (*EL* 25[2001] 35–48). Carol Siegel adopts Deleuze and Guattari's theories of deterritorialization, nomadism and rhizomatics in developing a strikingly original feminist reading of one of Lawrence's so-called 'problem' texts in her essay, 'With Lawrence in America, from House/Wife to Nomad: *The Plumed Serpent*', while (to note just two more of the essays here) M. Elizabeth Sargent and See-young Park both provide similarly original revisionary readings of other 'problem' works in, respectively, 'Thinking and Writing from the Body: Eugene Gendlin, D.H. Lawrence and "The Woman Who Rode Away"', and 'D.H. Lawrence Unbuttoned: *Aaron's Rod*, *Kangaroo* and the Influence of Lev Shestov'.

Two of this year's monographs pursue aspects of the above themes in elaborate detail. Drawing on Lacanian theorists such as Shoshana Felman, Peter Brooks and Jane Gallop, Earl G. Ingersoll's *D.H. Lawrence, Desire, and Narrative* applies a rigorously postmodern and post-structuralist psychoanalytical reading to Lawrence's major novels, and, as its title and approach suggest, it focuses on the complex ways in which desire 'energizes' narrative and how desire, sexuality and gender identities are coded by Lawrence's language and rhetoric. Most of the chapters in the book have been published previously as independent essays, and while, as essays, these are always stimulating and insightful, and suggestive of new ways of understanding each of the novels considered, it is a moot point as to whether the book (as monograph) generates anything greater than the sum of its parts.

Gerald Doherty's *Oriental Lawrence: The Quest for the Secrets of Sex* is actually a much more sophisticated book than its slightly lurid title may suggest, and this, too, addresses questions of language, representation, sexuality and otherness through its detailed exploration of Lawrence's affinities with and 'highly eclectic appropriations of' Eastern systems of thought (p. 140), especially yoga and Buddhism. This is an important and authoritative overview of some of the more obscure sources of Lawrence's writing and thinking about sex, language and the body, but it goes significantly beyond mere source-hunting in its closely argued and theoretically nuanced analyses of specific novels. Drawing on, amongst others, Barthes, Derrida, Foucault and Lacan, as well as on Eastern thought systems, Doherty develops some highly original perspectives on Lawrence's writing, and he provides fresh and compelling readings of some notoriously difficult scenes from the major novels. There are some important omissions in his otherwise well-informed engagement with relevant critical scholarship, and away from his main argument Doherty is sometimes a little cavalier in his judgements—for example, in his casually dismissive comments about Lawrence's plays and novels of the 1920s (pp. 65–6, 140)—but on the whole this is a valuable addition to work in the field. A useful brief companion-piece that might be mentioned here is Stephen Taylor's 'Lawrence the Mystic' (*JDHLS* [2001] 62–74). This makes a more general and more straightforward case about Lawrence's mysticism but also draws parallels with some of the Eastern sources cited by Doherty. The study of mysticism and spirituality in Lawrence is by no means new, of course (see, for example, Martin Wickramasinghe, *The Mysticism of D.H. Lawrence* (Colombo [1951]), but these two works, and also Zangenehpour's book (missed last year), *Sufism and the Quest for Spiritual Fulfillment in D.H. Lawrence's 'The Rainbow'*, may suggest a current resurgence of interest in the topic.

If defined in terms of Don Cupitt's 'solar ethics' (as he hints it should be in 'The Radical Christian Worldview': *CrosscurrentsJ* 50:i–ii[2000] 56–67: 60) as a form of radical humanism based on an ethics of flux, contingency and this-worldly living, then an interest in Lawrence's spirituality is certainly resurgent not only in the postmodern philosophical context of 'otherness' outlined by Watson, but also in the not unrelated context of ecology. This is explored in depth in Anne Odenbring Ehlert's monograph, *'There's a bad time coming': Ecological Vision in the Fiction of D.H. Lawrence*, and also in Keith Sagar's revised version of his 1992 essay, 'The Resurrection of Pan: Teaching Biocentric Consciousness and Deep Ecology in Lawrence's Poetry and Late Nonfiction' (in Sargent and Watson, eds., pp. 146–56). Sagar, in his shorter piece, makes the more compelling case for Lawrence as an exponent of holistic thinking and biocentric consciousness, and as a 'deep ecologist' *avant la lettre*—though Ehlert's more expansive (if more diffuse) study allows her more time to elaborate usefully on the background of ecological philosophy and the relatively recent development of ecocriticism. One of Sagar's main advantages is that, where Ehlert restricts herself to the fiction, he sensibly draws on the full range of Lawrence's writings, and especially on the poetry and non-fiction where Lawrence's spiritual engagement with the otherness of the natural world is often at its most intense and explicit. Clearly apposite here is David Ellis's probing scrutiny, in 'D.H. Lawrence: *Birds, Beasts and Flowers*' (in Roberts, ed., pp. 392–402), of the formal as well as philosophical problems facing Lawrence in his ongoing struggle to evoke an appropriate sense of non-human otherness in his poetry. Ellis here neatly grounds some of the more abstract discussions of this topic by working through concrete examples of how, in his poetry, Lawrence strives to negotiate the inherent difficulties of evoking non-human modes of being through an inevitably anthropomorphic medium (see also Ellis's 'Teaching Lawrence's Tortoise Poems as a Sequence', in Sargent and Watson, eds., pp.185–89). Ehlert's book begins with a quotation from Donald Gutierrez, one of the pioneers of an ecological approach to Lawrence. The quotation, in part, reads: 'Lawrence surely deserves attention as a prophet, poet, and a fictionalist of a 20th-century culture of ecology' (p. 11 in Ehlert), and it is therefore appropriate to end this 'ecological' section by noting a previously missed short essay by Gutierrez, 'Industrialization, Nature and Human Nature in D.H. Lawrence's Works' (*BR* 19:ii[1999] 12–13).

Although there is some unevenness among the fourteen essays of Fernihough, ed., *The Cambridge Companion to D.H. Lawrence*, the volume largely succeeds in its aims as a companion–reader and does indeed provide, as its blurb suggests, a well-contextualized range of 'diverse and stimulating readings' of Lawrence's major texts. Fernihough's introduction presents an insightful overview of the essays and makes some pertinent points of its own about the history of Lawrence's critical reception and reputation. Rightly, in my opinion, Fernihough particularly stresses the complexity of Lawrence's work, and the difficulty of doing critical justice to it given its radically transgressive and often self-contradictory nature, not to mention the 'astounding' quantity and generic diversity of Lawrence's output (p. 7). Among the essays themselves, there are solid overviews of the poetry by Helen Sword and of 'Lawrence's Critical and Cultural Legacy' by Chris Baldick, but three or four essays particularly stand out for striking just the right balance (for a book of this sort), between breadth and depth of analysis. Mark Kinkead-Weekes's superb essay, 'Decolonising Imagination: Lawrence in the 1920s', is exemplary in this respect, evincing both a masterly grasp of a wide range of contextual materials and a sure sense of how to relate these clearly and precisely to specific textual issues. Kinkead-Weekes skilfully maps out the full trajectory of Lawrence's 'American' thought and art in the first half of the 1920s and richly illuminates several key texts of the period from a carefully poised postcolonial perspective that is fully alive to many of the issues touched on earlier in relation to Lawrence's 'ethics of alterity'. Though relatively brief, these readings represent major critical statements on works such as *Quetzalcoatl*, *The Plumed Serpent* and 'The Woman Who Rode Away'. Michael Bell and Marianna Torgovnick, too, satisfyingly and stimulatingly negotiate the balance between the general and the specific in their respective essays, 'Lawrence and Modernism' and 'Narrating Sexuality: *The Rainbow*'. Both these essays, again, provide original perspectives on some of the terrain mapped out at the start of this review and, in particular, they have in common a central concern with questions of language and narrative representation. Finally here I would mention John Worthen's essay on 'Lawrence as Dramatist', which covers its field authoritatively while simultaneously maintaining a lively analytical focus on textual detail in exploring Lawrence's dramatic skills.

A small but welcome clutch of other essays on Lawrence's drama appeared this year and might conveniently be mentioned as potential complements to Worthen's essay. Amitava Banerjee provides a lucid and elegantly written introductory account of the colliery plays in 'D.H. Lawrence the Dramatist and his Tragic Vision' (*KCS* 47:iii[2001] 3–14), while Ian Clarke elucidates specific technical and linguistic elements of the same group of plays in 'Dialogue and Dialect in Lawrence's Colliery Plays' (*JDHLS* [2001] 39–61). Nora Foster Stovel presents one of the few detailed considerations of the rarely discussed (unfinished) play *Altitude*, in 'D.H. Lawrence's *Altitude*: A Taos Comedy' (*EL* 24[2001] 83–101), while another rarely discussed work, *David*, is briefly considered by Raymond-Jean Frontain in '"Man for Man": *David*, the Bible, and Gender Construction' (in Sargent and Watson, eds., pp. 230–2); also in Sargent and Watson, eds., is Hans-W. Schwarze, 'Teaching Lawrence's Early Plays with his Early Prose' (pp. 233–4).

Sargent and Watson, eds., *Approaches to Teaching the Works of D.H. Lawrence*, has many similar aims to the *Cambridge Companion* in trying to offer a broad contemporary overview of Lawrence's works, and this is again a very rich and diverse collection covering a wide range of texts and issues while also adopting an exhilarating range of theoretical approaches to Lawrence. The pedagogical emphasis of the book takes little from its scholarly value, and, if anything, gives it a greater unity of purpose and focus than the Cambridge volume. This is most evident in its use of a central organizing theme of 'otherness' for the main section of essays (there is also a section of shorter 'pragmatic' essays on specific teaching ideas, as well as an extremely useful section on materials and resources). Often taking their cue from the experience of teaching Lawrence and from actual student responses, all the essays in this main section maintain a reassuringly lively awareness of the dialogical complexity of Lawrence's texts, and they all invariably propose radically new perspectives on his work. Essays here are organized into four groups, 'Discovering Otherness: Lawrence Writing/Rewriting Himself', 'Psychoanalytic Approaches to Otherness', 'Cultural Criticism and Otherness' and 'Teaching Other Cultures and Religions'.

In the first group, Charles L. Ross and Donald Buckley, in 'Lawrence in Hypertext: A Technology of Difference for Reading/Writing *The Rainbow* and "Odour of Chrysanthemums"', present a fascinating account of using hypertext in the classroom, both to enable students actually to practise textual scholarship for themselves, and to create 'a more interactive environment in which to reinterpret and rewrite D.H. Lawrence' (p. 70). In the second group, intriguing new perspectives on *The Rainbow* are generated by three different forms of psychoanalytic discussion, including a particularly compelling one by Jorgette Mauzerall in 'Strange Bedfellows: D.H. Lawrence and Feminist Psychoanalytic Theory in *The Rainbow*'. Important feminist readings also feature in the third group of essays, with another typically imaginative and challenging piece by Carol Siegel on *Women in Love* and *Sons and Lovers* and yet another careful recontextualization of 'The Woman Who Rode Away' (to join those in earlier-mentioned essays by Sargent and Kinkead-Weekes) in Pamela L. Caughie's 'Teaching "Woman": A Cultural Criticism Approach to "The Woman Who Rode Away"'. In the other two essays in this rich group, Cynthia Lewiecki-Wilson presents a reader-response approach to *The Captain's Doll* and Isobel M. Findlay and Garry Watson discuss how to teach *Studies in Classic American Literature* self-reflexively *as* cultural criticism. I have already mentioned two of the essays from the final group (those by Sagar and Mills), but the theme of cultural otherness is perhaps most strongly represented here by Virginia Crosswhite Hyde's sophisticated discussion in 'Picking up "Life-Threads" in Lawrence's Mexico: Dialogism and Multiculturalism in *The Plumed Serpent*'. Again, this essay usefully complements earlier-mentioned essays on this novel and on the theme of postcolonialism; in this context, see also, later in the same collection, Theresa Mae Thompson's 'Unlearning Europe: Postcolonial Questions for Teaching *The Plumed Serpent*' and also, for a rather different if still pertinent perspective, Hugh Stevens, '*The Plumed Serpent* and the Erotics of Primitive Masculinity' (in Stevens and Howlett, eds., *Modernist Sexualities*, pp. 219–38). Before leaving *Approaches to Teaching the Works of D.H. Lawrence*, I should also mention the inclusion here of a revised version of Sandra M. Gilbert's important feminist reassessment, 'Some Notes toward a Vindication of the Rites of D.H. Lawrence' [1990].

Women in Love has recently been a set text for a major public examination in France and this has led to a spate of related critical publications in both French and English, including the fourth of the main essay collections this year, Pichardie and Romanski, eds., *Like a Black and White Kaleidoscope Tossed at Random: Essays on D.H. Lawrence's 'Women in Love'*. Once more, theoretical perspectives and issues of language, representation, dialogism and alterity loom large, as one might expect with this *locus classicus* of Lawrence's self-questioning fiction. Philippe Romanski perhaps best captures the dominant mood in his elegantly executed deconstructive reading in '"And we couldn't understand it": *Women in Love* or the Failure of Hermeneutics', while questions of identity and relationship are treated biographically, linguistically, philosophically and psychoanalytically by, respectively, Michael Squires and Lynn K. Talbot ('Art and Life in *Women in Love*'), Craig A. Hamilton ('"This fretful voyage of life": Figurative Language in *Women in Love*'), Gregory Tague ('Detachment and the Beyond as Concepts Integral to Identity') and Hervé Fourtina ('Lines, Boundaries, and the Borderline'). A Bakhtinian approach to the novel's carnivalesque satire is presented by Robert Burden and, interestingly, Garry Watson appears in this collection too, with a sort of counterbalancing dialogue to the essay I began with (by Sargent and Watson). Here, while he continues to tease out the philosophical and ethical implications of Lawrence's art of otherness and difference, Watson shifts his attention, through Foucault, and through careful textual analysis of Birkin's views in *Women in Love*, to 'the care of the self' in Lawrence, as his title indicates: 'The Lawrentian/Birkinian Version of the Care of the Self: Attending to the Demands of the Soul'.

Two volumes of *Études lawrenciennes* for 2001 together contain some sixteen essays, loosely thematized under the headings, 'The Dark Continent of the Soul' (*EL* 24[2001]) and 'An Ever Widening Circle' (*EL* 25[2001]), though this latter volume also has a particular emphasis on *Women in Love*, including, appropriately enough in the light of my preceding paragraph, an essay on 'Narrative Technique and the Dialogic Principle in *Women in Love*' by Stefana Roussenova (*EL* 25[2001] 85–94). The earlier volume is perhaps most notable for the attention it gives to Lawrence's poetry in Sandra M. Gilbert's 'Troth with the Dead: Lawrence's Poetry of Mourning' (*EL* 24[2001] 7–22) and Bethan Jones's 'Following the Starry Shelley: D.H. Lawrence and Lyric Poetry' (*EL* 24[2001] 55–67), as well as for the previously cited essay by Stovel on *Altitude*.

The *D.H. Lawrence Review*, meanwhile, was represented by only one number this year and contained only fairly meagre critical fare in the form of three essays on *The Lost Girl*. The loosely postcolonial perspective of Michael L. Ross's 'Losing the Old National Hat: Lawrence's *The Lost Girl*' (*DHLR* 30:i[2001] 5–14) might be noted, along with Jill Franks's interesting comparative study of how Lawrence and Forster utilize myth (and Italy) 'to support their own sexual mythopoeia' in 'Myth and Biography in *Where Angels Fear to Tread* and *The Lost Girl*' (*DHLR* 30:i[2001] 29–42).

Andrew Smith's 'Vampirism, Masculinity and Degeneracy: D.H. Lawrence's Modernist Gothic' (in Smith and Wallace, eds., pp. 150–66) is a spirited but ultimately strained reading of *Sons and Lovers*, though its focus on masculinity might be usefully linked to the essay by Hugh Stevens cited earlier, and to his other essay this year, 'Sex and the Nation: "The Prussian Officer" and *Women in Love*' (in Fernihough, ed., pp. 49–65). There may also be a potential link here with Ronald Granofsky's suggestive discussion of cannibalistic imagery in *Aaron's Rod*, in the essay 'Modernism and D.H. Lawrence: Spatial Form and Selfhood in *Aaron's Rod*' (*ESC* 26:i[2000] 29–51). Granofsky argues that such imagery relates to the self's fear of disintegration and of merging with a devouring other, and he connects it to a broader pattern of images in the novel to do with refection, selfhood and void. Granofsky's essay usefully summarizes a range of dominant motifs in the novel and relates them interestingly to a broader modernist context, though his view of modernism, and of Lawrence's relationship to it, is slightly dated. Fears of being devoured are pertinent too to Lawrence's short story 'Tickets, Please', which is given a competent but rather crude and over-generalized reading by Bernard-John Ramadier in 'Dubious Progress in D.H. Lawrence's "Tickets, Please"' (*JSSE* 35[2000] 43–54). Ramadier does, however, give a novel perspective to the climactic scene of the story in describing it as a form of 'aggravated date rape' (p. 50). The importance of memory to a sense of identity is the theme of another essay on the Lawrentian dialectic of integration and disintegration, Mary Ann Melfi's '"The Shake of the Kaleidoscope": Memory, Entropy, and Progress in Lawrence's *The Rainbow*' (*JEGP* 100:iii[2001] 355–76). Melfi's discussion of the novel is lucid and well informed, and her stress on the importance of truthful recollection in the process of spiritual growth is an unusual one in this context, but overall the essay remains within fairly well-trodden critical territory.

Two major books which lie largely outside the loose interpretative framework I established at the start of this section are Louis K. Greiff's *D.H. Lawrence: Fifty Years on Film* and the third edition of Warren Roberts' *A Bibliography of D.H. Lawrence* (revised by Paul Poplawski). Greiff's book is an engaging, informative and well-documented chronicle of the fifty-year history of Lawrence screen adaptations, concentrating mainly on cinema feature films but also covering television adaptations and some more recent experimental video productions. Lucidly written and full of fascinating factual information (including a comprehensive filmography, videography and bibliography), the book is rather more than just a documentary chronicle in that it also offers detailed analyses both of each individual adaptation and its reception, *and*, in an ongoing way, of the whole intertextual tradition of adapting Lawrence. Greiff provides a useful brief overview of theories of adaptation, and clearly sets out his own theoretical and methodological assumptions; he also maintains a sense of the broader historical and cultural context of each of the films (though I felt this contextualization was just a little thin at times). This is the first comprehensive study of Lawrence and film, and it tells a valuable and intriguing story, not only about the adaptations themselves but also about our epoch's continuing cultural engagement with Lawrence outside the academy and beyond print culture alone.

Roberts and Poplawski's *Bibliography of D.H. Lawrence* is, of course, the primary bibliography of the author and a key resource in the scholarly study of his works. In the revised edition every section of the book has seen a fairly massive increase in material, and there are now, for example, over 700 works listed in section F, 'Books and Pamphlets about D.H. Lawrence'. Partly thanks to the new texts in the Cambridge Edition of Lawrence, a great number of new entries have also been added to perhaps the most important section, section A, where full bibliographical descriptions are given to all first editions of Lawrence's texts (incidentally, this section is now nicely enhanced by a series of colour plates reproducing several of Lawrence's original dust-jackets). Section D, 'Translations', has seen an enormous expansion, too, reflecting the continuing and apparently growing popularity of Lawrence around the world.

An intriguing piece of scholarly research which I hope will find its way into the fourth edition of the above is reported in an essay by David Cram and Christopher Pollnitz, 'D.H. Lawrence as Verse Translator' (*CQ* 30:ii[2001] 133–50). Briefly, the original, previously unknown German source of some of Lawrence's verse ranslations from the 1910s has recently come to light and this makes it possible for the first time to evaluate Lawrence's skills as a translator of verse and also to trace more accurately the genesis and development of some of his early poetic manuscripts and typescripts. Finally, two other essays missed last year might be mentioned here for their reliance on bibliographical scholarship. The first again involves Christopher Pollnitz, this time looking at textual variants of Lawrence's later poetry, in 'D.H. Lawrence's *Last Poems*: Taking the Right Tack' (*JML* 23:iii–iv[2000] 503–17). The second is Neil Reeve's 'Two Lovely Ladies' (*English* 49[2000] 15–22), a finely wrought piece of detailed critical speculation based on textual variants of 'The Lovely Lady'. Although only brief, this essay cleverly activates a rich chain of associations which eddy out suggestively beyond the tale in question into related areas of Lawrence's life and work.

f) James Joyce

The most impressive contribution to Joyce studies in 2001 was undoubtedly the launch by Brepols of annotated versions of the *Finnegans Wake Notebooks at Buffalo*, an ongoing project of 'genetic criticism' edited by Vincent Deane, Daniel Ferrer and Geert Lernout. This year, three notebooks were released: VI.B.3, VI.B.10 and VI.B.29. Each provides an introduction to the history of the notebook and a high-resolution, scanned copy of each notebook page alongside transcriptions and source notes. All of the notebooks will in due course become available in this format. Even more ambitiously, the editors have proposed an electronic version of the notebooks that will include critical reactions and scholarly additions to the published volumes. This is, then, the beginnings of a massive new reference library for *Wake* scholars, providing a necessary supplement to the *Wake* sections of the James Joyce Archive. The new reproductions give smaller facsimiles (including a few in colour) which are better quality than those in the Archive. Each notebook entry is keyed to other notebooks and drafts as well as linked back to its source (in so far as this has been possible). It is with the inclusion of this source material that the new editions offer their most distinctive contribution, and it is also here that they become interpretative, not explicitly, but to the extent that they attempt to show Joyce's use of his library. For instance, I had no idea that while compiling VI.B.29 Joyce had used a history of the town I grew up in. This knowledge provides a starting-point, but also perhaps an implicit limit, for my reading of the relevant *Wake* passage. Thus 'Ouerlord's tithing' (*FW* 541.09) is shown to be derived from 'the tithing of our lord, the King' which took place in Hitchin at Michaelmas according to Reginald Hine's study, *The History of Hitchin* [1921]. (Lernout offers an intriguing suggestion for Joyce's interest in this volume in his introduction.) The point here is that this sumptuous and immensely useful scholarly production rests on the assumption that each element in Joyce's text can be traced back to his preparatory reading. That may be, but to what extent should those source-texts determine interpretations of the *Wake*? Perhaps the editorial practices that govern the electronic version will show to what extent the editors are prescriptive. Yet again, it seems, *Finnegans Wake* challenges its would-be readers to confront their own critical presuppositions. It may be that technological change will hasten the arrival of even better, full-colour notebooks at a cheaper price, but until then, the volumes of this new edition promise to keep *Wake* critics busy for many years. They

clearly represent a landmark achievement in Joyce studies and are great testament to
the editors and other researchers.

Going back a generation to the handful of enthusiasts who established many of
today's critical commonplaces and made possible the genetic endeavours
represented by the new *Notebooks* series, Adaline Glasheen stands out as perhaps
the single most devoted *Wake* reader of the 1950s and 1960s. Her *Third Census* is,
to my mind at least, the single most helpful work of exegetical *Wake* studies. Her
correspondence with Thornton Wilder, the playwright and a similarly pioneering
figure in early *Wake* criticism, has been published as *A Tour of the Darkling Plain:*
The Finnegans Wake Letters of Thornton Wilder and Adaline Glasheen, edited by
Edward Burns with Joshua Gaylord. This hefty tome is supported by fourteen
appendices, including several notes and essays by the two, and bibliographies of
their published and unpublished works. Towards the end of 1954, Wilder states that
he would 'like to fall into a Rip-van-Winkle sleep and wake up years later and read
all that our successors have discovered in the book' (p. 116). He would be
dumbstruck by the sheer volume of sourcing that has been traced from the
notebooks. To read these letters is to be transported to a different age of scholarly
activity: slower, but just as industrious; collaborative, but just as competitive ('I feel
Jim Atherton[']s intellectual equal and Matthew Hodgart[']s superior' says
Glasheen (p. 112)). Additional musings on the human interactions of the Joyce
community are provided by an international cast of critics in this year's *Joyce
Studies Annual*.

Despite proposing the ideal reader of *Finnegans Wake* as a sort of genetic
reader—the 'genreader' (p. 202)—Jean-Michel Rabaté still has a few critical words
for some genetic criticism in his *James Joyce and the Politics of Egoism*. The
archive promised by genetic studies must still be conceived as unstable, as work in
progress, and so not summarily dismiss as 'wrong' interpretations that it does not
sanction. For Rabaté, the 'genreader' 'should not be afraid of misreadings' (p. 207).
This book is a complex weaving of textual, genetic, biographical, psychoanalytic
and historical-contextual readings of both Joyce's writing and Joyce the man. It is an
arresting volume, strung together from some older material and with many
diversions along the way, but still a formidable series of readings that have been
brought into a fairly cohesive project more readily than many a collection of
previously published material (see Patrick McGee's *Joyce Beyond Marx*, below).
For Rabaté, egoism is certainly not an essentialist or narcissistic egotistic
individuality, it is more like 'a radical anarchism refusing any authority' (p. 67). It
has its own historical moment in modernism, located as the emergence of Dora
Marsden's *The Egoist*, launched from the pages of *The New Freewoman*, and in
which Joyce's ironic self-*Portrait* first appeared. There is also a discourse of
egoism—not far from anarchism—that Rabaté reads most fully in Max Stirner's *The
Ego and his Own* (the English translation appeared in 1907), and in Meredith's *The
Egoist*. This last text is read by Rabaté as a sort of parallel with *Ulysses*, each
showing 'how a female ego's realization both overcomes egoism and signifies its
culmination' (p. 66). Indeed a feminist egoism, embodied in Marsden, Weaver and
Beach, is seen by Rabaté to have sustained Joyce throughout his career. Rabaté'
notion of egoism leads him to discuss hospitality: the terms are not the opposites
they might appear, but are in fact similar. He shows that Joyce represents Irish
hospitality, through the figure of Gabriel Conroy, as a value fissured by its own

ambivalence, a 'fake universality': 'there is never far, indeed, from the position of the guest to the role of the sacrificial victim, a point which is crucial to understand why Stephen Dedalus refuses Bloom's hospitality' (p. 157). *Ulysses* 'is a great novel of hospitality because it demonstrates the impossibility of hospitality' (p. 160). Rabaté goes on to read the tale of Sodom as it is replayed in the novel, arguing that the sexual issue of *Ulysses* is manifest not only in the questions of paternity and incest but also in a 'strong undercurrent' (p. 164) of homosexuality that runs through the book. Sodomy, for Joyce, is mainly to be found in gossip, a transgression that is linguistic, as in the implied obscenities of *Finnegans Wake*. This chapter is based on an essay that came out in *Quare Joyce*, edited by Joseph Valente ([2000]; not reviewed last year), which provides a comprehensive and insistent coverage of same-sex desire in Joyce, of which Rabaté's essay is probably the best. Mostly predicated on Sedgwick's notion of 'compulsory heterosexuality', the essays in this volume find homosexual desire latent in the nebulous term 'homosociality', and readily decry any denial. However, there are also some very helpful investigations of Joyce's interest in several sexual scandals: those involving British civil servants in Dublin Castle, Casement, D.B. Murphy and, of course, Wilde. Another essay to treat this topic from a more historical perspective is Jack Morgan's 'Queer Choirs: Sacred Music, Joyce's "The Dead" and the Sexual Politics of Victorian Aestheticism' (*JJQ* 37:i–ii[2001] 127–52), which looks at the banning of women from Catholic choirs, lamented by Kate Morkan in 'The Dead'.

A collection that has built upon Valente's volume is van Boheemen-Saaf and Lamos, eds., *Masculinities in Joyce: Postcolonial Constructions*, published in the European Joyce Studies series. Mostly focusing on *Dubliners* and *Ulysses*, the variety of essays here supports the editors' contention that masculinity in Joyce is marked by a high degree of 'internal contradiction' (p. 8). Margot Norris adds to her highly provocative suggestion in *Quare Joyce* that the boy narrator of 'An Encounter' desires the 'old josser' by arguing, in 'Masculinity Games in "After the Race"', that the inveigling of Jimmy Doyle's friends displays 'the structure and devices of seduction and rape' (p. 13). In her typically clever analysis, Norris argues that this 'queering' or feminization of Doyle is mirrored by readers' over-haste to condemn him. We thus share in the narrator's deception by being trapped into mistakenly thinking we share in the male bonding promised by a false acquiescence to the inner circle of knowing and superiority. See also a similar argument about narratorial manipulation of the reader in Norris's 'Shocking the Reader in James Joyce's "A Painful Case"' (*JJQ* 37:i–ii[2001] 63–82).

Some of the essays in the *Masculinities* volume are on surer ground in their historical exploration of cultural constructions of masculinity. Richard Brown's '"As if a man were author of himself": Literature, Mourning, and Masculinity in "The Dead" and *Ulysses*' argues that Gabriel Conroy's chosen career could be seen as effeminate in his culture and that Stephen's attempted self-authoring is a kind of 'masculine birth' (p. 91) afforded by literature as opposed to the feminized Church. Stephen, Bloom and Gabriel are thus seen wrestling with an 'ambivalence towards the maternal' (p. 92) in their attempts to 'author' themselves. Another welcome attempt to marry historical and literary analyses is made by Tracey Teats Schwarz in '"Do you call that a man?": The Culture of Anxious Masculinity in Joyce's *Ulysses*'. She cites the cult of 'muscular Christianity' pioneered by Charles Kingsley as a hegemonic discourse for 1904 Dublin with serious implications for Irish nationalism.

Incidentally, the sloppy editing of this volume is instanced by the fact that both the author and the title of this last essay are spelt differently on the contents page and in the essay heading (in all, seven of the twelve pieces here have altered titles between the table of contents and essay heading). Similar inconsistencies are also evident in the other European Joyce Studies volume this year, the awkwardly entitled *James Joyce and the Fabrication of an Irish Identity*, edited by Michael Patrick Gillespie (perhaps the practice of providing camera-ready copy ought to have some reliable safeguards). Unfortunately, Gillespie's introduction is not much more coherent than his editing. He refers to the 'specific influence of the ethos of Irishness' and then says that 'Irishness' is 'a transient unstable creation' (p. 3). Some of the essays in this volume do make serious attempts to read the cultural complexities of Joyce's Ireland, including Vincent Cheng's analysis of the mutual dependence of cosmopolitanism and nationalism in '"Terrible queer creatures": Joyce, Cosmopolitanism and the Inauthentic Irishman' and John Rickard's discussion of the Revivalist trope of the wandering figure in his '"A quaking sod": Hybridity, Identity and Wandering Irishness'. Alongside these might be set two chapters from *Modernism and the Celtic Revival* by Gregory Castle, which deal with Joyce's critique of Revivalism, but seen as a reaction from within a shared ambition. The early fiction, Castle says, shares to a degree a Revivalist ethnographic project of representing the peasantry, while the later fiction enables a 'critique of both Revivalism and ethnography' and the formation of a new, 'empowering anthropological' writing (p. 207).

Another of the essays in Gillespie's volume treats a topic on which there has been some work this year: Joyce and film. Maria Pramaggiore's 'Unmastered Subjects: Identity as Fabrication in Joseph Strick's *A Portrait of the Artist as a Young Man* and *Ulysses*' shows that Strick offsets realist and avant-garde images in his films as a means of relaying the complexity of representing identities. Of two short books on Joyce and film this year, Kevin Barry's *The Dead* is an exemplary comparative study of Joyce's long short story and John Huston's film. Ever alert to the interpretative decisions of the filming process, as well as to the specificities of textual interpretation, Barry has chapters on the filming, lighting, setting and performing of Huston's version; its faithfulness (or otherwise); a wonderful comparison with Rossellini's *Voyage to Italy*; the film's overt nationalism (in which Miss Ivors leaves the party and 'is striding towards the Easter Rising' (p. 51)); the structure of the film; and, of course, the significance of the ending, where it seems clear, in Barry's view, that the greater ambiguity of the text, with its blank space, wins out over the film's voiceover and artificiality. The film's ending was actually shot in Kildare, Wicklow and at the Rock of Cashel, which were chosen as 'bits of Irish Irishness' (p. 79) according to the locations manager. As Barry argues, 'historical geography exceed[s] the nationalist iconography' of the West. If this reading is rather harsh on critics such as Luke Gibbons, it does at least show that the film concedes a 'material recognition of that symbolically empty space' (p. 80), the midlands. There are additional chapters on Huston's other films and on Joyce's cultural and political relationship with Revivalist Ireland around 1907.

Thomas Burkdall's *Joycean Frames: Film and the Fiction of James Joyce* offers a brief critical and biographical examination of a large and still under-researched topic. After a run-through of the generally known connections between Joyce and cinema, and a short chapter on the ways in which film altered structures of perception, Burkdall's thesis emerges. This is that a series of corresponding developments in film theory and Joyce's prose can be traced through the first three decades of the twentieth century. The microscopic realism of *Dubliners* has several features in common with Italian neo-realism and early documentary film (such as the work of the Lumières). Eisenstein's essays on montage are analysed in connection with *A Portrait* and Joyce's word-games. The fantastical quality of the films of Georges Méliès provides a starting point for a consideration of the 'protosurrealistic aspects of *Ulysses*' (p. xiv). In particular, Méliès's stop-motion trick, whereby a jammed camera led to the discovery that one image can be suddenly mutated into another (a bus into a hearse, men into women), is seen as an early forerunner of the hallucinations and dislocated perceptions of 'Circe'. One of the strengths of Burkdall's analysis is to employ the contemporaneous essays of early film critics, as here with the work of Vacel Lindsay. The final point of comparison is a reading of 'Nausicaa' in the light of the ideas of recent film theorists Laura Mulvey and Mary Ann Doane. This episode seems almost written for filmic analysis, playing as it does on scopophilia and voyeurism. To read the first half of 'Nausicaa' as parading Mulvey's analysis of the controlling male gaze is almost too neat. There is little awareness of the mutual perception at play in Joyce's chapter. In fact, Burkdall's analysis falls rather flat here: there is no sense of critical distance from the film theorists he utilizes, and the disappointment is that they offer nothing new to a reading of the text. While Burkdall has some useful information on early cinema, and successfully underlines the concomitant intertextual development of film techniques with Joyce's fiction, literary critics may find his readings somewhat limited and occasionally clichéd. The *James Joyce Broadsheet* published 'Joyce and Early Cinema' by Keith Williams, an informative placement of Joyce's technical innovations alongside developments in film, a piece that covers some similar ground to Burkdall.

The uneven Florida James Joyce series continues to account for a large proportion of books on Joyce, having produced three this year: *Joyce's Metamorphosis* by Stanley Sultan; Patrick McGee's *Joyce Beyond Marx: History and Desire in 'Ulysses' and 'Finnegans Wake'*; and *The Dublin Helix: The Life of Language in Joyce's 'Ulysses'* by Sebastian D.G. Knowles. In the first of these, Sultan has provided a useful tool for any future biographer of Joyce, for in reading the tangled career of the young writer he attempts to distinguish clearly—and to show the intense difficulties of distinguishing clearly—between historical autobiography and invented fiction. Taking as his focal point the period from the summer of 1904 to 1907, that is, the time surrounding and immediately following Joyce's departure from Dublin, Sultan reconstructs a close reading of the various versions of the early *Dubliners* stories, especially 'The Sisters' [1904–6] and relates these revisions to 'The Dead' and to the decision to rewrite *Stephen Hero* into *A Portrait* [both 1907]. Sultan's argument is that Joyce's 'stories of my childhood'—'The Sisters', 'An Encounter' and 'Araby'—owe much less to 'veridical autobiography' (p. 60) than has been supposed by some critics. 'The Sisters', Sultan contends, owes more to the earlier *Homestead* story sent to Joyce by George Russell than to anything in his own life. The centrepiece of this very brief book is a lengthy chapter that examines the various versions of 'The Sisters', showing that the rewritten story constitutes the beginning of Joyce's 'metamorphosis' of life into art. This transformational achievement is mirrored in the rewritten autobiographical novel and confirmed in Joyce's first work of maturity, 'The Dead'. A rather confusing analogy is drawn with D.H. Lawrence in the introduction and a long appendix on Lawrence's autobiographical practices; other than this Sultan does not venture beyond the texts of Joyce.

A rather more adventurous series of discussions is advanced by Patrick McGee in his collection of essays. *Joyce Beyond Marx* contains eleven essays: eight are modified versions of pieces already published, and one is forthcoming elsewhere. The two new pieces comprise, first, a discussion of the postcolonial conditions of Joyce's work, situated among recent fiction from other nations and recent readings of the historical conditions that determined Joyce's Ireland, and, second, an ambitious, lengthy, final essay that reads the spirit of Marxism in *Finnegans Wake*. The provocative closing lines of this essay—and so of the book itself—call for a recognition of the intersections of nationalism and internationalism, which McGee calls the 'desire that *Finnegans Wake* manifests and that we must learn to call communism' (p. 282). There is without exception something precious in the republication of old essays, always claiming to be substantially revised of course, and this collection sits awkwardly with McGee's call for Left academics to be more cognizant of the conditions of their work. When he chides Duffy and Nolan for not sufficiently acknowledging the historical embeddedness of their own (pathbreaking) readings of Joyce, it simply seems churlish. That said, McGee has produced some finely detailed theoretical readings with a keen ear for Joyce's language and a sharp eye for his cultural complexities. In addition, this collection charts the conflicts within McGee's own thought, between an earlier more post-structuralist position and a later more fully embraced postcolonialism (not 'semicolonialism' as he pointedly says). Throughout, 'history' hovers like a repeated mantra urging the reader on to yet more work.

The third Florida book this year is certainly the quirkiest, and readily admits that its argument is ludicrous. *The Dublin Helix* is a series of investigations into the 'enigmas and puzzles' of *Ulysses* that Joyce reportedly said would keep the professors busy for centuries. If M'Intosh and UP:up are the most celebrated of these, Knowles shows that there are many more where they came from. Among those lexical games de-riddled here are: the secret of Bloom's drawers; the use of Keller's Gothic poem by Othmar Schoek, then Joyce, and then Samuel Barber; eleven algebraic equations pertaining to the economics of the day; the fifteen sirens of episode eleven; the strange correspondence between *Frankenstein* and 'Penelope'; and the pertinence to 'Eumeaus' of the Tichborne Claimant. This is a lively and often instructive short book (some 130 pages of text), that, perhaps inevitably, has lots to say about 'Ithaca', but which some readers may find self-indulgent. However, Knowles manages to carry it off with good humour. His readings are teased through with panache, and even when most diverting (as in the *Frankenstein* chapter) the book is still faithful to the model set by Joyce. That is, Knowles has managed to produce amid the current portentous academic debates a text that is ludic and odd, treading the fine line between pedantry and fun, after the spirit of *Ulysses* itself (though Joyce knew, as Knowles appears not to, that 'Æ' is a pseudonym, not Russell's initials). One of the hard facts of reading *Ulysses*, to which Knowles is very much alive (witnessed in his excellent homage to the 1934 edition), is the materiality of the book, the physical arrangement of ink on paper and the importance of how it looks. The experience of reading is a physical and visual as well as an imaginative one, and this theme is also taken up by George Bornstein in his *Material Modernisms: The Politics of the Page*, which follows the work of Jerome McGann into the modern period. Bornstein has a chapter on 'Joyce and the Colonial Archive: Constructing Alterity in *Ulysses*', which shows that Joyce's allusions to cultural and ethnic diversity were usually added in revisions, thus transforming the extant text into a hybrid: the politics is literally on the page.

Stephen Sicari's *Joyce's Modernist Allegory: 'Ulysses' and the History of the Novel* argues that the latter half of *Ulysses* carefully rereads the opening naturalistic episodes in the same manner that theological allegory of the New Testament rereads the Old Testament. In this model—which Sicari locates initially in Dante and finally, ambitiously, attempts to apply to Eliot, Pound, and Stevens—the key chapter is 'Ithaca', which 'locates a fixed point capable of governing the meaning of the rest of the novel' (p. 8). From this Bloom emerges as a 'Christian hero' whose incarnation transcends the mundanities of daily life and whose 'shining example of Christian forgiveness' (p. 187) in wiping away the telltale crumbs of potted meat from his bedsheets is the true climax of the novel. This is an idiosyncratic and somewhat anachronistic argument that makes little or no mention of Bloom's complex relationship with Judaism, nor any serious attempt to investigate just what was so remiss in 'our culture' that Joyce sought to redress it. He did so, Sicari argues, by being 'a secret and subtle idealist' who fashioned a style fit to represent 'something ideal' (p. 2). That said, Sicari's book does offer a new perspective on the perennial topic of Joyce's styles, showing how he discarded the novel as genre, and then the epic, culminating in a mode of allegory derived from St Paul and Dante. This 'modernist allegory' is a fusion of the literal (or historical) with the transcendent and eternal, a style capable of expressing spirituality in a cynical age.

The form of allegory has been revisited, with greater success, by Lucia Boldrini, whose *Joyce, Dante and the Poetics of Literary Relations: Language and Meaning in 'Finnegans Wake'* stands out in a year that saw little by way of comparative studies. Concentrating for the most part on Joyce's use of Dante's *De Vulgari Eloquentia* in composing *Finnegans Wake*, Boldrini shows how the two writers shared a similar method of composition, and how each attempted to construct a new discourse from the languages available to him. Dante's treatise is seen as an 'important antecedent' (p. 100) for Joyce's universalizing idiom. Boldrini takes on Levin's distinction between four levels of meaning: the literal, anagogical, allegorical and moral. Including detailed readings of the Fall, the Letter, the washerwomen, and the geometry lesson, Boldrini's argument is that the literal and the allegorical collapse into one another. *Finnegans Wake*, then, has no literal level of reading. This book sets out both the affinities between Joyce's and Dante's poetics and Joyce's correspondence with medieval interpretation; it will surely be standard reading for future comparative work on the two writers.

The *James Joyce Quarterly* produced two double special editions this year. In 'Dublin and the Dubliners' (see also reviews of essays by Morgan and Norris, above), David Spurr has analysed 'Colonial Spaces in Joyce's Dublin' (*JJQ* 38:i–ii[2001] 23–42). He looks at the imposing authority of Dublin's architecture and the complex reactions it inspires in the consciousnesses of Joyce's city-dwellers. Spurr is particularly interested in 'The Dead', the depiction of Trinity College in *A*

Portrait and the route of the Viceregal cavalcade in 'Wandering Rocks'. A different approach to similar terrain is made by Luke Gibbons in '"Where Wolf Tone's statue was not": Joyce, Monuments and Memory' (in McBride, ed., *History and Memory in Modern Ireland*, pp. 139–59). Gibbons shows the complex ways in which cultural memory is built in to the city, in its buildings, streets and 'empty' spaces, as he follows the figure of the *flâneur* through cultural theory. Under colonial rule, popular memory is open to chance incursions, argues Gibbons, and hence the *flâneur* is not easily determined by public rituals: the oddest thoughts keep coming back, like a bad penny. The other *JJQ* special edition is devoted to 'Joyce and the Law'. There is some useful extra information in 'Sifting through Censorship: The British Home Office *Ulysses* Files (1922–1936)' (*JJQ* 38:iii–iv[2001] 479–508) by Carmelo Medina Casado, while Conrad L. Rushing has help for future biographers in 'The English Players Incident: What Really Happened?' (*JJQ* 38:iii–iv[2001] 371–88). In 'A Portrait of the Snob: James Joyce and the Anxieties of Cultural Capital' (*MFS* 47:iv[2001] 774–99) the new editor of the *James Joyce Quarterly*, Sean Latham, has written about the ironic undercutting of snobbery in Joyce's work, only to lament that it has itself become the subject of snobbery among a 'Stephen-like audience' (p. 795). Should we now expect to see 'Matcham's Masterstoke' in the *Quarterly*? One way to enhance the popularity of Joyce and maybe to encourage social inclusiveness in reading him might be to follow the hypermedia project under the guidance of Michael Groden. A long essay by Robert Bell offers a glimpse of how one *Ulysses* episode might look in hypermedia. Bell's '"Preparatory to anything else": Introduction to Joyce's "Hades"' (*JML* 24:iii–iv[2001] 363–500) sets out a series of different levels of annotation for different 'levels' of reader. This seems, if anything, to underscore the very difficulties of 'popularizing' Joyce.

(g) Virginia Woolf

Several years ago Jane Marcus called for a more thorough study of Virginia Woolf as a 'public intellectual', and some of the most important studies of Woolf published in 2001 can be usefully considered in this context. Naomi Black's scrupulous new edition of *Three Guineas*, the most recent volume in Shakespeare Head's series of scholarly editions of Woolf's writing, is certainly a major contribution to this effort since it has long been regarded as presenting the most 'explicit', though controversial, expression of Woolf's feminist politics. Arguing that the few corrections Woolf made in the first American edition are far outweighed by numerous 'outright errors' in this text, Black selected the 1938 edition produced by Hogarth Press rather than the version published by Harcourt-Brace, which is the edition most widely adopted for classroom use. Like other scholarly editions in this series, Black's volume documents the variants in the existing editions; it also reproduces the notes that Woolf originally appended, as well as the five 'satirical' photographs she included in Hogarth Press's first edition. In her thorough introduction, Black documents the complicated genesis and publication history of *Three Guineas*, using Woolf's diaries and scrapbooks from the period, and summarizes the initial critical response to it, noting that Maynard Keynes and Quentin Bell, among others, particularly objected to Woolf's inclusion of the photographs which, they felt, 'made a mockery not of men, but of institutions' (p. lvii). Black offers a persuasive analysis of Woolf's unique blend of defiant feminism and pacifism, contrasting it with the positions taken by her family and friends, by other feminists in the 1930s, and by men who were once in the Bloomsbury group.

Contributors to Pawlowski, ed., *Virginia Woolf and Fascism: Resisting the Dictators' Seduction*, have also helped to illuminate Woolf's self-defined role as a public intellectual, particularly in the 1930s as she contemplated the menace posed by the rise of fascism. Pawlowski has assembled an impressive collection of essays written by some of the most prominent American Woolf scholars. She begins this collection, after her brief introduction, with Quentin Bell's 'A Room of One's Own and Three Guineas', which reiterates his longstanding objections to Woolf's *Three Guineas* and to the feminist ideas it contains. Citing Leonard Woolf's famous remark that his wife was the 'least political animal that has ever been since Aristotle invented the definition' (p. 13), Bell argues that Virginia Woolf 'tended to forget that she had a vote; not only did she have one, every adult woman in the country had one too' by 1938 when this text was finally published (p. 16). The essays in this volume counter Bell's assessment of and arguments about *Three Guineas* in various ways. Jessica Berman, for example, in her superb 'Of Oceans and Opposition: *The Waves*, Oswald Mosley, and the New Party', shows convincingly how Woolf's 'aesthetic is bound up with the emergence of British fascism in the period of crisis from 1929–1932' (p. 106). Describing Oswald Mosley's split with the Labour party in 1930 and detailing Harold Nicholson's involvement as the editor of Mosley's New Party organ, *Action*, which included columns by Vita Sackville-West, Christopher Isherwood, and Francis Birrell, Berman both recognizes the powerful seductiveness of certain strands of fascist thought for British intellectuals in the early 1930s and demonstrates, through her reading of *The Waves*, that Virginia Woolf's politics showed her continuing allegiance to the Women's Co-operative Guild's 'agenda of international pacifism and to the Fabian socialist approach to economic equality' (p. 109). Drawing on Alice Kaplan's recent study of fascism and French literature, as well as on influential works by Klaus Theweleit and Walter Benjamin, Berman shows how Woolf in *The Waves* questions the 'promise of plenitude' held out by the proto-fascist nationalists in England through her contrast of Louis's business successes with Rhoda's suicide, and identifies the dangerous appeal of leaders like Percival, who inspire followers by their physical beauty and mindless charisma. Natalia Rosenfeld, author of *Outsiders Together: Virginia and Leonard Woolf* (PrincetonUP [2000]), presents a much more nuanced analysis than Bell's in her discussion of the politics of Virginia and Leonard Woolf in the 1930s in her excellent essay, 'Monstrous Conjugations: Images of Dictatorship in the Anti-Fascist writings of Virginia and Leonard Woolf'. Summarizing Virginia Woolf's interest in Freud's later work and describing her meeting with him in 1939, Rosenfeld charts her changing views of war, pacifism, and the efficacy of language and art as a response to the rhetoric of dictators and warmongers. Comparing Virginia's and Leonard's parallel explorations of the 'link between political dictatorship and verbal dictation' (p. 126) through a careful analysis of selected essays written in these years, Rosenfeld concludes by showing why Woolf's *Between the Acts* is a 'work that insists on its own fragmentedness, its disruptions and disjunctions as inseparable from its moments of harmony' (p. 129). Vara S. Neverow's essay in this volume complements Rosenfeld's by presenting a broader overview of Woolf's critique of Freudian thought throughout her career.

Other notable essays in *Virginia Woolf and Fascism* include Leigh Coral Harris's beautiful and evocative summary of Woolf's travels in Italy, which contrasts diary excerpts from her earlier trips, where she expressed her pleasure in the experience of 'anonymousness', with her comments during her later trip to Rome in 1935, where she noted with dismay the 'hyper-masculine identity' that had infused contemporary Italian art and impoverished its population. Harris thus offers a fresh context for Woolf's frequently cited remark in *A Room of One's Own* that 'poetry ought to have a mother as well as a father. The Fascist poem, one may fear, will be a horrid little abortion such as one sees in a glass jar in the museum of some country town' (p. 82). Molly Able Travis, in her trenchant, cleverly organized essay, documents the incipient fascism of some of the most famous male modernists of the period, including T.S. Eliot, Ezra Pound, D.H. Lawrence, H.G. Wells, and Oswald Mosley, and offers an analysis of the backlash directed at the Bloomsbury group in the criticism of F.R. and Queenie Leavis. Merry Pawlowski's essay, 'Toward a Feminist Theory of the State: Virginia Woolf and Wyndham Lewis on Art, Gender, and Politics', fills another gap in this survey of Woolf's intellectual concerns in the 1930s by illustrating the increasingly explicit fascism evident in Wyndham Lewis's 'malignant satire' on Woolf's 'Mr. Bennett and Mrs. Brown,' in his 1934 diatribe, *Men without Art*. Pawlowski argues that Lewis's critique provoked Woolf's anger and prompted her to write the essay that eventually became *Three Guineas*, which counters Lewis's self-aggrandizing model of the state headed by a masculine intellectual authoritarian leader who dominates the 'feminized masses' (p. 49) with Woolf's alternative model which allows space for women to escape such domination through an affiliation with the Outsider's Society. While Pawlowski's collection offers a good survey of Woolf's various responses to fascism in the public and private realms, and notes the importance of works such as Andrew Hewitt's *Political Inversions: Homosexuality, Fascism and the Modernist Imagination* (StanfordUP [1996]) and Erin G. Carlston's *Thinking Fascism: Sapphic Modernism and Fascist Modernity* (StanfordUP [1998]), none of the contributors to this volume fully considers Woolf's own writing in this context.

Fortunately, other scholars have ably evaluated Woolf's complex attitudes toward sexual identity in relation to her politics and aesthetics, including Gay Wachman in her excellent study, *Lesbian Empire: Radical Cross-Writing in the Twenties*, which compares Woolf with other writers of this decade in an analysis that is far more attentive to the contradictions evident in her treatment of gay and lesbian sexual identities, showing how they disrupt or even propel her changing theories of art and politics, perhaps most notably in *Mrs Dalloway* and *Orlando*. In other words, there is a kind of uniformity in the defence of Woolf's feminism and pacifism in *Virginia Woolf and Fascism* that might have been enlivened by the inclusion of a wider range of theoretical and political perspectives.

Readers interested in more materialist perspectives on Woolf's responses to fascism will applaud Karen Jacobs's elegant and profound analysis of her efforts to create an 'antidote to the spectacle of war' in *Between the Acts*, which is included as a chapter of Jacobs's fine comparative study, *The Eye's Mind: Literary Modernism and Visual Culture*. Drawing on some of the most theoretically sophisticated materialist analysis of *Between the Acts* by Patricia Klindiest Joplin (*SCR* 6[1989] 88–104), Catherine Wiley (*CLIO* 25:i[1995] 3–20), and Michael Tratner (in Pamela L. Caughie's *Virginia Woolf in the Age of Mechanical Reproduction* (Garland

[2000], pp. 115–34), Jacobs argues that Woolf attempted in this novel to imagine a 'means by which aesthetic spectacle can function as a palliative to violence' when it 'mystically serves as a conduit to collective, if momentary, apprehension' (p. 204). Miss La Trobe's play, Jacobs argues, uses the techniques of discontinuity and fragmentation to create the same 'flash of dialectical insight' that Benjamin describes in his influential essay, 'The Work of Art in the Age of Mechanical Reproduction', and in later works.

Emily Dalgarno's *Virginia Woolf and the Visible World*, which offers an impressive, broadly synthesizing analysis of Woolf's aesthetics through a survey of the entire corpus of her writing, also deserves notice. Dalgarno begins with Woolf's enigmatic remark that 'the main thing in beginning a novel is to feel, not that you can write it, but that it exists on the far side of a gulf, which words can't cross', and defines her subject as an exploration of the 'unrepresentable visible' in Woolf's writing (p. 2). Considering topics as apparently diverse as Woolf's study of Greek and her understanding of modern art, optics, and photography, Dalgarno offers an analysis of Woolf's changing aesthetic philosophy that is ambitious, well-informed, and refreshingly unpredictable. Dalgarno argues that Woolf's study of Greek with Janet Case allowed her to recognize the 'trope of the forever untranslatable' in *Agamemnon*, a discovery which allowed Woolf to claim a Cassandra-like authority to 'see beyond the bounds of the visible world' (p. 34). In what is arguably the most interesting chapter of this study, Dalgarno reconstructs a chronology of Woolf's reading of plays by Aeschylus, Sophocles, Aristophanes, and Euripides, as well as her study of the Platonic dialogues, and her translations of *Agamemnon*. She effectively shows how central Woolf's study of Greek was to her treatment of language and gender in *The Voyage Out*, Platonic love and beauty in *Jacob's Room*, war and transcendence in *Mrs Dalloway*, and vision and silence in *To the Lighthouse*. In considering Woolf's later works, Dalgarno turns her attention to optics and photography, arguing that Woolf moved beyond the limits of consciousness and language, as Lacan defines them, to construct an 'ethics of the imaginary' in *Three Guineas*, which invited women to take a position on the 'threshold of the symbolic'. Dalgarno's study complements Sibyl Oldfield's earlier analysis of Woolf's reading of *Antigone* (*SCR* 29[1996] 45–57), on one hand, and recent work on Woolf's aesthetics by, for example, Jane Goldman in *Feminist Aesthetics of Virginia Woolf* (CUP [1998]), on the other.

Another significant contribution to the field of Woolf studies in 2001 is Jessica Berman and Jane Goldman's well-edited collection, *Out of Bounds: Selected Papers from the Tenth Annual Conference on Virginia Woolf*, which incorporates selected papers from the conference held at the University of Maryland, Baltimore County, on 7–10 June 2000. While space will not permit a complete review of the forty short essays included in this volume, several should be noted. Maggie Humm's survey of Woolf's complex attitude towards photography, film, and modernist aesthetics (pp. 206–13) and Jennifer Wicke's theoretically sophisticated and delightfully witty 'Frock Consciousness: Virginia Woolf's Dialectical Materialism' (pp. 221–9) prompt readers to interrogate the limits of the 'iconic', high-fashion photographic images that Brenda Silver so persuasively analysed in *Virginia Woolf: Icon* (UChicP [1999]). Elizabeth Outka's 'The Shop Windows were Full of Sparkling Chains: Consumer Desire and Woolf's *Night and Day*' shows how Woolf's second and subsequent novels are 'neither above consumerism nor do they embrace it' (p. 234).

Several essays consider issues central to current feminist critical debates. Jane de Gray, for example, rereads *Orlando* to demonstrate how Woolf's use of 'theatrical' allusions reveals the 'performative' aspects of gender and sexuality (pp. 31–9). Patricia Moran, in her fine essay, 'Gunpowder Plots: Sexuality and Censorship in Woolf's Later Works', expands on her insights in *Word of Mouth* (UPVirginia [1996]) by tracing the patterns of 'traumatic memory' in Woolf's last three novels (pp. 6–12). Diana Swanson persuasively argues that Woolf's choice of a female narrator and her allusions to *Antigone* in *Jacob's Room* interrogate one of the basic boundaries that allowed women to be excluded from citizenship in the pre-war years by focusing exclusively on their roles as 'mothers' rather than 'sisters' (pp. 46–51). Michelle Barrett considers several excerpts from the typescripts for *A Room of One's Own* in order to demonstrate how Woolf deconstructs the concepts of truth and reason, as other members of the Bloomsbury group defined them (pp. 120–9). Jane Lilienfeld, in an intriguing essay, explores the contradictions that Woolf's anti-imperialist feminism posed for a postcolonial writer like the Canadian Alice Munro (pp. 92–6). Several essays push other standard boundaries in Woolf studies by considering new media and new perspectives on the organization of knowledge. Edward Bishop, for example, creatively uses Foucault's and Derrida's analysis of archival research as a means to compare Leonard Woolf's meticulously organized Hogarth Press archive with the scattered and variously organized collections of Virginia Woolf's manuscripts, books, and diaries in libraries in England and the United States. Todd Avery considers Woolf's critique of BBC broadcasts. Finally, in a superbly historicized reading of Virginia Woolf's essay, 'Middlebrow', which was originally written in response to J.B. Priestley's notorious essay, 'To a Highbrow' [1932], Melba Cuddy-Kean shows how Woolf 'exposes the complicity of unquestioning patriotism, capitalist values, media control of public discourse, and anti-intellectual complacency' which she found to be characteristic of the 'masculinized institutional discourse' of 'mass culture' (p. 64). The brevity of the essays in this volume makes them particularly accessible to the general reader, though most are also contextualized and annotated so as to provide satisfying reading for scholars of British modernism and specialists on Virginia Woolf.

Beth Rigel Daugherty and Mary Beth Pringle have also made a significant contribution to Woolf studies with their excellent collection, *Approaches to Teaching Woolf's 'To the Lighthouse'*, published as part of the MLA's series Approaches to Teaching World Literature, edited by Joseph Gibaldi. Perhaps the most valuable contribution in this volume is Daugherty and Pringle's concise, generous, brilliantly organized, and extraordinarily comprehensive survey of Woolf scholarship, which, along with their extensive, meticulously edited bibliography, provides an invaluable aid for specialists and non-specialists alike. The twenty-one essays included in this volume are written with an American educational context in mind; most describe how *To the Lighthouse* is used at various levels in the English, or occasionally the Women's Studies, curriculum in community colleges and public and private universities, and most describe teaching strategies designed to address the pedagogical challenges posed by inexperienced, ill-prepared, or resistant students. All of the contributors provide interesting practical suggestions for when and how to teach *To the Lighthouse*, what kinds of context can be provided, and how to design classroom activities that give students a greater sense of mastery and appreciation of Woolf's writing. As Patricia Laurence notes, in a wry understatement, 'Teaching Virginia Woolf isn't easy these days, perched as she is—a white, upper-middle-class British literary lady, with a whiff of experimentalism, feminism, lesbianism, and colonialism about her' (p. 66), yet she goes on to describe how she uses Bakhtin's theory of the novel's 'multi-voicedness' to help her students understand how to read the multiple voices and appreciate the rhythms of Woolf's prose style. Other contributors describe even more daring pedagogical experiments, such as Annis Pratt's inspiring description of her successful efforts to create a classroom where students learn to trust 'their own ability to develop close readings of the novel' (p. 73). Edward Bishop vividly describes his imaginative demonstration of a more 'materialist' approach to Woolf which involves retracing the steps that literally translated Woolf's manuscript of *To the Lighthouse* into 'real capital': he begins by recounting Woolf's involvement with the Hogarth Press, visits a print shop where students actually set and print type, and then reviews all the editing and marketing decisions that the Woolfs made in producing and distributing the novel in Great Britain, the US, and elsewhere. Several other contributors present various ways in which autobiographical or historical materials can be used to enhance students' appreciation of this novel. Louise DeSalvo, for example, explains how she uses excerpts from Woolf's diaries to highlight the class issues and silences in *To the Lighthouse*. Susan Yunis recounts how she creates a cultural context for Lily's painting through her display of Impressionist and post-Impressionist paintings of the period. Karen Levenback describes how she contextualizes *To the Lighthouse* as a 'civilian war novel' by introducing students to a range of historical materials about the First and Second World Wars, from newspaper accounts to standard studies of war literature to more recent works, for example by Jane Marcus, Allyson Booth, and Levenback herself. In short, it is hard to imagine that anyone who reads this collection will want to teach *To the Lighthouse* in exactly the same way again.

Although there have been numerous brief biographies published in the wake of Hermione Lee's splendid and monumental biography of Woolf, I would most confidently recommend the latest addition to this group, Mary Ann Caws's *Virginia Woolf*, to readers of all sorts. Published as part of the series of Penguin's lavishly illustrated biographies, it presents a clear, economical, comprehensive summary of Virginia Woolf's life and writing, illustrated with brilliantly chosen familiar and unfamiliar photographs of her, as well as intimate photographs and snapshots of the wide circle of her famous friends and family. Drawing on her extensive research and distinguished scholarship on modernist writers and painters in England and France, Caws also includes a marvellous selection of reproductions of paintings and drawings by Vanessa Bell, Duncan Grant, and Walter Sickert, a delightful sketch of Woolf by Richard Kennedy, and a sample of Woolf's book jackets designed by Vanessa Bell, bringing to light the rich visual dimensions of Woolf's cultural milieu in ways that no other recent biography has surpassed. Caws's study is organized more as an Impressionist painting than a conventional chronological narrative, though she succeeds admirably in identifying all the important strands in Woolf's life and art. Citing *The Waves*, 'Look. This is the truth' (p. 1), Caws characterizes her project as an effort to represent the 'visual scenes' of Woolf's life through a survey of 'the things that mattered the most' to her: 'friends, loves, travels, reading, correspondence, conversation … and her writing' (p. 91). Caws's masterful descriptions of Woolf's close relationships with Vanessa, Vita Sackville-West,

Roger Fry, and T.S. Eliot are especially illuminating. Perhaps her greatest contribution in this study, however, is that she considers Woolf in a more international and cosmopolitan context by summarizing her travels in Europe, and especially her fascination with Greece and southern France. She reminds readers of Woolf's appreciation not only of the works of Cézanne and the post-Impressionists, and of the writing of T.S. Eliot and Katherine Mansfield, which is, of course, well known, but also demonstrates her enthusiasm for the paintings of Simon Bussy and Jacques Ravenant, and for the poetry of Thomas Hardy and the prose of Marcel Proust. Caws eloquently evokes Woolf's vision and voice in her maturity, showing her confidence in her achievement in *The Waves*, where she felt able finally to 'shoot forth quite free and straight'. Her concluding chapter summarizes Woolf's brave defiance of loss, ageing, madness, and death.

Katherine Hill-Miller's *From the Lighthouse to Monk's House: A Guide to Virginia Woolf's Literary Landscapes* is also addressed to more general readers of Virginia Woolf; it is part analytical study of the centrality of landscapes in Woolf's creative process and part guidebook. Hill-Miller surveys Woolf's ongoing engagement with 'places' that she identifies as important in shaping Woolf's aesthetics, beginning with descriptions of St Ives, then moving to London and *Mrs Dalloway*, Vita Sackville-West's Knole and *Orlando*, Cambridge and *A Room of One's Own*, and ending with a lovely chapter about Monk's House and *Between the Acts*. Since she begins with *To the Lighthouse* and omits any discussion of place in Woolf's earlier novels, *The Voyage Out*, *Night and Day*, and *Jacob's Room*, Hill-Miller tries to explain this obvious problem with her organizational itinerary by observing, 'To begin with, an artist can't work until she has found her place' (p. 3). She notes that Woolf's first published essay was a 'travel piece' about a trip to the Brontës' Haworth Parsonage for the women's supplement of the *Guardian* (p. 2), and cites many familiar and lesser-known excerpts from Woolf's novels, short stories, diaries, and letters to illustrate her 'nearly mystical experience of transcendent union with things beyond the self' which involved 'a transcendent momentary union with nature, or of a vision of something indisputably "real" in the landscape around her' (p. 7). This study is unburdened by references to relevant theoretical discussions of space and modernism, unlike, for instance, Susan Stanford Friedman's important *Mappings: Feminism and the Cultural Geographies of Encounter* (PrincetonUP [1998]) or works in the emerging field of ecocriticism, and she only sparingly cites specific studies of Woolf's modernist aesthetics or representations of landscape. It is perhaps more useful, then, as a literary companion and guidebook rather than a scholarly analysis since it includes very practical details about how to follow the routes that Hill-Miller traced. It provides train times, road numbers, and detailed instructions for walkers, especially for a six-mile walk from Monk's House to Charleston. At the same time, Hill-Miller cites some of Woolf's most eloquent references to the sustaining beauty of the landscape, perhaps most memorably in her evocation of the Sussex Downs 'soaring, like birds' wings sweeping up and up' (p. 290).

Many fine articles of interest to Woolf's scholars have also appeared in literary journals in the past year, though space will allow the notice of only a few. Mark Wollaeger's superbly illustrated 'Woolf, Postcards, and the Elision of Race: Colonizing Women in *The Voyage Out*' (*Mo/Mo* 8[2001] 43–75), offers an innovative perspective on Woolf's treatment of women's bodies and the colonial culture depicted in this novel by considering it in the context of Malek Alloula's pioneering work with Algerian postcards, though Wollaeger does not address how the narrative describing Rachel's and Hewet's responses to the exoticized bodies of colonized women may also reflect Woolf's concerns with the relationship between sexuality and privacy. Wollaeger's essay is nicely complemented by Erica L. Johnson's 'Contours of Travel and Exile in *The Voyage Out*' (*JNT* 31:i[2001] 65–86), which also considers the 'orientalizing gaze' at work in this novel but argues that Rachel, unlike the other English tourists in this text, resists this discourse defining the imperial 'gendered subject in motion', though she also cannot escape from the Western model of individuality inscribed by it except through silence and death (p. 83). Karin E. Westman, in 'The First *Orlando*: The Laugh of the Comic Spirit in Virginia Woolf's "Friendships Gallery"' (*TCL* 47:i[2001] 39–71), shows how this early text anticipates Woolf's playful mixing of genres in *Orlando*. Woolf's treatment of the body and its relation to her modernist aesthetic is also the subject of Randi Koppen's sophisticated 'Embodied Form: Art and Life in Virginia Woolf's *To the Lighthouse*' (*NLH* 32[2001] 375–89). Finally, Andrew John Miller offers a bracing reading of *Between the Acts* (*SNNTS* 33[2001] 34–50), which demonstrates why the political conflicts represented in this novel 'cannot adequately be described in terms simply of repression or subversion, affirmation or negation, revolution or reaction' (p. 35). The *Woolf Studies Annual* has also published an invaluable 'Guide to Library Special Collections', which surveys major holdings of interest to Woolf scholars in libraries in the United States and Great Britain and will be of great help to Woolf scholars (*WStA* 7[2001] 115–28).

3. Post-1945 Fiction

Peter J. Conradi has published what is certain to be the definitive biography of Iris Murdoch. *Iris Murdoch: A Life* is a superbly researched and thoughtful book, which displays at every turn Conradi's diligence, and his warmth for Murdoch as a person and a writer. Conradi became friends with Iris Murdoch and John Bayley in the 1980s, and this obviously afforded him greater insight into her life and work, but it also means that his biography is a work of love. 'One task of the biographer must be to give the artist's "*mana*", power or prestige, back to herself', he writes, and this is what he does supremely well, and not without honest and critical commentary. Murdoch's complexity as a person, thinker and writer is explored conscientiously and meticulously. Conradi begins by resolving the issue of whether Murdoch could justifiably claim to be of Irish or Anglo-Irish stock, tracing the story of her Ulster Scots ancestors in County Down, although he remains aware of the ways in which Murdoch herself made use of a certain romantic notion of her Irishness. Her early encounters with religious, philosophical, literary and political issues are detailed exhaustively, but never dully. Her love affairs with Frank Thompson (brother of historian E.P. Thompson), Franz Steiner, Elias Canetti, and John Bayley are treated candidly but delicately, with much the same sensitivity as Murdoch herself treated her past relationships. The formative influences on her work, and the central theological, philosophical and psychological themes of her novels, are explained in an accessible and lucid manner, but they never interrupt a narrative which is determined to tell the story of a complex and rich life. Conradi is inspired by a certain sense of duty to record and honour a great individual, but this is never dutiful, and is as entertaining as it is informative. The intriguing and incidental titbits are also sprinkled through the narrative: she was a contemporary of Indira Gandhi at Badminton; when Murdoch signed in at the Bodleian Library for the first time, her name is written immediately before Philip Larkin's; Louis MacNeice, asked what he wanted on his deathbed, requested only an Iris Murdoch novel; Noel Coward told her at a lunch in 1971: 'I'm a screaming Murdoch fan!'; Murdoch purchased and sat writing at J.R.R. Tolkien's rolltop desk from the 1970s onwards. In the course of his narrative, Conradi surveys also the emerging critical reception of Murdoch's work, but what is made even more clear is that Murdoch was always her own most diligent critic. It is, as Conradi observes in his afterword, too early to surmise on whether Murdoch's writings will continue to be read and treasured, but what he celebrates is that she returns moral philosophy to the novel tradition, and that she remains 'subversively unfashionable' (p. 587). To coincide with the publication of the biography, Conradi has also issued the third, revised edition of his excellent study of Murdoch's novels, *The Saint and the Artist*. The revisions are made in the light of his biographical research, but do not alter the arguments articulated when this study was first published in 1986. He also extends his analyses to the three novels she published between 1989 and 1995. It remains the best critical study of Murdoch's fiction published to date.

Conradi's study features heavily in Barbara Stevens Heusel's discussion of critical responses to Murdoch's fiction. Heusel has written a lucid and authoritative study of the major critical approaches to Murdoch, entitled *Iris Murdoch's Paradoxical Novels: Thirty Years of Critical Reception*. It suffers somewhat from being repetitive, but it renders in a clear and accessible manner the history of how critics from A.S. Byatt to Deborah Johnson have understood Murdoch's work. According to Heusel, Murdoch criticism can be divided into three phases. Early critics writing between 1954 and 1976 tended to stay close to Murdoch's own statements about her literary and philosophical vision, and to argue that Murdoch is essentially a philosophical novelist. From 1977 to 1986, a new wave of criticism tended to move beyond Murdoch's statements and compare her with other writers, complicating the view that she was a philosophical novelist. Baldanza, Dipple, Conradi and Todd all emphasized instead Murdoch's interest in and complication of nineteenth-century realism. The more recent wave of criticism, including that of Heusel herself, tends to gather around issues concerning the postmodern leanings of Murdoch's writings, particularly the association of her work with ideas of magic realism, the carnivalesque, indeterminacy, and *mise-en-abyme* structures. Heusel narrates the progress of critical approaches to Murdoch in this book rather than offering any critical interventions herself. Indeed she states that her study attempts to 'stay out of the fray' (p. 168). This is a valuable summary of what has been written about Murdoch's novels, which will be useful to students and readers wanting to take stock of Murdoch's literary reputation.

Heusel identifies Lorna Sage as 'an influential transitional critic' in the study of Murdoch's literary career, who signalled a major shift in the direction of Murdoch studies with an essay which argued that Murdoch 'created intentionally unfinished, imperfect texts to disturb the reader's complacency' (p. 169). The reasons for Lorna Sage's importance as a critic abound in the collection of her writings published as *Moments of Truth: Twelve Twentieth-Century Women Writers*. Sage is renowned in particular as an exceptional critic of post-war women's writing, and there are incisive, indispensable essays here on Simone de Beauvoir, Christine Brooke-Rose, Iris Murdoch (an obituary), and Angela Carter. Much of this book, however, is concerned with women's writing prior to 1945, including pieces on Edith Wharton, Virginia Woolf, Katherine Mansfield, Jean Rhys, Christina Stead, Djuna Barnes, Violet Trefusis, and Jane Bowles. It was compiled by Sage shortly before her death in January 2001, mostly from introductions to reprinted editions of these authors' works, and from review articles written for the *Times Literary Supplement* and the *London Review of Books*. It is testimony to her clarity, precision and authority as a critic that these pieces fizz with insights and discerning readings, and hold together as a volume of essays rather well. There are recurring themes which reflect Sage's preoccupations neatly but unobtrusively: authors who departed from the social and cultural backgrounds they were born to, writings which emerge from displacement and mobility, women who discovered the craft of writing as a vocation and sometimes a salvation, the emergence of the anti-novel, the anti-biography, anti-art in twentieth-century writing, and the interpenetration of extraordinary lives and extraordinary writings. In almost every piece, it seems, Sage wrestles with the temptation that the lives of these women writers might make for more fascinating reading than their works, even though she is never less than fascinated by their works. Marina Warner's introduction to the volume summarizes Sage's implacable reputation: 'Lorna Sage's thinking about writing affected a whole generation of writers, publishers and, not least, readers' (p. xi).

Richard Bradford has written an intriguing biography of Kingsley Amis, *Lucky Him: The Life of Kingsley Amis*, which takes issue with the contention of Amis himself and of his authorized biographer, Eric Jacobs, that Amis's writings are not based upon his actual experiences. Bradford sets out, somewhat bizarrely, to prove, against the author's wishes, that we can read his works biographically. 'I shall treat Amis's fiction as one of the most entertaining and thought-provoking autobiographies ever produced' (p. 12), he writes, and in this he is largely successful. He tries, but sometimes fails, to avoid treating the work as a coded diary of Amis's life. Bradford's narrative is part biography, part biographical literary criticism, for at the heart of his book is a thesis that Amis worked to reflect and resolve the multiple facets of his personality and relationships through his writings. This fortunately goes beyond noting the correspondences between Amis's life and the situation of his principal characters. Bradford works largely from the letters, particularly those between Amis and Larkin, to show that Amis's laddish humour, gift for parody, and performance of multiple roles and selves, were as much a part of his life as his writings. The comic mispronunciations which are a recurring feature of Amis's parody of foreigners speaking English, for example, are shown to emerge from the playful, puerile exchanges with Larkin. The dips and turns in the styles Amis adopted in his fiction are shown to reflect the trends of his personal life: the double lives of the characters of his 1950s novels, for example, reflect his own double life as a settled husband and serial philanderer; *Take a Girl Like You* [1960] is for Bradford an exploration of Amis's marriage to Hilary Bardwell; the themes and styles of his writing between 1965 and 1980 reflect the influence of his second wife, the writer, Elizabeth Jane Howard; *Stanley and the Women* [1984] is a cruel, vindictive response to the break-up of his second marriage; his later novels reflect the reminiscent, introspective tone of his later years. Bradford's narrative is both predictable and illuminating, and perhaps what is most to be admired in it is that he succeeds in conveying the sense of a complex, difficult, restless man, at the same time as he situates and appreciates Amis as a writer who can be compared favourably to the comic and accessible forms of Pope, Swift and Fielding.

Amis's *Lucky Jim* is widely credited for establishing a taste for the provincial novel in post-war England, but Amis seems to be only playing with the provincial in comparison to a writer such as Stan Barstow, who has published his autobiography, *In My Own Good Time* with the West Yorkshire publishers Smith Settle. Barstow organizes his autobiography into two parts, the first of which recounts his life before he achieved literary fame with his first novel, *A Kind of Loving* [1960], and the latter part of which tells of time spent in 1962 earning his keep from writing novels, stories, plays, and television dramatizations. The latter part gives the impression of a whirlwind of meetings with writers, actors, directors, and BBC programmers, while at the same time Barstow displays his awareness that the taste for his literary forte—'lace-curtain' working-class realism, as he describes it so aptly—would never reach the heights of his first novel. For this reason, the first part of his autobiography is more enjoyable, and more rewarding, for here Barstow describes the social world in which he grew up, in West Riding in Yorkshire, with the solid conviction of its distinctiveness and worthiness which brought he and writers such as Sid Chaplin, Philip Callow, Keith Waterhouse, John Braine, Len Doherty, David Storey, and Willis Hall to a wide readership in the early 1960s. Moreover, Barstow's narrative is far from just memoir. It is invaluable as a reflection on the phenomenon of working-class writing in post-war England, the reasons for its emergence, and, in many ways, the frustrations with the metropolitan assumptions of the literary culture preceding its emergence. And it is an invaluable and illuminating account of the models and influences in Barstow's early career. His first steps into writing, for example, were encouraged by his reading of H.E. Bates: 'What Bates had done with his country people I could try to do with the semi-urban working class that I had known all my life' (p. 62). Yet Barstow's narrative is also tinged with melancholy in places, since the conditions which brought his 'real material', the little corner of the world he brought to fictional life, into existence, are also, he recognizes, the conditions which have brought about the disappearance of what is distinctive about a provincial way of life: 'I had no sooner begun to look at my heritage with the newly opened eyes of the writer than it started to disappear' (p. 71). For this reason, the trend for northern working-class realism in the early 1960s proved short-lived. Barstow and many of his literary contemporaries were always larger than this trend, however, and it is this implacable sense that Barstow has continued to write, and to represent the solid, unspoken provincial world of his upbringing, that he conveys so vividly in his autobiography. Of further note is that Smith Settle have also republished Barstow's fifth novel, *A Raging Calm.*

Bart Moore-Gilbert has written an authoritative overview of the writing career to date of Hanif Kureishi for the Contemporary World Writers series published by Manchester University Press. The first issue Moore-Gilbert tackles is the extent to which Kureishi is a 'world writer' in the same vein as writers such as Rushdie, Ngugi or Toni Morrison, since Kureishi's settings tend to be confined to London and south-east England, and his time-frames no earlier than the 1970s. Indeed, at one point Moore-Gilbert considers Kureishi within the more parochial context of the social realism of the 1950s, and the influence of Orwell and Priestley. Kureishi is essentially a London writer, but it is because London has become host to a wide variety of cultures from around the world that Kureishi has become a 'world writer'. This is the basis upon which Moore-Gilbert considers the seemingly paradoxical situation in which Kureishi has become associated with global discourses of diasporic identities and hybrid cultures, while all the while he has rarely ventured in his writing much beyond Bromley. Moore-Gilbert provides in this book a persuasive and balanced assessment of Kureishi's achievements to date, ranging from his early work in drama, to his screenplays and films, his novels, *The Buddha of Suburbia* and *The Black Album*, and his more recent plays and short stories. He does not flinch from commenting on the uneven quality of some of Kureishi's work, but is probably also Kureishi's most perceptive advocate. The comparison with Rushdie is illuminating and prudent, especially in the concluding chapter, in which Moore-Gilbert situates Rushdie in relation to contemporary critical debates about 'hybridity'. Kureishi has remained appropriately distant from the demands for his work to 'represent' Asian Britain, while his 'treatment of hybridity is itself hybrid and ambivalent' (p. 215). Moore-Gilbert finds that because of, not despite, this ambivalence, Kureishi's work has been a 'crucial catalyst' in the pluralization of British culture, and in rendering 'Asian Britain visible as a subject of cultural representation' (p. 216).

Northcote House continues to publish excellent short studies in the Writers and their Work series. A fine example of the strengths of this series is Sharon Monteith's study of the work of Pat Barker. This is the first critical book on Barker's oeuvre to date, although Karin Westman has also published a book-length reader's guide to *Regeneration* (New York: Continuum [2001]), regrettably not received for this publication. Monteith provides an accessible and lucid introduction to Barker's work, which situates her within a materialist tradition and argues that she has been one of the most rigorous, interrogative and political novelists in contemporary England. Monteith traces the recurring motifs and narrative strategies of Barker's oeuvre, consistently interweaving studies of each novel with allusions to the other novels, and thus builds up an impressive overview of the continuities and developments in her career. She counters the widespread fallacy that Barker shifted direction with her fourth novel, and provides a persuasive alternative account of how she became so popular with the *Regeneration* trilogy: '*Regeneration* is a watershed text, but its popularity reflects a change in direction not for Barker's writing but, more accurately, for the ways in which the popular-cultural history of the war has superseded its social history' (p. 4). All of Barker's major concerns and artistic signatures are considered in this short study: working-class identity and writing, materialist feminism, post-industrial dereliction, time, storytelling, memory, the relationship between language and identity, psychology and psychoanalysis, social taboos and norms, family and community. Monteith celebrates Barker principally as an iconoclastic novelist, a courageous and ground-breaking writer who has won huge critical acclaim and popularity. This assessment is considerably strengthened by Monteith's impressive knowledge of the literary, cultural and political contexts of Barker's work, which is deftly and pithily articulated within her analysis of Barker's nine novels.

Three studies of the work of J.R.R. Tolkien were republished in 2001, presumably to coincide with the release of the first part of the film version of *Lord of the Rings*. Jane Chance has revised and updated her *Tolkien's Art: A Mythology for England*, originally published in 1979, and *Lord of the Rings: The Mythology of Power*, which was first published in 1992. Chance, who published the volumes originally as Jane Chance Nitzsche, finds in her introduction to *Tolkien's Art* that the arguments she set out in 1979 have not been outdated, but in fact have been confirmed and extended. Both volumes are written with admirable lucidity, and offer persuasive interpretations of the development of Tolkien's vision, insightful commentaries on his use of mythological sources, and accessible arguments about the relationship between Tolkien's scholarship and his fiction, and about the contemporary contexts which explain the popularity of his fictions. The reason for the success of *Lord of the Rings*, Chance argues, 'derives from its giving voice to the dispossessed of the twentieth century, as epitomized in the marginal figure of the Hobbit' (p. 25). Chance guides her readers through the complex network of Foucauldian power relations in *Lord of the Rings* carefully, if sometimes too briefly. In *Tolkien's Art*, Chance quotes from a letter of Tolkien's which has been published since 1979 and which confirms her original argument that Tolkien intended to create in his writings a mythology for England which would rival the mythologies of the Greeks, Celts, and Scandinavians. She explores Tolkien's lectures, prefaces, *The Hobbit*, fairy stories, medieval parodies, *Lord of the Rings*, and *The Silmarillion*, in order to show that his studies of *Beowulf* and *Sir Gawain and the Green Knight* have a discernible inspiration on his desire to create an English mythology. Verlyn Flieger's study, *A Question of Time: J.R.R. Tolkien's Road to Faërie*, originally published in 1997 but now published in paperback, treads much the same ground as Chance. Flieger's analysis, which wears its scholarship more overtly, extends across a wider range of unpublished writings and lectures. In particular, unfinished works such as *The Lost Road* and *The Notion Club Papers* are considered, and his essay 'On Fairy-Stories', which Flieger examines as Tolkien's clearest statement of his artistic beliefs. Flieger's argument is that Tolkien immersed himself and his readers in a fantastical and elaborate faerie world, not as an escape from the tensions and crises of twentieth-century modernity, but instead as a critical register of the 'dissociation, dislocation, and psychological ravagement of modern life' (p. 2). Both Chance and Flieger rightly insist on placing Tolkien at the forefront of a critical response to the key cultural and political issues of the twentieth century, while at the same time recreating his wonder at the magical passage of language through time. Flieger concludes with a quotation from a letter Tolkien wrote to his son in 1944, marvelling at some lines of Anglo-Saxon: 'How these old words smite one out of the dark antiquity!' (p. 258). Tolkien's gift, both Chance and Flieger assert, is to enter fully, imaginatively, into the other worlds of the past and of fantasy while never straying from the dark and turbulent realities of European modernity.

Literatures of Memory: History, Time and Space in Postwar Writing by Peter Middleton and Tim Woods was published in 2000, but was not received in time for review in the last volume. It provides an innovative exploration of historical literature in British and American writing since 1945. Perhaps what is most impressive about the volume is the wide range of its literary and theoretical scope, which finds discussions of Stephen Hawking side by side with Margaret Atwood, Bernard Tschumi with Paul Auster, and Pat Barker situated in relation to postmodern debates about memory, to take just a few random examples. There are quite brilliant syntheses here of intelligent critiques of contemporary historicist (and futurist) theories, with detailed and persuasive readings of what the authors refer to ιs 'readily available texts', and yet include writers of whom there has been little if ιny critical discussion elsewhere. Middleton and Woods describe their book as provisional contributions to a cultural poetics of contemporary British and ιmerican literature' (p. 13). The nod towards the work of Stephen Greenblatt ιcknowledges that the book is partially indebted to new historicist paradigms, and ιndeed in its range of theoretical, political and philosophical reference, its insightful ιnd productive readings, and its engagement with the contemporary cultural ¯ascination with history, cultural geography and time, this book is an important :ontribution to understanding not just post-war literature, but also post-war culture. ¨ could single out chapters on historical drama, which begins with conservative ιolitical interventions in debates about the teaching of history, the excellent chapter ɔn poetry as memory, the final chapter on the city in contemporary fiction, or indeed ιny of the chapters on the general concepts of history, time and space which make ιp the first part of the book, but every chapter in this book is a rewarding, diligent :ontribution to the study of historical literature since 1945.

The Post-War English Novel is a new study of humanism in post-war writing by ₹udra Prasad Mahto, published by Prestige Books in New Delhi. The book analyses he theme of humanism, and the commitment to humanistic principles, in the ᴠritings of John Wain, Iris Murdoch, William Golding, Kingsley Amis, Doris ᴌessing and Angus Wilson. Humanism tends to get short shrift in contemporary iterary criticism, influenced as it tends to be by the prevailing anti-humanist tenets ɔf post-structuralist thinking. Post-structuralism is nowhere to be seen in this ᴠolume, however. Mahto's critical touchstones derive from the 1960s and 1970s; the nost recent critical study of English fiction cited is Patrick Swinden's *The English Novel of History and Society* [1984]. Mahto demonstrates persuasively that the ιumanist treatment of character and society in the novels he discusses goes against he grain of the anti-humanist trends in modernity, but his study would be greatly ɛnhanced by a sustained critical engagement with contemporary debates about anti-ιumanist and post-humanist modes of critical thinking.

Jeannette King's *Women and the Word: Contemporary Women Novelists and the ᴃible* is a superb and original study of the relationship between feminism and Christianity in the novels of Sara Maitland, Emma Tennant, Michèle Roberts, ᴊeanette Winterson, Angela Carter, Alice Walker and Toni Morrison. The work of ᴊulia Kristeva in particular informs the theoretical basis for King's understanding of :his relationship, although she also draws upon a wide range of mythological and :heological studies. King begins by tracing the emergence of a patriarchal ideology :hrough the shift from the mythic figure of Mother Goddess to the law and word of God the Father, and argues that this is the ideological context with which feminist ιovelists have had to engage. The title of King's study seems at first glance to ᵴuggest an obscure subject, but the range and depth of her analysis of such figures as ᴇve, 'Mrs Noah', Abraham's wife Sarah, the Virgin Mother, Mary Magdalene, and the female prophet, and the specific ways in which such figures may symbolize ɔppression, transgression or resistance in the work of contemporary women ιovelists, in fact makes the case for its importance. The two concluding chapters—on Angela Carter as a dissenting voice whose *The Passion of New Eve* deconstructs the 'original' gender division of Adam and Eve, and on Morrison and Walker's grappling with what can be recuperated for black women from the patriarchal and frequently racist discourses of Western Judaeo-Christianity—are rewarding and sophisticated studies of the ambivalent but productive relationship between feminist literary representations and religious discourses. The concluding lines to King's introduction make an excellent case for the novels she studies: 'Constructing alternatives to the myth of God the father represents a challenge not only to sexism but to a value system based on domination and power. And we do not have to be believers to find such challenges thought-provoking and constructive' (p. 9).

Neumeier, ed., *Engendering Realism and Postmodernism: Contemporary Women Writers in Britain*, is a welcome addition to the study of contemporary fiction. In part, it is welcome because the essays contained in the volume build upon the work of Andrej Gasiorek, Alison Lee and Amy Elias in delineating the particular ways in which British fiction since 1945 has tended to fuse the innovations and narrative strategies of postmodern fiction with the conventional forms of 'classic realism' Principally, however, it is worth consulting for its critical analyses of several women writers who are rarely recognized and debated in studies of contemporary British fiction. Of course, there are essays on A.S. Byatt, Jeanette Winterson, Fay Weldon and Michèle Roberts, but it is less common to find critical essays on Joan Riley Maureen Duffy, Eva Figes, Zoë Fairbairns, Emma Tennant, Sara Maitland Penelope Lively, Ravinder Randhawa, and Suniti Namjoshi. More importantly there are several essays on many of these writers—four on Joan Riley, for example—which gives the collection a coherence which is otherwise difficult to maintain in a volume containing twenty-two critical essays and eleven other contributions, mostly extracts from women's fiction. As to be expected in a collection of this size, some essays are slighter than others, but there are also important and substantial contributions here. Among the best are Monika Müller's treatment of the failure of love as a redemptive force in Winterson's novels, Reitz on Roberts's abandonment of realist narrative modes in *Daughters of the House*, Plummer on the same novel as 'a confident, multivocal rendering of the complexity of female identity' (p. 84), Bode's excellent overview of the career of prolific, innovative novelist Maureen Duffy, Stuby's overview of Figes, Anja Müller's essay on the relationship between feminism and deconstruction in Weldon's *Remember Me*, Palmer on the relationship between postmodern and lesbian/feminist perspectives in Winterson's work, Weedon on contemporary British Asian women's writing, Döring's examination of how commodities such as food and clothing function in Randhawa's fiction as emblems of the new realities of post-imperial England, Gohrisch's overview of Joan Riley's fiction, and Neumeier's own essay on madness and nomadism in Riley's *The Unbelonging*. Among the other contributions to the volume, Fairbairn's exploration of her own experience of 'writer's block' is searching, and the creative collaboration of Suniti Namjoshi and Gillian Hanscombe reflects on the split identity of migrant women from former colonies. Neumeier has arranged the essays and contributions in a very accessible order, and her introduction guides readers to the overlaps and interrelations within the volume.

Suzanne Keen mines a rich vein of literary narratives of the archive quest in her assiduous and persuasive study, *Romances of the Archive in Contemporary British Fiction*. Keen builds upon the work of David Leon Higdon, Frederick Holmes, Margaret Scanlan and Steven Connor in examining the relationship between contemporary British fiction and the themes and practices of historical narratives, but in a very specific and challengingly detailed way. She defines a sub-genre of historical fictions, which she calls 'romances of the archive', and which she argues possess common characteristics: characters engaged in doing research, romance adventures centred upon the activity of researching and the pleasure (sexual as well as intellectual) derived from researching, settings that contain archives such as libraries or country estates, material evidence of the past, and a more general evocation of the past. Any number of studies of contemporary British fiction have identified this fascination with and nostalgia for the past as a key characteristic of British novels since the decline of the empire, and so it was only a matter of time before critical studies began to emerge to define in more specific ways the particular forms which this fascination takes. What is so rewarding about Keen's study is that she manages to synchronize a number of disparate but related narratives—the archive narrative as antidote to postmodernism, the archive narrative as manifestation of postmodern textuality, the post-imperial mourning for the lost securities of the past, the postcolonial commitment to recovering the lost histories of the oppressed, the 'literary' novels which bring academic study and quest narrative into alignment, the 'popular' novel which situates the conventional detective, fantasy or realist narrative into the academic or scholarly setting—into one coherent and cogent whole. The thorough manner in which she approaches her subject is reflected in the structure of the book: an introduction which sets out its arguments and contexts is followed by a chapter which defines the characteristics of the genre through the paradigmatic model of A.S. Byatt's *Possession*. Two subsequent chapters trace the precursors of the genre to Edmund Spenser, Henry James, H.P. Lovecraft, Josephine Tey, and, of course, Umberto Eco, and explore the fictions of Barry Unsworth, Peter Ackroyd, and, more briefly, Penelope Lively, in the contexts of debates about history and heritage in post-war Britain. Three chapters then explore more 'popular' generic examples of fictions concerned with the archive quest, in fantasy, detective and realist novels respectively. The epilogue examines the ways in which fictions of archival research serve as vehicles for the search through issues of identity and history in postcolonial writing. Keen's book is an important contribution to the study of historical fiction in post-war England, and will serve as an exemplary model of how to define and map out a specific subgenre while remaining wholly attentive to the broader cultural contexts of post-imperial writing in which the past continues to be the source of deep divisions and searching explorations.

4. Pre-1950 Drama

In recent years there have been a number of publications which reappraise the work of popular dramatists or independent theatre groups, who aimed to take theatre of the period to non-traditional theatre audiences. Linda Mackenney's *The Activities of Popular Dramatists and Drama Groups in Scotland, 1900–1952* is one such example. Mackenney provides a detailed study of the interface between the playwright Joe Corrie and the production structures which controlled amateur and semi-professional theatre work in Scotland during the first half of the twentieth century. Careful to detail fully Corrie's own history and the political and ideological contexts of his work, Mackenney provides a critique of plays such as *In Time o' Strife* and assesses the way in which the predominant naturalism of the text is integrated with elements which borrow from more popular theatre forms such as melodrama and the comic sketch format of music-hall acts. Mackenney continually proposes that, although Corrie did not make use of the agitprop format utilized by political theatre groups in the 1930s and 1940s, his plays consistently focus on the Scottish working-class experience. The book also details the working practices of the various amateur and semi-professional theatre groups of the period, which she splits rather precariously into three categories: the mining community drama groups, the political or socialist groups, and the 'politicized' theatre groups, 'which comprises those community groups sufficiently motivated by the events of the 1930s to present plays concerning the burning issues of the day'. The contexts for the work of many of these groups were the performance festivals held by the Scottish Community Drama Association through the mid-1920s to the late 1930s. Such festivals hosted the work of playwrights such as Avrom Greenbaum, founder of the Glasgow Jewish Institute Players, whose popular play *The Bread of Affliction* was centred around pogroms in eastern Europe. By the late 1930s the SCDA had become more concerned with competition and formalizing what it considered to be stylistically and ideologically appropriate work thus many of the more political theatre groups and playwrights had to find other outlets for their work in a cultural economy which was moving away from community and popular live theatre by the 1950s.

Mackenney's book is detailed, although the theoretical framing is weak; this is in effect a documentation project which will prove useful for students and enthusiasts as it brings together a great deal of material that has hitherto been inaccessible but, much like Cecil Davies's *The Adelphi Players: The Theatre of Persons*, introduced and edited by Peter Billingham, it lacks a wider theoretical contextualization. *The Adelphi Players* is effectively an edited testimonial to the work of a touring theatre company active during the 1940s, whose work was based on humanist principles, and was toured to mostly non-theatre venues. Founded by Richard Ward, the company produced classical plays but also worked with non-commercial texts such as Susan Glaspell's *Bernice* and J.B. Priestley's *I Have Been Here Before*. The book is, again, a very useful document in terms of the way in which it adds to a growing body of work on non-commercial productions of plays written during the period. Similarly Peter Billingham's *Theatres of Conscience, 1939–1953*, is a reappraisal of the work of four touring British community theatres active from the beginning of the Second World War until the early 1950s: the companies included are the Adelphi Players, the Century Theatre, the Pilgrim Players, and the Compass Players. Such companies plugged 'gaps left by the decayed … commercial theatre', and as such the book is interesting for its documentation of non-commercial productions of plays by, amongst others, T.S. Eliot. Again, this monograph adds to the growing body of work on non-commercial mainstream theatre and drama of the period.

The republication of J.B. Priestley's *Dangerous Corner*, *Johnson Over Jordan* and *Eden End* is a welcome project from Oberon Books who have done much over the last few years to enable access to dramatic texts seen as somewhat unfashionable by more commercially minded publishers. These three volumes were published to coincide with the recent season of Priestley's work at the West Yorkshire Playhouse. Each of the plays reaffirms Priestley's skill in creating complex characters and plots which often play with ideas of time, memory and experience. Each shows his skill in creating psychologically complex human relationships on stage. Equally admirable is Oberon Books' continuing championing of the work of Rodney

Ackland. Born into a Jewish family—his father was a businessman and his mother a popular music-hall performer, Ackland was the darling of the West End commercial managements during the inter-war period. His plays have recently been revived, largely at the Orange Tree Theatre in Richmond under the directorship of Sam Waters, and at the National Theatre, with Judy Dench as the female lead in *Absolute Hell* (which was rewritten by the octogenarian Ackland in the early 1990s and based on the original play *The Pink Room*, first produced in 1951). Ackland was both an intriguing and a prolific playwright, and Oberon Books have added to their previous republication of Ackland's *The Dark River* and *After October* a second collection of his work. *Rodney Ackland: Plays Two* contains *Smithereens*, *Strange Orchestra*, *Before the Party* and *The Old Ladies*. Each play deals in some way with the shifting climate of sexual and social relations during the period from the end of the First World War to the 1950s. Ackland is a keen observer of human behaviour, with a Chekhovian skill for structure, character and humour, and *Strange Orchestra* in particular is interesting for the way in which it imagines and examines bohemian Chelsea in the early 1930s. *Before the Party* is based on a short story by Somerset Maugham and focuses on the superficiality of constructions of middle-class respectability. There are very few critical works on Ackland, and *The Playwright as Rebel: Essays in Theatre History* by Nicholas Dromgoole offers a useful if short biographical detailing of his work with a particular focus on *After October* and *The Dark River*. The level of analysis is not detailed, but the chapter provides a brief introduction to the work of one of the most intriguing and skilled dramatists who crossed over between film scripting and theatre through the 1920s to the post-1950s.

Helen Freshwater's 'Suppressed Desire: Inscriptions of Lesbianism in the British Theatre of the 1930s' (*NTQ* 68:iv[2001] 310–18), examines archival material in a theoretical framework which enables a revisioning of representations of lesbianism on the stage. Through looking primarily at *Love of Women*, a play by the highly successful husband-and-wife team Aimee and Phillip Stuart, Freshwater renegotiates the pathway between reading the past from a perspective fraught with contemporary preoccupations, and reconstructing it through an analysis of materials created within that past. Thus she proposes that, despite the lack of visibility of images of lesbianism in plays of the period, the censor's response to plays such as *Love of Women* suggests that in fact such images and representations were a cause of concern and thus a part of the cultural theatrical schema of the time. The censor's response to the play was to demand severe cuts, and these effectively resulted in the rewriting of the play, to the point where the dramatic and narrative structure was so damaged that the tamed allusions to lesbianism made no sense; as such the play confounded the critics. Lesbian desire on stage was susceptible to a system of censorship which graded the so-called potential harm of representing it, so much so that the censor claimed that he had 'no intention of seeing [the germ of] it fostered on the British stage'. Freshwater's is a very useful and thought-provoking article which, along with John Deeney's 'Censoring the Uncensored: The Case of *Children in Uniform*' (*NTQ* 63:iii[2000] 219–26), adds to a small cluster of research which is reopening the study of plays produced in commercial English theatres of the inter-war period, and the ways in which an interrogation of such dramatic texts, usually realist, usually concerned with the middle-class experience, can in fact provide material which helps us to revision the relationship between theatrical and cultural production and its social economic context.

Berg and Freeman, eds., *The Isherwood Century*, offers a further revisioning of Christopher Isherwood's life, although the book is mainly a collection which focuses on the (auto)biographical. William Ostrems chapter, 'The Dog Beneath the Schoolboy's Skin: Isherwood, Auden and Fascism', investigates some of Auden and Isherwood's theatre writing in the 1930s and will be useful for students new to the authors' dramatic works who have an interest in the intersection between Auden's and Isherwood's writing and their political and ideological positionings.

The problematics of (auto)biographical evidence are the focus of an article on the theatrical publicist turned historian Walter Macqueen-Pope, which asks for a reconsideration of the value and authenticity of his work and commentaries on theatre from the Edwardian period through to the 1950s. In 'Wistful Remembrancer': The Historiographical Problem of Macqueen-Popery' (*NTQ* 17:iv[2001] 299–309), Jim Davis and Victor Emeljanow use history-based theories of popular memory as a means of re-evaluating Macqueen-Pope as a historian of the transformation, over fifty years or so, of theatre as a business, a cultural phenomenon, and a form of entertainment. Macqueen-Pope wrote numerous books which detailed the sequence of plays produced, and although it is unreliable at times the writing of this industry insider is open to a variety of readings. His work is full of contradictions and changes in memory from one decade to another, and Davis and Emeljanow suggest that it is these contradictions and changes in perception or alteration of memory which are in fact of interest to the theatre historian.

Memory, or the reconstruction of it, plays a large role in Joan Plowright's *And That's Not All*. The book is a useful insider's insight into the early work at the Royal Court by the English Stage Company, which created the first productions of plays by new young playwrights such as Osborne, Wesker and Pinter, often grouped together as the 'new wave'. Plowright also, however, gives out a great deal of information about Laurence Olivier and his generation of actors which will be useful for anyone working in the field of theatre or drama from the 1930s to the 1950s in particular. Equally useful for the theatre scholar working through reconstruction is Devlin and Tischler, eds., *The Selected Letters of Tennessee Williams*, volume 1: *1920–1945*. The volume includes some 300+ letters, many of which are witty and enlightening about the early years of a writer who was to change the face of American drama. The volume ends with letters from 1945 at the point of his first Broadway success with *The Glass Menagerie*, and one can only hope that such a useful volume will have a sequel.

Irish studies has produced a great deal on Irish theatre and drama in recent years, and both Mary Trotter's *Ireland's National Theaters* and Lionel Pilkington's *Theatre and the State in Twentieth-Century Ireland: Cultivating the People* are useful additions to this body of scholarship. Trotter's book (also reviewed in section 1(b) above) is the less challenging of the two, although she revisits the early years of the Abbey Theatre and provides an analytic documentation of the work of the Daughters of Erin and other theatre and drama-producing groups in Ireland during the early years of the twentieth century. Trotter examines her materials in the context of theatre's role in nation formation, and looks at the intersections of class, gender, politics and ideology with cultural production. Pilkington's book is more detailed and complex in its analysis of the political climate of theatre in Ireland in the early part of the twentieth century. The minutiae of professional/political relationships and their effect on the kind of plays produced and the ways in which those productions were both constructed and received are argued in great detail. A clear distinction is made between pre- and post-independence drama in relation to textual analysis. In terms of drama up until the 1950s Pilkington provides close readings of plays by Synge and O'Casey amongst others, in a book which challenges easy analyses of the relationship between ideology, theatre and Irish culture. This is by far one of the best monographs on Irish theatre in the last few years.

5. Post-1950 Drama

Nineteen books on individual playwrights were received, with two or more on each of Alan Ayckbourn, Samuel Beckett, Alan Bennett, Harold Pinter and Tom Stoppard, together with a short text from Simon Gray and a study of the more distant figure of Emlyn Williams. Five more books examine broad aspects of recent theatre.

Paul Allen describes his *Alan Ayckbourn: Grinning at the Edge* as a biography, with Ayckbourn as his 'principal source' (p. vii). He then carefully traces a lonely child, interested in theatre, watching a disintegrating marriage. By page 67 Ayckbourn has written his first play, and after that the book is largely a description, a chirpy guide to about sixty plays. Allen soundly introduces Stephen Joseph, Peter Cheeseman, British theatre in the late 1950s, northern radio in the 1960s and the town of Scarborough. He sometimes attempts to parallel actual people and events with those found in the plays, for example, asking whether Ayckbourn's prep school headmaster is reflected in *Intimate Exchanges* (p. 15), how a real-life disastrous puppet show connects to *Season's Greetings* (p. 131), and whether Sarah and Reg in *Norman Conquests* were 'partly inspired by Daphne and Horace Ayckbourn' (p. 140).

Allen skilfully avoids monotony when summarizing the plays by interviewing actors, who provide insights into characters and anecdotes from rehearsals. His comments are good: is Colin in *Absent Friends* likeably nice or unlikeably shallow (p. 144)? *Woman in Mind* goes 'deeper and more bleakly into a single psyche than any other Ayckbourn play' (p. 213). Allen suggests that *Season's Greetings* 'goes further than previous explorations of domestic unhappiness' (p. 196)—further than *Just Between Ourselves*? He claims that Ayckbourn is 'our least politically engaged playwright (p. 4). Simon Gray, Christopher Hampton and Peter Shaffer have better claims to this position. Allen changes his mind, anyway, when he reaches *A Small Family Business*, writing that in an interview Ayckbourn made it clear that 'the play expressed his feelings about Thatcherite Britain' (p. 222). Further, Mark Ravenhill is quoted as presenting *Family Business* as '*the* political play of its time because it targeted the twin values of family and business' (p. 223). Allen is clear about Ayckbourn's achievements: 'He changed for ever the theatre's currency in relation to female characters' (pp. 63–4). He has also shown that tragedy and comedy are 'organically connected' (p. 64). Later plays are 'a remorseless exploration of the psyche' (p. 244) with 'cheerful despair' (p. 301). Allen is readable, accurate and informative.

Michael Holt's *Alan Ayckbourn* in the Writers and their Work series is only sixty-three pages, while the Pinter book in the same series is exactly twice as long: are no editorial guidelines given? Holt's bibliography is sloppy: John Bull's *Stage Right* [1994] and Duncan Wu's *Six Contemporary Dramatists* [1995] are missing. Holt lists *Mixed Doubles* for 'one-act play in a collection of five by various authors' (p. 66). Ayckbourn's six-page piece in this is a sketch, 'Countdown', and the book contains eight playlets. Holt begins with the nature of in-the-round theatre and comments on late twentieth-century audiences, so his starting point is performance. He places Ayckbourn as a 'visual playwright' (p. 34), explaining this clearly, identifying the 'filmic technique' (p. 38) of *Revenger's Comedies* and *Taking Steps*, in which 'the audience acts as camera and editor, switching shot from upstairs to down instantly' (p. 38). Holt looks at the four unpublished plays of 1958–61 to demonstrate Ayckbourn learning his craft. While Holt cannot comment on every play, he is astute and often original when he does. He shows *Way Upstream* as the first to focus on 'the abuse of power' (p. 48), while *'Wildest Dreams* explores the possibility that we are increasingly seeking an escape route in avoidance and through fantasy lives' (p. 55). Holt's insights include Ayckbourn's study of class difference, his affinity with the underdog, and his attention to the significance of chance in life, each of which could prompt substantial discussion.

On the cover of Glaap and Quaintmere, eds., *A Guided Tour through Ayckbourn Country* is a map of Britain with the titles of the plays randomly scattered, with *Comic Potential* at Berwick and *Communicating Doors* at John o'Groats. The organization within is equally whimsical, a programme, three acts with two intervals, and 'after the show', all wrongly described as 'a memoir' (p. 5). The bulk of the book is interviews with Ayckbourn conducted by Albert-Reiner Glaap between 1978 and 1998, commenting on about thirty-five of the plays, omitting *Norman Conquests*, *Just Between Ourselves* and *Revengers' Comedies*, presumably because Glaap has not asked questions about them. Ayckbourn, as usual, is articulate and speaks freely. *Time and Time Again* is 'the play when I first began to attend to people as well as plot' (p. 31). *Absurd Person Singular* shows 'the way certainly in this life the meek are very, very unlikely to inherit the earth' (p. 37). 'Mother Figure', a section of *Confusions*, is 'based entirely upon my wife bringing up two children and being at home while I was at work' (p. 53). The rest is made up of excerpts from articles by Glaap, who has the virtue of taking Ayckbourn seriously; Ayckbourn answering a few questions from directors and students and an essay he wrote for the *Independent* in 1988; a German student's account of discovering these plays; and a transcript of the discussion of *Season's Greetings* onstage at a German theatre.

Volumes 9 and 11 of the annual *Samuel Beckett Today* are to hand, both collections of essays, the first mainly with a clear theme, 'Beckett and Religion', the second with the open 'Endlessness in the Year 2000'. A substantial part of earlier volumes has been in French; only six of these seventy-six essays are in French. Volume 9 consists mainly of papers delivered at the 1999 conference in Stirling, and volume 11 of those given in Berlin in 2000. Wilhelm Fuger on the first Berlin presentation of *Godot* in 1953, Ciaran Ross on Beckett's own 1975 Berlin production of *Godot*, and Julian Garforth's view of all seven of Beckett's productions in German between 1967 and 1978 are all informative about styles of performance. Especially praiseworthy for a theatrical approach are Tom Bishop on recent productions in France and Annamaria Cascetta on Italian ones, and Shimon Levy quoting several actresses on the difficulties of performing *Not I*. James Knowlson summarizes the state of Beckett studies.

Alexander Games's biography of Alan Bennett, *Backing into the Limelight*, is not official or authorized (p. 4), so he has lacked the aid Allen had from Ayckbourn. Neither is the book biographical. Games has sought out every interview, no matter how brief. He has not listed these; they typically enter the text in the form 'an interview with Bennett appeared in *The Observer* on 28 May 1967' (p. 84). Games describes every work by Bennett, which some may find useful. He rarely adds any evaluation of his own, and when he does he confines comment to 'This writer has always felt strangely unmoved by *Talking Heads*' (p. 198), and he finds bad taste in *Lady in the Van* (p. 279). Games appears to lack familiarity with the worlds of television and theatre. Bennett is, in fact, the wrong match for Games. We learn more of Bennett from his *Writing Home* and *Telling Tales*, and his introductions to his texts, than anything in Games's superficial book.

Joseph O'Meahy, in his *Alan Bennett: A Critical Introduction*, gives little more than plot summaries, ignoring performance. Do any readers need twenty pages of exposition of the six monologues of the first *Talking Heads* series? Sustained descriptions are needed for the few unpublished pieces; elsewhere, I waited in vain for conclusions. Apart from earnestly suggesting that *Beyond the Fringe* draws on 'Beckett's comic absurdity' (p. 4) O'Meahy has just one angle, Erving Goffman's *The Presentation of the Self in Everyday Life*, which personally I found irrelevant. O'Meahy is a little more penetrating than Games, and knows more about Proust, the subject of *102 Boulevard Haussmann*. A few generalizations may enrich appreciation: Bennett's view is placed as 'a bracing kind of comic pessimism' (p. 156). His work is categorized under three headings: 'naturalistic studies of ordinary people' (p. xvi) in northern England; a 'metropolitan' voice engaging 'with larger political, literary, and social topics' (p. xvii), and monologues. O'Meahy's study is more 'introduction' than 'critical'.

Simon Gray's *Enter a Fox* is his fourth short self-portrait of the playwright as ageing, misanthropic, ex-alcoholic, and unlucky. He outlines the fate of his *The Late Middle Classes*—rejection by the Almeida, the National Theatre and even his publisher, success at Watford, the near-certainty of the West End, a bad review in the *Sunday Times* and closing in Richmond. He adds a few pages on *Japes*. He comments along the way on *Simon Gray: A Casebook*, 'I got the impression that it was mainly aimed at psychiatrists with a special interest in sexual abnormalities' (p. 94) and regrets the revisions he did for the four volumes of collected plays: 'I rewrote scenes and restructured acts that had worked perfectly well where it really counted—on the stage' (p. 90). Gray frequently digresses, too, about his cats and dogs and visiting a dying acquaintance—part of a carefully selected and contrived picture, I suppose, but suspiciously like padding.

Seven books about Harold Pinter have appeared in his seventieth-birthday year, three relatively slight. Richard Eyre's *Pinter: A Celebration* is the slightest, nineteen tributes and anecdotes, by David Hare, Ronald Harwood, and the like. John Pilger and Hilary Wainwright praise Pinter's political courage. We read of his professionalism as a director and slightly more memories of the man, as tennis player and batsman—his favourite stroke is leaning forward to drill the ball wide of mid-on.

I expected Gordon, ed., *Pinter at 70: A Casebook* would bring *Pinter at 60* up to date. But no, though a ten-year-old book with additions, the previous title was *Harold Pinter: A Casebook*, also edited by Lois Gordon [1990]. Four essays have been added. Mel Gussow has a note on Pinter as actor, Ann C. Hall surveys the work of the 1990s and Michael Billington is astute about *Celebration*. Kimball King observes that 'Pinter's assault on the ancient conventions of dramatic irony is his most radical yet enduring contribution to the stage' (p. 245). He illustrates changing fashions in studies of Pinter, how psychology, language and literary influences have followed each other in prominence. He concludes that many research opportunities 'for ambitious admirers' (p. 252) remain, pointing to *The Dwarfs*: 'Almost all of Pinter is there in that early novel, but almost no one writes about it (nor of the chapters in the archive that were not included in the published version)' (p. 252).

The booklet by Di Trevis, *Remembrance of Things Proust*, is explained on the title page, 'a commentary on the process of staging a production at the National Theatre, from first idea to first night'. This, curiously, is the staging of an unproduced film script based on a long novel. Trevis read Pinter's script before reading the novel, then had the opportunity to work with LAMDA students. She solved many problems with such devices as a half-curtain and overlapping scenes. Only then did she show Pinter the script she had created, and he made many changes and additions: in final form, twenty-six actors and 180 costumes were needed. Each actor was assigned responsibility for knowing the content of 200 pages of the novel. Quoting her 'rehearsal log', Trevis vividly re-creates the experience, ending with Pinter coming to a run-through and saying: 'I want to thank you all on behalf of Marcel Proust ... I have rarely seen a production as thrilling and as beautifully acted' (p. 43).

Gale, ed., *The Films of Harold Pinter*, is incomplete, for at least seven of his scripts are not mentioned. The book contains ten essays, seven on published film scripts and three about unpublished ones—of Isak Dinesen's *The Dreaming Child* and the rejected scripts of *Lolita* and *The Remains of the Day*. Eight of the contributors are American, one Korean and one British. Louis Marks asserts that Michael Billington's account of the making of *The Trial* is 'incorrect in many particulars' (p. 121). Most studies of the films of an individual concern a director or an actor, so I wonder whether, in an exceptional way, Pinter from the start of his career has had control of what is heard on screen. I note, too, that Americans here consider films in a self-contained way, rather than as a part of studies of media or popular culture.

Mark Batty, in his *Harold Pinter* for the Writers and their Work series, is less introductory than some readers of this erratic series might expect: he assumes the texts are known. He omits the film scripts, categorizing the works under three headings, each subdivided, 'Comedies of Menace', 'Tragedies of Isolation and Belonging' (fourteen plays are labelled as tragedies) and 'Politics at Play'. He can be harsh, faulting *The Room* and *A Slight Ache* more than is usual. He overstates in finding the Matchseller in *A Slight Ache* 'a manifestation of all the questions of existence that cannot be answered' (p. 26). Really? *Moonlight*, Batty suggests, affects us 'because Pinter sets in motion the acutely recognizable shapes of our own experience' (p. 89). Batty's approach is to consider what a play is trying to 'do' to those who witness it (p. 6), so he is alert to the impact of music in *Silence* and *Landscape*. Though Batty emphasizes how plays in performance operate on the mind and the sight (as in the visual 'images of power' in *One for the Road*, p. 102), he offers some aid to the newcomer and also traces Pinter's entire development and his recurring themes.

Raby, ed., *The Cambridge Companion to Harold Pinter*, is the most substantial of these books, though the content is made up of miscellaneous new essays, only three of which focus on performance. Steven H. Gale is alone in writing a lucid general survey suited to a 'companion', establishing Pinter as a major film scriptwriter, then looking at four scripts and finding *The French Lieutenant's Woman* the best. Peter Hall stays with generalizations in remarks on directing Pinter's plays: 'Pinter is essentially a poetic dramatist. He and Beckett have brought metaphor back to the theatre. ... Pinter actually *writes* silence, and he approaches it as a part of his dialogue' (pp. 147–8). Michael Pennington, chatty and anecdotal, communicates little about his experience of being directed by Pinter in Ronald Harwood's *Taking Sides* in 1995. Richard Allen Cave on body language starts with what he learned from Pinter's own performance in *The Collection* and scrutinizes intensely the physical in the 1991 revival of *The Caretaker*.

The best essay—and the best writing—is by Peter Raby, on Pinter's picturing and distillation of London, including 'the voices of the city, the languages of the capital' (p. 70), with *No Man's Land* more broadly 'a parodic exploration of Englishness' (p. 62). Harry Derbyshire explores an intriguing new approach: 'First, the playwright's capitalization on his fame as a means of promoting political causes is considered. Second, impressions of Pinter as they are created in the British press are explored, along with the dramatist's own reaction to them; and finally, unexpected, apparently random, citations of Pinter in popular culture are surveyed' (p. 231). Six more essays should be noted. John Stokes looks at early Pinter by way of racism and *Encore*, the little theatre magazine, and asserts that 'his seeming ritualised view of sexuality is taken for granted' (p. 33). Francesca Coppa shows how Pinter's jokes point to themes and meanings, claiming that 'many other writers have built their careers filling in Pinterian silences' (p. 52), naming Orton, Mamet and Stoppard. Ronald Knowles seeks influences and parallels in Beckett, then in Ionesco, Chekhov, Ibsen, Pirandello, Strindberg, T.S. Eliot and Joyce's *Exiles*. The effect is to place Pinter too tidily at the centre of twentieth-century drama. Yarl Zarhy-Levo traces how reviewers moved from exasperation with *The Birthday Party* to appreciation of Pinter's uniqueness, then had more difficulties when *A Kind of Alaska* and *Ashes to Ashes* failed to accord with expectations. Charles Evans explores the sideline of Pinter in Russia and Anthony Roche takes on Pinter in Ireland: touring with Anew McMaster, the influence of Yeats and, inevitably, Beckett, and a possible debt to a play by Lady Gregory. Most of these essays are original enough to be bricks in the never-to-be-completed edifice of Understanding Pinter's Work.

The reliable *Pinter Review* continues to offer, as its major contribution, a thorough bibliography, with an account of Pinter's activities, theatrical and political, by Ronald Knowles, reviews of relevant books and productions, an interview with Pinter ('Drama is a positive force and I certainly regard writing as an act of freedom', p. 95), and two short new Pinter texts, found in the archive and thoroughly assessed here. The volume is completed with assorted essays, on the influence of T.S. Eliot and Eugene O'Neill on Pinter; discussions of directing *The Lover* and *Ashes to Ashes*; Steven H. Gale, again, on the film scripts; Martin Esslin appraising the three plays of the 1990s; and Kimball King again on Pinter studies, listing such topics for research as 'women's issues' and 'political overtones' (p. 38). Michael Billington shrewdly sums up: 'What doesn't change is the obsession with memory, with space and territory, and with the insecurity of the moment, of the roles life forces us to adopt or play' (p. 46).

As with Beckett and Pinter, there are now far more studies of Tom Stoppard than anyone needs, and three more have arrived. New books don't seem to me to add a great deal to the existing ones, beyond being up to date to *The Invention of Love* [1997]. I have little sense of ongoing debate, rather of several people rushing in with overlapping commentaries. Billington, Jenkins and Whitaker remain the best introductions to most of Stoppard's career.

Kelly, ed., *The Cambridge Companion to Tom Stoppard*, uses a fancy name for some essays which between them cover much of Stoppard's work. Even the bibliography of books is incomplete, as those of Jim Hunter and Roger Sales and T. Bareham's 'Casebook' are missing. Only three of fourteen contributors are British, and they tend to be more down-to-earth than the Americans. John Bull and Neil Sammells are asked to cover subjects on which they have written before. The book is divided into two articles on background, nine on the works, two on 'culture and context'—and none on theatre and performance. Ira B. Nadel has dug in two new areas, Stoppard's film reviews for two Bristol papers between 1959 and 1961 (his reviews are 'witty, insightful and informative', p. 86) and the film scripts at the University of Texas, considering what film has contributed to his dramatic writing (p. 98). Elissa S. Guralnick—though she appears to believe that British radio drama *started* with *Under Milk Wood*—surveys Stoppard's radio and television work neatly in sixteen pages. Peter J. Rabinowitz applies narrative theory to the novel *Lord Malquist and Mr Moon*. Josephine Lee finds less well-trodden ground in pairing *In the Native State* and *Indian Ink*, while Paul Edwards works hard to explain 'Science in *Hapgood* and *Arcadia*'. Sammells studies the influence of Wilde, Beckett and James Saunders, and Jill L. Levenson gathers in her contribution all that is relevant about Shakespeare and Stoppard. Katherine Kelly's collection at times gave me a sense of a desperate search for new stones to turn over, especially for the major stage plays.

Hodgson, ed., *The Plays of Tom Stoppard for Stage, Radio, TV and Film: A Reader's Guide to Essential Criticism*, fails to find much forward movement in the understanding and appreciation of the dramas. For the curious series, Icon Readers' Guides, Hodgson is required to alternate excerpts from critics with linking bits which are sometimes his own views. Though his credit is as 'editor', at least half of the book is his own writing. Further, he quotes from the plays, interviews with Stoppard and reviews as well as the scholars. In his preface Hodgson gives his purpose as drawing attention to the 'smaller works' which 'have been, often unjustly, neglected' (p. 8). Thus his problem is to squeeze thirty-five scripts into 154 pages, followed by four sections on screenplays, 'Director, Actor and Author', remarks on character and dialogue, and an account of schools of criticism, featuring Alan Sinfield. Hodgson's stress on minor pieces leads him to over-intellectualize about the clever, funny *After Magritte* and to find the television play *Neutral Ground* [1968] 'powerful and successful' (p. 45). He finds space for a negative voice, citing Michael Stewart of *Tribune* defining Stoppard's role as the 'Great Comforter of the English middle class' (p. 119). While the formula of providing a 'guide to essential criticism' for a contemporary appears strange, Hodgson's approach ensures adequate attention is given to short and less celebrated texts.

John Fleming, in *Stoppard's Theatre: Finding Order amid Chaos*, has something new to report, describing what he found in Stoppard's papers at the University of Texas, several unperformed and unpublished plays preceding *Rosencrantz and Guildenstern*, and *Galileo*, a commissioned film script later adapted for possible performance at the London Planetarium. Passages I found particularly good were on *Jumpers* (both on the three texts and on the 'main perspectives on morality' found in it, p. 87) and on *Travesties*, such as the use of James Joyce and how Lenin's case is destroyed by the cuts made in 1993. Fleming sums up *The Real Thing* as 'Stoppard's most realistic, most personal, and most accessible play, the one in which audiences can most identify with the characters and their situations' (p. 155). Fleming tries intermittently to engage with performance, though he never makes clear what he has seen. He helpfully describes the differences between the London and New York sets for *The Real Thing* (p. 159) and the 1974 and 1993 sets for *Travesties* (p. 275). This study provides another sensible and informed account of the major plays.

British drama lacked outstanding writers for twenty-five years from Bernard Shaw's last major plays to the Osborne/Beckett/Pinter renaissance. Of the playwrights of that era, the survivors are Noel Coward, followed by J.B. Priestley, Terence Rattigan and Christopher Fry—all of whom were quickly placed as unfashionable and who may well have felt intimidated into silence. Russell Stephens directs attention to Emlyn Williams just before he sinks into obscurity. This book is largely biographical and well researched, with attention to Welshness and bisexuality (Williams wrote *He was Born Gay* in 1937—but about Louis XIII surviving in England in 1815!). Stephens points to what is omitted or may be inaccurate in Williams's two volumes of autobiography. I found too little about Williams as an actor, while evaluation of the plays is mainly by quotation from reviewers. Stephens is harsher towards the best work than I would be, and I especially wanted more about *Spring, 1600*. Stephens underlines Williams's limitations, that his objective was storytelling alone, that he was 'too conventionally naturalist' (p. 17) and that he wrote 'what he thought he could sell to the commercial theatre' (p. 15).

The most ambitious of the general texts is *Post-War British Drama: Looking Back in Gender*, by Michelene Wandor, a version of her 1987 book, which was more modestly entitled *Look Back in Gender: Sexuality and the Family in Post-War British Drama*. Instead of two parts, before and after censorship was abolished in 1968, she has five sections, one for each decade from 1950 to 2000. The core of both books is discussions of particular scripts (forty-five in the latest work), hence there are only two to three pages on each play, and the bulk of this is plot summary. Subheadings are changed: *The Romans in Britain* used to be 'The Taboo as Metaphor' and is now, less precisely, 'Chronicling Gender'. This is not what the title announces, as the starting date is 1955–6, not 1945, and some major figures, such as Stoppard and Shaffer, are absent. Some writing is sloppy: 'There is no direct subtext here' (p. 83: isn't all subtext indirect? Does she mean that there is no subtext?); 'In keeping with the plays of the 1970s, the locations shift as necessary' (p. 178). Footnotes are not used, and the bibliography is short, excluding—to name two— Michael Billington's *One Night Stands* and Richard Allen Cave's *New British Drama in Performance*. Wandor's problem is that she has far too little space to explain gender theory, describe social change in Britain and the rise of feminism, characterize five decades of theatre separately—and give most of her space to assessing scripts to fit with her framework. Her book is in a hurry, not so much to put out a topical message at high speed as for the author to complete it.

Turning to her commentaries on plays, she reminds readers of good 1950s plays such as Lessing's *Each his own Wilderness* and Jellicoe's *The Sport of My Mad Mother*. She approaches *Waiting for Godot* and *The Birthday Party* as realist, by way of character and what is shown of families. *Serjeant Musgrave's Dance* is a target as a male drama which has little place for women, yet the Arden of a play such as *Pearl* should be noted before he can be denounced as male chauvinist. Similarly, while the insignificance of women may usefully be recorded in Edgar's *Destiny* and *May Days*, it would be kind to point out that between these two he wrote *Teendreams* for the womens' group Monstrous Regiment. With Luckham's *Trafford Tanzi*, 'theatre becomes consciousness-raising' (p. 201), yet—contradiction?—on the next page 'the world, of course, remains the same'. Wandor zeroes in on only one facet of Griffith's *Occupations*, that Kabak refuses to stay with the dying Angelica. True, but Kabak leaves because of his duties, so the whole 'politics is personal' debate within Kabak and Griffiths is left out. Wandor states that she 'repositions the written text at the centre' (p. 5): I remain aware that my response to Hare's *Teeth'n' Smiles*, for example, was shaped by Helen Mirren's performance. Wandor at her best promotes a distinct way of looking at scripts, whether domestic, like Wesker's, or detached from family, like Harvey's *Beautiful Thing*. She asks: 'Who has the power?' and 'Is it always men?'

Aleks Sierz's *In-Yer-Face Theatre: British Drama Today* discusses most of the most publicized new dramatists of the 1990s, those who shocked in language and subject matter, especially in onstage sex and violence, with Sarah Kane's *Blasted* and Mark Ravenhill's *Shopping and Fucking* the most notorious cases. Sierz draws on his experiences in the theatre, plus interviews and alert reading of critics. Though he argues a thesis, he also introduces and explains. He finds that the 1990s were 'the most exciting decade for new writing since the heady days of the late 50s' (p. xi); 'New writing had rediscovered the angry oppositional and questioning spirit of 1956' (p. 12). In-yer-face theatre is marked by sensation, employing shock tactics, 'new in tone or structure', breaking taboos, questioning moral norms, and 'experiential, not speculative' (p. 4). So 'extremism became the new norm' (p. 233); such plays were 'privatized dissent' (p. 39). A dash through what Sierz sees as the pre-history follows: *Oedipus*, Webster, *Pygmalion, Saved*, the Living Theatre, the impact of feminism (*Once a Catholic*—the best example?), homosexuality (*Bent*) and violence (*The Romans in Britain*). Sierz credits Dominic Dromgoole with starting theatre of this kind as director at the Bush in 1990, followed by Stephen Daldry making the Royal Court's Theatre Upstairs 'a launching pad for young unknowns' (p. 38) and the landmark *Blasted* in January 1995.

The main exhibits are Kane, Ravenhill and Anthony Nielson, each of whom has a whole chapter. Sixteen others enter four by four, as early examples, 'boys together', 'sex wars' and plays of violence. Sierz names others, often little-known, and has diligently sought out new work at such places as the Bird's Nest in Deptford. His subtitle, *British Drama Today*, is misleading, as writers who were not in-yer-face (Conor McPherson, Shelagh Stephenson and Nicholas Wright, to pick three) are ignored, as well as a few who might fit, such as Helen Edmundson and her *The Clearing*. While Sierz emphasizes authors and scripts, he takes more note of directors and companies than Wandor does, and has one paragraph for actors (pp.

239–40). He downplays gay themes, only touches on writers from Ireland and Scotland, and ignores the black and Asian contribution. However, he provides a very good introduction to his chosen dramatists. In *The Beauty Queen of Leenane* he finds 'an eloquent, artificial, highly accentuated style that carries McDonagh's characteristic mix of savage irony and surreal humour' (p. 220). Of Nick Grosso's 1994 drama: 'In language as familiar as a pair of trainers, yet as hip as a trendy club, *Peaches* conjures up the urban lives and loves of Generation X' (p. 182). Sierz blends his enthusiasms with objectivity, setting out clearly the failings of Kane's *Phaedra's Love* and of the four scripts Ravenhill has written since his big success. As I read of these nineteen playwrights, I wonder how many are or may become major figures—Patrick Marber? Martin McDonagh? As shock as an approach is quickly exhausted, what are the rest going to find to write about? Which writers, what subjects, will matter in the early twenty-first century? What will follow in-yer-face theatre in the present decade?

Dramatists of the last thirty years feature in Edgar, ed., *State of Play: Playwrights on Playwriting*. This contains a substantial essay by Edgar, followed by two- or three-page comments by twenty-five contemporaries, remarks made at the annual Birmingham Theatre Conference from 1990 to 1999. Edgar's excellent opening notes the emergence of women dramatists in the early 1980s, the popularity of musicals, the focus on marketing, the role of television, and the new writing which Sierz describes. Edgar switches between well-known playwrights and obscure ones (such as Michael Punter, William Gaminara and Simon Bent) without introducing the latter group. Much of his collection provides provocative but fragmentary insights into the state of recent British theatre. Nicholas Wright believes that 'too many playwrights are given too public a platform too soon' (p. 106), while Peter Ansorge regrets that new plays are 'written for small spaces with tiny casts' (p. 39). Andy de la Tour makes good points about politics in plays, that 'the theatre establishment' lacks interest and that 'there is less and less real political debate in our political life' (pp. 62–3). Other writers illuminate their own work. Peter Whelan supplies the family sources for two of his plays and Christopher Hampton assures us that he made up more in his autobiographical *White Chameleon* than in such biographical work as *Total Eclipse*. In a chapter on Irish plays, Bill Morrison reports: 'I was 29 in 1969, and so violence became my subject whether I liked it or not.' This short book has many starting points for organizing ideas about the current theatre, as broad as Sierz is limited.

The two remaining texts are—in an old saying—neither use nor ornament. King, ed., *Modern Dramatists: A Casebook of Major British, Irish and American Playwrights*, takes one essay from each of the twenty-six Casebooks on playwrights published by Garland in the last thirteen years, claiming that somehow this provides 'an effective overview of recent theatre'. King's introduction comically forces links—Stoppard and David Storey as sportsmen, the former as 'cricketeer' (*sic*) and the latter as 'noted English athlete' (no, players for Leeds 2nd XIII are not 'noted'); the daisy chain is continued with a contrast, that Storey did not begin adult life as a dramatist while Wendy Wasserstein did. Eleven writers are American. The Britons featured are Arden and D'Arcy, Ayckbourn, Beckett, Brenton, Churchill, Friel, Gray, Hampton, Hare, Osborne, Pinter, Shaffer, Stoppard, Storey and Wesker. Libraries should have the original Casebooks: this pointless sampling has too much that is trivial and inadequate, even on single texts.

Why did Stephen Unwin and Carole Woddis write *A Pocket Guide to Twentieth-Century Drama* and why did Faber publish it? They outline fifty plays, one per author, with eighteen of them from Britain or Ireland, in the last fifty years. For each drama they provide a summary with a sketchy 'historical and theatrical context' and an even sketchier 'in performance'. So *A Pocket Guide* is no reference book—if you want to know about *Roots* or *Amadeus*, *Musgrave* or *Norman Conquests* this is no help. What use, indeed, is it? For a fair chance of a full account of a particular text, the student needs a reference work like the *International Dictionary of Theatre*, which Mark Hawkins-Dady edited in 1992. For a smaller number who would enjoy a personal, enthusiastic, idiosyncratic response to some scripts, try Nicholas Wright's *99 Plays* [1992] or Dominic Dromgoole's *The Full Room*, reviewed last year.

As the tomes on Pinter and Stoppard flood out and overviews are less common, I would like more on other prominent dramatists (David Hare, Howard Brenton, John Godber, and Timberlake Wertenbaker, to name four), a fresh look at some of the lesser figures of our times, more on companies (where do I go to find out about Paines Plough, Red Ladder and their authors?). And more attempts to make coherent sense of the recent past, especially the 1970s and 1980s.

6. Pre-1950 Poetry

Roberts, ed., *A Companion to Twentieth-Century Poetry*, is the most comprehensive of several overviews published in 2001. The *Companion* is ambitious in scope, attempting to cover every possible period, place and mode—an inclusivity which is achieved at some cost to the depth and originality of argument. The collection opens with essays on 'Topics and Debates', several of which rehearse familiar arguments about the writing of the period. There follow sections on 'Poetic Movements', 'International and Postcolonial Poetry in English' and 'The Contemporary Scene'. A sizeable proportion is dedicated to close readings of individual volumes of poetry, and Roberts is to be commended for ensuring that it is these, rather than dislocated iconic texts, which are reviewed. Roberts is aware that the 'Readings' section is susceptible to criticism and concedes that it 'is likely to provoke most debate, since any gesture towards canon formation (or reinforcement) is intensely controversial. The texts chosen are best considered as a selection of the most influential, widely discussed and characteristic poetry of the period; the concentration on specific volumes a recognition that even the most canonical poetry is born of a particular historical moment' (p. 3).

Turning to individual essays in the *Companion*: Hugh Witemeyer's 'Modernism and the Transatlantic Connection' examines the distinct material contexts of European and American modernism. In passing, he offers a lucid précis of Imagism. Jacob Korg offers a fuller account of the movement and its persistent influence later in the volume. Peter Brooker and Simon Perril's 'Modernist Poetry and its Precursors' brings key elements of Witemeyer's argument into sharper focus. They caution against the concept of 'modernism' and tactfully invoke the consensual view of a plurality of 'modernisms'. Brooker and Perril aim to 'disperse rather than determine any supposed point of origin' (p. 22)—hence their persuasive location of modernism in, amongst other places, *fin-de-siècle* attitudes towards masculinity,

Bergsonian philosophy and the dramatic monologue. David Goldie's 'The Non-Modernist Modern' discusses John Masefield and Rupert Brooke, restoring to the former elements of his radicalism and to the latter a sense of his 'self-reflexivity'. In 'Poetry and Science' Tim Armstrong indicates the importance of new technologies and modes of communication in the development of modernist poetics. Joanne Feit Diehl's 'Poetry and Literary Theory' is a welcome antidote to the absence in many of the works discussed this year of any sure sense of the relevance and potential of contemporary critical theories. In the 'Readings' section of Roberts's *Companion*, Tim Armstrong on 'Thomas Hardy: Poems, 1912–1913', John Haffenden on 'T.S. Eliot: *The Waste Land*', David Ellis on 'D.H. Lawrence: Birds, Beasts and Flowers' and Peter McDonald on 'W.H. Auden: *Poems*' all offer incisive commentaries. Certainly, the editor's aim that the readings should expand, illustrate and confirm points made elsewhere in the *Companion* is achieved.

Another overview of the field is represented by James Fenton's *The Strength of Poetry*, which includes essays on Wilfred Owen's juvenilia, D.H. Lawrence's early poems and W.H. Auden. Fenton resists the easy temptation of reading Owen purely in terms of his representation of war, and draws attention to the power of Eros on his imagination. In his essay on Lawrence, Fenton turns to the 'still somewhat shocking' early poems (p. 165). Here he adopts a rather well-worn perspective, reading Lawrence in terms of a series of dialectics (son/mother, spirit/body, Lawrence/Frieda). However, he also devotes time to tracing the textual relationship between his subject and Walt Whitman, asking how this transatlantic, transgenerational influence informs Lawrence's poetry thematically, structurally and tonally. In his three essays on Auden, Fenton is equitable and reassuring. He brings Auden, blinking, into the bright light of post-structuralist criticism (as, for example, when he gently suggests: 'I think that Auden would have been interested in Foucault's *The History of Sexuality*'). If anything, the tone here is a little too placatory. As Rainer Emig's recent *W.H. Auden: Towards a Postmodern Poetics* (see *YWES* 81[2002] 83–4) has shown, there are strong grounds for, and much to be gained by, reading Auden in terms of post-war cultural and critical theories.

Auden has otherwise attracted less attention this year than previously. Stan Smith mentions his influence on later poets and their sense of place in 'Suburbs of Dissent: Poetry on the Peripheries' (*SWR* 86[2001] 533–51). Susannah Young-Ah Gottlieb's learned exposition '"Reflections on the Right to Will": Auden's "Canzone" and Arendt's "Notes on Willing"' (*CL* 53:ii[2001] 131–50) explores the relationship between Auden's little-known poem 'Canzone', its source in Dante and Hannah Arendt's meditations on the will and its fulfilment.

Charles Ferrall's slim volume *Modernist Writing and Reactionary Politics* considers Lawrence, Eliot, Pound, Yeats and Wyndham Lewis. Ferrall discusses the aesthetics of modernism in terms of contemporary politics and the perceived attractions of fascism. His is a persuasive thesis which is cogently argued and represents a model of metacriticism, dealing with tact and precision with the work of other critics (Christopher Ricks, for example). Ferrall is alert to the modernist paradox by which primitivism and progress are simultaneously embraced, and he draws attention to the tension in the work of these writers between nostalgia and avant-gardism.

As Patrick J. Quinn and Steven Trout suggest in the introduction to *The Literature of the Great War Reconsidered*, there have been recent changes in critical opinion

about what constitutes war literature. The range of material discussed here—
journalism, fiction, autobiography, and poetry—exemplifies this change. The
collection is refreshingly international and feminist in perspective, offering a
salutary reminder of the dangers of seeing 'literature of the Great War' as a synonym
for the poetic endeavours of a small group of male British writers. Deborah Tyler-
Bennett's essay '"Lives mocked at by chance": Contradictory Impulses in Women's
Poetry of the Great War' considers Edith Sitwell, Iris Tree and the 'undeservedly
obscure' Phyllis M'egroz. Milton A. Cohen's chapter 'Fatal Symbiosis: Modernism
and the First World War' assesses the impact of the Great War on the logistics of
modernism (the exile of leading figures, the collapse of periodicals) and offers a
disturbing appendix of the fate of modernist writers and artists. The section of the
book which turns, seemingly inevitably, to the war poetry of Wilfred Owen and
Siegfried Sassoon does so with a refreshingly radical perspective. John Gibson's
'Mother's Boy and Stationmaster's Son: The Problem of Class in the Letters and
Poems of Wilfred Owen' identifies and disentangles a complex narrative of class,
place, gender and family. Malcolm Pittock, in 'The War Poetry of Wilfred Owen: A
Dissenting Reappraisal', reads previous generations' perceptions of Owen—
including recent dissenting views of his sentimentality and valorization of
machismo—in terms of each era's own perceptions of war. Patrick Campbell,
'"Thoughts that you've gagged all day": Siegfried Sassoon, W.H.R. Rivers and
"[The] Repression of War Experience"', offers subtle readings of Rivers's 1917
lecture on repression, alongside Sassoon's contemporaneous diaries and poetry. In
his concluding essay, 'Siegfried Sassoon: The Legacy of the Great War', Quinn
refocuses attention on the linguistic, metaphoric and syntactical strategies by which
Great War experience and resistance are represented on the page.

Turning now to single-author studies, John Hughes's '*Ecstatic Sound': Music and
Individuality in the Work of Thomas Hardy* combines a study of Hardy the music
enthusiast with close readings of musical elements in the poems themselves. Music
is the starting point here—as in Hardy's poetry—for a series of far-ranging
meditations on matters of subjectivity and identification, individuality and
collective experience, temporality and context, harmony and dissonance.

In *Thomas Hardy: Imagining Imagination in Hardy's Poetry and Fiction* [2000]
Barbara Hardy situates the poetry of Thomas Hardy in a long tradition of literary and
imaginative self-consciousness—a tradition which culminates in postmodern
metafiction. Barbara Hardy's attentive and lucid analysis of the poetry makes a
strong case for the sustained self-reflexivity of the work. She also offers an
interesting reading of the geographies of Hardy's poetry and its conflicting
metaphors of space and enclosure, seeing these as emblematic of the enticements
and 'failures' of the imagination.

Ivor C. Treby's *Music and Silence: The Gamut of Michael Field* [2000] is a useful
and enthusiastic—if inelegantly produced—collection. Treby offers an annotated
selection from 'the *entire* chronological range of the poetry of Katharine Harris
Bradley and Edith Emma Cooper [Michael Field]' and promises 'good clean
transgendering fun' (p. 15). One-third of the poems are published here for the first
time, and in making this material available Treby makes a worthy contribution to
Field scholarship. However, this is a limited edition of only 250 copies—a situation
which may be read as a sign of the timidity of current poetry publishing, or of the
persistent marginality of Field as a writer. Those unable to acquire the volume or

who might find Treby's enthusiasms and prejudices a little off-putting (he is particularly exercised by persistent uncertainty about the correct spelling of 'Katharine', excoriating 'in the main (female) writers less interested in factual accuracy and poetry than a platform for sexual politics', p. 16) might find Dorothy Mermin's review essay valuable (*VP* 39[2001] 621–6). Mermin discusses Treby's work in the context of Field publishing and scholarship and adds a much-needed theoretical inflection to the debate. Also of interest (and offering useful notes and a bibliography) is Vickie L. Taft's '*The Tragic Mary*: A Case Study in Michael Field's Understanding of Sexual Politics' (*NCC* 23[2001] 265–95).

In the consistently illuminating Writers and their Work series, John Lucas's *Ivor Gurney* appraises the work of this important, if often overlooked, poet. Lucas suggests that Gurney 'ought to be seen as *at least* as valid a presence in post-war poetry as Eliot'—potentially a more equivocal remark than may at first appear. Lucas's book sensitively locates Gurney's life and writing in the context of socialist and agrarian activism. He also indicates the importance to Gurney's writing of other personal and textual relationships, for example, with Edward Thomas and with the work of Walt Whitman. Like John Hughes in his study of Thomas Hardy and music, Lucas draws repeated attention to the musical idiom which sustains the poetry. Similarly, in a fascinating review of Gurney's setting of *Seven Sappho Songs* [2000], Roderic Dunnett discusses Gurney's musicality, as evidenced in his repertoire of over 300 songs (*PNR* 27:iv[2001] 77–8).

Also on Edward Thomas, Clive Wilmer's fine essay 'Edward Thomas: Englishness and Modernity' (*PNR* 27:iv[2001] 59–64) reads him as a modernist *manqué*. Wilmer compares Thomas's poetry, criticism and other prose and finds 'something remarkably innovative and renovative in both his style and sensibility'. The Cyder Press continues its valuable work in bringing back into print the work of Thomas and others associated with the Dymock and Georgian poets. Thomas's collection of children's stories *Four-and-Twenty Blackbirds* [1915] is reprinted in facsimile with an introduction by Richard Emeny. Charlotte Mew's *The Farmer's Bride* [1916] is made available for the first time in decades, here with a sensitive introduction by Deborah Parsons [2000]. Robert Frost's *North of Boston* (originally published in England [1914]) is also reissued with an introduction by Hugh Underhill [2000].

Helen Sword's chapter on 'Lawrence's Poetry' (in Fernihough, ed., *The Cambridge Companion to D.H. Lawrence*, pp. 119–35) insists that Lawrence 'granted a privileged status to poetic language and vision'. However, Sword maintains an admirably objective perspective, conceding that: 'the posthumously published *Complete Poems*, at more than 1000 pages long, functions better as a door-stop than as light bed-time reading' (p. 119). Sword sees Lawrence as the inheritor of Romantic lyricism, of modernism, and as an ancestor of confessionalism, and she is strongest on these proto-confessional elements (quoting Lawrence's description of his poetry as 'an essential story, or history, or confession, unfolding one from the other'). Elsewhere, in an exemplar of literary collaboration, David Cram and Christopher Pollnitz consider Lawrence's own practice of collaboration through translation. 'D.H. Lawrence as Verse Translator' (*CQ* 30:ii[2001] 133–50) speculates about the primary sources of the Egyptian folk songs which Lawrence translated (from their initial rendering into German) around 1910.

The paucity of material on T.S. Eliot noted by my predecessor (*YWES* 81[2002] 846] has amply been rectified this year. Jewel Spears Brooker's edited collection of essays, *T.S. Eliot and our Turning World*, declares three aims: to correct an accumulation of assumptions and prejudices which cloud readers' perceptions of Eliot's writing; to exploit the potential of recently published Eliot material, and to make productive use of new critical theories and practices. In this context, Brooker provocatively implies a fertile parallel between Eliot's philosophies and the relativism of postmodernism. Several chapters consider Eliot's philosophical and religious beliefs. A further section addresses his relationship to music and other arts and to the work of other poets. Randy Malamud's essay 'Shakespeare/Dante and Water/Music in *The Waste Land*' notably manages to do both. (The Dante–Eliot connection is also explored by David J. Ferrero in 'Ger(ont)yon: T.S. Eliot's Descent into the Infernal Wasteland' (*YER* 17:iii[2001] 2–9)). An equally important contribution is made in Teresa Gibert's 'T.S. Eliot and the Feminist Revision of the Modern(ist) Canon', a work of metacriticism which evaluates feminist readings of Eliot and modernism. Gibert mentions recent scholarship on the writing and influence of Eliot's first wife Vivienne—a relationship which is given full attention in Carole Seymour-Smith's biography *Painted Shadow: A Life of Vivienne Eliot*.

Of most interest in Brooker's collection are the chapters on Eliot and contemporary popular culture. David Chinitz's 'The Problem of Dullness: T.S. Eliot and the "Lively Arts" in the 1920s' lucidly delineates the profound boredom— Eliot's 'ennui of modern life'—against which his generation struggled. This is a nuanced and fertile essay which reads Eliot's perception of boredom against the background of anxieties about culture and class, and challenges the glib tendency to associate Eliot with elitism. In the same section Michael Coyle's 'T.S. Eliot on the Air: "Culture" and the Challenges of Mass Communication' traces the history of Eliot's collaboration with the BBC. Coyle reads Eliot's early and willing involvement with broadcast radio (he calculates that Eliot made at least eighty-one broadcasts) as a democratizing gesture, one born of his desire to share culture with the masses. Like Chinitz, Coyle reads against the grain of typical perceptions of Eliot as stubborn, reactionary defender of highbrow culture.

Three other journal articles discuss Eliot in the context of communication technology. In 'T.S. Eliot's *The Waste Land*, the Gramophone, and the Modernist Discourse Network' (*NLH* 32[2001] 747–68) Juan A. Suárez argues for the significance of the gramophone in and to Eliot's poem. In 'Sounding *The Waste Land*' (*PNR* 28:i[2001] 54–61), one of the most intriguing essays under review this year, Richard Swigg evaluates Eliot's newly discovered 1935 recording of *The Waste Land* (found by Swigg in the Library of Congress). He compares the new version with the widely known 1946 recording, suggesting that the multiplicity of voices, tones and emphases in the former suggests a host of new interpretative possibilities. Swigg reads with attentiveness and insight, and is to be applauded for the way in which he makes *The Waste Land* come alive to even the most jaded of eyes and ears. Pamela Thurschwell, in 'Supple Minds and Automatic Hands: Secretarial Agency in Early Twentieth-Century Literature' (*FMLS* 37[2001] 155– 68), provides a gendered perspective on these debates. She takes as her starting point the high-modernist 'collapse of the mechanical and the feminine' represented by Eliot's *Waste Land* typist.

Jewel Spears Brooker's own forceful contribution to *T.S. Eliot and our Turning World*, discussed above, writes back to Antony Julius's *T.S. Eliot, Anti-Semitism, and Literary Form* [1995]: her 'Eliot in the Dock' attempts to recuperate Eliot from the charge of anti-Semitism. Also entering, and broadening, the debate is Daniel T. McGee. 'Dada da da: Sounding the Jew in Modernism' (*ELH* 68[2001] 501–27) is a densely argued essay which discusses the multiple and apparently elusive languages of *The Waste Land*. McGee considers the relationship between Eliot's writing and African American modernism, seeing common ground in both traditions' linguistic heterogeneity and antipathy towards Jewishness.

Donald Childs has published two books on Eliot this year. The first, *Modernism and Eugenics: Woolf, Eliot, Yeats, and the Culture of Degeneration*, emphasizes the impact of eugenical discourse on the development of a certain kind of modernism. Eugenics, Childs suggests, is at the heart of the nexus of social, scientific and cultural change which defines modernity. Childs's practice is to 'draw attention to significant parallels between eugenical texts in general and particular texts by these writers' (p. 14). The strategy is relatively effective here (less so in *From Philosophy to Poetry*, discussed below), and Childs is able to identify specific connections between Eliot's close reading of the *Eugenics Review* during 1916 and 1917 and his subsequent writing. His analyses of Eliot's poetry in terms of its representation of eugenics-inflected concerns about biology, destiny, inheritance, disease, prostitution, degeneracy and miscegenation is informed and useful.

In *From Philosophy to Poetry: T.S. Eliot's Study of Knowledge and Experience*, Childs turns to Eliot's 1916 dissertation 'Experience and the Objects of Knowledge in the Philosophy of F.H. Bradley' [1964]. The Bradley dissertation is, however, merely the starting point, and Child's wider project is to examine a number of distinct philosophies with which Eliot has been identified. Thus in his introduction he characterizes an 'Anthropological Eliot', a 'Poststructuralist Eliot', an 'Existential Eliot' and a 'Bergsonian Eliot' amongst others. I find *From Philosophy to Poetry* troubling in a number of respects. First, the philosophical influence, particularly the impact of Bergson, rapidly seems overdetermined. This is particularly striking in the discussion of 'The Love Song of J. Alfred Prufrock', where the Bergsonian analysis neither informs nor supplements the text. Equally, the practice of seeking evidence of Bradley- or Bergson-influenced lines in Eliot's poetry becomes reductive, for example, in Childs's reading of 'Rhapsody on a Windy Night'. In both cases there is an unhappy conflation of dissertation and poetry such that the two are depicted as exercises—one in prose, one in verse—on the same theme. Moreover, the search for philosophical parallels dominates to the exclusion of other suggestive connections. Thus in chapter 4, 'The Death of Saint Narcissus', there is no mention of Milton's *Paradise Lost* and only the briefest mention of Freud. The best part of the volume, and the most out of place, is the final chapter, 'American Knowledge and Experience in Eliot's Puritan Jeremiad'. Here Childs sites Eliot's ostensibly 'impersonal' writing in the context of an American puritan tradition of self-disclosure. Similarly Liam Rector, in a polemical essay entitled 'Inheriting Eliot' (*APR* 30:v[2001] 11–12), considers Eliot's status and reputation in the American poetic tradition.

A number of essays on Eliot and his sources also merit attention. Cornelia Cook's deft 'Fire and Spirit: Scripture's Shaping Presence in T.S. Eliot's *Four Quartets*' (*L&T* 15:i[2001] 85–101) traces Pentecostal elements in Eliot's work. Christopher

Ricks, 'A Note on "The Hollow Men" and Stevenson's *The Ebb-Tide*' (*EIC* 51:i[2001] 8–17) draws attention to the two writers' shared vocabulary. In *Yeats Eliot Review* Robert Jungman, 'Augustinian Voices in Part 3 of *The Waste Land*' (*YER* 18:ii[2001] 28–32]), suggests new parallels between Eliot and the *Confessions* of St Augustine. In 'The Soul of Man under Psychoanalysis' (*LRB* 23:xxiii[2001] 19–23) psychotherapist Adam Phillips discusses Eliot and Freudian psychoanalysis (a 'dubious and contentious branch of science', as Eliot termed it) and identifies a number of areas of shared interest—including the fertile possibilities of uncertainty and incomprehensibility.

The New Casebook on Dylan Thomas—Goodby and Wigginton, eds., *Dylan Thomas: Contemporary Critical Essays*—performs the ultimate service to its subject: it returns one to the poetry. The rich allusiveness and often masked sophistication of Thomas's poetics are here rendered sympathetically and with precision. The volume opens with Stan Smith's authoritative and affectionate account of the relationship between Thomas and W.H. Auden. Smith explores Thomas's self-conscious testing of the boundaries/contiguities between old and new generations of poets, between Auden's work and his own. This informative and wide-ranging essay touches on a number of crucial themes (time, place, conflict, hope and despair, the body and its relation to the body politic) which subsequent essays develop. Katie Gramich, in '"Daughters of Darkness": Dylan Thomas and the celebration of the Female', also turns to the body, offering a nuanced reading of gender and sexuality which is influenced by contemporary psychoanalytical, feminist and post-structuralist perspectives. In '"Birth and copulation and death": Gothic Modernism and Surrealism in the Poetry of Dylan Thomas', Chris Wigginton places the 'miscegenation of modes and genres in Thomas's work' (p. 89) in the context of Metaphysical poetry, surrealism and nationalism. Essays by Ivan Phillips ('"Death is all metaphor": Dylan Thomas's Radical Morbidity') and Steve Vine ('"Shot from the locks": Poetry, Mourning, *Deaths and Entrances*') consider elegiac and melancholic tropes in Thomas's poetry. Phillips offers an uneasy combination of biographical and superficially psychoanalytic readings (which the editors tactfully label 'an impressionistic, free-flowing critical aesthetic', p. 138). Steve Vine deconstructs the refusal to mourn for which Thomas is so renowned. He offers an articulate and compelling analysis of the poems in *Deaths and Entrances* and their examination of presence and loss, meaning and aporia.

In a thoughtful and wide-ranging essay, 'Modernism, Male Intimacy, and the Great War' (*ELH* 68[2001] 469–500), Sarah Cole critiques the tendency to view the Great War as a crucible for the (positive) testing of male comradeship. Cole finds contradictory perspectives on friendship, comradeship, heterosexual love and male intimacy in David Jones, Siegfried Sassoon and T.S. Eliot. Such intimacy is seen to sustain Owen's 'Greater Love', although Cole wisely cautions against asserting a homosexual subtext: 'syntactically, the text's structure complicates simple binaries'. Allen J. Frantzen's article, '"Tears for Abraham": The Chester Plays of Abraham and Isaac and Antisacrifice in works by Wilfred Owen, Benjamin Britten and Derek Jarman' (*JMEMS* 31[2001] 445–76), discusses anti-sacrificial elements in all three artists' work—a feature which he sees as having common roots in their shared pacifism and homosexuality. Craig Hamilton's 'Genetic Criticism and Wilfred Owen's Revisions to "Anthem for Doomed Youth" and "Strange Meeting"' (*ELN* 39:ii[2001] 59–69) takes the opposite approach. Hamilton rejects recent tendencies towards biographical readings of Owen's poetry and speculative research into his sources in favour of close textual analysis of his meticulous and multiple drafts. Martin Dodsworth's 'Empson and the Trick of It' (*EIC* 51:i[2001] 101–18) is necessarily—given his subject—peppered with quaint critical terms: 'good', 'bad', 'force', 'truthfulness'. Dodsworth addresses Empson's desire to find a qualitative perspective on poetry which is simultaneously rational in its procedure and truthful in its object, which is scientific and aesthetic. Also published in 2001, although unavailable for review, is Haffenden, ed., *The Complete Poems of William Empson*.

A number of this year's essays are preoccupied with the problem of the marginality of their subjects. Elizabeth F. Judge's 'Notes on the Outside: David Jones's "Unshared Backgrounds" and (the Absence of Canonicity)' (*ELH* 68:i[2001] 179–213) reprises recent debates about Jones's exclusion from the modernist canon. Judge suggests that Jones's tendency to footnote his work led to his exclusion (that his marginalia led to his marginality perhaps)—a questionable premise given that such paratexts might be seen as quintessentially modernist. Barry Spurr's essay '"I Loved Old Tom": David Jones and T.S. Eliot' (*YER* 17:i[2001] 19–25) suggests significant parallels between Jones and Eliot. Spurr emphasizes both poets' mutual and seemingly contradictory belief in the value of innovation and of conservation. Hazel Hind's 'The Authority of Influence: John Davidson and Hugh MacDiarmid' (*SSR* 2:ii[2001] 77–93) is another attempt at recuperation, this time in an explicitly political and nationalistic context. Hugh MacDiarmid's *New Selected Letters*, edited by Dorian Grieve, O.D. Edwards and Alan Riach, provide a panoramic picture of MacDiarmid's development as a writer, and of the state of poetry and publishing in the period. The selection includes photographs, a chronology and a biographical list of correspondents, but is ill served by its discursive introduction.

In a brief retrospective, 'Hard Cider and Spam' (*PoetryR* 91:iv[2001] 15–17), John Lucas asserts the value of the work of George Fraser. Lucas is exercised by the critical neglect of Fraser and suggests that, in his case, chronology may have been a factor: 'the reputation of poets who are thought to be "of the forties" have still not recovered from the often malicious battering administered by those who succeed them'. Reviewing Robert Graves's *Complete Poems* [2000], Paul O'Prey puzzles over the current lack of recognition for Graves's work (*PNR* 28:ii[2001] 42–5). Like Lucas on Fraser, he posits Graves's chronological liminality—his output straddles both halves of the century—as a factor in his marginality. Finally, in an eloquent and personal commentary in the same journal (*PNR* 28:ii[2001] 62–4), Peter Scupham considers the work of Rudyard Kipling. The scholars mentioned above are preoccupied with their subjects' reputations, and here we find a minor model of restoration. Scupham sympathetically and persuasively describes a Kipling who had certainly been lost to me—a Kipling of restraint and understatement, a poet of proto-modernist, if not proto-postmodernist, 'darkness, blindfolds and warning', one concerned with 'failure, terror and the falling apartness of things'.

7. Post-1950 Poetry

Jeffries and Sansom, eds., *Contemporary Poems: Some Critical Approaches*, promises more and less than it delivers. The word 'some' in the subtitle indicates the patchy nature of the volume's critical coverage, and although a glossary provides explanations of Bakhtin, abjection, discourse and semiotic, among other terms, there is little attempt in the essays collected in the volume to address the ways in which critical theories and poetry can be read fruitfully together. Much more evident in some of the essays is a resistance to theory, best exemplified in Peter Sansom's melodramatic dismissal: 'Dr Freud might come in with his big boots, diagnosing something sinister, and he'd be wrong' (p. 84). Sansom explains in his preface that in the course of writing the essays in the volume, 'Exemplifying theory soon became less interesting to us ... than getting to grips with the work—with poems' (p. 7). At its best, this volume delivers some rewarding and entertaining engagements with contemporary poetry, and this is especially the case in Roy Mackay's 'subjective stylistic' analysis of Seamus Heaney's *The Spirit Level*, Peter Sansom's musings on how three Simon Armitage poems work by getting the literal detail 'right', Ian Gregson's essay on 'caricatural effects' in the poetry of Ian McMillan, Carol Ann Duffy and Geoff Hattersley, and Paul Mills's essay on the 'mercurial' poetry of Edwin Morgan. The sense that poetry opens the reader to experience, and that the study of poetry is the appreciation of the nuts and bolts which make a poem work, pervades the collection. This is valuable in itself, particularly in 'showing' rather than telling students how reading poetry can be enriched by a detailed engagement with its mechanics. Too often in the collection, however, the critical awareness of the contributors comes down to recognizing that, to borrow a line from one of the Armitage poems quoted, 'sometimes he did this, sometimes he did that'. There is much attention to the motivations of the poet in working out the forms for poetic expression, but there is less attention given to the motivations or mechanics of critical analysis.

The resistance to theory in poetry criticism continues apace, it seems, in Wade, ed., *Gladsongs and Gatherings: Poetry and its Social Context in Liverpool since the 1960s*. In his introduction to this miscellany of poems, interviews, critical essays, reflections, and social and cultural accounts, Wade states that the reluctance of poets Roger McGough and Brian Patten to explain their own poetics made it 'pointless to wrap these reflections and critical essays in the vocabulary of modern literary and cultural theory' (p. x). This seems to be an oddly anti-intellectual apology for the lack of insight and analysis offered in the volume. Wade correctly identifies that the strength of his collection is description, not analysis. His own essay on McGough reads like an extract from a biographical account. Against an academic context in which poetry seems to be struggling to find new readers and audiences, Peter Barry champions the relevance of the hard urban lyric of Liverpool poetry. Barry's essay is the only part of the collection to have been published previously, and it is the most substantial and valuable contribution. Reflections on the contexts in which poets began to write are provided by Michael Murphy, Deryn Rees-Jones, and Matt Simpson. David Bateman's interview with Adrian Henri and Wade's interview with Patten are prefaced with brief overviews of the significance of Liverpool in their respective careers as poets. Of the two interviews, Bateman elicits a more generous response from Henri. Wade's interview with Patten comes to just four pages, and Patten's responses are terse and awkward. The remainder of the collection comprises anecdotal reflections on the significance of Liverpool as a cultural scene for poetry and music. Wade alludes to Phil Bowen's *A Gallery to Play To* ([1999];

reviewed in *YWES* 80[2001] 692), which is a more focused and dependable critical source than the collection offered in *Gladsongs and Gatherings*.

Liverpool University Press is developing an interesting list of critical publications on contemporary British poetry, although Wade's collection is not included among its Liverpool English Texts and Studies series. Antony Rowland's *Tony Harrison and the Holocaust* is volume 39 of this series, and is a substantial and engaging study of Harrison's poetry in the context of Adorno's much-quoted remarks on the barbarism of post-Holocaust poetry. Rowland argues that Harrison is a 'post-Holocaust humanist', and argues that his poetry demonstrates Zygmunt Baumann's argument that culture and the barbaric 'remain caught in an inextricable dialectic' (p. 298). The book arrives at this conclusion through an intriguing tour of Harrison's work. In the first chapter, Rowland examines the centrality of the Second World War to Harrison's poetic imagination, and his specific allusions to the Holocaust imagery of Belsen and Hiroshima in *The Gaze of the Gorgon*, *The Loiners*, and *The Shadow of Hiroshima*. One of the most striking aspects of Rowland's analyses is his tendency to show the stresses in each poetic line he quotes, and indeed his attention to the relationship between Harrison's poetic form and historical representations is one of the strengths of the book. Subsequent chapters develop the idea that Harrison is a post-Holocaust humanist by examining how his poetry registers the altered contexts in which poetry strives to represent love, mourning, and memory after the watershed experiences of the war. Rowland occasionally draws the writings of Sylvia Plath, Geoffrey Hill, and Primo Levi into his analysis to situate Harrison's writings more clearly. The result is a persuasive and refreshing reading of Harrison as a central figure in the English poetic response to the post-war crisis in modernity.

Raphaël Ingelbien treads on well-worn ground in his study, *Misreading England: Poetry and Nationhood since the Second World War*. David Gervais, John Lucas and Neil Corcoran have all explored this subject in critical studies published in the 1980s and 1990s, and indeed focused on the same concentration of canonical male poets—Ted Hughes, Geoffrey Hill, Philip Larkin, and Seamus Heaney. But this is acknowledged by Ingelbien, and it is one of the strengths of his study that he finds an original and stimulating approach to his field. The key to his approach is in the title, for Ingelbien takes Harold Bloom's model of poetic interrelationships to account for the ways in which modern poets of English national identity have necessarily misread their precursors. Heaney seems at first an aberration in this model, but not after Ingelbien shows that his articulations of Irish nationhood themselves derive from his creative misreading of his English contemporaries, Hughes and Hill. Between them, according to Ingelbien's study, these three poets engage in a fascinating and somewhat risky attempt to reconnect contemporary national identity with an ancestral nation, thus bypassing the inflationary sense of identity inculcated by imperialism. Of course, Heaney has frequently been compared to Hughes, less so to Hill, but the idea that these three constitute something of a common response to post-imperial Englishness is innovative and instructive. Two chapters on Larkin begin and end Ingelbien's study. The first complicates the Movement stereotype of Larkin's poetry by reconsidering the relationship between Larkin and T.S. Eliot (it does so largely by revisiting the modernist stereotype of Eliot, too), and argues that Larkin shares the transcendental ambitions of Eliot's late poetry, but embodies finally a negative transcendence which makes his visions of England peculiarly aporetic. The final chapter continues this argument by analysing the validity of Heaney's representation of Larkin as the spokespoet of provincial, post-imperial Englishness, and finding that Larkin often operates within a 'nihilistic sublime that deconstructs those Englands' (p. 219). Ingelbien pays close attention to the historical contexts in which these poets have come to be associated with the meanings of contemporary national identity, and makes a good case for the ambivalent situation of Heaney between English and Irish traditions, but what is perhaps most notable about his study is his alertness to the ways in which poetry plays a role in deconstructing, rather than simply registering, national identity.

Ingelbien's study is published by Rodopi in its Costerus series. Volume 30 of its more familiar Studies in Literature series is McGonigal and Price, eds., *The Star You Steer By: Basil Bunting and British Modernism*. This is an excellent collection of essays, which makes a substantial contribution to the study of Bunting's significance for twentieth-century British literature. Roy Fisher writes about the influence of Bunting's poetry and personality on his own work. William Wootten explores Bunting's construction of a 'Northumbrian Modernism', examining the notion that *Briggflatts* works towards a nationalist vision which is at the same time more realist in its aspirations than Bunting's prose. Philip Hobsbaum expertly delineates the dominant English poetic tradition of iambic pentameter against which Bunting's verse seems strikingly original. Richard Caddel traces the emergence of Bunting's style of reading his poems, more fluid than his precursors Yeats and Pound. James McGonigal contributes a fascinating essay on Bunting's early reading experiences, what he learns and develops from E. Nesbit, Bunting's father's readings of Wordsworth, his own reading of the biblical books of Kings and the Song of Solomon, and proceeds to analyse the influence of romance narratives on Bunting's poetry. McGonigal's co-editor, Richard Price, examines Bunting's experiences and representations of patronage, including his involvement in and inevitable frustration with the machinery of arts subsidies. Ian Gregson explores how *Briggflatts* departs from the typical modernist preoccupation with masculine loss of power, and thus comes to 'a new acceptance of the collective shift in gender attitudes which had aroused such anxiety in his earlier work' (p. 114). David Annwn worries about the paucity of women poets contributing to published responses to and appreciations of Bunting's work, and so he interviews a handful of women writers, including Catherine Walsh, Maggie O'Sullivan, Geraldine Monk, Frances Presley, Elaine Randell, and Harriet Tarlo, to elicit their responses. Harriet Tarlo herself contributes an essay which considers the influence of Bunting on how contemporary poets write about the British landscape 'within the experimental tradition'. The next two essays discuss Bunting's translations. Parvin Loloi and Glyn Pursglove argue that Bunting's creative translations of the Persian poet Hafiz secularize Hafiz, and make English poems of erotic love out of Hafiz's Sufi poems. Harry Gilonis finds Horatian techniques abundant in Bunting's poetry, and argues that 'it is clearly the case that Bunting is at his most Horatian when not reading (or translating) Horace' (p. 230). Sister Victoria Forde quotes from Bunting's letters and poems to show how he represented and responded to the pleasures and pains of life in the twentieth century. Gael Turnbull's short piece considers Bunting's role of the poet as 'makar', no more and no less, reflecting Richard Price's earlier discussion of Bunting's desire to be paid as someone who works at poetry, who makes poems. Jonathan Williams shares Bunting's letters to him. In the final letter quoted, from February 1985,

Bunting comments that 'most people have very properly forgotten me. No doubt the *Times* has an acid obituary ready in its morgue, but three days after the funeral I'll be in Limbo for a long stay' (p. 284). The strength and pleasure of this volume is evidence that Bunting's readers knew better.

8. Irish Poetry

In the beginning there was *Writing Ireland*. *Inventing Ireland*, *Reinventing Ireland*, and *Visualizing Ireland* have all followed. Colin Graham's *Deconstructing Ireland* pushes the title trend to its only logical conclusion. After *Deconstructing Ireland: Identity, Theory, Culture* there is, presumably, nowhere left to go—not least because the theoretical sophistication of Graham's book is likely to render much that will postdate it already obsolete. Graham knows, of course, that there is no such thing as a last word on his subject; but that knowledge itself gives *Deconstructing Ireland* an authority often missing from more 'confident' studies.

Deconstructing Ireland 'tracks the processes by which Ireland becomes "Ireland", a "cited", quoted version of itself which is both excessive and phantasmal' (p. ix). Graham's concern is not with poetry in particular—on the contrary, his range of reference is vast, encompassing W.B. Yeats and Bart Simpson, Oscar Wilde and Judge Dredd—but his study has relevance for anyone with an interest in Irish literature and culture. His concern is with the ways in which an idea of 'Ireland' is produced and circulated through cultural forms which encompass kitsch as well as the canon, positing Ireland as a 'never-to-be-realised and thus never-to-be-broken promise' (p. 172). Graham's willingness to 'celebrate' Ireland, to become slightly 'punch-drunk' himself in the process of deconstruction gives an accessibility to what is a densely argued, important theoretical contribution to the field of Irish studies. His own evident delight in the 'leprechaun' which can 'continue eternally in his plastic bubble' renders what might otherwise have been a daunting read into a more enjoyable journey along the highways and byways of Irish culture. On that journey, Graham complicates 'the understanding of the representation of Ireland in British popular culture which is currently available in Irish Studies' (p. 157); subjects ideas of 'authenticity' in Irish culture to a scrutiny which 'potentially shifts Irish cultural criticism away from the often reified pre-existing terms of debate in literary studies' (p. 150); and, not least, re-examines the relationship of such enterprises as Field Day and Revisionism to a postcolonial subaltern studies position.

Graham's clear-sightedness here makes *Deconstructing Ireland* a crucial text for those with an interest in the literary and cultural debates, played out by such figures as Seamus Deane, R.F. Foster and Edna Longley, of the last twenty-five years. Thus, Graham sees Deane, for example, as balancing 'uneasily on the apex of the conceptual progression out of reliance upon the nation as the essential unit of culture—when he wavers it is to save what baggage he can from the crisis, to retain nationality as a liberating aspiration'(p. 89). If revisionism (based on a 'long goodbye to the sanctified centrality of the nation' p. 89) appears to take that extra step Deane and Field Day cannot manage, that view is also, Graham argues, too simplistic. Having analysed the terms of their disagreement, Graham moves towards 'a view of how ... connections which underlie both Field Day and revisionism ...

might be made to coalesce to produce a critique of Ireland in postcolonial terms which embodies the energy of both, while refuting to some extent their mutual problematics' (p. 92). Whether one accepts it or not, the gesture is worthy of ACAS, and should at least change some of the terms in which the disputes of the 1980s and 1990s raged.

Postcolonial criticism, for Graham, has to be a 'rigorous and precise' theoretical framework if it is to fulfil its potential—that is, if it is to be an adequate critical tool with which to examine 'the fractured range of complex cross-colonial affiliations which have existed within the British/Irish cultural axis' (p. 93). It is perhaps a pity that Dillon Johnston did not acquire that level of theoretical sophistication in dealing with the British/Irish axis before delving into *The Poetic Economies of England and Ireland, 1912–2000*. For most of this study Johnston finds himself in a cultural and theoretical quagmire, one which he seems unable to escape largely because he doesn't know he's in it. *Poetic Economies* pulls, inadvertently, in two different directions. Recognizing a shared marketplace for British and Irish poetry, he seems concerned, at the outset, to look for dialogue, influence, cross-cultural exchange. But Johnston is also deeply embedded in a concept of Irish (national) identity that wills the island of Ireland into cultural self-containment. That makes his book a prime example of a critical approach which uses some of the terms of postcolonial criticism, but is too invested in England-as-villain-of-history to be fully alert to the ambiguities inherent in both the English/Irish axis and in the ways in which the Irish nation itself has been invented and imagined. Where Deane, according to Graham, is unable to take that next conceptual step, Johnston seems to be having difficulty learning to walk in this new English/Irish territory he has marked out for himself.

It is worth noting at the outset that *Poetic Economies* makes only a very limited contribution to criticism of twentieth-century British poetry. Further, some of its assumptions are deeply problematical: the Irish poet, Johnston asserts, 'assumes the shovel or sounding rod with his responsibility to disclose and translate his culture'. (Presumably her culture as well?) The English poet, on the other hand, 'can ascend mountains and cast the empirical eye over dominions'. There is more. English poetry places 'a high premium on clarity'; Irish poetry might *seem* clear, but 'often contains keys that open different levels of access' (p. xiv). Even if one accepts Johnston's terms, he seems unaware that texts from a 'colonial' context are just as likely to encode subversive or hidden meanings as those written in a postcolonial context—if for different reasons. What Johnston reveals—here and elsewhere in the book—is his own failure to read English poetry with the attention he brings to bear on Irish poetry: to assume different levels of access aren't there in the former is tantamount to admitting his own inability to unlock or decode them. The result, in a study where English and Irish poetry are posited as bound together in a complex relationship, is that both are, by default, misread. If his view of England is coloured by prejudice in a negative way (by implication, everyone in England is a Protestant, and English poets are trapped in a condescending imperial mindset), his view of Ireland also suffers at times from sentimentality and reduction. Thus, he claims a multiculturalism for Irish society (prematurely perhaps) on the basis of Ireland's 'learning to accommodate refugees … in a spirit of restitution towards those who have accommodated the Irish diaspora over the centuries' (p. xiii). (Since one might reasonably claim that the treatment of refugees in Ireland has been appalling at both state and local levels, the sentimentality of Johnston's assumptions seems particularly ill advised.) Similarly, keen to distinguish spiritual, linguistically diverse Ireland from materialist, monoglot England, Johnston argues that '*even* Protestant poets' (emphasis added) in Ireland can be seen to share some of the virtues of their Irish Catholic counterparts (p. 170).

'Poetic economies', for Johnston, are understood as 'the interchange between bookseller and readers, the influence of one poet on another, the making of a canon'—all of which are 'enlargements of or digressions from the exchange between a reader and a poem' (p. xvii). While Johnston may be weaker on broad conceptual frameworks, that is not to say that this latter exchange between reader and poem is something which eludes him. For the last thirty years Johnston has successfully, through Wake Forest Press, promoted Irish poetry to an American audience, with an acute sense of what will and won't work in those publications. It is therefore on the home ground of publishing and reading contemporary Irish poets that *Poetic Economies* does make a valuable contribution to the field, notably in the chapters where Johnston is overtly playing to his own strengths and experience. The outstanding sections are those on publishing and poetry in Ireland in the 1960s (a discussion which he begins with the emergence of Kinsella and Montague in the 1950s). Johnston is sure of his ground here, and the use he makes of archive material gives the narrative an originality and authority missing from some other sections of the book.

Patrick Grant's *Literature, Rhetoric and Violence in Northern Ireland, 1968–98: Hardened to Death*, in contrast, offers a thoughtful and coherent conceptual framework for its subject. The book is also beautifully written, and expresses complex ideas with clarity and style. The title might suggest yet another 'Troubles literature' study, but although he revisits this heavily researched ground Grant has something new to bring to it. If violence and literature in Ireland is an old story, Grant tells it differently. He begins by taking Virgil's *Aeneid*, and the Bible's Passion story, as asymmetrical texts in their depiction of violence. He points up their historical as well as literary relevance to Northern Irish culture and politics, and uses them as a means of interrogating the relationship between literature and violence in contemporary writing—notably in the work of Longley, Heaney and Mahon. He also gives consideration to the work of playwrights and novelists, and to the rhetoric of politicians. Grant's concern is 'to re-situate Northern Ireland in a larger cultural history from which it is often too conveniently dislocated' (p. 5). He examines relationships between Christianity and imperialism, and also sets out to explain why Irish writers return so habitually to the paradigm that he proposes can be found in Virgil and the Gospels. In doing so, Grant's study uncovers the paradoxes that emerge from linking literature to violence, as well as the paradoxes inherent in the various forms of violence itself; such areas, he notes, 'prove tortuously difficult to adjudicate'. The debates thrown up range from the ethics of the legitimization of force in civilized society; literature as a mode of collusion and/or resistance, as, variously, propagandist or proposing instead an 'unmasking' of 'the over-simplification by which violence is perpetrated'; and poetry as either 'inherently political' or inhabiting its 'own sovereign realm, the aesthetic' (p. 5). These are 'big' questions, ones which have haunted criticism of 'poetry of the Troubles' since the first reviews of 'Ulster Poets' appeared in the early 1970s. They are linked to issues of responsibility (brooded over not only by critics but by the poets themselves), of the 'use or function of poetry', and of the relationship of poetry to history. Grant's is hardly likely to be the last word on these issues, but it is an intelligently and seductively argued intervention in the broad area of debate. Ultimately, Grant has a moral argument to propose, one particularly pertinent in view of recent world events. While he recognizes that we are all 'complicitous' in violence, as a means of maintaining social stability, he also recognizes that violence may simultaneously perpetuate the problems it sets out to solve. For Grant, it is literature, 'the educated imagination', which is 'a powerful moral agent', an 'antidote to the means by which violence is perpetrated'. He does not expect miracles, but does argue that literature provides an important site for non-propagandist language development, itself an antidote to what has been, in Northern Ireland, a 'war of words' as well as of physical violence.

Since war is the natural enemy of what it defends, attempts by 'civilized' societies to sustain themselves against the threat of barbarism by perpetrating acts of barbarism themselves are inevitably paradoxical. This also partly accounts for the paradoxical complexity of much twentieth-century war writing—both collusive and condemnatory. The problem is particularly acute—for political reasons—in Ireland. Jim Haughey's *The First World War in Irish Poetry* is the second study in recent years to subject Irish war poetry to sustained and detailed scrutiny, although in doing so it also demonstrates that what is meant by 'Irish war poetry' can vary widely. Haughey's dedication to his subject is such that he has gathered together here references to a wide range of material (he discusses over thirty poets), as well as immersing himself in the facts—and myths—circulating in relation to the Great War in Ireland. Although he does not explicitly say so, the model for Haughey (as it is profoundly influential on many studies of war poetry) is Fussell's *The Great War and Modern Memory*. As a consequence, Haughey's study opts for the detailed analysis of writing from the wartime period, and resurrects poets—the little-known Willoughby Weaving may be a prime example—who have at best only historical interest. But the application of a Fussell-type model to Ireland has some weaknesses, and causes Haughey some problems: thus, although he reads the case of Ireland as exceptional, he also at times validates the relevance of Irish poetry to the Great War by pointing out what it has in common with the myths circulating in England. Thus Yeats's elegies for Robert Gregory lose some of their Irish specificity to become poems 'about' the 'Lost Generation'. Haughey assures us that his pages are free of deconstruction and the like: those looking for such theoretical models will not find them here, which, of course, need not be seen as a problem. But those looking for consistency and clarity of argument might also encounter unexpected difficulties. The one consistent point hammered home throughout is the now generally accepted one that unionists and nationalists appropriated memory of the war in different ways, and that ideological premises continue to condition perceptions of the past. Outside of this, more complex threads of argument tend to get lost in the book's many—albeit interesting—examples. While some myths are exposed, others are recycled: Haughey comments in his introduction, for instance, on 'Yeats's ... exclusion of the more celebrated English war poets (Owen, Sassoon, *et al.*) from his *Oxford Book of Modern Verse*'. For the record, Sassoon, along with Blunden and Read, *are* included in that anthology. Haughey has done a phenomenal amount of research for this book: it is bound to be a useful resource in this respect, and it may well open up previously obscured areas of debate for an American audience. But in his anxiety to create polemical space for himself he argues on too many fronts; it is a valuable study, but—and it is a pity—it is also at times a rather confused and confusing read.

The year 2001 saw the reissue of what has been, for many years, a standard resource on Seamus Heaney, Curtis, ed., *The Art of Seamus Heaney*—now in its fourth edition. Its introduction, aimed particularly at a student audience, is largely descriptive and uncritical; happily, the collection itself has rather more 'bite' than this would suggest, containing as it does Edna Longley's well-known '*North*: "Inner Emigré" or "Artful Voyeur"?', as well as thoughtful essays by Bernard O'Donoghue, Patrick Crotty and Douglas Dunn, alongside the more usual praise-fest. As Tim Kendall points out in his excellent essay towards the close of the book, Heaney's 'natural mode' in his own critical prose 'consists of awe and delight rather than scepticism' (p. 230). His own readers have sometimes imitated that pattern, and there is, undoubtedly, much in Heaney to inspire awe and delight. But Goodby's phrase in his essay here, 'reverent disappointment', aptly captures the corner into which such a mode of criticism has driven itself. Perhaps as a result, the temptation, on returning to yet another edition of this book, is rather to delight in the moments of scepticism—in the moments, in other words, where it becomes apparent that reading Heaney has gradually, and rewardingly, become a more difficult enterprise.

The final essay here—and new to this edition—is by the medievalist Helen Phillips on the subject of Heaney's *Beowulf*. Since *Beowulf* appeared, many uninspiring journal articles have eagerly sought to plug one of the few gaps remaining in the oeuvre of Heaney criticism. Phillips, fortunately, is not reverential, but an acute and informed scholar whose essay seems to be designed precisely to meet the student needs that the introduction of Heaney's *Beowulf* into the Norton Critical Edition canon is likely to create. In other words, she recognizes that the translation has interest because of what it says about Heaney; but she also provides parallel text to discuss the original against the translation, and interprets the poem in its own right as much as through a Heaney lens. Her interpretation of *Beowulf*, in fact, is almost as stimulating as the translation itself. She is alert to what the translation loses, in choosing to formulate *Beowulf* as 'pre-eminently a narrative of heroic individual action and of dramatic encounters in dialogue'. Recognizing that the translation is shackled by forces from Heaney's own earlier writing, it is perhaps unsurprising that it is the treatment of females Phillips finds most disappointing (p. 275), since Heaney is tempted always to the most negative interpretation. Grendel's mother, for example, is turned into one of his own 'bog queens' or 'hell brides', thus losing much of the respect accorded to her in the original. Some of the specifics of translation are questioned—though Phillips is kinder than the *Beowulf* scholar who began his review with a simple but damning 'So.' The real service rendered in this essay is that she engages interest in *Beowulf* the poem rather more than in Heaney the poet—a service that the translation itself is, ultimately, designed to render too.

If the market has been saturated with studies of Heaney's poetry, that cannot be said of another Irish poet who has received attention in a full-length monograph this year—Thomas Kinsella. As Derval Tubridy notes in her *Thomas Kinsella: The Peppercanister Poems*, the reception of Kinsella's poetry has moved over the decades from 'early celebration to muted appreciation'. She might have added, in some cases, to active dislike. Kinsella's deliberate move away from an early lyricism to a more fragmented form may well have adversely affected his reputation. In one sense, therefore, the publication of this book continues a trend set by

University College Dublin Press in 2000, whereby it devoted much of its critical list to the work of Ireland's more 'modernist' or 'experimental' writers. In another sense, Tubridy picks up on another critical trend on the increase, apparent in Johnston's *Poetic Economies*, and apparent also in Chaudhry's study of Yeats (discussed below), whereby the aesthetics and politics of publishing come under scrutiny as well as the work itself. Tubridy concentrates on the Peppercanister poems, those issued from Kinsella's own Perppercanister Press from 1972 onwards. The pamphlets she discusses are themselves *objets d'art*, and her own text is illustrated to show the overall effect of this level of quality in presentation. She also contends that the Peppercanister poems offer a unique insight into the progress of Kinsella's poems, showing as they do his development into the larger collections published by OUP. They also allow for the development, in Kinsella's aesthetic, of the relationship between poetry and the visual arts.

Kinsella's direction in the Peppercanister poems, Tubridy argues, is one whereby he 'isolates the details under consideration, then constructs a framework of interrelationships through which the details cohere' (p. 226). Recognition of that method also makes for a particular kind of criticism—one that has to assume, in the reader, a vested interest in making those details cohere as well. (On such an issue the comparisons with Eliot, hinted at but never really developed, might have proved particularly illuminating.) Tubridy's knowledge of this material is phenomenal and exhaustive; she draws a great deal on specific details obtained from archive sources to show how the publications gradually take shape. That makes this a very specialized book likely to appeal first and foremost to dedicated Kinsella scholars. There is a great deal of examination of the texture of Kinsella's poems, without much consideration of where Kinsella might be situated in the broader, and possibly more accessible, contexts of debate surrounding Irish poetry (although that would of course make for an entirely different book). One problem with that might be that if the poems themselves leave the reader cold (as they do this one), the study is unlikely to encourage a change of mind. While Tubridy notes the increasingly lukewarm reception accorded to Kinsella, she does not take on that growing negativity directly. On the other hand, she may be rightly praised for taking the tack she also notes in Kinsella—the willingness to take one's own way regardless of convention. The sheer wealth of detail, and the length of the book, mean that there are occasional repetitions, and overall it may not be the most inspiring read. But its detailed chronological approach and close analysis of pamphlet after pamphlet in context makes it very unlikely to be superseded by any rival publication on the subject for some time to come.

Perhaps it lacks 'sexiness' or excitement, but the quality of Tubridy's research and her ability to write with some style, prove particularly appealing if one then encounters Sarah Fulford's *Gendered Spaces in Contemporary Irish Poetry*, which has more introduction than substance, and more questions than introduction. If Graham's *Deconstructing Ireland* is theory used well, Fulford's *Gendered Spaces* is theory apparently disguising a paucity of original thought. It is unlikely that this book, which posits itself as a continuation of, and correction of the sins of omission in, Clair Will's *Improprieties*, will warrant the attention rightly given to Wills's earlier, and in some ways seminal, text. Fulford writes: 'At first glance there are significant differences between the poets Seamus Heaney, Tom Paulin, Paul Muldoon, Eavan Boland, Medbh McGuckian and Sara Berkeley. It is necessary from the start to acknowledge the different social, political and ideological contexts existing between separate communities in the North and South of Ireland, while examining the relationship between the national, spatial, racial, religious and sexual as presented in the poetry.' This all sounds terribly sophisticated, but minus its unnecessary verbiage, is really saying something terribly simple. All her chosen poets write differently, and for fairly obvious reasons. So her rationale for linking them together is that 'what they hold in common is their revision of national and gendered identity to provide a different understanding of the poetic self in relation to the world' (p. 12). Do all poets hold this in common? Or just these?

The extraordinary number of repetitions of 'it is necessary to ask', 'it is important to ask', 'it is necessary to consider' and 'it is important to examine' should perhaps have been spotted by an editor; but they are indicative of broader problems. This book asks a series of questions. These are not always distinct from each other, and fail to culminate in a coherent argument (that the book is structured in a series of two- to three-page sections strikes this reader as indicative of an incapacity to sustain coherent thought); they are also posited in such a way that Fulford is, inevitably, unable to move beyond the act of questioning, instead becoming trapped in an endless cycle of words, words, words: 'How far can more flexible representations of identity be identified within the poems with the effect of establishing sophisticated ways of thinking about decolonization that take into account the way in which the nation is fragmented and discontinuous, rather than unified and uncontradictory?' (p. 22). Moments in this book require some effort on the reader's part to make them intelligible ('Critiquing Kearney's work, discussion problematizes how the notion of migration, introduced in the work of Heaney, is developed within contemporary Irish poetry as a whole'); at times its style renders it virtually unreadable. While the desire to open up the issues of gender and nationality in Irish poetry is admirable, Fulford's foray into 'new' territory is hampered by the number of questionable assumptions she uncritically takes with her: that a new generation has to be read in relation to Heaney; that various critical positions held by Longley, Graham and others can be easily identified and 'tagged' accordingly; that her own selection of writers is unproblematic. Fulford does have some useful things to say about her poets, notably Boland and Berkeley (she is more confident on women poets). But her approach is, essentially, to scour poems for the moments when they can be seen to illuminate an aspect of theory. As a result, *Gendered Spaces*, however well intentioned, does few favours to feminism, postcolonialism, or poetry.

Two publications appeared this year which make an important contribution to Yeatsian scholarship. Both illuminate, though in very different ways, Yeats in the context of the 1890s. Yug Mohit Chaudhry's *Yeats: The Irish Literary Revival and the Politics of Print* takes the important, and hitherto largely neglected, step of taking Yeats's contributions to periodicals and newspapers, many of which have been collected into various prose editions over the decades, and resituating—and re-reading—them in the time and place of their original publication. To limit knowledge of a text to its republication is, for Chaudhry, likely to lead to 'impaired and distorted readings of key Yeatsian poems' (p. 254). He makes that case partly through consideration of the poetry: 'September 1913' provides fodder for his forcefully argued opening case. But he is also concerned with the ways in which Yeats's prose writings are affected by the poet's consciousness of their original

publication outlet. All this is illuminating, and serves to make Yeats's writing seem
rather less sanctified: it is reassuring, perhaps, to know that the phase 17 poet who
could rise above the filthy modern tide was just as likely to cut his coat to suit his
cloth on occasion, subject as he was to pressures from partisan (and often opposed)
editors, as well as from the marketplace. While Chaudhry does not try and reduce
texts and poems to something less than they are aesthetically, he does make a
convincing case that Yeats's work may be more fully understood if his texts are
understood also as 'documents of their time, caught in the complexities of Irish
political and literary affairs' (p. 247). The 2001 Yeats Annual, a special issue
entitled *Yeats and the Nineties* edited by Warwick Gould, also casts new light on
early Yeats in the context of a network of social, artistic and occultist relations. As
always, the Annual is a valuable resource, and a good barometer of the current state
of play in Yeats scholarship and resources. R.A. Gilbert's essay on the Golden
Dawn takes the discovery of new papers to reach some tentative conclusions about
the movement's origins, and it seems the story is not likely to end here. Likewise
William F. Halloran's fascinating narrative concerning Yeats's relationship with
William Sharp/Fiona Macleod, also draws on recently discovered letters to shed
further light on a complex exchange of aesthetic ideas and principles. It has perhaps
been too easy to see Yeats's 1890s phase as shrouded in the veil he himself later
threw over it; this volume goes to show how much nevertheless remains to be
explored.

Books Reviewed

Ackland, Rodney. *Plays Two: Smithereens, Strange Orchestra, Before the Party
   and The Old Ladies.* Oberon. [2001] pp. 240. £12.99 ISBN 1 8400 2088 1.
Agnew, Kate, and Geoff Fox. *Children at War.* Contemporary Classics of
   Children's Literature. Continuum. [2001] pp. 194. hb £50 ISBN 0 8264 4849 6
   pb £14.99 ISBN 0 8264 4848 8.
Allen, Paul. *Alan Ayckbourn: Grinning at the Edge.* Methuen. [2001] pp. x + 337.
   illus. £19.99 ISBN 0 4137 3120 0.
Barfoot, C.C., ed. *Aldous Huxley Between East and West.* Studies in Comparative
   Literature 37. Rodopi. [2001] pp. 259. pb. €45 ISBN 9 0420 1347 8.
Barry, Kevin. *The Dead.* Ireland into Film. CorkUP. [2001] pp. x + 117. pb €10
   ISBN 1 8591 8285 2.
Barstow, Stan. *In My Own Good Time.* Smith Settle. [2001] pp. vii + 252. £11.95
   ISBN 1 8582 5153 2.
Batty, Mark. *Harold Pinter.* WTW. Northcote. [2001] pp. x + 134. £7.99 ISBN 0
   7463 0940 6.
Berg, James, and Chris Freeman, eds. *The Isherwood Century.* UWiscP [2001] pp.
   296. $34.95 ISBN 0 2991 6700 3.
Berman, Jessica, and Jane Goldman, eds. *Virginia Woolf: Out of Bounds: Selected
   Papers from the Tenth Annual Conference on Virginia Woolf.* PaceUP. [2001] pp.
   x + 313. $40 ISBN 0 9444 7355 5.
Bernhart, Walter, and Werner Wolf, eds. *Word and Music Studies: Essays on the
   Song Cycle and on Defining the Field.* Rodopi. [2001] pp. xii + 253. hb €57 ISBN
   9 0420 1575 6, pb €23 ISBN 9 0420 1565 9.

Beyers, Chris. *A History of Free Verse*. UArkP. [2001] pp. ix + 285. pb $22.95 ISBN 1 5572 8702 3.

Billingham, Peter, ed. *Theatres of Conscience, 1939–1959*. Routledge/Harwood. [2001] pp. 184. £30 ISBN 0 4152 7028 6.

Black, Naomi, ed. *Three Guineas* by Virginia Woolf. SHP/Blackwell. [2001] pp. lxxv + 253. £65 ISBN 0 6311 7724 8.

Boheemen-Saaf, Christine van. and Colleen Lamos, eds. *Masculinities in Joyce: Postcolonial Constructions*. European Joyce Studies 10. Rodopi. [2001] pp. 262. pb €18 ISBN 9 0420 1276 5.

Boldrini, Lucia. *Joyce, Dante and the Poetics of Literary Relations: Language and Meaning in 'Finnegans Wake'*. CUP. [2001] pp. xi + 233. £40 ISBN 0 5217 9276 2.

Bornstein, George. *Material Modernisms: The Politics of the Page*. CUP. [2001] pp. xii + 185. £40 ISBN 0 5216 6154 4.

Bolger, Dermot, ed. *Druids, Dudes and Beauty Queens: The Changing Face of Irish Theatre*. New Island. [2001] pp. 302. pb £14.99 ISBN 1 9026 0274 9.

Bradford, Richard. *Lucky Him: The Life of Kingsley Amis*. Owen. [2001] pp. 432. £22.50 ISBN 0 7206 1117 2.

Brake, Laurel. *Print in Transition, 1850–1910: Studies in Media and Book History*. Palgrave. [2001] pp. xv + 341. £47.50 ISBN 0 3337 7047 1.

Brearton, Fran, and Eamonn Hughes. *Last Before America: Irish and American Writing*. Blackstaff. [2001] pp. 233. £12.99 ISBN 0 8564 0701 1.

Brooker, Jewel Spears, ed. *T.S. Eliot and our Turning World*. Macmillan. [2001] pp. xix + 238. £45 ISBN 0 3337 1567 5.

Bucknell, Brad. *Literary Modernism and Musical Aesthetics: Pater, Pound, Joyce and Stein*. CUP. [2001] pp. xii + 288. £40 ISBN 0 5216 6028 9.

Buning, Marius, Matthijs Engelberts and Onno Kosters, eds. *Samuel Beckett Today*, vol. 9: *Beckett and Religion*. Rodopi. [2000] pp. 336. £18 ISBN 9 0420 1394 X.

Burkdall, Thomas L. *Joycean Frames: Film and the Fiction of James Joyce*. Studies in Major Literary Authors. Routledge. [2001] pp. xv + 114. £35 ISBN 0 8153 3928 3.

Burns, Edward M., with Joshua A. Gaylord, eds. *A Tour of the Darkling Plain: The Finnegans Wake Letters of Thornton Wilder and Adaline Glasheen*. UCDubP. [2001] pp. xxx + 732 + 10 plates. hb £69.99 ISBN 1 9006 2154 1, pb £28.99 ISBN 1 9006 2155 X.

Castle, Gregory. *Modernism and the Celtic Revival*. CUP. [2001] pp. viii + 312. £40 ISBN 0 5217 9319 X.

Caws, Mary Ann. *Virginia Woolf*. Penguin. [2001] pp. 144. £9.99 ISBN 0 1402 9160 1.

Chambers, Lilian, Ger FitzGibbon and Eamonn Jordan. *Theatre Talk: Voices of Irish Theatre Practitioners*. Carysfort. [2001] pp. 495. £15.75 ISBN 0 9534 2576 2.

Chance, Jane. *Lord of the Rings: The Mythology of Power*, rev. edn. UPKen. [2001] pp. xvii + 162. £15.95 ISBN 0 8131 9017 7.

Chance, Jane. *Tolkien's Art: A Mythology for England*, rev. edn. UPKen. [2001] pp. xiii + 262. £15.95 ISBN 0 8131 9020 7.

Chaudhry, Yug Mohit, *Yeats: The Irish Literary Revival and the Politics of Print*. CorkUP. [2001] pp. 292. pb. £16.95 ISBN 1 8591 8261 5.

Childs, Donald J. *From Philosophy to Poetry: T.S. Eliot's Study of Knowledge and Experience*. Athlone. [2001] pp. x + 223. £47.50 ISBN 0 4851 1550 6.

Childs, Donald J. *Modernism and Eugenics: Woolf, Eliot, Yeats, and the Culture of Degeneration*. CUP. [2001] pp. 266. £40 ISBN 0 5218 0601 1.

Cobley, Paul. *Narrative*. New CI. Routledge. [2001] pp. viii + 267. hb £40 ISBN 0 4152 1262 6, pb £9.99 0 4152 1263 4.

Conradi, Peter J. *Iris Murdoch: A Life*. HC. [2001] pp. xxx + 706. £9.99 ISBN 0 0065 3175 X.

Conradi, Peter J. *The Saint and the Artist: A Study of the Fiction of Iris Murdoch*, rev. edn. HC. [2001] pp. xxvi + 422. £9.99 ISBN 0 0071 2019 2.

Curtis, Tony, ed. *The Art of Seamus Heaney*, 4th edn. Seren. [2001] pp. 296. pb £12.95 ISBN 1 8641 1256 2.

Dalgarno, Emily. *Virginia Woolf and the Visible World*. CUP. [2001] pp. 240. £35 ISBN 0 5217 9299 1.

Daugherty, Beth Rigel, and Mary Beth Pringle, eds. *Approaches to Teaching Woolf's 'To the Lighthouse'*. MLA. [2001] pp. xiv + 211. hb $37.50 ISBN 0 8735 2765 8, pb $18 ISBN 0 8735 2766 6.

Davies, Cecil. *The Adelphi Players: The Theatre of Persons*. Routledge/Harwood. [2001] pp. 112. £30 ISBN 0 4152 7026 X.

Deane, Vincent, Daniel Ferrer and Geert Lernout. *The Finnegans Wake Notebooks at Buffalo*. Brepols. [2001]: *Notebook VI.B.10*, pp. 174. €85 ISBN 2 5035 0959 2; *Notebook VI.B.29*, pp. 230. €85 ISBN 2 5035 1307 7; *Notebook VI.B.3*, pp. 152. €85 ISBN 2 5035 1306 9; *Reader's Guide to the Edition*, pp. 16. €15 ISBN 2 5035 1308 5.

Devlin, Albert J., and Nancy M. Tischler, eds. *The Selected Letters of Tennessee Williams*, vol. 1: *1920–1945*. Oberon. [2001] pp. 452. £19.99 ISBN 1 8400 2226 4.

Doherty, Gerald. *Oriental Lawrence: The Quest for the Secrets of Sex*. Lang. [2001] pp. xi + 175. $54.95 (£36) ISBN 0 8204 5213 0.

Driver, Felix. *Geography Militant: Cultures of Exploration and Empire*. Blackwell. [2001] pp. viii + 258. pb £16.99 ISBN 0 6312 0112 2.

Dromgoole, Nicholas. *The Playwright as Rebel: Essays in Theatre History*. Oberon. [2001] pp. 150. £12.99 ISBN 1 8400 2147 0.

Edgar, David, ed. *State of Play: Playwrights on Playwriting*. Faber. [1999] pp. viii + 135. £9.99 ISBN 0 5712 0096 6.

Ehlert, Anne Odenbring. *'There's a bad time coming': Ecological Vision in the Fiction of D.H. Lawrence*. Uppsala. [2001] pp. 201. ISBN 9 1554 4931 X.

Eyre, Richard, ed. *Pinter: A Celebration*. Faber. [2000] pp. x + 73. £7.99 ISBN 0 5712 0661 1.

Farley, Fidelma. *This Other Eden*. CorkUP. [2001] pp. 93. $9.95 ISBN 1 8591 8289 5.

Fenton, James. *The Strength of Poetry*. OUP. [2001] pp. 266. £15.99 ISBN 0 1981 8707 6.

Fernihough, Anne, ed. *The Cambridge Companion to D.H. Lawrence*. CUP. [2001] pp. xx + 292. hb £37.50 ($54.95) ISBN 0 5216 2339 1, pb £13.50 ($19.95) ISBN 0 5216 2617 X.

Ferrall, Charles. *Modernist Writing and Reactionary Politics*. CUP. [2001] pp. viii + 202. £35 ISBN 0 5217 9345 9.

Fleming, John. *Stoppard's Theatre: Finding Order amid Chaos*. UTexP. [2001] pp. xvi + 325. $45 ISBN 0 2927 2533 7.

Flieger, Verlyn. *A Question of Time: J.R.R. Tolkien's Road to Faërie*. KentSUP. [2001] pp. x + 277. pb $18 ISBN 0 8733 8699 X.

Frost, Robert. *North of Boston*, introd. Hugh Underhill. Cyder. [2000] pp. viii + 154. £5 ISBN 1 8617 4103 0.

Fulford, Sarah. *Gendered Spaces in Contemporary Irish Poetry*. Lang. [2001] pp. 292. pb £30 ISBN 3 9067 6689 6.

Gale, Steven H., ed. *The Films of Harold Pinter*. SUNYP. [2001] pp. viii + 188, illus. £13.75 ISBN 0 7914 4932 7.

Games, Alexander. *Backing into the Limelight: The Biography of Alan Bennett*. Headline. [2001] pp. 312, illus. £18.99 ISBN 0 7472 7030 9.

Gillen, Francis, and Steven H. Gale, eds. *The Pinter Review: Collected Essays, 1999 and 2000*. UTampaP. [2000] pp. 242. ISBN 1 8798 5214 4.

Gillespie, Michael Patrick, ed. *James Joyce and the Fabrication of an Irish Identity*. European Joyce Studies 11. Rodopi. [2001] pp. 193. pb €18 ISBN 9 0420 1426 1.

Gillis, Alan A., and Aaron Kelly. *Critical Ireland: New Essays in Irish Literature and Culture*. FCP. [2001] pp. 221. £14.95 ISBN 1 8518 2598 3.

Glaap, Albert-Reiner, and Nicholas Quaintmere, eds. *A Guided Tour through Ayckbourn Country*. Trier: Wissenschaftlicher. [1999] pp. 195, illus. £10 ISBN 3 8847 6349 0.

Goodby, John, and Chris Wigginton, eds. *Dylan Thomas: New Critical Essays*. New Casebooks. Palgrave. [2001] pp. xiii + 235. £13.99 ISBN 0 3338 0395 7.

Gordon, Lois, ed. *Pinter at 70: A Casebook*. Routledge. [2001] pp. lxv + 342. $29.95 ISBN 0 4159 3630 6.

Gould, Warwick, ed. *Yeats and the Nineties*. Yeats Annual 14. Palgrave. [2001] pp. xxiii + 399. hb £55 ISBN 0 3337 1640 X, ISSN 0278 7687.

Graham, Colin. *Deconstructing Ireland: Identity, Theory, Culture*. EdinUP. [2001] pp. xv + 189. pb £16.99 ISBN 0 7486 0976 8.

Grant, Patrick, *Literature, Rhetoric and Violence in Northern Ireland, 1968–98: Hardened to Death*. Palgrave. [2001] pp. xi + 173. hb £42.50 ISBN 0 3337 9412 5.

Gray, Simon. *Enter a Fox*. Faber. [2001] pp. 121. £9.99 ISBN 0 5712 0940 8.

Greiff, Louis K. *D.H. Lawrence: Fifty Years on Film*. SIUP. [2001] pp. xviii + 352. $39.95 ISBN 0 8093 2387 7.

Grieve, Dorian, O.D. Edwards and Alan Riach, eds. *Hugh MacDiarmid: New Selected Letters*. Carcanet. [2001] pp. xxxvi + 572. £39.95 ISBN 1 8575 4273 8.

Halliwell, Martin. *Modernism and Morality: Ethical Devices in European and American Fiction*. Palgrave. [2001] pp. viii + 264. £45 ISBN 0 3339 1884 3.

Hardy, Barbara. *Thomas Hardy: Imagining Imagination in Hardy's Poetry and Fiction*. Athlone. [2000] pp. ix + 224. hb £55 ISBN 0 4851 1543 3, pb £14.99 ISBN 0 4851 2153 0.

Haughey, Jim, *The First World War in Irish Poetry*. BuckUP. [2001] pp. 309. $52.50 ISBN 0 8387 5496 1.

Hederman, Mark Patrick. *The Haunted Inkwell: Art and our Future*. ColUP. [2001] pp. 231. £9.99 ISBN 1 8560 7347 5.

Heusel, Barbara Stevens. *Iris Murdoch's Paradoxical Novels: Thirty Years of Critical Reception*. Camden House. [2001] pp. xi + 185. £40 ISBN 1 5711 3089 6.

Hill-Miller, Katherine C. *From the Lighthouse to Monk's House: A Guide to* *Virginia Woolf's Literary Landscapes*. Duckworth. [2001] pp. 200. £8 ISBN 0 7156 2995 6.

Hodgson, Terry, ed. *The Plays of Tom Stoppard for Stage, Radio, TV and Film: A Reader's Guide to Essential Criticism*. Icon. [2001] pp. 224. £9.99 ISBN 1 8404 6241 8.

Holt, Michael. *Alan Ayckbourn*. WTW. Northcote. [1999] pp. 70. £9.99 ISBN 0 7463 0859 0.

Hughes, Clair. *Henry James and the Art of Dress*. Palgrave. [2001] pp. x + 216. £35 ISBN 0 3339 1430 9.

Hughes, John. *'Ecstatic Sound': Music and Individuality in the Work of Thomas Hardy*. Ashgate. [2001] pp. ix + 246. £40 ISBN 1 8401 4633 8.

Humble, Nicola. *The Feminine Middlebrow Novel, 1920s to 1950s: Class, Domesticity, and Bohemianism*. OUP. [2001] pp. ix + 272. £45 ISBN 0 1981 8676 2.

Hunt, Peter, and Millicent Lenz. *Alternative Worlds in Fantasy Fiction*. Contemporary Classics of Children's Literature. Continuum. [2001] pp. vi + 174. hb £50 ISBN 0 8264 4936 0, pb £14.99 ISBN 0 8264 4937 9.

Hunter, Lynette. *Literary Value/Cultural Power: Verbal Arts in the Twenty-First Century*. UManP. [2001] pb £14.99. pp. xi + 156 ISBN 0 7190 6182 2.

Ingelbien, Raphaël. *Misreading England: Poetry and Nationhood since the Second World War*. Costerus ns 142. Rodopi. [2002] pp. ix + 252. €50 ISBN 9 0420 1123 8.

Ingersoll, Earl G. *D.H. Lawrence, Desire, and Narrative*. UFlorP. [2001] pp. xi +176. $55.00 (£46.50) ISBN 0 8130 1850 1.

Jacobs, Karen. *The Eye's Mind: Literary Modernism and Visual Culture*. CornUP. [2001] pp. viii + 311. $19.95 ISBN 0 8014 8649 1.

Jeffries, Lesley, and Peter Sansom, eds. *Contemporary Poems: Some Critical Approaches*. Smith/Doorstop. [2000] pp. 190. £9.99 ISBN 1 9023 8226 9.

Johnston, Dillon. *The Poetic Economies of England and Ireland, 1912–2000*. Palgrave. [2001] pp. xx + 252. hb £47.50 ISBN 0 3337 9046 4.

Keen, Suzanne. *Romances of the Archive in Contemporary British Fiction*. UTorP. [2001] pp. x + 288. £40 ISBN 0 8020 3589 2.

Kelly, Katharine E., ed. *The Cambridge Companion to Tom Stoppard*. CUP. [2001] pp. xvi + 244. £13.95 ISBN 0 5216 4592 1.

King, Jeannette. *Women and the Word: Contemporary Women Novelists and the Bible*. Palgrave. [2000] pp. x + 207. £47.50 ISBN 0 3339 1872 X.

King, Kimball, ed. *Modern Dramatists: A Casebook of Major British, Irish and American Playwrights*. Routledge. [2001] pp. xx + 396. £14.99 ISBN 0 8153 2349 2.

Knowles, Sebastian D.G. *The Dublin Helix: The Life of Language in Joyce's 'Ulysses'*. UPFlor. [2001] pp. xvi + 176. £46.50 ISBN 0 8130 1879 X.

Lázaro, Alberto, ed. *The Road from George Orwell: His Achievement and Legacy*. Lang. [2001] pp. 250. £25 ISBN 3 9067 6679 9.

Lea, Daniel, ed. *George Orwell—Animal Farm/Nineteen Eighty-Four: A Reader's Guide to Essential Criticism*. Icon. [2001] pp. 217. £9.99 ISBN 1 8404 6254 X.

Lucas, John. *Ivor Gurney*. Northcote. [2001] pp. xiv + 114. £9.99 ISBN 0 7463 0887 6.

Mackenney, Linda. *The Activities of Popular Dramatists and Drama Groups in Scotland, 1900–1952.* Mellen. [2001] pp. 320. $119.95 ISBN 0 7734 7905 8.

Mahto, R.P. *The Post-War English Novel.* Prestige. [2001] pp. 168. Rs400 ISBN 8 1755 1112 5.

Maslen, Elizabeth. *Political and Social Issues in British Women's Fiction, 1928–1968.* Palgrave. [2001] pp. viii + 248. £42.50 ISBN 0 3337 2953 6.

McBride, Ian, ed. *History and Memory in Modern Ireland.* CUP. [2001] pp. xi + 278. £40 ISBN 0 5217 9017 4.

McGee, Diane. *Writing the Meal: Dinner in the Fiction of Early Twentieth-Century Women.* UTorP. [2001] pp. viii + 221. £40 ISBN 0 8020 3541 8.

McGee, Patrick. *Joyce beyond Marx: History and Desire in 'Ulysses' and 'Finnegans Wake'.* UPFlor. [2001] pp. xii + 307. £46.50 ISBN 0 8130 1880 3.

McGonigal, James, and Richard Price, eds. *The Star You Steer By: Basil Bunting and British Modernism.* Studies in Literature 30. Rodopi. [2000] pp. 298. €68 ISBN 9 0420 1214 5.

Mew, Charlotte. *The Farmer's Bride*, introd. Deborah Parsons. Cyder. [2000] pp. x + 42. £5 ISBN 1 8617 4099 9.

Middleton, Peter, and Tim Woods. *Literatures of Memory: History, Time and Space in Postwar Writing.* ManUP. [2000] pp. viii + 323. £49.99 ISBN 0 7190 5949 6.

Monteith, Sharon. *Pat Barker.* Northcote. [2002] pp. xii + 130. £9.99 ISBN 0 7463 0900 7.

Moore-Gilbert, Bart. *Hanif Kureishi.* ManUP. [2001] pp. xvii + 266. £9.99 ISBN 0 7190 5535 0.

Moorjani, Angela, and Carola Veit, eds. *Samuel Beckett Today*, vol. 11: *Endlessness in the Year 2000.* Rodopi. [2001] pp. 493. ISBN 9 0420 1599 3.

Neumeier, Beate, ed. *Engendering Realism and Postmodernism: Contemporary Women Writers in Britain.* Rodopi. [2001] pp. 418. £48.70 ISBN 9 0420 1437 7.

O'Meahy, Joseph H. *Alan Bennett: A Critical Introduction.* Routledge. [2001] pp. xxii + 169. £50 ISBN 0 8153 3540 7.

Pawlowski, Merry M., ed. *Virginia Woolf and Fascism: Resisting the Dictators' Seduction.* Palgrave. [2001] pp. xiv + 241. $62 ISBN 0 3338 0115 6.

Peck, John. *Maritime Fiction: Sailors and the Sea in British and American Novels, 1719–1917.* Palgrave. [2001] pp. viii + 214. £40 ISBN 0 3337 9357 9.

Peters, John G. *Conrad and Impressionism.* CUP. [2001] pp. xiv + 206. £45 ISBN 0 5217 9173 1.

Pettitt, Lance. *December Bride.* CorkUP. [2001] pp. 94. $9.95 ISBN 1 8591 8290 9.

Pichardie, Jean-Paul, and Philippe Romanski, eds. *Like a Black and White Kaleidoscope Tossed at Random: Essays on D.H. Lawrence's 'Women in Love'.* URouen. [2001] pp. vi + 214. €19 ISBN 2 8777 5319 0.

Pilkington, Lionel. *Theatre and the State in Twentieth-Century Ireland.* Routledge. [2001] pp. 272. £19.99 ISBN 0 4150 6938 6.

Plowright, Joan. *And That's Not All.* Orion. [2001] pp. 302. £8.99 ISBN 0 7528 4840 2.

Poplawski, Paul, ed. *Writing the Body in D.H. Lawrence: Essays on Language, Representation, and Sexuality.* Greenwood. [2001] pp. xv + 240. $61.50 (£51.95) ISBN 0 3133 1517 5.

Priestley, J.B. *Dangerous Corner.* Oberon. [2001] pp. 107. £7.99 ISBN 1 8400 2251 5.

Priestley, J.B. *Eden End.* Oberon. [2001] pp. 108. £7.99 ISBN 1 8400 2254 X.

Priestley, J.B. *Johnson Over Jordan.* Oberon. [2001] pp. 104. £7.99 ISBN 1 8400 2248 5.

Quinn, Patrick J., and Steven Trout, eds. *The Literature of the Great War Reconsidered: Beyond Modern Memory.* Palgrave. [2001] pp. xiv + 246. £47.50 ISBN 0 3337 6459 5.

Rabaté, Jean-Michel. *James Joyce and the Politics of Egoism.* CUP. [2001] pp. x + 248. hb £40 ISBN 0 5218 0425 6, pb £14.95 ISBN 0 5210 0958 8.

Raby, Peter, ed. *The Cambridge Companion to Harold Pinter.* CUP. [2001] pp. xix + 272, illus. £13.95 ISBN 0 5216 5842 X.

Reynolds, Kimberley, Geraldine Brennan and Kevin McCarron. *Frightening Fiction.* Contemporary Classics of Children's Literature. Continuum. [2001] pp. vi + 134. hb £50 ISBN 0 8264 5309 0, pb £14.99 ISBN 0 8264 5310 4.

Roberts, Neil, ed. *A Companion to Twentieth-Century Poetry.* Blackwell. [2001] pp. xvii + 626. £80 ISBN 0 6312 1529 8.

Roberts, Warren, and Paul Poplawski. *A Bibliography of D.H. Lawrence,* 3rd edn. CUP. [2001] pp. xxiv + 847. £90 ISBN 0 5213 9182 2.

Rose, Jonathan. *The Intellectual Life of the British Working Classes.* YaleUP. [2001] pp. ix + 534. £29.95 ISBN 0 3000 8886 8.

Roston, Murray. *The Search for Selfhood in Modern Literature.* Palgrave. [2001] pp. vi + 248. £42.50 ISBN 0 3337 6334 3.

Rowland, Antony. *Tony Harrison and the Holocaust.* English Texts and Studies 39. LiverUP. [2001] pp. x + 326. £14.95 ISBN 0 8532 3516 3.

Rowland, Susan. *From Agatha Christie to Ruth Rendell: British Women Writers in Detective and Crime Fiction.* Palgrave. [2001] pp. x + 222. pb £13.99 ISBN 0 3336 8463 X.

Ryan, Marie-Laure. *Narrative as Virtual Reality: Immersion and Interactivity in Literature and Electronic Media.* JHUP. [2001] pp. xiii + 399. £31 ISBN 0 8018 6487 9.

Sage, Lorna. *Moments of Truth: Twelve Twentieth-Century Women Writers.* FE. [2002] pp. xx + 252. £7.99 ISBN 1 8411 5636 1.

Sargent, M. Elizabeth, and Garry Watson, eds. *Approaches to Teaching the Works of D.H. Lawrence.* MLA. [2001] pp. xviii + 270. hb $37.50 ISBN 0 8735 2763 1, pb $18 ISBN 0 8735 2764 X.

Schwarz, Daniel R. *Rereading Conrad.* UMissP. [2001] pp. xii + 194. hb £29.50 ISBN 0 8262 1327 8, pb £14.50 ISBN 0 8262 1327 8.

Seixo, Maria Alziro, ed. *Travel Writing and Cultural Memory / Écriture du voyage et mémoire culturelle.* Rodopi. [2000] pp. 293. pb $55 ISBN 9 0420 0470 3.

Seymour-Jones, Carole. *Painted Shadow: A Life of Vivienne Eliot.* Constable. [2001] pp. xx + 682. £20 ISBN 0 0947 9270 4.

Sicari, Stephen. *Joyce's Modernist Allegory: 'Ulysses' and the History of the Novel.* USCP. [2001] pp. xv + 252. £21.50 ISBN 1 5700 3383 8.

Sierz, Aleks. *In-Yer-Face Theatre: British Drama Today.* Faber. [2001] pp. xiii + 274. £9.99 ISBN 0 5712 0049 4.

Smith, Andrew, and Jeff Wallace, eds. *Gothic Modernisms.* Palgrave. [2001] pp. 248. £40 ISBN 0 3339 1873 8.

Steiner, George. *Grammars of Creation.* Faber. [2001] pp. 288. £16.99 ISBN 0 5712 0681 6.

Stephens, Russell. *Emlyn Williams: The Making of a Dramatist*. Seren. [2001] pp. 248, illus. £7.95 ISBN 1 8541 1264 3.

Stevens, Hugh, and Caroline Howlett, eds. *Modernist Sexualities*. ManUP. [2001] pp. ix + 276. hb £74.95 ISBN 0 7190 5160 6, pb £16.46 ISBN 0 7190 5161 4.

Sultan, Stanley. *Joyce's Metamorphosis*. UPFlor. [2001] pp. xv + 207. £46.50 ISBN 0 8130 2105 7.

Thomas, Edward. *Four-and-Twenty Blackbirds*, introd. Richard Emeny. Cyder. [2001] pp. vii + 112. £5 ISBN 1 8617 4111 1.

Treby, Ivor C., comp. *Music and Silence: The Gamut of Michael Field*. De Blackland. [2000] pp. 222. £13.50 ISBN 0 9074 0407 3.

Trevis, Di. *Remembrance of Things Proust*. National Theatre. [2001] pp. 46, illus. £5 ISBN 0 9519 9435 2.

Trotter, David. *Paranoid Modernism: Literary Experiment, Psychosis, and the Professionalization of English Society*. OUP. [2001] pp. 358. £35 ISBN 0 1981 8755 6.

Trotter, Mary. *Ireland's National Theaters: Political Performance and the Origins of the Irish Dramatic Movement*. SyracuseUP. [2001] pp. 207. £16.50 ISBN 0 8156 2889 7.

Tubridy, Derval. *Thomas Kinsella: The Peppercanister Poems*. UCDubP. [2001] pp. 273. pb £17.95 ISBN 1 9006 2153 3.

Tucker, Nicholas, and Nikki Gamble. *Family Fictions*. Contemporary Classics of Children's Literature. Continuum. [2001] pp. vi + 117. hb £50 ISBN 0 8264 4877 1, pb £14.99 ISBN 0 8264 4878 X.

Unwin, Stephen, with Carole Woddis. *A Pocket Guide to Twentieth-Century Drama*. Faber. [2001] pp. 300. £8.99 ISBN 0 5712 0014 1.

Valente, Joseph, ed. *Quare Joyce*. UMichP. [2000] pp. 312. $20.95 ISBN 0 4720 8689 8.

Wachman, Gay. *Lesbian Empire: Radical Cross-Writing in the Twenties*. RutgersUP. [2001] pp. xii + 237. $24 ISBN 0 8135 2942 5.

Wade, Stephen, ed. *Gladsongs and Gatherings: Poetry and its Social Context in Liverpool since the 1960s*. LiverUP. [2001] pp. xix + 196. £13.95 ISBN 0 8532 3727 1.

Wandor, Michelene. *Post-War British Drama: Looking Back in Gender*. Routledge. [2001] pp. x + 271. £17.99 ISBN 0 4151 3856 6.

Watkins, Susan. *Twentieth-Century Women Novelists: Feminist Theory into Practice*. Palgrave. [2001] pp. x + 218. pb. £14.50 ISBN 0 3336 8346 3.

Whitworth, Michael H. *Einstein's Wake: Relativity, Metaphor, and Modernist Literature*. OUP. [2001] pp. ix + 254. £45 ISBN 0 1981 8640 1.

Wilson, David L., and Zack Bowen. *Science and Literature: Bridging the Two Cultures*. UFlorP. [2001] pp. xiii + 252. £46.50 ISBN 0 8130 2283 5.

Woods, Tim. *Who's Who of Twentieth-Century Novelists*. Routledge. [2001] pp. x + 374. £19.99 ISBN 0 4151 6506 7.

Wykes, David. *Evelyn Waugh: A Literary Life*. Macmillan. [1999] pp. xii + 224. pb £16.99 ISBN 0 3336 1138 1.

Zangenehpour, Fereshteh. *Sufism and the Quest for Spiritual Fulfillment in D.H. Lawrence's 'The Rainbow'*. GothU. [2000] pp. vi + 241. ISBN 9 1734 6380 9.

XV

American Literature to 1900

HENRY CLARIDGE, ANNE-MARIE FORD AND THERESA SAXON

This chapter has three sections: 1. General; 2. American Literature to 1830; 3. American Literature, 1830–1900. Sections 1 and 2 are by Henry Claridge; section 3 is by Anne-Marie Ford and Theresa Saxon.

1. General

Current bibliographical listings for books in the field and period continue to be available quarterly in the 'Book Reviews' and 'Brief Mentions' sections of *American Literature*. Annually the *Modern Language Association International Bibliography* provides an exhaustive bibliography of books, articles, review essays, notes and dissertations that is an indispensable resource for scholars. *American Literary Scholarship: An Annual*, a narrative bibliography under the editorship of Gary Scharnhorst, casts its informed and attentive eye over the year's critical and scholarly writings: the editor and his contributors have an increasingly difficult job to do, given the sheer magnitude of the scholarship they are expected to review, yet *AmLS* remains the best and most thorough narrative bibliography in the field.

2. American Literature to 1830

To begin with three book-length contributions to the scholarship of the period: over a decade of work under the auspices of the American Antiquarian Society on the history of the book in colonial America and the United States begins to come to fruition with Amory and Hall, eds., *A History of the Book in America*, volume 1: *The Colonial Book in the Atlantic World*, the first in what is planned as a five-volume series. This volume is an important addition to recent work on both publishing and the place of the author. Here the emphasis is not merely on the culture of printing, readership, or the role of the book as an instrument of literate conversation—these issues are, indeed, addressed. But Amory and Hall are interested in the transnational character of colonial publishing and the book as an artefact of 'print capitalism'. Thus *The Colonial Book in the Atlantic World* contributes much to our understanding of the economic features of colonial America, especially relations between the church, the state, and the writer as they are interwoven with the determining characteristics of mercantile capitalism. The structure of this history is largely by way of chronology and region, and most of the individual chapters fall into the hands of either Amory or Hall, but there are 'specialist' chapters on issues such as printers' supplies, written by John Bidwell, periodicals, written by Charles Clark and Richard Brown, and literary culture, written by David S. Shields. It can be the case that single-author or joint-author literary histories have a coherence that comes from the 'singular' vision they offer, and that multi-author histories are shapeless and, potentially, fissiparous, but Amory and Hall seem to have exercised a firm editorial hand and this volume has the kind of coherence and narrative clarity that will make it an indispensable source for scholars for many decades to come. A major work of a related nature is Patricia Crain's *The Story of A: The Alphabetization of America from 'The New England Primer' to 'The Scarlet Letter'*. Crain's subject is the written word, its physical manifestation through the technology of the letter alphabet, and its role in the transatlantic culture of human communication. She argues that the letter alphabet brings with it the replacement of rhetoric by alphabetic instruction and that increasingly letters on the page give shape and structure to those human affairs where, in the past, rhetorical and oratorical modes of discourse had been dominant. She pursues her story through both the pedagogical and the imaginative modes by which print culture affects the lives of transatlantic readers (and, indeed, non-readers). This is a very important work of scholarship, even if one occasionally feels that Crain is saying obvious things in less than obvious ways.

Carretta and Gould, eds., *Genius in Bondage: Literature of the Early Black Atlantic*, brings together thirteen original articles on the transatlantic black literary tradition of the late eighteenth and early nineteenth centuries. The essays collected here discuss important figures, among them Olaudah Equiano, Ignatius Sancho and Phillis Wheatley. Collectively the essays are driven by the thesis that, until fairly recently, 'critical studies and anthologies of African American literature generally began with the 1830s and 1840s, as American abolitionism gained strength and the African American slave narrative proliferated largely in support of this movement'. Such a history, Carretta and Gould contend, inadequately recognizes the scholarly recovery of 'eighteenth century transatlantic literature by people of African descent writing in English'. These essays, therefore, seek to situate the African American tradition in a longer, and broader, historical perspective, and to show how the writings of Equiano and Wheatley, among others, have a value that is 'independent of the achievements of those who followed them'. The theoretical models of enquiry employed here emphasize the instability of more recent conceptual accounts of race and identity; thus Felicity Nussbaum's essay on 'Being a Man: Olaudah Equiano and Ignatius Sancho' argues that Equiano and Sancho challenged, or 'negotiated', the traditionally gendered stereotypes of black manhood, while the essays in part 3 of the volume, 'Language and the "Other": The Question of Difference', address the rhetorical processes by which African American writers relate to Anglo-American discourses. As with many collections of this kind, one sometimes finds the vocabulary of literary theory sits rather uneasily with the literature itself. In a related review essay, 'Slavery, Race, and American Literary Genealogies' (*EAL* 36[2001] 89–113), Robert S. Levine considers seven scholarly works that generate new methodologies for understanding, and developing, American literary genealogy between the Revolution and the Civil War, especially those that have race and slavery at 'their interpretive centers ... '.

Early American Literature continues to publish the best article work on the seventeenth century. Two articles, especially, are worthy of note. In 'Eaters and Non-Eaters: John Cotton's *A Brief Exposition of ... Canticles* (1642) in Light of Boston's (Linc.) Religious and Civil Conflicts, 1619–22' (*EAL* 36[2001] 149–81) Jesper Rosenmeier seeks to understand Cotton's poetics through the two series of sermons on Canticles, arguing that the political and theological controversies of Boston, Lincolnshire during 1619–22 (Cotton emigrated to Massachusetts in 1633), and Cotton's involvement in them, 'force us to radically revise the picture we have had of Cotton'. Far from being a 'Dimmesdale-like, somewhat timorous scholar, better fitted for the study than the affairs of the world, Cotton reveals himself involved in all aspects of Boston life, fiercely protective of his congregation, fearlessly willing to stand up to the authorities, politically astute, daring and skillful in giving his enemies only a moving target'. William J. Scheick, one of the most accomplished scholars in the field, discusses Increase Mather in his '"The captive exile hasteth": Increase Mather, Meditation, and Authority' (*EAL* 36[2001] 183–200). This essay rehearses many of Scheick's preoccupations with the period, notably his interest in the relations between authority, language, poetics and millennialism (see *YWES* 79[2000] 677–8). He reads Mather's *The Mystery of Israel's Salvation, Explained and Applied* [1667–9] as further evidence of an 'unresolved crisis in authority, as much Mather's as his culture's in the 1660s', a crisis in part generated by the 'seemingly relentless setbacks to the Reformation' and the destabilizing experience of exile. *EAL* also publishes two essays on the eighteenth-century Quaker, Elizabeth Ashbridge. Julie Siever's 'Awakening the Inner Light: Elizabeth Ashbridge and the Transformation of Quaker Community' (*EAL* 36[2001] 235–62) argues that Ashbridge's Quaker autobiography revivifies religious testimony by taking the 'tired language of the Society and making it *strange*, once again'. She does this by renewing the key terms of her faith and retrieving it from the increasingly scientific rationalism of the modern church. Siever's essay is interesting both for its brief, but informed, overview of the Quaker movement in the first half of the eighteenth century and for its account of the *Life*. In '"I had a religious mother": Maternal Ancestry, Female Spaces, and Spiritual Synthesis in Elizabeth Ashbridge's *Account*' (*EAL* 36[2001] 371–94) D. Britton Gildersleeve seeks to show how Ashbridge reaches beyond her maternal legacy and how her rejection of patriarchy and patristy connects her with modern writers such as Adrienne Rich and May Sarton in their articulation of a woman's desire for 'female spaces'. 'In her discovery of Quakerism', Gildersleeve concludes, 'and in the *Account* of that discovery which she leaves us, she refuses to be held captive even within the roomy theories of a sympathetic feminism'. This is an attempt to modernize Ashbridge's life and writings that for all its rhetorical inventiveness is ultimately very unconvincing.

Benjamin Franklin's 'theory of death' is, in effect, the subject of 'Death Effects: Revisiting the Conceit of Franklin's Memoir' (*EAL* 36[2000] 201–34) by Jennifer T. Kennedy. Her interest lies in what the genetic text of Franklin's *Autobiography*, edited by Leo Lemay and P.M. Zall, reveals as something approximating to the memoir that Franklin described in 'textual terms as a second "Edition" of his life'.

In the *Memoir*, Kennedy argues, 'Franklin is concerned about the preservation of his fantasy after-life and this is a fundamentally literary concern'; the *Memoir* seeks to answer the question: how durable is death? By examining the first part of the *Memoir* 'in light of its conceit of posthumousness', it becomes possible to 'give new life to this most famous of American texts'. The 'death effects' Kennedy describes have more to do with the literary than the material, for Franklin appears in various guises, and thus has many ghosts, one of which was that of commonsense author. Kennedy's Franklin thus becomes playfully postmodernist, though whether he would have recognized himself in this 'disguise' is quite another matter. Kennedy has pursued a similar theme in Thomas Jefferson's writings (see *YWES* 81[2002] 878–9).

There are two essays on Charles Brockden Brown in *EAL*. Edward Cahill's 'An Adventurous and Lawless Fancy: Charles Brockden Brown's Aesthetic State' (*EAL* 36[2000] 31–70) looks at Brown's novels through the 'models of aesthetic experience that inform them', especially those models that arise out of eighteenth-century theories of the imagination and their confusion of the distinction between the real and the ideal. For Brown, Cahill argues, the tensions in his fiction are 'realized in both the evanescence of his fiction's narrative reality and the substantiality of his characters' thoughts: the implied correlation between the "chain of audacious acts" described in his fiction and the "adventurous and lawless fancy" that describes them'. Cahill pursues his theme into areas that touch upon what he calls 'the geopolitical orientation of the discourse of the imagination in the eighteenth century'. Congress passed four legislative measures between June and July 1798, and Cahill sees these Alien and Sedition Acts of 1798 (although he misdates them to 1789) as expressions of 'a paranoid public discourse whose object was a national interior threatened by potential confusion'. Cahill argues that worry about national lawlessness helps us understand 'Brown's complex attitude toward the "lawless imagination" so often possessed and professed by his characters, the unrestrained thoughts and desires that propel them chaotically through their plots'. He concludes that the frequency with which characters leave their native country in Brown's fictions (for example, Clara leaving Pennsylvania for Montpellier in *Wieland* and Clithero's flight to America from Ireland in *Edgar Huntly*) suggests that this is a punishment 'meted out for the failure of the imagination' and is further evidence of the 'gap that remains between the real world of the early republic and the realm of the imagination, between the actual and the possible'. In 'The "Vulgar Thread of the Canvas": Revolution and the Picturesque in Ann Eliza Bleecker, Crevecoeur, and Charles Brockden Brown' (*EAL* 36[2001] 395–425) Larry Kutchen explores related issues. His interest in the origins of the American picturesque landscape leads him to challenge the view that the American picturesque is a product of 'romanticist notions of nature and a Turnerian definition of national development', and to offer, instead, an 'imperialist extension of the picturesque into eighteenth century North America, and thereby to suggest its functions as an English Atlantic aesthetic'. In the figure of Carwin in Brown's *Wieland* Kutchen suggests that it is the picturesque that mediates Carwin's 'revolutionary power of dissemblance', and he finds this in the Claudian landscape of the description of the elder Wieland's neoclassical temple. Relatedly, he argues that 'Carwin destroys Clara's serenity by exploiting her picturesque sensibility'. Ultimately both the picturesque and the pastoral are subverted in *Wieland*, for Brown writes at a turning-point where 'the energies of radical individualism' compete with 'the consolidating forces of American gentrification' in the arena of pictorial representation. The same issue of *EAL* includes further reflections on the visual arts in the revolutionary and early national period in Edward Larkin's 'Seeing through Language: Narrative, Portraiture, and Character in Peter Oliver's *The Origins & Progress of the American Revolution*' (*EAL* 36[2000] 427–56). Larkin read Oliver's 'Tory' history (first published in 1781) of the American Revolution through its presentation of satiric types and its poetic 'borrowings', notably from Dryden and Pope. He shows how Oliver's text forces us to re-examine 'the place of the written word and the public sphere in the Revolution' and to recognize that 'the public sphere was less a sociological phenomenon than it was a powerful idea that would be both strategically deployed and repeatedly challenged during the Revolution and the early national period'. This is an interesting and valuable essay.

Genius in Bondage, reviewed more generally above, offers two essays that bear centrally on Phillis Wheatley. Frank Shuffleton's 'On her own Footing: Phillis Wheatley in Freedom' shows how Wheatley's poetry negotiates the effects that the coming of the American Revolution had on her. Wheatley's sojourn in London in 1773 and her familiarity with both the contemporary British and American anti-slavery debates may, Shuffleton suggests, have prompted her to write and speak 'more boldly and explicitly about issues of race and slavery'. He argues that the political crisis Great Britain faced with her empire led Wheatley into complex, and sometimes contradictory, positions, and that by employing 'enlightened and Christian tropes of universal freedom' she sought to mediate the competing claims of conservative and radical politics, and to articulate more general terms for a 'principled emancipation'. In her short essay, '"Thou hast the Holy Word": Jupiter Hammon's "Regards" to Phillis Wheatley', Rosemary Fithian Guruswamy argues that the Bible provided Jupiter Hammon with discursive and rhetorical practices (to be found, also, in Wheatley herself) that turn his 'An Address to Phillis Wheatly' (*sic*) into a 'liberation discourse meant to empower his fellow slave poet with a sacred identification for herself as a writer and a heavenly commission to write on antislavery themes, even if she—like him—has to cloak them in hidden codes and patterns'.

Lucy Rinehart gives us a very informed and lucid account of the theatrical career of the playwright William Dunlap in her '"Manly Exercises": Post-Revolutionary Performances of Authority in the Theatrical Career of William Dunlap' (*EAL* 36[2000] 263–93). Dunlap began what was to become a versatile career at the age of 16 when he was employed professionally as a portrait painter; he studied in London under Benjamin West. But inspired by Royall Tyler's *The Contrast* [1787] he turned to the stage, and in 1789 his *The Father; or, American Shandyism* brought him great critical and commercial success. Rinehart's starting point is Dunlap's family portrait, *The Artist Showing a Picture from 'Hamlet' to his Parents* [1788], which she reads through the disposition of its figures as evidence of the father's disapproval of the son's (Dunlap's) theatrical ambitions. She follows Dunlap's life through the bankruptcy of his theatre in 1805 and the resumption of his career as a painter, focusing on his portrait and history paintings (*Christ Rejected* [1820–1] was one of the largest American historical paintings of its period). She sees Dunlap's waverings between theatre and painting as evidence of 'one of the most significant stylistic transformations of the of the nineteenth-century theater, as Martin Meisel describes it, the "shift in dramaturgy, from a rhetorical to a situational and pictorial mode" of representation'. And, she concludes, 'Dunlap highlights the transience of social and ethnic identity in the new nation'. This is a very good essay, notable for its intelligent discussion of a neglected figure and for its contribution to the equally neglected field of theatre history in the early national period.

An obscure work, Manuel's *The Florida Pirate*, first published in the April 1821 edition of *Blackwood's Edinburgh Magazine*, provides the subject of Daniel Williams's 'Refuge Upon the Sea: Captivity and Liberty in *The Florida Pirate*' (*EAL* 36[2000] 71–88). Williams argues that *The Florida Pirate* is a historically significant text, for Manuel's 'story of abuse and injustice offered antebellum readers a strong, unequivocal indictment of slavery', and no one who 'chanced upon the text during the 1820s could possibly have misread the inhumanity of the narrative's slave owners'. Williams's quotations are from the 1821 edition and, while the work he describes has little literary significance, it merits republication in a modern edition, if only for the enlargement it might offer to our understanding of the anti-slavery readership.

3. American Literature, 1830–1900

Bauer and Gould, eds., *The Cambridge Companion to Nineteenth-Century American Women's Writing* is a fascinating study. Divided into three sections, it begins by debating postcolonial culture, the public woman, antebellum politics and women's writing, thus investigating the historical and theoretical background underpinning the texts. Rosemarie Zagarri's discussion on postcolonialism reflects upon women's writing in the context of social and cultural change, a theme elaborated on in Dana D. Nelson's essay, 'Women in Public', which focuses on the notion of the woman's 'separate sphere'. Literary discourse became an important tool for women in their movement from the private world of the family into the public arena, a fact that Nelson discusses in some detail. The final chapter in this section studies texts written on women themselves. Illustrations are used to good effect in describing changes in clothing, most significantly the bloomers adopted by the 'new woman'. The second section of this study, 'Genre, Tradition, and Innovation', offers an insightful contribution from Kathryn Zabelle Derounian-Stodola on the subject of 'Captivity and the Literary Imagination'. Here she traces the discourses of oppression and emancipation in both autobiography and the novel. Elizabeth Perino discusses women's poetry, and specifically the critical premise that devalues the nineteenth-century woman as poet (with the notable exception of Emily Dickinson). Shirley Samuels's 'Women at War' challenges nineteenth-century assumptions about women within the literary, in which she traces examples of repressed rage, outright aggression and the refusal to submit to male authority. Anti-Catholicism in literary discourse, an enduring thread in the fiction of the nineteenth-century American woman, is the focus of Susan Griffin's essay. This vast and varied topic is investigated chiefly through a study of magazine articles and short stories, as well as a 'lost' novel by Louisa M. Alcott, *A Long Fatal Love Chase*, which remained unpublished until 1995. Themes of immigration and assimilation within the literary are the focus of Priscilla Wald's chapter, which discusses the ambivalent condition of the 'other' and the 'foreign' in contemporary literature. She also explores the voice of the female 'outsider', in texts such as *Incidents in the Life of a Slave Girl* [1861], by Harriet Jacobs, and 'Impressions of an Indian Childhood', by Zitkala-Sa, serialized in the *Atlantic Monthly* in 1900. The final part of the *Companion* is devoted to a series of case studies. Frederika J. Teute offers a detailed study of the way in which Margaret Bayard Smith used writing to reconcile conflicting impulses. Her diaries, letters and published works give voice to personal aspirations at odds with social strictures. The sentimental novel was an important form of liberation for women authors, and Gail K. Smith elaborates on this genre through the writings of Harriet Beecher Stowe. Stowe's vision was, it seems, in keeping with the national one, in her recollection of place as a significant shaping influence, and in her determined call for the abolition of slavery. But anti-slavery novels were only one kind of literary discourse that gave voice to the plight of African Americans. In the subsequent chapter, Yolanda Pierce discusses African American women's spiritual narratives, in which a new sense of freedom is experienced through religious conversion. The final chapters of the *Companion* study the powerful and challenging writings of Rebecca Harding Davis, Elizabeth Stuart Phelps, Elizabeth Stoddard and Frances Ellen Watkins Harper. Farah Jasmine Griffin reminds us that Harper, best known for *Iola Leroy* [1892], her anti-lynching novel, also wrote *Minnie's Sacrifice* [1869]. This text reflects Harper's own experiences under Reconstruction, and, Griffin argues, demonstrates a movement from an integrationist vision towards an emergent black nationalism. The careers of Harding Davis and Stuart Phelps are discussed by Lisa A. Long, who notes the critical acclaim both received for their first published writings. Following the appearance of Harding Davis's *Life in the Iron Mills* [1861], and Stuart Phelps's *The Gates Ajar* [1868], both were also to remain dedicated to the depiction of racial, gender and class conflict in their writing. Long reflects, however, that, despite being published and reviewed in the best journals of their time, neither is typically considered a 'major figure' of American literature. Her arguments for revision of the importance of these writers chime with those of Sandra A. Zagarell, whose chapter studies the novels of Elizabeth Stoddard. Focusing principally on Stoddard's first novel, *The Morgesons* [1862], Zagarell elaborates on the importance of this nineteenth-century woman writer's iconoclastic vision as an example of difference; difference, that is, which asks whether the writing of nineteenth-century American women was as coherent a process as we deem it to have been. The addition of a conclusion by Mary Kelley draws together the scholarship within this detailed study.

Nina Baym's *American Women of Letters and the Nineteenth-Century Sciences: Styles of Affiliation* also concerns itself with women's writing as a reflection of social conditions. The book is a fascinating study of responses to new scientific developments. Baym explores a range of writings by American women, among them Catharine Esther Beecher, Emily Dickinson, Sarah Hale and Almira Phelps. In addition, she investigates science in women's novels, writing by and about women doctors, and the scientific claims advanced by women's spiritualist movements. In a wide-ranging discussion Baym also observes the strongly gendered hierarchies of science. Conventional values figured science as a male domain, one which Phelps appears to have accepted. In *The Fireside Friend* [1840], she employs metaphors for women as spectators and consumers, rather than producers, of science. However, Phelps regarded scientific knowledge as an essential topic for study, as her writings on botany clearly indicate. The editor of *Godey's Lady's Book*, Sarah Hale, also comes under scrutiny. She began her editorial work, in 1828, by extolling the importance of scientific knowledge for women as well as men, but by the 1850s began to focus, instead, on women's redemptive spirituality. This rather more conventional focus on the woman's role was in accordance with Beecher's, who perceived science as a tool which enabled women to work more effectively in the home—quite simply, domestic science. Baym identifies the ideological conflict over women's proper sphere in the work of these women, and broadens the debate in a discussion of *Rural Hours* [1850], by Susan Fenimore Cooper. This writing privileges natural science above other forms of knowledge, but revisions that Cooper made over time shift the balance between nature and science. By 1868 she refers to changes in rural life brought about by such scientific items as the telegraph, gaslights and the railroad. Baym's study breaks new ground in its field of enquiry, deliberating, as it does, on the process of scientific change reflected through the literary. She describes the work of Elizabeth Cary-Agassiz, whose writings helped her scientific husband to achieve fame, and reflects that the role she adopted contributed to popular ideas about science and gender. In an era of scientific development only one woman was to be recognized for scientific achievement. Maria Mitchell had discovered a comet in 1847, yet she, Baym argues, was to see herself as an amateur, while other women, such as Emma Willard, were to make forays into the world of science that were doomed to failure and humiliation. One woman who refused to enter the public arena, yet who deployed scientific language liberally in her writings, was Emily Dickinson. Baym contends that Dickinson's scientific affiliations are provisional, and that they work as a strategy to critique the religious. There is detailed discussion of several of Dickinson's poems, followed by a study of women writers' responses to the scientific embedded within the fictional, including Susan Warner's *The Wide, Wide World* [1850] and Elizabeth Stoddard's *The Morgesons*. Baym then turns to the real, the actual, in references to women involved in medical science, a new branch of study for the nineteenth-century woman, concluding that the woman scientist inevitably struggled against social prejudice and limited opportunity. She completes her study by focusing on the popularity of spiritualism during the period, and specifically Mary Baker Eddy's Christian Science movement. Baym's wide-ranging debate is triumphant in its drawing together of a wide variety of texts, attitudes and affiliations, even as it identifies a common goal that all these women shared, that of mind over matter.

M. Giulia Fabi's *Passing and the Rise of the African American Novel* debates the variety of nineteenth-century American literature that focuses on tropes of miscegenation and passing. She investigates the white literary stereotypes of the tragic mulatto, alongside examples of slave narratives and texts authored by African Americans. The first chapter, 'The Mark Without', considers subversive mulattas and mulattos in the fiction of William Wells Brown and Frank J. Webb. While Brown's *Clotel, or the President's Daughter* [1853], possessed a sharp abolitionist thrust lacking in Webb's *The Garies and their Friends* [1857], both texts share a focus on the lives of black communities, and the trope of passing, which is discussed in detail. 'Race Travel in Turn-of-the-Century African American Utopian Fiction' reflects on the fiction of writers such as Pauline E. Hopkins and Frances E.W. Harper, in their visions of individual and collective ideological change, and the celebration of their own identity. Fabi continues to explore the theme of 'passing', and, moving towards the new century, she takes Charles W. Chesnutt's *The House behind the Cedars* [1900] as her principal focus in chapter 3. As Chesnutt's work is now being reclaimed, and his stories are once again in print, this chapter offers a timely consideration of his novels and short stories, in which the idea of 'passing' is a principal focus. Chesnutt's writings explore the meaning of identity and interrogate white perceptions of 'otherness', through carefully constructed narratives which subvert notions of racial difference. James Weldon Johnson's *The Autobiography of an Ex-Coloured Man*, first published anonymously in 1912, develops this theme in revising and reversing codes of racial difference, and Fabi's critical work concludes with 'Tres-passing in African American Literary Criticism'. In this chapter she re-evaluates the position of early African American authors, writers such as Mrs N.E. Mosell, whose *The Work of the Afro-American Woman* [1894] addresses a range of audiences, and does so successfully. Writing to the women of her race, the black men who wrote the introduction to the book, and are acknowledged in her preface, and the white 'sisters' of the suffrage movement, Mosell challenges limitations of both gender and race. However, by appearing to accept male authority and white supremacy, she actually celebrates the talents of African American womanhood, and their political, sometimes radical, writings, which are in conflict with patriarchy and white supremacy. The bibliography offers opportunities for further study, and widening the discussion of the role of the early African American novel.

Gidmark, ed., *Encyclopedia of American Literature of the Sea and the Great Lakes* (editorial board: Mary K. Bercaw Edwards, Attilo Favorini, Joseph Flibbert, Robert D. Madison, Mary Malloy, and Haskell Springer), aims to 'deepen awareness' of the impact that the marine environment and experience has had on American life, surveying the vast body of literature that has been motivated by the Great Lakes and the Pacific, Caribbean and Arctic Oceans. Well-known sea authors, such as Richard Dana, Herman Melville and Edgar Allan Poe, have been included, alongside those not necessarily considered writers of the sea, such as Stephen King and Gary Snyder. The 459 entries from 159 contributors cover a range of material, necessarily excluding some areas, such as non-English writings, but including entries concerned with women at sea, ghost legends, African American, American Indian, Asian American and Latino/a experiences. This volume, which also includes details of 'sea'-based locations such as Cape Cod and Nantucket, should appeal to scholars of American studies and the general reader alike.

The idea prevalent in antebellum America that the book can reveal the 'individuality' of the author, argues Barbara Hochman in *Getting at the Author: Reimagining Books in the Age of American Realism*, was challenged by the emergence of literary realism at the end of the nineteenth century, its project of narrative 'objectivity' questioning assertions of the presence of authorial personality in books. Hochman focuses on writers such as Henry James, Edith Wharton and Frank Norris, who were instrumental in 'removing' the author from the text, thus alienating themselves from a reading audience who expected the conventional, 'well-worn' relationship between the 'chatty authorial storyteller' and the reader, as provided during this turn-of-the-century period by popular writers such as Owen Wister, Francis Marion Crawford and Winston Churchill. Hochman also argues that the shift from the antebellum assertion of a cohesion between author and book to the impartial narration of the realist writers was informed by changes in the construction of the reading audience, specifically as a response to the new marketing and advertising techniques that emerged in the 1880s and 1890s, which created anxieties for the author about who had access to their work, in turn further consolidating the depersonalized narrative voice of the realist text. The divide that deepened at this time, argues Hochman, between 'serious' and 'popular' writers resonated throughout the twentieth century, where writers of the popular forms were largely forgotten or ignored in the classroom, having 'never received the academic stamp of approval'. Despite the cultural diversity that waves of immigration brought to America, Hochman contends that 'popular' writers aim to reproduce a sense of cultural cohesion, yet a closer reading reveals that the 'friendly reading habits' that had been part of the reading culture were no longer to be fully relied upon. This text is a useful and accessible guide to the history of reading practices in America and includes extensive notes and bibliography.

Mattingly, ed., *Water Drops from Women Writers: A Temperance Reader*, broadens our understanding of the connections between the call for woman suffrage and the temperance movement. This collection of writings by women, who used fiction as a tool to draw attention to social iniquities and inequalities, is a valuable resource. It sheds light on women's thinking, principally because such fiction is always about women. While the fictional framework deployed is that of temperance, the writers address legal, economic and social conditions that inhibit their lives, and those of their families. Although such fiction is limited in that it always deals with the evils of alcohol, it invariably elaborates on social injustices inflicted upon women. The collection includes works by Louisa May Alcott, Frances Dana Gage, Frances Ellen Watkins Harper, Elizabeth Stuart Phelps, Lydia Howard, Huntley Sigourney, Elizabeth Cady Stanton and Harriet Beecher Stowe. The book is organized into three sections which address family relationships, legal issues, and the role of women in society. The first section begins where so much romantic fiction ended—with marriage. These narratives emphasize the powerlessness of the woman whose husband becomes intemperate. Other issues are also examined, including the environmental conditions that make it difficult both for male victims to reform and for female victims to escape. The second part of this study focuses on the legal restrictions suffered by women, and the hypocrisy of the conventional wisdom of the time which declared that they were protected by the social system. Stories included in part 3 aim to critique and redefine gender roles, justifying women's participation in reform as a social benefit. Many women were only drawn into involvement with reform issues through the temperance movement, and such involvement belied an otherwise conventional existence; this study recognizes the complexity and variety of their engagements. Women such as Caroline Hyde Butler and Mary Dwinell Chellis, for example, wrote primarily about temperance issues, and seem to have been little engaged with wider issues of reform. Marietta Holley, however, was a novelist, and one who was not actively involved in reform causes, but she highlights the ills of intemperance in *Sweet Cicely* [1885]. Two excerpts from this popular novel are included here, as well as a story by the writer Caroline Lee Whiting Hentz, who, like Holley, did not engage in reform. An extract from the writings of Mrs E.N. Gladding offers a more challenging approach, in which her protagonist attempts to destroy portions of the liquor industry. Also included are a story by Sophia Louisa Robbins Little, who supported both the temperance movement and the abolition of slavery, an excerpt from Corra Lynn's *Durham*

Village: A Temperance Tale [1854], and a short story by Julia Perkins Ballard. The inclusion of these lesser-known writers in the study is significant, demonstrating the way that women from very different walks of life were drawn together, united in a common cause. The introduction contextualizes these works of fiction, locating them within the temperance movement, and a brief introductory discussion on the work and times of each woman writer, together with some line drawings and illustrations, enhance this collection.

Suzanne V. Shepard, *The Patchwork Quilt: Ideas of Community in Nineteenth-Century American Women's Fiction*, continues the theme of women's fiction, and literary responses to prevalent social conditions in the nineteenth century. In the introduction the image of quilting is considered as a metaphor for piecing together the narrative voices that speak to us over time. They recount women's ideas of community and of the family, as well as the threat to community brought by what Harriet Beecher Stowe reminded her readers was the sin of slavery, and the regionalist texts that recorded the loss of community. Shepard focuses on novels such as Sarah Hale's *Northwood: A Tale of New England* [1827], Susan Warner's *The Wide, Wide World* [1851] and Maria Cummins's *Mabel Vaughan* [1857] to elaborate on the significance of the family. She discusses the images of communal life portrayed in these narratives, as well as the way in which women writers were able to enter into literary discourse by deploying their intimate knowledge of family and community life. In a reflection upon the writings of Stowe, the discussion is broadened out to perceive the community as an extension of the family, with particular reference to *The Minister's Wooing* [1859] and *The Pearl of Orr's Island* [1862], as well as a consideration of some of her short stories, written for magazines of the period. Stowe's most famous novel, *Uncle Tom's Cabin* [1852], which articulates social anxieties with regard to slavery, is the subject of a chapter that investigates a lack of unity within the nation/family alongside Caroline Lee Hentz's *The Planter's Northern Bride* [1851]. Such important regionalist writers as Mary Wilkins Freeman, Sarah Orne Jewett and Susan Glaspell are the subject of Shepard's final chapter, which deliberates on the regionalist mode and its importance for a nation that was losing its sense of local community to a national and international vision. These texts celebrated the sense of family and unity that was, in reality, being subsumed by a new economic climate of growth and industrial development. This study is useful in providing an introduction to literary texts that respond to the themes of family, community and place in nineteenth-century America, and further research is facilitated through the bibliographical details.

Nancy A. Walker's *Kate Chopin: A Literary Life* is a fascinating study of a writer who displayed an astute professionalism in crafting an acceptable public identity. Her negotiations with the literary space accorded to her were disrupted, however, by the publication of *The Awakening* [1899], the novel for which she is now best remembered. Walker begins her analysis of Chopin's career by examining the short stories first published in St Louis newspapers, which made her something of a local celebrity, and widened her intellectual circle within the city. Although Chopin was to become, in her own period, best known for her 'local colour' fiction, her first published story, 'At Fault', is about an unconventional marriage. She followed this with 'Wiser than a God', the story of a woman artist who places her creativity before ideas of a conventional marriage. But as regionalism became a popular genre in the light of American industrial and economic development, and influenced by the writings of Sarah Orne Jewett and Mary Wilkins Freeman, Chopin began to produce her collections of 'local colour' stories. Garnered from her experiences of life as a married woman in Louisiana, her stories reflect both the cosmopolitan life of New Orleans and the rural, largely Cajun, culture of Cloutierville. *Bayou Folk* [1894], was followed by the even more successful *A Night in Acadie* [1887]. Perhaps because her 'local colour' work was so well received, it appears that her publisher did not baulk at the subject matter of *The Awakening*, which was published in the spring of 1899. An early review in April of that year, printed in the *St Louis Republic*, is openly scathing. Entitled, 'Kate Chopin's New Book is the Story of a Lady Most Foolish', the review employs quotations from the novel, carefully selected to emphasize the heroine's departure from the feminine ideal. Similar reviews quickly followed, and, perhaps as a result of this, some of her subsequent stories were rejected. Walker, in her concluding chapter, considers these unpublished works, and reflects on the publication of some of Chopin's short stories, which only appeared in print during the latter half of the twentieth century. A detailed chronology and useful list of materials for further reading enhance this study of a fascinating and daring woman writer.

Wendy Martin is the editor of *The Cambridge Companion to Emily Dickinson*, which includes eleven new essays by Dickinson scholars. Divided into three parts, it contextualizes Dickinson's writing, discussing the literary, cultural and political milieu of her time, as well as addressing, and provoking, new directions in Dickinson studies. Her stark style, ambiguous punctuation and word choices created complex, brilliant works that have led to startlingly different critical interpretations. Many of the essays in this study argue that contradiction lies at the heart of Dickinson's writings and her conception of herself as a poet. Commencing with Betsy Erkkila's 'The Emily Dickinson Wars', the early section of the book traces the battles within her family resulting from Dickinson's legacy, and publication of some of the poems. Critical response to her work is examined in detail by Christopher Benfey, who draws attention to the considerable praise southern critics express regarding her work, as early (or as late) as the 1920s. Dickinson's oblique use of words, waywardness, originality and embrace of freedom made her too startling a poet for her own time. This essay traces the growing realization of her importance, and centrality, as a major poet. Martha Nell Smith writes of another fascinating aspect of Dickinson's life, her letters, and more particularly those between Dickinson and her sister-in-law, Susan Gilbert Dickinson. The second section examines Dickinson's poetic strategy in Wendy Barker's close reading of some of her work, before exploring, in an essay by Fred D. White, 'Emily Dickinson's Existential Dramas'. The idea of performance, and, in particular, performance of gender, is interrogated in a fascinating discussion by Suzanne Juhasz and Cristanne Miller. Since gender was of crucial importance in constructing identity in nineteenth-century America, it provided a powerful focus for a woman poet whose sense of self was complex and deliberately contradictory. Shira Wolosky takes up this discussion of identity in 'Emily Dickinson: Being in the Body'. Pondering 'I am afraid to own a Body—' (Johnson 1090), Wolosky proposes that the body, or perhaps the problem of embodiment, is a central figure, or site, in Dickinson's work. Daneen Wardrop completes this section with a discourse on the Gothic, focusing on fascicle 16. In a close reading of the text Wardrop interprets such Gothicism as a platform, or jumping-off point, for Dickinson's exploded modernist self. The final part of the *Companion* considers Dickinson's cultural contexts. David S. Reynolds's view of the poet in relation to popular culture elaborates on this theme through a discussion of her letters in conjunction with her poetry. The letters of the 1850–3 period, for example, indicate a fascination with sensationalist literature. This, argues Reynolds, prepared the way for the haunted themes so prevalent in her work, although they clearly also expand on, and overlap with, the Gothic. Dickinson's responses to class structures is investigated by Domhnall Mitchell, who uses Dickinson's letters to reveal her attitudes to prevailing social and cultural values. The final chapter, by Paula Bernat Bennett, offers a fascinating comparison between Dickinson and her American women poet peers. Discussing common themes evident in the work of contemporaries, Bennett reminds us of the poetry of Rose Terry Cooke, Elizabeth Stoddard, Lucy Larcom and Harriet Prescott Spofford. This illuminates Dickinson's poetry, since her responses are often in opposition to those of her peers. In Stoddard's 'Before the Mirror' [1860], for example, the woman artist who is the central character of the poem is destroyed by the very situation that leaves Dickinson's speakers bursting with life. This excellent collection is of enormous scholarly interest, adding immeasurably to Dickinson studies. A detailed chronology and comprehensive guide to further reading also meet the needs of undergraduates.

The essays collected in Garvey, ed., *The Emerson Dilemma* focus particularly on the relationship between Emerson the transcendentalist and Emerson the social reformer, examining how, according to editor T. Gregory Garvey's substantial introduction, the transcendentalism that Emerson developed early in his writing career informed his involvement in reform movements in later life, particularly his complex relationships with abolitionist groups, women's rights activists and American Indian removal. Garvey's introductory essay addresses the 'dilemma' that Emerson faced between speaking as a reformer while at the same time exhibiting an unwillingness to act like one. *The Emerson Dilemma* is divided into three sections. The three essays in section 1, entitled 'Emerson's Other Inner Life', examine the psychological factors that influenced Emerson's reformism. In 'Reform and the Interior Landscape: Mapping Emerson's Political Sermons', Susan L. Robertson analyses Emerson's treatment of the American Indian removals and slavery in his sermons of 1830 and 1831, arguing that Emerson displaces the personal reality of his wife's tuberculosis into a public metaphor of a diseased body politic, contending that his hesitance to commit to reformist activism was at least in part due to his powerlessness to act in the face of his personal tragedy. T. Gregory Garvey's 'Emerson's Political Spirit and the Problem of Language' compares Emerson's 'organic theory of language' from his writing in 1835 and 1836 to the linguistic assumptions that he developed following the completion of *Essays: Second Series* in 1844, linking the development of language models to changes in his attitude towards reformism, and contending that Emerson formulated an 'internal logic' that allowed for his shift from a belief in universal reform towards the partisan reform movements of the 1850s. In 'Emerson, Thoreau's Arrest, and the Trials of American Manhood', Linck C. Johnson argues that, although Thoreau regarded his suffering and humiliation at his arrest as a reaffirmation of the individual's moral power in the face of unjust legislation, Emerson considered the event as far more problematic, as it both supported and disallowed the individual moral stance, a dilemma that had a dramatic resonance with his own increasingly active involvement in reformism at the time. The second section of this volume, entitled 'Emerson and Women's Rights', deals with Emerson's thoughts on the position of women in the public eye. In 'Pain and Protest in the Emerson Family', Phyllis Cole examines the 'idealist' reform of Mary Moody and the contrasting 'sentimental' stance of Lidian Emerson, arguing that Emerson's domestic environment was immersed in reformist rhetoric and that, although Emerson spoke out on behalf of women's rights, gaps emerge between his own commitment to reform and stances such as his wife's, which he regarded as unintellectual and lacking in substance. Armida Gilbert, in 'Pierced with the Thorns of Reform: Emerson on Womanhood', engages with Emerson's views on women's rights between the 1850s and 1870s, comparing his rhetoric on gender with that of women's rights convention organizers, and contending that, while Emerson recognized equality as essential to justice, he also maintained his belief in the 'selflessness' of an idealized womanhood. Jeffrey A. Steele focuses specifically on the relationship between Emerson and Margaret Fuller, in 'The Limits of Political Sympathy: Emerson, Margaret Fuller, and Women's Rights', arguing that Fuller's personal and spiritual transcendentalism throughout the early 1840s points up the limitations of Emerson's feminism, and reflecting that Emerson was unable to regard women as spiritually equal to men, thus exemplifying his gender-based interpretation of women's creativity. The third section, entitled 'Transitions in Antislavery', charts the changing relationship between Emerson and the abolitionist movement. In 'Emerson, Slavery and the Evolution of the Principle of Self-Reliance', Michael Strysick begins with an assessment of Emerson's journals from the 1820s, arguing that, as his thoughts on self-reliance become more concrete, so does his awareness of the materiality of the slave economy, exemplified by what Strysick regards as the 'translation' of the rhetoric of 'Self-Reliance' into the radial abolitionist discourse of Emerson's 1854 address 'The Fugitive Slave Law'. Len Gougeon, in 'Emerson's Abolition Conversion', examines Emerson's 1844 lecture on emancipation in the British West Indies, suggesting that the intensive study of the history of slavery undertaken by Emerson in preparation for this lecture resulted in his transformation from sympathizer to active participant. Harold K. Bush reflects on Emerson's response to John Brown's raid on Harper's Ferry in 'Emerson, John Brown, and "Doing the Word": The Enactment of Political Religion at Harper's Ferry', explaining that, in contrast to his ambivalent reaction to the arrest of Thoreau, Emerson was actively engaged in the rhetorical interpretation that led to John Brown being established as a martyr for the abolitionist cause. Bush looks particularly at Emerson's 'Speech at a Meeting to Aid John Brown's Family', which, he argues, shows how much Emerson's attitude towards reform had altered between 1846 and 1859. The final section, entitled 'Emerson's Thought and the Public Sphere', considers Emerson's development as a political theorist. In 'Emerson's "American Civilization": Emancipation and the National Destiny', David M. Robinson analyses Emerson's 1862 essay as it attempts to locate the Civil War in accordance with his theory of America's moral, cultural, physical, and technological development, an attempt that forced Emerson to adjust his transcendentalist thoughts into a consideration of the form and function of civilization more generally. In 'Power, Poise, and Place: Toward an Emersonian Theory of Democratic Citizenship', Stephen L. Esquith examines the influence of Emerson on political theorists, focusing on the recent evaluations of his understanding of Nature as delineating the individual's living conditions, and questioning the adaptability of his paradigms in the context of a technological global society. Also supplying a useful 'Photo Essay', this collection will provide the dedicated Emersonian with an informative and illuminating insight into the personal and ethical dilemmas that informed his writing throughout his career.

In line with the renewed critical interest in the works of Emerson, one of America's most influential writers and thinkers, the two volumes published as *The Later Lectures of Ralph Waldo Emerson, 1843–1871* (volume 1 covering 1843–54, and volume 2 1855–71), edited by Ronald A. Basco and Joel Myerson, provide an authoritative text for Emerson scholars and general readers alike. Drawing from manuscripts held at the Ralph Waldo Emerson Memorial Association Collection in the Harvard Library alongside recently published editions of Emerson's correspondence, journals, notebooks, sermons and early lectures, these volumes include forty-eight previously unpublished complete lectures from the middle period of Emerson's career, offering thoughts on such recurring subjects as New England and the 'Old World', poetry, education, and intellectual capacity and also covering Emerson's insights on race and women's rights. A valuable asset for the Emerson scholar, this two-volume set includes an extensive 'Historical and Textual Introduction' and an informative bibliography.

Jenine Abboushi Dallal, in 'American Imperialism UnManifest: Emerson's "Inquest" and Cultural Regeneration' (*AL* 73:i[2001] 47–84), argues that the ideology of US expansionism in the era of Manifest Destiny translated 'conquest' into 'inquest'—Emerson's definition of 'self-enquiry' as used in 'The American Scolar—indicating 'an inward search for what is already there', as the territories of the west were 'already there' to be explored, charted and located as 'document' rather than a 'material landscape', in other words to become 'unmanifest'. Dallal explains that Emerson very rarely engaged directly with issues of expansionism and generally spoke of land gains in connection with his discussions of slavery, where expansionism is criticized only as it contributes to an extension of slavery or is a tool of American Indian removal. Emerson's stance on expansionism, Dallal contends, is directly related to his thoughts concerning the structure of American culture, where 'expansionism is both the method and mark of a great civilization', but the continuations of slavery and American Indian removal are not justifiable acts of a 'civilized' culture. As Dallal points out, Emerson's remarks are ultimately addressed to a potential 'cultural regeneration' and the 'creative possibility' that exists in the American landscape, where 'beauty' is inspired by 'tangible nature' but is also to be found in the spiritual realm, forging a link between the material and the immaterial, connecting 'empire, beauty and self' which come together as functions of the 'production of culture'. Focusing also on the correlations between Kant's and Emerson's concepts of 'beauty', and briefly discussing Thoreau's thoughts on intangibility and beauty, Dallal conducts an examination of Agha Shadid Ali's poetry in an essay that will be of considerable value to the Emersonian as well as to the general student of American culture.

Robert N. Hudspeth's masterly edition, *'My Heart is a Large Kingdom': Selected Letters of Margaret Fuller*, offers a vivid portrayal of the life, times and passions of the intellectual Margaret Fuller. In doing so, it reminds us of her importance, as a literary critic, feminist theoretician, travel writer, journalist, editor and historian. Highly educated, Fuller, upon the sudden death of her father, became a teacher, then a translator and writer. She also began a series of 'Conversations' for Boston women which was extremely successful and provided her with a satisfactory income. The letters she wrote to her family and her many acquaintances, including Ralph Waldo Emerson, are full of passionate energy and vitality. The same passion colours those letters written during her travels in Europe, reflecting on the people she meets, the places she visits, and, above all, the cultural experiences Europe offers. Hudspeth's sensitive editing of these vibrant letters give the reader a fascinating insight into the world Fuller inhabited, and her passionate engagement with education, politics, and culture. The final chapter includes those letters from the last years of her life when she lived in Italy, deeply committed to the revolution and to her relationship with Giovanni Angelo Ossoli, whom she later married. These letters are an excellent introduction to Fuller, and convey, too, an understanding of the pre-eminent American woman of letters in the nineteenth century. Hudspeth has divided them into four sections, organized chronologically. The first, 'Hold on in Courage of Soul', traces Fuller's life in her letters from 1818 to 1839. From family exchanges to the early meetings of 'Hedge's Club', founded by Emerson, and later known as the Transcendentalists, Fuller's correspondence is lively and forceful. Her intense vision continues in 'Nature has Seemed an Ever Open Secret', which focuses on the years between 1840 and 1844, in which Fuller became editor of the *Dial*. The Transcendentalist journal, of course, brought Fuller and Emerson closer, and there are several of her letters to him in this section. She also published a book that resulted from her travels in the United States, *Summer on the Lakes*, in 1843. By 1845 Fuller had published her most famous work, *Woman in the Nineteenth Century*, and Hudspeth records the years 1845–7 in 'The Field which Opens Before Me'. Establishing herself in New York, Fuller began to write for the *Tribune*. Her life expanded in consequence, and among her friends were Edgar Allan Poe, William Cullen Bryant and Lydia Maria Child. In the following year she travelled in Europe, sending her letters home for publication. The final section of the book deals with the years 1848–50. In 'A Time Such as I Always Dreamed Of', Fuller's sympathy with the political aspirations of the revolutionary Giuseppe Mazzini, her relationship with Giovanni Angelo Ossoli, and the birth of their baby son are the main focus of her letters, and capture the most dramatic period of her life.

Reynolds, ed., *A Historical Guide to Nathaniel Hawthorne*, is part of a series that addresses a range of social, cultural and political topics in relation to various American authors. The series seeks to respond sensitively to the time and place in which these authors wrote, and offers, therefore, a broad base on which to investigate them and their creative art. This study of Hawthorne commences with an introduction by Reynolds and a brief biography of the author by Brenda Wineapple, before examining, in some detail, Hawthorne's response to mesmerism, popular in the antebellum period, and a shaping influence on his fiction. Samuel Chase Coale, in 'Mysteries of Mesmerism: Hawthorne's Haunted House', discusses the theme in relation to specific Hawthorne texts, including *The Blithedale Romance* [1852] and *The House of the Seven Gables* [1851]. He reflects upon Hawthorne's appropriation of mesmerism, linked with elements of the Gothic, to consider corrupt power. The violation of power is related to the male mesmerist, Hawthorne's Ethan Brand, Rappaccini, Chillingworth, Westervelt, and Matthew Maule, and their victims: Edith, Beatrice, Hester (and later, Arthur), Priscilla, and Alice Pyncheon. He concludes that Hawthorne's texts themselves partake of this mesmerism: as Hawthorne tells his tales of darkness and mystery he hypnotizes his readers with the power of language. In stark contrast to such themes was the social experience of middle-class family life, as Hawthorne himself lived it, in antebellum America, and the sentimental attitude adopted towards the child. In an age when educational reformers debated how to raise healthy, pious, gifted children, the Hawthornes decided to educate their three precious children at home. Hawthorne's literary talents were, as a result, also employed in writing for and about children. Gillian Brown's examination of this aspect of his creativity, 'Hawthorne and Children in the Nineteenth Century: Daughters, Flowers, Stories', reflects upon the sentimental and the educational stories Hawthorne published. She discusses, too, the influence of the idea of the child as a saviour, an instrument of moral goodness, often depicted in antebellum literature. But, in addition, Brown dissects the disturbing and powerful narratives of conflict between fathers and daughters that Hawthorne produced, stories such as 'Rappaccini's Daughter' and 'The Golden Touch'. 'Hawthorne and the Visual Arts', by Rita K. Gollin, studies the influence of portraits and artists upon Hawthorne's aesthetic vision, and chronicles his sojourn in Europe, between 1853 and 1860. His notebooks reflect his admiration of painters such as Turner, Rembrandt, Velasquez and Titian, and their ability to capture something of the essence of the people they painted. Gollin draws attention to the stories in which Hawthorne describes the power of a portrait, or the differing talents of artists, stories such as *The House of the Seven Gables* and, perhaps especially, *The Marble Faun* [1860]. This idea of the author as artist is so beguiling that it has been the primary focus of studies on Hawthorne, and his political stance has received rather less attention. In Jean Fagin Yellin's 'Hawthorne and the Slavery Question', his failure to participate in the abolitionist movement is closely interrogated. His notebooks, for example, reveal ambivalent racial attitudes, suggesting that, despite a lifetime of casual contacts with people of colour, he felt no common humanity with them. This chapter traces Hawthorne's responses to race through his published writing, his private notebooks, and his disinclination to involve himself in the abolitionist movement. Aspects of oppression, such as those in *The Scarlet Letter* [1850], are explored, alongside critical presentations of reformers in, for example, *The Blithedale Romance*. Concluding with a bibliographical essay, 'Hawthorne and History', by Leland S. Person, the book also includes a detailed bibliography and an extremely useful illustrated chronology, tracking Hawthorne's life against historical events.

W.D. Howells was 25 years old when he arrived in Venice as consul in 1862; he lingered there for four years and the city remained to him, as he departed, 'dream-like and unreal'. As entertaining, magical and enchanting now as it was when it was originally published in 1866, this edition of *Venetian Life* has been given an added dimension by the inclusion of illustrations by Joseph Pennell.

Daniel Mark Fogel notes, in his foreword to Ann Lillidahl's *Henry James in Scandinavia: His Literary Reputation*, that there is a 'proliferation of commentary' out there on a major writer like Henry James, who inspires ever-increasing critical attention. The bibliographical essays contained in this book cover the hundred-years-plus presence of Henry James in Sweden, Finland, Norway and Denmark, thus providing a summary that, if geographically specific, is invaluable and will be of benefit to all James scholars, while in addition offering an insight into the cultural and literary history of Scandinavia.

Henry James's short stories are crucial both to an understanding of his literary inheritance and to an awareness of the short story form itself, and Dewey and Horvarth, eds., *'The Finer Thread, The Tighter Weave' Essays on the Short Fiction of Henry James*, look specifically, as the title suggests, at short stories from the Jamesian canon, analysing some of his less well known, or less frequently anthologized, tales. The collection of essays is divided into two sections, the first dealing with 'Threads', and focusing on individual short tales, the second with 'Weaves', taking a broader look at some of the most prominent recurring themes, particularly those concerned with textual ambiguity. In the opening essay of the first section, 'The Ineluctability of Form: "The Madonna of the Future"', Adam Bresnick argues that the whiteness of the ancient canvas in the tale signifies a critique of the 'logical impasse of aesthetic formalism', as an acknowledgement of the impossibility of the Romantic ideal. Jeraldine Kraver, in 'All About "Author-ity": When the Disciple Becomes the Master in "The Author of *Beltraffio*"', reassesses the role of the apparently marginalized narrator, who is relocated by Kraver as deeply involved in the pathos of the tale. In '"The Deepest Depths of the Artificial": Attacking Women and Reality in "The Aspern Papers"', Jeanne Campbell Reesman locates a parallel between James's short story and the Orpheus legend, through an examination of the discourses of gender and sexuality so prevalent in James's writing. Rory Drummond, in 'The Spoils of Service: "Brooksmith"', argues that the class-conscious narrator, with his thinly veiled contempt for those from a lower social order, does at the same time 'romanticize' his butler, who by remaining silent and allowing the contradictory narrator to construct his image, emphasizes James's satiric attack on the unreliable narrative voice. The ambiguity of James's ghost fiction is explored by Karen Scherzinger's Freudian analysis in 'The (Im)Possibility of "The Private Life"', which argues that James's denial of coherence and resolution anticipates certain aspects of a postmodern imperative. In 'The Shining Page: "The Altar of the Dead" as Metafiction', Daniel Won-gu Kim contends that Stransom's altar itself constitutes a text from which the two main characters construct conflicting readings, negating the possibility of a fixed interpretation and thus pre-empting postmodern fiction. Patricia Laurence focuses on one of James's most ignored tales, in 'Collapsing Inside and Outside: Reading "The Friend of Friends"', claiming that the paranormal aspects of the text, its emphasis on uncertainty, gaps, silences and ellipses, exemplifies the unavailability of our 'emotional lives' to the writer, and the resultant frustration inherent to the narrative endeavour. The narrative process also forms the subject for Molly Vaux, in 'The Telegraphist as Writer in "In the Cage"', who locates the unnamed telegraphist as an articulation of the 'creative receptiveness' of the writer as she assimilates the experiences of others, weaving a narrative of her own, but one that can only survive in the cage itself. May Bartram is the beast, argues Lomeda Montgomery, in 'The Lady is the Tiger: Looking at May Bartram in "The Beast in the Jungle" from the "*Other* Side"', consuming Marcher, who becomes aware of the reality of his beast only in the ambiguous climax to the tale. In '"Some pantomimic ravishment": "Broken Wings" and the Performance of Success"', Annette Gilson examines the location of the artist within the moneyed classes, arguing that James's tale of resurrection articulates an opportunity for the artist to overcome the potentially damaging society of the art patron. Earl Rovit analyses the oppositions and antagonisms that feature in James's fiction, in 'The Language and Imagery of "The Jolly Corner"', focusing particularly on doublings in the narrative, where the conflicts set up are permanently unresolved and irresolvable. The last 'thread' of this section, Michael Pinker's 'Too Good to Be True: "Mora Montravers"', reassesses Sidney Traffle's romanticist reaction to his niece, which is wholly at odds with her morally ambiguous behaviour. The opening essay of the second section, '"A Landscape Painter" and "The Middle Years": Failures of the Amateur', by Brooke Horvath, is a deliberation on the failed artist, who, as James himself argued, was the only artist who could feature in fiction. Kristen Boudreau, in 'A Connection More Charming Than in Life: The Refusal of Consolation in "The Altar of the Dead"', contextualizes James's short fiction in an assessment of grief and mourning in the Victorian era, particularly the movement of the linguistic framework through the recollected memory of a historic event. A consideration of James's tales of artists, Phyllis van Slyck's essay 'Trapping the Gaze: Objects of Desire in James's Early and Late Fiction', examines the unreliable perception that formulates the characters' readings of each other, and how the ideal work of art becomes subject to the mockery of experience. Yet, Slyck argues, ultimately a more robust ethic emerges, articulating an awareness of the limited capacity of human understanding and an acceptance of inherent ambiguity in place of an unrealizable ideal. Joseph Wiesenfarth, in 'Metafiction as the Real Thing', contends that James's interest in the role of the writer is emphasized in the narrative strategy of his short fiction, which can be classified *en masse* as metafiction, commenting on the 'writerly dilemma', the struggle of the writer for a range of expression with which to deal with 'the sorry, sordid, squalid real'. The final 'weave' in the collection is Daniel Schwarz's 'Manet, "The Turn of the Screw", and the Voyeuristic Imagination', which interconnects James's ghost tale with later French Impressionism and the early Cubist movement and also assesses the relationship between the sexually repressed governess of the tale and the modernist experimentation that can be found in Lawrence, Joyce, Conrad, Wallace Stevens and Mann. Also drawing on the theoretical paradigms of Freud and Darwin and incorporating the technology of photography and atomic science, the essay provides a detailed conclusion to a compelling selection, which will be invaluable to dedicated James scholars.

In July 1997 a conference was organized in Volos, Greece, to debate the life and writings of Herman Melville. The 'international theme' was the primary requirement, and the interdisciplinary papers that are collected in *Melville 'Among the Nations'*, edited by Stanford E. Marovitz and A.C. Christodoulou, who are both contributors, cover a range of areas, including sources studies, visual arts, critical, theoretical and comparative approaches, philosophy, Melville's travels abroad, the influences of the world around him on his writings, and his literary heritage. Consisting of forty-five papers, the collection is divided into six sections, which focus on Melville's world-view, the major themes of his writings, sources and parallels in his works, his attitudes towards philosophical and religious thinking, the key motifs of his narrative work and his poetry, Melville and memory, and his appreciation of visual arts; the final section considers Melville's teaching and translation and the general study of his work. For the Melville scholar this collection will be of considerable use, containing as it does a wide-ranging selection of the various approaches that are out there on one of America's most vitally relevant writers.

Bennett, ed., *Palace-Burner: The Selected Poetry of Sarah Piatt* is the first collection of Piatt's poetry to fully incorporate her political poems within a whole body of work. Her published writings include novels, short stories for literary periodicals such as *Atlantic Monthly*, *Galaxy* and *Harper's Monthly*, and stories for children. Piatt was widely celebrated by her peers as a gifted stylist in the genteel tradition, yet some of her poetics caused discomfort, and were dismissed as 'deviant'. For her contemporaries, the fact that her poems began to move towards a new form of dramatic realism built on dialogue was unpopular, the more so since the language often lacked a certain smoothness of style. There are other ways in which Piatt can be seen as disruptive. As a native-born southerner and daughter of slaveholders, Piatt brought to her Civil War poetry a sense of political subjectivity. Equally, her early experiences were in conflict with her subsequent life as a northern bourgeois woman, and this is reflected in her poetry on gender issues. Interrogating the roles of lover, wife and mother, Piatt envisages the southern woman as deeply implicated in the war that destroys her country, her lover and herself. She also tests southern romanticism against the realities of life in the South for white landowners. Romanticism, in her poems, is a veil disguising the economic importance of relationships, in which both men and women are seen as complicit in seeing money and status as superior. Not only are marital relationships defiantly unromantic in Piatt's poetry, but, considering the gulf between male expectations and female desires, they are often close to farcical. Bennett argues that, to read Piatt as she should be read, we need to be aware of an ironic tone, present in her recounting of Civil War, bad-faith marriages, bad-faith politics and soured romanticism. This collection, reprinted with illustrations from the periodicals in which the pieces first appeared, is a powerful tribute to Piatt's work, and demands that we reread and reconsider it as a whole. Interestingly, when engaging on risky topics, such as elegies for dead children, Piatt adopts the use of a naive speaker. As Emily Dickinson employs a childlike voice to interrogate sensitive themes, so Piatt uses the child's penetrating perception to make her point more powerfully. 'The Palace-Burner', the title poem of this collection, makes use of a child's enquiry to question social evil, and the speaker's relationship to it. Extensive notes help to place the poet, both socially and historically, and the selected bibliography makes a useful contribution to this influential study.

Acknowledging a debt to Toni Morrison's claim that 'no early American writer is more important to the concept of American Africanism than Poe', the essays that constitute Kennedy and Weissberg, eds., *Romancing the Shadow: Poe and Race*, set out to assess Poe's position in the antebellum racial debate. Terence Whalen, in 'Average Racism: Poe, Slavery, and the Wages of Literary Nationalism', reconstructs the historical background to Poe and race with his discussion of the cultural climate of the 1830s, arguing that Poe's writing should be contextualized within the contemporary literary marketplace, particularly in connection with the relationship between the emerging publishing industry and an American nation that both depended on and excluded African Americans. Betsy Erkkila, in 'The Poetics of Whiteness: Poe and the Racial Imaginary', focuses specifically on 'The Raven', reading the imagery of the poem in accordance with the dominant racial discourses of the era, and arguing that this most popular of Poe's poems cannot be regarded without paying due attention to its inherent discourses of racial bigotry. In 'Edgar Allan Poe's Imperial Fantasy and the American Frontier', John Carlos Rowe also takes issue with Poe's racism, relating his comments to Poe's 'Journal of Julius Rodman' and *The Narrative of Arthur Gordon Pym* amongst others, drawing comparisons between Poe's fiction and other non-fiction exploration narratives, and contending that Poe's work can be regarded as intrinsic to the dominant imperialist rhetoric of the day, which situated the white explorer as superior to the black slave population and Native Americans. Joan Dayan addresses the acquisition of slaves in relation to legal discourses on property and ownership in 'Poe, Persons, and Property', arguing that racial structures in the antebellum era were intrinsic to legal definitions of property. In 'Black, White, and Gold', Liliane Weissberg concentrates on Poe's short tale 'The Gold-Bug' and its setting of Sullivan Island, discussing the history of the location as a point of entry for slaves, and also uses Poe's work as a tool with which to reconstruct the history of the island. Lindon Barrett, in 'Presence of Mind: Detection and Racialization in "The Murders in the Rue Morgue"', connects the genre of the detective story to discourses of race in an examination of Enlightenment ideas of 'Reason' as related to the construction of whiteness in Poe's tale. Elise Lemire also looks closely at 'The Murders in the Rue Morgue', in her essay of the same title, reading Poe's story as a political fable that incorporates and at the same time comments on the predominant anxieties about 'amalgamation' in antebellum America. Leland S. Person also pays attention to Poe and racial 'mixture' in 'Poe's Philosophy of Amalgamation: Reading Racism in the Tales', focusing on *The Narrative of Arthur Gordon Pym* and 'The Black Cat', amongst others, and charting a series of racial anxieties in Poe's work. In the concluding essay of this collection, '"Trust No Man": Poe, Douglass and the Culture of Slavery', J. Gerald Kennedy reads *Pym* alongside *The Narrative of the Life of Frederick Douglass*, pointing out that Poe and Douglass lived in the same neighbourhood in Baltimore for a short time, and reconstructing the contextual environment that informed the construction of both the novel and the slave narrative. As a collection dealing with the multiple perspectives of racial discourses, *Romancing the Shadow* will prove useful to the general scholar as well as the dedicated Poe specialist.

In the Student Companions to Classic Writers series, which aims to 'meet the needs of students and general readers', David E.E. Sloane's *Student Companion to Mark Twain*, written 'in a systematic way, at the level of the non-specialist and general reader', is specifically designed as an aid to secondary-school and undergraduate study. Sloane, in accordance with the series format, introduces his assessment with a biographical chapter, discussing the writer's life and times, then moves on to a discussion of 'Twain's career and contribution to American literature', tracing the literary heritage and commenting on the literary genres relevant to Twain's work, and specifically looking at definitions of American humour writing, local colour and realism. Sloane also examines Twain's travel narratives, specifically *The Innocents Abroad*, *Roughing It*, and *Life on the Mississippi*, briefly mentioning *A Tramp Abroad* and *Following the Equator*, before moving on to a study of the major novels, *The Adventures of Tom Sawyer*, *The Prince and the Pauper*, *Adventures of Huckleberry Finn*, *A Connecticut Yankee in the Court of King Arthur* and *Pudd'nhead Wilson*, concluding with an account of Twain's shorter fiction. Including an extensive bibliography, this critical assessment is exactly what it sets out to be, of use to the 'non-specialist' Twain student and the more generally interested reader.

One of a series of 'annotated' books issued by W.W. Norton, Hearn, ed., *The Annotated Huckleberry Finn*, offers an extensive background study to one of Mark Twain's most celebrated yet controversial novels. Hearn draws on letters, manuscripts and contemporary newspapers, Twain's own revisions and notes, the critical response to the novel, making use of material not previously published. Hearn's introductory essay constitutes a useful source of background material, discussing the problematic publishing history of the novel and also providing edifying biographical data. This edition also reintroduces the 175 original illustrations by E.W. Kemble in addition to some previously unpublished, and incorporates relevant photographs, drawings, prints, cartoons, and maps. Hearn's thorough research, including an extensive bibliography, collates much of the critical debate that continues to surround *The Adventures of Huckleberry Finn*, and this edition will be of considerable value to the Twain specialist as well to those more generally interested in American studies.

Ida B. Wells-Barnett and American Reform, 1880–1930 is a study of the African American activist, which offers a perceptive insight into Wells's legacy. Patricia A. Schechter discusses a variety of materials, speeches, published work, and personal letters, as she carefully considers Wells's demand for racial reform in the framework of its historical moment. Wells's fight for social change is probably best remembered through her anti-lynching campaign: although her pamphlet *Southern Horrors: Lynch Law in all its Phases* failed to achieve scholarly recognition until recently, its importance, both then and now, cannot be underestimated. Cited as a determining factor in developing American critical thought with regard to lynching and racism, the pamphlet is a powerful critique of southern society. Wells defines the iniquity of mob rule by revealing the way in which vigilante groups took the law into their own hands, lynching men who were often innocent of the crime of rape, of which they were accused. Wells understood lynching as the white male's means of terrorizing entire social groups, as well as a specific assault on the African American male. By documenting consensual, and sometimes illicit, sexual contact between white women and black men, as well as interrogating the historical and contemporary rape of black women by white men, Wells concluded they were of a piece with lynchings. They formed a web of sexual politics, she insisted, designed to subjugate all African Americans. Documenting Wells's battle for reform, Schechter broadens the debate by examining her relationship with other prominent social activists of the period, including Frederick Douglass, Ferdinand Barnett, and the temperance leader Frances Willard. These relationships were not always harmonious; Willard, for example, was unable to accept the possibility that a white woman might be sexually involved with a black man by choice. An acrimonious and long-running public exchange between these two women was the result, a detail which offers a wider historical perspective. Overall, Wells's campaign was informed not only by race, but also by gender, and women's suffrage was an important tool in her battle for equality and justice. As a reflection of enormous change in American social ideology over a fifty-year period in terms of race and gender parity, this study of Wells's crusade is absorbing. It also includes a variety of contextualized materials: the reprinting of posters for Wells's public appearances; cartoons reflecting racial and gender issues; and photographs from the period. These enhance the text and help to explore the significance of Wells's work. Extended research into the life and work of this important woman activist is facilitated through excellent and detailed notes, as well as a comprehensive bibliography.

Schmidgall, ed., *Intimate with Walt: Selections from Whitman's Conversation with Horace Traubel, 1888–1892*, forms part of the Iowa Whitman Series (general editor Ed Folsom), and condenses the mass of pages of Traubel's *With Walt Whitman in Camden*, cutting out much of the 'mundane and ephemeral' account that are contained in the original and focusing specifically on the words of the poet himself, giving us a useful insight into his life. Schmidgall's concise selection together with his informed and informative introductory essay, will be of particular benefit to the Whitman specialist but will also be of interest to the general reader of autobiographical writings.

Books Reviewed

Amory, Hugh, and David D. Hall, eds. *A History of the Book in America*, vol. 1: *The Colonial Book in the Atlantic World*. CUP. [2001] pp. xxiv + 638. $150 ISBN 0 5214 8256 9.

Basco, Ronald A., and Myerson, Joel, eds. *The Later Lectures of Ralph Waldo Emerson 1843–1871*, vol. 1: *1843–1854*; vol. 2: *1855–1871*. UGeoP. [2001] pp. lxii + 370 and viii + 432. £109 ISBN 0 8203 2295 4.

Bauer, Dale M., and Philip Gould, eds. *The Cambridge Companion to Nineteenth-Century American Women's Writing*. CUP. [2001] pp. xxix + 336. pb £14.95 ISBN 0 5216 6975 8.

Baym, Nina. *American Women of Letters and the Nineteenth-Century Sciences. Styles of Affiliation*. RutgersUP. [2001] pp. 268. hb £46.95 ISBN 0 8135 2984 0, pb £17.50 ISBN 0 8135 2985 9.

Bennett, Paula Bernat, ed. *Palace-Burner: The Selected Poetry of Sarah Piatt*. UIllP. [2001] pp. lviii + 200. £29.95 ISBN 0 2520 2626 8.

Carretta, Vincent, and Philip Gould, eds. *Genius in Bondage: Literature of the Early Black Atlantic*. UPKen. [2001] pp. 280. $34.95 ISBN 0 8131 2203 1.

Crain, Patricia. *The Story of A: The Alphabetization of America from 'The New England Primer' to 'The Scarlet Letter'*. Stanford UP. [2001] pp. 336. pb $27.95 ISBN 0 8047 3175 6.

Dewey, Joseph, and Brooke Horvath, eds. *'The Finer Thread, the Tighter Weave': Essays on the Short Fiction of Henry James*. PurdueUP. [2001] pp. x + 294. £27.50 ISBN 1 5575 3207 9.

Fabi, M. Giulia. *Passing and the Rise of the African American Novel*. UIllP. [2001] pp. 188. hb £32.50 ISBN 0 2520 2667 5.

Garvey, T. Gregory, ed. *The Emerson Dilemma: Essays on Emerson and Social Reform*. UGeoP. [2001] pp. xxxviii + 266. £33.95 ISBN 0 8203 2241 5.

Gidmark, Jill B., ed. *Encyclopedia of American Literature of the Sea and the Great Lakes*. Greenwood. [2001] pp. xxvi + 542. £93.95 ISBN 0 3133 0148 4.

Hearn, Michael Patrick, ed. *The Annotated Huckleberry Finn*. Norton. [2001] pp. clxviii + 486. £25 ISBN 0 3930 2039 8.

Hochman, Barbara. *Getting at the Author: Reimagining Books in the Age of American Realism*. UMassP. [2001] pp. 216. £23.50 ISBN 1 5584 9287 9.

Howells, W.D. *Venetian Life*, with illustrations by Joseph Pennell. NorthwesternUP. [2001] pp. 318. pb £12.95 ISBN 0 8101 6085 4.

Hudspeth, Robert N. *'My Heart is a Large Kingdom': Selected Letters of Margaret Fuller*. CornUP. [2001] pp. xviii + 336. £19.95 ISBN 0 8014 3747 4.

Kennedy, J. Gerald, and Weissberg, Liliane. *Romancing the Shadow: Poe and Race*. OUP. [2001] pp. xviii + 302. £30 ISBN 0 1951 3710 8.

Lillidahl, Ann. *Henry James in Scandinavia: His Literary Reputation*. AMS. [2001] pp. xii + 100. £46.95 ISBN 0 4046 1496 5.

Marovitz, Stanford E., and Christodoulou, A.C., eds. *Melville 'Among the Nations'*, proceedings of an international conference, Volos, Greece, 2–6 July 1997. KentSUP. [2001] pp. 594. £49.50 ISBN 0 8733 8696 5.

Martin, Wendy, ed. *The Cambridge Companion to Emily Dickinson*. CUP. [2001] pp. xvii + 248. pb £14.95 ISBN 0 5210 0118 8.

Mattingly, Carol, ed. *Water Drops from Women Writers: A Temperance Reader*. SIUP. [2001] pp. 292. £27.50 ISBN 0 8093 2399 0.

Reynolds, Larry J., ed. *A Historical Guide to Nathaniel Hawthorne*. OUP. [2001] pp. 224. pb £12.99 ISBN 0 1951 2414 6.

Schechter, Patricia A. *Ida B. Wells-Barnett and American Reform, 1880–1930*. UNCP. [2001] pp. xviii + 388. £42.95 ISBN 0 8078 2633 2.

Schmidgall, Gary. *Intimate with Walt: Selections from Whitman's Conversations with Horace Traubel, 1888–1892*. UIowaP. [2001] pp. xxxiii + 320. pb £17.95 ISBN 0 8774 5767 0.

Shepard, Suzanne V. *The Patchwork Quilt: Ideas of Community in Nineteenth-Century American Women's Fiction*. Lang. [2001] pp. 172. £29 ISBN 0 8204 4074 4.

Sloane, David E.E. *Student Companion to Mark Twain*. Greenwood. [2001] pp. x + 190. £24.95 ISBN 0 3133 1219 2.

Walker, Nancy A. *Kate Chopin: A Literary Life*. Palgrave. [2001] pp. 170. pb £15.99 ISBN 0 3337 3789 X.

XVI

American Literature: The Twentieth Century

VICTORIA BAZIN, BARRY ATKINS, JANET BEER, SARAH MACLACHLAN, NERYS WILLIAMS, STEVEN PRICE AND A. ROBERT LEE

This chapter has five sections: 1. Poetry; 2. Fiction 1900–1945; 3. Fiction Since 1945; 4. Drama; 5. Native, Asian American, Latino/a and General Ethnic Writing. Section 1 is by Victoria Bazin; section 2 is by Barry Atkins; section 3 is by Sarah MacLachlan and Nerys Williams; section 4 is by Steven Price; and section 5 is by A. Robert Lee. The material relating to Edith Wharton in section 2 is by Janet Beer. Alan Rice's section on African American Literature in *YWES* 83 will cover material published in 2001 as well as 2002.

1. Poetry

A cursory glance at the publications on American poetry this year suggests that a critical shift has taken place, resulting in fewer publications on poetic modernism. While there are monographs on both Wallace Stevens and William Carlos Williams, critical attention has, by and large, concentrated on poets writing in the wake of high modernism or writers on the margins of modernism. Thus the New York School of poets is the subject of two important publications, confessional poetry continues to generate discussion, and the Beat writers are considered in depth. There are also a number of important publications on what has been described as 'writing on the left', texts that reject the experiments of modernism in favour of overt political statement.

Elizabeth Bishop, a poet who fits uncomfortably into the above categories, is the subject of Camille Roman's *Elizabeth Bishop's World War II: Cold War View*. As Roman points out in her introduction, literary history frequently draws a line between the Cold War and the Second World War, refusing to acknowledge that Cold War anti-communist rhetoric was at least partly fuelled by a faith in the justness of the Second World War and in the apparent supremacy of American military power. In addition, there are still relatively few books that attempt to identify the political aspects of Bishop's postmodern verse. Roman manages to avoid simplifying the historical picture, as for her there is not simply one dominant ideology reinforcing American nationalism but a series of narratives that shift in response to the changing social, economic and political climate. Thus a poem like Bishop's 'Roosters', her famous indictment of fascism first published in 1935, is analysed in relation not only to events taking place in Europe but also to events literally taking place in Bishop's own backyard in Key West. While Roman doesn't find a great deal of archival evidence that directly supports her view that Bishop was deeply critical of US foreign and domestic policy, she is able to suggest, through a detailed examination of the poetry and its discursive contexts, that Bishop's poetry responded sometimes overtly, more often covertly, to the political issues that dominated this period of American history.

Jacqueline Vaught Brogan's 'Naming the Thief in "Babylon": Elizabeth Bishop and "The Moral of the Story"' (*ConL* 42[2001] 514–34) focuses on Bishop's late poem 'The Burglar of Babylon' as a highly subversive rewriting of the goodnight ballad (which was popular at the end of the nineteenth century and was the confession and warning of a criminal just before his execution). Bishop's inversion of this popular and moralistic poetic genre, argues Vaught Brogan, criminalizes society and its 'scripting of situations' rather than the condemned 'criminal'. This is a convincing argument, adding to the mounting evidence in support of Bishop as a politically and socially engaged poet attuned to the injustices of her times.

The group of poets known collectively as the New York School have, in the past two years, enjoyed something of a critical renaissance. Biographical and historical studies of their contribution to American poetry and poetics have begun to appear that reappraise the familiar and canonical figures such as John Ashbery but also confirm poets such as Kenneth Koch, James Schuyler and Barbara Guest as significant and weighty writers worthy of further study. Two important books were published this year that contribute to the critical reassessment of the New York School: William Watkin's *In the Process of Poetry: The New York School and the Avant-Garde* and Diggory and Miller, eds., *The Scene of My Selves: New Work on New York School Poets*. Watkins's monograph is an attempt to conceptualize the work of Koch, Ashbery, O'Hara and Schuyler in relation to what he describes as 'the avant-garde of everyday life'. His first chapter enters into a debate concerning the definition of the 'avant-garde' itself, which necessarily involves a detailed discussion of Peter Burger's seminal work on the subject. Watkins borrows from a range of post-structuralist theory to make his points, but is most convincing when he deals directly with the poetry itself. He is particularly illuminating on the subject of Schuyler's seemingly modest and self-effacing poems, convincingly arguing that Schuyler sets himself the daunting task of relating subject to object when both terms have been radically decentred. Watkins also examines unpublished material by these poets, such as Ashbery's *The Vermont Notebook*. It is in his examination of Ashbery's collaborative project with Joe Brainard that Watkins explores most fully what he refers to as 'the processual aesthetic' which characterizes, in some way, the work of all four poets he examines.

In Diggory and Miller's *The Scene of My Selves*, each of the aforementioned poets has a section of essays devoted to his work, and in addition there is a section on the work of Barbara Guest, a poet so often excluded from critical discussions of the New York School. The first essay, Diggory's 'Community "Intimate" or "Inoperative": New York School Poets and Politics from Paul Goodman to Jean-Luc Nancy', explores the political implications of this poetic 'school', focusing particularly on the work of Ashbery, who is so often approached in formalist terms. The next section of the book is devoted to Ashbery, beginning with Thomas Lisk's 'An Ashbery Primer', a very useful discussion of the difficulties of this poet's work. The following section on Frank O'Hara contains, among other essays, Andrew Epstein's '"I want to be at least as alive as the vulgar": Frank O'Hara's Poetry and the Cinema', an exploration of this poet's ambivalent response to film, as well as Susan Rosenbaum's 'Frank O'Hara, Flâneur of New York' that explores this poet's social engagement with urban culture through the cultural figure of the flâneur. While both Koch and Schuyler are well represented here, the marginalized figure of Barbara Guest receives considerable and well-deserved attention from, among others, Rachel Blau DuPlessis in her 'The Gendered Marvelous: Barbara Guest, Surrealism and Feminism Reception'. DuPlessis cites Kathleen Fraser in her opening paragraph, acknowledging Fraser's own attempts to recover Guest's work, and goes on to offer a fascinating account of this poet's reinterpretation of surrealism as 'fair realism'. Lyn Keller's 'Becoming "A Compleat Travel Agency": Barbara Guest's Negotiations with the Fifties Feminine Mystique' places the poet in the context of the post-war ideology of domesticity. In the last section of the book Charles Altieri's contribution, 'Contingency as Compositional Principle in Fifties Poetics', questions the critical categories that have emerged in response to poetry of the post-war period, suggesting the affinities between the supposedly 'confessional' Sylvia Plath and the work of Robert Creeley and Frank O'Hara. This is an impressive collection that adds to our understanding of a group of poets who have seemed less accessible and more demanding than their 'confessional' counterparts.

Marjorie Perloff has also contributed to the reassessment of post-war poetries in an interdisciplinary essay that examines the intersections between avant-garde poetry, music and painting. In 'Watchman, Spy, and Dead Man: Jasper Johns, Frank O' Hara, John Cage and the "Aesthetic of Indifference"' (*Mo/Mo* 8[2001] 197–223) Perloff examines John's 1961 painting *In Memory of My Feelings* in relation to the O'Hara poem that gave Johns his title. Here Perloff charts the shift from the confessional poetics of the post-war years to poetry which explores borrowed memories and assumes fake identities; this, she argues, runs parallel with the shift in the visual arts from abstract expressionism to the more conceptual art of the 1960s.

John Berryman, so often associated with the confessional mode, is the subject of 'Public Dreams: Berryman, Celebrity, and the Culture of Confession' (*AmLH* 13[2001] 716–36), in which David Haven Blake offers a fascinating reading of the production and consumption of 'confessional' poetry, seeing it as part of the celebrity industry emerging after the Second World War. Haven Blake's discussion of Berryman's *The Dream Songs* [1969] and *Love and Fame* [1970] argues that the poet embraces the 'language of publicity and hype' in order to promote the cultural value of his work but also, and more importantly, to encourage his readers to see him as 'a literary personality, a figure whose individuality appears as a general reflection of public life'. With its emphasis on public display and literary spectacle, Berryman's poetry reveals much about the relation between confession and celebrity, suggesting that the 'divide' separating the high art of poetry from its commercialized mass 'other' is not as wide as Berryman would have his readers believe.

It is the work of Sylvia Plath, of course, that has dominated critical discussions of post-war poetry and thereby inaccurately defined poetry of that period as largely autobiographical. Paul Giles's 'Plath and the Aesthetics of Transnationalism' (*Symbiosis* 5[2001] 103–20) suggests that Plath's poetry needs to be read in relation to her move from the United States to Britain. Her early work is suffused with a sense of the American landscape as well as American cultural values, while her late work is profoundly influenced by her experience of another culture. Giles argues that Plath's work cannot be easily assigned a cultural place but rather continually shifts between two different and at times conflicting cultural positions.

Gina Wisker's *Sylvia Plath: A Beginner's Guide* offers a practical and rather basic introduction to the main themes and issues surrounding Plath's poetry and prose. It includes discussions of 'family and relationships', 'writing and procreation/ death', and 'roles for women', together with a brief biographical sketch of Plath's life and an overview of the contemporary critical debates on Plath. It also has a chapter devoted to examining different theoretical frameworks for the study of Plath's writing that might prove helpful to students attempting to engage with literary theory in practice. Also included is a glossary of terms and a chronology of Plath's major works together with suggestions for further study. While Wisker's study is useful for students just beginning to explore Plath's writing, Tim Kendall's *Sylvia Plath: A Critical Study* is a more sophisticated approach aimed at undergraduates. Kendall's interpretative strategies pay attention to the circumstances of poetic production without becoming overly biographical. He therefore manages to convey a sense of the emotional crises Plath herself was contending with, but shows quite clearly how her poetry was not simply a reflection of these crises but an artistic transposition of them. There are in-depth discussions of many of Plath's most important poems such as 'The Rabbit Catcher', 'Daddy', 'Lady Lazarus' and the bee sequence of poems. There is also an engagement with other influential critics writing on Plath, though on occasion discussions of individual poems seem more concerned with the prevailing critical consensus than with the poems themselves. Kendall is clearly acutely aware of the competing critical discourses circulating around Plath, but seems overly preoccupied with these debates. However, this might be an inevitable consequence of writing on a poet who is still attracting a considerable amount of lively critical debate.

Plath is one of the poets considered in Harriet L. Parmet's *The Terror of our Days: Four American Poets Respond to the Holocaust*, along with William Heyen, Gerald Stern and Jerome Rothenberg. One of the central themes of this study is the way in which poets commemorate and remember history. However, post-structuralist debates around history and memory are not fully dealt with here; for example, in her introductory chapter, intended to provide an overview of Holocaust literature in the twentieth century, Parmet looks only cursorily at Adorno, simplifying his critique of Enlightenment thinking and failing to engage with some of the key issues in Holocaust studies. While Parmet is only claiming to deal with literary interpretations of the Holocaust, such interpretations seem meaningless without considering some of the recent work in cultural theory that has interrogated the meanings circulating around it. I am thinking in particular of work done by cultural theorists such as Shoshana Felman, whose psychoanalytical approach to the representation of testimony and witnessing needs to be acknowledged. As a result, readings of individual poets tend to reflect Parmet's general unwillingness to engage with the most ethically vexing questions relating to representations of the Holocaust.

Another study that attends to the poetic response to the Holocaust is Barbara Estrin's *The American Love Lyric after Auschwitz and Hiroshima*, which examines the political implications of the elegant formalisms of three post-war canonical poets. More specifically, this is a study of the late poetry of Wallace Stevens, Robert Lowell and Adrienne Rich that identifies a link between the formal conventions of the Petrarchan love lyric and the horrors of the Holocaust and the atomic bomb. Without wishing to distort the argument through simplification, Estrin's is a postmodern reading of the strategies adopted by three poets acutely conscious that the poetic forms they are drawn to make possible certain acts of violence in language. The form the love lyric takes, Estrin argues, erases the 'other' in an act of domination that is rhetorically related to the 'other-denying impulses of twentieth century genocide'. Thus complicity is signalled in the self-conscious return to the Petrarchan poetic tradition, while at the same time all three poets, in different ways, attempt to undermine or subvert the power relations implicit in the forms they use. Estrin provides lucid readings of Stevens's 'Auroras of Autumn' and 'An Ordinary Evening in New Haven' as well as Lowell's *The Dolphin* and *Day by Day* and Rich's most recent collections, *Dark Fields of the Republic* and *An Atlas of the Difficult World*. Also worth mentioning at this point is an article on Lowell that appears in *Symbiosis* this year. Christopher Pugh looks at his influence on contemporary British poetics in 'Robert Lowell, *Life Studies*, and the Father Poetry of Michael Hoffman' (*Symbiosis* 5[2001] 173–89). Crucial to understanding the construction of masculine identities in poetry, posits Pugh, is a sense of the part the Second World War played in the construction of notions of heroism and masculine agency.

While John Lardas, *The Bop Apocalypse: The Religious Visions of Kerouac, Ginsberg and Burroughs*, is largely concerned with prose, considerable attention is paid to Ginsberg's loose-limbed poetic lines. The thrust of Lardas's argument is that the spiritual dimension of Beat writing was politically motivated and offered one of the few genuinely subversive critiques of post-war American culture. The strength of this study is its ability to vividly describe the cultural politics of the period, thereby making sense of the Beat philosophy and practice. An example of this is the lengthy discussion of Beat writing in relation to the new criticism then dominating the literary scene. Lardas shows how Ginsberg evolved a poetic idiom that was resistant to new critical interpretation, allying himself to the Romantic, free-verse traditions of Whitman and William Carlos Williams.

Moving on to studies and collections that engage with contemporary poetry, there are two significant publications this year that focus on women's writing and two that explore what Gertrude Stein called the 'problem of identity'. First, Hinton and Hogue, eds., *We Who Love To Be Astonished: Experimental Women's Writing and Performance Poetics*, is a collection of essays that is acutely conscious not only of the experiments taking place in contemporary women's writing but also of the audience for that experimental writing. Thus when critics tackle the poetry of Susan Howe, for example, or Kathleen Fraser or the native American poet Joy Harjo, there is a concern to engage not only with the textual object of study but also with the reader. As a consequence, while many of these essays raise philosophical questions concerning the nature of being and knowing, they do so in a rather friendly and intimate way. A number of familiar poets are dealt with here, but there are also essays on the poets Harryette Mullen, Alice Notley (who was married to Ted

Berrigan) and Rosemary Waldrop, who are not particularly well known to most British readers. This collection engages with questions of poetic form, typography, and the relation between visual and verbal material, in addition to the political implications of writing from and representing cultural differences.

Aizenberg and Belieu, eds., *The Extraordinary Tide: New Poetry by American Women*, is a handsome anthology which offers students and critics an opportunity to read some of the most interesting and powerful women poets writing in the US. Among the 118 poets collected here are Jorie Graham, Adrienne Rich, Carolyn Forche, Rita Dove, Linda Hogan and Sharon Olds. It is easy and perhaps unfair to note omissions, but the absence of Kathleen Fraser, Cynthia Hogue and Susan Howe, to name only a few, suggests an antipathy towards avant-garde poetry. While omissions are inevitable and necessary, it seems that the turn away from the radically experimental and difficult poetry associated with the Language poets needs to be fully explained and justified.

Juliana Spahr, *Everybody's Autonomy: Connective Reading and Collective Identity*, focuses on a group of Language poets (Lyn Hejinian, Bruce Andrews, Harryette Mullen and Theresa Hak Kyung Cha) to explore and explain their disjunctive and fragmented poetic experiments. Spahr begins with a discussion of Gertrude Stein as a way of introducing the idea of an anti-grammatical language that implicitly undermines social hierarchies. After establishing Stein as the first Language poet, Spahr goes on to discuss Lyn Hejinian's *My Life*, interpreting this revisionary autopoetic text as 'narcissistic' yet also illustrating the 'possibilities for outward connection'. The chapter dealing with Haryette Mullen considers her abandonment of the lyric 'I' in *Trimmings*, *S*PeRM**K*T* and *Muse & Drudge*, and considers such texts as invitations to 'abandon standard ways of reading' and in turn to subvert the conventional racial and ethnic categories fixing identity. The fusion of collage, biography and Korean history in Cha's *DICTEE* [1995] is examined in Spahr's last chapter in relation to postcolonial theories of reading and writing. Spahr's discussions of the political debates taking place in poetry circles is, perhaps, the real strength of this book, as she maps out the contested sites of contemporary American poetry through four radically innovative writers.

While *Everybody's Autonomy* is principally concerned with the collective identities of readers and writers, Sontag and Graham, eds., *After Confession: Poetry as Autobiography*, is concerned with the fraught and contested site of the poetic 'self'. This is a collection of essays by contemporary poets and critics engaging with the politics, ethics and aesthetics of the confessional or autobiographical lyric poem. The collection opens with a poem by Sharon Olds, 'Take the I Out', and closes with a poem by Adrienne Rich, 'In Those Years', the former expressing love for the 'steel I-beam', the latter seeing poetry 'reduced to *I*'. As the editors of this collection point out, there is little critical consensus regarding the confessional mode; some are clearly sceptics while others regard the hostility towards the first person in poetry as misplaced or missing the point. For instance, Billy Collins, in his essay 'My Grandfather's Tackle Box: The Limitations of Memory-Driven Poetry', is clearly sceptical about the confessional mode, suggesting that poetry recalling past events sometimes limits the imaginative potential of the poem. However, David Graham feels that the use of autobiographical material need not be confined to acts of remembrance. In 'Voluminous Underwear: or, Why I Write Self-Portraits', he asserts that the avoidance of using the first person is no guarantee against 'egotism and self-enclosure'. Kate Sontag's 'Mother, May I? Writing with Love' examines the ethics of using the lives and experiences of others in poetry. Beginning with Lowell's appropriation of Elizabeth Hardwick's letters for *The Dolphin*, Sontag dramatizes the conflicts that arise for the poet wishing to use material that, in a sense, belongs to others. All the essays here are eminently readable and highly engaging, and suggest that interest in autobiographical poetry is by no means waning, despite the bad press it continues to receive.

Another study dedicated to contemporary poetry is Thomas Fink's *'A Different Sense of Power': Problems of Community in Late-Twentieth-Century U.S. Poetry*. Fink examines a number of poets who have come to prominence in the last twenty years who are not directly connected to the writers known as the Language poets. He considers clusters of poets around certain themes: the opening chapter is devoted to 'Problematizing Visibility', and includes discussions of Denise Duhamel, John Yau and Thylias Moss; the second engages with matters of history and includes critical analysis of the work of Carolyn Forché, Joseph Lease, Martín Espada and Gloria Anzaldúa; the final chapter considers issues relating to community and coalition, returning to the poetry of Anzaldúa and Lease together with readings of Melvin Dixon and Stephen Paul Miller. Fink's study is an insightful introduction to poets who will be unfamiliar to the majority of British readers, but also provides a useful overview of some recent developments in contemporary American poetry.

Thomas Gardner edits a special issue of *Contemporary Literature* this year on American poetry of the 1990s, and finds poetry in the United States alive and well. Gardner's own introduction to this number indicates that many American poets are practising a range of formal strategies and addressing a variety of political, philosophical and ethical issues. Both Gardner and Willard Spiegelman offer introductory overviews of the poetry of the last decade in 'American Poetry of the 1990s: An Introduction' (*ConL* 42[2001] 195–205) and 'The Nineties Revisited' (*ConL* 42[2001] 206–37) respectively. Another high-profile critic contributing to the difficult task of assessing poetry before the cultural dust has settled is Marjorie Perloff, whose essay '"Concrete Prose" in the Nineties: Haroldo de Campo's *Galáxias* and After' (*ConL* 42[2001] 270–93) explores the formal innovations of this emerging poet. One theme that recurs is the return to religious faith, as in Roger Gilbert's 'Awash with Angels: The Religious Turn in Nineties Poetry' (*ConL* 42[2001] 238–69) and Bonnie Costello's 'Charles Wright's *Via Negativa*: Language, Landscape, and the Idea of God' (*ConL* 42[2001] 325–46). Two essays on the poet Joan Retallack also appear: Burton Hatlen's 'Joan Retallack: A Philosopher among the Poets, a Poet among the Philosophers' (*ConL* 42[2001] 347–75) and Lynn Keller's '"Fields of Pattern-Bounded Unpredictability": Recent Palimpsests by Rosmarie Waldrop and Joan Retallack' (*ConL* 42[2001] 376–412).

In 'Between L=A=N=G=U=A=G=E and Lyric: The Poetry of Pink Collar Resistance' (*National Women's Studies Association* 13[2001] 22–39), Karen Kovacik discusses the poetry of Chris Llewellyn, Karen Brodine and Carol Tarlen, all clerical workers, together with Jan Beatty and Lenore Balliro, who are waitresses as well as poets. This socially and politically engaged poetry produced out of the experience of working in the service sector, so often already gendered as 'woman's work', is considered in terms of its formal innovations as well as its political content. Kovacik's article is a useful reminder of the ways in which certain kinds of poetry are effectively repressed by the judgements of dominant critical practices.

While there are fewer publications that specifically deal with American poetic modernism, there is an important and significant cluster of studies that engage with texts that either occupy the margins of modernism or operate in direct opposition to it. Cary Nelson's *Revolutionary Memory: Recovering the Poetry of the American Left* continues the ground-breaking work of his *Repression and Recovery: Modern American Poetry and the Politics of Cultural Memory, 1910–1945* (UWiscP [1989]). Here, though, Nelson extends his recovery project into the Cold War with an examination of the work of Edwin Rolfe, a Spanish Civil War veteran and left-wing poet. Nelson's interpretations of Rolfe's poetry combine historicist, biographical and formalist approaches in an effort to produce a sense of the complexity and density of the poetic text when read in relation to its discursive contexts. In the third section of the book Nelson argues persuasively that some of the writing produced in the 1930s in response to economic depression might best be read as contributions to a collective poetic 'chorus'. Thus the promotion of the individual poet's career becomes less important than the expression of a political and collective will. As Nelson suggests, this changes the way we might read some of this poetry, altering the critical paradigms that have consistently denigrated this kind of overtly political writing. The archival work Nelson has undertaken is very impressive, and so is his ability to provide the reader with the right amount of historical detail so that the poetry and the critical discussions of the poetry are never overwhelmed.

In addition to Nelson's study is Michael Thurston's *Making Something Happen: American Political Poetry between the World Wars*, a highly informative, well-written and compelling account of the work of four partisan poets: Edwin Rolfe, Ezra Pound, Langston Hughes and Muriel Rukeyser. As Thurston argues, while contemporary literary criticism has acknowledged the politicized nature of reading and writing, this has encouraged a critical reassessment of canonical texts never intended as political statements. 'We still have not turned much attention', writes Thurston, 'to those writers who wrote with direct political intentions, who wrote not only in the hope of having a political impact but also in the deep conviction that they would.' Though the inclusion of Ezra Pound in the study suggests that Thurston is still drawn, like so many, to the high modernists whose reputations are firmly established, nevertheless he opens the book with a lengthy and detailed discussion of Edwin Rolfe, whose reputation was destroyed during the Cold War years. Also included here is a chapter on Rukeyser's *The Book of the Dead*, a long sequence of poems that has suffered from neglect. Thurston's reading of this complex and powerful poetic series is subtle and persuasive, arguing that this poem employs a 'documentary modernism' to represent the case of the Union Carbide workers who died as a result of unsafe working conditions.

Another welcome addition to the body of work recovering writers on the left is Nancy Berke's *Women Poets on the Left: Lola Ridge, Genevieve Taggard, Margaret Walker*, which confronts the biases of feminist criticism that have resulted in the 'sidestepping of radical women poets'. In her introduction Berke is keen to emphasize not only the similarities but also the contrasts between these poets, divided as they were by race, class, ethnicity and generation. Yet because they speak from different political positions at different historical periods, reading them in conjunction provides a sense of the richness of American political culture. By reassessing the work of these three neglected poets, Berke demonstrates how feminist critical practices might be expanded and revised if directed at overtly political poetry. Thus the concept of 'the body', a familiar feminist trope, takes on an entirely different meaning if applied to the work of Lola Ridge, for example, a poet preoccupied with exploited working-class bodies. Berke's historically sensitive, close readings of individual poems will prove extremely useful to literature students and those interested in American cultural politics and history. Her book necessarily engages with some of the key historical moments of the first half of the twentieth century such as the Depression, the effects of the Great Migration, the terrors of lynching, race riots, and labour strikes.

Turning now to the more familiar canonical figures of modernism, Holmes, ed., *The Correspondence of Ezra Pound and Senator William Borah*, appeared this year. Ezra Pound began his six-year correspondence with Illinois Senator William Borah in 1933. Holmes has gathered previously unpublished letters between the two men and has done a thorough job of annotating Pound's letters, providing information concerning his shorthand references to various political figures. It remains a matter of debate whether we really need Pound's hysterical rantings to be preserved for posterity, though undoubtedly this publication will assist Pound scholars in their research on his turn towards fascism.

Michaela Giesenkirchen examines the influence of Browning on Pound in '"But Sordello,—and my Sordello?": Pound and Browning's Epic' (*Mo/Mo* 8[2001] 623–42), suggesting that it is Browning's use of montage which had the most profound influence on Pound's composition of his own 'bag of tricks', the *Cantos*. Another article that examines the Browning/Pound nexus is Stephen Brown's 'Preparing the Palette' (*Paideuma* 30[2001] 217–21), which looks at the incipient stages of Pound's preparation for the *Cantos*. Using Edward Said's *Beginnings: Intention and Method* (Granta [1998]) as a way of developing a critical language in response to Pound's self-conscious attempts to depart from his previous work, Brown suggests the poet was 'striving to discover his own intentions' as they were in the process of forming.

Naikan Tao's '"The Law of Discourse": Confucian Texts and Ideograms in the Pisan Cantos' (*Paideuma* 30[2001] 21–68) describes the intensely personal *Pisan Cantos* as the 'climax of [Pound's] interest in Confucian classics'. Tao notes that Pound was working on this section of his epic poem as he was simultaneously translating two Confucian texts. Aaron Loh's 'Decoding the Ideogram: The Chinese Written Character in the Cantos of Ezra Pound' (*Paideuma* 30[2001] 133–50) examines in detail Pound's use of Chinese ideograms in his work, arguing that, contrary to what both Pound and Fenollosa thought, significant portions of the Chinese language are not in any sense mimetic. Thus modernism's reconception of language is based on a Western misreading of Eastern difference. Another essay that deals with Pound's interest in Chinese language and culture is Lance Callahan's 'Signs of Life: Rethinking the Ideographic Method' (*Paideuma* 30[2001] 151–66). Here Callahan's thesis uses Pound's *Cathay* poems to demonstrate that for Pound the pictorial qualities of Chinese language demonstrated the essential randomness at the very heart of all language, rather than a secure and tight-fitting pattern of signification. Another essay concerned with translation is Michael Gooch's 'Authority and the Authorless Text: Ezra Pound's "The Seafarer"' (*Paideuma* 30[2001] 167–83). Here Gooch finds Pound's translation of this Anglo-Saxon poem to be lacking 'the dialogic ambiguity of its Old English source'. Rather than allowing both Christian and pagan aspects of the poem full expression, Pound silences the Christian elements, thereby collapsing the fruitful tensions embedded in the original.

In '"His fundamental passion": Hugh Selwyn Mauberley and the Ekphrastic Vortex of "The Eye"' (*Paideuma* 30[2001] 185–200), Julie Dennison traces the visual and verbal dimensions of *Hugh Selwyn Mauberley* in relation to both Imagism and Vorticism. Theresa Welford looks at the influence of a Thomas Wyatt poem on Pound in 'Echoes of Thomas Wyatt's "They flee from me" in Ezra Pound's "The Return"' (*Paideuma* 30[2001] 201–16).

Leon Surette's 'The Troubadours: A Romance of Scholarship' (*Paideuma* 30[2001] 3–20) explores Pound's use of two books by Josephin Péladan, *L'Origine et ésthétique de la tragédie* and *Le Secret des troubadours*. Pound's understanding of the troubadour tradition as a synthesis of mysticism, eroticism and subversive art is derived from Péladan rather than from his own first-hand knowledge of troubadour literary culture. In William McNaughton's 'The Secret History of St. Elizabeth's' (*Paideuma* 30[2001] 69–96) the author's own personal memories of visiting Pound at St Elizabeth's are woven into an account of the poet's increasing interest in mysticism in his later years. There are also anecdotal accounts of Pound's relationship with Sheri Martinelli, a figure who appears in the later cantos. Scott Eastham uses the *Leopoldine Cantos* to prove that Pound was deeply ambivalent about the forces of 'progress'. In 'Modernism Contra Modernity: The "Case" of Ezra Pound' (*Paideuma* 30[2001] 97–132) Eastham suggests that modernity, defined primarily in terms of free-market capitalism and its attendant ideologies, is what Pound sets his great poetic epic against. Also included in *Paideuma* this year is the original draft of Pound's 'European Paideuma' (*Paideuma* 30[2001] 225–45) as well as Pound's reading of Stanley Coffman's reading of the Imagist movement in Thomas Coles's 'Ezra Pound on the Imagist Movement, 1912–14' (*Paideuma* 30[2001] 247–54).

Also worth mentioning in relation to Pound is William Melaney's *After Ontology: Literary Theory and Modernist Poetics*, which serves as a theorized reading of modernist aesthetics based on a variety of philosophical approaches. Gadamer, Heidegger, Derrida, Lyotard and Nietzsche all figure in Melaney's discussion of modernism, and it is only in the last chapter of the book, 'Archaeology and Modernist Poetics', that he deals with modernism in practice. Of interest to Pound scholars is the examination of the epic poem as a 'site of translation'. Pound's use of Dante in the *Cantos* is, argues Melaney, a means of deconstructing the opposition between tradition and experiment.

Pound's nemesis, Amy Lowell, is the subject of Margaret Homans' 'Amy Lowell's Keats: Reading Straight, Writing Lesbian' (*YJC* 14[2001] 319–51), which suggests the ways in which the work of the earlier poet 'supplied and possibly also helped to create the changing needs of Lowell's life and literary career, including her recognition of her desire for women and her identification across an array of gendered positions'. Homans's interesting discussion disrupts the notion that women writers necessarily identify with female precursors, suggesting instead that imaginative identification can leap across gendered and sexualized boundaries. In the case of Lowell, the lesbian woman poet finds her voice via 'the mythic figure of the straight man'.

Other modernists receiving critical attention this year include H.D. and Robert Frost. Georgina Taylor's *H.D. and the Public Sphere of Modernist Women Writers, 1913–1946* uses the career of H.D. to chart the development of a 'gendered modernism'. Taylor's thesis suggests that the network of women writers that emerged during this period should not simply be read as a circle of close and supportive friends but rather as a 'public sphere'. Borrowing the term from Habermas, Taylor summarizes the public sphere as being a site of critical debate that is capable of influencing 'official decisions without being constrained by the official interests of the state itself or of the economy'. As Taylor shows, H.D. and other women writers form a public sphere partly in response to the difficulties they encounter as women writers. By uncovering a network of women writers, editors and critics all in contact with H.D., Taylor shows exactly how the formation of a female public sphere enabled them to publish and promote each other's work. What is distinctive about this approach is that it is a deliberate attempt to interpret H.D. as a resolutely public figure, a woman who is committed to fostering critical debate in a social context. Veering away from biographical interpretations, Taylor offers a refreshing and innovative perspective on H.D.'s work and on feminist modernism.

Another article that appears in the consistently excellent *Modernism/Modernity* is 'Thesmophoria: Suffragettes, Sympathetic Magic, and H.D.'s Ritual Poetics' (*Mo/Mo* 8[2001] 471–92). Here Edward P. Comentale explores the relation between feminist thinkers and modernism as well as the politics of classicism. For this, he turns to the political performances of protest enacted by the suffragettes as well as to the anthropologist Jane Ellen Harrison's exploration of ritual in order to understand more fully H.D.'s early poetry. The thrust of this argument is that H.D.'s work deliberately denies fulfilment: it arouses passions yet refuses to satiate them so that the reader returns to 'worldly praxis' having experienced the poem as a 'space of collective mediation'.

Readings of Robert Frost continue to explore the relation between his poetry and the philosophy of William James. Tyler Hoffman, *Robert Frost and the Politics of Poetry*, begins with a fascinating account of the years Frost spent living and working in London, associating with Pound, Hulme, George Bernard Shaw, May Sinclair and other literary luminaries. Between 1912 and 1915, Frost cultivated a network of contacts and liaisons that would help to establish his reputation in the United States; but Hoffman is not only concerned with Frost's promotional strategies, he is also identifying the discursive contexts in which Frost developed his prosodic theory. Hoffman argues that the poet's experience of English political culture informed his understanding of poetic form, offering an interpretation that identifies the ways in which Frost's poetry is socially and politically engaged in an egalitarian, left-leaning defence of individualism. He supports this with an examination of Frost's engagement with modern psychology and philosophy as it was theorized by both William James and Henri Bergson. However, Hoffman is careful to register the changes that take place in Frost's poetry as he responds to certain historical moments such as the Depression and the Cold War. In the latter part of the book Hoffman argues that Frost's 'theory of form attains crucial figurative significance and grows to express national political meanings as Frost grows to be a popular American poet'.

David H. Evans's 'Guiding Metaphors: Robert Frost and the Rhetoric of Jamesian Pragmatism' (*ArQ* 57[2001] 61–90) also explores pragmatist modernism but, rather than focusing only on the philosophical dimension of Frost's poetry, the critic attends to the poetic dimension of James's pragmatism. Beginning with a reading of James he demonstrates that, embedded in the philosopher's language, is a series of metaphors that undermine the power of metaphorical language itself. Then, turning to Frost's 'The Mountain', 'The Road Not Taken' and 'Directive', he suggests that in such poems there is an insistence on what he calls the 'ironic potential' of language that problematizes the choosing of paths and directions. As a result, the pragmatist acts of will that are so central to Jamesian philosophy are also problematized, because language interposes itself between the subject and his willed acts.

A number of general surveys of American poetry appear this year. Norman Finkelstein's *Not One of them in Place: Modern Poetry and Jewish American Identity* examines a cluster of Jewish American poets who explicitly engage with what might be loosely described as the twentieth-century experience of Jewishness in the United States. Yet Finkelstein resists defining a Jewish 'identity' as such, preferring instead to examine the various ways in which Jewishness is figured in and through poetry. Noting a relative paucity of critical writing on Jewish American poetry, Finkelstein provides a selective yet diverse range of poetic meditations on the relation between modernity, identity and Jewishness. Beginning with the Objectivists, Charles Reznikoff and Louis Zukofsky, Finkelstein's study suggests that modernist experiments with the fractured text appealed to a generation of writers familiar with the profound effects of exile and immigration, seeing in modernism 'a literature that acknowledges that history is accelerating to breaking point'. Going on to provide thoughtful critical analyses of the work of Allen Grossman, Jerome Rothenberg, Armand Schwerner, Harvey Shapiro, Michael Heller and Hugh Seidman, Finkelstein is clearly exploring a masculine tradition of Jewish writing, acknowledging only in passing the absence of poets such as Maxine Kumin, Denise Levertov and Muriel Rukeyser.

While David Bromwich's *Skeptical Music: Essays on Modern Poetry* is not exclusively devoted to American poets, reviews and articles on Wallace Stevens, John Ashbery and Elizabeth Bishop are included. 'Stevens and the Idea of the Hero' is a good introduction to the relation between pragmatist philosophies and Stevens's poetics. Also worth noting in a year in which no monograph on Hart Crane or Marianne Moore appears is Bromwich's interest in both these rather marginal modernists. There is a review here of Landon Hammer and Brom Weber, eds., *O My Land, My Friends: The Selected Letters of Hart Crane* (Four Walls and Eight Windows [1997]) which explores the myth of Crane, a poet closely associated with the reckless abandon of the 'jazz age', as well as an insightful essay comparing Eliot's 'La Figlia che Piange' to Crane's 'My Grandmother's Love Letters'. For students of modern poetry, this is a fine example of close formal analysis that shows the affinities between these two poets. Bromwich also pays considerable attention to Moore as a poet when he reviews her *Complete Poems* and when he discusses her friendship with Elizabeth Bishop.

In a similar vein to Bromwich's collection is Charles Tomlinson's *American Essays: Making It New*, which reflects on the critical reputations of some of the most important American poets of the twentieth century. The emphasis is on poetic modernism, and thus Pound, Williams, Moore, Stevens and Eliot are all represented, but so too are the relatively neglected figures of Lorine Niedecker and George

Oppen. Tomlinson's insights are not startlingly original, but they offer reminders of the various strands of canonical modernism from its first beginnings to its post-war incarnations. The essays included here are pithy, anecdotal, and idiosyncratic, reflecting Tomlinson's own tastes in poetry. In addition to the critical essays are four pieces that come under the heading 'Some Americans: A Personal Record', which includes the autobiographical essay 'Beginnings'. Here Tomlinson describes his early encounters with the poetry of Williams, Moore and Stevens and the literary alliances and affiliations he formed in the post-war years; particularly enjoyable is his account of his friendships with Moore, Williams and Lowell.

Though both Tomlinson and Bromwich offer elegant appraisals of American poets, they rarely surprise the reader. In *The Strength of Poetry* James Fenton, however, though not veering away from canonical poetry, offers some illuminating insights into the work of a number of canonical figures. Of interest to Americanists are the essays on three American women poets: 'Becoming Marianne Moore', 'The Many Arts of Elizabeth Bishop', and 'Lady Lazarus', an essay on Plath. Fenton perceptively avoids the caricatures of 'Miss Moore' that emerged in response to her later work. Instead, he concentrates on Moore's earlier poems such as 'Picking and Choosing', 'Silence' and 'Marriage'. Lamenting the fact that so little of this early work is now in print (though this is about to be rectified with the publication of Robin Schulze's *Becoming Marianne Moore: Early Poems, 1907–1924*), Fenton does much to promote Moore as a radical feminist not frightened to assert herself in the company of her male modernist peers. He also admires Bishop, but, for a poet so taken with these two very restrained and formally precise craftswomen, it is strange but fascinating to hear him on the subject of Plath. His reading of her as 'the phoenix-like, man-eating priestess poetess' of 'Lady Lazarus' is an excellent discussion of the extreme measures this poet went to in order to establish herself as a pre-eminent poetess.

A very useful textbook to appear this year is Roberts, ed., *A Companion to Twentieth Century Poetry*, which, though not offering particularly original readings, does provide a good introduction to some of the main themes and debates of the last century together with some solid and sensible essays on key poetic figures. Essays deal with the following individual poets: William Carlos Williams (by Lisa M. Steinman), Robert Frost (by Alex Calder), Wallace Stevens (by Phillip Hobsbawm), Marianne Moore (by Elizabeth Wilson), Elizabeth Bishop (by Jonathan Ellis), Sylvia Plath (by Sue Vice), Ezra Pound (by A.D. Moody), Robert Lowell (by Stephen Matterson) and John Ashbery (by David Herd). While many will argue that this is a rather homogenous selection that reinforces the whiteness of poetry at the expense of its more interesting and subversive 'others', there are essays on postcolonial poetry in English as well as the New Negro Renaissance. What is different and refreshing about the essays on individual poets is that each focuses on a particular collection rather than the whole poetic oeuvre. Thus the essay on Lowell, for instance, deals only with *Life Studies*, the essay on Pound considers the *Pisan Cantos*, and the essay on Stevens revisits *Harmonium*. This makes much more sense than trying to map the whole career of a poet who, if he or she is any good at all, adapts their work to respond to the changing times.

2. Fiction 1900–1945

There is an increasing dearth in academic publishing of single-author monographs not directed at a clearly identifiable undergraduate or general market, and the period 1900–45 appears to be suffering at least as much, if not more, than most from the increasing reluctance of many presses to publish what used to be the cornerstone of academic endeavour. Journal publication of some significant work remains strong, particularly in the case of writers who continue to excite substantial commentary in both formal and contextual terms (such as William Faulkner, and to a lesser extent Gertrude Stein), or those whose biographies excite as much interest as their works, such as F. Scott Fitzgerald and Ernest Hemingway. The most positive aspects of a year that seems to reflect what might well be an irreversible decline in the monograph have been a slight revival of interest in the treatment of Fitzgerald, and the continuing strength of academic interest in the works of Faulkner, even if both are best served by edited collections and, in Faulkner's case, by extensive coverage in a wide range of journals. Generally, however, this has been a disappointing year characterized by incremental additions to our understanding of what remains a significant period in American writing, and a crucial moment in the development and achievement of American modernism.

The critical and popular fascination with *The Great Gatsby* continues to drive Fitzgerald scholarship forwards, and Henry C. Phelps's 'Literary History/Unsolved Mystery: *The Great Gatsby* and the Halls–Mills Murder Case' (*ANQ* 14:iii[2001] 33–9) concentrates on Fitzgerald's incorporation of details that have their source in a (now largely forgotten) 1922 murder case. Rather than merely provide yet another extended footnote to the text, however, Phelps goes beyond the scholarly identification of specific details, borrowings, and parallels to produce a more generally interesting reading of the part the Wilsons play in Fitzgerald's text. In 'Undiscovering the Country: Conrad, Fitzgerald, and Meta-National Form' (*MFS* 47[2001] 356–90) Peter Mallios provides an intriguing addition to discussions of *The Great Gatsby*'s intertexts by focusing on Fitzgerald's fascination with Conrad, as well as on the two authors' shared preoccupation with the modern cultural problematics of nationality and nationhood, to produce an account of the formal and national intersections that can be traced between Fitzgerald's text and Conrad's *Nostromo*. Scott Donaldson's 'Possessions in *The Great Gatsby*' (*SoR* 37:ii[2001] 187–210) is, as might be expected from such an established critic, an accomplished essay that, through its focus on questions of materialism and consumption, actually manages that most difficult of things for a critic of Fitzgerald—saying something about *The Great Gatsby* that will be of interest to both the critical community and to the more general reader of Fitzgerald's works.

Interest in Fitzgerald is not entirely confined to the attention that continues to be paid to *The Great Gatsby*, however, with a welcome republication of the early work in Bruccoli and Baughman, eds., *Before Gatsby: The First Twenty-Six Stories*. As its title suggests, this collection directs almost all approaches to Fitzgerald through what the editors are hardly the first to identify as 'his great American novel', and will only reinforce the interpretation of the short stories as journeyman work produced as Fitzgerald moved towards the crowning triumph of his first novel. The continuing availability of works first published between 1919 and 1923 in such an attractive illustrated volume, however, can only be welcomed, even if the stories themselves remain in print in other collections. It should be remembered, and this volume provides the primary material for a timely reminder, that it was the Fitzgerald of *Flappers and Philosophers*, *Tales of the Jazz Age* and the stories published in the *Saturday Evening Post* who first caught the public imagination and produced work that seemed quintessentially representative of a historical moment in a way that has only rarely been repeated by subsequent authors, and that the short stories that made his initial reputation remain worthy of attention as something more than mere signposts on the way towards the production of the canonical colossus that *The Great Gatsby* has since become.

An impressive list of contributors has been gathered for Prigozy, ed., *The Cambridge Companion to F. Scott Fitzgerald*, including Kirk Curnutt, James L. West II, Bryant Mangum, Milton R. Stern, J. Gerald Kennedy, Rena Sanderson, Scott Donaldson, Alan Margolies, and Jackson S. Bryer. Organized more or less chronologically, but not slavishly mapping out yet another version of the Fitzgerald life and work according to the familiar trajectory of meteoric rise followed by slow and painful fall, the twelve individual chapters in this volume provide another pleasing addition to a CUP series that has served American writing of the period 1900–45 well in recent years, offering, in this case, some of the most insightful scholars in the field an opportunity to provide a useful composite account of the current state of Fitzgerald scholarship. Although all such collections are inevitably partial, there are no obvious absences from this as a general critical reader that will be of use to critics and students looking for a summary text, and Jackson R. Bryer's mapping of the critical reputation will be useful to many. These are accomplished essays in and of themselves, however, that have the capacity to look at Fitzgerald in relatively unusual contexts (such as Curnutt's examination of the relationship between Fitzgerald and 'the rise of American Youth Culture'), as well as to revisit areas of established interest, such as Prigozy's own return to the reception of the Fitzgerald marriage and its enduring fascination for both academic and general readers which has seen reconfirmation in another book-length treatment, Kendall Taylor's *Sometimes Madness is Wisdom: Zelda and Scott Fitzgerald, A Marriage* (Ballantine, not received). The *Cambridge Companion to F. Scott Fitzgerald* as a whole has a feeling of structural unity that is not always present in such volumes, loosely provided by the frequent double move of many of the contributors, who are looking not only at the work or the life (or lives), but at the textualization of life and work within the critical reception Fitzgerald has both enjoyed and endured.

A welcome addition to the study of the inviting intersection between Fitzgerald and Ernest Hemingway, that other emerging talent of post-First World War American writing whose own early promise was as often realized through a polished accomplishment within the apparent confinement of the writing of the short story as it was in his first forays into novel writing, is to be found in Ronald Berman's *Fitzgerald, Hemingway, and the Twenties*. This is familiar territory within both textual and biographical criticism, but Berman locates his subjects firmly in literary, cultural and popular contexts in an accomplished and informed manner that means that this is anything but a redundant addition to Hemingway and Fitzgerald criticism. There is little urgent need for yet another work that makes one of the most obvious pairings in American writing, and critical essays on the specific individual works are hardly thin on the ground (the focus is on *The Great Gatsby*, 'Bernice Bobs her Hair', 'The Diamond as Big as the Ritz', 'The Killers', *A Farewell to*

Arms, and *The Sun Also Rises*), but this is a sequence of intelligent readings offered by a critic in firm command of both primary and secondary material that will be of interest as much to those readers who are familiar with the critical traditions upon which it builds as to those who are looking for a lucid contextualizing introduction to either or both writers.

John Whittier-Ferguson's 'The Liberation of Gertrude Stein: War and Writing' (*Mo/Mo* 8[2001] 405–28) looks at Stein's Second World War writing and seeks to reconnect what critical consideration there has been of these late works with her earlier writings (and an earlier world war), arguing that for Stein it is 'modernity and the war that brings the twentieth century into the "modern composition"'. The Stein who emerges from Susan McCabe's '"Delight in Dislocation": The Cinematic Modernism of Stein, Chaplin, and Man Ray' (*Mo/Mo* 8[2001] 429–52) looks beyond the often acknowledged effect that modern art had on her writing to look at the contention that Stein's 'specific connections to film have been, for the most part, unexplored' and 'that avant garde cinema newly illuminates her strategies of representation and embodiment' and sees the comic and the hysteric overlapping in the 'cinematic aesthetic' of Stein, Chaplin, and Man Ray. In 'Gertrude Stein, Automatic Writing and the Mechanics of Genius' (*FMLS* 37:ii[2001] 169–75), Barbara Will sketches out some of the material covered in more detail in her *Gertrude Stein and the Problem of 'Genius'* (EdinUP [2000]), providing a short account of some aspects of Stein's attitude towards and understanding of 'genius' that will interest anyone who missed the longer work. Another interesting addition to Stein criticism can be found in Mark Goble, 'Cameo Appearances; or, When Gertrude Stein Checks into Grand Hotel' (*MLQ* 62:ii[2001] 117–63]. Also published this year, but not received for review, were Steven Meyer, *Irresistible Dictation: Gertrude Stein and the Correlations of Writing and Science* (StanfordUP) and Juliana Spahr, *Everybody's Autonomy: Connective Reading and Collective Identity* (UAlaP).

Matthew Stewart's *Modernism and Tradition in Ernest Hemingway's 'In Our Time'* is aimed not just at the reader but at the teacher of Hemingway, providing an accessible and readable account of a text that sits uneasily beside the received view of Hemingway's works as unproblematic celebrations of machismo, heavy drinking, and violence that so often finds its way into texts written with a student audience in mind. It is in *In Our Time* that Hemingway is most obviously engaged in the formal experimentation of modernism, with its fragmented and disjointed structure broken up by what have been variously described as 'chapters', 'interchapters' or 'vignettes' in a way that makes any contention that this is 'just' a collection of short stories hard to support. Stewart sensibly places *In Our Time* in both historical contexts (the First World War, what is known of Hemingway's biography, wider artistic and literary modernism, Hemingway's close relationship with Gertrude Stein during the period this work was written) to address the problems of classification that have attended *In Our Time* since the first reviews to recognize what Clinton S. Burhans had called its 'structural unity' appeared. This is a relatively short critical work, however, and in seeking a clear organization of his own the author follows many previous critics, most notably Philip Young, in seeing the presence of Nick Adams as the central vehicle for a developmental and progressive narrative that underlies the whole. Such an approach, that situates Hemingway in a position of tension between 'traditionalist' and 'experimentalist' impulses, has its appeal, but the space given to close consideration of the individual stories (less than half the volume) almost inevitably produces what amounts to a series of thumbnail sketches that do not always reflect the complexities and sophistication of Hemingway's project. This is a valuable work of Hemingway criticism admirably suited to teachers, but Stewart might have benefited from pursuing his arguments at greater length. Those interested in those elements of *In Our Time* such as the 'Greek' vignettes and 'On the Quai at Smyrna' might also be interested in Peter Lecouras, 'Hemingway in Constantinople' (*MQ* 43:i[2001] 29–41), which pays close and relatively extended attention to both context and Hemingway's formal experimentation within the limitations and possibilities of narrative representation; while the figure of Nick Adams is the subject of Howard L. Hunnam, '"Scared sick looking at it": A Reading of Nick Adams in the Published Stories' (*TCL* 47:i[2001] 92–113).

The essays in the 2001 issues of the *Hemingway Review* have more to say about the novels than they do about the short stories. *The Sun Also Rises* is the subject of four articles: C. Harold Hurley's '"But Bryant? What of Bryant in Bryan?": The Religious Implications of the Allusion to "A Forest Hymn" in *The Sun Also Rises*' (*Hemingway Review* 20:ii[2001] 76–89); Peter L. Hays's 'Hemingway's *The Sun Also Rises* and James's *The Ambassadors*' (*Hemingway Review* 20:ii[2001] 90–8); Michael Soto's 'Hemingway among the Bohemians: A Generational Reading of *The Sun Also Rises*' (*Hemingway Review* 21:i[2001] 5–21); and Greg Forter's 'Melancholy Modernism: Gender and the Politics of Mourning in *The Sun Also Rises*' (*Hemingway Review* 21:i[2001] 22–37). This novel's historical context is also the subject of William Adair, '*The Sun Also Rises*: A Memory of War' (*TCL* 47:i[2001] 72–91). Jeffrey A. Schwarz's '"The saloon must go, and I will take it with me": American Prohibition, Nationalism, and Expatriation in *The Sun Also Rises*' (*SNNTS* 33:ii[2001] 180–201) revisits some well-trodden territory in its reconsideration of what many have interpreted as a text almost obsessed with the representation of alcoholism.

Another relatively early Hemingway text, *A Farewell to Arms*, also comes in for reappraisal in the *Hemingway Review* in Gary Harrington's 'Partial Articulation: Word Play in *A Farewell to Arms*' (*Hemingway Review* 20:ii[2001] 59–75), and in Diane Price Hendl's 'Invalid Masculinity: Silence, Hospitals and Anesthesia in *A Farewell to Arms*' (*Hemingway Review* 21:i[2001] 38–52). As might be expected, the *Hemingway Review* continues to provide a source of serious, thorough, and impressive Hemingway scholarship, including Ron McFarland's 'Hemingway and the Poets' (*Hemingway Review* 20:ii[2001] 37–58), Charles J. Nolan Jr. 'Hemingway's "The Sea Change": What Close Reading and Evolutionary Psychology Reveal' (*Hemingway Review* 21:i[2001] 53–67), John Clark Pratt 'My Pilgrimage: Fishing for Religion with Hemingway' (*Hemingway Review* 21:i[2001] 78–92), and Dwight Eddins 'Of Rocks and Marlin: The Existentialist Agon in Camus's *The Myth of Sisyphus* and Hemingway's *The Old Man and the Sea*' (*Hemingway Review* 21:i[2001] 68–77).

Once again the annual 'Faulkner and Yoknapatawpha' conference held at the University of Mississippi (in this case the 1998 conference) provides a substantial resource for Faulkner scholarship and encouraging evidence of the continuing vibrancy of Faulkner criticism. Among the ten critical essays in Abadie and Urgo, eds., *Faulkner in America*, are contributions from Richard Godden, Catherine

Gunther Kodat, Charles A. Peek, Noel Polk, Hortense J. Spillers, Linda Wagner-Martin, and Charles Reagan Wilson. Such a conference title, and the resulting reworked papers, inevitably cover a broad range of material that demonstrates, once again, the problematical nature of any attempt to fix Faulkner firmly in terms of any secure sense of place, for all that his works appear to offer an unusually specific location in terms of a regional geography, a regional and national history, and a regional and national literary history. What emerges is a plural and complex range of approaches to Faulkner in the context of 'America' that recognizes Faulkner's twin and simultaneous positions as a writer of regional and national significance whose works still occupy a place within any account of national canon formation even as they insist on their very local reference.

In a special issue of *American Literature* on 'Violence, the Body and "The South"', Faulkner makes a not unexpected appearance in Laura Doyle's essay 'The Body against itself in Faulkner's Phenomenology of Race' (*AL* 73[2001] 339–64), which focuses on *Light in August* as a text 'that exposes race as the phantom that both promises and withdraws the body's unity—and the nation's', through careful consideration of the figures of Joe Christmas, Joanna Burden, and Gail Hightower. Peter Lurie's 'Some Trashy Myth of Reality's Escape: Romance, History, and Film Viewing in *Absolom, Absolom!*' (*AL* 73[2001] 563–98) sets romantic attitudes towards the history of the South against the influences on Faulkner's writing of both 'trashy' popular cinema, and the revisionism of films such as D.W. Griffith's *The Birth of the Nation*. Lurie sees the Faulkner of *Absolom, Absolom!* as both reproducing elements of the cinematic and critiquing it as a vehicle for a melancholic nostalgia for a dead past. Interest in the various forms of intersection between Faulkner and film also informs many of the essays in the two 2001 editions of the *Faulkner Journal*, unfortunately not received for review, with essays from Doug Baldwin, Dallas Hulsey, Gene M. Moore, Scott Yarbrough, Stephanie Li, and William Furry all addressing this area. In 'Flooded: The Excesses of Geography, Gender, and Capitalism in Faulkner's *If I Forget Thee Jerusalem*' (*AL* 73[2001] 811–35) Cynthia Dobbs seeks to refocus attention on a text that (since first publication as *The Wild Palms* in 1939) has been relatively ignored by scholars whose attention has been fixed on the 'four masterpieces of the 1920s and 1930s' (*The Sound and the Fury*, *As I Lay Dying*, *Light in August*, and *Absolom, Absolom!*). Dobbs makes an interesting case for Faulkner as struggling here with the same 'philosophical, psychological, sociopolitical and aesthetic issues' that have attracted the attention of scholars of the earlier works.

In seeking to make a new intervention in what she acknowledges to be the rather overcrowded area of criticism on *The Sound and the Fury*, Michelle Ann Abate directs her attention to what is usually considered to be a very minor character in 'Reading Red: The Man with the (Gay) Red Tie in Faulkner's *The Sound and the Fury*' (*MissQ* 54[2001] 293–313). In doing so Abate demonstrates the nuanced readings demanded of the critic who would attempt to bring something new to consideration of Faulkner. In 'Rereading Faulkner: Authority, Criticism, and *The Sound and the Fury*' (*MP* 98[2001] 604–28) Stacy Burton also recognizes the slippery nature of such a frequently revised (and appended) text, and through reference to figures such as Roland Barthes, Pierre Macherey and Mikhail Bakhtin makes a case for a reconsideration of the Compson Appendix that Faulkner prepared for Malcolm Cowley's *The Portable Faulkner*. Martyn Bone's '"All the confederate dead ... all of Faulkner the great": Faulkner, Hannah, Neo-Confederate Narrative and Postsouthern Parody' (*MissQ* 54[2001] 197–211) seeks to make an original intervention by looking at the question of Faulkner's influence on Barry Hannah not in terms of derivation or anxiety, but through the postmodern's preferred modes of irony, parody, and pastiche.

Alex Vernon's 'Narrative Miscegenation: *Absolom, Absolom!* as Naturalist Novel, Auto/biography, and African-American Oral Story' (*JNT* 31:ii[2001] 155–79) argues that *Absolom, Absolom!* can be read as 'a cross-breed of several literary forms', including those listed in his title. It is perhaps most interesting when reading this novel as, in Henry Louis Gates Jr.'s terms, a 'speakerly' text, and tracing the oral influences through the context of writers such as Toni Morrison and Zora Neale Hurston. Vernon concludes that 'Faulkner locates his solution to the debilitating aspects of Southern culture by affirming the South's African-American heritage.' Erik Dussere's 'Accounting for Slavery: Economic Narratives in Morrison and Faulkner' (*MFS* 47[2001] 329–55) is a useful addition to the study of both writers, arguing that 'Morrison's prose, so different in its calm eloquence from Faulkner's adjectival gush, nevertheless suggests a similar sense of imbalance, a sense that the American novel must strive to articulate the legacies of slavery, even if it cannot provide a final accounting for our reckoning with these legacies'. Dussere also has an essay in the *Faulkner Journal* entitled 'The Debt of History: Southern Honor, Affirmative Action, and Faulkner's *Intruder in the Dust*' (*Faulkner Journal* 17:i[2001] 37–58).

Not received for review, Dan H. Doyle's *Faulkner's County: The Historical Roots of Yoknapatawpha* (UNCP) aims to fill a possible void in Faulkner scholarship by looking in extended local detail at the relationship between his 'real' historical and geographical location and the fictional location that is Yoknapatawpha, a subject that has fascinated critics since Faulkner first laid claim to his 'postage stamp of native soil' and which is touched upon in Abadie and Ergo's *Faulkner in America*. R. Rio-Jellife's *Obscurity's Myriad Components: The Theory and Practice of William Faulkner* (BuckUP) and David L. Mintner's *Faulkner's Questioning Narratives: Fiction of his Major Phase, 1929–42* (CornUP) were also not received for review.

The more 'minor' figures of the period 1900–45 have had a generally patchy year. In 'Father's and Sons: *Winesburg, Ohio* and the Revision of Modernism' (*SAF* 29[2001] 209–31), Marc C. Conner traces the struggles that exist between fathers and sons in the process of locating Sherwood Anderson (an almost paternal influence on the young Ernest Hemingway and William Faulkner) at a transition point in our understanding of modernism, rejecting the father-slaying impulses of many modernists and interested in the reconciliation 'with the father-figure and moving toward a vision of harmony and understanding, rather than alienation and isolation' through which Anderson achieves his 'mature vision'. In 'The Plurality of Chronotopes in the Modernist City Novel: The Case of Manhattan Transfer' (*ES* 82[2001] 420–36) Bart Keunen utilizes Mikhail Bakhtin's notion of the chronotope in examining the expression of Dos Passos's 'literary imagination' in *Manhattan Transfer*, moving towards the conclusion that this novel 'can be seen as an attempt to construct out of the decaying fragments of the cultural images of modernity a world that is complex as our own'. The only other essay of note that pays attention to a writer who was once a fixture of the literary canon is Joe Nazare's 'Backtrack to the Future: John E. Stith's/John Dos Passos's *Manhattan Transfer*' (*Extrapolation* 42:i[2001] 37–52), which provides an unusual contextualization of Dos Passos within popular culture and genre fiction rather than within the literary high modernism in which he is usually fixed.

A more obvious intersection between literary and popular culture can be found in David A. Ullery, *The Tarzan Novels of Edgar Rice Burroughs: An Illustrated Reader's Guide*. As the title of this volume suggests, this is not an explicitly academic or critical work and the author (a writer and illustrator) communicates the kind of enthusiasm for his subject that one only rarely finds in academic publications. Despite some rather naive statements that seem oddly dated, such as the bald statement that the surprisingly polyglot Tarzan picked up the German language 'while living with civilized people', Ullery's work is thorough and accessibly organized in an almost encyclopedic fashion, and will provide a useful resource for anyone wanting to navigate their way around the twenty-four complete Edgar Rice Burroughs Tarzan novels and a range of peripheral material.

In 'Edith Wharton's Dream of Incest: *Ethan Frome*' (*SSF* 35:i[2001] 23–40), Ferda Aysa unfortunately yields to the desire to use Freudian analysis to reveal the repressed in the narrative of the New England novella where the origins of *Ethan Frome* are assigned to 'the writer's urge to confess the guilt that she unconsciously felt for her incestuous desire for her father'. Barbara Comins, in '"Outrageous Trap": Envy and Jealousy in Wharton's "Roman Fever" and Fitzgerald's "Bernice Bobs her Hair"' (*EWhR* 17:i[2001] 9–12), catalogues the instances of the two differentiated green emotions and concludes with the observation that 'in both tales the jealous character ensures, rather than spoils, her competitor's chance for success'. Phillip Barrish devotes a chapter of his *American Literary Realism, Critical Theory, and Intellectual Prestige, 1880–1995* to Wharton's too often neglected novel *Twilight Sleep* [1927]. The chapter entitled 'What Nona Knows' is a capacious and insightful discussion and theorization of the issues that drive the narrative, focusing on the part played by Nona Manford in the text. Barrish contends that 'Wharton's book ultimately accords to Nona a unique intellectual status, although one that is hard to think of as elevated because it is so oppressively heavy as literally to prostrate her.' In the same territory as Barrish, Melanie V. Dawson, in '"Too Young for the Part": Narrative Closure and Feminine Evolution in Wharton's '20s Fiction' (*ArQ* 57:iv[2001] 89–119), analyses the role played by the younger female protagonists in selected novels from the 1920s as caught between traditional mores and new opportunities, and forced into reaction by the imperative towards achieving family unity or some form of conventional closure.

Esch, ed., *New Essays on The House of Mirth* features four essays, two of which have been previously published, contradicting Emory Elliott's preface which claims that the essays in the collection were 'specifically commissioned'. Deborah Esch's introduction breaks no unfamiliar ground and the two new essays, Mary Nyquist's 'Determining Influences: Resistance and Mentorship in *The House of Mirth* and the Anglo-American Realist Tradition' and Thomas Loebel's 'Beyond Her Self', treat, respectively, the range and extent of literary influences on Wharton's text and— predictably enough—commodification. From a rather different standpoint in a year in which Wharton's novel of 1905 takes centre stage, David Herman conducts a socio-linguistic analysis of the text in 'Style-Shifting in Edith Wharton's *The House of Mirth*' (*L&L* 10:i[2001] 61–77), where he is concerned to demonstrate that 'style

is content' and 'content is style', in that the participants in the action of the novel take on and express selves *by* communicating, *by* stylizing'. Laura K. Johnson, in 'Edith Wharton and the Fiction of Marital Unity' (*MFS* 47[2001] 947–76), takes a scholarly overview of the social and legal significance of marriage in the American nineteenth century as expressed in *The House of Mirth*, and in the early twentieth as depicted in *The Glimpses of the Moon*, where Wharton's 'efforts to imagine a workable alternative to contract based on the principles of marital unity are unsuccessful.'

Helen Killoran provides both a survey and an overview of a century of Wharton criticism in *The Critical Reception of Edith Wharton*. Killoran proceeds chronologically, beginning with an analysis of the different critical trends and tendencies which have been applied to Wharton's work, from its reception at publication to contemporary approaches. She then apportions a chapter each to *The House of Mirth*, *Ethan Frome*, *The Custom of the Country*, *Summer*, *The Age of Innocence* and *Ghosts*, ending with a review of further sources and a comprehensive bibliography. This is a well-disciplined and capacious critical bibliography, partisan but clear-sighted and meticulous in its attention to the major issues which have both shaped and distorted critical approaches to Wharton's work, including the question of her relationship with Henry James.

Mary V. Marchand, in 'Cross Talk: Edith Wharton and the New England Women Regionalists' (*WS* 30:iii[2001] 369–95) uses the example of *Ethan Frome* to argue for a 'polemical intertextuality' in the expression of Wharton's representations of women as well as in her larger relationship to women's culture. Marchand stays in New England for her article, 'Death to Lady Bountiful: Women and Reform in Edith Wharton's *The Fruit of the Tree*' (*Legacy* 18:i[2001] 65–78), but is equally eager to demonstrate how the novel under discussion 'ties to the feminist debates of her day and to the tradition of women's literature'. Marchand identifies a sub-genre, the 'industrial novel'—drawing comparisons with the work of other women writers, from Rebecca Harding Davis's *Margret Howth* to Mary Wilkins Freeman's *The Portion of Labor*—which Wharton joins in *The Fruit of the Tree* only to change it, as 'much of the novel's vitality derives from its assimilation and transformation of the characters and idiom of this tradition'. William R. MacNaughton makes a series of small but telling points in his 'The Artist as Moralist: Edith Wharton's Revisions to the Last Chapter of *The Custom of the Country*' in discussion of the changes made between the draft of chapter 46 and the published version, changes which temper and fine-tune the presentation of Paul Marvell in a rare instance of Wharton narrating events from a child's perspective. In 'Compromising Realism to Idealize a War: Wharton's *The Marne* and Cather's *One of Ours*' (*ALR* 33:ii[2001] 157–67), John J. Murphy argues that greater critical respect should be given to these works. He examines their vexed relationship with realism and identifies their respective heroes as representing the 'imaginative poverty of American life and the need some feel to escape that life in fantasy'. Julie Olin-Ammentorp and Ann Ryan, in 'Undine Spragg and the Transcendental I' (*EWhR* 17:i[2001] 12–16), discuss *The Custom of the Country* as expressive of the tension in American culture 'between nostalgia for the purity of Emerson's aestheticism, and a deep, yet critical, fascination with the mechanisms of progress'. The ruthless, triumphant progress of Undine Spragg, it is argued, 'romanticizes, critiques, and realizes the promise of Emerson's Transcendentalism'. In 'Edgar Allan Poe and Edith Wharton: The Case of Mrs.

Mowatt' (*EWhR* 17:i[2001] 12–16), Carole M. Shaffer-Koros traces Wharton's literary relationship with Poe, and, like Olin-Ammentorp and Ryan, establishes links between Wharton's *The Custom of the Country* and the work of a distinguished precursor, specifically Poe, and his account of the work of the mid-nineteenth-century actress and playwright Anna Cora Mowatt. Gerard M. Sweeney, in 'Wharton's "The Other Two"' (*Expl* 59:ii[2001] 88–91), traces the appearances of typhoid—suffered in this story by Alice Waythorn's daughter, Lily—throughout Wharton's life and fiction in order to further demonstrate what we already knew: that 'Alice is not villainous or evil ... Alice is a mediocrity'. Edie Thornton's 'Selling Edith Wharton: Illustration, Advertising and *Pictorial Review*, 1924–25' (*ArQ* 57:iii[2001] 29–59) is, by contrast, an entirely engaging discussion of the interpretative complexities which arise when the illustrations accompanying the serialization of *The Mother's Recompense* are scrutinized. Thornton skilfully demonstrates the power of the magazine environment to 'introduce contradictions into [the novel's] tight little universe of age categories and controlled female sexuality'. 'Spectacular Homes and Pastoral Theaters: Gender, Urbanity and Domesticity in *The House of Mirth*' (*SNNTS* 33:iii[2001] 322–50), by Nancy Von Rosk, is an extremely insightful and scholarly treatment of the relationship between Lily Bart and social change as expressed by and through the series of settings in the novel. These latter two articles are the outstanding contributions to Wharton scholarship this year.

Deborah Lindsay Williams, *Not in Sisterhood: Edith Wharton, Willa Cather, Zona Gale, and the Politics of Female Authorship*, opens with a discussion of the correspondence between Gale and Wharton and Gale and Cather, there being no direct communication known to have taken place between Wharton and Cather. Williams denotes the epistolary relationship between Wharton and Gale as one that established itself along 'generational lines' with 'Wharton as mentor and literary mother' while the relationship between Cather and Gale is denoted as 'using geographical markers' which emphasize their physical distance while establishing their artistic community. Following this interesting consideration of a little-discussed range of correspondence, Williams devotes a chapter to an evaluation of Gale's work and social context before moving to a comparison of *The House of Mirth*, *My Ántonia*, and *Miss Lulu Bett* in the third chapter, which pinpoints the crucial difference between the work of Cather and Wharton on one side and Gale on the other—the positioning of the 'economically self-sufficient characters on the periphery of their novels' rather than at the centre. Chapter 4 examines the engagement with the war made by all three through their work, and Williams concludes this worthwhile study with a brief discussion of the disappearance of Gale from critical consideration in the twentieth century in the context of the revival of the reputations of Wharton and Cather.

3. Fiction Since 1945

(a) General

YES 31[2001], on 'North American Short Stories and Fictions', is an impressive collection dedicated to the poetics, aesthetics and politics of the short story incorporating historical and theoretical readings of a range of writers from both the

States and Canada. This volume includes a total of thirteen articles relevant to post-war American literature. A brief synopsis of their content will give a sense of the volume's diversity. The opening article by Judie Newman assesses the politics of Grace Paley's short fiction as a response to the Vietnam War. J. Gerald Kennedy and Robert Beuka consider the dispersal of community in the short-story cycles of Edward P. Jones's *Lost in the City* and Dagoberto Gibb's *The Magic of Blood*. Female Jewish American writers' response to the Holocaust is given a nuanced focus by Brauner. Religion and narcotics, Kevin McCarron suggests, form a potent cocktail in approaching the sacred and the absurd in the short fiction of Dennis Cooper, Dennis Johnson and Thom Jones. A preoccupation with the temporal configuration of the short story form emerges from two articles: T.J. Lustig examines the treatment of metonymy and ellipsis in Tim O'Brien's work, while David Seed concentrates on the representation of a 'historical destiny' in the story cycles of little-known science fiction writer Paul Linebarger (who published under the pseudonym Cordwainer Smith). Both Raymond Carver and Jayne Anne Phillips's short stories are considered in the light of their association with the 'Dirty Realism' movement by Charles E. May and Brian Jarvis respectively. In addition there are articles dedicated to the short fiction of Ben Marcus (by Peter Vernon), Rita Dove (by Pat Righelato), Tobias Wolff (by Martin Schofield), Sherman Alexie (by Andrew Dix), Jean Stafford (by Clare Hanson), John Updike (by Jay Prosser), and Eudora Welty (by Lionel Kelly). The publication of this volume indicates that the increased critical attention paid to the poetics of the American short story during the last decade shows no sign of diminishing. Moreover the diversity of texts included by the *Yearbook in English Studies* emphasizes that the genre still retains a potent cultural, political and aesthetic currency.

In *The Eye's Mind: Literary Modernism and Visual Culture*, Karen Jacobs widens understandings of modernist literature in exploring its connection to changing visual cultures. Jacobs contends that 'the modernist period is remarkable for its increasing cognizance of the body, itself grasped as an image, behind the neutral lens of the observer; the period may be understood as registering the emergence of that body as a kind of afterimage, exposed in repeated betrayals of its situated partiality, its culturally determined distortions, its will to dominance and even violence, that cumulatively have become the basis for anti-Enlightenment critique'. She goes on to state that recognition of the modernist loss of faith in the privileged subjectivity of the observer inevitably leads to a recognition of the struggle of traditional objects of gaze to redefine themselves. Of particular interest in this section are the chapters 'The Eye's Mind: Self-Detection in James's *The Sacred Fount* and Nabokov's *The Eye*' and 'One-Eyed Jacks and Three-Eyed Monsters: Visualizing Embodiment in Ralph Ellison's *Invisible Man*', as well as the 'Postscript: From "Our Glass Lake" to "Hourglass Lake": Photo/graphic Memory in Nabokov's *Lolita*'. With reference to Nabokov's *The Eye*, Jacobs charts the breakdown of the division between the narrator's and characters' gazes, arguing that the 'narrator unquestionably participates in the "fantasy of surveillance" said to characterize the function of the realist narrator, but fails adequately to represent the forms of discipline, regularization, and supervision normally associated with that narrative authority', while *Lolita* 'marks a mode of changing visual codes and visual relations … that cannily anticipates a postmodern view'. With reference to Ellison, Jacobs considers the relationships between the discourses that contribute to Ellison's development of invisibility as a racial construct—sociology, comparative anatomy, folklore, Emersonianism and Sartrean existentialism—to assert that his use of the metaphor 'begins to appear as overdetermined as it is inevitable, and as vexed'. Jacobs offers a sophisticated perspective that insightfully joins work on visual culture with literary studies.

In *From Richard Wright to Toni Morrison: Ethics in Modern and Postmodern American Narratives*, Jeffrey J. Folks explores the relationship of Southern and African American literature to contemporary ethical problems and debates. Tracing the neglect of ethics as a focus for literary criticism back to the 'disdain for traditional sources of belief accompanied by naive self-assurance in modern science and technology [that] arose forcefully in the decades after World War II', Folks asserts the need to consider the ways in which literature of the period addresses a failure of ethical understanding created by 'the legacy of a now lapsed religious culture and the uncertain promise of a modern secularism'. Writers considered are Richard Wright, Ernest J. Gaines and, of interest in this section, James Agee, Henry Roth, Flannery O'Conner, Walker Percy, Richard Ford and William Styron.

In *Archival Reflections: Postmodern Fiction of the Americas (Self-Reflexivity, Historical Revisionism, Utopia)* Santiago Juan-Navarro situates himself between the Spanish American and US literary traditions to explore a perceived distrust of comparative literary studies outside European models. He challenges the rigid borders that exist between academic disciplines in the Americas to assert that '"Americanness" is frequently approached from a narrow nationalist and Anglophone perspective, which can be seen in the appropriation of the word "America" as a synonym for the United States [while] many Latin Americanists ... look with suspicion on any attempt at connecting their own literary tradition to that of the United States, arguing that a history of economic and cultural domination stands in the way of any positive interaction between the two regions'. Putting the literary traditions of the Americas in dialogue, Juan-Navarro focuses on Spanish American and US literature of the 1970s to connect them in relation to their 'paradoxical combination of self-reflexivity and historiographic meditation', and the ways in which they 'foreground the act of writing, whilst simultaneously asserting their own historical condition'. Juan-Navarro evaluates postmodernism as an aesthetic sensibility, comparing the work of Carlos Fuentes, Ishmael Reed, Julio Cortázar, and, of interest in this section, E.L. Doctorow.

In 'Ellipsis, Ritual, and "Real Time": Rethinking the Rape Complex in Southern Novels' (*MissQ* 54[2001] 37–58) Laura S. Patterson foregrounds the elliptical history of Southern accounts of sexual violence. Referencing the work of W.J. Cash and Susan Brownmiller, Patterson explores the ways in which the literature of the South 'promotes multiple "dependent relationships" in the ways that reading audiences experience time, space and narrative sequences'. Patterson begins by asserting that 'the elliptical nature of the rape in William Faulkner's *Sanctuary* ... functions as this type of institutionalized rape, where the reader forms a dependent relationship with the textual flow of time and space, and that flow dictates not only the reader's sympathies, but also the degree of severity she reads into the sexual assault on Temple Drake', and charts the evolution of the narration of rape in Southern novels with reference to readings of Raymond Andrews's *Appalachee Red* and Dorothy Allison's *Bastard out of Carolina*.

Basso, McCall and Garceau, eds., *Across the Great Divide: Cultures of Manhood in the American West*, is an interdisciplinary volume bringing together individual essays on revisionist scholarship in Western history, multicultural research on gender construction, and analyses of masculinity. Within this broad-ranging agenda Craig Leavitt offers a cultural reading of the beatnik Western hero in his essay '*On the Road*: Cassady, Kerouac and Images of Late Western Masculinity'. Through his focus on Kerouac's novel Leavitt approaches Neal Cassady as both a literary artist and the persona of Dean Moriarty. This blurring of the boundary between fictional persona and individual history enables Leavitt to include a considerable amount of biographical material. He suggests that Kerouac's novel presents the West as a magnetic and mythic ideal, within which Moriarty initially serves as a potent figure of 'authentic' masculinity. Somewhat predictably the automobile is discussed as symbolic of power, freedom and virility. But the essay's crux lies in its reading of how Kerouac's text gradually inverts the historical representation of the Western hero. Moriarty is neither inexpressive nor inarticulate, and indeed his own heterosexuality is at points in question during the novel. Reading this revisionary masculinity through post-war American culture, Leavitt suggests that we could approach the novel's licentiousness through an understanding of 'sacrality'. This appreciation of a spiritual quality inherent in the material world is further examined as a flight from puritan guilt to a Western celebration of the unity of body, soul and land.

In *Coyote Kills John Wayne: Postmodernism and Contemporary Fictions of the Transcultural Frontier*, Carlton Smith brings together an impressive range of writers and critics of the American West in relation to theories of the postmodern. Although some of the writers considered (Leslie Marmon Silko, Louise Erdrich and Thomas King) are relevant to other sections of this chapter, of interest in this section are chapters on Thomas McGuane's Deadrock novels (part of the Montana Literary Renaissance), William Vollmann's *The Rifles* (the third volume of his *Seven Dreams* series) and possibly a chapter on the films of Sergio Leone. References to a number of critical figures familiar to readers of this section are also made (Leslie Fiedler, Richard Slotkin) and Smith's critical frame is informed by the work of Jacques Derrida, Jacques Lacan, Fredric Jameson, Jean-François Lyotard, Homi Bhabha and James Clifford, amongst others. Smith explores the terrain between cultural and critical theories to focus on representation of the frontier from the perspective of the 'other'.

On a similar theme, in *Mavericks on the Border: The Early Southwest in Historical Fiction and Film* J. Douglas Canfield explores the role of the American border hero in the midst of contending cultural forces, Indian, Hispanic and Anglo. Canfield is interested in a series of figures, portrayed by twentieth-century artists in historical fiction and film concerned with the period 1833–1917, who are '"exposed to some kind of ultimate test," are faced with cultural dilemmas that compel them to make extraordinary existential choices'. Drawing on the work of Sartre and Kristeva, in conjunction with Richard Slotkin's notion of regeneration through violence, Canfield brings together canonical and non-canonical works to explore representations of history and identity at the confluence of competing cultures. Writers considered include William Faulkner, Mariano Azuela, Carlos Fuentes, Laura Esquivel, Montserrat Fontes and, of particular interest in this section, Cormac McCarthy, Gore Vidal, Sam Peckinpah, L.D. Clark, Jane Candia Coleman, Robert

Houston and David Morrell. Acknowledging the impact of border studies and the contributions of critics such as Gloria Anzaldúa, Canfield states that, nevertheless, 'this is not a book about the border as liminal space for Chicanos' but rather an attempt to bring together a range of border fictions which focus on the moment of crossing from a range of cultural positions.

Placing conceptions of white middle-class Americans and the trope of the suburb into a considered animation, Catherine Jurca's *White Diaspora: The Suburb and the Twentieth Century American Novel* interrogates a range of novels from the 1900s to the present. Her introduction examines the phenomenon of suburbanization in post-Depression America and draws on sociological studies and political criticism. The overriding thesis of this work is that those two mutually dependent categories 'middle-class white America' and 'suburbanites' need careful examination and consideration. Jurca asserts that the term 'diaspora' characteristically evokes feelings of displacement in those who see themselves as disadvantaged and oppressed. This becomes an ironic point of reference for considering the dissatisfaction, alienation, and fear of conformity which haunts the representation of the suburb in twentieth-century literature. These sentiments lead to what Jurca characterizes as a form of 'sentimental dispossession'. The fantasy of victimhood and fraudulent identifications with cultural persecution fuel a desire for escape. Jurca argues that this position of victimization is usually articulated as the concern of the white male subject (as part of his loathing of encroachment/self-loathing in his alienation), obscuring the sexism and racism bound up with spatial organization while at the same time presenting a disabling view of white suburban privilege which conceives white flight as white diaspora. Jurca's study contributes an interesting new focus to the field of white studies. Individual chapters focus on the following novels: Edgar Rice Burroughs's *Tarzan of the Apes*, Sinclair Lewis's *Babbitt*, James M. Cain's *Mildred Pierce*, and Richard Wright's *Native Son*. Pertinent to this section for review is the final chapter, which considers Sloan Wilson's popular novel *The Man in the Grey Flannel Suit*. Entitled 'Sanctimonious Suburbanites and the Post War Novel', it examines the precarious relationship between individual, domestic space, work, marketing, press and publicity. Drawing on comparative readings with William H. Whyte's influential sociological treatise *The Organization Man* (Anchor–Doubleday [1956]) and novels such as Richard Yates's *Revolutionary Road* and Don Cousins's *It's Only Temporary*, Jurca proposes that *The Man in the Grey Flannel Suit* is the only novel that 'translates discontent into actual mobility'. Usefully *White Diaspora* closes by considering in brief contemporary novels by John Updike, Joyce Carol Oates, Frederick Bartheleme, Rick Moody, Richard Ford and David Gates. Provocatively Jurca suggests that the attention these novels now attract suggests that 'the suburb is understood to have contributed to the health of American letters rather than to its demise'.

In *Around Quitting Time: Work and Middle-Class Fantasy in American Fiction*, Robert Seguin addresses the perceived absence of class in the United States to question how this illusion continues to persist. He discusses the treatment of class in the fiction of Theodore Dreiser (*Sister Carrie*), Willa Cather (*A Lost Lady, The Professor's House*), Nathanael West (*The Day of the Locust*), John Barth (*The Floating Opera*) and, briefly, Don DeLillo (*White Noise*) and Ernest Hemingway (*The Old Man and the Sea*). Exploring the chosen writers' fictional treatment of the convergence of work and leisure, production and consumption, Seguin contends that the dynamics of social class are obscured (even as they are made central) by the blurring of the boundaries between these domains in the middle-class imaginary. In chapter 5, 'Into the 1950s: Fiction in the Age of Consensus', Seguin's reading of *The Floating Opera*, partly informed by Daniel Bell's *The End of Ideology: On the Exhaustion of Political Ideas in the Fifties*, argues that Barth's text depicts the middle classes as forming a 'serial culture', a culture in which 'things will indeed go on, but a silence, a strange inertia, will be at their heart'. In his postscript, Seguin considers *White Noise* as a descendant of the earlier texts discussed, a text which 'obsessively hovers over the problem of agency and in so doing produces a key literary presentation of the middle-class imaginary for our time'. This is a useful consideration of an under-represented topic.

Laura Hapke's accomplished study *Labor's Text: The Worker in American Fiction* spans over a century and a half of literary responses to workers and the work experience. Hapke contextualizes her readings within a crucial historical and political nexus. Crucially she places a keen emphasis on resisting the urge 'to defend manual toil by intellectualizing it'. This in itself reads as a provocative departure. The inclusive texture of this study, its detailing of the history of labour organization, industrial change and social transformations, succeeds in 'framing' an ambitious itinerary through shifting literary representations of the worker and the work environment. *Labor's Text* builds upon the pioneering work of critics such as Barbara Foley's revisionary feminist readings of 1930s proletarian literature. The final three chapters focus on post-war fiction, considering the representation of labour struggles during the Cold War, with its political backdrop of the House of Un-American Activities, the Civil Rights era and Vietnam. Approaching the fiction of the Cold War in the light of 1930s proletarian fiction, Hapke suggests there is a shift towards detailing 'the effects of social and economic forces on the individual rather than on the group psyche'. This psychological focus, she indicates, can be traced in the work of Willard Motley, Nelson Algren, Norman Mailer, Harriet Arnow and Ann Petry. The subsequent chapters chart how literary production, especially the development of 'magic realism', draws crucial attention to the frequently 'erased' labour histories of under-represented ethnic communities. Hapke also makes reference to representations of the blue-collar working class by examining the work of John Updike, John Cheever and, most prominently, Raymond Carver. Persuasively she suggests that we can approach Carver's stories as a site which interrogates the intersection of the self and work. *Labor's Text* acts as a compendium of extensive literary references. It also serves as an invaluable guide to any reader wishing to trace the dissipation of the radical political ambitions of 1930s fiction in post-war American writing.

In a similar cultural and historical vein M. Keith Booker's *Monsters, Mushroom Clouds and the Cold War* proposes that the science fiction of the post-war era can be read for signs of an incipient postmodernism. In many ways this is an interdisciplinary study since three chapters consider the political and social readings of alien invasion films and science fiction monster movies. But it also places a considerable focus on science fiction writing between 1946 and 1964. Interestingly Booker seeks to extend a definition of the 1950s as a neatly ring-fenced decade, arguing instead for a consideration of what he terms 'the long 50s'. In doing so he seeks to encompass a sense of continuity between post-war science fiction writing and the full range of American Cold War hysteria. He suggests that science fiction during this period chronicles a preoccupation with a sense of physical and social degeneracy and most importantly mirrors the anxieties of the cultural and political theorists of the period. The first chapter surveys the politics and the range of novels by major science fiction writers, such as Isaac Asimov's *Foundation Trilogy*, Frederik Pohl's *The Space Merchants* and Robert A. Heinlein's *Starship Troopers*. Considerable attention in this chapter is given to Philip K. Dick's novels *The World Jones Made* and *Time out of Joint*; Booker also examines the early science fiction writing in Kurt Vonnegut's *Player Piano*. The second chapter considers the post-Holocaust theme in both films and novels of the period and suggests how these works engage with issues such as alienation and conformity in addition to the more obvious reading of the threat of nuclear war. Amid the vast range of novels examined, considerable attention is given to George R. Stewart's *Earth Abides*, Bernard Wolfe's *Limbo* and Ray Bradbury's *Fahrenheit 451*. Usefully *Monsters, Mushroom Clouds and the Cold War* proposes that the tension between social conformity and a desire to assert individuation must be read as the erosion of polar oppositions which in turn anticipates the key tenets of the postmodern condition.

From one perspective Marcel Cornis-Pope's rigorous study *Narrative Innovation and Cultural Rewriting in the Cold War Era and After* investigates the development of an incipient postmodernism which *Monsters, Mushroom Clouds and the Cold War* closes upon. Cornis-Pope considers the Cold War in the light of competing political ideologies abroad and the tension between cultural uniformity and its disruption at home. He proposes that innovative American fiction during this period reflects a preoccupation with envisaging an 'alternative history of irreducible particularities, excluded middles and creative intercrossings'. His project is a vast and ambitious one since it chronicles the different narrative responses to problems of ontology, sociocultural division, realism and formalism. *Narrative Innovation* proposes that the tendency by literary critics to place in opposition deconstructive and representative or self-reflective practices creates a false dichotomy. Cornis-Pope encourages us to consider these two impulses as complementary approaches. By focusing on the novels of Thomas Pynchon and Robert Coover he initially examines how 'innovative' writing challenges Cold War 'narratives of containment' by subverting established master-narratives. He continues by considering the development of 'surfiction' and the postmodern feminist novel. Authors discussed are Walter Abish, George Chambers, Raymond Federman, Kenneth Gangemi, Madeline Gins, Marianne Hauser, Toni Morrison. Steve Katz, Clarence Major, Paul Metcalf, Ursule Molinaro, Gilbert Sorrentino and Ronald Sukenick. Cornis-Pope identifies two preoccupations in surfiction: first a sustained effort to dismantle the mimetic traditions of fiction, and second an attention to the process of the plot through self-reflexive digression or typographical design. Furthermore he suggests that post-feminism extends this project of disruption by creating narratives that rewrite cultural reality from alternative viewpoints. Common to all the chapters is an extensive reference to different theoretical approaches, ranging from postmodern representational theories and trauma psychology to performance theory.

In *Enemies Within: The Cold War and the AIDS Crisis in Literature, Film, and Culture*, Jacqueline Foertsch considers a correlation, which she initially locates in the late 1980s, between the symptoms of cultural hysteria as they relate to Cold War crisis in the Reagan years and the AIDS epidemic in America. Foertsch connects these responses in the American cultural imagination, which sees crises as 'plagues', to trace their treatment in a range of literary texts and films. She is particularly interested in the ways in which the AIDS-era text revises the Cold War text to cast 'a backward and insightful glance not only on its cold war original and the relationship between their respective eras but on problems and solutions from an earlier period that may bear significantly, curatively, on those of our own'. Writers considered include Margaret Atwood, Alan Hollinghurst, Tony Kushner, and—of interest in this section—Ray Bradbury, Kurt Vonnegut, Norman Mailer, Thomas Pynchon, Don DeLillo, Paul Auster, Tim O'Brien, Raymond Briggs, Armistead Maupin, Neil Bartlett, Peter Cameron, Robert Chelsey, Maggie Gee, Paul Monette and Philip Wylie. Foertsch discusses the 'doomsday' clock published in the atomic science journal *Bulletin*, a barometer of global nuclear threat, as a symbol of the countdown culture that characterizes contemporary America: 'In the shadow of this clock, life in the postbomb era itself is an endless counting down, an awareness of time and the momentousness of its movement towards midnight that bothers our dreams, diminishes our ability to care and love, and exacerbates our fears in the face of biological and environmental crises into hysterical searches for scapegoats and enemies within.' Describing recent American crises as 'postmodern nightmares', Foertsch discusses the ways in which 'postmodern plagues' infect contemporary culture and are central to the emergence and definition of specific literary genres: 'postapocalyptic and alterapocalyptic nuclear texts [and] pre-epidemic and intraepidemic AIDS texts'.

Foertsch is particularly interested in the gendered images of illness and the bomb in film and literary texts, which connects her work to that of Katie Hogan in a number of interesting ways. In *Women Take Care: Gender, Race and the Culture of AIDS*, centred on the impact of AIDS on American literature, Hogan explores stereotypes of 'good women' represented by the visual and print culture relating to AIDS: 'self-sacrificing mothers, caretaking sisters, nurselike lesbians, vigilant surrogate mothers, forgiving wives'. Hogan argues that AIDS texts reproduce a gendered paradigm of care that reinforces biases about race and sexuality. It is Hogan's contention that the validation of such female roles in connection to AIDS must be rejected in order to achieve an understanding of women's own health needs. She discusses the ways in which 'literary and visual responses to the pandemic, while breaking silence on women and AIDS, use traditional images of women to make the pandemic acceptable to white heterosexual Americans'. Hogan's focus is on how such images are formed in relation to epidemics, historically as well as in contemporary Western literature and culture. The writers she mentions include Harriet Beecher Stowe, Louisa May Alcott, Alice Walker, Toni Morrison, Sapphire and, briefly, Dorothy Allison. Hogan's text draws on a wide range of writers and critics of nineteenth- and twentieth-century literature and culture and will be of general interest to scholars in the field of American studies.

In Howe and Aguiar, eds., *He Said, She Says: An RSVP to the Male Text*, a range of women writers is discussed under the headings 'Religious Re-Inscripture', 'Sexual Re-Identification', 'Vintage Re-(Per)Versions' and 'Politically Re-Correct'. Howe and Aguiar address the ways in which women writers have responded to the male canon to 'enlarge, contest and re-animate the tradition itself', rather than merely forming their own canon. In the first section, Ruth Bienstock Anolik discusses female of retellings of Jewish tales with reference to the work of the contemporary Jewish American writers Allegra Goodman, Pearl Abraham, Rachel Goldstein, Marge Piercy and Cynthia Ozick. Unfortunately, due to a printing error, the essay is missing pages 33–41 in my edition and the second essay of the collection, on Lee Smith's *Fair and Tender Ladies*, is missing the first seven pages. Also of interest are the essays 'Lolita Talks Back: Giving Voice to the Object' by Timothy McCracken; 'I Will Not Wear That Coat: Cross-Dressing in the Works of Dorothy Allison' by Connie D. Griffin; 'Disobedient Daughters: (Dis)Inheriting the Kingdom of Lear' by Sarah Appleton Aguiar, in which there is a brief discussion of Anne Tyler and Jane Smiley; and 'To Speak with the Voices of Others: Kathy Acker and the Avant-Garde' by Svetlana Mintcheva.

In *Legacy of Rage: Jewish Masculinity, Violence, and Culture*, Warren Rosenberg presents a detailed study which connects the treatment of violence in foundational stories of Judaism with twentieth-century American literature. Rosenberg explores the stereotype that Jewish men are non-violent: 'erudite, comedic, malleable, nonthreatening, part nebbish, part schlemiel, Jewish men do not fight, they talk'. He complicates such stereotypes through his focus on 'sites where Western images of masculinity intertwine and clash with Eastern European Jewish proscriptions' as well as 'the powerful influence Westernization and Americanization have in engendering violent fantasies within Jewish men'. Rosenberg makes the point that violence is closely tied to construction of the other, and he feeds this observation into an exploration of gender, ethnicity and the repression of violence. For Rosenberg, an understanding of how oppositional images of masculinity are constructed might contribute to the transformation of gender roles, to the disconnection of traditional masculinity from violence. Drawing on men's studies, cultural studies, postmodern ethnic and Jewish studies, feminist film criticism and narrative theory, Rosenberg asks: 'What role does the representation of violence play in the formation of ethnic and gender identities, and, reciprocally, what role do these identities play in the creation of art, or any cultural product?' Writers considered include H. Leivick, Sholem Asch, Lamed Shapiro, Isaac Babel, Henry Roth, Philip Roth, Bernard Malamud, Saul Bellow, Norman Mailer, E.L. Doctorow, David Mamet, Mark Helprin, Cynthia Ozick and Tony Kushner.

In 'Recalling Home: American Jewish Women Writers of the New Wave' (*ConL* 42:iv[2001] 800–23) Janet Handler Burstein explores the ways in which recent writing by American Jewish women combines a postmodern awareness of the complexities of subjectivity (found in other American Jewish writing such as that of Philip Roth) with 'a persistent interest in the particular, constructive power of the search for origins' to rework discourses of 'home'. Writers and critics considered are Kim Chernin, Helen Epstein, Susan Rubin Suleiman, Eva Hoffman, Gerda Lerna, Marianne Hirsch, Rebecca Goldstein and Lilian Nattel.

The opening of David Brauner's *Post-War Jewish Fiction: Ambivalence, Self-Explanation and Transatlantic Connections* questions what exactly constitutes Jewishness and moreover whether a reply to this question grants us a clearer understanding of what characterizes American and British Jewish fiction. Brauner states that Jewishness itself is a multiplicity of often conflicting propositions: it can be a learned tradition, a belief system, a cultural construct, a race, a religion, a nationality, a sensibility, a historical legacy or even a metaphysical condition. Rather than presenting a definitive answer this study considers aspects of a shared transatlantic Jewish sensibility between American and British Jewish novelists of the post-war era. Brauner proposes that what they share is 'fundamental tension between self-assertion and self-denial' and a concern with protagonists who demonstrate an 'insatiable desire to acknowledge, advertise and *explain* their Jewishness'. His second chapter considers the representation of the relationship between Jews and anti-Semites in Arthur Miller's *Focus*, Bernard Malamud's *The Assistant* and Emily Praeger's *Eve's Tattoo*. These works are read in conjunction with novels by British Jewish authors: Frederic Raphael's *Lindmann* and Jonathon Wilson's *The Hiding*. Reflections on the Jewish anti-pastoral novel are discussed in relation to Saul Bellow's work with a reading of *Herzog*. Chapter 4 traces the emergence of the short story as a crucial genre for American and British Jewish women writers in addressing the aftermath of the Holocaust. Here Brauer pays specific attention to Cynthia Ozick's 'The Shawl' and 'Rosa', Lesléa Newman's 'A Letter to Harvey Milk', and Rebecca Goldstein's 'The Legacy of Raizel Kaidish'. *Post-War Jewish Fiction* concludes with a comparative reading of the fiction of Philip Roth and Clive Sinclair.

Christopher Douglas opens *Reciting America: Culture and Cliché in Contemporary U.S. Fiction* with a consideration of Bill Clinton's 1995 Loyalty Day Proclamation, a propagandistic call for Americans to take pride in a heritage of freedom through courage and sacrifice in which he connects anti-colonial struggle against the British with the Gulf War. Douglas states that his book 'begins with the premise that American identity is assumed by its citizens largely through the repetition, as recitation and performance, of different kinds of American discourses'. Drawing on Bakhtin's notion of heteroglossia as 'the stratifying, dialect-creating forces operating within a single language', Douglas discusses the ways in which seemingly oppositional political perspectives in the US are indebted to (and therefore absorbed by) the same kinds of clichéd discourses of Americanness as those recited by Clinton. He isolates four discourses at work in Clinton's speech: the first based on conceptions of the 'American Dream's' roots in the European Enlightenment's goal of progress; the second on the struggle against the tyranny of the British empire; the third on the moral heritage of the early revolutionaries; and the fourth on the virtues of the Constitution and the Bill of Rights. Douglas applies this model of the recitation of American discourses to four post-Second World War novels: Russell Banks's *Continental Drift*, Ralph Ellison's *Invisible Man*, Maxine Hong Kingston's *The Woman Warrior*, and T. Coraghessan Boyle's *East Is East*. He argues that Banks salvages an earlier ideal of the American Dream in order to reject its more recent degraded form, while Ellison rejects the discourse of the American Dream offered by Booker T. Washington, as well as the alternative discourse of the Communist party of the USA, in favour of the very individualism central to American founding fictions. Douglas contends that Kingston recites a narrative of Americanness, even as she revises it in relation to traditional Chinese stories, while T. Coraghessan Boyle's 'tale of cultural miscommunication' which brings together American clichés about the Japanese and Japanese clichés about America, 'is a type of "preoccupied" signification, a form of repeated semiotic material that short circuits its flexibility in representing the real . . . to form an impenetrable web of cultural and racial illusion'. Douglas makes the case that Banks and Boyle should be considered alongside 'classics' such as *Invisible Man* and *The Woman Warrior*, arguing that 'a productive dialogue can be held between ethnic minority and ethnic majority writers at the end of the twentieth century'. He also discusses the texts under consideration alongside a range of works by writers such as E.L. Doctorow, Norman Mailer, Richard Ford, Robert Stone, Raymond Carver, Don DeLillo and Robert Coover, historicist writers who question 'what America means and what it means to be American'. He concludes *Reciting America* with a discussion of the inaugural poems of Robert Frost and Maya Angelou, with reference to Sacvan Bercovitch's argument about the 'cultural self-sufficiency' of the United States. A somewhat familiar argument informs the project, but this is an interesting collection of material and comparison of texts.

In 'Teenage Wasteland: Coming of Age Novels in the 1980s and 1990s' (*Crit* 43:i[2001] 93–112) Kirk Curnutt interrogates the politics of despair that sets recent teenage novels apart from earlier novels such as J.D. Salinger's *Catcher in the Rye* and Sylvia Plath's *The Bell Jar*: 'Up through the 1970s, teenage resistance to social authority was such a pervasive motif in American fiction that the adolescent struggle for autonomy embodied for many critics the national struggle for self-reliance [whereas] in contemporary novels ... youth's disaffected disposition is credited not to the oppressiveness of adult authority but to a lack of it.' With reference to Brett Easton Ellis's *Less Than Zero*, Douglas Coupland's *Generation X* and Donna Tartt's *The Secret History*, Curnutt suggests that contemporary teenage novels counter an anti-authoritarian tradition to reassert the importance of the stability of home and family as part of a hunger to explain social crises, rescripting contemporary adolescent disaffection into a politics of repair.

In *Cop Knowledge: Police Power and Cultural Narrative in Twentieth-Century America* Christopher P. Wilson examines narratives of police power found in crime news, popular fiction and film to historicize methods of policing in America in relation to the police myths of American popular culture. Wilson is ultimately concerned with the ways in which such narratives support a climate of political conservatism. Of interest for this section is Wilson's consideration of Truman Capote, although Stephen Crane and Luis Rodriguez are also discussed.

James R. Giles opens *Violence in the Contemporary American Novel: An End to Innocence* with a discussion of the increasing involvement of children in violent crime in the US (as both victims and victimizers), which frames his focus on the work of a number of writers who are concerned with documenting and understanding the violence which has come to dominate perceptions of contemporary culture. Writers included are Sandra Cisneros, N. Scott Momaday, John Rechy and, of interest in this section, Don DeLillo, William Kennedy, Caleb Carr, Richard Price, John Edgar Wideman and Cormac McCarthy. Giles connects the work of the writers under consideration to the ways in which they 'explore the "systemic violence" originating in an oppressive and exploitive economic system that leaves blood in "every way of seeing" and, in so doing, give voice to the marginalized and seemingly voiceless "others" of America's inner cities'. Giles is concerned with the ways in which violence has ceased to seem extraordinary. He argues that contemporary texts which depict violence present it as 'a kind of random totalitarian force with roots in the very origins of the nation', and as such not intended to produce political change.

In *The American Thriller: Generic Innovation and Social Change in the 1970s* Paul Cobley discusses recent nostalgia for 1970s culture as a means of obscuring the social and political crises which dominated the decade and informed innovations in the genre of the thriller. Cobley defines the genre and attempts to recontextualize 1970s thrillers as texts in the process of transforming that genre in relation to their approaches to anxieties about crime, law enforcement, corruption and paranoia, as well as national crises such as Vietnam and Watergate. Taking a 'reader-oriented approach', he is keen to reconnect the 1970s thriller to its significance for readers during that decade, a significance he characterizes as various and multiple rather than monolithic. A range of films, television programmes and fiction is explored, and writers discussed include James Ellroy, Joseph Hansen, George V. Higgins, Elmore Leonard, Robert Ludlum, R.B. Parker, Ernest Tidyman and Joseph Wambaugh.

(b) Individual Authors
An extensive interest in revisionary readings of authors from the American South continued in 2001. The year marked a welcome addition to the existing body of scholarship published on the fiction of Flannery O'Connor. Two book-length studies, Cynthia L. Seel's *Ritual Performance in the Fiction of Flannery O'Connor* and Katherine Hemple Prown's *Revising Flannery O'Connor: Southern Literary Culture and the Problem of Female Authorship* tackle the author's work from decidedly different critical perspectives. Seel engages in close textual readings of O'Connor's short stories, and there are individual chapters dedicated solely to 'A Circle in the Fire', 'The Artificial Nigger', 'The Lame Shall Enter First', The River', 'The Temple of the Holy Ghost' and 'A Stroke of Good Fortune'. Drawing extensively on O'Connor's personal letters, marginalia and essays, Seel traces the use of ritual as a structural framework for the writing. She also considers ritual in terms of event or 'rites of passage'. Understanding ritual as a performative action in the text creates the opportunity to simultaneously evaluate O'Connor's own Catholicism and her interest in theological and psychological treatises. Approaches to O'Connor's work as a form of Southern 'grotesque' are by now established critical territory. *Ritual Performance* enervates this discussion by reflecting upon O'Connor's own interest in the less familiar theological enquiries of Teilhard de Chardin and Friedrich Hügel, the archetypal theory of Eric Neuman and William Lynch and, most importantly, the psychological investigations of Carl Jung. Drawing on this intertextual resonance in the texts, the book examines the sacred and profane. Cast in this light, ritual can be read in terms of initiation, mystery and even incarnation in the short stories. Illuminatingly the book closes with an extended discussion of how ritual patterns and archetypal structures perform a certain theatricality in O'Connor's work. Seel addresses how many of these texts have been translated into film versions and theatrical productions, and offers a comparative reading with the theatrical devices of Samuel Beckett and Antonin Artaud. This rigorous theosophical account of O'Connor's writing is unusual, yet does not shackle the author's work to a limited perspective, and the attention to individual stories is well judged.

Revising Flannery O'Connor addresses head-on O'Connor's ambivalent and often highly problematic representation of female gender within her short stories and fiction. Prown suggests that critical approaches have tended to valorize investigating a Southern regional identity and the influence of a Catholic credo as mutually exclusive preoccupations in O'Connor's work. While Prown certainly does not disavow the pertinence of these readings, she maintains that a problematic gap in the scholarship exists. She proposes that investigating O'Connor's ambivalent representations of female gender grants an expansive position from which to reconsider this problematic intersection of religion and Southern identity in the author's work. The study effectively places O'Connor within a discernible literary milieu, examining her relationship to the Southern agrarian and new critical movements. It delineates O'Connor's philosophical connections and strong identification with critics and writers associated with the Southern renaissance such as John Crowe Ransom, Allen Tate, Andrew Lytle and Robert Penn Warren. This linkage would appear to reinforce the perception of O'Connor as a latterday Southern conservative, but Prown deftly proposes that O'Connor's work orchestrates a certain muted if not 'encrypted' ambivalence towards the values espoused by these key figures. She argues that O'Connor's attempts to ally herself with a masculinist literary tradition were equally attempts to distance herself from a tradition of genteel women's writing. In Prown's words, we must read the author's use of violence and the grotesque, and her treatment of male and female characters, as strategies 'for transcending, neutralizing or denying her gendered self and its potential for upsetting the hierarchies on which her profession was built'. This reading of O'Connor as a subversive writer casts light on her writing's frequent resistance to a straightforward feminist analysis. Yet this evaluation is further complicated once one considers the self-consciously female-sexed voice which features in the manuscript versions of her writing. Initially it would seem that the published versions raise issues of misogyny, yet Prown reiterates that O'Connor's fiction demonstrates the use of masculinist narrative forms and male characters as vehicles for encoding representations of female identity and experience. Overall the book counterbalances situating O'Connor in a literary context with an extended textual analysis of both her longer fiction, *Wise Blood* and *The Violent Bear It Away*, and her short stories.

Extending the consideration of the relationship between the theological and O'Connor's work, Anne Carson tackles the apocalyptic texture of the author's writing. Her article '*Break forth and wash the slime from this earth!* O'Connor's Apocalyptic Tornadoes' (*SoQ* 40:i[2001] 19–27) focuses on three texts: *The Violent Bear It Away*, 'The Life You Save May Be Your Own', and 'Revelation'. She suggests that the symbol of the tornadoes in these three works must be read within the context of the grotesque and macabre as a form of 'ethical and spiritual regeneration'. Drawing on a sustained reference to Dante's *Divine Comedy* and O'Connor's correspondence, Carson proposes that the apocalyptic may be read as a regenerative force. This violence in the texts is compared to W.B. Yeats's formulation of the funnel-shaped 'gyre' as a symbol which illustrates both a historical cycle and its destruction. Paradoxically this explicit violence gestures towards the advent of an imminent spiritual possibility in O'Connor's work. Less insightful in considering the theological density of O'Connor's writing is a chapter in Jeffrey J. Folks's *From Richard Wright to Toni Morrison* (noticed above) entitled 'Physical Disability and the Sacramental Community in Flannery O'Connor's *Everything That Rises Must Converge*'. Folks assesses the relationship between the author's chronic illness, systemic *lupus erythematosus*, and her textual practice. Initially this would seem a productive line of enquiry: Folks does makes useful reference to O'Connor's correspondence and her attraction to the writings of de Chardin. But overall his argument that O'Connor's illness and creative practice serve a form of ethical enquiry is not articulated clearly enough. Indeed the weakness of this chapter is that its key terms, 'ethics' and 'morality' (or even O'Connor's own reference to a certain 'grace' in her writing), are not given a sustained focus. One is left wondering whether these terms, once applied to O'Connor's work, are as interchangeable as Folks's discussion implies.

Pollack and Marrs, eds., *Eudora Welty and Politics: Did the Writer Crusade?* attempts a concerted reappraisal of Welty's position as a woman writer of the American South. Pollack states that the volume stemmed from a frustration about Welty's critical reception as a minor regional writer, 'neither historically representative nor politically informed'. Taking its subtitle from an early essay by the author, this volume looks closely at how Welty's fiction and criticism can be read as a response to public and political corruption, racial apartheid in Mississippi, McCarthyism, and the Rosenberg trials. The ten essays attempt to develop a political vocabulary for approaching Welty's work, and unsurprisingly their perspectives on how the political is addressed and formulated in her fiction are markedly different. By focusing on *A Curtain of Green* Peggy Prenshaw investigates how political negotiations are rarely performed in the public domain in Welty's work. Instead she suggests they are displaced into the private sphere of domesticity, the traditional domain of women. Suzanne Mars chronicles Welty's unproclaimed lifetime of political reaction and the public views she expressed. In considering 'The Demonstrators' Suzan Harrison argues that Welty's short-story format is marked or 'encrypted' with various racial constructions. She proposes that the work can be simultaneously read as an attempt both to write race and also paradoxically to resist racial readings. Welty's fifteen years of composing *Losing Battle* (eventually published in 1970) are read in tandem with key events of the civil rights movement by Rebecca Marks, who proposes that, while race does not form an explicit rhetorical focus in the work, Welty's manipulation of narrative offers a coded and unsettling political commentary. Resistant to pigeonholing the author as a regionalist, Danielle Pitavy Souques considers the use of the self-portrait as an ambitious attempt to address American history, racial discrimination and social injustice. Barbara Ladd's study of Welty's non-fiction and photographs between 1935 and 1961 draws attention to her appeal to private life during times when fascist and totalitarian regimes threatened from abroad. This consideration is extended by Mars and Pollack's photographic 'essay', compiled from the Welty archive, which closes the volume. Remaining sections assess the relationship between the political, the private and the past in the author's work (Ann Romines), Welty's troubled view of the Rosenberg trial in *The Ponder Heart* (Sharon Baris), and a considered discussion of the relationship between pedagogy, politics and art in the light of Welty's own ambivalence to this triad (Noel Polk).

Taking his point of departure from T.S. Eliot's discussion of myth as a controlling strategy giving shape and significance to the 'futility and anarchy of contemporary history', Jim Owen examines the 'mythic method' of Eudora Welty's short fiction. His article 'Phoenix Jackson, William Wallace and King MacLain: Welty's Mythic Travellers' (*SLJ* 34:i[2001] 29–43) initially concentrates on the intertextual resonance of journeys undertaken in Welty's *Collected Stories*. Comparative readings of three short stories with epic Homeric journeys, Yeats's adaptation of 'The Song of the Wandering Aengus', romance, and classical mythology are introduced. Most importantly Owen insists that these allusions in Welty's stories are strategies for elevating the status of her protagonists, bringing into sharper focus the problems of memory and social readaptation. Moreover, in contrast to the modernist claim that myth somehow stabilizes a certain formlessness, Owen proposes that these allusions in the short stories impel a certain momentum, focusing on the process of the journey as opposed to its stated destination.

Welty's short fiction is given a further surprising contextual spin in Lionel Kelly's 'American Fat: Obesity and the Short Story' (*YES* 31[2001] 218–29). Kelly places Welty's short story 'A Memory' within the context of a comparative reading of contemporaneous work by Jean Stafford, Andre Dubus and Raymond Carver. The article in turn considers the various representations of obesity in the short-story form, ranging from the poetic, the parodic and the symbolic to obesity as a political motif and as an investigation of sexual hierarchies. Welty's work offers a consideration of the short-story form's preoccupation with moments of epiphany. The depiction of obesity in the story, Kelly suggests, brings into focus an ambivalent relationship between sexual sensibility and maternal intimacy. Indeed Kelly argues that this motif in the story emphasizes the adolescent protagonist's horror of the maternal and the familial. Also of interest is Géraldine Chouard's 'Ties That Bind: The Poetics of Anger in "Why I Live at the P.O." by Eudora Welty' (*SoQ* 39:iii[2001] 34–50).

Theodore R. Hovet and Grace-Ann Hovet address how, in Harper Lee's *To Kill a Mockingbird*, racial prejudice intersects with gender and class inequalities. Their article '"Fine Fancy Gentlemen" and "Yappy Folk": Contending Voices in *To Kill a Mockingbird* (*SoQ* 40:i[2001] 67–78) places an initial focus on the historical framing, critical reception and popular success of the novel. While the novel is set in the 1930s they suggest that the narrative refracts the civil rights campaigns of the 1950s in the American South. With some reference to the novels of Rebecca Harding Davies, Louisa M. Alcott, Harriet Beecher Stowe and Sarah Orne Jewett, the article investigates how the conventions of realism and regionalism combine with an essential dialogism to undermine the efforts of the narrator to impose a single narrative. This work poses a challenge to existing readings, which hold that the novel's 'poor white trash' characters are the primary cause and proponents of racism. The discussion contends that, in *To Kill a Mockingbird*, racism is 'part of a general pattern of exclusion and oppression which must be overcome before anyone can be said to be free'. Initially this statement may appear to dangerously generalize the novel into an all-inclusive humanism, but the critics back up their claim with an effective reading of the competing narratives which jostle in the novel, granting insight into its gender and class configurations.

Challenging configurations of race in the American South as a binary of black and white, Cynthia Wu urges the reader to reconsider Carson McCullers's strategies in her short-story collection *The Ballad of the Sad Café and Other Stories*. In 'Expanding Southern Whiteness: Reconceptualizing Ethnic Difference in the Short Stories of Carson McCullers' (*SLJ* 34:i[2001] 44–55) Wu proposes that the inclusion of European immigrant characters in the collection explores 'a new valence of race emerging in the New South'. The article draws certain parallels between McCullers's fiction and Southern labour history, making some reference to the socio-economic effects of the Great Migration. Wu focuses on two stories, the title story and 'Wunderkind', concentrating in particular on their representation of European Jewishness. Provocatively she argues that the absence of African

American characters in this volume mirrors a certain positioning of the Southern renaissance. More contentiously, she suggests that this absence is also an enabling device. In her words, the collection succeeds in 'isolating white ethnic difference' in order to 'reconceptualize white identities in the New South'.

Sarah Gleeson-White proposes that literary criticism has tended to frame the South's preoccupation with the grotesque in a negative light. The Southern grotesque, she suggests, has been read as closely allied to considerations of miscegenation and sexual deviance, and overall with a pessimistic vision of modernity. While her article 'Revisiting the Southern Grotesque: Mikhail Bakhtin and the Case of Carson McCullers' (*SLJ* 33:ii[2001] 108–23) does not dismiss the validity of these established claims, she urges us to reconsider the grotesque less in terms of alienation than of an *affirmative* quality focused on 'practices of regrowth, promise and transformation'. Mikhail Bakhtin's celebration of the carnivalesque forms the crucial premise for her argument. Drawing comparisons with the work of Truman Capote and Flannery O'Connor, the article considers McCullers's *The Heart is a Lonely Hunter*, *The Member of the Wedding* and *Clock Without Hands*. Her discussion centres on the grotesque as a focus on the body and as a repudiation of the classic ideal, with its indication of perfectibility and closure. The grotesque body, Gleeson-White argues, is transgressive: it disturbs but also 'challenges normative forms of representation'. This aspect of corporeality promotes considerations of gender construction and identity as both mutable, mobile and resistant to control.

Some less sustained attention was paid this year to contemporary Southern women writers. Essays included: '"You nothing but trash": White Trash Shame in Dorothy Allison's *Bastard Out of Carolina*' by J. Brooks Bouson (*SLJ* 34:i[2001] 101–23); 'Ellen Gilchrist's Women Who Would Be Queens (and Those Who Would Dethrone Them)' by Margaret D. Bauer (*MissQ* 55[2001–2] 117–31) and 'Into the Swamp at Oblique Angles: Mason's *In Country*' by Suzy Clarkson Holstein (*MissQ* 54[2001] 327–36).

Two essays appeared on William Styron's *Sophie's Choice*—Lisa Carstens' 'Sexual Politics and Confessional Testimony in *Sophie's Choice*' (*TCL* 47[2001] 293–324) and Bertram Wyatt Brown's 'William Styron's *Sophie's Choice*: Poland, the South, and the Tragedy of Suicide' (*SLJ* 34:i[2001] 56–67)—and three articles were published on Harry Crews: Anne Foata, 'Tragedy on the Road to Enigma: Ritual Death in Harry Crews's *The Gospel Singer*' (*SoQ* 39:iv[2001] 58–62); Jeff Abernathy, 'Agrarian Nightmare: Harry Crews' Dark Vision in *Naked in Garden Hills*' (*SLJ* 34:i[2001] 68–78); and Stephen Want, 'The (Over)exposed Body: Harry Crews's *Body*' (*Crit* 42:ii[2001] 155–66).

Vladimir Nabokov's *Lolita* is given a revisionary reading in 'Lolita Talks Back: Giving Voice to the Object', by Timothy McCracken (in Howe and Aguiar, eds., mentioned above). McCracken examines how Nabokov's narrative strives to manipulate a sympathetic response to Humbert Humbert. Mining the interstices of the text allows us to consider how Dolores Haze or 'Lolita' is framed as a fabricated object of male desire. McCracken argues persuasively that this dependency upon Humbert's narrative, combined with his flattery of the reader, essentially overwrites the history of a 12-year-old abused suburban schoolgirl. He suggests that Lolita 'becomes the eternally young *tabula rasa* upon which the older man may inscribe his new self'. Approaching *Lolita* in the light of Hélène Cixous's discussion of a female history written within the female body enables us to reconsider the young girl's perspective, which is silenced or buried in the text. Cixous's gesture to the 'white ink' of women's writing provides a useful strategy for reading a counter-memory against Humbert's personal romance of paedophilia. Usefully McCracken closes by considering female writers' responses to sexual abuse, in particular Paula Vogel's play *How I Learned to Drive* [1997], which he compares to Nabokov's novel.

A major study of Joseph Heller's *Catch-22* was published this year. Edited by Harold Bloom, *Heller's Catch-22: Modern Critical Interpretations* contains twelve new essays. Unsurprisingly perhaps the central preoccupations of this collection mirror the key tenets of *At Millennium's End*. The essays examine Yossarian's morality, the relationship between narrative and ethical commentary, and Heller's complex articulation of the ludic and the absurd in the novel. The moral education of Yossarian is given considerable attention in Mina Dosow's essay 'The Night Journey in *Catch-22*'. Drawing on the classical literary lineage of the *Odyssey*, the *Aeneid* and the *Divine Comedy*, Dosow examines Yossarian's itinerary as a symbolic journey to the Underworld. Challenging the preconception of Yossarian as the naive victim of a monolithic system, Stephen L. Sniderman argues that the character is the central crux on which the responsibility of the novel rests. Extending from this consideration of the ethical resonance in *Catch-22*, Leon F. Seltzer proposes that Heller's use of the comic or the absurd succeeds in exposing the inhumanities which are perpetrated by economic, social and political systems. Within this volume there are the more familiar intertextual and biographical analyses of the text. Marcus K. Billson reads the parallel between the novel and the biblical book of Genesis, and Walter James Miller charts the evolution of Heller's literary career, drawing attention to his later novels *Something Happened* and *Good as Gold*.

John Updike's work is given a specific interpretative focus in Marshall Boswell's *John Updike's Rabbit Tetralogy: Mastered Irony in Motion*. His study considers Updike's four-novel sequence which spans four decades: *Rabbit Run*, *Rabbit Redux*, *Rabbit is Rich* and *Rabbit at Rest*. Updike himself mentions that the sequence (built around his central character Harry 'Rabbit' Angstrom) was an attempt to create 'a coherent volume, a mega- novel'. Taking Updike's aim of a certain coherency and continuity as his starting point, Boswell initially considers the relationship between the novels and their historical background. Updike's use of found materials and popular culture is considered as an attempt to chronicle contemporary history in tandem with the experiences of the central character. But the primary thesis governing Boswell's study is the construction of an ironic commentary or investigation in Updike's work. Approaching the four novels as a composite whole, Boswell argues convincingly that we can trace the author's interest in the philosophy of Søren Kierkegaard, Paul Tillich, Karl Barth and Martin Heidegger throughout the tetralogy. Of central interest is Kierkegaard's proposition of 'mastered irony', which is drawn from the influence of Hegelian dialectics. Briefly, we can understand this term in Kierkegaard's work as an attempt to present two sides of an issue, leaving its paradox unresolved. In Kierkegaard's perspective the ironic author must deliberately master or control his irony. This control or mastery can be read as a deliberate organization of all the contradictory material so that the intended meaning of the work emerges from the differential play of its contradictory elements. Boswell argues that, applied to Updike's work, mastered irony can be approached as a device to 'inspire in the reader the process of existential self-questioning'. Above all, Boswell's nuanced treatment of the author's work insists on showing how the novels do not merely parrot or unpack Updike's philosophical interests. Rather, Boswell is interested in how these ideas are imbricated, transmuted and quietly activated within the fabric of Updike's novels. Also of interest is D. Quentin Miller's *John Updike and the Cold War: Drawing the Iron Curtain* (UMissP, not seen).

A sustained interest in the short stories and fiction of Kurt Vonnegut shows no signs of abating. Boone, ed., *At Millennium's End: New Essays on the Work of Kurt Vonnegut*, engages expansively with the author's work. Indeed the ten essays in this book are far from arid re-evaluations since they succeed in mobilizing earlier critical debates into startling new perspectives. This is above all a lively collection casting a wide net over many texts and extending the discussion from a focus on *Slaughterhouse-Five*. Importantly all these discussions share an impetus to update an evaluation of Vonnegut's work without immobilizing the fiction into predetermined theorizing. Jerome Klinkowitz assesses Vonnegut's undervalued role as an essayist, charting the evolution of the personal essay form in his work. He notes Vonnegut's increasing urge to anthologize his essay work alongside his shorter fiction, and pays particular attention to his collected volume *Palm Sunday*. The complex relationship between aesthetics, ethics, morality and responsibility forms the crux of the volume. Three essays address from various perspectives this complexity in Vonnegut's work. David Andrews, in 'Vonnegut and Aesthetic Humanism', examines *Bluebeard* as a response to the corruption of art. The seminal essay of the volume, Bill Gholson's excellent 'Narrative and Morality in the Writing of Kurt Vonnegut', identifies the author as a 'liberal ironist'. Drawing on Richard Rorty's term, Gholson proposes that the sheer indeterminacy and 'openness' of Vonnegut's texts challenge a prescriptive and predetermined moralizing. In this reading narrative technique has both an informing and a provisional mandate. Donald E. Morse extends this aspect of an ethical responsibility by focusing on Vonnegut's ambivalent relationship to ideas of human progress and evolution. Other essays compare the war experiences of Vonnegut and Hemingway (Lawrence R. Broer), and the relationship of his work to theories of quantum physics, technology, apocalypse, and science fiction (Loree Rackshaw, Harley S. Spratt, Todd F. Davis, and Jeff Karon respectively). Finally Kevin Boone and David Pringle examine film treatments of Vonnegut's work.

Challenging established approaches to William Burroughs's work, Jamie Russell's book-length study *Queer Burroughs* moves beyond considering the author solely in the light of the Beat movement, avant-gardism and postmodernity, addressing his work through a reading of sexual politics and what Russell suggests is the 'radical gay subjectivity' offered by the texts themselves. Surprisingly Russell's introduction alerts us that a queer critical reading of his novels virtually does not exist. Importantly Russell asserts that his project in this study is neither to 'dismantle' established readings of novels such as *Naked Lunch* and *Junkie* nor to inscribe Burroughs within the queer literary canon. Instead the volume presents an extended reading of Burroughs's novels in terms of queer thematics, gay political commitment and social concern. Provocatively he suggests that Burroughs's work can actually be read in opposition to the dominant tenets of gay American contemporary literature. The early novels *Junkie*, *Queer* and *Naked Lunch* are examined in terms of the gender identifications which they establish and their challenging of the dominant social paradigms of homosexuality in America at the time of writing. Interestingly Russell also considers Burroughs's interest in cut-ups not only as an inherited Dadaist aesthetic but as a metaphorical weapon with which gay men can reclaim control over both their bodies and their identities. This interconnection of both a sexual and textual poetics extends throughout the book. Overall *Queer Burroughs* proposes that William Burroughs's novels feed off the progressive expansion of the American gay rights movement, and moreover that the intersection of this history can be traced in the forty-year span of the author's career.

Burroughs himself grants us an insightful twist to the poetics of reading his work. He suggests that readerly reception is pure selection: 'The point is to scan out the message as it were, the message that is you.' Joseph McNicholas, in his article 'William S. Burroughs and Corporate Public Relations' (*ArQ* 57:iv[2001] 121–49), takes this proposition as a direction to examine the language, compositional strategies and social commentary of *Naked Lunch*. Convincingly he argues that Burroughs's writing must be read within the competing discourses of avant-garde experimentation and the corporate language of marketing, press and advertising. He suggests that the 'junk virus' and junkie of *Naked Lunch* operate as broad-ranging metaphorical critiques of consumer peddling, power lust, and mass hysteria. But, most importantly McNicholas emphasizes that there is a 'strategic' contradiction inherent in Burroughs's critique of advertising language and corporate image manipulation. One of the central paradoxes of *Naked Lunch* is that the critique of advertising culture and corporate jargon is situated or framed within the same linguistic codes and methods which govern these practices. The author deliberately leaves no space for ironic self-reflection or commentary. Essentially this clash of a system of values in the novel forces the reader to surrender any predetermined moral judgement. Moreover, the individual tasks set by advertising agencies, such as clipping, sorting, analysing, editing, proof-reading and typing, all coalesce within the novel's composition, while McNicholas also gives a useful commentary on the 'ephemerality' of the writing in *Naked Lunch* and the novel's sustained perseverance with narrative as a form of 'spectacle'. He argues in effect that individual events in the novel are there to be consumed independently of a totalizing structure.

Twelve years in its compilation, Lotringer, ed., *Burroughs Live: The Collected Interviews of William S. Burroughs, 1960–1997*, is a major additional resource to Burroughs scholars and researchers of the Beat generation. The volume contains nearly a hundred interviews with the author conducted over a period of thirty years. Two of its six sections are dedicated to introducing and contextualizing Burroughs's work. The remaining four sections are arranged chronologically and by location: 'Expatriate Journeys 1960–65'; 'London 1966–74'; 'New York 1974–81'; and 'Lawrence Kansas 1997'. These also include meditations in prose by Burroughs, reflecting on his poetics of composition, several translations from earlier European publications, and some contributions by Allen Ginsberg. This volume is a fascinating resource, extending to a compilation of obituaries published at the time of Burroughs's death, and one can appreciate the process of accumulation and revision which Lotringer's arduous project demanded.

Judie Newman's *Alison Lurie: A Critical Study* offers a comprehensive guide to Lurie's fiction, drawing on interviews, manuscript collections and Lurie's unpublished writings. Foregrounding Lurie's concern with utopianism, Newman explores the ways in which representations of community are consistently used to examine the 'boundaries between pragmatism and idealism, and to tackle issues of social conformity, engagement or detachment within a carefully circumscribed arena'. Newman argues against the widely held perception that Lurie's fiction is narrowly focused on marriage, the middle classes and morality to assert that she is profoundly engaged with questions of intellectual and social significance as they arise in the American context. A chapter is devoted to each of Lurie's nine novels, as they variously 'serve critical, even radical, aesthetic purposes within a popular form' to raise questions about transcendentalism and homosociality (*Love and Friendship*), homophobia (*The Last Resort*), the significance of popular culture (*The Nowhere City*), the religious cult (*Imaginary Friends*), domestic responses to Vietnam (*The War between the Tates*), remembering the American Depression (*Only Children*) and representations of transatlantic relations (*Foreign Affairs*).

Interest in Don DeLillo shows no signs of waning. A special edition of *Critique* (42:iv[2001]) is devoted to DeLillo, and includes six essays that cover the full range of his work to complicate its connection to postmodern frameworks of interpretation. In 'Wallpaper Mao: Don DeLillo, Andy Warhol, and Seriality' (*Crit* 42:iv[2001] 339–56) Jeffrey Karnicky discusses *Mao II* and *Underworld* with reference to DeLillo's interest in Andy Warhol, particularly as Warhol's presence in the texts raises questions about the connection between image proliferation in American visual culture and an understanding of social environment. Karnicky's discussion of Warhol seeks to expand discussions of image in DeLillo's work to move beyond the 'melancholy' frameworks provided by Walter Benjamin's formulation of 'aura' and Jean Baudrillard's discussion of simulacra: 'in the worlds of DeLillo's fiction, image proliferation is neither mourned not celebrated; it is strongly established as a matter of fact that cannot be ignored, as a creative force to be actively engaged'. Karnicky's essay asserts that, for both Warhol and DeLillo, there is a beauty and power revealed at the intersection between humanity and technology. In '"Like some endless sky waking inside": Subjectivity in Don DeLillo' (*Crit* 42:iv[2001] 357–66) Curtis A. Yehnert focuses on the ways in which DeLillo's attention to the details of his characters' inner lives contradicts critical perspectives which position DeLillo as a writer whose characters reflect the instability of the postmodern condition. For Yehnert, DeLillo 'uses his characters to contradict the poststructuralist claim that language constitutes subjectivity'. Arguing that DeLillo's characters are manipulating rather than manipulated, Yehnert suggests that DeLillo is concerned with representing the possibility of agency within (and despite) an uncertain and chaotic world, a position that is neither modernist or postmodernist. In '"Venerated Emblems": DeLillo's *Underworld* and the History-Commodity' (*Crit* 42:iv[2001] 367–83) Molly Wallace discusses *Underworld* to explore the representation of the 1950s in the 1990s, as well as the ways in which the text 'can be read to comment not only on the role of commodities in the construction of history, but also on the production of history as a commodity'. Wallace argues that *Underworld* not only explodes a nostalgia for the 1950s but also draws attention to the ways in which contemporary post-Cold War history effaces its own conditions of production. In 'Recycling Authority: DeLillo's Waste

Management' (*Crit* 42:iv[2001] 384–401) Jessie Kavadlo discusses Roland Barthes's familiar essay 'The Death of the Author' alongside DeLillo's foregrounding of his own reclusivity and refusal to discuss his work. Kavadlo argues that, although DeLillo ostensibly refuses the conventional role of author, 'his interviews, pictures, and personae suggest that perhaps the author as a figure, momentarily killed by poststructuralism, today seems ironically resurrected through DeLillo, as well as through the various adopted voices within his novels'. Kavadlo attends to the significance of waste in DeLillo's fiction to suggest that, just as his characters gain agency in the disposal of consumer goods, the author gains currency as a figure of authority through a process analogous to waste management. Kavadlo ends with the suggestion that DeLillo's position on silence reasserts Romantic and modernist constructions of the author with reflexivity and irony to construct an authorial stance which is 'unwilling to be diminished by poststructuralism and too smart to revive the authoritarianism of undemocratic modernism'. In 'Deft Acceleration: The Occult Geometry of Time in *White Noise*' (*Crit* 42:iv[2001] 402–15) Marion Muirhead employs the terminology of cybernetics, information theory and chaos theory alluded to in *White Noise* to consider the role of time in DeLillo's narrative strategies. Muirhead argues that 'use of time in *White Noise* conveys a sense of narrative pace and patterning that subverts the appearance of linearity and figures time as a multi-layered continuum ... the perception that technology is responsible for the acceleration of time and omnipotence of death evokes in Jack Gladney a nostalgia for the past and a terror of the future'. In 'Amazons in the Underworld: Gender, the Body, and Power in the Novels of Don DeLillo' (*Crit* 42:iv[2001] 416–36) Philip Nel takes a different tack in rereading DeLillo, which seeks to draw attention to the ways in which his fiction is concerned with the interaction of gender roles, media representations of the body and gendered power relations. While Nel argues that some of DeLillo's work has pornographic tendencies which support masculine structures of power, his fiction also explores how women are constructed by media images as well as critiquing violent masculinity as a cultural norm. Nel argues that when DeLillo 'approaches gender through media or investigates how masculinity and femininity interact with the performance of power ... [he reveals] the nuances of gender as a culturally enforced construct'. Nel's essay foregrounds a much neglected aspect of DeLillo's work and is a welcome contribution to this sophisticated collection of new readings.

Cormac McCarthy is considered this year by Susan Kollin in 'Genre and the Geographies of Violence: Cormac McCarthy and the Contemporary Western' (*ConL* 42[2001] 557–88) and John Blair, 'Mexico and the Borderlands in Cormac McCarthy's *All the Pretty Horses*' (*Crit* 42[2001] 301–7). Kollin explores the interconnected histories of the South and the West to discuss the development of the Western in relation to its dependence on the contributions and concerns of Southern literature, as well as offering a detailed critical discussion of McCarthy's contradictory position as writer of the Western/anti-Western. Blair's essay offers a fairly superficial reading of *All the Pretty Horses* as it relates to myths of American development and their frustration; the article suffers somewhat from a limited critical framework. Of interest and not reviewed last year is a special edition of *The Southern Quarterly* devoted to Cormac McCarthy's *Border Trilogy*, edited by Edwin T. Arnold and Diane C. Luce (*SoQ* 38:iii[2000]).

In *A Trauma Artist: Tim O'Brien and the Fiction of Vietnam*, Mark A. Heberle presents a detailed study of O'Brien's writing as it relates to theories of post-traumatic culture, exploring the 'psychic terrain ... that is variously linked to the war but not defined by it'. Heberle is interested in how O'Brien employs trauma as narrative device to reveal the ways in which Vietnam, as imaginative space, comes to stand for a post-war American condition of uncertainty and loss. Drawing on recent conversations with O'Brien, as well as previously published interviews, Heberle offers extremely useful and detailed readings of the full range of O'Brien's work.

Published on Kathy Acker this year is 'Voice in Kathy Acker's Fiction' (*ConL* 42[2001] 485–513) by Kathryn Hume, which problematizes established criticism that focuses on the ideological desirability of a lack of voice in Acker's work. Hume asserts that 'the voice in her fiction is so recognizable and so rabidly determined to resist all manipulation from outside that it troubles many assumptions about postmodern decentering ... the irreducibility, consistency, and repeated appearance of the voice suggest that Acker might usefully be studied as postmodern romantic'. Other contemporary writers who receive regular but limited coverage are John Barth, Charles Bukowski, William Gibson and Anne Tyler.

Also published this year are the following essays: Marjorie Worthington's 'Done with Mirrors: Restoring the Authority Lost in John Barth's *Funhouse*' (*TCL* 47:i[2001] 114–36); Tamas Dobozy's 'In the Country of Contradiction the Hypocrite is King: Defining Dirty Realism in Charles Bukowski's *Factotum*' (*MFS* 47[2001] 43–68); Tony Myers's 'The Postmodern Imaginary in William Gibson's *Neuromancer*' (*MFS* 47[2001] 887–909); Heidi Slettedahl Macpherson's 'Comic Constructions: Fictions of Mothering in Anne Tyler's *Ladder of Years*' (*SoQ* 39:ii[2001] 130–40); and Caren J. Town's 'Location and Identity in Anne Tyler's *Ladder of Years*' (*SoQ* 40:i[2001] 7–18).

Published this year but not received (to be reviewed next year): Paul Jahshan, *Henry Miller and the Surrealist Discourse of Excess: A Post-Structuralist Reading* (Lang) and Cyrus R. K. Patell, *Negative Liberties: Morrison, Pynchon and the Problem of Liberal Psychology* (DukeUP).

4. Drama

(a) General

The *Journal of American Drama and Theatre* 13:ii[2001] contains several essays on various periods of early American theatre. Maura L. Cronin, 'The Yankee and the Veteran: Vehicles of Nationalism' (*JADT* 13:ii[2001] 51–70) examines some post-revolutionary plays (Royall Tyler's *The Contrast* [1787], James Nelson Barker's *Tears and Smiles* [1808] and A.B. Lindsley's *Love and Friendship* [1810]) to look at how they contribute to the formation of national values and identity; Julian Mates, 'William Dunlap's *A Trip to Niagara*' (*JADT* 13:ii[2001] 85–96) is an account of Dunlap's last play [1828]; Walter J. Meserve and Mollie Ann Meserve outline some 'Aspirations, Challenges, and Accomplishments: American Literary Dramatists of the 1850s' (*JADT* 13:ii[2001] 1–22); and in 'Media Mania: The Demonizing of the Theatrical Syndicate' (*JADT* 13:ii[2001] 23–50) Vincent Landro offers such a convincing defence of the six men who virtually controlled the American theatre of a hundred years ago that his services should be retained by Enron. The remaining piece in this issue deals with a play of more recent vintage: Alice Petersen, '"Wishing on the Eye of the Horse": The Concept of "Entity" in Gertrude Stein's *Listen to Me*' (*JADT* 13:ii[2001] 71–84), provides a detailed reading of this 1936 play in the light of Stein's concept of 'entity', which refers to an object that, in Petersen's words, 'possesses a lucky autonomy and hermetic independence'. In another issue of the same journal, Marian Thomson outlines the formal properties and ideological contours of a popular sub-genre in 'The Crook Play' (*JADT* 13:i[2001] 1–35).

Oxford University Press's *American Theatre: A Chronicle of Comedy and Drama*, the previous volumes of which were written by Gerald Bordman, is completed by Thomas Hischak's fourth volume, which covers the period from 1969 to 2000. The title of the series is a little misleading, as in fact the volumes survey the New York theatre only, but this is otherwise an invaluable resource that allows one to situate a given play in relation to prevailing theatrical trends. In Hischak's case, of course, that means a survey not only of Broadway but also, more importantly in most respects, of off-Broadway and off-off-Broadway; as he puts it, 'theatre in New York during much of this period could be summarized as Neil Simon on Broadway, Sam Shepard Off Broadway, and the Ridiculous Theatrical Company Off Off Broadway'. As with all who seek to survey the American dramatic scene, Hischak faces a problem with the fluidity of generic boundaries: thus 'puppet presentations, magic shows, multi-media performance pieces, and musicals are not included', but a number of one-person shows are. Plot summaries and other factual information are incorporated within the text, but brief biographies of playwrights and some other individuals are placed in boxes, scattered throughout the text in an unsystematic and somewhat confusing way, since it is often unclear at what point in the survey a given playwright should be deemed to have become a significant figure. Bringing this material together in an appendix would have been more convenient. In other respects, however, Hischak has done a fine job in completing Bordman's mammoth undertaking.

It is a testament to the expansion of smaller-scale, non-Broadway playwriting, and to Hischak's industry, that at 504 pages his volume is longer than the third in Bordman's series, *American Theatre: A Chronicle of Comedy and Drama, 1930–1969*, which appeared in 1996; while a reminder, if any were needed, that the American theatre is defined as much by the musical as by the drama (to the latter's almost total erasure on Broadway) is provided by the appearance this year of the third edition of Bordman's *American Musical Theatre: A Chronicle*, which clocks in at over 900 pages. On the other hand, when one turns to Bordman's entry for a given recent season, the total number of new musicals mounted is invariably rather small, a necessary result of the oft-analysed economic conditions prevailing in the New York theatre that contribute so decisively to the product presented on stage. Another view of the history of Broadway theatre is to be found in Brooks McNamara, 'Broadway: A Theatre Historian's Perspective' (*TDR* 45:iv[2001] 125–8).

Early products of the American theatre economy form the subject of Roger A. Hall's *Performing the American Frontier, 1870–1906*, an account of the Wild West shows, dramas and melodramas that have previously been examined with exemplary lucidity in Jeffrey D. Mason's *Melodrama and the Myth of America* (Indiana UP [1993]). Hall covers a vast range of material to demonstrate that, although the received perception of these productions as gun-toting action stories of conflict between settlers and natives has some basis in fact, the reality is that the majority do not dramatize the confrontation with an indigenous Other but are instead sentimental romantic melodramas 'which happened to be set on the frontier'. Less surprising is that the plays almost invariably present derogatory portraits of all those of non-northern European descent, with the frontier becoming a site of both paradisal edenic promise and the descent into savagery. Where Hall claims new ground is in the interpretation and evaluation of these potential contradictions, arguing that what Mason regards as a collapse into mythologizing melodrama should instead be recognized as a productive exploitation of paradox. There is detailed discussion of the best-known works, including the Buffalo Bill shows, Frank Mayo's *Davy Crockett*, and David Belasco's *The Girl of the Golden West*, contextualized within a prodigious amount of material on the frontier dramas of the period as a whole. While Hall's account does little to change one's perspective, the wealth of detail makes this one of the essential guides to the subject.

American Drama 10:ii[2001] is a special issue on American drama and ethnicity. It includes interviews by Norma Jenckes with playwrights Jose Rivera (*AmDram* 10:ii[2001] 21–47) and Caridad Svich (*AmDram* 10:ii[2001] 88–103), and three essays. Jon D. Rossini, '*Marisol*, Angels, and Apocalyptic Migrations' (*AmDram* 10:ii[2001] 1–20) explores the relationship between subjectivity and environment in Rivera's play, arguing that in its treatment of New York as a 'border space' the eponymous protagonist 'is freed from her body and experiences a different form of bordered existence, one both ethnic and transcendent'. Rivera 'does offer a way out', in which 'something must be lost—identity, spatial orientation, life—in order to reach a possibility of transcendence in which to re-orient the self in relation to the world'. The title of Kurt Bullock's 'Famous/Last Words: The Disruptive Rhetoric of Historico-Narrative "Finality" in Suzan-Lori Parks' *The America Play*' (*AmDram* 10:ii[2001] 69–87) threatens a tough read, a fear not dispelled by the opening clause: 'History, itself an index of time and space, of individual and event, finds itself supported by, if not constructed upon, a series of sub-indexical markers.' As often happens, once one gets past the self-conscious theoretical camouflage one discovers an illuminating article, in this case the treatment of Parks's meditation on notions of finality encapsulated in such phenomena as 'last words' and endnotes. It should be noted, however, that the essay is not really about ethnicity at all, and therefore one has to feel that it has been included in this special issue largely because of Parks's ethnicity, which seems a retrograde step. Çigdem Üsekes, '"You always under attack": Whiteness as Law and Terror in August Wilson's Twentieth-Century Cycle of Plays' (*AmDram* 10:ii[2001] 48–68), points out that, despite the relatively few white characters on Wilson's stage, there are many offstage, associated with a persecuting legal authority. There is a certain crudity to the language ('In his plays, Wilson denounces Euro-Americans who implement and carry out a twisted system in the name of law and order and who act on their infinite greed') that tends to produce a troublingly simplistic view of a highly complex playwright: Üsekes thinks Wilson has a 'format' and 'knows how to get his message across without having to agitate and alienate his white audience'. With friends like these, does Wilson need Robert Brustein?

For a more persuasive range of responses to the currently critical issues in African American drama one need look no further than Elam and Krasner, eds., *African*

American Performance and Theater History: A Critical Reader, which is perhaps the single most useful collection on African American theatre yet to have appeared. The crucial word here is 'theatre': as Elam notes in his introduction, the anthology 'proceeds from the assertion that, at its inception, the American "race question" is inherently theatrical', and thus the emphases of the book fall rather more on questions of performance and 'constructedness' than on analyses of dramatic texts, as indicated in the headings the editors have given to the book's four sections: 'Social Protest and the Politics of Representation', 'Cultural Traditions, Cultural Memory, and Performance', 'Intersections of Race and Gender', and 'African American Performativity and the Performance of Race', with a concluding 'roundtable discussion with senior scholars'. Each section has some discussion of playwrights, however. Margaret B. Wilkerson argues for Lorraine Hansberry as a more politically radical dramatist than is often conceded, while Sandra D. Shannon, in examining 'Audience and Africanisms in August Wilson's Dramaturgy', argues for the need to understand Wilson's plays in the light of what the editors refer to as 'cultural memory', here the memory of Africa in the imaginative and performative world of Wilson's African American characters and audiences, whom Wilson sees as Africans first and Americans second. 'Cultural memory' is also a term used by Kimberly D. Dixon, here in reference to the experience of migration, which she treats as a metaphor for the transgression of boundaries of gender and race that help to constitute the 'creative nomadism' informing the work of several contemporary African American playwrights, among whom Suzan-Lori Parks is prominent. And Elam himself offers a rare study of Charles Gordone's Pulitzer-winning *No Place To Be Somebody* in a nuanced examination of how performance attests to yet undermines persisting notions of 'blackness'. These studies of plays and playwrights mesh with several broader concerns of Elam and Krasner's book: for example, in 'Uncle Tom's Women', Judith Williams notes the persistence of certain representations of racial difference deriving from the nineteenth century, while the contested legacy of the Black Arts movement, often regarded as troublingly essentialist and misogynistic, is also evident. Mike Sell argues for the movement's productive effects as political agitation (see also Sell's '[Ed.] Bullins as Editorial Performer: Textual Power and the Limits of Performance in the Black Arts Movement', *TJ* 53[2001] 411–28); but Henry Louis Gates, in a reprinted essay ('The Chitlin Circuit'), questions the claims to 'authenticity' that tends to inform debates around the movement, instead arguing for the merits of a different, widely derided set of theatre practices visible in the 'Chitlin circuit'.

   The dominant issues in African American theatre studies, as this volume attests, are still invigorated by the continuing fallout from the Wilson–Brustein debate of January 1997, an event whose ramifications also inform Angela C. Pao, 'Changing Faces: Recasting National Identity in All-Asian(-)American Dramas' (*TJ* 53[2001] 389–409), which discusses the effects of Asian casts performing 'non-Asian' roles in productions of Arthur Miller's *Death of a Salesman* and Eugene O'Neill's *Long Day's Journey into Night* and *Ah! Wilderness*. As with Elam and Krasner's collection, Pao's analysis is informed by an interdisciplinary approach to questions of ethnicity, performance and America drama. Another essay on non-traditional casting to begin with reference to August Wilson's speech on 26 June 1996, which so incensed Brustein, is Glenda E. Gill's 'The Triumphs and Struggles of Earle Hyman in Traditional and Non-Traditional Roles' (*JADT* 13:i[2001] 52–72). For a sympathetic discussion of the problems facing a now little-regarded, white Southern playwright creating African American characters in the 1920s, see James Potts, 'Dubose Heyward and the Politics of Representation: A Mote in the Critical Eye' (*JADT* 13:i[2001] 82–98).

Related topics are also raised in several pieces on dramatists in *African American Review* 35[2001]. Elizabeth J. Heard, 'August Wilson on Playwriting: An Interview' appears in *AAR* 35[2001] 93–102, while Wilson's *Joe Turner's Come and Gone* is examined in James R. Keller's 'The Shaman's Apprentice: Ecstasy and Economy in Wilson's *Joe Turner*' (*AAR* 35[2001] 471–9), which argues for 'the centrality of shamanism to the structure of the drama'. In the same issue, Joy L. Abell's 'African/American: Lorraine Hansberry's *Les Blancs* and the American Civil Rights Movement' (*AAR* 35[2001] 459–70) qualifies the widespread view that Hansberry's play is principally an indictment of colonialism in Africa by noting that 'it was written by an African *American* for an *American* audience', and thus should also be seen 'as a commentary on race relations in early 1960s America'. Since the play was written in the early 1960s Abell can make the case without difficulty, though she does stick her neck out in suggesting that Hansberry may have set the play in Africa to enable her implicitly to criticize Martin Luther King and Malcolm X while tracing connections between the struggles on the two continents.

It was a quiet year for *Modern Drama* on the American front. Markus Wessendorf, 'The (Un)Settled Space of Richard Maxwell's *House*' (*MD* 44[2001] 437–57) provides a close reading of a play by a new dramatist whose style Wessendorf characterizes as 'minimalist, formally rigorous, and anti-expressive … run[ning] the risk of being mistaken for heightened amateurism or bad theatre'. The best-known play of a much more familiar figure, Maria Irene Fornes, is considered in the same issue in Piper Murray, '"They are well together. Women are not": Productive Ambivalence and Female Hom(m)osociality in *Fefu and her Friends*' (*MD* 44[2001] 398–415). Murray seeks to qualify what she considers the two dominant readings of the play—the first arguing that 'the psyches of Fefu and her friends have been inscribed by male dominance' and that therefore 'the most significant bond that exists between the play's all-female cast would seem to be their common interest in making a place for themselves within that structure'; the second 'see[ing] Fefu and her friends as a positive presence in their own right'—and argues instead that central to the play is an ambivalence revolving around the question of performance, and how performance relates to what Murray sees as a relatively untheorized arena of 'female homosociality from the point of view of homosocial (including, but not exclusively, homosexual) desire'.

(b) Individual Dramatists

Brenda Murphy's *O'Neill: Long Day's Journey into Night* appears in Cambridge's now well-established Plays in Production series. Restrictions of space in the series format compel a selective approach to the production history: here Murphy has decided to devote around a third of the book to the play's development from conception to first production, the emphasis falling on Carlotta's role in negotiating with publishers and producers and, fascinatingly, on the actors' preparations for the premiere. Following this, Murphy provides an inevitably sketchier overview of several major productions, first in English and then in translation, and concludes with a survey of some of play's transformations into other media. Those familiar with other volumes in the series will recognize the constraints it places on interpretation—Murphy's account is largely factual, although conducted with her usual elegance—and as she remarks, the volume will serve as a basis for further research, not as the last word. One would have welcomed a more expansive treatment of some of the archival material Murphy examines in her first chapter, but this is a solid contribution to a useful series, and to the study of O'Neill's play. I have not yet seen Zander Brietske, *The Aesthetics of Failure: Dynamic Structure in the Plays of Eugene O'Neill* (McFarland [2000]) or Madeline C. Smith and Richard Eaton, *Eugene O'Neill: An Annotated International Bibliography, 1973 through 1999* (McFarland [2001]).

In a note on 'O'Neill's *The Rope*' (*Expl* 60:i[2001] 35–6), Michele Valerie Ronnick suggests that the phrase 'dirt puncher', coined in this play, may owe something to the 1870s noun 'cowpuncher'. Lorna Fitzsimmons, in 'Capitalist Dispossession in O'Neill's *More Stately Mansions*' (*NConL* 31:ii[2001] 8–10) briefly offers a range of defences of this little-regarded, unfinished play, suggesting that as autobiographical self-revelation it complements *Long Day's Journey into Night*, and that 'O'Neill succeeds in exposing significant threads within capitalist ideology—secularized Calvinism, pragmatism, and materialism—as potentially internecine when greed predominates'.

In recent years the *Eugene O'Neill Review* has placed less emphasis than previously on biographical pieces, and more on critical discussion of single plays. The trend is continued in the latest issue, which is largely given over to essays of the latter kind. These include Diya M. Abdo, 'The Emperor Jones: A Struggle for Individuality' (*EONR* 24[2000] 28–42), a competent if not especially original close reading of the play that argues for Jones as 'an individual', as opposed to a representation of African American men in general; and Zander Brietzke, 'Tragic Vision and the Happy Ending in *Anna Christie*' (*EONR* 24[2000] 43–60), which walks a well-trodden road in identifying the melodramatic propensities of O'Neill's endings, but argues that *Anna Christie*, a play in which this awkwardness is particularly marked, contains seeds of the mature vision of the late, major plays. Miriam M. Chirico, 'Moving Fate into the Family: Tragedy Redefined in *Mourning Becomes Electra*' (*EONR* 24[2000] 81–100), is a lucid account of 'four significant revisions in [O'Neill's] manuscripts as he moved from a classical paradigm to a more contemporary application of tragedy: the deliberate elimination of the word "fate," the emphasis on self-punishment, the use of questions that lead to self-examination, and the removal of the figure of Cassandra. These four revisions register O'Neill's gradual transformation from a classical understanding of tragedy, revolving around unseen gods, to one that locates tragedy within the immediate setting of the family.' Lisa Miller carefully disentangles some of the Greek source material of the same play in 'Iphigenia: An Overlooked Influence in *Mourning Becomes Electra*' (*EONR* 24[2000] 101–12). Another essay in this issue that takes Greek myth as its starting point is Daniel Larner, 'Dionysus in Diaspora: O'Neill's Tragedy of Muted Revelries' (*EONR* 24[2000] 13–19), which takes O'Neill's tragedies, especially *The Iceman Cometh*, to be dramatizations of 'the Dionysian Living Death'. Larner makes good use of a comparison to *King Lear*, but the familiar dangers of approaching particular texts by way of mythic paradigms are well illustrated in Julia White, '*The Iceman Cometh* as Infertility Myth' (*EONR* 24[2000] 113–20), which draws on Jungian archetypes and Joseph Campbell's *The*

Hero with a Thousand Faces (PrincetonUP [1949]) in elucidating what she sees as the 'mythic world' of the play. Such accounts are rarely incisive because, by definition, Campbell's 'monomyth' is universally applicable and therefore lacks persuasive force at the level of detail.

The issue also contains a short biographical account by Madeline C. Smith and Richard Eaton of a tangential figure, John Francis, as well as three performance-based pieces, of which two are given over to interviews: James R. Fleming, 'O'Neill Beyond Borders: A Bengali *Desire Under the Elms*' (*EONR* 24[2000] 61–72), is a discussion with the play's adapter, Sudipto Chatterjee, while Sharon O. Watkinson, 'Two Journeys to Wilderness' (*EONR* 24[2001] 73–80), contains conversations with the directors of two productions of *Ah! Wilderness*. Also included is Sheila Hickey Garvey's 'New Myths for Old: A Production History of the 2000 Broadway Revival of O'Neill's *A Moon for the Misbegotten*' (*EONR* 24[2000] 121–33).

The remaining essay in this issue, Robert E. Byrd's 'Unseen, Unheard, Inescapable: Unseen Characters in the Dramaturgy of O'Neill' (*EONR* 24[2000] 20–7), has some interesting local observations to make on the plays; but it is revealing that, for Byrd, 'In America, the first major writer to vigorously explore and use the unseen character was Eugene O'Neill.' There are those who would give that honour to Susan Glaspell; and Byrd's argument could be seen as a late example of the tendency to marginalize Glaspell in pursuit of the creation of O'Neill as 'father' of serious American drama. More widespread publication of Glaspell's plays (or at least of *Trifles*), and a developing body of critical analyses, have gone some way towards redressing the balance but, as Barbara Ozieblo demonstrates this year in *Susan Glaspell: A Critical Biography*, Glaspell is in many ways her own worst advocate. She tended to subordinate herself in her relationships with men, and one might extend this to include the literary relationship with O'Neill, whose relentless construction of himself as a major figure could hardly form a starker contrast. Similarly, while there is any amount of material that can be used by the biographer of O'Neill, Ozieblo's research is hampered by the relative paucity of documentation: Glaspell destroyed her letters and left behind little that was not characterized by the tendency towards self-effacement that ironically contributes to the patriarchal narrative of American theatre history which those advancing Glaspell's claims are attempting to resist. Given the peculiar difficulties associated with her subject, Ozieblo does a fine job in carving out a distinctive identity for Glaspell alongside O'Neill, George Cram Cook, and the other men in her life.

J. Ellen Gainor, *Susan Glaspell in Context: American Theater, Culture, and Politics, 1915–48* provides a broad range of perspectives on Glaspell's plays. Each chapter is dedicated to a single play (or, in one chapter, a group of one-act plays). Gainor commendably avoids any totalizing narrative or theoretical perspective, instead 'making social/political/historical connections with the plays and discussing issues of literary form or subgenre and theatre history that they represent'. Gainor's approach is distinctive in emphasizing the oft-overlooked humour of the plays, although one might have hoped for a more detailed engagement with the texts themselves. For example, while there is a valuable chapter on the one-act play in America, one the one hand it is symptomatic of a tendency to give greater priority to a historical and theoretical analysis of form and genre than to questions of 'culture and politics' (though these are certainly present); on the other, this formalist emphasis nevertheless leads at times towards treating the plays at too great a remove, with too much space given to general questions of genre and to summarizing and combating the secondary material, and not enough given to keeping the plays themselves in the foreground. And the debate about whether or not Glaspell was a feminist soon becomes sterile. But these qualifications should not detract from a recognition of Gainor's achievement: this is a most impressive book, looking well beyond the limited scope of previous studies to position Glaspell as a writer actively engaged with the theatrical, social and political contexts of her time.

Duffy, ed., *The Political Plays of Langston Hughes*, brings together four dramatic works—*Harvest, Angelo Herndon Jones, De Organizer*, and *Scottsboro, Limited*—by this key figure of the Harlem Renaissance. Duffy structures her introductory discussions of the plays within a debate about whether Hughes as a professional writer found leftist causes convenient because they provided him with ready material and a paying audience, or whether instead the plays demonstrate a more heartfelt commitment to left-wing ideas. This is not very promising; neither is Duffy's deeply strange revelation that 'In the preparation of this manuscript, I was strongly encouraged to employ a semiotic approach to Hughes' scripts, basing the analysis of the texts on the interpretive guidelines of Umberto Eco.' She does not reveal the name of the weirdo who gave her this idea, but fortunately he or she is soon forgotten as Duffy much more sensibly decides to ground the ensuing discussions of the plays in terms of genre, rhetoric, and the left-wing circles and causes that engaged Hughes throughout the 1930s. The book is most valuable, of course, for bringing together four previously unpublished works. Also on Hughes is Carme Manuel's '*Mule Bone*: Langston Hughes and Zora Neale Hurston's Dream Deferred of an African-American Theatre of the Black Word' (*AAR* 35[2001] 77–92). For Manuel, what made the collaboration most potentially fruitful (although a notorious disagreement between the two writers meant that it was not staged in their lifetimes) was a shared interest in folklore and oral tradition, an interest that Manuel situates within the contexts of the Harlem Renaissance and Alain Locke's 'New Negro'; he also considers the piece in the context of today's 'Black Aesthetics'.

Critical discussion of Tennessee Williams in recent years has tended to focus on questions of miscegenation and cannibalism, tropes of incorporation and abjection that explore boundaries of self and Other. Some of these concerns inform Rachel van Duyvenbode's 'Darkness Made Visible: Miscegenation, Masquerade and the Signified Racial Other in Tennessee Williams' *Baby Doll* and *A Streetcar Named Desire*' (*JAmS* 35[2001] 203–15). Van Duyvenbode concentrates on the characters of Silva Vacarro and Stanley Kowalski, who are of foreign origin yet consider themselves American; on to them, van Duyvenbode argues, Williams maps his 'own veiled fantasies of the dark Africanist other' and a history of fascination by and fear of miscegenation that finds its outlet in the Southern Gothic that infuses Williams's sensibility. Less ambitious is 'The Metaphysics of Tennessee Williams' (*AmDram* 10:i[2001] 11–37), in which Robert Siegel suggests that the ancient philosophical duality of mind and body is ever present in the playwright's work. Although one might have doubts about this approach, and indeed about other binary oppositions which, as Siegel correctly states, have characterized much discussion of this playwright (and which receive their necessary deconstruction in analyses such as van Duyvenbode's), his analysis does place the treatment of sexual and gender identity, for example, in potentially productive contexts.

Another noticeable trend in Williams scholarship in recent years, symptomatic of a general reorientation in the field as a whole, is the shift away from considering dramatic texts in isolation, and towards looking at the drama as but one, albeit dominant, mode in which the major writers in this area work. This flight to interdisciplinarity is perhaps one reason for the (perhaps temporary) falling-off of studies of Arthur Miller, Edward Albee and Sam Shepard, for example, and the turn towards figures such as Williams and David Mamet, who are prominent in more than one field. Recently there has been an extensive range of articles on Williams's screenplays and short stories, for example, while this year saw two essays that place Williams's drama in interdisciplinary contexts: Philip C. Kolin, '"A Play about Terrible Birds": Tennessee Williams's *The Gnädiges Fraulein* and Alfred Hitchcock's *The Birds*' (*SoAR* 66:i[2001] 1–22) and Gary Richards, 'Scripting Scarlett O'Goldberg: Margaret Mitchell, Tennessee Williams, and the Production of Southern Jewishness in *The Last Night of Ballyhoo*' (*SoQ* 39:iv[2001] 5–16), which explores some of the many connections between Alfred Uhry's 1997 play and Williams's work. There is an account of some 'Korean Productions of *A Streetcar Named Desire*' by Byungho Han (*JADT* 13:i[2001] 36–51).

In *Richard Foreman*, the editor Gerald Rabkin brings together a generous selection of previously published material, including critical essays, reviews and interviews, as well as several essays by Foreman. Some brief notes on one of Foreman's plays are to be found in Kenneth Bernard's 'Bad Boy Foreman: Some Observations on Richard Foreman's *Bad Boy Nietzsche!*' (*AmDram* 10:i[2001] 87–90).

Leslie Kane has edited or co-edited two books on David Mamet this year. *David Mamet in Conversation* provides an excellent scholarly resource, bringing together twenty-six interviews with the playwright from a wide range of sources and from all stages of his career. Mamet is a provocatively lucid commentator on his work and suggests innumerable connections with all manner of texts. Many of the radio and television conversations appear for the first time in print in this volume, and Kane has taken an unusual course in transcribing the hesitations and circumlocutions of the discussions, making Mamet a warmer, more vulnerable and personable interviewee than the fearsomely articulate and confident figure he can appear to be either in print or when appearing in public.

With Christopher C. Hudgins, Kane has also edited *David Mamet: Gender and Genre*. The editors' introduction notes the accusations of misogyny that have so often surrounded this playwright's work, accusations that are well represented in Kellie Bean's essay on *Oleanna* in this volume. The standard rebuttal—that women exert power over the men in various ways and, in particular, that their marginalization on his stage reveals the emptiness of his male characters' lives—is illustrated here in the contributions of Imtiaz Habib and Karen C. Blansfield, while Robert Skloot's essay, also on *Oleanna*, typifies a third position that notes the ambivalence in Mamet's treatment of gender relations. While the question of misogyny is certainly a pertinent consideration for many of the contributors, it has always appeared a reductive way of looking at such a rich body of material, and the volume in fact offers multiple approaches to Mamet's work while giving a fair indication of the range of genres he has explored. For example, Ilkka Joki writes on Mamet's first novel, *The Village*, while in the first substantial essay to deal extensively with Mamet's plays for children Thomas P. Adler notes that in fact they deal with the imaginative dream-life and desire for communion of adult audiences, and that all owe a debt to Thornton Wilder. Adler's discussion of *The Frog Prince* is especially helpful. Janet V. Haedicke pays particular attention to *American Buffalo* and *Speed-the-Plow* in arguing that the attraction to the Oedipal narrative that characterizes much of Mamet's formal organization and treatment of adult relationships is undermined by a parodic or ironic treatment that problematizes the plays' overt masculinity. Also alert to the element of parody in Mamet's work is Richard Brucher, who notes that the spectator is distanced from the eponymous hero of *Edmond*, the play operating less as realistic tragedy than as a dark urban comedy informed by the ironic sensibility of Thorstein Veblen's critique of capitalism. Brucher also makes productive use of a comparison to Eugene O'Neill's *The Hairy Ape*. Several essays discuss Mamet's first film as director, *House of Games*, including Hudgins, Steven Price (alongside *Speed-the-Plow*), and Diane M. Borden, in a challenging essay rooted in psychoanalysis and semiotics. Borden argues that *House of Games* and Mamet's third film, *Homicide*, stimulate the desire for meaning while finally thwarting it, producing effects that she situates within the Freudian uncanny or 'the sublime, where meaning is constructed by, yet ineffably lost in, language'. Relationships between parents and children, which have come to the foreground in some of Mamet's more recently staged works, are explored in essays by Leslie Kane and Linda Dorff, both of whom write persuasively on *The Cryptogram*. The book as a whole at first sight threatens to restrict itself too tightly to an already well-rehearsed debate about gender; in practice, genre is much more to the fore, and the volume gives a good sense of the scope of Mamet's writing and the range of interpretative possibilities it provokes.

In 'Differing Dramatic Dynamics in the Stage and Screen Versions of *Glengarry Glen Ross*' (*AmDram* 10:i[2001] 38–55), Robert I. Lublin notes that Mamet's screenplay for James Foley's 1992 film reduces the complexity of the play by introducing a new character whose success in salesmanship indicates possibilities of achievement unavailable to the characters in the stage version. This is true enough; but the suggestion that such a character in any way contradicts 'the epic theme of an entire society on its progression towards decay' is curious, unless one believes that the possession of an expensive watch is proof against the decline of the West. In the same issue, Steve Ryan's 'David Mamet's *A Wasted Weekend*' (*AmDram* 10:i[2001] 56–65) is an enjoyable and all too short discussion of Mamet's excellent teleplay for an episode of *Hill Street Blues*. Ryan notes that the published script is probably an earlier draft of the screened episode, argues for the success of the script as a teleplay, and situates it within some of the thematic emphases of Mamet's work in general.

Robert Combs compares Mamet to one of his contemporaries in 'Slaughtering Lambs: The Moral Universe of David Mamet and Wallace Shawn' (*JADT* 13:i[2001] 73–81), focusing on *Edmond* and *Aunt Dan and Lemon*. Combs accurately states that these playwrights 'have created characters who identify themselves with the destructive forces operating in their societies' yet who 'do not quite realize what they have done'; it does not quite follow from this, I think, that members of the audience cannot understand them 'without admitting to themselves their own moral confusion and complicity with evil'. Shawn's plays seem to generate this kind of excessive affective claim: there is something similar in Robert M. Post, 'Theater as Persuasion: The Plays of Wallace Shawn' (*AmDram* 10:i[2001]

66–86), which aims 'to explore major ways in which Shawn tries to get his audience to think and possibly act by dramatizing some of the harsher realities of life'. The mimetic and humanistic assumptions here are somewhat at odds with the Brechtian techniques Post rightly sees as characteristic of Shawn's drama; the danger that this will lead to both contradiction and an unsatisfactorily simplistic chain connecting 'life', play and affective response is ever present, not least in Post's conclusion that Shawn 'believes the remedy to the sad condition of the world mirrored in his plays is to better ourselves, to become truly moral, to improve our inner landscape so the world around us will echo this purified inner life'.

The play that more than any other has dominated critical discussion of American theatre in the 1990s is considered from yet another angle in Dennis A. Klein, '*Angels in America* as Jewish-American Drama' (*Modern Jewish Studies* 12:iv[2001] 34–43), while the title of Roger Bechtel's '"A Kind of Painful Progress": The Benjaminian Dialectics of *Angels in America*' (*JDTC* 16:i[2001] 99–121) immediately brings to mind the most powerful critique of Tony Kushner's keynote work: David Savran's 'Ambivalence, Utopia, and a Queer Sort of Materialism: How *Angels in America* Reconstructs the Nation' (*TJ* 47[1995] 207–27). Savran's essay explored Kushner's appropriation of Walter Benjamin's figure of the 'angel of history' in arguing that any play which achieves the near-unanimous approval of critics must be failing if it aims at political radicalism, a failure Savran locates in its evasion of dialectics. Bechtel is unimpressed by what he sees as the 'idealized leftist agenda' behind such criticism, finding it to be drawn from a nostalgic desire for Marxist revolution, and arguing that 'Claims that *Angels* is insufficiently dialectical or opposed to Benjamin's derisory notion of progress prove false upon a closer reading of Benjamin and the play, which ... exhibits a historical sensibility very much akin to Benjamin's.' For Bechtel, both writers find themselves in a historical situation in which the left is in danger of disappearing altogether, with Kushner's response lying in the counter-hegemonic possibilities of 'identity politics'.

A valuable corrective to the tendency to restrict comment on Kushner to *Angels in America* is provided by James Fisher, *The Theater of Tony Kushner: Living Past Hope*, which includes chapters on each of the dramatist's four longer plays as well as detailed coverage of his shorter pieces, adaptations, unpublished pieces, poetry and essays. In this wide-angle perspective the controversy over Kushner's appropriation of Benjamin appears too narrowly focused: Brecht (and not Benjamin's study of Brecht) emerges as the central figure, accompanied by Tennessee Williams and Thornton Wilder. Fisher's prose seems a little dry, his explication of influences and contexts perhaps too dutiful and polite given the vehement arguments Kushner's work has provoked; but as the first book to cover the whole career, and as a level-headed introduction to a writer of dazzling complexity, it could hardly be bettered.

5. Native, Asian American, Latino/a and General Ethnic Writing

The too early recent death of Louis Owens, novelist, essayist and critic of mixed Choctaw, Cherokee and Irish background, deprives Native American writing of one of its leading presences. His *I Hear the Train: Reflections, Inventions, Refractions* therefore turns out to be a last *omnium gatherum*, a reminder not only of his best strengths but of what would likely have been still in prospect. Its twenty or so pieces of autobiography, fiction and critique, together with some compelling photography, offer a wide sweep to embrace considerations of mixedblood family legacy (his 'Finding Gene', a memoir of his brother, could not read more affectingly); life in the Choctaw rural south, and then in California and the Washington Cascades as firefighter and ranger; his academic career; overseas travel in Paris, Italy and Spain; coyote and other storytelling, and literary analysis of contemporaries from Gerald Vizenor to Michael Dorris. Owens's special gift was hard-won intellectual clarification, an ability to use life and theory (and there is plenty, ranging from Fanon to Barthes) in the interests of understanding both his own history and that of the different self-expressions of art and word of a Native America which both shaped him and which, in turn, he helped shape.

Jace Weaver's *Other Words: American Indian Literature, Law, and Culture* offers interdisciplinary soundings, discursive essay-work for the most part conceived and published through the 1990s. As strong a piece as any is to be found in the book's opening chapter, 'In Other's Words: Literature and Community', a rebuttal of any 'supposed, singular Native worldview'. He argues for what he calls 'communitism': the Native writer if in one sense self-voice, then also, overlappingly, and by history, the community-participant voice. The collection has its unevennesses, not least in the occasional nature of some of the reprinted reviews. But there remains plenty to get your teeth into, notably chapters on Karl May and Indians, the Native American Graves Protection and Repatriation Act (NAGPRA), and the role in Native story and belief-systems of trickster as Sacred Fool.

Nelson and Nelson, eds., *Telling the Stories: Essays on American Indian Literatures and Cultures*, thirteen essays derived from the American Culture Association's 1997 meeting in San Antonio, Texas, and given over to analysis of oral and written Native texts, yields a steady if not exceptional trove. The language essays include a spirited piece on trickster resistance to post-Columbian evisceration of indigenous speech (by Scott Manning Stevens), an anatomy of Alaskan Haida narrative (by Jeane C. Breinig), storytelling and gender in the Makitare creation myth as told in the *Watunna* (by Heather Brooke Bucher), and oral subtexts in Mari Sandoz's *These were the Sioux* (by Malcolm A. Nelson) and Leslie Marmon Silko's *Ceremony* (by Robert M. Nelson). In other pieces on recent written literary work, Jeri Zulli argues for an anti-essentialist, and beyond Native as against white binary, reading of D'Arcy McNickle's *The Surrounded*; Blanca Chester shows how James Welch in *Fool's Crow* uses landscape to complicate, and undermine, usual white-frontier ideology; John K. Donaldson develops a helpful anatomy of Native American sleuth fiction, including Tony Hillerman's dozen Navajo-centred novels, Sherman Alexie's *Indian Killer* [1996] and Louis Owens's *The Sharpest Sight* [1992], along with writing by A.A. Carr, Martin Cruz Smith, James D. Doss and Mercedes Lackey; and Tom Machie argues, rather too briefly, for the intertextual link between Louise Erdrich's *Tales of Burning Love* [1996] and Hawthorne's *The Scarlet Letter*.

Paradoxa: Studies in World Literary Genres 15[2001] devotes its entire issue to 'Native American Literature: Boundaries and Sovereignties' under the editorship of Kathryn W. Shanley. It has a lively span of more than thirty essays, interviews and reviews. Of the literary-critical contributions there should especially be noted Louis Owens's 'As If an Indian were Really an Indian: Uramericans, Euramericans, and

Postcolonial Theory' (*Paradoxa* 15[2001] 170–83), which, with typical incisiveness, shows how 'the colonizing gaze' as developed in the work of Homi Bhabha, Gayatri Spivak and Dipesh Chakrabarty can be reworked to apply to Native America and its best-known texts of subversion and resistance by the likes of Momaday, Vizenor, Silko and Erdrich. More locally focused readings include Simona Fojtova on Gerald Vizenor's *Manifest Manners* as Bakhtinian and transgressive text (*Paradoxa* 15[2001] 86–97) and Elvira Pulitano on his *Darkness in Saint Louis Bearheart* as not only about the envisioning of a Native America caught up in hyper-real history but itself hyper-real text (*Paradoxa* 15[2001] 241–62); Peter Alan Froehlich and Joy Harris Philpott on Leslie Marmon Silko's *Ceremony* as reverse captivity narrative (*Paradoxa* 15[2001] 98–113); and Jane Haladay in a well-taken reading of the comic vein in the poetry of Simon Ortiz and Carter Revard (*Paradoxa* 15[2001] 114–31). A further bonus is Kathryn Shanley's interview with James Welch (*Paradoxa* 15[2001] 17–37), an attractive, and vernacularly delivered, overview of both his own writing from *Winter in the Blood* [1974] onward and the landscape of contemporary Native literature.

Three literary-historical volumes bear witness to the extending breadth of scholarship on Native American culture. Neil Schmitz's *White Robe's Dilemma: Tribal History in American Literature* examines Mesquakie cultural tradition, from its origins in the Great Lakes area and its encounter with the French through to the eventual, and against the odds, settlement in Iowa. The account does scrupulous good service, placing Mesquakie tribal perception and values at the working centre, whether in its consideration of White Robe as early culture hero, or its depiction of the Mesquakie people as a longtime self-financing community, or its discussion of a literary tradition which has shown every scepticism about anthropological case-study, and to include both literary forerunners such as Black Hawk and Black Elk and contemporaries such as Ray Young Bear and Georges Sioui. The upshot amounts to savvy scholarship, full of edge and provocation.

Joni Adamson's *American Indian Literature, Environmental Justice, and Ecocriticism: The Middle Place* explores a grid of ecological and Native reference: on the one hand spatial-geographic writings such as Edward Abbey's *Desert Solitaire* [1968], and on the other literary texts, including Simon Ortiz's *Fight Back* (reprinted in *Woven Stone* [1992]), Louise Erdrich's *Tracks* [1988], the verse of Joy Harjo's *In Mad Love and War* [1990] and Leslie Marmon Silko's *Almanac of the Dead* [1991]. The account at times risks earnestness, not to say rather indulgent self-positioning about teaching and the classroom. But it does open up—Chiapas to Black Mesa, Laguna to Chippewa country—the ways in which Native fiction has taken up the politics of environment in an America too often seemingly bent upon its despoliation.

Shari M. Huhndorf's *Going Native: Indians in the American Cultural Imagination* examines, in detail, and with a raft of telling examples, how 'Indians' have been assigned a slew of stereotypical roles in the 'performance of national identity'. She takes off from *Dances with Wolves* as Hollywood fabrication into an interlinking deconstruction of government-held artefacts, popular cinema like *Nanook of the North*, Forrest Carter's literary fakery in *The Education of Little Tree* [1968], New Age 'Indian' film and lore, and National Museum of the Indian exhibits. Her account is bracing, much of the nostalgia and desire built into 'If only

I were an Indian' (the phrase taken from a Czech documentary film) shown up as a dependence on false 'Indians', and so, accusingly, on false US history.

In *Sifters: Native American Women's Lives*, Theda Perdue assembles thirteen brief bio-histories, each written by a different hand. The gallery runs from Pocahontas as a mythic but actually little-known Powhatan woman, dead at 21 on her return from London to Virginia, through to Ada Deer, born on the Menominee reservation in Wisconsin, widely admired for her lifetime's activism in the name of tribal sovereignty and an eventual stalwart in the Bureau of Indian Affairs. Other portraiture looks to Molly Brant as revolutionary-era Mohawk clan mother; Mourning Dove, the Salish-Okanogan woman who wrote under the pen-name of Christine Quintasket; and Alice Lee Jemison, a leading Seneca nation presence in fighting for Native land and treaty rights. Each of these accounts acts as a working synopsis, a tribute to a line of historic Native women as players in the making of America.

A long and rightly recognized prime focus in the writings of Alexander Posey, Muskogee Creek poet and journalist, is landscape, whether his sense of it is in high Romantic terms or, contrarily, in terms of mock-epic. In 'Alexander Posey's Nature Journals: A Further Argument for Tribally-Specific Aesthetics' (*SAIL* 13:ii–iii[2001] 49–66) Craig Womack gives the issue a keen, not to say combative, airing. He looks, in turn, at the Creek–Oklahoma 'homeland' dimensions of Posey's river journals, his folkloric Rabbit tales, and the shrewd deadpan-folksy satire of the Fus Fixico letters. Each is used to urge Native-centred readings, with a number of swipes feistily aimed at 'the postcolonial lobby', MLA committees on Native culture, and non-Native criticism in general.

In *The Novels of Louise Erdrich: Stories of her People*, Connie A. Jacobs writes a dutiful, highly conscientious, overview of the six fictions to date, replete with maps and a helpful foray into Turtle Mountain Ojibway history. The account can at times veer too close to plot summary and conscientious annotation. But that is not to underestimate Jacobs's insights into, say, *The Beet Queen* as a 'connected web of family tales', or *Love Medicine* as the story portraiture of 'a culture in transition', or the narrative uses of Anishinaabe twin mythology in *The Antelope Wife*. Jacobs offers a reader's companion to Erdrich and her fiction, in both contour and detail.

Julie Barak begins her 'Un-Becoming White: Identity Transformation in Louise Erdrich's *The Antelope Wife*' (*SAIL* 13:iv [2001] 1–23) with a reprise of the expanding domain of 'whiteness studies' before bearing down upon how Erdrich deals with their implications for *The Antelope Wife*. Focusing on the figure of Scranton Roy, a rare white presence in Erdrich's fiction, she tracks 'whiteness' in its different degrees and manifestations in the lives of Klaus and Mary Shawano, Richard Whiteheart Beads, Rozin, and Callie and Zosie Roy. A mixedblood dynasty this may be, shadowed, and often enough embattled and hexed, by inter-racial genetics. Nonetheless, and as Barak convincingly demonstrates, it evolves through the generations into its own kind of dynastic self-possession. The upshot, as the essay very intelligently conveys, amounts to an eclectic Native family 'web' replete with its own 'beading and quilling and weaving stories'.

In another well-taken piece of excavation Jeff Karem's 'Keeping the Native on the Reservation: The Struggle for Leslie Marmon Silko's *Ceremony*' (*American Indian Culture and Research Journal* 25:iv [2001] 21–34) begins with Silko's relationship with her novel's publisher, Richard Seaver. Her resistance to Seaver's initial attempt to excise the 'world-historical' dimensions in *Ceremony* was amply justified: it gives a confirming larger resonance to Tayo's healing quest. In this Karem goes against standard interpretation, such as that of Alan Velie or Shamoon Zamir, regarding them as infinitely too localist. Tayo's 'flow of consciousness' extends beyond Laguna country, which is anything but to deny its own specific cultural complexity, to a more epic remit of nuclear war and destruction, the witchery of global eco-damage and transnational power politics.

For Page Rozelle in 'The Teller and the Tale: History and the Oral Tradition in Elizabeth Cook-Lynn's *Aurelia: A Crow Creek Trilogy*' (*AIQ* 25:ii[2001] 203–15) the constituent three novels connect 'political history with everyday tribal stories and traditional myths'. Cook-Lynn, the argument suggests, is best situated within the tradition of Dakotah tribal storytelling. Her protagonist in *Aurelia*, Aurelia Blue, moreover, serves as fictional self-refraction. Not the least of this lies in Aurelia's concern to act as the story-custodian of family, joining the figures of Jason and Blue as the trilogy's other key co-storytellers. For Cook-Lynn, in other words, 'story', oral-into-scriptural, serves two overlapping ends: narrative as performative energy in its own right while, at the same time, supplying the means by which the Dakotah Nation looks to speak, to write, and always to remember, its own historic meaning.

Herman Melville as intertextual presence in the fiction of Thomas King is given challenging exposition in Robin Riley's 'Babo's Great-Great Granddaughter: The Presence of *Benito Cereno* in *Green Grass, Running Water*' (*American Indian Culture and Research Journal* 25:iii[2001] 27–46). Riley moves well beyond evident echoes in naming, like Babo Jones and Sergeant Cereno, into a consideration of how the story is told, whose view presides, and who, finally in the novel, exerts authority over whom. Babo Jones, on this reckoning, differs from his Melvillian namesake in not retreating into silent stare, a head upon a pole. Rather, Jones assumes Coyote's trickster stance, playful, feisty, and always transformational in tactics of voice and defiance of arbitrary rule. To an extent this does less than full justice to Melville's own story trickeries, but it throws up a genuinely stimulating comparison.

In becoming a leading, if controversial, heir to the generation of Momaday, Erdrich, Silko, Vizenor and Welch, Sherman Alexie has increasingly begun to win scholarly dues. Stephen F. Evans's '"Open Containers": Sherman Alexie's Drunken Indians' (*AIQ* 25:i[2001] 46–72) tackles head-on some of the negative criticism which designates his writing as 'gadfly' (Kenneth Lincoln) or too given to 'the deficit model of Indian reservation life' and thereby 'trash or fraudulent or pop' (Elizabeth Cook-Lynn). Evans seizes upon the issue of the 'drunken Indian' figure to be met with in Alexie, whether Michael White Hawk in *Reservation Blues*, or the uncles in the poem 'Futures' (in *The Business of Fancydancing*), or, notably, Dirty Joe in *The Lone Ranger and Tonto Fistfight in Heaven*. For Evans, to see these figures as mere stereotype is a serious misreading of the irony at work throughout, of each careful undercutting of drink and its consequences, and with it of Alexie's genuine if unsentimental fund of sympathy. The essay speaks persuasively of 'critical misunderstanding': too easy a reduction of Alexie's characterizations.

In 'Another Fine Example of the Oral Tradition? Identification and Subversion in Alexie Sherman's *Smoke Signals*' (*SAIL* 13:i[2001] 23–38) Jhon Warren Gilroy addresses the film version of *Smoke Signals*. If indeed it is a buddie road movie, it at the same time lays about Native stereotype with well-turned fervour. Gilroy uses a

sequence of case-instances: the Arizona police chief's surprise at being told that in
Victor he has an Indian who does not drink and his bafflement at his 'mock-warrior'
pose alongside Thomas Builds the Fire; Thomas's response that the two of them
would better be regarded as Tonto and Tonto rather than the Lone Ranger and
Tonto; the reverse car-driving as a send-up of 'otherness' on the Coeur d'Alene
reservation; and the parodic, roistering 'John Wayne Song'. Thomas Builds the
Fire's own proliferation of stories, in addition, can be seen as a yet further kind of
narratorial bridge to the reader, at once canny, inventive, and always disruptive of a
fixed 'Indian' image.

Stuart Christie takes on Alexie's controversial portrait of John Smith in
'Renaissance Man: The Tribal "Schizophrenic" in Sherman Alexie's *Indian Killer*'
(*American Indian Culture and Research Journal* 25:iv [2001] 1–19). He sees in
Smith not just a figure of displacement but 'the ultimate postmodern signifier of
mixed-blood madness: the nothing of nothing'. He alights on Smith's experience as
orphan, his being twice adopted, the mentoring he receives from the schizoid priest
Father Duncan, and his recurrent homelessness. Smith's suicide leap, argues
Christie, indeed confers upon him a negative 'Indian' death, a bitterly ironic 'brown'
destiny. But the essay also asks if it is too easy a line to think Alexie may have
played into cliché by so dooming Smith, figuring mixedblood birth as predestined
blight, anonymity, or even murderousness. This, its author suggests, would be to
miss Alexie's much subtler point: the historical non-necessity, as against the
inevitability, of Smith's fate.

In her *Contemporary Chicana Literature: Bernice Zamora, Ana Castillo, Sandra
Cisneros, Denise Chávez, Alma Luz Villanueva and Lorna Dee Cervantes*, which
arrived too late for inclusion last year, Deborah L. Madsen does an exemplary job in
setting out the landscape of achievement of these six authorial mainstays of
literatura chicana. She elucidates, accessibly and with great local acuity, contextual
issues of a feminism of colour, Chicano patriarchy and canons of femininity, and the
stock of female myth to include La Malinche and La Llorona. The individual
readings do great justice, whether to the flourish of Bernice Zamora's poetry in
Restless Serpents [1976], Ana Castillo's epistolary-postmodern verve in *The
Mixquiahuala Letters* [1996], Sandra Cisneros's intimacy and rite-of-passage
nuance in her story cycle *Woman Hollering Creek* [1991], Denise Chávez's vision
of the Latina body in *The Last of the Menu Girls* [1986], Alma Luz Villanueva's
unflinching eco-feminist writing, from poetry like *Bloodroot* [1977] to the novel
The Ultraviolet Sky [1988], or Lorna Dee Cervantes's important uses of class and
gender dynamics, and of the West Coast as inner location, begun in her landmark
poetry collection *Emplumada* [1981]. The intelligence with which Madsen maps
this range of Chicana literary voice deserves every credit.

Charles M. Tatum proffers *Chicano Popular Culture: Que Hable el Pueblo* as
essentially a classroom primer, to include essay topics: a mapping of everyday
cultural sights, sounds and words throughout the Chicano spectrum. In music he
invokes *corrido* tradition, the Tex-Mex singing of Selena and the historic West
Coast sound of Richie Valens. Film calls up landmarks such as *The Ballad of
Gregorio Cortez* [1982], *El Norte* [1984] and what Tatum calls 'Hollywood
Hispanic films' such as *Zoot Suit* [1981] and *American Me* [1992], in which the
actor Edward James Olmos has long been a presiding force. The volume makes a
real contribution in its account of media: newspapers from the *La gaceta de Texas*

(*The Texas Gazette*) to the United Farm Workers' journal, *El malcriado* (*The Brat*) and the television and cable of widely viewed Spanish-language channels like Univisión. The literary sections look to an established cast list of Gary Soto, Tomás Rivera, Rudolfo Anaya, Rolando Hinojosa, Estela Portillo Trambley and Sandra Cisneros, but also to Chicano mystery writing by Michael Nava and Manuel Ramos. The visual dimensions of *chicanismo* are given their focus in the analysis of church, muralist, and home-decorative art, of which not the least important aspect has been the design features and adaptations of lowrider cars. The book yields a compendium of helpful annotation, a genuine pathway into the inside popular-cultural tracks and fashionings of Chicano life.

The 1990s can justly be thought an era of woman-centred stage work, a Latina efflorescence. The point is amply borne out in *Stages of Life: Transcultural Performance and Identity in U.S. Latina Theater* by Alberto Sandoval-Sánchez and Nancy Saporta Sternbach. One confirmation lies in the thirteen-page bibliography of playtexts, along with the showbill posters and performance illustrations which accompany the critical narrative. In spanning New York to West Coast theatre, straight and gay dramaturgy, and the leading names of Chicana, Puertorriqueña and Cubana-Americana theatre authorship, Sandoval-Sánchez and Sternbach indeed leave little doubt of a Latina renaissance. Key dramatists include Dolores Prida, Cherrié Moraga, Janis Astor del Valle, Josefina López, Elaine Romero, Denise Chávez (especially her one-woman shows), Alina Troyana, Marga Gomez and Migdalia Cruz. Each is given specific attention, as are theatre venues and productions, issues of Latina identity-formation and gender politics, and the representation of migrancy and family across, as they call it, *la transfrontera*. The authors make a good case, as busy as it is persuasive.

In 'A Sojourn of Desire. Cuando lleguemos: Chicano/a Literature, a Historical Reflection' (*Aztlán* 26:ii[2001] 125–51), Jesús Rosales argues for the persistence of indigenous (and with it mestizo) consciousness in Chicano literary tradition from the earliest *corridos* through to, among others, the fiction of Tomás Rivera, Ron Arias, Alejandro Morales and Ana Castillo, the autobiography of Oscar Zeta Acosta, and the poetry of Lorna Dee Cervantes. He especially highlights 'Cuando lleguemos' ('When We Arrive') as the culminating sequence in Rivera's classic migrant labour story cycle, *Y no se lo tragó la tierra / And the Earth Did Not Part* [1971]. His account argues for the text as a perfect working example of Aztec metaphor, and links it to Guillermo Gómez-Peña's later, and clever, performance-art notion of *Naftazteca*. Rosales persuasively insists that Chicano writing, for all the hybridities of modern literary forms and culture, has not lost its sedimentation in a shared community past.

Juan E. de Castro, in 'Richard Rodriguez in "Borderland": The Ambiguity of Hybridity' (*Aztlán* 26:i[2001] 101–26), tackles the thorny issue of Rodriguez's cultural-political standing within discussions of Chicano ethnicity. Is he simply the assimilationist opposed to bilingual education and affirmative action? Or, in the writing within, and since, *Days of Obligation: An Argument with My Mexican Father* [1992], has he actually helped redefine *chicanismo* in his affirmations of 'Mexican and border hybridity', of which not the least part have been his activities as a defender of gay rights? The argument that, on account of migration and intermarriage, US 'racial difference' is actually dissolving lays down a challenge to easy divisions of mainstream and margin. Castro makes an intriguing case for recognition of Rodriguez's contribution to the need for far more nuanced ethnic terms of reference.

A full, lively interview comes to hand in '"Carrying the Message: Denise Chávez on the Politics of Chicana Becoming' (*Aztlán* 26:i[2001] 127–56), conducted by Marilyn Mehaffy and AnaLouise Keating. The topics addressed include Chicano/a identity politics, the issue of *chicanismo* as explored in Chávez's novel *Face of an Angel* [1994], the role of so ethnically unmarked a figure as Rocio in *The Last of the Menu Girls* [1986], the relationship of *chicanismo* to Christianity, the degree to which Chávez's own experiences feed into the fiction, and her relationship with contemporaries such as Gloria Anzaldúa, Cherrié Moraga, Ana Castillo and Sandra Cisneros.

'A literary history of narrative experimentation in the Puerto Rican colonial diaspora.' So Lisa Sánchez González offers a well-taken prospectus for her timely, and greatly pioneering, *Boricua Literature: A Literary History of the Puerto Rican Diaspora*. She opens with the overlooked figure of Luisa Capetillo [1879–1922], a founding worker-feminist literary voice who took her literary bow with *Ensayos libertarios / Libertarian Essays* [1904–7], and who points to an ensuing line of *riqueño* writing in New York and, eventually, in a further America. An inspired chapter looks at Arturo Schomberg and William Carlos Williams as Boricua luminaries, respectively the Puerto Rico-raised major bibliophile who gives his name to Harlem's 135th Street branch of the New York Public Library, and the other, of Puerto Rican origin through his mother, the stalwart of poetic modernism. Subsequently González examines the bilingual fiction and folklore of Pura Teresa Belpré, the key Nuyorican orbit of Piri Thomas (a helpful analysis of *Down These Mean Streets*) and of Nicholasa Mohr (whose *Nilda* [1973] as Manhattan autofiction remains a landmark), the novel-writing of Judith Ortiz Cofer, Carmen de Monteflores and Esmeralda Santiago, and the song-poetry of such figures as Juan Luis Guerra and Willie Colón. Be it, further, the poetry of Tato Liviera or Sandra María Esteves, or the fiction of Luis Rafael Sanchez, González is able to demonstrate a broad contextual flourish, the literary voicing of, as she aptly calls it, 'Boricua cultural citizenship'.

Wong and Sumida, eds., *A Resource Guide to Asian American Literature*, containing twenty-five essays issued under MLA auspices, is a well-conceived state-of-the-art scholarly contribution. Summaries, with attached bibliographies, of fifteen key fictions, from Meena Alexander's *Nampally Road* [1991] to Amy Tan's *The Joy Luck Club* [1989] open the bidding. Drama, including Frank Chin, David Henry Hwang and Wakako Yamauchi, is covered, followed by overviews of literary anthologies, short fiction and Asian American poetry. Accounts, of necessity, tend to be synoptic, angled to serve as a teaching and reference aid. But they cannot do other than remind us how imaginatively rich, not to say plural, Asian American literary terrain has become.

The point finds busy, and wholly engaging, confirmation in Srikanth and Iwanaga, eds., *Bold Words: A Century of Asian American Writing*. Its selections from over sixty authors, under the headings of memoir, poetry, fiction and drama, well cover much of the literary waterfront. The mix is as rich in genre as in its crossover of literary generation, whether discursive pieces from Carlos Bulosan's 'How My Stories were Written' to Chang-rae-Lee's 'The Faintest Echo of our Language', poetry from Mitsuye Yamada to Marilyn Chin, or stories from Hisaye

Yamamoto's 'Seventeen Syllables' to Jhumpa Lahiri's 'Mrs Sen's'. Anthologies at their best serve to highlight the talent to hand while supplying overall maps, a latest literary cartography. True to its title *Bold Words* does both, a selection shrewdly chosen and edited, a timely resource.

Two further book publications add their own confirmation to the increasingly recognized depth and breadth of the Asian American literary roster. Rutgers University Press has reissued Hisaye Yamamoto's *Seventeen Syllables and Other Stories*, long a landmark collection. If the introduction by King-Kok Cheung, rightly observant of how Yamamoto's storytelling 'exemplifies precision and restraint', and the select bibliography, imply something of a move towards textbook status, that in its own way gives emphasis to the importance of Yamamoto as a pioneer Japanese American literary voice.

Diana Birchall's *Onoto Watanna: The Story of Winnifred Eaton* yields a full, scrupulously researched biography of her own 'unknown fairy grandmother'. The contour embraces the woman born Eurasian in Montreal of an English father and a Chinese mother, who published her novels, from *Miss Nume of Japan* [1899] onwards, under an adopted Japanese name, whose career as best-selling author was mirrored by her sister, Edith Eaton (writing under the name Sui Sin Far), and who would lead an odd, but always bold, thread of lives as Hollywood screenwriter (not least for *Shanghai Lady* [1929] and *East is West* [1930]) and Canadian westerner in Calgary, Alberta. Birchall is particularly acute in exploring Eaton's different kinds of self-masking: Canadian begetter of Asian American texts, vexed (and vexing) wife, mother of a family as large as her literary output, and, always, a Westerner playing Easterner. The portrait not only helps situate Eaton across the board but fills in much hitherto missing biographical family and professional detail, a contribution to be saluted.

An old-time interest in archetype is to be found in M. Dick Osumi's 'Jungian and Mythological Patterns in Wakako Yamauchi's "And the Soul Shall Dance"' (*AmasJ* 27:i[2001] 87–98). Rightly urging the claims of the story as 'one of the most significant works in Asian American literature' Osumi proceeds, with no small amount of determined Jungianism, to discern in Mrs Oka, within the context of her 1930s farm life in California's Imperial Valley, the embodying of the ego in search of 'psychic wholeness'. Tendentious this may be, but it makes for a lively account.

Wing Tek Lum, the Chinese Hawaiian poet, and an outstanding figure of Hawaii's Bamboo Ridge literary generation, joins with Gregory Yee Mak of California State University to produce a verse-text-image sequence of one of Hawaii's Chinese family generations (*AmasJ* 27:ii[2001] 50–61). Rich in itself, their collage underscores the point that, in consequence of the Exclusion Laws, this one family, like others, could be 'united only through photography'. *Amerasia Journal* 27:iii[2001] and 28:i[2002], a double issue given over to 'After Words: Who Speaks on War, Justice, Peace?', amounts to a sizeable consideration of how, since 9/11 and the twin towers assault, America has taken on a new consciousness of ethnicity. Jewish or Arab American ethnicity, inevitably, has been to the fore, but so also has the more general relationship of groups to wholes. Among a considerable roll-call of contributors the literary names include *Amerasia Journal*'s editor, the poet Russell Leong, together with Jessica Hagedorn, Frank Chin, Janice Mirikitani and Roshni Rustomi-Kerns.

Literature Interpretation Theory dedicates a special double issue (12:i[2001] and 12:iii[2001]) to Asian American literature. A number of the contributions especially invite attention. In 'The Precision of Persimmons: Hybridity, Grafting and the Case of Li-young Lee' (*LIT* 12:i[2001] 1–23) Steven G. Yao focuses on Lee's early lyric poem 'Persimmons'. He gives sharp, well-argued attention to how, throughout, Lee renders a rite of passage of migrant activity in mastering, and often enough being mastered by, English pronunciation and, not unconnectedly, in the dynamics of inter-racial sexual relationships. These, Yao suggests, become tropes, in all their challenge and vexation, of the American multicultural self. In '"Mocking my own ripeness": Authenticity, Heritage, and Self-Erasure in the Poetry of Marilyn Chin' (*LIT* 12:i[2001] 25–45) John Gery argues that the verse of Chin's *Phoenix Gone, the Terrace Empty* [1994] represents 'a crafty combination of self-erasure and assertion'. This back-and-forth tactic on Chin's part, he suggests, works to subvert the Chinawoman stereotype, be it warrior or concubine, and helps to create a claim to an infinitely cagier richness of self-voice.

Min Hiyoung Song's 'A Disaporic Future? *Native Speaker* and Historical Trauma' (*LIT* 12:i[2001] 79–98) analyses Chang-rae Lee's novel of Korean American politics in the New York borough of Queens in terms of three styles of diaspora: that which fails the narrator's father by locking him into groceryman isolation; that of assimilationism as practised by the doomed politician Johnny Kwang; and that which situates the protagonist, Henry Park, as distanced spy/observer, and which finally returns him to private domesticity as aide to his wife in her speech therapy practice. The essay bears down with considerable shrewdness on a genuinely consequential Asian American work of fiction.

Cynthia Franklin's 'Turning Japanese/Returning to America: Problems of Gender, Class, and Nation in David Mura's Use of Memoir' (*LIT* 12:iii[2001] 235–65) gives a none-too-flattering reading of Mura's *Turning Japanese: Memoirs of a Sansei* [1991] as modernist 'detachment and self-absorption'. She accuses him of an American provincialism in cherry-picking that which he favours, and that which he does not, both from within Japanese culture and from the span of Japanese American culture. To Eleanor Ty in 'A Filipino Prufrock in an Alien Land: Bienvenido Santos's *The Man Who (Thought He) Looked Like Robert Taylor*' (*LIT* 12:iii[2001] 267–83) Santos's novel portrays Sol, the hero, as a comic Prufrock, neither wholly outside nor wholly inside US society, always the would-be assimilationist and yet, whether by his own choice or otherwise, always not. Lavina Dhingra Shankar's 'Postcolonial Diasporics. "Writing in Search of a Homeland": Meena Alexander's *Manhattan Music, Fault Lines*, and *The Shock of Arrival*' (*LIT* 12:iii[2001] 285–312) explores the three texts for 'the multifarious transnational identities which have accompanied [Alexander's] constantly shifting locations'. This emphasis on the dialectic of location and dislocation opens up a genuinely useful pathway into the trajectories of Alexander's verse, fiction, autobiography and discursive writing, her imaginative transformation of migrancy into literary word.

Beginning Ethnic American Literatures, in the 'Beginnings' series from Manchester University Press, delivers a four-part guide to Native American fiction (Martin Padget), African American fiction (Maria Lauret), Asian American fiction (Helena Grice) and Chicano/a fiction (Candida Hepworth). Following a shared formula of overview, theory, three case studies, further investigation and short bibliography, each section supplies its own succinct, and generally well turned, route-marker into the ethnic-multicultural literary traditions addressed. The volume occasionally risks expository flatness, some deflation of the buoyant self-fashioning, ideological risk and contentiousness of a number of the writers in play (Toni Morrison in *Jazz*, for instance). But, overall, the upshot is a necessary working primer, conscientious and intelligently student-oriented: the laying out of ground.

Ihab Hassan's 'COUNTERPOINTS: Nationalism, Colonialism, Multiculturalism, and Spirit' (in Grabes, ed., *Innovation and Continuity in English Studies*, pp. 171–86; the proceedings of the fiftieth jubilee of the International Association of University Professors of English), offers, as its author describes it, 'a record of passages and crossings'. Well it might, for Hassan, an established name since the appearance of his *Radical Innocence: Studies in the Contemporary American Novel* [1961], ponders an Egyptian birth, 'mixed Arab, Turkic and Albanian' roots, an education in English, French and Arabic, and a long American professional career, in the light of current multicultural interests and preoccupations. He writes challengingly on migrancy as gain as much as loss, the diversity of the self within, and a weighing of societies which, however multicultural in make-up, are anything but multiculturalist in practice.

Books Reviewed

Abadie, Ann J., and Joseph R. Ergo, eds. *Faulkner in America*. UPMissip. [2001] pp. 248. hb $46 ISBN 1 5780 6375 2, pb $22 ISBN 1 5780 6376 0.

Adamson, Joni. *American Indian Literature, Environmental Justice, and Ecocriticism: The Middle Place*. UArizP. [2001] pp. 250. $19.95 ISBN 0 8165 1792 4.

Aizenberg, Susan, and Erin Belieu, eds. *The Extraordinary Tide: New Poetry by American Women*. ColUP. [2001] pp. xxix + 464. £35.50 ISBN 0 2311 1962 3.

Barrish, Phillip. *American Literary Realism, Critical Theory, and Intellectual Prestige, 1880–1995*. CUP. [2001] pp. 213. $55 ISBN 0 5217 8221 X.

Basso, Matthew, Laura McCall, and Dee Garceau, eds. *Across the Great Divide: Cultures of Manhood in the American West*. Routledge. [2001] pp. 304. pb £13.99 ($22.95) ISBN 0 4159 2471 5.

Berke, Nancy. *Women Poets on the Left: Lola Ridge, Genevieve Taggard, Margaret Walker*. UFlorP. [2001] pp. viii + 202. £46.50 ISBN 0 8130 2115 4.

Berman, Ronald. *Fitzgerald, Hemingway, and the Twenties*. UAlaP. [2001] pp. 192. $19.95 ISBN 0 8173 1255 2.

Birchall, Diana. *Onoto Watanna: The Story of Winnifred Eaton*. UIllP. [2001] pp. 252. $29.95 ISBN 0 2520 2607 1.

Bloom, Harold, ed. *Joseph Heller's Catch-22: Modern Critical Interpretations*. Roundhouse. [2001] pp. 182. £29.95 ISBN 0 7910 5927 8.

Booker, M. Keith. *Monsters, Mushroom Clouds and the Cold War*. Greenwood. [2001] pp. 232. £49.50 ISBN 0 3133 1873 5.

Boone, Kevin. *At Millennium's End: New Essays on the Work of Kurt Vonnegut*. SUNYP. [2001] pp. 224. pb £18.95 ISBN 0 7914 4930 0.

Bordman, Gerald. *American Musical Theatre: A Chronicle*, 3rd edn. OUP. [2001] pp. 917. ISBN 0 1951 3074 X.

Bordman, Gerald. *American Theatre: A Chronicle of Comedy and Drama*. vol. 3: *1930–1969*. OUP. [1996] pp. 472. ISBN 0 1950 9079 9.

Boswell, Marshall. *John Updike's Rabbit Tetralogy: Mastered Irony in Motion*. UMissP. [2001] pp. 312. £29.50 ISBN 0 8262 1310 3.

Bradbury, Nicola *et al.*, eds. *North American Short Stories and Short Fictions*. Yearbook of English Studies 31. Maney. [2001] pp. 342. pb £55 ISBN 1 9026 5315 7.

Brauner, David. *Post-War Jewish Fiction: Ambivalence, Self-Explanation and Transatlantic Connections*. Palgrave. [2001] pp. 240. £47.50 ISBN 0 3337 4035 1.

Bromwich, David. *Skeptical Muse: Essays on Modern Poetry*. UChicP. [2001] pp. 288. pb £11.50 ISBN 0 2260 7561 3.

Bruccoli, Matthew J., and Judith S. Baughman, eds. *Before Gatsby: The First Twenty-Six Stories*. USCP. [2001] pp. 584. $24.95 ISBN 1 5700 3371 4.

Canfield, J. Douglas. *Mavericks on the Border: The Early Southwest in Historical Fiction and Film*. UPKen. [2001] pp. ix + 238. £20.95 ISBN 0 8131 2180 9.

Cobley, Paul. *The American Thriller: Generic Innovation and Social Change in the 1970s*. Palgrave. [2000] pp. 256. pb £17.99 ISBN 0 3337 7669 0.

Cornis-Pope, Marcel. *Narrative Innovation and Cultural Rewriting in the Cold War Era and After*. Palgrave. [2001] pp. 336. £37.50 ISBN 0 3122 3837 1.

Diggory, Terence, and Stephen Paul Miller, eds. *The Scene of My Selves: New Work on New York School Poets*. NPF. [2001] pp. 417. pb £23 ISBN 0 9433 7350 6.

Douglas, Christopher. *Reciting America: Culture and Cliché in Contemporary U.S. Fiction*. UIllP. [2001] pp. x + 203. £35 ISBN 0 2520 2603 9.

Duffy, Susan. *The Political Plays of Langston Hughes*. SIUP. [2000] pp. xi + 221. hb $39.95 ISBN 0 8093 2295 1, pb $16.95 ISBN 0 8093 2296 X.

Elam, Harry J., and David Krasner, eds. *African American Performance and Theater History: A Critical Reader*. OUP. [2001] pp. xiv + 367. hb £34 ISBN 0 1951 2724 2, pb £17.95 ISBN 0 1951 2725 0.

Esch, Deborah, ed. *New Essays on The House of Mirth*. CUP. [2001] pp. 162. £10.95 ISBN 0 5213 7833 8.

Estrin, Barbara. *The American Love Lyric after Auschwitz and Hiroshima*. Palgrave. [2001] pp. xv + 253. £37.50 ISBN 0 3122 3865 7.

Fenton, James. *The Strength of Poetry*. FS&G. [2001] pp. 272. $25 ISBN 0 3742 2845 0.

Fink, Thomas. *'A Different Sense of Power': Problems of Community in Late-Twentieth-Century U.S. Poetry*. FDUP. [2001] pp. 239. £30 ISBN 0 8386 3897 X.

Finkelstein, Norman. *Not One of them in Place: Modern Poetry and Jewish American Identity*. SUNYP. [2001] pp. 194. £39 ISBN 0 7914 4983 1.

Fisher, James. *The Theater of Tony Kushner: Living Past Hope*. Routledge. [2001] pp. 268. $80 ISBN 0 8153 3150 9.

Foertsch, Jacqueline. *Enemies Within: The Cold War and the AIDS Crisis in Literature, Film, and Culture*. UIllP. [2001] pp. viii + 239. $29.95 ISBN 0 2520 2637 3.

Folks, Jeffrey J. *From Richard Wright to Toni Morrison: Ethics in Modern and Postmodern American Narrative*. Lang. [2001] pp. x + 199. pb $29.95 ISBN 0 8204 5105 3.

Gainor, J. Ellen. *Susan Glaspell in Context: American Theater, Culture, and Politics, 1915–48*. UMichP. [2001] pp. 327. $52.50 ISBN 0 4721 0650 3.

Giles, James R. *Violence in the Contemporary American Novel: An End to Innocence*. USCP. [2000] pp. xiii + 161. £24.95 ISBN 1 5700 3328 5.

González, Lisa Sánchez. *Boricua Literature: A Literary History of the Puerto Rican Diaspora*. NYUP. [2001] pp. viii + 216. $18.50 ISBN 0 8147 3147 3.

Grabes, Herbert, ed. *Innovation and Continuity in English Studies*. Lang. [2001] pp. ix + 329. pb $47.95 ISBN 0 8204 5427 3.

Grice, Helena, Candida Hepworth, Maria Lauret, and Martin Padget. *Beginning Ethnic American Literatures*. ManUP. [2001] pp. 255. £9.99 ISBN 0 7190 5763 9.

Hall, Roger A. *Performing the American Frontier, 1870–1906*. CUP. [2001] pp. xii + 281. $54.95 ISBN 0 5217 9320 3.

Hapke, Laura. *Labor's Text: The Worker in American Fiction*. RutgersUP. [2001] pp. 544. pb £23.50 ISBN 0 8135 2880 1.

Heberle, Mark A. *A Trauma Artist: Tim O'Brien and the Fiction of Vietnam*. UIowaP. [2001] pp. xxvii + 344. pb £15.50 ISBN 0 8774 5761 1.

Hinton, Laura, and Cynthia Hogue, eds. *We Who Love To Be Astonished: Experimental Women's Writing and Performance Poetics*. UAlaP. [2001] pp. xii + 308. pb £21.50 ISBN 0 8173 1095 9.

Hischak, Thomas S. *American Theatre: A Chronicle of Comedy and Drama*, vol. 4: *1969–2000*. OUP. [2001] pp. 504. £53 ISBN 0 1951 2347 6.

Hoffman, Tyler. *Robert Frost and the Politics of Poetry*. UNewE. [2001] pp. xiii + 263. pb £15.95 ISBN 1 5846 5150 4.

Hogan, Katie. *Women Take Care: Gender, Race and the Culture of AIDS*. CornUP. [2001] pp. xvi + 179. pb £10.95 ($15.95) ISBN 0 8014 8753 6.

Holmes, Sarah C., ed. *The Correspondence of Ezra Pound and Senator William Borah*. UIllP. [2001] pp. xxv + 95. $24.95 ISBN 0 2520 2630 6.

Howe, Mica, and Sarah Appleton Aguiar, eds. *He Said, She Says: An RSVP to the Male Text*. FDUP. [2001] pp. 292. £36 ($45) ISBN 0 8386 3915 1.

Hudgins, Christopher C., and Leslie Kane, eds. *David Mamet: Gender and Genre*. Palgrave. [2001] pp. 265. £37.50 ISBN 0 3122 3869 X.

Huhndorf, Shari M. *Going Native: Indians in the American Cultural Imagination*. CornUP. [2001] pp. xiv + 220. $16.95 ISBN 0 8014 8695 5.

Jacobs, Connie A. *The Novels of Louise Erdrich: Stories of her People*. Lang. [2001] pp. xix + 260. £19 ISBN 0 8204 4027 2.

Jacobs, Karen. *The Eye's Mind: Literary Modernism and Visual Culture*. CornUP. [2001] pp. viii + 311. pb £12.95 ($19.95) ISBN 0 8014 8649 1.

Juan-Navarro, Santiago. *Archival Reflections: Postmodern Fiction of the Americas (Self-Reflexivity, Historical Revisionism, Utopia)*. AUP. [2000] pp. 367. £40 ISBN 0 8387 5427 9.

Jurca, Catherine. *White Diaspora: The Suburb and the Twentieth Century American Novel*. PrincetonUP. [2001] pp. viii + 238. pb £12.42 ISBN 0 6910 5735 4.

Kane, Leslie, ed. *David Mamet in Conversation*. UMichP. [2001] pp. xiv + 248. hb £30 ($50) ISBN 0 4720 9764 4, pb ISBN £10.50 ($16.95) 0 4720 6764 8.

Kendall, Tim. *Sylvia Plath: A Critical Study*. Faber. [2001] pp. xii + 235. pb £9.99 ISBN 0 5711 9235 1.

Killoran, Helen. *The Critical Reception of Edith Wharton*. Camden House. [2001 pp. 184. £40 ISBN 1 5711 3101 9.

Lardas, John. *The Bop Apocalypse: The Religious Visions of Kerouac, Ginsberg, and Burroughs*. UIllP. [2001] pp. x + 316. $39 ISBN 0 2520 2599 7.

Lotringer, Sylvère, ed. *Burroughs Live: The Collected Interviews of William S. Burroughs 1960–1997*. Semiotext(e). [2001] pp. 848. pb £19.95 ISBN 1 5843 5010 5.

Madsen, Deborah L. *Contemporary Chicana Literature: Bernice Zamora, Ana Castillo, Sandra Cisneros, Denise Chávez, Alma Luz Villanueva and Lorna Dee Cervantes*. USCP. [2000] pp. 283. £25 ISBN 1 5700 3379 X.

Melaney, William D. *After Ontology: Literary Theory and Modernist Poetics*. SUNYP. [2001] pp. x + 260. pb £13.50 ISBN 0 7914 4958 0.

Miller, D. Quentin. *John Updike and the Cold War: Drawing the Iron Curtain*. UMissP. [2001] pp. xi + 192. pb £22.95 ISBN 0 8262 1328 6.

Murphy, Brenda. *O'Neill: Long Day's Journey into Night*. Plays in Production. CUP. [2001] pp. xvii + 250. hb £45 ISBN 0 5216 6197 8, pb £16.95 ISBN 0 5216 6575 2.

Nelson, Cary. *Revolutionary Memory: Recovering the Poetry of the American Left*. Routledge. [2001] pp. 270. £30 ISBN 0 4159 3004 9.

Nelson, Elizabeth Hoffman, and Malcolm A. Nelson, eds. *Telling the Stories: Essays on American Indian Literatures and Cultures*. Lang. [2001] pp. xi + 186. $24.95 ISBN 0 8204 3954 1.

Newman, Judie. *Alison Lurie: A Critical Study*. Rodopi. [2001] pp. 220. pb £27 ISBN 9 0420 1222 6.

Owens, Louis. *I Hear the Train: Reflections, Inventions, Refractions*. UOklaP. [2001] pp. 265. $29.95 ISBN 0 8061 3354 6.

Ozieblo, Barbara. *Susan Glaspell: A Critical Biography*. UNCP. [2001] pp. 345. hb £42.95 ($55) ISBN 0 8078 2560 3, pb £17.50 ($22.50) ISBN 0 8078 4868 9.

Parmet, Harriet L. *The Terror of our Days: Four American Poets Respond to the Holocaust*. LehighUP. [2001] pp. 268. £35 ISBN 0 9342 2363 7.

Perdue, Theda, ed. *Sifters: Native American Women's Lives*. OUP. [2001] pp. xii + 260. £15.99 ISBN 0 1951 3081 2.

Pollack, Harriet, and Suzanne Mars, eds. *Eudora Welty and Politics: Did the Writer Crusade?* LSUP. [2001] pp. 208. £31.50 ISBN 0 8071 2618 7.

Prigozy, Ruth, ed. *The Cambridge Companion to F. Scott Fitzgerald*. CUP. [2001] pp. 294. hb £42.50 ISBN 0 5216 2447 9, pb £14.95 ISBN 0 5216 2474 6.

Prown, Katherine Hemple. *Revising Flannery O'Connor: Southern Literary Culture and the Problem of Female Authorship*. UPVirginia. [2001] pp. 208. £27.50 ISBN 0 8139 2012 4.

Rabkin, Gerald, ed. *Richard Foreman*. JHUP. [1999] pp. 248. hb $45 ISBN 0 8018 6113 6, pb $19.95 ISBN 0 8108 6114 4.

Roberts, Neil, ed. *A Companion to Twentieth Century Poetry*. Blackwell. [2001] pp. 648. £80 ISBN 0 6312 1529 8.

Roman, Camille. *Elizabeth Bishop's World War II: Cold War View*. Palgrave. [2001] pp. xiii + 173. £37.50 ISBN 0 3122 3078 8.

Rosenberg, Warren. *Legacy of Rage: Jewish Masculinity, Violence, and Culture*. UMassP. [2001] pp. xi + 312. £26.95 ($34.95) ISBN 1 5584 9303 4.

Russell, Jamie. *Queer Burroughs*. Palgrave. [2001] pp. 262. pb £13.99 ISBN 0 3122 3923 8.

Sandoval-Sánchez, Alberto, and Nancy Saporta Sternbach. *Stages of Life: Transcultural Performance and Identity in U.S. Latina Theater*. UArizP. [2001] pp. 260. $21.95 ISBN 0 8165 1829 7.

Schmitz, Neil. *White Robe's Dilemma: Tribal History in American Literature*. UMassP. [2001] pp. x + 181. £15.50 ISBN 1 5584 9291 7.

Seel, Cynthia. *Ritual Performance in the Fiction of Flannery O'Connor*. Camden House. [2001] pp. 285. £40 ISBN 1 5711 3196 5.

Seguin, Robert. *Around Quitting Time: Work and Middle-Class Fantasy in American Fiction*. DukeUP. [2001] pp. ix + 210. pb £12.95 ($17.95) ISBN 0 8223 2670 1.

Smith, Carlton. *Coyote Kills John Wayne: Postmodernism and Contemporary Fictions of the Transcultural Frontier*. UPNE. [2001] pp. x + 167. pb $18.95 ISBN 1 5846 5020 6.

Sontag, Kate, and David Graham, eds. *After Confession: Poetry as Autobiography*. Graywolf. [2001] pp. 341. pb $17.95 ISBN 1 5559 7355 8.

Spahr, Juliana. *Everybody's Autonomy: Connective Reading and Collective Identity*. UAlaP. [2001] pp. xiii + 224. hb £42.50 ISBN 0 8173 1053 3, pb £16.95 ISBN 0 8173 1054 1.

Srikanth, Rajini, and Esther Y. Iwanaga, eds. *Bold Words: A Century of Asian American Writing*. RutgersUP. [2001] pp. xxiv + 442. £21.50 ISBN 0 8135 2965 4.

Stewart, Matthew. *Modernism and Tradition in Ernest Hemingway's 'In Our Time': A Guide For Students and Readers*. Camden House. [2001] pp. 130. $55 ISBN 1 5711 3017 9.

Tatum, Charles. *Chicano Popular Culture: Que Habla el Pueblo*. UArizP. [2001] pp. 212. $14.95 ISBN 0 8165 1983 8.

Taylor, Georgina. *H.D. and the Public Sphere of Modernist Women Writers, 1913–1946: Talking Women*. Clarendon. [2001] pp. ix + 228. £40 ISBN 0 1981 8713 0.

Thurston, Michael. *Making Something Happen: American Political Poetry between the World Wars*. UNCP. [2001] pp. viii + 272. hb £39.50 ISBN 0 8078 2654 5, pb £15.95 ISBN 0 8078 4979 0.

Tomlinson, Charles. *American Essays: Making It New*. Carcanet. [2001] pp. xi + 200. pb £12.95 ISBN 1 8575 4476 5.

Ullery, David A. *The Tarzan Novels of Edgar Rice Burroughs: An Illustrated Reader's Guide*. McFarland. [2001] pp. 298. $45 ISBN 0 7864 0825 1.

Watkin, William. *In the Process of Poetry: The New York School and the Avant-Garde*. BuckUP. [2001] pp. 314. £38 ISBN 0 8387 5467 8.

Weaver, Jace. *Other Words: American Indian Literature, Law, and Culture*. UOklaP. [2001] pp. 381. $34.95 ISBN 0 8061 3352 X.

Williams, Deborah Lindsay. *Not in Sisterhood: Edith Wharton, Willa Cather, Zona Gale, and the Politics of Female Authorship*. Palgrave. [2001] pp. 225. £35. ISBN 0 3122 2921 6.

Wilson, Christopher P. *Cop Knowledge: Police Power and Cultural Narrative in Twentieth-Century America*. UChicP. [2000] pp. xii + 281. pb £11.50 ISBN 0 2269 0133 5.

Wisker, Gina. *Sylvia Plath: A Beginner's Guide*. H&S. [2001] pp. viii + 88. pb
  £5.99 ISBN 0 3408 0040 2.
Wong, Sau-ling Cynthia, and Stephen H. Sumida, eds. *A Resource Guide to Asian
  American Literature*. MLA. [2001] pp. 345. $22 ISBN 0 8735 2272 9.
Yamamoto, Hisaye. *Seventeen Syllables and Other Stories*, rev. edn. RutgersUP.
  [2001] pp. xxiii + 179. £13.50 ISBN 0 8135 2953 0.

XVII

New Literatures

FEMI ABODUNRIN, IAN HENDERSON, BERNADETTE
BRENNAN, RICHARD LANE, CHESTER ST H. MILLS, ASHOK
BERY AND NELSON WATTIE

This chapter has six sections: 1. Africa; 2. Australia; 3. Canada; 4. The Caribbean; 5. India; 6. New Zealand. Section 1 is by Femi Abodunrin; section 2 is by Ian Henderson and Bernadette Brennan; section 3 is by Richard Lane; section 4 is by Chester St H. Mills; section 5 is by Ashok Bery; section 6 is by Nelson Wattie.

1. Africa

(a) General
The journals with special themes covered in this review include *African Literature Today* 23[2001] on 'South and Southern African Literature' edited by Eldred D. Jones and Marjorie Jones; *African Theatre* 22[2001] on 'Playwrights and Politics' edited by Martin Banham, James Gibbs and Femi Osofisan; *Research in African Literature* 31:iv[2000] on 'Poetics of African Art'; *Matatu* 20[1999] on 'New Theatre in Francophone and Anglophone Africa'; and *Matatu* 21–2[2000] on 'FonTomFrom: Contemporary Ghanaian Literature, Theatre and Film'. With nearly 6,000 entries, Bernth Lindfors's *Black African Literature in English, 1992–1996*, following on from *Black African Literature, 1987–1991* and its predecessors, continues the task of making research in African literatures less daunting. Lindfors's previous four volumes have been described on these pages as a compendium with which researchers, students and teachers of African literature can approach the field with less trepidation. The present volume provides information on books and articles published between 1992 and 1996, and the intention remains 'to provide comprehensive coverage of major scholarly books and periodicals as well as selective coverage of other relevant sources of informed commentary'. Similarly, James Gibbs's 'Edua Theodora Sutherland: A Bibliography of Primary Materials, with a Checklist of Secondary Sources' (*Matatu* 21–2[2000] 117–23) is a comprehensive list of the primary works—selected poems, short stories, letters, essays, articles, plays and other works—and secondary sources of one of Africa's foremost poets and playwrights, Efua Sutherland (1924–96).

Ngugi wa Thiong'o's 'Europhonism, Universities and the Magic Fountain: The Future of African Literature and Scholarship' (*RAL* 31:i[2001] 1–11), and his seminal collection of essays *Penpoints, Gunpoints, and Dreams: Towards a Critical Theory of the Arts and the State in Africa* [1998] (the latter being reviewed belatedly in this section), revisit the language question in African literature, describing language as 'a product of a community in its economic, political and cultural evolution in time and space'. While the former is the Ashby Lecture given at Clare Hall, Cambridge in May 1999, the latter are the Clarendon Lectures in English Literature organized by the Oxford University English Faculty. The four lectures in *Penpoints* are entitled 'Art War with the State: Writers and Guardians of a Post-Colonial Society' (pp. 7–35), 'Enactments of Power: The Politics of Performance Space' (pp. 37–69), 'The Allegory of the Cave: Language, Democracy and a New World Order' (pp. 71–101), and 'Oral Power and Europhone Glory: Orature, Literature and Stolen Legacies' (pp. 103–28). They are among the clearest and probably the most historicist of Ngugi's endeavours on the language issue that has consumed so much of his critical and creative energy for more than three decades now. In the Ashby Lecture, Ngugi describes the creative and critical issues at stake as follows: 'In most of my publications, principally in *Decolonizing the Mind*, *Penpoints, Gunpoints and Dreams*, and *Writers in Politics*, I have tried to argue that the language question is so crucial because language occupies a significant position in the entire hierarchy of the organization of wealth, power and values in a society.' His claim that no African society can become fully aware of itself as an entity, combined with the contention that 'language is what most helps in the movement of a community from the state of being for itself when it becomes aware of itself as an entity', and his consideration of the ways in which this self-consciousness gives the community 'its spiritual strength to keep on reproducing its being as it continually renews itself in culture, in its power relations and in its negotiation with its environment', have been at the centre of Ngugi's arguments on the language question. The complicity of the postcolonial states—and Ngugi doubts 'if there is a single country in our continent which is free of this stigma'—with what 'Engels calls that "special public power"' over society that was largely introduced by colonialism to control and keep the colonized in their place is, according to Ngugi, coterminous with 'the four features of art which would illuminate the conflict and give a clue to why the creative state of art is always at war, actually or potentially, with the crafty art of the state'. The project that he started in 1976—a literacy and cultural programme with theatre at the centre—has been a defining moment in Ngugi's life and career as a committed artist. He describes his effort to assist the community reclaim their historical space as 'The attempt to locate theatre among the people [which] would raise new questions and answers about the content, form, and language of African theatre. But in November 1976 I did not realize that the attempt to locate culture where it belongs would raise even more problems and questions, not only about the performance space of the artist but about that of the state as well'. However, in 'Culture, Cultivation, and Colonialism in *Out of Africa* and Beyond' (*RAL* 31:i[2000] 63–79), Simon Lewis examines Karen Blixen's writerly exploitation of Africa and Africans against the background of what he describes as 'Ngugi's allegation of racist continuity between the colonial and postcolonial, initially through an analysis of *Out of Africa* in terms of the European tradition of pastoral, and then through an examination of the wider question posed by that analysis concerning the occupation and commodification of tracts of African land, both in Kenya and South Africa'.

Odile Cazenave's *Rebellious Women: The New Generation of Female African Novelists* examines what she describes as a new generation of women writers and considers in 'what sense one can speak of a new feminine novel'. Focusing on the novel from the early 1980s to the mid-1990s by Francophone African women, Cazenave describes the phenomenal entry of young Francophone African women writers whose writing was 'wilful, combative, and full of a new energy that was typical of their generation'. These dominant characteristics of their mode of writing transcended the boundaries of 'a single testimonial work—as Calixthe Beyala, Angele Ramiri and Veronique Tadjo demonstrate'. Mariama Ba, Aminata Sow Fall, and Myriam Warner-Vieyra are the other major contributors to a list that is by no mean exhaustive, but one that, according to Cazenave, 'is a selection representative of thematic and narrative strategies used since the mid-1980s by the new generation of women writers. This generation is characterized by its youth as of 1994–5—most of the women in question are in their thirties—and, perhaps as a consequence, by the forcefulness of its tone'. One of Cazenave's primary conclusions is that, even when they are treating themes that are not new in African literature, such as the character of the white woman, for example, 'the nature and function of this character differ significantly (. . .). '[I]n the texts of women writers, the foreigner or the imposed wife paradoxically becomes a symbolic vehicle for the difficulties facing young African women'. As in the discussion of their foreign counterparts, the part of the book assigned to 'Women in the Margins' includes studies on 'Prostitutes and Prostitution' as well as on the ubiquitous subject of 'Madness and "Mad" Women'. The theme of prostitution is one of the most commonly treated subjects in modern literature, whether in Europe, the United States, or the countries of Asia. In Africa the prostitute has functioned as an instrument of political critique 'aimed at the newly empowered African bourgeoisie and its haunts—whitened Africans and their night clubs, balls and other places of corruption'. Like the treatment accorded to her equally archetypal counterpart who 'live[s] in the midst of depression and fall[s] prey to madness', the prostitute has been portrayed with a comparable intensity and dimension with the advent of female novelists such as Angele Raviri and Calixthe Beyala: 'The traditional character dissolves, giving way to woman-as-object and body-as-merchandise.' In this highly readable account of the exploits of the Francophone African novel of the feminine mode in the past fifteen years, Cazenave observes that one of the major achievements of the mode is that it 'has freed itself from the forms of simple testimony and been able to report experiences and present the current state of African societies'.

Annie Gagiano's *Achebe, Head, Marachera: On Power and Change in Africa* examines what it calls the existential urgency with which the questions of power and change are addressed by novelists from Africa. According to Gagiano, in spite of the persistent habit of reading them reductively as providing mere anthropological or socio-political evidence—'not only in "Western" texts, but, unfortunately also in some works by scholars who are themselves of African origin'—it is by means of their fineness as literary artefacts that Achebe, Head and Marachera have produced works that depict the 'tragedy and loss to humanity [that would occur] if we fail to adjust global imbalances'. The first imagined context to be problematized is 'Africa' itself, and, according to Gagiano, 'use of the inclusive continental name "Africa" is both unavoidable and appropriate as a basket term to contain studies of the writings of Nigerian, South African-Botswanan, and Zimbabwean novelists'. Gagiano urges us to see the fifteen representative texts discussed in this rigorously theorized account, which includes the study of Head's, Marachera's and Achebe's depictions of power and change, and the societies they depict, as not isolated and hermetically sealed, but as offering a 'variety of ways of experiencing and coping with power and change, in social personal and political contexts, *variously* African' (original italics). In three central chapters and a lengthy introductory consideration, Gagiano presents the chosen novelists as analysts of the societies they depict: 'By this I mean that they are "primary" thinkers who concern themselves with the investigation of social, psychological, and political realities and issues, and are not mere recorders, or providers of material for the theories of scholarly writing—though the material they provide may be at one remove from raw data.' Besides the attempt to demonstrate the social density, literary richness and subtlety of political analysis implicit in these works, another *raison d'être* of Gagiano's study is 'the attempt to investigate whether the novelist's depictions of colonial and postcolonial conditions are not more complex, compelling, and significant than many of the more derivative theoretical presentations of such conditions'. Achebe's portrayal of an earlier Igboland, Marachera's surrealism, and Head's plunge into psychic depths are some of the 'variously African' conditions inherent in the continent's colonial and postcolonial experiences, and, according to Gagiano, they 'do not attempt to avoid or seek to escape from the circumstances in which the authors and the many others who are similarly located find themselves'.

Similarly, Patrick Colm Hogan's *Colonialism and Cultural Identity: Crises of Tradition in the Anglophone Literatures of India, Africa, and the Caribbean* examines the universal concept of cultural identity, a phenomenon which, according to Hogan 'is at the centre of world politics today, and has been for some time now'. Despite the broad differences among Africa, India and the Caribbean, the colonial condition provides the basis for a general theory of cultural identity that could be employed to explore the dialectical tension that defines postcolonial literature. To the extent that colonial contact disrupts indigenous culture, often radically, one of Hogan's primary objectives is 'to provide a positive account of cultural identity after colonization'. In Africa, colonial contact distorted Igbo culture in general and Igbo gender identity in particular, as it did with most other African indigenous cultures. In *Things Fall Apart*, Achebe explores this distortion, which, though sometimes subtle, is nevertheless 'so severe that it may undermine one's entire sense of purpose, one's entire imagination of a future life, and thus result in complete and psychologically devastating despair, as it does in the case of the main character'. If 'Culture and Despair', according to Hogan, is the main theme of Achebe's exploration of colonial contact and their distortions, Buchi Emecheta's overriding concern, even while addressing the loss of indigenous masculinity after colonization, is the 'Lives of Women in the Region of Contact', including the way in which colonization degraded the condition of indigenous women: 'In each case the author examines how the development or intensification of colonial contact precipitates a crisis in cultural identity in general, and gender identity in particular, and thereby generates a specifiable range of conflicting attitudes toward an enactment of that tradition.'

Epstein and Kole, eds., *The Language of African Literature*, is a collection of articles that were originally published in *Language and Style: An International Journal*. According to Edmund L. Epstein, the sixteen articles in the present collection, dealing with the language structures and narrative conventions of sub-Saharan African authors writing in English, 'represent only a handful of recent and current issues of the journal'. Reinforcing Hogan's useful demarcation between 'assimilation' and 'mimeticism', and examining the degree to which assimilation could be described as 'the full acceptance and internalization of the other basic culture', he observes that, in linguistic terms, the nature and characteristics of literature in English by African authors could be described in two ways: 'One employs the most sophisticated means of linguistic and cultural analysis on the works of African writers. The other way analyses the rich influence of indigenous African languages on African writers in English.' With over 3,000 indigenous languages, many of the articles in *The Language of African Literature* describe the effect of indigenous African languages on the varieties of English spoken in sub-Saharan Africa. Tony E. Efejuku's 'Language as Sensation: The Use of Poetic and Evocation Language in Five African Autobiographies' (pp. 3–7) and Oluwole Adejare's 'Translation: A Distinctive Feature of African Literature in English' (pp. 19–38) focus on the general area. While the former treats five novelists from West, East, and Southern Africa, analysing the use of poetic and evocative language in the works of these five novelists, 'mainly in terms of speech, rhythms, incantations and "musical" intonations', the latter revisits the issue of the ubiquitous status of translation in African Literature in English (ALE). West African literature is the subject of eleven articles, and while three, analysing the works of Okot p'Bitek and Taban lo Liyong, cover the East African sub-region, Benjamin Magura's long article examines the function of register in Southern Africa. The regional articles are discussed under the different sub-regions.

Linguanti, Casotti and Concilio, eds., *Coterminous Worlds: Magical Realism and Contemporary Post-Colonial Literatures in English*, examines the literary phenomenon known as 'magical realism', which has manifested itself in such large variety of forms across so many Anglophone cultures. In her introduction to the volume, Elsa Linguanti raises all the pertinent questions around the dichotomous subject, including magical realism's sufficiently difficult and enticing ability 'to excite interest, if not fascination'. According to Linguanti, the variants are numerous and quite distinct, and range from the 'destabilizing tendencies within the still dominant mode of narrative realism itself—in the unusual yokings of the "ordinary" and the "extraordinary" in the language of Patrick White, for instance', to the coexistence of '*naturalia* and *mirabilia*' in the novels of Jack Hodgins and the epic writing of Syl Cheney-Coker. In Africa, the preponderance of hybridity and syncreticity, which have been described as constituent elements of postcolonial literature, contributes to the continent's reputation as a place still open to a magic-mythic world-view, 'where one can still find oneself in daily contact with something that could be defined as the marvellous real, and where "an entire mythology is preserved by an entire people"'. African writers, according to Linguanti, seem to share what Wilson Harris calls 'a shamanic yearning for a break-through from a predatory coherence or stasis'. Renato Oliva's 'Re-Dreaming the World: Ben Okri's Shamanic Realism' (pp. 171–96), Paolo Bertinetti's 'Reality and Magic in Syl Cheney-Coker's *The Last Harmattan of Alusine Dunbar*' (pp. 197–207), Pietro

Deandrea's '"History never walks here, it runs in any direction": Carnival and Magic in the Fiction of Kojo Laing and Mia Couto' (pp. 209–25) and Valeria Guidotti's 'Magical Realism Beyond the Walls of Apartheid? *Missing Persons* by Ivan Vlandislavic' (pp. 227–43) are critical articulations of the African writer's response to modes of cultural apprehension whose definition of reality is less rigid than that of the Western world, for example. While Ben Okri's narratives revive, among other African beliefs, the African conception of time as 'eternal return', and the perception of history as psychohistory, in Syl Cheney-Coker's attempt to fictionalize the contradictory history of his native Sierra Leone, which covers 200 years of history replete with the mingling of the story of native Africans with the history of the slaves in America, he does not think in terms of the historical novel, a well-established genre in literatures in English. 'He [thinks], rather, of the fictional form adopted by García Márquez, where history is transfigured by myth and where character and incident, with the complete liberty of the literary imagination, contain the ultimate meaning of the history that is taking place alongside them.' The same organizational principle is at work in Kojo Laing's writing, 'where the extraordinary setting is not severed from social issues belonging to postcolonial Ghana'. Finally, focusing on Vlandislavi's collection of short stories, *Missing Persons*, Guidotti's attempt to trace the existence of a fictional mode identifiable as magical realism, in a South Africa that was until recently a divided and unnaturally fragmented nation, has led to the description of magical realism as 'a mode suited to exploring—and transgressing—boundaries, free from conventionalism, narrowness and hate', and one which 'might function as a catalyst in the development of a new, national and cross-cultural post-apartheid literature'.

Another belated review is the coverage of 'New Theatre in Francophone and Anglophone Africa' in *Matatu* 20[1999], edited by Anne Fuchs. 'Divergent trends', persistence of traditional elements in forms of 'syncretic' theatre, and 'popular' in the true sense of the word, are the terms and perspectives used by contributors of these essays, most of which originate from a conference held at Mandelieu on the French Riviera in June 1995, to describe the variety and richness of new theatre in Africa. The volume brings together theorists as well as practitioners of theatre issuing out of the contexts of both British and French colonial systems. According to Fuchs, 'the concentration of work on the Cameroon, the predestined theatrical meeting-ground or battlefield reflecting political or linguistic divisions between the societies which had been produced by the different paradigms of colonial rule' epitomizes the nature of the problem. Conditions of production and production problems play different debilitating roles in stifling the potential and growth of African theatre: while the former concerns the emergence or lack of new theatrical forms due to a plethora of factors, from political and economic conditions once imposed by the colonial powers to the different dictatorial regimes on the continent, the latter encapsulates 'the precariousness prevailing in most African countries at organizational levels'. Fuchs has compiled a series that, according to her, speaks for itself: 'Indeed after eighteen months' hard work trying to find subsidies and persuading African troupes to participate in what we hoped would be a festival of African theatre, four of the scheduled performances had to be cancelled for a variety of reasons. These included a French cultural service cutting off funds at the last minute (for political reasons?), an African Ministry of Culture ordering an actor to attend a Festival in Canada (whereas he had already received his air-ticket from

Nice), economic problems which prevented a troupe from beginning their rehearsals in time to be ready for Mandelieu (once again the subsidy for their fares had been granted for the festival), and finally another engagement on the Côte d'Azur fell through for a performer who was obliged to take on other contracts for June.'

Eckhard Breitinger's 'Divergent Trends in Contemporary African Theatre' (*Matatu* 20[1999] 3–16), Godfrey Tangwa's 'Anglophone Theatre in a Francophone City: The Flame Players and Other Anglophone Troupes in Yaounde' (*Matatu* 20[1999] 155–68), Geoffrey Davis's 'Of "Undesirability": The Control of Theatre in South Africa During the Age of Apartheid' (*Matatu* 20[1999] 183–208), Christopher Balme's 'Syncretic Theatre: The Semiotics of Postcolonial Drama and Wole Soyinka's *Death and the King's Horseman*' (*Matatu* 20[1999] 209–28), Christine Fioupou's 'Variations on Wole Soyinka's *Death and the King's Horseman*' (*Matatu* 20[1999] 229–40), and James Gibbs's 'Soyinka and a Tattered Power: Notes on Wole Soyinka's Contacts with France, 1955–95' (*Matatu* 20[1999] 259–74) are some of the choice essays focusing on the conditions of production, and problems of production in relation to the whole issue of 'newness' in the field of African theatre from the Anglophone perspective alone. The 'divergent trends' that Breitinger observes in contemporary African theatre, for example, render any generalization about Africa, whether it be 'in the field of politics, culture or economics', at best misleading. Nevertheless, in the domain of theatre, there are a number of common trends that distinguish modern African theatre from other theatrical traditions. For instance, a 'common trend in present-day African theatre seems to be that the formerly strong traditions of touring the country with travelling troupes has more or less come to a standstill'.

Finally, in spite of their many connections, African literatures and African arts, according to Mineke Schipper, have mostly been studied apart. *Research in African Literatures* 31:iv[2000] is a special issue on the 'Poetics of African Art', edited by Schipper. It is a collection of essays that examines parallels and differences in form, meaning and function between productions in the two fields, 'as well as developments, intercultural contacts, and reflections on aesthetic norms, concept and methods of research'. African literature and African art have also endured a complicated relationship, both having been 'used as historical, sociological or anthropological material that can inform us about village life, colonization, the position of women, political or social change etc.'. An integral aspect of that complicated relationship is the fact that, until the 1960s, oral literature was not considered as literature, and it was anthropologists and 'folklorists' who rescued the genre so that it was never completely lost. Schipper's lucid introduction to the volume raises all the potential areas of complication, including the question of 'beauty' or how to pass aesthetic judgement, how to appreciate an art object or a text as performance: 'Since the nineteenth century, in the Western world, there has been a tendency to isolate "the arts" as well as "literature" aesthetically as "messages for their own sake," referring to themselves, mainly exclusively. But words and images are embedded in history, in past and present social and cultural contexts, and aesthetics have become a subject for debate.'

Wilfried van Damme's 'African Verbal Arts and the Study of African Visual Aesthetics' (*RAL* 31:iv[2000] 8–20), Dennis Duerden's 'The "Discovery" of the African Mask' (*RAL* 31:iv[2000] 29–47) and Antonia Kalu's 'African Literature and the Traditional Arts: Speaking Art, Molding Theory' (*RAL* 31:iv[2000] 48–62) examine, in varying degrees, what van Damme describes as 'what the opinions that are expressed in various literary types may teach us about the aesthetics informing the creation and evaluation of the visual arts in African cultures' in practical and theoretical terms. While several forms of verbal art may express views on aesthetics, and may contribute significantly to the study of African aesthetics as well as philosophies of art, one of van Damme's primary conclusions is that 'in the study of aesthetics, the relevant opinions that surface in these literary forms may be used as a confirmation or supplement to findings yielded by other means, such as the results of examining art criticism'. In his discussion of the "discovery" of African art, Duerden uses four terms that 'previous writers have used in a very confused manner', to advance the central thesis that 'visual cognition must be distinguished from verbal cognition and that the thesis of localized linguistic particularity does not apply to visual understanding'. Kalu's essay, on the other hand, explores the purposeful use of oral narratives, 'by purposefully inserting fragments from traditional archives into the new', as a contemporary African literary technique with positive implications for the development of an African literary theory. Mineke Schipper's 'The Verbal and the Visual in a Globalizing Context: African and European Connections as an Ongoing Process' (*RAL* 31:iv[2000] 139–54) extends Kalu's discussion of the colonized African's conscious efforts to increase 'the match between the oral tradition and Western scriptocentric incursions into existing African temporal and spatial realities', as an ongoing process of negotiating power, along the lines of their own imagination, which a number of European and African intellectuals, artists and writers have been actively involved in as a result of the history of colonization. Within the context of the ensuing process of negotiation and appropriation, one of Schipper's primary conclusions is that 'there will certainly be more differences than similarities, but are not differences as relevant in such a globalizing *rendezvous du donner et du reçevoir?*'

(b) West Africa

'FonTomFrom: Contemporary Ghanaian Literature, Theatre and Film' (*Matatu* 21–2[2000]), edited by Kofi Anyidoho and James Gibbs, is a collection that recalls the cultural landscape of Ghana as seen in her literary and performing arts—a phenomenon which, according to Kofi Anyidoho, 'is dominated by an amazing range of metaphors and symbols, of which a certain core group constitute various patterns of recurrence'. 'National Identity and the Language of Metaphor' (*Matatu* 21–2[2000] 1–22) is the title of Anyidoho's characteristically lucid introduction to the collection of articles, interviews, creative writing and book reviews. From the Sankofa bird, through Ananse the Spiderman, to the primal drum, and the slave fort or castle, even a cursory glance at the metaphors that dominate the Ghanaian cultural landscape would reveal that the constant interplay between antiquity and modernity, between past and present/future time, as the divine drummer 'takes us on a voyage of exploration on which we follow the path/road as a symbol of the probing, perhaps intrusive, spirit of human civilization', points to the fact that 'The path has crossed the river/The river has crossed the path'. Reiterating the pre-eminence of the Sankofa principle in the development of Ghanaian national literature, and the manner in which the Sankofa bird stands 'as a defining metaphor for the question of methodology or approach to artistic practice as a pointer to the nation's search for direction and self-definition', one of Anyidoho's primary conclusions is that the emphasis on written literature 'is an anomaly in the definition of a national literature which focuses unduly on printed texts mostly written in a foreign language'. The oral contexts of Ghanaian literature, literature in Ghanaian languages, (video)film, and dance are the other aspects of this cultural landscape often neglected within the purview of such a definition. The total corpus of Ghanaian literature, according to Anyidoho, 'emerges as a more complex phenomenon than formal academic studies have so far indicated', and he identifies five broad and often overlapping forms of literary expression in Ghana: 'Oral literature, (mostly in the various local languages); popular literature (some of it written, some of it in oral forms, in both English and local languages); literature written in Ghanaian languages; literature written in English; and the special category of children's literature, in both English and Ghanaian languages.'

Conversely, the twenty-one articles, three essays on different aspects of what is described broadly as 'Marketplace: The Media', five interviews, all of which are interspersed with creative extracts from a crop of writers, described by Anyidoho as 'a generation of creators who have since become ancestral figures, even though many of them are indeed alive and still full of creative energy', and book reviews, introduce us to new works by some older writers as well as works by new artists. However, 'it is also a celebration of the coming together of several new scholarly voices for the common purpose of giving greater visibility to and appreciation of a nation trying to come to terms with its identity in the complex theatre of the modern world'.

Kwadwo Opoku-Agyemang's 'Cape Coast Castle: The Edifice and the Metaphor' (*Matatu* 21–2[2000] 23–8), and Ebow Daniel's 'In Celebration of a Harvest of Contemporary Ghanaian Writing' (*Matatu* 21–2[2000] 29–35) begin the celebration of the theme of identity in the complex theatre of the modern world, articulated by Anyidoho above. While Opoku-Agyemang examines the ubiquitous roles of the Cape Coast Castle, both the metaphor and the edifice in its context as 'a society in itself, a society of experiences, a system or order whose fundamental concepts are planted in the disordering of our society', Ebow Daniel makes a bold appeal for a recognizable format, of the sort that accompanies 'ship launches', to be accorded the launching or harvesting of books as well. John K. Djisenu's 'The Art of Narrative Drama in Ghana' (*Matatu* 21–2[2000] 37–43) and Efua Theodora Sutherland's 'The Second Phase of the National Theatre Movement in Ghana' (*Matatu* 21–2[2000] 45–57) are also two sides of the same theatrical narrative. The former was first published in 1975, and the latter in 1965. Besides its popularity in Ghana, narrative drama, according to Djisenu, remains the country's greatest contribution to world theatrical forms. Efua Sutherland, Ama Ata Aidoo, Asiedu Yirenkyi, Martin Owusu and Mohammed Ben-Abdallah are among the leading practitioners of the theatrical form in which Ananse, the spider about whom folktales are told and who is known for his endless tricks, predominates. Sutherland's 1965 essay has gone down in the annals of Ghanaian literary history as the document that raises all the pertinent issues 'which are very much a concern of the ongoing debate about arts and culture in Ghana today'. Drawing on the lessons from the first phase of the national theatre movement in Ghana, Sutherland writes, 'Of all the factors signifying the end of the first phase of the National Theatre Movement, the most disquieting is the slowdown in output of creative material, particularly dramatic literature.' Again, Anne V. Adams's 'Revis(it)ing Ritual: The Challenge to the Virility of Tradition in Works by

Efua Sutherland and Other African Writers' (*Matatu* 21–2[2000] 85–94) recalls
Sutherland's pioneer position in contemporary African literature: she describes her
as a 'Path-Finding Mother', and asserts that her aesthetic point of view and her work
constitute part of the 'foundation on which the contemporary production of written
literature by Africans rests'. W. Ofotsu Adinku's 'The Early Years of the Ghana
Dance Ensemble' (*Matatu* 21–2[2000] 131–4) revisits the pulsating moment in
1962 when the National Dance Company was formed, an event that 'was in line with
Kwame Nkrumah's nation-building policy and his programme for the cultural
emancipation of Ghana and Africa'. Kofi Anyidoho's 'Dr. Efua Sutherland: A
Biographical Sketch' (*Matatu* 21–2[2000] 77–81) and 'Mother Courage: A Tribute
to Auntie Efua from all her Children in the Arts' (*Matatu* 21–2[2000] 83–4) pay
further tribute to Sutherland's legacy and giant vision. 'Textual Deviancy and
Cultural Syncretism: Romantic Fiction as Subversive Strain in Black Women's
Writing' (*Matatu* 21–2[2000] 155–64), by Jane Bryce and Kari Dako, Irene M.
Danysh's 'Ama Ata Aidoo's *Changes*: The Woman's Voice in African Literature'
(*Matatu* 21–2[2000] 165–72), Francis Ngaboh-Smart's 'Narrative as Tactics in
Armah's *Two Thousand Seasons*' (*Matatu* 21–2[2000] 173–87), A.N. Mensah's
'Counting the Ways: The Love Poetry of Kofi Anyidoho' (*Matatu* 21–2[2000] 217–
26) and M.E. Kropp-Dakubu's 'Kojo Laing's Poetry and the Struggle for God'
(*Matatu* 21–2[2000] 235–41) are essays on various aspects of the creative output of
Ghanaian writers who, according to Anyidoho, 'work primarily and directly in the
colonial heritage language of English. However, to achieve formal, structural,
ideological and aesthetic relevance, each one draws on various aspects of African
traditional arts as well as on certain characteristic features of their mother tongue
and possibly other African languages'. Interspersed with interviews with leading
writers, such as Mohammed Ben-Abdallah, Bill Marshall, and Kwaw Ansah, are
creative writings by Ama Ata Aidoo, Efua Sutherland, Kofi Awoonor, Abena Busia,
and Kwesi Brew, as well as book reviews, which make 'FonTomFrom: Ghanaian
Literature, Theatre and Film' is a welcome publication, and one that gives, in
Anyidoho's words, 'greater visibility' to and appreciation for 'a nation trying to
come to terms with its identity in the complex theatre of the modern world'.

Stephanie Newell's 'Redefining Mimicry: Quoting Techniques and the Role of
Readers in Locally Published Ghanaian Fiction' (*RAL* 31:i[2000] 33–49) and
African Theatre's focus on two Ghanaian playwrights, Joe de Graft and Mohammed
Ben-Abdallah, complete this coverage of Ghanaian writing. The latter comprises
Obi Maduakor's 'Joe de Graft and the Ghana Cultural Revival' (*African Theatre*
22[2001] 65–71), James Gibbs's 'Joe de Graft: Theatrical Prophet with Strange
Honours—A Response to a Profile by Kofi Agovi' (*African Theatre* 22[2001] 72–
83), 'Mohammed Ben-Abdallah at Fifty' (*African Theatre* 22[2001] 84–8) by
Anthony A Aidoo and James Gibbs, and James Gibbs's 'Land of a Million
Magicians' (*African Theatre* 22[2001] 89–94).

Ahmed S. Bangura's *Islam and the West African Novel: The Politics of
Representation* revisits what he describes as the image of Arabs and Muslims that 'I
had in my head', including its source and its enduring influence on African letters
and thought. The question of representation, ideology, and the relationship between
literary and religio-political systems are, according to Bangura, at the heart of 'the
debate on the "worldliness" of the literary system: the politics of textuality and
representation, as well as the politics of interpretation'. Bangura's book examines

the representation of Islam and Muslims in the sub-Saharan novel, including the critical discourse it has generated. The 'Othering' of Islam, and the habit of opposing it with African traditional wisdom or with materialist Marxism, combined with a reluctance or inability to situate the questions discussed within an Islamic paradigm, have led to 'a failure or refusal to recognize the diversity in unity of Islam and the myriad voices that Islam can accommodate, and hence the possibility of conflict emanating from varying emphases and interpretations'. The book has five chapters, a lucid introduction and a concluding chapter that summarizes some of the more obvious distortions of Islam in the novels studied and the criticism that pertains to them. The works analysed include novels by Cheikh Hamidou Kane [1961], selections from the works of Sembene Ousmane, Aminata Sow Fall, Ahmadou Kourouma [1968] and Ibrahim Tahir [1984], as well as the major critical works on these novels, such as those by Mohamadou Kane [1982] and Debra Boyd-Buggs [1986]. The central thesis of Bangura's study emphasizes 'the ideological character of the textualization of Islam in the novels and of the criticism the novels have generated'. Proceeding from the premise of the most virulent attack to date on Western scholarship on the Muslim Orient, Edward Said's paradigmatic *Orientalism*, chapter 2, entitled 'Africa, Islam, and the Legacies of Colonialism', discusses the concomitant effects of the distortions and self-perpetuating body of 'truths' about Islam by scholar-administrators, or at least by those closely linked with administration. While Said's attack on Orientalism is to a large extent applicable to colonial scholarship on Muslim societies in sub-Saharan Africa, it is regrettable that 'Africanists and African literary critics of African literature, as well as some African writers, continue to make generalizations about Islam and Islamic history based on ideas borrowed from politically overdetermined European Orientalist sources'. Bangura's subsequent delineation of the extent to which the survival of colonial perceptions and attitudes contributes to what he calls 'outright misreadings of sub-Saharan fiction of the Islamic traditions' begins with 'Islam and Africanist Literary Criticism' in chapter 3 and continues with 'Critical (Mis)Readings' of the novels of Sembene Ousmane, Aminata Sow Fall, and Ibrahim Tahir, among others. According to Bangura, he is attempting to examine 'many key arguments on the characteristics of contemporary African(ist) writings on Islam and Muslims in black Africa'.

Femi Ojo-Ade's *Ken Saro-Wiwa: A Bio-Critical Study* is written, on its own admission, partly to 'exorcise the feeling of cowardliness and betrayal consequential to Saro-Wiwa's challenge in that hotel room'. Best known for his political activism on behalf of his Ogoni people of the Niger Delta of Nigeria, Saro-Wiwa was hung by the Nigerian military junta on 10 November 1995. According to Ojo-Ade, controversy 'has continued to swirl over the man's personality and political purposes'. A distinguished Nigerian artist and academic himself, Ojo-Ade met Saro-Wiwa 'at one of those academic get-togethers included on his [Saro-Wiwa's] itinerary as a 1990 distinguished Visiting Fellow of the United States Information Agency'. The consequent 'senseless slaying of a patriot and fellow artist', Ojo-Ade reveals, was another reason why he set out to buy as many of Saro-Wiwa's books as he could find: 'Upon reading those books that, interestingly enough, never attracted my attention while Saro-Wiwa was alive, I have come to understand why he laughed so loudly on that cold North American night. Tragically, I have come to know why his killers were so single-minded in their plan to "pacify" his Ogoni people (think of the European's pacification of Africa) by ridding the land of his immensely powerful presence.' The 300-page book comprises lengthy chapters devoted to each of Saro-Wiwa's novels, as well as to his short stories, poetry and the hilarious popular TV series *Basi and Company* in its print and televised versions. The 'bio-critical study', as Ojo-Ade subtitles the book, is an attempt to decipher the enigma that Saro-Wiwa represents within Nigerian arts and politics: 'Yet the questions remain because, in spite of it all, Saro-Wiwa's books reveal a deep affinity for the Nigerian military. His is symptomatic of the dilemma of the potentially progressive elements within the African intelligentsia, confused in their quest for change by their inexplicable and often fatal attraction to the military, whose objectives, ever retrogressive, have always been geared towards self-perpetuation in power.'

The penultimate chapter, entitled 'The Ogoni Tragedy and Saro-Wiwa's Commitment' (pp. 259–83), discusses Saro-Wiwa's last two books, *Genocide in Nigeria* [1992] and *A Month and a Day* [published posthumously in 1995], in the same bio-critical fashion as the previous chapters and indeed the entire book. It summarizes Ojo-Ade's critical angst, directed at not just Saro-Wiwa's own paranoia, but also at the local gamesters and gangsters at the helm of power who facilitated Saro-Wiwa's brutal death: 'Oil, one must agree, is the cause of the country's curse. If Saro-Wiwa can be criticized for paranoia, the Nigerian vultures are guilty of much worse, from arrogant insensitivity to absolute inhumanism.' The politics of oil and its international dimension have produced what Ojo-Ade describes further as something akin to 'colonial situations, [in which] a combination of the government's unforgivable ignorance of the oil industry, and the Ogoni's understandable naiveté, gave the oil company a free hand to exploit the land. By every reckoning, Shell-BP is a perfect example of international capitalism in its worst character of cruelty, stupidity and racism.'

Tayo Olafioye's *The Poetry of Tanure Ojaide: A Critical Appraisal* is a book-length study of the oeuvre of one of the prominent Nigerian writers of the post-Soyinka/Achebe generation. Like Saro-Wiwa, Ojaide hails from the Niger Delta of Nigeria, and, according to Olafioye, in order to appreciate the 'spiritual energy that excites Tanure Ojaide's poetic manifestation', one must look at the iroko tree—a cultural metaphor of stability and strength, and the delta, a feature of physical geography imbued with mythical connotations. Both the iroko and the delta 'symbolize nature's rich endowment in the natal habitat whose cultural waters bathe him [Ojaide]'. Ojaide's first volume of poetry, *Labyrinths of the Delta* [1986], is suggestive of 'a maze, a myth, an intricate structure of interconnectedness—convoluted in character and composition'. The iroko metaphor, on the other hand, is given detailed treatment in Ojaide's collection, *Children of Iroko*, in which the topography of the delta vegetation, where the iroko is a monarch, is explored in its traditional/cultural as well as postcolonial settings. In the traditional setting, protective prayers are procured through the traditional articles of purification so that the 'children [of iroko] are saved from pythons and puff-adders'; in postcolonial terms, however, 'the pythons and puff-adders are the politicians, business marauders, greedy interlocutors and such effete knobs of society'. In spite of the various charges levelled by some critics of African literature who argue that 'with a few exceptions … Ojaide's poems are mostly "messages from the front", imagistically flat but loud with rhetorical outrage', Olafioye insists that what has eluded these critics is 'Ojaide's African linguistic approach to poetic cadence, assonance and resonance'.

Three essays from *African Theatre*'s focus on 'Playwrights and Politics' discuss the plays of Femi Osofisan: Sam Ukala's 'Politics of Aesthetics' (*African Theatre* 22[2001] 29–41); Victor Ukaegbu's '*Once Upon Four Robbers*: Continuing the Intercultural Debate' (*African Theatre* 22[2001] 42–56) and Awo Asiedu's '*Once Upon Four Robbers*: A Review' (*African Theatre* 22[2001] 57–61). In his study of Osofisan's plays and the politics of aesthetics in which they are caught, Ukala describes Osofisan's art as an integral aspect of the alternative African tradition of exploring 'largely political issues, which makes Osofisan a playwright in politics from the perspective of subject matter'. Ranked within the alternative theatre tradition that is distinct from Western theatre, which was taught by the colonialists 'to the African student as *the* literature while most African artistic creations were denigrated or even banned' (original italics), Osofisan's plays, by his own admission, aim to contribute to what he describes as 'new patterns of dramaturgy, derived from our "African traditions"'. The plays, according to Ukala, can be studied 'in relation to the aesthetics of the alternative theatre and the crucial issue of mass appeal and mobilisation'. Through its dismantling of the European or Brechtian aesthetic hegemony in Africa, Osofisan's dramaturgy is engaged in a mode of subversion that is 'the cornerstone of the politics of aesthetics required to totally free the African mind from the cultural shackles of colonialism'. Similarly, focusing on Osofisan's *Once Upon Four Robbers*, Ukaegbu examines the relevance of theatre that crosses cultures: 'These theatrical elements do not limit *Once Upon Four Robbers* to its traditional landscape as much as they render it a blueprint capable of different interpretations and adaptations.' While Ukaegbu's contribution examines the *modus operandi* of such adaptability through the theatrical experience of the Jawi Collective, an organization formed by four lecturers in Drama and Performance Studies at University College, Northampton (UK), Awo Asiedu's review, from the perspective of a researcher in African theatre, raises all the potential critical and creative apprehensions that could exist around the producers' attempt to adapt the play to suit a Northampton context and audience. In the context of the growing interest in intercultural theatre, it must be observed that *Once Upon Four Robbers* was Osofisan's response to a specific situation, and, according to Asiedu, 'it also has unique features and is very different from the European plays with which the students are familiar. It is not surprising therefore that the Jawi collective would choose it, if for no other reason than to demonstrate how it might be performed.' Finally, from the perspective of an active member of the collective, Ukaegbu suggests that the choice of text was predicated on two main considerations: Besides the challenge of adapting African theatre to a Western setting, 'Osofisan's aesthetics and its similarities to Brechtian theatre had mouth-watering prospects: the adaptation presents numerous specific challenges for its multi-racial cast, and has serious implications for intercultural theatre in general.'

Eckhard Breitinger's 'Bole Butake's Strategies as a Political Playwright' (*African Theatre* 22[2001] 7–17) and Foluke Ogunleye's 'Ife Convocation Plays as Politics: An Examination of Some Past Productions' (*African Theatre* 22[2001] 18–25) complete this issue's coverage of the West Africa sub-region. Against the background of Butake's declaration not to say things in a blunt manner 'simply because I want to be politically committed', Breitinger observes that while the thematic points of departure for most of Butake's plays are taken from current political issues—'a case of sexual abuse and corruption for *The Rape of Michelle*, the Lake Nyos gas eruption in 1986 for *Lake God*, the maladministration of international relief for *The Survivors*, students riot and police brutality for *Shoes and Four Men in Arms*'—the issues in which Butake is really interested go beyond pure topicality. Ogunleye's discussion of the Convocation plays goes back to the first of the productions, the world premiere of Wole Soyinka's *Death and the King's Horseman*, which coincided with the establishment of the Department of Dramatic Arts in 1976 at the then University of Ife. During the period from 1976 to 1998, which witnessed among others the production of Rasaki Bakare's *Drums of War*, the playwrights and directors of the Convocation plays, according to Ogunleye, have taken advantage of 'the freedom of artistic enterprise in a locale which has been relatively free from political pressure to put forward their socio-political commentaries through drama'.

(c) East and Central Africa
Tirop Peter Simatei's *The Novel and the Politics of Nation Building in East Africa* examines what it describes as a literature that is 'not only about the history of imperialist subjugation of African peoples and their resistance to it; it is also its product'. Within the context of the complex process of nation-building in East Africa, the novelists have not only responded with a certain urgency to the need to decolonize the minds of the citizens, but, perhaps more importantly, also reveal the subtle and undisguised forms which oppressive power has taken in the postcolonial era. Simatei's study delineates a process in which East African novelists have moved from affirmation to delegitimation. Having supported the aspirations of African nationalism, and the idea of nation-building that animated these aspirations, according to Simatei, 'the partnership between the writer and the nationalist politician could not hold in the post-colonial period'. The change in African literature's orientation in general, from nationalist to revolutionary, has been approached in different ways by both the critics and the creative writers themselves: while the Kenyan critic Neil Lazarus 'tends to overemphasize what he perceives as the short-sighted perspective of African writers that leads them to "experience decolonisation as a time of massive transformation"', Simon Gikandi argues that what may appear as confusion in the outlook of the writers 'is the outcome of attempts to represent situations which were themselves incoherent and still forming'. Ostensibly, the writers from the three East African countries studied here have approached the whole notion of East African identity differently. For Leonard Kibera, Robert Serumaga and, in spite of the ideological dimension of his literary project, Ngugi wa Thiong'o, the creative temperament remains animated by the collapse of the dream of independence, while for the trio of Oludhe-MacGoye, Peter Nazareth and M.G. Vassanji, Homi Bhabha's 'politics of migrating metaphors' can be regarded as the organizing principle. With the latter group, an understanding of the Asian presence in East Africa helps to contextualize the kind of issues that animate their creative discourses. One of Simatei's primary conclusions is that, within the context of the politics of nation-building in which it is obviously implicated, the novel in East Africa has functioned as a challenge to national projects just as it is inspired by them: the novel 'antagonizes the national project

precisely because it activates the disparate and at times discordant identities and voices within the national space'.

One East African country or nation-state that has developed 'the different political conditions' that render a regional approach to the study of East African literatures and cultures untenable is Tanzania. Alain Ricard's *Ebrahim Hussein: Swahili Theatre and Individualism*, translated from the French by Naomi Morgan, examines the peculiarities of this milieu against the backdrop of the corpus of theatrical materials produced by Ebrahim Hussein, the best-known Swahili playwright, dramatist and theorist. Proceeding by allusion, images, and ellipses, but always in the same direction, Hussein's texts, according to Ricard, 'interpolate us as they interpolate the pupil, the student and the Tanzanian intellectual'. In Tanzania, as in the case of most African countries, a totalizing concept of culture tried to take root: 'Tanzania's socialist and cultural and political unity-project was a totalising one and it left very little space for the autonomy of artistic creation—Ebrahim's space'. Tanzanian critics, according to Ricard, are for ever reproaching Hussein 'for his *ubinafsi* (individualism)'—a position that Ricard employs to posit one of the central hypotheses of his study: 'The question about autonomy of artistic creation leads to that of autonomy of the individual. Today Ebrahim is alone: does that make him an individualist?' Hussein, as Ricard observes, epitomizes the experience and dilemma of a generation, a phenomenon that can be seen in his early plays, and if his compulsive *oeuvre* could be described as contemporaneous with the development and planning of standard Swahili—Kiswahili Sanifu—the question arises, 'Why, in all the French and English writings on Tanzania, is there little interest in literature in general and in Ebrahim's work in particular?' Ricard's hypotheses, he reveals, have undergone several stages of gestation and germination, and the gradual development of Hussein's work has modified and invalidated a few of them. 'But the central thesis was validated: that there had been a divorce between the sixties activist, and the socialist Tanzanian regime. This break could be understood from Ebrahim's comments and his erratic behaviour, according to my Tanzanian interlocutors.' Ricard's interpretative study traces the ubiquitous role that the Swahili language has played, not only in the evolution of Tanzanian, but also of East African social, cultural and political consciousness, eventually leading to its imposition as the national language imbued with the goal of building socialism: 'Finally, *Kwenye Ukingo wa Thim*, expresses the triumph of Kiswahili, a truly international language capable of describing the condition of the Luo and Gikuyu of Nairobi. It is also the admission of the failure of the dream of the fusion of the ethnic groups within a national melting-pot, a dream which Hussein shared with the great Kenyan writer Ngugi.'

Another writer whose life and personality are unusual in many respects, yet who represents 'a sort of summary of the troubles and strife of many artists from the African continent', is the Somali novelist Nuruddin Farah. *Research in African Literature*'s 'Roundtable on Nuruddin Farah' comprises Jacqueline Bardolph's 'On Nuruddin Farah' (*RAL* 31:i[2000] 119–21); '*Secrets*: Farah's "Things Fall Apart"', by Ousseina D. Alidou and Alamin M. Mazrui (*RAL* 31:i[2000] 122–8); Francis Ngaboh-Smart's '*Secrets* and a New Civic Consciousness' (*RAL* 31:i[2000] 129–36); and Said S. Samatar's 'Are There Secrets in *Secrets*?' (*RAL* 31:i[2000] 137–43). According to Bardolph, Farah's life is unusual 'in the number of languages, alphabets, and worldviews that shaped him as a youth: Somali, Arabic, Amharic,

English, Italian, Punjabi, to which he later added other African and European languages'. From the moment the politics of nation-building, to use Simatei's phrase quoted above, forced him out of his native Somalia during the regime of the dictator Siyad Barre and into exile for over twenty years, to the moment he finally returned to Mogadishu in 1996 to discover a shattered nation, Farah has kept alive the country in his mind and in his books. Bardolph's short but lucid overview of Farah's nomadic life and writing has dwelt on all the paradigmatic aspects of his baffling, hard-to-categorize life and creativity. Not part of the canon and not very familiar in Africa or in Anglophone countries, three factors, according to Bardolph, are at the core of the lasting power of Farah's fiction: 'Farah's novels have a way of never reflecting dominant accepted thinking. From his first novel, his stance has not been the expected one. *From a Crooked Rib* is the story of a young country woman who comes to town to escape from marriage to an old man. The simple tale has been read as a national allegory or as a feminist tract … Another characteristic of his production is the sheer skill of the writing. The craft of storytelling is mastered and even foregrounded in the display of a wide range of technical devices that change totally from book to book … Finally, Farah's work is distinctive because, for all its varied modes, it has created an imaginary world that is immediately recognizable, and that is the mark of the major novelist.'

The theme of the failed state animates the contribution by Alidou and Mazrui, and to a significant extent, those of Ngaboh-Smart and Samatar. According to Alidou and Mazrui, the way in which, in his award-winning novel *Secrets*, Farah grapples with this theme in the context of Somalia and makes it generalizable to the rest of Africa 'offers what amounts to a "moralistic" explanation that shows certain parallels with the one advanced by Chinua Achebe to explain how things came to fall apart in the Igbo "state" of Umuofia'. However, while sounding as laudatory as the other commentators, and perhaps more so as a fellow Somali compatriot in celebration and vindication of a badly demoralized Somalia, Samatar concedes that integrity in assessing a work of fiction is another matter; 'and on the latter basis it must be said that *Secrets* arouses, at least in this reader, certain concerns of context and credibility'. A work of fiction, according to Samatar, must stand or fall by the measure of its plausibility, and Samatar offers a running sample of the various grounds for complaint, concluding: 'All in all, this is a fiercely non-Somali novel … "Persistence and determination alone are omnipotent". Farah has persistence and determination in abundance. And therein lies the guarantee of his fame.'

Ogo A. Ofuani's 'Lexical Cohesion in Okot p'Bitek's *A Song of Prisoner*' (pp. 205–28) and 'The Stylistic Significance of the Graphological Structure of Taban lo Liyong's *Another Nigger Dead*' (pp. 229–49), as well as F. Odun Balogun's 'Taban lo Liyong's *The Uniformed Man*: A Reconstructionist and Metafictional Parody of Modernism' (pp. 251–62), are the three essays from Epstein and Kole, eds., *The Language of African Literature*, which focus on the East African sub-region. Ofuani's essay on Okot p'Bitek explores the effectiveness and aesthetic use of language in p'Bitek's *Song of Prisoner* [1971], by focusing on some of its special properties, and argues that it is only 'by looking at the lexical cohesive properties of a specific text' that the semantic concept of cohesion can be employed to reveal that, 'in spite of the length of this monologue, the poem is a coherent unit. Cohesion, particularly lexical cohesion, helps to make the poem what it is.' In his second contribution to the volume, Ofuani examines the role played by the peculiar nature of the typographic/graphological shape in Taban lo Liyong's poetic form, particularly in *Another Nigger Dead*. An evaluation of lo Liyong's free verse, according to Ofuani, would reveal that a significant relationship exists 'between lo Liyong's graphological deviation in *Another Nigger Dead* and his conception of poetic art, particularly the significance he attaches to this process'. Similarly, Odun Balogun examines lo Liyong's short-story collection *The Uniformed Man* [1971]. One of his primary conclusions is that the reader who prefers the realistic mode of writing could easily be upset by lo Liyong's iconoclastic postmodernist experimentation: 'Taban lo Liyong disturbs and disorients this class of readers with his confident assertive ego; his frank treatment of subject matter; his irreverence toward traditional religious beliefs, philosophies, literary luminaries, critics and the establishment; his parodies of ostentatious modernist erudition; and the liberty he takes with his intrusive and digressive narrative technique, which produces fragments and collages rather than smooth chronological narrations.'

(d) Southern Africa

This year's special issue of *African Literature Today* 23[2001], edited by Eldred Durosimi Jones and Marjorie Jones, focuses on 'South and Southern African Literature'. The dismantling of legal apartheid and the consequent liberation of the culture as well as the language and literatures of South Africa into the outside world, and the end of the war of liberation and consequent independence of Zimbabwe, are two momentous events with telling implications for the direction of South and Southern African literature today. In Zimbabwe alone, 'uncomfortable questions of inequality—privileged versus underprivileged, men versus women, black on black oppression', according to Eldred Jones, form the basis of the work of such writers as Chenjerai Hove and Yvonne Vera. There is an urgent need for the literature of South Africa to assume a deeper responsibility, with the removal of the dominating influence of apartheid and 'its stark polarities of black versus white, oppression versus liberty and poverty versus opulence' which produced a literature of protest, limiting even in its compelling necessity. Eldred Jones cites Njabulo Ndebele's seminal *Rediscovery of the Ordinary* [1991], especially its suggestion that 'an injection of irony, hitherto largely absent from the output of South African writers', may be appropriate, and discusses the ways in which the ordinary could contribute to the production of an artistic tradition: 'South African literature should rediscover the "ordinary" which includes a concern with the rural environment, and liberate itself from the mesmerising lure of the township: the "Jim come to Johannesburg" syndrome.'

Lekan Oyegoke's '"Renaissance" and South African Writing' (*ALT* 23[2001] 1–10), Ritske Zuidema's 'The Changing Role of Poetry in the Struggle for Freedom, Justice and Equality in South Africa' (*ALT* 23[2001] 11–22) and Michael Carklin's 'Dramatic Excavations and Theatrical Explorations: Faustus, Ubu and Post-Apartheid South African Theatre' (*ALT* 23[2001] 23–33) are three articles that critique, in varying degrees, what Oyegoke has described as 'the place of history in African culture, with South Africa as a specific example, by looking at change as an inevitable part of history and hence culture'. Among the germane questions raised by the spectre of history, and one that remains largely unresolved, concerns the issue of commitment; according to Oyegoke, the question still remains; 'Should commitment mean one thing for a writer from the political vantage point of post-independence West or East Africa and another thing for a writer operating under the rank burden of oppression, repression and exploitation in apartheid South Africa?' Against the backdrop of the word 'renaissance' that has surfaced in the South African political vocabulary recently, Oyegoke's critique remonstrates with the critical tendency to shift perspectives in talking about South African literature: 'Prior to 1994 South African writing had been treated by the rest of Africa mostly as black South African writing, which had the effect of either excluding liberal white writers who were sympathetic to the black cause or accommodating them in an uneasy kind of relationship.' The consequences of the 'change', for which the word 'renaissance' is perhaps a synonym, require that allowance be made for the 'ontological difference between the modern writer and the oral traditional bard'. The former, according to Oyegoke, will not come about as dramatically as the first interracial elections: 'It will be slower but steadier as old self-destructive prejudices and passions melt away and get replaced with more humane and civilized attitudes which recognize and respect the right of all human beings to life, dignity and decent treatment.' Similarly, in order to arrive at the changing role of poetry in the new South Africa, Zuidema revisits the history of black protest and resistance to apartheid and the ways in which 'poetry started to play a significant role in South Africa's social and political struggles at the time when Steve Biko's Black Consciousness Movement came to dominate black opposition politics in South Africa, in the late 1960s and early 1970s'. From Don Mattera's Black Consciousness-inspired poem, 'No Time, Black Man', through James Matthews's 'Freedom's Child' and the Umkhonto wa Sizwe fighter Dikobe wa Mogale, the pre-eminence of poetry in the struggle against apartheid came about, according to Zuidema, largely because 'poems could be performed orally in front of large audiences, and because of their brevity and density they could be turned into effective carriers of urgent political messages'. However, the need to build a new world for themselves and their children, and the public discovery of common needs, are at the heart of the poetry produced in the 1990s, and 'one of the poems that has to be seen in the light of this new commitment to constructivism and reconciliation is Mogane Wally Serote's *Come and Hope with Me* which was published shortly before the elections of 1994'. Also, focusing on the two paradigmatic examples, *Faustus in Africa* and *Ubu and the Truth Commission* by William Kentridge and the Handspring Puppet Company, Michael Carklin argues that, contrary to the approach of the dramatic historian, it is perhaps more useful to understand the work of the theatre-makers as 'a process of theatrical archaeology in which we explore with them layers of imaginative debris, or excavate tangible fragments that could lead us to new insights into the manifold human experiences that constitute our past'. The other choice essays on different aspects of the South African historical and contemporary experience are C.R. Botha's 'The Stereotyping of Whites in Xhosa Prose Fiction' (*ALT* 23[2001] 34–45), Noleen S. Turner's 'The Dynamic and Transformational Nature of Praising in Contemporary Zulu Society' (*ALT* 23[2001] 46–62), Duncan Brown's '"Structures of Feeling" and Construction of History: Mazisi Kunene's *Emperor Shaka the Great*' (*ALT* 23[2001] 63–78) and Dan Wylie's '"Speaking Crystals": The Poetry of Lionel Abrahams and South African Liberalism' (*ALT* 23[2001] 101–9).

M.T. Vambe's 'Popular Songs and Social Reality in Post-Independence Zimbabwe' (*ALT* 23[2001] 79–90), Jo Dandy's 'The Representation of Violence, the Individual, History and the Land in Chinodya's *Harvest of Thorns* and Nyamfukudza's *The Non-Believer's Journey*' (*ALT* 23[2001] 91–100) and Sophia Obiajulu Ogwude's 'Personality and Self-Re-Creation in Bessie Head's Art' (*ALT* 23[2001] 100–22) articulate, again in varying degrees, what Vambe has described as 'the broadened market situation' in the other post-independence Southern African countries of Zimbabwe and Botswana. According to Vambe, during the Zimbabwe liberation struggle in the 1970s, the link between the popularity of a song and the quest for the political freedom the song espoused was a foregone conclusion. In the post-independence era, however, like other aspects of popular culture such as local film, television and theatre, songs, especially in the context of the late 1980s and 1990s 'attempted to "name" reality in ways that more openly interrogate and oppose "official truths and accounts" of both the war and independence, even when the songs reveal an awareness of uneven forms of consciousness among the rank and file of the masses themselves'. The same politics of representation is at work in Dandy's articulation of how the private and public realms of consciousness interact in the novels of Chinodya and Nyamfukudza, and of the predominance of themes relating to history and the land. While both novels reveal a deep preoccupation with history, *Harvest of Thorns* remonstrates with different and conflicting ways of writing and telling history: for Nyamfukudza, however, history 'is essentially linked to the land, because of both traditional dependency of the local people on the land and their dispossession by the colonizers'. Finally, in her examination of the ways in which Bessie Head's psychoanalytic interests have been manifested in her artistic creations, Ogwude observes that Head 'did not write anything for which she is known and remembered today until she broke finally with South Africa and settled in Botswana'. The quest that Head began when she left South Africa for Botswana, when examined against the backdrop of the major preoccupation of psychoanalysis 'to see the work of art as a product of an individual psyche within the context of a particular historical and cultural setting', is, according to Ogwude, indicative of the fact that, 'for a character and writer who is as humane as Bessie Head, the South African society is to say the least maddening'.

Craig MacKenzie's seminal *The Oral-Style South African Short Story in English: A.W. Drayson to H.C. Bosman* is concerned with a certain tradition or sub-genre of South African short story, or what he has defined as the 'oral-style story'. The nineteenth century, according to MacKenzie, was in fact dominated by this kind of story, and the investigation in this study 'is primarily concerned with the period from the 1860s to the 1950s'. In this exploration of the oral-style story, from A.W. Drayson's fireside tales in 1862 to Bosman's bushveld stories of the 1930s, 1940s, and 1950s, MacKenzie's primary argument 'is the notion that, in the diachronic view of human history, writing (hence written literature) was preceded by many thousands of years of cultural life rooted in oral discourse'. In South Africa, the short story was dominated by the oral-style tale in the period 1860–1950: it 'took the form of the oral anecdote or frame narrative, and ... this kind of story grew in sophistication with the passing years until it became "artful"—at which point layers of irony and greater narrational complexity were introduced to the oral-style story'. The leading practitioners of the 'artful' tale are Perceval Gibbon and Herman Charles Bosman, and two central arguments are involved in the transformation or displacement of the artful tale by what may be called the 'modern short story': 'The first ... pertains to the internal shift in the oral-style story itself—the shift from the "artless" to the "artful" oral-style story ... The second concerns the broader transition from oral tale to modern short story, which, in historical terms, occurs after the rise to prominence of the "artful" oral-style story.' The shift is similar to the kind of social shift discussed by Walter Benjamin in relation to nineteenth- and early twentieth-century Europe. The focus of MacKenzie's study is 'the South African oral-style story from its beginning in the mid-nineteenth century to its most sophisticated and celebrated form in Bosman's Schalk Lourens stories of the 1930s, through the 1950s'.

Isidore Diala's 'Biblical Mythology in Andre Brink's Anti-Apartheid Crusade' (*RAL* 31:i[2000] 80–94) and Susan Pearsall's '"Where the Banalities are Enacted": The Everyday in Gordimer's Novels' (*RAL* 31:i[2000] 95–118) examine, respectively, Brink's frequent depiction of the 'characteristic Afrikaner reduction of the Bible to a White mythology that complements the materiality of apartheid', and the rendition of the political into everyday life that arose from apartheid's microscopic definitions of human behaviour with which Gordimer's novels are laden. According to Diala, like historiography and cartography, 'theology too has become a species of myth-making, annexed into the formidable machinery specifically created to empower the Afrikaner Establishment through the presentation of an authorized version of reality'. Like Gordimer's, the heroes and heroines of Brink's political novels—Bernard Franken (*Rumours of Rain*), Ben du Toit (*A Dry White Season*), Thomas Landman and Nina Jordeans (*An Act of Terror*)—must renounce kindred and political rights, and take upon themselves 'the grim burden of testifying to Afrikaner highmindedness and nobility in defiance of persecution and even death. They re-enact in Brink's fiction the role played in the struggle of South African liberation by prominent Afrikaners like Jan Hendrik Hofmeyr, Beyers Naude, Bram Fischer, and others.' Similarly, the rigidly defined power relations structuring her society, and the ways in which they manifest themselves in the most minor circumstances, have been the *raison d'être* of Gordimer's novels. Laden with political issues and catalogues of details revealing South African life in its mundane specificity, the novels, according to Pearsall, 'render accounts of the intrusions of the political into the everyday that arose from apartheid's microscopic definitions of criminal behaviour'.

2. Australia

(a) Australian Story-Telling, Australia's Telling History

The year began with celebrations for the centenary of federation, 1 January 2001 marking one hundred years to the day since the British colonies in Australia became states of a single nation. In Sydney, New Year's Day, usually one for recovery from the fireworks, drink and dance parties of the night before, was newly burdened with a family-oriented street parade and pageant in Centennial Park. While continuing to highlight increased appreciation of Australia's complex of Aboriginal cultures, the celebrations lacked the vibrant vulgarity of the bicentenary of British settlement/ invasion [1988] and the capital-fuelled brilliance of the 2000 Sydney Olympics. Significantly, the prime minister had to suffer continued calls, even catcalls, during his speech in the park, for an official apology for the stolen generations.

Indeed it was a year which saw world attention turned to Australia generally for far less celebratory reasons: the *Tampa* dispute received CNN airplay, the government refusing to allow the Norwegian freighter *Tampa* to disembark 433 asylum-seekers, rescued from their sinking boat, at Christmas Island. The subsequent controversy resulted in the 'Pacific solution': a bankrupt island nation, Nauru, was encouraged to house these refugees at Australia's expense. Fuelling growing fears in Australia of invasions by the world's undeserving poor, and with an election looming, the government next widely publicized the 'children overboard' affair, wherein another boatload of asylum-seekers allegedly threatened to throw their children off their sinking vessel, with the perceived objective of gaining entry to Australia by obliging the Royal Australian Navy to rescue them. That the story was entirely lacking in corroborative evidence from the navy was first hinted at in the press only on the morning of the federal election. The election, held in November, was fought, and won, by the incumbent conservative government largely on the issue of border protection. The end result saw the demise of Pauline Hanson's neo-conservative One Nation party, but for some it seemed Hanson's overt xenophobia had simply dissipated into the 'decent' exterior of government policy and tacitly endorsed by the federal opposition. All this in the wake, too, of 9/11.

These events politicized Australia's cultural community in ways similar to the 1997 National Inquiry into the Separation of Aboriginal and Torres Strait Islander Children from their Families. Indeed the 'stolen generations' and asylum-seeker controversies seemed linked. Both Aboriginal culture from 'within' and asylum-seekers from 'without' were characterized as threats to 'ordinary' (predominantly white, lower-middle-class) Australians, so 2001's debates about what 'is' and 'is not' Australian, what constitutes the 'in' and the 'out' (manifest in border disputes), are in many ways a continuation of a culture war over the *Bringing Them Home* report. If reaction to the report raised questions of what constitutes the 'Australian', it also prompted arguments about how 'truth' is constituted, and together these remain the principal debates pervading the year's literary scholarship. The 'truth' of fiction, the fiction of truth—postmodernism's premise and literature's age-old surmise—found new political relevance through controversies about the value and significance of oral history and legend, all freighted with new legal and material consequences, all further blurring the boundaries between Australian literature, history and anthropology.

Even so this section will limit its survey to scholarly analyses of 'literature' proper, situating many important cultural studies of Australia 'outside' its borders. An example of what might be excluded is Peggy Brock's anthology of essays by anthropologists, historians and lawyers, *Words and Silences: Aboriginal Women, Politics and Land*. The volume is anchored to the controversy over 'secret women's business', which arose over the Hindmarsh Island court battles, providing a foundation for the articulation of strategies for affirming women's land claims while protecting culturally sensitive knowledge from publication. The anthology foregrounds gender in its history and analysis of land rights and native title campaigns, but while it is all about the telling of stories, its focus is not on Australian 'literature' as such. Where does it go? In or out?

The decision is clearer with Julie Carr's *The Captive White Woman of Gipps Land: In Pursuit of the Legend*. This monograph details and analyses a persistent rumour about a woman living with the Kurnai people in south-eastern Victoria during the 1840s. Despite numerous reports, and a publicly funded expedition to discover her, she was never found. Carr is preoccupied with the mobilization of the legend for various political ends, such as to confirm the belief that Aboriginal people were 'savage' to justify seizing their land, or to affirm white masculinity in the pursuit of a damsel in distress. She also outlines controversies over the cultural 'ownership' of the legend, between local and regional versions, between oral narrative and textual record, and attempts to insert its relevance as a legend into contemporary black-white relations in Australia. While the book is principally a detailed history, Carr also discusses a dozen literary treatments of the legend (a chapter which includes some fascinating illustrations), half of them from the nineteenth century, ranging from 'A Lay of Lament' by 'J.R.M.' [1846] in the *Port Phillip Herald*, to Liam Davison's novel *The White Woman* [1994]. Carr also refers to other treatments of the 'white captive' theme in Australian literature, such as those by Patrick White, Rodney Hall and David Malouf.

Fatal Collisions: The South Australian Frontier and the Violence of Memory is co-authored by Robert Foster, Rick Hosking and Amanda Nettelbeck, who identify themselves as 'scholars in the fields of History, English and Cultural Studies'. They write that their shared project, 'the way in which European accounts of frontier violence have been mythologised over time', embodies 'that fluid zone where history, memory and myth meet in popular consciousness'. Their work is not 'a history of violence on the South Australia [*sic*] frontier, but rather an exploration of the ways in which violence has been remembered' (p. vii). Or not remembered, as the accounts of various whitewashings reveal. Given the transformation of history itself as a discipline in the last decade, the authors might be splitting hairs to position this datey volume outside it. Evidently they do not want to lay claim to a comprehensive account of frontier violence in South Australia: it must be worse than it already sounds. Rather, each chapter 'traces the way a specific event in the history of the South Australian frontier has been transmitted in, and transformed by, the folk-memory of the South Australian community' (p. 11). Certainly less historically 'sound' documents, in the traditional sense, are analysed here, as are oral legends; the making of history is interrogated. But (or maybe thus) *Fatal Collisions* is still a history in the best sense of the word. And it tells directly on the field of Australian literature, for example, contextualizing adventure romances like Simpson Newland's *Paving the Way* [1893], which fictionalizes the 'legend' of South Australian settler James Brown. The authors articulate Brown's reputation in various accounts for having poisoned and shot Aboriginal people, accounts which lack corroborative evidence yet which may be true, or, as they speculate, may simply associate Brown with crimes committed by other settlers in his time. Of related interest is Amanda Nettelbeck, 'South Australian Settler Memoirs' (*JAS* 68[2001] 97–104).

The premise of Atwood and Magowan, eds., *Telling Stories: Indigenous History and Memory in Australia and New Zealand*, is that indigenous stories challenge not only colonial accounts of history but the nature of history itself. Contributors to *Telling Stories* generally analyse the cultural, political and legal implications of indigenous life stories, genealogy, 'myths', song, dance and paintings. The editors' introduction also highlights the increasingly prominent role of indigenous culture in national pageants and celebrations and the frequency of disputes over ownership of indigenous material culture or archaeological deposits. Contributions demonstrate and some discuss directly the often fraught cross-cultural work of the recovery of indigenous histories by indigenous and non-indigenous peoples in collaborative projects (for example, through editorial arrangements) with various parties affiliated or not with institutions such as universities, museums and art galleries. Of further interest is the increasing legal (to say nothing of moral) responsibilities of anthropologist consultants working on indigenous land claims.

Again, in focusing on 'telling stories', this volume is by definition part of Australian literary studies, although ostensibly it situates itself on the border of anthropology and history. Penny van Toorn, however, whose essay 'Indigenous Australian Life Writing: Tactics and Transformations' opens the collection, works in an English department and uses postcolonial theories and practices to illuminate historic indigenous forms of autobiography ('life-writing') when it appears in unorthodox (from a literary-historical perspective) forms. Van Toorn selects various fragments of writings from as far back as 1796, and argues that together they may be viewed as a 'fragmented, collectively produced autobiography of a people'. She traces patterns of connection, as well as differences, which link early colonial writings with contemporary Aboriginal life-writing, beginning with Bennelong's letter [1796], through to the *Flinders Island Chronicle* [1836–7], legal testimony [1880–90] and Ruby Langford Ginibi's *Haunted by the Past* [1999], to demonstrate the strategic means by which indigenous authorial agency has worked within colonial power relations. (Of related interest, Susan Hosking opens a special section on 'Writing From and About Australia' in *CRNLE* with 'Breaking the Silence: Aboriginal Life Narratives' (*CRNLE* [2001] 9–24)).

Basil Sansom wants to resist the notion that the surge in publication, since the 1970s, of Aboriginal life stories constitutes an emergent genre. In 'In the Absence of Vita as Genre: The Making of the Roy Kelly Story' (in Atwood and Magowan, eds., pp. 99–122), he insists that the proliferation of stories should be viewed as an 'active movement'. He looks briefly at Stephen Muecke's successful collaboration with Paddy Roe to initiate discussion about the problems of cross-cultural translation and interference in Aboriginal storytelling by non-Aboriginal editors. Sansom notes that the preservation of self in photographs and the tape-recording of oral narratives offer a way forward in the transmission of Aboriginal knowledge. He articulates the significance of mechanical reproduction in disseminating stories beyond the reach of their source communities, examining changes to perceptions of the self and issues of public continuity. Jeremy Beckett, in 'Autobiography and Testimonial Discourse in Myles Lalor's "Oral History"' (pp. 123–43), revisits the controversy that surrounded the publishing success of Sally Morgan's *My Place* [1987] as an introduction to his own narrative of recording the life story of Myles Lalor, an elderly, dying Aboriginal man. He sets up Myles's story in opposition to that told by Morgan while dealing with similar issues of racial discrimination. Beckett acknowledges the role that he, as a 'middle-class white academic', has played in the recording and editing process and states that he regards that role as a privilege and a gift.

Telling Stories also includes a transcription of 'The Saga of Captain Cook', as told by Hobbles Danaiyarri from the Victoria River district of the Northern Territory, a work worthy of literary as well as historical-anthropological analysis (if a distinction can still be made among the three), a process which would not take away from its status as 'truth' though it may focus on its skilled manipulation of epic, poetic and dramatic effects. Not unlike a literary historian, Deborah Bird Rose begins her analysis of this 'Saga' by distinguishing its genre from that of a 'Dreaming myth' on the grounds of her research-based knowledge of different understandings of time usually operating in each category according to the speaker's culture. Bain Atwood's contribution, a study of what he terms 'the stolen generations narrative', is an excellent account of the story's (or stories') changing value and use over time and the implications of its telling. In '"Learning about the Truth": The Stolen Generations Narrative' (pp. 183–212), he investigates the role played by new fields of historical study in the 1960s and 1970s, the interest in family history and the rise of feminism, in shaping the narrative. Atwood suggests that, by the early 1990s, 'narrative accrual' or 'coalescence' was occurring: stories of removal were being reproduced and were being interpreted in terms of the 'stolen generations'. While he critiques the methodologies of the National Inquiry, his aim is not to dispute the truth of the stories but rather to argue their importance as a collective memory and acknowledge the vital role they play in constructing identity. There remains, nonetheless, much work to be done placing *Bringing Them Home* in a literary-historical context, perhaps one stretching back to the political mobilization of sentiment in such texts as Harriet Beecher Stowe's *Uncle Tom's Cabin* [1851–2], work which might elucidate the report's undoubted symbolic power, whatever its purported flaws in its historicism.

Stephen Muecke and Adam Shoemaker, non-indigenous editors of David Unaipon's *Legendary Tales of the Australian Aborigines*, have much to say on the subject of non-Aboriginal editorial interference in Aboriginal stories. In their introduction to this beautifully produced volume they trace the complex and dramatic history of Unaipon's missed opportunity to publish his stories through A&R in the 1920s and the resultant appropriation and publication of those stories by William Ramsay Smith in the 1930s with no mention of their real author. As editors Muecke and Shoemaker aim to restore Unaipon's work in two ways: to return it to a version as close as possible to the manuscript he produced in 1924–5, and to restore it as intellectual property to the Ngarrindjeri community of South Australia and to Unaipon's descendants (who were involved in the editorial process).

Disturbed by the wave of historical writing on indigenous Australia that has flourished since 1997, Wendy Brady, in 'Indigenous Insurgency against the Speaking for Others' (*UTS Review* 7:i[2001] 23–8), argues for the need and right for Aborigines to write their own histories. In 'Stolen Children, Invisible Mothers and Unspeakable Stories: The Experiences of Non-Aboriginal Adoptive and Foster Mothers of Aboriginal Children' (*Social Semiotics* 2:ii[2001] 149–54), Denise Cuthbert investigates an important, though largely overlooked, chapter in the tragic story of child separation. Writing from a non-Aboriginal, feminist perspective, Cuthbert outlines some of the ways in which the assimilationist policies of forced child removal impacted on the lives of the men, women and children who adopted or fostered Aboriginal and Torres Strait Islander children. Cuthbert continues her investigation in 'Holding the Baby: Questions Arising from Research into the Experiences of Non-Aboriginal Adoptive and Foster Mothers of Aboriginal Children' (in Levy and Murphy, eds., *Story/telling, The Woodford Forum*, pp. 180–200; discussed further below).

Sue Hosking, in 'Homeless at Home, Stolen and Saved: Three Colebrook Autobiographies' (*Westerly* 46[2001] 65–73), also taps into the continuing debate about social outcomes for Aboriginal and Torres Strait Islander children affected by the policies of separation. Hosking reads three somewhat contradictory autobiographies of Aboriginal women raised in the Colebrook Home at Eden Hills: Nancy Barnes's self-published *Munyi's Daughter: A Spirited Brumby* [2000], Doris Kartinyeri's *Kick the Tin* [2000], and Molly Lennon's *That's How It Was* [1989]. Barnes's story differs from the other two largely because she considers herself 'saved' not 'stolen'. Hosking raises important questions about preferred narratives and about censorship in terms of perceptions and expectations of Aboriginal stories.

Again, relating more to history than literature but worthy of mention is the publication of 'Indigenocide and the Massacre of Aboriginal History', a long essay by historians Raymond Evans and Bill Thorpe, which offers a comprehensive, scholarly counter-interpretation to the *Quadrant* group's sustained attacks on the issue of Aboriginal and settler deaths (*Overland* 163[2001] 21–39). Melissa Lucashenko's 'More Migaloo Words', John McLaren's 'A Scribbling Generation of the Right' and Jennifer Rose's 'Manne's Rightness' (*Overland* 163[2001] 15–20), all offer ringing endorsements of Robert Manne's *In Denial: The Stolen Generations and the Right* [2001].

Issues of 'whiteness' were also important in 2001. Alison Ravenscroft, in 'The Production of Whiteness: Revisiting Roberta Syke's *Snake Dreaming*' (*UTS Review* 7:ii[2001] 163–72), considers the ways in which 'white' readers have produced racialized meanings from the text, in particular how whiteness, blackness and Aboriginality have been read in Sykes's work, and by what signifiers. She argues that *Snake Dreaming*, in dramatizing the proximity of Aboriginality in white Australia's history, uncovers a repressed or hidden (sexual) history of black and white contact that destabilizes the notion of whiteness as identity. Of related interest is Sonia Kurtzer, 'Identity Dilemmas in Roberta Sykes's Autobiographical Narratives, *Snake Cradle* and *Snake Dancing*' (*AuFS* 16:i[2001] 101–11). Penelope Ingram's 'Racializing Babylon: Settler Whiteness and the "New Racism"' (*NLH* 32:i[2001] 157–76) theorizes the role played by whiteness in the formation of dominant subjectivities. Ingram argues that whiteness in postcolonial white settler texts is marked or 'racialized' and that, rather than suggesting a respect for difference, is the 'new racism'. She reads David Malouf's *Remembering Babylon* [1994] as 'less an encounter with Aboriginal difference than an encounter with the possibility of white difference'. Clare Bradford argues a similar point in her exhaustive investigation of children's literature, written predominantly by non-Aboriginal authors. In *Reading Race: Aboriginality in Australian Children's Literature*, she examines the representation of Aboriginality in popular and literary children's books of all genres, from late nineteenth-century texts through to the present, in terms of how those representations work towards constructions of white identity and notions of Australianness. Of related interest is Penny van Toorn's 'Hegemony or Hidden Transcripts?' (*UTS Review* 7:i[2001] 44–58) in which she investigates the oppression of Aboriginal people in reserves across Australia, conjecturing hegemonic pressures may have worked less on Aboriginal minds than on whites who did not want to admit moral culpability for Aboriginal suffering.

The making of convict rather than Aboriginal history is at issue in Rickard, ed., *George Barrington's Voyage to Botany Bay: Retelling a Convict's Travel Narrative of the 1790s*, a fully annotated edition of *The Impartial and Circumstantial Narrative of the Present State of Botany Bay* [*c*.1793]. This is the fourth title in the excellent Leicester University Press series Literature of Travel, Exploration and Empire. The original work, allegedly written by England's most famous pickpocket, George Barrington, was in fact 'skilfully manufactured' (p. 5) by publishers with a view to sales built on the purported author's notoriety, enhanced by the (true) story of his later reform. Further blurring the disciplines of history and literary studies, Rickard notes how Barrington's narrative (one of many in the bibliography) offered 'kernels of truths, peripheral visions', and that the 'contribution' it made 'to increasing public knowledge cannot be underestimated' (p. 56). Then, as now, the image of Australia becomes its land, and story becomes its history. Of related interest is Michael Ackland's 'Imprisoned Voices: Forgotten Subtexts of Colonial Convict Fiction' (*Westerly* 46[2001] 136–51), in which he seeks to uncover the concealment, in the form of covert or encoded subtexts, operating in colonial convict fiction. An appreciation of these techniques casts light on the interpretative dilemmas raised by the writings of Henry Savery and James Tucker, 'whose fictional tales of individual reformation, so often read as vindications of the imperial establishment, implicitly attest to the constraints under which each man wrote'.

Each of the chapters in Frost and Maxwell-Stewart, eds., *Chain Letters: Narrating Convict Lives*, aims to recover the biography of an individual convict, or group of convicts, from a range of sources usually considered too scanty, too 'official', or too 'numerical' to bear much fruit, or too personal to be of much general interest. It is a project, as the editors note, arising from the successful 'Colonial Eye' conference in Hobart in 1999, and the consequent formation of an International Centre for Convict Studies. Scholars associated with this project redress a general absence of individual convict voices in the 'grand narrative' of Australian history, or even (as noted in the final chapter) in the displays at the Port Arthur Museum. Certainly this volume indicates the enormous potential the tracing of individual histories has to offer our understanding of Australia's historical and contemporary culture. And *Chain Letters* maintains the emphasis on the racial, national, social and political diversity of the convicts that characterizes other recent work in the area. Some contributions to the anthology succeed in piecing together a speculative 'life', either through a meticulous chasing of names through numerous lists, or by offering 'likely' scenarios pilfered from an awareness of general social and economic changes in particular localities. All are conscious of the tentative nature of this enterprise, and most give accounts of the frustrations associated with the process of constructing lives from the archives. But by far the most successful of the contributors employ the more traditional methodology of reading sources as subject to historically specific generic conventions and moulded to the expectations of their first readers. In one such stand-out contribution, Hamish Maxfield-Stewart refers to the 'search' for readers as 'a more profitable task' than seeking to authenticate texts, and the results in his chapter are fascinating, helping to identify a particular narrative as specifically addressed to other convicts. It is unfortunate that this volume provides little insight into 'unofficial' interactions between convicts and Aboriginal people: escaped convicts who joined or fought with Aboriginal tribes, or who were assigned near or even in Aboriginal missions. These would have made interesting figures to select for re-narration, an important contribution to postcolonial discourse otherwise ignored. The gap is partly filled by Jan Kociumbas

in '"Mary Ann", Joseph Fleming and "Gentleman Dick": Aboriginal–Convict
Relationships in Colonial History' (*JACH* 3:i[2001] 28–54), though there is more
work to be done in the area.

Chris Eley addresses the 1901 federation directly in 'Deep Rooted in the
Commonwealth? Australian Artists and Writers and the Sydney Federation
Celebrations 1901' (*New Federalist* 7[2001] 62–70). A century later, 'On the
Occasion of the Centenary of Federation', Bruce Bennett provides a guest editorial
for the first issue in 2001 of the *Journal of Commonwealth Literature*, commenting
on 'Australian Writing: A View from 2001' (*JCL* 36:i[2001] 1–6). Bennett notes the
past propensity for 'the metaphor for stages in the human life-cycle' by
commentators, and contemporary attempts to proffer a more sober, fact-based
history of federation in various celebratory events and exhibitions. He articulates
how issues of race were fundamental to this union of the states and the contemporary
reassessment of non-indigenous Australia's past and present relationship with the
country's indigenous peoples, not least through the publication of their writing. He
observes that the 'rise and fall of the bushman figure' is 'the chief among many
changes in white Australian literary culture' (p. 3), noting, in relation to this, the
equivocal reception of Peter Alexander's biography of Les Murray, and of the work
of Murray himself. 'In the longer run, Murray's sheer brilliance as a writer, and his
growing international reputation will probably see him through, as the way of life he
has represented withers on the vine. But nothing is certain' (p. 4). Bennett also notes
the resurgence of women's writing in the 1970s and the 'foothold in Australian
literary publishing' being gained by Asian Australians (p. 4).

Ommundsen, ed., *Bastard Moon: Essays on Chinese-Australian Writing* explores
the history and complexity of the engagement with Australian culture by Chinese
Australian intellectuals. Their writing, stretching back to the gold rush, appeared in
many different forms, from poetry to petitions. Alison Broinowski's essay on the
latter, protesting racism encountered in the goldfields (the first in 1855), recalls Van
Toorn's recovery of Aboriginal writing and history in the form of petitions from
missions. Kam Louie and Yong Zhong concentrate on the more recent migrant
experience and how issues of race interact with those of gender, in particular
masculinity. Shen Yuanfang, in 'Confucians Down Under', focuses on
autobiography, specifically *My Life and Work* by Taam Sze Pui [1925] and Tam
Sie's memoirs from the 1920s. Other chapters include readings of work by Asian
Australian writers and Ouyang Yu's interviews with Brian Castro and Lillian Ng,
and Rodney Noonan's with Arlene Chai. Kirpal Singh discusses the work of Ee
Tiang Hong and Beth Yahp in terms of the anxiety inspired by the 'crossing borders'
experience. In the introduction Ommundsen acknowledges that Australian writing
in Chinese is 'largely unknown and thus considered nonexistent within the literary
life of Australia' (p. 3), though many writers are well known in their own
communities and in the reading communities of the countries where their work is
published. Ommundsen's subsequent essay focuses on the co-authored 'stories of
modern China' published in the 1990s by Trevor Hay and Fang Xiangshu,
highlighting these writers' refusal to exoticize their subjects. Anne McLaren writes
on the theme of loneliness and isolation in Chinese writing on Australia, while an
essay in translation by Qian Chaoying focuses on 'Death in the "New Chinese
Literature"', the literature of mainland Chinese migrants who arrived in Australia as
'overseas students' and were later allowed to stay, men and women whose

immigration trajectory and national background are different to those of many other Chinese Australians. Collections such as this one tip the iceberg of non-Anglo-Celtic, non-indigenous Australian literature, let alone that not written in English.

Ang, Chalmers, Law and Thomas, eds., *Alter/Asians: Asian-Australian Identities in Art, Media and Popular Culture*, was first published in 2000, but its engagement with questions of Australian and 'Asian Australian' identity make it an important text that warrants inclusion in this year's survey. *Alter/Asians* explores the diverse and changing meanings of 'Asia' and being 'Asian' in Australia in these uncertain post-Hanson times of rapid social, economic and cultural change. It asks what the cultural implications are of the shift which sees Australia's location and destiny as part of Asia, and challenges the categorical otherness that is still imputed to 'Asia' and 'Asians' in Australia. There is a wealth of material in this book for those interested in constructions and performances of otherness, specifically 'Asian' otherness, in Australian art, art criticism, popular culture and the media. Suvendrini Perera ('Futures Imperfect', pp. 3–24) explores the possibilities of the term 'coexistence' within the space-time context of Australia on the brink of the twenty-first century and stresses the importance of complicating the relationship between Australia and 'Asia' with an Aboriginal presence. She cites Bruce Pascoe's *Ruby-Eyed Coucal* [1996] and its narrative of relationship and trade between China, Indonesia, Papua New Guinea and the peoples of Arnhem Land prior to 1770 as an example of a counter-history of international and regional relations. Pascoe's narrative goes against any suggestion that Australia was and is a separate entity from Asia. It is, according to Perera, a narrative of coexistence, and such narratives are to be celebrated because they open up new possibilities of relationships and belonging.

The second section of *Alter/Asians* is concerned with cultural negotiations in the visual, written and performing arts. Wenche Ommundsen's discussion of the new literature produced by Chinese Australian writers dramatizes the intensity and complexity of the migrant experience, especially of the generation of mainland Chinese writers who settled in Australia after the 1989 Tiananmen Square massacre. In 'Birds of Passage? The New Generation of Chinese-Australian Writers' (pp. 89–106) Ommundsen, remarks on the difficulty that the unapologetically raw and disturbing voices of Ouyang Yu, Sang Ye and Lillian Ng pose for non-Chinese readers, and looks forward to the impact these writers and their work will have on Australian literature and culture. Of related interest to students of Chinese writing is Victor Ye's 'East or West: An Inquiry into Identity in Today's Chinese Literature' (*Westerly* 46[2001] 51–60), which explores the effects of modern capitalism on contemporary Chinese writers and their work.

In *Dragon Seed in the Antipodes: Chinese-Australian Autobiographies*, Shen Yuanfang offers a compelling narrative of the changing perspectives Chinese migrants have had of themselves, of Australia and of their country of origin, over the last 150 years. These autobiographical accounts chart personal as well as national histories. Significantly Australia's year of federation was also the one in which the Boxer rebellion 'brought disaster to the Chinese empire', so on one level, although somewhat indirectly, *Dragon Seed in the Antipodes* illuminates 'the underlying tensions between two sets of social and political revolutions that were taking place in Australia and China from the mid-19th century to the present' (p. v).

Also addressing questions of belonging and otherness is Saadi Nikro's 'The Self as Stranger: Re-Viewing *The Cars That Ate Paris*' (*Southerly* 61:i[2001] 13–17).

Nikro argues that Peter Weir's 1974 film radically questions the very basis by which Australian identity may be secured and defined. In its exploration of how strangeness is irredeemably woven into the fabric of Australian forms of culture and social life, the film takes its Australian audience beyond any simplistic division between 'us' and 'them'.

The advance of ethics, usually disguised as politics, into literature (noted in this section in 1999) continues to gain momentum. An issue of *Southerly* (61:iii[2001]) is entitled 'Lines of Concern' and focuses on critical and creative writing that addresses social, political and ethical issues. In the editorial Noel Rowe affirms his belief that 'good writing' not only helps us think differently, 'it can invite difference into our ways of thinking'. The critical essays in this volume examine issues of race, class, sexuality and gender. Rosalind Smith's '*Clara Morison*: The Politics of Feminine Heterotopia' (*Southerly* 61:iii[2001] 40–51) examines the feminist credentials of Catherine Helen Spence's novel in terms of the feminine politics of mid-nineteenth-century Adelaide, as opposed to much contemporary criticism that reads *Clara Morison* within a liberal feminist framework. Fiona Morrison, in 'On Foreign Ground: Expatriate Masculinity and the Unhomely Woman in Henry Handel Richardson's *Maurice Guest*' (*Southerly* 61:iii[2001] 64–79), argues that *Maurice Guest* thematizes deviant masculinity, wherein the male expatriate is undone through his failure to possess the 'unhomely' woman. Deirdre Moore's 'Remembering Muir Holborn' (*Southerly* 61:iii[2001] 125–34) seeks to redress a perceived neglect of Holborn, poet, author and literary critic. Moore ruminates on Holborn's life, and critiques some of his more substantial works written in the 1940s and 1950s in terms of their literary value and how they read Australian society of their time.

Also concerned with ethics, David Palmer's 'Injustice in Black and White' (*Overland* 162[2001] 21–30) asks if fiction, specifically historical fiction, can shed any light on Australia's deepening human rights crisis. Palmer reads two vastly different texts, Ian Callinan's *The Lawyer and the Libertine* [1997] and Don Fuller's *Payback at the Capricornia Casino* [1998], in order to make some sense of present political mindsets and demonstrate how the crisis has come about. Both authors, he argues, consider their novels to be statements of moral values in the political realm. Both novels engage with the politics of exclusion and inclusion. Here, however, the similarities end. Palmer asserts that Callinan's novel dramatizes the way in which Australian political conservatives view history—as a struggle between order and morality on the one hand and anarchy, corruption and licentiousness on the other. He derides such a simplistic view, and suggests that Fuller's more complex and messy understanding of history looks forward to the prospect of hope and reconciliation.

Although only in part dealing with 'Australian literature', one of the year's major publications was Robert Dixon's *Prosthetic Gods: Travel, Representation, and Colonial Governance*. *Prosthetic Gods* focuses on instances of white Australia's own imperialism in its relationship with Melanesia, 'particularly the Torres Strait Islands, Papua and New Guinea, during the first half of the twentieth century' (p. 1). Each chapter consists of 'case studies organized around exemplary careers, institutions, policies, and texts' (p. 1), including the work of individuals such as tropical medicine experts J.S.C. Elkington and Raphael Cilento, film-maker Frank Hurley, writer Ion Idriess, travel writer Frank Clune and poet James McCauley, all of whom had notable interactions with or roles within colonial administrative bodies. The strength of the volume is in each of these case studies on its own account, perhaps more so than in analysis drawn across the collection. In his introduction Dixon expresses concern at postcolonial studies which too readily conflate the representation and the governance of other peoples: 'theories of postcolonial discourse have an insidious tendency to overdetermine the evidence' (p. 2). Opposing the abstracting and generalizing gestures of Homi Bhabha's work, Dixon turns to the writing of anthropologist Nicholas Thomas, who warns against 'too instrumental a view of the relation between culture and governance' (p. 3), reiterating Thomas's arguments from *Colonialism's Culture* [1994] which, Dixon argues, 'has not ... had the impact on Australian studies, especially on the disciplines of literary and historical studies, that it ought to have had' (p. 4).

Dixon also sets out to establish a connection between 'colonialism and modernity, or the colony and suburbia' (p. 9), since the modernity of 'the Western world' implicates its other, supporting this aim by indicating scholarship which has made this connection in French cultural history. Dixon's work, citing Freud's *Civilisation and its Discontents* [1929], frames the argument that 'modernism produced an image of the colonial body defined by its capacity to incorporate mechanical processes—notably the aeroplane, the gun and the camera—and that these prostheses set it apart from the native body, which is required to be naked' (p. 19), no matter, as Dixon makes clear, if it is actually decorated. Meanwhile, Dixon, taking up Paul Carter's term from *The Road to Botany Bay* [1987], contends that incursions of the native in or on the modern body induce a 'spatial nausea', which he identifies as arising from 'a sense of the violation or, imagined violation, of "here" by "there"'. It is this nausea, Dixon argues, which the travel writer suffers for his 'sedentary readers' as a self-sacrificial act enabling stable white Australia ('here') to be brought into being as distinct from 'there' (p. 21).

More clearly 'literary', Ralph Pordzik's *The Quest for Postcolonial Utopia* describes itself as 'a comparative introduction to the Utopian novel in the New English literatures'. Its focus is the contemporary (post-1970) fictions of Australia, New Zealand, Canada, Africa and India, and the various portrayals they contain of utopic and dystopic worlds. Australian authors addressed include David Ireland, Peter Carey, Rodney Hall and Gerald Murnane. Pordzik argues that 'the utopian novel has a particular interest in ... problems created by disenchantment with cultural nationalism and decolonization on the one hand and the disillusionment with Marxism and utopian idealism that followed the end of the socialist world order on the other', somewhat pessimistically claiming that they 'make available perceptual alternatives to the poor future prospects of many postcolonial societies and cultures today' (p. 9). Rather than extended readings of individual novels, say, in the context of an author's other work, the focus is on analysis of generic attributes and their development with the transition 'from a colonial to a postcolonial or postmodern frame of reference' (p. 172).

Catronia Elder's 'Ambivalent Utopias: Representing Colonisation and Assimilation in *Naked Under Capricorn*' (*JAS* 68[2001] 135–43) argues that the 'political critique of white colonisation ... and the destruction of Aboriginal people and cultures' in Olaf Ruhe's 1957 novel 'collapses back into a sympathy and pity for the white man struggling for redemption' (p. 143). Addressing older utopias, Paul Longley Arthur discusses Robert Paltock's *The Life and Adventures of Peter Wilkins* [1751], an account of an imaginary voyage to the southern hemisphere, in

'Capturing the Antipodes: Imaginary Voyages and the Romantic Imagination' (*JAS* 67[2001] 186–95). Also clearly 'literary' in its postcolonialism, Martin Crotty writes on 'Frontier Fantasies: Boys' Adventure Stories and the Construction of Masculinity in Australia, 1870–1920' (*JACH* 3:i[2001] 55–76), distinguishing his analysis from that of Robert Dixon in *Writing the Colonial Adventure* [1995] and John Docker's *The Nervous Nineties* [1981] 'by adopting a slightly broader time span that reveals more clearly how the masculinities promoted within the adventure genre evolved, and by focusing on children's literature' (p. 56). These changes, Crotty argues, were effected by changing 'constructions of the Australian nation and in particular changing fears and hopes for the fate of white Australian society' between 1870 and 1920 (p. 76).

General cultural studies framing Australian literature include the first part of a special issue of the *Journal of Australian Studies* entitled 'Romancing the Nation' and, as the blurb has it, emphasizing 'fragmented notions of Australian identity and nationalisms' (*JAS* 70[2001]). The issue reflects both the publishing pressure to thematize and the increasingly blurred boundary between scholarly journals and essay anthologies. Andrew McGann heads the collection with an article on 'Romanticism, Nationalism and the Myth of the Popular in William Lane's *The Workingman's Paradise*' (*JAS* 70[2001] 1–12). McGann observes that Australian literature is 'still … a form of nationalist pedagogy' and identifies the 'easy simultaneity of text and populace' as a 'recurring trope in the writing of Australian cultural history' (p. 1). He critiques the assumption that realism's perceived 'exorcism' of Romanticism 'is constitutive of a national literary culture' (p. 1), proposing instead that 'the nation, with its attendant notions of organically bonded community, locality and autochthony (in short *Gemeinschaft* as opposed to *Gesellschaft*) is not simply haunted by Romanticism, it is fundamentally Romantic' (pp. 1–2). To back the claim, McGann pursues Lane's *Workingman's Paradise* [1892], a 'socialist-realist novel' (p. 2) as 'paradigmatically Romantic, and hence symptomatic of the ways in which the persistence of Romanticism organizes popular political consciousness in deeply, but constitutively contradictory ways' (p. 2).

In the same issue Paul Genoni embarks on a comparative postcolonial reading in 'Subverting the Empire: Exploration in the Fiction of Thea Astley and Peter Carey' (*JAS* 70[2001] 13–21), linking exploration as a trope (in the context of postcolonial analyses of the explorer's journal) to 'personal search' (p. 13), in particular the failures inherent in both enterprises. With inevitable reference to *Voss*, Genoni moves on to discuss a number of novels by Astley, who 'commenced writing in the wake of White's achievement' (p. 15), and Carey's *Oscar and Lucinda* [1988]. Ian Bickerton's breathless assessment of Les Murray's *Fredy Neptune* follows, 'Why Australian, and American, Why Indeed All, Historians Should Read Les Murray's *Fredy Neptune*' (*JAS* 70[2001] 23–32), recommending it to all historians: '[To] say that this verse novel is a poetic masterpiece is to sell it short'. His article addresses the question of whether 'poetry (or prose fiction) provides a form of distinctive knowledge about society which differs from that provided by historical writing' (p. 24), one which resonates with the many other debates about the value and significance of 'story' to 'history' published this year. Other contributions are cultural/historical studies and perhaps, by their quantity, demonstrate the place of Australian literature in this 'broader' (inter)discipline, even when it speaks of 'romance': Perrie Ballantyne writes on the Australian ghost town in 'Unsettled Country: Reading the Australian Ghost Town' (*JAS* 70[2001] 33–8); James Gore has an article 'Historical Collections in Australian Museums 1800–1975' (*JAS* 70[2001] 33–47); Anne Beggs Sunter surveys monuments, celebrations and performances in 'Remembering Eureka' (*JAS* 70[2001] 49–56); Lynette Russell addresses an 1860 exhibition of two intellectually disabled siblings as 'Wild Australian Children' in '"The wonderful beings they had captured": Reading the Exhibition of the Australian Wild Children' (*JAS* 70[2001] 57–62); while Peter Davies has contributed 'A Cure for All Seasons: Health and Medicine in a Bush Community' (*JAS* 70[2001] 63–72).

Worthy of mention, even if containing more examples of cultural studies than of Australian literary criticism, is the annual publication of *The Best Australian Essays* edited by Peter Craven, a stimulating and valuable text for readers seeking insight into some of the year's preoccupations. Essays dealing with 9/11 and asylum-seekers in Australia were an obvious choice to begin the collection. Also to be found are essays from David Marr, Amanda Lohrey, Helen Garner, Benda Niall and Margaret Scott, to name a few, which deal with issues as diverse as Native title rights, the Boyd dynasty, ageing, and wedding dresses. Clive James, in 'The Great Generation of Australian Poetry' (pp. 418–29) ruminates, from a personal perspective, on the deaths of Judith Wright and A.D. Hope, with passing reference to the work of McAuley, Murray, Harwood, Slessor and Brennan.

The power and relevance of stories and their telling form the basis of Levy and Murphy, eds., *Story/telling: The Woodford Forum*. This collection ranges over diverse topics, from enigma and creativity to the impact of digital technology on how films are made, from stories told in rural and urban Australia to histories of mothering, narratives of indigenous and migrant experience, and a variety of Australian music traditions. Bronwen Levy, in 'Writing Someone/Somewhere Else' (pp. 233–40), looks at how women in Australia today are writing 'Australia' and writing themselves. David Walker's 'Travelling Asia: Home and Away' (pp. 87–98) examines images of the East portrayed in Australian travel literature from the 1880s through the next hundred years. Humphrey McQueen ponders the valuable books published after his 700-page biography of Tom Roberts which he wishes he had read beforehand. In 'Prospectus for the Next Life Story of Tom Roberts (But Not By Me)' (pp. 201–15), he argues the case for rethinkng the relationship between history and biography and suggests that biographers need to employ the empathy and self-awareness when writing about their subjects that novelists use in creating characters. Richard Nile's 'Kathy Come Home: The Dubious Cartographies of a Young Novelist' (pp. 223–32) charts the personal and public literary career of Katharine Susannah Prichard.

Another text devoted to the power of stories is *Storykeepers*, in which Marion Halligan as editor has collected eighteen literary responses to deceased Australian authors or texts of the past. Tom Griffiths celebrates Francis Ratcliffe's *Flying Fox and Drifting Sand* [1938], Beverley Farmer is moved by Katherine Susannah Prichard's *Coonardoo* [1929] and Rodney Hall laments a perceived lack of interest in Joseph Furphy's *Such Is Life* [1903]. Dorothy Porter writes on Barbara Baynton's work. Bill Gammage considers Mrs Aeneas Gunn's *We of the Never Never* [1907]. Brian Matthews, meanwhile, juxtaposes Henry Lawson and Pauline Hanson.

Thinking of 'storytelling' not as the stuff of political history but as a distortion of and comment on literary history, K.K. Ruthven's *Faking Literature* argues for the legitimacy of literary forgeries because they underscore the inauthenticity of all literature. They are characterized here as creative cultural critiques, throwing light on dubious practices in cultural institutions rather than themselves representing fault. 'Fakes' discussed include Ern Malley and, more contentiously, Helen Demidenko-Darville and Mudrooroo. Of related interest are Maureen Clark, 'Unmasking Mudrooroo' (*Kunapipi* 23:ii[2001] 48–62), and Hilary Gow, 'Faking It: Representations of Arts in the News', addressing the print media (*JAS* 70[2001] 89–97). Kylie O'Connell discusses the work of Elizabeth Durack, who painted as Aboriginal artist 'Eddie Burrup' and invented his autobiography in '"A Dying Race": The History and Fiction of Elizabeth Durack' (*JAS* 67[2001] 44–54). O'Connell argues Durack's art retraces 'the history of colonial relationships between indigenous and non-indigenous Australians' and 'contributed to the erosion of Aboriginal identity and difference' (p. 44).

Michael Ackland's *Damaged Men: The Precarious Lives of James McAuley and Harold Stewart* is the story of how 'Ern Malley' shadows the lives of his creators. Issues of rational control, modernist incoherence, alienation and performance, central to the hoax, become guiding threads for this doubled biography. Ackland also shows how each life becomes a different realization of Ern's potential. McAuley begins to favour the public effect, Stewart the work of secret composition. Stewart abandons the quest for an enduring self, taking the no-path of Buddhist emptiness. McAuley hopes through sacrifice to obtain his true self, taking the path that leads to Catholic doctrine. Stewart and McAuley are, then, loosely held together by the divisions Ackland finds within them. However, in seeking to show these divisions, *Damaged Men* reveals a division within itself, becoming uneven in its sympathies. McAuley's foibles and dishonesties become evidence of hypocrisy, whereas Stewart's are accepted as part of his humanity. This means that the portrait of McAuley is still very close to that conjured by Cassandra Pybus in *The Devil and James McAuley* [1999]. Nevertheless, Ackland's study will hopefully generate renewed interest in Harold Stewart and his poetry. *The Devil and James McAuley* was reissued in 2001 complete with Pybus's strongly worded defence of her professional credentials. In this second edition she gives more extensive consideration to McAuley's time as editor of *Quadrant* in order to 'flesh out the extent of the CIA's covert cultural patronage in Australia between 1954 and 1967'.

(b) Commemoration: Biography, Letters, Reissues

If 2000 was the year for letters by or relative to Henry Handel Richardson, scholarship on the history of Australian women's writing continued with the publication of North, ed., *Yarn Spinners. A Story in Letters: Dymphna Cusack, Florence James, Miles Franklin*. These missives, chronologically arranged to read 'like a novel', include details of these women's collaborative writing and refer to many other prominent figures in the Australian and expatriate literary scene during the second quarter of the twentieth century (including, for example, Xavier Herbert and Christina Stead). North's commentary is perhaps lacking in critical distance, her footnotes sometimes chatty or even superfluous, but the letters themselves provide insight into the process of collaboration and, in the details of these authors' extended and not always benign negotiations with publishers, into the history of the book in

Australia. In supplementing Jill Roe's two-volume edition of Franklin's letters, *My Congenials*, this collection is some ways an acknowledgement of the centenary of Franklin's outstanding first novel, *My Brilliant Career* [1901], and her important role as one-woman central communication agency for so many Australian authors. Nonetheless, it is perhaps the correspondence between Cusack and James over *Come in Spinner* which is the centrepiece for North's edition. This novel is also discussed alongside Henrietta Drake-Brockman's *The Fatal Days* [1947] and Zora Cross's *This Hectic Age* [1944] by Donna Coates in 'Damn(ed) Yankees: The Pacific's Not Pacific Anymore' (*Antipodes* 15:ii[2001] 123–8), comparing these women writers' representations of Americans in wartime Australia with accounts by male historians. Sylvia Martin's monograph *Passionate Friends: Mary Fullerton, Mabel Singleton, Miles Franklin* also inserts Franklin into a web of relationships among women writers, though poet Mary Fullerton is the central figure. In this self-reflexive work, Martin discusses the difficulty of labelling the types of relationship Fullerton developed with the other women, but acknowledges the desire to do so as a means of illuminating the writing and Fullerton's life in particular. Martin's delicate negotiation of this ambiguity is summed up in her statement: 'Mary Fullerton struggled in her poetry to find a language to articulate her desire for Mabel Singleton; I have tried to suggest my own readings of these poems' (p. 178).

Of course, Miles Franklin had one other surprise up her sleeve when she died: the provision she made in her will for the establishment of Australia's richest literary prize. A site of controversy over the years, the prize also acts as a thermometer measuring changing literary and cultural values since it was first awarded (to Patrick White for *Voss*) in 1957. All this is recounted in Harry Heseltine's *The Most Glittering Prize: The Miles Franklin Award, 1957–1998*. Heseltine charts the growth, development and public perception of the award during the second half of the twentieth century. There is a sense of anxiety and perhaps justification in his tone when he states at the outset that, despite being a member of the judging panel from 1978 to 1998, his intention in this study is 'to place on the record, as objectively and straightforwardly as possible' the award's judging processes and management and 'the means by which those responsible for its management and administration have sought to realize and perpetuate Miles Franklin's own intentions' (p. xi). Franklin's will is inserted in one of Heseltine's useful appendices, which also list winners, the amount of the prize, judges, number of entries and the publishers of winning novels. While Heseltine details a few of the machinations involved in the judging process, readers hoping to gain some inside knowledge of the controversies of 1994, when the eligibility of Frank Moorehouse's *Grand Days*, Elizabeth Jolley's *The Georges' Wife* and Maurilla Meehan's *Fury* was questioned, and 1995, when the prize was awarded to Helen Demidenko/Darville for *The Hand that Signed the Paper*, will be disappointed. Heseltine engages briefly with Robert Manne's *The Culture of Forgetting: Helen Demidenko and the Holocaust* [1996] and Andrew Riemer's *The Demidenko Debate* [1996], but refuses to be drawn into the public debate surrounding the 1995 decision and the culpability of the judges. The 'Personal Postscript', a testament to his professionalism, offers a coded justification for his own conduct. He insists that 'the maintenance of silence' is the appropriate mode of conduct for a judge, even a retired judge, and states that he has no intention of revealing 'the substance, tenor and course' of the deliberations in 1995.

Contextualizing Franklin's work, Susan Magarey's *Passions of the First-Wave Feminists* attempts to dispel the reputation of early feminists for wowserism and sexual repression. Magarey highlights their 'passions' instead, their political 'fervour' and the centrality of sexuality to their 'campaigns concerning marriage, work, and citizenship': 'rather than being repressed they were utopian visionaries' (p. 2), thinking and acting outside the square of heterosexual marriage, even if that sometimes (if certainly not always) entailed or resulted in physical sexual abstinence. Franklin and other Australian women writers of fiction are referenced directly in this book, though it is principally a history of feminism in Australia in the context of world debates about marriage, morality and women's rights around the start of the twentieth century.

Further extending awareness of Franklin's oeuvre, Margaret Bettison and Jill Roe have taken selections from her extensive writings for journals and magazines to produce *A Gregarious Culture: The Topical Writings of Miles Franklin*. These they also outline comprehensively in their article 'Miles Franklin's Topical Writings: A Listing' (*ALS* 20:i[2001] 94–105). Halstead Classics, meanwhile, has reissued Franklin's study (in association with Kate Baker) of *Joseph Furphy: The Legend of a Man and his Book*, presumably (it is not sufficiently explicit) a facsimile of the original 1944 edition, and unfortunately lacking a new introduction. Joseph Furphy's *The Buln Buln and the Brolga* [1948] has also been reissued with commentary, a textual note, and annotations by Frances Devlin Glass. Speaking of Furphy, one of few articles this year to address his work also examined its interaction with 1890s feminism: Raymond Driehuis's '"The Coming Australienne": Landscape and Gender in Furphy's Nationalist Thought' (*JAS* 67[2001] 144–51). Halstead also issued rather basic editions of Judah Waten's *Distant Land* [1964], and Vance Palmer's *The Passage* [1930], sporting afterwords by novelist Hsu Ming Teo and publisher Neil James respectively. Meanwhile Elizabeth Webby reviews the 'A&R Classics' released this year by HarperCollins Australia (Angus & Robertson now being their subsidiary) in 'Classic Reissues' (*AuBR* 232[2001] 44–5). These include, appropriately, Miles Franklin, *My Brilliant Career*, in addition to Henry Lawson, *Selected Stories*, Dymphna Cusack and Florence James, *Come in Spinner*, Kylie Tennant, *Ride on Stranger*, Eve Langley, *The Pea Pickers*, Mudrooroo, *Wild Cat Falling*, Tom Keneally, *The Chant of Jimmie Blacksmith*, and George Johnston, *Clean Straw for Nothing* and *A Cartload of Clay*. Webby rightly emphasizes the boon to the teaching of Australian literature that these reissues represent.

On a different level altogether from the Halstead Classics is the continuing series of Academy Editions of Australian Literature published by the University of Queensland Press. These highly important and handsome critical editions include scholarly introductions and essays contextualizing each work, as well as full accounts of textual variations, notes and maps. Lurline Stuart's edition of *His Natural Life* is particularly welcome. Stuart has chosen the revised edition of Marcus Clarke's masterpiece, as it was first published in volume form, probably a wise decision (if not without considerable disappointment for some) granted that Stephen Murray-Smith's 1970 Penguin Classics edition of the substantially augmented and original serial version is still readily available. One day we will wish for a full comparative edition, but that would be a very large and complicated volume indeed: it is a more appropriate task for a future editor/creator of hypertext.

Stuart's edition is supplemented by an essay by Michael Roe on Clarke and convictism, and a contribution from Elizabeth Webby on adaptations of the tale from stage to film to television mini-series and comic strip. Accounts of fiddly textual variations across the volume editions in Australia, America and Britain, as well as a table of rearrangements of chapter order from the serial version (or omissions where an entire chapter is removed), are indispensable for future scholarship on Clarke.

Also released is Henry Handel Richardson's memorable second novel, *The Getting of Wisdom*, edited by Clive Probin and Bruce Steele. Though its bibliographic history is not as complex as that of *His Natural Life*, the work had lost its original Nietzsche epigraphs along the way, which are here restored. Also released this year was the late Axel Clark's *Finding Herself in Fiction: Henry Handel Richardson, 1896–1910*, sequel to his *Henry Handel Richardson: Fiction in the Making* [1990]. This volume takes the story of Richardson's life from 1896, when the author began writing *Maurice Guest*, to the reception of *The Getting of Wisdom* [1910].

The major literary biography for the year was Nadia Wheatley's *The Life and Myth of Charmian Clift*, which naturally also provides details on her partner George Johnston. Wheatley begins with an apology for her 'old-fashioned combination of chronological method and third-person narrator', used in reaction to 'a considerable blurring of the boundaries of fact, fiction and myth' in other 'tellings' of Clift's life (p. xvii). There were two related reissues in 2001, *Charmian Clift: Selected Essays*, edited by Wheatley, and in a single volume Clift's *Mermaid Singing* [1956] and *Peel Me A Lotus* [1959].

Meanwhile Meg Tasker gives Francis Adams the full critical biographical treatment in *'Struggle and Storm': The Life and Death of Francis Adams*. Adams is portrayed as a 'self-styled modern' who saw himself as 'bringing together three important strands of late nineteenth-century life—socialism, science and art'. His work, writes Tasker, 'was engaged in reconciling the contradictions implied by the simultaneous commitment to socialist ideals and those of high culture' (p. 1). Tasker also critiques her own biographical project, noting in her introduction Adams's statement at the end of his life requesting that no one write his story: 'If a bare outline … is required', wrote Adams, 'it can be given: the rest concerns no one but myself' (p. 2). But, as Tasker observes, 'Most readers are (even despite ourselves) interested in the lives of writers, and in the connections between their lives and texts' (p. 6). Her account includes the now *de rigueur* personal interventions in the conventional history, printed in a different type.

Pauline Armstrong largely resists personal interventions but cannot disguise her personal investment in Frank Hardy as a man (or perhaps hero) and a subject for biography. Her *Frank Hardy and the Making of Power Without Glory* charts the tumultuous and passionate times experienced by Hardy and members of the Communist Party of Australia and the Eureka Youth League in the 1940s and 1950s. The biography focuses on Hardy's life up to and including his acquittal on a charge of criminal libel. Armstrong offers much detail on the trial and investigates claims made against Hardy, posthumously, that he did not write *Power Without Glory*. Of related interest, and addressing Armstrong's work, is Jenny Hocking's 'Marketing Frank Hardy: The Revival of Biography as Scandal' (*JAS* 68[2001] 146–53).

Gregory Kratzmann has edited *A Steady Storm of Correspondence: Selected Letters of Gwen Harwood, 1943–1995*, on an epic scale, 400 of them gathered up into a doorstopping 500 pages, large and packed with print—and this is only a selection. Justifying the paper is the assertion in the preface that they represent 'the most valuable letters of Australia's literary culture' (p. ix), an audacious claim given the unforgettable brilliance and hilarious acidity of Patrick White's efforts collected by David Marr and the aforementioned edition of Richardson's correspondence. But as with that of Miles Franklin, Harwood's correspondence adds a whole new and important string to her literary bow, a body of work worthy of attention for its own sake.

So too for the correspondence of John Shaw Neilson. Hewson, ed., *John Shaw Neilson: A Life in Letters*, establishes a social background and a literary context, which demonstrate the complexity of Shaw Neilson as a man and a poet. Helen Hewson's comprehensive selection of letters to, from, and about Neilson provides a vivid personal and social history, making this text a valuable literary and cultural source. Readers are treated not only to Shaw Neilson's voice but the voices and thoughts of writers such as Robert Bridges, Mary Gilmore, Christopher Brennan and Vance and Nettie Palmer. The selection begins in 1906 and continues over thirty-five years. The letters cover family, social and publishing correspondence, in addition to the detailed letters about writing poetry that passed among Shaw Neilson and his three editorial advisers, A.G. Stephens, Robert H. Croll and James Devaney.

Jobling and Runcie, eds., *Matters of the Mind: Poems, Essays and Interviews in Honour of Leonie Kramer* is neither a biography nor a collection of letters, but it is designed to celebrate a significant literary life. Leonie Kramer was the Professor of Australian Literature at the University of Sydney for twenty-one years, retiring as chancellor of that university in 2001. In *Matters of the Mind*, thirty-four eminent academics, artists, politicians and writers trace developments in their various fields of expertise over the second half of the twentieth century. Poems by Clive James and Vivian Smith operate as bookends for contributions which discuss philosophy, government, law, medical research, archaeology, Asian studies, trade unionism and music. Scholars of Australian literature will be interested in Harry Heseltine's discussion of the role Leonie Kramer has played in Australian literary studies.

(c) History of the Book, the Oz Lit Historical Moment

The most compelling book of the year is part memoir, part cultural history: Hilary McPhee's *Other People's Words*. McPhee recounts her development as a reader, her early editing work for Penguin Australia, and how she established an independent publishing house—the famous McPhee Gribble imprint—with Diana Gribble in 1975. In the fifteen years of its life, McPhee Gribble published such landmark works of Australian literature as Helen Garner's *Monkey Grip*, Brian Matthew's *Louisa*, Tim Winton's *Cloudstreet* and Drusilla Modjeska's *Poppy*, becoming well known for an emphasis on quality born of time committed to authors, as well as for nurturing (unconsciously in McPhee's account) new models of workplace conditions and management. McPhee spent much time and effort lobbying against the carving up of global copyright between Britain and America, which leaves Australian publishers unable to publish and promote Americans who have already signed British rights to British publishers. In her view Australia remains a colonial backwater to the British, who show little awareness of the needs, wants, and conditions of Australian readers but rather see the country as a convenient dumping ground for surplus stock. McPhee can name a few success stories where American publishers and agents recognized her call, signing Australian rights where certain American writers and their relevance to Australians had been overlooked by the British. The rise and fall of McPhee Gribble is recounted in a fascinating narrative; the company was finally sold off to Penguin thanks to the machinations of a globalized (and, in McPhee's view, less book-centred) publishing industry. McPhee sounds a warning about the consequences of lack of care and quality in this new market where books are simply another product (they might as well be lipstick, she observes), concluding with the parable of a young author who is talked up at publishers' meetings but deprived of anything like proper editorial support before being dumped on the conveyor belt of a $3,000 promotional budget and abandoned once her rough first novel has been panned by the critics. A disquieting glimpse into the industry on which all the other scholarship reviewed here depends, McPhee's is probably the most important work on Australian literature published this year.

Of related interest is Anne Galligan, 'Cultural Determinants: The Publishing House and the Australian Literary Estate, 1960–1980' (*JAS* 67[2001] 162–71), which addresses 'the specific shifts or disjunctions in the structure of the publishing and literary fields, the historic moments of struggle when the culture of a publishing house ... collides with an overriding determinate force from the external economic or political fields' (p. 162). And another of the year's important biographies, Jacqueline Kent's *A Certain Style*, focuses on another high-profile Australian editor, Beatrice Davis, among other things editor with Angus & Robertson from 1937 to 1973. Tracing a rise and fall in the spirit of McPhee's memoir is Laurie Hergenhan's editorial for the first issue of *ALS* for 2001, the final year of his epic editorial reign (*ALS* 20:i[2001] 3–4). Hergenhan notes how *ALS* was founded thirty-nine years ago 'with the first main growth in the secondary and tertiary teaching of Australian literature as well as a growth in the production of Australian books and a growing audience for them', a favourable situation that 'quickened in the seventies' due to 'university expansion' but now looks 'much less promising'. Hergenhan cites internal and external reasons: 'developments in the study itself' ('texts' to 'contexts') and 'unfriendly economic and cultural conditions'. 'The gains have been in the refinement of notions of both text and context and their interaction; the loss is that literary texts have become subordinate to materialist approaches, that literary study is not interested in questions of art and aesthetics, in the appreciation and empathy that used to be encouraged as a way of entering into the imaginative world that the text opens up, apart from the contexts which have helped to shape it' (p. 3). While acknowledging periodic change in critical approaches, Hergenhan regrets the erosion of a specifically literary 'value' and the aversion to speaking of 'spiritual needs' (p. 4), or indeed of 'appreciation' at all, going on to note the effect of economic rationalism on the discipline generally but also specifically in the bureaucratic funding nightmare faced by this centrally important journal itself.

In the same issue Anthony Hassall takes on 'Australian Literary Criticism: Future Directions' (*ALS* 20:i[2001] 88–93), outlining 'three urgent issues' facing the discipline: 'finding a place for the teaching of literature (and specifically Australian literature) in the academy; finding an appropriate audience for that teaching; and finding a voice in which to articulate the critical scrutiny of that literature' (p. 88). Hassall calls for literature to 'disentangle itself from the disciplines which have grown up parasitically around it', stating that its difference demands it be 'separate' (p. 91), and arguing that student numbers are inflated because literature has been 'oversold' and should be allowed to reduce to the truly passionate and interested (p. 92). Affirming the discipline, stapling it together, or cataloguing its demise, depending on your outlook, Delys Bird, Robert Dixon and Christopher Lee have selected and edited a collection of 'key documents' in Australian literary criticism, *Authority and Influence: Australian Literary Criticism, 1950–2000*. Immensely useful for students and lecturers alike—its express purpose is to enable the 'systematic study of the history of Australian literary criticism' (p. xiii)—the collection includes extracts from diverse sources (almost) chronologically arranged, from A.D. Hope's 'Standards in Australian Literature' [1956] to Leigh Dale's 'Canonising Queer' [1999]. Contrasting Hassall's call, and signing on rather than off as editor, is Sonia Mycak at Australian Canadian Studies in 2001 ('Editorial: Signing On', *ACS* 19:ii[2001] 3–16). In her inaugural editorial, Mycak embraces change and writes of the loss of the hyphen in the journal's title which bespeaks 'a broad and inclusive perspective' relevant to 'a wider Asia-Pacific region and from the widest Canadian studies network'. The other change signalled is from an inter- to a multi-disciplinary approach, 'so that scholars engaged in discipline-based approaches feel equally welcome' (p. 4).

This year the University of Queensland Press inaugurated its three-volume edition of *A History of the Book in Australia* with the release of volume 2, *1891–1945: A National Culture in a Colonised Market*, edited by Martyn Lyons and John Arnold. The volume's title encapsulates an economic and cultural condition still deplored by McPhee several decades later. It is 'not an encyclopedia' but sets out to be 'a useful reference instrument' and a 'solid base' for future research (p. xix). It is divided into four parts ('Publishing and Printing', 'Bookshops and Libraries', 'Genres and their Place in the Market' and 'Reading'), with each part organized into chapters with thematic titles (for example 'Bookshops and Retailing'), occasionally punctuated by case studies that take more specific topics applicable to the chapter in question (for example 'Radical Bookshops'). Lyons's introduction opens with an appealing account of the literary career of Clive Bleeck, writer of such memorable titles as *Invasion of the Insectoids*, using his example (Bleeck is 'one of the most prolific and successful fiction writers Australia has produced', p. xiii) to illustrate the kind of relevant cultural data which slip through traditional literary histories but not, we can be assured, this broader, material culture-focused study. Lyons comments on how this volume begins in the 'mythologized decade' of the 1890s and, although it provides 'plenty of ammunition' for those 'who insist that Australian literary culture between the wars' was 'derivative' in comparison (p. xvi), this is 'only one side of the story' (p. xviii). Children's books led the way for a national literary culture, the publishing house Angus & Robertson was established as a market leader, and fiction titles increased. 'Strenuous efforts by a dedicated minority to obtain recognition for Australian writers began to bear fruit' (p. xviii), leading overall to a 'schizophrenic nationalism ... in which there was little perceived contradiction between imperial and Australian loyalties' (pp. xviii–xix).

In other chapters, Richard Nile and David Walker write on 'the importance of London as a production centre for Australian literature' (p. 3) in the period, while Lyons himself addresses the importance of Australia as an export market for British books (providing the historical context for what McPhee deplores), before Jennifer

Alison discusses the rise of A&R. Deana Heath writes on literary censorship in the context of imperialism and the White Australia policy, and Debra Adelaide, herself a writer of fiction, asks the sixty-four-thousand-dollar question: 'How Did Authors Make a Living?' (p. 83). On a more technical front, John Arnold writes on 'Printing Technology and Book Production' (pp. 104–15) and Raelene Frances on print workers; these are followed by the section on retailing books and public, circulating, Mechanics' Institute and private libraries, with a chapter for each of these categories. In the third section, Nile and Walker debate the 'bestseller' as 'an intriguing and still largely unexplored phenomenon in Australian literature' (p. 235); John Arnold writes on newspapers as well as on 'Reference and Non-Fiction Publishing' (pp. 282–97), and Heather Scutter turns to 'Children's Fiction' (pp. 298–309), Kerry Kilner very briefly to 'Drama Publishing' (pp. 310–13) (what *can* be said before the advent of Currency Press?), and Leigh Astbury to 'Art Publishing' (pp. 314–22). In the final section, on 'Reading', Patrick Buckridge continues his interesting work on the idea of 'Serious Reading' and reading guides (pp. 325–34), Peter Pierce looks at criticism, and Martyn Lyons follows with 'Reading Practices in Australia' (pp. 335–58), and later with 'Reading Models and Reading Communities' (pp. 370–88) and with a discussion of the commemoration of literary anniversaries (pp. 389–400), before supplying the concluding chapter on 'The Book Trade and the Australian Reader in 1945' (pp. 401–7). Overall this is an entertaining, varied, well-illustrated and extremely informative work.

Among the few articles to address readers rather than writers was Bill Bell's 'Bound for Australia: Shipboard Reading in the Nineteenth Century' (*JAS* 68[2001] 5–18), arguing that these 'books, tracts, letters, and newspapers ... provided vital connections with familiar social values, serving for many to organize an otherwise unpredictable environment into recognisable patterns' (p. 18). Another is John Arnold's 'The Left Book Club in Australia: Achieving Reform and Change through Reading and its Attempted Suppression' (*JAS* 69[2001] 103–12), which looks at 'a significant educational institution' in Britain and Australia which provided 'the left and the left-leaning with cheap informative reading', similar to the nineteenth century's Mechanics' Institutes but more overtly political (p. 111). Christopher Lee discusses 'Civic Virtue and the Monumental Pleasures of Poetic Work: Margaret Curren and Toowoomba's Ladies' Literary Society' (*Coppertales* 7[2001] 56–64). The Toowoomba Ladies' Literary Society, Lee writes, was 'originally conceived as a self-improvement society for young women', though 'it quickly evolved into an important custodian of Toowoomba's literary heritage', Toowoomba being home at various times to 'Steele Rudd', A.G. Stephens and Margaret Curran, the poet and president of the society, who is Lee's focus in this fine article.

(d) Covering the Field: UQP Studies in Australian Literature
University of Queensland Press continues its Studies in Australian Literature, unfortunately also continuing to sport its unappealing covers. Crisis in academic publishing or not, need cheap production necessarily mean ugly design? The issue is not without its serious side. What effect do such covers have on the idea of 'Studies in Australian Literature'? Can it be anything other than unglamorous, 'economical', 'worthy'? Granted, looking within, things usually improve. But why look at all? These covers have the answer written all over them: 'have to' (for school).

Lyn Jacobs provides the first full-length study of a very deserving author, Beverley Farmer, in *Against the Grain: Beverley Farmer's Writing*. In contrast to the 'grainy', out-of-focus, unflattering cover photograph of Farmer, Jacobs's content is as clear and comprehensive as her previous work on Farmer. This is a thorough and useful survey, opening with a chronology of the author's life and work and ending with a good bibliography (excellent for Farmer's own published and unpublished writing). Well known for her exploration of the interface of life and art, particularly in *A Body of Water* [1990], Farmer's writing responds well to the intricacies of feminist criticism with its notions of *écriture feminine* and ficto-criticism. Jacobs is careful, however, to underscore the breadth of Farmer's work, in criticism, reviews, poetry and photography as well as fiction, and the significance of her fiction (which Jacobs compares, for example, to Patrick White's) for its exploration of Greek–Australian cultural relations, and even the history of queer writing in *Alone* [1980]. Chapters are basically arranged in chronological order of Farmer's major publications, so this is an account of the writer's life as well as of her work and its critical reception. Overall this study obviously is most useful for high-school and undergraduate students (not least for its handy subheadings), at the price, perhaps, of brand new and controversial insight, but in spite of this a very firm foundation has been provided for future debates about Farmer's contributions to Australian literature.

Toning with the yellowish brown of *Against the Grain*'s spine is the dead brown of Dennis Haskell's *Attuned to Alien Moonlight: The Poetry of Bruce Dawe*, the poet looking vacantly in the same direction as Farmer out of another terrible photograph. Dawe, doubtless 'Australia's most popular and widely studied poet', as the blurb claims, is also somewhat ignored by academe, generally abandoned to high-school teachers and their pupils, so again, this comprehensive survey is welcome. In the same vein as others in the series, it offers 'introductions' to and study notes on this writer. Haskell does want to get away from the School Certificate reading of Dawe as a 'social satirist', so while, like Jacobs, he provides a chronology, survey, life and (yet more extensive) bibliography, he sets out to focus on the lyrical qualities of Dawe's poetry. Dawe's social satire remains, however, the most compelling aspect of his work. And celebrating the 'ordinary', even if you do play with the concept, is even more fraught politically in Australia after Hanson. Perhaps academic support for, or interest in, Dawe will remain split along political lines. Haskell devotes a chapter to Dawe's response to politics, including Hansonism, and, elsewhere, issues regarding Aboriginal Australians. Like Jacobs's, Haskell's is a book full of explanations of the 'canon', of critical approaches and theories, and is therefore useful more than controversial.

Bruce Bennett is awarded a slightly less unsightly green cover for his *Australian Short Fiction: A History*, and a pleasant oil-on-canvas beach scene illustrating Stead's reference to an 'ocean of story'. A straightforward historical survey, with chapters demarcated by chronological periods, and under such a title, there can be few surprises here. Not at all as dreary or superficial as it sounds, its succinct analysis is enhanced by many contemporary quotes. Bennett's stress is on 'range and depth' (p. 2). He discusses older writing growing into, out of, or now understood as in reaction to the *Bulletin* 'tradition', before moving on to modernism and the new writing of the 1970s and the present 'States of the Art' (final diagnosis: 'alive and well', p. 318), with historic events and critical shifts outlined along the way, though the focus is on aesthetic differences and each writer's themes. Bennett's survey appears impressively comprehensive, and it is little wonder, since he acknowledges that the book has been his 'companion' throughout the 1990s and into the present century. Even so, considering the short story is a genre in which many Australians have achieved undoubted excellence, it is surprising that this should be its 'first extended study'. Of related interest is David Coad's 'The Australian Short Story: An Overview' (*EA* 54:ii[2001] 233–44).

On the subject of covers, Alison Ravenscroft compares Kathleen Mary Fallon's *Working Hot* [1989], published under the imprint of Sybylla Press, with the Vintage/ Random House edition [2000], and questions the conditions under which the text now takes its meaning. In *'Working Hot*: A Book, its Publishers, the Author and her Reader' (*Meanjin* 60:ii[2001] 74–82), Ravenscroft warns readers not to judge the new publication by its cover. *Working Hot* is much more than the sexy 'cult classic' its cover makes it out to be.

Also sporting colourful quality covers is the new series of *Heat*, launched in 2001. Still under the editorship of Ivor Indyk and published by Giramondo but with the backing of Newcastle University (Australia), *Heat* 1 and 2, with their stunning photographs, generous margins and uncluttered page layout, are a visual as well as an intellectual treat. The emphasis in these two editions is, however, weighted heavily towards creative writing rather than critical essays.

(e) The Novel

This section and those following cover scholarship on Australian novels, poetry, and drama that have not already been discussed in different contexts above. Predictably, Peter Carey attracted more attention than any other single Australian novelist, with attention focused predominantly on issues relevant to 'hi-story/telling', Carey's practice (and the ethics of his practice) of blending myth and history such as in his *True History of the Kelly Gang* [2000]. Andreas Gaile discusses this in 'Re-Mythologizing an Australian Legend' (*Antipodes* 15:i[2001] 37–9). Leading into his discussion of a similar topic, Bill Ashcroft takes *Oscar and Lucinda* as his text to address 'the status of settler colonies', which he describes as the most 'contentious area of discussion in post-colonial studies' (p. 129) in his monograph *On Post-Colonial Futures: Transformations of Colonial Culture*. 'The relevance of the cultural hegemony of empire is obvious to anybody who grows up in these countries', writes Ashcroft, 'but to others, their relative prosperity and officially monolingual character excludes all except their indigenous inhabitants from post-colonial discourse', leaving them, in their ambivalence and contradictoriness, according to his argument, 'supreme examples of post-colonial transformation' (p. 129). Ashcroft outlines how categories of 'Truth, Fiction and the Real' are brought into question in these exemplary cultures and discusses how this is addressed in Carey's fiction. Dorothy Lane uses *Oscar and Lucinda* as a recurring reference point in '"Deliver their land from Error's chain": Conversion, Convictism and Captivity in Australian Fiction' (in Scott and Simpson-Housley, eds., *Mapping the Sacred: Religion, Geography and Postcolonial Literatures*, pp. 92–108), suggesting that Carey's novel is 'the clearest fictional examination of mission in Australia' (p. 95), although Lane focuses on Clarke's *His Natural Life* [1874] and Mudrooroo's *Master of the Ghost Dreaming* [1991] to discuss 'how the Christian mission adopts seemingly contradictory associations of imprisonment and liberation in several writings, both literary and historical' (p. 95).

Douglas Kerr, in 'History and Theirstories: A Review of Some Recent Australian and Asian Fiction' (*Westerly* 46[2001] 190–203), argues the case for an acceptance of novels as historiography, as ways of seeing lives. In his fulsome review of Carey's *True History of the Kelly Gang*, Kerr asks what cultural need is being answered by the choice, now, of this 'romantic victim of oppression' for an ancestor. Andrew Dowling also casts a critical eye over *True History* and notes, in 'Truth and History' (*Heat* 1[2001] 249–54), the inherent contradiction in attempting to use history to create fiction and using fiction to reveal the 'truth' about history. Dowling celebrates Carey's use of transvestism to delve beneath the icons of masculinity, but he is disappointed that Carey, having pitted the dress against the suit of armour, explains the dress away in terms of ancient Celtic warrior traditions. 'The dress', writes Dowling, 'is an excellent metaphor for the fears against which manliness defines itself' (p. 252).

Christer Larsson's *'The Relative Merits of Goodness and Originality': The Ethics of Storytelling in Peter Carey's Novels* links 'formal and thematic patterns' across Carey's novels to assert an 'ethics of storytelling' pervading his works. Whereas much scholarship on Carey focuses on the unreliability of his narrators—and, through the relativity of narrative this seems to champion, the suggestion that all writing is fiction—Larsson seeks 'to extricate Carey's novels from the postmodern and post-colonial discussions', arguing the author is careful to delineate the borderline between fiction and non-fiction, 'refusing to resist closure'. Larsson uses the speech act theory of John R. Searle to link formal analysis to the question of ethics. On a similar subject but with different conclusions Xavier Pons, in 'The Novelist as Ventriloquist: Autobiography and Fiction in Peter Carey's *True History of the Kelly Gang*' (*CE&S* 24:i[2001] 61–72), reads Carey's work as a 'significant departure' for the author in that 'we are supposed to hear the authentic voice of a genuine historical figure'. Pons outlines the work's 'reality effects' and articulates an 'uneasy tension' between these and its fictional nature (p. 62), between the historian and the writer of fiction. He notes how Carey privileges 'the fictional representation of Kelly over strict adherence to the known facts about him' through a 'hyperrealistic approach' (p. 72) which 'deconstructs itself' (p. 61), the effect of which is to 'fictionalise Ned's autobiography as much as to historicise Peter's fictions' (p. 72).

Addressing similar themes, and citing Carey's *Kelly Gang* in her introduction, is Renate Howe in 'Oral Sex and the League of Nations: The Genre of Faction in *Grand Days* and *Dark Palace*' (*JAS* 71[2001] 101–6). Howe takes Frank Moorhouse's *Dark Palace* [2000] as 'a case study of this developing genre [faction]', providing 'an opportunity to explore the issues raised for the historian in the postmodern era of interpretation' (p. 101). Howe argues that 'researched historical fiction should be more accountable to its sources and open to assessment by historians', and laments 'the belittling of the endeavours of women' from the League of Nations movement in Moorhouse's account and the 'ignoring of the extensive networks that supported their endeavours and the worth of the women's agenda that they pursued' (p. 106). Also reviewing *Dark Palace* is Nicole Walker's 'A Brilliant Career' (*LitR* 45:i[2001] 181–3). Elsewhere Collette Selles provides a more benign if less memorable survey of Moorhouse's work in 'Frank Moorhouse and the "Oscillation" between Biography, Autobiography and Fiction: Reconciling Contradictions' (*CE&S* 24:i[2001] 53–60), noting that the author has written both conventional novels and more experimental discontinuous narratives. Selles focuses on their 'referential, or even self referential value' (p. 53), inducing for the reader 'a puzzling, humorous in-betweenness' (p. 60).

Christina Stead attracted attention in the lead up to the centenary of her birth in 1902. Ann Blake discusses 'A "Very Backward Country": Christina Stead and the English Class System' (in Blake, Gandhi and Thomas, eds., *England through Colonial Eyes in Twentieth-Century Fiction*, pp. 104–15). Written late in her career after leaving England, Stead's English fiction, Blakes notes, 'construct[s] a damning analysis of the country' (p. 104). Her discussion in this chapter centres on Stead's *Cotter's England* [1966] and *Miss Herbert (The Suburban Wife)* [1976]. Overall the volume examines 'England and representations of England, English life and English people as a "contact zone"' (p. 2), and is written in reaction to the marginalization of the 'voices' discussed in recent scholarship on the construction of Englishness (p. 3). Teresa Petersen's *The Enigmatic Christina Stead: A Provocative Re-Reading* lives up to its name by uncovering lesbian eroticism and male homosexuality in Stead's work, despite a preoccupation with heterosexual relationships, which is here reduced to a 'façade'. 'Stead's model family', writes Petersen, 'is the Oedipal family (by which I mean the traditional family unit), which is dependent on the heterosexual norm for its sustenance.' She goes on: 'Lying in the shadow of the dominant heterosexual signifier, masked by the incongruencies and verbosity of Stead's narratives, lies the almost imperceptible lesbian signifier' (p. 4). Not any more. Petersen argues that Stead uses the 'brother-sister trope' to 'examine lesbian love' (p. 232) because 'publishers were then loath to publish novels about lesbians' (p. 231).

Nicole Moore is also interested in Stead's depiction of eroticism. In '"A Monster of Indecision": Abortion, Choice and Commodity Culture in Christina Stead's *The Beauties and Furies*' (*Southerly* 61:ii[2001] 142–57), she suggests that the sexual and the material are complexly interwoven in Stead's exploration of commodified erotics. Elsewhere Moore argues that cliché and taboo operate as opaque narrative devices that work against a realist or revelatory promise in narrative. In 'The Politics of Cliché: Sex, Class and Abortion in Australian Realism' (*MFS* 47:i[2001] 69–88), she examines the cliché of abortion plots for working-class women, specifically in terms of women's bodily experiences, in Ruth Park's *The Harp in the South*, Dymphna Cusack's *Jungfrau* and Katherine Susannah Prichard's *Winged Seeds*.

Meanwhile Carole Ferrier discusses the life and works of Australian writer Eleanor Dark in 'Focus on Eleanor Dark' (*Hecate* 27:i[2001] 6–10), outlining the consequences of her being denounced in parliament as 'an underground worker for the Communists'. Barbara Brooks, '"A Writer with a Last Story to Write ...": From an Unfinished Novel by Eleanor Dark', provides background information and excerpts from Dark's manuscript (*Hecate* 27:i[2001] 67–73). Other articles dealing with Australian women writers include Brian Dribble's 'Plus ça change ... An Early Elizabeth Jolley Story' (*Overland* 163[2001] 55–8), in which he comments on the way in which Jolley's earliest stories, specifically 'Lehmann Sieber', written when she was 17, employ certain of her trademark techniques and anticipate many of the central concerns of her later fiction. Sue Kossew recovers a first novel overshadowed by the author's second, *Leaning Towards Infinity* [1996], in

'Murdering the Muse: Creativity and Violence in Sue Woolf's *Painted Woman*' (*CRNLE* [2001] 32–41), the latter first published in 1990 but reissued by Allen & Unwin Australia in 1999. Robert Darby, in 'Reflective Imagery in the Fiction of M. Barnard Eldershaw' (*Southerly* 61:iii[2001] 146–59), suggests that the prominence of mirrors in Majorie Barnard's stories (and in some works written with Flora Eldershaw) 'arises from the confluence of two streams: from a personal preoccupation with beauty, ageing and sexual disappointment; and from the intellectual influence of the 1930s literary theory, which held that fiction should be true to life'. Bronwyn Cran wonders if the fairytale or the domestic romance written by a woman represents a retreat from political engagement. In '"The Private is Political": Women's Writing and Political Fiction' (*Overland* 162[2001] 35–40), she notes that a number of recent novels—Amanda Lohrey's *Camille's Bread* [1995], Sara Dowse's *Digging* [1996], Dorothy Johnston's *One for the Master* [1997] and Dorothy Hewett's *Neap Tide* [1999]—shift ground from earlier political fiction to more 'domestic and feminized canvasses' (p. 39). Cran asks if these works will be seen as 'political fiction' or 'women's writing' in the Australian literary canon.

In 'Writers Behaving Badly: Stead, Bourdieu and Australian Literary Culture' (*ALS* 20:i[2001] 76–87), Brigid Rooney outlines a Pierre Bourdieu-influenced interpretation of the role of public intellectuals in Australia, opening with a discussion of Les Murray, making a case study of Christina Stead, and concluding by reflecting on the interventions of Helen Garner in public life. The latter invites a critique of Mark Davis's *Gangland* [1999]. In this self-reflexive essay, Rooney articulates 'a logic to the practice of such writers who behave badly' (p. 86), writers who all have a reputation for being 'difficult'. Also discussing public intellectuals is David Carter, in 'Public Intellectuals, Book Culture, and Civil Society' (*AuHR* 24[2001]), noting the changes wrought in Australian book culture 'double'-handedly, as he puts it, by Drusilla Modjeska and Robert Dessaix, and addressing such issues as the rise of the essay collection and literary memoir, and the reformulation and assertion of 'Good Books, Good Taste, Good Readers'. Speaking of Dessaix, Paolo Bartolini gives a critical overview of the writer's second book of fiction [1996] in 'Travelling with Mortality: Robert Dessaix's *Night Letters*' (*Antipodes* 15:ii[2001] 107–9).

Despite its ubiquity in tourist advertisements, David Callahan notes the relative absence of the rainforest from Australian literary iconography before discussing the work of Janette Turner Hospital in 'Rainforest Narratives: Janette Turner Hospital and the Ethics of Interference' (*Antipodes* 15:i[2001] 31–5). 'The rainforest', observes Callahan, 'becomes as complex a metaphoric site' in Turner Hospital's writing 'as it is a complex biological site, so that the rainforest both invites symbolic exploration and confounds it, just as its exuberance invites physical exploration and confounds it' (p. 31). Fiona Coyle, 'A Third Space? Postcolonial Australia and the Fractal Landscape in *The Last Magician* (1993) and *Oyster* (1996)' (in Scott and Simpson-Housley, eds., pp. 110–30), argues that the 'disparate worlds' of 'chaos theory and Aboriginal land rights' meet in the textual space of Turner Hospital's novels (p. 111). Roslynn Haynes, 'Romanticism and Environmentalism: The Tasmanian Novels of Marie Bjelke-Petersen' (*ALS* 20:i[2001] 62–75), recovers and surveys the Tasmanian novels of Marie Bjelke-Petersen, nine of them written between 1917 and 1937 and 'immensely popular' (p. 62) in their day, noting their interest in conservation.

One of few articles to focus on Murray Bail's innovative and complex novel *Eucalyptus* [1999] is Lyn Jacobs's 'The "Good Oil": Eucalypts and Murray Bail's *Eucalyptus*' (*Antipodes* 15:i[2001] 40–6). It outlines the novel's historical context, noting that, while 'the mindscapes of the nation have been surveyed via the binaries of desert and sea, the treatment of real and representative "gum trees" also evidences changing cultural values' (p. 40), which it relates to 'Indigenous custodianship of environmental heritage' (p. 43). Jacobs includes a 'Glossary and Guide' to Murray's novel. Returning to the more traditional landscape of the Australian psyche Alison Bartlett discusses 'Desire in the Desert: Exploring Contemporary Australian Desert Narratives' (*Antipodes* 15:ii[2001] 119–23). Works discussed include Susan Hawthorne's *The Falling Woman* [1990], Evas Sallis's *Hiam* [1998], Helen Garner's filmscript *The Last Days of Chez Nous* [1992], Nikki Gemmell's *Cleave* [1998], Kim Mahood's *Craft for a Dry Lake* [2000], Julia Blackburn's *Daisy Bates in the Desert* [1994] and Muriel Lenore's *Travelling Alone/Together* [1998]. One of few articles to address the work of Patrick White invokes his 'Great Australian Emptiness', Charles Lock's 'Patrick White: Writing towards Silence' (*Stand* 2:iv–3:i[2001] 72–84). Despite the lack of articles, White scholarship was considerably advanced in 2001 with the publication of James Bulman-May's *Patrick White and Alchemy*, a highly scholarly work which reads White's novels up to, and including, *The Solid Mandala* in light of the alchemical tradition. Bulman-May discusses aspects of White's work not only in terms of alchemy but also with reference to Jewish kabbalistic thought, French Symbolism, contemporary literary theory and Jungian psychology.

In an interesting comparison in 'Fractal Intricacies: A Queer Map of Ethnicity, Sexuality and Class in Christos Tsiolkas's *Loaded* and Ana Kokkinos's *Head On*' (*CRNLE* [2001] 153–64), Josh Peisach argues that, by 'employing similar techniques to those of postcolonial critical practice, queer theory has the potential to engage in a productive critique of the material effects of ethnicity and class, and to re-examine their relationship to the construction of sexual subjects' (p. 163).

Other articles on Australian novels and novelists include Madeleine Byrne's 'How Australian Is It? (Reading *Benang*)' (*Antipodes* 15:ii[2001] 110–15), in which she provides a sensitive reading of Kim Scott's 1999 work. Elsewhere Byrne interviews Elliot Perlman, in '"The world is closing in": An Interview with Elliot Perlman' (*Antipodes* 15:i[2001] 10–12). Russell McDougall, in 'On the Track: Travels Outback with Xavier Herbert, 1927' (*Antipodes* 15:ii[2001] 130–4), discusses Herbert's earliest publications (written under the names of Alfred or A.X. Herbert or even 'Herbert Astor'). In 'Immigrant Irony and Embarrassment' (*JAS* 67[2001] 109–17), Mary Besemeres 'addresses the central role of embarrassment, as a concept bound up with significant cultural values' in Andrew Riemer's memoir *The Habsburg Café* [1993]. Teri Merlyn surveys the work of Australian post-war communist writer Eric Lambert in 'The Hero's Journey: Marxism, Morality and the Literature of Eric Lambert' (*JAS* 67[2001] 67–74). Providing a critical reading of a first novel is Michael Deves's '"Casual Kindness and Causeless Cruelty": Michael Meehan's *The Salt of Broken Tears* [1999]' (*CRNLE* [2001] 53–9). Noel Henricksen, naming a Latin hymn cited in Dante and by his focus author, discusses Christopher Koch's work in '*Vexilla regis prodeunt*: Myth and Allusion in *Out of*

Ireland (*ALS* 20:i[2001] 33–48), the latter a novel disguised as the nineteenth-century Vandemonian journal of 'an Irish insurrectionist' (p. 33). Bronwen Morrison relates details of a dialogue between Michael Ondaatje and Thomas Keneally in 'Running in the Family—Novels, Films and Nations—with Michael Ondaatje and Thomas Keneally' (*ACS* 19:ii[2001] 17–20).

(f) Poetry

Paul Kane, poetry editor of *Antipodes*, surveys 'A Geology of Contemporary Australian Poetry' (*AuBR* 233[2001] 43–5), noting that his position has enabled him access to much 'bad' Australian poetry that is 'quite illuminating: it tells us something about common perceptions of poetry in Australia, and it can be taken as a virtual critique of much contemporary poetry' (p. 43). Such poetry, he observes, nearly always rhymes, is set in the Bush or on the beach, and is often elegiac and uncomplicated. Given these characteristics, Kane moves on to the work of two 'exemplary' poets whose work also meets these criteria, Gwen Harwood and Philip Hodgins. Kane also asserts that the most common metaphor heard in Australian poetry is 'the romantic trope of organic growth' (p. 44). Brendan Ryan also surveys the poetry of Philip Hodgins, specifically his rural poetry, in 'Vulnerable Landscapes: Pastoral in the Poetry of Philip Hodgins' (*Antipodes* 15:i[2001] 26–30), claiming Hodgins broadens 'the possibilities of the Virgilian pastoral form' by adding a 'tension' to his better pastoral poems reminiscent of his 'cancer poems' (p. 30). Responding to Kane's *Australian Poetry: Romance and Negativity* [1996] in 'Francis Webb's White Swan of Trespass: *A Drum for Ben Boyd* and Australian Modernism in the 1940s' (*JCL* 36.i.27–43), Andrew Lynch identifies Webb as occupying the modernist literary persona Kane associates with Ern Malley, concluding that Webb's poem *A Drum for Ben Boyd* embodies 'within its personal and eclectic form, the local complexities of an art in crisis', enabling Webb to 'represent the condition of his own Australian modernity' (p. 41).

Brian Lloyd discusses 'Ern Malley and his Rivals' (*ALS* 20:i[2001] 20–32), taking up Michael Heyward's statement in *The Ern Malley Affair* [1993] that Malley's *Darkening Ecliptic* was 'the most decisive piece of literary criticism ever produced in Australia'. Lloyd supports this claim, adding that the way in which it has been taken up by reviewers of Heyward's book 'amounts to an impasse in these affairs' because the meaning of the hoax is taken as 'self-evident, and positions within the scenario—superior or inferior—are always clear and distinct' (p. 20). Lloyd prefers a dialogic reading, adopting the 'relational view' suggested, he believes, by Heyward's statement, thus enabling an investigation 'of differences and unacknowledged *similarities* between the two groups involved' (p. 20), between, that is, the supporters and detractors of poetic modernism. Lloyd concludes that *Angry Penguins* was 'a kind of "source" or "influence"' for McAuley's and Stewart's involvement with the *No.1* magazine series, 'and the *resentment* expressed in Ern Malley is a direct result of the hoaxers' desire to obscure this "debt"' (p. 31). Meanwhile Michael Ackland, in 'Writing the East and the Epic Endeavour of Harold Stewart' (*Antipodes* 15:i[2001] 18–21), asserts that Harold Stewart 'looked to poetry to counterbalance the humiliations he experienced as a homosexual, and to Eastern philosophies to justify his life-choices' (p. 18). Ackland calls for a reassessment of Stewart on the basis of two epic poems, *By the Old Walls of Kyoto* [1981] and 'Autumn Landscape Roll: A Divine Panorama' [1995].

Jeffrey Poacher discusses 'The Drowned World of Kenneth Slessor' (*ALS* 20:i[2001] 5–19), marking the centenary of the poet's birth by revisiting one of his 'central preoccupations'. 'For Slessor', writes Poacher, 'the drowned were proof of human insignificance', going on to articulate this statement in terms of their appearance in much of Slessor's poetry and prose, and not just in 'Five Bells', voted 'Australia's favourite poem' in 1998 for the Australian Broadcasting Corporation's inaugural 'National Poetry Day' (p. 5). Of 'Five Bells', Poacher newly emphasizes the 'positive aspects' in the face of the critical tradition which stresses its 'pessimism' (p. 16).

Readers of contemporary Australian poetry will find much of interest in Alan Urquhart's 'New Poetry—2001' (*Westerly* 46[2001] 109–25), a lengthy and detailed review of a diverse range of poetry published in 2001. Martin Duwell's 'Contemporary Australian Poetry' (*Heat* 2[2001] 241–8) and Greg McLaren's 'Blowing Dandelions' (*Heat* 2[2001] 249–55) offer two further significant reviews of contemporary Australian poetry. In 'Contemporary Australian Poetry', Duwell reviews *Calyx: Thirty Contemporary Australian Poets* [2001] and *New Music: An Anthology of Contemporary Australian Poetry* [2001], and recommends that these texts, read together, are a valuable source for readers who wish to gain an overview of Australian poetry over the last decade. He notes that the strength of *New Music*, which offers brief samples of nearly a hundred poets, is its lengthy focus on young poets. Both Duwell and McLaren note the prevalence of 'language' poetry in *Calyx*. Both are 'surprised' by, and favourably draw attention to, the poetry of Nick Riemer and Noel Rowe.

In other critical reviews Fay Zwicky's 'Past and Present Worlds' (*Heat* 1[2001] 243–7) celebrates the poetic depth and range of Rosemary Dobson's *Untold Lives and Later Poems* [2000], in which Dobson reminds us of the 'emotional resilience, and openness to change, of old age' (p. 247). Carmel Macdonald Grahame, in 'Dorothy Hewett's Faith in Doubt' (*ALS* 20:i[2001] 49–61), reads Hewett's work in the light of changes in how modernism and feminism have been 'conceptualized', seeking to articulate a 'sublime aesthetic' in her writing which moves beyond the usual interpretation of it in terms of 'a privileging of desire' (p. 49). Drawing out Hewett's 'uncertainty' in prose and poetry (drama is not discussed), Grahame argues this 'links her writing with a modest postmodernism' (p. 49). Sarah Attfield, in 'The Invisible Force: Working Class Voices in Contemporary Australian Poetry' (*Overland* 165[2001] 21–8), asserts the importance of contemporary working-class poetry, but laments that poetry in Australia seems to be produced for an elite, educated audience. She canvasses a diverse range of 'working-class' poets, from traditional male, blue-collar workers through to those of migrant or non-English-speaking backgrounds, Aboriginal people, and single mothers: the Adelaide-based Geoff Goodfellow (known as the 'builder poet' or 'prison poet'), Caterina Passoni, Mick Searles, po, and Lionel Fogarty. 'If it is being written', asks Attfield, 'why can't we read it in *Southerly*, *Meanjin* or anthologies?' (Notably *Southerly* 62:ii[2002] features Lionel Fogarty and other less well known Aboriginal poets.) Under the editorship of David Brooks another issue of *Southerly* (61:i[2001]), entitled 'That Fatal Song: Judith Wright and A.D. Hope', is a commemoration of the life and work of two major figures in Australian literature. Brooks has included a four-year correspondence between A.D. Hope and Vincent Buckley, Hope's 'verse response' to Valéry's *Le Jeune Parque* and a memoir of Wright by Barbara

Blackman, along with tributes, photographs of each poet (many not previously seen) and essays. Veronica Brady, in 'Judith Wright: The Politics of Poetics' (*Southerly* 61:i[2001] 82–8), argues the case for reading Wright on 'her own terms', terms that not only recognized but insisted upon the political nature of poetry. Brady insists that, since Wright understood the role of a poet to be both an ethical and an imaginative one, both concerns should be acknowledged in her work. John Hawke suggests that the central thematic concerns of Australian poets 'lie firmly within the metaphysical traditions of Romanticism and its adaptation in French Symbolism'. In 'The Moving Image: Judith Wright's Symbolist Language' (*Southerly* 61:i[2001] 160–78), he outlines the way in which Wright identified these concerns in the work of Kendall, Harpur and Brennan, and goes on to argue that Wright's own concept of the symbol was much influenced by the linguistic philosophy of her husband, J.P. McKinney. This is a valuable article for Wright scholars and for those wanting to know more about McKinney's published writings, particularly *The Challenge of Reason* [1950] and *The Structure of Modern Thought* [1970]. Hawke convincingly demonstrates the relevance of McKinney's arguments on primordial consciousness to Wright's work, both as a poet and as a conservationist. David McCooey investigates, in '"What are we doing here?": A.D. Hope's "Ascent into Hell"' (*Southerly* 61:i[2001] 112–16), the 'disturbing character' of Hope's poem. He notes that the poem's repeated inversions, of time, traditional cosmology and heaven and hell, and its unanswered, perhaps unanswerable, questions operate powerfully to unsettle the reader.

Disruption is also the theme of Alexis Harley's between-the-lines reading of Robert Harris's *JANE, Interlinear* [1992]. In her article of the same name (*Southerly* 61:ii[2001] 180–8), she suggests that the historiographic exchanges between the sixteenth and twentieth centuries are designed to disturb the smooth linearity of history and entangle past and present. Kate Lilley, guest editor for the second issue of *Southerly* for 2001, publishes her interview with John Tranter from May that year, in which she discusses Tranter's establishment of *Jacket* and the role of electronic publication in poetry and literature generally (*Southerly* 61:ii[2001] 7–23). *Jacket* turned 4 in 2001. In 'Old Wine in New Bottles' (*Meanjin* 60:ii[2001] 167–70), Tranter notes with satisfaction that over 275,000 people have visited *Jacket*'s webpage. The two great advantages of internet publishing, according to Tranter, are its ability to incorporate audio files and its ability to overcome the cost and difficulty of distributing poetry. Hazel Smith also celebrates off-the-page publication of poetry. In 'Poetry in Performance and the New Media' (*Meanjin* 60:ii[2001] 169–71), she argues that future poetry anthologies should routinely include a CD or CD-ROM to showcase work (as this edition of *Meanjin* does).

In their introduction to 'The Poetry of Les Murray: Critical Essays' (special issue of *ALS* 20:ii[2001]), Laurie Hergenhan and Bruce Clunies Ross remark on 'the disparity in Australia between Murray's acknowledged stature as the leading poet and the relatively small amount of criticism of his work'. In 2001 that perceived disparity seems to have been redressed. In addition to this collection of nine critical essays from both local and overseas scholars, 2001 has seen the publication of Steven Matthews's *Les Murray* and John Kinsella's 'Heavy Machinery' a two-part, lengthy interview conducted with Murray in September 2000 (*Meanjin* 60:i[2001] 187–203; 60:ii[2001] 152–65).

Contributors to the *ALS* issue chose their own subjects. Both Peter Steele, 'Les Murray: Watching with his Mouth' (*ALS* 20:ii[2001] 1–14), and Nils Eskestad, 'Dancing "on bits of paper": Les Murray's Soundscapes' (*ALS* 20:ii[2001] 64–75), read Murray's poetry in conversation with that of Gerard Manley Hopkins. While Steele comments on the similarity of approach of the two poets: 'the prominence of the construing mind', 'the appetite for the particular' and the attunement to metamorphosis, Eskestad takes up Murray's notion of 'Wholespeak' to explore the interplay between mind and body, and map out a relationship between sound, rhythm and embodiment. Murray's 'sprung' lines, he suggests, enable his poetry to model a variety of experience. Charles Lock also reads Murray in terms of Hopkins and embodiment, but he explores, in '*Fredy Neptune*: Metonymy and the Incarnate Preposition' (*ALS* 20:ii[2001] 122–41), another important dimension to Murray criticism, the question of suffering.

As noted in last year's essay, Peter Alexander's *Les Murray: A Life in Progress* [2000] revealed that Murray's 'The Steel' was guilty of historical inaccuracy: the ambulance that might have saved the mother was delayed more by the father's reticence than the doctor's resistance. As a contribution to subsequent discussion about the ethics of Murray's poem, Noel Rowe's 'Justice, Sacrifice and the Mother's Poem' (*ALS* 20:ii[2001] 142–56) argues that a careful reading will show that the poem does not quite believe its own attempt to sacrifice the doctor to justice and that a concern about historical accuracy needs to be balanced against a recognition that the 'mother's poem' is still crucial to Murray's theology of sacrifice. Elsewhere Christopher Pollnitz, in 'Criticism, Biography and Les Murray' (*Heat* 1[2001] 229–42), reviews Peter Alexander's *Les Murray: A Life in Progress* and offers a personal insight into the difficulties Murray's biographers and critics face. Pollnitz's contribution to the *ALS* issue, 'Folie, Topography and Family in Murray's Middle-Distance Poems' (*ALS* 20:ii[2001] 1–14), focuses on the figure of the 'holy fool' in some of Murray's 'middle distance poems' defined as 'those more than one or two pages but less than 50 to 100'.

Discussion of *Fredy Neptune* features prominently in this collection of essays. In 'The Art of "Cracking Normal"' (*ALS* 20:ii[2001] 110–21), Bruce Clunies Ross celebrates the complex multiplicity of *Fredy Neptune* both as an Australian poem and as a fable for the twentieth century. *Fredy Neptune*, he writes, is both a 'fully dialogical novel and a true poem'. Line Henriksen, in '"Big Poems Burn Women": *Fredy Neptune*'s Democratic Sailor and Walcott's Epic *Omeros*' (*ALS* 20:ii[2001] 87–109), reads Murray in conversation with Walcott and Dante. Peter Pierce's 'Les Murray's "Narrowspeak"' (*ALS* 20:ii[2001] 76–86) applauds the way in which the public, political concerns addressed in Murray's prose—an Australian republic, patronage of the arts, declining university standards, socio-economic class, depression—operate to interpret Australian life to ourselves.

Explanations as to the role of place, specifically Bunyah, in Murray criticism is, according to Martin Leer, somewhat commonplace. In '"This Country is my Mind": Les Murray's Poetics of Place' (*ALS* 20:ii[2001] 15–42), he seeks to go beyond such criticism and describe phenomenologically the notion of place in Murray's work. Leer examines the way in which Bunyah, a peripheral location, is complexly reconceptualized as a centre of the world, and argues that a poetics of place is established and developed from Murray's earliest collections.

Steven Matthews's *Les Murray* is part of the Contemporary World Writers series, which seeks to locate individual writers within their specific cultural contexts. Matthews offers a broadly chronological reading of Murray's work. He locates the poet and his poetry within the context of a postcolonial Australian landscape, and examines Murray's engagement with the tensions and ambiguities raised by Australia's colonial history. This study seeks to articulate the many and varied voices—Boetian, Aboriginal orality, Gaelic, republican, Catholic—and impulses operating in Murray's poetry. Murray's sense of the sacredness of place, his empathy with Aboriginal people and their history of dispossession, and his concern for the rural poor are all discussed with close reference to his poetry. So too is his emergent democratic poetics, his use of the vernacular and his understanding of nationalism.

(g) Drama

One of the finest books of the year is Julian Meyrick's *See How It Runs: Nimrod and the New Wave*. More than just a history of the Nimrod Theatre, Meyrick's work seems to capture a whole cultural moment of excitement and change in Australian drama, the fervour of university students and experimental actors contextualized by the vigour of inner-city renewal centred on Kings Cross and the inner eastern suburbs of Sydney. He traces the rise, decline, and fall of the theatre, and the partial transformation into the less edgy but still marketably 'alternative' Belvoir Street Theatre of the present day. While the importance of the Nimrod to changing what Australians knew of and expected from an experience in the theatre is undoubted, soberly articulated by Meyrick's precise analysis, a (minor) quibble might be the ignoring of nearby commercial enterprises (like 'Les Girls'), which had brought a tradition of international but locally inflected burlesque into the Cross for years. How did some of the new skills and genres performed by these excited middle-class radicals compare with what the drag queens were up to two blocks away? And which of the Nimrod set would *not* have seen their shows? This is a really handsome production, nicely illustrated, including a catalogue of the Nimrod's seasons, and boasting tables of figures (for example of attendances) to back the claims. Tracing a meticulous history, Meyrick also deftly handles the theories driving decisions and shaping performances, further offering penetrating insight into individual productions and plays. But he never loses sight of the main plot, the human story of a theatrical enterprise set in the fun context of 1970s Sydney and, more broadly, of the international radical theatres from which the Nimrod actors borrowed or by which they were inspired.

Tim Robertson could boast that 'he was there' ('He lived it', as Helen Garner puts it in her foreword) for his comparable though eccentric memoir of *The Pram Factory: The Australian Performing Group Recollected*. The work sets out to balance the volume of writing on the APG's playwrights with accounts of its performers' contribution to theatrical history. This is a far less meaty and entirely untheorized affair that pays off with its entertainment value, large format and proliferation of photographic illustrations. It may be non-academic but it contains, as does *See How It Runs*, a useful chronology of productions, and even an idiosyncratic, Johnsonian dictionary of who was who in the APG. There is a bibliography (beginning with Abehsera, Michael, *Zen Macrobiotic Cooking*) but no notes, and doubtless everyone in the who's who will contest some part of its tale.

Garner has it that Robertson 'combines the intellectual abilities of a scholar with the imagination of a joyful lunatic' (p. v).

Alan Filewod and David Watt discuss protest theatre in Australia, Canada and Britain as it emerged *after* its heyday in *Workers' Playtime: Theatre and the Labour Movement since 1970.* Players have had to be strategic to cope with a loss of funding and an erosion of the value placed on theatre in the workplace. This, write Filewod and Watt, 'has led to the collapse of the "company" as an ensemble' and also 'to the disappearance of another feature once thought central to the viability of a theatrical venture—the theatre building itself' (p. 2). 'Politically engaged' artists, 'who understand the historical changes affecting their working environments' are the 'most effective' because they can 'develop appropriate new structures to meet those changes' (p. 3). Of the four case studies of strategic ventures Filewod and Watt examine, two are Australian: the Melbourne Workers' Theatre, 'based in a temporary pre-fab shed beside the tracks at the Jolimont Train Maintenance Depot', 'rehearsing in the midst of a busy train yard' (p. 128), and the Northern Territory Trades and Labour Council, which 'organises performance-based work through a shifting group of individuals hired by a purpose-formed committee' (p. 3). Currency Press continues to produce excellent reissues of 1970s Australian drama. Jennifer Compton's *Crossfire*, Ron Blair's *The Christian Brother*, John O'Donoghue's *A Happy and Holy Occasion* and Louis Nowra's *Inner Voices* can all be found in *Plays of the 70s*, edited by Katherine Brisbane.

First in a Peter Lang series on 'Dramaturgies' comes Marc Maufort and Franca Bellarsi's edited comparative collection of essays on postcolonial drama, *Siting the Other: Re-Visions of Marginality in Australian and English-Canadian Drama.* Contrasting the British 'settler-invader' colonies of Australia and Canada with the 'assimilationist model of the American melting pot', Maufort's introduction notes the 'continuous negotiation of the boundaries between "Self" and "Other"' in these 'multicultural' countries, negotiation intensified by increasingly 'contentious internal polarities between First Nations aborigines, various marginal ethnic groups and the mainstream' (p. 1). Multicultural 'reinvention', Maufort argues, is 'especially visible in the field of theatre', although, in contrast to the novel in both countries, it is 'an emergent art' (p. 1). Maufort sustains an organic model in arguing for the 'maturation' of Australian and Canadian drama 'concomitant ... with the development of a multicultural fabric', such that 'the articulation of otherness forms a central concern in the drama of the two countries' (p. 2). The marginality of the title extends from indigenous to non-Anglo-Celtic and even gay perspectives. For Australian drama, Maufort surveys 'First Nations playwriting', Australia's indigenous people using theatre to promulgate their 'forgotten history' (p. 8), decentring 'the certainties of Western realistic perception' through the 'use of sporadic/extended magic realism' (p. 21). Helen Thomson, referencing *Bringing Them Home*, continues by analysing women's stories in the Australian theatre, characterized as 'staged autobiography' (p. 23). She speculates that the apparent gender inflection of such work results from the way in which 'the extremity of social subjugation, occupying the lowest position in Australia's social hierarchy, requires the unmediated subjectivity and powerful claim of truth that is uniquely found in autobiography' (p. 33). It could also be claimed that white audiences are not prepared to sit comfortably with the potentially more confrontational, even threatening, subjectivities of Aboriginal males. Thomson discusses the autobiographical plays of Tom E. Lewis as a 'break' from the usual focus on women. It seems questionable, however, whether Jack Davis's plays (if one thinks of Dolly in *The Dreamers*) do not, as is claimed, deal with the 'gendered subaltern' (p. 35) at the same time as they showcase the plight (and humour) of Aboriginal men.

Elsewhere in this collection, Gerry Turcotte writes on 'Dis/possession in *The Book of Jessica* and *The Mudrooroo/Müller Project*' (p. 175), while Helena Grehan discusses the white women's stories of *Tiger Country* by Sarah Cathcart and Andrea Lemon. Maryrose Casey surveys indigenous Australian theatre companies, their political contexts and the identity of 'individual artists living as indigenous Australians' (p. 67). Jacqueline Lo examines the representation of Asianness in contemporary Australian drama. Susan Pfisterer recovers and analyses women's suffrage plays (Miles Franklin apparently wrote twenty), also discussing, for example, Oriel Gray's *The Torrents* [1955], set in a newspaper office in the Western Australia of 1890 (p. 91), the script that tied with *The Doll* in the famous Playwright's Advisory Board competition of 1954, as well as more recent drama set in the suffrage era. Of related interest is Sue Thomas, '"What happens to the spectator of hysteria's realism?": The Reception of Elizabeth Robins and Florence Bell's *Alan's Wife* (1893)' (*ADS* 38[2001] 68–82), which deals with an independent woman and an unwanted baby portrayed on the late nineteenth-century stage.

Back in *Siting the Other*, Bruce Parr gives a queer reading of Nick Enright's drama, as does Peta Tait of some recent Australian circus and physical theatre productions. Tom Burvill discusses the urban theatre projects sited in Sydney's geographically, socially and culturally marginalized western suburbs, while Paul Makeham elucidates the work of Brink, Brisbane's visual theatre company. Peter Fitzpatrick writes more generally on multiculturalism in mainstream Australian theatre. Also on the topic of physical theatre, Adele Chynoweth analyses 'Post-Feminist Physical Theatre: The Abject and the Split Subject in *My Vicious Angel* by Christine Evans' (*ADS* 38[2001] 44–57), referring to a positively received work based on the life of a Circus Oz trapeze artist, which premiered in Adelaide in 1998. This piece is offered as 'an alternative to the phallocentric formula of the singular male protagonist within the conventional linear narrative' (p. 55). Work of the year's most memorable street-theatre performer is analysed by Lawrence M. Bogad in 'Electoral Guerrilla Theatre in Australia: Pauline Hanson vs. Pauline Pantsdown' (*TDR* 45:ii[2001] 70–93).

Peter Fitzpatrick, in 'Whose Turn to Shout? The Crisis in Australian Musical Theatre' (*ADS* 38[2001] 16–28), identifies a 'crisis in Australian musical theatre' despite the achievements of *The Boy from Oz* and *Shout!*, noting the dependence of these shows on a local market (and knowledge) for success and downplaying their export potential. Fitzpatrick refers to their genre as an offshoot of the musical, the 'bioconcert' (p. 17), and notes that both were released into a 'critical vacuum, lacking in both historical knowledge of the Australian musical and an understanding of procedures for its formal analysis' (p. 27). In 'The Movie as Museum' (*Meanjin* 60:iv[2001] 212–17), Brian McFarlane credits Baz Luhrmann with reimagining the film musical, and applauds *Moulin Rouge* for taking the art of bricolage to dizzying new heights where anything and everything goes.

Wesley Enoch, resident director of the Sydney Theatre Company, where he has directed *Black Medea* and *The Cherry Pickers*, surveys indigenous theatre from a personal perspective in '"We want hope": The Power of Indigenous Arts in Australia Today', a transcription of the Sixth Annual Rex Cramphorn Memorial Lecture (*ADS* 38[2001] 4–15). Russell McDougall, in 'Sugar, Land and Belonging' (*ADS* 38[2001] 58–67), presents an original, fascinating, and genuinely productive postcolonial perspective on *Summer of the Seventeenth Doll* [1955] by reading it in conjunction with Jack Davis's *No Sugar* [1985], drawing out the racialized context of Roo's and Barney's labour in the 'plantation economy' of the Queensland canefields. He also provides an insightful reading of the symbolism of characters' names in Lawler's play (p. 60).

On a more cultural studies front, Delyse Ryan, 'Proscenium Arches and Fashion Columns: Brisbane Theatre and the Role of Women During the Wars' (*ADS* 38[2001] 83–97), discusses the importance of images of fashion and beauty in Brisbane during both world wars (on stage and in newspaper accounts of the audience's finery) for ensuring the theatre's appeal to women. *ADS* also released a special issue (39[2001]) focusing on pedagogy, 'Performance Studies in Australia', edited by Gay McAuley, Glenn D'Cruz and Alison Richards, with definitions and surveys of the field, comments on future directions, discussions of the interaction of Performance Studies with feminism and cross-cultural issues, and articles on various methodologies deployed in the Australian context.

In 2001 Veronica Kelly edited a special issue of *Theatre Research International* focusing on 'Theatre in Aotearoa/New Zealand and Australia' (*TRI* 26:i[2001]). Kelly provides an introductory overview, 'The Globalized and the Local' (*TRI* 26:i[2001] 1–14), discussing the final report of the Performing Arts Enquiry in Australia [1999]. She sees 'the financial viability of Australian live performance as deeply affected by the impact of globalization, especially by ... escalating technical, administrative and wage costs' while revenue remains fixed (p. 1). However, Kelly reviews the government response favourably (a $70 million shot in the arm 'to undertake a defined period of stabilizing and repositioning of companies') and credits it to the 'astute use of economic rhetoric' by the report's author Helen Nugent (p. 1). Smaller companies, however, receive 'no or sporadic project funding' (p. 3). Kelly also notes that the 'emergent "sexy" experimental forms in Australia in the 1990s are usually identified as Aboriginal performance and physical theatre' (p. 5), with multicultural theatre not far behind. She concludes that, in economically 'small countries' like Australia and New Zealand, with increasing globalization 'we may have to turn once again to our "non-major" theatre ... to keep alive vital expressions of specific knowledges of histories and place' (p. 11).

In the 'Australia' section of the issue, Joanne Tompkins addresses '"Homescapes" and Identity Reformations in Australian Multicultural Drama' (*TRI* 26:i[2001] 47–59), using for her case studies William Yang's *Sadness*, Janis Balodis's *The Ghost Trilogy* and Noëlle Janaczewska's *The History of Water*, while Helen Gilbert writes on 'Cultural Frictions: John Romeril's *The Floating World*' (*TRI* 26:i[2001] 60–70), looking at revivals of this 'new wave' play first performed in 1974. Mary Ann Hunter discusses 'Anxious Futures: Magpie2 and "New Generationalism" in Australian Youth-Specific Theatre' (*TRI* 26:i[2001] 71–81). Referring to a 'youth-specific company' once 'attached to the State Theatre Company of South Australia', Hunter notes that 'new generation' approaches attempted to respond to young people's own 'preferences in cultural activity', but that this has been complicated as 'youth' comes to be perceived as a sector in major

companies' marketing strategies (p. 71). Concluding the 'Australia' section is
Rachel Fensham's 'Farce or Failure? Feminist Tendencies in Mainstream Australian
Theatre' (*TRI* 26:i[2001] 82–93), which discusses Elizabeth Coleman's successful
play *Secret Bridesmaids' Business* [1999]. In the 'Performance Analyses' section of
the issue, Bruce Parr writes on Brisbane 'Rock 'n' Roll Circus' production
'*Sweetmeats* as Space of Desire' (*TRI* 26:i[2001] 94–105) and Helena Grehan
focuses on indigenous Australian theatre company Kooemba Jdarra's production of
a play by Wesley Enoch and Deborah Mailman, raising many of the issues faced
elsewhere in dealing with indigenous storytelling: 'Faction and Fusion in *The 7
Stages of Grieving*' (*TRI* 26:i[2001] 106–16).

This was a productive publishing year for Helena Grehan. In addition to the two
articles already cited, her *Mapping Cultural Identity in Contemporary Australian
Performance* is the second title in Peter Lang's Dramaturgies series. Here she offers
detailed critical readings of four Australian performance pieces: *Tiger Country,
Ningali, The 7 Stages of Grieving* and *The Geography of Haunted Places*. Grehan
takes as her point of departure issues of place, belonging and cultural identity,
acknowledging at the outset that such concerns are complicated by Australia's
colonial history and positioning of Aboriginal and Torres Strait Islander peoples.
She demonstrates the ways in which the performance pieces share a deep concern
with imagining and reimagining responses to the Australian landscape, be it
figurative or literal. Her analysis also demonstrates how performance can facilitate
consideration of issues such as erasure, the moral responsibility of belonging and the
process by which non-Indigenous Australians, including migrants, inscribe
themselves onto or into this landscape. Significantly Grehan insists that belonging is
not an issue that we should be aiming to resolve. Rather, in the interest of cultural
diversity it should be left open and continually interrogated.

Shakespeare features strongly in this year's Australian drama scholarship. In
'Teaching Shakespeare in Locked Facilities' (*ADS* 38[2001] 29–43) Philippa Kelly
discusses the teaching of Shakespeare in prisons, drawing on her own experiences
'in context with current theory on education and dramatherapy in locked facilities.
Of related interest is the same author's '"How may I compare I this prison where I
live unto the world?": Shakespeare in a Changi Prison' (*AUMLA* 95[2001] 13–26).
Clay Djubal, '"That men may rise on stepping stones": Walter Bentley and the
Australasian Stage, 1891–1927' (*JAS* 67[2001] 152–61), recovers the life and work
of Walter Bentley, associated with Shakespearian theatre in Australia.

Most importantly John Golder and Richard Madelaine have produced the
anthology of new essays *O Brave New World: Two Centuries of Shakespeare on the
Australian Stage*. This valuable and fascinating text presents an impressive selection
of critical pieces arranged to offer a broadly chronological overview of the role
Shakespeare has played in the cultural evolution of Australia during the past 200
years. Golder's and Madelaine's stated aim is to begin the much-needed analysis of
Shakespeare on the Australian stage and to explore the relationship between
Shakespeare and Australian national culture. Included are sixty archival
photographs, many not previously published, a chronology of premieres of
professional productions of Shakespeare's plays in Australia, an impressive
nineteen pages of notes, and essential bibliography.

Richard Waterhouse's 'High Culture and Low Culture: The Changing Role of
Shakespeare, 1833–2000' (pp. 17–39) provides a history of the appreciation of

Shakespeare in terms of class, of the educated elite versus the ignorant masses, and the strategies employed by Australian Shakespeare companies from the 1920s to the present day to build bridges successfully between Shakespeare and contemporary popular culture. Most recently film has shown the way forward in spanning this gap. Waterhouse takes pleasure in the notion that Baz Luhrmann's presentation of his 1993 'exotic' production of Benjamin Britten's operatic version of *A Midsummer Night's Dream* to British audiences represents 'an elegantly symmetrical example of reverse cultural imperialism'. In 'Shakespeare in Australia: The Early Years, *c*.1830–50' (pp. 40–55), Elizabeth Webby considers some of the ways in which 'the cultural icon called "Shakespeare" together with his dramatic works, circulated in early colonial Australia'. Shakespeare's popularity was evident 'at the booksellers' and in the burlesques and parodies that often preceded productions'. Webby goes beyond that popularity to comment on the influence Shakespeare's work had on some of the earliest writers and critics of Australian literature.

In his perceptive essay, '"Sir, I am a tragedian": The Male Superstars of the Melbourne Stage, 1850–1870' (pp. 56–71), Harold Love notes that the patriarchal tragedian 'embodied notions of patriotism and imperial ardour, while at the same time projecting a vision of life as a serious, heroic matter. This was particularly appropriate for audiences engaged in the earnest, though often far-from-heroic, business of subjugating new territories of the world in the name of civilisation.' But what about the women? Janette Gordon-Clark's contribution, 'From Leading Lady to Female Star: Women and Shakespeare 1855–88' (pp. 72–86), seeks to reinstate three significant (Australian) Shakespearian actors—Fanny Cathcart, the leading lady; Louisa Cleveland, the tragedienne; and Essie Jenyns, the popular star—to their rightful place in this literary discussion. Essie Jenyns was greatly influenced by the visiting American actor Louise Pomeroy. Douglas McDermott's '"This isle is full of noises": American Players of Shakespeare in Australia, 1879–89' (pp. 87–102) offers insight into the performances of and audience response to Pomeroy and her compatriots William H. Leake, George Crichton Miln and William E. Sheridan.

The logistics involved in staging national tours in the early twentieth century must have been daunting yet Oscar Asche, between 1909 and 1924, staged three. Richard Madelaine, in 'Substantial Pageant: Oscar Asche, Latter-day Pictorialism and Australian Audiences, 1909–24' (pp. 103–20), examines some crucial questions about the perception and reception of Asche's 'pictorialism and orientalism' over the course of these Australian tours, and suggests that Asche's melodramatic productions of *Othello* and *The Merchant of Venice* demonstrated his 'imperialist, racist and Tory attitudes'. Asche's rival was Allan Wilkie, 'cultural crusader and imperialist', who formed his own Shakespeare company in 1920. John Golder captures a sense of Wilkie's passion as he went about his moral crusade to instruct Australian audiences through exposure to Shakespeare. In 'A Cultural Missionary on Tour: Allan Wilkie's Shakespearean Company, 1920–30' (pp. 121–42), Golder offers detailed readings of a number of Wilkie's productions.

Discussions on 'Australianness' are necessarily complicated by questions of regional diversity. Alan Brissenden, Bill Dunstone and Richard Fotheringham all explore the issue of regional diversity with relation to Shakespeare. Brissenden's 'Shakespeare in Adelaide: Professionals and Progressive Amateurs' (pp. 143–62) offers an overview of the history of (largely amateur) performance and theatre spaces in Adelaide from the first Shakespearian production in 1841 to the present.

From Adelaide we move to Perth and 'Dinkum Shakespeare? Perth, Empire and the Bard' (pp. 163–79), where Dunstone notes that Shakespeare seemed to have 'tapped into racial and gender repression in colonial masculine subjectivity'. Touring British productions were welcomed by the insecure west Australian colonists as a sign of their continuing ties with Britain. As in Perth, the performance of Shakespeare in Brisbane was considered as indicating the city's sophistication and worth. In 'Shakespeare in Queensland: A Cultural-Economic Approach' (pp. 218–35), Fotheringham considers the early infrequent performances before moving on to ponder the extent to which new Shakespeare performance texts are created to respond to different economic, educational and cultural policy agendas.

Penny Gay's 'International Glamour or Home-Grown Entertainment? 1948–64' (pp. 180–99) introduces serious glamour to this study in the form of Laurence Olivier and Vivien Leigh, and notes the impact they, and a little later Anthony Quayle, made on the Australian theatre scene. Gay charts the history and production styles of the John Alden Company (established 1948) until Alden's death in 1962. She concludes with a discussion (and photograph) of the 1964 AETT production of *Henry V*, in which the 22-year-old John Bell made his debut as the King to Anna Volska's Princess Katherine.

Two chapters are devoted to 'Experiments in Shakespeare'. The first, by Mark Minchinton, 'Rex Cramphorn and *Measure for Measure*, 1973–88' (pp. 200–8), celebrates Cramphorn's creativity and openness to interpretation discovered through the physical actuality of rehearsal. The second, John Senczuk's 'The DSI Elizabethan Experiments, 1986–93' (pp. 209–17), offers a fascinating insight into the experimentation undertaken by Philip Parsons in conjunction with Wayne Harrison, which involved a return for modern actors to Elizabethan methods, styles and working conditions. The imaginative freedom that transition provided has since been carried over into other forms of Australian theatre.

Golder and Madelaine are at pains to emphasize the need for more extensive research on the history of Shakespeare in Australia. One future area of study that receives only a passing mention in their introduction would be the way in which Aboriginal Australians have appropriated Shakespeare for their own purposes. There has been to date only one all-indigenous production of Shakespeare: Noel Tovey's *A Midsummer Night's Dream*, offered as part of the Festival of Dreaming in 1997. That production, in which the cast were dressed in full Elizabethan costume (with the requisite stiff white collars), raised important 'postcolonial' issues of performance as appropriation.

It is fitting that the concluding chapter of *O Brave New World* is devoted to a study of John Bell's career (and the history of the Nimrod Theatre) and the impact his work has had on Australian theatre. Adrian Kiernander's 'John Bell and a Post-Colonial Australian Shakespeare, 1963–2000' (pp. 236–55) directly addresses the issue of Australianness in the context of Bell's (and more recently Kosky's) work over more than thirty years. The political dimension of performance is neatly underscored by an anecdote: the actors in *Richard III* (directed by Richard Wherrett), which opened on the night of Gough Whitlam's dismissal (11 November 1975) apparently rushed offstage at every opportunity and huddled over a radio to keep up with the latest developments. John Tasker 'regretted that after the high political drama in Canberra the costumes were not thrown away and the play presented in pin-stripe suits and sensible tweeds'. In Australia's centenary of federation year, and as a fitting final note to this survey of the year's literary scholarship, it is salutary to remember the proposal of King O'Malley, Minister for Home Affairs in Australia's first federal parliament, that the chosen site for the national capital be named 'Shakespeare'.

3. Canada

(a) General

Situated in the Pacific Northwest, and with the recent rise in interest in ecocriticism, it is no mere coincidence that *Canadian Literature* 170/1[2001] should explore the issue of nature/culture. Guest editor Iain Higgins, 'Nature/Culture: Scenes from a North American Boyhood' (*CanL* 170/1[2001] 5–16), notes that his own editorial crosses myriad boundaries in prose and verse, as well as in his use of academic, playful and autobiographical modes of writing, in order to explore experiences of birth and death, and their natural/cultural constructions. J'Nan Morse Sellery, 'Robert Kroetsch and Aritha van Herk on Writing and Reading Gender and Genres' (*CanL* 170/1[2001] 21–55), situates these two famous Canadian authors as boundary-crossing 'writers, teachers, critics, and performers' (p. 21). The three-way interview explores the western Canadian writing that Kroetsch and van Herk have produced, with specific topics such as gender difference and the erotics of writing being related to the *CanL* theme issue; the interview is divided into three sections: 'I. Writing, Reading, and Interpreting the Canadian West and the North', 'II. Gender and Differences: Bodies, Minds, and Sexualities', 'III. Reading and Writing Story: Voices, Genres, and Criticism'. A relatively neglected text of Canadian nature writing is analysed by Christoph Irmscher, 'Nature Laughs at our Systems: Philip Henry Gosse's *The Canadian Naturalist*' (*CanL* 170/1[2001] 58–86). Irmscher's central argument is that Gosse's *The Canadian Naturalist* [1840] is an early example of Canadian environmental writing, where the human subject is questioned and decentred; Frye's infamous and resounding question, 'Where is here?', is reworked by Irmscher in relation to Gosse to become 'What exactly is here?'. This important paper shows how myriad theorists of Canadian writing, who regard the latter as a response to the environment, need also to be mindful of the conversion of 'natural history' into 'natural theology' as performed by Gosse. Anne Compton, 'Physics and Poetry: The Complex World of Alan R. Wilson' (*CanL* 170/1[2001] 91–107), interviews the author of *Before the Flood* [1999]. Wilson was co-winner of the Chapters/Books in the Canada First Novel Award in 2000. The centrality of rivers to environmental writing is explored by Charles Dawson in 'Reading Mark Hume and the River: Conditional Lyricism, Disappearing Salmon and the Braided Voice' (*CanL* 170/1[2001] 110–34). Dawson argues that rivers are overdetermined contested sites of interpretation, where 'ideas of nature and culture blur or might be revisioned' (p. 110). Hume's *River of the Angry Moon* [1998] is the focus for an essay that interweaves an extensive body of riverine non-fiction, explicating content and form, with emphasis upon the lyrical mode and epiphany as undercut by scientific narratives of loss and ecological destruction. Susie O'Brien, 'Articulating a World of Difference: Ecocriticism, Postcolonialism and Globalization' (*CanL* 170/1[2001] 140–58), attempts a speculative combination of postcolonial and ecocritical thought as driven by the demands of globalization (its interlinkings and the new politics of protest); O'Brien charts the genealogy of postcolonialism and ecocriticism and how their different scopes have converged, through a close reading of Anita Rau Badami's *The Hero's Walk* [2000]. I.S. MacLaren, in '*Splendor sine occasu*: Salvaging Boat Encampment' (*CanL* 170/1[2001] 162–87), examines the intersection of cultural and technological history in his attempt to retrace the site of Boat Encampment, an important 'rendezvous point' for the nineteenth-century transcontinental fur-trade route. The essay neatly completes the theme issue, which should be of great use for the teaching of and research in ecocriticism with a focus on Canadian literature, culture and ecology.

Conny Steenman-Marcuse posits the centrality of pioneer women for questions of Canadian identity in her *Re-Writing Pioneer Women in Anglo-Canadian Literature*. Chapters 1 and 2 address theoretical issues of postmodernism, postcolonialism, feminism in Canada, and Canadian identity, while there are further chapters on Carol Shields's *Small Ceremonies* [1976], Daphne Marlatt's *Ana Historic* [1988] and Susan Swan's *The Biggest Modern Woman of the World* [1983]. Steenman-Marcuse regards the latter three novels as sharing 'female experiences of alienation' and exile (p. 24) from the perspectives of the various narrators and the protagonists. Her book serves as a useful, clearly written, but ultimately rather too basic introduction to critical issues in Canadian literature and feminist readings of pioneer writing. Gerald Lynch, *The One and the Many: English–Canadian Short Story Cycles*, offers an in-depth survey and specific analyses of the short story and story cycle. The radical thesis is that not only has the short-story cycle become a distinct genre, but that it is one which is also distinctively Canadian. Lynch gives a brief history of the Canadian short story and examines the conceptual differences between short story and story cycle, arguing that the latter 'came into its own at the end of the nineteenth century and is in the main a twentieth-century form' (p. 23). The introduction covers a wide range of Canadian and other short-story writers, before turning to focused chapters on Duncan Campbell Scott (chapter 1), J.G. Sime (chapter 2), F.P. Grove and Emily Carr (chapter 3), George Elliott (chapter 4) and Alice Munro (chapter 5). The recuperation of little-known authors, such as Sime, is a major part of Lynch's project. The conclusion, or 'L'Envoi: Continuity/Inclusion/ Conclusion', returns to the seminal influence on the short-story genre of Stephen Leacock, and also performs an interesting analysis of a book usually thought of as a novel, Thomas King's *Medicine River* [1989]. Lynch's study makes an important contribution to the history and development of Canadian literary genres.

Major Canadian short-story writers are covered in Fallon et. al., eds., *A Reader's Companion to the Short Story in English*, where each chapter provides a brief biography, survey of criticism and analysis of key concepts and themes in the author's work. Linda H. Straubel and Gayle Elliott, 'Margaret Eleanor Atwood', focus on the structuring binaries in Atwood's work and the ways in which she resists a scientific, machine-like view of nature and humanity with an anti-Cartesian way of thinking and writing. Grant Tracey, 'Morley Callaghan', argues that all of Callaghan's characters 'seek love and tolerance' (p. 83). Michael Trussler, 'Mavis Gallant', argues that Gallant's use of form is significant to a general readership since she uses it 'to investigate the reciprocity between private constructions of memory and the overall cultural imaginary that is historical remembrance' (p. 177). Trussler concludes that, as with other key practitioners of the short story, Gallant utilizes fragmentary form as a resistance to totalization and as mimetic of human cognition.

J.R. (Tim) Struthers, 'Alice Munro', takes a genealogical approach to the development of Munro's writing, tying this in with the main critical works. Allan Weiss, 'Michael Ondaatje', examines the 'blending of fact and fiction' as well as generic conventions, arguing that Ondaatje's shorter prose even resists being characterized as 'short stories'.

Elizabeth Waterston's *Rapt in Plaid: Canadian Literature and Scottish Tradition*, attempts to recuperate a tradition of writing, in this case, of Scottish writing in Canada; such a project is personal and autobiographical, and explores questions of place via a lifetime's *enjoyable* reading and studying of Scottish Canadian literature. Controversially, Waterston's overall aim goes beyond the academic projects of mapping influences and exploring ethnic categories to suggest that her most important contribution is in reliving the pleasures of the act of reading itself. As such, *Rapt in Plaid* functions counter-discursively in an unusual sense, writing back against 'post-literate' or notions of hyperreal multi-media texts and culture. As with Lynch, Waterston also manages to recuperate many lesser-known Canadian writers, and she utilizes the concept of the 'cycle' but in relation to the connections between literature and life; the notes and books cited provide a useful reference tool for those who wish to take the Scottish Canadian literature readings further.

(b) Fiction

Two books in the Reappraisals: Canadian Writers series from the University of Ottawa Press were published this year, La Bossière and Morra, eds., *Robertson Davies: A Mingling of Contrarieties*, and Staines, ed., *Margaret Laurence: Critical Reflections*. Camille R. La Bossière, in her 'Introduction: Davies Tristram-gistus', examines Davies's changing relationship with the work of Aldous Huxley as a way of revealing the complexities of Davies as a writer. La Bossière notes how the collection of essays derives from the first-ever conference on him at the University of Ottawa in 1998, before summarizing the various contents of the volume. The eleven further chapters provide a wide range of perspectives on Davies, starting with his own multi-perspectival presentations to the world in Michael Peterman's 'The Concert of his Life: Perspectives on the Masks of Robertson Davies'. Peterman takes a biographical approach to sort out the conceptual shifts in his theatrical masks that Davies developed and discarded throughout his life. Faith Balisch, '"A hint of the basic brimstone": The Humour of Robertson Davies', suggests that the comic mode which functions as 'the illuminating medium' of Davies's work has been little explored or understood; the chapter attempts a deeper critical understanding of the dark and serious sides or functions of humour. David Creelman, 'Undermining Comedy: Shadows of Determinism in the Salterton Novels', looks at the Salterton trilogy as an 'anxious investigation' into the realm of determinism. Todd Pettigrew, 'Magic in the Web: Robertson Davies and *Shamanstvo*', accounts for the myriad opposing and contradictory reader responses to Davies with reference to strategies of 'enchantment' and 'monologic domination of the reader' in Davies's work (p. 59). Pettigrew provides a useful way of making sense of the extreme reactions to the Deptford trilogy by replacing the concept of didacticism in Davies's work with that of patterning. K.P. Stich, 'The Leaven of Wine and Spirits in the Fiction of Robertson Davies', takes the motif of alcohol as a serious pursuit, placing Davies's references to alcohol in a historical and cultural context. Lois Sherlow, 'Metadrama and Melodrama: Postmodern Elements in the Plays of Robertson Davies', provides a useful summary of Davies's career as a playwright, starting with the scripts he attempted to get produced in London, and his isolation from early Canadian theatre developments. Ironically, as Sherlow suggests, Davies's theatre has more in common with 1980s and 1990s postmodern and postcolonial Canadian theatre. Mark Silverberg, '"Where there's a will, there are always two ways": Doubling in *World of Wonders*', examines doubling in relation to narrative content and structure, Bakhtin and Jung; he concludes that there is a debate in the novel between monologue and dialogue and that the doubling relates to Davies's Magian world-view. David Hallett, 'Authentic Forgeries: Hermeneutics, Artifice, and Authenticity in Robertson Davies's *What's Bred in the Bone*', approaches Davies via Hans Robert Jauss, Hans-Georg Gadamer and Stanley Fish; the sophisticated reading that results argues that Davies's fiction is central to Canadians' definitions of self. Tatjana Takseva Chorney, 'The Myth and Magic of a Textual and/or a Metaphorical Reading of the Deptford Trilogy', draws on Jung, and Tzvetan Todorov's *The Fantastic: A Structural Approach to a Literary Genre* [1973], among other sources, to produce a reading sensitive to the 'enchantment' and magic that Davies regards as central to the gift of reading. Andrea C. Cole, '"Converting the Clerisy": Quest/ioning, Contradictions, and Ethics in the Cornish Triptych', looks at the processes of writing and questing as central in Davies's work; she also examines the counter-discursivity of Davies's writing in relation to colonial literary precursors. Rick Davis, M.D. and Peter Brigg, '"Medical Consultation" for *Murther and Walking Spirits* and *The Cunning Man*', is an intertextual exploration of cross-disciplinary knowledge, in this case Davies consulting a physician about medical details that would eventually find their way, through the creative process, into his literature. In conclusion, this collection of essays provides wide enough scope for students and researchers to begin to explore the main critical questions about Davies's work, and proceed in some new directions.

David Staines's introduction to *Margaret Laurence: Critical Reflections* provides a brief biography of Laurence and summary of the chapters that follow. The collection contains critical essays, responses to Laurence's work by creative writers, and new biographical research. John Lennox, 'The Spirit and the Letter: The Correspondence of Margaret Laurence', regards communication as 'the theme that fills Laurence's work' (p. 9) and he provides a glimpse of the vast archive of letters between Laurence and Adele Wiseman (450 letters) and Laurence and Al Purdy (300 letters). Noting that this correspondence has not yet been selectively ordered by any major biographer, Lennox also charts the ways in which it helped Laurence define herself as a writer. Correspondence is also central to Christl Verduyn, 'Cavewomen Div(in)ing for Pearls: Margaret Laurence and Marian Engel', where Laurence's *The Diviners* [1974] is read in conjunction with Engel's *The Glassy Sea* [1978]. Verduyn argues that both novels share parallel experiences, and both novelists experienced similar conditions in post-war Canada and England. Helen M. Buss, 'Reading Margaret Laurence's Life Writing: Toward a Postcolonial Feminist Subjectivity for a White Female Critic', reads Laurence's two autobiographical works, *The Prophet's Camel Bell* [1963] and *Dance on the Earth: A Memoir* (completed [1987]). Buss utilizes the polyphony of women's voices to perform a critique of postcolonial theory that denies a place for white feminist critics and/or mainstream authors such as Laurence. W.H. New, 'Margaret Laurence and the City', argues that cities function variously in Laurence's work, as 'signs of power, signs of social alternatives, the external confirmation of the difference between physical desire and spiritual grace, and embodiments of energy and imperfection, aspiration and decay' (p. 60). New examines a wide range of fiction, including Laurence's children's writing, to analyse the thematics and function of cities, in particular in relation to biblical intertext. Birk Sproxton, 'The Figure of the Unknown Soldier: Home and War in *The Fire-Dwellers*', addresses the ways in which war is the 'matrix' of Laurence's *The Fire-Dwellers*, with specific reference to the uncanny figure of the unknown soldier operating as 'multiple and transtextual'. A contextualization and close reading of one of Laurence's most famous novels is performed by Nora Foster Stovel in '*(W)rites of Passage*: The Typescript of *The Diviners* as Shadow Text'. Starting with comments on the typescript, Stovel moves through the editing process via biographical information, analysis of the metafictional framework, the embedded *Kunstlerroman*, and final remarks on the excised material; the analysis suggests that further valuable archival work on the 'shadow text' of *The Diviners* remains to be done. Three creative responses to Laurence follow, from Canadian authors: Kristjana Gunnars, 'Listening: Laurence's Women'; Robert Kroetsch, 'Sitting Down to Write: A Discourse of Morning'; and Aritha Van Herk, 'Margaret Laurence: The Shape of the Writer's Shadow'. Gunnars reads Laurence through French feminism to hear the pain, the unhappiness and the politics in her fictional worlds; Kroetsch reads the third paragraph of *The Diviners* to produce a post-structuralist meditation on writing, subjectivity and technology; Van Herk also addresses the act of writing, via thoughts on anatomy, painting and the writer's shadow. Janet Lunn's useful chapter on Laurence's less well covered children's writing, 'To Find Refreshment in Writing Children's Books: A Note on Margaret Laurence's Writing for Children', broadly condemns her dissociation from her audience, and makes some interesting comments about the British contexts of her reading and writing in this area. Two biographical pieces end the collection, Lois Wilson, 'Faith and the Vocation of the Author', and Joyce Marshall, 'Margaret Laurence: A Reminiscence'. Wilson includes excerpts from a discussion between Laurence and herself on vocation, ethics and God, and traces Laurence's 'faith and vocation' throughout key parts of her fiction; Laurence's return to the United Church is also discussed. Marshall somewhat counters Wilson's interpretation by suggesting that the United Church phase did not provide Laurence with 'serenity or spiritual peace' (p. 164). She situates Laurence as a major Canadian author, generous of spirit and a profound portrayer of women. Staines has edited a collection that encompasses many aspects of Laurence's writing and life, providing a useful addition to critical surveys of Laurence.

A close reading of Laurence's fiction set in Africa is provided by Wendy Roy in 'Anti-Imperialism and Feminism in Margaret Laurence's African Writings' (*CanL* 169[2001] 33–57). Roy argues that there is a tension between Laurence's feminist representation of women, particularly with reference to the issue of female genital mutilation, and her 'imperialist discursive inheritance' (p. 52). Roy also usefully situates Laurence's feminist critical contexts in relation to what theoretical models and discourses were available to her at the time of writing her African material.

A book-length introduction to Carol Shields's prizewinning novel was published by Abby Werlock: *Carol Shields's The Stone Diaries*. Written for the Continuum Contemporaries series, the book covers 'The Novelist', 'The Novel', 'The Novel's

Reception', 'The Novel's Performance', and 'Further Reading and Discussion Questions'. While there is necessarily a thematic approach to this introductory account of *The Stone Diaries*, there is also a good deal of insightful analysis, written in clear and accessible prose. The short chapters on the novel's reception and performance analyse not just the increasing interest in Shields's work, but also the ways in which Shields is situated in three main English-speaking publishing markets: Canada, the US and Britain. The tripartite analysis of sales figures relates to Werlock's discussion in the biographical section of Shields's national identities, where the point is made that American-born Shields is read as a Canadian author, and herself identifies with both countries. The bibliography is a useful starting point for researching mainly journalistic essays and reviews of Shields's work.

Contemporary writing is also the subject of a theme issue of *Essays on Canadian Writing*, 'Recent Canadian Fiction' (*ECW* 73[2001]). The issue opens with Jennifer Andrews's timely updating of the Canadian Gothic in relation to First Nations writing, 'Native Canadian Gothic Refigured: Reading Eden Robinson's *Monkey Beach*' (*ECW* 73[2001] 1–24). Through a discussion of Margot Northey's *The Haunted Wilderness: The Gothic and Grotesque in Canadian Fiction* [1976] and recent reviews of Haisla author Eden Robinson's *Monkey Beach* [2000], Andrews suggests that the Canadian Gothic is in effect deconstructed and reconfigured by Native authors such as Robinson, where the uncanny and alien threat comes not from some supernatural or primitive other, but from the colonial presence in an indigenous land and community. Andrews's work also raises some important questions concerning critical receptions of contemporary Trickster writing. Canadian expatriate writing is covered in John Clement Ball, 'Spaces of Postimperial Dwelling: Metropolitan Life and Colonial History in Kate Pullinger's Fiction' (*ECW* 73[2001] 25–50). Pullinger, who originated from Cranbrook, British Columbia, writes of the Canadian expatriate experience in *When the Monster Dies* [1989] and *The Last Time I Saw Jane* [1996]; Ball utilizes Doreen Massey's notions of four-dimensional urban space as well as a Foucauldian approach to read and analyse Pullinger's novels. Peter Dickinson, 'Derek McCormack: In Context and Out' (*ECW* 73[2001] 51–71), develops a queer theory approach to Canadian literature, locating McCormack's fiction in relation to 'a continuum of queer literary and cultural production from the 1920s to the present' (p. 51). McCormack's own critique of Anne Michael's *Fugitive Pieces*, and the ensuing row in critical and reviewing circles, also enable Dickinson to comment on the competing and radically different styles of Canadian literary production that have been notable in recent years. Postmodern Canadian fiction and the environment is the subject of an essay by Allan Hepburn, '"Enough of a wonder": Landscape and Tourism in Thomas Wharton's *Icefields*' (*ECW* 73[2001] 72–92). Hepburn situates Wharton's novel in the 'international postmodern tradition' (p. 73) in order to argue that *Icefields* functions quite differently from the work in the Canadian realist tradition of major Canadian authors such as Atwood or Wilson; although the essay argues for landscape as a 'socially constructed space', the close reading of the novel's textual excesses and strategies reveals it to be not only distorting various categories of containment, but ultimately positing a notion of 'wonder' which retains a surprising link with a notion of authenticity. A subtle teasing apart of racialized reading strategies and responses is allied with 'overcoming whiteness' in Mark Libin, '"Some of my best friends ...": Befriending the Racialized Fiction of Hiromi Goto'

(*ECW* 73[2001] 93–121). Through a reading of feminist and postcolonial theory that explores the issues of a reader's racial positioning and power, Libin develops a notion of literary-critical 'befriending' for productively reading Goto's work. The 'disavowal of race' is one of the problematic notions explored by Rita Wong, but this time not in relation simply to readers, but to a Chinese Canadian author, Evelyn Lau. Wong's 'Market Forces and Powerful Desires: Reading Evelyn Lau's Cultural Labour' (*ECW* 73[2001] 122–40) is highly critical of the commodification of the literary text, both its content and form; she produces a doubled reading that situates Lau and her texts as commodities, and which critiques the representation of sexuality and race in her texts as commodification. Philip Marchand, 'Confession and Critique: The Work of Lynn Crosbie' (*ECW* 73[2001] 141–50), posits a chiastic movement between Crosbie's fictional and poetic worlds; the worlds of popular culture and the notion of the public persona are explored. An American perspective is positively used to gain insight into a Canadian author who 'doesn't fit into any of the preconceived categories of Canadian literature' (p. 151); thus Robert Murray Davis, 'Everything Old/New is New/Old Again: The Fiction of Russell Smith' (*ECW* 73[2001] 151–65), examines the ways in which the popular-cultural, urban voice of Smith rejects notions of small-town, nature-based Canadian 'authenticity'. Davis contextualizes and positions Smith culturally before moving on to close readings of his books *How Insensitive* [1994], *Noise* [1998] and *Young Men: Stories* [1999]; the genre, or sub-genre, of the *Kunstlerroman*, as reworked by Smith, is explored. The fiction of another recent author, David Bergen, is the subject of Neil Besner, 'Bergen's Beginnings' (*ECW* 73[2001] 166–83). Focusing on 'the meanings of faith' and 'the hope for redemption' (p. 168) in Bergen's work, Besner analyses closely the literary style and strategies of this subtly and powerfully expressive new author who is gaining in popularity across North America and Canada. Tamas Dobozy, 'Lhasa Unlimited: The Metaphysics of Death in Steven Heighton's *The Admen Move on Lhasa* and "Translations of April"' (*ECW* 73[2001] 184–207), is in similar territory to Besner, exploring the self-consciously essentialist movement in Heighton's work, and the author's realization that a metaphysics of presence is always potentially undermined by mediation and self-consciousness. The essay is not only a sustained examination of the search for an authentic expression of being via an awareness of post-structuralist literary-critical theory and philosophy in Heighton's writing, but it also illuminates key issues of writing spaces inside/outside late capitalism via Eagleton and Jameson. The issue of *ECW* closes with T.F. Rigelhof's 'Catherine Bush and the Other Talent in the Room' (*ECW* 73[2001] 208–26). Rigelhof celebrates and situates Bush, mainly through a reading of her novel *Minus Time* [1993], and with reference to her *Rules of Engagement* [2000]; Rigelhof argues that Bush maintains a balance between realist description (of the Toronto environment) and 'intellectual robustness' (i.e. the theories of Debord and McLuhan). The essay is a solid and positive introduction to Bush's work.

Mainstream Canadian authors continue to get in-depth critical coverage: Margaret Atwood, in Magali Cornier Michael, 'Rethinking History as Patchwork: The Case of Atwood's *Alias Grace*' (*MFS* 47:ii[2001] 421–47); Rudy Wiebe, in Ervin Beck, 'Postcolonial Complexity in the Writings of Rudy Wiebe' (*MFS* 47:iv[2001] 855–86); and Alice Munro, in Klaus P. Stich, 'Letting Go with the Mind: Dionysus and Medusa in Alice Munro's "Meneseteung"' (*CanL* 169[2001]

106–25). Michael writes a textbook essay on postmodernism and history in Atwood's *Alias Grace*, reading theorists such as Hayden White, Dominic LaCapra and Susan Stanford Friedman to explain the feminist 'history as patchwork' trope at work throughout Atwood's novel. Patchwork quilting is theorized as 'the metaphor and model for an alternative form with which to think about and reconstruct the past … a revaluation of a form traditionally associated with women and disassociated from the serious and valued realms of official history and art' (p. 426). Beck engages in a lengthy and complex unravelling of critical charges put to Wiebe about his novel's religious content and his 'representation of indigenes' (p. 855); the resulting essay argues that Wiebe is a postcolonial writer via analysis in the sections headed 'Wiebe and Settler Culture'; 'Representing the Historical Indigene', 'Representing the Contemporary Indigene', and 'Representing Menonites'; 'Religion and Postcoloniality'; and 'Toward a Postcolonial Canadian Literature'. The 'radical universalism' of Wiebe's work is placed in the postcolonial contexts out of which it emerges in terms of representing marginalized Menonite culture and beliefs. Stich finds critical analysis of myths and archetypes in Munro's work wanting (bar a few exceptions), and sets out to redress the situation, analysing the story 'Meneseteung' which 'thrives on intimations of Dionysus and Medusa' (p. 107). Mennonite Catholic Métis writing is the focus of Isla Duncan's '"The profound poverty of knowledge": Sandra Birdsell's Narrative of Concealment' (*CanL* 169[2001] 85–101). Duncan uses a narratological approach to resist the critical 'pigeonholing' of Birdsell's writing, yet also to attempt an understanding of the ellipses and aporias at the heart of her narratives. In another ideological and social world, science fiction author William Gibson is the subject of Tony Myers, 'The Postmodern Imaginary in William Gibson's *Neuromancer*' (*MFS* 47:iv[2001] 887–909), where a genealogy of Gibson's highly influential ideas concerning cyberpunk and virtual worlds is elaborated upon.

(c) Poetry and Drama
Two related, and important reassessments of Canadian poets are Susan Gingell, 'Claiming Positive Semantic Space for Women: The Poetry of Dorothy Livesay' (*ECW* 74[2001] 1–25) and Tony Tremblay, '"git yr I eye of Canada I and onto internat criteria I": Exploring the Influence of Ezra Pound on the Cultural Production of Louis Dudek' (*ECW* 74[2001] 26–52). The question of Livesay's feminism has not been critically resolved, and Gingell aims to clarify the situation by accepting the contradictions and potentialities in Livesay's own notion of her subjectivity via a post-structuralist reading which is also open to historical contextualization. Gingell provides ample biographical analysis which she relates to the scarcity of feminist authors, and argues that Livesay's project was to 'clear and claim more positive semantic space for women through feminist counterdiscourse and discursive reconstruction' (p. 6). Close readings of the poems are integrated in a thoughtful and commanding essay. The critical neglect of Louis Dudek and his association with Ezra Pound are the subjects of Tremblay's essay. Tremblay mentions the critics who have worked on Dudek, such as Trehearne and Goldie, before arguing that analysis of the Pound–Dudek association is an important part of the history of Canadian poetry. He takes an archaeological approach to the correspondence and other materials concerning Pound and Dudek, and supplies an analysis and commentary on the poetical development that ensued. *Canadian*

Literature published a number of significant review essays of Canadian poetry, the most wide-ranging being R.W. Stedingh, 'A Poetic Potpourri' (*CanL* 168[2001] 122–5), exploring work by Alfred G. Bailey, Mark Cochrane, George Amabile, Leonard Gasparini, Seymour Mayne, Ted Plantos, George Swede, François Charron, and Robin Skelton. New poetry by Susan Musgrave, Lorna Crozier and Libby Scheier is reviewed and analysed by Susan Knutson in 'The Questions Posed to Life by Death: A Canon for Three Voices' (*CanL* 169[2001] 152–4), and the reprinting of Alden Nowlan's celebrated poetry is reviewed by Heather Sanderson in 'On Life, Love and Cats' (*CanL* 169[2001] 159–61).

Drama received considerable and wide-ranging coverage in terms of national and international appeal and exposure. Maufort and Bellarsi, eds., *Siting the Other*, brings together twenty-three chapters and one interview; the chapters on Canadian drama and those taking comparative approaches are reviewed here. Marc Maufort, 'Siting the Other: Cross-Cultural Re-Visions of Marginality', argues for shared historical and cultural experiences between Australia and Canada, with an ongoing 'multicultural reinvention' being highly visible in the field of theatre, which is still emergent. Maufort, 'Forging an "Aboriginal Realism": First Nations Playwriting in Australia and Canada', compares and contrasts established and new indigenous dramatists; he argues that the Eurocentric term 'magic realism' is better replaced with Mudrooroo Narogin's term 'Aboriginal realism' to comprehend the extended range of Aboriginal drama and its interaction with, and critique of colonial theatrical forms. Another comparative chapter is by Gerry Turcotte, 'Collaborating with Ghosts: Dis/possession in *The Book of Jessica* and *The Mudrooroo/Müller Project*'. Both theatrical texts are records of collaborative projects; Turcotte examines from a postcolonial perspective the dynamics and inequalities of collaboration and the demands of mainstream publishing. The resulting chapter analyses collaborative processes and regards them as synecdochic for 'Indigenous/non-Indigenous interaction' (p. 189). Anne Nothof, 'Canadian "Ethnic" Theatre: Fracturing the Mosaic', regards the figure of the 'cultural mosaic' as a master narrative that has been deconstructed by ethnic theatres via identity politics, iconoclastic fracturing of the mosaic, transcultural communication and the establishment of intercultural dialogue. Nothof investigates community plays and audience reception to reveal further such deconstructive practices. Albert-Reiner Glaap offers an insightful survey and overview, 'Drew Hayden Taylor's Dramatic Career', with critical summaries of key plays. Robert Appleford, 'Making Relations Visible in Native Canadian Performance', looks at the ways in which Native Canadian performance destabilizes audiences and resists audience expectations; he argues that, instead of looking at this destabilization in a negative way, the mismatch between performance objectives and audience responses can be positively utilized to make relations between Natives and non-Natives visible. Ric Knowles, 'Translators, Traitors, Mistresses, and Whores: Monique Mojica and the Mothers of the Métis Nations', looks at the revisioning that has occurred in the performance histories of *Princess Pocahontas and the Blue Spots* and its accompanying radio play, *Birdwoman and the Suffragettes*. Knowles argues that it is precisely the contested site of the representation of Native women that can be traced in this performance history, and he is careful to examine the implications of non-Native criticism and positioning in such a tracing. African Canadian drama is the subject of Ann Wilson, '*Beatrice Chancy*: Slavery, Martyrdom and the Female Body', the critical argument being that in George Elliott Clarke's play the heroine is reconfigured problematically as the 'phallic avenger'. Alan Filewod, '"From Twisted History": Reading *Angélique*', situates Lorena Gale's play within the context of a wider argument about the absence of African Canadians from 'the narrative of theatre history'. The production pre-history, with seven workshop productions and one fully staged production in Canada, is indicative, for Filewod, of the ways in which the play exceeds commercial and critical capacities to contain its subversive reconfiguring of the Canadian denial of a history of slavery. Robert Wallace, 'Defying Category: Re/ viewing John Herbert's *Fortune and Men's Eyes*', recuperates gay drama in terms of sociological analysis and aesthetic categories that have largely been ignored by mainstream critics of Canadian literature. The subject of incarceration is explored via Herbert's play and biography; strategies of reading are devised to resituate Herbert within the history of Canadian drama. Permeable borders and margins are the subjects of Robert Nunn's analysis, 'Crackwalking: Judith Thompson's Marginal Characters', revealing through close readings of a series of Thompson's plays how the marginalized other is not actually something separate or separable from the mainstream society. Reid Gilbert, 'Escaping the "Savage Slot": Interpellation and Transgression in George F. Walker's *Suburban Motel*', has a complex notion of audience reception as open subjectivities; he argues that a reading of Walker's plays can illuminate the 'postmodern and postcolonial dramaturgy increasingly evident in Canada' (p. 327). Gilbert specifically reads Walker's *Suburban Motel* and 'companion plays' *Problem Child* and *Risk Everything* to resist binary thinking. The chapter offers analysis of Walker's plays through complex Althusserian and Lacanian theory in a clearly written, critically useful way. Finally, a comparative chapter, which also takes a Lacanian approach, is Joanne Tompkins, '"Fatherlands and Mother-Tongues": Family Histories and Futures in Recent Australian and Canadian Multicultural Theatre'. Four plays are explored, two from Australia and two from Canada, to analyse contemporary multicultural theatre. In conclusion, this edited volume is timely and comprehensive: teachers and lecturers have long been in need of a critical volume that brings together up-to-date readings of Australian and Canadian Aboriginal theatre.

Four special issues of *Canadian Theatre Review* were published: 'Canada on the World Stage', edited by Ann Wilson (*CTR* 105[2001]); 'Youth. Theatre. Politics', edited by Alan Filewod and Eleanor Crowder (*CTR* 106[2001]); 'Stage Lighting in Canada', edited by Harry Lane and Allan Watts (*CTR* 107[2001]); and 'Tours, Remounts and Co-Productions', edited by Ric Knowles and Skip Shand (*CTR* 108[2001]). Jennifer Harvie, 'Canadian Drama and Performance in the UK: Featuring Quebec and a Canon' (*CTR* 105[2001] 5–9), asks why UK productions of Canadian drama are dominated by work from Quebec and overall by canonical Canadian plays. She argues that Québécois theatre is particularly resonant for the UK's regions, particularly Scotland, thanks to shared cultural experiences and populations and issues of dialect and translation, as well as being heavily promoted by the cultural attaché in London. Moving to the other side of the Atlantic, Erin Hurley, 'Canadian Theatre in New York City: Two Case Studies' (*CTR* 105[2001] 10–15), looks at the relatively small number of Canadian plays put on in this cultural centre. She examines work produced by the Brooklyn Academy of Music (BAM) and the Ubu Repertory Theatre, arguing that 'Canada is mined for the new' in different ways by the two companies: 'BAM looks for practical innovation. Ubu

Rep looks for French waves to anglicize' (p. 14). Issues of translation are also covered in some depth by Christiana Ziraldo in 'Lepage's *Polygraphe* in Italy' (*CTR* 105[2001] 16–19), where the play's themes and technological innovations are seen to encourage an enthusiastic audience response; the subject of translation versus technological effects is also explored, leading to questions concerning whether the play is ultimately read as Canadian or Québécois. Marc Maufort studies the first English Canadian play produced in French translation in Belgium, 'A Passage to Belgium: George F. Walker's "Problem Child" in Brussels' (*CTR* 105[2001] 20–3); Maufort analyses the play's structure and themes, and gives a critique of the cast's handling of language. He argues that the play's specific 'Canadian subtext' never comes to the surface in performance, although he says that this was nonetheless a 'significant production' in terms of Canadian performance overseas. Geeta Budhiraja, 'A Glimpse of Canada in India' (*CTR* 105[2001] 24–6), looks at M.S. University Baroda's productions of Sharon Pollock's *Generations* and George F. Walker's *Love and Anger*. Arguing that the plays, developed through workshops run by Robert Fothergill, stretched inexperienced actors, Budhiraja also regards them as allowing glimpses into 'the Canadian way of life'. Practical pedagogical issues are discussed in Joanne Tompkins, 'Teaching Canadian Plays in Australia' (*CTR* 105[2001] 27–8), ranging from difficulties in acquiring expensive texts, to the need to supplement students' historical knowledge; she questions why students appear more open towards Canadian rather than Australian postcolonial issues raised by the plays. Judy Van Rhijn, 'Pamela Rabe: Nurturing a Trans-Pacific Career' (*CTR* 105[2001] 29–31), is a largely descriptive account of actress Pamela Rabe's career in Australia and her return to Canada, while Deborah Cottreau, 'Homage to a Master' (*CTR* 105[2001] 32–9), is an archival collection of quotations from and about Jacques Lecoq. The special issue also contains a 'script', Thomas King's 'Five Episodes from the Dead Dog Café Comedy Hour' (*CTR* 105[2001] 40–66), which will be of use to students and lecturers who are unable to hear King's broadcast material, or, who wish to perform closer analysis of his text.

In the editorial to 'Youth. Theatre. Politics' (*CTR* 106[2001] 3–4), Eleanor Crowder notes how charges of having 'too much fun' in the world of theatre are doubled when it comes to 'artists working with young people' (p. 3); she argues that there are serious issues raised by working with youth, including the continual renewal of pedagogic practices. Practical youth theatre programmes are explored throughout the issue; Edward (Ted) Little and Rachael Van Fossen, 'Pedagogies, Politics and Practices in Working with Youth' (*CTR* 106[2001] 5–10), explore the ways in which the undergraduate programme in Drama for Human Development (DFHD) at Concordia University actively seeks to interact with social groups or communities and engage in a wide range of contemporary issues such as environmentalism. Overall, Little and Fossen explain how the DFHD programme is concerned with promoting the notion of 'theatre artists as cultural workers' (p. 5). David Fancy, 'Productive Transgressions: The Marsh Fire People's Theatre Company' (*CTR* 106[2001] 11–15), narrates and analyses a week-long production of the *Great Big Mosquito Show*, an inaugural project that performs the intersecting, but 'competing and contested', historical narratives of the Tantramar marshes at the Bay of Fundy, New Brunswick. Emphasis is given to the therapeutic approaches taken in and via the production and the establishment of an interactive performance space 'geared towards increased community health resulting from collective and individual creativity' (p. 13). The development of a community arts organization is explored and explained in Wolfgang Vachon, 'The Political Spaces of Open City' (*CTR* 106[2001] 21–3); the facilitation of 'spaces for expression' for people in transition is the key issue, alongside how such spaces can be positively transformative. Therapeutic theatre continues to be lauded in John Lazarus, 'ICE: Beyond Belief' (*CTR* 106[2001] 24–8), in relation to the frustrations and delights of producing a piece of youth theatre, *ICE: Beyond Cool*. The production, concerning youth suicide, was premiered in a downtown Vancouver shopping mall, and after funding struggles, went on tour across Canada. The article gives an insider's view of youth production, and how different members of the business community react to youth issues, given that young people form a large consumer group. Ann Wilson, 'Reaching Out: Soulpepper, Youth and the "Classics"' (*CTR* 106[2001] 29–34), appears torn between the positive side of youth involvement with theatre professionals and a dislike of canonical theatre. Wilson utilizes Jacqueline Rose's work on *Peter Pan* to address the problematic of the representation of young people by adults, and suggests that Soulpepper attempts to resist this appropriation of young people's actual perspectives; she also explores the issue of 'the classics' via Alan Sinfield's work on Shakespeare and pedagogy in Britain, also accusing Soulpepper's approach of being 'Leavisite'. After an extended critique of Soulpepper, Wilson uses Freud to perform a critique of the category of youth itself. The article raises some genuine, compelling theoretical and pedagogic issues, especially in defence of Canadian theatre, yet bizarrely draws on a whole host of British and European critics to reject the mentoring of students within a Eurocentric canon. This begs the question of why Wilson does not draw upon significant Canadian criticism to make the same points. Shannon Hengen, 'First Teller of Tales' (*CTR* 106[2001] 35–8), addresses briefly the notion of Native stories as being non-commercial, indigenous property, while at the same time discussing the mandate of the Debajehmujig Theatre of Wikwemikong Unceded Reserve on Manitoulin Island, which is to revitalize the Anishinaabe 'Culture, Language and Heritage' through education and a creative dialogue between Natives and non-Natives. The therapeutics of theatre continue to be of concern for Laura J. Forth and Mixed Company, 'On the Streets with Cobblestone Youth Troupe: A Dossier' (*CTR* 106[2001] 39–45), following the work done with street youth. Forth creates a montage of Cobblestone Youth Troupe members' poems and testimonials in charting the history and development of the troupe; unusually, audience voices are also given room for expression. Eleanor Crowder, '*Uncertain Sacrifice*: Then and Now' (*CTR* 106[2001] 46–7) and Claire Tansey, 'Returning to *Uncertain Sacrifice* (*CTR* 106[2001] 48), explore the process of producing and writing the *Uncertain Sacrifice* script with Salamander Theatre (launched in 1993 around the youth theatre project). Crowder's article follows the successes and then the budgetary and educational policy restrictions, whereas Tansey is more concerned with the existential issues of 'a raw, youthful text that documents … the politicization of a group of young actors' (p. 48). Julie Salverson, 'Questioning an Aesthetics of Injury: Notes from the Development of *Boom*' (*CTR* 106[2001] 66–9), discusses the problematic representation and 'erotics of suffering' in youth theatre. She charts the context of the play, commissioned by the Canadian Red Cross, about 'anti-personnel landmines'; there is an in-depth discussion of conceptual and performative issues, followed by the script of *Boom* by Julie Salverson and Patti Fraser (*CTR* 106[2001] 70–81).

The editorial to *CTR* 107, Harry Lane and Allan Watts, 'The Paradox of Stage Lighting in Canada: Sometimes So Transparent that it's Invisible' (*CTR* 107[2001] 3–4), makes the case for lighting designers being key to the visual and perceptual experience of theatre. The editors also stress that, in order to get the voices of lighting designers heard, they used a significant number of interviews for the issue; these include Allan Watts, 'Learning to Be Bold with Lighting: A Conversation with Andrea Lundy' (*CTR* 107[2001] 11–15); Emmy Alcorn, 'Notes from a Maritime Kitchen Talk on Lighting: Leigh Ann Vardy in Conversation with Emmy Alcorn' (*CTR* 107[2001] 16–20); John Cooper, 'When the Canvas Isn't Blank: An Interview with Marsha Sibthorpe' (*CTR* 107[2001] 26–31); Allan Watts, 'Discipline Makes Better Art: Michael J. Whitfield Talks about Repertory and Opera Lighting with Allan Watts' (*CTR* 107[2001] 32–6); and Allan Watts, 'Lighting Reflections: Philip Silver Interviewed by Allan Watts' (*CTR* 107[2001] 43–9). The interviews form a useful archive of reflections and analyses from some of Canada's most experienced and prestigious lighting designers. An authoritative examination of the discourses of lighting design is performed in Ric Knowles, 'Looking for Enlightened Lighting: The Discourses of Lighting Design, Training and Practice' (*CTR* 107[2001] 5–10), while Duncan McIntosh, 'Lighting from Character: The Art of Jeffrey Dallas' (*CTR* 107[2001] 21–5), focuses on the influence of a single 'master light designer who … created some of the most memorable productions in Canadian theatre' (p. 21). Another focused piece on a single influential designer is Ana Cappeluto and Edward Little, 'Seeing the Light: Montreal's Axel Morgenthaler' (*CTR* 107[2001] 37–42), where artistic and technical innovation are examined and celebrated. In comparison with the big technical productions of Morgenthaler, Tim Fort, 'Lighting in Miniature' (*CTR* 107[2001] 50–4), examines lighting design in the small theatre and within its historical context; he argues for the aesthetic potential of lighting design first, with technical developments seen as secondary to this potential. Fort gives site-specific instances of learning and application, revealing the fundamentals of the lighting design processes and how they can be used in different contexts and budgets. Judy Van Rhijn, 'Lights Up at the Registry Theatre' (*CTR* 107[2001] 58–107), describes the lease and redesign of a venue, the Registry Office in downtown Kitchener, and the key role played in its development by lighting designer Alex Kordics. Finally, the script of *The Vic* by Leanna Brodie (*CTR* 107[2001] 58–107) completes the issue. This special issue is undoubtedly a major attempt to open up the world of lighting design to a wider critical audience, and provides a valuable archive of comments and analyses by practitioners and other experts.

Another major issue is introduced by Ric Knowles and Skip Shand in their editorial to *CTR* 108, where they observe that tours, remounts and co-productions 'constitute an increasing percentage of theatrical activity in Canada'. They raise the issue of a sense of place in relation to the impact of tours, remounts and co-productions as the latter often posit an international aesthetic, and ask: 'Whose theatre is it … when it comes to visit, or when it is mounted here for performance there?' (*CTR* 108[2001] 3). Alvina Ruprecht is in interview with Marti Maradeu, director of English-language theatre at the National Arts Centre, in 'Co-production and the NAC' (*CTR* 108[2001] 4–9); generally the discussion takes a positive approach to co-productions. Reid Gilbert, 'Speaking from the Pre-Symbolic: Morris

Panych and Wendy Gorling's *The Overcoat'* (*CTR* 108[2001] 10–16), looks at co-production processes in relation to Studio 58 productions, at Vancouver's Langara College, and co-production with the Vancouver Playhouse Theatre. Gilbert examines both negative and positive sides of co-production, the latter including the financial support of the playhouse and the 'apprentice-like experience for the student actors' (p. 12). Skip Shand, 'Co-producing *A Dream*: Are Two "Pucks" Better than One?' (*CTR* 108[2001] 17–23), is concerned with 'interpretive choice' in a co-production of paid professionals and senior acting students; he looks at the 'inspired accident' of having two 'Pucks' mirroring and shadowing one another, one professional and one amateur. David Burgess looks at conversations with playwright Michael Healer and Layne Coleman, artistic director at Passe Muraille and director of their touring production *The Drawer Boy*, in 'The Writer Boy and the Director Boy' (*CTR* 108[2001] 24–8). Gerhard Hauck, 'Redrawing *The Drawer Boy*' (*CTR* 108[2001] 29–34), asks how Canadian production and artistic success stories are handled with remounts and tours; he argues that the notion of the remount being essentially a lesser version leads to a cycle of disappointments. Guillaume Bernardi, 'Inventing *Kopernikus*: A Retrospective Journal' (*CTR* 108[2001] 35–9), looks at the ironies of a French cast performing Claude Vivier's opera *Kopernicus* in a large Montreal venue when this Canadian opera (and the works of this composer) are usually performed abroad. Bernardi writes a retrospective journal of cross-cultural difficulties in production, and the positive energies of the Banff Centre production in 2000 that gave the later performances a coherent identity. Judy Van Rhijn examines the economics of co-production in south-western Ontario in 'Joining Forces in Summer Theatre' (*CTR* 108[2001] 40–2), and Emmy Alcorn follows Mulgrave Theatre, Guysborough, NS, and its mandate to 'develop and tour plays' for the local community in 'The Economy versus God (Everything Comes with Fries)' (*CTR* 108[2001] 43–7). The 1998 tour of Ojibway playwright Ian Ross's *fareWel* to largely First Nations audiences is the subject of Christine Leuze, '"The whole thing you're doing is white man's ways": *fareWel*'s Northern Tour' (*CTR* 108[2001] 48–51); Leuze argues that notions of orality and story, as well as radical changes in performance venue/space, all lead to revised notions of how the theatre is experienced and interpreted. Interestingly, the indigenous audiences play a major part in rethinking what performance means. Two scripts complete the issue, *SMUDGE* by Alex Bulber (*CTR* 108[2001] 52–67) and *RADIO: 30* by Chris Earle (*CTR* 108[2001] 68–79). The issue as a whole raises concerns about the shifting priorities of Canadian theatre performance, mainly due to the positive economics of tours, remounts and co-productions; these issues will only become more urgent and important as theatre funding dwindles, to be replaced by market forces and economics.

4. The Caribbean

(a) General

Each year, new chapters of Caribbean literature emerge to inform the literary world of a distinct Caribbean cultural identity born out of a colonial past, raised in exile, now embracing a pluralistic environment, with a universal theme of place, and with a greater understanding of self. The literature of the Caribbean may be likened to a sleeping giant. It has now awakened to take its place in the annals of literature, establishing its own literary canon, recognizing its own fate, and marching toward its own destiny. This journey has resulted in several journal articles about the Caribbean and Caribbean writers. Dissertations, which can be found in this year's *DAIA*, have also been produced, and a number of books have been published. Indeed, in 2001 writers from the Caribbean, and work about writers from the Caribbean, have become accepted and respected, and validated by the literary community. The present review section, though it attempts to be as complete as possible, cannot therefore be exhaustive. The entries here are to stimulate and encourage the journey of discovery into this oeuvre and determine the path to take.

(b) Dissertations
'Performative Metaphors in Caribbean and Ethnic Canadian Writing (Derek Walcott, St Lucia, David Dabydeen, Austin Clarke, Barbados, M.G. Vassanji, Sky Lee)', by Heike Härting, suggests that 'Postcolonial theorists tend to read metaphor generally as a trope of power that synthesizes its inherently binary structure of tenor and vehicle to produce totalizing meanings.' She goes on to say that her dissertation attempts to combine Judith Butler's feminist theory of performativity with postcolonial theory, and with Caribbean and Canadian literary criticism. Härting examines the works of Walcott, Dabydeen, Austin Clarke, M.G. Vassanji and Sky Lee to show that 'metaphor is one of the most important tools for a postcolonial critique of identity and nation formation'. I would imagine that if one can get past the arcane language of the first paragraph of Härting's abstract, the rest of the dissertation would be readable.

Apparently, Donna Weir goes beyond binaries. In her dissertation, 'Beyond Binaries: Creolized Forms of Resistance in African-American and Caribbean Literatures (Aimé Césaire, Louise Bennett, Toni Morrison, Opal Palmer Adisa, Martinique, Jamaica)', Weir uses only Toni Morrison's *Beloved* in her attempt to establish a commonality between African American literatures and Caribbean literatures. On the other hand, she chooses three Caribbean writers—Aimé Césaire, Louise Bennett and Opal Palmer Adisa—to represent Caribbean writers 'who deal with creolized forms of cultural resistance in their texts'.

Edward Sackey, in 'Michelle Cliff's Poetics of Negation: A Telephone to Africa (Jamaica)', also tries to find some way to link Caribbean literature to African American literature, arguing that Africa provides the energizing as well as the enervating force of Cliff's poetics. Sackey further points out in his abstract that 'Cliff resorts to Africa as an alternative to Euro-America presumably because she considers the Euro-American epistemological impetus spent.' Thus, he maintains, Africa assumes a 'universalist function in Cliff's poetics'.

Laura Issen's dissertation, 'Expressions of Socioeconomic and Cultural Complexities in Works by Derek Walcott, Jamaica Kincaid, and Michelle Cliff (St Lucia, Antigua)', seems to be more straightforward and less histrionic. According to her abstract, Issen counters the argument of Edward Sackey and Donna Weir. She considers the 'cultural complexities and contradictions' of the three writers mentioned, and suggests that 'Their narratives address how the Caribbean's histories and cultures are interconnected with the histories and cultures of England and America.' Issen calls the economically powerful regions and peoples of the world 'the center', the less economically powerful regions and people 'the periphery'. Her dialectic is that the multiple affiliations of these writers, and the subjects of their works, show them to be of the 'center' and 'periphery' at the same time.

Fadwa AbdelRahman's dissertation, 'Hybridity and Assimilation: The Effect of the Racial Encounter on V.S. Naipaul and Chinua Achebe', uses Achebe's *No Longer at Ease* [1960] and Naipaul's *A Bend in the River* [1979], to explain Naipaul's 'controversial ideas about mimicry and hybridity in Africa'.

Donette Francis's 'Cosmopolitan Patriots: West Indian Intellectuals between Home and Metropole' discusses the intellectual and cultural history of the Caribbean Artists' Movement, founded by Kamau and Doris Brathwaite, Andrew Salkey and John LaRose in London in 1966. Francis contends that the movement influenced the cultural and political life of the newly independent Caribbean nations. She further maintains that the intellectual framework of the movement in the Caribbean during the 1960s was heavily influenced by a strong feminist tradition.

Suzanne Develter's dissertation, 'Ritual Embodiment: A Study in the Caribbean Grotesque', tries to use myth to resolve the controversial issue of place. 'Because of its situation of diversity', says Develter, 'the Caribbean defies atavistic notions of community. The situation of the islands is one of "impurity" and this disallows the possibility of sustaining myths based on traceable origins.' Apparently Develter did not consider the Anansi stories prevalent in the Caribbean to this day. Nevertheless, she uses the works of Césaire and Brathwaite, 'who portray their islands as diseased and depleted', as myth-invokers. The rest of her thesis is based on her interpretation of the works of Césaire (*Cahier d'un retour au pays natal*), Brathwaite (*Mother Poem*) and Joseph Zobel (*Rue Cases Nègres*).

Victor Figueroa's 'Each Man is an Island: The Archipelago of Luis Pales Matos, Aime Cesire [*sic*], and Derek Walcott' examines 'the articulation of a lyric subjectivity in these poems, and how this articulation interacts with the imperative of engaging the social, political, and cultural complexities and conflicts of this heterogeneous region'.

(c) Articles in Journals

The *Journal of Caribbean Studies* continues its foray into the literary canon. Volume 15:iii [Winter 2000–Spring 2001] is dedicated to C.L.R. James, and to the people of Haiti. All well and good, but the articles in it seem long-winded, pompous and soporific. Many of the contributors seem to have run amok with the number of notes they append to their articles. One, for example, has 125 notes that the reader must consult while examining the essay. Such a large number of notes leaves the reader unbalanced and perplexed as to what is being stated. One noteworthy article, however, 'Historical Context of a Nation's Folklore', by Angela Rhone (*JCSt* 15:iii[2000–1] 171–86), recounts the Anansi folktales in Jamaica. Rhone traces the history of Anansi, the trickster, the rascal, to West Africa. She maintains that Anansi reappears in the Caribbean, brought there through the oral tradition of the slaves, where he survives in his new environment by his wits. What Rhone may have missed, however, is that the figure of the trickster or rogue is prevalent in the folktales of most national literatures, and does not have its archetype only in West Africa. In Italy Anansi is known as the *buffatore* or *bricone*, in Spain as the *pícaro*, in France as the *coquin*. Examples of the rascal also emerge in *The Pickwick Papers*.

Nevertheless, in her article, Rhone bemoans the fact that the Anansi stories have lost their historical significance. 'What was left,' she states, 'was a Brer Anancy or Brer Rabbit whose persona was no longer that of the slave struggling to outwit his master or even struggling to survive.'

JCSt 16:i–ii[2001] is dedicated to 'the people of Vieques Island ... And those who continue to endure in Haiti, Jamaica, Guyana ... ', whatever that means. Some articles of note in this volume come from José Javier Lopez, Miguel A. De La Torre and Leon and Colwick Wilson. Lopez's 'Vieques Island: The Politics of Military Maneuvers in the Caribbean' (*JCSt* 16:i–ii[2001] 1–22) fulminates against the use of the inhabited Puerto Rican island for bombing practice by the US navy; De La Torre, 'Cuban Classism on Both Sides of the Florida Straits: A Theological Perspective' (*JCSt* 16:i–ii[2001] 23–44), presents his readers with an interesting rendition of 'classism' in Cuba; and the Wilsons' 'A Historic Review and Empirical Profile of Caribbean Immigrant Domestic Workers in New York City' (*JCSt* 16:i–ii[2001] 61–80) discusses the immigrant experience of English-speaking domestic workers from the Caribbean.

In her article, 'Decolonizing the Tongue: Reading Speech and Aphasia in the Work of Michelle Cliff' (*L&P* 47:i–ii[2001] 94–108), Marian Aguiar makes an attempt to interpret Cliff's 'Journey into Speech' from a psychoanalytic viewpoint. Aguiar suggests that Cliff cannot come to terms with her self, and with a language that she uses but is not her own—it is the language of the oppressor. The dilemma created becomes a representation of aphasia that, according to Aguiar, appears and is discussed frequently in postcolonial theory and in the literature of the African diaspora. Aguiar then tries to 'work through the nuances, assumptions and possibilities of a representation of speechlessness'. She presents a lengthy and detailed argument replete with a spate of psychoanalytic theoreticians (Breuer, Freud, Derrida, Kristeva), as well as some post-structuralist ideas, to show that Cliff is depressed. 'The depressed speaker', argues Aguiar, 'gradually finds words irrelevant ... speaks below a level of communication, and then slips into progressive periods of silence.' Aguiar's prolix work is divided into two parts: 'Theoretical Readers of Speech and Aphasia', and 'Aphasia as Bodily Strategy'.

Aguiar may be spot on with her psychoanalytic interpretation of Michelle Cliff and the aphasia issue, and the dilemma is truly characteristic of many writers in this brave new world. As Aguiar suggests, Michelle Cliff is certainly interested in (in Cliff's words) 'mixing in the forms taught us by the oppressor, undermining his language and co-opting his style and turning it to our purpose'. Gregory Alles, however, puts a different spin on this idea of Aguiar's. Cliff's desire is brought to fruition, and is seen, in the new language of the Caribbean people. In his essay, 'The Greeks in the Caribbean: Reflections on Derek Walcott, Homer, and Syncretism' (*Historical Reflections/Réflexions Historiques* 27:iii[2001] 425–52), Alles writes that his interest is in the Caribbean 'because during the last half century it has emerged as a contemporary paradigm of syncretism—or hybridization, or creolization'. He further writes that he is 'particularly interested in Walcott because he, as much as anyone, has consciously worked with the kinds of models that generally interest students of Greek religions the most, that is, Greek models'. But Walcott does not write only in pure or *hoch* English. Like Louise Bennett, Jean Binta Breeze and Mickey Smith, Walcott also lets the mixture that characterizes Caribbean speech shine through in his works. This new Caribbean language gives new vigour, growth and identity to the 8.5 million people who inhabit the region. Alles's essay is well worth reading. It demonstrates the energy of the Caribbean, seen through the eyes of its writers, who take elements of English literature and European culture and blend them with Caribbean and African cultural forms in order to establish a new world view, and a new world order.

In 'Pride and Prejudice: West Indian Men in Mid-Twentieth-Century Britain' (*JBS* 40:xiii[2001] 391–419), Marcus Collins describes the perceptions of West Indian men in England between 1930 and 1970. Collins explains the differences in perspective by detailing the negative characterizations held by mainland British who, during this period, described West Indian men as promiscuous, violent, neglectful as fathers, patriarchal, and 'insolent and indolent'. He simultaneously informs the reader how West Indian men describe themselves as they talk about employment discrimination and social subjugation due to colonial stereotypes, and fear and competition among British labourers. Collins explains that, during the early period of immigration, West Indians thought of the British as gentlemanly and admirable. They therefore desired to emulate 'Britishness'. He argues that this population of immigrants, after experiencing chronic and debasing discrimination and self-negation, created a new black identity that provided a 'constituency for the Black Power movement in Britain'. Collins's work illustrates the pioneering efforts of West Indian men in England who fought to discover and claim a definition of black masculinity in a foreign and hostile location where white masculinity was viewed as the standard-bearer for manhood.

In 'The Postcolonial Chickens Come Home to Roost: How *Yardie* has Created a New Postcolonial Subaltern' (*SAQ* 100:i[2001] 287–305), Grant Farred argues that the recent fictionalized versions of Anglophone postcolonial life in black Britain produce an innovative literary canon that not only attracts the cellphone generation of black Brits but also acts as a resource for detectives in Scotland Yard seeking to understand the underground drug culture. This fiction, represented by Victor Headley's *Yardie*, is controversial because of its inherent negative image and stereotyping of black males in London. However, the work is valued as a narrative that tells the story of those individuals from the peripheral 'yards of Kingston's ghetto' who enter London without any hope of participating in the mainstream economy, which is seen simply as 'indentured servitude for Afro-Saxons'. This type of fiction tells through its narrative of England's 'dis-ease' with the huge demand for the drugs provided by the opportunistic and impoverished postcolonial underclass of the Jamaican diaspora. Farred suggests that this type of fiction is marginalized, creating and maintaining an 'out of sight, out of mind' location in literature and, thus, in English life. Although this article is a bit lengthy, it is nonetheless loaded with interesting history about postcolonial life for Caribbean people migrating to England. It details the new ways of self-definition and presence by vulnerable Caribbean people in their wealthy stepmother country.

Cynthia James, in 'Gender and Hemispheric Shifts in the Caribbean Narrative in English at the Close of the Twentieth Century: A Study of Paule Marshall's *Daughters* and Erna Brodber's *Louisiana*' (*Jouvert* 5:iii[2001]), presents a fascinating picture of the interaction among gender, American and West Indian identities as represented in the works of Paule Marshall and Erna Brodber. James looks at *Daughters* and *Louisiana*, the literary works of Marshall and Brodber that portray interdependent, enduring, productive and complementary relationships between women of the Caribbean and America. She suggests that these novels illustrate female resilience and agency even though the West Indian immigrant woman in the US suffers from 'triple invisibility': as a black, as a foreigner, and as a woman. Simultaneously, these female writers of Caribbean ancestry make themselves notably visible and vocal through their popular classic novels.

The *New West Indian Guide* touts itself as the oldest scholarly journal on the Caribbean. It publishes works in the social sciences and in the humanities. The articles in volume 75[2001] examine several socio-political issues such as drug control and labour and economic differences in Barbados, Jamaica, and Trinidad/Tobago, as well as the debate concerning bilingualism in Puerto Rico. This volume also includes a book review article about the US presence in the Caribbean; however, this article seems misplaced since the rest of this volume is dedicated to book reviews.

In his article 'Between the Death Penalty and Decriminalization: New Directions For Drug Control in the Commonwealth Caribbean' (*NWIG* 75[2001] 193–227), Axel Klein examines drug control policies and activities in the Caribbean. He argues that pressure from the United States, the European Union and the Caribbean elite shape the development of drug trafficking and drug use policies and practices that create costly stiff penalties with a number of unintended consequences. He shows how the focus on funding the prevention of illegal drug activities allows other criminal activities that impact on people in the Caribbean to be ignored, while increased arrests of drug abusers create a vacuum of available therapeutic resources. According to Klein, in Jamaica, the response to crack cocaine use and marijuana use directs us to the cultural meaning of these two different drugs: crack cocaine is demonized, while marijuana is considered to be more benign. In the light of this bipolar interpretation of drug use, the Jamaican Ganja Commission recommends decriminalization of marijuana use with stiff penalties for crack cocaine trafficking. Klein argues that this trend towards a new policy is being closely watched by other Caribbean countries, as it represents a more complex response to a complicated and thorny issue, especially for the United States, where simplistic 'Just Say No' rhetoric drives unsophisticated policy formulation.

The second essay, 'Labor and Place in Barbados, Jamaica, and Trinidad: A Search for a Comparative Unified Field Theory Revisited' by Karen Dhanda (*NWIG* 75[2001] 229–56), records its author's quest to examine the differences among labour markets in Barbados, Jamaica, and Trinidad, and to suggest a common theoretical framework that explains the disparity within these markets. Dhanda traces the post-emancipation era of these 'sugar colonies' to describe how these countries responded to new-found economic independence. She suggests that the interaction of geographic location, labour patterns, and the dynamic relationship between global and local markets can create a portrait that contributes to understanding the current economic picture in these countries. Dhanda's view on labour patterns, geography, and what she calls 'path dependence' provides the reader with a productive way of examining differences in the current economic status of each of the three countries.

Erna Kerkhof's 'The Myth of the Dumb Puerto Rican: Circular Migration and Language Struggle in Puerto Rico' (*NWIG* 75[2001] 257–88) is an attention-grabbing essay which explains the meaning assigned to the retention and loss of the Spanish language due to the revolving émigré process between Puerto Rico and the

United States, and the subsequent incorporation of English in Puerto Rico. Kerkhof maintains that the struggle for cultural and identity preservation is central to understanding bilingualism in Puerto Rico. Popular stories related to the loss of the Spanish language and identity for returning Puerto Rican children fuel these myths as 'Neoricans and Nuyoricans' (derogatory terms used to describe Puerto Ricans who return from the US mainland and from New York) enter the formal education system. Kerkhof explains how cultural elites establish and maintain identity narratives that glorify Spanish while mocking English and Puerto Ricans who speak 'Spanglish'. One popular song, *El Nietecito* [1996], illustrates the struggle. It tells the tale of an intelligent Spanish child sent to the US by his grandfather to learn English. According to the song, after seven years, the grandson begs to return to Puerto Rico, reporting that he has not learned English, and is forgetting Spanish and his roots. His grandfather's retort is 'Hurry up and move back before you end up dumb!' Kerkhof argues that this politically charged and time-consuming issue circumvents national dialogue about a failing educational system and serious economic matters in Puerto Rico.

A fourth article, 'Security, Insecurity, and the U.S. Presence in the Caribbean', by William Walker (*NWIG* 75[2001] 289–95), analyses the American presence in the Caribbean by reviewing five books written about the United States, Cuba and the Caribbean. Walker argues that Cuba and other Caribbean countries have not been passive participants in what appear to be US-dominated actions in Cuba and the Caribbean. He suggests that Cuba and other Caribbean countries are actively involved in shaping their own history, although the story of many of US–Cuban–Caribbean events is told from the viewpoint of the United States.

The remaining sixty pages of this volume are dedicated to book reviews which cover various Caribbean works from 1997 to 2002. The volume details some important issues for the Caribbean, although discussed, perhaps, by writers outside the Caribbean community. Even though some authors in this volume conduct ethnographic studies as outsiders, there is a missing perspective that can only be narrated by insiders from the Caribbean region.

Barbara Baumgartner, in 'The Body as Evidence: Resistance, Collaboration, and Appropriation in *The History of Mary Prince*' (*Callaloo* 24:i[2001] 253–75), argues that *The History of Mary Prince*, an autobiographical narrative dictated by Mary Prince, a slave in the British West Indies, is the subject and object of scholarly dialogue, in part because of the voice given to those individuals wounded by slavery in the colonies, and likewise because of the representation of Prince's abused body as an instrument of passive resistance in the battle between slave and master. Baumgartner suggests that several scholars, including Henry Louis Gates Jr. and Moira Ferguson, interpret the narrative in a way that challenges the original scribe, Thomas Pringle, an abolitionist, who published the account in 1831. Baumgartner's work focuses on the physical pain expressed by Mary Prince and how that pain, pivotal in her story, creates a cultural narrative of the representation of women's bodies as a source of economic power that benefits others, and a mechanism to achieve power that benefits the person. Baumgartner details Prince's journey, from an enslaved life in the Caribbean islands to England, where she seeks to purchase freedom from a hideously oppressive and psychologically brutal existence. At the same time, Baumgartner employs the interpretation of other scholars to illustrate the potency of Mary Prince's narrative, which indicates the necessity for scholars to examine, clarify and reinterpret the life of Mary Prince.

(d) Volumes in Series

Bardolph, ed., *Telling Stories: Postcolonial Short Fiction in English*, was finalized for publication by André Viola and Jean-Pierre Durix, on account of Jacqueline Bardolph's untimely death. It is volume 47 in Rodopi's Cross/Cultures series, and presents us with the work of thirty-five contributors, who write about Commonwealth literature and Commonwealth writers. Their essays are grouped in seven 'geographical zones'. Five writers contribute to the section entitled 'The West Indies'. Louis James's 'Writing the Ballad: The Short Fiction of Samuel Selvon and Earl Lovelace' (pp. 103–8) discusses the emergence of West Indian literature as a world force in the 1950s, and the development of the Caribbean short story that begins with C.L.R. James's *La Divina Pastoral* [1927]. François Charres, in her contribution, 'Neither Fish Nor Fowl: A Reading of Paule Marshall's Earlier Short Stories from a Caribbean Perspective' (pp. 109–18), discusses the 'process of acculturation of the rural Bajan migrant to the American metropolis'. Charras follows the literary development of Paule Marshall, her involvement in the Caribbean Arts Movement, and her eventual recognition as a Caribbean writer by Kamau Brathwaite, Wilson Harris and Derek Walcott. 'The Poetics of Death: Olive Senior's "Tears of the Sea"' (pp. 119–28), by Claude Maisonnat, is about the theme of death, the language used in 'Tears of the Sea', and the three 'signifiers sea/shell/ sand', in Senior's short story.

In 'Colonial Literature or Caribbean Outure? *Creole Chips* by Edgar Mittelholzer' (pp. 129–43), Frances Williams makes a courageous attempt to revivify Edgar Mittelholzer, the Guyanese writer who, now almost completely forgotten, was hailed 'as the giant of Caribbean literature' in the 1950s. Williams writes, 'That we should deny him the quality of his early, or Caribbean, works is the result of that very same ostracism that he has been condemned for.' Williams refers to the racist and fascist overtones of Mittelholzer's later output, which alienated him from the Caribbean and Anglo-American intellectual community, but makes a strong case for 're-examination and perhaps re-assessment' of Mittelholzer's works. Finally in this volume is Thorunn Lonsdale's article 'Literary Foremother: Jean Rhys's "Sleep It Off Lady" and Two Jamaican Poems' (pp. 145–54). Lonsdale sees 'Sleep It Off Lady' not so much as a collection of short stories, but 'as a kind of autobiography'. He follows with an explication of the text.

Volume 48 of Cross/Cultures is Scott and Simpson-Housley, eds., *Mapping the Sacred* (also noticed above), which contains three articles on the Caribbean. Joscelyn Moody's 'Unsentimental Journeys: Christian Landscapes of Slavery' (pp. 155–78) discusses the 'number of common characteristics' in the autobiographies of Mrs Nancy Prince and Mary Prince—the former black, free, and American, the latter black, a slave, and West Indian. Moody suggests that, although both women 'represent different nations and caste and class systems, these ... narratives indicate that both women were "social dissidents"'. Victoria Carchidi continues the theme of Christianity-cum-spirituality in the Caribbean. Her essay, '"Heaven is a green place": Varieties of Spiritual Landscape in Caribbean Lifestyles' (pp. 179–98), should generate much controversy among the academic community in the Caribbean. Her first broadside is to state that the 'gulf separating the ... notions that have ... fueled the "conquest" of these lands ... might well have stripped the peoples now inhabiting them of any connection between their spiritual beliefs and the land'. Carchidi then uses Walcott's *Omeros* to show that the land (in this case, St Lucia) creates a 'living spirituality out of its peoples' various heritages'. 'The land', continues Carchidi, 'supports and nurtures the physical and spiritual elements of its varied population, thereby forming a harmonious site for a new and syncretic spirituality.' A number of Caribbean heads would be nodding approval, and a number of Caribbean voices would say 'amen' to the statement. But the disagreement begins when Carchidi uses Viamen's *Of Nuns and Punishment* to argue that organized religion 'frequently offered the only way to acquire the education needed by anyone hoping to participate in governance and to have a voice in the way the land was treated'. In her discussion of organized religion Carchidi does not make the distinction between the Spanish and French Caribbean and the Catholic Church, on the one hand, and the English-speaking Caribbean and its Protestant counterpart, on the other hand. The third essay, '"Monstrous prodigy": The Apocalyptic Landscapes of Derek Walcott's Poetry' by Yvette Christiansë (pp. 199–224), discusses 'apocalypticists' and 'apocalypticism' in Walcott's *Another Life*.

Bucknell Review 44:ii[2001] is dedicated to the theme of 'Caribbean Cultural Identities', and contains essays by some well-known Caribbean writers. Richard Allsopp, George Lamming and Gordon Rohlehr are among the list of eight contributors who respond to the question, 'What does it mean culturally and philosophically, to be a Caribbean person?' As Glyne Griffith maintains in the introduction, 'the common thread uniting this collection into a coherent whole is the intellectual concern with the complex and oftentimes vexed question of identity in a Caribbean cultural and philosophical context.' This volume of the *Bucknell Review* is relevant to the issues being discussed today, and should be among the books read by students and scholars of Caribbean literature.

The *Jamaican Historical Review* contains numerous articles about various aspects of slavery in Jamaica. It provides an account of slave life according to historical documents and informs the reader about the diverse black and white immigrants who populated the island in the seventeenth and eighteenth centuries. This volume also tells us about health care during this period, and about the dissemination of relief to victims of the 1730 hurricane in Jamaica. The remainder of the journal focuses on reviews of books about Jamaica and the Caribbean and on aspects of slavery and resistance.

The first article, 'John Taylor's Ideas about Seventeenth-Century Jamaican Slavery' by David Buisseret (*JHR* 21[2001] 1–7), provides a brief report gleaned from John Taylor, a would-be slave trader who recorded slave life during his two years in Jamaica. Buisseret provides documentation about slave life during this period with specific notes on health, marriage, and weekend and religious activities. He suggests that Taylor's documents inform historians about the diverse origins of Jamaican slaves, discussed more fully by Trevor Burnard in the next article. His '*E pluribus plures*: African Ethnicities in Seventeenth- and Eighteenth-Century Jamaica' (*JHR* 21[2001] 8–22) argues that, during the seventeenth and eighteenth centuries, Jamaica was an immigrant society that included diverse European migrants who were outnumbered by people of African descent by 20:1. Burnard suggests that the demographics of Jamaica created 'Africanization', even though 'whites, who monopolized political and cultural power attempted to replicate English culture in a new Anglicized settlement'. Burnard adds that African slaves came from various regions, making heterogeneity a striking characteristic of the African slave population in Jamaica. He suggests that the current national dictum 'From Many One', which describes the Jamaican people, in no way acknowledges people from many different African countries who create Jamaica's multinational identity.

The next essay, John Campbell's 'Reassessing the Consciousness of Labour and the Role of the "Confidentials" in Slave Society: Jamaica 1750–1834' (*JHR* 21[2001] 23–30), signals its content with the following epigraph: 'Though I was born a slave, with a slave's name, My Mind is my own, and I should like to be ranked Among the noble slaves … '. Campbell suggests that Confidentials hired by white management to maintain the status quo became agents who advanced resistance strategies in the enslaved community. He argues further that, although the English aristocracy in Jamaica disliked labour negotiation, they engaged in it, often facilitated by Confidentials, in order to maximize sugar returns on their plantations.

'The Health Care of Jamaican Urban Slaves, 1780–1838', by Lorna Simmonds (*JHR* 21[2001] 31–7), describes the illnesses, disease and medical care of slaves in Kingston, Jamaica in the eighteenth and nineteenth centuries. Simmonds discusses the segregated medical care system that was part of a larger troubled health-care system on the island. She illustrates the use of 'illness marks' to identify runaway slaves, and the use of slaves in the formal medical system as nurses and hospital attendants. She contends that the combination of folk medicine administered by slaves and by ex-slave black doctors provided much-needed service for the black population during this period.

The final essay, 'The 1780 Hurricane Donation: "Insult offered instead of relief"', by Linda E. Sturtz (*JHR* 21[2001] 38–46), illustrates the tragedy of the 1780 storm not just for the economic system in Jamaica but for the homeless and traumatized families who had to prove their worthiness in order to receive relief supplies. Sturtz suggests that, as a result of their faulty relief system, the English maltreated hurricane victims, and that these victims were neglected by the Jamaican Commission, which distributed relief using unfair and unjust practices. During this period, victims were required to justify their deserving status, and advantage was predicated on skin colour in Jamaica. Sturtz reports that humanitarian relief to the wealthy was viewed as 'wealthfare'. She also suggests that black Jamaicans and middle-class white Jamaicans responded to the selectively parsimonious British with social activism.

(e) Literary Criticism

In *Charting Caribbean Development*, Anthony Payne and Paul Sutton write about and analyse the various strategies used by the Commonwealth Caribbean countries in their attempt to develop economically after independence. Although they explore the alternative 'destinies' for the Caribbean communities, their particular focus is on Jamaica, Grenada, and Trinidad and Tobago. Payne and Sutton examine the different models of development promoted by Eric Williams, for Trinidad and Tobago, and by Michael Manley and Edward Seaga, for Jamaica. They also include discussions on the Grenada revolution. *Charting Caribbean Development* will be an important source book for the student interested in the history of the economic development of the Commonwealth Caribbean countries.

In *C.L.R. James: A Life*, Farrukh Dhondy writes about James and his life in England, including the activist philosophy of this political theorist, who wrote for the *Manchester Guardian*. The book's sixteen chapters tell of James's scholarly output, his travels, his meeting with Trotsky, his literary relationship with his Trinidadian countryman, Naipaul, and his love of cricket.

Nicole King's *C.L.R. James and Creolization: Circles of Influence* takes a different tack. King struggles with the definition of creolization to show how that definition fits into James's fiction; she even considers the etymology of the word, and spends twenty-seven pages of her first chapter working towards a definition. Perhaps her book was in press before the *Dictionary of Caribbean English Usage* was published. Had she considered the definition given there, her first chapter, 'Mapping Creolization', could have been shortened.

Dawes, ed., *Talk Yuh Talk*, is a literary goldmine of interviews with nineteen Anglophone Caribbean poets who share their views on poetry and poetics from a Caribbean perspective. They discuss the tension arising from using a language that is not their own, as well as the difficulty of writing in their own countries. Dawes introduces each poet with a brief biographical sketch.

Victor Chang, in 'West Indian Poetry' (in Roberts, ed., *A Companion to Twentieth-Century Poetry*), gives further and persuasive explanation to the issues raised in Dawes's book. Chang argues that, 'while it is true that the poetry of the Anglophone Caribbean reveals shifts in approach and variations in style, much as the islands themselves have differences and nuances, still one can discern a similarity and a general pattern which is largely the result of a shared kinship, a shared history and a common heritage of slavery, indentureship, and colonialism'. He then explores and examines the Caribbean poets and writers who share the 'Caribbean experience', and who must write in the language of the conquerors. Brathwaite, Walcott, McKay, and many other Caribbean writers are considered in this chapter.

More about Walcott can be found in *Nobody's Nation: Reading Derek Walcott* by Paul Breslin, which discusses Walcott and his works. Each of the ten chapters (plus epilogue, notes, and index) contains lots of notes, and the authorial 'asides' help to give the book significance.

A refreshing departure from Walcott, Brathwaite, *et al.* is a new publication, *In Praise of New Travelers: Reading Caribbean Migrant Women's Writing*, by Isabel Hoving. Hoving suggests that 'Caribbean women's writing is irreducibly *different*. One reason for this difference lies precisely in the fact that their writing takes shape by their engagement in complex, vehement dialogues with their many audiences, dialogues inevitably structured by power, violence and resistance.' The rest of her work is structured around the theme of 'Place, Voice, and Silence'.

The year 2001 again brings Naipaul to our attention with Lillian Feder's *Naipaul's Truth: The Making of a Writer*. Feder looks at the truth according to Naipaul, and at his attempt and commitment 'to deliver the truth' to the rest of the world. However, with Brathwaite's seventieth birthday this year, Timothy Reiss allows many people to celebrate Brathwaite's works and Brathwaite's truth. Reiss, ed., *For the Geography of a Soul: Emerging Perspectives on Kamau Brathwaite* is a rich compilation of contributions honouring Brathwaite's birthday. Well-known

Caribbean authors and scholars such as Maryse Condé, Cynthia James and Erna Brodber share appreciative reflections about Brathwaite, while personal testimonials reveal another aspect of this renowned Caribbean scholar. Writers across the generations provide the reader with thrilling poetry, narratives and interpretation of works that serve as a kaleidoscopic panegyric to this multi-talented writer, historian and mentor.

A lovely departure from English-speaking Caribbean writers to the French-speaking Caribbean is the work by Jeannie Suk, who looks at the Francophone Caribbean in her book *Postcolonial Paradoxes in French Caribbean Writing*, in much the same way Chang, Dawes, Griffith and Alles examine the Anglophone Caribbean. The same view of the paradoxes and tensions associated with postcoloniality in the English-speaking Caribbean are also found in French Caribbean literature. The issues of *négritude*, *antillanité*, and *créolité* are similar, and the same themes of 'in-between', and 'incompleteness' are modes central to the Caribbean, regardless of language. Suk, however, focuses on the works of Aimé Césaire (*Cahier d'un retour au pays natal*), Édouard Glissant (*Le Discours antillais*), and Maryse Condé (*Moi, Tituba, sorcière ... Noire de Salem*).

5. India

(a) General

Shyamala A. Narayan's annual bibliography 'India' (*JCL* 36:iii[2001] 39–71) lists creative and critical writing published in 2000. In the introduction, which is mainly devoted to a survey of creative writing, Narayan notes that fine collections of poetry appeared from Keki N. Daruwalla, Tabish Khair and Sunita Jain. Significant drama included Mahesh Dattani's *Collected Plays* and works by Manjula Padmanabhan, Poile Sengupta and Dina Mehta. Among the fiction highlights were Amitav Ghosh's *The Glass Palace* and Shashi Deshpande's *Small Remedies*.

Amit Chaudhuri has edited *The Picador Book of Modern Indian Literature*, an anthology of prose from the nineteenth-century Bengal renaissance to the present day. His note on the selection asserts that 'this anthology is not a riposte to any other anthology', but it will inevitably be compared with Salman Rushdie and Elizabeth West's *Vintage Book of Indian Writing, 1947–1997*. Like Rushdie and West, Chaudhuri excludes poetry 'for reasons of space'. Although there is an extract from Vikram Seth's *The Golden Gate*, Chaudhuri sees it as 'an example of hybridized narrative fiction, rather than of poetry'. Unlike Rushdie and West, Chaudhuri includes a substantial amount of work translated from Indian languages. The anthology has its own imbalance, however, since the emphasis falls heavily on Bengali and English. Hindi is represented by three pieces, Urdu by four, and the homogenized category 'the South' by four as well. Despite this imbalance, the volume contains much interesting material. In addition to fiction (by Tagore, Premchand, Manto, Anantha Murthy and Rushdie, amongst others), it includes autobiographical writing and literary and cultural essays. Notable nineteenth-century essays include Michael Madhusudan Dutt's 'The Anglo-Saxon and the Hindu', a paean to the English language, and two pieces by Bankimchandra Chatterjee debating the conflict of cultures in his time. Later criticism is represented by Arvind Krishna Mehrotra's 'The Emperor Has No Clothes', an incisive analysis of the multilingual situation within which many Indian writers work, and by A.K. Ramanujan's well-known 'Is There an Indian Way of Thinking?'. Each writer's work is preceded by a brief but helpful introduction and the selection is prefaced by two essays that were originally published in the *TLS*: 'Modernity and the Vernacular' notes how Western conceptions of Indian literature and culture are skewed by an emphasis on writing in English; 'The Construction of the English Novel in English' argues that particular features of Salman Rushdie's style, such as non-linearity and fantasy, are taken by critics to be 'emblematic of a non-Western mode of discourse, of apprehension, that is at once contemporaneously postcolonial and anciently, inescapably Indian', but Indian fiction, and Indian literature in general, are more heterogeneous than such constructions allow for.

A number of books deal with the diaspora. Crane and Mohanram, eds., *Shifting Continents/Colliding Cultures: Diaspora Writing of the Indian Subcontinent* [2000], covers film and Sri Lankan and Bangladeshi writing, in addition to work by writers of the Indian diaspora. The editors' introduction outlines the effects of migration on ideas of identity, home, the body and sexuality, and sketches the main themes of the collection: history, the negotiation of South Asian identities in Western spaces and its converse, diaspora and the canon, and the role of diasporic women. An essay by Satendra Nandan reflects on the situation in Fiji and assesses some of the writing produced by Fijian Indians in response to the 1987 coup. A dissenting Afterword by Makarand Paranjape opposes the contention that 'diaspora, expatriation, dispossession and exile are the definitive features of postcolonial identity'.

Paranjape is also the editor of *In Diaspora: Theories, Histories, Texts*. In his introduction he questions the romanticization of diasporic identities and, following Vijay Mishra, distinguishes between the old South Asian diaspora, which involved forced migration through processes such as the indenture of labour, and the new voluntary diaspora. The first produced 'orature and para-literature' and sacralized the homeland; the second is producing texts that describe the homeland but also justify the decision to leave it. Mishra himself, in one of the three general essays which open the book, stresses the significance of an 'impossible mourning' for the homeland that 'congeals round quite specific moments of trauma'. Shiva Kumar Srinivasan expresses unease about celebratory models of diaspora. K. Satchidanandan interrogates the diasporic paradigm through a consideration of factors such as class and language, and explores the notion of diasporas within India. Other essays deal with a variety of subjects and areas. Paranjape provides an account of South Asian Canadian writing. Vijay Mishra and Satendra Nandan reflect on the Indian experience in Fiji. Nandan's essay also discusses Gandhi's experiences in South Africa, a subject taken up by Sudhir Kumar as well. There are essays, too, on film, the 'digital diaspora', the Indo-Malaysian situation, and Punjabi diasporic writing. R. Raj Rao contributes a piece on gay South Asian identity in the diaspora, arguing that the primary identification of gays should be with their sexuality rather than their ethnicity. C. Vijaysree discusses the specific co-ordinates of women's experiences of migration and how these are represented. 'Survival', she argues, 'is the central paradigm.' Writers discussed include Meena Alexander and Bapsi Sidhwa. Alexander is also the subject of two essays in a third, less substantial, book, Dhawan, ed., *Writers of the Indian Diaspora*. All three of these collections on the diaspora also contain essays which deal primarily with fiction and which are reviewed in section 5(b) below.

Graham Huggan's *The Postcolonial Exotic: Marketing the Margins*, a study of the 'global commodification of cultural difference', contains much that relates to Indian writing in English. The chapter entitled 'Consuming India' examines the packaging of India for metropolitan consumption. One section discusses various events and publications commemorating the fiftieth anniversary of Indian independence in 1997 (see *YWES* 79[2000] 883 for further details). The chapter goes on to analyse the reception of *Midnight's Children*, Vikram Seth's *A Suitable Boy* and Arundhati Roy's *The God of Small Things*, arguing that, while their authors may have taken advantage of the packaging of their work as 'exotic', they also display a self-conscious critique of exoticism. Huggan also explores some of the anxieties engendered by the high visibility of writing in, and translation into, English (particularly of works by diasporic writers) in a context where only a small proportion of India's population is literate in English. Other parts of this book are dealt with in section 5(b) below.

In 'Fixing the Language, Fixing the Nation' (*Jouvert* 5:iii[2001] 39 paras.), Nandita Ghosh explores the language question in India through an analysis of selected journalism and fiction, arguing that by foregrounding linguistic tensions these texts expose the hegemony of English and Hindi and the marginalization of other languages. This allows subaltern subjects to formulate their own narratives instead of being absorbed into the 'middle-class discourse of the nation'. Fiction discussed includes Anita Desai's *In Custody*, Mahasweta Devi's *Imaginary Maps* and Upamanyu Chatterjee's *English August*.

A number of significant contributions to the study of Indian poetry appeared in 2001. The revised edition of Bruce King's *Modern Indian Poetry in English* (first published in 1987 and updated in 1989) adds five new chapters to the text of the original book. The first of these chapters, 'The Diaspora: Agha Shahid Ali's Tricultural Nostalgia', discusses Ali's poetry book by book, focusing on loss and nostalgia and exploring the interweaving of Islamic and American motifs and poetic modes in his work. The other new chapters are more broadly based and, perhaps for that reason, lack the coherence of the chapter on Ali. They do, however, provide solid and informative accounts of their subjects. 'Publishing 1987–99' takes stock of Indian poetry in English through a survey of Indian publishers' involvement in poetry and by discussing a number of recent anthologies. A third chapter focuses on poets discussed in the original book, such as Dom Moraes and A.K. Ramanujan, but brings the story up to date by looking at their work since the late 1980s. Another chapter surveys the work of women poets who have emerged in the last fifteen years, including Imtiaz Dharker and Sujata Bhatt, while the final chapter discusses the work of male poets who have been published since the mid-1980s, suggesting that, while 'they were not always as serious or successful as the earlier poets ... they widened the range of emotions and areas of Indian life that were the subject of poetry'.

A.K. Ramanujan's *Uncollected Poems and Prose*, edited by Molly Daniels-Ramanujan and Keith Harrison, complements Ramanujan's *Collected Poems* [1995] and *Collected Essays* [1999] by bringing together material not published in his lifetime. Two interviews convey Ramanujan's views on a variety of subjects, such as exile, translation, folktales, the Indian writer's multilingualism and the status of contemporary Indian poetry in English. There is a characteristically open-ended essay by Ramanujan, 'The Ring of Memory: Remembering and Forgetting in Indian

Literatures'. Molly Daniels-Ramanujan's concluding note comments briefly on a number of the poems included in this volume. In 'The Ambivalence of Poetic Self-Exile: The Case of A.K. Ramanujan' (*Jouvert* 5:ii[Winter 2001] no pagination), Rajeev S. Patke explores the relationship between Ramanujan's poems in English and his translations. While translation provides a sense of a past plenitude lacking in the diasporic present, it also looks forward to the possibility of redeeming the experience of migration.

Jahan Ramazani's *The Hybrid Muse: Postcolonial Poetry in English* contains a chapter on 'Metaphor and Postcoloniality: The Poetry of A.K. Ramanujan', a slightly modified version of an article published in 1998 and reviewed in *YWES* (79[2000] 886–7). The introduction to the book explores features common to postcolonial poetry from different parts of the world: the recuperative quest for the precolonial past and the hybridity of language and form such texts display, particularly the interaction between literary and oral traditions. The Indian poets briefly discussed in this introduction are Ramanujan, Eunice de Souza, Adil Jussawalla and Agha Shahid Ali. Another, slightly different version of the introduction can be found in Ramazani's 'Contemporary Postcolonial Poetry', his contribution to Roberts, ed., *A Companion to Twentieth-Century Poetry* (pp. 596–610).

The *Companion* also includes Vinay Dharwadker's essay 'Poetry of the Indian Subcontinent' (pp. 264–80), which surveys work in English from the early nineteenth century to the present, discussing pioneers such as Henry Derozio, Michael Madhusudan Dutt and Toru Dutt, as well as twentieth-century writers. A section on post-partition poets explores different constructions of Indianness in writers such as Nissim Ezekiel and A.K. Ramanujan, the postcolonial critique found in Adil Jussawalla and the 'postmodernist internationalism' of Agha Shahid Ali, Vikram Seth and others. Dharwadker suggests that the most important poetic development in post-independence India may be the formation of a body of women's poetry in English and the indigenous languages. The essay includes a brief survey of Pakistani and Sri Lankan poetry.

Satchidanandan, ed., *Indian Poetry. Modernism and After: A Seminar*, is based on an event organized by the Sahitya Akademi (India's national academy of letters). The contributions cover a variety of Indian languages, but there are some essays on, or otherwise relevant to, Indian poetry in English. Dilip Chitre's keynote address, 'A Home for Every Voice', expresses concerns about the erosion of India's pluralism, going on to ask whether the story of Indian poetry since independence has been one of 'a levelling of iniquitous hierarchies and dominant traditions' or one of 'parochial elitism'. K.D. Kurtkodi's 'Tradition and Modernity: Modern Kannada Poetry' includes a brief discussion of A.K. Ramanujan's Kannada poems. Makarand Paranjape's 'Reflections on the Changing Identity of Indian English Verse' contends that debates on the identity and validity of writing in English are really debates about national identity. Three different phases of Indian poetry in English can be distinguished—proto-nationalistic, nationalistic and post-nationalistic. Nissim Ezekiel is the focus of a paper by Jagdish V. Dave, who sees the poet as extending Upanishadic tradition. In 'The Testament of the Tenth Muse: A Perspective on Feminine Sensibility and Sexuality among Indian Women Poets in English', Rukmini Bhaya Nair argues that the emancipatory potential of feminism in literature comes through a rejection of strong heterosexual boundaries and a nurturing of 'hermaphrodite awareness'. Two contributors consider the problems of translating poetry into English, Shama Futehally through an examination of her own and others' translations of Meerabai, and M. Asaduddin through a survey of Urdu poetry in translation. In 'Sujata Bhatt in Conversation', an interview published in *Poetry and Nation Review* (27:iv[2001] 36–43), Bhatt discusses a variety of subjects, including her background, multilingualism and women's writing.

There are several useful contributions to the study of Indian drama. Mee, ed., *DramaContemporary: India*, contains the texts of a number of plays in English translation—including Girish Karnad's *The Fire and the Rain* and Usha Ganguli's *Rudali*—and one originally written in English, Mahesh Dattani's *Tara*. The editor's introduction offers a general survey of the movements out of which these plays emerged: theatre of roots, women's theatre, street theatre and Dalit literature. There are brief accounts of each of the plays, offering biographical information about their authors, discussions of their themes and comments on their social and formal contexts. Particularly interesting are the discussions of their relationship to Indian theatrical traditions. Gilbert, ed., *Postcolonial Plays: An Anthology* includes two Indian plays, Girish Karnad's *Hayavadana* (originally in Kannada) and Manjula Padmanabhan's *Harvest*. Helen Gilbert's introduction to the anthology offers some reflections on the concept of postcolonialism, as well as on the language, reception and performance traditions of the plays. Each play is preceded by an introduction discussing its themes and forms.

Although it says little about drama in English, Ralph Yarrow's *Indian Theatre: Theatre of Origins, Theatre of Freedom* is a helpful resource for work on Indian drama in general. A wide-ranging and ambitious book, it sets out to look at Indian theatre in the context of 'contemporary philosophical and scientific understandings which imply dimensions to human experience which most western post-Enlightenment thought has ruled out'. In looking at Eastern answers to Western questions, it provides stimulating discussions of Indian views on text, the many forms of Indian performance, gender, and various Indian and Western aesthetic, ethical and political theories which have been applied to the analysis of Indian theatre. A lengthy chapter, 'Indian Theatre in the Contemporary World: Cultural Politics in India', discusses contemporary theatre practice in India in the light of a number of questions about identity, including the relationship between English and the regional languages. The chapter provides a good overview of the many theatre companies, drama schools and other institutions that constitute theatrical activity in India today.

(b) Fiction

This section reviews criticism that focuses on prose fiction, but readers should also refer to Section 5(a) above for work that considers fiction along with other forms.

One of the Grand Old Men of Indian fiction, R.K. Narayan, died in 2001, and a number of assessments of his life and work appeared. In 'R.K. Narayan: An Indian Perspective' (*JCL* 36:ii[2001] 117–21), Ranga Rao takes issue with some of V.S. Naipaul's comments on Narayan, who is presented as a writer grounded in reality and attentive to social issues. John Thieme's editorial in the same issue reassesses a number of elements in Narayan's work (*JCL* 36:ii[2001] 1–4). Malgudi, he suggests, 'was always a hybrid site', not an India insulated from the outside world. In 'Everything but the Kitchen Sink: R.K. Narayan Remembered (1906–2001)'

(*TLS* 5124[2001] 14), Michael Gorra notes that Narayan's fiction 'raises questions of form that criticism has yet fully to address', such as the impact of the concept of *maya* on literary realism, or the effect of the idea of *dharma* on plot and character. Amit Chaudhuri, 'A Bottle of Ink, A Pen and a Blotter' (*LRB* 23:xv[2001] 21–2), suggests that the true subject of Narayan's fiction is 'the fictionality of "timeless India"' and that individual novels rarely seem self-sufficient, because Narayan's interest lies in the 'recycling of familiar, used material'.

Pankaj Mishra, 'The Great Narayan' (*NYRB* 48:iii[2001] 44–7), argues that, despite the paucity of overt political references, Narayan's novels 'map out an emotional and intellectual journey that many middle-class people in formerly colonial societies have made'. Ian Almond's article, 'Darker Shades of Malgudi: Solitary Figures of Modernity in the Stories of R.K. Narayan' (*JCL* 36:ii[2001] 107–16), questions the idea of Narayan's India as an enduring, essentially Hindu location. He shows how Hinduism is extolled in some of Narayan's stories and presented as a stultifying tradition in others. A number of the stories reveal a dark side to his work, presenting us with solitary characters who can find solutions to their dilemmas neither in tradition nor in modernity.

Scott and Simpson-Housley, eds., *Mapping the Sacred: Religion, Geography and Postcolonial Literatures*, contains Chelva Kanaganayakam's 'Charting a Secular Ganges: Revisiting R.K. Narayan's Malgudi and "Little India" in the Malaysian Fiction of K.S. Maniam and Lee Kok Liang' (pp. 317–34) and Clara Joseph's 'The Hindu Mother's Space in Nayantara Sahgal's *Mistaken Identity*' (pp. 297–316). Kanaganayakam argues that Narayan's *The Man-Eater of Malgudi* presents a hierarchical, Brahmin-dominated world which is homogeneous and unified, but does so through underplaying or ignoring gender, caste and class. Narayan is contrasted with two Malaysian writers, K.S. Maniam and Lee Kok Liang, who, in their representations of Indian life in Malaysia, portray a religion under stress from transplantation. Joseph's essay on Sahgal examines how *Mistaken Identity* resists the nationalist Gandhian ideology that restricts women to motherhood and the home.

Translating Partition: Stories, Essays, Criticism, edited by Ravikant and Tarun K. Saint, is a useful contribution to the growing body of work on the partition of India. It reproduces a number of Hindi and Urdu short stories in English translation, including work by Saadat Hasan Manto, Kamleshwar and Bhisham Sahni. English-language fiction on partition is represented by Attia Hosain's 'Phoenix Fled'. Some of the stories are accompanied by critical commentaries. The editors' introduction to the volume offers an overview of the events leading up to partition and surveys the main outlines of the fiction it generated. The volume also contains a number of essays on the literature of the partition. Naiyer Masud's 'Partition and the Urdu Short Story' provides a brief categorization of the main themes of Urdu writing about partition. In 'Partition Narratives: Some Observations', Arjun Mahey looks at the rhetorical tropes used by narrative histories and short stories to portray partition, concluding with a detailed analysis of Manto's 'Toba Tek Singh'. Ravikant's 'Partition: Strategies of Oblivion, Ways of Remembering' contrasts the voice of the state, emphasizing unity and progress, with other voices which resist elite narratives. Bodh Prakash's 'The Woman Protagonist in Partition Literature' examines the representation of women in selected Hindu and Urdu fiction, concluding that responses vary from an 'incipient feminist gesture' to significant alterations in their relationships with men. The book concludes with some useful reference material, including an annotated bibliography.

Manto, who appears prominently in *Translating Partition*, is a central figure in Alex Tickell's article '"How Many Pakistans?" Questions of Space and Identity in the Writing of Partition' (*ArielE* 32:iii[2001] 155–79), which 'reasserts the salience of space alongside issues of temporality and historical becoming' in a number of partition narratives. Although the main emphasis falls on Manto, there are brief discussions of two English-language novels, Khushwant Singh's *Train to Pakistan* and Bapsi Sidhwa's *Cracking India*.

A significant contribution to the study of fiction is Tabish Khair's *Babu Fictions: Alienation in Contemporary Indian English Novels*, which examines a central but under-explored aspect of Indian fiction written in English: the consequences of the fact that its practitioners come from the 'Babu' class—that is, the Westernized, urban, Brahminized, educated upper and middle classes fluent in English (a tiny proportion of India's population)—while India itself presents a 'huge and heterogeneous Coolie and non-Babu population' (the 'Coolies', in Khair's formulation, being 'non-English speaking, not or not significantly "westernized", not or less Brahminized, economically deprived, culturally marginalized and, often, rural or migrant-urban populations'). This situation produces alienation. The question Khair asks is how the Coolie can be constituted in English, a language with 'a different socio-economic and discursive siting', without denying him voice and agency. Section 1 of the book consists of a number of general and theoretical chapters discussing the socio-economic and discursive positioning of writers of Indian English fiction. A chapter on language explores the dilemmas created by the use of English, particularly the problems involved in using the language to depict Indian realities and in 'transcreating' dialogues from other Indian languages into English. Section 2 deals with three specific areas of tension within Indian English fiction: caste, urban and industrial landscapes, and gender. The Babu attitude to the Coolie, Khair finds, is one of 'proscription and prescription regarding Coolie discursive and physical realities'. Section 3 examines the work of Raja Rao, R.K. Narayan, V.S. Naipaul, Salman Rushdie and Amitav Ghosh in the light of the analysis developed in the previous sections. The first two of these are seen as participating in 'national/indigenous Brahminized Babu discourses', while Naipaul and Rushdie are exponents of different types of international Babu discourses, Naipaul being 'colonial Babu (largely modernist)' and Rushdie 'cosmopolitan Babu (heavily post-modern)'. Khair views Ghosh's *The Calcutta Chromosome* as a text which productively negotiates the problems of Babu fiction. The Afterword, finally, suggests that alienation can be enabling; Khair argues that 'it is in the spaces created by the conflict of discourses that one can begin to fashion a narrative that, in spite of one's Babu heritage, may allow for subaltern agency and pay close attention to subaltern speech'. Mukul Kesavan's novel *Looking through Glass* [1995] is seen as a text that achieves this goal. Although somewhat laboured at times, *Babu Fictions* highlights an aspect of Indian writing in English which is becoming increasingly important.

Diasporic fiction is discussed in Crane and Mohanram, eds., *Shifting Continents/ Colliding Cultures* (see also section 5(a) above). Crane's essay on Leena Dhingra's *Amritvela* stresses the fluidity and in-between nature of diasporic identity. Nilufer Bharucha surveys the literature of the Parsi diaspora, including work by Cornelia

Sorabji, Bapsi Sidhwa and Rohinton Mistry. Susheila Nasta describes the evolution and diversity of South Asian writing in Britain. Women's writing—particularly the work of Bharati Mukherjee—is analysed in essays by C. Vijaysree, Radhika Mohanram and Zohreh T. Sullivan. Debjani Ganguly relates Salman Rushdie's *The Moor's Last Sigh* and Taslima Nasreen's *Lajja* to the upsurge of Hindu and Muslim fundamentalism on the subcontinent. An essay by Susan Spearey, which lends its title to the book as a whole, analyses 'spatial operations' in diasporic writing, particularly Naipaul's *The Enigma of Arrival*.

Another work on the diaspora mentioned in section 5(a) above—Paranjape, ed., *In Diaspora*—also contains material primarily on fiction. Jasbir Jain's essay 'The New Parochialism: Homeland in the Writings of the Indian Diaspora' makes a variety of points, including a typology of the constructions through which post-independence diasporic writers work. She argues that, although diasporic writers are inevitably drawn to the homeland, there is in this appropriation of space at home the danger of 'parochial affiliations'. Alka Kumar and Harish Narang's 'Writing South Asian–Canadian Diaspora: *Amriika* and Ideology' points to the dangers of critical homogenization and commercial commodification of diaspora experiences and writings, before turning its attention to M.G. Vassanji's *Amriika*, particularly its critique of the United States in the 1960s and 1970s. In 'Footnoting History: The Diasporic Imagination of Amitav Ghosh', Brinda Bose analyses the relationship between history and fiction in Ghosh's work. One of Ghosh's settings, Malaya, is the focus of three contributions to the book. K.S. Maniam discusses the problems of the Indian community in Malaya and of writing in English, concluding that the writer 'has to accept exile in a land that continually denies him a sense of belonging'. Maniam's own fiction is the subject of essays by Susanna Checketts and Shanthini Pillai.

Dhawan, ed., *Writers of the Indian Diaspora*, includes some essays of variable quality on Salman Rushdie and Jhumpa Lahiri (see also section 5(a)). C.N. Ramachandran pursues an anti-Rushdie line, arguing that the writer is legitimized by British and US institutions, and that the Indian response largely follows the Anglo-American lead. Joel Kuortti provides two essays about various positions on the *Satanic Verses* controversy. Essays on *The Moor's Last Sigh* complete the Rushdie section. David Myers examines it as an 'allegory of the fall of India, and specifically Bombay, from multicultural tolerance to fanatical sectarianism'. P. Balaswamy looks at Rushdie's revision of the 'Mother India' figure. The essays on Lahiri are somewhat unfocused surveys of *The Interpreter of Maladies*.

Bardolph, ed., *Telling Stories: Postcolonial Short Fiction in English*, includes a section on India, Sri Lanka and the diaspora. Padmini Mongia argues that the stories in the Kali for Women anthology *In Other Words* reflect middle-class worlds and a constricted consciousness, features characteristic of much writing in English by Indian women. Martina Ghosh-Schellhorn surveys stories from other well-known anthologies of Indian women's writing and concludes that a repeated theme is the inevitable failure of rebellion. Cynthia Carey-Abrioux looks at the liberating effect of competing discourses in Salman Rushdie's story 'The Courter'. Rocío G. Davis discusses short-story cycles by Rohinton Mistry, V.S. Naipaul and M.G. Vassanji, concentrating on the significance of place as a way of negotiating identity and community.

David Punter's *Postcolonial Imaginings: Fictions of a New World Order* [2000] links postcolonialism with approaches to texts derived from psychoanalysis and deconstruction. He sets out to investigate how elements such as the uncanny, the phantom, trauma, melancholy and loss manifest themselves in the postcolonial. Among other things, this wide-ranging book probes at the problems of using 'Western' theories in this field and questions dominant paradigms within postcolonial criticism. Punter discusses a large number of texts from different areas, although none at great length. Among the Indian writers he comments on are Narayan, Rushdie, Arundhati Roy, Vikram Chandra and Kiran Desai.

Ann Blake, Leela Gandhi and Sue Thomas's *England through Colonial Eyes in Twentieth-Century Fiction* addresses itself to representations of England and Englishness. In the chapter '"Learning me your language": England in the Postcolonial *Bildungsroman*', Leela Gandhi examines the conditions under which the *Bildungsroman* manages to travel successfully to areas outside Europe. Texts discussed include autobiographies (Mahatma Gandhi's and Nirad Chaudhuri's) and novels (Desani's *All About H. Hatterr*, Upamanyu Chatterjee's *English, August*, Amit Chaudhuri's *Afternoon Raag*, Arundhati Roy's *The God of Small Things*, Amitav Ghosh's *The Shadow Lines* and Pankaj Mishra's *The Romantics*). In '"Ellowen, Deeowen": Salman Rushdie and the Migrant's Desire', Gandhi concentrates on *The Satanic Verses* but situates its analysis in the context of Rushdie's fiction as a whole. She argues that the political implications of Rushdie's celebrations of migrancy and attacks on nationalism are constrained by his libidinal, private subtexts. Through its self-contradictions, *The Satanic Verses* 'demonstrates the impossibility of a "pure politics"'.

The flood of Rushdie criticism shows few signs of abating. Jaina C. Sanga's *Salman Rushdie's Postcolonial Metaphors: Migration, Translation, Hybridity, Blasphemy, and Globalization* is a book-length study which contends that Rushdie's novels are held together by metaphors of the five themes singled out in her subtitle. Each theme is allotted a chapter, although the introduction cautions that this is for analytic purposes only; they are, in fact, intertwined with each other. Sanga's book is a thorough and detailed discussion of Rushdie's work, but its interpretations of the novels go over ground that is already well trodden and add little that is new to the existing body of criticism. It is also rather uncritical in its assessment of Rushdie's oeuvre and achievements, often repeating his line on ideas—for instance, his celebrations of migrant identity and hybridity—without evaluating them. In contrast, an awareness of the potential difficulties with these concepts characterizes Minoli Salgado's 'Migration and Mutability: The Twice Born Fiction of Salman Rushdie' (in Davies and Sinfield, eds., *British Culture of the Postwar: An Introduction to Literature and Society, 1945–1999* [2000] pp. 31–49).

Rushdie is a recurrent point of reference in Graham Huggan's *The Postcolonial Exotic* (see also section 5(a) above). The chapter 'Staging Marginalities: Rushdie, Naipaul, Kureishi' discusses Naipaul's *The Enigma of Arrival*, Rushdie's *The Satanic Verses* and Kureishi's *The Buddha of Suburbia* and screenplays as examples of 'staged marginality ... the process by which marginalized individuals or minority groups dramatize their "subordinate" status for the imagined benefit of a majority audience'. Staged marginality, Huggan concludes, is an ambivalent strategy. It can be both subversive and a 'reconfirmation of relative powerlessness' in relation to the dominant culture. 'Prizing Otherness: A Short History of the Booker' uses

Midnight's Children as one of its examples in its discussion of how prizes such as the Booker '*contain*' (self-)critique by endorsing the commodification of a glamorized cultural difference'. The chapter also discusses Booker prizewinners who have used India as a setting—Paul Scott, J.G. Farrell and Ruth Prawer Jhabvala.

In 'Does Saleem Really Miss the Spittoon? Script and Scriptlessness in *Midnight's Children*' (*JCL* 36:ii[2001] 127–45), Helga Ramsey-Kurz draws attention to some of the implications of the fact that Padma, Saleem Sinai's audience in *Midnight's Children*, is illiterate. Linking this to contrasting Muslim and Western assumptions about writing, Ramsey-Kurz argues that Padma, along with a number of other characters, signifies the erasure of parts of Indian history. Padma is also central to Teresa Heffernan's essay 'Apocalyptic Narratives: The Nation in Salman Rushdie's *Midnight's Children*' (*TCL* 46[2000] 470–91], which argues that this novel is suspicious of the 'apocalyptic underpinnings' of the modern nation and that it explores another—also apocalyptic—model, the Islamic *umma*. Both these models of the nation, however, are dependent on the 'figure of the (un)veiled woman', Padma, to whom Saleem Sinai tells his story. Rosalia Baena's 'Telling a Bath-Time Story: *Haroun and the Sea of Stories* as a Modern Literary Fairy Tale' (*JCL* 36:ii[2001] 65–76) explores Rushdie's use of formal and thematic elements from fairy-tales. In 'Allegories of Woman, Nation, and Empire in Salman Rushdie s *East, West Stories*' (*Kunapipi* 23:ii[2001] 121–44), Asha Sen argues that, while some of the stories replicate the victim paradigm of women for which Rushdie has been criticized, or incorporate women into nationalist allegory, others point to a subversive space outside, or opposed to, this allegory. Brian May's 'Memorials to Modernity: Postcolonial Pilgrimage in Naipaul and Rushdie' (*ELH* 68[2001] 241–65) discusses *The Satanic Verses* along with Naipaul's *An Area of Darkness* as books which both attack and memorialize modernity, displaying an openness that reaches across the boundary between colonizer and colonized. Mariam Pirbhai's 'The Paradox of Globalization as an "Untotalizable Totality" in Salman Rushdie's *The Ground Beneath her Feet*' (*IFR* 28[2001] 54–66) examines the 'paradox of globalization' in the novel: while it opens up the world to heterogeneity, globalization, she suggests, also brings hegemonic practices which must be challenged. John Docker's *1492: The Poetics of Diaspora*, an exploration of the consequences of the ending of Moorish Spain and the expulsion of the Jews in that year, contains a chapter on *The Moor's Last Sigh*. 'The Disaster of 1492: Europe and India' (pp. 215–26) suggests that Rushdie's novel does not allow the opposition between ethnic nationalism and secular cosmopolitanism to settle. The chapter also considers the idea that the novel might be 'slightly superficial'. Two collections of interviews with Rushdie are worth noting: Chauhan, ed., *Salman Rushdie: Interviews. A Sourcebook of his Ideas*, and Reder, ed., *Conversations with Salman Rushdie*.

A less discussed writer is the focus of Priyamvada Gopal's '"Curious Ironies": Matter and Meaning in Bhabhani Bhattacharya's Novel of the 1943 Bengal Famine' (*ArielE* 32:iii[2001] 61–88), which analyses Bhattacharya's *He Who Rides a Tiger*. Gopal argues that the novel engages with 'the role of language in shaping both oppression and resistance'.

Joel Kuortti has conducted two interviews with Indian women writers. '"The Double Burden": The Continual Contesting of Tradition and Modernity. Geeta Hariharan interviewed by Joel Kuortti' (*JCL* 36:i[2001] 7–26) ranges widely, covering Hariharan's own life and fiction, as well as broader issues such as the problems faced by women writers and the relationships between Indian writing in English and writing in indigenous languages. In '"Years of Silence Came to an End": Interview with Shashi Deshpande' (*Kunapipi* 23:ii[2001] 145–66), Kuortti questions Deshpande about a similar range of topics.

Amitav Ghosh's *In an Antique Land* is the subject of a number of essays taking contrasting approaches to the text. Neelam Srivastava's 'Amitav Ghosh's Ethnographic Fictions: Intertextual Links between *In an Antique Land* and his Doctoral Thesis' (*JCL* 36:ii[2001] 45–64) argues that the book rewrites the ethnographic material of Ghosh's D.Phil. thesis, and undermines the ethnographer's authority, replacing it with 'a dialogue between Ghosh and his native informants'. The text's syncreticism is seen as a search for alternatives to narratives of cultural segregation. Kathleen Beddick's 'Translating the Foreskin' (in Burger and Kruger, eds., *Queering the Middle Ages*, pp. 193–212) deploys theories of fetishism to read *In an Antique Land*, which is a central piece of evidence in a wider argument about historical periodization and 'queering the Middle Ages'. She contends that Ghosh's construction of a medieval golden age disrupted by the violence of modernity occludes the violence and homoeroticism within the institution of medieval slavery. Shirley Chew's 'Texts and Worlds in Amitav Ghosh's *In an Antique Land*' (in Bell et al., eds., *Re-Constructing the Book: Literary Texts in Transmission*, pp. 197–209) examines a variety of forms of loss and retrieval in Ghosh's text, suggesting that it is an experiment in recovering ground appropriated by colonialism. In the course of a general argument about globalization taking the form of a 'dismantling of subaltern nationalisms by dominant nationalisms', R. Radhakrishnan, 'Globalization, Desire and the Politics of Representation' (*CL* 53[2001] 315–32), uses another book by Ghosh, *The Shadow Lines*, as an example of a text which points to a different, dialogic model of the relationship between nations and cultures.

In 'Duelling with the Crown: On Literature and Language in Shashi Tharoor's *The Great Indian Novel*' (*Wasafiri* 33[2001] 58–61), Ralph J. Crane argues that Tharoor represents India as a nation which 'has emerged from a variety of contexts including a recent colonial or British Indian one, rather than from any pure indigenous context'. Tabish Khair's 'Remembering to Forget Abu Taleb' (*Wasafiri* 34[2001] 34–8) looks at a travel account in Persian by Mirza Abu Taleb Khan, an Indian nobleman who visited Europe, Africa and Persia in the late eighteenth and early nineteenth centuries. Examining his view on gender and other issues, Khair concludes that Abu Taleb defends Eastern customs while being ready to borrow from European culture without any sense of inferiority. The article also discusses Indian amnesia concerning the past hegemony of the Persian language and briefly compares Abu Taleb to the better-known Dean Mahomet.

6. New Zealand

F.W. Nielsen Wright's bibliographical study, *An Account of Noel Farr Hoggard as Georgian Editor and Writer in Aotearoa, 1931–1953*, does not claim to be totally comprehensive but covers its topic more fully than any other publication to date. It is part of a long project on the part of Wright to reinstate the importance of Georgianism in New Zealand poetry.

John Thomson's annual survey of New Zealand literature (*JCL* 36:iii[2000] 73–92) is regularly the most acute comment on developments, analysing individual books within the framework of an awareness of general trends, as they are modified over the years. His summary of publications in 2000 makes sobering reading. In the novel he finds 'not quite a famine': although quantity is maintained quality seems lower than even a year before. In poetry the concentration on domestic and often quite personal subject-matter at the expense of anything more visionary clearly depresses him. He asks of Jenny Bornholdt's *These Days*, 'Is it material appropriate for publication?' and implies that the question could be asked of almost all poetry published in 2000. Significantly, he finds no criticism at all worthy of comment.

In 'Imaginary Toads in Real Gardens: Poets in Christchurch' (in Howard, ed., *Complete with Instructions*) Jack Ross discusses the nature of regionalism in a series of interviews with Christchurch poets—Julia Allen, John Allison, Kenneth Fea, David Gregory, Rob Jackaman, Graham Lindsay, Mike Minehan and John O'Connor. The responses are various. Allen remarks that the location of her poems is her head, rather than a geographic region; others speak of their relationships with European poets; only John O'Connor really emphasizes the importance of place. Although the interviews begin with an idea of regionalism, that idea seems very diluted at the end of the project. There are echoes of all of this and more in the wide-ranging interview with David Howard that follows in the same book, 'Magic, Murder and the Weather: Richard Reeves Interviews David Howard' (pp. 62–9). For him, the poet is dwelling in a language that embraces many times and places rather than being limited by locality, and memory is what links those disparate experiences.

Carmen Zamorano Llena, in her article 'The Location of Identity in Interstitial Spaces: The Poetry of Fleur Adcock in a Multicultural Britain' (*JNZL* 18/19[2000–1] 161–72), examines Fleur Adcock's estrangement from both New Zealand and Britain, and places her in this regard together with the other immigrants to Britain from Commonwealth countries, who have created a multicultural society there. Adcock's New Zealand family background, childhood in England, youth and early adulthood in New Zealand and later adulthood in London have left her with a sense of identity that inhabits 'interstitial spaces' rather than some essentialist construct of home.

Paul Millar's vast project on the life and poems of James K. Baxter, a project that is likely to be pursued for many years, was continued in 2001 with the publication of two volumes. The first of these was Millar's edition of *New Selected Poems*. Its first part is a new selection from published volumes, presenting an updated image of the poet in the remarkable range of his styles and subject matter, but focusing, it would seem, largely on the colloquial poet of ballads and seemingly laconic lyrics. The second part presents poems published in scattered places and, even more interesting, poems never published before. Some of these—notably 'The Maori Jesus'—have already caught the popular imagination, as Baxter's verse is apt to do. That there are more riches to discover is common knowledge among literary people, and it is to be expected that Millar will continue to present new aspects of his subject in coming years. *New Selected Poems* has a general introduction, which claims that 'The poems in this selection place James K. Baxter among the major poets of the twentieth century. They show him emphatically as being more than a New Zealand poet.' Millar's broadest purpose is to give Baxter a place in English-language poetic history that he has not yet acquired. There are also short introductions throughout the first part succinctly describing the basic features of each phase in Baxter's output.

Millar's second publication is *Spark to a Waiting Fuse: James K. Baxter's Correspondence with Noel Ginn, 1942–1946*. This is more than its title suggests. Not only does it uncover an important correspondence with a fellow poet at an early stage of Baxter's life—colouring our understanding of later phases, too—but it also includes 255 Baxter poems, written at the time of the correspondence and discussed therein. Most of them have never been published before. In addition, Millar's extensive introduction and editorial comments are major contributions to literary and social history. Noel Ginn did not develop as a poet, as Baxter did, although Millar has also edited a volume of Ginn's poetry, but the correspondence treats the two men as equals, and reveals much about the concerns that were to shape a major New Zealand poet's future (that of a world poet, if we are to accept Millar's evaluation). Baxter's readings of major poets of the past are stimulating in themselves.

Lawrence Jones has provided a short but original overview of the New Zealand literature relating to the First World War in 'The Shadow of that Earlier War: World War I in the Writing of the 1930s' (*JNZL* 18/19[2000–1] 67–82). Its originality lies largely in giving more space to pacifist writing than to war reminiscence and, in particular, emphasizing the anti-war poetry of Basil Dowling. This poetry is said to trace 'a Christian pacifist version of the history of a decade'. Dowling's poetry has been ignored in much writing about poetry and it is timely for his point of view to be recalled. Together with Archibald Baxter and Robin Hyde, Dowling is said to have commented on the First World War while anticipating the Second, and criticizing the social and political structures that led from one war to the next.

Sarah Quigley, who is engaged in writing a biography of Charles Brasch, uses this project as a background to her essay, 'No Names: Notes on a Biography of Charles Brasch' (*Landfall* 202[2001] 33–41). Her central concern is with aspects of biography in itself. Particularly in the case of a man who, like Brasch, was extremely reticent about his private life, the task of the biographer can seem intrusive and indiscreet, not only to readers but also to the biographer. The biography of a writer can be more problematic than others, in spite of the large quantities of written records they are likely to leave. Such records, like the creative work that justifies the biography in the first place, may well conceal as much as they reveal. Writers are skilled at using words to hide their innermost personalities even while seeming to speak in a frank and personal manner.

The death of Allen Curnow, by consensus the most important New Zealand poet of the century, led to a number of tributes. Contributions going beyond the qualities of an obituary by adding to our understanding of the poet are mainly to be found in *JNZL* 18/19. 'Publishing Curnow' (*JNZL* 18/19[2000–1] 1–13), by Elizabeth Caffin, provides some fascinating vignettes of the poet at work, adding, for example, poems to a collection already 'complete' without disturbing the overall unity of the collection. Caffin also demonstrates by example the meticulous attention to detail that made each Curnow publication an event. Peter Simpson has compiled a most useful 'Chronological List of Curnow's Poems' (*JNZL* 18/19[2000–1] 14–35) listed by the first date of publication. This first step in a bibliographical study of Curnow already reveals much of interest, in particular the wide range of international journals in which poems first made their appearance before being absorbed into the structure of the carefully crafted volumes Caffin discusses. An essay by Leigh Davis, 'Notes on *Yes* and *No*' (*JNZL* 18/19[2000–1] 39–66), also uses Curnow as a central feature, but only to exemplify a more wide-ranging philosophical speculation on the relationship between place and poetry which makes the phrase 'New Zealand poetry' seem to have a fault-line running between its two elements.

Michael King's otherwise massively informative biography of Janet Frame [2000] says all too little about the relationship between her life and her work. In a discussion of the biography, first presented as a talk in the National Library and now published under the title 'Janet Frame's Life and Fiction' (*Kite* 20[2001] 4–10), Patrick Evans takes some interesting steps towards bridging that gap. He analyses Frame's techniques for concealing the authorial voice behind a kaleidoscopically changing narrative consciousness, seducing the reader into taking pleasure only in the highly coloured narrational veils, while slipping through them nevertheless to introduce elements from her life, often extremely personal elements, which only she or her intimates could be aware of. His half-paragraph on the narrative strategy of *Living in the Maniototo*, for example, is a masterly illumination of complexity, retaining clarity of style, while exploring deliberately unclear narrative prose. Evans is so deeply saturated in knowledge of Frame's work that he is able to pick up small signs in it that relate to moments almost as slight in King's biography and to cast his own light on the interconnections. His awareness of these issues permits him to say, as perhaps no other critic might, that 'parts of Frame's fiction begin to seem considerably less fictional when read in the light of King's biography'. At the same time, he points out, for example, that her way of taking intimate characteristics of Frank Sargeson and giving them to Turnlung in *Daughter Buffalo* is modified by having Turnlung suffer from the death of sisters in precisely the way Frame did herself, so that Turnlung cannot be said to 'be' Sargeson, for all the similarities. Evans argues that King's biography has a transforming effect on the reader's perception of Frame's novels, even though King himself makes none of the connections explicit. So dense is this concealment of self that when Frame comes to write autobiography, Evans argues, she uses certain fictional strategies even more intensively than in her fiction: 'to present a self to us she is going to have to make one up'. The most controversial part of Evans's argument is his application of all this to King's biography. In Evans's view, King's narrative voice is yet another strategy behind which the authorial voice of Frame is almost but not totally concealed. King almost becomes a character in a Frame book, or, as Evans repeatedly says, a ventriloquist's dummy. Frame has not commented in public on this suggestion but King has denied the image vigorously. Evans justifies it by pointing out that there are significant continuities between Frame's autobiography and King's biography—notably the virtual absence from both of Frame's brother, a man, according to Evans, so forceful and crude in his manner that he could only be evaded deliberately. Similarly, Frame's father loses colour in both biographical studies and, speaking of *Intensive Care*, Evans says, 'I would guess that there is more emotional "truth" about Frame's father in this novel than in the autobiography and the biography put together.' This is bold, but it makes a strong attempt to fill the gap between life and work that many readers have felt in King's book. Bruce Harding's essay, 'The Nativization of Feeling: Motifs of Bonding to the Past and to the Land in Janet Frame's *A State of Siege* (1966) and in *The Carpathians* (1988)'

(*JNZL* 18/19[2000–1] 114–37), takes a much simpler approach by ignoring the complexities of narrative structure and taking the narrator's view to be Frame's. On this basis he makes some interesting comments on 'Frame's' relationship to landscape, but these can only be of limited value when one considers that 'Frame' in this construction is in fact a complex of narrative voices.

Brian Easton's *The Nationbuilders* examines the growing sense of national independence by using exemplary figures with strong voices, who articulated the various stages of the growth forcibly. Of the seventeen representative voices, remarkably, only one is a poet: Denis Glover. The essay on Glover focuses on his poems 'Home Thoughts' and 'The Magpies', demonstrating the poet's respect for the English tradition and his sturdy insistence that its local variant has a value of its own. The most interesting aspect of the essay is, perhaps, its context, where Glover is placed in relationship to economists, politicians, union bosses and sociologists rather than in a 'pure' literary tradition, so that his voice is given a broader significance, even, than in Ogilvy's standard biography of the poet.

Dennis McEldowney's *A Press Achieved: The Emergence of the Auckland University Press, 1927–1972* is more memoir than history. Nonetheless it presents an interesting picture of the place of a university press among a variety of forces: the university authorities, the authors and those who make and sell books—designers, printers and distributors. It goes back to a time before its author's appointment as editor in 1966, covering the work of E.H. McCormick, M.K. Joseph and J.C. Reid. Of particular interest are McEldowney's encounters with Auckland University authors such as Allen Curnow, Kendrick Smithyman, C.K. Stead and Albert Wendt. There is also a valuable list of Auckland University Press publications 1927–2000, compiled by Katrina Duncan.

Katherine Mansfield's knowledge of Russian literature and her reception in Russia have been studied by Joanna Woods, now at book length in *Katerina: The Russian World of Katherine Mansfield*. Frequently compared with Chekhov as a short-story writer, Mansfield in fact read widely in Turgenev, Tolstoy and Dostoevsky as well, guided by her devoted friend S.S. Koteliansky, who was responsible for some of the translations of these writers into English. She shared this interest with other friends, such as A.R. Orage and, indeed, with many writers and critics of the time. The Russian reception of her work began even before her death and shortly afterwards, in 1923–4, two collections of her work were published by the State Publishing House. Stalinist Russia was less friendly to her work, viewing her as one of the 'decadent' writers of the West. Woods presents a solid account of all this material without adding greatly to previous works of scholarship. Some of the bibliographical material, such as a list of fifteen Russian theses on Mansfield, represents the largest expansion of our knowledge.

Since the publication of *The Katherine Mansfield Notebooks*, edited by Margaret Scott, in 1997, scholars have been aware that Middleton Murry's edition of Mansfield's *Journal* is practically a compilation of scraps manipulated into the semblance of coherence—Mansfield did not in fact write a 'journal' at all. In 'The *Notebooks, Journal* and Papers of Katherine Mansfield: Is Any of This her Diary?' (*JNZL* 18/19[2000–1] 83–99), Anna Jackson discusses the qualities of Scott's edition in a more critical way than that, and shows that the act of transcription followed by the printing and publication process transforms Mansfield's chaotic scraps—where, for example, a shopping list may be central and a poetic stanza peripheral—in more subtle ways. The Mansfield who emerges from all of this, says Jackson, is a 'Kitchen KM', who is distracted by the needs of daily living and constantly forces herself to be 'poetic'. In 'Katherine Mansfield: Distance, Irony and the Vertigo Perception' (*JNZL* 18/19[2000–1] 100–13), Renata Casertano views the turning point in many stories as a moment of vertigo, leading to an imbalance or fall.

Elizabeth Glanville, in her essay 'Familiars: R.A.K. Mason, Jenny Barrer and James K. Baxter in 1963–64' (in Howard, ed., pp. 114–37), has added some biographical detail to the public image of R.A.K. Mason by examining his association with Jenny Barrer, in her diaries and in his correspondence with her. Jenny Barrer was a schoolteacher and actress, who met Mason when she was 22 and he 58. They had an intimate correspondence and Mason's play *Strait is the Gate* appears to have been based on her life. She directed its first performance after his death. Glanville's article also quotes a letter to Barrer from Baxter, in which he talks of the need for a poet or actor to forget criticism and rise above it.

Geoffrey de Montalk, who preferred to use the name Potocki, relating himself thus to the Polish aristocracy, besides making insistent claim to the Polish throne, is one of the eccentrics of New Zealand writing. His poetry, though prolific, and despite his self-proclamation as a divinely inspired genius, is unremarkable, and it is his life that provides the greater interest. Consequently a biographical approach seems most appropriate in this case, and his niece, Stephanie de Montalk, who has also established a reputation as a poet, has now published *Unquiet World: The Life of Count Geoffrey Potocki de Montalk*. In addition to family knowledge, de Montalk is able to draw on extended interviews with the ageing poet and pretender in both New Zealand and Europe and on the confusion of papers deposited in the Alexander Turnbull Library. His journey from Auckland milkman to king of Poland, self-crowned with a crown of his own design, is entertaining, but for students of literature there is possibly more interest in his encounters with fellow poets Fairburn and Mason. A glimpse of the restrictive culture of the time is provided by Alan Mulgan's refusal to have Potocki's first book reviewed in the *Auckland Star* on the grounds that its author was obtaining a divorce. Later, in 1932, he was charged with obscenity for a book published in Britain and spent six months with hard labour in Wormwood Scrubs. The Woolfs, Yeats, Wells, Eliot, Forster and Aldous Huxley all spoke out in his defence. Some of them may have been less willing to support his later fascist writings, published in his own journal, *Right Review* and expressing great hatred of England as well as of Jews. It seems, however, that any support for him was due to the witty and lively prose in which he expressed his unwelcome ideas. Unfortunately this prose is available to the reading public only in small doses and de Montalk quotes too little of it for its effect to be judged. Her book nonetheless provides a colourful account of a curious life with passing reference to matters of broader literary interest. At worst it depresses with its account of fascist attitudes; at best it raises the spirits with its account of a man who refused to be silenced by censorship and neglect.

The connection between the eponymous character in C.K. Stead's novel *Talking about O'Dwyer* and the New Zealand novelist and Oxford publisher Dan Davin is examined in an essay by Janet Wilson, 'The Portrait of Dan Davin in C.K. Stead's *Talking about O'Dwyer*' (*Kite* 20[2001] 13–16). The word 'portrait' in the title seems to beg the question, and it is a question central to many discussions of New Zealand literature: what is the relationship between fact and fiction? Wilson's thesis is carried by a belief that the 'portrait' is 'an act of retribution' for Davin's negative review, in 1984, of an earlier Stead book, *In the Glass Case*. Her essay seems to add little to an understanding of the novel, since O'Dwyer is by no means simply a negative character but rather a man of courage and integrity with some tragic flaws. Wilson does, however, reveal something of the relationship between Stead and Davin and presents her own portraits of the two men, which have some interest in themselves. She presents Davin as the representative of a New Zealand generation impatient of the 'modernism' embraced by Stead. The difference is more than generational, however, since a major contrast is Davin's long absence from New Zealand and Stead's constant contact with the country, often situating himself at the heart of developments—such as the concern with 'open form'—that seem barely to have touched Davin. Wilson suggests that their 'dispute' has long passed any hope of resolution and that the future will pass on beyond it rather than revisit this problematic area.

Books Reviewed

Ackland, Michael. *Damaged Men: The Precarious Lives of James McAuley and Harold Stewart*. A&UA. [2001] pp. x + 326. $A45 ISBN 1 8650 8445 X.

Ang, Ien, Sharon Chalmers, Lisa Law, and Mandy Thomas, eds. *Alter/Asians: Asian-Australian Identities in Art, Media and Popular Culture*. Pluto. [2000] pp. xxx + 323. pb $A32.95 ISBN 1 8640 3176 X.

Armstrong, Pauline. *Frank Hardy and the Making of Power Without Glory*. MelbourneUP. [2001] pp. xix + 249. $A43.95 ISBN 0 5228 4888 5.

Ashcroft, Bill. *On Post-Colonial Futures: Transformations of Colonial Culture*. Continuum. [2001] pp. 170. $A49.95 ISBN 0 8264 5226 4.

Atwood, Bain, and Fiona Magowan, eds. *Telling Stories: Indigenous History and Memory in Australia and New Zealand*. A&UA. [2001] pp. xvii + 269. pb $A35 ISBN 1 8650 8554 5.

Bangura, Ahmed S. *Islam and the West African Novel: The Politics of Representation*. Lynne Rienner. [2000] pp. 171. $59.95 ISBN 0 8941 0863 8.

Bardolph, Jacqueline, ed. *Telling Stories: Postcolonial Short Fiction in English*. Rodopi. [2001] pp. xiii + 477. hb £75 (€114) ISBN 9 0420 1534 9, pb £22 (€34) ISBN 9 0420 1524 1.

Bell, Maureen, *et al.*, eds. *Re-Constructing the Book: Literary Texts in Transmission*. Ashgate. [2001] pp. xi + 231. £37.50 ISBN 0 7546 0360 1.

Bennett, Bruce. *Australian Short Fiction: A History*. UQP. [2001] pp. xix + 379. pb $A29.95 ISBN 0 7022 3301 3.

Bettison, Margaret, and Jill Roe, eds. *A Gregarious Culture: The Topical Writings of Miles Franklin*. UQP. [2001] pp. 280. $A29.95 ISBN 0 7022 3237 8.

Bird, Delys, Robert Dixon, and Christopher Lee, eds. *Authority and Influence: Australian Literary Criticism, 1950–2000*. UQP. [2001] pp. xxxviii + 401. pb $A30 ISBN 0 7022 3203 3.

Blake, Ann, Leela Gandhi, and Sue Thomas. *England through Colonial Eyes in Twentieth-Century Fiction*. Palgrave. [2001] pp. x + 207. £47.50 ISBN 0 3337 3744 X.

Bradford, Clare. *Reading Race: Aboriginality in Australian Children's Literature*. MelbourneUP. [2001] pp. 283. pb $A34.95 ISBN 0 5228 4954 7.

Breslin, Paul. *Nobody's Nation: Reading Derek Walcott*. UChicP. [2001] pp. vii + 333. $50 ISBN 0 2260 7426 9.

Brisbane, Katherine, ed. *Plays of the 70s*. Currency. [2001] pp. x + 211. pb $A29.95 ISBN 0 8681 9599 5.

Brock, Peggy, ed. *Words and Silences: Aboriginal Women, Politics, and Land*. A&UA. [2001] pp. ix + 210. pb $A29.95 ISBN 1 8644 8947 2.

Bulman-May, James. *Patrick White and Alchemy*. ASP. [2001] pp. 332. pb $A29.95 ISBN 1 8756 0697 1.

Burger, Glenn, and Steven F. Kruger, eds. *Queering the Middle Ages*. UMinnP. [2001] pp. xxiii + 318. hb £34.50 ($54.95) ISBN 0 8166 3403 3, pb £14 ($19.95) ISBN 0 8166 3404 1.

Carr, Julie. *The Captive White Woman of Gipps Land: In Pursuit of the Legend*. MelbourneUP. [2001] pp. xvii + 309. pb $A29.95 ISBN 0 5228 4930 X.

Cazenave, Odile. *Rebellious Women: The New Generation of Female African Novelists*. Lynne Rienner. [2001] pp. 257. hb $55 ISBN 0 8941 0884 0, pb $19.95 ISBN 0 8941 0892 1.

Chaudhuri, Amit, ed. *The* Picador *Book of Modern Indian Literature*. Picador. [2001] pp. xxxiv + 638. hb £16.99 ISBN 0 3303 4363 7, pb £7 ISBN 0 3303 4364 5.

Chauhan, Pradyumna S., ed. *Salman Rushdie: Interviews. A Sourcebook of his Ideas*. Greenwood. [2001] pp. xx + 320. £64.95 ($82.95) ISBN 0 3133 0809 8.

Clark, Axel. *Finding Herself in Fiction: Henry Handel Richardson, 1896–1910*. ASP. [2001] pp. viii + 161. pb $A49.95 ISBN 1 8756 0687 4.

Clift, Charmian. *Mermaid Singing* and *Peel Me a Lotus*. Flamingo. [2001] pp. 422. pb $A24.95 ISBN 0 7322 6886 9.

Crane, Ralph J., and Radhika Mohanram, eds. *Shifting Continents/Colliding Cultures: Diaspora Writing of the Indian Subcontinent*. Rodopi. [2000] pp. xv + 262. hb £43 (€59) ISBN 9 0420 1271 4, pb £15 (€21) ISBN 9 0420 1261 7.

Craven, Peter, ed. *The Best Australian Essays 2001*. Black Inc. [2001] pp. xvii + 593. pb $A29.95 ISBN 1 8639 5091 5.

Daniels-Ramanujan, Molly, and Keith Harrison, eds. *A.K. Ramanujan: Uncollected Poems and Prose*. OUPI. [2001] pp. xii + 109. £13.50 (Rs325) ISBN 0 1956 5631 8.

Davies, Alistair, and Alan Sinfield, eds. *British Culture of the Postwar: An Introduction to Literature and Society, 1945–1999*. Routledge. [2000] pp. x + 211. hb £45 ISBN 0 4151 2810 2, pb £15.99 ISBN 0 4151 2811 0.

Dawes, Kwame, ed. *Talk Yuh Talk*. UPVirginia. [2001] pp. vii + 244. $50 ISBN 0 8139 1945 2.

de Montalk, Stephanie. *Unquiet World: The Life of Geoffrey Potocki de Montalk*. VictUP. [2001] pp. 336. $32.95 ISBN 0 8647 3414 X.

Devlin Glass, Frances, ed. *Joseph Furphy's The Buln Buln and the Brolga*. Halstead. [2001] pp. 159. $A18.95 ISBN 1 8756 8459 X.

Dhawan, R.K., ed. *Writers of the Indian Diaspora*. Prestige. [2001] pp. 160. Rs400 ISBN 8 1755 1111 7.

Dhondy, Farrukh. *C.L.R. James: A Life*. Pantheon. [2001] pp. vii + 224. $24 ISBN 0 3754 2100 9.

Dixon, Robert. *Prosthetic Gods: Travel, Representation, and Colonial Governance*. UQP. [2001] pp. xi + 191. pb $A30 ISBN 0 7022 3270 X.

Docker, John. *1492: The Poetics of Diaspora*. Continuum. [2001] pp. 256. hb £45 ISBN 0 8264 5131 4, pb £16.99 ISBN 0 8264 5132 2.

Easton, Brian. *The Nationbuilders*. AucklandUP. [2001] pp. vi + 318. £15.49 ($24.95) ISBN 1 8694 0260 X.

Epstein, Edmund L., and Robert Kole, eds. *The Language of African Literature*. Africa World Press. [2000] pp. 298. $21.95 ISBN 0 8654 3535 9.

Fallon, Erin, R.C. Feddersen, James Kurtzleben, Maurice A. Lee, and Susan Rochette-Crawley, eds. *A Reader's Companion to the Short Story in English*. Greenwood. [2001] pp. 432. $99.95 ISBN 0 3132 9104 7.

Feder, Lillian. *Naipaul's Truth: The Making of a Writer*. R&L. [2001] pp. vii + 271. $28 ISBN 0 7425 0808 0.

Filewod, Alan, and David Watt. *Workers' Playtime: Theatre and the Labour Movement since 1970*. Currency. [2001] pp. viii + 278. pb $A39.95 ISBN 0 8681 9631 2.

Foster, Robert, Rick Hosking, and Amanda Nettelback. *Fatal Collisions: The South Australian Frontier and the Violence of Memory*. Wakefield. [2001] pp. vii + 168. $A24.95 ISBN 1 8625 4533 2.

Franklin, Miles, and Kate Baker. *Joseph Furphy: The Legend of a Man and his Book*. Halstead. [2001] pp. 207. $23.95 ISBN 1 8756 8458 1.

Frost, Lucy, and Hamish Maxwell-Stewart, eds. *Chain Letters: Narrating Convict Lives*. MelbourneUP. [2001] pp. xiv + 248. pb $A32.95 ISBN 0 5228 4977 6.

Gagiano, Annie. *Achebe, Head, Marachera: On Power and Change in Africa*. Lynne Rienner. [2001] pp. 306. $44.95 ISBN 0 8941 0887 5.

Gilbert, Helen, ed. *Postcolonial Plays: An Anthology*. Routledge. [2001] pp. xiv + 469. hb £65 ISBN 0 4151 6448 6, pb £18.99 ISBN 0 4151 6449 4.

Golder, John, and Richard Madelaine, eds. *O Brave New World: Two Centuries of Shakespeare on the Australian Stage*. Currency. [2001] pp. xiii + 306. pb $A39.95 ISBN 0 8681 9613 4.

Grehan, Helena. *Mapping Cultural Identity in Contemporary Australian Performance*. Lang. [2001] pp. 167. pb £25 ISBN 9 0520 1947 9.

Griffith, Glyne, ed. *Caribbean Cultural Identities*. BuckUP. [2001] pp. 178. $28 ISBN 0 8387 5475 9.

Halligan, Marion, ed. *Storykeepers*. D&S. [2001] pp. 279. pb $A25 ISBN 1 8766 3110 4.

Haskell, Dennis. *Attuned to Alien Moonlight: The Poetry of Bruce Dawe*. UQP. [2001] pp. xv + 265. pb $A29.95 ISBN 0 7022 3238 6.

Hergenhan, Laurie, and Bruce Clunies Ross, eds. *The Poetry of Les Murray: Critical Essays*. UQP. [2001] pp. viii + 176. pb $A14.20 ISBN 0 7022 3291 2.

Heseltine, Harry. *The Most Glittering Prize: The Miles Franklin Award, 1957–1998*. Permanent. [2001] pp. xi + 108. pb $A19.95 ISBN 0 7317 0386 3.

Hewson, Helen, ed. *John Shaw Neilson: A Life in Letters*. Miegunyah. [2001] pp. xxiii + 503. $A69.95 ISBN 0 5228 4920 2.

Hogan, Patrick Colm. *Colonialism and Cultural Identity: Crises of Tradition in the Anglophone Literatures of India, Africa, and the Caribbean*. SUNYP. [2000] pp. 353. pb $17.25 ISBN 0 7914 4460 0.

Hoving, Isabel. *In Praise of New Travelers: Reading Caribbean Migrant Women's Writing*. StanfordUP. [2001] pp. vii + 374. $55 ISBN 0 8047 2947 6.

Howard, David, ed. *Complete with Instructions*. Firebrand (Christchurch NZ). [2001] pp. 96. ISBN 0 4730 7646 2.

Huggan, Graham. *The Postcolonial Exotic: Marketing the Margins*. Routledge. [2001] pp. xvi + 328. hb £60 ISBN 0 4152 5033 1, pb £16.99 ISBN 0 4152 5034 X.

Human Rights and Equal Opportunity Commission. Bringing Them Home: National Inquiry into the Separation of Aboriginal and Torres Strait Islander Children from their Families. HREOC. [1997] pp. 689. pb $A59.95 ISBN 0 6422 6954 8

Indyk, Ivor, ed. *Heat*. New series. Giramondo. [2001]: *Heat 1*, pp. 254. pb $A23.95 ISBN 0 9578 3111 0; *Heat 2*, pp. 255. pb $A23.95 ISBN 0 9578 3112 9.

Ismond, Patricia. *Abandoning Dead Metaphors: The Caribbean Phase of Derek Walcott's Poetry*. UWI. [2001] pp. vii + 309. $29.95 ISBN 9 7664 0107 1.

Jacobs, Lyn. *Against the Grain: Beverley Farmer's Writing*. UQP. [2001] pp. xiv + 258. $A29.95 ISBN 0 7022 3157 6.

Jobling, Lee, and Catherine Runcie, eds. *Matters of the Mind: Poems, Essays and Interviews in Honour of Leonie Kramer*. USydP. [2001] pp. 365. pb $A49.95 ISBN 1 8648 7362 0.

Kent, Jacqueline. *A Certain Style: Beatrice Davis, A Literary Life*. Viking. [2001] pp. 344. $A45 ISBN 0 6709 1131 3.

Khair, Tabish. *Babu Fictions: Alienation in Contemporary Indian English Novels*. OUPI. [2001] pp. xvi + 407. £23.50 ISBN 0 1956 5296 7.

King, Bruce. *Modern Indian Poetry in English*, rev. edn. OUPI. [2001] pp. x + 416. £25 ISBN 0 1956 5616 4.

King, Nicole. *C.L.R. James and Creolization: Circles of Influence*. UPMissip. [2001] pp. ix + 168. $40 ISBN 1 5780 6364 7.

Kratzmann, Gregory, ed. *A Steady Storm of Correspondence: Selected Letters of Gwen Harwood, 1943–1995*. UQP. [2001] pp. xxi + 507. pb $A40 ISBN 0 7022 3257 2.

La Bossière, Camille R., and Linda M. Morra, eds. *Robertson Davies: A Mingling of Contrarieties*. UOttawaP. [2001] pp. 175. $21.95 ISBN 0 7766 0531 3.

Larsson, Christer. *'The Relative Merits of Goodness and Originality': The Ethics of Storytelling in Peter Carey's Novels*. Studia Anglistica Upsaliensia. [2001] pp. 173. pb €207 ISBN 9 1554 5158 6.

Levy, Bronwen, and Ffion Murphy, eds. *Story/telling: The Woodford Forum*. UQP. [2001] pp. viii + 279. pb $A22 ISBN 0 7022 3202 5.

Lindfors, Bernth. *Black African Literature in English, 1992–1996*. Zell. [2001] pp. 654. £90 ($140) ISBN 0 8525 5565 2.

Linguanti, Elsa, Francesco Casotti, and Carmen Concilio, eds. *Coterminous Worlds: Magical Realism and Contemporary Post-Colonial Literature in English*. Rodopi. [2000] pp. 282. hb €89 ($83) ISBN 9 0420 0448 7, pb €28 ($26.50) ISBN 9 0420 0438 X.

Lynch, Gerald. *The One and the Many: English–Canadian Short Story Cycles*. UTorP. [2001] pp. 239. £30 ($50) ISBN 0 8020 3511 6.

Lyons, Martyn, and John Arnold. *A History of the Book in Australia*, vol. 2: *1891–1945: A National Culture in a Colonised Market*. UQP. [2001] pp. 444. $A50 ISBN 0 7022 3234 3.

MacKenzie, Craig. *The Oral-Style South African Short Story in English: A.W. Drayson to H.C. Bosman.* Rodopi. [2000] pp. 223. hb €65 ($61) ISBN 9 0420 0527 0, pb €21 ($19) ISBN 9 0420 0517 3.

Magarey, Susan. *Passions of the First-Wave Feminists.* UNSWP. [2001] pp. xii + 250. pb $34.95 ISBN 0 8684 0780 1.

Martin, Sylvia. *Passionate Friends: Mary Fullerton, Mabel Singleton, Miles Franklin.* Only Women. [2001] pp. 192. pb $A34.95 ISBN 0 9065 0064 8.

Matthews, Steven. *Les Murray.* ManUP. [2001] pp. xv + 184. pb $A29.95 ISBN 0 7190 5448 6.

Maufort, Marc, and Franca Bellarsi, eds. *Siting the Other: Re-Visions of Marginality in Australian and English-Canadian Drama.* Dramaturgies. Lang. [2001] pp. 374. $43.95 ISBN 9 0520 1934 7.

McEldowney, Dennis. *A Press Achieved: The Emergence of the Auckland University Press, 1927–1972 with a Brief Epilogue to 1986 and a List of Auckland University College, University of Auckland and Auckland University Press Publications, 1927–2000.* AucklandUP. [2001] pp. 166. $9.95 ISBN 1 8694 0239 1.

McPhee, Hilary. *Other People's Words.* Macmillan. [2001] pp. 312. pb $A21 ISBN 0 3303 6342 5.

Mee, Erin B. ed. *DramaContemporary: India.* JHUP. [2001] pp. 362. hb £40.50 ($55) ISBN 0 8018 6621 9, pb £16.50 ($22.50) ISBN 0 8018 6622 7.

Meyrick, Julian. *See How It Runs: Nimrod and the New Wave.* Currency. [2001] pp. vi + 312. pb $A39.95 ISBN 0 8681 9651 7.

Millar, Paul, ed. *New Selected Poems by James K. Baxter.* OUPNZ. [2001] pp. 294. ISBN 1 9558 429 5.

Millar, Paul, ed. *Spark to a Waiting Fuse: James K Baxter's Correspondence with Noel Ginn, 1942–1946.* VictUP. [2001] pp. 567. $32.95 ISBN 0 8647 3400 X.

Muecke, Stephen, and Adam Shoemaker, eds. *Legendary Tales of the Australian Aborigines by David Unaipon.* Miegunyah. [2001] pp. xlviii + 232. $A44.95 ISBN 0 5228 4905 9.

Ngugi wa Thiong'o. *Penpoints, Gunpoints, and Dreams: Towards a Critical Theory of the Arts and the State in Africa.* OUP. [1998] pp. 160. $39.95 ISBN 0 1981 8390 9.

North, Marilla. *Yarn Spinners. A Story in Letters: Dymphna Cusack, Florence James, Miles Franklin.* UQP. [2001] pp. xi + 441. pb $A35 ISBN 0 7022 3192 4.

Ojo-Ade, Femi. *Ken Saro-Wiwa: A Bio-Critical Study.* Africana Legacy Press. [1999] pp. 300. pb £16.95 ($27.95) ISBN 0 9663 8371 0.

Olafioye, Tayo. *The Poetry of Tanure Ojaide: A Critical Appraisal.* Malthouse Press. [2000] pp. 175. pb £ 8.95 ($14.95) ISBN 9 7802 3125 0.

Ommundsen, Wenche, ed. *Bastard Moon: Essays on Chinese-Australian Writing.* Overland. [2001] pp. v + 245. pb $A30 ISBN 0 9578 9740 5.

Palmer, Vance. *The Passage,* afterword by Neil James. Halstead. [2001] pp. 208. $A23.95 ISBN 1 8756 8453 0.

Paranjape, Makarand, ed. *In Diaspora: Theories, Histories, Texts.* Indialog. [2001] pp. vi + 351. hb $13.95 ISBN 8 1879 8105 9, pb $10.95 ISBN 8 1879 8106 7.

Payne, Anthony, and Paul Sutton. *Charting Caribbean Development.* UPFlor. [2001] pp. ix + 284. $55 ISBN 0 8130 2092 1.

Petersen, Teresa. *The Enigmatic Christina Stead: A Provocative Re-Reading*. MelbourneUP. [2001] pp. ix + 253. pb $A29.95 ISBN 0 5228 4922 9.

Pordzik, Ralph. *The Quest for Postcolonial Utopia*. Lang. [2001] pp. vii + 179. £34 ISBN 0 8204 5193 2.

Probin, Clive, and Bruce Steel, eds. *Henry Handel Richardson's The Getting of Wisdom*. UQP. [2001] pp. lv + 282. $65 ISBN 0 7022 3179 7.

Punter, David. *Postcolonial Imaginings: Fictions of a New World Order*. EdinUP. [2001] pp. viii + 238. pb £16 ISBN 0 7486 0856 7.

Pybus, Cassandra. *The Devil and James McAuley*, rev. edn. UQP. [2001] pp. xvii + 332. pb $A28 ISBN 0 7022 3124 X.

Ramazani, Jahan. *The Hybrid Muse: Postcolonial Poetry in English*. UChicP. [2001] pp. x + 223. hb £35 ($50) ISBN 0 2267 0342 8, pb £12.50 ($17.50) ISBN 0 2267 0343 6.

Ravikant and Tarun K. Saint, eds. *Translating Partition: Stories, Essays, Criticism*. Katha. [2001] pp. xxx + 238. pb £12.50 (Rs250) ISBN 8 1876 4904 6.

Reder, Michael R., ed. *Conversations with Salman Rushdie*. UPMissip. [2000] pp. xvi + 238. hb $46 ISBN 1 5780 6184 9, pb $18 ISBN 1 5780 6185 7.

Reiss, Timothy J., ed. *For the Geography of a Soul: Emerging Perspectives on Kamau Brathwaite*. AWP. [2001] pp. ix + 501. $29.95 ISBN 0 8654 3904 4.

Ricard, Alain. *Ebrahim Hussein: Swahili Theatre and Individualism*. Mkuki na Nyota. [2000] pp. 160. pb £8.95 ($14.95) ISBN 9 9769 7381 0.

Rickard, Suzanne, ed. *George Barrington's Voyage to Botany Bay: Retelling a Convict's Travel Narrative of the 1790s*. LeicUP. [2001] pp. xxiv + 181. pb £18.99 ISBN 0 7185 0186 1.

Roberts, Neil, ed. *A Companion to Twentieth-Century Poetry*. Blackwell. [2001] pp. ix + 626. £80 ISBN 0 6312 1529 8.

Robertson, Tim. *The Pram Factory: The Australian Performing Group Recollected*. MelbourneUP. [2001] pp. 178. pb $A39.95 ISBN 0 5228 4983 0.

Ruthven, K.K. *Faking Literature*. CUP. [2001] pp. x + 237. pb $A49.95 ISBN 0 5216 6965 0.

Sanga, Jaina C. *Salman Rushdie's Postcolonial Metaphors: Migration, Translation, Hybridity, Blasphemy, and Globalization*. Greenwood. [2001] pp. xvi + 176. £49.50 ($62.95) ISBN 0 3133 1310 5.

Satchidanandan, K., ed. *Indian Poetry. Modernism and After: A Seminar*. SA. [2001] pp. xviii + 370. Rs175 ISBN 8 1260 1092 4.

Scott, Jamie S., and Paul Simpson-Housley, eds. *Mapping the Sacred: Religion, Geography and Postcolonial Literatures*. Rodopi. [2001] pp. xxxiii + 486. hb £75 (€114) ISBN 9 0420 1554 3, pb £23 (€37) ISBN 9 0420 1544 6.

Simatei, Tirop Peter. *The Novel and the Politics of Nation Building in East Africa*. Bayreuth African Studies 55. Bayreuth. [2000] pp. 182. DM29.90 (€14.95) ISBN 3 9275 1070 X.

Staines, David, ed. *Margaret Laurence: Critical Reflections*. UOttawaP. [2001] pp. 169. $19.95 ISBN 0 7766 0446 5.

Steenman-Marcuse, Conny. *Re-Writing Pioneer Women in Anglo-Canadian Literature*. Rodopi. [2001] pp. 246. $46 ISBN 9 0420 1305 2.

Stuart, Lurline, ed. *Marcus's Clarke's His Natural Life*. UQP. [2001] pp. lx + 686. pb $A80 ISBN 0 7022 3177 0.

Suk, Jeannie. *Postcolonial Paradoxes in French Caribbean Writing*. Clarendon. [2001] pp. 206. $70 ISBN 0 1981 6018 6.

Tasker, Meg. *'Struggle and Storm': The Life and Death of Francis Adams*. MelbourneUP. [2001] pp. xii + 259. pb $A39.95 ISBN 0 5228 4946 6.

Waten, Judah. *Distant Land*, afterword by Hsu Ming Teo. Halstead. [2001] pp. 192. $A22.95 ISBN 1 8756 8469 7.

Waterston, Elizabeth. *Rapt in Plaid: Canadian Literature and Scottish Tradition*. UTorP. [2001] pp. 344. £40 ($45) ISBN 0 8020 4785 8.

Werlock, Abby. *Carol Shields's The Stone Diaries*. Continuum. [2001] pp. 94. £5 ($8.95) ISBN 0 8264 5249 3.

Wheatley, Nadia. *The Life and Myth of Charmian Clift*. Flamingo. [2001] pp. xix + 739. pb $A35.95 ISBN 0 7322 6912 1.

Wheatley, Nadia., ed. *Charmian Clift: Selected Essays*. HCAus. [2001] pp. vii + 408. pb $A24.95 ISBN 0 7322 6886 9.

Woods, Joanna. *Katerina: The Russian World of Katherine Mansfield*. PenguinNZ. [2001] pp. 320. ISBN 0 1430 1805 1.

Wright, F.W. Nielsen. *An Account of Noel Farr Hoggard as Georgian Editor and Writer in Aotearoa, 1931–1953*. Monographs of Aotearoa Literature 51. Cultural and Political Booklets (Wellington NZ). [2001] ISBN 1 8693 3513 9.

Yarrow, Ralph. *Indian Theatre: Theatre of Origins, Theatre of Freedom*. Curzon. [2001] pp. xiv + 231. £55 ISBN 0 7007 1412 X.

Yuanfang, Shen. *Dragon Seed in the Antipodes: Chinese-Australian Autobiographies*. MelbourneUP. [2001] pp. 196. pb $A32.95 ISBN 0 5228 4941 5.

XVIII

Bibliography and Textual Criticism

PAUL WEBB AND WILLIAM BAKER

The year's work in bibliography and textual criticism continues the pattern of previous years. There are an increasing number of monographs concerned with editorial theory and the history of the book as well as bibliographies devoted to the works of individual writers. This year's survey will draw our readers' attention to useful enumerative, analytical and descriptive bibliographical labours. The review also describes materials of interest to students of various areas of librarianship, book collecting and antiquarianism as well as English literature.

The variety and diversity of journals devoted to bibliography and textual criticism continue to flourish. *The Papers of the Bibliographical Society of America* (95[2001]) contains William Robins, 'Antonio Pucci's *Contrasto delle donne* and the Circulation of Fourteenth-Century Florentine Dramatic Poetry' (*PBSA* 95[2001] 5–19); Eric Rasmussen, 'The Date of Q4 *Hamlet*' (*PBSA* 95[2001] 21–29); Don-John Dugas, 'The London Book Trade in 1709 (Part One)' (*PBSA* 95[2001] 31–58); J.A. Leo Lemay, 'An Attribution of Reflections on Courtship and Marriage (1746) to Benjamin Franklin' (*PBSA* 95[2001] 59–96); Robert D. Armstrong, 'The Only Alternative Course: Incidents in Nevada Printing History' (*PBSA* 95[2001] 97–156); Don-John Dugas, 'The London Book Trade in 1709 (Part Two)' (*PBSA* 95[2001] 157–72); Paul Needham, 'Copy Description in Incunable Catalogs' (*PBSA* 95[2001] 173–239); MacD. P. Jackson, 'Late Webster and his Collaborators: How Many Playwrights Wrote *A Cure for a Cuckold*?' (*PBSA* 95[2001] 295–313); Paul Werstine, 'Scribe or Compositor: Ralph Crane, Compositors D and F, and the First Four Plays in the Shakespeare First Folio' (*PBSA* 95[2001] 315–39); Keith Arbour, 'Solomon Stoddard's Addition to *The Safety of Appearing* (Boston, 1729) and the Attribution of its Printing, with a Note on "Reilly 695"' (*PBSA* 95[2001] 341–7); Peter Isaac, 'The English Provincial Book Trade: A Northern Mosaic' (*PBSA* 95[2001] 410–441); Christian Y. Dupont, 'Collecting Dante in American at the End of the Nineteenth Century: John Zahm and Notre Dame' (*PBSA* 95[2001] 443–81); R. Carter Hailey, '"Geuyng light to the reader"': Robert Crowley's Editions of *Piers Plowman* (1550)' (*PBSA* 95[2001] 483–502); William Searle, '"By foule authority": Miscorrection in the Folio Text of Shakespeare's *Troilus and Cressida*' (*PBSA* 95[2001] 503–19).

The latest volume of *Studies in Bibliography* (52[2001]) contains a diverse range of articles dealing with bibliographies, textual criticism, marginalia and watermarks, and transcription, among many others. Selections include: G. Thomas Tanselle, 'The Treatment of Typesetting and Presswork in Bibliographical Description' (*SB* 52[2001] 1–58); Andrew Galloway, 'Uncharacterizable Entities: The Poetics of Middle English Scribal Culture and the Definitive *Piers Plowman*' (*SB* 52[2001] 59–88); Joseph A. Dane and Alexandra Gillespie, 'Back at Chaucer's Tomb-Inscriptions in Two Early Copies of Chaucer's *Workes*' (*SB* 52[2001] 89–96); Daniel W. Mosser, 'Corrective Notes on the Structures and Paper Stocks of Four Manuscripts Containing Extracts from Chaucer's *Canterbury Tales*' (*SB* 52[2001] 97–114); Peter Rolfe Monks, 'The Diptych by the Rolin Master Detached from Autun, Bibliothèque Municipale, MS.110 (S. 133)' (*SB* 52[2001] 115–28); Adrian Weiss, 'Watermark Evidence and Inference: New Style Dates of Edmund Spenser's *Complaints* and *Daphnaida*' (*SB* 52[2001] 129–54); Laurie E. Maguire, 'The Printer and Date of Q4 *A Looking Glass for London and England*' (*SB* 52[2001] 155–60); James E. May, 'A Joint-Purchase Agreement for Books in Eighteenth-Century Massachusetts' (*SB* 52[2001] 161–8); David Chandler, '"A Sort of Bird's Eye View of the British Land of Letters": The *Monthly Magazine* and its Reviewers, 1796–1811' (*SB* 52[2001] 169–80); Nicholas A. Joukovsky, 'Leigh Hunt's Contributions to the *Guide*' (*SB* 52[2001] 181–6); Gillian Kyles, 'Alteration of Leading within Editions' (*SB* 52[2001] 187–92); Arthur Sherbo, '*The Cambridge Review*' (*SB* 52[2001] 193–200); David L. Vander Meulen and G. Thomas Tanselle, 'A System of Manuscript Transcription' (*SB* 52[2001] 201–12); G. Thomas Tanselle, 'Bowers's *Principles* at Fifty' (*SB* 52[2001] 213–14); David L. Vander Meulen, 'Revision in Bibliographical Classics: "McKerrow" and "Bowers"' (*SB* 52[2001] 215–46).

The Library: The Transactions of the Bibliographical Society (7th series[2001]) includes Margaret Lane Ford, 'A New Addition to the Corpus of English Incunabula: Wynkyn de Worde's *Proprytees & Medicynes of Hors (c*.1497–98)' (*Library*, 7th series[2001] 3–9); Julian Pooley, 'The Papers of the Nichols Family and Business: New Discoveries and the Work of the Nichols Archive Project' (*Library*, 7th series[2001] 10–52); Andrew Nash, 'The Serialization and Publication of *The Return of the Native*: A New Thomas Hardy Letter' (*Library*, 7th series[2001] 53–9); Lotte Hellinga, 'The Interpretation of Measurements of Pinholes and Analysis of Ink in Incunabula' (*Library*, 7th series[2001] 60–4); Martin Holmes, 'A Song Attributed to Dryden: A Postscript' (*Library*, 7th series[2001] 65–8); Richard Beadle and Lotte Hellinga, 'William Paston II and Pynson's *Statutes of War* (1492)' (*Library*, 7th series[2001] 107–19); Peter Beal, 'Alexander Dicsone, Elizabethan Philosopher, Propagandist, Spy: A Checklist of his Writings' (*Library*, 7th series[2001] 120–30); Victoria E. Burke and Sarah C.E. Ross, 'Elizabeth Middleton, John Bourchier, and the Compilation of Seventeenth-Century Religious Manuscripts' (*Library*, 7th series[2001] 131–60). Also included is a fine review article by Donald D. Eddy and Robert J. Berry on J.D.F. Freeman's important *Bibliography of the Works of Samuel Johnson* (*Library*, 7th series[2001] 161–78); Satoko Tokunaga, 'The Sources of Wynkyn de Worde's Version of "The Monk's Tale"' (*Library*, 7th series[2001] 223–35); Timothy Raylor, 'Moseley, Walkley, and the 1645 Editions of Waller' (*Library*, 7th series[2001] 236–65); Harold Love, 'The Intellectual Heritage of Donald Francis McKenzie' (*Library*, 7th series[2001] 266–80); Lynette Hunter, 'The Dating of Q4 *Romeo and Juliet* Revisited' (*Library*, 7th series[2001] 281–5); B.J. McMullin, 'A Scottish Sexto in

Fours and Twos' (*Library*, 7th series[2001] 286–9); R.J. Fehrenbach, 'A Pre-1592 English Faust Book and the Date of Marlowe's *Doctor Faustus*' (*Library*, 7th series[2001] 327–35); Jacqueline Glomski, '*Incunabula Typographiae*: Seventeenth-Century Views on Early Printing' (*Library*, 7th series[2001] 336–48); Arthur and Janet Ing Freeman, 'Did Halliwell Steal and Mutilate the First Quarto of *Hamlet?*' (*Library*, 7th series[2001] 349–63); Clare Hutton, 'Reading *The Love Songs of Connacht*: Douglas Hyde and the Exigencies of Publication' (*Library*, 7th series[2001] 364–93).

The final volume of *Analytical and Enumerative Bibliography* (12[2001]) contains the following: William P. Williams and William Baker, '*Caveat Lector*: English Books 1475–1700 and the Electronic Age' (*AEB* 12[2001] 1–29); Paul Menzer, '"'Tis heere, 'tis heere, 'tis gone": Q1 *Hamlet* and Degenerate Texts' (*AEB* 12[2001] 30–49); Edward Ragg, 'The Oxford Shakespeare Re-Visited: An Interview with Professor Stanley Wells' (*AEB* 12[2001] 73–101); Candice L. Hart, 'Georgette Heyer and *The Queen's Book of the Red Cross*' (*AEB* 12[2001] 102–11). *AEB* 12[2001], numbers iii–iv, is a final double issue and is devoted to essays on 'Shakespeare's Stationers', introduced by Thomas L. Berger (*AEB* 12[2001] 150–2). Other contributions include Kirk Melnikoff, 'Richard Jones (fl. 1564–1613): Elizabethan Printer, Bookseller and Publisher' (*AEB* 12[2001] 153–84); Jean R. Brink, 'William Ponsonby's Rival Publisher' (*AEB* 12[2001] 185–205); Terri Bourus, 'Shakespeare and the London Publishing Environment: The Publisher and Printers of Q1 and Q2 *Hamlet*' (*AEB* 12[2001] 206–28); Lori Humphrey Newcomb, 'Literary Restoration: Francis Kirkman and the Canons of Pre-War Drama and Romance' (*AEB* 12[2001] 229–40); and Andrew Murphy, 'Shakespeare Goes to School: Educational Stationers' (*AEB* 12[2001] 241–63). The last two articles in the final *AEB* are Thomas L. Berger and George Walton Williams, 'Notes on Shakespeare's *Henry V*' (*AEB* 12[2001] 264–87); James E. May, 'Who Will Edit the ESTC? (and Have you Checked OCLC Lately?)' (*AEB* 12[2001] 288–304). May's is a detailed amplification of Williams and Baker's 'Caveat Lector: English Books 1475–1700 and the Electronic Age' (*AEB* 12[2001] 1–29). *AEB* then closes its pages with reviews by Brian Vickers, Kenneth Womack, Paul F. Gehl, John C. Ross, Terri Bourus and Jan Fergus, and 'A Note from the Editor', William Proctor Williams. After twenty-five years' publication 'the rest is silence': a unique and important bibliographical journal is no more.

The *Bulletin of Bibliography* (58[2001]) includes Seth Whidden, 'Marie Krysinska: A Bibliography' (*BB* 58[2001] 1–10); Allan Metz, 'Blondie and Deborah Harry: A Comprehensive Bibliography, 1975–2000' (*BB* 58[2001] 11–48); James C. Fairfield, '*Slaughterhouse-Five*: A Selected Guide to Scholarship and Resources, 1987–1999' (*BB* 58[2001] 49–58); Linda Capps Boyd, 'Folklore in Hawthorne's Work: An Annotated Bibliography' (*BB* 58[2001] 59–86); James F. Collins, 'The High Points So Far: An Annotated Bibliography of Ursula K. LeGuin's *The Left Hand of Darkness* and *The Dispossessed*' (*BB* 58[2001] 89–100); William L. Svitavsky, 'Geek Culture: An Annotated Interdisciplinary Bibliography' (*BB* 58[2001] 101–8); Christopher D. Lewis, '*Tender is the Night* and the Critics: From 1982 to the Present' (*BB* 58[2001] 109–24); Julia Stephens, 'Caroline Lee Hentz: Antebellum Scenes and Settings' (*BB* 58[2001] 125–34); Lawrence J. Mykytiuk, 'Did Bible Characters Really Exist? Part 3: An Annotated Bibliography of Northwest-Semitic Monumental Inscriptions from before 539 BC, Concluded'

(*BB* 58[2001] 135–42); Bert Chapman, 'Assessments of China's Military: A Resource Guide' (*BB* 58[2001] 145–58); Allan Metz, 'First-Term Retrospective of the Clinton Presidency' (*BB* 58[2001] 159–226); Jacqueline F. Johnson, 'Joshua Lawrence Chamberlain: A Select and Annotated List of Sources' (*BB* 58[2001] 227–34); Kevin W. Jett, 'A Checklist and Brief Publishing History of Incunable and Early German Dictionaries, 1450–1550' (*BB* 58[2001] 239–54); Peter Dollard, 'A Bibliography of the Poems and Essays of Adah Isaacs Menken' (*BB* 58[2001] 255–8); A. Carolyn Carpan, 'Twentieth-Century Girls Series Books: A Selected Bibliography' (*BB* 58[2001] 259–66); George Monteiro, 'David H. Hirsch: A Primary Bibliography' (*BB* 58[2001] 267–70); Caroline Weaver, 'Jean Vigo (26 April 1905 to 5 October 1934)' (*BB* 58[2001] 271).

Antiquarian Book Monthly (28:vi[2001]) includes Michael Seeney on 'Three Wilde Exhibitions' (*ABM* 28:i[2001] 8–10); Eric Ford 'America's Very Own Winston Churchill' (*ABM* 28:i[2001] 14–19); Lucy Gordan 'William Blake: The Exhibition' (*ABM* 28:i[2001] 20–4) which is an account of the William Blake exhibition at Tate Britain and the Metropolitan in New York; Michael Holman's 'Booksellers of Our Time' focuses upon Bromlea and Jonkers (*ABM* 28:i[2001] 36–37); Boris Wertz's 'Online Offline' discusses the impact of the Internet on the antiquarian book world (*ABM* 28:ii[2001] 14–17); Peter Frost writes on 'A.H. Mackmurdo' (*ABM* 28:ii[2001] 33–6); William H.P. Crewdson writes on the boys' adventure writer 'Hylton Cleaver' (*ABM* 28:iii[2001] 20–4); Roy Davids postulates on 'Manuscripts on Endangered Species' (*ABM* 28:iv[2001] 15–17); Janice Peters writes on 'Donald MacCormick' who specializes in Gaelic antiquarian materials (*ABM* 28:iv[2001] 22); David Ashford writes on 'R.D. Blackmore and *Lorna Doone*' (*ABM* 28:iv[2001] 23–8); Michael Holman speaks on the antiquarian bookseller who specializes in maps and prints 'Philip Burden'(*ABM* 28:iv[2001] 30); Lucy Gordan writes on the Italian nationalist 'D'Annunzio: Man, Hero, Poet' (*ABM* 28:v[2001] 12–13); William H.P. Crewdson writes on 'The Real Treasure Island' (*ABM* 28:v[2001] 29–35); in the June issue Osric Allen of the distinguished London booksellers 'Robert Temple' writes on the vagaries and unreliable of internet sites in his appropriately titled 'Obituary!' (*ABM* 28:vi[2001] 18–20); Lucy Gordan's focus is the '[oldest] firm in the world in the field of image making' in her 'At 150 Ever-Modern Fratelli Alinari Goes Online' (*ABM* 28:vi[2001] 32–6); Gordan also writes on 'Claudio de Polo Saibanti' (*ABM* 28:vii[2001] 12–15); Carol Grossman discusses 'A Reflection of Shropshire: Mary and Nicholas Parry's Tern Press' (*ABM* 28:vii[2001] 16–21); Lucy Gordan reflects on 'Travels to Italy: A Passion Five Centuries Long' (*ABM* 28:vii[2001] 24–7); Eric Ford's 'Much More than a Mohican Man' focuses on James Fenimore Cooper (*ABM* 28:viii[2001] 9–13); Rosie Speno's 'Biblion.com and the Future of the British Book Trade' contains an interview with Leo Harrison, founder of Biblion (*ABM* 28:viii[2001] 15); Michael Holman focuses on a wood-engraving specialist in 'Booksellers of our Time: Geraldine Waddington' (*ABM* 28:ix[2001] 12–15); Cynthia A. Burgess focuses on Baylor University's 'The Armstrong Browning Library Observes its Golden Jubilee: By Honouring the Past and Embracing the Future' (*ABM* 28:ix[2001] 16–22); in 'Louise McDermott's Italica Books' (*ABM* 28:ix[2001] 26–8) Lucy Gordan discusses rare books on Italy in English; Steven E. Ericson focuses on the development of the science fiction genre in 'Science Fiction: From Chronic Affliction to Full-Blown Mania' (*ABM* 28:x[2001] 12–16); Barry R. Levin discusses views related to author-signed books in 'Is Flat Signed Better' (*ABM* 28:x[2001] 17–18); Lucy Gordan writes on the city of Leipzig in 'Literary Leipzig: City of the Black Art Since 1481' (*ABM* 28:x[2001] 21–5), and on 'Along the Märchenstrasse: Germany's Fairy-Tale Road' (*ABM* 28:xi[2001] 13–17); Joe McCann describes 'At Swim Two Books or the Bookshops of Dublin' (*ABM* 28:xi[2001] 24); William H.P. Crewdson writes on 'Walter Crane' (*ABM* 28:xi[2001] 36–40) in what is the final article in the *Antiquarian Book Monthly*, which will subsequently appear under the title *Antiquarian Book Review*.

The *Book Collector* (50[2001]) includes Neil Harris, 'A Review of *The Diario*' (*BC* 50[2001] 10–32); Melissa Conway, 'A Reply to Professor Harris's Review' (*BC* 50[2001] 33–41); Jonathan Smith, 'John Gould, Charles Darwin, and the Picturing of Natural Selection' (*BC* 50[2001] 51–76); John Commander, 'Blake at the Millennium' (*BC* 50[2001] 77–84); 'Obituaries: Harry Oppenheimer' (*BC* 50[2001] 117–19); 'Obituaries: Hylton Henry Bayntun-Coward' (*BC* 50[2001] 119–21); 'Ireland, Where Booksellers Cannot Pretend to Any Property' (*BC* 50[2001] 165–85); Roger Eliot Stoddard, 'François Hemsterhuis: Some Uncollected Authors LVIII' (*BC* 50[2001] 186–201); Jan Storm van Leeuwen, 'Frans Hemsterhuis' Binders and Some Bindings on *Lettre sur l'Homme*' (*BC* 50[2001] 202–16); David Pearson, 'The Howard Collection of Bibles and Liturgical Books in the Alexander Turnbull Library' (*BC* 50[2001] 217–34); 'Obituaries: William O'Sullivan' (*BC* 50[2001] 269–71); 'Obituaries: Frederick B. Adams, Jr.' (*BC* 50[2001] 271–3); 'Obituaries: Lawrence Clark Powell' (*BC* 50[2001] 273–4); 'Obituaries: Will Carter' (*BC* 50[2001] 275–7); 'Obituaries: Horst Kunze' (*BC* 50[2001] 277–8); Richard Garnett, 'Rupert Hart-Davis Limited, A Brief History: Part 1' (*BC* 50[2001] 329–46); James S. Dearden, 'The Chace, Hunting for Somerville' (*BC* 50[2001] 347–64); Asya Haikin, 'Investigating Two Cranach Miniatures' (*BC* 50[2001] 365–78); 'Obituary: David Foxon' (*BC* 50[2001] 416–19); 'Typography and Design' (*BC* 50[2001] 449–70); Mark Purcell, 'Master Petypher's Virgil: The Anatomy of a Tudor School Book' (*BC* 50[2001] 471–92); Richard Garnett, 'Rupert Hart-Davis Limited, A Brief History: Part 2'(*BC* 50[2001] 493–506); Marvin Spevack, ' "Truth" Discovered' (*BC* 50[2001] 507–14). This is followed by the *Book Collector*'s hilarious and sometimes embarrassing 'Christmas Catalogue No. 9' which should be compulsory reading for all word-processors, typists, proof-readers and others! (*BC* 50[2001] 515–544). Volume 50 concludes with 'Obituaries: Robert Rivington' (*BC* 50[2001] 570–2); 'Obituaries: Philip Gaskell' (*BC* 50[2001] 572–4); Obituaries: Kenneth Evan Hill' (*BC* 50[2001] 574).

The *East Central Intelligencer* (15:i[2001]) includes E. Richard McKinstry, 'Resources for Eighteenth-Century Studies at the Winterthur Library' (*ECIntell* 15:i[2001] 19–22); Elaine Smyth, 'Eclectic and Underadmired: 18th-Century Holdings in the LSU Libraries' (*ECIntell* 15:i[2001] 23–5); William C. Horne, 'Eighteenth Century Accounts of Hudson's Bay and the Phenomenology of Samuel Hearne's Journey (1795)' (*ECIntell* 15:ii[2001] 3–7); Hermann J. Real, 'Gulliver and the Moons of Mars, Once More' (*ECIntell* 15:ii[2001] 7–8); Hermann J. Real, 'That 'Flower of Swift's Cynicism', *The Lady's Dressing Room*, Again' (*ECIntell* 15:ii[2001] 8–13); Máire Kennedy, 'Dublin in 1738: Compiling a Directory of Dubliners' (*ECIntell* 15:ii[2001] 13–16); 'The Children's Books History Society' (*ECIntell* 15:ii[2001] 16–19); Cheryl Wanko, 'Love Arm'd, Aphra Behn and her Pen: A Performance by Karen Eterovich' (*ECIntell* 15:ii[2001] 19–21); James J.

Kirschke, 'Teaching the American Revolutionary Era Founders: An Interdisciplinary Approach' (*ECIntell* 15:ii[2001] 21–8); Harry Keyishian, '18th Century Studies at Fairleigh Dickinson U. Press' (*ECIntell* 15:ii[2001] 28–30); Peter Berg, 'Eighteenth-Century Holdings at Michigan State University' (*ECIntell* 15:iii[2001] 4–9).

The *Journal of Scholarly Publishing* (32[2000/2001]), includes Sanford G. Thatcher, 'Fair Use: A Double-Edged Sword' (*JScholP* 32[2000] 3–8); Jennifer M. Siler, 'From Gutenberg to Gateway: Electronic Publishing at University Presses' (*JScholP* 32[2000] 9–23); Manzurul Islam, 'Academic Publishing and the University Presses: The Case in a Developing Region (Saudi Arabia)' (*JScholP* 32[2000] 24–32); Ruth Panofsky, 'The Editor as Gap-Filler: The Letters of Margaret Laurence and Adele Wiseman' (*JScholP* 32[2000] 33–42); Hazel Bell, 'Personalities in Publishing: Ian Norrie' (*JScholP* 32[2000] 43–9); Albert N. Greco, 'The General Reader Market for University Press Books in the United States, 1990–9, with Projections for the Years 2000 through 2004' (*JScholP* 32[2001] 61–86); Theresa M. Liu, 'Notes from Down Under: Musings of a Junior Staff Member' (*JScholP* 32[2001] 87–90); Maggie Hivnor, 'Adventures in Reprint Rights' (*JScholP* 32[2001] 91–101); Fredrika J. Teute, 'To Publish and Perish: Who Are the Dinosaurs in Scholarly Publishing?' (*JScholP* 32[2001] 102–12); Hazel Bell, 'Personalities in Publishing: John Vickers' (*JScholP* 32[2001] 113–18); David Henige, 'Mis/Adventures in Mis/Quoting' (*JScholP* 32[2001] 123–35); Ibironke Lawal, 'Scholarly Communication at the Turn of the Millennium: A Bibliographic Essay' (*JScholP* 32[2001] 136–54); Amadio Arboleda, 'The Gutenberg Syndrome: An Illusion of International Research' (*JScholP* 32[2001] 155–63); Merina Hew, 'Scholarly Journal Publishing in Malaysia' (*JScholP* 32[2001] 164–8); Hazel Bell, 'Personalities in Publishing: Maeve O'Connor' (*JScholP* 32[2001] 169–75); George Meadows, 'The Twentieth-Century Erasmus' (*JScholP* 32[2001] 179–81); Bill Harnum, 'The Characteristics of the Ideal Acquisition Editor' (*JScholP* 32[2001] 182–8); Marcel Danesi, '"Schoeffling" the Editorial Deck: A Tongue-in-Cheek Personal Note on Editing Two University Press Series with Ron Schoeffel' (*JScholP* 32[2001] 189–94); Francis Sparshott, 'Two-Faced at the Interface: Meditations on the Manuscript Review Committee' (*JScholP* 32[2001] 195–203); Frances G. Halfpenny, 'Living a Project' (*JScholP* 32[2001] 204–20). Halfpenny's article discusses, among other projects undertaken by the University of Toronto Press, the *Collected Works of Erasmus*, the *Records of Early English Drama* and the *Collected Works of John Stuart Mill*. *JScholP* 33:i[October 2001] includes Benjamin R. Beede's 'Editing a Specialized Encyclopedia' (*JScholP* 33[2001] 1–10), and David Henige explores the nature of reviewing scholarly publications in his 'Reviewing Reviewing' (*JScholP* 33[2001] 23–36). The importance of design in scholarly publishing is discussed in 'Why Design is Important: Five Designers Speak to Non-Designers' with an introduction by Robert Tombs (*JScholP* 33[2001] 37–46). John Taylor is the subject of Hazel Bell's 'Personalities in Publishing' (*JScholP* 33[2001] 47–52); William Germano writes on 'Surviving the Review Process' (*JScholP* 33[2001] 53–69).

Book History (4[2001]) includes John Barnard, 'London Publishing, 1640–1660: Crisis, Continuity, and Innovation' (*BoH* 4[2001] 1–16); Eugenia Roldán Vera, 'Reading in Questions and Answers: The Catechism as an Educational Genre in Early Independent Spanish America' (*BoH* 4[2001] 17–48); Thomas Cragin, 'The

Failings of Popular News Censorship in Nineteenth-Century France' (*BoH* 4[2001] 49–80); Elaine Hoag, 'Caxtons of the North: Mid-Nineteenth-Century Arctic Shipboard Printing' (*BoH* 4[2001] 81–114); Helen Williams, 'Ringing the Bell: Editor–Reader Dialogue in Alexander Herzen's *Kolokol*' (*BoH* 4[2001] 115–32); Robert Darnton, 'Literary Surveillance in the British Raj: The Contradictions of Liberal Imperialism' (*BoH* 4[2001] 133–76); Eric Lupfer, 'Before Nature Writing: Houghton, Mifflin and Company and the Invention of the Outdoor Book, 1880–1900' (*BoH* 4[2001] 177–204); Troy J. Bassett and Christina M. Walter, 'Booksellers and Bestsellers: British Book Sales as Documented by *The Bookman*, 1891–1906' (*BoH* 4[2001] 205–36); Matthew Skelton, 'The Paratext of Everything: Constructing and Marketing H.G. Wells's *The Outline of History*' (*BoH* 4[2001] 237–76); Chris Baggs, 'How Well Read Was My Valley? Reading, Popular Fiction, and the Miners of South Wales, 1875–1939' (*BoH* 4[2001] 277–302); Rimi B. Chatterjee, 'Canon Without Consensus: Rabindranath Tagore and *The Oxford Book of Bengali Verse*' (*BoH* 4[2001] 303–34); Paul C. Gutjahr, 'Sacred Texts in the United States' (*BoH* 4[2001] 335–70).

Of interest to students of bibliography and textual criticism is the following item in *Textual Practice*: Peter Middleton and Tim Woods, 'Textual Memory: The Making of the *Titanic*'s Literary Archive' (*TPr* 15[2001] 507–26). *The Proceedings of the British Academy* (111[2001]), entitled 'Lectures and Memoirs', contains the following of interest to readers of *YWES*: Michael Lapidge, '*Beowulf* and Perception' (*PBA* 111[2001] 61–98); Graham Bradshaw, 'Shakespeare's Peculiarity' (*PBA* 111[2001] 99–126); Peter Holland, 'Beginning in the Middle' (*PBA* 111[2001] 127–56); Margaret Kean, 'Waiting for God: John Milton's Poems of 1671' (*PBA* 111[2001] 157–78); Helen Vendler, 'Wallace Stevens: Hypotheses and Contradictions' (*PBA* 111[2001] 225–44). Amongst the memoirs presented are E.A.J. Honigmann on 'Harold Jenkins, 1909–2000' (*PBA* 111[2001] 553–74) and Claire Lamont on 'Mary Madge Lascelles, 1900–1995' (*PBA* 111[2001] 575–94).

Text Technology: The Journal of Computer Text Processing (10:i[2001]) contains Geoffrey Rockwell, 'The Visual Concordance: The Design of Eye-ConTact' (*Text Technology* 10:i[2001] 73–86). This paper proposes that text-hyphen analysis tools represent a text or corpus by rearranging the text according to a user's question. Penelope J. Gurney and Lyman W. Gurney , 'Authorship Attribution: A Computer-Based Approach to a Literary Crux in Late Roman Historiography' (*Text Technology* 10:i[2001] 87–104), although focused on the late Roman period has relevance to English scholars wrestling with the problems of multiple versus single authorship of printed text or manuscripts.

The *Bibliographical Society of Australia and New Zealand Bulletin* (25:i and ii[2001]) is a special issue in memory of Donald Francis McKenzie (1931–99), entitled *Printers and Readers*. It includes Sydney J. Shep, 'Book History and the Practice of Material Culture: The Example of Wai-te-Ata Press' (*BSANZB* 25[2001] 3–7) ; J.E. Traue, 'The Two Histories of the Book in New Zealand' (*BSANZB* 25[2001] 8–16); Noel Waite, 'Printers' Proof: The Dunedin Master Printers' Association 1889–1894' (*BSANZB* 25[2001] 17–42); Lydia Wevers, 'The Sociology of Travel Texts' (*BSANZB* 25[2001] 43–9); Roderick Cave, 'John Buckland Wright, Engraver and Book Illustrator' (*BSANZB* 25[2001] 50–66); MacDonald P. Jackson, 'Finding the Pattern: Peter Short's Shakespeare Quartos Revisited' (*BSANZB* 25[2001] 67–86); Keith Maslen, 'Puritan Printers in London:

The Dawes Family 1627–1737' (*BSANZB* 25[2001] 87–106); B.J. McMullin, 'John Hayes, Printer to the University of Cambridge 1669–1705, and *The Book of Common Prayer*' (*BSANZB* 25[2001] 107–16); Kathleen Coleridge, 'Sir William Dawes's *Sermons* of 1707, and Henry Hills the Pirate' (*BSANZB* 25[2001] 117–20); Ross Harvey, 'A Music Publisher's Response to Competition: Henry Playford, 1690–1702' (*BSANZB* 25[2001] 121–34); John C. Ross, 'Comedy Elevating its Voice': Tragic Intertextualities in Congreve's *The Double Dealer*' (*BSANZB* 25[2001] 135–44); Shef Rogers, 'Uncovering Wycherley's *Miscellaneous Remains*' (*BSANZB* 25[2001] 145–56); J.E. Traue, 'Don McKenzie: Books, Libraries and Scholarship' (*BSANZB* 25[2001] 165).

Moving from serials to monographic publications and essay collections, the latest reprint of Jacob Abbott's original 1855 publication, *The Harper Establishment*, features a new and informative introduction by Joel Myerson and Chris L. Nesmith that places the original work in its proper historical context. In presenting their views of the historical importance of the work, Myerson and Nesmith assert its valuable role in serving as the premier source on the basic concepts associated with nineteenth-century American bookmaking. Bibliophiles will be heartened to find that this latest edition of Abbott's work retains the numerous illustrations found in the original. In *The Kynoch Press: The Anatomy of a Printing House, 1876–1981*, Caroline Archer traces the rise and evolution of one of Britain's main printing houses. Based on archival research, and supported by personal accounts from surviving staff, Archer's work is a revealing look at what it meant and took to rise to prominence in the highly competitive printing industry. Additionally, illustrations and listings are present throughout the book, including illustrations of the typefaces held by Kynoch Press and a listing of these typefaces from 1920 to 1970.

Brown and Stalker, eds., *Getting Ready for the Nineteenth-Century: Strategies and Solutions for Rare Book and Special Collections Librarians: Proceedings of the Thirty-Ninth Annual Preconference of the Rare Books and Manuscripts Section*, features the following contributors and contents: William E. Brown Jr., 'Introduction'; John Y. Cole and Nancy E. Gwinn, 'Debating National Culture in Nineteenth-Century Washington: The Library of Congress and the Smithsonian Institution'; Alice Schreyer, 'Common Cause: Collaborating to Preserve Printed and Primary Source Materials'; Paul Conway, 'Preserving the Nineteenth Century: Challenges and Possibilities'; Abby Smith, 'Setting a National Agenda: A Collaborative Plan' ; James N. Green, 'Revaluing the Nineteenth Century'; James G. Neal, 'The Future of the Nineteenth Century: Preparing the Research Library for a Renaissance in Cultural and Historical Studies'; and Laura Stalker, 'Afterword'.

The latest instalment of the material text series published by the University of Pennsylvania Press is *Books and Readers in Early Modern England*, by Jennifer Andersen and Elizabeth Sauer. They have compiled a useful guide to the intellectual history of books, literature, and reading society in sixteenth- and seventeenth-century England. Divided into three sections, their work chronicles selectively the social context and preferences of sixteenth- and seventeenth-century authors and readers, while also discussing the publishing and book trade medium that brought them together.

In Gutjahr and Benton, eds., *Illuminating Letters: Typography and Literary Interpretation*, a further volume in the University of Massachusetts Press's enterprising Studies in Print Culture and the History of the Book series, the editors have brought together a series of essays challenging conventional views on typographic and visual page arrangement. In their 'Introduction: Reading the Invisible' they consider 'the relationship between a text's typography and its literary interpretation'. 'The Letter(s) of the Law: Four Centuries of Typography in the King James Bible' by Paul C. Gutjahr is the first chapter. The second chapter, by Sarah A. Kelen, discusses '*Peirs Plouhman* [*sic*] and the "formidable array of blackletter" in the Early Nineteenth Century'. Megan L. Benton's topic in chapter 3 is 'Typography and Gender: Remasculating the Modern Book', while in chapter 4 Beth McCoy writes on 'Perpetua(l) Notion: Typography, Economy, and Losing Nella Larsen'. Harlem Renaissance author Nella Larsen's novel *Passing* was first published by Knopf in 1929 and then republished in an entirely different font by Rutgers University Press in 1986; McCoy uses this typographical change to explore 'typography as a maker of meaning'. Samuel Richardson as author and printer is the focus of chapter 5, Steven R. Price's 'The Autograph Manuscript in Print: Samuel Richardson's Type Font Manipulation in *Clarissa*'. In chapter 6, Leon Jackson, '"The italics are mine": Edgar Allen Poe and the Semiotics of Print', argues that Poe 'was, in essence, fighting a rearguard action against the encroaching forces of industrialization'. In the final chapter, 'Graphic Text, Graphic Context: Interpreting Custom Fonts and Hands in Contemporary Comics', Gene Kannenberg, Jr., moves from Poe to the world of the cartoonist and the study of comics in America. *Illuminating Letters* is well supported with accompanying black and white illustrations of typography and spatial settings. All in all, this is a most challenging volume.

The publication of African American literature and criticism has been a hallmark of American literary studies for several decades. The appearance of *The Concise Oxford Companion to African American Literature*, by William L. Andrews, is a vitally relevant reference tool to present the wide-ranging subjects that have comprised African American literature and criticism. Encyclopedic in scope, this work contains over 400 entries ranging from at least half a page up to several pages for each entry. Entries deal with major authors, literary characters, and notable cultural figures from the African American community. Each entry is further supported by a brief citation of the source material used that may be consulted for further reading. In the *Dictionary of Literary and Dramatic Censorship in Tudor and Stuart England*, Dorothy Auchter has compiled a unique and highly resourceful reference source. Dealing with censorship in sixteenth- and seventeenth-century England, Auchter's entries are copiously detailed and include title of censored work, author, date of issue, date of censorship, the type of work, and the overriding offending issue that resulted in the work being censored and banned. Each entry also provides a running commentary regarding the historical context of the work and further reading suggestions. There are also a number of useful appendices, including the following: 'Classification of Censored Topics'; 'Prohibiting Unlicensed Printing of Scripture'; 'Queen Mary's Proclamation Against Wicked and Seditious Books'; 'Proclamation Against Seditious, Popish, and Puritanical Books and Pamphlets'; 'Proclamation to Restrain the Spreading of False News and Licentious Talking of Matters of State and Government'; 'The Judgment and Decree of the University of Oxford'; and the 'Refusal of the House of Commons to Renew the Licensing Act'. In *A Potencie of Life: Books in Society*, its distinguished editor Nicolas Barker brings together a series of essays by leading bibliographic scholars, each dealing with a unique topic related to the history of the book. Based on a series of lectures given at the William Andrews Clark Library, contributors and contents include: John Bidwell, 'American Papermakers and the Panic of 1819'; Mirjam M. Foot, 'Bookbinding and the History of Books'; Thomas R. Adams and Nicolas Barker, 'A New Model for the Study of the Book'; Lotte Hellinga, 'The Codex in the Fifteenth Century: A Manuscript and Print'; W.B. Carnochan, 'The 'Trade of Authorship' in Eighteenth Century Britain'; and Nicolas Barker, 'Libraries and the Mind of Man'.

Baron, Walsh and Scola, eds., *The Reader Revealed*, published in conjunction with the exhibition of the same title at the Folger Shakespeare Library, presents a view of books and reading in the sixteenth and seventeenth-centuries. A compilation of nine essays, selections include: Steven N. Zwicker, 'The Reader Revealed'; Sabrina Alcorn Baron, 'Red Ink and Black Letter: Reading Early Modern Authority'; Anthony Grafton, 'John Doe Reads Books of Magic'; Evelyn B. Tribble, 'Godly Reading: John Foxe's *Actes and Monuments* (1583)'; Arthur F. Marotti, 'Folger MSS V.a 89 and V.a 345: Reading Lyric Poetry in Manuscript'; Kevin Sharpe, 'Uncommonplaces? Sir William Drake's Reading Notes'; Jennifer Andersen, 'Posh Print and the Polemicization of William Dugdale's *Monasticon Anglicanum* (1655)'; Anna Battigelli, "To Conclude Alright Within Ourselves': Narcissus Luttrell and the Burden of the Protestant Reader, 1678–88'; William H. Sherman, '"Rather soiled by use": Renaissance Readers and Modern Collectors'. In *Five Hundred Years of Book Design*, Alan Bartram reviews and analyses books generally considered classic examples of quality design and production. Bartram pulls no punches in his analysis, and resolutely argues that the modern emphasis on readability and function represents a tremendous improvement in the practice of bookmaking.

In her first book, *Remember Me to Harlem: The Letters of Langston Hughes and Carl Van Vechten, 1925–1964*, Emily Bernard has collected the correspondence between Car Van Vechten and Langston Hughes. The result is a series of exchanges that reveals not only the complex and subtle relationship between the two, but also provides a picture of the vibrant and frenetic Harlem Renaissance and the figures that dominated both its epicentre and its fringes. The latest volume in the Black Studies series published by the Edwin Mellen Press, Bennett, ed., *An Annotated Bibliography of Mary McLeod Bethune's Chicago Defender Columns*, presents a vivid portrayal of the journalistic life's work of Mary McLeod. Largely completed just on the cusp of the emerging national civil rights movement in America, what some might refer to as the Brown era, her work is organized into twenty-one general categories. Each entry contains an abstract, a listing of citations in each specific category, and excerpts from that category. Categories include the following: women; integration; youth; Bethune herself; civil rights; war and the military; citizenship; 'Recognitions'—people, action, ideas, places, events, days; 'Called by the Spirit'; freedom; the Negro press; religion and Christianity; democracy; 'International, Peace'; Bethune–Cookman College, 'Negro People—The Race'; labour and economics; the National Council of Negro Women; communism; social ills; education. An index is included.

The Crime Files series, edited by Clive Bloom and published by Palgrave, has issued two recent additions to its growing collection of works devoted to detective fiction. In *The Noir Thriller*, Lee Horsley has compiled an impressive bibliography related to the continued popularity of the noir thriller in popular culture. Of particular noteworthy mention is the bibliography dealing with primary and secondary sources. In *Contemporary American Crime Fiction*, compiled by Hans Bertens and Theo D'Haen, readers are presented with a goldmine of commentary regarding authors whose works were particularly notable and popular in the 1990s.

The most recent edition of E.C. Bigmore and C.W.H. Wyman's classic, *A Bibliography of Printing: With Notes and Illustrations*, issued by Oak Knoll Press and the British Library, includes the original text and illustrations, and also contains a newly added comprehensive index regarding titles, subjects, and authors, as well as a new introduction by Henry Morris. In *Material Modernism: The Politics of the Page*, George Bornstein cogently argues that the physical forms of books are themselves intrinsically important, and with this view, he re-examines the work of such notable authors as Yeats, Pound, Brooks and Joyce, and presents a thought-provoking argument. Brake, Bell and Finkelstein, eds., *Nineteenth-Century Media and the Construction of Identities*, assembles an impressive collection of essays that use both theoretical and empirical approaches to discuss the development and rise of a mass culture in the nineteenth century. Focusing mostly on periodicals and printed matter, the work is divided into five main sections. The essays are individualistic enough to serve as stand-alone pieces of scholarship and information, while read together they serve to demonstrate the unique diversity of the emerging nineteenth-century press. Contributors and contents include: Kate Jackson, 'George Newnes and the "Loyal Tit-Bitties": Editorial Identity and Textual Interaction in *Tit-Bits*'; Richard Salmon, 'A Simulacrum of Power: Intimacy and Abstraction in the Rhetoric of the New Journalism'; Kate Campbell, 'Journalistic Discourses and Constructions of Modern Knowledge'; Margaret Linley, 'A Centre That Would Not Hold: Annuals and Cultural Democracy'; Andrew King, 'A Paradigm of Reading the Victorian Penny Weekly: Education of the Gaze and *The London Journal*'; Michael Hancher, 'From Street Ballad to Penny Magazine: "March of Intellect" in the Butchering Line'; Brian E. Maidment, '"Penny" Wise, "Penny" Foolish? Popular Periodicals and the "March of Intellect" in the 1820s and 1830s'; Lynne Warren, '"Women in Conference": Reading the Correspondence Columns in *Woman*, 1890–1910'; Robert L. Patten, 'Dickens as Serial Author: A Case of Multiple Identities'; Alexis Easley, 'Authorship, Gender and Power in Victorian Culture: Harriet Martineau and the Periodical Press'; Joanne Shattock, 'Work for Women: Margaret Oliphant's Journalism'; Meri-Jane Rochelson, 'Israel Zwangwill's Early Journalism and the Formation of an Anglo-Jewish Literary Identity'; Amy Beth Aronson, 'America's First Feminist Magazine: Transforming the Popular to the Political'; Anne Humpherys, 'Coming Apart: The British Newspaper Press and the Divorce Court'; Mark W. Turner, '*Saint Pauls Magazine* and the Project of Masculinity'; Margaret Beetham, 'The Agony Aunt, the Romancing Uncle and the Family of Empire: Defining the Sixpenny Reading Public in the 1890s'; Laurel Brake, '"Gay Discourse" and *The Artist and Journal of Home Culture*'; Leslie Williams, 'Bad Press: Thomas Campbell Foster and British Reportage on the Irish Famine, 1845–1849'; Aled Jones, 'The Nineteenth-Century Media and Welsh Identity'; David Finkelstein, '"Long and Intimate Connections": Constructing a Scottish Identity for *Blackwood's Magazine*'; Dean de la Motte, 'Making News, Making Readers: The Creation of the Modern Newspaper Public in Nineteenth-Century France'; Toni Johnson-Woods, 'The Virtual Reading

Communities of the *London Journal*, the *New York Ledger* and the *Australian Journal*; the index is by Drusilla Calvert.

A collection of nineteen essays dealing with the historical practices of punctuation, Bray and Henry's *Ma(r)king the Text: The Presentation of Meaning on the Literary Page* had its original impetus in a 1998 Cambridge conference dealing with the same topic. The overriding theme of the essays is the argument that punctuating a text is a form of 'marking' that lends nuanced and more overt meanings to the overall tone of any work, altering it and shaping it in a multitude of ways. Authors whose texts are discussed include Austen, Castiglione, Richard Edwards, George Eliot, Alasdair Gray, Keats, Tom Robertson, Shakespeare, Charlotte Smith, Stendhal, Sterne, and James Whistler.

The history of the American bookplate and efforts related to its collection and design is the subject of William E. Butler's *American Bookplates*. Profiled are over 140 American bookplate designers, as well as more than 800 American artists of the bookplate. Butler also discusses how to form a bookplate collection and how to join societies devoted to the topic of the American bookplate. In *The Plays of Shakespeare: A Thematic Guide*, Victor L. Cahn attempts to identify recurring themes that appear throughout Shakespeare's canon with an eye to relating the relevance of these themes to contemporary life. Themes developed and presented include acting, appearance versus reality, clerics, commoners, cynicism, divine right, fate, fathers and daughters, fidelity, fools, forgiveness, gender, generations, and honour. In Cain, ed., *The Poetry of Mildmay Fane, Second Earl of Westmorland*, the editor has shepherded over 500 recently discovered poems by Mildmay Fane, second earl of Westmorland, written between 1625 and 1665, into one convenient collection. In doing so, he provides early modern literature scholars with a valuable new resource while the social and political content of Fane's poetry presents cultural and political historians with an equally valuable resource. A.M. Challinor's *The Achievement of Francis Bacon: A Complete Subject and Author Index to Baconiana, 1886–1999*, represents a masterful and major accomplishment regarding indexing the works by and about Bacon. Covering the period from 1886 to 1999, it represents a thorough and comprehensive effort to fill in gaps left by prior indexing attempts, while also making all manner of Baconiana accessible to current and future researchers. Serious scholars and those with a general interest in Bacon will want to become familiar with this pioneering work. In *Censorship in Canadian Literature*, Mark Cohen posits the provocative thesis of viewing censorship as a practice of judgement and less an overt tool of oppression by authoritative bodies. Cohen develops his idea by examining the views and reactions to censorship of five Canadian writers, including Margaret Atwood, Beatrice Culleton, Timothy Findley, Margaret Lawrence, and Marlene Novrbese.

De Grazia and Wells, eds., *The Cambridge Companion to Shakespeare*, contains over nineteen essays devoted to the historical, literary, and performance-oriented aspects of Shakespeare's work. It contains numerous illustrations and a considerable reading list, as well as an informative biographical essay. Also included is useful information related to online internet resources devoted to Shakespeare and his body of work.

Davies, ed., *Incunabula: Studies in Fifteenth-Century Printed Books Presented to Lotte Hellinga*, contains an impressive array of papers by friends and colleagues of Hellinga, covering topics as diverse as library and printing history, binding, collecting, and illustration. The essays range widely from highly individual accounts of specific printers to more thematic studies encompassing the book trade itself. Readers interested in wide-ranging and provocative works dealing with rare and hermetic book studies would be well advised to become familiar with this collection, which treats its subject with a scholarly respect. Contributors include Luigi Balsamo, Elly Cockx-Indestege, Margaret Lane Ford, John Flood, Gerard van Thienen, Piero Scapecchi and Paola Veneziana, A.K. Offenberg, Dennis Rhodes, Paul Needham, Roland Folter, Georges Colin, Anthony Hobson, Mirjam Foot, Lilian Armstrong, Ursula Baurmeister, A.S.G. Edwards, J.B. Trapp, Peter Amelung, Julian Martin Abad, James Walsh, and Kristian Jensen.

Oxford University Press continues its tradition of publishing quality reference books with the appearance of *The Oxford Dictionary of Allusions*. A co-effort by editors Andrew Delahunty, Sheila Dignen, and Penny Stock, *The Oxford Dictionary of Allusions* contains a list of themes and special entries, along with a useful index. Entries are arranged thematically in the style of a thesaurus and are further defined by referring to passages of literary text that demonstrate their origin and use. Dobson and Wells, eds., *The Oxford Companion to Shakespeare*, represents an encyclopedic approach to all things Shakespeare-related that general readers and scholars will find helpful and useful. The work contains over 3,000 entries and over 100 photographs. Additionally, major review articles are included regarding Shakespeare's theatrical works.

Scholars and devotees of the life and work of Theodore Dreiser will be pleased with the collection of his early magazine and freelance work contained in Hakutani, ed., *Theodore Dreiser: Art, Music and Literature, 1897–1902*. The editor's compilation allows Dreiser's quick-witted observations on the cultural milieu of his day to shine clearly through. Also, period illustrations and Hakutani's notes regarding the biographical details of the individuals Dreiser profiled add clarity for students and those not too familiar with the period.

Emerson et al., eds., *The Culture of the Book in the Scottish Enlightenment: An Exhibition*, is a collection of essays based on the materials in the University of Toronto's Thomas Fisher Library dealing with the history of the book in Scotland, with a particular emphasis on the eighteenth century. For researchers, a useful annotated list of texts held at the library can be found at the end of the text. The essays in the volume are wide-ranging and deal with such diverse topics as the library catalogue of Archibald Campbell, third duke of Argyll, the publication history of David Hume's *Essays and Treatises on Several Subjects*, and the marginalia of John Robinson, professor of natural philosophy at the University of Edinburgh. In *Feminism: Critical Concepts in Literary and Cultural Studies*, volumes 1–4, Mary Evans seeks to firmly root feminism in the intellectual history of modern Europe and introduce basic concepts, ideas, and works representative of the feminist literary canon to readers with varied levels of interest. Each volume includes a useful chronological table of reprinted articles and chapters to assist readers in familiarizing themselves with significant feminist works while aiding further research efforts.

In Fernihough, ed., *The Cambridge Companion to D.H. Lawrence*, leading scholars present new perspectives on Lawrence and his work. Included are useful listings of primary and secondary sources, as well as an unannotated bibliography. In a major achievement, *The Rivers of America: A Descriptive Bibliography*, Carol

Fitzgerald has compiled a meticulously researched bibliography of the sixty-five titles published between 1937 and 1974 regarding America's major river systems. An excellent reference source, Fitzgerald's bibliography is also noteworthy for the biographies of the series' sixty authors, fifty-three illustrators, and eight series editors. The entries not only deal with the sixty-five titles that comprise the series, but also cover the over 400 printings of those titles. Oak Knoll Press is to be congratulated for publishing such a delightfully produced and important descriptive bibliography.

In *Graffiti and the Writing Arts of Early Modern England*, Juliet Fleming explores previously unknown, neglected, and discarded writing practices outside the traditional venues of print and manuscript formats. Highly unique and original, Fleming's work serves as a cogent reminder that what is often considered worthy of preservation and historical study typically stems from the vantage point of the observer. In Pearson, ed., *For the Love of the Binding*, a compilation of essays presented to Mirjam Foot, themes connected with placing bookbinding in its historical context are discussed. Essays include: Robin Myers, 'Mirjam Foot'; David Pearson, 'Bookbinding in Cambridge in the Second Half of the Sixteenth Century'; Nicholas Pickwood, 'Tacketed Bindings: A Hundred Years of European Bookbinding'; Marianne Tidcombe, 'The Mysterious Mr. de Santy'; Anthony Hobson, 'Plaquette and Medallion Bindings: A Second Supplement'; Nicholas Barker, 'Some Unrecorded Sixteenth-Century French Bookbindings'; and Lotte Hellinga, 'Fragments Found in Bindings and their Role as Bibliographic Evidence'.

In Fargnoli and Golay, eds., *William Faulkner A to Z*, readers will find a convenient and detailed source regarding the life and work of Faulkner. Material includes entries regarding Faulkner's novels, short fiction, poetry, essays and reviews, as well as personal biographical information related to Faulkner's family, the reception of his work, and the events and issues that influenced that work. Ian Gibson, *The Erotomaniac: The Secret Life of Henry Spencer Ashbee*, relying extensively on Ashbee's diaries and family archives, argues persuasively that Ashbee may have been the secret author of the infamous *My Secret Life*, a work that narrates in detail the sexual proclivities, habits, and liaisons of an unnamed Victorian gentleman. Gibson has produced a well-argued account that provides insights into the Victorian age and its dual-minded and repressive approach to sexuality and desire. The work contains numerous references and an informative bibliography, as well as illustrations. In *Family Business: Selected Letters Between a Father and Son*, Michael Schumacher has provided a unique and revealing portrait not only of the relationship between Allen and Louis Ginsberg, but also of a nation in social and economic flux. Representing the correspondence between father and son spanning over thirty years, Schumacher's work is a must-have for those seeking new material on Allen Ginsberg and the social context of his work.

The expanded and revised version of *American Watermarks, 1690–1835*, by Thomas L. Gravell, George Miller and Elizabeth Walsh yields over 300 new watermark entries which, along with the 700 contained in the previous edition, have all been digitally enhanced for clarity and better identification. As a piece of concise and specialized scholarship, Gravell and Miller's work remains the pre-eminent source regarding the type and history of American watermarks and their production.

Hadfield, ed., *Literature and Censorship in Renaissance England*, brings together the efforts of leading scholars of censorship in sixteenth- and seventeenth-century

England. The views contributed represent wide-ranging and diverse conclusions. The work includes an extensive primary and secondary listing of selective sources, as well as an unannotated bibliography. In *Texts, Ideas, and the Classics*, S.J. Harrison brings together scholars who range widely in their views but agree on the central tenet that traditional classical scholarship and modern ideas regarding literary theories should both be utilized to interpret classical literature texts. In *The Theory and Criticism of Virtual Texts: An Annotated Bibliography, 1988–1999*, Lory Hawkes, Christina Murphy, and Joe Law annotate works on the history, theoretical underpinnings, and critique of virtual texts. They focus their efforts on the last decade, a period in which the internet has emerged as the dominant form of global communication. The bibliography is divided into fifteen sections, each representing a dominant mode of research and critique. These include: history and development; theories and critiques of hypertext; visualization studies; information design; discourse studies; textual analysis; computer-mediated communication; computer-mediated education; research, service, and scholarly projects; professional concerns; (cyber)cultural studies; gender and sexuality studies; literacy studies; legal and political issues; and future trends. There is a detailed index.

Getting at the Author: Reimagining Books and Reading in the Age of American Realism, by Barbara Hochman, is an analysis of the motivations of the adherents of the American literary realist movement to objective storytelling that focuses on the shifting of the traditional relationship between reader and author that mirrored the contemporary shifting of American society in the late nineteenth century. Hochman convincingly argues that this literary response to the shift in the traditional make-up of American society and culture created the now familiar rift in American literature between serious and popular reading cultures.

In *Maxine Hong Kingston: A Critical Companion*, E.D. Huntley provides a critical study of Kingston's three main prose works, focusing on the talk story narrative device utilized by Kingston. Huntley begins by providing an introduction to Kingston's life and placing her literary output in the context of the Asian American literary tradition. Huntley should be commended both for this, and for highlighting the general appeal of Kingston's work for readers with diverse backgrounds and experiences. The balance of the book examines each of her three main prose works, and a useful bibliography and index are provided as well. David Norbrook, professor of English at the University of Maryland, presents the seventeenth-century epic poem *Order and Disorder* in its entirety for the first time in print. Norbrook attributes the authorship of the epic poem to one of the seventeenth century's well-known and prolific female writers, the republican Lucy Hutchinson. His efforts are a welcome addition to the field of seventeenth-century poetry, as well as to the field of early modern women's writing. In the fifth volume of the Print Network series, Isaac and McKay, eds., *The Moving Market: Continuity and Change in the Book Trade*, brings together seventeen contributions from scholars regarding the intricacies of the provincial book trade in England. Contributions include: Jeffrey Smith, 'Books and Culture in Late Eighteenth- and Early Nineteenth-Century Newcastle'; Philip Henry Jones, 'The First World War and Welsh-Language Publishing'; John Hinks, 'The Beginning of the Book Trade in Leicester'; David Hounslow, 'A Moving Market: The Influence of London Books of Street Cries on Provincial Editions to *c.*1830'; Richard B. Sher with Hugh Amory, 'From Scotland to the Strand: the Genesis of Andrew Millar's Bookselling Career';

Iain Beavan, '"What Constitutes the Crime Which it is Your Pleasure to Punish so Mercilessly?": Scottish Booksellers' Societies in the Nineteenth Century'; Wallace Kirsop, 'From Curry's to Collins Street, or How a Dubliner Became the "Melbourne Mudie"'; Michael Powell and Terry Wyke, '"Aristotle to a Wery Tall Man": Selling Secondhand Books in Manchester in the 1830s'; Diana Dixon, 'New Town, New Newspapers: The Development of the Newspaper Press in Nineteenth-Century Middlesborough'; Lisa Peters, 'The Troubled History of a Welsh Newspaper Publishing Company: The North Wales Constitutional Newspaper Company Limited, 1869–1878'; Barry McKay, 'John Atkinson's "Lottery" Book of 1809: John Locke's Theory of Education Comes to Washington'; Peter Isaac, '*Splendide mendax*: Publishing Landscape Illustrations of the Bible'; Maureen Bell, 'Reading in Seventeenth-Century Derbyshire: The Wheatcrofts and their Books'; Janet Phipps, 'Book Availability in Ipswich over the Years'; and Sydney J. Shep, 'Mapping the Migration of Paper: Historical Geography and New Zealand Print Culture'. The essays are topically and geographically diverse and represent views on the provincial book trade from the seventeenth to the nineteenth centuries. While they are diverse in terms of subject, locale, and period, all serve to further establish that the provincial book trade was a thriving and autonomous enterprise that stood on its own merits, rather than simply a smaller and marginal part of a trade centred in cities such as Cambridge, London, and Oxford. The collection also reinforces the notion that the study of the history of the book trade yields valuable historical and cultural insights into how reading and culture are historically formed and transmitted to later generations. It also contains useful and interesting information regarding the historical role of book illustrating, as well as the evolving relationship between authors, illustrators, and publishers.

In *Marginalia: Readers Writing in Books*, H.J. Jackson provides a groundbreaking, thoroughly engrossing, and sometimes humorous account on the common practice of note-writing in the margin of books. Her efforts cover a wide range of annotated books, and she seeks to classify and categorize the types and forms of marginalia in an attempt to illuminate the psychological motivations of the reader. Jackson's solid work strongly reinforces the notion that reading is an interactive and emotion-laden process. Her superb efforts strongly suggest that the act of creating marginalia represents an attempt at communication between the reader and the author, between the reader and the self, and between the present reader and future readers.

In an *Encyclopedia of American War Literature*, Philip K. Jason and Mark A. Graves have compiled a unique and long overdue source that brings together the diverse American literary treatments chronicling the consequences of war. The bulk of material contained in this volume represents selections from fiction, poetry, and drama. Entries are arranged alphabetically, and sample topic entries include African American war literature, the Civil War, women's diaries in the Civil War, the First World War, Indian captivity narratives, the Korean War, revolutionary war, the Spanish–American War, the Spanish Civil War, and the Vietnam War.

Joseph Sheridan Le Fanu's *The Cock and Anchor* is reprinted in a fine new edition by Jan Jedrzejewski. Jedrzejewski's efforts bring Le Fanu's engaging tale of mid-eighteenth-century Dublin back to the forefront of Victorian Irish literature studies. Updated with new material, the second edition of Ben Jonson's *Plays and Masques*, edited by Richard Harp, is divided into three main parts: the first includes the texts of the plays and masques; the second deals with the context of Jonson's work; and the third deals with criticisms of his work. This new edition features nine new commentaries by Jonson scholars, including Anne Barton, Ian Donaldson, Robert C. Evans, D.J. Gordon, Richard Hays, Leah S. Marcus, John Mulryan, Stephen Orgel, and Robert Watson. In *From Baltimore to Bohemia: The Letters of H.L. Mencken and George Sterling*, S.T. Joshi has compiled a useful book for Mencken admirers and scholars by making accessible the correspondence between Mencken and largely forgotten Californian poet George Sterling. Apart from providing revealing personal glimpses of both men, the tone and content of the letters help illuminate the American era between the First and Second World Wars. In *A Historical Guide to Edgar Allan Poe*, J. Gerald Kennedy has added a valuable and useful contribution to the growing field of Poe studies. Contributors and contents include: J. Gerald Kennedy, 'Introduction: Poe in Our Time'; J. Gerald Kennedy, 'Edgar Allan Poe, 1809–1849: A Brief Biography'; Terence Whalen, 'Poe and the American Publishing Industry'; David Leverenz, 'Spanking the Master: Mind–Body Crossings in Poe's Sensationalism'; Leland S. Person, 'Poe and Nineteenth-Century Gender Constructions'; Louis A. Renza, 'Poe and the Issue of American Privacy'; Scott Peeples, 'Bibliographical Essay: Major Editions and Landmarks of Poe Scholarship', and includes an illustrated chronology.

The ninth volume of *The Cambridge History of Literary Criticism*, edited by Christa Knellwolf and Christopher Norris, compiles a wide range of commentary on twentieth-century literary criticism. Each development is presented in its historical context with an emphasis on critically examining the historical and philosophical approaches that have dominated literary criticism in the twentieth century. There is a detailed but unannotated primary and secondary bibliography that complements the two main sections of the book dealing with the topics of history and Marxism and post-Marxism. This is a solid work and highly recommended.

In the useful *Shakespeare and Minorities: An Annotated Bibliography, 1970–2000*, Parvin Kujoory brings together over 900 items from a wide variety of disciplines, the central criterion for inclusion being items that fall into three broad schools of literary criticism: feminism, new historicism, and cultural materialism. Following these parameters, Kujoory has divided her bibliography into six chapters reflecting various aspects of minority group status. These are, in order of precedence, women, Blacks, Jews, homosexuals, slaves, and 'other' (defined as the 'oppressed' or the 'underprivileged'). Entries included represent books, articles, book chapters, reviews, and critical correspondence from disciplines such as anthropology, history, literature, philosophy, psychology, and sociology. The work contains both a subject and a name index to assist in locating entries.

Leitch, ed., *The Norton Anthology of Theory and Criticism*, brings together in one volume some of the best scholarship regarding literary theory and criticism from the ancient world up to the present. Richly annotated with informative headnotes, this volume will find a ready audience for its eclectic contents. Readers will greet the concise but information-packed *Literature Lover's Companion: The Essential Reference to the World's Greatest Writers—Past and Present, Popular and Classical* with great enthusiasm. Spanning over 3,000 years of published writing, with over 10,000 novels, plays, poetry and short story collections profiled, this A–Z source will delight serious scholars and the general interested reader alike. Useful indexes aid user navigation by author, period, nationality, and genre.

In *John Quinn: Selected Irish Writers from his Library*, Janis and Richard Londraville present a selection, by no means complete, of the Irish writers that John Quinn collected in his personal library and whose financial largesse over the years helped turn literary ambitions into literary careers. In *A History of the Book in Australia, 1891–1945: A National Culture in a Colonised Market*, Lyons and Arnold, eds., have compiled a series of essays and case-studies that trace the development of Australian writing, publication, editing, distribution, libraries, and reading habits from the 1890s to the end of the Second World War. Much of the commentary in the book focuses on the distancing of Australia from its heavily British influence in all manner of areas related to books and reading. The result is an informative and highly scholarly read that is recommended reading.

In *The Year's Work in Critical and Cultural Theory*, volumes 8 and 9, covering work published in 1998 and 1999 respectively, editor Kate McGowan has compiled an excellent source regarding essays devoted to bibliographic work. Contributors and contents for volume 8 include: David Walker, 'Critical Theory: General'; Ann-Marie Smith, 'Psychoanalysis'; Patrick Williams, 'Colonial Discourse, Postcolonial Theory'; Angela Werndly, 'Cultural Studies: General'; Jeffrey Walsh, 'Media Studies'; Hillegonda C. Rietveld, 'Popular Culture'; Tara Brabazon, 'Australian Popular Culture and Media Studies'; David Buckley, 'Popular Music'; Ian Saunders, 'Virtual Cultures'; Susan Purdie, 'Film and Film Theory'; Angelica Michelis, 'Art Histories and Visual Cultural Studies'; Robin Trotter, 'Cultural Policy'; Kate Cregan et al., 'Aboriginal Identity, Art and Culture'; Vijay Mishra, 'Multiculturalism'. Volume 9 includes: Bella Adams, 'Critical Theory: General'; Kate McGowan, 'Feminisms'; Glyn Daly, 'Marxism(s) and Postmarxism(s)'; Patrick Williams and Nahem Yousaf, 'Colonial Discourse, Postcolonial Theory'; Simon Malpas and Kate McGowan, 'Postmodernism'; Angela Werndly, 'Cultural Studies: General'; Hillegonda C. Rietveld, 'Popular Culture'; Tara Brabazon, 'Australian Popular Culture and Media Studies'; David Buckley, 'Popular Music'; Ian Saunders, 'Virtual Cultures'; Susan Purdie, 'Film Theory'; Angelica Michelis, 'Art Histories and Visual Culture Studies'; Vijay Mishra, 'Multiculturalism'; Robin Trotter, 'Cultural Policy'.

In *The First Quarto of Othello*, Scott McMillin argues that the earliest version of the 1622 *Othello* represents a written account based on cuts and actors' interpolations during performance, all the effort of an anonymous chronicler who wrote down the text as it was being performed. Besides serving as window on how *Othello* was spoken during the seventeenth century, McMillin's compelling thesis also has ramifications for general Shakespeare textual studies and for those interested in the early English theatre. The book also contains an introduction, a quarto text, and collation and textual notes.

In *Sigrid Undset in America: An Annotated Bibliography and Research Guide*, Marie Maman admirably fills a gap in studies devoted to Norwegian author Sigrid Undset. Maman's bibliography is divided into two parts, the first dealing with primary sources and the second with secondary sources. The first part includes novels set in the Middle Ages, contemporary novels, and articles and chapters in books; the second includes biographies, literary criticism, dissertations at American universities, articles about Sigrid Undset in the United States, 1940–5, correspondence and archival material, internet resources, and recent studies published in Scandinavia. An appendix listing the American edition of Undset's novels is also included.

Alastair Mann's *The Scottish Book Trade, 1500–1720: Print Commerce and Print Control in Early Modern Scotland*, provides an informative accounting of the Scottish book trade and the political and economic circumstances that affected that trade. Political, economic, and social historians, as well as scholars of book publishing, will find his efforts a useful read. Included are appendices regarding a list of copyrights granted from 1540 to 1708, a listing of officially banned books from the 1570s to the 1700s, and financial information relating to Scottish book traders. In *Critical Times: The History of the Times Literary Supplement*, Derwent May provides a cogent and revealing history of one of the most important literary journals. Based largely—almost exclusively—on the files of the *TLS* itself, May's clearly written account profiles the many famous personalities who either reviewed or were reviewed in its pages, including T.S. Eliot, Aldous Huxley, Philip Larkin, George Orwell, Ezra Pound, Virginia Woolf, and many more. Contents include: 'The Beginnings'; 'The First Year: 1902'; 'Edwardian Peace: 1903–1907'; 'Storm Clouds Over the Empire: 1908–13'; 'War and Independence: 1914–18'; 'Northcliffe Passes, Eliot Arrives: 1919–1922'; 'Peace Among the Vile Bodies: 1923–29'; 'Richmond's Twilight Years: 1930–1937'; 'D.L. Murray Faces the Dictators: 1938–45'; 'Stanley Morison's Hard Read: 1945–47'; 'The World Pours In: 1948–58'; 'The Gaiety of Nations: 1959–74'; 'Coming Out: 1974–81'; 'The Trouble with Theory: 1982–90'; 'Debates and Deaths: 1991–2001'. There is a detailed index.

A new edition of Thomas Middleton's *Michaelmas Term*, edited by Gail Kern Paster and published by Manchester University Press, was published in 2001. This new edition of Middleton's satiric commentary on early modern London contains detailed explanations of the play's bawdy dialogue and will serve as a useful tool for students and scholars of Middleton and the theatrical culture of early modern London.

The Routledge 'Who's Who' series has added two more volumes to its expanding publications list. In *Who's Who in Contemporary Women's Writing*, editor Jane Eldridge Miller has assembled an impressive collection of over 1,000 entries by international contributors. International and contemporary in its coverage and focus, this volume serves as an excellent general introduction to contemporary female authors. In the *Who's Who of Twentieth-Century Novelists*, Tim Woods has compiled a useful reference source on largely post-1945 writers. Selections are international in scope, although the work is slanted towards English-speaking countries. Authors of popular fiction such as science fiction, romance, mystery, and thrillers are present. A useful appendix of literary prizes is available at the end of the book.

The topic of Middle English poetry is given thorough consideration in *Middle English Poetry: Texts and Traditions: Essays in Honour of Derek Pearsall*, compiled by A.J. Minnis. Contributors and contents include: Christopher Cannon, 'The Unchangeable Word: The Dating of Manuscripts and the History of English'; Estelle Stubbs, 'Clare Priory, the London Austin Friars and Manuscripts of the *Canterbury Tales*'; Elizabeth Solopova, 'The Survival of Chaucer's Punctuation in the Early Manuscripts of the *Canterbury Tales*'; Charlotte C. Morse, 'What the *Clerk's Tale* Suggests about Manly and Rickert's Edition—and the *Canterbury*

Tales Project'; Siân Echard, 'Dialogues and Monologues: Manuscript Representations of the Conversation of the *Confessio Amantis*'; Kate Harris, 'The Longleat House Extracted Manuscript of Gower's *Confessio Amantis*'; John Scattergood, 'Iste liber constat Johanni Mascy: Dublin, Trinity College, MS 155'; Carole M. Meale, 'Romance and its Anti-Type? *The Turnament of Totenham*, the Carnivalesque, and Popular Culture'; S.S. Hussey, 'Langland the Outsider'; Kathryn Kerby-Fulton, 'Langland in his Working Clothes?: Scribe D, Authorial Loose Revision Material, and the Nature of Scribal Intervention'; J.A. Burrow, 'Scribal Mismetring'; John J. Thompson, 'Reading Lydgate in Post-Reformation England'; Martha W. Driver, 'Medievalizing the Classical Past in Pierpont Morgan MS M 876'; Linne R. Mooney, 'Scribes and Booklets of Trinity College, Cambridge, Manuscripts R.3.19 and R.3.21'; A.S.G. Edwards, 'The Middle English Translation of Claudian's *De Consulatu Stilichonis*'; Julia Boffey, '"Twenty Thousand More": Some Fifteenth- and Sixteenth-Century Responses to *The Legend of Good Women*'.

The newly revised *Penguin Roget's College Thesaurus in Dictionary Form*, edited by Philip Morehead, contains over 1,500 new entries, including contemporary colloquial and slang terminology. Categories contained include brief descriptions, antonyms, informal and colloquial use, slang, and related words, as well as quotes and phrases used in their historical and modern forms. In *The Public Face of Modernism: Little Magazines, Audiences, and Reception, 1905–1920*, Mark Morrison convincingly argues that lesser-known American and British magazines reflected wider social realities in often unexpected ways, but failed to achieve mass appeal in terms of circulation owing to advertising restrictions and the difficulty of selling avant-garde aesthetics to a mainstream reading public. In Myers, Harris and Mandelbrote, eds., *Libraries and the Book Trade: The Formation of Collections from the Sixteenth to the Twentieth Century*, bibliographical scholars discuss the evolving relationship between those involved in the book trade and those involved with libraries, from the sixteenth century to the beginning of circulation libraries in the early nineteenth century. Essays are contributed by Leslie Morris, Esther Potter, Keith Manley, and Julian Roberts, among others.

With the publication of her *Shakespeare's Unorthodox Biography: New Evidence of an Authorship Problem* Diana Price enters the fray in the debate over whether the historical Shakespeare wrote the many works attributed to him. Readers will want to examine Price's introduction of new evidence and determine for themselves the validity of her conclusions. Marilyn Randall's *Pragmatic Plagiarism: Authorship, Profit, and Power*, offers a thought-provoking and challenging thesis regarding the notion of plagiarism and the evolving concepts that define what it is and how to identify it. Relying heavily on Foucault's concepts related to authorship, Randall posits the notion that accusations of plagiarism are often not objectively defined, but represent a power struggle often initiated by those concerned with protecting profit and prestige. Structurally, Randall's book is divided into three sections: 'Authoring Plagiarism', 'Reading Plagiarism', and 'Power Plagiarism'. Randall's thesis is sure to generate much debate and deserves a wide reading.

The latest edition of Warren Roberts's *A Bibliography of D.H. Lawrence* continues as an unsurpassed guide regarding Lawrence's literary output. This latest edition, the third, was revised and carried through to publication by Paul Poplawski following Robert's death in 1998. While every section has been expanded, like its predecessors, this edition is divided into six sections: 'Books and Pamphlets'; 'Contributions to Books'; 'Contributions to Periodicals'; 'Translations'; 'Manuscripts'; plus an important section dealing with books and pamphlets about Lawrence. The latest edition also has most useful appendices and an extensive index. In Rollyson and Paddock, eds., *Herman Melville A to Z*, readers will find a convenient and detailed source regarding the life and work of Melville. Drawing freely on useful earlier works, material contained includes entries regarding Melville's novels, short fiction, poetry, essays and reviews, as well as personal biographical information related to Melville's family, the reception of his work, and the events and issues that influenced that work.

As long-standing personalities of significance in the antiquarian book trade, Leona Rostenberg and Madeleine Stern have written a highly personal and poignant account of their friendship, relationship, and lives spanning over half a century in *Bookends: Two Women, One Enduring Friendship*. Readers who were captivated by their account in their prior publication, *Old Books, Rare Friends*, will want to seek out this decidedly unique and colourful presentation of their personal lives and insights into the antiquarian book world. In *Books have their Fates* Rostenberg and Stern present a less personal but thoroughly professional account as they follow the path of thirty outstanding books from their inception through their evolution into the realm of the unique and classic. While neither stoically scholarly nor revealing to a significant degree, the narrative and the light which the authors shed on both the books and the people who write, read, and enjoy them will be appreciated by readers.

In the latest instalment of the Crime File series published by Palgrave and edited by Clive Bloom, Susan Roland has compiled a valuable resource regarding the works of six seminal authors in the detective fiction genre. In *From Agatha Christie to Ruth Rendell: British Women Writers in Detective and Crime Fiction*, Rowland covers the work of Agatha Christie, Dorothy Sayers, Margery Allingham, Ngaio Marsh, P.D. James, and Ruth Rendell/Barbara Vine. Analysing over forty important novels, Rowland's comparative work provides key insights for enthusiastic fans and scholars of the detective fiction genre. A useful appendix is located at the end of the work detailing work by each author. Also included are interviews with Ruth Rendell/Barbara Vine and P.D. James.

Using both traditional and electronic sources, Marie-Laure Ryan argues, in *Narrative as Virtual Reality: Immersion and Interactivity in Literature and Electronic Media*, that contemporary culture is driven by the idea of interactivity. The work echoes themes in modern literary studies that interaction between reader and text results in a creative process that informs the meaning of the text. Ryan's challenging work is divided into four main parts: 'Virtuality', 'The Poetics of Immersion', 'The Poetics of Interactivity', and 'Reconciling Immersion and Interactivity'. Numerous figures and tables are presented throughout.

Lewis O. Saum provides a valuable work on the life and times of journalist Eugene Field (1850–95) in *Eugene Field and his Age*. Saum's work presents a vivid picture of the man and his times and draws out well the themes and energy that Field reflected in his columns regarding the promise and ascendancy of America at the close of the nineteenth century. In the paper version *British Wood-Engraved Book Illustration, 1904–1940: A Break with Tradition*, a volume first published in hardback in 1998, Joanna Selborne presents a fascinating history of British book illustration and the role British wood-engravers played in breaking with the patterns and practices of the nineteenth century. By breaking with traditional book illustrative practices these engravers laid the early foundation on which modern British book illustration would build and evolve. Selborne utilizes a number of resources in her book, including unpublished material such as art school records, publishers' and print societies' archives, and correspondence from and between important artists prominent in the transition she discusses. She has been well served by her publishers, Oxford University Press, who have republished a stoutly bound volume worthy of the subject.

L.E. Semler provides a critical and thorough introduction to readers of *Elizas Babes: Or the Virgin's-Offering* [1652]. Semler's study is organized into three main sections: an introduction, the text itself, and commentary regarding the text. The care Semler has taken regarding annotations and references yields a bounty of information useful for pursuing further study. Examples of commentary provided include that dealing with bibliographic sources and quotations, instances of the text affected by editorial changes, and issues dealing with obscure syntax and archaic words.

Sitter, ed., *The Cambridge Companion to Eighteenth-Century Poetry*, brings together a series of essays devoted to what many might consider non-traditional themes and practices of English poets writing from 1700 into the 1790s. There is an extensive unannotated bibliography. A useful reference tool is Slusser, Parrinder and Chatelain, eds., *H.G. Wells's Perennial Time Machine*, which brings together sixteen essays and commentaries on Wells's masterful novel, often credited with establishing the science fiction genre. Contributors include Brian Aldiss, Paul Alkon, Larry W. Caldwell, Daníele Chatelain, Robert Crossley, Kirby Farrell, J.R. Hammond, Sylvia Hardy, David Leon Higdon, John Huntington, Carlo Pagetti, Patrick Parrinder, W.M.S. Russell, Frank Scafella, George Slusser, and Joshua Stein. The volume has an extensive but unannotated bibliography.

The latest volume of Dr Chester W. Topp's important and definitive bibliography of publishers specializing in Victorian yellowbacks and paperbacks is found in *Victorian Yellowbacks and Paperbacks, 1849–1905*, which covers the firms of Macmillan and Smith Elder. Apart from information related to publisher, year published, and month and date of publication, there are also valuable introductory histories of publishers mentioned, a colour section of photographs, and a useful author, title, and series index. In *The Title Page: Its Early Development, 1460–1510*, Margaret Smith examines an interesting area of publishing history by recounting the rise and use of the title page in book publishing. The first major study of the topic since the late 1890s, Smith's work fills a niche long neglected in the history of publishing and book design. Smith does a good job of demonstrating how the rise of the printing press led to the opportunity to include title pages that were more instructive than ornamental, and how the title page eventually assumed a marketing role beyond its original information purpose.

In an expansive and wide-ranging reference work, Dawn B. Sova, *Edgar Allan Poe, A to Z: The Essential Reference to his Life and Work*, has compiled an impressive array of material related to the life and work of Poe. Topics covered include short fiction, poetry, reviews, essays and articles. Additional material is included that deals with Poe's family background, the characters of his fiction, where he lived and worked and where he was employed, as well as an assessment of the critical and popular reception of his work during his life and following his death. Apart from the wealth of information contained in the book, serious researchers will find the index and cross-references valuable, as well as the listing of Poe research collections.

While much has been written about Shakespeare and his works, little has been written about those whose dedication to all things Shakespearian has kept his work modern and relevant to contemporary readers. In the detailed *James Orchard Halliwell-Phillipps: The Life and Works of the Shakespearean Scholar and Bookman*, Marvin Spevack does a wonderful job of redressing that imbalance in his biography of James Orchard Halliwell-Phillipps (1820–89), generally considered the greatest Shakespeare scholar of his age. Apart from presenting a fascinating biography of an eminent scholar, Spevack's work also presents an exacting portrait of Victorian literary theory and practice. In *John Bewick: Engraver on Wood, 1760– 1795*, Nigel Tattersfield presents the first biography of wood-engraver John Bewick, the younger brother of the better-known Thomas Bewick. Divided into two sections, the first part deals with Bewick's biography, drawing heavily on unpublished correspondence only recently discovered. The second part provides a comprehensively annotated bibliography of Bewick's illustrations, most of which were commissioned to appear in children's books. The British Library has produced a nicely illustrated volume worthy of its subject.

Taylor and Wingquist, eds., *Encyclopedia of Postmodernism*, is an essential work that provides comprehensive coverage regarding a varied and multifaceted topic. Entries are arranged alphabetically, and general readers and serious scholars will find the work useful. Each entry is followed by suggested further reading, and the book will assist users with immediate research needs while encouraging further study. In *The Memory of Mankind: The Story of Libraries Since the Dawn of History*, by Don Heinrich Tolzmann, the role of libraries and their importance to the societies and civilizations that created and supported them is discussed from the earliest beginnings up to the modern era. While societies and their basic patterns of organization and evolution have been many and varied, the library as an institution of knowledge, learning, and power has remained a remarkably constant fixture. Much of Tolzmann's work is based on the classic German-language work *The History of Libraries* by Alfred Hessel (published in 1925 and translated into English in 1950), and additional original text is provided covering developments in the last fifty years. Tolzmann's work is also richly illustrated and will serve as a valuable introduction to students, librarians, and bibliophiles.

Daniel Berkeley Updike's classic two-volume work, *Printing Types: Their History, Forms, and Use*, has been reprinted in a third edition, this latest edition combined into one book with a new introduction by Martin Hutner. Daniel Berkeley Updike was the founder of the Merrymount Press in Boston in 1893, and for upward of half a century produced printing and typography of the highest standards. Admirers of his seminal work will be pleased to know that all 367 typographical illustrations have been retained, as well as the commentary regarding the historical significance of each. Oak Knoll and the British Library are to be congratulated on the republication of this classic text, which traces the development of typography from the earliest years of printing through to the twentieth century.

Richard Wall's impressive reference work *An Irish Literary Dictionary and Glossary* provides the first large-scale effort to organize and present the Anglo-Irish dialect featured so prominently in the Irish literary revival. Useful for general readers and scholars alike, entries provide a concise definition that is further illustrated by citing examples from major works of Irish literature. Also present are a useful abbreviation guide and a detailed bibliography. A critical and appreciative appraisal of children's books written in English is provided in *The Cambridge Guide to Children's Books in English*. Editor Victor Watson has included entries on drama, television, comics, adventure-game books, and the ever-expanding realm of electronic media. The entries are divided into four main categories, by author, title, topic, and technical terms, all arranged alphabetically. Cross-references and headwords are provided, as well as a list of abbreviations and applicable literary prizes for the field.

Unusual and unique in its purpose, Toby Widdicombe's *A Reader's Guide to Raymond Chandler* is an information-packed guide for fans and serious researchers of Chandler's fiction. Entries are alphabetical and arranged in the format of a traditional dictionary. Included are appendices which deal with subjects such as Marlowe on film, television, and radio, Chandler as a screenwriter, Chandler resources, and other writers' versions of Chandler's work. Widdicombe's book is highly recommended for all library collections that seek to support their detective fiction reference collection.

The genre of supernatural fiction receives a thorough treatment in two fine publications, Neil Wilson's *Shadows in the Attic: A Guide to British Supernatural Fiction, 1820–1950*, and S.T. Joshi's *The Modern Weird Tale*. Through Wilson's efforts, the work of authors both good and bad, sometimes both, are presented to demonstrate the evolving character of British supernatural fiction. While the time-frame of Wilson's work ends at 1950, later works by authors who also published prior to that date are included, up to 1999. All of the entries are representative of either novels or short stories in which the bulk of the plot could be subject to a supernatural explanation. Authors are all given a brief biography and notes on their output, giving readers less familiar with the field the historical context of their writing. A useful 'Sources Consulted' section may be found at the end of the book. Joshi's volume represents a successful attempt to establish and separate those writers of weird fiction whose work is meritorious if not universally acclaimed in the realm of popular culture. This criterion allows Joshi to present the work of such writers as Shirley Jackson, Ramsey Campbell, Robert Aickman, T.E.D. Klein, Thomas Ligotti, William Peter Blatty, Thomas Tryon, Robert Bloch, and Thomas Harris. The book includes bibliographies of these writers.

In *Seeing Shelley Plain: Memories of New York's Legendary Phoenix Book Shop*, Robert Wilson offers an intimate and highly personal account not only of his association with a legendary bookstore, but also of his friendships and observations of some of the leading literary personages of the twentieth century. The book is divided into three sections. The first and third deal with the history of the Phoenix Book Shop and the second contains essays on W.H. Auden; Ted Berrigan; Robert Creely, Robert Duncan, and Denise Levertov; Diane di Prima; William Faulkner; Jean Garrigue; H. Rider Haggard; Barbara Howes; Michael McClure; Eve Merriam; Marianne Moore; Fernanda Pivano; Ezra Pound; Laura Riding; Delmore Schwartz; Gary Snyder; Alice B. Toklas; Glenway Wescott; and Louis Zukovsky.

In *Reading History in Early Modern England*, D.R. Woolf presents the reader with a 'history book about the history of history books' by analysing the relationships between printers, publishers, collectors, customers, and others in the production and dissemination of historical texts from roughly 1475 to 1730. Analysing marginal annotations, diaries, and manuals, among other source material, Woolf successfully increases the accepted scholastic understanding regarding reading practices and book production for the years of his study.

In *Love Letters: Leonard Woolf and Trekkie Ritchie Parsons, 1941–1968*, the editor Judith Adamson brings together for the general public a series of letters which only a few scholars have previously seen. Remarkable for their compassionate, longing nature and their humorous and playful undertones, these letters provide a unique and compelling picture of the mysterious and multifaceted nature of human love and devotion, and the extent some people go to in their attempts to satisfy that need while being mindful of the constraints and mores of society.

A significant addition to this year's account of recent bibliographical and textual studies is Wood, ed., *The Culture of the Book in the Scottish Enlightenment: An Exhibition*, published by the Thomas Fisher Rare Book Library at the University of Toronto. Essays included are Roger Emerson, '*Catalogus Librorum* A.C.D.A.', or, the Library of Archibald Campbell, Third Duke of Argyll (1682–1761)'; Richard Sher, 'The Book in the Scottish Enlightenment'; Stephen Brown, 'William Smellie and the Culture of the Edinburgh Book Trade, 1752–1795'; and Paul Wood, 'Marginalia on the Mind: John Robison and Thomas Reid'.

Other bibliographical, textual and reference works of interest to students of literature include Barbara Backus McCorkle's *New England in Early Printed Maps, 1513 to 1800: An Illustrated Carto-Bibliography*, with a foreword by Edward H. Dahl. McCorkle's work is a comprehensive and detailed listing of printed New England maps from America and all over the world. The listing of over 800 maps is arranged chronologically, and numerous useful indexes are supplied throughout, including indexes arranged by title, publisher, cartographer, engraver, printer, and artist. Of the maps profiled, more than half (about 450), are illustrated. Also included is a useful bibliography of related secondary works.

Bell et al., eds., *Re-Constructing the Book: Literary Texts in Transmission*, brings together an eclectic grouping of essays dealing with the process of how meaning in literary works is transmitted from author to reader. The topics covered deal with diverse historical periods and contributors and contents include: Maureen Bell, 'Introduction: The Material Text'; Lynette Hunter, 'Why has Q4 *Romeo and Juliet* Such an Intelligent Editor?'; Paul Hammond, 'Marvell's Coy Mistress'; D.F. McKenzie, 'Congreve and the Integrity of the Text'; C.Y. Ferdinand, 'The Economics of the Eighteenth-Century Provincial Book Trade: The Case of Ward and Chandler'; Roger Lonsdale, 'Thomas Gray, David Hume and John Home's *Douglas*'; David Fairer, 'Texts in Conversation: Coleridge's *Sonnets from Various Authors* (1796)'; Inga-Stina Ewbank, 'Reading the Brontës Abroad: A Study in the Transmission of Victorian Novels in Continental Europe'; Simon Eliot, 'Sir Walter, Sex and the SoA [the Society of Authors]'; David Richards, 'Making (Pre-)History: Mycenae, Pausanias, Frazer'; James L.W. West III, 'Editing Private Papers: Three Examples from Dreiser'; Martin Dodsworth, 'Coercive Suggestion: Rhetoric and Community in *Revaluation*'; Hermione Lee, 'Re-reading Elizabeth Bowen'; Alistair Stead, '"Drastic Reductions": Partial Disclosures and Displaced Authorities in Muriel Spark's *The Driver's Seat*'; Peter D. McDonald, '"Not Undesirable": J.M. Coetzee and the Burdens of Censorship'; Martin Butler, 'Prospero in Cyberspace';

and Shirley Crew, 'Texts and Worlds in Amitav Ghosh's *In An Antique Land'*. The final contribution, Christopher Ricks's 'Congratulations', not unsurprisingly is a highly witty exposition of the multiple meanings and historical ramifications of the word 'congratulations'.

Skillion, ed., *The New York Public Library Literature Companion*, is a reference source dealing with significant literary figures and their works. Coverage is international in scope and extends over historical periods, although English-language literature and international works in English translation predominate. The main section headings include 'Creators', 'Works of Literature', and 'Literary Facts and Resources'. Additional sources of information include web-based resources, libraries with large and important literary collections, and literary factbooks and handbooks of particular merit.

In Roberts, ed., *A Companion to Twentieth Century Poetry*, readers will find a wide-ranging source, which is largely balanced between work traditionally considered standard fare and work at one time considered marginal and postmodern, such as feminist or post-colonial poetry. There are many excellent individual contributions and an extensive unannotated bibliography of primary and secondary works. Readers will find a revealing and authoritative voice in *Pursuit: The Uncensored Memoirs of John Calder*. An important figure in the publishing world known for his willingness to bring to press the works of such notable literary figures as Henry Miller, William Burroughs, Samuel Beckett, and Ann Quinn, among others, Calder's memoirs make fascinatingly informative reading, while also providing key insights regarding major literary personalities publishing and the social issues of their times.

Daybell, ed., *Early Modern Women's Letter Writing, 1450–1700*, assembles a solid collection of essays dealing with female English letter-writers from the late medieval to early modern periods, roughly representing the late fifteenth century up to the early eighteenth century. Contributors and contents include James Daybell's introduction; Roger Dalrymple, 'Reaction, Consolation and Redress in the Letters of the Paston Women'; Jennifer C. Ward, 'Letter-Writing by English Noblewomen in the Early Fifteenth Century'; Alison Truelove, 'Commanding Communications: the Fifteenth-Century Letters of the Stonor Women'; James Daybell, 'Female Literacy and the Social Conventions of Women's Letter-Writing in England, 1540–1603'; Alison Wall, 'Deference and Defiance in Women's Letters of the Thynne Family: the Rhetoric of Relationships'; Vivienne Larminie, 'Fighting for Family in a Patronage Society: The Epistolary Armoury of Anne Newdigate (1574–1618)'; Sara Jayne Steen, '"How subject to interpretation": Lady Arbella Stuart and the Reading of Illness'; Rosemary O'Day, 'Tudor and Stuart Women: Their Lives through their Letters'; Jacqueline Eales, 'Patriarchy, Puritanism and Politics: the Letters of Lady Brilliana Harley (1598–1643)'; Claire Walker, '"Doe not supose me a well mortified Nun dead to the world": Letter-Writing in Early Modern English Convents'; Susan Whyman, 'Gentle Companions: Single Women and their Letters in Late Stuart England'; Anne Laurence, '"Begging pardon for all mistakes or errors in this writeing I being a woman & doing itt myselfe": Family Narratives in Some Early Eighteenth-Century Letters'.

Editions of correspondence include Holmes, ed., *The Correspondence of Ezra Pound and Senator William Borah*, with a foreword by Daniel Pearlman. The edition consists of thirty-one previously unpublished letters which provide a revealing glimpse into two strong-willed and passionate individuals. Holmes allows Pound and Borah to present their respective views on political and economic issues in their own words, providing helpful annotations to further elucidate the ideas, thoughts, individuals, and organizations that each address in their frank correspondence.

In *The Element of Lavishness: Letters of Sylvia Townsend Warner and William Maxwell, 1938–1978*, Michael Steinman chronicles the enduring and remarkable friendship of two important literary figures, one British, the other American. The new edition of James Hogg's *The Private Memoirs and Confessions of a Justified Sinner*, edited by Peter Garside, with an afterword by Ian Campbell, is the latest volume of *The Collected Works of James Hogg*. The textual, cultural, geographical, and theological contexts of Hogg's novel are explained in Garside's useful annotations, while Garside also recounts Hogg's struggle to see his novel to publication without major revisions.

Spanning sixteen centuries of women's travel writing, Jane Robinson, in *Wayward Women: A Guide to Women Travelers*, has edited and compiled a unique annotated bibliographic account full of perceptive and humorous observations. Robinson's book covers over 400 English-speaking women whose travels took them beyond their homeland. A brief biographical sketch of each profiled travel writer is included, as well as an author and a geographical index. A list of related reference books is also included.

Pelayo, ed., *Gabriel García Márquez: A Critical Companion*, brings together into one source much information related to one of Latin America's best known and acclaimed authors. Readers are presented with a listing of García Márquez's works in English translation, including a full analysis of six of his novels and five of his best short stories. Pelayo introduces and assists the reader in understanding the historical context of the work, its character and its literary themes; he also successfully places García Márquez in the canon of Western literature and ably discusses his literary techniques, particularly his use of magical realism.

In the *Dictionary of Midwestern Literature*, volume 1: *The Authors*, general editor Philip A. Greasley presents in a survey format the lives and collected works of about 400 midwestern authors, as well as criticism of their work. This is the first volume in a projected four-volume series sponsored by the Society for the Study of Midwestern Literature, and the goal of the series is to reflect the experience, views, and character of the Midwest as reflected in its literature. Both well-known and lesser-known authors are profiled. Entries are alphabetically arranged and include author name, birth and death dates, pseudonyms used if applicable, biographical information, literary significance, and major works, along with references to the most important commentaries on the author.

In *Hugh Kenner: A Bibliography*, with a foreword by Guy Davenport, Willard Goodwin has produced a comprehensive bibliography of the distinguished literary critic. Contents include: 'Books and Pamphlets by Hugh Kenner'; 'Books and Pamphlets with Contributions by Hugh Kenner'; 'Periodical Contributions'; 'Broadcasts and Recordings'; 'Translations of Kenner's Work'; 'Gists and Piths: A Selection of Blurbs'; and 'Miscellany'.

Books that seek to rank the stature and greatness of authors become the source of debate and are interesting to read if for no other reason than to confirm or inflame one's own reading passions. In *The Literary 100: A Ranking of the Most Influential*

Novelists, Playwrights, and Poets of All Time, author Daniel S. Burt has fulfilled both of those expectations. Based on the assessment and considered opinions of leading literary scholars, the entries examine the life and achievements of each author and their contribution to literature. A bibliography and 'Honourable Mention' list are also included.

One of the most important contributions to our understanding of the history of bibliography which has come the reviewer's way is the delightfully produced and well-edited *The Stationers' Company: A History of the Later Years, 1800–2000*. Robin Myers, the honorary archivist and author of work on the early history of the Stationers' Company, contributes an introduction on the significance of the company. This is followed by contributions from Myers herself (who contributes two essays), Michael Berlin, Michael Harris (who contributes two essays), David Whitaker, Richard Bowden, Penelope Hunting (who contributes two essays), and Ann Saunders. There are six appendices and an extensive index to this volume which has an impressive list of subscribers who justifiably supported its publication.

Appropriately, the final work mentioned in this survey is P.D.A. Harvey's excellent *Editing Historical Records*, an impressive but not lengthy work about editing historical and documentary texts. While not an instruction manual, it enumerates the critical and theoretical principles related to editing historical texts. These include such issues as selection of documents, the need for accuracy, translation and punctuation, the need for consistency, and good practices related to creating a useful glossary and index.

Books Reviewed

Abbott, Jacob. *The Harper Establishment*. OakK. [2001] pp. 182. $29.95 ISBN 1 5845 6058 4.

Adamson, Judith, ed. *Love Letters: Leonard Trekkie Woolf and Ritchie Parsons, 1941–1968*. C&W. [2001] pp. xxiii + 312. £20 ISBN 0 7011 6927 3.

Archer, Caroline. *The Kynoch Press: The Anatomy of a Printing House*. OakK. [2001] pp. 240. $49.95 ISBN 1 5845 6046 0.

Andersen, Jennifer, and Elizabeth Sauer. *Books and Readers in Early Modern England: Material Studies*. UPennP. [2001] pp. vi + 305. $24.95 ISBN 0 8122 1794 2.

Andrews, William L. *The Concise Oxford Companion to African American Literature*. OUP. [2001] pp. 512. £10.99 ISBN 0 1951 3883 X.

Auchter, Dorothy. *Dictionary of Literary and Dramatic Censorship in Tudor and Stuart England*. Greenwood. [2001] pp. xxxiv + 403. $91 ISBN 0 3133 1114 5.

Baker, Nicholson. *Doublefold: Libraries and the Assault on Paper*. RandomH. [2001] pp. xxi + 370. £15.85 ISBN 0 3755 0444 3.

Barker, Nicolas. *A Potencie of Life*. OakK. [2001] pp. 216. $29.95. ISBN 1 5845 6054 1.

Baron, Sabrina Alcorn, Elizabeth Walsh, and Susan Scola. *The Reader Revealed*. Folger/UWashP. [2001] pp. 158. $29.95 ISBN 0 2959 8183 0.

Bartram, Alan. *Five Hundred Years of Book Design*. YaleUP. [2001] pp. 192. $35 ISBN 0 3000 9058 7.

Bell, Maureen, Shirley Chew, Simon Eliot, Lynette Hunter and James L. W. West III, eds., *Re-constructing the Book: Literary Texts in Transmission*. Ashgate. [2001] pp. xi + 231. $59.95 ISBN 0 7546 0360 1.

Bernard, Emily. *Remember Me To Harlem: The Letters of Langston Hughes and Carl Van Vechten, 1925–1964*. Knopf. [2001] pp. xxxiv + 356. $30 ISBN 0 6794 5113 7.

Bennett, Carolyn LaDelle. *An Annotated Bibliography of Mary McLeod Bethune's Chicago Defender Columns*. Mellen. [2001] pp. xiii + 126. $69.95 ISBN 0 7734 7590 7.

Bertens, Hans, and Theo D'Haen. *Contemporary American Crime Fiction*. Palgrave. [2001] pp. ix + 233. $62 ISBN 0 3336 7455 3.

Bigmore, E.C., and Wyman, C.W.H. *A Bibliography of Printing: With Notes and Illustrations*. OakK. [2001] pp. xx + 333. $85 ISBN 1 5845 6061 4.

Bornstein, George. *Material Modernism: The Politics of the Page*. CUP. [2001] pp. xii + 185. $55 ISBN. 0 5216 6154 4.

Brake, Laurel, Bill Bell and David Finkelstein, eds. *Nineteenth-Century Media and the Construction of Identities*. Palgrave. [2000] pp. xv + 387. £47.50 ISBN 0 3336 8151 7.

Bray, J., M. Handley and A.C. Henry. *Ma(r)king the Text: The Presentation of Meaning on the Literary Page*. Ashgate. [2000] pp. xxiv + 341. £55 ISBN 0 7546 0168 4.

Brown, William E. Jr., and Laura Stalker, eds. *Getting Ready for the Nineteenth Century: Strategies and Solutions for Rare Books and Special Collections Librarians: Proceedings of the Thirty-Ninth Annual Preconference of the Rare Books and Manuscripts Section*. Association of College and Research Libraries/ American Library Association. [2000] pp. 107. $18 ISBN 0 8389 8117 8.

Burt, Daniel S. *The Literary 100: A Ranking of the Most Influential Novelists, Playwrights, and Poets*. Facts on File. [2001] pp. xv + 400. $45 ISBN 0 8160 4382 5.

Butler, William E. *American Bookplates*. Primrose Hill Press. [1999] pp. 64. £29.95 ISBN 1 9016 4808 7.

Cahn, Victor L. *The Plays of Shakespeare: A Thematic Guide*. Greenwood. [2001] pp. xiii + 361. $49.95 ISBN 0 3133 0981 7.

Cain, Tom, ed. *The Poetry of Mildmay Fane, Second Earl of Westmorland*. ManUP. [2001] pp. xii + 465. $95 ISBN 0 7190 5984 4.

Calder, John. *Pursuit: The Uncensored Memoirs of John Calder*. Calder/CBS. [2001] pp. 621. £24.99 ISBN 0 7145 4313 6.

Challinor, A.M. *The Achievement of Francis Bacon: A Complete Subject and Author Index to Baconiana, 1886–1999*. Francis Bacon Society. [2001] pp. 165. £25 ISBN 0 9540 4380 4.

Cohen, Mark. *Censorship in Canadian Literature*. McG-QUP. [2001] pp. xii + 205. $55 ISBN 0 7735 2214 X.

De Grazia, Margreta, and Stanley Wells. *The Cambridge Companion to Shakespeare*. CUP. [2001] pp. xx + 328. £40 ISBN 0 5216 5094 1.

Davies, Martin, ed. *Incunabula: Studies in Fifteenth-Century Printed Books Presented to Lotte Hellinga*. BL/UTorP. [1999] pp. xviii + 650. £50 ISBN 0 7123 4507 8.

Daybell, James, ed. *Early Modern Women's Letter Writing, 1450–1700*. Palgrave. [2001] pp. xiv + 213. $62 ISBN 0 3339 4579 4.

Delahunty, Andrew, Sheila Dignen, and Penny Stock. *The Oxford Dictionary of Allusions*. OUP. [2001] pp. xii + 453. $27.50 ISBN 0 1986 0031 3.

Dobson, Michael, and Stanley Wells. *The Oxford Companion to Shakespeare*. OUP. [2001] pp. xxix + 541. $45 ISBN 0 1981 1735 3.

Emerson, Roger. et al. *The Culture of the Book in the Scottish Enlightenment: An Exhibition*. Thomas Fisher Rare Book Library/UTorP. [2000] pp. x + 160. $CAN20 ISBN 0 7727 6035 7.

Evans, Mary. *Feminism: Critical Concepts in Literary and Cultural Studies*, vols. 1–4. Routledge. [2001] pp. 1976. £475 (complete set) ISBN 0 4151 9283 8.

Fargnoli, Nicholas A., and Michael Golay, eds. *William Faulkner A to Z*. FOF. [2001] pp. 352. £9.79 ISBN 0 8160 3860 0.

Fernihough, Anne. *The Cambridge Companion to D.H. Lawrence*. CUP. [2001] pp. xx + 292. $22 ISBN 0 5216 2617 X.

Fitzgerald, Carol. *The Rivers of America: A Descriptive Bibliography*. OakK. [2001] pp. 1,020. $124 ISBN 1 5845 6032 0.

Fleming, Juliet. *Graffiti and the Writing Arts of Early Modern England*. UPennP. [2001] pp. 224. $35 ISBN 0 8122 3629 7.

Garside, Peter, ed. *The Private Memoirs and Confessions of a Justified Sinner*, by James Hogg. EdinUP. [2001] pp. 366. pb. £8.99 ISBN 0 7486 6315 0.

Gibson, Ian. *The Erotomaniac: The Secret Life of Henry Spencer Ashbee*. Faber. [2001] pp. xv + 285. £12.99 ISBN 0 5711 9619 5.

Goodwin, Willard. *Hugh Kenner: A Bibliography*. Whitston. [2001] pp. 485. $49.95 ISBN 0 8787 5524 1.

Gravell, Thomas L., George Miller and Elizabeth Walsh. *American Watermarks, 1690–1835*. OakK. [2001] pp. xxxii + 363. $85 ISBN 1 5845 6068 1.

Greasley, Philip A., ed. *Dictionary of Midwestern Literature*. IUP. [2001] pp. 678. £45 ISBN 0 2533 3609 0.

Gutjahr, Paul C., and Megan L. Benton. *Illuminating Letters: Typography and Literary Interpretation*. UMassP. [2001] pp. xii + 198. $34.95 ISBN 1 5584 9288 7.

Hadfield, Andrew. *Literature and Censorship in Renaissance England*. Palgrave. [2001] pp. xii + 234. $62 ISBN 0 3337 9410 9.

Hakutani, Yoshinobu, ed. *Theodore Dreiser: Art, Music and Literature, 1897–1902*. UIllP. [2001] pp. xxiv + 298. $39.95 ISBN 0 2520 2625 X.

Harp, Richard, ed. *Ben Jonson: Plays and Masques*. Norton. [2001] pp. 534. £8.95 ISBN 0 3939 7638 6.

Harrison. S.J. Texts, Ideas, *and the Classics*. OUP. [2001] pp xiii + 330. $74 ISBN 0 1992 4746 3.

Harvey, P.D.A. *Editing Historical Records*. BL. [2001] pp. 104. £15.95 ISBN 0 7123 4684 8.

Hawkes, Lory, Christina Murphy and Joe Law. *The Theory and Criticism of Virtual Texts: An Annotated Bibliography, 1988–1999*. Greenwood. [2001] pp. xiii + 334. $80 ISBN 0 3133 1224 9.

Hochman, Barbara. *Getting at the Author: Reimagining Books and Reading in the Age of American Realism*. UMassP. [2001] pp. xi + 185. $29.95 ISBN 1 5584 9287 9.

Holmes, Sara C., ed. *The Correspondence of Ezra Pound and Senator William Borah*. UIllP. [2001] pp. xxv + 95. $24.95 ISBN 0 2520 2630 6.

Horsley, Lee. *The Noir Thriller*. Palgrave. [2001] pp. xi + 305. £42.50 ISBN 0 3337 2045 8.

Huntley, E.D. *Maxine Hong Kingston: A Critical Companion*. Greenwood. [2001] pp. xi + 204. $35 ISBN 0 3133 0877 2.

Isaac, Peter, and Barry McKay, eds. *The Moving Market: Continuity and Change in the Book Trade*. OakK. [2001] pp 206. $39.95 ISBN 1 5845 6052 5.

Jackson, H.J. *Marginalia: Readers Writing in Books*. YaleUP. [2001] pp. 328. £19.95 ISBN 0 3000 8816 7.

Jason, Philip K., and Graves, Mark A. *Encyclopedia of American War Literature*. Greenwood . [2001] pp. xiv + 424. $95 ISBN 0 3133 0648 6.

Jedrzejewski, Jan. *Joseph Sheridan Le Fanu: The Cock and Anchor*. Smythe. [2000] pp. xxviii + 489. $55 ISBN 0 8614 0423 8.

Joshi, S.T. *From Baltimore to Bohemia: The Letters of H.L. Mencken and George Sterling*. FDUP. [2001] pp. 284. $45 ISBN 0 8386 3869 4.

Joshi, S.T. *The Modern Weird Tale*. McFarland. [2001] pp. x + 278. $34.95 ISBN 0 7864 0986 X.

Kennedy, Gerald. *A Historical Guide to Edgar Allan Poe*. OUP. [2001] pp. 256. $15.95 ISBN 0 1951 2150 3.

Knellwolf, Christa, and Christopher Norris, eds. *The Cambridge History of Literary Criticism*. CUP. [2000] pp. xii + 493. $70 ISBN 0 5213 0014 2.

Kujoory, Parvin. *Shakespeare and Minorities: An Annotated Bibliography, 1970–2000*. Scarecrow. [2001] pp. xii + 403. $65 ISBN 0 8108 3900 8.

Leitch, Vincent, ed. *The Norton Anthology of Theory and Criticism*. Norton. [2001] pp. xxxviii + 2624. $63 ISBN 0 3939 7429 4.

Londraville, Janis, and Richard Londraville. *John Quinn: Selected Irish Writers from his Library*. Locust Hill. [2001] pp. xxx + 462. $48 ISBN 0 9339 5193 0.

Lyons, Martyn, and John Arnold. *A History of the Book in Australia, 1891–1945: A National Culture in a Colonised Market*. UQP. [2001] pp xix + 444. $50.95 ISBN 0 7022 3234 3.

McCorkle, Barbara Backus. *New England in Early Printed Maps 1513 to 1800: An Illustrated Carto-Bibliography*. John Carter Brown Library (RI). [2001] pp. 354. $185 ISBN 0 9166 1753 X.

McGowan, Kate. *The Year's Work in Critical and Cultural Theory*, vols. 8 and 9. OUP. [2001] ISBN 0 1985 0851 4, ISBN 0 1985 1526 X.

McMillin, Scott. *The First Quarto of Othello*. CUP. [2001] pp. xi + 148. $50 ISBN 0 5215 6257 0.

Maman, Marie. *Sigrid Undset in America: An Annotated Bibliography and Research Guide*. Scarecrow. [2000] pp. xvi + 112. $35 ISBN 0 8108 3738 2.

Mann, Alastair J. *The Scottish Book Trade, 1500–1720: Print Commerce and Print Control in Early Modern Scotland*. Tuckwell. [2000] pp. 308. £25 ISBN 1 8623 2115 9.

May, Derwent. *Critical Times: The History of the Times Literary Supplement*. HarperCollins. [2001] pp. 606. $35 ISBN 0 0071 1449 4.

Miller, Jane Eldridge. *Who's Who in Contemporary Women's Writing*. Routledge [2001] pp. xxi + 385. $29.95 ISBN 0 4151 5980 6.

Minnis, A.J., ed. *Middle English Poetry: Texts and Traditions: Essays in Honour of Derek Pearsall*. UYork/Boydell. [2001] pp. xv + 304. $85 ISBN 1 9031 5309 3.

Morehead, Philip, ed. *The Penguin Roget's College Thesaurus in Dictionary Form*. Penguin Reference. [2001] pp. x + 1,782. $40 ISBN 0 6700 3016 3.

Morrison, Mark. *The Public Face of Modernism: Little Magazines, Audiences, and Reception, 1905–1920*. UWiscP. [2001] pp. 279. $50 ISBN 0 2991 6920 0.

Myers, Robin, ed. *The Stationers' Company: A History of the Later Years, 1800–2000*. The Worshipful Company of Stationers and Newspaper Makers. [2001] pp. xxii + 265. £29.99 ISBN 1 8607 7140 8.

Myers, Robin, Michael Harris and Giles Mandelbrote, eds. *Libraries and the Book Trade: The Formation of Collections from the Sixteenth to the Twentieth Century*. OakK. [2001] pp. 191. $39.95 ISBN 1 5845 6034 7.

Norbrook, David, ed. *Order and Disorder* by Lucy Hutchinson. Blackwell. [2001] pp. lviii + 272. $68.95 ISBN 0 6312 2060 7.

Paster, Gail Kern, ed. *Thomas Middleton: Michaelmas Term*. ManUP. [2000] pp xv + 205. $69.95 ISBN 0 7190 1552 9.

Pearson, David. *For the Love of the Binding: Studies in Historical Bookbinding Presented to Mirjam Foot*. OakK. [2001] pp. 392. $135 ISBN 1 5845 6035 5.

Pelayo, Ruben, ed. *Gabriel García Márquez: A Critical Companion*. Greenwood. [2001] pp. xiii + 179. $35 ISBN 0 3133 1260 5.

Prentice Hall Press, Editors of. *Literature Lover's Companion: The Essential Reference to the World's Greatest Writers—Past and Present, Popular and Classical*. PHI. [2001] pp. 704. $20 ISBN 0 7352 0229 X.

Price, Diana. *Shakespeare's Unorthodox Biography: New Evidence of An Authorship Problem*. Greenwood. [2001] pp. xvi + 357. $45 ISBN 0 3133 1202 8.

Randall, Marilyn. *Pragmatic Plagiarism: Authorship, Profit, and Power*. UTorP. [2001] pp. xviii + 321. $60 ISBN 0 8020 4814 5.

Roberts, Neil, ed. *A Companion to Twentieth Century Poetry*. Blackwell. [2001] pp. xvii + 626. $124.95 ISBN 0 6312 1529 8.

Roberts, Warren, and Paul Poplawski. *A Bibliography of D.H. Lawrence*. CUP. [2001] pp. xxiv + 847. $130 ISBN 0 5213 9182 2.

Robinson, Jane, ed. *Wayward Women : A Guide to Women Travelers*. OUP. [2001] pp. xi + 344. $15.95 ISBN 0 1928 0233 X.

Rollyson, Carl E., and Lisa Paddock. *Herman Melville A to Z: The Essential Reference to his Life and Work*. FOF. [2000] pp. 261. $65 ISBN 0 8160 4160 1.

Rostenberg, Leona, and Madeleine Stern. *Bookends: Two Women, One Enduring Friendship*. FreeP. [2001] pp. ix + 246. $24 ISBN 0 7432 0245 7.

Rostenberg, Leona, and Madeleine Stern. *Books Have Their Fates*. OakK. [2001] pp. 218. $34.95 ISBN 1 5845 6048 7.

Rowland, Susan. *From Agatha Christie to Ruth Rendell: British Women Writers in Detective and Crime Fiction*. Palgrave. [2001] pp. x + 222. $59.95 ISBN 0 3336 7450 2.

Ryan, Marie-Laure. *Narrative as Virtual Reality: Immersion and Interactivity in Literature and Electronic Media*. JHUP. [2001] pp. xiii + 399. $45 ISBN 0 8018 6487 9.

Saum, Lewis O. *Eugene Field and his Age*. UNebP. [2001] pp. xii + 324. $50 ISBN 0 8032 4287 5.

Schumacher, Michael, ed. *Family Business: Selected Letters Between a Father and Son* by Louis and Allen Ginsberg. Bloomsbury. [2001] pp. xxxii + 412. $37.50 ISBN 1 5823 4107 9.

Selborne, Joanna. *British Wood-Engraved Book Illustration, 1904–1940: A Break With Tradition*. OUP. [2001] pp. 458. pb $59.95 ISBN 1 5845 6059 2.

Semler, L.E., ed. *Elizas Babes, or The Virgins Offering: A Critical Edition*. FDUP. [2001] pp. 202. $37.50 ISBN 0 8386 3872 4.

Sitter, John, ed. *The Cambridge Companion to Eighteenth-Century Poetry*. CUP. [2001] pp. xix + 298. pb £13.95 ISBN 0 5216 5885 3.

Skillion, Anne. *The New York Public Library Literature Companion*. FreeP. [2001] pp. xii + 772. $40 ISBN 0 6848 6890 3.

Slusser, George, Patrick Parrinder, and Daniele Chatelain, eds. *H.G. Wells's Perennial Time Machine*. UGeoP. [2001] pp. 232. $40 ISBN 0 8203 2290 3.

Smith, Margaret. *The Title Page: Its Early Development, 1460–1510*. OakK. [2000] pp. 176. $39.95 ISBN 1 5845 6033 9.

Sova, Dawn B. *Edgar Allan Poe, A to Z: The Essential Reference to his Life and Work*. FOF. [2001] pp. x + 310. $65 ISBN 0 8160 3850 3.

Spevack, Marvin. *James Orchard Halliwell-Phillipps: The Life and Works of the Shakespearean Scholar and Bookman*. OakK. [2001] pp. 624. $49.95 ISBN 1 5845 6051 7.

Steinman, Michael, ed. *The Element of Lavishness: Letters of Sylvia Townsend Warner and William Maxwell, 1938–1978*. Counterpoint. [2001] pp. xxvii + 356. $27.50 ISBN 1 5824 3118 3.

Tattersfield, Nigel. *John Bewick: Engraver on Wood, 1760–1795: An Appreciation of his Life Together with an Annotated Catalogue of his Illustrations and Designs*. BL. [2001] pp. 192. $75 ISBN 1 5845 6053 3.

Taylor, Victor E., and Charles E. Winquist. *Encyclopedia of Postmodernism*. Routledge. [2001] pp. 496. £75 ISBN 0 4151 5294 1.

Tolzmann, Don Heinrich. *The Memory of Mankind: The Story of Libraries Since the Dawn of History*. OakK. [2001] pp. 212. $39.95 ISBN 1 5845 6049 5.

Topp, Chester W. *Victorian Yellowbacks and Paperbacks, 1849–1905: Smith Elder and Macmillan & Co*. Hermitage. [2001] pp. xiii + 326. $150 ISBN 0 9633 9204 2.

Updike, Daniel Berkeley. *Printing Types: Their History, Forms, and Use*, 3rd edn. OakK. [2001] pp. 1,088. $85 ISBN 1 5845 6056 8.

Wall, Richard. *An Irish Literary Dictionary and Glossary*. Colin Smythe. [2001] pp. 374. $55 ISBN 0 8614 0442 4.

Watson, Victor. *The Cambridge Guide to Children's Books in English*. CUP. [2001] pp. xi + 814. $75 ISBN 0 5215 5064 5.

Widdicombe, Toby, *A Reader's Guide to Raymond Chandler*. Greenwood. [2001] pp. xix + 211. $75 ISBN 0 3133 0767 9.

Wilson, Neil. *Shadows in the Attic: A Guide to British Supernatural Fiction 1820–1950*. BL. [2001] pp. xvii + 554 ISBN 0 7123 1074 6.

Wilson, Robert. *Seeing Shelley Plain*. OakK. [2001] pp. 256. $39.95 ISBN 1 5845 6050 9.

Wood, Paul, ed. *The Culture of the Book in the Scottish Enlightenment: An Exhibition*. Thomas Fisher Rare Book Library/UTorP. [2000] pp. x + 160. $20 ISBN 0 7727 6035 7.

Woods, Tim. *Who's Who of Twentieth-Century Novelists*. Routledge. [2001] pp. x + 374. $29.95 ISBN 0 4151 6506 7.
Woolf, D.R. *Reading History in Early Modern England*. xvi + 360. CUP. [2000] pp. 379. $65.95 ISBN 0 5217 8046 2.

Index I. Critics

Notes
(1) Material which has not been seen by contributors is not indexed.
(2) Authors such as A.S. Byatt, who are both authors of criticism and subjects of discussion, are listed in whichever index is appropriate for each reference.
(3) Authors of multi-authored works, all of whom may not be mentioned in the text, are listed with the name of the first author in brackets.

Index II. Authors and Subjects Treated

Chardin, Teilhard de 784, 785

Charles II 471

Charron, François 885

charters: Anglo-Saxon 120

Chartist fiction 577

Chartist poetry 589

Chatterjee, Sudipto 800

Chatterjee, Upamanyu: *English August* 903, 909

Chatterton, Thomas 479

Chaucer, Alice 146

Chaucer, Geoffrey 150, **190–223**, 296, 297, 477; and Boece 206; and Caxton 204; and Giotto 220; and Gower 198-9; and Henryson 179; and Hoccleve 176; and Junius 203; and Langland 199, 219; and Lydgate 172, 210; and Plautus 210; and Shakespeare 202; and Spenser 244; and Wynken de Worde 204–5; and classroom nostalgia 196; and cultural tradition 220; and cyberspace 220–1; and England 192; and landscape 198; and Wycliffism 217; alliteration 201; ambiguity in 209; antisemitism 216; apocrypha 203; bibliography 190; characters 209; Christian feminism in 213; churchmen in 211; circulation of money and language 206–7; contemporary politics in 218–19; criticism 191; death in 214; dream poetry 191, 196; editing 202–3; editions 195–6, 942; electronic texts 138; epitaph 204; female agency in 211; feminine audience 221; forms of address in 205; gender in 214; guides 191–2; illustrations 211–12; language 60, 206, 209–10, 216–17; legal fiction 193–4; marriage contracts 193; medieval psychology in 207; music in 201; narrative voice 213; nature in 221; non-Christian other in 207–8; oxymoron in 175; philosophy 220; places in 198; poetics 157–8; professional readers 140; prosody 201–2; punctuation 195; rape and 143, 194–5; reception 200–1; as religious writer 199; sartorial signs in 219; secular marvels 211; social commentaries 145; social context 190–1; speech in 205; spelling 205–6; story of Lucretia in 194; suicide in 196–7; theology in 153, 208–9; as translator 221; typography 203–4; vision in 207; walking in 200; widows in 193; *ABC* **221–2**; *Anelida and Arcite* 199; *Book of the Duchess* 192, 198, 200, **219-20**; *Canterbury Tales* 190–1, 192,

193, 196, 201, 202–3, 205, **206–18**, 238, 361, 925, 942–3; *Canon's Yeoman's Tale* 207; *Clerk's Prologue* 191; *Clerk's Tale* 195–6, 197–8, 210, 211, 214, 218, 942; *Franklin's Tale* 194, 196–7, 206, 209, 211, 215; *General Prologue* 209, 212, 215–16; *Knight's Tale* 197, 207, 244; *Man of Law's Prologue* 191; *Man of Law's Tale* 195, 198–9, 200, 206, 213; *Manicple's Tale* 217; *Merchant's Tale* 157, 210, 211, 214; *Miller's Tale* 144, 197, 202, 211, 212; *Monk's Tale* 199, 217; *Nun's Priest's Tale* 145, 202, 208, 217; *Pardoner's Tale* 198, 208, 210, 215–16; *Parson's Tale* 198, 207, 217; *Physician's Tale* 195; *Ploughman's Tale* 203; *Prioress's Tale* 199, 208, 212, 216; *Reeve's Tale* 194, 195, 208, 212–13; *Retraction* 218; *Second Nun's Tale* 207, 208, 217; *Shipman's Tale* 194; *Squire's Tale* 173, 199, 208, 211, 214; *Summoner's Tale* 196, 197; *Tale of Melibee* 209, 216–17; *Wife of Bath's Tale* 138, 192, 195, 209; *House of Fame* 192, 194, **220–1**; *Legend of Good Women* 145, 191, 192, 195, 196–7, 218, **221**, 943; *Legend of Hypermnestra* 221; *Parliament of Fowls* 192, **221**, 353; *Troilus and Criseyde* 180, 191, 192–3, 195, 197, 202, 205, 206, **218–19**; *Works* 925

Chaudhuri, Amit: *Afternoon Raag* 909

Chaudhuri, Nirad 909

Chaumpaigne, Cecily 194

Chávez, Denise 810, **811**; interview 811; *Face of an Angel* 811; *Last of the Menu Girls, The* 809, 811

Cheever, John 778

Chekhov, Anton 697, 915

Chellis, Mary Dwinell 737

Chelsey, Robert 780

Cheney-Coker, Syl: *Last Harmattan of Alusine Dunbar, The* 824–5

Chernin, Kim 781

Cheshire: place-names 65

Chesnutt, Charles W.: *House Behind the Cedars, The* 736

Chester Plays 183, 708

Chevalier de la Charrette, Le

Chicago Shakespeare Theatre 320

Chicano/a literature **809–11**; fiction 813–14

Chichewa 83

Child, Lydia Maria 743

childhood: 19C women 554; vocation of 496–7